PAGE
48

ON THE ROAD

YOUR COMPLETE DESTINATION GUIDE
In-depth reviews, detailed listings
and insider tips

DEC 12 2014

PUBLIC LIBRARY

D0027379

Health

THIS EDITION WRITTEN AND RESEARCHED BY

Carolyn McCarthy

Carolina A Miranda, Kevin Raub, Brendan Sainsbury,

Luke Waterson

welcome to
Peru

All Things Ancient

A visit to South America isn't complete without a pilgrimage to the glorious Inca citadel of Machu Picchu, but, the truth is, this feted site is just a flash in a 5000-year history of peoples. Walk through the dusted remnants of a vast ancient city at Chan Chan, the largest pre-Columbian ruins in all the Americas. Fly over the puzzling geoglyphs etched into the arid earth at Nazca. Or venture into the rugged wilds that hem the stalwart fortress of Kuelap. Lima's great museums, with priceless ceramics, gold and some of the finest textiles in the world, reveal in full detail the sophistication, skill and passion of these lost civilizations. Visit remote communities and see how old ways live on. Immerse yourself, and you will leave Peru a little closer to the past.

Pleasure & the Palate

Some cultures are haunted by the existential. For many Peruvians, the question that gnaws at them daily would seem simple: what to eat? Ceviche with slivers of fiery chili and corn, stews simmered for hours in beer and cilantro, velvety Amazonian chocolate. In the capital of Latin cooking, so many choices can be perplexing. Great geographic and cultural diversity has brought ingredients – ranging from highland tubers to tropical jungle fruits – to a

Peru is as complex as its most intricate weavings. Festivals mix ancient pageantry with stomping brass bands. The urban vanguard beams with artistry and innovation. Trails mark the way from dense jungle to glacial peaks.

(left) San Antonio Pass, Cordillera Huayhuash Circuit (p384)
(below) Traditionally dressed indigenous girl, Cuzco (p194)

cuisine created with the complex history of Spanish, indigenous, African and Asian influence. The truth is, fusion existed here long before it came with airs. Treat your taste buds with missions to the chaotic markets. Sample grilled *anticuchos* (beef skewers) on the street corners and splurge a little on exquisite *novoandina* (Peruvian *nouvelle*) cuisine. Because going hungry was never an option.

Oh, Adventure

Giant sand dunes, chiseled peaks and Pacific breaks a few heartbeats away from the capital's rush-hour traffic: from downtown Lima to smack-dab nowhere, this vast country translates to paradise for the active traveler. All the usual suspects – rafting, paragliding, zip lines and bike trails – are present. But that doesn't mean your adventure has to be an Olympic event. It could be spotting scarlet macaws and following big cat tracks in the Amazon, watching the sun set over the dusty remnants of an ancient civilization, or joining a holy pilgrimage to an Andean peak believed to be a god. Our advice? Don't rush. Set out to do less than you think you should. Delays pop up. Festivals can swallow you whole for days. And that's when you realize: the adventure is getting there.

Máncora
Warm waters and
ripping waves (p350)

Chan Chan
The Americas' largest
pre-Columbian city (p323)

Reserva Nacional
Pacaya-Samiria
A massive national park (p471)

Kuélap
An extraordinary
stone fortress (p424)

Parque Nacional Manu
A great rainforest
experience (p457)

Machu Picchu
The planet's most-famous

BRAZIL

COLOMBIA

ECUADOR

QUITO

Guayaquil

Machala

Loja

Macará

Zumba

La Tina

San Ignacio

Huancabamba

Bagua

Pedro Ruiz

Kuélap

Celendín

Cajamarca

Chan Chan

Trujillo

Tayabamba

Río Marañón

Chachapoyas

Moyobamba

Tarapoto

Yurimaguas

Lagunas

Reserva Nacional
Pacaya-Samiria

Río Marañón

Río Tigre

Río Napo

Iquitos

Requena

Río Amazonas

Leticia

Santa Rosa

Tabatinga

Río Ucayali

Contamana

Pucallpa

Cruzeiro do Sul

Máncora

Talara

Tumbes

Sullana

Piura

Chiclayo

Equator

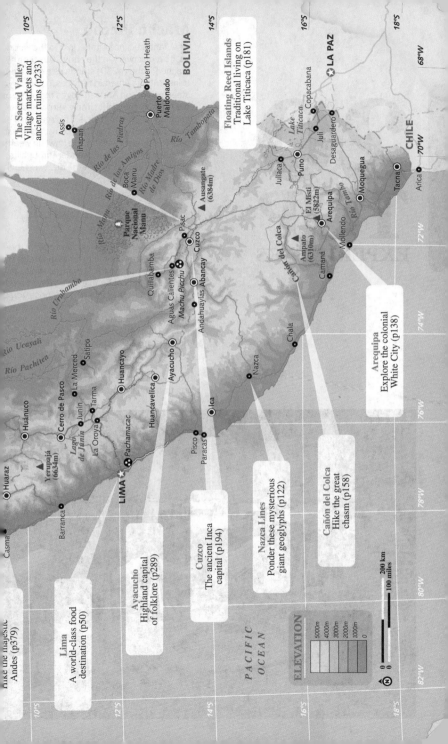

The Sacred Valley
Village markets and ancient ruins (p233)

Floating Reed Islands
Traditional living on Lake Titicaca (p181)

Arequipa
Explore the colonial White City (p138)

Cañón del Colca
Hike the great chasm (p158)

Nazca Lines
Ponder these mysterious giant geoglyphs (p122)

Cuzco
The ancient Inca capital (p194)

Ayacucho
Highland capital of folklore (p289)

Lima
A world-class food destination (p50)

Hike the majestic Andes (p379)

BOLIVIA

LA PAZ

CHILE

PACIFIC OCEAN

ELEVATION

5000m
4000m
3000m
2000m
1000m
0

200 km
100 miles

0
0

N

Puerto Heath
Assis
Iñapari
Puerto Maldonado
Río Tambopata
Río Madre de Dios
Río de las Piedras
Río de los Amigos
Boca Manu
Río Manu
Parque Nacional Manu
Río Urubamba
Río Ucayali
Río Pachitea
Ausangate (6384m)
Pisac
Cuzco
Quillabamba
Aguas Calientes
Machu Picchu
Andahuaylas
Abancay
Copacabana
Lake Titicaca
Juli
Desaguadero
Juliaca
Puno
El Misti (5822m)
Arequipa
Cañón del Colca
Ampato (6310m)
Mollendo
Río Tambo
Moquegua
Tacna
Arica
Camaná
Chala
Nazca
Ica
Pisco
Paracas
Ayacucho
Huancavelica
Huancayo
Satipo
La Merced
Tarma
La Oroya
Junín
Lago de Junín
Cerro de Pasco
Huánuco
Huaraz
Yerupajá (6634m)
Barranca
LIMA
Pachacamac
Casma

20 TOP EXPERIENCES

Machu Picchu

1 A fantastic Inca citadel lost to the world its rediscovery in the early 20th century. Machu Picchu (p250) stands as a ruin amo ruins. With its emerald terraces, backed by steep peaks and Andean ridges that echo o the horizon, the sight simply surpasses the imagination. Beautiful it is. This marvel of er gineering has withstood six centuries of ear quakes, foreign invasion and howling weath Discover it for yourself, wander through its stone temples, and scale the dizzying heigh Wayna Picchu.

Floating Reed Islands, Lake Titicaca

2 Less a lake than a highland ocean, the T caca area is home to fantastical sights, none more so than the surreal floating islan crafted entirely of tightly woven *totora* reed Centuries ago, the Uros people constructed the Islas Uros (p181) in order to escape mor aggressive mainland ethnicities, such as the Incas. The reeds require near-constant reno tion and are also used to build thatched hor elegant boats and even archways and childr swing sets. See this wonder for yourself wit homestay visit that includes fishing and lea ing traditional customs.

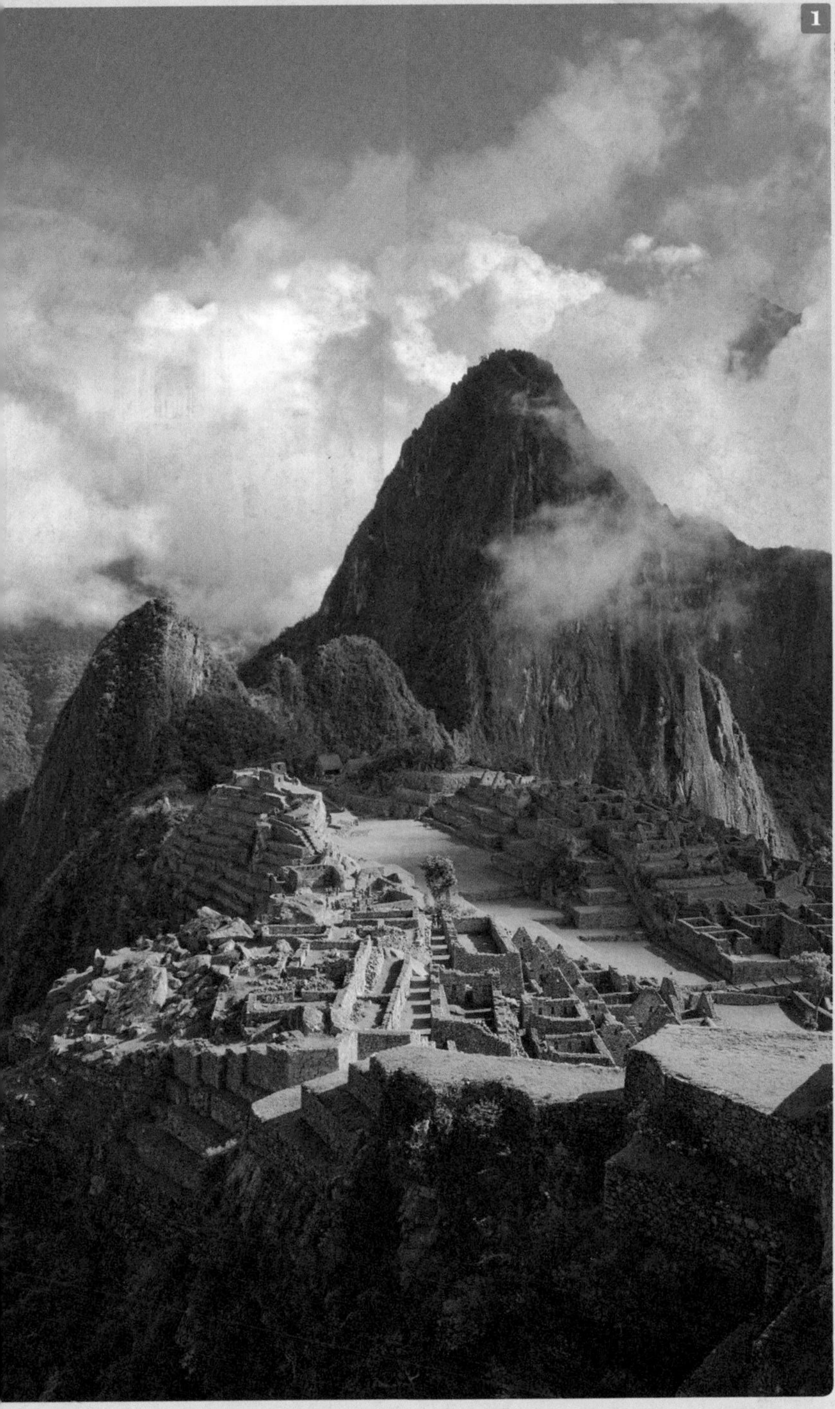
1

ALFREDO MAQUEZ/GETTY IMAGES©

Hiking in the Cordillera Blanca

3 The dramatic peaks of the Cordillera Blanca (p379) stand sentinel over Huaraz and the surrounding region like an outrageously imposing granite Republican Guard. The range is the highest outside of the Himalayas, and 16 of its ostentatious summits breech 6000m, making it the continent's most challenging collection of summits-in-waiting. Glacial lakes, massive *Puya raimondii* plants and shards of sky-pointed rock all culminate in Parque Nacional Huascarán, where the Santa Cruz trek rewards the ambitious with a living museum of razor-sharp peaks.

Colonial Arequipa

4 Peru's second-largest metropolis bridges the historical gap between the Inca glories of Cuzco and the clamorous modernity of Lima. Crowned by some dazzling baroque-*mestizo* architecture hewn out of the local white *sillar* rock, Arequipa (p138) is primarily a Spanish colonial city that hasn't strayed far from its original conception. Its ethereal natural setting, amid snoozing volcanoes and the high *pampa* is complemented by a 400-year-old monastery, a huge cathedral and some interesting Peruvian fusion cuisine eloquently showcased in traditional *picanterías* (spicy restaurants). Arequipa's cathedral (p142)

Parque Nacional Manu

5 Traverse three climatic zones from rearing Andean mountains to mist swathed cloud forest on the lower slopes en route to the bowels of the jungle in Parque Nacional Manu (p457), the Amazon's best adventure. Manu has long been Peru's best-protected wilderness, brimming with opportunities to see fabled jungle creatures such as the anaconda, tapir, thousands of feasting macaws festooning clay licks with their colors, and jaguar. In this deep forest, tribespeople li as they have for centuries, with barely any contact wit the outside world.

FRANS LEMMENS/GETTY IMAGES©

nca Trail

The continent's most famous pedestrian adway, the Inca Trail (p36) akes 43km, up stone steps d through thick cloud for-t mists. A true pilgrimage, e four- to five-day trek ends the famous Intipunku – or n Gate – where trekkers t their first glimpse of the travagant ruins at Machu cchu. While there are untless ancient roads all er Peru, the Inca Trail, with mix of majestic views, aggering mountain passes d clusters of ruins, remains e favorite of travelers. View om Runkurakay (p256)

MICHAEL TAYLOR/GETTY IMAGES©

Cuzco

7 With ancient cobblestone streets, grandiose baroque churches and the remnants of Inca temples with centuries-old carvings, no city looms larger in Andean history than Cuzco (p194), a city that has been inhabited continuously since pre-Hispanic times. Once the capital of the Inca empire, tourist-thronged Cuzco also serves as the gateway to Machu Picchu. Mystic, commercial and chaotic, this unique city is still a stunner. Where else would you find ornately dressed women walking their llamas on leashes, a museum for magical plants, and the wildest nightlife in the high Andes? Iglesia de La Compañía de Jesús (p197)

Lima Cuisine

8 Some cities are known for their parks, o even their politics, but Lima (p81) is a ci where life is often planned around the next meal. Consider it an experience worth savoring. The coastal capital is replete with option ranging from street carts to haute cuisine restaurants offering exquisite interpretation: of Peru's unique fusion cuisine. Dishes are a complex blend of Spanish, indigenous, Africa and Asian influences (both Chinese and Japanese). There's a reason that magazines such as *Bon Appetit* are feting Lima as the 'next great food city.' Appetizers at La Rosa Nautica (p87)

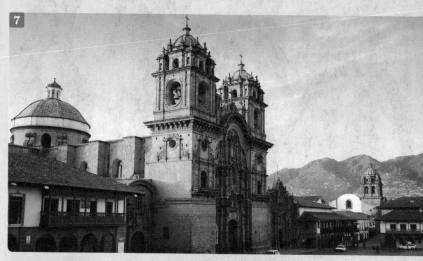

RALPH LEE HOPKINS/GETTY IMAGES©

CHRIS BEALL/GETTY IMAGES©

PEP ROIG/ALAMY©

he Sacred
Valley

9 Ragtag Andean villages, crumbling Inca military outposts and agricultural terraces used since time immemorial are linked by the Río Urubamba as it curves and dens, coursing through the Sacred Valley (p233). A strategic location between Cuzco and Machu Picchu makes his picturesque destination an ideal base to explore the area's famed markets and ins. Accommodations range from inviting inns to top resorts, and adventure options include horseback riding, rafting and treks that take you through remote weaving and agricultural villages. Mercado de Chinchero (p241)

Nazca Lines

10 Made by aliens? Laid out by prehistoric balloonists? Conceived as a giant astronomical chart? No two evaluations of Southern Peru's giant geoglyphs, communally known as the Nazca Lines (p122), are ever the same. The mysteries have been drawing in outsiders since the 1940s when German archaeologist Maria Reiche devoted half her life to studying them. But, neither Reiche nor subsequent archaeologists have been able to fully crack the code. The lines remain unfathomed, enigmatic and loaded with historic intrigue, inspiring awe in all who pass.

Chavín de Huántar

11 The Unesco recognized ruins of Chavín de Huántar (p396) were once a righteous ceremonial center. Today, the exceptional feat of engineering, dating between 1200 BC and 800 BC, features striking temple-like structures above ground and a labyrinthine complex of underground corridors, ducts and chambers that invite clambering through. Nearby, the outstanding Museo Nacional de Chavín, home to the lion's share of the intricate and horrifyingly carved *tenon* heads that once embellished Chavín's walls, helps piece together the enigma.

Semana Santa in Ayacucho

12 As if a week wasn't enough for a party, Ayacucho's Semana Santa (p294) lasts 10 days (from the Friday before Palm Sunday until Easter Sunday). The religious spectacle is moving, with vivid re-enactments of scenes like the procession of Christ on a donkey through streets of flowers and palm fronds. But the after-show parties are the highlight. Fairs, feasts and spectacular pre-dawn fireworks take place on Easter Sunday after a Saturday during which it is believed, as Christ died Friday and rose again Sunday, that no sin can be committed.

Kuélap

13 Lacking the marketing budget, Unesco branding and – drum roll, please – the crowds of Machu Picchu, the extraordinary stone fortress at Kuélap (p424) is second to Peru's most famous ruins in little else. Tucked away deep in cloud forested territory at 3100m above the Río Urubamba near Chachapoyas, this remarkably preserved citadel is a testament to the enigmatic and strong-willed 'People of the Clouds.' Some 400 circular dwellings, some ornately adorned and surrounded by a towering rock wall, highlight this beautiful and mysterious stone beast in the clouds.

Islas Ballestas

14 A collection of barren, guano-covered rocks protruding out of the Pacific Ocean, the Islas Ballestas (p112) support an extraordinary ecosystem of birds, sea mammals and fish (most notably anchovies). They also represent one of Peru's most successful conservation projects; guano is managed by the Ministry of Agriculture while the archipelago is protected in a national reserve. Boat trips around the island's cliffs and arches allow close encounters with barking sea lions, huddled Humboldt penguins and tens of thousands of birds.

Trujillo

15 Rising from the sand-strewn desert like a kaleidoscopic mirage of colonial color, old Trujillo (p313) boasts a dazzling display of preserved splendor. The city's historical center is chock-full of elegant churches, mansions and otherwise unspoiled colonial constructions, which are steeped today in a modern motif that lends the city a lovely, livable feel. Tack on the vicinity of impressive Chimú ruins such as Chan Chan and Moche Huacas del Sol y de la Luna and Trujillo easily trumps its northern rivals in style and grace.
Plaza de Armas (p313)

GRANT DIXON/GETTY IMAGES©

Cañón del Colca

16 It's deep, very deep, but the Colca Canyon (p158) is about far more than mere statistics. In an area colonized by pre-Inca, Inca and Spanish civilizations, the culture here is as alluring as the endless trekking possibilities. Stretching 100km from end to end and plunging over 3400m at its deepest part, the canyon has been embellished with terraced agricultural fields, pastoral villages, Spanish colonial churches and ruins that date back to pre-Inca times. Hike it, bike it, raft it or zipline it, just keep your eyes peeled for the emblematic condors.

Lima Museums

17 Want to understand what Peru's ancient civilizations were all about? Begin your trip here. Lima's museums hold millennia worth of treasures, from sublime ceramics and carved rock stelae to breathtaking textiles made centuries ago. Some of the best collections are at Museo Larco (p65), Museo Andrés del Castillo (p62) and the Museo Nacional de Antropología, Arqueología e Historía del Perú (p65). Extended evening hours at Museo Larco offer an alternative to conventional nightlife. Inca ceramic vessel, Museo Nacional de Antropología, Arqueología e Historía del Perú (p65)

Chan Chan

18 The extraordinary Chimú capital of Chan Chan (p323) is the largest pre-Columbian city in the Americas and the largest adobe city in the world. Once home to some 60,000 inhabitants and a trove of treasures, Chan Chan today is a work in progress, with the Tschudi complex being the only one of the 10 walled citadels within restored to near its former glory. Despite numerous weather-batterings courtesy of El Niño over the years, Chan Chan's ceremonial court-yards, decorative walls and labyrinthine audience rooms resonate resilience.

urfing on the orth Coast

9 Surfers hellbent on an endless summer flock to Peru's north coast for the ance to catch some of the world's longest d most consistent breaks. The coast's surf ene culminates in rowdy Máncora (p350), ru's only tried and true beach resort. Not be confused with the world's other famous rth Shore, Máncora holds its own as far as uth America is concerned, drawing surfers d sand worshippers alike to its crescent-aped coast for year-round fun in the sun. rfing Los Organos, Piura (p343)

Reserva Nacional Pacaya-Samiria

20 Peru's biggest national park (p471) is home to weird and wonderful creatures rarely glimpsed elsewhere: Amazon manatees, pink river dolphins, 6m caimans and giant river turtles. Just getting here is challenge enough – the park is up to a day's journey by boat from the nearest towns. But unlike other Peruvian reserves, this is a walk on the *really* wild side. Transport is by dug-out canoe, there are no fancy lodges and you'll need to spend several days roughing it to see the best stuff: welcome to pure, unadulterated nature.

19

PAUL KENNEDY/GETTY IMAGES ©

20

VILLE PALONEN /ALAMY ©

need to know

Currency
» Nuevo sol (S)

Language
» Spanish, Aymara & Quechua

When to Go

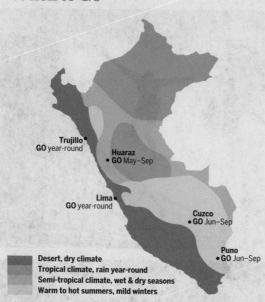

Trujillo
GO year-round

Huaraz
• GO May–Sep

Lima •
GO year-round

Cuzco
• GO Jun–Sep

Puno
• GO Jun–Sep

Desert, dry climate
Tropical climate, rain year-round
Semi-tropical climate, wet & dry seasons
Warm to hot summers, mild winters

High Season
(Jun–Aug)

» Dry season in Andean highlands and eastern rainforest

» Best time for festivals and highland sports, including treks

» Busiest time due to North American and European holidays

Shoulder
(Sep–Nov & Mar–May)

» Spring and fall weather in the highlands

» Ideal for less-crowded visits

» September to November for good rainforest trekking

Low Season
(Dec–Feb)

» Rainy season in the highlands

» The Inca Trail closes during February for clean up

» High season for the coast and beach activities

» Very rainy in the Amazon, lasting through May

Your Daily Budget

Budget less than
S130

» Inexpensive hotel room or dorm bed: S25-85

» Set lunches: less than S10; supermarkets have takeout

» Entry fee to historic sights: average S10

Midrange
S130–390

» Double room in midrange hotel: S130

» Multicourse lunch at midrange restaurant: S30

» Group tours from: S104

Top End more than
S390

» Double room in top-end hotel: S250

» Private city tour: from S150 per person

» Fine restaurant dinner: from S70

Money

» ATMs widely available in larger cities and towns. Credit cards accepted widely. Traveler's checks *not* widely accepted.

Visas

» Generally not required for stays of up to 90 days.

Cell Phones

» Local SIM cards (and top-up credits) are cheap and widely available, and can be used on unlocked triband GSM 1900 world phones.

Transport

» Internal flights and buses are convenient and frequent. Drive on the right.

Websites

» **Lonely Planet** (www. lonelyplanet.com) Good for pre-planning.

» **Expat Peru** (www. expatperu.com) Useful for government offices and customs regulations.

» **Latin America Network Information Center** (www.lanic. utexas.edu) Diverse, informative links.

» **Living in Peru** (www. livinginperu.com) An English-speaking guide.

» **Peru Links** (www. perulinks.com) In Spanish and English.

» **Peruvian Times** (www.peruviantimes. com) The latest news, in English.

Exchange Rates

Australia	A$1	S2.72
Canada	C$1	S2.67
Europe	€1	S3.40
Japan	¥100	S3.28
New Zealand	NZ$1	S2.15
UK	UK£1	S4.22
USA	US$1	S2.60

For current exchange rates, see www.xe.com.

Important Numbers

Peru country code	☑51
International access code	4-digit carrier + 00 + country code
Directory assistance	☑103
National tourist information (24hr)	☑511-574-800
Police	☑105

Arriving in Peru

» **Aeropuerto Internacional Jorge Chávez**

Many flights arrive in the wee hours, so be sure to have a hotel booked ahead. For more, see p543.

» **Bus**

The *combi* company La S (per person S2 to S3) runs various routes to Miraflores and beyond. It's found heading south along Av Elmer Faucett.

» **Taxi**

S45, 30 minutes to one hour (rush hour) to Miraflores, Barranco or San Isidro, faster for downtown Lima.

Don't Leave Home Without

» A passport valid for six months beyond your trip and, if necessary, a visa.
» All recommended immunizations and medical items.
» Reservations for trekking the Inca Trail or alternative route.
» Warm waterproof gear – indispensable year-round in the Andes.
» Essentials such as a Swiss Army knife, head lamp and duct tape.
» Earplugs to combat onboard bus videos and noisy hotels.
» Toilet paper – public toilets and most restaurants don't supply it.
» Chargers and adaptor.
» Cleaning out your cloud server for on-the-road photo storage.
» Photocopies of your passport, travel insurance policy, and other important documents; store copies in your email.

what's new

For this new edition of Peru, *our authors have hunted down the fresh, the transformed, the hot and the happening. These are some of our favorites. For up-to-the-minute recommendations, see* lonelyplanet.com/peru.

Transoceanic Highway, Amazon Basin

1 Peru's biggest construction project put a controversial paved highway from Cuzco to the southern Amazon, connecting Brazil and creating access to formerly isolated rainforest. (p441)

Noche en Blanco, Lima

2 Lima's take on White Nights, this nighttime art and music festival encompasses parks and venues throughout Miraflores in early May. (p22)

Huellas de los Dinosaurios, near Huaraz

3 A 2009 excavation by highway builders turned up more than 100 footprints and fossilized remains of at least 12 species of prehistoric animals. (p398)

Casa-Hacienda San José, near Chincha

4 Reopening post-2007 earthquake, this ex–slave estate has been sympathetically renovated with true artisanal skill. Worth a detour from Lima. (p107)

Selvámanos

5 The country's most innovative music festival mesmerizes with renegade *cumbia* and rock-electronica in a gorgeous Central Amazon national park. (p462)

La Sirena d'Juan, Máncora

6 Serving yellow curry *tiradito* (sashimi) and grilled fish with mango-pepper chutney, this seafood restaurant is a delicious addition to Máncora. (p353)

Northern Highlands Lodges

7 New to this rugged region, decked-out jungle lodges make overnighting a treat. Check out the Gocta Andes Lodge (p423), Kentitambo (p426) and Pumarinri Amazon Lodge (p432).

Los Tambos Hostal, Arequipa

8 This fine new boutique hotel with gourmet breakfasts and thoughtful touches sits just off Arequipa's main square. (p148)

Ayacucho's Food Scene

9 Barrio Gastronómico is a whole city neighborhood dedicated to Andean cuisine: from rustic eateries known as *recreos* to Plaza Moré, a courtyard full of sensational eats. (p295)

Museo Julio C Tello, Paracas Reserve

10 Opened in 2012, this refurbished museum contains ancient artifacts found at the adjacent archaeological site and necropolis. (p112)

Lake Titicaca Lodges

11 On a remote island, Casa Andina Isla Suasi (p184) pampers with spa services immersed in nature. Luxury boutique option Titilaka (p186) is both whimsical and wondrous.

Hotel El Molino, Lunahuana

12 This plush new hotel is set in lush grounds with swimming pools, on the edge of Lunahuaná right next to the Río Cañete. (p106)

if you like...

Ancient Ruins

Beyond the obvious must-see of Machu Picchu, a cache of incredible ruins throughout Peru possess stark beauty, ancient mystery and nary a crowd. If in Lima, you don't have to enter a museum to encounter history – a few ancient sites are scattered throughout the city.

Kuélap Perched atop a limestone mountain, this monumental stone-fortified city is the best-preserved site of Chachapoyas (p424)

Tambo Colorado An understated gem on the south coast, it's worth going with a guide for a fuller appreciation (p114)

Cahuachi When in Nazca, it's worth checking out these expansive 2000-year-old pyramids and other ruins (p125)

Wari For an off-the-beaten-path adventure, head to the capital of the empire that ruled the roost in the highlands before the Inca invaded (and share the experience with just a few snuffling hogs; p298)

Ollantaytambo Wonderful ruins (some free, some paid) surround this Inca-built Sacred Valley village (p242)

Hiking

At the heart of the Andes, Peru has some of the best hiking on the continent, and taking to the trail isn't just about achieving alpine heights. Try a jungle trek or descend to the depths of canyon country.

El Clásico The best trek in the Colca Canyon for seeing a bit of everything except for a paved road (p164)

Ausangate In a stunning arena of tumbling glaciers, turquoise lakes and rural hamlets, the most challenging trek in the Cuzco region is also the most worthy if you have four to five days to spend exploring (p264)

Santa Cruz trek This five-day favorite journeys through Andean hamlets and valleys, with excellent views of Huascarán, Peru's highest peak (p379)

Lares Beautiful Andean landscapes are just a by-product, since the main draw here is learning about village life in remote parts of the Sacred Valley (p38)

Peruvian Delicacies

By now, everyone has heard of ceviche and *cuy* (guinea pig), but the incredible diversity of Peruvian cuisine means your taste buds are making new and delicious discoveries all the time.

Cooking courses Become a gastro-boffin like Gastón Acurio, attending well-organized courses in Arequipa (p146)

Patarascha A jungle dish consisting of giant prawns or fish cooked with tomatoes, sweet peppers, onions, garlic and *sascha culantro,* wrapped in a bijao leaf; try it in Tarapoto at the restaurant of the same name (p433)

Café Tostado With picnic tables and old iron stewpots, this lunch spot is Lima's authentic take on down-home cooking. Pre-order the rabbit or join locals for the Sunday *chicharrónes* (fried pork) breakfast (p88)

Chocolate Luxuriant Andean-style hot cocoa is served with chilis and honey at Cuzco's new Choco Museo (p197)

Picanterias Arequipa's ultimate salt-of-the-earth eateries emphasize authenticity and spices (p150)

» A traditionally dressed weaver at work in Cuzco (p194)

Time-Traveling Cultures

In Peru, culture isn't something you enter a dusty museum to find. It's all around you. The strong traditions of indigenous cultures are easily witnessed in many religious or seasonal festivals. To get a more in-depth experience, check these out:

Colca homestays Rustic homestays in the Colca Canyon villages of Sibayo and Yanque offer a taste of rural canyon life (p162)

Weaving villages Cuzco-based tour operators can provide access to the more remote traditional villages around the Sacred Valley towns of Ollantaytambo and Pisac (p210)

Nazca Beyond sighting the famous 'Lines,' the highly distinctive and colorful pottery amazes too (p121)

Community tourism Sustainable tour operators can help connect visitors with locals in the area of Huaraz (p367)

Parque Nacional Manu You won't find it on official itinerary lists, but a trip deep into the jungle here has often been known to yield sightings of so-called 'uncontacted' tribes (p457)

Into the Wild

Potent scenery is not hard to find in Peru, where ecosystems range from parched desert to lush Amazonian rainforest and glaciated Andean peaks.

Cordillera Huayhuash Circuit Rivaling the big Himalayan treks, this 10-day odyssey takes you among alpine lakes, with condors circling the surrounding 6000m peaks (p384)

The source of the Amazon Only unequivocally authenticated as the real source in 2007, this three-day hike from the Colca Canyon takes you to the genesis of the world's longest river (p160)

Cotahuasi The 12-hour road journey from Arequipa plus spartan facilities scare off all but the brave from the world's deepest canyon (p165)

Choquequirau These remote ruins are a sister site to Machu Picchu, but require four days of hard trekking (p265)

Río Heath To enjoy a little-known Amazonian wonder, the magical Parque Nacional Bahuaja-Sonene is one of Peru's largest, wildest, most biodiverse regions (p451)

Pisco

Emblematic of Peru, this potent grape brandy is best known in sours – paired with sugar and lime juice and prepared with artistry (*and* pageantry) by Peruvian bartenders. New fusions (think macerated jungle fruit, coca leaves and herbs) make it even more quaffable. Follow its journey from producer to cocktail hour.

Tacama Offering the best of Ica's wine and, by definition, pisco, this place lays on free tours and tastings at its lovely colonial hacienda (p117)

Museo del Pisco A chic Cuzco bar with a knowledgeable staff who can guide you through an encyclopedic list of piscos and original cocktails that wow (p226)

Lima bars Do a DIY tour, tasting pisco sours at the historic bar that first made it, El Bolivarcito, and discovering the best bastard incarnations at the hipster bar-mansion Ayahuasca (p89)

Luanahuná Taste industrial-strength pisco (or sweet wines) at the Bodega Santa Maria – a doable day trip from Lima (p105)

month by month

Top Events

1 **Q'oyoriti**, May/June

2 **Semana Santa**, March/April

3 **Carnaval**, February/March

4 **Verano Negro**, February/March

5 **Fiesta de la Vendimia**, March

January

January through March is the busiest (and most expensive) season on the coast, also the best time to find beach facilities open and festivals rocking. In the mountains and canyons, it's rainy season and best avoided by trekkers and mountaineers.

 Año Nuevo
New Year's Day, January 1, is particularly big in Huancayo, where the fiesta continues until Epiphany (January 6; p280).

 Dance of the Blacks
Revelers wear costumes with black masks to commemorate slave forefathers who worked the area mines. In the central highlands town of Huánuco (p303).

 Fiesta de la Marinera
Trujillo's national dance festival (p317) is held the last week in January.

February

The Inca Trail is closed all month. Many Peruvian festivals echo the Roman Catholic calendar and are celebrated with great pageantry, especially in indigenous highland villages, where Catholic feast days are often linked with traditional agricultural festivals.

 La Virgen de la Candelaria
Held on February 2, this highland fiesta, also known as Candlemas, is particularly colorful around Puno, where folkloric music and dance celebrations last for two weeks (p172).

 Carnaval
Held on the last few days before Lent (in February/March), this holiday is often 'celebrated' with weeks of water fights, so be warned. It's popular in the highlands, with the fiesta in Cajamarca being one of the biggest (p409). It's also busy in the beach towns.

 Lunahuaná Adventure Sports Festival
Lunahuaná has an active and growing adventure sports scene, especially river running. Check out this festival in late February/early March.

March

Beach resort prices go down and crowds disperse though the coast remains sunny. Orchids bloom post–rainy season on the Inca Trail and Amazonian birds enact their mating rituals.

 Fiesta de la Vendimia
Celebrated big on the south coast's two main wine regions, Ica (p118) and Lunahuaná (p105). These harvest festivals involve some grape stomping.

 Verano Negro
A must for anyone with an interest in Afro-Peruvian culture, this festival in Chincha (p107) features plenty of music and dancing. It takes place in late February or early March.

April

Crowds and high season prices mark Holy Week, a boon of national tourism in March or April.

⭐ Semana Santa
The week before Easter Sunday, Holy Week is celebrated with spectacular religious processions almost daily, with Ayacucho recognized as the biggest celebration in Peru, lasting a full 10 days. Arequipa and Huancayo also have Easter processions. (p274)

May

Trekking season starts in Huaraz and around Cuzco, with the return of drier weather.

⭐ Noche en Blanco
Inspired by Europe's White Nights, the streets of Miraflores in Lima are closed to cars while arts, music and dance take over. Held in early May.

⭐ Q'oyoriti
A fascinating indigenous pilgrimage to the holy mountain of Ausangate, outside of Cuzco, in May/June (p266). Though known by few outsiders, it's well worth checking out.

⭐ Festival of the Crosses
This festival is held on May 3 in Lima, Apurímac, Ayacucho, Junín, Ica and Cuzco. (p288)

June

High season for international tourism runs June through August, with Machu Picchu requiring advance reservations for train tickets and entry. It's also the busiest time for festivals in and around Cuzco.

⭐ Corpus Christi
Processions in Cuzco are especially dramatic. Held on the ninth Thursday after Easter. (p213)

⭐ Inti Raymi
The Festival of the Sun; also the Feast of St John the Baptist and Peasant's Day, it's the greatest of Inca festivals, celebrating the winter solstice on June 24. It's certainly the spectacle of the year in Cuzco (p213), attracting thousands of Peruvian and foreign visitors. It's also a big holiday in many jungle towns.

⭐ Selvámanos
Reggae, *cumbia* and electronica rock the jungle at this new music festival (p462) held near Oxapampa, in a spectacular national park setting.

⭐ San Juan
The feast of San Juan (p475) is all debauchery in Iquitos, where dancing, feasting and cockfights go until the wee hours on the eve of the actual holiday of June 24.

⭐ San Pedro y San Pablo
The feasts of saints Peter and Paul provide more fiestas on June 29, especially around Lima and in the highlands.

July

The continuation of high-season tourism. In Lima the weather is marked by *garúa*, a thick, grey sea mist that lingers over the city for the next few months and brings a chill.

⭐ La Virgen del Carmen
Held on July 16, this holiday is mainly celebrated in the southern sierra, with Paucartambo and Pisac (p235) near Cuzco, and Pucará near Lake Titicaca being especially important centers.

⭐ Fiestas Patrias
The National Independence Days are celebrated nationwide on July 28 and 29; festivities in the southern sierra begin with the Feast of St James on July 25. (p280)

August

The last month of high visitation and the most crowded at Machu Picchu.

⭐ Feast of Santa Rosa de Lima
Commemorating the country's first saint, major processions are held on August 30 in Lima, Arequipa and Junín to honor the patron saint of Lima and of the Americas. (p73)

September

Low season everywhere, September and October can still offer good weather to highland trekkers without the crowds, while migrating

birds become another attraction.

Mistura

For one week in September, this massive food festival with international acclaim is held in Lima (p51).

El Festival Internacional de la Primavera

A don't miss, the International Spring Festival features supreme displays of horsemanship, as well as dancing and cultural celebrations during the last week of September in Trujillo (p317).

October

The best time to hit the Amazon runs from September to November when drier weather means better wildlife-watching.

Great Amazon River Raft Race

The longest raft race in the world flows between Nauta and Iquitos in September or early October.

La Virgen del Rosario

On October 4, this saint's celebration comes to Lima, Apurímac, Arequipa and Cuzco. Its biggest event is

held in Ancash, with a symbolic confrontation between Moors and Christians.

El Señor de los Milagros

A major religious festival, the Lord of the Miracles celebration (p73) is held in Lima on October 18, around which time the bullfighting season starts.

November

A good month for festivals, it's worth checking out the wild celebrations held in Puno.

Todos Santos

All Saints' Day is November 1, a religious precursor to the following day.

Día de los Muertos

All Souls' Day is celebrated on November 2 with gifts of food, drink and flowers taken to family graves. It's especially colorful in the Andes where some of the 'gift' food and drink is consumed, and the atmosphere is festive rather than somber.

Puno Week

Starting November 5, this week-long festival (p173) involves several days of spectacular

costumes and street dancing to celebrate the legendary emergence of the first Inca, Manco Cápac.

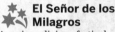

December

Beach season returns with warmer Pacific temperatures. Skip the Amazon, which experiences heavy rains from the end of the month through early April.

Fiesta de la Purísima Concepción

The Feast of the Immaculate Conception is a national holiday celebrated with religious processions in honor of the Virgin Mary. It's held on December 8.

Christmas Day

Held on December 25, Christmas is less secular and more religious, particularly in the Andean highlands.

La Virgen del Carmen de Chincha

Frenzied dancing and all-night music in the *peñas* (bars or clubs featuring live folkloric music) of El Carmen on December 27.

itineraries

Whether you've got six days or 60, these itineraries provide a starting point for the trip of a lifetime. Want more inspiration? Head online to lonelyplanet.com/thorntree to chat with other travelers.

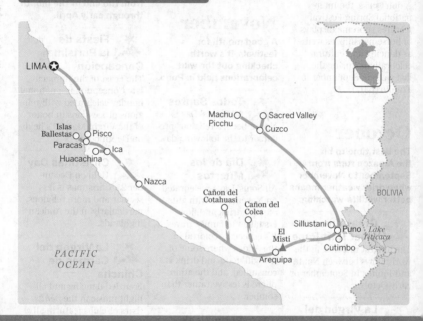

Two to Four Weeks
The Gringo Trail

This trip hits some of the pre-eminent highlights of the continent. Leaving **Lima**, journey south to **Pisco** and **Paracas**, where you can boat to the wildlife-rich **Islas Ballestas**. Then it's on to **Ica**, Peru's wine and pisco capital, and the palm-fringed, dune-lined oasis of **Huacachina**, famous for sandboarding. Next is **Nazca** for a flight over the mysterious Nazca Lines.

Turn inland for the 'White City' of **Arequipa**, with its colonial architecture and stylish nightlife. Lace up your boots to trek the incredible **Cañón del Colca** or **Cañón del Cotahuasi** – perhaps the world's deepest – or climb **El Misti**, a postcard-perfect 5822m volcano. Continue upwards to **Puno**, Peru's port on **Lake Titicaca**, one of the world's highest navigable lakes. From here you can boat to traditional islands and explore the strange *chullpas* (ancient funerary towers) at **Sillustani** and **Cutimbo**.

Wind through the Andes to **Cuzco**, South America's oldest continuously inhabited city. Browse colorful markets and explore archaeological sites in the **Sacred Valley**, then trek to **Machu Picchu** via an adventurous alternative route.

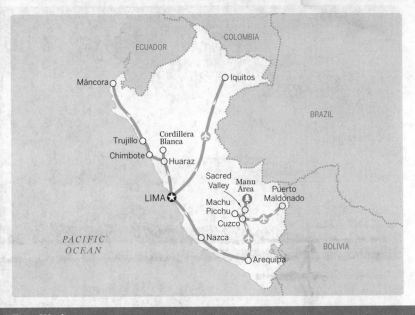

Four Weeks
The Best of Peru

> If you're set on getting a taste of everything, this whirlwind tour hits Peru's top must-see attractions. Give yourself a full month to fully take it all in.

Conquer your jet lag by becoming acquainted with the exquisite tastes of Peru in the restaurants of **Lima**, strolling parks and museums between meals. Head south through the coastal desert for a flyover of the **Nazca Lines** before arriving in stylish, cosmopolitan **Arequipa**, with its mysterious monasteries, deep canyons and smoking volcanoes.

Fly high into the Andes to reach the ancient Inca capital of **Cuzco** for a few days of acclimatization, exploring the cobblestone city and visiting **Sacred Valley** villages to check out colorful markets selling textiles, talismans and dozens of types of tubers. Then board the train to **Machu Picchu**, the most visited archaeological site in South America.

From Cuzco, fly to **Puerto Maldonado** (or brave the 10-hour bus ride) where you can kick back at a wildlife lodge along one of the mighty rivers of the Amazon Basin. Alternatively, you can take an overland tour from Cuzco to the **Manu area**, with remote tracts of virgin forest holding diverse animals from kinkajous to caimans, it's one of the most biodiverse areas of the planet. Another option for exploring the Amazonian *selva* (jungle) is to first fly back to Lima, then onward to **Iquitos**, a bustling port that will launch you deeper into the jungle.

Back in Lima, take a bus or fly north to the adventurers' base camp of **Huaraz**, where a short trek will take you to the precipitous peaks of the **Cordillera Blanca**. A day trip to Chavín de Huántar will lead you to one of Peru's oldest ancient sites. Rumble back down to the coast at **Chimbote**, then dash north to historic **Trujillo**, which offers spicy northern dishes, surrounded by a cornucopia of archaeological sites. These include the ruins of the largest pre-Columbian city in the Americas, Chan Chan, and the fascinating Huacas del Sol y de la Luna. Finish up the journey by taking a seaside break at the bustling surf town of **Máncora**.

AXEL FASSIO/GETTY IMAGES ©

» (above) A traditional boat made of totora reeds on Lake Titicaca (p176)
» (left) Inca burial chullpas (funeral towers) in Cutimbo (p179)

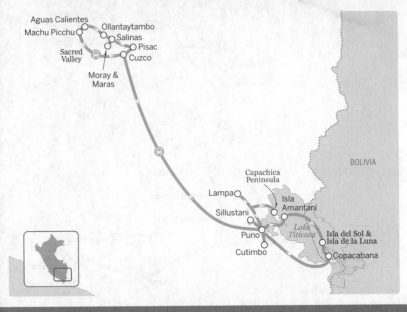

Two Weeks Plus
The Inca Heartland

From Lima, fly to Cuzco but move on to the lower **Sacred Valley** to spend your first three to four days acclimating to the altitude. Visit the bustling market of **Pisac**, see the ruins and ride horses at **Moray** and **Maras**. The best accommodations are in the quaint Inca village of **Ollantaytambo**, at a swank valley resort or area B&B.

From Ollantaytambo, hike the town ruins in the morning or visit the cool salt pans of **Salinas** and take an afternoon train to **Aguas Calientes**. Enjoy a leisurely dinner and tuck in early to take the first bus to the great Inca citadel of **Machu Picchu**. Spend the day browsing the ruins.

The following morning, hop the train to **Cuzco**. Now that you're acclimated, spend a few days enjoying the colonial charms of this former Inca capital, taking a walking tour, visiting a few museums, admiring the splendors of **Qorikancha**, the Inca's most spectacular temple, and enjoying the city's outstanding cuisine.

Grab a comfortable tourist bus (or take the historic train) to the altiplano city of **Puno**. If you can coincide with a festival, this is the place to do it, with wild costumes, brass bands and fervent merriment. Otherwise, take in folkloric music at a dinner show or adventure to aquatic accommodations on the retired steamship *Yavari*.

From your base in Puno, the funerary towers of the Colla, Lupaca and Inca cultures can be found at **Sillustani** and **Cutimbo**, an easy day trip, and worth combining with lovely **Lampa** and its historic church. Take a boat tour of **Lake Titicaca**, visiting the famous reed islands and staying overnight in traditional family lodgings on **Isla Amantaní**. If you have a few extra days, take a catamaran tour, which also visits the Bolivian islands of **Isla del Sol** and **Isla de la Luna**, landing you in **Copacabana**, from where you can take a tourist bus back to Puno.

Returning to Puno, explore the rural coast of the **Capachica Peninsula**, home to places still steeped in the ancient traditions of the altiplano with nary another traveler in sight.

Get ready for the culture shock of big city living, and fly back to Lima.

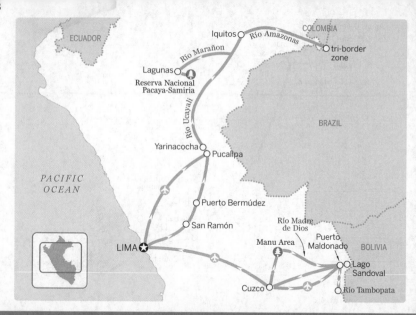

Two to Four Weeks
Exploring Amazonia

More than half of Peru is jungle, populated by spectacular wildlife and tribal peoples. Go overland and drop dramatically away from the eastern slopes of the Andes to slip deep into the Amazon Basin, which stretches all the way to the Atlantic. This entire itinerary takes a month, or it can be divided by region into one- or two-week segments.

The most popular excursion starts from **Cuzco** and heads to the **Manu area**, itself the size of a small country, albeit one with kingdoms of jungle lodges. Another option is to fly from Cuzco to **Puerto Maldonado** and kick back in a thatch-roofed bungalow with a view, either along the **Río Madre de Dios**, the gateway to lovely **Lago Sandoval**, or along the **Río Tambopata**, where a national reserve protects one of the country's largest clay licks. The dry season (July and August) is traditionally the best time to return overland back to Cuzco, although the recent paving of this route means it's possible outside these months.

Or turn your focus to the north. The easiest way to get there is to fly from Lima to **Pucallpa**, staying in a lodge or bungalow in the nearby **Yarinacocha**. The lovely oxbow lake is ringed by tribal villages. You can visit some of these, including those of the matriarchal Shipibo people, renowned for their pottery. Hardcore overland travelers can opt to reach Pucallpa from Lima via the coffee-growing settlement of **San Ramón** and the miniscule village of **Puerto Bermúdez**, the stronghold of Peru's largest Amazon tribe, the Asháninka.

From Pucallpa, begin the classic slow riverboat journey north along the **Río Ucayali** to **Iquitos**, the world's largest city with no road access! This northern jungle capital has a floating market and a bustling port, where you can catch a more comfortable cruise into Peru's largest national park, **Reserva Nacional Pacaya-Samiria**, via **Lagunas**. It's also tempting to float over into Brazil via the unique **tri-border zone**.

It's best to fly if your time is limited; if not, lose yourself for weeks on epic river and road journeys through jungle terrain. Bring bucket loads of patience and self-reliance – and a lot of luck never hurts.

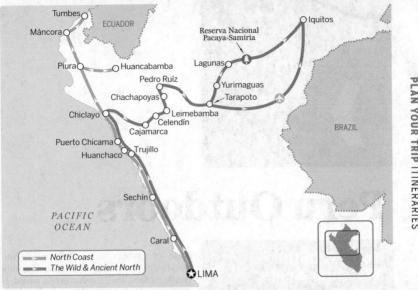

10 Days to Two Weeks
North Coast

The first stop north of **Lima** could be **Caral**, where the oldest known civilization in South America arose about 5000 years ago. Further north, spy ancient engravings of human sacrifice at **Sechín** and continue to **Trujillo**. Nearby attractions include the Moche pyramids of **Huacas del Sol y de la Luna** and ruins of the once-mighty **Chan Chan**.

Off the sleepy beaches at **Huanchaco**, surfers paddle out to the breakers while local fishers trawl the coast. To the north, the surf spot of **Puerto Chicama** boasts one of the world's longest left-hand breaks. Then it's **Chiclayo**, with world-class museums nearby showcasing riches from the important archaeological site of **Sipán**.

Craft-market hub **Piura** boasts great dining possibilities, while the witch doctors of **Huancabamba** are hidden away in the Andes. Peru's best beaches lie along the Pacific shoreline further north, with resorts such as **Máncora**, where you can feast on fresh seafood and dance the balmy nights away.

The journey ends at **Tumbes**, a gateway to Ecuador and jumping-off point to Peru's endangered mangrove swamps, which teem with wildlife (mind the crocs!).

Two to Four Weeks
The Wild & Ancient North

From **Lima**, head to **Trujillo**, sampling the fiery coastal cuisine and exploring nearby ruins at **Chan Chan** and **Huacas del Sol y de la Luna**. Head further north to spy ancient ruins and the witches' market of **Chiclayo**.

From here, brave the wild route to the lovely highland town of **Cajamarca**, where the conquistadors captured Inca Atahualpa. In the dry season, adventure on the slow, spectacular route to friendly **Celendín** and on to **Leimebamba** to see the Marvelous Spatuletail Hummingbird. Continue on to **Chachapoyas** where the cloud forest obscures the fantastic monolithic fortress of **Kuélap**.

From Chachapoyas, journey via **Pedro Ruíz** to **Tarapoto**, where you can hike in lush forest to waterfalls. Next, fly to the jungle city of **Iquitos** or continue via **Yurimaguas**, where cargo boats make the rugged two-day trip to Iquitos via the village of **Lagunas**, the entry point to the **Reserva Nacional Pacaya-Samiria**, for an unforgettable glimpse of the world's greatest river basin. At Iquitos, you can arrange boat trips that go deeper into the rainforest and on to Brazil or Colombia.

Peru Outdoors

Top 5 Wildlife Watching Spots

Parque Nacional Manu Jaguars, tapirs and monkeys inhabit this expansive rainforest park, among the continent's wildest, deep in the Amazon

Cañón del Colca Andean condors glide over this rugged canyon, the second deepest in the world

Islas Ballestas Colonies of honking sea lions and penguins claim these rocky Pacific outcrops off Peru's south coast

Parque Nacional Huascarán Giant Puya raimondii plants burst with flowers while vicuñas and viscachas bustle around the high alpine landscape of the Cordillera Blanca

Tumbes A rare mangrove forest on the northernmost coast, home to crocodiles, seabirds, flamingos and crabs

Scale icy Andean peaks. Raft one of the world's deepest canyons. Surf the heavenly Pacific curlers. Walk the flanks of a smoldering volcano known locally as a living deity. With its breathtaking, diverse landscapes, Peru is a natural adventure hub. History goes deep here—you may be mountain biking routes used by Inca messengers or hiking through terraced fields along ancient trade routes. Yet even then, the fledgling status of some outdoor activities here means that, in certain times and places, you can get a whole mountain, sandy shore or complex of ruins to yourself. So gear up and take the Band-Aids. You're in for one wild ride.

Hiking & Trekking

Pack the hiking boots because the variety of trails in Peru is downright staggering. The main trekking centers are Cuzco and Arequipa in the southern Andes, and Huaraz in the north. Hikers will find many easily accessible trails around Peru's archaeological ruins, which are also the final destinations for more challenging trekking routes.

Peru's most famous trek is the Inca Trail to Machu Picchu. Limited permits means this guided-only trek sells out months in advance. For those who haven't planned so far in advance, there are worthwhile alternative routes. In addition, other possibilities around Cuzco include the spectacular six-day trek around the venerated Ausangate (6372m), which will take you over 5000m passes, through huge herds of alpacas, and past tiny

TOUCHING THE VOID

What inspires a person to endure inhospitable climes, hunger, exhaustion and a lack of oxygen in order to conquer forbidding mountain peaks? It's a question explored at length by Joe Simpson in his celebrated book, *Touching the Void: The True Story of One Man's Miraculous Survival.* This gripping narrative tells the story of a climb that Simpson undertook with his climbing partner, Simon Yates. The climb began well enough – with an extremely challenging and, ultimately, successful ascent on the jagged and steep Siula Grande in the Cordillera Huayhuash. But it ended in an accident that almost claimed one man's life. The book examines the thrills, rewards and agony of mountaineering. *Touching the Void* became an award-winning British documentary in 2003.

hamlets unchanged in centuries. Likewise, the isolated Inca site of Choquequirau is another intriguing destination for a trek.

In nearby Arequipa, you can get down in some of the world's deepest canyons – the world-famous Cañón del Colca and the Cañón del Cotahuasi. The scenery is guaranteed to knock you off your feet, and it's easier going than some higher-altitude destinations. During the wet season, when some Andean trekking routes are impassable, Colca is invitingly lush and green. It's also the best place in Peru for DIY trekking between rural villages. The more remote and rugged Cañón del Cotahuasi is best visited with an experienced local guide and only during the dry season.

Outside Huaraz, the Cordillera Blanca can't be beat for vistas of rocky, snowcapped mountaintops, while the remote and rugged Cordillera Huayhuash is similarly stunning. The classic and favorite trekking route is the four-day journey from Llanganuco to Santa Cruz, where hardy mountaineers climb the 4760m Punta Union pass, surrounded by ice-clad peaks. Longer treks include the northern route around the dazzling Alpamayo, which requires at least a week. Shorter overnight trips in the area go to mountain base camps, alpine lakes and even along an old Inca road.

Cuzco and Huaraz (and, to a lesser degree, Arequipa) have outfitters that can provide equipment, guides and even *arrieros* (mule drivers). If you prefer to trek ultralight, you might want to purchase your own gear, especially a sleeping bag, as old-generation rental items tend to be heavy. Whether you'll need a guide depends on where you trek. Certain areas of Peru, such as along the Inca Trail, require guides; in other places, such as in the Cordillera Huayhuash, there have been muggings, so it's best to be with

a local. Thankfully, scores of other trekking routes are wonderfully DIY. Equip yourself with topographic maps for major routes in the nearest major gateway towns or, better yet, at the Instituto Geográfico Nacional (IGN) or at the South American Explorers Club in Lima.

Whatever adventure you choose, be prepared to spend a few days acclimating to the dizzying altitudes – or face a heavy-duty bout of altitude sickness.

Trekking is most rewarding during the dry season (May to September) in the Andes. Avoid the wet season (December to March), when rain makes some areas impassable.

Mountain, Rock & Ice Climbing

Peru has the highest tropical mountains in the world, offering some absolutely inspired climbs, though acclimatization to altitude is essential. The Cordillera Blanca, with its dozens of snowy peaks exceeding 5000m, is one of South America's top destinations. The Andean town of Huaraz has tour agencies, outfitters, guides, information and climbing equipment for hire. Still, it's best to bring your own gear for serious ascents. Near Huaraz, Ishinca (5530m) and Pisco (5752m) provide two ascents easy enough for relatively inexperienced climbers. For experts, these mountains are also good warm-up climbs for bigger adventures such as Huascarán (6768m), Peru's highest peak. Other challenging peaks include the stunning, knife-edged Alpamayo (5947m) and Yerupajá (6634m), Peru's second-highest mountain, located in the Cordillera Huayhuash. Rock and ice climbing are also taking off around Huaraz, where a few outfitters have indoor

» (above) Mountaineering in Cordillera Blanca (p379)
» (left) Rafting in Caraz (p390)

TODD LAWSON/GETTY IMAGES©

RESPONSIBLE TREKKING

» Don't depend on open fires. Cook on a lightweight camp stove and dispose of butane cartridges responsibly.

» Carry out all rubbish.

» Contamination of water sources by human waste can lead to the transmission of all sorts of nasties. Where there is a toilet, use it. Where there is none, bury your waste. Dig a small hole 15cm deep and at least 100m from any watercourse. Cover the waste with soil and a rock. Pack out toilet paper.

» For washing, use biodegradable soap and a water container at least 50m away from any watercourses. Disperse the waste water widely to allow the soil to filter it fully.

» Do not feed the wildlife.

» Some trails pass through private property. It's polite to ask residents before crossing their property and leave all livestock gates as you found them.

» Don't give children money, sweets or gifts. This encourages persistent begging, which has become a major problem on some busy routes. If you wish to help, consider donating directly to local schools, NGOs and other volunteer organizations (p365).

» Keep a low profile: the gear you are carrying costs more than many locals earn in a month (or a year!). Stow everything inside your tent at night.

climbing walls, rent out technical equipment and organize group trips.

In southern Peru, the snowy volcanic peaks around Arequipa can be scaled by determined novice mountaineers. The most popular climb is El Misti (5822m), a site of Inca human sacrifice. Despite its serious altitude, it is basically a very long, tough walk. Chachani (6075m) is one of the easier 6000m peaks in the world – though it still requires crampons, an ice ax and a good guide. Other tempting peaks tower above the Cañón del Colca.

For beginners looking to bag their first serious mountains, Peru may not be the best place to start. Not all guides know the basics of first aid or wilderness search and rescue. Check out a prospective guide's credentials carefully and seek out those who are personally recommended. Carefully check any rental equipment before setting out.

As with trekking, high-elevation climbing is best done during the dry season (mid-June to mid-July).

Rafting & Kayaking

River running is growing in popularity around Peru, with trips that range from a few hours to more than two weeks.

Cuzco is the launch point for the greatest variety of river-running options. Choices range from a few hours of mild rafting on the Urubamba to adrenaline-pumping rides on the Santa Teresa to several days on the Apurímac, technically the source of the Amazon (with world-class rafting between May and November). A river-running trip on the Tambopata, available from June through October, tumbles down the eastern slopes of the Andes, culminating in a couple of days of floating in unspoiled rainforest.

Arequipa is another rafting center. Here, the Río Chili is the most frequently run, with a half-day novice trip leaving daily between March and November. Further afield, the more challenging Río Majes features class II & III rapids. On the south coast, Lunahuaná, not far from Lima, is a prime spot for beginners and experts alike. Between December and April, rapids here can reach class IV.

Note that rafting is not regulated in Peru. There are deaths every year and some rivers are so remote that rescues can take days. In addition, some companies are not environmentally responsible and leave camping beaches dirty. Book excursions only with reputable, well-recommended agencies and avoid cut-rate trips. A good operator will have insurance, provide you with a document indicating that they are registered, and have highly experienced guides with certified first-aid training who carry a properly stocked medical kit. Choose one that provides top-notch equipment, including self-bailing rafts,

US Coast Guard–approved life jackets, first-class helmets and spare paddles. Many good companies raft rivers accompanied by a kayaker experienced in river rescue.

For more on river running in Peru, visit www.peruwhitewater.com.

Surfing

With consistent, uncrowded waves and plenty of remote breaks to explore, Peru has a mixed surfing scene that attracts dedicated locals and international die hards alike.

Waves can be found from the moment you land. All along the southern part of Lima, surfers ride out popular point and beach breaks at Miraflores (known as Waikiki), Barranquito and La Herradura. Herradura's outstanding left point break gets crowded when there is a strong swell. In-the-know surfers prefer the smaller crowds further south at Punta Hermosa. International and national championships are held at nearby Punta Rocas as well as Pico Alto, an experts-only 'kamikaze' reef break with some of the largest waves in Peru. Isla San Gallán, off the Península de Paracas, also provides experts with a world-class right-hand point break only accessible by boat; ask local fishermen or at hotels.

Peru's north coast has a string of excellent breaks. The most famous is Puerto Chicama, where rides of more than 2km are possible on what's considered the longest left-hand break in the world. Also, very consistent waves can be found at Pacasmayo, and outside Chiclayo at Pimentel and Santa Rosa.

The water is cold from April to mid-December (as low as 15°C/60°F), when wet suits are generally needed. Indeed, many surfers wear wet suits year-round (2/3mm will suffice), even though the water is a little warmer (around 20°C, or 68°F, in the Lima area) from January to March. The far north coast (north of Talara) stays above 21°C (70°F) most of the year.

Though waves are generally not crowded, surfing can be a challenge – facilities are limited and equipment rental is expensive. The scene on the north coast is the most organized, with surf shops and hostels that offer advice, rent boards and organize surfing day trips. Huanchaco is a great base with these services. Serious surfers should bring their own board.

The best surfing sites include www.peruazul.com, www.vivamancora.com and www.wannasurf.com, with a comprehensive, highly detailed list of just about every break in Peru. Good wave and weather forecasts can be found at www.magicseaweed.com and www.windguru.com.

Sandboarding

Sandboarding down the giant desert dunes is growing in popularity at Huacachina and around Nazca, on Peru's south coast. Nazca's Cerro Blanco (2078m) is the highest known sand dune in the world. Some hotels and travel agencies offer tours in *areneros* (dune buggies), where you are hauled to the top of the dunes, then get picked up at the bottom. (Choose your driver carefully; some are notoriously reckless.)

For more information on sandboarding worldwide, check out *Sandboard Magazine* at www.sandboard.com.

Mountain Biking & Cycling

In recent years mountain biking has exploded in popularity, but it is still a fledgling sport in Peru. There is no shortage of incredible terrain. Single-track trails ranging from easy to expert await mountain bikers outside of Huaraz, Arequipa and even Lima. If you're experienced, there are incredible mountain-biking possibilities around the Sacred Valley and downhill trips to the Amazon jungle, all accessible from Cuzco. Easier cycling routes include the wine country around Lunahuaná and in the Cañón del Colca, starting from Chivay.

Mountain-bike rental in Peru tends to be basic; if you are planning on serious biking it's best to bring your own. (Airline bicycle-carrying policies vary, so shop around.) You'll also need a repair kit and extra parts.

Swimming

Swimming is popular along Peru's desert coast from January to March, when the Pacific Ocean waters are warmest and skies are blue. Some of the best spots are just south of Lima. Far more attractive is the stretch of shore on the north coast, especially at laid-back Huanchaco, around Chiclayo and the perennially busy jetset resorts of Máncora.

Only north of Talara does the water stay warm year-round. Watch for dangerous currents and note that beaches near major coastal cities are often polluted.

Scuba Diving

Scuba diving in Peru is limited. The water is cold except from mid-December to March. During these months the water is at its cloudiest, due to runoff from mountain rivers. Dive shops in Lima offer PADI certification classes, rent scuba equipment and have trips to sea-lion colonies along the coast.

Horseback Riding

Horse rentals can be arranged in many tourist destinations, but the rental stock is not always treated well, so check your horse carefully before you saddle up. For a real splurge, take a ride on a graceful Peruvian *paso* horse. Descendants of horses with royal Spanish and Moorish lineage, like those ridden by the conquistadors, are reputed to have the world's smoothest gait. Stables around Peru advertise rides for half a day or longer, especially in the Sacred Valley at Urubamba.

Paragliding

Popular paragliding sites include the coastal clifftops of suburban Miraflores in Lima and various points along the south coast, including Pisco and Paracas (even, possibly, over the Nazca Lines). There are few paragliding operators in Peru. Book ahead through the agencies in Lima.

Trekking the Inca Trail

Alternative Routes to Machu Picchu

Two-day Inca Trail A guided overnight route with the top highlights of the trail. Permits are limited, so book far in advance.

Lares Best done with a guide, this culturally oriented option is a flexible multiday trek through quaint Andean villages, combined with train travel from Ollantaytambo to Aguas Calientes.

Salcantay Trek A scenic, but demanding, five-day hike that ranges from jungle to alpine terrain, peaking at 4700m. It's possible to do independently or with a guide.

The Inca Jungle Trail With hiking, biking and rafting options, this guided multisport route stages to Machu Picchu via Santa Teresa.

You have pictured its deep green gorges, the lost citadels and misty peaks that ebb in and out of view. It is nothing less than mind-bending to climb these stone stairways laid millennia ago, following the Andean route that evaded the Spanish for centuries. There is no doubt: trekking the Inca Trail is a traveler's rite of passage and the adventure of a lifetime. Since logistics can be confusing, this chapter offers the absolute essentials to get your boots on the trail.

Planning Your Trek

When to Go

Organized groups leave year-round except in February, when the Inca trail is closed for maintenance and it rains so much that nobody in their right mind goes trekking. The coldest, driest and most popular months are June to August. But those who are well prepared with proper gear can enjoy the trail during any month it's open.

To skip the crowds, consider going before and after the rainy season: from March to May (best vegetation, orchids and birdlife) or September to November.

What to Expect

Even if you are not carrying a full backpack, this trek requires a good level of fitness. In addition to regularly exercising, you can

WARNING!

Due to the Inca Trail's overwhelming popularity, you must book at least six weeks in advance for trips outside of high season and six months to a full year beforehand for departures between late May and early September. The same goes for the abbreviated two-day route.

And if it's already booked for your dates? Check out the alternative routes.

get ready with hikes and long walks in the weeks before your trip (also a good time to test out your gear). Boots should be already worn in by the time you go. On the trail, you may have to deal with issues like heat and altitude. Just don't rush it, keep a reasonable pace and you should do fine.

Booking Your Trip

It is important to book your trip at least six months in advance for dates between May and August. Outside these months, you may get a permit with a few weeks' notice, but it's very hard to predict. Only licensed operators can get permits, but you can check general availability at www.camino-inca.com.

Consider booking a five-day trip to lessen the pace and enjoy more wildlife and ruins. Other positives include less-crowded campsites and being able to stay at the most scenic one – Phuyupatamarka (3600m) – on the third evening.

Take some time to research your options – you won't regret it. It's best to screen agencies for a good fit before committing. Also make sure you have international travel insurance that covers adventure activities.

Regulations & Fees

The Inca Trail is the only trek in the Cuzco area that cannot be walked independently – you must go with a licensed operator. Prices range from US$480 to US$600 and above.

Only 500 people each day (including guides and porters) are allowed to start the trail. You must go through an approved Inca Trail operator. Permits are issued to them on a first-come, first-served basis. You will need to provide your passport number to get a permit, and carry the passport with

you to show at checkpoints along the trail. Be aware that if you get a new passport but had applied with your old, it may present a problem.

Also, permits are nontransferrable: no name changes.

Choosing an Inca Trail Operator

While it may be tempting to quickly book your trek and move onto the next item on your To Do list, it's a good idea to examine the options carefully before sending that deposit. If price is your bottom line, keep in mind that the cheapest agencies may cut corners by paying their guides and porters lower wages. Other issues are substandard gear (ie leaky tents) and dull or lackadaisical guiding.

Yet paying more may not mean getting more, especially since international operators take their cut and hire local Peruvian agencies. Talk with a few agencies to get a sense of their quality of service. You might ask if the guide speaks English (fluently or just a little), request a list of what is included and inquire about group size and the kind of transportation used. Ensure that your tour includes a tent, food, a cook, one-day admission to the ruins and the return train fare.

If you have special dietary requirements, state them clearly before the trip, being clear about allergies (versus preference issues). Vegans will meet with a lot of quinoa and lentils. If possible, get confirmation in writing that your specific requirements will be met.

Porters to carry group gear – tents, food etc – are also included. You'll be expected to carry your own personal gear, including sleeping bag, unless you pay extra for a personal porter; this usually costs around US$50 per day for about 10kg.

Part of the fun may be meeting other travelers from other parts of the world in your trekking group. Keep in mind that

WATER

When hiking the Inca trail, get your next day's water hot in a well-sealed bottle; you can use it as a sleeping bag warmer and it will be cool to drink by the time you're hiking.

individual paces vary and the group dynamic requires some compromise.

For those who prefer more-exclusive services, it's possible to organize private trips with an independent licensed guide (US$1250 to US$2000 per person). This can be expensive but for groups of six or more it may in fact be cheaper than the standard group treks. Prices vary considerably, so shop around.

Porter welfare is a major issue in the Cuzco region (see boxed text, p39). Porter laws are enforced through fines and license suspensions by Peru's Ministerio de Trabajo (Ministry of Work).

The operators listed here have not been sanctioned in the past year. Of course, there are other conscientious operators out there. The following companies offer treks as well as tours around Peru. For more Cuzco-based options, see p207.

Amazonas Explorer (☎84-25-2846; www. amazonas-explorer.com) Cuzco's longest-standing outfitter, with socially and environmentally responsible practices. Offers five-day classic and alternative treks.

Aracari (☎in Lima 01-651-2424; www.aracari. com) A reputable Lima-based agency with high-end tours.

Aventours (☎84-22-4050; www.aventours. com; Saphi 456, Cuzco) A responsible outfitter with a long-tenured team.

Culturas Peru (☎84-24-3629; www.cultur asperu.com; Tandapata 354-A, Cuzco) A highly knowledgeable and reputable, locally owned and run outfitter with sustainable practices.

Explorandes (☎in Lima 01-715-2323; www. explorandes.com) Offers five-day itineraries and a luxury version; ISO certified.

Intrepid Adventures (☎in Australia 61-3-9473-2626; www.intrepidtravel.com) A reputable Australian outfitter with sustainable practices.

Peruvian Odyssey (☎84-22-2105; www. peruvianodyssey.com; Pasaje Pumaqchupan 204, Cuzco) Operator with 20 years experience; also offers alternative route via Santa Teresa.

Tambo Trek (☎84-23-7718; www.tambotreks. net) A pioneer outfitter, does classic and alternative routes, supports clean-up initiatives.

What to Bring

Trekking poles are highly recommended, as the Inca Trail features a cartilage-crunching number of downhill stone steps. Other items that will come in handy: first-aid kit, sunscreen, sandals or crocs for camp, a down jacket for cold nights, a waterproof jacket, a warm hat and gloves, sun hat, travel towel, broken-in hiking boots, warm trekking socks, thermal underwear top and bottom, a fleece, water bottle or hydration pack, insect repellent, long pants and sunglasses. Make sure that your pack is comfortable with weight and that you have enough camera batteries – there are no electrical outlets on the way.

Take cash (in Peruvian soles) for tipping; an adequate amount is S100 for a porter and S200 for a cook.

For more information on packing for treks in the Cuzco region, see p207.

Alternative Routes to Machu Picchu

For more information on the following hikes, the *Alternative Inca Trails Information Packet* from the South American Explorers Club (p229) is a great resource.

Two-Day Inca Trail

This 10km version of the Inca Trail gives a fairly good indication of what the longer trail is like. It's a real workout, and passes through some of the best scenery and most impressive ruins and terracing of the longer trail.

It's a steep three- or four-hour climb from Km 104 to Wiñay Wayna, then another two hours or so on fairly flat terrain to Machu Picchu. You may be on the trail a couple hours more, just to enjoy the views and explore. We advise taking the earliest train possible.

The two-day trail means overnighting in Aguas Calientes, and visiting Machu Picchu the next day, so it's really only one day of walking. The average price is US$400 to US$535.

Lares Valley Trek

This is not a specific track as such, but a walk along any of a number of different routes to Ollantaytambo through the dramatic Lares Valley. Starting at natural hot springs, the route wanders through rural Andean farming villages, lesser-known Inca archaeological sites, lush lagoons and river gorges. You'll finish by taking the train from

PORTER WELFARE

In the past, Inca trail porters have faced excessively low pay, enormous carrying loads and poor working conditions. Relatively recent laws now stipulate a minimum payment of S170 to porters, adequate sleeping gear and food, and treatment for on-the-job injuries. At checkpoints on the trail, porter loads are weighed (each is allowed 20kg of group gear and 5kg of their own gear).

Yet there is still room for improvement and best way to help is to choose your outfitter wisely. Conscientious operators do exist, but only a few are confident enough to charge the price that a well-equipped, well-organized, well-guided trip requires. A quality trip will set you back at least US$500. The cheaper trips cut costs and most often impact on porter welfare – on the Inca Trail and other trekking routes. Go with a well-recommended company, such as those listed in this chapter and on p207.

There's more you can do on the trail:

» Don't overpack. Someone will have to carry the extra weight and porters may have to leave their own essential gear behind.

» Don't occupy the dining tent until late if it's where the porters sleep.

» Tip the cooks if you liked the food, and always tip your porters.

» Tip individuals directly and in soles. Don't leave it to the company or a guide to distribute.

» If you don't plan to use your gear again, items such as good sleeping bags are like gold to porters. Warm jackets, pocket tools and headlamps also make thoughtful end-of-trip tips.

» If you don't like what you see, complain to your guide and to the agency, and register an official complaint with iPerú (www.peru.info), either at a branch or online. Though guides and outfitters are subject to annual review, it can take time to deactivate a company that has acted irresponsibly. It is important for trekkers to give feedback. To learn more about the life of porters, look for the documentary *Mi Chacra*, winner of the 2011 Banff Film Festival Grand Prize.

Ollantaytambo to Aguas Calientes. Although this is more of a cultural trek than a technical trip, the mountain scenery is breathtaking, and the highest mountain pass (4450m) is certainly nothing to sneeze at. The average price is US$460.

Salkantay Trek

A longer, more spectacular trek, with a slightly more difficult approach to Machu Picchu than the Inca Trail. Its highest point is a high pass of over 4700m near the magnificent glacier-clad peak of Salkantay (6271m; 'Savage Mountain' in Quechua). From here you descend in spectacular fashion to the vertiginous valleys of the subtropics. It takes five to seven days to get to Machu Picchu, and the average price is US$400.

For a luxury approach, **Mountain Lodges of Peru** (☑84-26-2640; mountainlodgesofperu. com; per person US$2390-2990) offers high-quality guiding with accommodations in comfortable lodges with outdoor Jacuzzis. Prices vary according to high and low seasons.

Inca Jungle Trail: Back Door to Machu Picchu

Dreamed up by outfitters and guides, this multisport route between Cuzco and Machu Picchu travels via Santa Teresa with options to bike, hike and raft your way in two to five days. The number of days and activities vary, but the backbone of tours on offer is the same.

The trip starts with a long, four- to five-hour drive from Cuzco to Abra Málaga – the high (4350m) pass between Ollantaytambo and the Amazon Basin. Somewhere on the Amazon side you'll board mountain bikes for the long ride down to Santa María. Starting on a paved road that turns to dirt after about 20km, it's an incredibly scenic descent from the glacial to the tropical, up to 71km total.

Some operators walk the 23km from Santa María to Santa Teresa; others send you by vehicle (one hour), arguing that it's not a particularly interesting hike, though there is a short section of preconquest *camino de hierro* (iron road) – the Inca version of a superhighway.

Either way you'll arrive in Santa Teresa to the welcome spectacle of the Cocalmayo hot springs. Some companies include rafting near Santa Teresa; see p208.

From Santa Teresa, you can walk the 20km to Machu Picchu, 12km of it along train tracks. There's nice river scenery but no particular attraction and it's usually dusty and hot. Alternatively, you can catch a bus and a train. You may reverse this route to get back to Cuzco, but it's much quicker to catch the train via the Sacred Valley.

Many varieties of this trip exist, and bare-bones versions may not include hotels or entry fees, so read the fine print. Whether you stay in a tent or a hostel, key factors in the trip price are bike quality, professional English-speaking guides and whether you walk or catch the train to Aguas Calientes. A three-day/two-night trip costs around US$379, and usually includes a guided tour of Machu Picchu and return train ticket to Ollantaytambo.

Gravity Peru (☎84-22-8032; www.gravity peru.com; Santa Catalina Ancha 398, Cuzco) offers the best-quality bikes. Other respected operators include **Reserv Cusco** (☎84-26-1548; www.reserv-cusco-peru.com; Plateros 326, Cuzco) and **X-treme Tourbulencia** (☎84-22-4362; www.x-tremetourbulencia.com; Plateros 358, Cuzco).

Travel with Children

Best Regions for Kids

Lima

Kids dig the Parque del Amor, Circuito Mágico del Agua, visiting markets and joining outdoor family events.

Cuzco & the Sacred Valley

Whether exploring the narrow passageways of the ancient city of Cuzco, visiting a traditional market or climbing high on the Via Ferrata, there's something here for all ages.

The Coast

Seaside resorts like Paracas and Huanchaco provide beach fun and some surf. A gentle, sunny climate here helps keep your plans on target.

Machu Picchu

What could be more intriguing for teens than the mysteries of the Incas? Nearby, smaller sites like Ollantaytambo, Pisac and Maras also offer intrigue.

Travel with children to Peru and you will find that it brings some distinct advantages. A family-oriented society, little ones are treasured. For parents, it's an easy conversation-starter with locals and ultimately an aid in breaking down cultural barriers. In turn, Peru can be a great place for kids to explore and interact with.

This chapter describes the range of possibilities to help you plan for all stages of your trip.

Peru for Kids

Peru is welcoming to kids, though it's best to take all the same travel precautions you would at home. Be sure kids have the appropriate vaccinations. Free or reduced admission rates are often given at events and performances.

Practicalities

In Peru, kids are no stranger to public transportation. Often someone will give up a seat for a parent and child or offer to put your child on their lap. On buses, children aren't normally charged if they sit on their parent's lap.

Expecting mothers enjoy a boon of special parking spaces and grocery store lines. Breastfeeding in public is not uncommon, but most women discreetly cover themselves. Babysitting services or children's

ROCK PERU KID-STYLE

The country has many ways to please young adventurers; here are a few highlights.

Adventure

» Rafting near Cuzco
» Horseback riding in the Andean foothills
» Splashing about in the hot pools in Cañon del Colca's La Calera
» Canopy zipline in the Sacred Valley
» Climbing the 'super Mario' steps of Moray ruins
» Exploring ruins in Chachapoyas, Sacred Valley and Machu Picchu
» Spying wildlife in the Amazon

Entertainment

» Fiestas with traditional dances
» Bungee tramps and climbing walls in summer
» Llamas and alpacas at farms and petting zoos

Dining

» *Quintas* (places serving Andean food) with oversized grills and backyard ambience
» Picnics on rocky outcrops with a view to the world

Rainy Day Refuges

» Chiquity Club in Cuzco and *ludotecas* (educational centers) in Lima
» Making chocolates at the Choco Museos in Lima and Cuzco

activity clubs tend to be limited to upmarket hotels and resorts.

In general, public toilets are poorly maintained. Always carry toilet paper. While a woman may take a young boy into the ladies' room, it would be socially unacceptable for a man to take a girl into the men's room.

Health & Safety

The main issue is diet. Drink only filtered/bottled water for starters. It's also best to avoid raw vegetables unless you are assured they have been properly prepared. When traveling with young children, be particularly careful about their diet, because diarrhea can be especially dangerous to them and because the vaccines for the prevention of hepatitis A and typhoid fever are not approved for children under two.

Sun exposure can be dangerous, particularly at high altitudes, so make sure kids are adequately covered up and using sunscreen. Altitude can also be an issue, so make sure the family acclimates slowly. It's safer not to take children under three to high altitudes.

Children under nine months should not be brought to lower-altitude jungle areas because yellow-fever vaccine is not safe for this age group.

The two main malaria medications, Lariam and Malarone, may be given to children, but insect repellents must be applied in lower concentrations.

Since street dogs are common, it's good to be up to date with rabies vaccinations. Most dogs are mild-mannered, but avoid those that seem aggressive.

For more information, see the Health chapter (p551).

Dining

While restaurants don't offer special kids' meals, most offer a variety of dishes suitable for children or may accommodate a special request. You can always order it *sin picante* (without spice). It is perfectly acceptable to split a dish between two children or an adult and a child. Don't wait to eat until everyone is too hungry – service can be quite slow. High chairs are available in some larger restaurants.

Adventure

Routine travel, such as train rides or jungle canoe trips, can amount to adventure for kids. In rural areas, community tourism can be a great option. Many of the activities aimed at adults can be scaled down for children. Activities such as guided horseback rides and canyoning usually have age limits (usually eight and up), but are invariably OK for teenagers. Some rivers may be suitable for children to float or raft; make sure outfitters have life vests and wet suits in appropriate sizes.

Planning
When to Go

Summer (between December and February) offers the most opportunities for good weather and beach fun, though the coast is enjoyed year-round. Avoid the highlands during the rainiest months (December to March). The highland dry season, between June and August, is ideal for exploring Cuzco and Machu Picchu, though these are also the busiest times.

Accommodations

Most midrange and top-end hotels will have reduced rates for children under 12 years of age, provided the child shares a room with parents. Cots are not normally available, except at the most exclusive hotels. Cabins or apartments, more common in beach destinations, usually make a good choice with options for self-catering.

What to Pack or Rent

If you're traveling with an infant, stock up on diapers in Lima or other major cities before heading to rural areas. Other things to pack: infant medicines, a thermometer and, of course, a favorite toy. Formula and baby food are easily found.

Kids should have comfortable outdoor clothing, a bathing suit, hats for the sun, a shell jacket and warm clothing for chilly days and nights. Before your trip, make sure everyone has adequate, broken-in shoes. Sandals or Crocs can also be useful for the coast. A cheap digital camera or pair of binoculars can provide lots of entertainment. It's possible to rent children's bikes with helmets, as well as surf gear.

Strollers are unlikely to be convenient in most places beyond cities. Baby backpacks are handy for market visits or getting onto the trails with tots or babies over six months old.

Electronic games and tablet computers are bound to attract a lot of attention if used in public – it's probably best to limit their use to the hotel.

Before You Go

Keep the kids in mind as you plan your itinerary or include them in the trip planning from the get-go. If renting a car, communicate ahead if you will need a child's seat, they are not always available. Lonely Planet's *Travel with Children* provides good information, advice and anecdotes.

Children under the age of 12 receive discounts on airline travel, while infants under two pay only 10% of the fare provided they sit on their parent's lap.

If you don't want to be tied down to a schedule while traveling, plenty of activities can be booked just a few days in advance.

regions at a glance

With parched coastal desert, jagged Andean peaks and the lush expanse of the Amazon rainforest, the regions of Peru feature cultures and landscapes rich in diversity. In Lima, urban life is among the most sophisticated on the continent. In remote areas, cultures still follow age-old traditions. In this dazzling mosaic, solemn pilgrimages honor gods both Christian and indigenous, neon clubs pulse with reveling youth, and ancient ruins bring us back to prehistory. And then, there is the food – sublime creations that alter with the landscape, made from ingredients both native and contemporary. Welcome to Peru – a blast to the senses.

Lima

Food ✓✓✓
Culture ✓✓✓
Nightlife ✓✓

Food
Setting the foodie world on fire, Lima's signature pan-cultural cuisine introduces fresh, indigenous ingredients to sophisticated preparations. For a mere sampling, join the half-million attending Mistura, Lima's prestigious food festival.

Culture
Founded way back in the 15th century, Lima boasts culture in spades, from its colonial catacombs and many museums to cool art galleries throughout the funky *barrio* (neighborhood) of Barranco.

Nightlife
When the sun sets behind the Pacific, a million lights pop on in Lima. Time to enjoy a little Latin nightlife. Start with a pisco sour or *chilcano* in a weathered bar or velvet lounge. Then hit a club to shake it 'til the wee hours to *cumbia*, house, techno, Latin rock or *reggaeton*.

p50

South Coast

History ✓✓
Adventure ✓✓
Wine ✓

Arequipa & Canyon Country

Trekking ✓✓✓
Architecture ✓✓
Food ✓✓

Lake Titicaca

Festivals ✓✓✓
Culture ✓✓✓
Detouring ✓✓

History
Two crucially important pre-Inca civilizations once existed on the coast of southern Peru. The Nazca left their mark in the famous geoglyphs etched into the desert landscape south of Ica. The Paracas buried intricately decorated textiles in necropolises near Pisco.

Adventure
Some of the best river running in Peru happens in Lunahuaná, while equally white-knuckle sand-boarding opportunities are available in the desert oasis of Huacachina and on nearby Cerro Blanco, the world's tallest sand dune.

Wine
A relative newcomer to the viticulture world, Peru's best grapes are grown in its well-irrigated southern desert. Ica is the nation's wine capital, but you'll also find decent wineries in Lunahuaná close to Lima, and Moquegua, a few hours south of Arequipa.

p102

Trekking
For many travelers, trekking in Peru begins and ends on the Inca Trail. But, if you're the kind of walker who gets claustrophobic after seeing more than 25 hikers in any given day, come to the Colca and Cotahuasi Canyons where spectacular, isolated trails stretch for kilometers.

Architecture
Arequipa is widely touted as one of the best-preserved Spanish colonial cities in the Americas, crafted uniquely out of white volcanic *sillar* rock. Less heralded are the exquisitely preserved baroque churches in Colca Canyon villages.

Food
Long before Peru became the 'Gastronomic Capital of the Americas,' Arequipa was fusing Quechua, Spanish and Chinese influences to concoct a unique hybrid cuisine best showcased in the city's traditional *picanterías* (informal local restaurants).

p137

Festivals
With wild costumes and more than 300 traditional dances, Puno is serious about its festivals. Not every city can boast a patron virgin; perhaps that's reason enough why the Virgen de Candelaria (celebrated February 2) should feature a thunderous street party that's the event of the year.

Culture
Community tourism is the best way to get a feel for life on this great blue expanse almost 4000m high. You could say islanders live in another dimension – from the surreal reed-made Uros to the rural rhythms of Isla Amantani.

Detouring
Splurge on a visit to the nature preserve of Isla Suasi or spend a few days in rural homestays on the lakeshores to experience timeless Titicaca.

p167

Cuzco & the Sacred Valley

Ruins ✓✓✓
Adventure ✓✓✓
Culture ✓✓

Ruins

People day trip from Cuzco, but consider lacing up your boots to trek an alternate route. You'll be thankful you took the time to immerse yourself in the Andean culture and landscape before the grand finale.

Adventure

With outfitters galore, Cuzco rivals Huaraz as Peru's adventure center. Whiz from the high Andes to the jungle on a mountain bike, ascend sheer rock on the *via ferrata* (iron way) or trek the wild wilderness around Ausangate.

Culture

Inca culture is everywhere, in ruins and museums, but living indigenous cultures have just as much to offer. Engage in community tourism, join the fervor of a festival or do the culturally fascinating Lares trek through remote Andean villages.

p192

Central Highlands

Architecture ✓✓
Detouring ✓✓
Festivals ✓✓✓

Architecture

Forgotten cities such as Ayacucho and Huancavelica offer better insights into Peru's colonial heyday than the likes of Cuzco: they may lack preservation funds but haven't been spoilt by Western chain stores either: wander the ancient streets and be transported back in time.

Detouring

The Central Highlands still resembles the Andes of the good old days: proper adventures through spectacular gorges on wheezing buses along abysmal roads to towns or temples seldom seen by tourists.

Festivals

When just one valley boasts a festival for every day of the year, you know a party is likely. Here they take their revelry seriously – as would be expected from the region responsible for South America's best Semana Santa celebrations. Río Mantaro towns are the most fiesta-prone.

p269

North Coast

Ruins ✓✓✓
Food ✓✓✓
Beaches ✓✓

Ruins

It's not hard to channel your inner Indiana Jones along Peru's North Coast, where practically under every grain of sand this sweeping dune desertscape reveals yet another largely intact antediluvian ruin.

Food

Peru's iconic dish, ceviche (raw fish marinated in citrus juices and chili pepper, served with onions, corn and sweet potato), was a major player in the country's gastronomic renaissance and there's no better stretch of sand for a seafood crusade than Peru's North Coast.

Beaches

It would be odd to come all the way to Peru for a beach vacation, but once you're here, you might be pleasantly surprised as you dip your toes into the ample sands of Huanchaco, Colán, Máncora or Punta Sal.

p307

Huaraz & the Cordilleras

Trekking ✓✓✓
Outdoors ✓✓
Ruins ✓✓

Trekking

The majestic peaks of the Cordillera Blanca, Cordillera Negra and Cordillera Huayhuash peer down on some of the most iconic trails in South America, offering a near endless array of treks over a plethora of varied terrains and postcard-perfect scenery.

Outdoors

Opportunities in the Cordilleras aren't limited to trekking – these stately mountains afford a bounty of open-air adventures, from casual mountain biking, horseback riding and rock-climbing day trips to more serious ice climbing and mountaineering endeavors.

Ruins

Highlighted by the don't-miss Unesco ruins at Chavín de Huántar, one of Peru's most important and fascinating primordial sites, there are wonderful opportunities in the Cordilleras to break up the outdoor lovefest with a little ancient culture.

p362

Northern Highlands

Nature ✓✓✓
Ruins ✓✓
Food ✓✓

Nature

From the impressive 771m Gocta waterfall to birding opportunities galore and numerous new nature lodges, the Northern Highlands holds its own when it comes to getting out and about into some of Peru's most impressive landscapes.

Ruins

Second only to Machu Picchu in awe, the excellently preserved ruins of Kuélap, tucked away in misty-eyed cloud forest near Chachapoyas, is reason alone to venture into this neck of the woods.

Food

Peru's coastal cuisine is more famous, but the jungle-influenced recipes of Tarapoto and Chachapoyas will raise the hairs on your taste buds as well. Wash it all down with regional elixirs soaked in wild roots and vines and toast to La Selva.

p403

Amazon Basin

Adventure ✓✓✓
Wildlife ✓✓✓
Festivals ✓✓

Adventure

Trekking amid foliage so thick you have to slice through it; navigating rivers in dug-out canoes like 17th-century explorers; soaring through the canopy on ziplines. The Amazon is synonymous with adventure and it's hard to come here without having one.

Wildlife

It's not just anacondas or giant creepy-crawlies, nor is it rose-colored river dolphins, the scarlet flash of cock-of-the-rocks found only in Manu's cloud forests, or jaguar sightings – it's the search for these creatures, and the fun you'll have en route that makes Amazon wildlife-watching unmissable.

Festivals

Only one thing to do in all that heat? Enjoy yourself! The Amazon's two premier parties are among Peru's best – conveniently occurring within a week of each other in June: San Juan (Iquitos) and Selvámanos (Oxampampa).

p436

> Every listing is recommended by our authors, and their favorite places are listed first

> Look out for these icons:

 TOP CHOICE Our author's top recommendation

 A green or sustainable option

 FREE No payment required

On the Road

Lima

Includes »

Best Places to Eat

» Central (p84)
» Astrid y Gastón (p84)
» El Verídico de Fidel (p82)
» El Rincón que no Conoces (p89)
» El Enano (p84)

Best Places to Stay

» 3B Barranco B&B (p80)
» Backpacker's Family House (p77)
» DUO Hotel Boutique (p75)

Why Go?

With fog bundling its colonial facades and high rises, it takes a little imagination to get beyond the grit of Lima's first impression. After Cairo, this sprawling metropolis is the second-driest world capital, rising above a long coastline of crumbling cliffs. To enjoy it, climb on the wave of chaos that spans from high-rise condos built alongside pre-Columbian temples, and fast Pacific breakers rolling toward noisy traffic snarls. Think one part southern Cali doused with a heavy dose of *America Latina*.

But Lima is also a sophisticate, with civilization that dates back millennia. Stately museums display sublime pottery; galleries debut edgy art; solemn religious processions date back to the 18th century and crowded nightclubs pulse with tropical beats. No visitor can miss the capital's culinary genius, part of a gastronomic revolution more than 400 years in the making.

This is Lima. Shrouded in history, gloriously messy and full of aesthetic delights. Don't even think of missing it.

When to Go

Lima

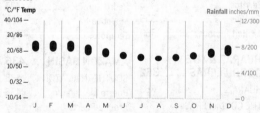

°C/°F Temp / Rainfall inches/mm

Dec–Mar The hottest, blue-sky months ideal for surf and sun on the coast.

Year-round A mild and dry climate means comfortable capital visits throughout the year.

Late Aug Colorful processions mark the festival of Santa Rosa de Lima, the country's first saint.

City Cuisine

In Lima, food inspires as much reverence as religion. So, the agonizing question is, what to eat? Start by sampling these local staples:

Lima's most tender beef-heart skewers, *anticuchos*, can be found in a simple street cart (Anticuchos de la Tía Grima, p85) and a posh Miraflores eatery (Panchita, p87).

Sublime renditions of the country's most seductive dish, ceviche, can be found in places both economical (El Verídico de Fidel, p82) and upscale (Pescados Capitales, p84); for something truly different, try it seared (Fiesta, p85).

The country's fusion cuisine, Criollo cooking – a singular blend of Spanish, Andean, Chinese and African influences – is without parallel at neighborhood cheapie Rincón Chami (p86), El Rincón que No Conoces (p89) and the super-chic Restaurant Huaca Pucllana (p85).

First-rate service, encyclopedic wine lists, and sculptural dishes that blend the traditional and the nouveau find their apex at Astrid y Gastón (p84) and Malabar (p83).

Celebrating the humble potato, *causas* are cold potato dishes that are as beautiful as they are delectable, and are found in any traditional restaurant.

DON'T MISS

One serious eating event, **Mistura** (www.mistura.pe) is Lima's prestigious weeklong international food fair held every September. Get a ticket and sample an astonishing diversity of delicacies, from the finest restaurants to the best street food.

Lima's Best Museums

» Museo Larco (p65), with its naughty erotic pots, is anything but routine. The world's largest private collection of pre-Columbian art now offers night-time visits, with dining and an illuminated courtyard.

» Fundación Museo Amano (p67) only takes private tours, so this appointment-only collection offers the most intimate glimpse of ancient textiles and ceramics.

» Museo de Arte de Lima (p63) has undergone a total renovation infusing this grande dame of belle arts with new energy.

» Monasterio de San Francisco (p57) is a trove of centuries-old catacombs but also houses texts dating from before the conquest and astonishing colonial fittings.

» Museo Pedro de Osma (p68) provides visitors with a taste of colonial times in a gorgeous setting decorated with exquisite Cuzco School canvases and relics from the viceroyalty.

MAIN POINTS OF ENTRY

International flights arrive at Lima's Aeropuerto Internacional Jorge Chávez. There is no main bus terminal. Buses for regional and international destinations leave through their respective terminals throughout Lima.

Fast Facts

» Population: 8.5 million
» Area: 800 sq km
» Elevation: sea level

Top Tip

The same street can have several names as it traverses Lima, such as Av Arequipa (aka Garcilaso de la Vega or Wilson). Some names reappear in different districts, so indicate the right neighborhood to taxi drivers. Streets also may change names – for practicality we have used the most common names.

Resources

» www.lonelyplanet.com/peru/lima
» www.livinginperu.com
» www.peru.travel
» www.saexplorers.org
» www.munlima.gob.pe
» lima.dailysecret.com

Lima Highlights

1 Biting into Peruvian delicacies at the innovative restaurants of **Miraflores** (p84)

2 Sipping potent pisco cocktails at the vintage bars and chic lounges of **Barranco** (p90)

3 Admiring pre-Columbian masterpieces, from sublime tapestries to intricate goldwork at **Museo Larco** (p65)

4 Exploring sandy ruins with several civilizations' worth of temples at **Pachacamac** (p99)

5 Leaping off the Miraflores cliff tops and **paragliding** (p72) among the high-rises with the Pacific Ocean filling the horizon

6 Gazing upon the skulls of some of Latin America's most celebrated saints at the **Iglesia de Santo Domingo** (p57) in Central Lima

7 Strolling or cycling the colonial neighborhoods of **Barranco** (p68) and the lush coastal parks of **Miraflores** (p67)

History

As ancient as it is new, Lima has survived regular apocalyptic earthquakes, warfare and the rise and fall of civilizations. This resilient city has welcomed a rebirth after each destruction. In pre-Hispanic times, the area served as an urban center for the Lima, Wari, Ichsma and even the Inca cultures in different periods.

When Francisco Pizarro sketched out the boundaries of his 'City of Kings' in January of 1535, there were roughly 200,000 indigenous people living in the area. By the 18th century, the Spaniards' tumbledown village of adobe and wood had given way to a vice-regal capital, where fleets of ships arrived to transport the golden spoils of conquest back to Europe. After a disastrous earthquake wiped out much of the city in 1746, it was rebuilt with splendorous baroque churches and ample *casonas* (mansions). The city's prominence began to fade after independence in 1821, when other urban centers were crowned capitals of newly independent states.

In 1880, Lima was ransacked and occupied by the Chilean military during the War of the Pacific (1879–83). As part of the pillage, the Chileans made off with thousands of tomes from the National Library (they were returned in 2007). Postwar expansion meant that by the 1920s Lima was crisscrossed by a network of broad boulevards inspired by Parisian urban design. When another devastating earthquake struck in 1940, the city again had to rebuild.

By the mid-1900s the population was growing exponentially. An influx of rural poor took the metro area from 661,000 inhabitants in 1940 to 8.5 million by 2007. The migration was particularly intense during the 1980s, when armed conflicts in the Andes displaced many people. Shantytowns mushroomed, crime soared and the city fell into a period of steep decay. In 1992, the terrorist group Sendero Luminoso (Shining Path) detonated deadly truck bombs in middle-class Miraflores, marking one of Lima's darkest hours.

Today's Lima has been rebuilt to an astonishing degree. A robust economy and a vast array of municipal improvement efforts have repaved the streets, refurbished parks and created safer public areas to bring back a thriving cultural and culinary life.

LAY OF THE LAND

With over 30 municipalities, Lima's historic heart is Lima Centro (Central Lima). Av Arequipa, one of the city's principal thoroughfares, plunges southeast toward well-to-do San Isidro, the contemporary seaside neighborhood of Miraflores, and Barranco to the south.

The principal bus routes connecting Central Lima with San Isidro and Miraflores run along broad avenues such as Tacna, Garcilaso de la Vega and Av Arequipa. These neighborhoods are also connected by the short highway Paseo de la República or Vía Expresa, known informally as *el zanjón* (the ditch).

◉ Sights

The city's historic heart, Lima Centro (Central Lima) is a grid of crowded streets laid out in the 16th-century days of Francisco Pizarro, and home to most of the city's surviving colonial architecture. Well-to-do San Isidro is Lima's banking center and one of its most affluent settlements. It borders the contiguous, seaside neighborhood of Miraflores, which serves as Lima's contemporary core, bustling with commerce, restaurants and nightlife. Immediately to the south lies Barranco, a former resort community transformed into a hip bohemian center with hopping bars and nice areas to stroll.

CENTRAL LIMA

Bustling narrow streets are lined with ornate baroque churches in the city's historic and commercial center, located on the south bank of the Río Rímac. Few colonial mansions remain since many have been lost to expansion, earthquakes and the perennially moist weather.

Plaza de Armas Area

Plaza de Armas   PLAZA

(Map p58) Lima's 140-sq-meter Plaza de Armas, also called the Plaza Mayor, was not only the heart of the 16th-century settlement established by Francisco Pizarro, it was a center of the Spaniards' continent-wide empire. Though not one original building remains, at the center of the plaza is an impressive bronze fountain erected in 1650.

Surrounding the plaza are a number of significant public buildings: to the east resides the **Palacio Arzobispal** (Archbishop's Palace), built in 1924 in a colonial style and boasting some of the most exquisite Moorish-style balconies in the city. To the northeast is the block-long **Palacio de Gobierno**, a grandiose baroque-style building from 1937 that serves as the residence of Peru's president. Out front stands a handsomely uniformed presidential guard (think French Foreign Legion, c 1900) that conducts a changing of the guard every day at noon – a ceremonious affair that involves slow-motion goose-stepping and the sublime sounds of a brass band playing 'El Cóndor Pasa' as a military march.

Though the palace is no longer regularly open to visitors, it hosts occasional public exhibits, which require a 48-hour advance reservation. Check the website for a schedule and reserve through the **Office of Public Relations** (☑311-3900; www.presiden cia.gob.pe; ☺8:30am-1pm & 2:30-5:30pm Mon-Fri). The web page offers a virtual tour (click on 'Visita Virtual') showing the building's lavish interiors.

La Catedral de Lima CATHEDRAL
(Map p58; ☑427-9647; museum S10; ☺9am-5pm Mon-Fri, 10am-1pm Sat) Next to the Archbishop's palace, the cathedral resides on the plot of land that Pizarro designated for the city's first church in 1535. Though it retains a baroque facade, the building has been built and rebuilt numerous times: in 1551, in 1622 and after the earthquakes of 1687 and 1746. The last major restoration was in 1940.

A craze for all things neoclassical in the late 18th century left much of the interior (and the interiors of many Lima churches) stripped of its elaborate baroque decor. Even so, there is plenty to see. The various chapels along the nave display more than a dozen altars carved in every imaginable style, and the ornate wood **choir**, produced by Pedro de Noguera in the early 17th century, is a masterpiece of rococo sculpture. A **museum**, in the rear, features paintings, vestments and an intricate sacristy.

By the cathedral's main door is the **mosaic-covered chapel** with the remains of Pizarro. Their authenticity came into question in 1977, after workers cleaning out a crypt discovered several bodies and a sealed lead box containing a skull that bore the inscription, 'Here is the head of the gentleman Marquis Don Francisco Pizarro, who found and conquered the kingdom of Peru…' After a battery of tests in the 1980s, a US forensic scientist concluded that the body previously on display was of an unknown official and that the brutally stabbed and headless body from the crypt was

---

LIMA IN...

Two Days

Start with a walking tour of the city's colonial heart. For lunch, try the historic **El Cordano** (p82) or the lovely **Domus** (p82). Afterwards, view the Chancay pottery inside a pristine historic mansion at the **Museo Andrés del Castillo** (p62) and end the day with a most important pilgrimage: a pisco sour at **El Bolivarcito** (p89), the renowned bar inside the Gran Hotel Bolivar.

On the second day, you can go pre-Columbian or contemporary: view breathtaking Moche pottery at the **Museo Larco** (p65) or see a gripping exhibit on the Internal Conflict at the **Museo de la Nación** (p64). In the afternoon, grab an espresso from **Café Bisetti** (p88) and stroll through the clifftop gardens of **Barranco** (p68); you could also visit **Huaca Pucllana** (p68), the centuries-old adobe temple in the middle of Miraflores. Spend the evening sampling *novoandina* cuisine at one of the city's many fine restaurants.

Three Days

Seeking something colonial? In the morning, visit the exquisite **Museo Pedro de Osma** (p68) in Barranco to view some of the most intriguing Cuzco School canvases and an abundance of relics from the days of the viceroyalty. Otherwise, make the day trip to **Pachacamac** (p99) to stand amid arid ruins dating back almost two millennia. Spend the afternoon haggling for crafts at the **Mercado Indio** (p92) in Miraflores.

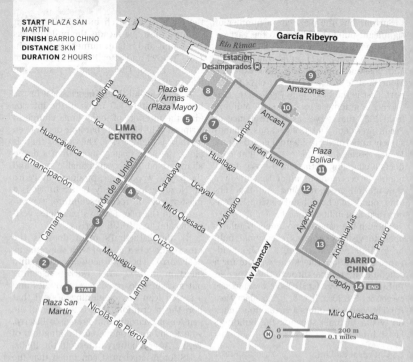

START PLAZA SAN MARTÍN
FINISH BARRIO CHINO
DISTANCE 3KM
DURATION 2 HOURS

Walking Tour
Downtown Lima

Begin your day in ❶ **Plaza San Martín**, and imbibe the faded grandeur of ❷ **Gran Hotel Bolívar**, the city's first fine hotel. Walk the pedestrian street of ❸ **Jirón de la Unión**; once the heart of aristocratic city life, it's now lined with cinemas and bargain shoe stores. To the right is ❹ **Iglesia de la Merced**, originally built in 1541. It held the first Mass in Lima. Peek inside for a glimpse of the impressive mahogany altars.

The boulevard ends at the centerpiece of the city, the ❺ **Plaza de Armas**, surrounded by palms and ornate canary-yellow buildings. In the era of the viceroys it served as market, bullpen and even execution site for the condemned. The restored ❻ **La Catedral de Lima** houses the once-misplaced remains of conquistador Francisco Pizarro in an inscribed lead box. On the adjacent corner, the ❼ **Palacio Arzobispal** (Archbishop's Palace) has some of the city's best-preserved ornate Moorish balconies, perfectly designed for absconding people-watchers.

To the northeast, the grandiose baroque ❽ **Palacio del Gobierno** serves as Peru's presidential palace – pass at noon for the ceremonious changing of the guard with a brass band tapping out 'El Condor Pasa.'

The palace backs up against the Río Rimac. Follow behind it to ❾ **Parque de la Muralla**, a spacious city park installed alongside remains of the original city wall. Return via Amazonas to Lampa and ❿ **Monasterio de San Francisco** to check out the monastery's compelling catacombs that hold skulls and bones laid out in geometric designs.

Cross the avenida to ⓫ **Plaza Bolívar** and Congress, passing the ghoulish ⓬ **Museo de la Inquisición**, where only wax figures are tortured in the basement. Follow Ayacucho two blocks to the ⓭ **Mercado Central**, with stalls of goods from soccer jerseys to piles of tropical and Andean fruit. Take the pedestrian street Capón to ⓮ **El Barrio Chino** (Chinatown) for tea or lunch at a Cantonese eatery.

Pizarro's. Head and body were reunited and transferred to the chapel, where you can also view the inscribed lead box.

Guide services in Spanish, English, French, Italian and Portuguese are available for an additional fee.

Iglesia de Santo Domingo CHURCH
(Map p58; ☑427-6793; cnr Camaná & Conde de Superunda; church free, convent S5; ⊙9am-1pm & 5-7:30pm Mon-Sat) One of Lima's most storied religious sites, the Iglesia de Santo Domingo and its expansive **monastery** are built on land granted to the Dominican Friar Vicente de Valverde, who accompanied Pizarro throughout the conquest and was instrumental in persuading him to execute the captured Inca Atahualpa. Originally completed in the 16th century, this impressive pink church has been rebuilt and remodeled at various points since. It is most renowned as the final resting place for three important Peruvian saints: San Juan Macías, Santa Rosa de Lima and San Martín de Porres (the continent's first black saint). The convent – a sprawling courtyard-studded complex lined with baroque paintings and clad in vintage Spanish tiles – contains the saints' tombs. The church, however, has the most interesting relics: the skulls of San Martín and Santa Rosa, encased in glass, in a shrine to the right of the main altar. (For background on the saints of colonial Peru, see boxed text, p492.)

Monasterio de San Francisco MONASTERY
(Map p58; ☑426-7377; www.museocatacum bas.com; cnr Lampa & Ancash; adult/child under 15 S7/1; ⊙9:30am-5:30pm) This bright yellow Franciscan monastery and church is most famous for its bone-lined catacombs (containing an estimated 70,000 remains) and its remarkable library housing 25,000 antique texts, some of which predate the conquest. But this baroque structure has many other treasures: the most spectacular is a geometric Moorish-style cupola over the main staircase, which was carved in 1625 (restored 1969) out of Nicaraguan cedar. In addition, the refectory contains 13 paintings of the biblical patriarch Jacob and his 12 sons, attributed to the studio of Spanish master Francisco de Zurbarán.

Admission includes a 30-minute guided tour in English or in Spanish. Tours leave as groups gather.

FREE **Iglesia de la Merced** CHURCH
(Map p58; ☑427-8199; cnr Jirón de la Unión & Miró Quesada; ⊙10am-noon & 5-7pm) The first Latin Mass in Lima was held in 1534 on a small patch of land now marked by the Iglesia de la Merced. Originally built in 1541, it was rebuilt several times over the course of the next two centuries. Most of today's structure dates to the 18th century. The most striking feature is the imposing granite facade, carved in the *churrigueresque* manner (a highly ornate style popular during the late Spanish baroque period). Inside, the nave is lined with more than two-dozen magnificent baroque and Renaissance-style altars, some carved entirely out of mahogany.

To the right as you enter is a large silver cross that once belonged to Father Pedro Urraca (1583–1657), renowned for having had a vision of the Virgin. This is a place of pilgrimage for Peruvian worshippers, who come to place a hand on the cross and pray for miracles.

FREE **Santuario de Santa Rosa de Lima** CHURCH
(Map p58; ☑425-1279; cnr Tacna & Callao; ⊙7:30am-noon & 5-8pm) Honoring the first saint of the Americas, this plain, terracotta-hued church on a congested avenue is located roughly at the site of her birth. The modest adobe sanctuary in the gardens was built in the 17th century for Santa Rosa's prayers and meditation.

FREE **Casa-Capilla de San Martín de Porres** CHURCH
(Map p58; ☑423-0707; Callao 535; ⊙9am-1pm & 3-6pm Mon-Fri, 9am-1pm Sat) Right across the street from the Santuario de Santa Rosa de Lima, this building (now a center of religious study) commemorates the birthplace of San Martín. Visitors are welcome to view the bright interior patios and diminutive chapel.

FREE **Iglesia de las Nazarenas** CHURCH
(Map p58; ☑423-5718; cnr Tacna & Huancavelica; ⊙7am-1pm & 5-9pm) One of Lima's most storied churches was part of a 17th-century shantytown inhabited by former slaves. One of them painted an image of the Crucifixion on a wall here. It survived the devastating earthquake of 1655 and a church was built around it (the painting serves as the centerpiece of the main altar) in the 1700s. The church has been rebuilt many

Centro Histórico

0 — 400 m
0 — 0.2 miles

RIMAC

LIMA CENTRO

BARRIO CHINO

To Convento de los Descalzos (700m)

Río Rímac

Estación Monserrate (FFCC)

Alfonso Ugarte

Plaza Castilla

Plaza 2 de Mayo

Av Colonial de Mayo

Iglesia Nuestra Señora de Monserrate

Iglesia de Santo Domingo

Puente Santa Rosa

Puente de Piedra

Puente Ricardo Palma

Puente Balta

Parque de la Muralla

Monasterio de San Francisco

Estación Desamparados

Plaza de Armas (Plaza Mayor)

Plaza Bolívar

Congreso

Pasaje de los Escribanos

García Ribeyro

Streets
Jr Hualgayoc
Cajamarca
Patáz
Libertad
Lambayeque
Loreto
Chiclayo
Marañón
Trujillo
Pataz
Ayabaca
Conde de Superunda
Callao
Riviera Bravo
Oroya
Tayacaja
Angaraes
Ica
Cañete
Chancay
Tacna
Huancavelica
Emancipación
Moquegua
Ocoña
Nicolás de Piérola (Colmena)
Zepita
Chota
Quilca
Pinillos
Rufino Torrico
Camaná
Caylloma
Jirón de la Unión
Camaná
Carabaya
Lampa
Ucayali
Miró Quesada
Cuzco
Azángaro
Ancash
Huallaga
Jr Junín
Av Abancay
Ayacucho
Paruro
Capón
Andahuaylas
Amazonas
R Benavides

Numbered markers
48, 18, 3, 17, 44, 59, 20, 1, 36, 55, 19, 12, 23, 14, 53, 21, 10, 38, 26, 34, 52, 39, 32, 31, 49, 37, 7, 5, 9, 29, 11, 47, 41, 28, 54, 50, 57, 42, 27, 35, 61, 15, 60, 30, 33, 2, 25, 6, 8, 16, 51, 43, 4

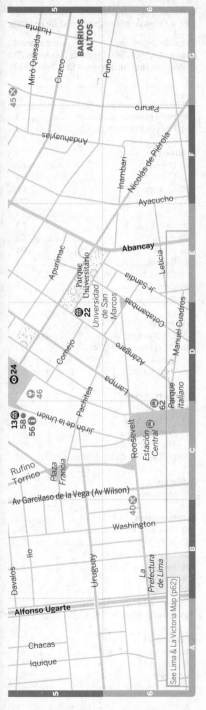

times since but the wall endures; on October 18 each year a representation of the mural, known as 'El Señor de los Milagros' (Christ of Miracles), is carried around in a tens-of-thousands-strong procession that lasts for days.

FREE **Iglesia de San Pedro** CHURCH

(Map p58; ☑428-3010; www.sanpedrodelima.org; cnr Azángaro & Ucayali; ⊙8:30am-1pm & 2-4pm Mon-Fri) This small 17th-century church is considered to be one of the finest examples of baroque colonial-era architecture in Lima. Consecrated by the Jesuits in 1638, it has changed little since. The interior is sumptuously decorated with gilded altars, Moorish-style carvings and glazed tiles.

FREE **Iglesia de San Agustín** CHURCH

(Map p58; ☑427-7548; cnr Ica & Camaná; ⊙8-9am & 4:30-7:30pm Mon-Fri) This church has an elaborate *churrigueresque* facade (completed in 1720), replete with stone carvings of angels, flowers, fruit and, of course, St Augustine. Limited operating hours can make it a challenge to visit. The interiors are drab, but the church is home to a curious woodcarving called 'La Muerte' (Death) by 18th-century sculptor Baltazar Gavilán. As one (probably fictional) story goes, Gavilán died in a state of madness after viewing his own chilling sculpture in the middle of the night. The piece sometimes travels, so call ahead.

Palacio Torre Tagle HISTORIC BUILDING

(Map p58; Ucayali 363; ⊙closed Sat & Sun) The most immaculate of Lima's historic *casonas* was completed in 1735, with its ornate baroque portico (the best one in Lima) and striking Moorish-style balconies. Unfortunately, it is now home to Peru's Foreign Ministry, so entry is restricted. Groups and educational organizations, however, can request a tour in advance via the **oficina cultural** (☑311-2400).

Casa Aliaga HISTORIC BUILDING

(Map p58; http://casadealiaga.com; Jirón de la Unión 224; ⊙9:30am-1pm, 2:30-5:45 Mon-Fri) Innocuously tucked on a side street by the post office is Casa Aliaga, which stands on land given in 1535 to Jerónimo de Aliaga, one of Pizarro's followers, and which has been occupied by 16 generations of his descendants. It may not look like much from the outside, but the interiors are lovely, with vintage furnishings and tile work. It can also be visited via organized excursions with Lima Tours (p96).

Casa de la Riva HISTORIC BUILDING
(Map p58; Ica 426; admission S5; ☺10am-1pm & 2-4pm Mon-Fri) This handsome, 18th-century

mansion features beautiful wooden balconies, an elegant patio and period furnishings.

Casa de Oquendo HISTORIC BUILDING
(Map p58; ☎427-7987; Conde de Superunda 298; ☺9am-5pm Mon-Fri, 9am-noon Sat) Two blocks

to the north of the Casa de la Riva, the cornflower blue Casa de Oquendo is a ramshackle turn-of-the-19th-century house (in its time, the tallest in Lima) with a creaky lookout tower that, on a clear day, has views of Callao. Arrange tours for small groups ahead of time with a suggested donation.

Casa de Riva-Aguero HISTORIC BUILDING
(Map p58; ☑626-6600; Camaná 459; admission S2; ☺10am-1pm, 2-7pm Mon-Fri) Toward the center of downtown, this traditional *casona* houses the small Museum of Art & Popular Tradition.

FREE **Casa de Pilatos** HISTORIC BUILDING
(Map p58; ☑427-5814; Ancash 390; ☺8am-1pm & 2-5pm Mon-Fri) East of the plaza, the lovely red Casa de Pilatos is home to offices for the Tribunal Constitucional (Supreme Court). Access is a challenge: visitors are only allowed into the courtyard provided there aren't official meetings going on. Enter through the side door on Azángaro.

Elsewhere in Central Lima

FREE **Parque de la Muralla** PARK
(Map p58; ☑427-4125; Amazonas, btwn Lampa & Av Abancay; ☺9am-9pm) During the 17th century, the heart of Lima was ringed by a *muralla* (city wall), much of which was torn down in the 1870s as the city expanded. However, you can view a set of excavated remains at the Parque de la Muralla, where, in addition to the wall, a small on-site museum (with erratic hours) details the development of the city and holds a few objects.

More interestingly, the park is home to a bronze statue of Francisco Pizarro created by American sculptor Ramsey MacDonald in the early 20th century. The figure once commanded center stage at the Plaza de Armas, but over the years has been displaced as attitudes toward Pizarro have grown critical. The best part: the figure isn't even Pizarro – it's an anonymous conquistador of the sculptor's invention. MacDonald made three copies of the statue. One was erected in the US; the other, Spain. The third was donated to the city of Lima after the artist's death in 1934 (and after Mexico rejected it). So now, Pizarro – or, more accurately, his proxy – sits at the edge of this park, a silent witness to a daily parade of amorous Peruvian teens.

FREE **Museo Banco Central de Reserva del Perú** MUSEUM
(Map p58; ☑613-2000, ext 2655; www.bcrp.gob.pe/proyeccion-institucional/museo.html; cnr Lampa & Ucayali; ☺10am-4:30pm Tue-Fri, 10am-1pm Sat & Sun) Housed in a graceful bank building, the Museo Banco Central de Reserva del Perú is a well-presented overview of several millennia of Peruvian art, from pre-Columbian gold and pottery to a selection of 19th- and 20th-century Peruvian canvases. Don't miss the watercolors by Pancho Fierro on the top floor, which provide an unparalleled view of dress and class in 19th-century Lima. Identification is required for admittance.

FREE **Museo Postal y Filatélico** MUSEUM
(Postal & Philatelic Museum; Map p58; ☑428-0400; Conde de Superunda 170; ☺9am-5pm Tue-Fri, 9am-1pm Sat & Sun) Everything you've ever wanted to know about the Peruvian mail system can be found at the Museo Postal y Filatélico next to the main post office.

FREE **Museo de la Inquisición** MUSEUM
(Map p58; ☑311-7777, ext 5160; www.congreso.gob.pe/museo.htm; Jirón Junín 548; ☺9am-5pm) A graceful neoclassical structure facing the Plaza Bolívar houses this diminutive museum, where the Spanish Inquisition once plied its trade. In the 1800s, the building was expanded and rebuilt into the Peruvian senate. Today, guests can tour the basement, where morbidly hilarious wax figures are stretched on racks and flogged – to the delight of visiting eight-year-olds. The old 1st-floor library retains a remarkable baroque wooden ceiling. Entry is by half-hour guided tours, conducted in Spanish and English, after which you are free to wander.

Jirón de la Unión HISTORIC SITE
(Map p58) In the late 19th and early 20th centuries, the five pedestrian blocks on Jirón de la Unión, from the Plaza de Armas to Plaza San Martín, was *the* place to see and be seen. The street has long since lost its aristocratic luster, but the shells of neocolonial and art-deco buildings survive. Watch out for pickpockets who work the crowds during street performances.

Plaza San Martín PLAZA
(Map p58) Built in the early 20th century, Plaza San Martín has come to life in recent years as the city has set about restoring its park and giving the surrounding beaux-arts

Lima & La Victoria

architecture a much-needed scrubbing. It is especially lovely in the evenings, when it is illuminated. The plaza is named for the liberator of Peru, José de San Martín, who sits astride a horse at the center of the plaza. At the base, don't miss the bronze rendering of Madre Patria, the symbolic mother of Peru. Commissioned in Spain under instruction to give the good lady a crown of flames, nobody thought to iron out the double meaning of the word flame in Spanish (*llama*), so the hapless craftsmen duly placed a delightful little llama on her head.

The once-stately **Gran Hotel Bolívar** (p74), built in the 1920s, presides over the square from the northwest.

Museo Andrés del Castillo   MUSEUM
(Map p58; ☏433-2831; www.madc.com.pe; Jirón de la Unión 1030; admission S10; ☺9am-6pm, closed Tue) Housed in a pristine 19th-century mansion with Spanish-tile floors, this worthwhile new private museum showcases a vast

collection of minerals, as well as breathtakingly displayed Nazca textiles and Chancay pottery, including some remarkable representations of Peruvian hairless dogs.

Panteón de los Próceres   MONUMENT
(Map p58; ☏427-8157; Parque Universitario; ☺10am-5pm) Located inside a little-visited 18th-century Jesuit church, this monument pays tribute to Peruvian battle heroes, from Túpac Amaru II, the 18th-century Quechua leader who led an indigenous uprising, to José de San Martín, who led the country to independence in the 1820s. The mosaic-lined crypt holds the remains of Ramón Castilla, the four-time Peruvian president who saw the country through a good piece of the 19th century. The impressive baroque altar, carved out of Ecuadorean mahogany, dates to the 1500s.

Museo de la Cultura Peruana   MUSEUM
(Museum of Peruvian Culture; Map p58; ☏423-5892; http://museodelacultura.perucultural.org.

Lima & La Victoria

pe; Alfonso Ugarte 650; admission S3.60; ⊘10am-5pm Tue-Fri, 10am-2pm Sat) About half-a-dozen blocks west of the Plaza San Martín, on a traffic-choked thoroughfare, resides the Museo de la Cultura Peruana, a repository of Peruvian folk art. The collection, consisting of elaborate *retablos* (religious dioramas) from Ayacucho, historic pottery from Puno and works in feathers from the Amazon, is displayed in a building whose exterior facade is inspired by pre-Columbian architecture.

Museo de Arte de Lima   MUSEUM
(Map p62; ☎204-0000; www.mali.pe; Paseo Colón 125; adult/child S12/4; ⊘10am-5pm, closed Wed) Known locally as MALI, Lima's principal fine-art museum is housed in a striking beaux-arts building that was recently renovated. Subjects span from pre-Columbian to contemporary art, and there's also guided visits to special exhibits. On Sunday, entry is just S1. A satellite museum is under construction in Barranco.

Parque de la Cultura   PARK
(Map p62) Originally known as Parque de la Exposición, this newly revamped park has gardens and a small amphitheater for outdoor performances. Two of Lima's major art museums reside here.

Museo de Arte Italiano   MUSEUM
(Italian Art Museum; Map p62; ☎423-9932; Paseo de la República 250; adult/child S3/1; ⊘10am-5pm Mon-Fri) Just north of MALI, the Museo de Arte Italiano exhibits a tepid collection of 19th- and 20th-century Italian academic art.

Its best attribute is the glittering Venetian mosaics on the exterior walls.

El Circuito Mágico del Agua   FOUNTAIN
(Map p62; Parque de la Reserva, Av Petit Thouars, cuadra 5; admission S4; ⊘4pm-10pm) This indulgent series of illuminated fountains is so over the top it can't help but induce stupefaction among even the most hardened traveling cynic. A dozen different fountains – all splendiferously illuminated – are capped, at the end, by a laser light show at the 120m-long Fuente de la Fantasía (Fantasy Fountain). The whole display is set to a medley of tunes comprised of everything from Peruvian waltzes to ABBA. Has to be seen to be believed.

Museo de Historia Natural   MUSEUM
(Natural History Museum; off Map p62; ☎471-0117; http://museohn.unmsm.edu.pe; Arenales 1256, Jesús María; adult/child S7/5; ⊘9am-5pm Mon-Sat, 10am-1:30pm Sun) One block west of cuadra 12 off Av Arequipa, south of the Parque de la Reserva, the Museo de Historia Natural run by the Universidád de San Marcos, has a modest taxidermy collection that's a useful overview of Peruvian fauna.

RÍMAC
Rímac can be a rough neighborhood. Taxis or organized tours are the best options for the following sights:

Museo Taurino   MUSEUM
(Bullfight Museum; Map p58; ☎481-1467; Hualgayoc 332; admission S5; ⊘9am-6pm Mon-Fri) Plaza

STRANGEST SADDEST CITY

Visit Lima in winter (April through October) and you will likely find it steeped – day after day – in the fog known as *garúa*. It is relentless, a mist that turns the sky an alabaster white and leaves the city draped in a melancholy pall. Interestingly, this otherworldly microclimate has been the source of much literary inspiration. The most famous citation is in none other than *Moby Dick* by Herman Melville, who visited Lima in the 1800s. It is 'the strangest saddest city thou can'st see,' he wrote. 'For Lima has taken the white veil; and there is a higher horror in this whiteness of her woe.'

Countless Peruvian writers have also chronicled *garúa*, including the Nobel-winning Mario Vargas, a native *limeño*. In his 1964 treatise, *Lima la Horrible* (Lima the Horrible), essayist Sebastián Salazar Bondy describes the mist as a 'tenacious *garúa*, a floating powder, a cold fog.' Novelist Alfredo Bryce Echenique compared it to 'the belly of a dead whale,' while Daniel Alarcón depicted it as 'heavy, flat and dim, a dirty cotton ceiling.'

So why would the Spanish build the capital of their Andean empire at the one point on the coast regularly blanketed by this ghostly fog? Well, they likely wouldn't have known. Francisco Pizarro established the city on January 18 – right in the middle of summer – when the skies are blue every day.

de Acho, Lima's bullring, was built on this site north of the Río Rímac in 1766. Some of the world's most famous toreadors passed through here, among them the renowned Manolete from Spain. A visit includes a free guided tour inspecting cluttered displays of weapons, paintings, photographs and the gilded outfits worn by a succession of bullfighters – gore holes, blood stains and all.

Cerro San Cristóbal   LOOKOUT

This 409m-high hill to the northeast of Central Lima has a **mirador** (lookout) at its crown, with views of Lima stretching off to the Pacific (in winter expect to see nothing but fog). A huge **cross**, built in 1928 and illuminated at night, is a Lima landmark and the object of pilgrimages during Semana Santa (Holy Week) and the first Sunday in May. There is a small **museum** (admission S1). From the Plaza de Armas, taxis can take you to the summit (from S16) or you can wait for the **Urbanito bus** (☎428-5841; www.urbanito.com.pe; Jr Manoa 391, Breña; per person S5; ☺10am-/pm), on the southwest corner of the plaza, which does a one-hour round-trip tour to the summit. Buses run every 30 minutes.

Convento de los Descalzos   MUSEUM

(Map p58; ☎481-0441; Alameda de los Descalzos s/n; admission S6; ☺10am-1pm & 3-6pm, closed Tue) At the end of the attractive Alameda de los Descalzos, forgotten, is this 16th-century convent and museum, run by the Descalzos ('the Barefooted,' a reference to Franciscan friars). Visitors can see old winemaking equipment in the kitchen, a refectory, an infirmary and the monastic cells. There are also some 300 colonial paintings, including noteworthy canvases by renowned Cuzco School artist Diego Quispe Tito. Spanish-speaking guides give 45-minute tours. Taxis from the Plaza de Armas start at about S10.

EAST LIMA

The city begins to rise into the foothills of the Andes as you turn east, an area carpeted with government buildings and teeming residential districts.

Museo de la Nación   MUSEUM

(Museum of the Nation; ☎476-9878; Av Javier Prado Este 2466, San Borja; admission S7; ☺9am-6pm Tue-Sun) A brutalist concrete tower houses the catch-all Museo de la Nación, which provides a cursory overview of Peru's civilizations, from Chavín stone carvings and the knotted-rope *quipus* (used for record-keeping) of the Incas to artifacts from the colony. Large traveling international exhibits are also shown here (often for an extra fee), but if there is a single reason to visit this museum, it is to view a permanent installation on the 6th floor called **Yuyanapaq** (www.pnud.org.pe/yuyana paq/yuyanapaq.html). The exhibit, named after the Quechua word meaning 'to remember,' is a moving and beautifully installed photographic tribute to the Internal Conflict (1980–2000) created by Peru's Truth & Reconciliation Commission in 2003. For students of contemporary Latin American history it's an absolute must-see. (For more on the Commission, see the boxed text, p503.)

From San Isidro, you can catch one of the many buses or *combis* (minivans) heading east along Av Javier Prado Este toward La Molina.

Museo de Oro del Perú   MUSEUM
(Gold Museum of Peru; ☑345-1292; www.museor operu.com.pe; Alonso de Molina 1100, Monterrico; adult/child under 11 S33/16; ☺10:30am-6pm) The now notorious Museo de Oro del Perú, a private museum, was a Lima must-see until 2001, when a study revealed that 85% of the museum's metallurgical pieces were fakes. It reopened with an assurance that works on display are bona fide, though descriptions classify certain pieces as 'reproductions.' The cluttered, poorly signed exhibits still leave something to be desired.

Of greater interest (and, in all likelihood, of greater authenticity) are the thousands of weapons presented in the Arms Museum, on the museum's ground floor. Here, in various jumbled rooms, you'll find rifles, swords and guns from every century imaginable, including a firearm that once belonged to Fidel Castro.

Go via taxi or *combi* Museum of the Nation heading northeast on Angamos toward Monterrico and get off at the Puente Primavera. From there, it's a 15-minute stroll north to the museum.

Asociación Museo del Automóvil   MUSEUM
(Automobile Museum; ☑368-0373; www.museo delautomovilnicolini.com; Av La Molina, cuadra 37, cnr Totoritas, La Molina; adult S20; ☺9:30am-7pm) The Asociación Museo del Automóvil has an impressive array of classic cars dating back to 1901, from a Ford Model T to a Cadillac Fleetwood used by four Peruvian presidents.

SAN ISIDRO & POINTS WEST

A combination of middle- and upper-class residential neighborhoods offer some important sights of note.

Museo Larco   MUSEUM
(☑461-1312; http://museolarco.org; Bolívar 1515, Pueblo Libre; adult/child under 15 S30/15; ☺9am-10pm) An 18th-century viceroy's mansion houses this museum, which has one of the largest, best-presented displays of ceramics in Lima. Founded by Rafael Larco Hoyle in 1926, a dedicated collector and cataloguer of all things pre-Columbian, the collection is said to include more than 50,000 pots (thousands are housed in glass storerooms, which visitors can also see). The museum showcases ceramic works from the Cupisnique, Chimú, Chancay, Nazca and Inca cultures, but the highlight is the sublime Moche portrait vessels, presented in simple, dramatically lit cases. Equally astonishing is a Wari weaving in one of the rear galleries that contains 398 threads to the linear inch – a record. There's also gold and jewels. Many visitors are lured here by a separately housed collection of pre-Columbian erotica illustrating all manner of sexual activity with comical explicitness. Don't miss the vitrine that depicts sexually transmitted diseases.

The highly recommended on-site Café del Museo (mains S28-40) faces a private garden draped in bougainvillea and is a perfect spot for ceviche.

Catch a bus from Av Arequipa in Miraflores marked 'Todo Bolívar' to Bolívar's 15th block. A painted blue line on the sidewalk links this building to the Museo Nacional de Antropología, Arqueología e Historía del Perú, about a 15-minute walk away.

Museo Nacional de Antropología, Arqueología e Historía del Perú   MUSEUM
(National Anthropology, Archaeology & History Museum; ☑463-5070; http://museonacional.peru cultural.org.pe; Plaza Bolívar, cnr San Martín & Vivanco, Pueblo Libre; adult/child S10/1; ☺9am-5pm Tue-Sat, 9am-4pm Sun) The Museo Nacional de Antropología, Arqueología e Historía del Perú traces the history of Peru from the pre-ceramic period to the early republic. Displays include the famous Raimondi Stela, a 2.1m rock carving from the Chavín culture, one of the first Andean cultures to have a widespread, recognizable artistic style. The building was once the home of revolutionary heroes San Martín (from 1821 to 1822) and Bolívar (from 1823 to 1826) and the museum contains late-colonial and early republic paintings, including an 18th-century rendering of the *Last Supper* in which Christ and his disciples feast on *cuy* (guinea pig).

From Miraflores, take a 'Todo Brasil' *combi* from Av Arequipa (just north from Óvalo) to cuadra 22 on the corner of Vivanco, then walk seven blocks up that street. A blue line connects this museum with Museo Larco.

Huaca Huallamarca   RUIN
(Map p76; ☑222-4124; Nicolás de Rivera 201, San Isidro; adult/child S5.50/1; ☺9am-5pm Tue-Sun)

Miraflores

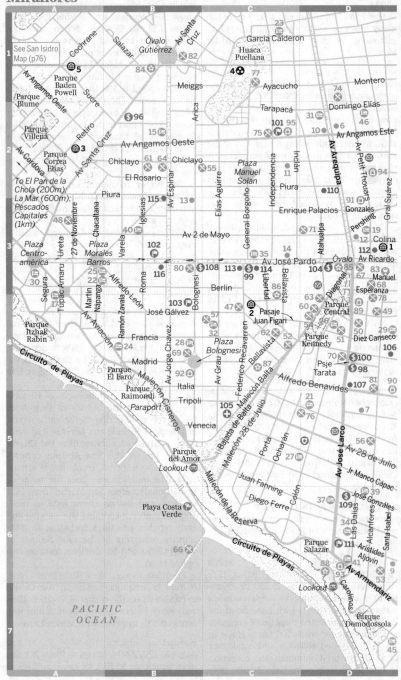

Av Santa Cruz
Cochrane
Salazar
Óvalo Gutiérrez
García Calderón
23
Huaca Puellana
84
4
77
See San Isidro Map (p76)
5
Parque Baden Powell
Meiggs
Ayacucho
Montero
74
Av Angamos Oeste
Parque Blume
Sucre
Retiro
Tarapacá
Domingo Elías
31
6
46
Parque Villena
96
Av Santa Cruz
15
Av Angamos Oeste
101 95
75
10
Av Angamos Este
3
Chiclayo
61 64
Chiclayo
55
Plaza Manuel Solan
Inclán
11
Piura
110
91
94
Av Cordova
Parque Correa Elias
El Rosario
Av Espinar
Enrique Palacios
Gonzales
Pershing
To El Pan de la Chola (200m); La Mar (600m); Pescados Capitales (1km)
48
Chacaltana
Piura
13
115
40
Iglesias
Av 2 de Mayo
General Borgoño
71
Atahualpa
19
12
Plaza Centro-américa
Ureta
27 de Noviembre
Plaza Morales Barros
Varela
102
35
14
Av José Pardo
Óvalo
Av Ricardo
112
1
104
85
83
67
68
78
30
25
22
Martín Napanga
Alfredo León
Roma
116
80 108
113 114
99
Bellavista
Libertad
86
Berlin
Diagonal
63
89
49
Segura
Túpac Amaru
Ramón Zavala
103
José Gálvez
47
2 Pasaje Juan Figari
60
Parque Central
50
29
106
Parque Itzhak Rabin
Av Aviación
Francia
28
57
32
69
62
52
Parque Kennedy
51
Diez Canseco
Parque El Faro
Madrid
92
Plaza Bolognesi
Bellavista
87
70 100
98
Malecón Cisneros
Italia
105
21
107
81
90
Parque Raimondi
Paraport
Tripoli
76
7
Venecia
Malecón 28 de Julio
Malecón Balta
Alfredo Benavides
Psje Tarata
Parque del Amor Lookout
Porta
Ochirán
27
56
Av 28 de Julio
Av José Larco
Playa Costa Verde
Juan Fanning
Colón
37
Jr Manco Cápac
José Gonzáles
39
109
Diego Ferre
Malecón de la Reserva
34
Las Dalias
Alcanfores
Santa Isabel
66
Parque Salazar
111
88
93
41
Aristides Aljovin
9
Circuito de Playas
Lookout
Carolinas
Av Armendáriz
PACIFIC OCEAN
Parque Domodossola
45

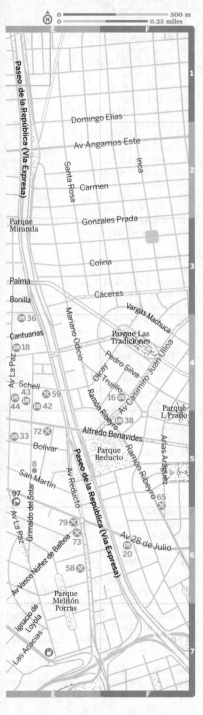

Nestled among condominium towers and sprawling high-end homes, the simple Huaca Huallamarca is a highly restored adobe pyramid, produced by the Lima culture, that dates to somewhere between AD 200 and 500. A small on-site museum, complete with mummy, details its excavation.

Bosque El Olivar   PARK

(Map p76) This tranquil park, a veritable oasis in the middle of San Isidro, consists of the remnants of an old olive grove, part of which was planted by the venerated San Martín de Porres in the 17th century.

MIRAFLORES

The city's bustling, modern hub – full of restaurants, shops and nightspots – overlooks the Pacific from a set of ragged cliffs.

FREE Fundación Museo Amano   MUSEUM

(Map p66; ☎441-2909; www.museoamano.org; Retiro 160; ☺3-5pm Mon-Fri, by appointment only) The well-designed Fundación Museo Amano features a fine private collection of ceramics, with a strong representation of wares from the Chimú and Nazca cultures. It also has a remarkable assortment of lace and other textiles produced by the coastal Chancay culture. Museum visits are allowed by a one-hour guided tour only, in Spanish or Japanese.

Museo Enrico Poli Bianchi   MUSEUM

(Map p66; ☎422-2437; Cochrane 400; admission S50; ☺4-6pm Tue-Fri, by appointment only) The pricey, private Museo Enrico Poli Bianchi holds a lavish collection of gold textiles, colonial silver and paintings featured in *National Geographic,* and is only available for visits by prearranged tours in Spanish.

Choco Museo   MUSEUM

(Map p66; ☎445-9708; Berlin 375; www.chocomuseo.com; admission S2; ☺10:30am-8:30pm) On-site chocolate production is the seducing factor of this new 'museum' selling fondue and fair-trade hot cocoa. French-owned (with an outlet in Cuzco), it is already well known for organic chocolate-making workshops (S70 per person).

Casa de Ricardo Palma   HISTORIC BUILDING

(Map p66; ☎617-7115; Gral Suárez 189; adult S6; ☺10am-1pm & 3-5pm Mon-Fri) This house was the home of the Peruvian author Ricardo Palma from 1913 until his death in 1919. A listless tour is included in the price.

Miraflores

Huaca Pucllana RUIN
(Map p66; ☎617-7138; cnr Borgoño & Tarapacá; admission S7; ⊙9am-4:30pm Wed-Mon) Located near the Óvalo Gutiérrez, this *huaca* is a restored adobe ceremonial center from the Lima culture that dates back to AD 400. In 2010, an important discovery of four Wari mummies was made, untouched by looting.

Though vigorous excavations continue, the site is accessible by regular guided tours in Spanish (for a tip). In addition to a tiny on-site museum, there's a celebrated restaurant (p85) that offers incredible views of the illuminated ruins at night.

BARRANCO

A tiny resort back at the turn of the 20th century, Barranco is lined with grand old *casonas,* many of which have been turned into eateries and hotels.

Puente de los Suspiros BRIDGE
(Bridge of Sighs; Map p70) A block west of the main plaza, look for this narrow, wooden bridge over an old stone stairway that leads to the beach. The bridge – especially popular with couples on first dates – has inspired many a Peruvian folk song.

Museo Pedro de Osma MUSEUM
(Map p70; ☎467-0141; www.museopedrodeosm .org; Av Pedro de Osma 423; admission S20;

⊗10am-6pm Tue-Sun) Housed in a lovely beaux-arts mansion surrounded by gardens, this undervisited museum has an exquisite collection of colonial furniture, silverwork and art, some of which dates back to the 1500s. Among the many fine pieces, stand-outs include a 2m-wide canvas that depicts a Corpus Christi procession in turn-of-the-17th-century Cuzco.

Galería Lucía de la Puente   GALLERY
(Map p70; ☑477-9740; www.gluciadelapuente.com; Sáenz Peña 206; ⊗10:30am-8pm Mon-Fri, 11am-8pm Sat) A magnificent two-story *casona* is home to Lima's most prestigious contemporary art gallery. Look for works by cutting-edge painters such as Fernando Gutiérrez, whose canvases often skewer Peruvian culture.

WEST LIMA & CALLAO
To the west of downtown, cluttered lower-middle-class and poor neighborhoods eventually give way to the port city of Callao, where the Spanish once shipped their gold. Travelers should approach Callao with caution, since some areas are dangerous, even during the day.

Parque de Las Leyendas   PARK
(☑717-9878; www.leyendas.gob.pe; Av Las Leyendas 580-86, San Miguel; adult/child S10/5; ⊗9am-6pm) Located between Central Lima and Callao, the zoo covers Peru's major geographical

Barranco

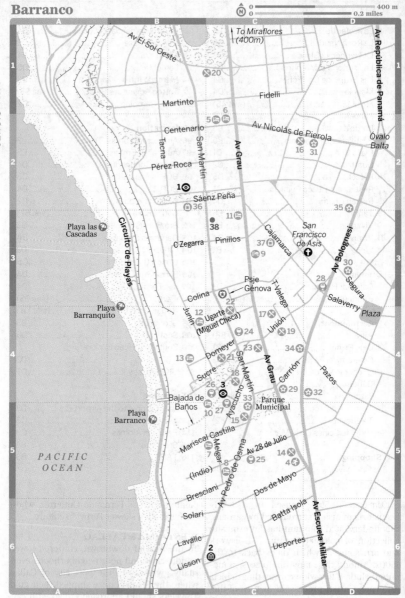

To Miraflores
(400m)

Av El Sol Oeste

Av República de Panamá

Martinto

Fidelli

Centenario

Av Nicolás de Piérola

Tacna

San Martín

Av Grau

Óvalo Balta

Pérez Roca

Playa las Cascadas

Sáenz Peña

San Francisco de Asís

Av Bolognesi

Plaza

C Zegarra

Pinillos

Cajamarca

Segura

Salaverry

Playa Barranquito

Colina

Psje Génova

T Valega

Junín

Ugarte (Miguel Checa)

Unión

Domeyer

San Martín

Carrión

Pazos

Sucre

Av Grau

Playa Barranco

Bajada de Baños

Ayacucho

Parque Municipal

Mariscal Castilla

Melgar

Av 28 de Julio

(Indio)

Av Pedro de Osma

Bresciani

Dos de Mayo

PACIFIC OCEAN

Solari

Batta Isola

Av Escuela Militar

Lavalle

Deportes

Lisson

Circuito de Playas

---

divisions: coast, mountains and jungle. There are 210 native animals, with a few imports (such as hippos). The conditions are OK, and the zoo is well maintained.

In Central Lima, catch buses and *colectivos* (shared taxis) that travel past the park at Av Abancay and Garcilaso de la Vega. These run roughly every 30 minutes.

Fortaleza del Real Felipe   FORT
(☎429-0532; Plaza Independencia, Callao; admission S1; ⊙9am-2pm) In the 1820s, the Spanish

Barranco

royalists made their last stand during the battle for independence at this historic fort, which was built in 1747 to guard against pirates. It still houses a small military contingent. Visits are by guided tours in Spanish only.

On the western flank of the fort, don't miss an opportunity to stroll through the truly bizarre **Parque Temático de la Policía** (Police Park), a nicely landscaped garden that is dotted with police tanks and life-size statues of policemen in riot gear – a perfect place for those surreal family vacation photos.

Note that the nearby dock area is quite a rough neighborhood; travel by taxi.

LA PUNTA

A narrow peninsula that extends west into the Pacific Ocean, La Punta was once a fishing hamlet, and later, in the 19th century, an upscale summer beach resort. Today this pleasant upper-middle-class neighborhood, graced with neocolonial and art-deco homes, is a great spot to stroll by the ocean and enjoy a seafood lunch.

You can take a taxi from Miraflores (about S30). In Central Lima, *combis* traveling to Callao run west along Av Colonial from the Plaza 2 de Mayo. Take the ones labeled 'La Punta.' A good spot to get out is Plaza Gálvez; from here, you can head west all along the waterside Malecón Figueredo, which offers magnificent views of craggy Isla San Lorenzo, just off the coast.

🏃 Activities

Cycling

Popular excursions from Lima include the 31km ride to Pachacamac, where there are good local trails open between April and December. Expert riders can inquire about the stellar downhill circuit from Olleros to San Bartolo south of Lima. For general information (in Spanish) on cycling, try **Federación Deportiva Peruana de Ciclismo** (📞346-3493; www.fedepeci.org; Av San Luis 1308, San Luis) or the online portal **Ciclismo Sin Fronteras Miraflores** (www.ciclismosinfronteras.com). For organized cycling tours from abroad, see international tour companies, p545.

Dozens of bike shops are listed in Lima's Yellow Pages under 'Bicicletas.' Check out the following places:

Bike Tours of Lima
GUIDED TOUR
(Map p66; ☑445-3172; www.biketoursoflima. com; Bolívar 150, Miraflores; ◉9am-7pm Mon-Sat) Highly recommended for organized day tours around Barranco, Miraflores and San Isidro, as well as Sunday excursions into downtown (from S65). Rentals available (from S30 for a half-day).

Perú Bike
GUIDED TOUR
(☑260-8225; www.perubike.com; Punta Sal D7, Surco; ◉9am-1pm & 4-8pm Mon-Sat) A recommended shop that offers mountain-biking tours and repairs.

Paragliding
For paragliding off the Miraflores cliff tops, contact **Peru Fly** (☑993-086-795; www.perufly. com) or **Andean Trail Peru** (http://andean trailperu.com). Flights take off from the cliff-top 'paraport' at the Parque Raimondi (Map p66), starting at S150 for a 15-minute tandem flight. Paragliding companies do not have offices on-site, so if you want to fly, make a reservation in advance – then wave at the bemused shoppers at the cliffside LarcoMar mall as you glide past.

Swimming & Water Sports
Despite the newspaper warnings about pollution, *limeños* hit the beaches in droves in summer (January through March). **Playa Costa Verde** in Miraflores (nicknamed Waikiki) is a favorite of local surfers and has good breaks year-round. Barranco's beaches have waves that are better for long boards. There are seven other beaches in Miraflores and four more in Barranco. Serious surfers can also try **Playa La Herradura** in Chorrillos, which has waves up to 5m high during good swells. Do not leave your belongings unattended as theft is a problem.

The following stores carry surfing equipment:

Big Head
SURFING
(Map p66; ☑818-4156; www.bighead.com.pe; LarcoMar, Malecón de la Reserva 610, Miraflores; ◉11am-10pm) A popular mall chain that sells fashion and gear.

Focus
SURFING
(☑475-8459; www.focussurf.com; Leonardo da Vinci 208, Surquillo; ◉8am-8pm Mon-Fri, 9am-1pm Sat) An established board fabrication outlet, they also run a surf camp south of Lima.

Wayo Whilar
SURFING
(Map p70; ☑247-6343; www.wayowhilar.com.pe; Av Grau 111, Barranco; ◉9am-7pm Mon-Thu, 9am-4pm Fri & Sat) The shop of a longtime Peruvian surfer who sells his own line of hand-shaped surf boards.

Perú Divers
DIVING
(☑251-6231; www.perudivers.com; Santa Teresa 486, Chorrillos) Deep-sea diving off Peru's southern coast is reasonably priced. Luis Rodríguez, a PADI-certified instructor, owns this excellent dive shop with equipment for sale, and offers certification and diving trips. There are regular excursions to Islas Palomino, off the coast of Callao, to see a year-round sea-lion colony.

Courses
Lima has plenty of language schools. The following places are recommended:

Centro de Idiomas
LANGUAGE COURSE
(Map p76; ☑421-2969; www.up.edu.pe/idiomas; Prescott 333, San Isidro) Overseen by the Universidad del Pacífico, it offers a 40-hour semester-long course, available in five levels.

El Sol
LANGUAGE COURSE
(Map p66; ☑242-7763; http://elsol.idiomasperu. com; Grimaldo del Solar 469, Miraflores) Private classes are S65 per hour; one-week courses start at S410.

Idiomas Católica
LANGUAGE COURSE
(Map p76; ☑626-6500; www.idiomas.pucp.edu.pe; Av Camino Real 1037, San Isidro) Managed by the prestigious Catholic University, this program offers five two-hour group classes per week.

Instituto Cultural Peruano-Norteamericano
LANGUAGE COURSE
(ICPNA; ☑706-7000; www.icpna.edu.pe) Central Lima (Cuzco 446); Miraflores (Map p66; Av Arequipa 4798) The institute's various branches offer Spanish courses from qualified instructors.

Museo de la Cultura Peruana
CULTURE COURSE
(Map p58; ☑423-5892; http://museodelacul tura.perucultural.org.pe; Alfonso Ugarte 650) The museum runs limited classes on some Peruvian instruments and folk dances such as the *marinera*.

Tours & Guides
For guided tours of Lima and nearby archaeological sites such as Pachacamac, as well as trips around Peru, try these companies. In

addition, travel agencies (see p95) organize local, regional and national tours. It may be helpful to look for guides registered with **Agotur** (www.agotur.com), the Peruvian guide organization. Another resource is www. leaplocal.com. Telephone numbers are for Peruvian daytime use only.

Aventours ADVENTURE TOUR
(Map p66; ☎444-9060; www.aventours.com; Av Arequipa 4799, Miraflores) Private tours, guided trips and treks throughout the country.

Condor Travel TOUR
(off Map p76; ☎615-3000; www.condortravel.com; Blondet 249, San Isidro) Recommended for top-end touring and custom itineraries throughout the Andes.

Ecoaventura Vida CULTURAL TOUR
(☎461-2555; www.ecoaventuravida.com) Focused on sustainable travel throughout the country, Ecoaventura organizes trips that include homestays with Peruvian families.

Explorandes ADVENTURE TOUR
(Map p66; ☎715-2323; www.explorandes.com; Aristides Aljovín 484, Miraflores) Outdoors travel is the focus, with a specialty in trekking, biking and adventure sports.

Inkanatura ADVENTURE TOUR
(Map p76; ☎203-5000; Manuel Bañon 461; San Isidro) Quality tours throughout Peru, including Chachapoyas and the jungle.

Lima Vision TOUR
(Map p66; ☎447-7710; www.limavision.com; Chiclayo 444, Miraflores) Lima Vision has various four-hour city tours (S70), as well as day trips to the ruins at Pachacamac.

Peru Expeditions ADVENTURE TOUR
(Map p66; ☎447-2057; www.peru-expeditions.com; Colina 151, Miraflores) Books trips and organized tours around the region and beyond, and also specializes in 4WD excursions.

Peru Hands On TOUR
(☎999-542-728; www.peruhandson.com; apt 401, Av La Paz 887, Miraflores) A locally run agency specializing in standard and custom itineraries around Peru.

Respons TOUR
(Map p66; ☎989-526-095; www.responsibletravel peru.com; Arica 329, Miraflores) High-end tours all over Peru, specializing in sustainable tourism.

Arturo Rojas GUIDED TOUR
(☎99-738-9276; www.limatastytours.com) In addition to regular guide services, Arturo can arrange gastronomic tours; speaks English.

Jorge Riveros Cayo GUIDED TOUR
(jorgeriveros@yahoo.com) A fluent English speaker offering city excursions, longer custom trips and gastronomic tours.

Mónica Velásquez GUIDED TOUR
(☎99-943-0796; www.monicatoursperu.com) Reader recommended; speaks English.

Tino Guzman GUIDED TOUR
(☎420-1723, 99-909-5805) Speaks English; member of SAE.

Toshie Matsumura de Irikura GUIDED TOUR
(☎225-6518, 99-757-3924) Speaks Japanese.

✯ Festivals & Events

See p21 for major festivals and special events, and p534 for national holidays. For other events, see local newspapers or visit *The Peru Guide* (www.theperuguide.com). Holidays specific to Lima:

Festival of Lima GENERAL
Celebrates the anniversary of Lima's founding on January 18.

Feast of Santa Rosa de Lima SAINT'S DAY
Held on August 30, this feast has processions in honor of Santa Rosa, the venerated patron saint of Lima and the Americas.

El Señor de los Milagros RELIGIOUS
(Christ of Miracles) The city drapes itself in purple during this massive religious procession on October 18 in honor of the Christ from the Nazarenas church; smaller processions occur other Sundays in October.

🛏 Sleeping

From diminutive family *pensións* to glassy hotel towers armed with spas, Lima has every type of accommodations imaginable. It is also one of the most expensive destinations in the country (other than the tourist mecca of Cuzco).

The favored traveler neighborhood is Miraflores, where you'll find a bounty of hostels, inns and upscale hotel chains. The former seaside resort of Barranco nearby has become a hot neighborhood and is certainly one of the most walkable areas, with lots of gardens and colonial architecture. More upscale – and generally more tranquil – is the financial hub of San Isidro. The best value spots can be found in Central Lima, though it is a little removed from the city's hopping restaurants and nightclubs.

If arriving at night, it's worth contacting hotels in advance to arrange for airport pickup; even budget hostels can arrange this – sometimes for a few dollars less than the official airport service.

CENTRAL LIMA

The city's congested historic heart offers good-value lodging and proximity to some of the most storied attractions. But keep in mind that it's mainly alive during the day. Central Lima has seen its high-end business slip away as upscale establishments have shifted to San Isidro and Miraflores. Although security in downtown has improved greatly, it is advisable to take taxis at night and not to display expensive camera gear or jewelry.

TOP CHOICE **1900 Backpackers** HOSTEL $
(Map p62; ☑424-3358; www.1900hostel.com; Av Garcilazo de la Vega 1588; dm S21-29, d/tw/tr incl breakfast 74/80/111; @🛜) A sudden new hot spot in downtown Lima, this old mansion designed by Gustavo Eiffel has been revamped with modern design touches, though it maintains the marble floors and other turn-of-the-century flourishes. For a hostel it's downright gorgeous. Rooms are smart and simple, with bunks shoulder-to-shoulder. There's a tiny kitchen and cool common spaces, like a pool room with bar and red chandelier. Though the location is riddled with traffic exhaust during the day, there's the plus of having a premier museum right across the street.

Clifford Hotel HOTEL $$
(Map p62; ☑433-4249; www.thecliffordhotel. com.pe; Parque Hernán Velarde 27; s/d/tr/ste incl breakfast S143/169/208/247; @🛜) On a quiet cul-de-sac, this smart hotel occupies an elegant 1930s *casona*. Relax in the common areas with Spanish baroque touches. By contrast, the 21 carpeted rooms are modern, and come equipped with fans, cable TV and telephones. There's a bar, a restaurant and a lovely garden with a fountain.

Gran Hotel Bolívar HISTORIC HOTEL $$
(Map p58; ☑619-7171; Jirón de la Unión 958; s/d/tr S169/195/234; @) For anyone chasing the retro atmosphere of a gilded age, check out this venerable 1924 hotel on the Plaza San

Martín. Figures like Clark Gable, Mick Jagger and Robert Kennedy all tucked in here, once among the most luxurious accommodations in Latin America. Today, it is frayed at the edges, but possesses the rare finesse of a grand dame. It's also employee-owned, a rarity in the hotel world, which translates to impeccable and entertaining service even from the bellhop.

Familia Rodríguez HOMESTAY $
(Map p58; ☑423-6465; jotajot@terra.com.pe; No 201, Nicolás de Piérola 730, apt 201; d incl breakfast S70; @🛜) An early-20th-century building west of the Plaza San Martín houses a sprawling old apartment with parquet floors and spotless bathrooms in this tranquil, well-recommended family homestay. All bathrooms are shared.

Hostal Iquique HOTEL $
(Map p62; ☑433-4724; www.hostaliquique.com; Iquique 758; s/d without bathroom S38/63, s/d/ tr incl breakfast S55/70/82; @) Recommended Iquique is basic but clean and safe, with small, dark, concrete rooms sporting remodeled bathrooms with hot showers. The rooftop terrace features a pool table, and guests get to use shared kitchen facilities. Credit cards are accepted.

Hotel Kamana HOTEL $$
(Map p58; ☑426-7204, 427-7106; www.hotelka mana.com; Camaná 547; s/d/tr incl breakfast S120/150/180; ✳@🛜) Popular with tour groups and business travelers, this secure hotel has 46 tidy, carpeted rooms enlivened by colorful bedspreads. English and French are spoken. Credit cards accepted. An onsite restaurant-cafe is open 24 hours. Overall, very good value.

Pensión Ibarra GUESTHOUSE $
(Map p58; ☑427-8603; pensionibarra@gmail.com; 14th fl, No 152, Tacna 359; s/d without bathroom from S25/35) Inside a scruffy concrete apartment block, the helpful Ibarra sisters keep seven basic guest rooms that are clean and stocked with firm beds. There is a shared kitchen and laundry service. A small balcony has views of the noisy city.

Hostal Bonbini HOTEL $$
(Map p58; ☑427-6477; www.hostalbonbini.com; Cailloma 209; s/d/tr incl breakfast S105/135/165; @) On a street cluttered with print shops, this comfy, 15-room hotel features simple, carpeted rooms, spick-and-span bathrooms

and cable TV. Service could be more attentive, but credit cards accepted.

Hostal Roma HOTEL $
(Map p58; ☑427-7576; www.hostalroma.8m.com; Ica 326; s with/without bathroom S43/35, d S66/53; ☷☎) The 22 tidy rooms here are dull (some are windowless), but they are quiet and set around a sunny interior courtyard. Beds sag – it's hard to expect more from a bargain – but some units feature cable TV. An on-site cafe serves breakfast.

La Posada del Parque HOTEL $$
(Map p62; ☑433-2412, 99-945-4260; www.inca country.com; Parque Hernán Velarde 60; s/d/tr incl breakfast S96/127/164; ☷☎) This graceful Spanish colonial sits on a tranquil, tree-lined oval that once served as Lima's dog-racing track. Small, carpeted rooms have folk-art touches, while public areas display colonial-style paintings and Ayacucho *retablos*. It's run by the very chatty Mónica and her daughter. All rooms have cable TV and luggage storage is available.

Hotel Maury HOTEL $$
(Map p58; ☑428-8188; hotmaury@amauta.rep.net. pe; Ucayali 201; s/tw/d incl breakfast S150/190/240; ☷☷☎) A longtime Lima outpost renowned for cultivating a new-fangled cocktail known as the pisco sour (grape brandy cocktail) back in the 1930s. While public areas retain old-world flourishes such as gilded mirrors and Victorian-style furniture, the 76 simple rooms are modern, some equipped with Jacuzzi tubs and lockboxes. Credit cards accepted.

Lima Sheraton HOTEL $$$
(Map p62; ☑619-3300; www.sheraton.com.pe; Paseo de la República 170; d S1039; ☷☷☎☀) Housed in a brutalist high-rise that overlooks the equally dour Palacio de Justicia (Supreme Court), downtown's top hotel has more than 400 rooms and suites decorated in an array of desert tones. In addition to 24-hour room service, there are concierge services, two on-site restaurants, a bar, a gym, a swimming pool and a beauty salon.

WEST LIMA
Mami Panchita INN $$
(☑263-7203; www.mamipanchita.com; Av Federico Gallesi 198, San Miguel; s/d/tr incl breakfast S69/98/127; ☷☎) In a pleasant neighborhood near Miraflores, this Dutch–Peruvian guesthouse occupies a comfortable and sprawling

Spanish-style house. The owners run an on-site travel agency. It's a great option for families, with rooms that are large and homey, a crib option and a flower-bedecked patio ideal for relaxing.

SAN ISIDRO
Want to fit into San Isidro? Carry a tennis racket. With a hyper-exclusive golf course at its heart, this is the cradle of Lima's elite who inhabit expansive modernist homes and sip cocktails at members-only social clubs. Accommodations are unapologetically upscale, though there are a few other options tucked away among the tree-lined streets.

TOP CHOICE **DUO Hotel Boutique** BOUTIQUE HOTEL $$$
(off Map p76; ☑628-3245; www.duohotelperu. com; Valle Riesta 576; s/d/ste incl breakfast S305/398/437; ☷☷☎☀) With minimalist chic, this intimate hotel features 20 monochromatic rooms outfitted with fresh flowers, soft sheets, slippers and marble baths. Service is excellent and the on-site restaurant offers evening meals that marry the best of Peruvian and Italian flavors. It's on a serene residential street, two blocks west of the Lima Golf Club. Credit cards accepted.

Malka Youth Hostel HOSTEL $
(Map p76; ☑222-5589; www.youthhostelperu.com; Los Lirios 165; dm with/without bathroom S42/30, d S85/70; ☷☎) A quiet hostel in a nice neighborhood just a block from a park, Malka is run by an amiable mother–daughter team. The house features 10 clean rooms, a nice garden space and rock-climbing wall. Breakfast is included. There is a large shared kitchen and laundry facilities, a TV room with DVD player, luggage storage, free wi-fi and a small on-site cafe serving light meals. It's near the transit hub of Av Arequipa and Av Javier Prado.

Country Club Lima Hotel LUXURY HOTEL $$$
(Map p76; ☑611-9000; www.hotelcountry.com; Los Eucaliptos 590; d from S1678; ☷☷☎☀) Set on a sprawling lawn dotted with palms, this regal hotel occupies one of Lima's finest buildings, a sprawling 1927 structure built in the Spanish tradition. Clad in colorful tiles, wood-beam ceilings and replica Cuzco School paintings, its signature feature is a round stained-glass atrium where breakfast is served. The 83 rooms replete with amenities range from the luxurious Master Room to the opulent Presidential Suite. Credit cards accepted.

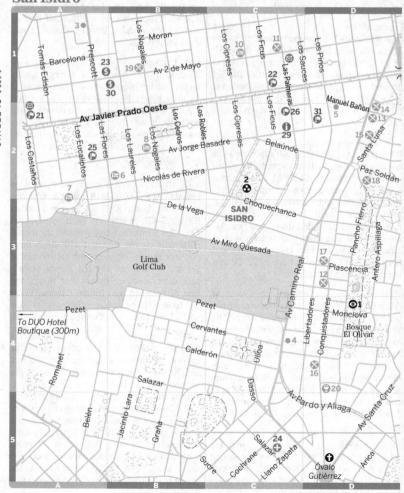

Casa Bella Perú
GUESTHOUSE **$$**

(Map p76; ☑421-7354; www.casabellaperu.net; Las Flores 459; s/d/tr incl breakfast S183/199/262; @🖘) A great midrange option in a relentlessly expensive area, this expansive former 1950s home has contemporary rooms accented by indigenous textiles. Fourteen varied units have comfy beds, firm pillows, oversized plasma TVs and remodeled bathrooms. There is a kitchen, an ample garden and a lounge. Credit cards accepted.

Hotel Basadre Suites
HOTEL **$$**

(Map p76; ☑442-2423; www.hotelbasadre.com; Jorge Basadre 1310; s/d/ste incl breakfast S154/164/197;

🟥@🌊) A good option, this attentive inn has 20 attractive contemporary rooms, some quite spacious. Built around a former private home, each room has a minibar, hair-dryer, cable TV and lockbox. Breakfast, served in a small room by the garden, is abundant. Credit cards accepted; check the website for excellent special offers.

Suites Antique
APARTMENT **$$$**

(Map p76; ☑222-1094; www.suites-antique.com; Av 2 de Mayo 954; s/d/ste incl breakfast S276/315/368; 🟥@) Central and low-key, this small hotel features smart and bright decor. The 23 spotless suites are spacious, with small

San Isidro

kitchenettes equipped with microwaves and a minifridge. Breakfast is served at the cozy in-house cafe.

MIRAFLORES

Overlooking the ocean, this neighborhood's pedestrian-friendly streets teem with cafes, restaurants, hotels, high-rises, banks, shops and nightclubs that pump everything from disco to *cumbia*. There are many quiet blocks, too.

TOP CHOICE Backpacker's Family House HOSTEL **$**
(Map p66; ☎447-4572; www.backpackersfamily house.com; Juan Moore 304; dm/d incl breakfast S27/81; @🛜) This refreshing design hostel occupies a small brick home with parquet floors and graffiti murals. It's vibrant, super clean and uncluttered, with games like foosball and ping-pong and an attentive owner.

TOP CHOICE Miraflores Park Hotel LUXURY HOTEL **$$$**
(Map p66; ☎242-3000; www.miraflorespark. com; Malecón de la Reserva 1035; d from US$921; ✳@🛜🏊) The best of Lima's small luxury hotels, this Orient Express property enjoys

a glorious oceanside setting and every frill. The spiral grand staircase, gorgeous library and infinity pool help foster the fairy-tale atmosphere. Want to indulge? For US$55, the bath butler will run an a salt-infused, petal-strewn, candlelit aphrodisiac bath – with champagne and fresh strawberries. Mesa 18, the on-site restaurant, is currently one of the hottest reservations in town.

Casa San Martín
INN $$

(Map p66; ☏241-4434, 243-3900; www.casasan martinperu.com; San Martín 339; s/d/tr incl breakfast S156/218/273; @🖥🤖) Among the more atmospheric options, this Spanish Revival building is modern and uncluttered, with 20 pleasant, high-ceiling rooms with terra-cotta tiles and Andean textiles. Breakfast is served in a bright cafe that faces the terrace. Credit cards accepted.

Inka Frog
HOTEL $$

(Map p66; ☏445-8979; www.inkafrog.com; Iglesias 271; s/d incl breakfast S103/127; @🤖) As budget lodgings go, this is one of Lima's best. Subdued and friendly, it features ample and spotless modern rooms with fans and flat-screen TVs, some on a cute roof patio. Enjoy the complimentary coffee hour on plush sofas. Staff is helpful and the street is refreshingly quiet.

Hotel Antigua Miraflores
INN $$$

(Map p66; ☏241-6116; www.peru-hotels-inns.com; Av Grau 350; s/d/tr incl breakfast S216/257/351; ✷@🤖) In a converted early-20th-century mansion, this quiet, atmospheric hotel with a lovely courtyard channels colonial charm. Rooms are equipped with the expected modern amenities, but the furnishings display baroque touches. Units vary in size and style; the more expensive ones have Jacuzzi tubs and kitchenettes.

JW Marriott Hotel Lima
HOTEL $$$

(Map p66; ☏217-7000; www.marriotthotels.com/limdt; Malecón de la Reserva 615; d from US$320; ✷@🤖🏊) The lively five-star Marriott has a superb seafront location by the LarcoMar shopping mall, ideal for watching paragliders float outside the glass walls. And if you're nervous about your next flight, you can check the departure and arrival board in the lobby. The rooms sparkle and sport every amenity (though wi-fi costs extra): think minibar, plasma TV and whirlpool bath. There is also an executive lounge, restaurants, a bar, a casino and an open-air tennis court, sauna and pool.

Ekeko Hostel
HOSTEL $

(Map p66; ☏635-5031; Garcia Calderon 274; dm/s/d incl breakfast S27/42/85; @🤖) Tucked into a comfortable middle-class neighborhood, this well-run hostel is a find. A spacious home with a huge kitchen and oversized breakfast table, it also features nonstandard amenities, like hairdryers, and a Japanese-speaking host. Guests will enjoy the nice backyard and impeccable service.

Casa Andina
HOTEL $$$

(☏213-9739; www.casa-andina.com) San Antonio (off Map p66; ☏241-4050; Av 28 de Julio 1088; d incl breakfast S289; ✷@🤖); Miraflores Centro (Map p66; ☏447-0263; Av Petit Thouars 5444; d incl breakfast S397; ✷@🤖); Colección Privada (Map p66; ☏213-4300; Av La Paz 463; d/ste incl breakfast from S982/1291; ✷@🤖🏊) This upmarket Peruvian chain has three hotels at various price points scattered around Miraflores. The San Antonio and Miraflores Centro branches are more affordable, with 50-plus rooms decorated in contemporary Andean color schemes. Colección Privada is the luxury outpost, situated in a tower that once served as the home of the now-defunct Hotel César (where Frank Sinatra once stayed). In a nod to its history, the elegant lobby lounge maintains the grand piano from the storied César. The hotel's 148 chic, earth-palette rooms are spacious, sporting pre-Columbian flourishes and organic bath products. For nightly turndown service, staff leave a deliriously stupendous *cocada* (coconut cookie).

Hotel Ibis
HOTEL $$

(Map p66; ☏634-8888; www.ibishotel.com; Av José Larco 1140; d incl breakfast S183; @🤖) New to Lima, this French hotel chain is a good option with a great location. There's a chic Ikea look, blackout curtains and soundproof windows. The hotel is cleverly divided into smoking and nonsmoking floors, though all rooms are on the small side. Biodegradable toiletries and water-saving policies are a plus. Breakfast is extra.

Albergue Miraflores House
HOSTEL $$

(Map p66; ☏447-7748; www.alberguemiraflore shouse.com; Av Espinar 611; d/tr/q incl breakfast S110/150/190; @🤖) The owner's wanderlust sets the tone for this welcoming hostel tucked into a busy street. For those traveling in groups, it's well worth it, otherwise singles pay the double rate. Guests can make free international calls, there's plenty of on-site games and the location is central.

Hitchhikers
HOSTEL $

(Map p66; ☑242-3008; www.hhikersperu.com; Bolognesi 400; dm/s/d without bathroom S28/64/70, s/d incl breakfast S70/84; @☎) Occupying an enormous century-old *casona*, this longtime hostel has a wide array of rooms. Secure and sleeper-friendly, it includes a lounge with cable TV and a DVD library, while a bare outdoor patio has barbecue facilities and ping-pong. Overall, a good choice.

Pensión Yolanda
GUESTHOUSE $

(Map p66; ☑445-7565; pensionyolanda@hotmail.com; Domingo Elías 230; r per person without bathroom S40, with bathroom S60; @☎) A humble family house with small, basic rooms, some with worn bunk beds and kitchen use. Proprietor Erwin is helpful and versed in languages. Breakfast included.

El Faro Inn
HOTEL $$

(Map p66; ☑242-0339; www.elfaroinn.com; Francia 857; s/d/tr incl breakfast S106/159/212; @☎) You'll find this quiet option behind a row of international flags (there is no sign) close to the relaxing cliff-top park on the north side of Miraflores. Rooms are airy and well appointed; only some have wi-fi.

La Casa Nostra
INN $$

(Map p66; ☑241-1718; www.lacasanostraperu.com; Grimaldo del Solar 265; s/d/tr incl breakfast S110/140/180; @☎) All the charm of this Spanish-style *casona* goes into the shared spaces, including a vintage wood-beamed ceiling in the lobby. By contrast, the seven rooms are clean but not very interesting, with mattresses that are a bit flat and narrow single beds.

Hotel Esperanza
HOTEL $$

(Map p66; ☑444-2411; www.hotelesperanza.com.pe; Esperanza 350; s/d/tr incl breakfast S119/146/186; ☎) A friendly spot. Baroque-style furniture and satin bedspreads provide an unusual juxtaposition to the somewhat monastic 39 brick rooms. Advantages: it is clean, functional and has a central location.

Hostal El Patio
GUESTHOUSE $$

(Map p66; ☑444-2107; www.hostalelpatio.net; Diez Canseco 341A; s/d incl breakfast S126/156, s/d superior S156/186; @☎) On a quiet side street just steps from the Parque Kennedy, this gem of a guesthouse is named for its plant-filled courtyard with a trickling fountain. With a cheery English- and French-speaking owner, it features small, spotless rooms with cast-iron beds and colonial-style art. A few are equipped with small kitchenettes and minifridges. Check the website for special offers.

Hotel Alemán
HOTEL $$

(Map p66; ☑445-6999; www.hotelaleman.com.pe; Av Arequipa 4704; s/d/tr incl breakfast S143/169/195; @☎) A rowdy boulevard gives way to the surprisingly charming 23-room hotel built around a Spanish *casona*. Simple, stuccoed rooms are decorated with Peruvian textiles and colonial-style furnishings and cable TV, telephones, desks and minifridges. Credit cards accepted.

Condor's House
HOSTEL $

(Map p66; ☑446-7267; www.condorshouse.com; Napanga 137; dm S28-33, d/tr S98/140; @☎) In a good location, this hostel fosters mild chaos, with weekend barbeques and live music, ping-pong and a bar. Be warned: private doubles feature bunks, and baths have electric showers. There's a nice back patio for lounging, but not much locked storage space.

Hotel San Antonio Abad
HOTEL $$

(Map p66; ☑447-6766; www.hotelsanantonioabad.com; Ramón Ribeyro 301; s/d incl breakfast S159/199; @☎) A bright yellow mansion from the 1940s houses this pleasant, reader-recommended hotel. There are 24 ample dark-paneled rooms (some with air-con) with cable TV and soundproofed windows. Breakfast is served on a terrace facing the garden. Free airport pickup can be arranged with advance reservation. Credit cards are accepted.

Hotel Señorial
HOTEL $$$

(Map p66; ☑445-7306, 445-1870; www.senorial.com; José González 567; s/d/tr incl breakfast S191/267/333; @☎) This longtime hotel features over 100 rooms and a pleasant grassy courtyard. Think standard, with cable TV and perfunctory stabs at decoration. Credit cards accepted.

Hostal Torreblanca
HOTEL $$

(Map p66; ☑447-3363; www.torreblancaperu.com; Av José Pardo 1453; s/d/tr incl breakfast S159/195/240) The lobby may be cramped and the hallways narrow, but the clean, modern rooms in this Spanish-style building are comfortable. A few on the top floor have wood-beamed ceilings, red tilework and fireplaces. Rooms have down duvets and feature cable TV, minibars and telephones. Credit cards are accepted.

Hotel Bayview
HOTEL **$$**

(Map p66; ☎445-7321; www.bayviewhotel.com.pe; Las Dalias 276; s/d/tr incl breakfast S169/221/229; @🖤) A simple, pleasant hotel with restaurant, painted salmon pink. It has carpeted rooms adorned with folksy Peruvian paintings and amenities like minibars and cable TV. It tends to fill up.

Hotel El Doral
HOTEL **$$$**

(Map p66; ☎242-7799; www.eldoral.com.pe; Av José Pardo 486; s/d incl breakfast S237/264; ❄@🖤💧) All business on the outside, these 39 shiny suites (think 1980s) face a pleasant, plant-filled interior. All units have cable TV, minibars and sitting areas – plus double-glazed windows to block out the noise. Breakfast is served on a rooftop terrace that faces the pool.

Hotel Ariosto
HOTEL **$$$**

(Map p66; ☎444-1414; www.hotelariosto.com.pe; Av La Paz 769; s/d/tr incl breakfast S286/312/364; ❄@🖤) This seven-story hotel has colonial-meets-the-1960s Peruvian formality. A sprawling modernist lobby sports oversized leather couches and baroque art flourishes, while the 96 spacious, carpeted rooms are equipped with king-size beds. There is a small business center and a lounge area, and the buffet breakfast is immense. Rates include free airport pickup.

La Castellana
INN **$$**

(Map p66; ☎444-4662; www.castellanahotel.com; Grimaldo del Solar 222; s/d/tr incl breakfast S167/199/233; 🖤) In a stucco mansion, this 42-room inn has pleasant but dark rooms, many around a lovely garden courtyard where breakfast is served. Rooms sport an '80s decor, some without wi-fi signals, so check ahead when booking.

La Paz Apart Hotel
APARTMENT **$$$**

(Map p66; ☎242-9350; www.lapazaparthotel.com; Av La Paz 679; s/d ste incl breakfast S336/420, 2-bedroom ste S700; ❄@🖤) This modern high-rise may have a businesslike demeanor, but the service is attentive and the rooms comfortable. Twenty-five super-clean suites, all equipped with kitchenettes, minifridges and separate sitting areas, are tastefully decorated. The most spacious sleeps up to five. The hotel also has a minigym and a small conference room.

Flying Dog Hostel
HOSTEL **$$**

(Map p66; ☎444-5753; www.flyingdogperu.com; Lima 457; dm S30, d with/without bathroom S90/66;@🖤) Of Flying Dog's four Lima hostels, this is the best, featuring a lovely outdoor garden bar and 3rd-floor lounge area with expansive views over Parque Kennedy. Two kitchens make for a shorter cooking queue, and the included breakfast is taken at the terrace restaurant across the park.

Albergue Turístico Juvenil Internacional
HOSTEL **$$**

(Map p66; ☎446-5488; www.limahostell.com.pe; Av Casimiro Juan Ulloa 328; dm S48, s/d S124/135; @💧) This first-generation youth hostel caters mostly to groups. Dorms are spotless, and ample private rooms feature homey decorations, but the vibe is a little dull (save for the friendly pooches). Infrastructure is a strength, with ample kitchen facilities and a spacious backyard with a pool.

Friend's House
HOSTEL **$**

(Map p66; ☎446-6248; friendshouse_peru@yahoo.com.mx; Jirón Manco Cápac 368; dm/d incl breakfast S20/S50) Overtaken by young dudes, this backpacker haunt is unpretentious and sociable, though dorms are cramped and a little worn. There's kitchen privileges and a small lounge with cable TV.

Explorer's House
HOSTEL **$**

(Map p66; ☎241-5002; evaaragon_9@hotmail.com; Alfredo León 158; dm/s/d without bathroom S28/64/70, s/d incl breakfast S70/84; @) Bare bones, this hostel is somewhat frayed and busy with Spanish-speaking guests. The management is very sweet and there's a shared kitchen, wi-fi and a rooftop terrace with views.

BARRANCO

At the turn of the 20th century, this was a summer resort for the upper-crust. In the 1960s, it was a center of bohemian life. Today, it is cluttered with restaurants and bustling bars, its graceful mansions converted into hotels of every price range.

TOP CHOICE 3B Barranco B&B
B&B **$$**

(Map p70; ☎247-6915; www.3bhostal.com; Centenario 130; s/d incl breakfast S146/175; @🖤) Cool, clean and modern, this new service-oriented boutique hotel is poised to be a traveler favorite. A common area charged with Warholesque pastiche art leads to 16 minimalist rooms with plush burlap-colored bed covers, polished concrete vanities and windows opening on lightboxes of tended greenery. For the price, it's great value.

TOP CHOICE One Hostel Peru
GUESTHOUSE $$

(Map p70; ☎247-7989; www.operu.com; Av Grau 717; dm S35, s with/without bathroom S120/70, d with/without bathroom S120/90; @☜) This old home with patterned tiles, high ceilings and cozy spaces is more of a comfortable home-away-from-home than a party hostel. But what makes the difference is Melissa, the smiling owner with an arsenal of insider tips. Breakfast includes fresh fruit and juice; there are also bikes for guests to use.

Second Home Perú
B&B $$$

(Map p70; ☎247-5522; www.secondhomeperu. com; Domeyer 366; d/ste incl breakfast S286/325; @☜⊠) With a fairy-tale feel, this lovely five-room Bavarian-style *casona* has claw-foot tubs, sculpted ironworks, a swimming pool and breathtaking views of the ocean. Run by the children of artist Victor Delfín, it features private gardens with his taurine sculptures, works of other artists and a sculpting studio available for rent. Credit cards accepted.

Backpackers Inn
HOSTEL $

(Map p70; ☎247-1326; www.barrancobackpack ersinn.com; Mariscal Castilla 260; dm/tw incl breakfast S27/92) A standout option, this British-run eight-room backpacker hang-out is housed in a renovated mansion on a quiet street with 24-hour security. Dorms are ample, some with ocean views. There's a kitchen, help with trips and tours, a TV lounge and convenient access to Bajada de Baños, leading to the beach.

Aquisito B&B
GUESTHOUSE $$

(Map p70; ☎247-0712; www.aquisito.com.pe; Centenario 114; s incl breakfast S65-80, d incl breakfast S95-110; @☜) Eight simple, immaculate rooms of various sizes make up this cozy, modern B&B in a convenient location. Rooms on the street are louder. Shared spaces are a little cramped but the staff is amenable and it's excellent value. There is no sign.

D'Osma B&B
B&B $$

(Map p70; ☎251-4178; www.deosma.com; Av San Pedro de Osma 240; d/tr incl breakfast from S95/111; @☜) A tranquil family home with a cute patio, this five-room B&B has small carpeted rooms with skylights and fans. Some English and German are spoken. The only drawback is the noisy street outside – try for a back room. There is no obvious sign; look for the wooden gate.

Hostal Gémina
HOTEL $$

(Map p70; ☎477-0712; hostalgemina@yahoo.com; Av Grau 620; s/d/tr incl breakfast S135/175/216; @☜) Tucked into a small shopping gallery, this welcoming surprise offers 31 spacious units. Though tacky and somewhat dated, they're ship-shape. There's an ample living room, and clean, modern rooms feature TVs and folksy textiles. Credit cards accepted.

Hostal Kaminu
B&B $

(Map p70; ☎252-8680; www.kaminu.com; Bajada de Baños 342; dm S25-30, d without bathroom S70-100; @) Tiny and rambling, this hostel sits in the thick of Barranco nightlife – for better or worse. Highlights include an ambient rooftop deck.

Point Lodge
HOSTEL $

(Map p70; ☎247-7997; www.thepointhostels.com; Junín 300; dm S27-35, d with shared bathroom S70; @☜) Reminiscent of a well-worn fraternity house, this long-running party hostel is equipped with all the toys that backpackers love: cable TV, a DVD collection, free internet, pool and ping-pong, a garden with hammocks and a convenient in-house bar.

✖ Eating

The gastronomic capital of the continent, Lima is where you will find some of the country's most sublime culinary creations: from simple *cevicherías* (ceviche counters) and corner *anticucho* (beef-heart skewer) stands to fusion meccas where the cuisine is bathed in foam. Lima's prime position on the coast gives it access to a wide variety of staggeringly fresh seafood, while its status as a centralized capital assures the presence of all manner of regional specialties.

You'll find cocktails infused with Amazon berries, nutty chicken stews from Arequipa (*ají de gallina*) and one of the country's most exquisite renderings (outside of Chiclayo) of Chiclayo-style *arroz con pato* (rice and duck), slowly simmered in cilantro, garlic and beer. The city has such a vast assortment of cuisine, in fact, that it's possible to spend weeks here without beginning to taste it all. Pack your appetite; you'll need it.

CENTRAL LIMA

Miraflores and San Isidro may have the city's trendiest restaurants, but Central Lima's downtown spots offer cheap deals and history, from functional *comedores* (simple dining rooms) packed with office workers to atmospheric eateries that count Peruvian presidents among the clientele. *Menús* (set meals) in the vicinity of S10 can be found at many of the cheaper restaurants.

TOP CHOICE El Verídico de Fidel
CEVICHE $$

(www.elveridicodefidel.com; Abtao 935, La Victoria; ceviches S20-40; ⊗noon-5pm) Not just a *cevichería* but a place of pilgrimage, this hole-in-the-wall across from the Alianza Lima stadium is renowned for its *leche de tigre* (ceviche broth), served not in the typical shot glass but in a soup bowl, studded with fresh seafood. The ceviches are equally spectacular. This is a rough neighborhood; take a taxi – even in the daytime.

Cevichería la Choza Nauticà
CEVICHE $$

(Map p62; ☑423-8087; www.lachozanautica. pe; Breña 204; ceviches S20-36, mains S19-39; ⊗8am-11pm Mon-Sat, 8am-9pm Sun) A surprisingly bright spot in a slightly dingy area, this popular *cevichería*, tended to by bow-tied waiters, offers more than a dozen types of ceviches and *tiraditos* (Japanese-style ceviche, without onions). There is also a long list of soups, seafood and rice dishes. Live music plays on busy nights.

Domus
PERUVIAN $

(Map p58; ☑427-0525; Miró Quesada 410; 3-course menús S16; ⊗9am-4:30pm Mon-Fri) A restored 19th-century mansion houses this modern-yet-intimate two-room restaurant that caters to journalists from the nearby offices of *El Comercio*. There is no à la carte dining, just a rotating daily list of well-executed Peruvian–Italian specialties that always includes a vegetarian option in the mix. Freshly squeezed juices accompany this well-tended feast. Excellent value; highly recommended.

A LA LIMEÑA

Many restaurants in Lima tone down the spices on some traditional dishes for foreign travelers. If you like your cooking spicy *(picante)*, tell them to turn up the heat by asking for your food *a la Limeña* – Lima-style.

El Cordano
CAFETERIA $

(Map p58; ☑427-0181; Ancash 202; mains S8-26; ⊗8am-9pm) A Lima institution since 1905, this old-world dining hall has served practically every Peruvian president for the last 100 years (the presidential palace is right across the street). It is known for its skillfully rendered *tacu tacu* (pan-fried rice and beans) and *butifarra* (French bread stuffed with country ham).

L'Eau Vive
FRENCH $$

(Map p58; ☑427-5612; Ucayali 370; mains S30, 3-course menús S15-30; ⊗12:30-3pm & 7:30-9:30pm Mon-Sat) In an 18th-century building, this very simple and somewhat unusual eatery is run by French Carmelite nuns. Expect French and other continental specialties (think *coquilles St Jacques*) – with various Peruvian influences. The food isn't jaw-dropping, but the real reason to come is to enjoy the strange serenade. Every night, after dinner (at around 9pm), the nuns gather to sing 'Ave Maria.'

Wa Lok
CHINESE $$

(Map p58; ☑447-1329, 427-2750; Paruro 878; mains S10-80; ⊗9am-11pm Mon-Sat, 9am-10pm Sun) Serving seafood, fried rice as light and fresh as it gets, and sizzling meats that come on steaming platters, Wa Lok is among the best *chifas* (Chinese restaurants) in Chinatown. The 16-page Cantonese menu includes dumpling, noodles, stir-fries and a good selection of vegetarian options (try the braised tofu casserole). Portions are enormous; don't over-order.

El Chinito
SANDWICHES $

(Map p58; ☑423-2197; Chancay 894; sandwiches S10; ⊗8am-10pm Mon-Sat, 8am-1pm Sun) Nearly half a century old, this venerable downtown outpost, clad in Spanish tile, is *the* spot for heaping sandwiches stuffed with a bevy of fresh-roasted meats: turkey, pork, beef, ham – and the most popular, *chicharrón* (fried pork) – all served with a traditional marinade of red onions, hot peppers and cilantro.

Tanta
CAFE $$

(Map p58; ☑428-3115; Pasaje de los Escribanos 142; mains S21-46; ⊗9am-10pm Mon-Sat, 9am-6pm Sun) One of several informal bistros in the Gastón Acurio brand, Tanta serves Peruvian dishes, fusion pastas, heaping salads and sandwiches. Though service is a little uppity, the food is generally good (if

BEST CHEAP EATS

» Heaping sandwiches at El Enano (p84)

» Open-air ceviche at Canta Ranita (p88) or El Rincón del Bigote (p86)

» Hearty breads paired with olives and cheese at El Pan de la Chola (p86)

» Exotic herb and juice blends from Kulcafé (p86)

» DIY picnics from gorgeous grocery store Vivanda (p88 and p84)

overpriced). Desserts are better: try a heavenly passion-fruit cheesecake mousse, nicely paired with a stiff espresso.

Pastelería San Martín　　　　　BAKERY $
(Map p58; ☎428-9091; Nicolás de Piérola 987; snacks S5; ⊙9am-9pm Mon-Sat) Founded in 1930, this bare-bones bakery serves what is considered Lima's finest *turrón de Doña Pepa,* a dessert associated with the religious feast of *El Señor de Los Milagros* (see p23): flaky, sticky and achingly sweet, it is best accompanied by a stiff espresso.

Salon Capon　　　　　　　　CHINESE $$
(Map p58; ☎426-9286; Paruro 819; mains S10-45; ⊙9am-10pm Mon-Sat, 9am-7pm Sun) Across the street from Wa Lok, the smaller Salon Capon also has a lengthy Cantonese menu, good dim sum and a traditional bakery that makes scrumptious, flaky egg tarts.

Queirolo　　　　　　　　　PERUVIAN $
(Map p58; ☎425-0421; Camaná 900; mains S10-33; ⊙9:30am-1am Mon-Sat) Lined with wine bottles, Queirolo is popular with office workers for cheap *menús* (S9) featuring staples such as *papa rellena* (stuffed potatoes). It is also popular for evening gatherings, when locals pop in for *chilcano de pisco* (pisco with ginger ale and lime juice) and chit-chat.

Rovegno　　　　　　　　　　DELI $
(Map p62; ☎424-8465; Arenales 456; mains S13-25, buffet S28; ⊙7am-10pm Mon-Sat) This cluttered bakery-deli-restaurant sells an assortment of decent wine, breads, cheeses, ham and olives, plus plenty of pastries in a rainbow of colors. Restaurant dishes are typical Peruvian specialties such as *lomo saltado* (beef stir-fried with onions and peppers).

La Merced　　　　　　　　PERUVIAN $
(Map p58; ☎428-2431; Miró Quesada 158; menús S10-18; ⊙9am-8pm Mon-Sat) Bustling with businesspeople at lunchtime, the bland, unsigned exterior gives little clue to the gorgeous baroque wood ceiling inside. The menu is long on traditional dishes; at busy times you may have to wait for a table.

Metro　　　　　　　　SELF-CATERING $
(Map p58; cnr Cuzco & Lampa; ⊙9am-10pm daily) In Central Lima, the best supermarket is the block-long Metro in downtown, which also stocks prepared foods.

SAN ISIDRO

Chic dining rooms, frothy cocktails and fusion haute cuisine: San Isidro is a bastion of fine dining – and not much else. Those on a budget may prefer to prepare their own meals, or head to nearby Miraflores, which is generally cheaper.

TOP CHOICE **Malabar**　　　　　FUSION $$$
(Map p76; ☎440-5200; www.malabar.com.pe; Av Camino Real 101; mains S52-68; ⊙12:30-4pm & 7:30-11pm Mon-Sat) Rising culinary star Pedro Miguel Schiaffino is the chef at this hot destination restaurant at the heart of San Isidro. Influenced, in particular, by Amazonian produce and cooking techniques, Schiaffino's seasonal menu features deftly prepared delicacies such as crisp, seared *cuy* and Amazonian river snails bathed in a sauce made with spicy chorizo. Do not forego the cocktails (the chef's father, a noted pisco expert, consulted on the menu) or desserts – perhaps the lightest and most refreshing in Lima.

Matsuei　　　　　　　　JAPANESE $$
(Map p76; ☎422-4323; Manuel Bañon 260; maki S30-49; ⊙12:30-3:30pm & 7:30-11pm Mon-Sat) None other than the venerated Japanese super-chef Nobu Matsuhisa once co-owned this diminutive sushi bar, now situated on a San Isidro side street. Don't let the modest appearance fool you: it's some of the most spectacular sashimi and *maki* (sushi rolls) in Lima. A must-have: the 'acevichado,' a roll stuffed with shrimp and avocado, and then doused in a house-made mayo infused with ceviche broth. It will make your brain tingle in all the right places.

Segundo Muelle　　　　　CEVICHE $$$
(Map p76; ☎421-1206; www.segundomuelle.com; Conquistadores 490; mains S23-69; ⊙noon-5pm) A mainstay of impeccable service and

LIMA EATING

renowned ceviches with innovative twists. Try the *ceviche de mariscos a los tres ajíes,* a stack of mixed fish and shellfish bathed in three types of hot pepper sauce. The menu also features heaping rice and other seafood dishes, including a recommended *parrilla marina* (seafood grill).

Punta Sal
CEVICHE $$

(Map p76; ☑441-7431; www.puntasal.com; Conquistadores 958; mains S30-40; ⊙11am-5pm) Another great seafood restaurant (it's been around for 20 years), Punta Sal serves at least nine different kinds of ceviche. Try the assassin ceviche – a paradisiacal mix of octopus, squid, crawfish, crab, flounder and mangrove cockles. Reader recommended.

Hanzo
JAPANESE $$

(Map p76; ☑422-6367; www.hanzo.com.pe; Conquistadores 598; mains S23-37; ⊙12:30-4pm & 7:30pm-11:30pm Mon-Sat, 12:30-4pm Sun) With a full bar, this atmospheric fusion house is a lively place for sushi that doesn't break the bank. But it's not for purists. *Maki* acevichado and butter rolls made with fried rice are playful nods to Peruvian influence.

Vivanda
SELF-CATERING $

(Map p76; www.vivanda.com.pe; Av 2 de Mayo 1420; ⊙8am-10pm) Lima's top supermarket has luscious arrays of meats, cheeses, vegetables, baked goods, prepared foods and even a cafe.

Antica
PIZZERIA $$

(Map p76; ☑222-9488; Av 2 de Mayo 732; mains S24-42; ⊙noon-midnight) On a street littered with European restaurants, this is one of the most reasonable: a woody, candle-bedecked spot serving house-made pastas, gnocchis and pizzas from a wood-fired oven. It's popular with local families. There is antipasto, as well as a decent wine list strong on South American brands (from S40).

News Café
CAFE $$

(Map p76; ☑421-6278; Santa Luisa 110; sandwiches S9-26, mains S18-36; ⊙9am-11pm) Bursting with local office types at lunchtime, this casual cafe serves up bounteous pastas, pastas, traditional Peruvian dishes and a wide gamut of international newspapers. The ice-cream stand serves delectable scoops made with Andean fruits such as chirimoya and lúcuma.

Tanta
CAFE $$

(Map p76; ☑421-9708; Pancho Fierro 115) The San Isidro outpost of Acurio's restaurant-cafe chain (see p82).

MIRAFLORES

By far the most varied neighborhood for eating, Miraflores carries the breadth and depth of Peruvian cooking at every price range imaginable, from tiny *comedores* with cheap lunchtime *menús* to some of the city's most revered gastronomic outposts. Pavement cafes are ideal for sipping pisco sours and people-watching.

Casual places with cheap *menús* abound on the tiny streets east of Av José Larco just off the Parque Kennedy.

TOP CHOICE Central
NOVOANDINA $$$

(Map p66; ☑242-8515; www.centralrestaurante.com.pe; Santa Isabel 376; mains S52-88; ⊙) Toast of Lima, Central has impressed many a critic with its seductive creations. Chef Virgilio Martinez spent a decade in the top kitchens of Europe and Asia, but coming home meant reinventing local traditions. Seafood – like the charred octopus starter – is a star, but Peruvian classics like suckling pig dazzle, reinvented with pears, mustard and *tomate de arbol.* A menu supplied by sustainable fish and a rooftop herb garden enhance the ultra-fresh appeal.

TOP CHOICE Astrid y Gastón
NOVOANDINA $$$

(Map p66; ☑444-1496, 242-5387; www.astridgaston.com; Cantuarias 175; mains S53-89; ⊙12:30-3:30pm & 6:30pm-midnight Mon-Sat) Now one of the older outposts of *novoandina* cooking in Lima, Gastón Acurio's French-influenced standard-bearer remains a culinary force to be reckoned with. His seasonal menu is equipped with traditional Peruvian fare, but it's the exquisite fusion specialties – such as the seared filets of *cuy,* served Peking-style, with fluffy purple-corn crêpes – that make this such a sublime fine-dining experience. There is a first-rate international wine list.

TOP CHOICE El Enano
SANDWICHES $

(Map p66; Chiclayo 699; sandwiches S7-10; ⊙6am-3am) Grab a stool at the open-air counter and watch the masters at work making fresh-roasted chicken, ham, turkey and *chicharrón* sandwiches on French bread dressed with marinated onions and chilies. If you've had one too many piscos, these will cure what ails you. An array of fresh juices are oversized and served in glass jars.

Pescados Capitales
SEAFOOD $$$

(off Map p66; ☑421-8808; www.pescadoscapitales.com; Av La Mar 1337; mains S35-50; ⊙12:30-

5pm) On a street once home to nothing but clattering auto shops, this contemporary destination (think artsy warehouse meets Peruvian rustic) serves some of the finest ceviche around. Try the 'Ceviche Capital,' a mix of flounder, salmon and tuna marinated with red, white and green onions and bathed in a three-chili crème. A nine-page wine list offers a strong selection of Chilean and Argentinean vintages.

Fiesta
PERUVIAN $$$

(off Map p66; ☎242-9009; www.restaurantfiesta gourmet.com; Av Reducto 1278; mains $40-50; ☻dinner & lunch) Anyone in search of the finest northern Peruvian cuisine in Lima should make a reservation at this busy establishment on Miraflores' eastern edge. Not only do they cook up an *arroz con pato a la chiclayana* (duck and rice Chiclayo-style) that is achingly tender, they also serve *ceviche a la brasa,* traditional ceviche that is given a quick sear before being served, resulting in a fish that is lightly smoky, yet tender. It has to be eaten to be believed. There is a sister restaurant in Chiclayo (p335).

Anticuchos de la Tía Grima
BARBECUE $

(Map p66; ☎99-849-3137; www.anticuchosdelatia grima.com; cnr Enrique Palacio & 27 de Noviembre; anticucho $8; ☻7-11pm Mon-Sat) This corner cart produces the most venerated *anticuchos* in all of Lima, tended to by the legendary Doña Grimanesa for over 30 years. With tender meat and homemade hot sauces, it's no wonder the wait often surpasses an hour. The best bet: show up at 6:45pm and wait for Doña Grimanesa to roll up, or phone in your order.

La Mar
SEAFOOD $$$

(off Map p66; ☎421-3365; www.lamarcebicheria. com; Av La Mar 770; mains $29-69; ☻noon-5pm Mon-Fri, 11:45am-5:30pm Sat & Sun) A *cevichería* done Gastón Acurio–style, La Mar is a polished cement patio bursting with VIPs (note the security guards outside). Choose from 10 types of ceviche and almost as many varieties of *tiraditos* or just try the *degustación,* with five different kinds. There are grills, rice dishes and soups, but it's the ceviche that sings. Cocktails here include Lima's best coca-leaf sour.

Las Brujas de Cachiche
PERUVIAN $$$

(Map p66; ☎444-5310; www.brujasdecachiche. com.pe/ibien.html; Bolognesi 460; mains $35-80; ☻12:30-5pm & 7pm-11pm Mon-Sat, 12:30-5pm Sun) A staple of quality Peruvian cooking,

Brujas' menu has all the popular dishes (such as *ají de gallina*), as well as lesser-known specialties such as *carapulcra,* a dried potato stew. To try a bit of everything, hit the lunch buffet ($89).

Mesa 18
FUSION $$$

(Map p66; ☎610-4000 ext 224; www.mesa18restau rant.com; Av Malecón de la Reserva 1035; 6-course meal $98; ☻12:30-3pm & 7-10:30pm Mon-Fri, 7-11pm Sat & Sun) Featuring traditional Japanese fare with a nod to Peruvian ingredients, this top-notch restaurant spells treat. Grilled squid, conger eel in chardonnay and airy tempura are masterfully crafted, no surprise since chef Toshiro has celebrity status. Best known are the *tiraditos* and the ceviches. The ambience, in Miraflores Park Hotel, is cool modern.

Restaurant Huaca Pucllana
PERUVIAN $$

(Map p66; ☎445-4042; www.resthuacapucl lana.com; Gral Borgoño, cuadra 8; mains $18-60; ☻12:30pm-midnight Mon-Sat, 12:30-4pm Sun) This sophisticated establishment overlooks the illuminated ruins at Huaca Pucllana. The menu consists of a skillfully rendered and beautifully presented array of contemporary Peruvian dishes (from grilled *cuy* to seafood chowders), along with a smattering of Italian-fusion specialties. Portions are large. Save room for the pisco and lemon parfait come dessert.

El Punto Azul
CEVICHE $$

(Map p66; ☎445-8078; San Martín 595; mains $22-30; ☻noon-5pm) Awash in Caribbean blues, this pleasant family eatery dishes up super-fresh ceviches and *tiraditos,* as well as big-enough-to-share rice dishes. Try their risotto with parmesan, shrimp and *ají amarillo* (yellow chili) – and don't miss the line-up of tasty desserts. It gets packed on weekends, so show up before 1pm if you want a table. Excellent value.

Rafael
NOVOANDINA $$$

(Map p66; ☎242-4149; http://rafaelosterling.com; San Martín 300; mains $35-68; ☻1-3:30pm & 8pm-midnight) Don't let the demure exterior fool you: this is *the* place in Lima to see and be seen. Here, Chef Rafael Osterling produces a panoply of fusion dishes, such as *tiradito* bathed in Japanese citrus or suckling goat stewed in Madeira wine. For those who make it past the generously poured cocktails, there is a decent and lengthy international wine list.

Quattro D
ICE CREAM $

(Map p66; ☑445-4228; Av Angamos Oeste 408; mains S16-32, ice cream from S7; ☺6:30am-11:45pm Mon-Thu, 6:30am-12:30am Fri & Sat, 7am-11am Sun) A bustling cafe that serves hot pressed sandwiches, pasta and other dishes, in addition to a diabetes-inducing assortment of sweets and the city's best gelato (including a few sugar-free flavors).

El Rincón del Bigote
CEVICHE $$

(Map p66; José Galvez 529; S21-28; ☺noon-4pm Tue-Sun) On weekends, locals line up for seating in this bare-bones ceviche house. The specialty is *almejas in su concha:* pair these marinated clams with a side of crisp yucca fries and a bottle of cold pilsner and you're in heaven.

El Pan de la Chola
CAFE $

(off Map p66; Av La Mar 918; mains S8-15; ☺8am-8pm Tue-Sat, 9am-1pm Sun) In South America, finding real, crusty whole-grain bread is rarer than striking gold. Enter this small brick cafe baking four scrumptious varieties, with organic coffee from the Peruvian Amazon, greek yogurt and sweets. There's European-style seating at big wooden tables, grab a sandwich or share the tasting plate with bread, olives, hummus and fresh cheese (S9).

La Pascana de Madre Natura
CAFE $

(Map p66; Chiclayo 815; mains S5-16; ☑) This natural-food store, bakery and cafe is herbivore Eden, serving up salads, pizza and other treats in a Zen courtyard. The divine veggie burgers are world-class and the carrot cake is a close second.

Kulcafé
CAFE $

(Map p66; ☑993-325-5445; Bellavista 370; mains S8-12; ☺9:30am-6:30pm Tue-Sun; 🖥) For German sweets, coffee drinks and smoothies, this is the spot. Don't go conventional – the 'sweet green' smoothie makes spinach, watermelon and mango delectable together. There are also organic foods and beautiful whole-grain bagels served in a cozy living-room atmosphere.

Dédalo Arte y Cafe
CAFE $

(Map p66; Benavides 378; snacks S3-9; 8am-10pm Mon-Fri, 10am-11pm Sat; 🖥) Caffeine fiends find their way to this discreet cafe on Parque Kennedy where coffee is as serious as a sacrament. You'll find the usual suspects plus rarer *ristretto* and Australian takes like a flat white. It's owned by the same family as the tasteful Barranco home-decor and accessories shop, which houses a branch upstairs.

La Trattoria di Mambrino
ITALIAN $$

(Map p66; ☑446-7002; Manuel Bonilla 106; mains S30-50; ☺1-3pm & 8-11pm Mon-Sat, 12:30-4pm Sun) One of the top Italian restaurants in town, whose kitchen is overseen by Ugo Plevisani and his wife Sandra, this white-tablecloth spot has traditional house-made pastas (think ravioli stuffed with veal and porcini) as well as delectable gnocchi.

Bodega Miraflores
CAFE $

(Map p66; Diez Canseco 109; coffee S3; ☺9:30am-1pm & 3:30-7:30pm Mon-Sat) A frumpy spot with a grumpy counterman that serves strong, inky *cortados* (espresso with a dollop of steamed milk) made with coffee grown in Chanchamayo. Bagged, whole-bean coffee is available to take home.

Pastelería San Antonio
CAFE $

(Map p66; ☑241-3001; Av Vasco Núñez de Balboa 770; sandwiches S10-16; ☺7am-11pm) A cross-section of Miraflores society jams into this 50-year-old institution for an infinite variety of sandwiches, as well as a wide selection of baked goods, including a dreamy chocolate croissant (ask for it warm).

Rincón Chami
PERUVIAN $

(Map p66; ☑444-4511; Esperanza 154; mains S6-27; ☺8am-8:30pm Mon-Sat, noon-5pm Sun) A classic, this simple, 40-year-old dining hall serves a rotating selection of Peruvian specialties. Chami is renowned for skillfully prepared dishes such as *cau cau* (tripe stew), tasty *pastel de choclo* (maize casserole) and *milanesa* (breaded steaks) as big as a platter.

Helena Chocolatier
SWEETS $

(Map p66; ☑242-8899; http://helenachocolatier.com; Iglesias 498; chocolates from S3; ☺10:30am-7:30pm Mon-Fri) A longtime artisanal chocolate shop that crafts scrumptious 'Chocolates D'Gala,' each stuffed with fillings made from pecans, marzipan or raspberries and individually gift-wrapped.

Haiti
CAFE $

(Map p66; ☑445-0539; Diagonal 160; snacks S12) This nearly half-century-old cafe is like stepping into 1960s Lima: waiters in green jackets tend to coiffed ladies and chattering businessmen. It's a perfect spot to order dessert or a pressed pork sandwich and watch the world go by. Be forewarned: the innocent-looking pisco sours pack a wallop.

La Lucha Sanguacheria SANDWICHES $
(Map p66; ☑241-5953; Benavides 308; sandwiches S10-15; ⊕8am-1am Sun-Thu, 8am-3am Fri & Sat) This all-hours corner sandwich shop is the perfect fix for the midnight munchies. *Lechon a la leña* (roasted pork) is their specialty, but there's also roast chicken or ham served in fluffy rolls.

Bircher Benner VEGETARIAN $
(Map p66; ☑446-5791; 2nd fl, Av José Larco 413; mains S15-22; ⊕9am-11pm Mon-Sat) A long-time vegetarian restaurant and shop that produces a lengthy list of dishes, including veg-only versions of Peruvian staples such as *lomo saltado,* as well as a worthy 'ceviche' crafted with marinated mushrooms, onions, cilantro, tomato and ricotta.

Manolo CAFE $$
(Map p66; ☑444-2244; www.manolochurros.com; Av José Larco 608; mains S15-50, churros S4; ⊕7am-1am Sun-Thu, 7am-2am Fri & Sat) Quite popular, this all-hours sidewalk cafe serves a long list of sandwiches, pasta and pizza. But it is best known for its piping-hot churros, which go smashingly well with a *chocolate caliente espeso* (thick hot chocolate) – perfect for dipping.

AlmaZen VEGETARIAN $$
(Map p66; ☑243-0474; Federico Recavarren 298; mains S30; ⊕11am-11pm Mon-Fri, 5-11pm Sat) Vegetarian restaurant and teahouse, this soothing spot features a rotating daily selection of organic dishes such as sweet-potato and ginger soup, as well as tarts and risottos. Wheat-free and vegan items are also available.

Panchita PERUVIAN $$
(Map p66; ☑242-5957; Av 2 de Mayo 298; mains S33-56; ⊕12:30-9pm Mon-Sat, 12:30-5pm Sun) This Gastón Acurio restaurant pays homage to Peruvian street food in a contemporary setting of folklore-laced decor. *Anticuchos* are grilled over an open flame to melt-in-your-mouth perfection. Also worth the cholesterol: the crisp suckling pig with *tacu tacu.* The lengthy wine list (heavily South American) will help wash it all down.

La Tiendecita Blanca EUROPEAN $$
(Map p66; ☑445-9797; Av José Larco 111; mains S39-53) A Miraflores landmark for more than half a century, fans of Swiss cuisine will find potato *röstis,* fondues and a terrific selection of apple tarts, Napoleons and

MORE, PLEASE

Want to eat like a local? When eating in homes, local *fondas* or *quintas* (informal family restaurants) you can ask for a generous portion by ordering it *'bien taipa.'* If you want seconds, say *'yapa!'* – it roughly translates as 'more, please.'

quiches at this graceful beaux-arts bistro on the square.

La Rosa Nautica SEAFOOD $$$
(Map p66; ☑445-0149; Circuito de Playas; mains S36-75, 3-course menús S110) Location, location, location. Though you can get the same (or better) seafood elsewhere for less, the views at this eatery on the historic pier are unparalleled. Go during happy hour (5pm to 7pm), when you can watch the last of the day's surfers skim along the crests of the waves. Take a taxi to the pier and walk the last 100m.

Tanta CAFE $$
(Map p66; ☑447-8377; Av 28 de Julio 888) The Miraflores outpost of Gastón Acurio's restaurant-cafe chain (see p82).

Pardo's Chicken PERUVIAN $
(Map p66; ☑446-4790; www.pardoschicken.pe; Alfredo Benavides 730; mains S15-30) Lima is littered with rotisserie chicken chains; this one is, hands down, the best.

Café Z CAFE $
(Map p66; ☑444-5579; Diagonal 598; sandwiches S15-23; ⊕7am-midnight) Lima hipsters and *bricheros* (locals keen to romance a tourist) gather at this busy cafe with live music, delicious sandwiches (try the *Butifarra Z*) and a mind-boggling number of coffees and herbal teas – in addition to the world's most uncomfortable chairs.

Govinda VEGETARIAN $
(Map p66; ☑445-8487; Schell 630; mains S12-16; ⊕noon-8pm Mon-Fri, noon-7pm Sat & Sun) Run by the Hare Krishna, this cheerful cafe serves a Peruvian–Indian fusion of vegetable curries and nonmeat versions of dishes such as *lomo saltado.*

Self-Catering

On Saturdays, a small green market sets up at Parque Reducto, off Alfredo Benavides and Ribeyro. Likewise, try the neighborhood's excellent supermarkets:

La Preferida
SELF-CATERING $$

(Map p66; 445-5180; Arias Araguez 698; mains S13-30, tapas S5; 8am-5pm Mon-Sat) Located a couple of blocks north of Av 28 de Julio, just east of the Vía Expresa, this charming take-out place has gorgeous *causas* and fresh seafood specialties such as *pulpo al olivo* (octopus in olive sauce) and *choros a la chalaca* (mussels with a corn and tomato salsa) served in tapas-sized portions. A few stools accommodate diners.

Plaza VEA
SUPERMARKET

(Map p66; 625-8000; www.plazavea.com.pe; Av Arequipa 4651; 8am-10pm) Big supermarket.

Vivanda
SUPERMARKET

(620-3000; www.vivanda.com.pe) Alfredo Benavides (Map p66; Alfredo Benavides 487; 24hr); José Pardo (Map p66; Av José Pardo; 8am-10:30pm) Supermarket with some gourmet items available.

Wong
SUPERMARKET

(Map p66; 625-0000, ext 1130; www.ewong.com; Óvalo Gutiérrez, Av Santa Cruz 771) A massive supermarket built around the courtyard of a vintage home; look out for the baroque-style staircase.

BARRANCO
Even as Barranco has gone upscale in recent years, with trendy restaurants serving everything fusion, the neighborhood still holds on to atmospheric, local spots where life is no more complicated than ceviche and beer.

A number of informal restaurants serving *anticuchos* and cheap *menús* line Av Grau around the intersection with Unión.

Café Bisetti
CAFE $

(Map p70; 713-9565; Av Pedro de Osma 116; coffee S8-16; 8am-9pm Mon-Fri, 10am-11pm Sat, 3-9pm Sun) Locals park their designer dogs out front of this roasting house with the finest lattes in town, well matched with fresh pastries or bitter chocolate pie. Check out the courses on roasting and tasting.

La 73
INTERNATIONAL $$

(Map p70; 247-0780; Av El Sol Oeste 175; mains S34-39; noon-midnight) Named for an iconic local bus, this contemporary bistro has an uncomplicated Peruvian–Mediterranean menu that incorporates sustainable fish. The menu isn't long but it has several standouts, including homemade artichoke ravioli stuffed with goat cheese, and a lovely duck risotto.

Quench your thirst with the amazing *herba luisa* iced tea. A pleasant bar serves wine, in addition to eight types of pisco. To end on a sweet note, split the crisp, warm churros for dessert.

Café Tostado
PERUVIAN $$

(Map p70; 247-7133; Av Nicolás de Pierola 222; mains S8-32, set menu S20; 12:30-9pm Mon-Sat, 7:30am-6pm Sun) Call it a cultural experience. This barely converted auto repair shop long ago transformed into a bastion of traditional cooking, with long wooden tables and an open kitchen surrounded by scarred iron pots and drying noodles. Daily specials rotate but the sought-after signature dish is rabbi – which feeds up to three people for S45. Award-winning Tunki coffee is served with *chicharrónes* on Sunday for a typical Peruvian breakfast.

Canta Ranita
CEVICHE $

(Map p70; Unión s/n; mains S16-20; 12:30-4pm Wed-Mon) Just getting here is a treasure hunt – look for Mercado Capullo in front of the Chung Yion and follow the stalls of trinkets and soccer shirts to the rear. This open-air grill is no-fuss wonderment, with locals drinking jars of *chicha* (corn beer) and drinking cold artisan beer biding the time until the *ceviche apaltado* (with avocado), chicken or blackened octopus doused with olive oil appears. It's run by the son of the formal restaurant of the same name.

Las Mesitas
PERUVIAN $

(Map p70; 477-4199; Av Grau 341; menús S10; noon-2am) A vintage spot with terra-cotta tile floors that serves cheap Peruvian classics and an array of recommended desserts. If you've been thinking about dipping into *suspiro limeño* (a caramel-meringue sweet), this would be the place to do it.

La Canta Rana
CEVICHE $$

(Map p70; 247-7274; Psje Génova 101; mains S25-38; 8am-11pm Tue-Sat) Around for decades, this unpretentious spot draped in flags and plastered in photos packs in the locals with its offering of more than 17 different types of ceviche.

Burrito Bar
MEXICAN $

(Map p70; 987-352-120; Av Grau 113; mains S12-15; noon-11pm Tue-Sat, noon-5pm Sun) Young Londoner Stew is an unlikely purveyor of Mexican fast food, but it works like a smash. Try the Baja-style fish tacos served with fresh salsa in homemade flour tortillas.

The fresh mint limeade may be the best in the city, but you'll probably want one of the Sierra Andina microbrews. For dessert, the chocolate tamal is a no-brainer.

La Bodega Verde CAFE $
(Map p70; ☑247-8804; Sucre 335A; mains S10-23; ☺9am-10pm Mon-Sat, 9am-8pm Sun; 🛜) Set in a walled garden, this cafe and gallery is a pleasant spot to linger. Grab the Scrabble (or toys set out for kids) and order up a salad, lucuma milkshake (from the garden fruit tree), tea served in a ceramic pot or organic coffee. Breakfast includes whole-grain breads and the sweets, such as carrot cake, are especially good.

Chifa Chung Yion CHINESE $$
(Map p70; ☑477-0550; Unión 126; mains S7-37; ☺noon-5:30pm & 7pm-midnight) Known locally as the 'Chifa Unión,' this bustling restaurant is known for its heaping bowls of wonton soup and well-rendered fried rice with prawns. Ample veggie options as well.

Chala FUSION $$$
(Map p70; ☑252-8515; www.chala.com.pe; Bajada de Baños 340; mains S36-59; ☺1-4pm & 8pm-midnight Mon-Sat, 1-4pm Sun) A charming *casona* with a broad terrace houses this local favorite serving modern dishes that blend Peruvian and Asian flavors. Not to be missed: chicken ravioli bathed in *ají de gallina* and topped with seared prawns. It's at the top of the narrow stairway that leads to the beach.

LINCE

TOP CHOICE / El Rincón que no Conoces PERUVIAN $$
(☑471-2171; Av Bernardo Alced 363; mains S21-35; ☺12:30-5 Tue-Sun) Worth the taxi trek, this mecca of *comida criolla* was founded by the late Teresa Ocampo de Chincha, a home-trained cook who grew into a beloved national icon. It's *all* good. Try the creamy *ahí de gallina, causas* and heaping plates of *cordero al seco,* a tender lamb dish. Accompany it with *chicha morada,* a sweet corn drink served by the jar. Just save room for the *pícarones,* airy pumpkin pastries dipped in sweet molasses. Go early and be prepared to wait, as it's wildly popular.

🍷 Drinking

Lima is overflowing with establishments of every description, from rowdy beer halls to high-end lounges to atmospheric old bars. Downtown has the cheapest prices while

---

SEAFOOD AT LA PUNTA

A quiet residential neighborhood with great views of the water, La Punta is perfect for a leisurely lunch. At the humble fish house **Manolo** (☑429-8453; Malecón Pardo s/n, cuadra 1; ☺lunch only), seafood die-hards line up for fresh ceviche, grilled fish and hearty soups. Or dine in style at the waterfront **La Rana Verde** (☑429-5279; Parque Gálvez s/n; mains S29-55; ☺lunch only), ideal for Sunday dinner within view of the Isla San Lorenzo. Dishes are all deftly prepared and the *pulpo al olivo* is one of the best in Lima. It's located on the pier inside the Club Universitario de Regatas. A taxi ride from Miraflores runs at around S30.

San Isidro, Miraflores and Barranco feature trendier lounges charging up to S15 to S20 a cocktail.

CENTRAL LIMA

Nightlife in central Lima is for the nostalgic, composed largely of vintage hotel bars and period halls.

El Bolivarcito BAR
(Map p58; ☑427-2114; Jirón de la Unión 958) Facing the Plaza San Martín from the Gran Hotel Bolívar, this frayed yet bustling spot is known as 'La Catedral del Pisco' for purveying some of the first pisco sours in Peru. Order the double-sized *pisco catedral* if your liver can take it.

Hotel Maury BAR
(Map p58; ☑428-8188; Ucayali 201) Another vintage bar renowned for popularizing pisco sours. Intimate and old-world, it's lined with stained-glass windows and tended to by a battalion of bow-tie-clad waiters.

El Estadio Fútbol Club SPORTS BAR
(Map p58; ☑428-8866; Nicolás de Piérola 934; ☺noon-11pm Mon-Thu, noon-2am Fri & Sat) Another good evening place, this soccer-fanatic hangout is an old-timey spot.

SAN ISIDRO

Bravo Restobar COCKTAIL BAR
(Map p76; ☑221-5700; www.bravorestobar.com; Conquistadores 1005) With a backlit bar and stone and wood interiors, Bravo's able bartenders stir up an encyclopedic cocktail

menu (try the *aguaymanto* sour, made with pisco and Amazonian berries). An excellent selection of small-batch piscos make this mellow San Isidro lounge a good spot to sip and be seen. Also serves lauded Italian–Peruvian fusion fare.

MIRAFLORES

Old-world cafes where suited waiters serve frothy pisco sours, or raucous watering holes blaring techno and salsa – Miraflores has a little bit of everything. The area around the Parque Kennedy is particularly suited for sipping and people-watching.

Café Bar Habana   CAFE
(Map p66; ☎446-3511; www.cafebarhabana.com; Manuel Bonilla 107; ⊗6pm-late Mon-Sat) Boisterous Cuban proprietor Alexi García and his Peruvian wife, Patsy Higuchi, operate this homey establishment with delicious *mojitos*. The couple, both of whom are artists, sometimes display their works in the adjacent gallery.

Huaringas   LOUNGE
(Map p66; ☎447-1883; Bolognesi 460; ⊗9pm-late Tue-Sat) A popular Miraflores bar and lounge located inside the Las Brujas de Cachiche restaurant, Huaringas serves a vast array of cocktails, including a well-recommended passionfruit sour. On busy weekends, there are DJs.

BARRANCO

Barranco's bars and clubs are concentrated around the Parque Municipal, which is thronged with revelers on Friday and Saturday nights.

Cinemas, theaters, traveling art exhibits and concerts are covered in the daily *El Comercio,* with the most detailed listings found in Monday's 'Luces' section. Likewise, the informational portal *Living in Peru* (www.livinginperu.com) maintains an up-to-date calendar of events. More youth oriented is *Oveja Negra* (www.revistaovejanegra. com), a pocket-sized directory distributed free at restaurants and bars, which provides monthly listings of cultural and nightlife happenings.

Ayahuasca   COCKTAIL BAR
(Map p70; ☎247-6751; www.ayahuascabar.com; San Martín 130; ⊗8pm-late) Lima's of-the-moment lounge resides in a stunning restored *casona* full of Moorish architectural flourishes. Not that anyone's looking at the architecture – everyone's checking out everyone

else, in addition to the hyper-real decor that includes a dangling mobile made with costumes used in Ayacucho folk dances. There's a long list of contemporary pisco cocktails, like the tasty Ayahuasca sour made with jungle fruit *tambo* and coca leaves.

Bar Piselli   BAR
(Map p70; ☎252-6750; Av 28 de Julio 297; ⊗10am-11pm Mon-Thu, 10am-3am Fri & Sat) This neighborhood bar reminiscent of old Buenos Aires beats all for ambience. There's live music on Thursdays provoking boisterous sing-alongs of Peruvian classics.

La Posada del Mirador   BAR
(Map p70; ☎256-1796; Ermita 104; ⊗5pm-midnight) A low-key, 2nd-story drinking establishment, the cliff-top Posada del Mirador has outdoor tables great for catching the sunset.

Santos   LOUNGE
(Map p70; ☎247-4609; Jirón Zapita 203; ⊗5pm-1am Mon-Thu, 5pm-3am Fri & Sat; ☎) In a creaky old mansion, this funky and congenial bar has multiple rooms and a balcony with sea views (also perfect for people-watching). Local 20- and 30-somethings start their night out here with tapas and the daily two-for-one that goes until 9pm.

Wahio's   BAR
(Map p70; ☎477-4110; Plaza Espinosa; ⊗Thu-Sat) A large and lively bar with a fair share of dreadlocks and a classic soundtrack of reggae, ska and dub.

☆ Entertainment

Some of the best events in the city – film screenings, art exhibits, theatre and dance – are put on by the various cultural institutes, some of which have several branches. Check individual websites, newspapers or the web portal *The Peru Guide* (www.theperuguide. com) for listings.

Live Music

Many restaurants and bars feature small local acts, while bigger bands tend to play at the casinos or sporting arenas. The following venues are the current best-known live-music spots.

El Dragón   LIVE MUSIC
(Map p70; ☎477-5420; www.eldragon.com.pe; Av Nicolás de Pierola 168, Barranco; cover up to S20; ⊗Thu-Sat) With live music or DJs, this popular venue draws a diverse crowd for Latin rock, *tropicalismo,* soul and funk.

Cocodrilo Verde LIVE MUSIC
(Map p66; ☎242-7583; Francisco de Paola 226, Miraflores; minimum tab S20; ☺6:30pm-late Mon-Sat) With great bands that range from popular music to jazz and bossa nova, this hip lounge is good for a night out.

La Noche LIVE MUSIC
(Map p70; ☎247-1012; www.lanoche.com.pe; Av Bolognesi 307, Barranco) Get ready to groove! This well-known tri-level bar is *the* spot to see rock, punk and Latin music acts in Lima.

La Estación de Barranco CLUB
(Map p70; ☎247-0344; www.laestaciondebarranco. com; Av Pedro de Osma 112, Barranco) A middling space that hosts a variety of jazz, cabaret, musical and comedy performances.

Jazz Zone CLUB
(Map p66; ☎241-8139; www.jazzzoneperu.com; Centro Comercial El Suche, Av La Paz 656, Miraflores; cover from S5) A variety of jazz, folk, *cumbia,* flamenco and other acts at this intimate, well-recommended club on the eastern side of Miraflores.

PEÑAS
Peruvian folk music and dance is performed on weekends at *peñas.* There are two main types of Peruvian music performed at these venues: *folklórica* and *criollo.* The first is more typical of the Andean highlands; the other, a coastal music driven by African-influenced beats. Admission varies; dinner is sometimes included in the price.

Las Brisas del Titicaca TRADITIONAL MUSIC
(Map p62; ☎715-6960; www.brisasdeltiticaca.com; Wakuski 168, Central Lima; cover from S25) The best *folklórica* show in Lima is at this *peña* near Plaza Bolognesi in downtown.

La Candelaria TRADITIONAL MUSIC
(Map p70; ☎247-1314; www.lacandelariaperu.com; Av Bolognesi 292, Barranco; admission from S31) In Barranco, a show that incorporates both *folklórica* and *criollo* music and dancing.

La Oficina TRADITIONAL MUSIC
(☎247-6544; www.laoficinabarranco.com; Enrique Barron 441, Barranco) A locally recommended traditional *criollo* performance space located near the intersection of Avs Grau and El Sol.

Don Porfirio TRADITIONAL MUSIC
(☎477-3119; www.donporfirio.com; Calle Manuel Segura 115, Barranco) ☺Fri & Sat) A *peña criollo* that's popular with the local crowd.

Nightclubs
The club scene gets started well after midnight and keeps going until the break of dawn. Barranco and Miraflores are the best neighborhoods to go clubbing, but spots come and go, so ask around before heading out. Music styles and cover charges vary depending on the night of the week.

For other options, hit 'Pizza Street' (Pasaje Juan Figari) in Miraflores, where a row of raucous clubs regularly spin their wares.

Aura CLUB
(Map p66; ☎242-5516, ext 210; www.aura.com.pe; LarcoMar, Malecón de la Reserva 610, Miraflores; admission S40) Located in the LarcoMar shopping mall, Lima's most exclusive club is minimalist chic, featuring house and guest DJs who spin a mix of house, hip-hop, electronica and Latin. Dress to the nines or you're not getting in.

Gótica CLUB
(Map p66; ☎628-3033; www.gotica.com.pe; LarcoMar, Malecón de la Reserva 610, Miraflores; admission S40) A fashionable, high-energy dance spot with a churchy interior and a mix of DJs playing electronica, hip-hop and pop. It sometimes serves as a venue for live Latin dance bands.

Sargento Pimienta CLUB
(Map p70; ☎247-3265; www.sargentopimienta.com; Av Bolognesi 755, Barranco; admission S20) More accessible is this reliable spot in Barranco, whose name means 'Sergeant Pepper.' The

TELETICKET

A handy place to buy tickets is **Teleticket** (☎613-8888; www.teleticket.com.pe), a one-stop shopping broker that sells tickets to sporting events, concerts, theatre and some *peñas,* as well as the tourist train to Huancayo. The most convenient Teleticket offices can be found on the 2nd floor of the Wong supermarket at Óvalo Gutiérrez (p88) and inside the Metro supermarket in Central Lima (p83). The website has a full listing of locations all over Lima.

barnlike club hosts various theme nights and occasional live bands.

Déjà Vu
CLUB

(Map p70; ☑247-3742; Av Grau 294, Barranco) A bar that also has dancing, this vintage place has two tiers: upstairs, expect thumping international beats; downstairs you'll find traditional Peruvian acts.

Cinemas

The latest international films are usually screened with Spanish subtitles, except children's movies, which are always dubbed. Some cinemas offer reduced admission midweek. Listings can be found online or in the cultural pages of the local newspapers.

Cine Planet
CINEMA

(☑624-9500; www.cineplanet.com.pe); Central Lima (Map p58; Jirón de la Unión 819; admission S5-9); Miraflores (Map p66; Av Santa Cruz 814; admission S9-17) Large cinema.

Cinerama El Pacífico
CINEMA

(Map p66; ☑243-0541; www.cine.peru.com; Av José Pardo 121, Miraflores; admission S11)

UVK Multicines
CINEMA

(www.uvkmulticines.com); LarcoMar (Map p66; ☑446-7336; LarcoMar, Malecón de la Reserva 610, Miraflores; admission S9-17); Plaza San Martín (Map p58; ☑428-6042; Ocoña 110, Central Lima; admission S6.50-8.50) The LarcoMar branch has a 'CineBar,' where, for S23, you can sit in a theater with bar tables and have cocktails delivered to your seat.

Theater

Pickings are slim, but the following theaters are worth noting. Built in 1909, the **Teatro Segura** (Map p58; ☑426-7189; Huancavelica 265, Central Lima) puts on opera, plays and ballet, while the **Teatro Británico** (Map p66; ☑615-3434; www.britanico.edu.pe; Bellavista 527, Miraflores) puts on a variety of works, including plays in English.

Sports

Estadio Nacional
STADIUM

(Map p62; Central Lima) *Fútbol* is the national obsession, and Peru's Estadio Nacional, off *cuadras* 7 to 9 of Paseo de la República, is the venue for the most important matches and other events. Teleticket (see boxed text, p91) has listings and sales.

Plaza de Acho
SPECTATOR SPORT

(Map p58; ☑481-1467; Jr Hualgayoc 332, Rímac) Bullfighting remains popular in Lima. The height of the season is in October, during the religious feast of *El Señor de los Milagros,* when Peru's best toreadors arrive to take on the baddest of the bulls. Teleticket has listings (see boxed text, p91).

Jockey Club of Peru
HORSE RACING

(☑610-3000; www.jcp.org.pe; Hipódromo de Monterrico) Located at the junction of the Panamericana Sur and Av Javier Prado, the horse track has races three to four days a week.

🔒 Shopping

Clothing, jewelry and handicrafts from all over Peru can generally be found in Lima. Shop prices tend to be high, but those with less capital can haggle their hearts out at the craft markets. Shopping hours are generally 10am to 8pm Monday to Saturday, with variable lunchtime hours. Credit cards and traveler's checks can be used at some spots, but you'll need photo identification.

Quality pisco can be bought duty-free at the airport just prior to departure.

Handicrafts

Small shops selling crafts dot the major tourist areas around Pasaje de los Escribanos in Central Lima, and near the intersection of Diez Canseco and La Paz in Miraflores. To buy crafts directly from artisans, visit the Ichimay Wari collective in Lurín (p100).

A number of Miraflores boutiques sell high-quality, contemporary alpaca knits.

Mercado Indio
MARKET

(Map p66; Av Petit Thouars 5245, Miraflores) The best place to find everything from pre-Columbian-style clay pottery to alpaca rugs to knock-offs of Cuzco School canvases. Prices vary; shop around.

Feria Artesanal
MARKET

(Av de la Marina, Pueblo Libre) Slightly cheaper is this crafts market in Pueblo Libre.

Centro Comercial El Suche
MARKET

(Map p66; Av La Paz, Miraflores) A shady passageway with a jumble of handicrafts, antiques and jewelry stores.

Dédalo
HANDICRAFTS

(Map p70; ☑477-0562; Sáenz Peña 295, Barranco; ⊙10am-7pm Mon-Sat) A vintage *casona* houses this contemporary crafts store with a lovely courtyard cafe.

Las Pallas
HANDICRAFTS

(Map p70; ☑477-4629; www.laspallasperu.com; Cajamarca 212, Barranco; ⊙10am-7pm Mon-Sat) For special gifts, check out this handicrafts shop featuring a selection of the highest-quality products from all over Peru; it's even on the radar of Sotheby's. Ring the bell if the gate is closed during opening hours.

La Casa de la Mujer Artesana Manuela Ramos HANDICRAFTS
(☎423-8840; www.casadelamujerartesana.com; Av Juan Pablo Fernandini 1550, Pueblo Libre; ☺11am-1pm & 2-6pm Mon-Fri) Crafts cooperative whose proceeds support women's economic development programs, at cuadra 15 of Av Brasil.

Local Markets
Both of these places get crowded; watch your wallet.

Mercado Central MARKET
(Map p58; cnr Ayacucho & Ucayali, Central Lima) From fresh fish to blue jeans, you can buy almost anything at this crowded market close to the Barrio Chino.

Polvos Azules MARKET
(Map p62) Need a socket wrench, a suitcase and a T-shirt of Jesus Christ wearing an Alianza Lima soccer jersey? Then Polvos Azules is the place for you. This multilevel, popular market attracts people of all social strata for a mind-boggling assortment of cheap goods.

Shopping Malls
In San Isidro, Conquistadores street is cluttered with high-end boutiques. For the full-blown Peruvian mall-rat experience, try these two popular spots.

Jockey Plaza MALL
(Av Javier Prado Este 4200, Monterrico) A huge, relentlessly upscale mall bursting with department stores, boutiques, movie theaters and a food court.

LarcoMar MALL
(Map p66; Malecón de la Reserva 610, Miraflores) A well-to-do outdoor mall wedged into the cliff top beneath the Parque Salazar, full of high-end clothing shops, trendy discotheques and a wide range of eateries. There's also a bowling alley.

Camping Equipment
These shops sell specialized clothing, backpacks and a variety of other gear:

Alpamayo OUTDOOR EQUIPMENT
(Map p66; ☎445-1671; 2nd fl, Av José Larco 345, Miraflores) Outdoor supplies.

Tatoo Adventure Gear OUTDOOR EQUIPMENT
(Map p66; ☎242-1938; www.tatoo.ws; LarcoMar, Malecón de la Reserva 610, Miraflores) Tatoo brand outdoor clothes, some accessories.

Todo Camping OUTDOOR EQUIPMENT
(Map p66; ☎242-1318; Av Angamos Oeste 350, Miraflores) Sells fuel stoves and also climbing equipment.

Other Shopping

El Virrey BOOKS
(Map p66; ☎444-4141; www.elvirrey.com; Bolognesi 510, Miraflores; ☺10am-7pm) Includes a room stocked with thousands of rare vintage editions.

CompuPalace ELECTRONICS
(Map p66; Av Petit Thouars 5358, Miraflores) You'll find rechargeable and lithium batteries, as well as computer parts, supplies and replacements at CompuPalace, a block-long electronics arcade.

ⓘ Information
Dangers & Annoyances
Like any large Latin American city, Lima is a land of haves and have-nots, something that has made stories about crime here the stuff of legend. To some degree, the city's dangers have been overblown. Lima has improved greatly since the 1980s, when pickpockets, muggers and carjackers plied their trade with impunity. Even so, this is a big city, in which one in five people live in poverty, so crime is to be expected. The most common offense is theft, and readers have regularly reported muggings. You are unlikely to be physically hurt, but it is nonetheless best to keep a streetwise attitude.

Do not wear flashy jewelry, and keep your camera in your bag when you are not using it. It is best to keep your cash in your pocket and take only as much as you'll need for the day. And, unless you think you'll need your passport for official purposes, leave it at the hotel; a photocopy will do. Blending in helps, too: *limeños* favor a muted wardrobe of jeans and sweaters. Hitting the streets in designer sneakers or brand-new trekking gear will get you noticed.

Be wary at crowded events and the areas around bus stops and terminals. These bring out pickpockets – even in upscale districts. Late at night, it is preferable to take taxis, especially in downtown, or if you've been partying until late in Barranco. The areas of Rímac, Callao, Surquillo and La Victoria can get quite rough so approach with caution (taxis are best). The most dangerous neighborhoods are San Juan de Lurigancho, Los Olivos, Comas, Vitarte and El Agustino.

In addition, be skeptical of unaffiliated touts and taxi drivers who try to sell you tours or tell you that the hotel you've booked is a crime-infested bordello. Many of these are scam artists who will say and do anything to steer you to places that pay them a commission. For more tips on safe travel in Peru, see p537.

Emergency

Policía Nacional head office (460-0921; Moore 268, Magdalena del Mar; 24hr)

Tourism Police (Policía de Turismo, Poltur; Map p66; 460-0844; Colón 246; 24hr) A division of the Policía Nacional (National Police) that usually has English-speaking officers who can provide theft reports for insurance claims or traveler's-check refunds. In heavily touristed areas, it is easy to identify members of Poltur by their white shirts.

Immigration

For general information about visas, stay extensions and a list of embassies, see p540.

Arrive first thing in the morning at the **oficina de migraciónes** (immigration office; off Map p62; 200-1000; www.migraciones.gob.pe; Prolongación España 734, Breña; 8am-1pm Mon-Fri) if you want to get your tourist-card extension (US$20) on the same day. Rights to the specially stamped paperwork can be bought beforehand at the nearby Banco de la Nación (S12.25). You will need a copy of form F-007 (available for download on the website, in the section titled *Prórroga de Residencia*), along with your passport and the immigration slip you received upon entry into Peru. Make an extra photocopy of each to make the process faster. If you don't have the original immigration slip, you may be fined and have status delayed. You may have to show a return ticket out of the country, or proof of sufficient funds. The more formally attired you look, the less hassle you'll have. Process your paperwork only with officials inside the office; do not accept offers of help from people on the street.

Maps

Canada-based **ITBM** (www.itbm.com) features a city map. For far more detail, opt for *Lima Plan Metro*, produced by the Peruvian company Editorial Lima 2000.

In downtown, the top spot for maps is the **Caseta el Viajero Kiosk** (Map p58; 423-5436; Jirón de la Unión 1002), a cluttered stand facing Plaza San Martín.

Medical Services

The following clinics have emergency service and some English-speaking staff. Consultations start in the vicinity of S80 and climb from there, depending on the clinic and the doctor. Treatments and medications are an additional fee, as are appointments with specialists.

Clínica Anglo-Americana (www.clinanglo americana.com.pe) La Molina (436 9933; Av La Fontana 362); San Isidro (Map p76; 616-8900; Salazar 350) A renowned (but expensive) hospital. There's a walk-in center in La Molina, near the US embassy.

Clínica Good Hope (Map p66; 610-7300; www.goodhope.org.pe; Malecón Balta 956) Quality care at good prices; there is also a dental unit.

Clínica Internacional (Map p62; 619-6161; www.clinicainternacional.com.pe; Garcilaso de la Vega 1420, Central Lima) A well-equipped clinic with specialties in gastroenterology, neurology and cardiology.

Clínica Montesur (317-4000; www.clinica montesur.com.pe; Av El Polo 505, Monterrico; fees vary) Devoted exclusively to women's health.

Clínica San Borja (475-4000; www.clinica sanborja.com.pe; Av Guardia Civil 337, San Borja) Another reputable clinic, with cardiology services.

Other medical options:

Instituto de Medicina Tropical (482-3903, 482-3910; www.upch.edu.pe/tropicales; Hospital Nacional Cayetano Heredia, Av Honorio Delgado 430, San Martín de Porras) Good for treating tropical diseases. The immediate area around the hospital is safe, but the surrounding neighborhood can be rough.

Instituto Nacional de Salud del Niño (330-0066; www.isn.gob.pe; Brasil 600, Breña) A pediatric hospital; gives tetanus and yellow-fever jabs.

Pharmacies abound in Lima. **Botica Fasa** (Map p66; 619-0000; www.boticafasa.com.pe; cnr Av José Larco 129-35, Miraflores) and **InkaFarma** (Map p66; 315-9000, deliveries 314-2020; www.inkafarma.com.pe; Alfredo Benavides 425, Miraflores) are well-stocked chains and open 24 hours. They often deliver free of charge.

You can have eyeglasses made cheaply by one of the opticians along Miró Quesada in the vicinity of Camaná in Central Lima or around Schell and Av José Larco in Miraflores.

Money

Banks are plentiful and most have 24-hour ATMs, which tend to offer the best exchange rates. Many of the big supermarkets also have ATMs. Use caution when making withdrawals late at night.

Lima's *casas de cambio* (foreign-exchange bureaus) give similar or slightly better rates than banks for cash, although not traveler's checks. They're found downtown on Ocoña and Camaná, as well as along Av José Larco in Miraflores. Consider using street moneychangers carefully as counterfeits are a problem. See the boxed text, p536, for tips on how to avoid fakes.

The following are some of the most useful options:

American Express/Travex (Map p66; ☑630-9800; www.amextravelresources.com/offices; Av Santa Cruz 873, Miraflores; ⊗8:30am-6pm Mon-Fri, 9am-1pm Sat) Buy traveler's checks or replace lost ones.

Banco Continental (BBVA; ☑595-0000; www.bbvabancocontinental.com; ⊗9am-6pm Mon-Fri, 9:30am-12:30pm Sat) Central Lima (Map p58; Cuzco 290); Miraflores (Map p66; Av José Larco 631) A representative of Visa; its ATMs also take Cirrus, Plus and MasterCard.

Banco de Crédito del Perú (BCP; www.viabcp.com; ⊗9am-6:30pm Mon-Fri, 9:30am-1pm Sat) Central Lima (☑427-5600; cnr Lampa & Ucayali, Central Lima); José Gonzales (Map p66; cnr Av José Larco & José Gonzales, Miraflores); José Pardo (Map p66; ☑445-1259; Av José Pardo 425, Miraflores) Has 24-hour Visa and Plus ATMs; also gives cash advances on Visa, changes Amex, Citicorp and Visa traveler's checks. The Central Lima branch has incredible stained-glass ceilings.

Citibank (☑221-7000; www.citibank.com.pe; ⊗9am-6pm Mon-Fri, 9:30am-1pm Sat) San Isidro (Map p76; Av 2 de Mayo 1547); Miraflores (Map p66; Av José Pardo 127, Miraflores) These locations have 24-hour ATMs operating on the Cirrus, Maestro, MasterCard and Visa systems; they cash Citicorp traveler's checks.

LAC Dólar (⊗9:30am-6pm Mon-Fri, 9am-2pm Sat) Central Lima (Map p58; ☑428-8127; Camaná 779); Miraflores (☑242-4069; Av La Paz 211) A reliable exchange house; can deliver cash to your hotel in exchange for traveler's checks.

Scotiabank (☑311-6000; www.scotiabank.com.pe; ⊗9:15am-6pm Mon-Fri, 9:15am-12:30pm Sat) San Isidro (Map p76; Av 2 de Mayo 1510-1550); Miraflores Larco (Map p66; Av José Larco 1119); Miraflores Pardo (Map p66; cnr Av José Pardo & Bolognesi, Miraflores) ATMs (24-hour) operate on the MasterCard, Maestro, Cirrus, Visa and Plus networks and dispense soles and US dollars.

Post

Serpost, the national postal service, has outlets throughout Lima. Mail sent to you at Lista de Correos (Poste Restante), Correo Central, Lima, can be collected at the main post office in Central Lima. Take identification.

Serpost (www.serpost.com.pe; ☑511-5000) Central Lima (Main post office; Pasaje Piura s/n, Central Lima; ⊗8am-9pm Mon-Sat); San Isidro (Map p76; ☑422-0985; Las Palmeras 205; ⊗9am-1pm & 2-5:40pm Mon-Fri, 9-11:40am Sat); Miraflores (Map p66; Av Petit Thouars 5201; ⊗8am-8:45pm Mon-Sat, 9am-1:30pm Sat, 9am-2pm Sun); Larco (Map p66; Av José Larco 868; ⊗8am-7:30pm Mon-Sat)

Other shipping services:

DHL (Map p76; ☑652-2194; www.dhl.com.pe; Av Dos de Mayo 595, San Isidro; ⊗9am-6pm Mon-Fri, 9am-1pm Sun)

Federal Express (FedEx; Map p66; ☑242-2280; www.fedex.com.pe; BSC Miraflores, Pasaje Olaya 260, Miraflores; ⊗9am-7pm Mon-Fri, 10am-3pm Sat)

Tourist Information

iPerú (www.peru.travel) Aeropuerto Internacional Jorge Chávez (☑574-8000; Main Hall; ⊗24hr); Miraflores (Map p66; ☑445-9400; Module 14, by movie theater box office, LarcoMar, Malecón de la Reserva 610; ⊗noon-8pm); San Isidro (Map p76; ☑421-1627; Jorge Basadre 610; ⊗9am-6pm Mon-Fri) The government's reputable tourist bureau dispenses maps, offers good advice and can help handle complaints. The Miraflores office is tiny but is highly useful on weekends.

Municipal tourist office (Map p58; ☑315-1542; www.munlima.gob.pe; Pasaje de los Escribanos 145, Central Lima; ⊗9am-5pm Mon-Fri, 11am-3pm Sat & Sun) Of limited use; check the website for a small number of listings of local events and info on free downtown tours.

Trekking & Backpacking Club (☑423-2515; www.angelfire.com/mi2/tebac; Huascar 1152, Jesús María) Provides information, maps, brochures, equipment rental and guide information for independent trekkers.

Travel Agencies

For companies in Lima offering local and regional tours, see p72. For travel agencies to organize airline bookings and other arrangements, try the following agencies:

Fertur Peru Travel (www.fertur-travel; ⊗9am-7pm Mon-Fri, 9am-noon Sat) Central Lima (Map p58; ☑427-2626, 427-1958; Jirón Junín 211, Central Lima); Miraflores (Map p66; ☑242-1900; Schell 485, Miraflores) A highly recommended agency that can book local, regional and international travel, as well as create custom group itineraries. Discounts available for students and SAE members.

InfoPerú (Map p58; ☑431-0117; http://infoperu.com.pe; Jirón de la Unión 1066, Central Lima; ⊗9:30am-6pm Mon-Fri, 10am-2pm Sat)

SOUTH AMERICAN EXPLORERS

Now more than three decades old, the venerable **South American Explorers Club** (SAE; Map p66; ☎445-3306; www.saexplorers.org; Piura 135, Miraflores; ☉9:30am-5pm Mon-Tue, Thur-Fri, 9:30am-8pm Wed, 9:30am-1pm Sat) is an indispensable resource for long-term travelers, journalists and scientists spending long periods in Peru, Ecuador, Bolivia and Argentina. It has an extensive library as well as a vast array of guides and maps for sale, from topographic plans to trail maps for the Inca Trail, Mt Ausangate, the Cordillera Blanca and Cordillera Huayhuash. You can also get useful information on travel conditions in remote areas, research volunteer opportunities and pick up a copy of the *Lima Survival Kit* (US$35), a handy guide for new long-term residents.

The club is a member-supported, nonprofit organization (it helped launch the first clean-up of the Inca Trail and has supported local medicine drives). Annual dues are US$60 per person (US$90 per couple); special discounts are available for ISIC holders and volunteers. Members receive full use of the clubhouse and its facilities, including luggage storage, poste restante, a book exchange, access to the online magazine *South American Explorer*, and discounts on items sold on-site. Members are also eligible for discounts at participating businesses throughout Peru. There are additional clubhouses in Cuzco, Quito and Buenos Aires (find contact information online). You can sign up in person at one of the offices or via the website.

Nonmembers are welcome to browse some of the information and purchase guides or maps.

Books bus and plane tickets and dispenses reliable information on hotels and sightseeing.

Intej (Map p70; ☎247-3230; www.intej.org; San Martín 240, Barranco) The official International Student Identity Card (ISIC) office, Intej can arrange discounted air, train and bus fares, among other services.

Lima Tours (Map p58; ☎619-6901; www.limatours.com.pe; Jirón de la Unión 1040, Central Lima; ☉9:30am-6pm Mon-Fri, 9:30am-1pm Sat) A well-known agency that handles all manner of travel arrangements. Also organizes gay-friendly trips and basic gastronomic tours of Lima.

Tika Tours (Map p66; ☎719-9990; www.tikagroup.com.pe; José Pardo 332-350, Miraflores) Tour operator and travel agent, helpful for local information, as well as travel all over Peru.

❶ Getting There & Away

Air

Lima's **Aeropuerto Internacional Jorge Chávez** (code LIM; ☎517-3100; www.lap.com.pe; Callao) is stocked with the usual facilities plus a pisco boutique, a post office and luggage storage. Internet access is available on the 2nd floor. For information on international flights, see p543.

The principal domestic destinations from Lima are Arequipa, Ayacucho, Cajamarca, Chiclayo, Cuzco, Iquitos, Juliaca, Piura, Pucallpa, Puerto Maldonado, Tacna, Tarapoto, Trujillo and Tumbes. You can get flight information, buy tickets and reconfirm flights online or via telephone,

but for ticket changes or problems, it is best to go to the airline office in person.

For general information on air travel in Peru, see p543. The international departure tax of US$31 should be included in your ticket, along with domestic departure taxes.

The following are the Lima offices of current domestic operators:

LAN (Map p66; ☎213-8200; www.lan.com; Av José Pardo 513, Miraflores) LAN goes to Arequipa, Chiclayo, Cuzco, Iquitos, Juliaca, Piura, Puerto Maldonado, Tacna, Tarapoto and Trujillo. Additionally it offers link services between Arequipa and Cuzco, Arequipa and Juliaca, Arequipa and Tacna, Cuzco and Juliaca, and Cuzco and Puerto Maldonado.

LC Peru (☎204-1313; www.lcperu.pe; Av Pablo Carriquirry 857, San Isidro) Flies to Andahuaylas, Ayacucho, Cajamarca, Huancayo, Huánuco, Huaraz and Jauja on smaller turbo-prop aircraft.

Peruvian Airlines (Map p66; ☎716-6000; www.peruvianairlines.pe; Av José Pardo 495, Miraflores) Flies to Arequipa, Cuzco, Piura, Iquitos and Tacna.

Star Perú (Map p66; ☎705-9000; www.starperu.com; Av Espinar 331, Miraflores) Flies to Arequipa, Ayacucho, Cuzco, Huanco, Iquitos, Juliaca, Pucallpa, Puerto Maldonado, Talara, Tarapoto and Tumbes; with link service between Tarapoto and Iquitos.

TACA (Map p66; ☎511-8222; www.taca.com; Av José Pardo 811, Miraflores) Flies to Cuzco.

Bus

There is no central bus terminal; each company operates its ticketing and departure points independently. Some companies have several terminals, so always clarify from which point a bus leaves when buying tickets. The busiest times of year are Semana Santa (the week before Easter Sunday) and the weeks surrounding Fiestas Patrias (July 28–29), when thousands of *limeños* make a dash out of the city and fares double. At these times, book well ahead.

Some stations are in rough neighborhoods. If possible, buy your tickets in advance and take a taxi when carrying luggage.

There is an infinite number of bus companies. These are the most reliable:

Civa (Map p62; ☎418-1111; www.civa.com.pe; cnr 28 de Julio & Paseo de la República 575, Central Lima) For Arequipa, Cajamarca, Chachapoyas, Chiclayo, Cuzco, Ilo, Máncora, Nazca, Piura, Puno, Tacna, Tarapoto, Trujillo and Tumbes. The company also runs a more luxurious sleeper line to various coastal destinations called **Excluciva** (www.excluciva.com).

Cruz del Sur (☎311-5050; www.cruzdelsur. com.pe) Central Lima (Map p58; ☎431-5125; Quilca 531); La Victoria (☎311-5050; Av Javier Prado Este 1109) One of the biggest companies, serving the coast – as well as inland cities such as Arequipa, Cuzco, Huancayo and Huaraz – with three different classes of service: the cheaper Ideal, and the more luxurious Imperial and Cruzero. The more expensive services usually depart from La Victoria.

Movil Tours (Map p62; ☎716-8000; www. moviltours.com.pe; Paseo de la República 749, Central Lima) For Chachapoyas, Chiclayo, Huancayo, Huaraz and Tarapoto.

Oltursa (off Map p76; ☎708-5000, 225-4495; www.oltursa.pe; Av Aramburu 1160, Limatambo) A short distance from San Isidro lies the main terminal for this very reputable company, which travels to Arequipa, Chiclayo, Ica, Máncora, Nazca, Paracas, Piura, Trujillo and Tumbes.

Ormeño (☎472-1710; www.grupo-ormeno. com.pe) Central Lima (Map p62; Carlos Zavala Loayza 177); La Victoria (off Map p76; Av Javier Prado Este 1059) A huge Lima bus company offering daily service to Arequipa, Ayacucho, Cajamarca, Cañete, Chiclayo, Chincha, Cuzco, Huaraz, Ica, Ilo, Nazca, Paracas, Puno, Tacna, Trujillo and Tumbes, all of which leave from the terminal in La Victoria. It has three classes of service: Econo, Business and Royal. The Central Lima terminal is for buying tickets or arranging transport on one of the smaller subsidiaries: Expreso Continental (northern Peru), Expreso Chinchano (south coast and Arequipa) and San Cristóbal (Puno and Cuzco).

PeruBus (Map p62; ☎226-1515; www.perubus. com.pe; Carlos Zavala Loayza 221, Central Lima) Frequent buses to Cañete, Chincha, Ica and Nazca.

Tepsa (☎202-3535; www.tepsa.com.pe) Central Lima (Map p58; ☎427-5642, 428-4635; Paseo de la República 151-A, Central Lima); Javier Prado (☎617-9000; Av Javier Prado Este 1091) Comfortable buses that travel to

BUS INFORMATION

DESTINATION	COST* (S)	DURATION (HR)
Arequipa	101-143	15
Ayacucho	50-95	10
Cajamarca	80-130	16
Chiclayo	40-125	12-14
Cuzco	130-175	21
Huancayo	57-175	7
Huaraz	35-100	8
Ica	22-76	4½
Nazca	50-86	8
Piura	59-144	12-16
Puno	140-170	18-21
Tacna	50-144	18-22
Trujillo	25-100	8-9
Tumbes	132-165	19

* prices are general estimates for normal/luxury buses

Arequipa, Cajamarca, Chiclayo, Cuzco, Ica, Lambayeque, Máncora, Nazca, Piura, Tacna, Trujillo and Tumbes.

Car

Lima has major intersections without stoplights, kamikaze bus drivers, spectacular traffic jams and little to no parking. If you still dare to get behind the wheel, the following companies have 24-hour desks at the airport. Prices range from about S130 to S338 per day, not including surcharges, insurance and taxes (of about 19%). Delivery is possible.

Budget (☑442-8706; www.budgetperu.com)
Dollar (☑444-3050; www.dollar.com)
Hertz (☑447-2129; www.hertz.com.pe)
National (☑575-1111; www.nationalcar.com.pe)

Train

The **Ferrocarril Central Andino** (☑226-6363; www.ferrocarrilcentral.com.pe) railway line runs from Estación Desamparados in Lima inland to Huancayo, climbing from sea level to 4829m – the second-highest point for passenger trains in the world – before descending to Huancayo at 3260m. There is no regular passenger service, but the train makes the journey a couple of times a month as a tourist attraction – a 12-hour odyssey along Andean mountainscapes and vertigo-inducing bridges. The round-trip costs S130 to S350. Check the schedule in advance since the rail lines aren't always operational. Tickets can be purchased through Teleticket (see the boxed text, p91).

❶ Getting Around

To & From the Airport

The airport resides in the port city of Callao, about 12km west of downtown or 20km north-west of Miraflores. As you come out of customs, inside the airport to the right is the official taxi service: **Taxi Green** (☑484-4001; www.taxi green.com.pe; Aeropuerto Internacional Jorge Chávez; 1-3 people to Central Lima, San Isidro, Miraflores & Barranco S50). Outside the airport perimeter itself, you will find 'local' taxis. Taking these does not always save you money, and safety is an issue – local hustlers use this as an opportunity to pick up foreign travelers and rob them. It is best to use the official airport taxis, or arrange pickup with your hotel.

The cheapest way to get to and from the airport is via the *combi* company known as **La S** (per person S2-3) – a giant letter 'S' is pasted to the front windshields – which runs various routes from the port of Callao to Miraflores and beyond. From the airport, these can be found heading south along Av Elmer Faucett. For the return trip to the airport, La S *combis* can be found traveling north along Av Petit Thouars and east along Av Angamos in Miraflores. The most central spot to find them is at the *paradero* (bus stop) on Av Petit Thouars, just north of Av Ricardo Palma (Map p76). Expect to be charged additional fares for any seats that your bags may occupy. *Combi* companies change their routes regularly, so ask around before heading out.

In a private taxi, allow at least an hour to the airport from San Isidro, Miraflores or Barranco; by *combi*, expect the journey to take at least two hours – with *plenty* of stops in between. Traffic is lightest before 6:30am.

Bus

El Metropolitano (www.metropolitano.com.pe), a new trans-Lima electric express bus system, is the fastest and most efficient way to get into the city center. Routes are few, though there are intentions to expand coverage to the northern part of the city. Ruta Troncal (S1.50) goes through Barranco, Miraflores and San Isidro to Plaza Grau in the center of Lima. Users must purchase a 'tarjeta intelligente' (card S4.50) that can be credited for use.

Otherwise, traffic-clogging caravans of minivans hurtle down the avenues with a *cobrador* (ticket taker) hanging out the door and shouting out the stops. Go by the destination placards taped to the windshield. Your best bet is to know the nearest major intersection or landmark close to your stop (eg Parque Kennedy) and tell that to the *cobrador* – he'll let you know whether you've got the right bus. *Combis* are generally slow and crowded, but startlingly cheap: fares run from S1 to S3, depending on the length of your journey.

The most useful routes link Central Lima with Miraflores along Av Arequipa or Paseo de la República. Minibuses along Garcilaso de la Vega (also called Av Wilson) and Av Arequipa are labeled 'Todo Arequipa' or 'Larco/Schell/Miraflores' when heading to Miraflores and, likewise, 'Todo Arequipa' and 'Wilson/Tacna' when leaving Miraflores for Central Lima. Catch these buses along Av José Larco or Av Arequipa in Miraflores.

To get to Barranco, look for buses along Av Arequipa labeled 'Chorrillos/Huaylas/Metro' (some will also have signs that say 'Barranco'). You can also find these on the Diagonal, just west of the Parque Kennedy, in Miraflores.

Taxi

Lima's taxis lack meters, so negotiate fares before getting in. Fares vary depending on the length of the journey, traffic conditions, time of day (evening is more expensive) and your Spanish skills. Registered taxis or taxis hailed outside a tourist attraction charge higher rates. As a (very) rough guide, a trip within Miraflores costs around S5 to S8. From Miraflores to Central Lima is S10 to S15, to Barranco from S5 to S10, and San Isidro from S6 to S12. You can haggle fares – though it's harder during rush hour. If there are two or more passengers be clear on whether the fare is per person or for the car.

The majority of taxis in Lima are unregistered (unofficial); indeed, surveys have indicated that no less than one vehicle in seven here is a taxi. During the day, it is generally not a problem to use either. At night it is safer to use registered taxis, which have a rectangular authorization sticker with the word SETAME on the upper left corner of the windshield. Registered taxis also usually have a yellow paint job and a license number painted on the sides.

Registered taxis can be called by phone or found at taxi stands, such as the one outside the Sheraton in Central Lima or outside the Larco-Mar shopping mall in Miraflores. Registered taxis cost about 30% to 50% more than regular street taxis and can be hired on a per-hour basis from S25.

The following companies all work 24 hours and accept advance reservations:

Moli Taxi (☏479-0030)

Taxi América (☏165-1960)

Taxi Lima (☏271-1763)

Taxi Móvil (☏422-6890)

Taxi Real (☏470-6263; www.taxireal.com) Recommended.

Taxi Seguro (☏241-9292)

AROUND LIMA

On weekends and holidays, *limeños* head for the beach or the hills. From exploring ancient ruins to beach bumming, there is much to do outside of the city that is worthy of exploration if you have a few extra days.

Pachacamac

☏01

Situated about 31km southeast of the city center, the archaeological complex of **Pachacamac** (☏430-0168; http://pachacamac.peru cultural.org.pe; admission S6; �9am-5pm Mon-Fri) is a pre-Columbian citadel made up of adobe and stone palaces and temple pyramids. If you've been to Machu Picchu, it may not look like much, but this was an important Inca site and a major city when the Spanish arrived. It began as a ceremonial center for the Lima culture beginning at about AD 100, and was later expanded by the Waris before being taken over by the Ichsma. The Incas added numerous other structures upon their arrival to the area in 1450. The name Pachacamac, which can be variously translated as 'He who Animated the World' or 'He who Created Land and Time,' comes from the Wari god, whose wooden, two-faced image can be seen in the on-site **museum**.

Most of the buildings are now little more than piles of rubble that dot the desert landscape, but some of the main temples have been excavated and their ramps and stepped sides revealed. You can climb the switchback trail to the top of the **Templo del Sol** (Temple of the Sun), which on clear days offers excellent views of the coast. The most remarkable structure on-site, however, is the Palacio de las Mamacuna (House of the Chosen Women), commonly referred to as the **Acllahuasi**, which boasts a series of Inca-style trapezoidal doorways. Unfortunately, a major earthquake in 2007 has left the structure highly unstable. As a result, visitors can only admire it from a distance. Without funding to repair the extensive damage, it has been listed as one of the planet's most endangered sites.

There is a visitors center and cafe at the site entrance, which is on the road to Lurín. A simple map can be obtained from the ticket office, and a track leads from here into the complex. Those on foot should allow at least two hours to explore. (In summer, take water and a hat – there is no shade to speak of once you hit the trail.) Those with a vehicle can drive from site to site.

NEW DISCOVERIES IN PACHACAMAC

The widespread looting of Peru's archaeological treasures has left many ruins with more puzzling questions than answers. So the discovery in May, 2012 of an untouched 80-person burial chamber in Pachacamac is considered nothing less than a coup. Archaeologists from the Free University of Brussels discovered an 18m (60ft) oval chamber in front of the Temple of Pachacamac, hidden under newer burials. The perimeter was laced with infants and newborns encircling over 70 skeletons in the center of the tomb. The mummies were wrapped in textiles and buried with valuables, offerings, and even dogs and guinea pigs. According to *National Geographic*, investigators think the tomb may contain pilgrims who were drawn to the site to seek cures for serious illnesses.

ARTISAN STUDIOS OF LURÍN

Lurín is a working-class enclave 50km south of Central Lima on the Panamericana. At its southern edge, crafts collective **Ichimay Wari** (☎430-3674; www.ichimaywari.org; Jr Jorge Chávez, Manzana 22, Lote A; ☉8am-1pm & 2-5pm Mon-Fri) has its studios. Here, talented artisans from Ayacucho produce traditional *retablos* (religious dioramas), pottery, Andean-style Christmas decorations and the colorful clay trees known as *arbolitos de la vida* (trees of life). Your best bet is to make an appointment 24 hours in advance to tour individual studios and meet the artisans.

A taxi from Lima costs around S70. By bus from the Puente Primavera, take one headed to Lurín, San Bartolo or San Miguel. Get off at the main stoplight in Lurín. From there, hail a *mototaxi* (motorcycle taxi) and ask them to take you south to the Barrio Artesano. The cost will be S2. Parts of Lurín can get rough; take taxis and keep your cameras stowed.

Various agencies in Lima (see p72) offer guided tours (half-day around S115 per person) that include transport and a guide. Mountain-bike tours can be an excellent option. Alternatively, catch a minibus signed 'Pachacamac' from the sunken roadway at the corner of Andahuaylas and Grau in Central Lima (S2, 45 minutes); minibuses leave every 15 minutes during daylight hours. From Miraflores, take a taxi to the intersection of Angamos and the Panamericana, also known as the Puente Primavera, then take the bus signed 'Pachacamac/Lurín' (S1 to S2, 30 minutes). For both services, tell the driver to let you off near the *ruinas* (ruins) or you'll end up at Pachacamac village, about 1km beyond the entrance. To get back to Lima, flag down any bus outside the gate, but expect to stand. You can also hire a taxi per hour (from S25) from Lima.

Southern Beaches

♪01

Every summer, *limeños* make a beeline for the beaches clustered along the Panamericana to the south. The exodus peaks on weekends, when, occasionally, the road is so congested that it becomes temporarily one way. The principal beach towns include El Silencio, Señoritas, Caballeros, Punta Hermosa, Punta Negra, San Bartolo, Santa María, Naplo and Pucusana. Don't expect tropical resorts; this stretch of barren, coastal desert is lapped by cold water and strong currents. Inquire locally before swimming, as drownings occur annually.

Popular with families is **San Bartolo**, which is cluttered with hostels at budget to midrange rates during the busy summer. Sitting above the bay, **Hostal 110** (☎430-7559; www.hostal110.com; Malecón San Martín Nte 110; d S100-130, additional person S30; ✿), has 14 spacious and neat tiled rooms and apartments – some of which sleep up to six – staggered over a swimming pool on the cliffside. Guests pay the higher rate on Saturdays. On the far southern edge of town (take a *mototaxi*), facing the soccer field, the recommended **Restaurant Rocío** (☎430-8184; www.restaurant-rocio.com; Urb Villa Mercedes, Mz A, Lte 5-6; mains S15-38; ☉11am-11pm) serves fresh fish grilled, fried and bathed in garlic.

Further south, **Punta Hermosa**, with its relentless waves, is *the* surfer spot. The town has plenty of accommodations. A good choice is the compact **Punta Hermosa Surf Inn** (☎230-7732; www.puntahermosasurfinn.com; Bolognesi 407, cnr Pacasmayo; dm/s/d incl breakfast S45/60/120; @), which has six rooms, a cozy hangout area with hammocks and cable TV. Note: weekend rates are S30 higher for private rooms and S10 higher for shared rooms. The largest waves in Peru, which can reach a height of 10m, are found nearby at **Pico Alto** (at Panamericana Km 43).

Punta Rocas, a little further south, is also popular with experienced surfers (annual competitions are held here), who generally crash at the basic **Hostal Hamacas** (☎88-104-144; www.hostalhamacas.com; Panamericana Km 47; s/d with air-con S104/117, with fan S60/78, 2-person apt S143), right on the beach. There are 15 rooms and five bungalows (which sleep six), all with private bathrooms, hot water and ocean views. There is an on-site restaurant during the high season (October to April). It also rents boards. Generally, however, surfboard rental is almost nonexistent; best to bring your own.

To get to these beaches, take a bus signed 'San Bartolo' from the Panamericana Sur at the Puente Primavera in Lima. You can get off at any of the beach towns along the route, but in many cases it will be a 1km to 2km hike down to the beach. (Local taxis are usually waiting by the road.) A one-way taxi from Lima runs between S70 and S80.

For beaches to the south, such as Pucusana, see p103.

Carretera Central

The Carretera Central (Central Hwy) heads directly east from Lima, following the Rímac valley into the foothills of the Andes and on to La Oroya in Peru's central highlands.

Minibuses to Chosica leave frequently from Arica at the Plaza Bolognesi (Map p62). These can be used to travel to Puruchuco (S2 to S3, 50 minutes) and Chosica (S3 to S4, two hours).

Colectivo taxis also make the journey from the corner of Arequipa and Av Javier Prado in San Isidro for S8. Recognizing sites from the road can be difficult, so let the driver know where you want to get off.

PURUCHUCO

📍01

The site of **Puruchuco** (📞494-2641; http://museopuruchuco.perucultural.org.pe; admission S5; ⊙9am-4pm Tue-Sun) hit the news in 2002 when about 2000 well-preserved mummy bundles were unearthed from the enormous Inca cemetery. It's one of the biggest finds of its kind, and the multitude of grave goods included a number of well-preserved *quipu*. The site has a highly reconstructed chief's house, with one room identified as a guinea-pig ranch. Situated amid the shantytown of Túpac Amaru, Puruchuco is 13km from Central Lima. (It is best to take a taxi.) A signpost on the highway marks the turn-off, and from here it is several hundred meters along a road to the right.

CAJAMARQUILLA

📍01

Another pre-Columbian site, **Cajamarquilla** (admission S5; ⊙9am-4pm) is a crumbling adobe city that was built up by the Wari culture (AD 700–1100) on the site of a settlement originally developed by people of the Lima culture. A road to the left from Lima at about Km 10 (18km from Central Lima) goes to the Cajamarquilla zinc refinery, almost 5km from the highway. The ruins are located about halfway along the refinery road; take a turn to the right along a short road. There are signs, but ask the locals for the *zona arqueológica* if you have trouble finding them.

CHOSICA

📍01

About 40km from Lima lies the rustic mountain town of Chosica, which sits at 860m above sea level, above the fog line. In the early half of the 20th century, it was a popular weekend getaway spot for *limeños* intent on soaking up sun in winter. Today its popularity has declined, though some visitors still arrive for day trips. The plaza is lined with restaurants, and in the evenings *anticucho* vendors gather along some of the fountain-lined promenades. From Chosica, a minor road leads to the ruins of Marcahuasi (see p272).

South Coast

Includes »

Best Places to Eat

» Café Da Vinci (p133)

» As de Oro's (p110)

» Via La Encantada (p127)

» El Chorito (p115)

Best Places to Stay

» Casa-Hacienda San José (p107)

» Hotel El Huacachinero (p120)

» Hotel El Molino (p106)

» Nazca Lines Hotel (p126)

Why Go?

The main mystery that preoccupies outsiders as they inspect the barren, foggy, uncompromisingly dry desert that infests Peru's southern coastline for the first time (usually from the window of a crowded bus) is, how does anyone live here? It, thus, comes as a surprise to discover that people don't just live here, they positively thrive – check out Ica's wine industry or Chincha's Afro-Peruvian culture if you want proof. What's more, they've been thriving for millennia. The perplexing Nazca Lines, a weird collection of giant geoglyphs etched into the desert, date from 400–650 AD, while intricate cloths unearthed on the Paracas peninsula were woven 1000 years before Pachacuti led the Incas out of Cuzco. Though Machu Picchu hogs most of the limelight in Southern Peru, the south coast is pierced by a lesser 'gringo trail' whose obligatory stops include adventure nexus Lunahuaná, wildlife obsessed Paracas, Nazca and the desert oasis of Huacachina.

When to Go
Nazca

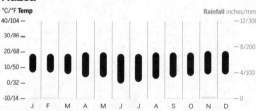

Jan–Mar High summer means main coastal beach resorts are open and pulsating with energy.

Mar Grape harvest and accompanying wine festivals in Lunahuaná and Ica.

Jun & Jul Cooler temperatures, fewer tourists and esoteric festivals in Chincha and Ica.

Pucusana

✈ 01 / POP 10,000

Materializing out of the fog and grime that hangs over Lima's southern suburbs, Pucusana marks the first genuinely worthwhile stop on the coast. Superficially, it's a typical Peruvian fishing village: clamorous, a little grubby and packed with literally hundreds of wooden boats bobbing around in its protected harbor. But there's an innate soulfulness here too. If you've just waltzed out of Miraflores thinking you'd arrived in a Latin American version of LA, this will feel more like the real warts-and-all Peru.

The small Pucusana and Las Ninfas beaches are on the town's seafront or you can catch a boat (S1) to La Isla, an offshore island with a lofty hill and a strand of sand. The most exclusive beach in the area is Naplo, 1km away and reached through a tunnel. The **Gremio de Pescadores de Puscana** (fishing port) is quite a scene at any time of day with oil-skinned fishermen battling with huge whale-sized fish while snappy-beaked pelicans inspect their work from close quarters. Just outside the entrance, boats gather offering fishing trips and tours of the marina (from S40).

The best of the simple hotels in Pucusana, **El Mirador de Pucusana** (✆ 430-9228; s/d/tr S30/40/55) enjoys a lofty perch atop the bayfront with good views. Rooms are basic, but do have hot water. If you're hankering for fresh seafood, you'll find it in the *cevicherías* (restaurants serving ceviche) that line the boardwalk below. **Restaurante Jhony** (mains S20-30) is the best of the cluster; try the *tortillita de camarones,* a thick tasty omelet full of prawns with most of their anatomy still intact.

From central Lima, *combis* (minibuses) run frequently to Pucusana from Plaza Bolognesi (S5 one way). An alternative is to take a taxi from Lima to the Puente Primavera bridge at the intersection of Av Primavera and Carr Panamericana Sur. Southbound coastal buses along Carr Panamericana Sur leave from here and can drop you off at Km 57, from where minibuses shuttle during daylight hours to central Pucusana (S1, 10 minutes).

For beaches closer to Lima, see p99.

Asia

✈ 01 / POP 4000

With a growth rate that could emulate anywhere on the Asian side of the Pacific Rim, Peru's namesake 'Asia' is a nebulous commercial area south of Lima that incorporates more than 30 beaches, thousands of pricey holiday homes, and a humungous shopping mall known as El Sur Plaza Boulevard which opened in 2003. Most of the action is centered around the 97.5km marker of Carr Panamericana Sur, although clubs, restaurants and condos are now spreading as far north as Pucusana and as far south as Cerro Azul. Traditional Peru this most certainly isn't (think more mini-Dubai), though it's a lively place with young moneyed Limeños dropping by for nightlife and beach bumming opportunities in season (January to March). The rest of the year, it can be pretty dead.

Almost any bus along Carr Panamericana Sur can drop you here upon request. There are some basic guesthouses on the main boulevard that are quite expensive, but Lima is less than an hour away with countless buses leaving 24/7. Fares start at S16.

Cañete & Cerro Azul

✈ 01 / POP 37,000

The full name of this small market town and transport nexus, about 145km south of Lima, is San Vicente de Cañete. Most Peruvian holidaymakers head north of town to Cerro Azul, a beach that's popular with experienced surfers. It's a 15-minute walk west of Km 131 on Carr Panamericana Sur, about 15km north of town. There's a small Inca sea fort in the area, known as **Huarco**, but it's in a poor state.

In Cerro Azul, the surfer-friendly **Hostal Cerro Azul** (✆ 271-1302; www.cerroazul hostal.com; Puerto Viejo 106; d/tr/q/ste S150/185/200/220) is less than 100m from the shoreline. If you're hungry, beachfront restaurants all serve fresh seafood. **Restaurant Juanito** (✆ 335-3710; Rivera del Mar; mains S20-25; ☺8am-9pm) is a popular local pick.

From Lima, buses for Pisco or Ica can drop you at Cañete and sometimes Cerro Azul (S18 to S21, 2½ hours). Buses back to Lima are invariably crowded, especially on Sunday from January to April. There are also *combis* between Cañete and Cerro Azul (S1, 30 minutes) or south to Chincha (S2, one hour).

South Coast Highlights

1 Deciphering the mysteries of the **Nazca Lines** (p122) from an overflight or a tour on terra firma

2 Observing sea lions and birdlife, and dodging guano on a boat trip to the **Islas Ballestas** (p112)

3 Watching the sun set atop a giant sand dune overlooking the desert oasis of **Huacachina** (p120)

4 Watching live Afro-Peruvian music and dance at **Casa-Hacienda San José** (p107) in El Carmen

5 Rafting the angry rapids of Río Cañete in adventure nexus **Lunahuaná** (p105)

6 Tasting some of Peru's best wines and piscos at the **Bodega Tacama** (p117) near Ica

7 Hiking across the deserted Paracas peninsula for a seafood lunch in **Lagunillas** (p112)

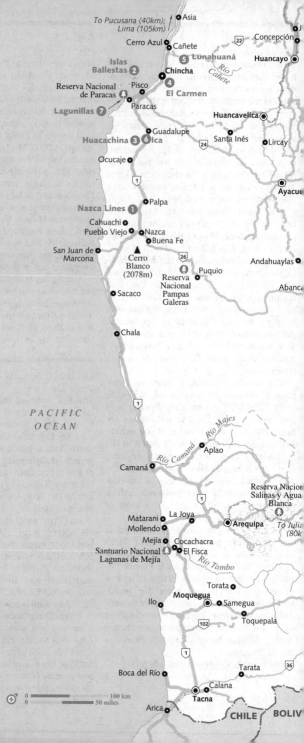

Lunahuaná

📍01 / PO 3600 / ELEV 1700M

The small town of Lunahuaná rises like a slice of desert romance above the foggy and grubby coastal strip south of Lima. Reached via a winding 38km road that tracks east from the noisy settlement of Cañete, it appears almost magically, a thin strip of broccoli green amid the dusty desert that gleams with a touch of Middle Eastern promise. But, there are no Bedouin tents or wailing minarets here. Instead, Lunahuaná's raison d'être is split between wine-production and river running. Both owe their existence to the seasonally turbulent Rio Cañete, whose class IV rapids provide cheap thrills for brave rafters and a vital form of irrigation for the local vineyards.

Some people incorporate Luanahuaná into an overnighter from Lima and it's certainly worth the effort. The best time to show up is during the second week of March for the grape harvest, Fiesta de la Vendimia. An adventure-sports festival is usually held in late February or early March.

👁 Sights

Lunahuaná is small with little of architectural significance outside of its main square, which is crowned by the Iglesia Santiago Apostal dating from 1690. The square's arched *portales* hide bars and shops that specialize in wine and pisco. From here, it's a five-minute walk up to a scenic mirador with great views of the town and its surrounding greenery.

Bodega Santa Maria   WINERY
(www.bodegasantamaria.com; Km 39 Carr Cañete-Lunahuaná) A very civilized semi-industrial winemaker 1km north of the town whose flowery grounds and large wooden casks retain the air of an Andalucian sherry bodega. Free samples of the sweet-ish wine (red, white and rosé) and powerful pisco varietals are laid on in an aromatic tasting room. It also sells locally made honey.

Catapalla   VILLAGE
A tiny settlement 6km further up the valley from Lunahuaná, Catapalla is notable for one of the valley's oldest artisanal wineries, the venerable La Reyna de Lunahuaná (📞99-477-7117; admission & tours free; ⏰7am-1pm & 2-5pm) which presides over the main plaza. The owners here can teach you the ABCs of pisco (Peruvian grape brandy) and wine production. The village's other main feature is its Puente Colgante (suspension bridge) that hangs precariously over the Río Cañete's angry rapids. A one-way taxi ride to Catapalla from Lunahuaná should cost from S6, but you may have to wait until a car shows up for the return.

Incahuasi   RUINS
(Km 39 Carr Cañete-Lunahuaná; admission S3.50; ⏰9am-5pm) The most notable archaeological site in the Cañete Valley is Incahuasi, the rough-walled ruins of the military headquarters of the 10th Inca king Túpac Yupanqui, located on the western outskirts of Lunahuaná. It is thought that the original buildings date from 1438-ish, soon after the ascension of Emperor Pachacuti. You won't find a lot of signage or fellow travelers here, but therein lies the attraction. The ruins are on the main road 10km west of Lunahuaná. A taxi should cost S10 to S12 round-trip.

🏃 Activities

River running

River running (rafting) can be done year-round, but the best time is between December and April, the rainy months in the Andes when the Río Cañete runs high. Adventure-sport championships, including river running, are held here in late February or early March. For rafting purposes, the river is split into three sections. The hardest (Ruta Alta) is the section east of Lunahuaná up to the village of Catapalla which is graded III-IV in summer. The easier sections to the west between Lunahuaná and Paullo, and Paullo and Socsi are graded I-III and are only doable in the summer.

Reputable rafting companies include Río Cañete Expediciones (📞284-1271; www.riocanete.com.pe) based at Camping San Jerónimo (p106) and Laberinto Explorer (📞284-1057; Av Grau 365) a couple of blocks from Lunahuaná's main plaza.

Zip-lining

Satisfying a growing international craze for zip-lining (canopy tours), Luanahuaná has come up with a real corker fitted out with five cables that shoot vertigo-shunners over the Río Cañete for a total 'zip' distance of 2500m – one of Latin America's longest. The price for the full five lines is S100. Zippers launch into thin air from Camping San Jerónimo.

SOUTH COAST LUNAHUANÁ

Abseiling

For a more vertical drop, you can abseil (rappel) down a cliff face overlooking the Cañete river approximately 7km north of town. Most agencies in Av Grau organize excursions.

Cycling

Located high above the car-crazed coast, Luanahuaná is easily cycled; indeed bikes are a handy way of visiting some of the outlying sites and wine bodegas. Decent machines with gears generally cost S40 for two hours and can be procured from most of the travel companies on Av Grau.

🛏 Sleeping

TOP CHOICE Hotel El Molino   HOTEL $$$

(☎378-6061; www.hotelelmolino.com.pe; Malecon Araoz Km 39 Carretera Cañete-Lunahuana; s/d/ste S260/280/340; ❄🌐🎔🏊) Not far from the 'beast' of Lima's southern suburbs lies the 'beauty' of El Molino, a lovingly tended hotel complex set on the banks of the Cañete river on the cusp of Luanahuná. The hotel opened in 2011 with boutique-style rooms encased in glassy river-facing units. There are two pools, table football, and a fine restaurant in the beautifully landscaped grounds where tranquility reigns bar the odd triumphant whoop of a passing rafter.

Refugio de Santiago   HOTEL $$$

(☎436-2717; www.refugiodesantiago.com; Km 31 Carr Cañete-Lunahuaná; r per person incl meals adult/child S200/100) This renovated colonial home a few kilometers west of Lunahuaná is the ultimate relaxing getaway. Rooms are rustic but elegant and the grounds feature a fragrant botanical garden and a restaurant that serves textbook local specialties (mains S32 to S48). The prices include breakfast, lunch and dinner, and guided walks through the local orchards.

Hostal Río Alto   HOTEL $$

(☎284-1125; www.rioaltohotel.com; Km 39 Carr Cañete-Lunahuaná; s/d S91/147; 🎔🏊) About 1km along the highway east of Lunahuaná, this friendly guesthouse looks down to the river from a shady terrace overrun with plants. Rooms, though plain, are modern and have hot showers.

Camping San Jerónimo   CAMPGROUND $

(☎284-1271; Km 33 Carr Cañete-Lunahuaná; per person S15) This campground borders the river at the far west of town. Base camp for

Río Cañete Expediciones, it has good facilities and a free artificial rock-climbing wall for guests.

Hostal Los Andes   HOTEL $

(☎284-1041; Los Andes; s/d/tr S40/50/70) A basic but dependable three-storied yellow block with some 2nd-floor rooms offering peek-a-boo river views. There's hot water and cable TV, but no wi-fi.

🍴 Eating

Sabores de mi Tierra   PERUVIAN $

(Bolognesi 199: meals from S6) Cheap, earthy flavors served up for as little as S6 for a main plus starter. Try the chicken stew and prawn chowder.

Don Ignacio La Casa del Pisco   PERUVIAN $

(Plaza de Armas; mains from S10) One of the best pisco-biased restaurants on the main square where you can dilute the local 'rocket fuel' with typical food from the area, including memorable crawfish.

ℹ Getting There & Away

From Cañete, catch a *combi* to Imperial (S1, 10 minutes), from where *combis* also run to Lunahuaná (S3.50, 45 minutes). Faster *colectivos* (shared taxis) wait for passengers on the main road, just downhill from the plaza in Lunahuaná, and then race back to Imperial (S4, 25 minutes).

Chincha

☎056 / POP 194,000

Gloriously chaotic or frustratingly anarchic (depending on your tolerance for dust and noise), Chincha is Peru uncut and unpackaged, an unregulated mess of buses, taxis and jay-walking humanity. On the surface it could be any Peruvian town in any south coast province, but closer scrutiny unearths some engrossing details: sugar cane juice sellers, black African figurines offered as souvenirs, and menus advertising *criolla* specialties (*sopa seca* anyone?). Chincha is the font of Afro-Peruvian culture, a small and little-known component of the national whole that testifies to a brutal slave past.

⊙ Sights

There's not much to see in the city center, although the main square with its terracotta church and tall, sinuous palm trees is surprisingly salubrious. The local wine industry is evident in the shops that line Av Benavides between the square and the bus station. **La Plazuela** (Av Benavides 501) will pour a few gratis miniglasses of the eye-wateringly sweet local wine and the mega-strong pisco. The owners run a restaurant next door should you fancy further top-ups.

El Carmen District   VILLAGE

Veterans of Cuba have been known to double take in El Carmen, a place where African and Latin American cultures collide with hip-gyrating results. The small rustic 'village' is famous for its rhythm-heavy Afro-Peruvian music heard in the *peñas* (bars and clubs featuring live folkloric music) which lie about 15km outside town. The best times to visit are during the cultural festivals. Festival or no festival, there's usually something going on at the **Ballumbrosio Estate** (San José 325). The house of El Carmen's most famous dancing family is a museum to Afro-Peruvian culture and music breaks out here spontaneously most weekends. Pop in if you're in the village to view the photos and paintings and see what's up.

TOP
CHOICE **Casa-Hacienda San José**   MUSEUM
(☏31-3332; www.casahaciendasanjose.com; El Carmen) Providing reason alone to make the trip down from Lima, this former slave plantation with its stately hacienda offers a rare opportunity for Afro-Peruvian historical immersion – some of it gilded, some of it gruesome. You can even stay overnight, in heady colonial-era opulence – the hacienda reopened as a 12-room **hotel** (r S210-250; ❈❈) in 2012 after a five-year hiatus following the 2007 earthquake. For nonguests, one hour tours of the hacienda and its famous catacombs cost S20 – just ring the bell at the main gate. The original building with its fine baroque chapel dates from 1688. Surviving artifacts include frescos, agricultural equipment, and brutal remnants of a system once used to subjugate the slaves including an extensive web of catacombs and underground tunnels (which you explore with a candle). Should you arrive on a Sunday be sure to stay for the dinner buffet show (S70) which is accompanied by athletic Afro-Peruvian dancing in the shaded courtyard. A spectacularly ruined cotton factory, dating from 1913, sits next door.

Archaeological Sites

In ancient times, the small Chincha empire flourished in this region until it was clobbered by the Incas in the late 15th century. The best surviving archaeological sites in the area are **Tambo de Mora**, on the coast about 10km from Chincha, and the temple of **La Centinela** northwest of the city, about 8km off Carr Panamericana Sur. Both can be visited by taxi (about S15 one way).

★ Festivals & Events

The abundance of local festivals includes the **Verano Negro** (late February/early March), **Fiestas Patrias** (National Independence, in late July) and **La Virgen del Carmen de Chincha** (the festival in honor of the patron Virgin, on December 27). During these times, minibuses run from Chincha to El Carmen all night long, and the *peñas* are full of frenzied *limeños* and locals dancing. One traditional dance not to try at home: 'El Alcatraz,' when a gyrating male dancer with a candle attempts to set fire to a handkerchief attached to the back of his partner's skirt.

🛏 Sleeping & Eating

Bare-bones cheap hotels and *chifas* (Chinese restaurants) surround Chincha's main plaza. Most fill up and double or triple

---

AFRO-PERUVIAN MUSIC & DANCE

The mesmerizing beats and lightning-speed movements of this traditional art form are guaranteed to make you want to get up and dance. During the colonial period, when Spanish colonizers banned the use of drums, African slaves working on Peruvian plantations began using hollow wooden crates (now called a *cajón*) and donkey jawbones to create percussion that now forms the base of this distinct musical style. Often music is accompanied by an impressive flamenco-style dance called *zapateo* and impassioned singing.

Over the past few decades, groups such as Perú Negro and the Ballumbrosio family have garnered quite a following both nationally and internationally, making it their mission to preserve Peru's African heritage through the performance of its music and dance. If you're in the right place at the right time, you can catch one of these shows in the community that is famous for it, El Carmen.

their prices during festivals, though you can always avoid this problem by dancing all night and taking an early morning bus back to Lima or further south along the coast.

In El Carmen, a few local families will take in overnight guests and cook meals for between S10 and S20 per person per night – ask around. Or you can stay in the town's only hotel, the **Parador Turístico** (☏27-4060; Plaza de Armas; s/d S25/40).

Casa Andina –
Chincha Sausal   BOUTIQUE HOTEL **$$$**
(☏213-9739; www.casa-andina.com; Carr Panamericana Sur Km 197.5; d/tr S261/290; ✹@☞☒)
A rather odd outpost of Peru's plushest hotel chain, glued to the frankly horrible Carr Panamericana Sur 1km north of Chincha's bus station, the Sausel is aimed at the corporate business market and is thus a bit stuffy and officious. Facilities are nonetheless, upper-crust with flowered grounds, luxury bed-linens and a decent restaurant.

Hostal El Condado   HOTEL **$$**
(☏26-1424; Pan Am Km195; r from S100; ☞) Another air freshener on the congested Carr Panamericana Sur, El Condado rarely disappoints with super clean rooms, welcoming service and a rather nice restaurant where the portions aren't small.

Restaurant Doña Jita   PERUVIAN **$**
(Av Benavides 293; mains from S6) Set menus are the order of the day here in a communal atmosphere not far removed from an Arequipa *picantería* (traditional spicy restaurant). Choose from the two-course *ejecutivo* (S10) or *económico* (S6) menus. The garbanzo soup and *lomo saltado* (strips of beef stir-fried with onions, tomatoes, potatoes and chili) are among the best (and cheapest) you'll taste this side of Lima.

❶ Getting There & Around

There are many companies based on Carr Panamericana Sur with buses running through Chincha en route between Lima (S20 to S23, 2½ hours) and Ica (S7 to S10, two hours). If you're headed to Pisco, most southbound buses can drop you off at the San Clemente turnoff on Carr Panamericana Sur (S4), from where you can catch frequent *colectivos* and *combis* for the 6km trip into Pisco (S3). From Chincha, *combis* headed north to Cañete (S2, one hour) and south to Paracas (S3, one hour) leave from near Plazuela Bolognesi.

Combis to El Carmen (S2, 30 minutes) leave from Chincha's central market area, a few blocks from the main plaza.

The plaza is 500m from Carr Panamericana Sur where the coastal buses stop.

Pisco
☏056 / POP 58,200

Crushed by a 2007 earthquake which destroyed its infrastructure but not its spirit, Pisco is a town on the rebound, reinventing itself almost daily with the resilience of an immortal phoenix. Irrespective of the substantial damage, the town remains open for business, promoting itself along with nearby beach resort of El Chaco (Paracas), as a base for forays to the Paracas Reserve and Islas Ballestas, although El Chaco trumps it in terms of location and choice of facilities.

Pisco shares its name with the national beverage, a brandy that is made throughout the region. The area is of historical and archaeological interest, having hosted one of the most highly developed pre-Inca civilizations – the Paracas culture from 700 BC until AD 400. Later it acted as a base for Peru's revolutionary fever in the early 19th century.

Although the Pisco-Paracas area is spread out, it's easy to get around. Public transportation between Pisco and the harbor at Paracas, 15km further south along the coast, leaves from Pisco's market area or the main plaza in the El Chaco beach area of Paracas.

◉ Sights

Post-earthquake, Pisco's main **Plaza de Armas** is a mishmash of the vanquished and the saved. The equestrian **statue of José de San Martín**, sword bravely raised in defiance falls into the latter category. Another survivor is the Moorish **Municipalidad** building (town hall) dating from 1929 whose wrecked shell awaits a major refurb. Pisco's biggest earthquake casualty was the colonial **San Clemente Cathedral**. A new modern red-bricked church has gone up in its place, financed with Spanish money – not so pretty, but an achievement all the same. Commerce has returned to pedestrianized San Martin which runs west from the plaza and is beautified with benches, flower-covered trellises and a refreshing fountain.

🏃 Activities

It is still perfectly viable to use Pisco as a base for tours of the Paracas Peninsula and the Islas Ballestras. Various agencies dot the central area.

Aprotur TOUR
(📞50-7156; www.aproturpisco.webs.com; San Francisco 112) The stoic boys at Aprotur run a laid-back but businesslike travel company from an office on the main square organizing

Pisco

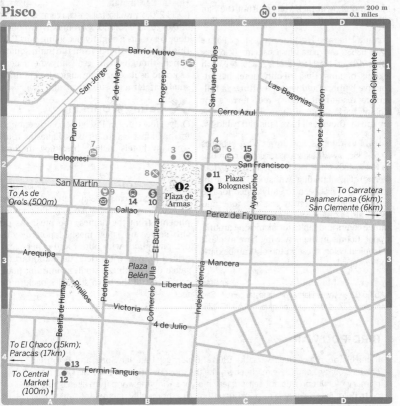

Pisco

◎ Sights
1 San Clemente Cathedral C2
2 Statue of José de San Martín B2

✪ Activities, Courses & Tours
3 Aprotur B2

🛏 Sleeping
4 Hostal La Casona C2
5 Hostal Residencial San Jorge B1
6 Hostal Villa Manuelita............................ C2
7 Posada Hispana Hotel A2

✕ Eating
8 El Dorado B2

🍷 Drinking
9 Taberna de Don Jaime............................ B2

ⓘ Information
10 Interbank B2
11 Muncipalidad C2

ⓘ Transport
12 Colectivos to Paracas and the
   San Clemente turnoff on
   the Panamerica A4
13 Combis to Paracas A4
14 Flores B2
15 Ormeño.. C2

trips to all the local sights, including Islas Ballestras (S45), Paracas peninsula (S25) and Tambo Colorado (S20). Guides speak six languages, including Hebrew.

🛏 Sleeping

Many hotels will pick you up from the San Clemente turnoff on Carr Panamericana Sur.

Posada Hispana Hotel
HOTEL $

(☎53-6363; www.posadahispana.com; Bolognesi 236; s/d/tr incl breakfast US$15/25/35; @) With legions of fans, this friendly hotel has attractive bamboo and wooden fittings, a full-service restaurant, and a roof terrace for kicking back. Some of the well-worn rooms are musty, though all have fans and cable TV.

Hotel Residencial San Jorge
HOTEL $$

(☎53-2885; www.hotelsanjorgeresidencial.com; Barrio Nuevo 133; s/d/tr incl breakfast S85/110/130; @🌐🌊) This building withstood the earthquake, but it has been recently added to. The breezy, modern entryway sets the tone and there's also a bright cafe, and back garden with lounge chairs and tables for picnicking around a pool. Rooms in the new wing have a splash of tropical color; those in the old can be dark and cramped.

Hostal Villa Manuelita
HOTEL $$

(☎53-5218; www.villamanuelitahostal.com; San Francisco 227; s/d/tr incl breakfast S70/95/125; @) While it had to be heavily renovated post-earthquake, this hotel still retains the grandeur of its colonial foundations. Plus, it's very conveniently located only half a block from the plaza.

Hostal La Casona
HOTEL $

(☎53-2703; www.hostallacasona.com; San Juan de Dios 252; s/d S55/80; 🌐) A massive wooden door serves as a slightly deceiving portal to this hotel half a block from the main square which, though clean, isn't anywhere near as grand as its entryway suggests. There's a small cafeteria on site for meals.

🍴 Eating & Drinking

Only a few cafes in Pisco open early enough for breakfast before an Islas Ballestas tour, so many hotels include breakfast in their rates.

TOP CHOICE As de Oro's
PERUVIAN $$

(www.asdeoros.com.pe; San Martín 472; mains S30-50; ⏲noon-midnight Tue-Sun) Talk about phoenix from the flames; the plush As de Oro serves up spicy mashed potato with octopus, plaice with butter and capers, and grilled prawns with fried yucca and tartare sauce overlooking a small swimming pool, as the rest of the town struggles back to its feet.

BIRD-POO WAR

In the history of pointless wars, the 1864–66 skirmish between Spain and its former colonies of Peru and Chile might seem like the most pointless of them all. Ostensibly, its primary motivation was not self-preservation or saving the world from aliens, but guano, or, to put it less politely, bird-poo. But, although a thoroughly unpleasant substance when dropped from a great height onto your head, guano has long been a vital contributor to the Peruvian economy, and a resource worth protecting from prying outsiders. In the early 19th century, German botanist Alexander von Humboldt sent samples of it to Europe where innovative British farmers found it to be 30 times more efficient that cow dung when used as a fertilizer. By the 1850s a rapidly industrializing Britain was importing 200,000 tons of the crap annually to bolster its agriculture. Suddenly the white droppings that covered Peru's bird-filled Pacific Islands were worth the lion's share of the GDP. Spain understood as much in 1864 when in an act of post-colonial petulance it occupied the guano-rich Chincha Islands in an attempt to extract reparations from Peru over a small domestic incident in Lambayeque. Peru didn't hesitate to retaliate. A protracted naval war ensued that dragged in Chile, before the islands and their precious bird-pooh were wrenched back from Spain in 1866.

In the conflict-free present, the industry remains lucrative. Layers of sun-baked, nitrogen-rich guano still cover the Chincha Islands, as well as the nearby Islas Ballestas, although the overfishing of anchovies (the bird's main food source) in the 1960s and '70s led to a worrying decline in supplies. Today guano production is closely (and peacefully) regulated by Peru's Ministry of Agriculture.

La Concha de Tus Mares
PERUVIAN $

(Calle Muelle 992; mains S15-25) Old pictures of what Pisco used to look like pre-2007 adorn the walls of this nostalgic place next to the Colegio Alexander Von Humboldt about 1km south of the center. The fish comes in big portions and is lauded by the locals.

El Dorado
BREAKFAST, INTERNATIONAL $

(☑53-4367; Progreso 171; mains S10-20; ☺6:30am-11pm) Nothing fancy, and popular because of it, the Dorado advertises no pretensions with its Nescafé granule coffee, excellent *tres leche* cake and simple but effective breakfasts on the main square.

Taberna de Don Jaime
BAR

(☑53-5023; San Martín 203; ☺4pm-2am) This clamorous tavern is a favorite with locals and tourists alike. It is also a showcase for artisanal wines and piscos. On weekends, the crowds show up to dance to live Latin and rock tunes into the small hours.

ℹ Information

There's no tourist office in Pisco, but travel agencies on the main plaza and **police** (☑53-2884; San Francisco 132; ☺24hr) help when they can. Everything else you'll need is found around the Plaza de Armas, including internet cafes.

Dangers & Annoyances

On its knees after the earthquake, Pisco acquired a reputation for crime, but the curtain is lifting. The commerce-packed streets should be fine during the daytime (there's a notable police presence in the city center). Nonetheless, it is best to utilize taxis after dark, particularly around the bus station and market areas. If you arrive late, get the ticket agent at your bus company office to hail you a reputable cab.

Money

Interbank (San Martín 101) has a 24-hour global ATM.

ℹ Getting There & Around

Pisco is 6km west of Carr Panamericana Sur, and only buses with Pisco as the final destination actually go there. **Ormeño** (☑53-2764; San Francisco), **Flores** (☑79-6643; San Martín) and **Soyuz** (www.soyuz.com.pe; Av Ernesto R Diez Canseco 4) offer multiple daily departures north to Lima and south to Ica, Nazca and Arequipa.

If you're not on a direct bus to either Pisco or Paracas, ask to be left at the San Clemente turnoff on Carr Panamericana Sur, where fast and frequent *colectivos* wait to shuttle passengers to central Pisco's Plaza de Armas (S3, 10

PISCO BUSES

DESTINATION	COST (S)	DURATION (HR)
Arequipa	60-144	12-15
Ica	4-15	1½-2
Lima	28-76	4½
Nazca	17-35	4

minutes) or Paracas (S10, 20 minutes). In the reverse direction, *colectivos* for the San Clemente turnoff leave frequently from near Pisco's central market. After dark, avoid the dangerous market area and take a taxi instead (S5). From the San Clemente turnoff, you can flag down buses, which pass frequently heading either north or south.

Transportation from Pisco to Paracas is possible via *combi* (S1.50, 30 minutes), or *colectivo* (S2.50, 20 minutes), which leave frequently from near Pisco's central market.

Paracas (El Chaco)

The Paracas peninsula's main village, El Chaco – often referred to erroneously as 'Paracas' – is a mishmash of half demolished and half repaired buildings that pepper a motley 'resort' strip shared by youthful backpackers, middle-aged ornithologists and a growing band of moneyed Limeños. On potholed streets still recuperating from the 2007 earthquake stray dogs bark, waiters hold open fish-inspired menus and hungry pelicans stakeout the harbor like vultures searching for fresh carrion. Tourism is the village's raison d'être, though the posh new hotels and Lima-like condos that have recently embellished the town's periphery have yet to forge a collective personality. On the road north to Pisco a collection of large fish factories emit a distinctive and stomach-churning pong.

◉ Sights

The reserve's essential business is the de rigueur boat tour of the Islas Ballestros and the one-day sojourn around the bald deserted Paracas peninsula. Birds and sea mammals are the lures here, but, lest we forget, this is also one of Peru's most important archaeological sites thanks primarily to the pre-Inca treasures unearthed by one of the country's most important archaeologists, Julio Tello in the 1920s.

EL CHACO

Paracas History Museum MUSEUM
(Av Los Libertadores; admission S10; ⊙9am-5.30pm) Since most of the archaeological booty dug up nearby has been carted off to Lima, Paracas' tiny museum is left with only a few scraps, the most striking of which are the elongated human skulls.

ISLAS BALLESTAS

Although grandiosely nicknamed the 'poor man's Galapagos,' the Islas Ballestas make for a memorable excursion. The only way to get there is on a boat tour, offered by many tour agencies (p114). While the tours do not actually disembark onto the islands, they do get you startlingly close to an impressive variety of wildlife. None of the small boats have a cabin, so dress to protect against the wind, spray and sun. The sea can get rough, so sufferers of motion sickness should take medication before boarding. Wear a hat (cheap ones are sold at the harbor), as it's not unusual to receive a direct hit of guano (droppings) from the seabirds.

On the outward boat journey, which takes about 30 minutes, you will stop just offshore to admire the famous Candelabra geoglyph.

A further hour is spent cruising around the islands' arches and caves and watching large herds of noisy sea lions sprawl on the rocks. The most common guano-producing birds in this area are the guanay cormorant, the Peruvian booby and the Peruvian pelican, seen in colonies several thousand strong. You'll also see cormorants, Humboldt penguins and, if you're lucky, dolphins. Although you can get close enough to the wildlife for a good look, some species, especially the penguins, are more visible with binoculars.

Back on shore, you can grab a bite to eat at one of the many waterfront restaurants near the dock in El Chaco, or you can continue on a tour of the Reserva Nacional de Paracas.

RESERVA NACIONAL DE PARACAS

This vast desert reserve occupies most of the Península de Paracas. For tour operators, see p114. Alternatively, taxi drivers who function as guides often wait beyond the dock where passengers disembark in Paracas' beach village of El Chaco, and can take groups into the reserve for around S50 for a three-hour tour. You can also walk from El Chaco – just make sure to allow lots of time, and bring food and plenty of water. To get there, start at the obelisk commemorating the landing of the liberator General José de San Martín that lies near the entrance to El Chaco village, and continue on foot along the tarmac road that heads to the south.

Centro de Interpretación MUSEUM
(⊙7am-6pm) Located 1.5km south of the park-entry point, where a S5 entrance fee is charged, this modest center's displays kick off with a 12-minute rather twee video aimed, it would seem, at wide-eyed teenagers. The subsequent exhibits on fauna, archaeology and geology are weightier and more inspiring. The new Museo Julio C Tello next door, which opened in July 2012, has upped the ante significantly. The bay in front of the complex is the best spot to view Chilean flamingos, and there's now a walkway down to a mirador (lookout), from where these birds can best be spotted from June through August.

Paracas Necropolis ARCHAEOLOGICAL SITE
A few hundred meters behind the visitor complex on Cerro Colorado are the 5000-year-old remains of a necropolis related to the Paracas culture, which predated the Incas by more than a thousand years. A stash of more than 400 funerary bundles was found here, each wrapped in many layers of colorful woven shrouds for which the Paracas culture is famous. There's little to see now; indeed signs warn you off the site. Lima's Museo Larco (p65) and Ica's Museo Regional de Ica (p115) exhibit some of these exquisite textiles and other finds from the site.

Beyond the visitor complex, the tarmac road continues around the peninsula to Puerto General San Martín, which has a pongy fish-meal plant and a port on the northern tip of the peninsula.

Lagunillas VILLAGE, BEACH
Turkey vultures feast on the washed-up remains of yesterday's marine carcasses on the lonely beach at Lagunillas, 5km south of the Centro de Interpretación, where three almost identical salt-of-the-sea restaurants constitute 'the village'. La Tia Fela (mains S35; ⊙9am-5pm) does an excellent corvina a la plancha (grilled sea bass) which you can enjoy while watching pelicans squabble over

Reserva Nacional de Paracas

Reserva Nacional de Paracas

yesterday's cast offs. Warning: this is a basic place. Ask the way to the loos and they'll point at a nearby sand dune. Bring the hand-sanitizer!

Punta Arquillo   LOOKOUT

From Lagunillas, the road continues a few kilometers to a parking area near this clifftop lookout, which has grand views of the ocean, with a sea-lion colony on the rocks below and plenty of seabirds gliding by.

Other seashore life around the reserve includes flotillas of jellyfish (swimmers beware!), some of which reach about 70cm in diameter with trailing stinging tentacles of 1m. They are often washed up on the shore,

where they quickly dry to form mandala-like patterns on the sand. Beachcombers can also find sea hares, ghost crabs and seashells along the shoreline, and the Andean condor occasionally descends to the coast in search of rich pickings.

La Mina Beach   BEACH

This beach is short drive or walk south of Lagunillas on a dirt road. Sunbathers come here in summer (January to March) when you may find the odd mobile drinks concession set up. Camping is also allowed. Plan to bring all the water you will need, and never camp alone as robberies have been reported. Adjacent is the rockier **El Raspón beach**.

Yumaque Beach & La Catedral
BEACH, LANDMARK

The reserve protrudes south a fair few kilometers below the Paracas Peninsula. Dirt roads branch off just east of Lagunillas to Yumaque beach and La Catedral. The latter – a majestic natural arch that jutted out into the sea – was destroyed by the 2007 earthquake. Formed over hundreds of thousands of years of wind and wave erosion, it got toppled in less than a minute. Today it is little more than a sea stack.

Candelabra Geoglyph
ARCHAEOLOGICAL SITE

A giant three-pronged figure etched into the sandy hills, which is more than 150m high and 50m wide. No one knows exactly who made the glyph, or when, or what it signifies, but theories abound. Some connect it to the Nazca Lines, while others propound that it served as a navigational guide for sailors and was based on the constellation of the Southern Cross. Some even believe it to have been inspired by a local cactus species with hallucinogenic properties.

TAMBO COLORADO

This early Inca lowland **outpost** (admission S8.50; ☉dawn-dusk), about 45km northeast of Pisco, was named for the red paint that once completely covered its adobe walls. It's one of the best-preserved sites on the south coast and is thought to have served as an administrative base and control point for passing traffic, mostly conquered peoples.

From Pisco, it takes about an hour to get there by car. Hire a taxi for half a day (S50) or take a tour from Pisco (S60, two-person minimum). A *combi* through the village of Humay passes Tambo Colorado 20 minutes beyond the village; it leaves from the Pisco market early in the morning (S8, three hours). Once there, ask the locals about when to expect a return bus, but you could get really stuck out there, as transportation back to Pisco is infrequent and often full.

🧭 Tours & Guides

Prices and service for tours of Islas Ballestas and Reserva Nacional de Paracas are usually very similar. The better tours are escorted by a qualified naturalist who speaks Spanish and English. Most island boat tours leave daily around 8am and cost around S35 per person, but do not include S6 in dock fees. The number of tours and departure times varies, so it is recommended to reserve a day in advance. Less-than-interesting afternoon land tours of the Península de Paracas (S25) briefly stop at the national reserve's visitor center, breeze by coastal geological formations and spend a long time having lunch in a remote fishing village. Tours of the reserve can be combined with an Islas Ballestas tour to make a full-day excursion (S60).

Established tour operators:

Paracas Explorer
GUIDED TOURS

(✆53-1487, 54-5089; www.pparacasexplorer.com; Paracas 9) In the El Chaco village of Paracas, this backpacker travel agency offers the usual island and reserve tours, as well as multiday trips that take you to Ica and Nazca (US$48 to US$175 per person).

Paracas Overland
GUIDED TOURS

(✆53-3855; www.paracasoverland.com.pe; San Francisco 111) Popular with backpackers, this agency offers tours of the Islas Ballestas with its own fleet of boats, as well as to the Reserva Nacional de Paracas and Tambo Colorado. It can also arrange sandboarding trips to nearby dunes.

🛏 Sleeping

If arriving directly to Paracas, most hotels and hostels will pick you up from the bus terminal upon request.

Hotel Gran Palma
HOTEL $

(✆665-5933; www.hotelgranpalma.com; Calle 1 lot 3; d S48; ❄☎) The newest hotel in on-the-up Paracas is this brain-surgery-clean abode that offers breakfast on a pleasant rooftop terrace. The functional minimalist rooms sparkle, but leave little space for embellishment or storage.

Hotel Libertador Paracas
RESORT $$$

(✆in Lima 01-518-6500; www.libertador.com.pe; Av Paracas 178; r from US$230; ❄@☀) A dreamscape plucked from a tourist brochure with puffed cushions, permanently smiling staff, excellent kid's facilities and a luxuriously raked beach. Accommodation with all the trimmings is provided in two-storey ocean-facing villas, and the grounds are tranquil and elegant.

La Hacienda Bahia Paracas
RESORT $$$

(✆213-1000; www.hoteleslahacienda.com; Santo Domingo lot 25; s/d US$220/260; ❄☎☀) The luxury Hacienda, 2km south of El Chaco, has the air of an all-inclusive resort with some welcome local touches such as (non-original) Inca murals. Lovely terraces overlook curvaceous swimming pools and a nice private slice of beach kisses Paracas Bay. Going head to head with the Hilton next door there's also a classy restaurant, spa, Jacuzzi, and sauna splayed across the well-watered grounds.

Hostal Santa Maria
HOTEL $$

(☎54-5045; www.santamariahostal.com; Av Paracas s/n; s/d/tr incl breakfast S80/100/120; @) Rooms here are functional and admirably clean, all with cable TV. The staff is knowledgeable and can help arrange tours, though is sometimes preoccupied with looking after the restaurant next door.

Paracas Backpackers House
HOSTEL $

(☎77-3131; www.paracasbackpackershouse.com. pe; Av Los Libertadores; dm/d/tr S20/70/100, dm/s/d/tr without bathroom S17/35/40/55; ☎) A very friendly, eager-to-please *hombre* called Alberto presides over this simple but adequate hostel which offers plenty of privacy in a variety of double, triple or quadruple rooms, plus one dorm. Water is hot, wi-fi is reliable and Alberto is a font of local info.

Hostal Refugio del Pirata
HOTEL $$

(☎54-5054; www.refugiodelpirata.com; Av Paracas 6; s/d/tr incl breakfast S60/70/90; @) Rooms are bland here but get the job done, and some have ocean views. The upstairs terrace provides a pleasant setting to sip a pisco sour while watching the sunset. Ask to borrow kitchen facilities.

✖ Eating & Drinking

On the waterfront there are loads of lookalike beachfront restaurants serving fresh seafood throughout the day.

⦿TOP CHOICE El Chorito
SEAFOOD, PERUVIAN $$

(Paracas; mains S20-30; ⊙noon-9pm) The Italians come to the rescue in the clean, polished Chorito – part of the Hostal Santa Maria – where a welcome supply of *Illy* coffee saves you from the otherwise ubiquitous powdered Nescafé. The cooked-to-order fish dishes aren't bad either – all locally caught, of course.

Juan Pablo
SEAFOOD $$

(Blvd Turístico; mains S15-40; ⊙7am-9pm) Probably the best of the restaurants with a waterfront view, Juan Pablo is a winner for fresh seafood and offers breakfast for those departing early to the Islas Ballestas.

Punta Paracas
CAFE, INTERNATIONAL $

(Blvd Turístico; mains S15-35; ⊙7am-10pm) Coffee and chocolate brownies hit the spot at this open-all-day cafe that remains lively after most other places have closed.

ℹ Getting There & Around

A few buses run daily between Lima and the El Chaco beach district of Paracas (S40 to S55, 3½ hours) before continuing to other destinations south. These include **Cruz del Sur** (☎53-6336) and **Oltursa** (☎in Lima 01-708-5000; www. oltursa.com.pe); the latter company also runs direct buses to Nazca, Ica, Arequipa and Lima from Paracas. Prices are the same as from Pisco. Most agencies in El Chaco sell bus tickets including **Paracas Explorer** (☎53-1487, 54-5089; www.pparacasexplorer.com; Paracas 9).

Transportation from Paracas to Pisco is possible via *combi* (S1.50, 30 minutes), or *colectivo* (S2.50, 20 minutes).

Ica

☎056 / 125,000 / ELEV 420M

Just when you thought the landscape was dry enough for Martians, out jumps Ica, Peru's agricultural 'miracle in the desert' that churns out Californian amounts of asparagus, cotton and fruits, as well as laying claim to being the nation's leading (and best) wine producer. Ica, like Pisco, sustained significant earthquake damage in 2007 – the graceful cathedral, though still standing, has been condemned, while two other churches are undergoing lengthy repairs. Most people who make it this far bed down in infinitely more attractive Huacachina 4km to the west, but Ica has reasons to be cheerful too: the south coast's best museum (outside Arequipa) resides here, plus – arguably – the finest winery in Peru. If Nazca seems too much of a circus, it's also possible to organize Nazca Line excursions from Ica – the desert etchings lie 1½ hours to the south.

⦿ Sights & Activities

Ica's main square has been repainted post-Earthquake in generic mustard-yellow to reflect its 'city of eternal sun' moniker. The two sinuous obelisks in its center are supposed to signify the Nazca and Paracas cultures. Elsewhere, bustling commerce has returned.

Museo Regional de Ica
MUSEUM

(Ayabaca cuadra 8; admission S10; ⊙8am-7pm Mon-Fri, 9am-6pm Sat & Sun) In the suburban

Ica

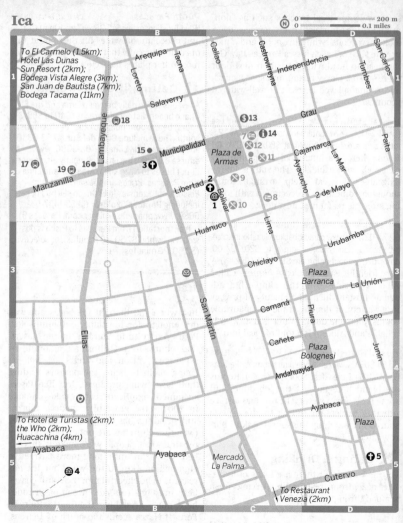

neighborhood of San Isidro, Ica pulls out its trump card: a museum befitting of a city three times the size. While it might not be the British Museum in terms of layout and design, this understated gem catalogues the two key pre-Inca civilizations on Peru's southern coast, namely the Paracas and Nazca cultures, the former famed for its intricate textiles and the latter for its instantly recognizable ceramics. Any attempt to understand the region's ancient history should begin here where a whole gamut of locally excavated artifacts is on display.

Unfortunately, the museum's famous riches have attracted malign as well as benign interest. In 2004, the building was robbed, with thieves making off with three priceless textiles. As of 2012 only one of these has been found. 'Wanted' posters and blurry photos sit where the other two once hung.

The museum is 2.5km southwest of the city center. Take a taxi from the Plaza de Armas (S3). You could walk, but it's usually not safe to do so alone, and even larger groups may get hassled.

Ica

SOUTH COAST ICA

Iglesia de La Merced CHURCH
(cnr Bolívar & Libertad) Ica's cathedral was the last church the Jesuits built in Peru before their expulsion. It was rebuilt in the late 19th century and contains a finely carved wooden altar. The effects of the 2007 earthquake caused a steeple and part of the roof to collapse. At the time of writing the church was still closed with talk of it being demolished. Various campaigns are being formulated to save it.

Santuario de El Señor de Luren CHURCH
(Cutervo) This fine church has an image of the patron saint that is venerated by pilgrims during Semana Santa and again in October. The streets surrounding the Plaza de Armas display a few impressive Spanish colonial mansions, including along the first block of Libertad. The church tower fell in the 2007 earthquake, but the dome survived. It was still undergoing extensive renovation five years later.

Iglesia de San Francisco CHURCH
(cnr Municipalidad & San Martín) Third in an ecclesial trio, this hulking church withstood the earthquake and continues to show off its fine stained-glass windows.

FREE Centro Cultural de la Unica GALLERY
(Calle Bolívar 232; ◷9am-5pm) A new temporary art gallery off a recently restored courtyard next to the condemned cathedral; expositions inside are small but packed with local talent.

Wineries
Ica is Peru's largest and most revered wine producer, though it's desert defying vineyards are unlikely to get any Euro wine-snobs jumping on a plane anytime soon. The main drawback is 'sweetness'. Even Peru's *semi-seco* (medium-dry) wines are sweet by most yardsticks. Nonetheless, tours around the vineyards can be novel and worthwhile diversions. Most offer free sampling. Bodegas can be visited year-round, but the best time is during the grape harvest from late February until early April.

The countryside around Ica is also scattered with family-owned artisanal bodegas, including **San Juan de Bautista** about a 7km taxi (S7 one way) or *colectivo* (S1.50) ride from Ica's center. *Colectivos* leave from the corner of Municipalidad and Loreto.

FREE Bodega Tacama WINERY
(www.tacama.com; ◷9am-4:30pm) Possibly the most professional and lauded of Ica's wineries, Tacama is run out of a sprawling pink hacienda backed by striped fields lined by vines. Eschewing Peru's penchant for sickly sweet wines, Tacama produces some rather good chardonnays and malbecs that might one day give the Chileans a run for their money. The free tour and sampling includes a mirador (lookout), a guide through the ageing process (in French oak barrels, no less) and a glimpse of an old chapel damaged in the 2007 earthquake. Situated 11km northwest of town, you'll have to hire a taxi to get here (S15 each way).

FREE Bodega Ocucaje   WINERY
(www.hotelocucaje.com; Av Principal s/n; ⊘tastings 9am-noon & 2-5pm Mon-Fri, 9am-noon Sat, tours 11am-3pm Mon-Fri) Some of Peru's finest wine is said to come from this bodega, but, unfortunately, it's fairly isolated, more than 30km south of Ica off Carr Panamericana Sur. Hiring a taxi to reach the winery costs around S30 each way, or you can join a local tour leaving from Ica.

Bodega Vista Alegre   WINERY
(Camino a La Tinguina, Km 2.5; admission S5; ⊘8am-noon & 1:45-4:45pm Mon-Fri, 7am-1pm Sat) About 3km northeast of Ica in the La Tinguiña district, this is the easiest of the large commercial wineries to visit (taxi one way S5). It's best to go in the morning, as the winery occasionally closes in the afternoon.

☞ Tours

Travel agencies around the Plaza de Armas offer city tours, winery excursions and trips further afield to Paracas and Nazca. **Desert Travel** (✆22-7215; Calle Lima 171) has an office in the rather alluring Tejas Don Juan chocolate shop on the Plaza.

★☆ Festivals & Events

Ica has more than its share of fiestas. February inspires the water-throwing antics typical of any Latin American **carnaval**, plus dancers in beautiful costumes. In early to mid-March, it's time for the famous grape-harvest festival, **Fiesta de la Vendimia**, with all manner of processions, beauty contests, cockfights and horse shows, music and dancing, and of course, free-flowing pisco and wine. The founding of the city by the Spanish conquistadors on June 17, 1563 is celebrated during **Ica Week**, while **Tourist Week** happens during mid-September. In late October, the religious pilgrimage of **El Señor de Luren** culminates in fireworks and a traditional procession of the faithful that keeps going all night.

⌷ Sleeping

Beware that hotels fill up and double or triple their prices during the many festivals.

Most budget travelers head for Huacachina, 4km west of the city, but Ica has several options.

El Carmelo   HISTORIC HOTEL **$$**
(✆23-2191; www.elcarmelohotelhacienda.com; Carr Panamericana Sur Km 301; s/d/tr/q from

S100/150/200/250; @🛜🏊) This romantic roadside hotel on the outskirts of town inhabits a delightful 200-year-old hacienda that has undeniable rustic charm. There's a good restaurant plus a winery onsite. Take a taxi from the city center (S3).

Hotel Las Dunas Sun Resort   RESORT **$$$**
(✆25-6224; www.lasdunashotel.com; Av La Angostura 400; d/tr from S333/376; ❄@🛜🏊) By far the most luxurious hotel in town, the sprawling Las Dunas resort is equipped with a swimming pool, sauna, tennis courts, minigolf course, business center, restaurants and bars. Various excursions are offered (for an additional fee), including cycling, horseback riding, sandboarding and winery tours. Service can be haphazard, however. The resort is located off Carr Panamericana Sur Km 300.

Hotel Sol de Ica   HOTEL **$$**
(✆23-6168; www.hotelsoldeica.com; Lima 265; s/d/tr incl buffet breakfast S110/140/190; @🛜) This dazzlingly white, three-story central hotel is hidden down a long dark passage behind reception that delivers more than it initially promises. Remarkably small rooms have unusual wood paneling, TVs and phones. The hotel has a sauna and two swimming pools.

Hotel Colón Plaza   HOTEL **$**
(✆21-6487; Av Grau 120; s/d/ste S50/80/100; @🛜) Worthwhile only if you bag one of the corner suites (there are four of 'em) which are radically superior to the rest of the rooms with cinema-sized flat-screens, antique furniture, king-sized beds, power showers and plaza views.

Hostal Soyuz   HOTEL **$**
(✆22-4743; Manzanilla 130; s/d/tr S40/50/70; ❄) Sitting directly over the Soyuz bus terminal, this handy option for late arrivals or early departures has carpeted rooms with air-con and cable TV, but is only for heavy sleepers on account of the rumpus below. Check in is at the bus ticket desk.

✕ Eating

Several shops in the streets east of the plaza sell *tejas* (caramel-wrapped sweets flavored with fruits, nuts etc) including **Helena** (Cajamarca 139).

Anita   BAKERY, PERUVIAN **$$**
(Libertad 135; menús from S12, mains S15-36; ⊘8am-midnight) True, the bow-tied waiters

are a bit OTT (this ain't the Ritz), but Anita does a mean stuffed avocado and the bakery counter knocks out some hard-to-resist cakes. Best restaurant in the main square by far.

El Otro Peñoncito PERUVIAN, INTERNATIONAL $$
(Bolívar 225; mains S9-26; ☺8am-midnight Mon-Fri) Ica's most historic and characterful restaurant serves a varied menu of Peruvian and international fare that includes plenty of options for vegetarians. The formal bartenders here shake a mean pisco sour, too.

Restaurant Venezia ITALIAN $$
(☎21-0372; San Martín 1229; mains S12-29; ☺lunch & dinner Tue-Sun) In a suburban location about 2.5km south of the town center, Venezia is a popular family-run Italian restaurant. Allow plenty of time as all plates are made fresh upon ordering.

Plaza 125 PERUVIAN $
(Lima 125; mains S10-16) Your quick stop on the main square backs up homespun *lomo saltado* with more internationally flavored spag bol and chicken fillets. It's riotously popular with locals in a hurry.

Drinking

There's not much happening in Ica outside of fiesta times, though if its gringo-dominated nightlife you're after, Huacachina (p121) calls like a desert siren. On Ica's Plaza de Armas, you'll find several wine and pisco tasting rooms to pop into for a quick tipple. South of the plaza along Lima, local bars and clubs advertise live music, DJs and dancing, but they're pretty rough. The craziest late-night disco, called the **Who** (Av de Los Maestros 500; admission S10), is situated on the north side of the Hotel de Turistas, 3km southwest of the plaza; it's a S3 taxi ride.

Information

Tour agencies and internet cafes abound in the area around the Plaza de Armas.
BCP (Plaza de Armas) Has a Visa/MasterCard ATM and changes US dollars and traveler's checks.
DIRCETUR (☎21-0332; www.dirceturica.gob.pe; Grau 148) Government-sponsored office of tourism.
Hospital (☎23-4798, 23-4450; Cutervo 104; ☺24hr) For emergency services.
Police (☎23-5421; Elías cuadra 5; ☺24hr) At the city center's edge.
Serpost (☎23-3881; San Martín 156) Southwest of the Plaza de Armas.

Dangers & Annoyances
Ica experiences some petty theft. Take the normal precautions, particularly around the bus terminals and market areas.

Getting There & Away

Ica is a main destination for buses along Carr Panamericana Sur, so it's easy to get to/from Lima or Nazca. Most of the bus companies are clustered in a high-crime area at the west end of Salaverry, and also Manzanilla west of Lambayeque.

Soyuz (☎23-3312; Manzanilla 130) run the 'Perubus' to Lima via Chincha and Cañete with services leaving every 15 minutes. **Cruz del Sur** (☎22-3333; Lambayeque 140) and **Ormeño** (☎21-5600; Lambayeque s/n) offer more luxurious services going north and south.

Some faster, but slightly more expensive *colectivos* and *combis* heading for Pisco and Nazca leave when full from near the intersection of Lambayeque and Municipalidad in Ica.

Ormeño as well as some small companies may serve destinations around Peru's central highlands, such as Ayacucho and Huancavelica.

ICA BUSES

DESTINATION	COST (S)	DURATION (HR)
Arequipa	50-144	12
Ayacucho	40	8
Cañete	12-15	3
Chincha	7-10	2
Lima	22-76	4½
Nazca	7-35	2½
Pisco	4-15	1½-2

Huacachina

⏺ 056 / POP 200

Imagine.... It's 6pm and you're sitting atop a giant wind-sculpted sand dune watching the sun set psychedelically over a landscape of golden yellows and rusty reds. Two hundred meters below you lays a dreamy desert lagoon ringed by exotic palm trees, and furnished with a clutch of rustic yet suitably elegant hotels. It took you 20 exhausting minutes to climb up to this lofty vantage point, but with a well-waxed sand-board wedged beneath your belly you'll be down in less than one.

While not as famous as Nazca to the south, Huacachina, an aesthetically perfect desert oasis 4km west of Ica, is a firmly established stopover on Southern Peru's well-trampled Gringo Trail, and with good reason. Sand-boarding, dune buggie rides and good-old romantic idling are the orders of the day here. Not surprisingly, you'll find backpacker-dom and all its attendant paraphernalia on full display – dreadlocks, tie-die T-shirts, all-night discos, and sinewy dudes with wispy beards clutching well-thumbed copies of *Shantaram*. Yet, despite the nightlife noise and the surfeit of banana pancake cafes, the spot remains a sublime place to spend a day or three, and a dead cert to enhance your dune climbing skills.

🏃 Activities

Sand is an essential ingredient in most Huacachina activities.

Sandboarding

You can rent sandboards for S5 an hour to slide, surf or ski your way down the dunes, getting sand lodged into every bodily orifice. Snowboarding this isn't. There are no tow ropes or chair-lifts here. Instead you must stagger up the sugary dunes for your 45-second adrenalin rush. Make sure you are given wax (usually in the form of an old candle) when you hire your board as they are pretty useless without regular rub-downs. Start on the smaller slopes and don't be lulled into a false sense of security – several people have seriously injured themselves losing control of their sandboards. Most riders end up boarding belly down with their legs splayed out behind as emergency brakes. Don't forget to keep your mouth shut.

Dune Buggies

Many hotels offer thrill-rides in **areneros** (dune buggies) which head out early morning (8am-ish) and late afternoon (4pm-ish) to avoid the intense sun. They then stop at the top of the soft slopes, from where you can sandboard down and be picked up at the bottom. Word on the street is that some drivers take unnecessary risks, so ask around before choosing an operator. Make sure cameras are well protected, as sand can be damaging. The going rate for tours is S45 but ask first if sandboard rental is included and how long the tour lasts. Tours do not include a fee of S3.60 that must be paid upon entering the dunes (this doesn't apply to those entering on foot).

Litter is an issue on Huacachina's dunes, as it is in much of Peru. It ought to go without saying, but pack out all your rubbish when you visit these beautiful sandy behemoths.

Swimming & Boating

The lagoon's murky waters supposedly have curative properties, though you may find **swimming** in the hotel pools (of which there are half a dozen) more inviting. You can also hire boats – both rowing and pedal-powered – at a couple of points on the lagoon for S12 an hour.

👉 Tours

Pretty much all the hotels can organize dune buggy rides. A handful of others run trips to Paracas, Islas Ballestras and Nazca. An excellent option is **Pelican Travel & Service** (⏺22-5211; Perotti) which has an office next to El Huacachinero Hotel and another one in Ica.

🛏 Sleeping & Eating

TOP CHOICE **Hotel El Huacachinero**   HOTEL $$
(⏺21-7435; www.elhuacachinero.com; Perotti; s/d/tr incl breakfast S100/110/140; ✳🛜🏊) Recently upgraded, the Huacachinero logs the finest restaurant in the oasis (by a stretch), a relaxing pool area (no blaring music), and immediate dune access via the back gate if you're up for a 45° one-step-forward-two-steps-back climb to the sunset of your dreams. Agreeably rustic rooms have super-comfortable beds but no TVs – then again, who needs them?

Hotel Mossone   HISTORIC HOTEL $$$
(⏺21-3630; Balneario de Huacachina; s/d/ste S200/260/315; ✳@🛜🏊) There's a wonderfully neglected air about this once posh balneario that was formerly the only hotel to

grace Huacachina's fertile oasis. Rooms are huge – in fact you get two of them, a sala and a high-ceiling bedroom – and there's a private pool across the road. The atmospheric central courtyard with its chipped paving stones and wire-mesh aviary looks like something out of Fidel Castro's time-warped Cuba.

Hostería Suiza   HOTEL $$
(☎23-8762; www.hosteriasuiza.com.pe; Balneario de Huacachina; d S172-215; ❋ 🛜 🏊) The oasis' top end hotel has a Swiss air of cleanliness about it meaning the amply furnished suites are popular with families and older travelers. Positioned strategically at the far end of the lagoon it remains out of earshot of Huacachina's rowdiest bars – a blessing for some.

Desert Nights   HOSTEL, INTERNATIONAL $
(☎22-8458; Blvd de Huacachina; dm from S15; @🛜) The menu might have been ripped off from Ko Samui or anywhere else on the banana pancake trail, but this international hostel with a decent and very popular cafe out front is somewhere you're guaranteed to meet other travelers. The excellent shade-grown Peruvian coffee is backed up by peanut butter and jam sandwiches, burgers, pizza and brownies. The shared dorms are basic but the owners are friendly.

Casa de Arena   HOTEL $
(☎21-5274, 23-7398; www.casa-de-arena.com; Balneario de Huacachina; r per person without/ with bathroom S40/50; @🛜🏊) Cast with a rowdy reputation, the Arena's well-worn rooms come with or without baths, allowing scrimpers to.... well.... scrimp. The boisterous Friday night disco gets a sneer from other operators nearby who feel their precious tranquility is being violated. If you want peace, go elsewhere. If you want to party, this is the place.

Hostal Curasi   HOTEL $$
(☎21-6989; www.huacachinacurasi.com; Balneario de Huacachina; s/d S80/110; 🛜🏊) Strangely, Huacachina's newest hotel doesn't look as spiffy as some of the older stalwarts, though it has the obligatory pool and restaurant and journeymen rooms, and the price is right.

 Drinking & Entertainment

Bars and discos in Huacachina are generally attached to the various hotels and clientele is 95% foreign. Fame and infamy belong to the boisterous **Casa de Arena** and its weekend discos. Next door, the **Pub** (Balneario

de Huacachina) is a cool new bar/restaurant owned by the same people as Desert Nights. The **House of Avinoam** (☎21-5439; Perotti) in the Carola del Sur Lodge has a decent pizza restaurant and one of the oasis' larger and more atmospheric bars.

 Information

Dangers & Annoyances

Though safer than Ica, Huacachina is not a place to be lax about your personal safety or to forget to look after your property. Some guesthouses have reputations for ripping off travelers and also harassing young women with sexual advances. Check out all of your options carefully before accepting a room. Also, the few small stores around the lake offer plenty of souvenirs but are often out of the basics; come prepared!

ℹ Getting There & Away

The only way to get to Huacachina from Ica is by taxi (S5 to S7 one-way).

Palpa

☎056 / POP 7200 / ELEV 300M

From Ica, Carr Panamericana Sur heads southeast through the small oasis of Palpa, famous for its orange groves. Like Nazca, Palpa is surrounded by perplexing geoglyphs, the so-called **Palpa Lines** that are serially overshadowed by the more famous, but less abundant, Nazca Lines to the south. The Palpa Lines display a greater profusion of human forms including the **Familia Real de Paracas**, a group of eight figures on a hillside. Due to their elevated position, the figures are easier to view from terra firma at a **mirador** 8km south of the town. A small museum hut onsite offers further explanations in English and Spanish. The best way to see more of these lines is on a combined overflight from Nazca (p125).

Nazca & Around

☎056 / ELEV 590M

It's hard to say the word 'Nazca' without following it immediately with the word 'Lines,' a reference not just to the ancient geometric lines that crisscross the Nazca desert, but to the enigmatic animal geoglyphs that accompany them. Like all great unexplained mysteries, these great etchings on the pampa, thought to have been made by a pre-Inca civilization between 450–600 AD, attract a variable fan base of archaeologists,

Nazca

Nazca

scientists, history buffs, New Age mystics, curious tourists, and Peru pilgrims on their way to (or back from) Machu Picchu. Question marks still hang over how they were made and by whom, and the answers are often as much wild speculation as pure science (aliens? prehistoric balloonists?). Documented for the first time by North American scientist Paul Kosok in 1939 and declared a Unesco World Heritage site in 1994, the lines today are the south coast's biggest tourist attraction meaning the small otherwise

insignificant desert town of Nazca (population 57,500) can be a bit of a circus.

⦿ Sights

NAZCA LINES
The best-known lines are found in the desert 20km north of Nazca, and by far the best way to appreciate them is to get a bird's-eye view from a *sobrevuelo* (overflight).

Mirador   LOOKOUT
(observation tower; admission S1) You'll get only a sketchy idea of the Lines at this lookout

on Carr Panamericana Sur 20km north of Nazca, which has an oblique view of three figures: the lizard, tree and hands (or frog, depending on your point of view). It's also a lesson in the damage to which the Lines are vulnerable: Carr Panamericana Sur runs smack through the tail of the lizard, which from nearby seems all but obliterated. Signs warning of landmines are a reminder that walking on the Lines is strictly forbidden. It irreparably damages them, and besides, you can't see anything at ground level. To get to the observation tower from Nazca, catch any bus or *colectivo* northbound along Carr Panamericana Sur (S1.50, 30 minutes). Some tours (from S50 per person, p125) also combine a trip to the *mirador* with visits to another natural viewpoint and the Maria Reiche Museum. About 1km south of the man-made *mirador* there a **Mirador Natural** on a small knoll-like hill with a close up view of one of the geometric lines made by removing reddish pebbles from the grey earth.

Museo Maria Reiche
MUSEUM

(admission S5; ☺9am-6pm) When Maria Reiche, the German mathematician and long-term researcher of the Nazca Lines, died in 1998, her house, which stands 5km north of the *mirador* along Carr Panamericana Sur, was made into a small museum. Though disappointingly scant on information, you can see where she lived, amid the clutter of her tools and obsessive sketches, and pay your respects to her tomb. Though the sun can be punishing, it's possible to walk here from the mirador in a sweaty hour or so, or passing *colectivos* can sometimes take you

(S1). To return to Nazca, just ask the guard to help you flag down any southbound bus or *colectivo*. A visit to the museum can also be arranged as part of a tour to the nearby *mirador*.

Museo Didáctico Antonini
MUSEUM

(http://digilander.libero.it/MDAntonini; Av de la Cultura 600; admission S15, cameras S5; ☺9am-7pm) On the east side of town, this excellent archaeological museum has an aqueduct running through the back garden, as well as interesting reproductions of burial tombs, a valuable collection of ceramic pan flutes and a scale model of the Lines. You can get an overview of both the Nazca culture and a glimpse of most of Nazca's outlying sites here. Though the exhibit labels are in Spanish, the front desk lends foreign-language translation booklets for you to carry around. To get to the museum follow Bolognesi to the east out of town for 1km, or take a taxi (S2).

Planetarium Maria Reiche
PLANETARIUM

(☏52-2293; Nazca Lines Hotel, Bolognesi; admission S20) This small planetarium is in the Nazca Lines Hotel and offers scripted evening lectures on the Lines with graphical displays on a domed projection screen that last approximately 45 minutes. Call ahead or check the posted schedules for show times in Spanish or English (French and Italian by reservation only).

OUTLYING SIGHTS

All of the sights listed here can be visited on tours from Nazca (see p125), although individual travelers or pairs may have to wait a day or two before the agency finds enough people who are also interested in going.

Chauchilla Cemetery
ARCHAEOLOGICAL SITE

(admission S7.50; ☺8am-2pm) The most popular excursion from Nazca, this cemetery, 30km south of Nazca, will satisfy any urges you have to see ancient bones, skulls and mummies. Dating back to the Ica-Chinca culture around AD 1000, the mummies were, until recently, scattered haphazardly across the desert, left by ransacking tomb-robbers. Now they are seen carefully rearranged inside a dozen or so tombs, though cloth fragments and pottery and bone shards still litter the ground outside the demarcated trail. Organized tours last three hours and cost US$10 to US$35 per person.

THE NAZCA LINES: ANCIENT MYSTERIES IN THE SAND

Spread across an incredible 500 sq km of arid, rock-strewn plain in the Pampa Colorada (Red Plain), the Nazca Lines remain one of the world's great archaeological mysteries. Consisting of more than 800 straight lines, 300 geometric figures (geoglyphs) and, concentrated in a relatively small area, some 70 spectacular animal and plant drawings (biomorphs), the Lines are almost imperceptible at ground level. It's only when viewed from above that they form their striking network of enormous stylized figures and channels, many of which radiate from a central axis. The figures are mostly etched out in single continuous lines, while the encompassing geoglyphs form perfect triangles, rectangles or straight lines running for several kilometers across the desert.

The Lines were made by the simple process of removing the dark sun-baked stones from the surface of the desert and piling them up on either side of the lines, thus exposing the lighter, powdery gypsum-laden soil below. The most elaborate designs represent animals, including a 180m-long lizard, a monkey with an extravagantly curled tail, and a condor with a 130m wingspan. There's also a hummingbird, a spider and an intriguing owl-headed person on a hillside, popularly referred to as an astronaut because of its goldfish-bowl-shaped head, though some are of the opinion that it's a priest with a mystical owl's head.

Endless questions remain. Who constructed the Lines and why? And how did they know what they were doing when the Lines can only be properly appreciated from the air? Maria Reiche (1903–98), a German mathematician and long-time researcher of the Lines, theorized that they were made by the Paracas and Nazca cultures between 900 BC and AD 600, with some additions by the Wari settlers from the highlands in the 7th century. She also claimed that the Lines were an astronomical calendar developed for agricultural purposes, and that they were mapped out through the use of sophisticated mathematics (and a long rope). However, the handful of alignments Reiche discovered between the sun, stars and Lines were not enough to convince scholars.

Later, English documentary maker Tony Morrison hypothesized that the Lines were walkways linking *huacas* (sites of ceremonial significance). A slightly more surreal suggestion from explorer Jim Woodman was that the Nazca people knew how to construct hot-air balloons and that they did, in fact, observe the Lines from the air. Or, if you believe author George Von Breunig, the Lines formed a giant running track.

A more down-to-earth theory, given the value of water in the sun-baked desert, was suggested by anthropologist Johann Reinhard, who believed that the Lines were involved in mountain worship and a fertility/water cult. Recent work by the **Swiss-Liechtenstein Foundation** (SLSA; www.slsa.ch) agrees that they were dedicated to the worship of water, and it is thus ironic that their theory about the demise of the Nazca culture suggests that it was due not to drought but to destructive rainfall caused by a phenomenon such as El Niño!

About the only thing that is certain is that when the Nazca set about turning their sprawling desert homeland into an elaborate art canvas, they also began a debate that will keep archaeologists busy for many decades, if not centuries to come.

FREE **Pardeones Ruins** RUINS
The Pardeones ruins, 2km southeast of town via Arica over the river, are not very well preserved, primarily because they were constructed from adobe rather than stone. Their position on a slope above the town is commanding which is probably why the Incas used it as an administrative control center between the mountains and the coast.

Cantallo Aqueducts ARCHAEOLOGICAL SITE
(admission S10) About 2km further from the ruins are the 30-plus underground Cantallo aqueducts, which are still in working order and essential in irrigating the surrounding fields. Though once possible to enter the aqueducts through the spiraling *ventanas* (windows), which local people use to clean the aqueducts each year, entry is now prohibited; instead, you can take note of the Nazca's exceptional stonework from outside.

It's possible, but not necessarily safe, to walk to the aqueducts; at least, don't carry any valuables. Alternatively you can hire a taxi to take you there (and perhaps tie in the Paredones ruins as well). This should cost around S40 to S50 round-trip. Tours from Nazca that take 2½ hours, cost from US$5 per person and may be combined with a visit to see **El Telar**, a geoglyph found in the town of **Buena Fe**, and visits to touristy gold and ceramics workshops.

 FREE Cahuachi RUINS

(⊙9am-4pm) A dirt road travels 25km west from Nazca to Cahuachi, the most important known Nazca center, which is still undergoing excavation. It consists of several pyramids, a graveyard and an enigmatic site called Estaquería, which may have been used as a place of mummification. Tours from Nazca take three hours, cost US$15 to US$50 per person, and may include a side trip to **Pueblo Viejo**, a nearby pre-Nazca residential settlement.

Reserva Nacional Pampas Galeras
WILDLIFE RESERVE

This national reserve is a vicuña (threatened wild relatives of alpacas) sanctuary high in the mountains 90km east of Nazca on the road to Cuzco. It is the best place to see these shy animals in Peru, though tourist services are virtually nonexistent. Every year in late May or early June is the **chaccu**, when hundreds of villagers round up the vicuñas for shearing and three festive days of traditional ceremonies, with music and dancing, and of course, drinking. Full-day or overnight tours from Nazca cost US$30 to US$90 per person.

Cerro Blanco
ADVENTURE TOUR

Stand down all other pretenders. Cerro Blanco, 14km east of Nazca, is the highest sand dune in the world: 2078m above sea level and – more importantly – 1176m from base to summit, that's higher than the tallest mountain in England and numerous other countries. If Huacachina's sand didn't irrevocably ruin your underwear, this could be your bag. Due to the dune's height and steepness it's best to organize an excursion from Nazca. Trips leave at about 4am to avoid the intense heat. The arduous climb to the top of the dune (buggies can't climb this behemoth) takes approximately three hours. Going down is counted more in minutes with some clear runs of up to 800m. Many agencies in Nazca offer this trip, including Kunan Tours.

☞ Tours

Most people fly over the Lines then leave, but there's more to see around Nazca. If

---

OVERFLIGHTS OVERVIEW

Bad publicity wracked the Nazca Lines in 2010 when two small aircraft carrying tourists on *sobrevuelos* (overflights) crashed within eight months of each other causing a total of 13 fatalities. The crashes followed an equally catastrophic 2008 accident that killed five French tourists, along with another incident when a plane was forced to make an emergency landing on the Carr Panamericana Sur in 2009.

In reaction to the incidents some changes have been made. Fifteen plane companies have been streamlined into half a dozen, all planes now fly with two pilots, and prices have gone up to ensure that companies don't cut corners with poorly maintained aircraft or over-filled flights.

Nonetheless, it still pays to put safety before price when choosing your overflight company. Question anyone who offers less than US$80 for the standard 30-minute excursion and don't be afraid to probe companies on their safety records and flight policies. **Aeroparacas** (www.aeroparacas.com) is one of the better airline companies. Other longstanding operators include **Aerodiana** (☎444-3057; www.aerodiana.com.pe) and **Alas Peruanas** (☎52-2497; www.alasperuanas.com). Some countries, including the UK and USA, still place warnings about overflights on their foreign office websites.

If you do opt for a flight, bear in mind that, because the small aircraft bank left and right, it can be a stomach-churning experience, so motion-sickness sufferers should consider taking medication. Looking at the horizon may help mild nausea.

Most airline companies use **Maria Reiche Neuman Airport** 4km southwest of Nazca, although you can also depart from Pisco and Lima. On top of the tour fee the aerodrome normally charges a departure tax of S20.

you take one of the many local tours, they typically include a torturously long stop at a potter's and/or gold-miner's workshop for a demonstration of their techniques (tips for those who show you their trade are expected, too).

Hotels and travel agencies tirelessly promote their own tours. Nazca Lines Hotel and Casa Andina are good options. Other agencies include:

Alegría Tours
ADVENTURE TOUR

(☑52-3775; www.alegriatoursperu.com; Hotel Alegría, Lima 168) Behemoth agency offers all the usual local tours, plus off-the-beaten-track and sandboarding options. The tours are expensive for one person, so ask to join up with other travelers to receive a group discount. Alegría can arrange guides in Spanish, English, French and German in some cases.

Kunan Tours
GUIDED TOUR

(☑52-4069; www.kunantours.com; Arica 419) Based out of the Kunan Wasi hotel with another office in Miraflores, Lima, this comprehensive travel company offers all the Nazca tours, plus excursions to Islas Ballestras, Huacachina and Chincha.

🛏 Sleeping

Prices drop by up to 50% outside of peak season, which runs from May until August.

TOP CHOICE Nazca Lines Hotel
HOTEL $$$

(☑52-2293; www.peru-hotels.com/nazlines.htm; Bolognesi s/n; s/d/tr/q incl buffet breakfast S288/337/399/459; ✺@🛜🌊) Exceedingly tranquil considering its city center location, this lauded hotel is arranged around a large courtyard complete with lovely swimming pool and fountain. Classy touches include Seville-like tilework, an onsite planetarium (with daily shows), a shop, a comfy lounge, and efficient but not officious service.

Kunan Wasi Hotel
HOTEL $

(☑52-4069; www.kunanwasihotel.com; Arica 419; s/d/tr S40/50/60; @🛜) Very clean and very bright with each room conforming to a different color scheme. Kunan Wasi is run by English speaking Yesenia who has lived in LA and has nailed the budget end of the market with facilities that more than justify the asking price. Welcome to a perfectly packaged Nazca bargain.

Casa Andina
BOUTIQUE HOTEL $$$

(☑52-3563; www.casa-andina.com; Bolognesi 367; r incl breakfast buffet from S272; ✺@🛜🌊) This newly renovated Peruvian chain hotel, poised midway between the bus stations and the Plaza de Armas, offers the best value for money of any of Nazca's upmarket hotels. Rooms have eminently stylish, modern furnishings with bold color schemes, air-con and cable TV.

Hotel Oro Viejo
HOTEL $$

(☑52-3332, 52-1112; www.hoteloroviejo.net; Callao 483; s/d/tr/ste incl buffet breakfast S100/140/170/315; ✺@🛜) This charming hotel retains a familial atmosphere and has airy, well-furnished rooms, a welcoming common lounge, an exquisitely tended garden and even a souvenir shop.

Hotel Nuevo Cantalloc
HOTEL $$$

(☑52-2283; www.hotelnuevocantalloc.com; s/d incl breakfast S299/516; ✺@🛜🌊) Previously in Italian hands but now being run by new Peruvian owners, the rechristened Nuevo Cantalloc (formerly Hotel Cantayo Spa & Resort) is out-of-town and feels more like a posh retreat than a hotel. Rooms in the hacienda-style building are huge with some antique furnishings and the extensive grounds are replete with such esoteric attractions as peacocks, ostriches, a meditation circle and a 200-year-old ficus tree with supposed mystical properties.

Hotel La Encantada
HOTEL $$

(☑52-2930; www.hotellaencantada.com.pe; Callao 592; s/d/tr S95/115/140; @🛜) A good, clean and new hotel that's associated with the equally professional Via La Encantada restaurant around the corner, this place has made the opposition look over its shoulder with bright, freshly painted rooms and a pleasant terrace out front.

Hotel Alegría
HOTEL $$

(☑52-2702; www.hotelalegria.com; Lima 168; s/d incl breakfast S100/130; ✺@🛜🌊) This is a classic travelers' haunt with a restaurant, manicured grounds and pool. It has narrow, carpeted rooms with TVs and fans, and its own tour company. Rates include a free half-hour of internet access and a pickup from the bus stations, where you should ignore touts from the Hotel Alegría II.

Hospedaje Yemayá
HOTEL $

(☑52-3146; www.hospedajeyemaya.com; Callao 578; s & d/tr incl breakfast S55/75; @🛜) An indefatigably hospitable family deftly deals with all of the backpackers that stream through their doorway. They offer a few floors of small but well-cared-for rooms with hot showers and cable TV. There's a sociable terrace with a handy washing machine and dryer.

Hotel Sol del Sur
HOTEL **$$**

(☑52-3716; www.hotelsoldelsur.com; Av Guardia Civil 120; s/d S70/100; ☜) A cut above your standard bus station dive (though it's right next to it), this new gaff with an associated restaurant downstairs has clean rooms, and windows thick enough to keep out the sound of screeching 10-tonne buses.

Hotel Nazca
HOTEL **$**

(☑52-2085; marionasca13@hotmail.com; Lima 438; s/d/tr S35/45/65) A rock-bottom, bargain basement place with friendly, elderly owners. Army barracks-style rooms offer bare bones facilities; some have private baths.

✖ Eating & Drinking

West of the Plaza de Armas, Bolognesi is stuffed full of foreigner-friendly pizzerias, restaurants and bars.

TOP CHOICE Via La Encantada
EUROPEAN, PERUVIAN **$$**

(www.hotellaencantada.com.pe; Bolognesi 282; mains S20-40) The best restaurant in the 'Boulevard' (Bolognesi), La Encantada sparkles in Nazca's dusty center with well-placed wine displays, great coffee and courteous and friendly wait-staff. The extensive menu mixes Europhile food (pasta et al) with Peruvian favorites.

Rico Pollo
PARRILLA **$**

(Lima 190; mains from S12) A local lunchtime phenomenon, this very cheap, very crowded parrilla offers some of the best barbecued meat cuts on the south coast. For S12 you get a filling meal of chicken breast with fries and vegetables. Cakes and salads (S10) provide an excellent supporting act.

El Porton
PERUVIAN **$**

(www.elportonrestaurante.com; Ignacio Moreseky 120; mains S20-30) Fed with a regular diet of Nazca Lines tour groups, single diners could get lonely in this rambling place. The menu is anchored by above-average potatoes in a Huancayo sauce, stuffed avocados and some fancier mains. Musical trios drop by with *El Condor Pasa* on default setting.

La Taberna
PERUVIAN **$**

(☑52-3803; Lima 321; menús S6, mains from S15; ☺lunch & dinner) It's a hole-in-the-wall place: the scribbles covering every inch of wall are a testament to its popularity. Try the spicy fish, challengingly named '*Pescado a lo Macho*' ('macho fish') or chose from a list of vegetarian options.

La Kañada
PERUVIAN **$**

(☑52-253; Lima 160; menús S10, mains S12-16; ☺8am-11pm) Handy to the bus stations, this old standby still serves bog-standard Peruvian food. A decent list of cocktails includes *algarrobina,* a cocktail of pisco, milk and syrup from the *huarango* (carob) tree.

Plaza Mayor I
PARRILLA **$$**

(cnr Calle Bolognesi & Arica; meals S15-25) A coal grill with a rustic wood and bamboo mezzanine seating area overlooking Plaza de Armas – barbecued meats dominate.

❶ Information

BCP (Lima 495) Has a Visa/MasterCard ATM and changes US dollars and traveler's checks.

DIRCETUR (Parque Bolognesi, 3rd fl) Government-sponsored tourist information office; can recommend local tour operators. There's an information booth in the park itself.

Hospital (☑52-2586; Callao s/n; ☺24hr) For emergency services.

Post office (Castillo 379) Two blocks west of the Plaza de Armas.

Dangers & Annoyances

The town of Nazca is generally safe for travelers, though be wary when walking at night near either bridge to the south of town. Travelers arriving by bus will be met by persistent *jaladores* (agents) trying to sell tours or take arriving passengers to hotels. These touts may use the names of places listed here but are never to be trusted. Never hand over any money until you can personally talk to the hotel or tour-company owner and get a confirmed itinerary in writing. It's best to go with a reliable agency for land tours of the surrounding area, as a few violent assaults and robberies of foreign tourists have been reported.

❶ Getting There & Around

Nazca is a major destination for buses on Carr Panamericana Sur and is easy to get to from Lima, Ica or Arequipa. Bus companies cluster at the west end of Calle Lima, near the *óvalo* (main roundabout) and about a block towards town on the same street. Buses to Arequipa generally originate in Lima, and to get a seat you have to pay the Lima fare.

NAZCA BUSES

DESTINATION	COST (S)	DURATION (HR)
Arequipa	40-144	10-12
Camaná	45	7
Chala	15	3½
Cuzco	120-180	14
Lima	50-86	8
Ica	7-35	2½
Pisco	5-15	1½-2
Tacna	70-120	15

Most long-distance services leave in the late afternoon or evening. Located on Av Los Incas, **Cruz del Sur** (☏52-3713) and **Ormeño** (☏52-2058) have a few luxury buses daily to Lima. Intermediate points such as Ica and Pisco are more speedily served by smaller, *económico* (cheap) bus companies, such as **Flores** and **Soyuz** (☏52-1464), which run buses to Ica every half-hour from Av Los Incas. These buses will also drop you at Palpa (S3, one hour).

To go direct to Cuzco, several companies, including Cruz del Sur, take the paved road east via Abancay. This route climbs over 4000m and gets very cold, so wear your warmest clothes and bring your sleeping bag on board if you have one. Alternatively, some companies also offer direct buses to Cuzco via Arequipa.

For Ica, fast *colectivos* (S15, two hours) and slower minibuses leave when full from near the gas station on the *óvalo*. On the south side of the main roundabout, antiquated *colectivos* wait for enough passengers to make the run down to Chala (S15, 2½ hours).

A taxi from central Nazca to the aerodrome, 4km away, costs about S4.

Chala

☏054 / POP 2500

The tiny, ramshackle fishing village of Chala, about 170km from Nazca, presents intrepid travelers with an opportunity to break the journey to Arequipa and visit the archaeological site of **Puerto Inca** (admission free; ⊙24hr), from whence fresh fish was once sent all the way to Cuzco by runners – no mean effort! The well-marked turnoff is 10km north of town, at Km 603 along Carr Panamericana Sur, from where a dirt road leads 3km west to the coastal ruins.

Near the ruins, **Hotel Puerto Inca** (☏25-8798; www.puertoinka.com.pe; Carr Panamericana Sur Km 603; s/d/tr/q S96/153/202/242; @⊕) is a large resort set on a pretty bay. It has a campground that costs S13 per person, with a shower complex by the sea. It also offers horseback riding and rents bodyboards, kayaks, and jet skis.

Colectivos to Chala (S15, 2½ hours) leave from the *óvalo* in Nazca when full from the early morning until mid-afternoon. Onward buses to Arequipa (S35, eight hours) stop in Chala at small ticket offices along Carr Panamericana Sur, with most buses departing in the evening.

Camaná

☏054 / POP 14,600

After leaving Chala in the dust, Carr Panamericana Sur heads south for 220km, clinging tortuously to sand dunes dropping down to the sea, until it reaches positively urban Camaná. This coastal city has long been a summer resort popular with *arequipeños* (inhabitants of Arequipa) who flock to its beaches, about 5km from the center.

The main plaza is about a 15-minute walk toward the coast along the road where all the buses stop. To get to the coast, *colectivos* to La Punta beach (S1, 10 minutes) leave from the intersection where Av Lima turns into a pedestrian walkway.

At the beach there are a few sparse restaurants and hotels, some bearing scars from a 2001 tsunami. Hotels get busy on summer weekends from January to April, even in the city center. A cut above the competition, **Hotel de Turistas** (☏57-1113; Lima 138; s/d/tr incl breakfast S90/115/155; @⊕) is housed in a large elegant building set in spacious gardens. It has a restaurant and is just a short walk or taxi ride from the bus stations.

Frequent bus services to Arequipa (S12 to S45, 3½ hours) are provided by several companies, all of which are found along Lima, including luxurious **Cruz del Sur** (📞57-1491; Lima 474), and the always economical **Flores** (📞57-1013; Lima 200). Cruz del Sur and other smaller bus companies also have daily services to Lima (S35 to S135, 12 hours) that stop at most intermediate coastal points, such as Chala (S15, 4½ hours) and Nazca (S45, seven hours).

Mollendo

📞054 / POP 22,800

The gringo trail takes a sharp left turn south of Camaná as it heads inland toward Arequipa, leaving the next stop on the coast, Mollendo, to diehard locals plus a seasonal influx of beach-starved *arequipeños*. Don't expect any Huacachina-style banana pancake restaurants here, although the beaches are ample, if a little lacking in atmosphere outside of the summer season (January to April). Mollendo's history testifies to occupations by the Incas and the Chileans. More notoriously, it was the birthplace of Abimael Guzmán, aka Presidente Gonzalo, the philosophy professor turned political agitator who became leader of the Sendero Lumioso (Shining Path) in 1980. Among nonsunbathers, Mollendo is revered for its bird reserve at the nearby Lagunas de Mejía.

🄾 Sights & Activities

When temperatures are searing from January through to at least March, the beachside aquatic park (adult/child S4/2) opens alongside the sea, and beachfront discos stay thumping until the small hours of the morning. But Mollendo can be like a ghost town throughout the rest of the year.

El Castillo de Forga was built in 1908 on a crag between beach numbers two and three by a rich *arequipeño* in love with Eu-

ropean architecture. Once an eye-catching stately home, it is currently unoccupied. There have been proposals to turn it into a casino.

🛏 Sleeping & Eating

Mollendo has a clutch of nothing-to-write-home-about hotels, none of which appear to offer breakfast. Reservations are a must during the high season, January to April.

Hotel Bahia del Puerto   HOTEL $$
(📞53-2990; Ugarte 301; s/d incl breakfast S50/90; ✳@🛜) Mollendo's cleanest bargain has some rooms with peek-a-boo ocean views and has benefited from recent renovations. There's an unattached *chifa* (Chinese restaurant) below.

Hostal La Casona   HOTEL $
(📞53-3160; Arequipa 188-192; s/d S30/40; 🛜) The handiest town center option, La Casona has high-ceilinged, bright rooms with cable TV and hot water. The staff can be stiff necked, but the atmosphere is casual.

Marco Antonio   PERUVIAN $$
(📞53-4258; Comercio 258; mains S15-24; ⊗8am-8pm Mon-Sat, 8am-7pm Sun; 🛜) A good no-thrills Peruvian cafe that gets the basics right; bank on a well-presented *lomo saltado*.

❶ Getting There & Around

The *terminal terrestre* (bus station) is about 2km northwest of the center; there's a S1 departure tax. **Santa Ursula** (📞53-2586) have frequent bus departures throughout the day for Arequipa (S8, two hours). *Colectivos* wait outside the terminal to whisk arriving passengers down to the town's plazas and the beach (S1, 10 minutes) or you can walk.

Combis (S1.20, 20 minutes) and *colectivos* (S2, 15 minutes) to the beach resort of Mejía leave from the corner of Valdivia and Arequipa. Unfortunately, there are no direct buses onward to Moquegua or Tacna. *Colectivos* and minivans marked 'El Valle' leave Mollendo

SANTUARIO NACIONAL LAGUNAS DE MEJÍA

About 6km southeast of Mejía along an unbroken line of beaches this 690-hectare sanctuary (Carretera Mollendo, Km 32; admission S5; ⊗dawn-dusk) protects coastal lagoons that are the largest permanent lakes in 1500km of desert coastline. They attract more than 200 species of coastal and migratory birds, best seen in the very early morning. The visitor center has maps of hiking trails leading through the dunes to *miradors*. From Mollendo, *colectivos* pass by the visitor center (S3, 30 minutes) frequently during the daytime. Ask the staff to help you flag down onward transportation, which peters out by the late afternoon.

from the top end of Mariscal Castilla, by a gas station, and pass through Mejía and the Río Tambo Valley to reach Cocachacra (S4, 1½ hours). There you can immediately jump into a *colectivo* heading for El Fiscal (S3, 15 minutes), a flyblown gas station where crowded buses heading to Moquegua, Tacna, Arequipa and Lima regularly stop.

Moquegua

📞053 / 56,000 / ELEV 1420M

Clinging to the northern limits of the world's driest desert, Moquegua defies near zero annual rainfall by supporting a thriving wine industry and a valley full of green fields replete with grazing cows that look like they might have been peeled off the surface of northern France (it's the rivers, you know). The town itself has a picturesque main square (supposedly designed by Frenchman Gustav Eiffel), but there is little else to detain you from a fleeting, but by no means unpleasant, overnight stop.

◉ Sights & Activities

PLAZA DE ARMAS & AROUND

The town's small and shady plaza boasts a 19th-century wrought-iron fountain, thought by some to have been designed in a workshop run by Gustave Eiffel (of eponymous tower fame), and flower gardens that make it a welcome oasis away from the encroaching desert.

The foreign-funded **Museo Contisuyo** (www.museocontisuyo.com; Tacna 294; adult/child S1.50/0.50; ⊙8:30am-1pm & 2:30-5:30pm) is an excellent little repository of local archaeological artifacts, including photographs of recent excavations, along with exhibitions of new works by local artists. The labels are in Spanish and English.

Opposite the facade of the town's oldest **church**, which mostly collapsed during a massive earthquake in 1868, is an 18th-century Spanish **colonial jail**, with intimidating iron-grilled windows. At one corner of the Plaza de Armas, visitors can enter the **Casa Posada de Teresa Podesta** (cnr Ancash & Ayacucho; admission S2; ⊙10am-3pm Mon-Fri), a stately colonial mansion with its innards still intact.

Walk around the town center to see some of the typical sugarcane thatching, especially along Calle Moquegua, and have a peek inside **Catedral Santa Catalina** (Ayacucho),

which houses the body of 18th-century St Fortunata, whose hair and nails are said to be still growing.

A park on a cliff high above the town is dominated by the **Cristo Blanco**, a white statue of Christ raised in 2002. There are swinging seats, a small suspension bridge, and expansive views over the Moquegua oasis and the surrounding desert.

CERRO BAÚL

A worthwhile excursion outside the city is to the flat-topped and steep-sided hill of **Cerro Baúl**, 18km northeast of Moquegua, once a royal brewery built by the Wari people. As was the case with succeeding Inca traditions, it was upper-class Wari women who were the skilled brewers here. Archaeologists who are still at work excavating the site believe that it was ceremonially destroyed by fire after one last, drunken *chicha* (fermented corn beer) bash, though why it was abandoned in such a rush remains a mystery so far. The rugged walk to the top of the site, which boasts panoramic views, takes about an hour. From Moquegua, a round-trip taxi costs about S30, or simply catch a *combi* (S1.50) or *colectivo* (S3) headed for Torata from central Moquegua and ask to be let off at Cerro Baúl.

🛏 Sleeping & Eating

It's best to pass up the cheap hostels near the bus stations in lieu of a safer option closer to the center of town.

Hostal Plaza   HOTEL $
(📞46-1612; Ayacucho 675; s/d/tr S35/45/55; 🛜) This is a neat spot by the plaza where some of the upstairs rooms have pretty views of the cathedral. The good-value digs are airy and sport large-screen cable TVs.

Hostal Arequipa   HOTEL $
(📞46-1338; Arequipa 360; s/d/tr S37/48/59) Located on a busy main street not far from the plaza, the Arequipa has clean and inviting rooms with hot showers and cable TV. Service here is reasonably friendly and helpful.

Vissios Pizzeria   PIZZERIA $
(Plaza de Armas 343; mains S13-23) A little more chic than your average pizza joint, Vissios has bright red walls, waiter service and modish photo prints on the wall. The roaring eat-in, take-out trade is spearheaded by pizzas, pastas, and iffy super-sweet Moquegua wine.

MOQUEGUA BUSES

DESTINATION	COST (S)	DURATION (HR)
Arequipa	30	3½-4
Ilo	7	1½
Lima	50-144	16-20
Puno	25	9
Tacna	10	3

Naples it isn't. Nonetheless, it's a welcome sight in the middle of the Peruvian desert.

Roda Fruta
BREAKFAST $
(Moquegua 439; breakfast S8-12) Grab your eggs, granola, yogurt and fruit salad in this salubrious breakfast place with casual seating. There's another branch in Calle Arequipa.

ⓘ Information
BCP (Moquegua 861) Has a 24-hour Visa/MasterCard ATM.
Municipal tourist office (Casa de la Cultura, Calle Moquegua; ◷7am-4pm) Local government-run tourist office located next to BCP.

ⓘ Getting There & Away
Buses leave from several small terminals downhill southwest of the Plaza de Armas. There you'll also find faster, though less safe and more expensive *colectivos* that leave when full for Ilo (S12, 1½ hours) and Arequipa (S30, 3½ hours).

Quality **Ormeño** (☎76-1149; Av La Paz 524) buses and cheaper **Flores** (☎46-2647; Av Ejercito s/n) run north serving Lima via Nazca and Ica, and south to Tacna. Flores and a couple of other companies also head west to Ilo. Numerous companies serve Arequipa.

Several smaller companies, including **San Martín** (☎95-352-1550; Av La Paz 175), take a mostly paved route to Puno (S25, nine hours) via Desaguadero on the Bolivian border (S18, six hours), usually departing in the evening.

Ilo
☎053 / POP 58,700
Ilo is the ugly departmental port, about 95km southwest of Moquegua, used mainly to ship copper from the mine at Toquepala further south, and wine and avocados from Moquegua. Ilo does offer a pleasant boardwalk and a few beachside luxury hotels that fill with Peruvian vacationers in the summertime, but though the beach is long and

curving, the waters are murky and unappealing for swimming.

⊙ Sights
Museo Municipal de Sitio MUSEUM
(Centro Mallqui; adult S5; ◷10am-3pm Mon-Sat, 10am-2pm Sun) About 15km inland at El Algarrobal is the Museo Municipal de Sitio, which hosts a surprisingly noteworthy collection of exhibits on the area's archaeology and agriculture, including ceramics, textiles, a collection of feather-topped hats and a mummified llama. A round-trip by taxi costs around S30.

🛌 Sleeping & Eating
There's no need to stay overnight, but if you get stuck there are plenty of options, including:

Hotel Kristal Azul HOTEL $
(☎48-4050; www.hotelkristalazul.com; Av 28 de Julio 664; s/d S60/70; ☎) Above a pizza restaurant two blocks from bus station, this place is clean, if unremarkable, with breakfast included.

Los Corales SEAFOOD $$
(Malecón Miramar 504; mains S14-30; ◷lunch & dinner; ☎) The prime shorefront position pretty much guarantees fresh seafood including local favorite, *pulpo al olvia* (octopus in olive oil), a cold appetizer.

ⓘ Getting There & Away
Most buses leave from a terminal in the town center, a couple of blocks from the plaza and the beach.

Flores (☎48-2512; cnr Ilo & Matará) covers Tacna (S10, 3½ hours), Moquegua (S8, 1½ hours) and Arequipa (S18, 5½ hours) where you can connect for onward journeys.

Faster, slightly pricier *colectivos* to Tacna and sometimes Moquegua leave when full from the side streets near the smaller bus stations.

Tacna

☎052 / POP 262,700 / ELEV 460M

Patriotism puts up a steely rearguard action in Tacna (population 262,700), Peru's most southerly settlement, a city that belonged to Chile as recently as 1929 (a young Salvador Allende lived here for eight of his childhood years), but is now proudly and unequivocally part of Peru. Just in case you forget, there's an earnest flag-raising ceremony every Sunday morning in the main plaza, plus a raft of heroic statues, leafy avenues and hyperbolic museum exhibits all dedicated to Peru's glorious past.

For outsiders, Tacna's primary role is as a staging post on the way to its former nemesis, Chile. Cordial modern relations between the two countries make the border crossing a comparative breeze. If you're delayed in town, a trio of small museums and some Europhile bars and restaurants will smooth the wait.

◉ Sights & Activities

Plaza de Armas   SQUARE

Tacna's main plaza, which is studded with palm trees and large pergolas topped by bizarre mushroom-like bushes, is a popular meeting place and has a patriotic flag-raising ceremony every Sunday morning. The plaza, famously pictured on the front of Peru's S100 note, features a huge arch – a monument to the heroes of the War of the Pacific. It is flanked by larger-than-life bronze statues of Admiral Grau and Colonel Bolognesi. Nearby, the 6m-high bronze **fountain** was created by the French engineer Gustave Eiffel, who also designed the **cathedral**, noted for its small but fine stained-glass windows and onyx high altar.

Museo Ferroviario   MUSEUM

(admission S5; ⊙8am-6pm) This museum located inside the train station – just ring the bell at the southern gates – gives the impression of stepping back in time. You can wander amid beautiful though poorly maintained 20th-century steam engines and rolling stock, most of them British. The shed-like salons by the station are filled with historic paraphernalia, including a curious collection of international postage stamps.

About a 15-minute walk south of the train station, a British locomotive built in 1859 and used as a troop train in the War of the Pacific is the centerpiece of **El Parque de la Locomotora**, an otherwise empty roadside park.

Casa Museo Basadre   MUSEUM

(Plaza de Armas 212; admission by donation; ⊙9am-5pm) Named for a local historian born in 1903, this place is more convincing as a cultural center than a museum (though there's a handful of old photos and exhibits). Check out the posters inside for upcoming music and art shows.

FREE **Museo de Zela**   MUSEUM

(Zela 542; ⊙8am-noon & 3-5pm Mon-Sat) The small, musty Museo de Zela provides a look at the interior of one of Tacna's oldest colonial buildings, the Casa de Zela. It houses a motley collection of 19th-century paintings of stately folk.

Museo Histórico Regional   MUSEUM

(Casa de la Cultura, Apurímac 202; admission S5; ⊙8am-noon & 1:30-5pm Mon-Fri) Patriotic like everything in Tacna, this museum above the town library broadcasts a grand somewhat triumphant air. Five huge canvases adorn the walls and busts of erstwhile heroes such as Zela, Bolognesi and Ugarte sit among old swords, yellowed letters and details about the War of the Pacific against former foe Chile.

⊨ Sleeping

There's no shortage of hotels catering to Tacna's cross-border traffic. That said, almost all are overpriced and fill up very fast, especially with Chileans who cross the border for weekend shopping trips.

Dorado Hotel   HOTEL $$

(☎41-5741, 42-1111; www.doradohoteltacna.com; Av Arias Aragüez 145; s/d/tr incl breakfast S100/130/165; @ ⊛) Posing as Tacna's grandest hotel, the Dorado is the sort of place where the curtains are heavy, the lobby sports shiny balustrades, and a bellboy will carry your bags to your room. While it can't emulate the classy exclusivity of a European city hotel, it makes a good job of trying.

Gran Hotel Tacna   HOTEL $$

(☎42-4193; www.granhoteltacna.com; Bolognesi 300; s/d incl breakfast S214/244; @ ⊛ ⊠) Bringing the feeling of a 'resort' to the city center, the architecturally uninteresting Gran Hotel Tacna is certainly large with numerous bars and restaurants, a shop, a pool and waist-coated waiters running around looking busy. It's not the classiest joint in town but it's certainly the most comprehensive (and expensive).

Maximo's Hotel
HOTEL $$

(☎24-2604; Av Arias Aragüez 281; s/d/tr incl breakfast S90/115/130; ☏) Quirky Maximo's has a lobby that's overladen with plants, balconies and candelabra, all suffused by green-tinted light. There's also a snack bar and good clean rooms with fans. The novel hotel sauna (S8 for guests) is open from 2pm to 10pm daily.

Hostal Le Prince
HOTEL $

(☎42-1252; Zela 728; r from S70; ☏) New economical but modern place next to the scruffier Hostal Universo that's hard to resist if you can cough up the extra cash.

Hotel Camino Real
HOTEL $$

(☎42-1891; San Martín 855; s/d/tr incl breakfast S100/130/165; ☏) Stay in the Camino Real and you're on a *camino* (path) back to the 1970s, not the cool, retro '70s of repackaged Stones CDs, but the fraying-round-the-edges '70s that cries out 'give me a paint-job!' That said, the basics are all here: large rooms, comfy beds, and a restaurant and cafeteria onsite.

Hostal Universo
HOTEL $

(☎41-5441; Zela 724; s/d/tr S30/40/60) Next door to Hostal Le Prince, this broken-in hotel is a secure option with accommodating staff, hot showers and cable TV, though rooms are on the small side.

 Eating

Popular local dishes include *patasca a la tacneña,* a thick, spicy vegetable-and-meat soup, and *picante a la tacneña,* hot peppered tripe (it's better than it sounds). A surprising number of hole-in-the-wall cafes serve fresh fruit and yogurt, as well as other healthy, vegetarian snacks.

TOP CHOICE Café Da Vinci
EUROPEAN, PERUVIAN $$

(cnr Calle Arias Aragüez & San Martín; mains S23-40; ⏰11am-11pm) There's a Euro-feel to the food and decor in this wood-paneled domain where well-dressed wait staff give out Mona Lisa smiles along with menus that highlight fabulous baguettes, pizzas, generous glasses of dry red wine, and decent Peruvian staples. Pride of place goes to the real Italian espresso machine.

Uros Restaurante
PERUVIAN, FUSION $$

(www.restauranteuros.com; Av San Martín 608; mains S22-35) Tacna's stab at *novoandina* cuisine avoids too many pretensions, if you can get past the (admittedly photogenic) photos of the food on the menu. There's another branch on the town's periphery.

Café Verdi
CAFE $

(Vigil 57; menús S7.50, snacks S3-8; ⏰8:30am-9pm Mon-Sat) Verdi's an old school cafe with baked goods and desserts, as well as affordable fixed lunches served at perennially busy tables. Half the clientele looks as if they've been coming here for 50 years. They probably have.

La Mia Mama
ITALIAN $

(☎24-2022; Av Arias Aragüez 204; mains S10-18; ⏰6-11pm Mon-Sat) This little Italian joint is a great place to sip a glass of *vino de chacra* (local table wine) over one of the menu's classic pizzas or pastas. Tables fill up quickly.

BORDER CROSSING: CHILE VIA TACNA

Border-crossing formalities are relatively straightforward. There are three main transport options: train, public bus or *colectivo* (shared taxi), with the latter proving to be the most efficient. The five-passenger taxis are run by professional companies with desks inside Tacna's international bus terminal. They charge approximately S18 to take you the 65km to Arica in Chile with stops at both border posts. Most of the paperwork is done before you get in the car. On a good day the trip should take little more than an hour. The public bus is cheaper (S10), but slower, as you have to wait for all the passengers to disembark and clear customs.

The Chilean border post is open 8am to midnight from Sunday to Thursday, and 24 hours on Friday and Saturday. Note that Chile is an hour ahead of Peru, or two hours during daylight-saving time from the last Sunday in October to the first Sunday in April. From Arica, you can continue south into Chile by air or bus, or northeast into Bolivia by air or bus. For more information, consult Lonely Planet's *South America on a shoestring, Chile & Easter Island* and *Bolivia.*

Tacna

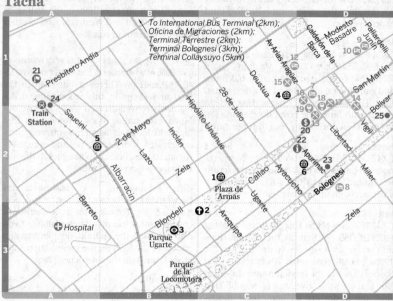

To International Bus Terminal (2km);
Oficina de Migraciones (2km);
Terminal Terrestre (2km);
Terminal Bolognesi (3km);
Terminal Collaysuyo (5km)

Tacna

Mushna　　　　INTERNATIONAL, FUSION **$$**
(Av Arias Aragüez 204; mains S25-35) A post-modern resto-bar that looks like it has drifted across from Arica, Chile. Food is presented with artistic panache in an interior that is more nightclub than restaurant. Cocktails abound.

 Drinking

The small pedestrian streets of Libertad and Vigil are ground zero for Tacna's limited nightlife. There you'll find a couple of pubs and clubs, some with live music and dancing on weekends. Beer geeks imbibe at the flashy **München Brauhaus** (☏24-6125; ◷8pm-late) while rockers get to compare

To Bolivian
Consulate
(1km)

hair grease at **Jethro Pub**; both are on Av Arias Aragüez.

ℹ Information

Internet cafes are everywhere, and most offer inexpensive local, long-distance and international phone calls. Chilean pesos, Peruvian nuevos soles and US dollars can all be easily exchanged in Tacna. There's a global ATM at the *terminal terrestre*.

BCP (San Martín 574) Has a Visa/MasterCard ATM, changes traveler's checks and gives cash advances on Visa cards.

Bolivian consulate (☎24-5121; Bolognesi 1721; ☺8am-3:30pm Mon-Fri) Some nationalities (American included) will need to solicit a visa one month in advance and pay a US$130 entry fee; there's another Bolivian consulate located in Puno.

Chilean consulate (☎42-3063; www.minrel.cl; Presbítero Andía at Saucini; ☺8am-1pm Mon-Fri) Most travelers don't need a Chilean visa and head straight for the border instead.

Hospital (☎42-2121, 42-3361; Blondell s/n; ☺24hr) For emergency services.

iPerú (☎42-5514; iperutacna@promperu.gob.pe; San Martín 491) National tourist office, provides free information and brochures.

Oficina de Migraciones (immigration office; ☎24-3231; Circunvalación s/n, Urb Él Triángulo; ☺8am-4pm Mon-Fri)

Police (☎41-4141; Calderón de la Barca 353; ☺24hr)

ℹ Getting There & Away

Air

Tacna's **airport** (code TCQ; ☎31-4503) is 5km west of town. **LAN** (www.lan.com; Calle Apurímac 101; ☺8.30am-7pm Mon-Fri, 9am-2pm Sat) and **Peruvian Airlines** (www.peruvian.pe; Av Bolognesi 670) both offer daily passenger services to Lima, and some seasonal services to Arequipa and Cuzco.

Bus

Most long-distance departures leave from the **terminal terrestre** (☎42-7007) on Hipólito Unánue, at the northeast edge of town, with the exception of some buses to Juliaca, Desaguadero and Puno, which leave from **Terminal Collaysuyo** (☎31-2538), located in the district of Alta Alianza to the north of town.

Frequent buses (S10) to Arica, Chile, leave between 6am and 10pm from the international terminal across the street from the *terminal terrestre*.

A few companies, including **Sagitario** (☎952-843-439) and **San Martín** (☎952-524-252), run overnight *económico* and luxury bus services to Puno via Desaguadero on the Bolivian border, finally ending up in Cuzco. These mostly leave in the evening from Terminal Collaysuyo. When choosing this route, opt for the nicest bus, or you could be in for a cold, bumpy ride with few bathroom breaks – trust us! Alternatively, you can also return to Arequipa and transfer there.

Long-distance buses are frequently stopped and searched by immigration and/or customs officials not far north of Tacna. Have your passport handy.

A S1 terminal-use tax is levied at the *terminal terrestre*. The usual suspects head to all destinations north including **Ormeño** (☎42-3292) and more economical **Flores** (☎74-1150).

Taxi

Numerous *colectivos* (S18, one to two hours) to Arica, Chile, leave from the international terminal across the street from the *terminal terrestre* in order to cross the **Chilean border** (☺8am-midnight Sun-Thu, 24hr Fri & Sat). For border crossing formalities, see p133.

Fast, though notoriously unsafe, *colectivos* to Moquegua (S15, 2½ hours), and sometimes Ilo, leave when full from Mercado Grau, a short walk uphill from the *terminal terrestre*. Be sure to keep your wits about you in the dangerous market area.

Train

Trains between Tacna's **train station** (☎42-4981; Av 2 de Mayo) and Arica, Chile

TACNA BUSES

DESTINATION	COST (S)	DURATION (HR)
Arequipa	15-35	7
Cuzco	60-125	17
Ilo	10	3½
Lima	50-144	18-22
Moquegua	10	3
Puno	25-45	10

(S10/C$2000, 1½ hours) are the cheapest and most charming but also the slowest way to cross the border. Your passport is stamped at the station before boarding the train in Tacna. There is no stop at the actual border and you receive your entry stamp when you arrive in Chile near Arica's Plaza de Armas. Though this historic railway is a must for train buffs, service can be erratic and inconveniently timed. At the time of writing two trains a day were departing Tacna at 4am and 6am. Return trains leave Arica at 4pm and 6pm. Always double check at the station for the latest schedules.

Getting Around

A taxi between the airport and the city center costs about S5. A taxi from the center to the bus terminals costs about S3.

Arequipa & Canyon Country

Best Places to Eat

» Zingaro (p151)
» Tradición Arequipeña (p151)
» Zig Zag (p151)
» Chicha (p151)

Best Places to Stay

» Hostal Casona Solar (p148)
» Los Tambos Hostal (p148)
» Colca Lodge (p162)
» Casa Andina (p149)

Why Go?

Arequipa province is Peru's big combo ticket. Authentic historical immersion and white-knuckle Andean adventure inhabit the same breathing space here. Imagine the cultural riches of one of South America's finest colonial cities just a few hours' drive from the world's two deepest canyons and you'll get a hint of the dramatic contrasts. Ample urban distractions can be found in Arequipa, the arty, audacious, unflappably resilient metropolis that lies in the shadow of El Misti volcano. Beckoning to the northwest lie the Colca and Cotahuasi canyons whose depth, while impressive, is a mere statistic compared to the Andean condors, epic treks, and long-standing Spanish, Inca and pre-Inca traditions that lurk in their midst. Other unusual apparitions include the lava encrusted Valle de los Volcanes, the haunting Toro Muerto petroglyphs, and the barren Paso de Patopampa where a main road ascends to 4910m, higher than any point in Western Europe or North America.

When to Go

Arequipa

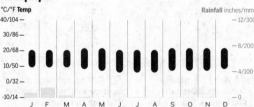

Mar–Apr Arequipa puts on a Semana Santa parade to rival the cities of former colonial power, Spain

Apr–Dec Outside of the rainy season, hiking in the Colca and Cotahuasi canyons is sublime

Jun–Sep Your best chance of seeing Andean condors gliding above the Colca Canyon

AREQUIPA

054 / POP 864,300 / ELEV 2350M

It's hard playing second fiddle to Cuzco and Machu Picchu on Peru's international tourist circuit, not that this little detail makes the average *arequipeño* jealous. Other Peruvians joke that you need a different passport to enter Peru's second-largest city, a metropolis one-tenth of the size of the capital Lima but pugnaciously equal to it in terms of cuisine, historical significance and confident self-awareness. Guarded by not one but *three* dramatic volcanoes, the city enjoys a resplendent, if seismically precarious setting – earthquakes regularly wrack this region, the last big one causing significant damage in 2001. Fortunately, the city's architecture, a

Arequipa & Canyon Country Highlights

❶ Watching massive Andean condors catch thermal uplifts above the almost sheer walls of the **Cañón del Colca** (p158)

❷ Wandering way off the beaten track in the isolated **Cañón del Cotahuasi** (p165)

❸ Getting a glimpse of austere, monastic life behind the high stone walls of the **Monasterio de Santa Catalina** (p139) in Arequipa

❹ Dining the traditional way in one of Arequipa's **picanterías** (p151)

❺ Making a summit attempt on the almost perfectly symmetrical cone of **El Misti volcano** (p157)

❻ Studying the frozen remains of Juanita in the **Museo Santuarios Andinos** (p140)

❼ Pondering the meaning of the mysterious **Toro Muerto petroglyphs** (p164)

formidable ensemble of baroque-*mestizo* buildings grafted out of the local white *sillar* rock, has so far withstood most of what Mother Earth has thrown at it. In 2000 the city's central core earned a well-deserved Unesco World Heritage listing and the sight of the gigantic cathedral, with the ethereal image of 5825m El Misti rising behind it, is worth a visit alone. Pretty cityscapes aside, Arequipa has played a fundamental role in Peru's gastronomic renaissance; classic spicy dishes such as *rocoto relleno, chupe de camarones* and *ocopa* best enjoyed in the city's communal *picantería* restaurants, all hail from here. *Arequipeños* are also a proud people fond of intellectual debate, especially about their fervent political beliefs, which find voice through regular demonstrations in the Plaza de Armas. Not surprisingly, the city has produced one of Latin America's most influential novelists, Mario Vargas Llosa, the literary genius who ran unsuccessfully for the Peruvian presidency in 1990.

History

Evidence of pre-Inca settlement by indigenous peoples from the Lake Titicaca area leads some scholars to think the Aymara people first named the city (*ari* means 'peak' and *quipa* means 'lying behind' in Aymara; hence, Arequipa is 'the place lying behind the peak' of El Misti). However, another oft-heard legend says that the fourth *inca* (king), Mayta Cápac, was traveling through the valley and became enchanted by it. He ordered his retinue to stop, saying, '*Ari, quipay,*' which translates as 'Yes, stay.' The Spaniards refounded the city on August 15, 1540, a date that is remembered with a week-long fair.

Arequipa is built in an area highly prone to natural disasters; the city was totally destroyed by earthquakes and volcanic eruptions in 1600 and has since been rocked by major earthquakes in 1687, 1868, 1958, 1960 and, most recently, in 2001. For this reason, many of the city's buildings are built low for stability. Despite the disasters, many fetching historic structures survive.

◉ Sights

Monasterio de Santa Catalina MONASTERY, MUSEUM
(☏22-9798; www.santacatalina.org.pe; Santa Catalina 301; admission S35; ⊙9am-5pm, last entry 4pm, plus 7-9pm Tue & Thu) Even if you've already overdosed on colonial edifices, this convent shouldn't be missed. Occupying a whole block and guarded by imposing high walls, it is one of the most fascinating religious buildings in Peru. Nor is it just a religious building – the 20,000-sq-meter complex is almost a citadel within the city. It was founded in 1580 by a rich widow, Doña María de Guzmán.

There are two ways of visiting Santa Catalina. One is to wander around on your own, soaking up the meditative atmosphere and getting slightly lost (there's a finely printed miniature map on the back of your ticket if you're up for an orienteering challenge). Alternatively, informative guides who speak Spanish, English, French, German, Italian and Portuguese are available for S20. The tours last about an hour, after which you're welcome to keep exploring by yourself, until the gates close. The monastery is also open two evenings a week so that visitors can traipse through the shadowy grounds by candlelight as nuns would have done centuries ago.

For visitors who undertake a self-tour of Santa Catalina, a helpful way to begin is to focus a visit on the three main **cloisters**. After passing under the *silencio* (silence) arch you will enter the **Novice Cloister**, marked by a courtyard with a rubber tree at its center. After passing under this arch, novice nuns were required to zip their lips in a vow of solemn silence and resolve to a life of work and prayer. Nuns lived as novices for four years, during which time their families were expected to pay a dowry of 100 gold coins per year. At the end of these four years they could choose between taking their vows and entering into religious service, or leaving the convent – the latter would most likely have brought shame upon their family.

Graduated novices passed onto the **Orange Cloister**, named for the orange trees clustered at its center that represent renewal and eternal life. This cloister allows a peek into the **Profundis Room**, a mortuary where dead nuns were mourned. Paintings of the deceased line the walls. Artists were allotted 24 hours to complete these posthumous paintings, since painting the nuns while alive was out of the question.

Leading away from the Orange Cloister, **Córdova Street** is flanked by cells that served as living quarters for the nuns. These dwellings would house one or more nuns, along with a handful of servants, and ranged from austere to lavish depending on the wealth of the inhabitants. Ambling

JUANITA – THE 'ICE MAIDEN'

In 1992 local climber Miguel Zárate was guiding an expedition on Nevado Ampato (6310m) when he found curious wooden remnants, suggestive of a burial site, exposed near the icy summit. In September 1995 he convinced American mountaineer and archaeologist Johan Reinhard to climb the peak, which following recent eruptions of the nearby Sabancaya volcano had been coated by ash, melting the snow below and exposing the site more fully. Upon arrival, they immediately found a statue and other offerings, but the burial site had collapsed and there was no sign of a body. Ingeniously, the team rolled rocks down the mountainside and, by following them, Zárate was able to spot the bundled mummy of an Inca girl, which had tumbled down the same path when the icy tomb had crumbled.

The girl had been wrapped and almost perfectly preserved by the icy temperatures for about 500 years, and it was immediately apparent from the remote location of her tomb and from the care and ceremony surrounding her death (as well as the crushing blow to her right eyebrow) that this 12- to 14-year-old girl had been sacrificed to the gods at the summit. For the Incas, mountains were gods who could kill by volcanic eruption, avalanche or climatic catastrophes. These violent deities could only be appeased by sacrifices from their subjects, and the ultimate sacrifice was that of a child.

It took the men days to carry the frozen bundle down to the village of Cabanaconde, from where she was transported, on a princely bed of frozen foodstuffs, in Zárate's own domestic freezer to the Universidad Católica (Catholic University) in Arequipa to undergo a battery of scientific examinations. Quickly dubbed 'Juanita, the ice maiden,' the mummy was given her own museum in 1998 (Museo Santuarios Andinos; see below). In total, almost two dozen similar Inca sacrifices have been discovered atop various Andean mountains since the 1950s.

down **Toledo Street** leads you to the cafe, which serves up fresh-baked pastries and espresso drinks, and finally to the communal washing area where servants washed in mountain runoff channeled into huge earthenware jars.

Heading down **Burgos Street** toward the cathedral's sparkling *sillar* tower, visitors may enter the musty darkness of the communal kitchen that was originally used as the church until the reformation of 1871. Just beyond, **Zocodober Square** (the name comes from the Arabic word for 'barter') served as a site where nuns gathered on Sundays to exchange their handicrafts such as soaps and baked goods. Continuing on, to the left you can enter the **cell** of the legendary Sor Ana, a nun renowned for her eerily accurate predictions about the future and the miracles she is said to have performed until her death in 1686.

Finally, the **Great Cloister** is bordered by the **chapel** on one side and the **art gallery**, which used to serve as a communal dormitory, on the other. This building takes on the shape of a cross. Murals along the walls depict scenes from the lives of Jesus and the Virgin Mary.

TOP CHOICE **Museo Santuarios Andinos** MUSEUM
(☎20-0345; www.ucsm.edu.pe/santury; La Merced 110; admission S20; ☺9am-6pm Mon-Sat, 9am-3pm Sun) There's an escalating drama to this theatrically presented museum, dedicated to the preserved body of a frozen 'mummy,' and its compulsory guided tour which starts with a beautifully-shot 20-minute film about how Juanita, the so-called 'Ice Maiden,' was unearthed atop Nevado Ampato in 1995. Next, well-versed student guides from the university lead you through a series of atmospheric, dimly lit rooms filled with artifacts from the expedition that found the 'mummy.' The climax is the vaguely macabre sight of poor Juanita, the 12-year-old Inca girl sacrificed to the gods in the 1450s and now eerily preserved in a glass refrigerator. Tours take about an hour and are conducted in Spanish, English and French.

Plaza de Armas SQUARE
Arequipa's main plaza, unblemished by modern interferences (save for the ubiquitous honking taxis) is a museum of the city's *sillar* architecture – white, muscular and aesthetically unique. Impressive colonnaded balconies line three sides. The fourth is given over to Peru's widest cathedral, a

Arequipa

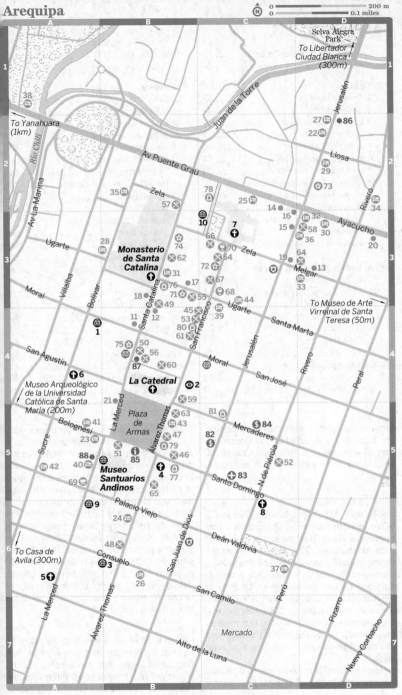

Arequipa

humungous edifice with two soaring towers. Even this is dwarfed by the duel snow-capped sentinels of El Misto and Chanchani, both visible from various points in the central park.

FREE **La Catedral** CATHEDRAL
(⊙7-11:30am & 5-7:30pm Mon-Sat, 7am-1pm & 5-7pm Sun) The history of the cathedral that dominates Arequipa's main plaza is filled with doggedness. The original structure, dating from 1656, was gutted by fire in 1844. Consequently rebuilt, it was then promptly flattened by the earthquake of 1868. Most of what you see now has been rebuilt since then. An earthquake in 2001 toppled one enormous tower, and made the other slump precariously, yet by the end of the next year the cathedral looked as good as new once again.

The cathedral is the only one in Peru that stretches the length of a plaza. The interior is simple and airy, with a luminous quality, and the high vaults are uncluttered. It also has a distinctly international flair; it is one of less than 100 basilicas in the world entitled to display the Vatican flag, which is to the right of the altar. Both the altar and the 12 columns (symbolizing the 12 Apostles) are made of Italian marble. The huge Byzantine-style brass lamp hanging in front of the altar is from Spain and the pulpit was carved in France. In 1870, Belgium provided the impressive organ, said to be the largest in South America, though damage during shipping condemned the devout to wince at its distorted notes for more than a century.

Iglesia de la Compañía CHURCH
(⊙9am-12:30pm & 3-6pm Mon-Fri, 11:30am-12:30pm & 3-6pm Sat, 9am-noon & 5-6pm Sun) One could argue that Arequipa's cathedral is just *too* big. Providing an interesting antidote (and proving that small really can be

beautiful) is this diminutive Jesuit church on the southeast corner of the Plaza de Armas. The front facade is an intricately carved masterpiece of the *churrigueresque* style (think baroque and then some – a style hatched in Spain in the 1660s). The equally detailed altar, completely covered in gold leaf, takes the style further and will be eerily familiar to anyone who has visited Seville cathedral in Spain. To the left of the altar is the San Ignacio chapel (admission S4), with a polychrome cupola smothered in unusual jungle-like murals of tropical flowers, fruit and birds, among which mingle warriors and angels.

Next door and accessed via Calle Santo Domingo, the Claustros de la Campañía continues the ornate theme. This wonderful double courtyard is ringed by cloisters held up by shapely *sillar* columns etched with skillful carvings. These days the cloisters house what must be one of South America's most elegant shopping centers. You'll find a wine bodega, an ice-cream outlet, numerous alpaca wool shops and a couple of elegant cafes here.

Monasterio de la Recoleta   MONASTERY
(La Recoleta 117; admission S5; ⊙9am-noon & 3-5pm Mon-Sat) A short cab ride from the city center in a dicey neighborhood, this musty monastery was constructed on the west side of the Río Chili in 1648 by Franciscan friars, though now it has been completely rebuilt. Scholarship was an integral part of the Franciscans' order, and bibliophiles will delight in the huge library, which contains more than 20,000 dusty books and maps; the oldest volume dates back to 1494. The library is open for supervised visits; just ask at the entrance. There is a well-known museum of Amazonian artifacts (including preserved jungle animals) collected by the missionaries, and an extensive collection of pre-Conquest artifacts and religious art

of the *escuela cuzqueña* (Cuzco School). Guides who speak Spanish, English, French and Italian are available; a tip is expected.

Museo de Arte Virreinal de Santa Teresa
MUSEUM

(Melgar 303; admission S10; ⊙9am-5pm Mon-Sat, 9am-1pm Sun) This gorgeous 17th-century Carmelite convent was opened to the public as a living museum a few years back. The colonial-era buildings are justifiably famed for their decoratively painted walls and restored rooms filled with priceless votive *objets d'art,* murals, precious metalworks, colonial-era paintings and other historical artifacts. It is all capably explained by student tour guides who speak Spanish, English, French, German and Portuguese; tips are appreciated. A charming shop at the front of the complex sells baked goods and rose-scented soap made by the nuns.

Casa de Moral
HISTORIC BUILDING

(Moral 318; admission S5; ⊙9am-5pm Mon-Sat) Built in 1730, this stylized baroque-*mestizo* house is named after the 200-year-old mulberry tree in its central courtyard. Owned by BCP (a bank) since 2003 it is essentially a museum notable for its antique maps, heavy furniture, religious art, and extensive coin and banknote collection (courtesy of BCP). Notes are in Spanish and English.

FREE Casa Ricketts
HISTORIC BUILDING

(Casa Tristán del Pozo; San Francisco 108; ⊙9:15am-12:45pm & 4:30-6:30pm Mon-Fri, 9:30am-12:45pm Sat) Built in 1738, the ornate Casa Ricketts has served as a seminary, archbishop's palace, school and home to well-to-do families. Today it is the most splendiferous working bank in the city – possibly even Peru. Even if you're not here for a transaction, it's worth nosing around its dual interior courtyards with their puma-headed fountains.

La Mansión del Fundador
HISTORIC BUILDING

(admission S10; ⊙9am-6pm) This 17th-century mansion was once owned by Arequipa's founder Garcí Manuel de Carbajal, has been restored with original furnishings and paintings, and even has its own chapel. The mansion is in the village of Huasacache, 9km from Arequipa's city center, most easily reached by taxi (round-trip S20). Local city tours occasionally stop here.

Iglesia de San Francisco
CHURCH

(Zela cuadra 1; admission S5; ⊙church & convent 9am-12:30pm & 3-6:30pm Mon-Fri) Originally built in the 16th century, this church has been badly damaged by several earthquakes. It still stands, however, and visitors can see a large crack in the cupola – testimony to the power of quakes. Other colonial churches around the city center include San Agustín, La Merced and Santo Domingo.

Museo Arqueológico de la Universidad Católica de Santa María
MUSEUM

(Cruz Verde 303; voluntary donation; ⊙9am-5pm Mon-Fri) This university-run museum has interesting little displays on local excavation sites, as well as some artifacts, including surprisingly well-preserved ancient ceramics. Guided tours are available in Spanish and English; tips are expected.

Museo Histórico Municipal
MUSEUM

(Plazuela San Francisco 407; admission S5; ⊙9am-5pm Mon-Sat, 9am-1pm Sun) Arequipa's and, by definition Peru's, historical trajectory is showcased in this educational, if unexciting museum that is split into different rooms dedicated to different epochs. There's pre-Hispanic, the independence era, the republic era and the War of the Pacific. Once you're done counting the dead heroes (and there are many), pop into the adjacent Museo Arqueológico Chiribaya (included in entry fee) which houses an impressive collection of artifacts from the pre-Incan Chiribaya civilization, including well-preserved textiles and the only pre-Inca gold collection in southern Peru.

Museo de la Universidad Nacional de San Agustín (UNAS)
MUSEUM

(Álvarez Thomas 200; admission S5; ⊙9am-4pm Mon-Fri) Another small university-run museum, this one's a little more esoteric with themes jumping between archaeological remains, baroque furniture and colonial art from the Peruvian Cuzco School.

FREE Casona Editora Peru
MUSEUM

(Consuelo 202; ⊙9am-noon) In another of those gorgeous colonial houses lies this homage to the newspaper *El Peruano,* founded in 1825 by legendary politician and South American liberator Simón Bolívar (it's the oldest surviving newspaper in Latin America). The small museum includes old printing presses, and some yellowed front pages. A separate room showcases temporary art expositions.

YANAHUARA

The peaceful neighborhood of Yanahuara makes a diverting excursion from the Arequipa city center. It's within walking distance: go west on Av Puente Grau over the Puente Grau (Grau Bridge) and continue on Av Ejército for half a dozen blocks. Turn right on Av Lima and walk five blocks to a small plaza, where you'll find the **Iglesia San Juan Bautista** (admission free), which dates from 1750. It housed the highly venerated Virgen de Chapi after the 2001 earthquake brought her church tumbling down about her ears. The popular Fiesta de la Virgen de Chapi is held on May 1. At the side of the plaza there's a *mirador* (lookout) with excellent views of Arequipa and El Misti.

Head back along Av Jerusalén, parallel to Av Lima, and just before reaching Av Ejército you'll see the well-known restaurant Sol de Mayo (p152), where you can stop for a tasty lunch of typical *arequipeño* food. The round-trip walk should take around two hours, but there are also *combis* (minibuses) to Yanahuara from along Av Puente Grau (and returning from Yanahuara's plaza to the city) every few minutes to speed you along (S1, 10 minutes).

🏃 Activities

Arequipa is the centerpoint for a raft of nebulous sights and activities dotted around the high country to the north and east of the city. Trekking, mountaineering and river running are the big three activities, but there are plenty more.

Trekking & Mountaineering

ℹ️ INFORMATION

The spectacular canyons around Arequipa offer many excellent hiking options. Trekking agencies can arrange off-the-beaten-track routes to suit your timeline and fitness level.

Trekking solo in the well-traveled Cañón del Colca area is popular and easy, but, if you're nervous about hiking without guides or want to tackle more untrammeled routes, there are dozens of tour companies based in Arequipa that can arrange guided treks.

Superb mountains for climbing surround Arequipa. Adequate acclimatization for this area is essential and it's best to have spent some time in Cuzco or Puno immediately before a high-altitude expedition. Cold temperatures, which sometimes drop to -29°C at the highest camps, necessitate very warm clothing.

The Association of Mountain Guides of Peru warns that many guides are uncertified and untrained, so climbers are advised to go well informed about medical and wilderness-survival issues. Most agencies sell climbs as packages that include transport, so prices vary widely depending on the size of the group and the mountain, but the current cost for a guide alone is around US$70 per day.

WHEN TO GO

Although you can trek year-round, the best (ie driest) time is from April to December.

MAPS

Maps of the area can be obtained from **Colca Trek** (☎20-6217, 9-60-0170; www.colcatrek.com.pe; Jerusalén 401-B) in Arequipa or the Instituto Geográfico Nacional (see p535) and South American Explorers Club (see boxed text, p96) in Lima.

EQUIPMENT & RENTALS

Carlos Zárate Adventures (☎20-2461; www.zarateadventures.com; Santa Catalina 204) and **Peru Camping Shop** (☎22-1658; www.perucampingshop.com; Jerusalén 410) rent tents, ice axes, crampons, stoves and boots.

River Running

Arequipa is one of Peru's premier bases for river running and kayaking. Many trips are unavailable during the rainy season (between December and March), when water levels can be dangerously high. For more information and advice, surf www.peruwhitewater.com.

The **Río Chili**, about 7km from Arequipa, is the most frequently run local river, with a half-day trip suitable for beginners leaving almost daily from April to November (from US$35). Further afield, you can also do relatively easy trips on the **Río Majes**, into which the Río Colca flows. The most commonly run stretches pass class II and III rapids.

YOU'VE TASTED IT, NOW COOK IT

If you recognize the name Gastón Acurio and concur that Peru is the gastronomical capital of Latin America, you may be inspired to enroll in an Arequipa **cooking course**. Local guide and qualified chef Miguel Fernández who runs Al Travel (p147) organizes **Peru Flavors**, a four-hour cooking course (S50) where you will learn to prepare a trio of appetizers and mains from the three different geographical regions of Peru: Amazonia, the Andes and the Coast. Dishes include *rocoto relleno* (stuffed spicy red peppers), *lomo saltado* (beef stir-fried with onions and peppers) and *chupe de camerones* (prawn chowder).

Another popular option is the **Peruvian Cooking Experience** (www.peruviancook ingexperience.com; San Martín 116, Vallecito), based out of the Casa de Avila hotel (p150) four blocks southwest of Plaza de Armas. Three-hour courses (11am to 2pm) run Monday, Wednesday and Friday and cost S45 (S35 if you're staying at the hotel). You can study the art of ceviche preparation or even opt for vegetarian recipes. Courses are available in Spanish and English. Maximum group size is six.

A more off-the-beaten-track possibility is the remote **Río Cotahuasi**, a white-water adventure – not for the fainthearted – that reaches into the deepest sections of what is perhaps the world's deepest known canyon. Expeditions here are infrequent and only for the experienced, usually taking nine days and passing through class IV and V rapids. The **Río Colca** was first run back in 1981, but this is a dangerous, difficult trip, not to be undertaken lightly. A few outfitters will do infrequent and expensive rafting trips, and easier sections can be found upriver from the canyon.

Mountain Biking

The Arequipa area has many mountain-biking possibilities. Many of the same companies that offer trekking or mountain-climbing trips (see earlier) also organize downhill volcano mountain-biking trips at Chachani and El Misti or can arrange tailor-made tours. If you have the experience and wherewithal, these agencies can rent you high-end bikes and offer expert trip-planning advice to help get you started on your own. For more basic machines, try **Peru Camping Shop** (www.perucampingshop.com; Jerusalén 410) which rents bikes by the half-day for S35 including helmet, gloves and a map of the area. It also organizes downhill cycling blasts in the vicinity of El Misti for S68 (one day) with transport.

🎓 Courses

Want to learn to speak Spanish? Immersion is the best way and Arequipa provides plenty of opportunities to hook up on a course while practicing with the locals in the evenings. Book in with one of the following agencies and you'll be reading Mario Vargas Llosa in the original before you know it.

CEPESMA   LANGUAGE

(☎9-59-961-638; www.cepesmaidiomasceci.com; Puente Grau 108) You can organize courses from two ($16) to eight hours ($64) per day. Cooking, dancing and volunteer opportunities are also available.

Juanjo   LANGUAGE

(www.spanishlanguageperu.com; 2nd epata C-4, Urb Magisterial, Yanahuara) Recommended by travelers, it arranges individual, small-group classes from S300 per week. Homestays and volunteer work can also be arranged.

ROCIO   LANGUAGE

(☎22-4568; www.spanish-peru.com; Ayacucho 208) Charges S18 per hour for an individual class, while small group lessons cost S290 per 40-hour week. Ring bell number 21 at the communal entrance.

Centro Cultural Peruano Norteamericano   LANGUAGE

(ICPNA; ☎39-1020; www.cultural.edu.pe; Melgar 109) Aside from offering a raft of cultural activities (theater, music and the like), the well-established Peru-North American cultural center bivouacked in a pleasant 'casona' in the city center can organize Spanish lessons for foreigners from S35 for a 90-minute session.

Instituto Cultural Peruano Alemán   LANGUAGE

(ICPA; ☎22-8130; www.icpa.org.pe; Ugarte 207) The Peruvian-German cultural center also offers Spanish lessons in the city center at similar rates.

👉 Tours & Guides

The streets of Santa Catalina and Jerusalén harbor dozens of travel agencies offering ho-hum city tours and excursions to the canyon country, most with daily departures. While some agencies are professional, there are also plenty of carpetbaggers muscling in on the action, so shop carefully. Never accept tours from street touts and, where possible, tours should be paid for in cash, as occasional credit-card fraud is reported.

The standard two-day tour of the Cañón del Colca costs S65 to S225 per person, depending on the season, group size and the comfort level of the hotel you choose to stay at in Chivay. All tours leave Arequipa between 7am and 9am. Stops include the Reserva Nacional Salinas y Aguada Blanca, Chivay, Calera hot springs, an evening *peña* (bar or club featuring live folkloric music) plus a visit to the Cruz del Cóndor.

Day Tours

Al Travel Tours CULTURE
(☑22-2052; www.aitraveltours.com; Santa Catalina 203) Owner Miguel Fernández offers some unique tours including a popular Reality Tour (from S40 per person depending on group size) which visits a poor Arequipan neighborhood of stonemakers. A large part of your fee goes to the local workers' coops.

Tours Class Arequipa BUS TOUR
(www.toursclassarequipa.com.pe; Portal de San Agustín 103, Plaza de Armas) This open-top bus tour (two/four hours S35/45) is actually a handy way of seeing some of Arequipa's outer sights. The Campiña (countryside) tour includes stops at Cayma, Yanahuara and the Mansión del Fundadaor.

Hiking & Mountaineering

Carlos Zárate Adventures TREKKING, ADVENTURE
(☑20-2461; www.zarateadventures.com; Santa Catalina 204) This company was founded in 1954 by Carlos Zárate, the great-grandfather of climbing in Arequipa. One of his sons, Miguel, was responsible, along with archaeologists for unearthing Juanita 'the Ice Maiden' atop Mt Ampato in 1995. Another son, Carlos Zárate Flores, also an experienced guide, runs this highly professional outfit. Zárate's guides generally speak Spanish or English, but are available in French when prearranged. The company offers all manner of treks, and climbs all the local peaks with prices varying depending on group size and method of transportation; they charge around S250 per person for a group of four to climb El Misti, and S365 for a three-day trek in the Cañón del Colca with private transport. They also rent all kinds of gear to independent climbers and hikers including ice axes, crampons and hiking boots.

Colca Trek TREKKING, ADVENTURE
(☑20-6217, 9-60-0170; www.colcatrek.com.pe; Jerusalén 401-B) Colca Trek is an ecoconscious adventure-tour agency and shop run by the knowledgeable, English-speaking Vlado Soto. In addition to trekking tours, it organizes mountaineering, mountain-biking and river-running trips; and it is one of the few shops selling decent topographical maps of the area. It is a venerable source of information for those hoping to explore the area on their own. Be careful of copycat travel agencies that use the Colca Trek name and/or web addresses that are similar to the agency's official site.

Naturaleza Activa TREKKING, ADVENTURE
(☑69-5793; Santa Catalina 211) A favorite of those seeking adventure tours, and offering a full range of trekking, climbing and mountain-biking options. Guides speak English, French and German.

Pablo Tour TREKKING, ADVENTURE
(☑20-3737; www.pablotour.com; Jerusalén 400 AB-1) Consistently recommended by readers, Pablo Tour's guides are experts in trekking and cultural tours in the region, and can furnish trekkers with all the necessary equipment and topographical maps.

River Running

Casa de Mauro RAFTING
(☑9-59-336-684; www.lacasademaurotoursperu.com; Ongoro Km 5) This convenient base camp for rafting the Río Majes is in the village of Ongoro, 190km by road west of Arequipa. The lodge offers one- to three-hour trips for beginner to experienced rafters (per person S60 to S240). The lodge offers camping (per person S15) or rooms with private bathrooms (per person S30). It is cheapest to take a Transportes del Carpio bus from Arequipa's *terminal terrestre* to Aplao (S10, three hours, hourly) and then a *combi* (S1.50) or a taxi (S12) to Ongoro.

Majes River Lodge RAFTING
(☑83-0297, 9-59-797-731; www.majesriver.com) Offers easy one-hour rafting trips (S70) or more challenging three-hour trips that pass

through class IV rapids (S120) on the Río Majes. Overnight accommodations in bungalows with solar hot-water showers cost S70/100 per single/double; camping, meals of fresh river shrimp and tours to the nearby Toro Muerto petroglyphs are also available. Take a taxi (S10) or a *combi* (S1.50) from Aplao to the Majes River Lodge.

Ecotours ADVENTURE TOURS
(☑20-2562; Jerusalén 409) Twenty years in the business, Arequipa-based Ecotours organizes half-day trips (US$35) on the Río Chili's II-IV-class rapids, or three-day excursions to the Cañon de Colca (US$250).

✦✦ Festivals & Events

Semana Santa RELIGIOUS
(Holy Week) *Arequipeños* claim that their Semana Santa celebrations leading up to Easter are similar to the very solemn and traditional Spanish observances from Seville. Maundy Thursday, Good Friday and Holy Saturday processions are particularly colorful and sometimes end with the burning of an effigy of Judas.

Fiesta de la Virgen de Chapi RELIGIOUS
Arequipa also fills up for this festival, celebrated on May 1 in the Yanahuara district.

August 15 CULTURAL
The founding day of the city is celebrated with parades, dancing, beauty pageants, climbing competitions on El Misti and other energetic events over the course of several days. The fireworks show in the Plaza de Armas on the evening of August 14 is definitely worth catching.

🛏 Sleeping

Central Arequipa is peppered with hotels of all shapes, sizes and prices. Due to the nature of the architecture in this Unesco World Heritage zone, many of them inhabit attractive, thick-walled *sillar* buildings. Cable TV and free wi-fi are pretty much a given in all but the bottom-rung places. Breakfast is also usually included though it is little more than bread, jam and coffee in the cheaper joints. Prices listed are for high season (June to August), but fluctuate greatly even during these months.

TOP CHOICE **Hostal Casona Solar** HOTEL $$
(☑22-8991; www.casonasolar.com; Consuelo 116; r from S104; 🛜) You can live like a colonial *caballero* (gentleman) in this 'secret garden'

of gorgeousness situated – rather incredibly given its tranquility – only three blocks from the main square. Grand 18th-century rooms are crafted from huge *sillar* stones and some come with mezzanine bedrooms. The service (same-day laundry, bus reservations, free airline check-in) is equally dazzling. Then there's the price. Best bargain in the city – maybe even Peru.

Los Tambos Hostal BOUTIQUE HOTEL $$$
(☑60-0900; www.lostambos.com.pe; Puente Bolognesi 129; d S219-289; ❄@🛜) Breaking the mold in historic Arequipa is this modern boutique hotel, a marble roll from the main square, where small but significant extras and above-and-beyond service justify every *sole* of the asking price. Luring you in are free bottles of water, chocolates on your pillow, aromatic soap selections, huge gourmet breakfasts (included in rates), and free transportation to and from the airport or bus terminal.

Casablanca Hostal HOTEL $$
(☑22-1327; www.casablancahostal.com; Puente Bolognesi 104; s/d/tr incl breakfast S80/120/160; @) The *New York Times'* 'Frugal Traveler' wasn't the only budget-seeker to marvel at what he was getting for his money in this place. Bank on prime corner-of-main-plaza location, beautiful exposed *sillar* brickwork, and rooms large enough to keep a horse (or two) in. Service is discreet and breakfast is taken in a lovely sun-filled cafe.

Libertador Ciudad Blanca LUXURY HOTEL $$$
(☑21-5110; www.libertador.com.pe; Plaza Bolívar s/n, Selva Alegre; r S400-600, ste S500-775; ❄@🛜⛱) This is the grand dame of Arequipa's hotels, situated 1km north of the center. The stylish building is perfectly set in gardens with a pool and playground. It has spacious rooms and opulent public areas, plus its spa boasts a sauna, Jacuzzi and fitness room. The sedate restaurant serves a fine Sunday brunch. Neighboring Selva Alegre park is beautiful, but don't wander too far from the crowds, and avoid it after dark.

La Hostería HOTEL $$
(☑28-9269; www.lahosteriaqp.com.pe; Bolívar 405; s/d incl breakfast S140/165; 🛜) Worth every *sole* is this picturesque colonial hotel with a flower-bedecked courtyard, light and quiet rooms (with minibar), carefully chosen antiques, a sunny terrace and a lounge. Some rooms suffer from street noise, so request one in the back. Apartment-style suites

(US$68) on the upper floors have stellar city views. Prices include airport pickup.

Casona Terrace Hotel   HOTEL $$

(☑21-2318; www.hotelcasonaterrace.com; Álvarez Thomas 211; s/d S120/170; ❋@☎) Another lovely old colonial home reopened as a hotel in 2012 with rooms that have opted for modern simplicity over old-world splendor. The secure facility is one block from the main square and has a roof terrace and buffet breakfast included.

Casa Arequipa   BOUTIQUE HOTEL $$

(☑28-4219; www.arequipacasa.com; Av Lima 409, Vallecito; s/d S150/235; ☎) Inside a cotton-candy pink colonial mansion in the gardens of suburban Vallecito, this gay-friendly B&B offers more than half a dozen guest rooms with fine design touches such as richly painted walls, pedestal sinks, antique handmade furnishings and alpaca wool blankets. A sociable cocktail bar is in the lobby.

La Casa de Melgar   HOTEL $$

(☑22-2459; www.lacasademelgar.com; Melgar 108; s/d incl buffet breakfast US$120/150; ☎) Housed in an 18th-century building, this hotel is nonetheless fitted with all the expected modern comforts. High-domed ceilings and unique decor lend the entire place an old-world feel. Comfy beds and tucked-away inner patios help make this a romantic hideaway within the city limits.

La Posada del Puente   HOTEL $$$

(☑25-3132; www.posadadelpuente.com; Bolognesi 101; s/d S437/492; @☎) Dipping down to the river, the extensive gardens of this high-end hotel make for a tranquil setting that's surprisingly removed from the bustling traffic above. Staying here gives you free access to the sports facilities and swimming pool at the nearby Club Internacional sports complex.

Sonesta Posada del Inca   HOTEL $$$

(☑21-5530; www.sonesta.com; Portal de Flores 116; s/d/ste incl breakfast S695/730/925; ❋@☎) OK, but ridiculously overpriced, Plaza de Armas' Sonestra has a lovely terrace with fabulous El Misti views, but some less beguiling interior hiccups: eg rough, industrial carpets and dodgy brown leather sofas in its communal areas. It's time to join the 2010s or knock the price down.

La Casa Blanca   HOTEL $

(☑28-2218; Jerusalén 412; r without/with bathroom S35/70; @☎) The second Casa Blanca in Arequipa (note: two words as opposed to one), this one is another reasonably priced 'find' with a fantastic coffee bar in the courtyard out front. Rooms are quite basic, but the staff is friendly and eager to please.

La Casa de Sillar   HOTEL $

(☑28-4249; www.thecasadesillar.com; Rivero 504; s without/with bathroom S35/45, d S60/70; @☎) Another of those thick-walled colonial mansions made – as the name implies – out of *sillar* rock hewn from El Misti, this one doesn't pretend to be boutique, but it does offer a fine bargain, especially if you're prepared to share a bathroom. Huge maps and an equally huge TV adorn a communal lounge.

Wild Rover Hostel   HOSTEL $

(☑21-2830; www.wildroverhostels.com; Calle Ugarte 111; dm from S25; @☎❋) If halfway through your Peruvian sojourn you get a sudden compulsion to consume bangers and mash with Swedish backpackers in the familiar confines of an Irish pub, then the Wild Rover awaits you with open arms.

Le Foyer   HOTEL, HOSTEL $

(☑28-6473; www.hlefoyer.com; Ugarte 114; dm/s/d without bathroom S25/35/55, s/d/tr with bathroom S50/65/90; @☎) There's a distinct New Orleans look to this cheap hostel-y hotel where its wrap-around upstairs verandah where you can enjoy a standard bread and jam breakfast overlooking busy Calle Jerusalén. Rooms are nothing to brag about but the proximity to plenty of restaurants and nightlife (there's an alluring Mexican place downstairs) means you don't need a GPS-phone app to work out what's where.

Los Andes Bed & Breakfast   HOTEL, B&B $

(☑33-0015; www.losandesarequipa.com; La Merced 123; s/d without bathroom S31/50, with bathroom S48/72; @☎) There's a bit of a hospital feel to this hotel's giant rooms and ample communal kitchen which are popular with climbing groups and long-term stays. But the pricing's good and it's a font of information for the surrounding 'outdoors.'

Casa Andina   BOUTIQUE HOTEL $$$

(☑213-9739; www.casa-andina.com; Jerusalén 603; s/d/ste S270/365/426; ❋@☎) Like most of the Casa Andina chain, this place flirts with boutique decor, but feels a tad overpriced when you factor in the rather dark restaurant, officious service and rooms that are basically just motel rooms with some deft color accents. The onsite spa claws back a little credibility with massages offered for S90 (one hour).

La Posada del Parque
HOTEL, B&B $

(☎21-2275; www.parkhostel.net; Deán Valdivia 238A; dm/s/d S25/50/70; @🖥🛜) The slightly frosty welcome quickly melts away at this B&B bargain near the market whose high-ceilinged rooms sit beneath a wonderfully weathered terrace where El Misti appears so close you could almost hug it. There's a kitchen available and the owners can organize onsite Spanish lessons for S6 per hour.

Point Hostel
HOSTEL $

(☎28-6920; www.thepointhostels.com; Palacio Viejo 325; dm S19-24; @🛜) One of five Point backpackers hostels in Peru, this one has recently moved into the city center (two blocks from the main square) from the suburb of Vallecito. It still has its popular billiards/pool tables and bar; but beware, this is a place for people who like to socialize and don't necessarily need to be tucked up in bed quietly by 10pm. Breakfast is included.

Hostal Núñez
HOSTEL $

(☎21-8648; www.hotel_nunez.de; Jerusalén 528; s/d without bathroom S30/45, s/d/tr S45/80/90, all incl breakfast; @) On a street full of not-so-great guesthouses, this secure, friendly hostel is always stuffed with gringos. The colorful rooms sport frilly decor and cable TV, though the singles are a bit of a squeeze.

La Posada del Cacique
HOTEL $

(☎20-2170; Jerusalén 404; s/d/tr S30/50/60; @🛜) This 2nd-floor hostel has spacious, sunny rooms, a well-equipped shared kitchen, reliable hot water, and a tranquil rooftop sitting area. The father-son owners are great resources for local info and make guests feel right at home.

Casa de Avila
HOTEL $$

(☎21-3177; www.casadeavila.com; San Martín 116, Vallecito; s/d/tr/q S70/90/120/150; @🛜) If the spacious courtyard garden doesn't swing it for you, the congenial personalized service ought to – this is no 'yes sir, no sir' chain hotel. The place also hosts Spanish language courses and a more unique cooking course (see boxed text, p146) in the sunny garden three times a week.

Colonial House Inn
GUESTHOUSE $

(☎22-3533; colonialhouseinn@hotmail.com; Av Puente Grau 114; s/d incl breakfast S48/72; @) Peaceful, if slightly run-down, colonial house with friendly staff. Rooftop terrace with a garden and striking views of El Misti on clear days.

Hostal Solar
HOTEL $$

(☎24-1793; www.hostalsolar.com; Ayacucho 108; s/d incl breakfast S90/150; 🛜) This snazzy pick is clean and airy, with contemporary decor. Prices include touches like airport pickup and a buffet breakfast served on the rooftop terrace.

Hostal las Torres de Ugarte
HOTEL $$

(☎28-3532; www.hotelista.com; Ugarte 401A; s/d/tr incl breakfast S96/128/144; @🛜) This is a friendly hostel in a quiet location behind the Monasterio de Santa Catalina. It has immaculate rooms with TVs and colorful wooly bedspreads. You'll just have to ignore the cacophonous echoing hallways. Rates drop considerably in the low season.

Hotel La Posada del Monasterio
HOTEL $$

(☎40-5728; www.posadadelmonasterio.com.pe; Santa Catalina 300; s/d/tr incl buffet breakfast from S160/205/260; @🛜🖥) On a prime pedestrian corner, this hotel gracefully inhabits an architecturally mix-and-match building combining the best of the Old and New Worlds, especially popular with European tour groups. The comfortable modern rooms here have all the expected facilities. From the rooftop terrace you can peer into the Santa Catalina convent across the street.

Posada Nueva España
HOTEL $$

(☎25-2941; www.nuespana.com; Antiquilla 106, Yanahuara; s/d/tr incl breakfast S75/100/125; @) This distinguished 19th-century colonial house has just more than a dozen rooms with solar hot showers. It's in the quaint suburb of Yanahuara; call for free pickups. Spanish, French, German and English are spoken.

Hostal El Descanso del Fundador
HOTEL $

(☎20 2341; www.eldescansodelfundador.com; Jerusalén 605; s/d S70/80; 🛜) In a charming, pale-blue house on the cusp of the colonial core, this old mansion has a more classical feel than the heavier baroque abodes further south. Rooms are a little past their refurb date, but service is cute and helpful.

🍴 Eating

Hunker down. If you want to truly 'get' Arequipa, you've got some serious food sampling to enjoy. Start with the basics: *rocoto relleno* (stuffed spicy red peppers) and *chupe de* camarones (prawn chowder) and work up to the stuff you'll never find east of the Amazon (at least on a dinner plate) – guinea pig, anyone? Trendy upscale restaurants line Calle San Francisco north of the Plaza de Armas, while touristy outdoor cafes huddle together on Pasaje Catedral behind the cathedral.

TOP CHOICE Zingaro
PERUVIAN, PARRILLA $$
(www.zingaro-restaurante.com; San Francisco 309; mains S25-45; ⊘noon-11pm Mon-Sat) In an old *sillar* building with wooden balconies, stained glass and a resident pianist, culinary legends are made. Zingaro has taken on Zig Zag and Chicha as a font of gastronomic innovation, meaning it's an ideal place to try out *nouveau* renditions of Peruvian standards including alpaca ribs, ceviche, or perhaps your first *cuy* (guinea pig). Two doors down, a new venture under the same ownership (Lazos – Parrilla de Zingaro) specializes in Argentinian-style meats with equally splendid results.

Zig Zag
PERUVIAN, EUROPEAN $$
(☏20-6020; www.zigzagrestaurant.com; Zela 210; mains S33-40; ⊘6pm-midnight) Upscale but not ridiculously pricey, Zig Zag is a Peruvian restaurant with European inflections that inhabits a two-story colonial house with an iron stairway designed by Gustave Eiffel (blimey, that bloke must have been busy). The menu classic is a meat selection served on a unique volcano-stone grill with various sauces. The fondues are also good. Some heretics claim it's even better than Gastón Acurio's Chicha.

Tradición Arequipeña
PERUVIAN $
(☏42-6467; www.tradicionarequipena.com; Av Dolores 111; meals S18-40; ⊘11:30am-6pm Mon-Fri, 11:30am-1am Sat, 8:30am-6pm Sun) This locally famous restaurant has mazelike gardens, live *folklórica* and *criollo* music (upbeat coastal music), and offers a Sunday morning breakfast of *adobo de cerdo*, a traditional slow-cooked pork dish. It's 2km southeast of the center; a taxi ride here should cost S4.

Chicha
PERUVIAN, FUSION $$$
(☏28-7360; www.chicha.com.pe; Santa Catalina 210; mains S26-58; ⊘noon-midnight Mon-Sat, to 9pm Sun) Peru's most famous chef, Gastón Acurio owns this wildly experimental place whose menu never veers too far from Peru's Inca-Spanish roots. River prawns are a highlight in season (April to December), but

Acurio prepares the Peruvian staples – *tacu tacu, lomo saltado*, ceviche – with equal panache, along with tender alpaca burgers and pastas earthy enough to placate even the most fastidious Italian. Like many 'celeb' places, Chicha divides opinion between food snobs and purists. Step inside its fine colonial interior and join the debate.

Crepisimo
CREPERIE $
(www.crepisimo.com; Alianza Francesa, Santa Catalina 208; mains S6-16; ⊘8am-11pm Mon-Sat, noon-11pm Sun; 🞲) For a truly great cafe you need all the essential components – food, setting, service, ambience et al – to come together in a blockbusting whole. Crepisimo succeeds by taking the simple crepe and offering it with 100 different types of filling, from Chilean smoked trout to exotic South American fruits. Furthermore, it wraps them up in a chic colonial setting in the local French cultural center where casual wait staff serve you coffee as good as in Paris.

Cafe Fez-Istanbul
MIDDLE EASTERN $
(San Francisco 229; mains S6-11; ⊘7:30am-11pm) The name suggests two cities, but the food is distinctly Middle Eastern rather than Moroccan. Falafels are the main draw – in a crepe or in a sandwich – served in a rather trendy resto-bar with a people-watching mezzanine floor. Other favorites include hummus, fresh cut fries and various sandwiches. Portions are snack fodder mainly, but in a cool environment.

Nina-Yaku
PERUVIAN, FUSION $$
(San Francisco 211; menús S35, mains S25-36; ⊘3-11pm) Escaping the tumult of 'happening' Calle San Francisco, Nina Yaku offers an atmosphere of whispered refinement along with affordable Arequipan specialties such as broccoli soufflé, potatoes in Huatacay sauce, and fettuccine pesto with alpaca.

Ras El Hanout
MOROCCAN $$
(www.raselhanout40.com; Santa Catalina 300B; mains S28-40) Alright, you probably didn't come to Peru to feast on classic Moroccan food, but, just in case the notion of guinea pig and raw fish was too out-of-the-box, you can fall back on more comforting exoticisms in this cool North African resto-lounge whose name means 'blend of spices.' Leading lights include lamb tagine, kefta and an energy restoring 4pm to 6:30pm Moroccan 'tea time.'

La Trattoria del Monasterio
ITALIAN, FUSION $$

(☎20-4062; www.latrattoriadelmonasterio.com; Santa Catalina 309; mains S18-33; ⊘lunch from noon daily, dinner from 7pm Mon-Sat) A helping of epicurean delight has descended upon the Monasterio de Santa Catalina. The menu of Italian specialties was created with the help of superstar Peruvian chef Gastón Acurio, and is infused with the flavors of Arequipa. Reservations are essential.

La Nueva Palomino
PERUVIAN $$

(Leoncio Prado 122; mains S14-29; ⊘lunch) Definitely the local favorite, the atmosphere at this *picantería* is informal and can turn boisterous even during the week when groups of families and friends file in to eat local specialties and drink copious amounts of *chicha de jora*. The restaurant is in the Yanahuara district 2km northwest of the city center.

Café y Más
DESSERTS $

(Portal de Flores 122; cakes S7-9) Five tiny tables but a choice of twice as many giant cakes teases you into this diminutive cafe on the Plaza de Armas for a post-dinner sweetener under the colonial arches.

El Charrua
ARGENTINE $$

(☎34-6688; www.elcharrua.com; Cuesta del Olivo 318; mains S30-50) This new Argentine-Uruguayan grill with its dark wood, gentlemen's club-style cocktail bar is bivouacked in the Yanahuara quarter just off leafy Plaza Yanahuara. Its terrace enjoys one of the best views in the city with the symmetrical hump of El Misti, looking like an upturned Christmas pudding, seemingly close enough to touch. The heavily meat-biased menu is well complemented by some robust malbec reds. Not surprisingly, it ain't cheap.

El Tio Dario
SEAFOOD $$

(☎27-0473; Callejon de Cabildo 100; mains S22-50) Like fish? Like intimate secret garden settings? Then, hook up with a taxi (or walk) out to the pleasant Yanahuara district for the ultimate in ceviches or grilled fish dishes served in a flower-rich garden that frames superb volcano views. It's a two-minute walk from the Yanahuara mirador.

Hatunpa
PERUVIAN $

(Ugarte 208; dishes S7-12; ⊘11am-10pm Mon-Fri, 5-11pm Sat) With just four tables and the common garden spud as its star ingredient, Hatunpa probably doesn't sound promising, but it has a fervent and fast-growing following. The trick? Potatoes originate in Peru and the *arequipeños* know how to embellish them with imaginative sauces and toppings. Even better, they're cheap (and filling) too.

Sol de Mayo
PERUVIAN $$

(www.restaurantsoldemayo.com; Jerusalén 207, Yanahuara; menú S14, mains S18-47; ⊘11:30am-6pm) Serving good Peruvian food in the Yanahuara district, this *picantería* has live *música folklórica* every afternoon from 1pm to 4pm. Book a table in advance. You can combine a visit here with a stopoff at the *mirador* in Yanahuara (see boxed text, p145).

Café Casa Verde
CAFE $

(Jerusalén 406; snacks S2-6; ⊘8am-6pm) This nonprofit courtyard cafe staffed by underprivileged kids is the perfect spot for a morning or afternoon break. It dishes up yummy German-style pastries and sandwiches, though service can be slow. Attached to the cafe is a local handicraft store where proceeds also go to helping kids in need.

Lakshmivan
ASIAN

(Jerusalén 400; menús S4-6; ⊘9am-9pm) Set in a colorful old building with a tiny outdoor courtyard, this place has various *menús* (set meals) and an extensive à la carte selection, all with a South Asian flair.

Restaurante Gopal
PERUVIAN, VEGETARIAN $

(Melgar 101B; menús S5, mains S4-11; ⊘8am-9pm; ⊘) This basic, health-conscious vegetarian cafe specializes in traditional Peruvian dishes made with imitation meats, so you can enjoy *lomo saltado* meat-free.

Ribs Café
BARBECUE, BREAKFAST $

(Álvarez Thomas 107; ribs & empanadas S5-18; ⊘8am-6pm) This surprising storefront cooks up barbecue ribs in a rainbow variety of sauces, ranging from chocolate to honey-mustard to red wine, as well as empanadas (meat or cheese turnovers) and solid American breakfasts.

El Turko
TURKISH $

(www.elturko.com.pe; San Francisco 225; mains S6-14; ⊘7am-midnight Sun-Wed, 24hr Thu-Sat) Part of an ever-expanding Ottoman empire, this funky little joint serves a hungry crowd late-night kebabs and vegetarian Middle Eastern salads, with excellent coffee and sweet pastries during the day.

Inkari Pub Pizzeria
PIZZERIA $

(Pasaje Catedral; pizzas from S14; ☺8am-midnight) You're pretty much guaranteed to meet a gringo at this predictably popular place behind the cathedral which pampers to Western palates with a happy-hour special of a personal pizza and a *copa de vino* (glass of wine) for S14.

Manolo's
PERUVIAN $

(Mercaderes 107 & 113; mains S10-30; ☺7:30am-midnight) Seeing double? Well, yes, actually. There are two Manolo's 20m apart in Arequipa's pedestrianized shopping thoroughfare, Calle Mercaderes. Shagged-out shoppers find it hard to resist the hiss of the coffee machine and the glint of the glass display case stuffed with thickly sliced cakes.

Café Restaurant Antojitos de Arequipa
CAFE $

(Moran Cuadra 1; mains S14-32; ☺24hr) Unadulterated, unrefined Arequipan favorites served on the corner of the main square with zero pampering to tourist palates. Home in on the *rocoto relleno* and anything else with potatoes in it. The same menu is served at Restaurant at the Top around the corner for slightly inflated prices (due to the view).

Mixtos
ITALIAN, SEAFOOD $

(Pasaje Catedral 115; mains S15-36; ☺11:30am-9:30pm) Tucked away in the alley behind the cathedral on the Plaza de Armas is this popular and quaint restaurant that serves mainly Italian and *criollo* (spicy Peruvian fare with Spanish and indigenous influences) seafood dishes. Try the enormous and flavorful *sudado de pescado* (fish stew) while enjoying the view from the outdoor balcony.

Cevichería Fory Fay
CEVICHE $$

(Álvarez Thomas 221; mains S20-25; ☺lunch) Small and to-the-point, it serves only the best ceviche (raw seafood marinated in lime juice) and nothing else. Pull up a chair at a rickety table and crack open a beer – limit one per person, though! By the way, the name is a phonetic spelling of how Peruvians say '45' in English.

El Viñedo
PERUVIAN $$

(www.vinedogrill.com; San Francisco 319; mains S20-50; ☺noon-midnight) A Calle San Francisco stalwart that looks more formal than it actually is, this place does Arequipa specialties with varying degrees of success. For a taste overview, go for the *Americano* platter which offers a medley of five potato-heavy samples including *ocupa* (potatoes in spicy sauce) and *pastel de papas* (potato cake). The wine list features South American varietals.

El Carpriccio
CAFE $

(Santa Catalina 120; snacks from S10; ☺9am-midnight; ☎) Coffee, carrot cake and wi-fi; this is where you come to write up your holiday blog.

El Super
SELF-CATERING $

(☺9am-2pm & 4-9pm Mon-Fri, 9am-9pm Sat, 9:30am-1:30pm Sun); Plaza de Armas (Portal de la Municipalidad 130); Piérola (N de Piérola, cuadra 1) Pick up groceries at El Super.

🍷 Drinking

The nocturnal scene in Arequipa is pretty slow midweek but takes off on weekends. Many of the bars along Calle San Francisco offer happy-hour specials worth taking advantage of.

Cusco Coffee Company
CAFE

(La Merced 135; drinks S5-11; ☺8am-10pm Mon-Sat, noon-7pm Sun; ☎) If you're missing chocolate chip muffins, bucket-sized lattes and sofas full of noncommunicative wi-fi nerds, this Starbucks-wannabe is undoubtedly your bag.

Déjà Vu
BAR

(San Francisco 319B; ☺9am-late) With a rooftop terrace overlooking the church of San Francisco, this eternally popular haunt has a long list of crazy cocktails and a lethal happy hour every evening. After dark, decent DJs keep the scene alive on weekdays and weekends alike.

Farren's Irish Pub
PUB

(Pasaje Catedral; ☺noon-11pm) Where would any city be without its themed Irish pub? Tucked behind the cathedral, this gringo haven has – guess what? – Guinness, pub grub and soccer on satellite TV.

Brujas Bar
BAR

(San Francisco 300; ☺5pm-late) Nordic-style pub with Union Jack flags, happy hour cocktails and plenty of local and expat chinwaggers.

☆ Entertainment

Arequipa's nightlife is as vital as Lima's, but confined to a smaller downtown area. Anyone who's anyone can be seen strolling Calle San Francisco sometime after 9pm on a

Friday or Saturday. The 300 block (between Ugarte and Zela) has the highest concentration of places to compare fashion notes. Another hotspot is Av Dolores, 2km southeast of the center (a taxi costs around S3 one way) where salsa and *cumbia* (Colombian salsa-like dance and musical style) music and dancing predominate.

Café Art Montréal
LIVE MUSIC

(Ugarte 210; ⊙5pm-1am) This smoky, intimate little bar with live bands playing on a stage at the back would be equally at home as a bohemian student hangout on Paris' Left Bank.

Las Quenas
LIVE MUSIC

(Santa Catalina 302; ⊙Mon-Sat) An exception to the rule, this traditional *peña* features performances almost nightly starting around 9pm. The music varies, although *música folklórica* predominates. It also serves decent *arequipeño* food starting at 8pm.

La Quinta
LIVE MUSIC

(Jerusalén 522; ⊙10am-10pm) Another good spot for local food and melodic *folklórica* music. Live bands are featured daily during the high season (June to August) when the place fills up for lunch, but it's potluck as to whether you get live music on other days.

Casona Forum
CLUB

(www.casonaforum.com; San Francisco 317) A five-in-one excuse for a good night out in a *sillar* building incorporating a pub (Retro), pool club (Zero), sofa bar (Chill Out), nightclub (Forum) and restaurant (Terrasse).

Zoom
CLUB

(Santa Catalina 111) They're dancing by 8pm on a Saturday night in this youthful upstairs pub/club a block from the main square with enough sectioned-off parts to find your own favored nook. Beware of the tuneless karaoke.

Sports
Conducted *arequipeño* style, *peleas de toros* (bullfights) here are less bloodthirsty than most. They involve pitting two bulls against each other for the favors of a fertile female until one realizes he's beaten. The fights take place on Sundays between April and December. Ask at your hostel for the location of fights – they usually take place at stadiums on the outskirts of town. The three most important fights are in April, mid-August and early December (admission S15).

Shopping
Arequipa overflows with antique and artisan shops, especially on the streets around Monasterio de Santa Catalina. High-quality alpaca, vicuña (threatened wild relative of alpacas) and leather goods, and other handmade items, are what you'll see being sold most often.

Casona Santa Catalina
CLOTHING, SOUVENIRS

(www.santacatalina-sa.com.pe; Santa Catalina 210; ⊙most shops 10am-6pm) Inside this polished tourist complex, you'll find a few shops of major export brands, such as Sol Alpaca and Biondi Piscos.

Patio del Ekeko
CLOTHING, SOUVENIRS

(⌨21-5861; www.patiodelekeko.com; Mercaderes 141; ⊙10am-9pm Mon-Sat, 11am-8pm Sun) This high-end tourist mall has plenty of expensive but good alpaca- and vicuña-wool items, jewelry, ceramics and other arty souvenirs.

Galería de Artesanías 'El Tumi de Oro'
CRAFT MARKET

(126 Portal de Flores; ⊙10am-6pm) A small artisan market under the *portales* on Plaza de Armas.

Fundo El Fierro
CRAFT MARKET

The city's primary craft market occupies a beautiful colonial *sillar* courtyard next to the San Francisco church. Garments, paintings, handmade crafts and jewelry predominate, but you can also procure rare alpaca carpets from Cotahuasi. There's an artisanal fair with special stalls held here over the month of August.

Librería el Lector
BOOK

(San Francisco 221; ⊙9am-noon Mon-Sat) Two-for-one English book exchange and an excellent selection of new local-interest titles, guidebooks and music CDs.

ℹ Information
Dangers & Annoyances
Petty theft is often reported in Arequipa, so travelers are urged to hide their valuables. Most crime is opportunistic, so keep your stuff in sight while in restaurants and internet cafes. While the area south of the Plaza de Armas is reportedly safe after dark, be wary of wandering outside of touristy zones at night. Take great care in Parque Selva Alegre, north of the city center, as muggings have been reported there. Instead of hailing a cab on the street, ask your hostel or tour operator to call you an official one; the extra time and money are worth the added safety. Only pay for tours in a recognized agency

and never trust touts in the street – they bamboozle cash out of a surprisingly high number of travelers.

Emergency

Policía de Turismo (Tourist Police; ☎20-1258; Jerusalén 315-317; ☺24hr) May be helpful if you need an official theft report for insurance claims.

Immigration

Oficina de migraciónes (immigration office; ☎42-1759; Parque 2, cnr Bustamente & Rivero, Urb Quinta Tristán; ☺8am-3:30pm Mon-Fri) Come here for a visa extension.

Internet Access

Most internet cafes charge about S1.50 per hour. Many also offer cheap local and international phone calls. All but the cheapest hotels offer free wi-fi as do many cafes.

Medical Services

Clínica Arequipa (☎25-3424, 25-3416; Bolognesi at Puente Grau; ☺8am-8pm Mon-Fri, 8am-12:30pm Sat) Arequipa's best and most expensive clinic.

Hospital Regional Honorio Delgado Espinoza (☎21-9702, 23-3812; Av Daniel Alcides Carrión s/n; ☺24hr) Emergency 24-hour services.

InkaFarma (☎20-1565; Santo Domingo 113; ☺24hr) One of Peru's biggest pharmacy chains; it's well stocked.

Paz Holandesa Policlinic (☎43-2281; www.pazholandesa.com; Av Jorge Chávez 527; ☺8am-8pm Mon-Sat) This appointment-only travel clinic provides vaccinations as well. Doctors here speak English and Dutch. Profits go toward providing free medical services for underprivileged Peruvian children.

Money

There are moneychangers and ATMs on streets east of the Plaza de Armas. Global ATMs are easy to find in most areas frequented by travelers, including inside the Casona Santa Catalina complex, the bus terminal and the airport.

Both banks listed exchange US traveler's checks.

BCP (San Juan de Dios 125) Has a Visa ATM and changes American dollars.

Interbank (Mercaderes 217) Has a global ATM.

Post

DHL (☎22-5332; Santa Catalina 115; ☺8:30am-7pm Mon-Fri, 9am-1pm Sat)

Main post office (Moral 118; ☺8am-8pm Mon-Sat, 9am-1pm Sun)

Tourist Information

Indecopi (☎21-2054; Hipólito Unanue 100A, Urb Victoria; ☺8:30am-4pm Mon-Fri) This is the national tourist-protection agency that deals with complaints against local firms, including tour operators and travel agencies.

iPerú airport (☎44-4564; 1st fl, Main Hall, Aeropuerto Rodríguez Ballón; ☺10am-7:30pm); Plaza de Armas (☎22-3265; iperuarequipa@ promperu.gob.pe; Portal de la Municipalidad 110; ☺8:30am-7:30pm) Government-supported source for objective information on local and regional attractions.

 Getting There & Away

Air

Arequipa's **Rodríguez Ballón International Airport** (code AQP; ☎44-3458) is about 8km northwest of the city center.

LAN (☎20-1224; www.lan.com; Santa Catalina 118C) has daily flights to Lima and Cuzco. **Sky Airline** (☎28-2899; www.skyairline.cl; La Merced 121) also offers flights to Arica and Santiago de Chile.

Bus

Night buses provide a convenient means to reach many far-off destinations in a city where options for air travel are limited, although some routes do have histories of accidents, hijackings and robberies. Paying a bit extra for luxury bus services is often worth the added comfort and security. Exercise extreme care with your belongings on cheaper buses and refrain from keeping baggage in overhead luggage racks. It is also recommended to carry extra food with you on long bus rides in case of a breakdown or road strike.

International

From the Terrapuerto bus terminal, **Ormeño** (☎42-7788) has two buses a week to Santiago, Chile (US$130, 2½ days), and three a week to Buenos Aires, Argentina (US$190, three days).

Long-distance

Most bus companies have departures from the *terminal terrestre* or the smaller Terrapuerto bus terminal, both of which are together on Av Andrés Avelino Cáceres, less than 3km south of the city center (take a taxi for S5). Check in advance which terminal your bus leaves from and keep a close watch on your belongings while you're waiting there. There's an S1 departure tax from either terminal. Both terminals have shops, restaurants and left-luggage facilities. The more chaotic *terminal terrestre* also has a global ATM and a tourist information office.

Dozens of bus companies have desks in the terminal so shop around. Prices quoted in the boxed text show a range between super-luxury **Cruz del Sur** (☎42-7375) and **Ormeño** (☎42-3855) with 180-degree reclining 'bed' seats, and no-thrills **Flores** (☎42-9905, 43-2228) which travels to a greater variety of destinations including Mollendo, Moquegua and Ilo.

AREQUIPA BUSES

DESTINATION	COST (S)	DURATION (HR)
Cabanaconde	17	6
Camaná	45	7
Chivay	15	3
Cotahuasi	30	12
Cuzco	25-126	9-11
Ica	40-114	13-15
Juliaca	15-72	6
Lima	50-144	14-16
Mollendo	15	2
Moquegua	18	4
Nazca	40-144	10-12
Pisco	40-144	15
Puno	15-72	6
Tacna	20-57	6

Regional Services

Many buses useful for sightseeing in the canyon country also leave from the *terminal terrestre* and Terrapuerto. Travel times and costs can vary depending on road conditions. During the wet season (between December and April), expect significant delays.

The best companies serving the Cañón del Colca (Cabanaconde and Chivay) are **Andalucía** (☑44-5089) and **Reyna** (☑43-0612). Try to catch the earliest daylight departure, usually around 5am, and reserve tickets in advance if possible.

For buses to Corire (S10, three hours) to visit the Toro Muerto petroglyphs, both Transportes del Carpio and Eros Tour run hourly daytime services, from where you can continue on to Aplao in the Valle de Majes (S10, three hours) for river running. **Transportes Trebol** (☑42-5936) usually has a service departing around 4pm that continues on to Andagua (S25, 10 to 12 hours) to visit El Valle de los Volcanes. The bus leaves Andagua for the return trip to Arequipa at around 5:30pm.

For the Cañón del Cotahuasi (S30, 12 hours), Reyna has a 4pm departure and **Transportes Alex** (☑42-4605) has a 4:30pm departure.

ℹ Getting Around

To/From the Airport

There are no airport buses. An official taxi from downtown Arequipa to the airport costs around S15. It is possible to take a *combi* marked 'Río Seco' or 'Zamacola' from Av Puente Grau and Ejército that will let you off in a sketchy neighborhood about 700m from the airport entrance.

Leaving the airport, *colectivo* (shared) taxis charge around S6 per person to drop you off at your hotel.

Bus

Combis and minibuses go south along Bolívar to the *terminal terrestre* (S2, 20 minutes), next door to the Terrapuerto bus terminal, but it's a slow trip via the market area.

Taxi

You can often hire a taxi with a driver for less than renting a car from a travel agency. Local taxi companies include **Tourismo Arequipa** (☑45-8888) and **Taxitel** (☑45-2020). A short ride around town costs around S3, while a trip from the Plaza de Armas out to the bus terminals costs about S4. Whenever possible, try to call a recommended company to ask for a pickup as there have been numerous reports of travelers being scammed or assaulted by taxi drivers. If you must hail a taxi off the street, pick a regular size saloon (sedan) or estate (station wagon) over a compact yellow cab.

CANYON COUNTRY

Going to Arequipa and missing out on the Colca Canyon is like going to Cuzco and neglecting to visit Machu Picchu. For those with more time there's a whole load of other excursions that merit attention, including climbing the city's guardian volcano El Misti, rafting in the Majes canyon and visiting the petroglyphs at Toro Muerto, exploring

El Valle de los Volcanes, and trekking down into the world's deepest canyon at Cotahuasi. Most of these places can be visited by a combination of public bus and hiking. Alternatively, friends can split the cost of hiring a taxi or 4WD vehicle and driver; a two-day trip will set you back more than US$150.

Reserva Nacional Salinas y Aguada Blanca

The trouble with all those organized Colca Canyon tours is that they rush through one of southern Peru's finest protected reserves (☏054-25-7461; admission free; ⊘24hr), a vast Andean expanse of dozing volcanoes and brawny wildlife forging out an existence against the odds several kilometers above sea level. Drives here take you up to an oxygen-deprived 4910m where, in between light-headed gasps for air, you can ponder weird wind-eroded rock formations, trek on old Inca trails and watch fleet-footed vicuñas run across the desolate pampa at speeds of up to 85kmh. As a national reserve, Salinas y Aguada Blanca enjoys better protection than the Colca Canyon, primarily because no one lives here bar the odd isolated llama-herder. Its job is to protect a rich raft of high-altitude species such as the vicuñas, tarucas envinados (Andean deer), guanacos and various birds, most notably flamingos. Both El Misti and Chachani volcanoes are included in the reserve.

AREQUIPA TO CHIVAY

Patahuasi   LANDMARK
The only civilization between Arequipa and Chivay, save for a few scattered farmsteads, is this fork in the road that acts as a kind of truck/bus stop and fill-up point (buses head southeast for Puno every hour). A few snack shacks pepper the scruffy byway while a kilometer or so beyond the Puno turning you'll run into El Chinito (snacks from S5), the favored breakfast stop for early morning tour buses. Next door to the restaurant sit various handicraft stores. Close by and accessible via a short off-piste drive is the Bosque de Piedras, a surreal collection of mushroomlike stones eroded by the wind that stand sentinel over the Río Sumbay.

Pampa de Toccra   LOOKOUT
The high plains (pampa) that lie between El Misti/Chachani and the Colca Canyon have an average height of around 4300m and support plentiful bird and animal life. All four members of the South American camelid family thrive here: the domesticated llama and alpaca, and the wild vicuña and guanaco. You're almost certain to see vicuñas roadside in the 'Zona de Vicuñas' on the approach to Patahuasi; guanacos are more timid and rare. Later on, at a boggy and sometimes icy lake on the Pampa de Toccra, waterfowl and flamingos reside in season. A bird-watching *mirador* is being constructed nearby. You'll also find the Centro de Interpretación de la Reserva Nacional Salinas (admission free; ⊘9am-5pm) here with more detailed notes in English and Spanish about the area's geology and fauna.

Paso de Patopampa   VIEWPOINT
The highest point on the road between Arequipa and Chivay is this almost lifeless pass which, at 4910m, is significantly higher than Europe's Mt Blanc and anywhere in North America's Rocky Mountains. If your red blood cells are up to it, you can disembark into the rarefied air at the Mirador de los Volcanes to view a muscular consortium of eight snow-capped volcanoes: Ubinas 5675m, Misti 5822m, Chachani 6075m, Ampato 6310m, Sabancaya 5976m, Huaca Huaca 6025m, Mismi 5597m and Chucura 5360m. Less spectacular but no less amazing is the scrubby Yareta, one of the few plants that can survive in this harsh landscape. Yaretas can live for several millennia and their annual growth rate is measured in millimeters rather than centimeters. Hardy ladies in traditional dress discreetly ply their wares at the *mirador* during the day – the world's highest shopping center?

EL MISTI
Looming 5822m above Arequipa, the city's guardian volcano El Misti is the most popular climb in the area. It is technically one of the easiest ascents of any mountain of this size in the world, but it's hard work nonetheless and you normally need an ice axe and, sometimes, crampons. Hiring a guide is highly recommended. A two-day trip will usually cost between US$50 to US$70 per person. The mountain is best climbed from July to November, with the later months being the least cold. Below the summit is a sulfurous yellow crater with volcanic fumaroles hissing gas, and there are spectacular views down to the Laguna de Salinas and back to the city.

WORTH A TRIP

LAGUNA DE SALINAS

This lake (4300m above sea level), east of Arequipa below Pichu Pichu and El Misti, is a salt lake that becomes a white salt flat during the dry months of May to December. Its size and the amount of water in it vary from year to year depending on the weather. During the rainy season it is a good place to see all three flamingo species, as well as myriad other Andean water birds.

Buses to Ubinas (S12, 3½ hours) pass by the lake and can be caught on Av Sepulveda. A small ticket booth on Sepulveda sells tickets, and schedules vary so it is a good idea to inquire a day before you wish to go. You can hike around the lake, which can take about two days, then return on the packed daily afternoon bus at around 3pm (expect to stand) or try to catch a lift with workers from the nearby mine. One-day minibus tours from Arequipa cost about S150 per person; mountain-biking tours are also available.

The ascent can be approached by many routes, some more worn-in than others, most of which can be done in two days. The Apurímac route is notorious for robberies. One popular route starts from Chiguata, and begins with a hard eight-hour slog uphill to reach base camp (4500m); from there to the summit and back takes eight hours, while the sliding return from base camp to Chiguata takes three hours or less. The Aguada Blanca route is restricted to a handful of official tour operators and allows climbers to arrive at 4100m before beginning to climb.

Determined climbers can reach the Chiguata route via public transportation. Buses going to Chiguata leave from Av Sepulveda in Arequipa (S7 one way, one hour) hourly beginning at 5:30am and will drop you off at an unmarked trailhead, from where you can begin the long trek to base camp. On the return trip, you should be able to flag down the same bus heading the opposite way. The more common method to reach the mountain is hiring a 4WD vehicle for around S200 that will take you up to 3300m and pick you up on the return.

CHACHANI

One of the easiest 6000m peaks in the world is Chachani (6075m), which is as close to Arequipa as El Misti. You will need crampons, an ice ax and good equipment. There are various routes up the mountain, one of which involves going by 4WD to Campamento de Azufrera at 4950m. From there you can reach the summit in about nine hours and return in under four hours. Alternatively, for a two-day trip, there is a good spot to camp at 5200m. Other routes take three days but are easier to get to by 4WD (US$110 to US$160).

OTHER MOUNTAINS

Sabancaya (5976m) is part of a massif on the south rim of the Cañón del Colca that also includes extinct Hualca Hualca (6025m) and Nevado Ampato (6310m). Sabancaya has erupted in recent years, and should only be approached with a guide who understands the geologic activity of the area; neighboring Ampato is a fairly straightforward, if strenuous, three-day ascent, and you get safer views of the active Sabancaya from here.

Other mountains of interest near Arequipa include Ubinas (5675m), which used to be the easiest mountain to summit but is currently spewing enough toxic ash that it is not recommended for climbing. Nevado Mismi (5597m) is a fairly easy three- or four-day climb on the north side of the Cañón del Colca. You can approach it on public transportation and, with a guide, find the lake that is reputedly the source of the Amazon. The highest mountain in southern Peru is the difficult Nevado Coropuna (6613m).

Cañón del Colca

It's not just the vastness and depth of the Colca that make it so fantastical, it's the shifts in its mood. There are more scenery changes along its 100km passage than there are in most European countries; from the barren steppe of Sibayo, through the ancient terraced farmland of Yanque and Chivay, into the steep-sided canyon proper beyond Cabanaconde that wasn't thoroughly explored until the 1980s. Of course one shouldn't turn a blind eye to the vital statistics. The Colca is the world's second-deepest canyon, a smidgeon shallower than near neighbor, the Cotahausi, and twice as deep as the more famous Grand Canyon in the US. But, more than that, it is replete with history, culture, ruins, tradition and – rather like Machu Picchu – intangible Peruvian magic.

Despite its depth, the Cañón del Colca is geologically young. The Río Colca has cut into beds of mainly volcanic rocks, which were deposited less than 100 million years ago along the line of a major fault in the earth's crust. Though cool and dry in the hills above, the deep valley and generally sunny weather produce frequent updrafts on which soaring condors often float by at close range. Viscachas (burrowing rodents closely related to chinchillas) are also common around the canyon rim, darting furtively among the rocks. Cacti dot many slopes and, if they're in flower, you may be lucky enough to see tiny nectar-eating birds braving the spines to feed. In the depths of the canyon it can be almost tropical, with palm trees, ferns and even orchids in some isolated areas.

The local people are descendants of two conflicting groups that originally occupied the area, the Cabanas and the Collagua. These two groups used to distinguish themselves by performing cranial deformations, but nowadays use distinctively shaped hats and intricately embroidered traditional clothing to denote their ancestry. In the Chivay area at the east end of the canyon, the white hats worn by women are usually woven from straw and are embellished with lace, sequins and medallions. At the west end of the canyon, the hats have rounded tops and are made of painstakingly embroidered cotton.

For guided tours of the canyon leaving from Arequipa, see p147.

Upper Canyon

The Upper Canyon (really still a valley at this stage) has a colder and harsher landscape than the terraced fields around Chivay and Yanque, and is only lightly visited. Pierced by a single road which plies northeast through the village of Tuti to Sibayo, the grassy terrain is inhabited by livestock while the still young river is ideal for rafting and trout-fishing.

SIBAYO
Sitting at an altitude of 3900m at the head of the canyon, Sibayo is a traditional rural village little touched by tourism. Many of the adobe houses still have old-fashioned straw roofs while the diminutive main plaza is framed by the recently restored Iglesia

San Juan Bautista. Northeast of the town a quiet spot by the river has been embellished by a small suspension bridge crossing the Colca called the **Puente Colgante Portillo**, and a lookout, the **Mirador de Largarta**, named for a lizard-shaped mountain up the valley. It is possible to hike southwest down the canyon to Tuti and, ultimately, Chivay from here.

Sibayo has a handful of very basic homestays available in traditional houses. One such place is **Samana Wasi** (990-049-5793; Av Mariscal Castilla; r S25) where the eager-to-please owners can rustle up dinner (S14) and take you trout fishing.

TUTI
Tuti is another tourist-lite village situated only 19km northeast of Colca-hub Chivay. With an economy centered on broad bean cultivation and clothes-making, it is surrounded by some interesting sights all connected by hiking trails. The easiest excursion is to a couple of caves in the hills to the north clearly visible from the main road and accessible via a 3.5km grunt uphill from the village. From the same starting point, you can also hike 8km to an old abandoned village dating from the 1600s known colloquially as **Ran Ran** or 'Espinar de Tuti.' Continue beyond Ran Ran and you'll join the trail to the source of the Amazon on the north side of Nevado Mismi. Down in the valley you can catch a taxi or *colectivo* from Chivay to Tuti and hike back to Chivay on a well-marked trail alongside the Río Colca. This stretch of the river is popular with rafters.

Middle Canyon

Behold the most accessible and popular segment of the canyon, a landscape dominated by agriculture and characterized by some of the most intensely terraced hillsides on earth. The greenery and accessibility has led this to becoming the canyon's busiest region with the bulk of the business centered in the small town of Chivay.

CHIVAY
054 / POP 6300 / ELEV 3630M
Chivay is the Colca Canyon's unashamedly disheveled nexus, a traditional town that has embraced tourism without (so far) losing its unkempt high country identity. Long may it continue!

Around the market area and in the main square are good places to catch a glimpse the decorative clothing worn by local

SOURCE OF THE AMAZON TREK

For centuries it remained one of the world's greatest mysteries. Humans had landed probes on Mars and split the atom before they got around to finding and – more importantly – agreeing upon the source of the world's most voluminous and (debatably) longest river, the mighty Amazon. Everyone from Alexander von Humboldt to Jean-Michel Cousteau pitched in with their thoughts and theories (often backed up with expensive expeditions) before the headwaters were finally pinpointed unequivocally in 2007: a fissure in a steep cliff situated at 5170m on the northern slopes of Nevado Mismi 6992km from the Amazon's river mouth on Brazil's Atlantic coast. Here glacial melt-waters collect in Laguna McInytre before flowing into the Apacheta, Apurímac, Ucayali and Marañón rivers whereupon they form the Amazon proper.

It is surprisingly easy to hike to the Amazon's source (marked inauspiciously by a wooden cross) from the Cañón del Colca. Paths ply north from the villages of Lari or Tuti. It's a two-day out-and-back hike from the latter village though some people prefer to undertake a three-day circuitous route starting in Lari and ending in Tuti, thus making a complete circle of Nevado Mismi. Alternatively, in the dry season, it is possible to get a 4x4 to within 30 minutes hike of the Apacheta cliff. Carlos Zárate Adventures (p147) in Arequipa organizes memorable guided hikes. Soloists should come equipped with maps, food, tents and cold-weather clothing.

women. The town itself affords enchanting views of snowcapped peaks and terraced hillsides, and serves as a logical base from which to explore smaller towns further up the valley.

☉ Sights & Activities

Astronomical Observatory OBSERVATORY
(Huayna Cápac; admission S25) No light pollution equals excellent Milky Way vistas. The Casa Andina hotel has a tiny observatory which holds nightly sky shows in Spanish and English. The price includes a 30-minute explanation and chance to peer into the telescope. It can be hard to catch a night with clear skies between December and April.

La Calera Hot Springs THERMAL BATHS
(admission S15; ☉4:30am-7pm) If you've just bussed or driven in from Arequipa, a good way to acclimatize is to stroll 3km to La Calera Hot Springs and examine the canyon's slopes (surprisingly shallow at this end) alfresco while lying in the famous pools. This isn't your average shopping mall spa (forget the pampering), but the water's warm, the setting's idyllic and you'll be spontaneously entertained by the whoops of zip-liners as they sail overhead. *Colectivos* from Chivay cost S1 to S2.

HIKING

Chivay is a good starting point for canyon hikes, both short and long. The view embellished 7km path to Coporaque on the north side of the canyon starts on the north edge of town. Fork left on the La Calera Hot Springs road, cross the Puente Inca, and follow the fertile fields to the village. Rather than retracing your steps, you can head downhill out of Coporaque past some small ruins and descend to the orange bridge across the Río Colca. From Yanque, on the southern bank, passing buses or *colectivos* return the 7km to Chivay (or you can walk along the road). For a quicker sojourn rent a mountain bike in Chivay (see p161).

To penetrate further west it's possible to continue on up the northern side of the canyon from Coporaque to the villages Ichupampa, Lari and, ultimately, Madrigal. Occasional *combis* run to these villages from the streets around the main market area in Chivay. Another option is to pitch northeast from near the Puente Inca and follow a path along the river to the villages of Tuti and Sibayo.

ZIPLINING

You can dangle terrifyingly over the Río Colca while entertaining bathers in La Calera Hot Springs (who relax below) doing the canyon's newest sport – ziplining. The start point is just past La Calera Hot Springs, 3.5km from Chivay, but you can organize rides with one of the agencies in town or directly with Colca Zip-lining (☎95-898-9931; www.colcaziplining.com; 2/4 cables S50/100).

🛏 Sleeping

Though it's a tiny town, Chivay has plenty of budget guesthouses to choose from.

TOP CHOICE ⟩ Hotel Pozo del Cielo HOTEL $$

(☏34-6547; www.pozodelcielo.com.pe; Huascar; d/ste S88/135; 🛜) Looking a bit like something Gaudi might have crafted, 'Heaven's Well,' as the name translates, is all low doorways, weirdly shaped rooms and winding paths. One half expects the seven dwarfs to come marching out. But, surrealism aside, this place works, a functional yet comfortable abode with an almost boutique-y feel to its individually crafted rooms and fine '*mirador*' restaurant.

Hostal La Pascana HOTEL $

(☏53-1001; Siglo XX 106; s/d/tr incl breakfast S55/70/87; 🛜) La Pascana is a good old-fashioned crash-pad that will probably seem like luxury after a few days hiking in the canyon. Simple rooms have blankets (thank heavens!), the staff is gracious and there's a small but decent restaurant. It's several notches above the other more modest guesthouses and lies adjacent to the plaza.

Casa Andina BOUTIQUE HOTEL $$$

(☏53-1020, 53-1022; www.casa-andina.com; Huayna Cápac; s/d incl breakfast from S250; 🛜) Purposefully rustic rooms inhabit thatched-roof stone cottages in neatly sculpted grounds, but the main grab-you features here are the unusual extras which include an observatory, oxygen (should you be feeling lightheaded for a lack of it) and nightly culture shows where local musicians and artisans mingle, and a shaman tells fortunes with coca leaves.

Hostal Estrella de David HOTEL $

(☏53-1233; Siglo XX 209; s/d/tr S20/20/40) A simple, clean *hospedaje* (small, family-owned inn) with bathrooms and some rooms with cable TV. It's a few blocks from the plaza in the direction of the bus terminal.

Hostal Anita HOSTEL $

(☏53-1114; Plaza de Armas 607; s/d/tr S20/40/50) With a pretty interior courtyard, this friendly hostel smack on the main plaza has hot showers and affable owners. Breakfast is available upon request.

✗ Eating & Drinking

Innkas Café PERUVIAN, CAFE $

(Plaza de Armas 705; mains S12-20; ⊙7am-11pm) An old building with cozy window nooks warmed by modern gas heaters (and boy do you need 'em). Maybe it's the altitude, but the lomo saltado tastes Gastón Acurio–good here. The sweet service is backed up by even sweeter cakes and coffee.

Cusi Alina PERUVIAN $$

(Plaza de Armas 201; buffet S25) One of a couple of restaurants in Chivay that offers an all-you-can-eat lunchtime buffet. The food represents a good Peruvian smorgasbord with plenty of vegetarian options. It's popular with tour buses, so get in before 1pm to enjoy more elbow room.

Aromas Caffee CAFE

(www.aromascaffeecolca.com; Plaza de Armas cnr Av Salaverry) The tiny cappuccino machine in this diminutive 'three's-a-crowd' cafe takes the conscientious barista about 10 minutes to manipulate, but your Peruvian coffee, when it emerges, is worth the wait.

🛈 Information

There's a helpful **information office** (☏53-1143; Plaza de Armas 119; ⊙8am-1pm & 3-7pm) right on the main plaza. The police station is next to the *municipalidad* (town hall) on the plaza. There is one ATM in town located on Calle Salaverry one block west of the main plaza. Some of the higher-end hotels and a few shops around town exchange US dollars, euros and traveler's checks at unfavorable rates. Internet access is available from a few internet cafes near the plaza.

🛈 Getting There & Around

The bus terminal is a 15-minute walk from the plaza. There are nine daily departures to Arequipa (S15, three hours), while buses to Cabanaconde (S5, 2½ hours), stopping at towns along the southern side of the canyon and at Cruz del Cóndor, leave four times daily.

BOLETO TURÍSTICO

To access the sites in the Colca Canyon you will need to purchase a *boleto turístico* (tourist ticket; S70) from a booth on the Arequipa road just outside Chivay. If you are taking an organized tour, the cost of the tour usually does not include this additional fee. If you are traveling alone, tickets can be purchased on most public buses entering or leaving Chivay, or in the town of Cabanaconde. Half of the proceeds from this ticket go to Arequipa for general maintenance and conservation of local tourist attractions, while the other half goes to the national agency of tourism.

Combis and *colectivo* taxis run to the surrounding villages from street corners in the market area, just north of the main plaza, or you can arrange a private taxi. Mountain bikes in varying condition can be readily hired from travel agencies on the plaza or at **BiciSport** (✆9-58-807-652; Zaramilla 112; ☺9am-6pm) behind the market for about S5 per day.

Traveling onward to Cuzco from Chivay may be possible, but it's overly complicated and not recommended. Although some travelers have managed to catch *combis* to Puente Callalli and flag down a bus there, it's much safer and probably just as fast to return to Arequipa instead.

YANQUE
✆054 / POP 1900

Of the canyon's dozen or so villages, Yanque, 7km west of Chivay, has the prettiest and liveliest main square, and sports its finest church (from the exterior, at least); the **Iglesia de la Inmaculada Concepción** whose ornate baroque-*mestizo* doorway has an almost *churrigueresque* look. Local women in traditional costume dance to music in the main square most mornings at around 7 o'clock, catching tourists on their way to the Cruz del Cóndor.

☉ Sights

Museo Yanque   MUSEUM
(admission S5; ☺9am-5pm Mon-Sat) Opposite the church on the plaza sits this university-run museum, unexpectedly comprehensive for a small village, which explains the culture of the Colca Canyon in conscientious detail. Exhibits include information on Inca fabrics, cranial deformation, local agriculture, ecclesial architecture and a mini-exposé on Juanita, the 'Ice Maiden.'

Baños Chacapi   THERMAL BATHS
(admission S10; ☺4am-7pm) From the plaza, a 30-minute walk down to the river brings you to these hot springs, a kind of poor-man's La Calera. The early-bird opening time is mainly for locals, many of whom don't have hot water in their houses.

🛏 Sleeping

In Yanque, a number of simple, family-run guesthouses have joined in a local development project; they are scattered around town, and offer lodging from S15 per night. **Sumaq Huayta Wasi** (✆83-2174; www.casabellaflor.com; Cusco 303), also known as 'Casa Bella Flor,' just two blocks from the main plaza, provides an excellent balance between tradition and comfort. A more upscale option is **Hotel Collahua** (✆22-6098;

www.hotelcollahua.com; Av Collahua Cuadro 7; s/d/tr S65/85/95; ☎) whose bright rooms are encased in independent bungalows over largeish grounds where alpacas roam. There's a comprehensive restaurant onsite.

COPORAQUE
Noncommercialized Coporaque has the valley's oldest church and not a lot else, unless you count the splendiferous views of canyon slopes covered in terraced fields.

☉ Sights

Nonguests can use the Colca Lodge's thermal baths for S30 (price includes one meal in the lodge restaurant).

Oyu Oyu   RUIN
Though not visible from the road, the remnants of this pre-Incan settlement are reachable by a half-hour uphill hike, after which you can continue on to a waterfall whose source is the runoff from Nevado Mismi. Guides can be procured at the Colca Lodge.

🛏 Sleeping

TOP CHOICE **Colca Lodge**   LUXURY HOTEL $$$
(✆53-1191; www.colca-lodge.com; d/ste with breakfast S546/852; ❄☎☻☻) Expensive but utterly romantic, this is the Colca Canyon packaged for the decadent where the artistically manicured grounds appear like a shot of oxygen aside the rippling Río Colca. Lavish rooms come loaded with Noel Coward-esque dressing gowns, wood-burning stoves, candles, coffee machines and king beds, but the real carrot is the alfresco thermal baths (37°C to 39°C) sculpted into whimsical pools aside the river. For advance reservations, visit the **Arequipa office** (✆054-20-2587, 054-20-3604; Benavides 201).

La Casa de Mamayacchi   INN $$
(www.lacasademamayacchi.com; d/tr incl breakfast from S192/250) Hidden away downhill from the main plaza, this inn is built with traditional materials and resides over terraced valley views. The cozy rooms have no TVs, but there's a games library, fireplace and bar that make it sociable. Make advance reservations through the **Arequipa office** (✆24-1206; Jerusalén 606).

LARI

Sleepy Lari, 16km west of Corporaque on the north side of the river, has the canyon's largest church. It is also a potential start point for the Source of the Amazon trek (p160) which can be looped back round to Tuti in

AREQUIPA & CANYON COUNTRY CAÑÓN DEL COLCA

the northeast. There's a rock-bottom hotel in the main square and a couple of bare-bones restaurants, but you're better off forging on to Chivay or Cabanaconde for an overnighter.

MADRIGAL

Madrigal is the last village on the canyon's north side reachable by road (unpaved by this point). Aside from its oversized church and scruffy digs at the **Hostal Municipalidad** (Plaza de Armas; r S12), Madrigal is a bucolic backwater perfect for a slow unflustered digestion of traditional Colca life. You can forge west on foot from here to two nearby archaeological sites: the **Fortaleza de Chimpa**, a walled Collagua citadel atop a hill, and the **Pueblo Perdido Matata**, some long-abandoned ruins.

PINCHOLLO

Pinchollo, about 30km from Chivay, is one of the valley's poorer villages. From here, a trail climbs toward **Hualca Hualca** (a snow-capped volcano of 6025m) to an active geothermal area set amid wild and interesting scenery. Though it's not very clearly marked, there's a four-hour trail up to a bubbling geyser that used to erupt dramatically before a recent earthquake contained it. Ask around for directions, or just head left uphill in the direction of the mountain, then follow the water channel to its end.

CRUZ DEL CÓNDOR

Some much hyped travel sights are anticlimactic in the raw light of day, but this is *not* one of them. No advance press can truly sell the **Cruz del Cóndor** (admission with boleto turístico), a famed viewpoint, also known locally as Chaq'lla, about 50km west of Chivay. A large family of Andean condors nests by the rocky outcrop and, weather and season permitting, they can be seen between approximately 8am and 10am gliding effortlessly on thermal air currents rising from the canyon, swooping low over onlookers' heads (condors rarely flap their wings). It's a mesmerizing scene, heightened by the spectacular 1200m drop to the river below and the sight of **Nevado Mismi** reaching over 3000m above the canyon floor on the other side of the ravine.

Recently it has become more difficult to see the condors, mostly due to air pollution, including from travelers' campfires and tour buses. The condors are also less likely to appear on rainy days so it's best to visit during the dry season. You won't be alone at the lookout. Expect a couple of hundred people for the 8am 'show' in season. Afterwards, it

is possible to walk 12.5km from the viewpoint to Cabanaconde.

Lower Canyon

The narrow lower canyon is the Colca at its deepest. It runs roughly from Cabanaconde down to Huambo. Fruit trees can be found around Tapay and Sangalle, but otherwise the canyon supports no real economic activity.

CABANACONDE
☏054 / POP 2700 / ELEV 3290M

Only approximately 20% of Colca Canyoners get as far as ramshackle Cabanaconde (most organized itineraries turn around at the Cruz del Cóndor). For those who make it, the attractions are obvious – less people, more authenticity and greater tranquility. Welcome to the *true* canyon experience. The Colca is significantly deeper here with steep, zigzagging paths tempting the fit and the brave to descend 1200m to the eponymous river. There are no ATMs in Cabanaconde. Stash some cash.

🏃 Activities

You've only half-experienced Colca if you haven't descended into the canyon by foot (the only method anywhere west of Madrigal). The shortest way in is via the spectacular two-hour hike from Cabanaconde down to **Sangalle** (also popularly known as 'the oasis') at the bottom of the canyon, where four sets of basic bungalows and camping grounds have sprung up, all costing from about S10 to S15 per person. There are two natural pools for swimming, the larger of which is claimed by Oasis Bungalows, which charges S5 (free if you are staying in its bungalows) to swim. Paraíso Bungalows doesn't charge for the smaller swimming pool, and there is a local dispute over whether travelers should be charged to use the pools at all. Do not light campfires as almost half of the trees in the area have been destroyed in this manner, and cart all trash out with you. The return trek to Cabanaconde is a stiff climb and thirsty work; allow 1½ hours (superfit), two to 2½ hours (fit), three hours plus (average fitness). There's drink and food available in Sangalle.

👉 Tours & Guides

Local guides can also be hired by consulting with your hostel or the *municipalidad* in Cabanaconde. The going rate for guides is S30 to S60 per day, depending on the type of trek, season and size of the group. Renting a horse or mule, which is an excellent way

'EL CLÁSICO' TREK

Short on time? Confused by the complicated web of Colca paths? Couldn't stand the crowds on the Inca Trail? What you need is 'El Clásico,' the unofficial name for a circular two- to three-day hike that incorporates the best parts of the mid-lower Colca Canyon below the Cruz del Cóndor and Cabanaconde. Commence by walking out of Cabanaconde on the Chivay road. At the San Miguel viewpoint, start a long 1200m descent into the canyon on a zigzagging path. Cross the Río Colca via a bridge and enter the village of **San Juan de Chuccho** where accommodations are available at the **Casa de Rivelino** (r S10) with bungalows with warm water and a simple restaurant. Alternatively, you can ascend to the charming village of **Tapay** where camping or overnight accommodations are available at **Hostal Isidro**, whose owner is a guide and has a shop, satellite phone and rental mules. On day two descend to the Cinkumayu Bridge before ascending to the villages of **Coshñirwa** and **Malata**. The latter has a tiny **Museo Familiar**, basically a typical local home where the owner will explain about the Colca culture. From Malata, descend to the beautiful **Sangalle** oasis (crossing the river again) with more overnight options before ascending the lung-stretching 4km trail back to Cabanaconde (1200m of ascent).

Though it's easy to do solo, this classic trek can be easily organized with any reputable Arequipa travel agency.

to carry water into the canyon and waste out, can be arranged easily for about S60 per day.

🛏 Sleeping & Eating

Accommodation options are limited in Cabanaconde. Most people eat where they're sleeping, although there are a couple of cheap local restaurants near or on the main plaza.

TOP CHOICE Hotel Kuntur Wassi   HOTEL $$
(☎81-2166; www.arequipacolca.com; Cruz Blanca s/n; s/d/ste incl breakfast US$125/150/190; @🖘) As upmarket as Cabanaconde gets, Kuntur Wassi is actually rather charming and is built into the hillside above town, with stone bathrooms, trapezoidal windows overlooking the gardens and a nouveau-rustic feel. Suites have enormous bathtubs. There's also a bar, restaurant, library, laundry and foreign-currency exchange. The food served here is top-notch city standard.

Pachamama Backpacker Hostal   HOSTEL $
(☎9-59-316-322, 25-3879; www.pachamama home.com; San Pedro 209; dm S15, d without/ with bathroom S35/50, all incl breakfast; @) Run by the ultra-friendly and helpful Ludwig (who's fluent in English), Pachamama has plenty of room options (dorms, doubles and other combos), a pizza oven, a fantastic crepe breakfast and an unexpectedly warmhearted bar. One-way bike excursions can be organized from the Cruz del Cóndor for S25.

La Posada del Conde   HOTEL $
(☎40-0408, 83-0033; www.posadadelconde.com; San Pedro s/n; s/d incl breakfast S35/50; 🖘) This small journeyman hotel mostly has double rooms, but they are well-cared-for with clean bathrooms. The rates often include a welcome *mate* (herbal tea) or pisco sour in the downstairs restaurant. The same people run a smaller, slightly plusher and pricier lodge up the road.

Restaurante Las Terrazas   INTERNATIONAL $
(☎958-10-3553; www.villapastorcolca.com; Plaza de Armas; snacks S10-15; @) Pizza, pasta, sandwiches and cheap Cuba Libres are offered here overlooking the main square and its bucolic donkey traffic. There's also a computer terminal charitably offering free internet. Rooms are available.

❶ Getting There & Away

Buses for Chivay (S5, 2½ hours) and Arequipa (S17, six hours) via Cruz del Cóndor leave Cabanaconde from the main plaza seven times per day with **Andalucia** (☎44-5089) and **Reyna** (☎43-0612). Departure times change frequently though, so check with the bus company office on the main plaza. All buses will stop upon request at towns along the main road on the southern side of the canyon.

Toro Muerto Petroglyphs

A fascinating, mystical site in the high desert, Toro Muerto (meaning 'Dead Bull') is named for the herds of livestock that commonly died here from dehydration as they were escorted from the mountains to the coast. A barren hillside is scattered with white volcanic boulders carved with stylized people, animals and birds. Archaeologists have documented more than 5000 such petroglyphs spread over several square kilometers of desert. Though the cultural origins of this site remain unknown, most archaeologists date the mysterious drawings to the period of Wari domination, about 1200 years ago. Interpretations of the drawings vary widely; a guide can fill you in on some of the most common themes, or you can wander among the boulders yourself and formulate your own elaborate interpretation of the message these ancient images aim to tell.

To reach the site by public transportation, take a bus to Corire from Arequipa (S10, three hours). If you don't want to sleep in Corire, take an early bus (they start as early as 4am) and get off at a gas station just past the sign that denotes the beginning of the town of Corire. From there, you can walk the hot, dusty road about 2km uphill to a checkpoint where visitors must sign in. Otherwise, continue on into Corire, from where you can catch a taxi to take you to where the petroglyphs start (from S40 round-trip if the taxi waits). In Corire, Hostal Willy (☏054-47-2046; Av Progresso; r per person from S35) has basic accommodations and can provide information on reaching the site. Bring plenty of water, sunblock and insect repellent (as there are plenty of mosquitoes en route).

Buses return from Corire to Arequipa once an hour, usually leaving at 30 minutes past the hour. The Toro Muerto petroglyphs can also be visited more conveniently on expensive full-day 4WD tours from Arequipa.

El Valle de los Volcanes

El Valle de los Volcanes is a broad valley, west of the Cañón del Colca and at the foot of Nevado Coropuna (6613m), famed for its unusual geological features. The valley floor is carpeted with lava flows from which rise many small (up to 200m high) cinder cones, some 80 in total, aligned along a major fissure, with each cone formed from a single eruption. Given the lack of erosion of some cones and minimal vegetation on the associated lava flows, the volcanic activity occurred no more than a few thousand years ago, and some was likely very recent – historical accounts suggest as recently as the 17th century.

The 65km-long valley surrounds the village of Andagua, near the snowy summit of Coropuna. Visitors seeking a destination full of natural wonders and virtually untouched by travelers will rejoice in this remote setting. From Andagua, a number of sites can be visited by foot or car. It is possible to hike to the top of the perfectly conical twin volcanoes which lie about 10km from town, though don't expect a clear-cut trail. Other popular hikes are to a nearby *mirador* at 3800m and to the 40m-high Izanquillay falls which are formed where the Río Andahua runs through a narrow lava canyon to the northeast of town. There are some *chullpas* (funerary towers) at Soporo, a two-hour hike or half-hour drive to the south of Andagua. En route to Soporo are the ruins of a pre-Columbian city named Antaymarca. Topographical maps of the area are available at Colca Trek (☏054-20-6217, 9-60-0170; www.colcatrek.com.pe; Jerusalén 401-B) in Arequipa. An alternative way to enter the valley is by starting from Cabanaconde, crossing the Cañón del Colca, then hiking over a 5500m pass before descending into El Valle de los Volcanes. This trek requires at least five days (plus time for proper acclimatization beforehand), and is best to attempt with an experienced guide and pack mules.

There are several cheap and basic hostels and restaurants in Andagua, including the recommended Hostal Trebol (Calle 15 de Agosto; r S20). Camping is also possible, though you will need plenty of water and sun protection. To get to the valley from Arequipa, take a Reyna bus to Andagua (S40, 10 to 12 hours) which departs from Arequipa around 4pm. Return buses leave Andagua around 2pm. Some tour companies also visit El Valle de los Volcanes as part of expensive tours in 4WD vehicles that may also include visits to the Cañón del Cotahuasi and Chivay.

Cañón del Cotahuasi

While the Cañón del Colca has stolen the limelight for many years, it is actually this remote canyon, 200km northwest of Arequipa as the condor flies, that is the deepest known canyon in the world. It is around twice the depth of the Grand Canyon, with stretches dropping down below 3500m. While the depths of the ravine are only accessible to experienced river runners, the rest of the fertile valley is also rich in striking scenery and trekking opportunities. The canyon also shelters several traditional rural settlements that currently see only a handful of adventurous travelers.

◉ Sights & Activities

The main access town is appropriately named Cotahuasi (population 3800) and is at 2620m above sea level on the southeast side of the canyon. Northeast of Cotahuasi and further up the canyon are the villages of Tomepampa (10km away; elevation 2500m) and Alca (20km away; 2660m), which also have basic accommodations. En route you'll pass a couple of thermal baths (admission S2).

Buses to the Sipia bridge (S3, one hour) leave the main plaza of Cotahuasi daily at 6:30am, from where you can begin a number of interesting hikes into the deepest parts of the canyon. Forty-five minutes up the trail, the Sipia waterfall is formed where the Río Cotahuasi takes an impressive 100m tumble. Another 1½ hours on a well-trodden track brings you to Chaupo, an oasis of towering cacti and remnants of pre-Incan dwellings. Camping is possible here. From here a dusty path leads either up to Velinga and other remote communities where sleeping accommodations are available, or down to Mallu, a patch of verdant farmland at the river's edge where the owner, Ignacio, will allow you to pitch tents and borrow his stove for S10 per night. To get back to Cotahuasi, a return bus leaves the Sipia bridge around 11:30am daily.

Another possible day trip from Cotahuasi is to the hillside community of Pampamarca. From here, a two-hour hike up a steep switchbacking trail will bring you to an interesting group of rock formations, where locals have likened shapes in the rocks to mystical figures. A short walk from town brings you to a viewpoint with a view of the rushing 80m high Uscune falls. To get to Pampamarca, *combis* leave the main square in Cotahuasi twice daily in the early morning and afternoon (S5, two hours), and return shortly after arriving.

Trekking trips of several days' duration can be arranged in Arequipa (p147); some can be combined with the Toro Muerto petroglyphs, and, if you ask, they may return via a collection of dinosaur footprints on the west edge of the canyon.

🛏 Sleeping & Eating

In Pampamarca, ask around for basic family guesthouses (per person S10) that provide travelers with beds and meals.

Hotel Vallehermoso   HOTEL $$
(☑054-58-1057; www.hotelvallehermoso.com; Calle Tacna 106-108, Cotahuasi; s/d S70/100) Just what you probably wanted after a dusty 12-hour bus ride, Cotahuasi's poshest joint offers divine comfort in the middle of nowhere while never straying too far from rustic tradition. An onsite restaurant even tries its spin on Novoandina cuisine.

Hostal Hatunhuasi   HOTEL $
(☑054-58-1054, in Lima 01-531-0803; www.hatunhuasi.com; Centanario 309, Cotahuasi; s/d S25/50) A notch above the other options in town, this friendly guesthouse has plenty of rooms situated around a sunny inner courtyard and hot water most of the time. Food can be made upon request, and the owners are good sources of hard-to-get information for travelers.

Hospedaje Casa Primavera   INN $
(☑054-28-50-89; primaverahostal@hotmail.com; Calle Union 112, Tomepampa; r per person S20) A good find in the tiny village of Tomepampa, this oldish hacienda-style building has a balcony, some floral embellishments and views. There is a variety of simple but clean rooms of different sizes and breakfast is included.

Hostal Alcalá   GUESTHOUSE $
(☑054-83-0011; Plaza de Armas, Alca; s/d S25/40, dm/s/d without bathroom S10/15/25) In Alca, this guesthouse has a good mix of clean rooms and prices, including some of the most comfortable digs in the whole valley. There is 24-hour hot water here.

❶ Getting There & Away

The 420km bus journey from Arequipa, half of which is on unpaved roads, takes 12 hours if the going is good (S25). Over three-quarters of the way there, the road summits a 4500m pass between the huge glacier-capped mountains of Coropuna and Solimana (6323m) before dropping down to Cotahuasi. Wild vicuña can also be spotted here running on the high altiplano. Reyna (☑43-0612) and Transportes Alex (☑42-4605) both run buses that leave Arequipa around 4pm. Buses return to Arequipa from Cotahuasi at around 5pm.

There are hourly *combis* from the Cotahuasi plaza up to Alca (S3, one hour) via Tomepampa (S2, 30 minutes). For Pampamarca, there are two daily buses (S5, two hours) departing in the early morning and again mid-afternoon.

Lake Titicaca

Best Places to Stay & Eat

» Titilaka (p186)

» Casa Andina Isla Suasi (p184)

» Casa Panq'arani (p173)

» Capachica community homestays (p184)

» Mojsa (p176)

Best Festivals

» La Virgen de la Candelaria (p172)

» Puno Week (p173)

» Fiesta de San Juan (p173)

» Alacitas (p173)

» Feast of Saint James (p173)

Why Go?

In Andean belief, Titicaca is the birthplace of the sun. In addition, it's the largest lake in South America and the highest navigable body of water in the world. Banner blue skies contrast with bitterly cold nights. Enthralling and in many ways singular, the shimmering deep blue Lake Titicaca is the longtime home of highland cultures steeped in the old ways.

Pre-Inca Pukara, Tiwanaku and Collas all left their mark upon the landscape. Today the region is a mix of crumbling cathedrals, desolate altiplano and checkerboard fields backed by rolling hills and high Andean peaks. In this world, crops are still planted and harvested by hand. *Campesinos* wear sandals recycled from truck tires, women work in petticoats and bowler hats, and llamas are tame as pets.

It might first appear austere, but ancient holidays are marked with riotous celebrations where elaborately costumed-processions and brass bands ripcord a frenzy that lasts for days.

When to Go

Puno

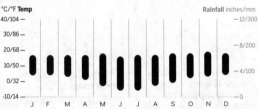

Early Feb For the marvelous spectacle of the festival of La Virgen de la Candelaria.

Jun–Aug Winter's dry season heralds cold, clear nights and bright sunny days.

Early Nov Puno Week celebrates the birth of Mánco Capac, the first Inca, in wild style.

❶ Getting There & Around

There are daily flights to Juliaca (one hour from Puno) from Lima and Cuzco. Regular buses travel from Arequipa, Cuzco and Lima to Juliaca and Puno. There's also an iconic train route from Cuzco (see p178). If arriving from sea level, it's best to travel overland in order to better acclimate to the altitude; flying straight from Lima can serve up quite a headache.

It's also possible to arrive from Bolivia by bus or a packaged island tour of Lake Titicaca.

Juliaca

📞 051 / TRANSPORT HUB / ELEV 3826M

The region's only commercial airport makes Juliaca, the largest city on the altiplano, an unavoidable transit hub. The city bustles

Lake Titicaca Highlights

❶ Boat the serene blue expanse to the mystical **islands** (p181) of Lake Titicaca

❷ Celebrate festivals with blaring brass bands and crazy costumes in **Puno** (p174), Peru's *capital folklórico*

❸ Admire the elaborate temples that dwarf Lake

Titicaca's bucolic **south-shore towns** (p186)

❹ Hike across farmland and climb hills to overgrown ruins in **Ichu** (p186)

❺ Visit awe-inspiring funerary towers at **Sillustani** (p179) and **Cutimbo** (p179)

❻ Recharge your batteries on the sunny, somnolent **Capachica Peninsula** (p184)

❼ Stargaze and sleep on board the historic steamship **Yavari** (p176)

❽ Cross into Bolivia to explore the legendary **Isla del Sol** (p190)

BUS INFORMATION

DESTINATION	COST* (SOLES)	DURATION (HRS)
Arequipa	15/72	6
Cuzco	20	5-6
Puno	3.50	1
Lima	130/170	20
Tacna	25/45	10-11

* Prices are general estimates for normal/luxury buses

with commerce (and contraband) due to its handy location near the border. Daytime muggings and drunks on the street are not uncommon. Since Juliaca has little to offer travelers, it is advisable to stay in nearby Lampa or move on to Puno.

Hotels, restaurants, *casas de cambio* (money exchangers) and internet cafes abound along San Román, near Plaza Bolognesi. ATMs and banks are also nearby on Nuñez.

If you are in a pinch, Royal Inn Hotel (32-1561; www.royalinnhoteles.com; San Román 158; s/d/tr S100/130/150) is an excellent choice for the price. This towering hotel boasts recently revamped modern rooms with hot showers, heating and cable TV, plus one of Juliaca's best restaurants (mains from S18).

❶ Getting There & Away
Air

The **airport** (32-8974) is 2km west of town. **LAN** (32-2228; San Román 125; 8am-7pm Mon-Fri, to 6pm Sat) has daily flights to/from Lima, Arequipa and Cuzco. **Taca** (32-7966; Centro Comercial Real Plaza, Jr. San Martín, cuadra 1) flies to Lima, as does **Star Peru** (32-3816; San Román 154).

Official airport taxis go to Puno (S80) and Juliaca (S10). A cheaper option are the *colectivos* (S15), bus shuttles which go direct to Puno and drop passengers at their hotels.

Bus & Taxi

The **terminal terrestre** (Cnr Jr. San Martín & Av Miraflores) houses long-distance bus companies. Buses leave for Cuzco every hour from 5am to 11pm, and for Arequipa every hour from 2:30am to 11:30pm.

Buses to the coast leave from within walking distance of Plaza Bolognesi, on and around San Martín over the railway tracks; *combis* (minibuses) to Puno leave from Plaza Bolognesi.

Julsa (32-6602, 33-1952) has the most frequent departures to Arequipa; Power (32-1952) has the most frequent to Cuzco. Civa, Ormeño and San Cristobal run to Lima.

Sur Oriente has a daily bus to Tacna at 7pm. More centrally located, **San Martín** (32-7501) and other companies along Tumbes between Moquegua and Piérola go to Tacna (S25, seven hours) via Moquegua.

Combis to Puno (S3.50, 50 minutes) leave from Plaza Bolognesi when full. *Combis* for Lampa (S2.50, 30 minutes) leave from Jirón Huáscar when full. *Combis* to Huancané (S3, one hour) leave every 15 minutes from Ballón and Sucre, about four blocks east of Apurímac and 1½ blocks north of Lambayeque. *Combis* to Capachica (S4, 1½ hours) leave from the **Terminal Zonal** (Av Tacna, cuadra 11). *Combis* to Escallani (S3, 1½ hours), via an incredibly scenic, unpaved back road, leave from the corner of Cahuide and Gonzáles Prada. All of these terminals are a S2 *mototaxi* (three-wheeled motorcycle rickshaw taxi) ride from the center of town.

❶ Getting Around

Mototaxi is the best option for getting around. A ride to local destinations, including bus terminals, will cost under S3. Bus line 1B cruises around town and down Calle 2 de Mayo before heading to the airport (S0.60).

Around Juliaca
LAMPA
051 / POP 1655 / ELEV 3860

This charming little town, 36km northwest of Juliaca, is known as La Ciudad Rosada (the Pink City) for its dusty, pink-colored buildings. A significant commercial center in colonial days, it still shows a strong Spanish influence. It's an excellent place to kill a few hours before flying out of Juliaca, or to spend a quiet night.

STRANGEST SIGHTS

Even if you don't believe in tales of alien colonies and strange sightings, Lake Titicaca has no shortage of the surreal.

» Islands made of reeds (p181)
» Michaelangelo's *Pietà* faked (p170)
» An age-old tradition of edible clay (p179)
» Enormous stone phalluses (p186)

⊙ Sights

Iglesia de Santiago Apostol CHURCH
(tour S10; ⊗9am-12:30pm, 2-4pm) Well worth seeing and the pride of locals, this beautifully constructed lime-mortar church is rife with fascinating features. Among other things, a life-sized sculpture of the Last Supper; a model of Santiago (St James) atop a real stuffed horse, returning from the dead to trample the Moors; creepy catacombs; secret tunnels; and a huge domed tomb topped by a wonderful copy of Michelangelo's *Pietà*. It's also lined with hundreds of skeletons arranged in a ghoulishly decorative, skull-and-crossbones pattern. It truly has to be seen to be believed. Excellent Spanish-speaking guides are on hand daily.

Museo Kampac MUSEUM
(☑951-82-0085; cnr Ugarte & Ayacucho; admission S5; ⊗7am-6pm) Staff at the shop opposite this museum, two blocks west of the Plaza de Armas, will give you a Spanish-language guided tour of the museum's small but significant collection of mostly pre-Inca ceramics, monoliths, and one mummy, and may show you a unique vase inscribed with the sacred cosmology of the Incas.

Lampa Municipalidad TOWN HALL
(Town Hall; admission S2; ⊗8am-12:45pm & 1:30-4pm Mon Fri; 9am-1pm Sat & Sun) In the small square beside the church, is recognizable by its murals depicting Lampa's history – past, present and future. Inside there's a gorgeous courtyard, another replica of the *Pietà*, and a museum honoring noted Lampa-born painter Víctor Humareda (1920–86).

Just out of town is a pretty colonial **bridge**, and about 4km west is **Cueva de los Toros**, a bull-shaped cave with prehistoric carvings of llamas and other animals. The cave is on the right-hand side of the road heading west. Its entrance is part of a large, distinctive rock formation. En route you'll see several *chullpas* (funerary towers), not unlike the ones at Sillustani and Cutimbo.

🛏 Sleeping & Eating

Lampa isn't all that geared up for overnight stays, but there are a few basic accommodations available.

Casa Romero GUESTHOUSE
(☑952-65-1511, 952-71-9073; casaromerolampa.com; Aguirre 327; s/d/tr incl breakfast S50/80/120) Recommended, with friendly service, warm down duvets and well-appointed rooms. Full board is available with advance booking. There are a couple of restaurants around the Plaza de Armas.

ℹ Getting There & Away

Combis for Lampa (S2.50, 30 minutes) leave when full from Jirón Huáscar in Juliaca. If you have time to kill after checking in at Juliaca airport, get a taxi to drop you off in Lampa (S4).

PUCARÁ
☑051 / POP 675 / ELEV 3860M
More than 60km northwest of Juliaca, the sleepy village of Pucará is famous for its celebrations of **La Virgen del Carmen** on July 16 and its earth-colored pottery – including the ceramic *toritos* (bulls) often seen perched on the roofs of Andean houses for good luck. Several local workshops are open to the public and offer classes where you can make your own ceramics. Try the reader-recommended **Maki Pucará** (☑951-79-0618), on the highway near the bus stop.

The **Museo Lítico Pucará** (Jirón Lima; ⊗8:30am-5pm Tue-Sun), by the church, displays a surprisingly good selection of anthropomorphic monoliths from the town's pre-Inca site, **Kalasaya**. The ruins themselves sit above the town, a short walk up Jirón Lima away from the main plaza. Just S8 gets you into both sites, though there's nobody to check your ticket at the ruin.

If you get stuck, there are some simple accommodations near the bus stop. Buses to Juliaca (S3.50, 1 hour) run from 6am to 8pm.

ABRA LA RAYA
From Ayaviri, the route climbs for almost another 100km to this Andean **mountain pass** (4470m), the highest point on the trip to Cuzco. Buses often stop here to allow passengers to take advantage of the photogenic view of snowcapped mountains and the cluster of handicrafts sellers. The pass also

marks the departmental line between Puno and Cuzco. For points of interest north of here, see p258.

Puno

📞 051 / POP 120,200 / ELEV 3830M

With a regal plaza, concrete block buildings and crumbling bricks that blend into the hills, Puno has its share of both grit and cheer. It serves as the jumping-off point for Lake Titicaca and a convenient stop for those traveling between Cuzco and La Paz. But it may just capture your heart with its own rackety charm.

Smoke from unvented fires wafts through Puno's streets, along with jangling waves of traffic, including *mototaxis* and *triciclos* (three-wheeled cycles) that edge pedestrians to the narrow slivers of sidewalks. Its urban center can feel contaminated and cold. But Puno's people are upbeat, cheeky and ready to drop everything if there's a good time to be had.

As a trade (and contraband) hub between Peru, Bolivia and both coasts of South America, Puno is overwhelmingly commercial and forward-looking. For a glimpse of its colonial and naval identity, you only have to peruse the spots of old architecture, the colorful traditional dress worn by many inhabitants and scores of young cadets in the streets.

Puno is known as Peru's *capital folklórica* (folkloric capital) – its Virgen de la Candelaria parades are televised across the nation – and the associated drinking is the stuff of legend (see p172). Good times aren't restricted to religious festivals, though: some of Peru's most convivial bars are found in Puno.

⊙ Sights & Activities

Puno is handily compact. If you've got energy to spare, you can walk into the center from the port or the bus terminals; otherwise, hop into a *mototaxi*. Everything in the town center is within easy walking distance. Jirón Lima, the main pedestrian street, fills in the early evening as *puneños* (inhabitants of Puno) come out to promenade.

FREE **Catedral de Puno** CHURCH
(admission free; ☺8am-noon & 3-6pm) On the western flank of the Plaza de Armas, Puno's baroque cathedral was completed in 1757.

The interior is more spartan than you'd expect from the well-sculpted facade, except for the silver-plated altar, which, following a 1964 visit by Pope Paul VI, has a Vatican flag to its right.

FREE **Casa del Corregidor** HISTORIC BUILDING
(📞35-1921; www.casadelcorregidor.pe; Deustua 576; ☺9:30am-7:30pm Mon-Fri, 12:30-7pm Sat) An attraction in its own right, this 17th-century house is one of Puno's oldest residences. A former community center, it now houses a small fair-trade arts-and-crafts store.

Museo Carlos Dreyer MUSEUM
(Conde de Lemos 289; admission with English-speaking guide S15; ☺9:30am-7pm Mon-Sat) Around the corner from Casa del Corregidor, this museum houses a fascinating collection of Puno-related archaeological artifacts and art. Upstairs there are three mummies and a full-scale fiberglass *chullpa* (funerary tower).

Coca Museum MUSEUM
(📞36-5087; Deza 301; admission S5; ☺9am-1pm & 3-8pm) Tiny and quirky, this museum offers lots of interesting information – historical, medicinal, cultural – about the coca plant and its many uses. Presentation isn't that interesting, though: reams of text (in English only) are stuck to the wall and interspersed with photographs and old Coca-Cola ads. The display of traditional costumes is what makes a visit to this museum worthwhile.

Though the relation between traditional dress and coca is unfathomable, it's a boon for making sense of the costumes worn in street parades.

☞ Tours

It pays to shop around for a tour operator. Agencies abound and competition is fierce, leading to touting in streets and bus terminals, undeliverable promises, and prices so low as to undercut fair wages. Several of the cheaper tour agencies have reputations for ripping off the islanders of Amantaní and Taquile, with whom travelers stay overnight, and whose living culture is one of the main selling points of these tours.

Island-hopping tours, even with the better agencies, are often disappointing: formulaic, lifeless and inflexible, the inevitable result of sheer numbers and repetition. Seeing the islands independently is recommended – you can wander around freely and spend longer in the places you like.

Puno

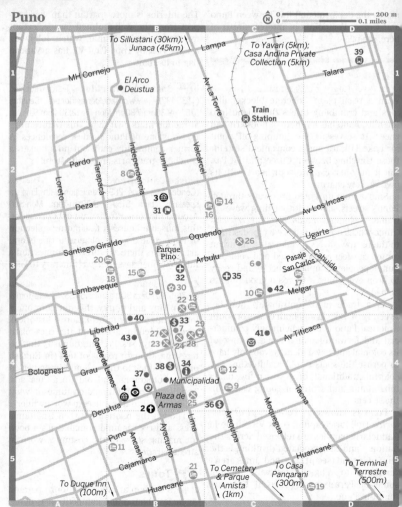

To Sillustani (30km);
Junaca (45km)

Lampa

To Yavari (5km);
Casa Andina Private
Collection (5km)

MH Cornejo

El Arco
Deustua

Train
Station

Pardo

Tarapacá

Independencia

Junín

Valcárcel

Av La Torre

Ilo

Loreto

Deza

3

31

14

16

Av Los Incas

Santiago Giraldo

Oquendo

Arbulu

26

Ugarte

Cahuide

20

18

15

Parque
Pino

32

6

Pasaje
San Carlos

17

Av Los Incas

Lambayeque

5

35

22 **13**

10 **42** Melgar

Libertad

40

33

7

29

27

43

23

24 **28**

41

Av Titicaca

Conde de Lemos

Illave

Grau

37

38 **34**

12

9

Municipalidad

Bolognesi

4 **1**

Deustua

2

Plaza de
Armas

25

36

Tacna

Arequipa

Moquegua

Puno

Ancash

Ayacucho

Lima

11

Cajamarca

21

To Cemetery
& Parque
Amista
(1km)

To Casa
Panqarani
(300m)

Huancané

19

To Terminal
Terrestre
(500m)

Huancané

To Duque Inn
(100m)

LAKE TITICACA PUNO

The following agencies offer responsible tours of the region:

All Ways Travel   TOURS
(☑35-3979; www.titicacaperu.com; Deustua 576, 2nd fl) Offers both classic and 'non-touristy' tours.

Edgar Adventures   TOURS
(☑35-3444; www.edgaradventures.com; Lima 328) Longtime agency with positive community involvement.

Las Balsas Tours   TOURS
(☑36-4362; www.balsastours.com; Tacna 240) Offers classic tours on a daily basis.

Nayra Travel   TOURS
(☑36-4774, 975-1818; www.nayratravel.com; Lima 419, Office 105) Local package tour operator.

✦ Festivals & Events

No list of regional holidays and fiestas could ever be exhaustive. Most are celebrated for several days before and after the actual day. All of these festivals feature traditional music and dancing, as well as merry mayhem of all sorts.

La Virgen de la Candelaria   FESTIVAL
The region's most spectacular festival spreads out for several days around the actual date

Puno

⊙ **Sights**
1 Casa del Corregidor B4
2 Catedral de Puno B4
3 Coca Museum B2
4 Museo Carlos Dreyer B4

🌀 **Activities, Courses & Tours**
All Ways Travel ....(see 1)
5 Edgar Adventures B3
6 Las Balsas Tours C3
7 Nayra Travel B4

🛏 **Sleeping**
8 Casa Andina Classic..........................B2
9 Casona Plaza Hotel C4
10 Colón Inn C3
11 Conde de Lemos Inn B5
12 Hostal La Hacienda C4
13 Hostal Pukara...................................B3
14 Hostal Uros......................................C2
15 Hotel El Buho....................................B3
16 Hotel Italia C2
17 Inka's Rest C3
18 Intiqa Hotel B3
19 Mosoq Inn..D5
20 Posada Don Giorgio B3
21 San Antonio Suites............................B5

🍴 **Eating**
22 Balcones de Puno B3
23 Café Tunki B4
Colors ....(see 5)

IncAbar..(see 5)
24 La Casona B4
25 Mojsa B4
26 Supermercado Central C3
27 Tulipans...B4
28 Ukuku's B4

🍷 **Drinking**
29 Kamizaraky Rock Pub.........................B4

🎭 **Entertainment**
30 Ekeko's B3

ℹ **Information**
31 Bolivian Consulate B2
32 Botica Fasa B3
33 Interbank..B4
34 iPerú B4
35 Medicentro Tourist's Health
Clinic C3
36 Moneygram.......................................C4
37 Oficina de Migraciónes B4
38 Scotiabank.......................................B4

ℹ **Transport**
39 Capachica Bus Stop D1
40 Crillon Tours B4
41 Inka Express.....................................C4
42 LAN C3
Star Peru ....(see 23)
43 Transturin B4

LAKE TITICACA PUNO

(February 2), depending upon which day of the week Candlemas falls. If it falls between Sunday and Tuesday, things get under way the previous Saturday; if Candlemas occurs between Wednesday and Friday, celebrations will get going the following Saturday.

Puno Week FESTIVAL
A huge celebration marking the legendary birth of Manco Cápac, the first Inca. Events are held the first week of November, centered on Puno Day (November 5).

Epiphany FESTIVAL
Held on January 6.

Fiesta de San Juan FESTIVAL
The Feast of St John the Baptist is held on March 8.

Alacitas FESTIVAL
With the blessing of miniature objects, such as cars or houses, supplicants pray that the

real thing will be obtained in the coming year. Features a miniature handicrafts fair in Puno on May 2.

Las Cruces FESTIVAL
Held from May 3 to 4, with celebrations on Isla Taquile and in Huancané.

Feast of St James FESTIVAL
Celebrated mostly on Isla Taquile on July 25.

Our Lady of Mercy FESTIVAL
Held on September 24.

🛏 Sleeping

TOP CHOICE **Casa Panq'arani** B&B $$
(☎36-4892, 951-677-005; www.casapanqarani. com; Jirón Arequipa 1086; s/tw/d incl breakfast S70/120/130; ☎) A delightful find, this traditional Puno home has a flower-filled courtyard and inviting rooms lining a second-floor balcony. But the real draw is the

FIESTAS & FOLKLORE AROUND LAKE TITICACA

The folkloric capital of Peru, Puno boasts as many as 300 traditional dances and celebrates numerous fiestas throughout the year. Although dances often occur during celebrations of Catholic feast days, many have their roots in precolonial celebrations usually tied in with the agricultural calendar. The dazzlingly ornate and imaginative costumes worn on these occasions are often worth more than an entire household's everyday clothes. Styles range from strikingly grotesque masks and animal costumes to glittering sequined uniforms.

Accompanying music uses a host of instruments, from Spanish-influenced brass and string instruments to percussion and wind instruments that have changed little since Inca times. These traditional instruments include *tinyas* (wooden hand drums) and *wankaras* (larger drums formerly used in battle), plus a chorus of *zampoñas* (panpipes), which range from tiny, high-pitched instruments to huge bass panpipes almost as tall as the musician. Keep an eye out for *flautas* (flutes): from simple bamboo penny-whistles called *quenas* to large blocks of hollowed out wood. The most esoteric is the *piruru*, which is traditionally carved from the wing bone of an Andean condor.

Seeing street fiestas can be planned, but it's often simply a matter of luck. Some celebrations are localized to one town, but with others the whole region lets loose. Ask at the tourist office in Puno about any fiestas in the surrounding area while you're in town. The festivals listed here are particularly important in the Lake Titicaca region, but many countrywide fiestas are celebrated here, too.

If you plan to visit during a festival, either make reservations in advance or show up a few days early, and expect to pay premium rates for lodgings.

---

sincere hospitality of owners Edgar and Consuelo. Rooms are ample, with comfortable beds with crocheted bedspreads and fresh flowers. There are ample sunny spots for lounging. Don't miss the opportunity to try Consuelo's gourmet altiplano cooking (meals S30 with advance request).

Casa Andina Private Collection
LUXURY HOTEL $$$

(☏213-9739; www.casa-andina.com; Av Sesqui Centenario 1970; d incl breakfast from US$446; @🛜) On the outskirts of Puno, with lovely lakeside ambience, the exclusive version of this upscale chain features 46 rooms, gardens and a gourmet restaurant. It even has its own train stop for those coming from Cuzco. The look is rustic chic. Rooms feature impeccable white linens and subtle decor, some with chimneys and all with oxygen to help acclimatize. Credit cards accepted.

Colón Inn
HOTEL $$

(☏35-1432; www.coloninn.com; Tacna 290; s/d/tr incl breakfast S150/180/225; @🛜) An elegant European-owned *casona* with helpful staff, part of its charm is the Republican-era building, decorated with Cuzco-school paintings, frescos and a covered courtyard. The onsite restaurant specializes in Belgian and French cuisine; reservations are recommended. Rooms are smallish but with all amenities, while shared spaces are sumptuously colonial.

Casa Andina Classic
HOTEL $$$

(☏213-9739; www.casa-andina.com; Jirón Independencia 143; d incl breakfast S258; @🛜) The classic version of this fashionable Peruvian chain features snappy service and 50 tasteful rooms with muted colors, decorated with Andean folk motifs. Rooms feature heat, lockboxes, blackout curtains and flat-screen TVs. Guests also get free oxygen and *mate* to help acclimate. A cozy dining space serves pizzas and soups post-excursion. Credit cards accepted.

Mosoq Inn
HOTEL $$

(☏36-7518; www.mosoqinn.com; Jr Moquegua 673; s/d/tr incl breakfast S106/133/1/2; @🛜) Recommended, this modern hotel features 15 rooms distributed in three stories. High-quality mattresses ensure sound sleeping in ample, tangerine-hued rooms. There are also big closets, cable TV and space heaters, in addition to a business center.

Hotel Italia
HOTEL $$

(☏36-7706; www.hotelitaliaperu.com; Valcárcel 122; s/d/tr S110/150/190; @🛜) Snug rooms have parquet floors, cable TV, hot showers and heating but vary in quality at this large, well-established spot. The long-serving staff is efficient, and the delicious buffet breakfast includes salty black olives and Puno's own triangular anise bread. Credit cards are accepted.

Intiqa Hotel   HOTEL **$$**
(☏36-6900; www.intiqahotel.com; Tarapacá 272; s/d incl breakfast S159/186; @☏) Finally, a midrange Puno hotel with a sense of style. The 33 large, heated rooms feature snug duvets and earth tones, extra pillows, desks, flat-screen TVs and a safe box. The elevator is somewhat of a rarity in Puno. With free pickups from the *terminal terrestre*. Credit cards accepted.

Hostal Pukara   HOTEL **$$**
(☏78-4240/28; www.pukaradeltitikaka.com; Libertad 328; s/d S75/120; @☏) Bright and cheery, Pukara leaves no corner undecorated, with an eye-catching four-story relief, murals and other touches. Rooms all have cable TV, phones, heating and are soundproofed. There's a glass-covered rooftop cafe with a great view.

Casona Plaza Hotel   HOTEL **$$**
(☏36-5614; www.casonaplazahotel.com; Arequipa 655; s/d incl breakfast S212/239; @☏) This well-run, central hotel with 64 rooms is one of the largest in Puno, but is often full. All rooms are good and bathrooms are great, but this one is especially for lovers – most of the *matrimoniales* (matrimonial suites) are big enough to dance the *marinera* (Peru's national dance) between the bed and the lounge suite.

Inka's Rest   HOSTEL **$**
(☏36-8720; www.inkasresthostel.com; Pasaje San Carlos 158; dm/d incl breakfast S24/60; @☏) Tucked into a small alley, this hostel earns high marks for service. Very clean, it features bunks with down duvets, attractive old tile and parquet floors. There's a cute breakfast area as well as a guest kitchen and room with a huge flat screen, among other shared spaces. Privates are less attractive. Take a taxi if arriving at night.

Duque Inn   HOTEL **$**
(☏20-5014; Ayaviri 152; r per person with/without bathroom S20/15) Cordial but kooky, this budget lodging is spruced up with satin bedspreads and chandeliers. Archaeologist owner Ricardo Conde is eccentric gold, offering free tours. All in all, it's a steal for budget

travelers and serious trekkers. If you're not up for splurging on taxis, consider the long haul up an endless hill to get here.

To find it, continue along Ilave for three blocks beyond Huancané and then turn right into Ayaviri.

Hostal La Hacienda   HOTEL **$$$**
(☏35-6109; www.lahaciendapuno.com; Deustua 297; d/tr S239/292; @☏) This colonial-style hotel has lovely, airy common spaces, a mind-bending *Vertigo*-style spiral staircase, and a 6th-floor dining room with panoramic views. After all that, rooms are a bit generic, but they're warm and comfortable with cable TV and phones. Some have bathtubs.

Hostal Uros   HOTEL **$**
(☏35-2141; www.hostaluros.com; Valcárcel 135; s/d/tr incl breakfast S30/50/75; @☏) Serene but close to the action, this friendly, good-value hostel has its best rooms on the upper floors. The roomy light-filled patio can store bicycles or motorbikes. Ask for a room with a window. If you're counting pennies, those with shared bathroom are S5 cheaper per person.

San Antonio Suites   HOTEL **$$**
(☏35-1767; www.sanantoniosuitespuno.com; Huancané 430; s/d/tr incl breakfast S66/93/119; @☏) This very accommodating budget hotel is praised by guests, though on the surface it's your average hotel, with a plastic runner on the stairs and so-so rooms with cable TV, phones and heat.

Hotel El Buho   HOTEL **$$**
(☏36-6122; Lambayeque 142; www.hotelbuho.com; s/d incl breakfast S98/172; @☏) This quiet hotel features nice (but somewhat dull) rooms with paneled walls and carpets. The staff is helpful and there's a tour agency on-site.

Posada Don Giorgio   HOTEL **$$**
(☏36-3648; dongiorgio@titicacalake.com; Tarapacá 238; s/d/tr S90/155/180; @☏) A mellow spot with a barrage of cultures and exceptionally comfy rooms, Don Giorgio offers super-clean standard rooms. It's small enough to provide personal service, and rooms have phones, cable TV and deep armchairs.

Conde de Lemos Inn   HOTEL **$$**
(☏36-9898; www.condelemosinn.com; Puno 675-681; s/d incl breakfast S122/159; @☏) Housed in a startlingly jagged, glass-fronted ziggurat on the Plaza de Armas, this small hotel has been recommended by many travelers for its

SWEET STEAMSHIP DREAMS

The oldest steamship on Lake Titicaca, the famed Yavari (☑36-9329; www.yavari.org; museum admission by donation; ☺8am-1pm, 3-5:30pm; B&B per person incl breakfast S99) has turned from British gunship to a museum and recommended bed & breakfast, with bunk-bed lodging and attentive service under the stewardship of its captain. And no, you don't have to be a navy buff reflecting on Titicaca. It's probably the most tranquil spot in Puno.

Its passage here was not easy. In 1862 the Yavari and its sister ship, the Yapura, were built in Birmingham and shipped as parts around Cape Horn to Arica (now northern Chile), moved by train to Tacna, and finally hauled by mule over the Andes to Puno. The incredible undertaking took six years.

After its assembly, the Yavari was launched on Christmas Day 1870. The Yapura was later renamed the BAP Puno and became a Peruvian Navy medical ship; it can still be seen in Puno. Both had coal-powered steam engines, but due to a shortage of coal, they were fuelled with dried llama dung.

After long years of service, the ship was decommissioned by the Peruvian Navy and the hull was left to rust on the lakeshore. In 1982, Englishwoman Meriel Larken visited the forgotten boat and decided to attempt to save this piece of Peruvian history. The Yavari Project was formed to buy and restore the vessel.

The Yavari is moored behind the Sonesta Posada Hotel del Inca, about 5km from the center of Puno. Its devoted crew happily gives guided tours. With prior notice, enthusiasts may even be able to see the engine fired up. Now with a restored engine, the Yavari motors across the lake seven times a year – though you will have to find out for yourself if it's still powered on llama dung.

personable staff and high standards. Ask for a corner room with balcony.

✖ Eating

Mojsa
TOP CHOICE   PERUVIAN $$

(☑36-3182; Lima 394; mains S18-35; ☺8am-10pm) The go-to place for locals and travelers alike, Mojsa lives up to its name, Aymara for 'delicious.' It has a thoughtful range of Peruvian and international food, including innovative trout dishes and a design-your-own salad option. All meals start with fresh bread and a bowl of local olives. In the evening, crisp brick-oven pizzas are on offer.

La Casona
PERUVIAN $$

(☑]35 1108; http://lacasona-restaurant.com; Lima 423, second fl; mains S12-36) Another solid choice, with upscale *criollo* and international food and portions on the small side. Trout comes bathed in garlic or chili sauce. There's also pasta, salad and soup.

Tulipans
PIZZERIA $$

(☑35-1796; Lima 394; mains S12-22) Highly recommended for its yummy sandwiches, big plates of meat and high-piled vegetables, this cozy spot is warmed by the pizza oven in the corner. It also has a selection of South American wines. The courtyard patio is attractive for warm days – whenever those happen! Pizzas are only available at night.

Café Tunki
CAFE $

(Lima 394; ☺10am-7pm Mon-Sat) This closet-sized cafe serves hot cups of coffee, brewed with acclaimed beans from the tropical side of Puno province and available for purchase by the kilo.

Balcones de Puno
PERUVIAN $$

(☑36-5300; Libertad 354; mains S14-32) Dinner-show venue with traditional local food. The nightly show (7:30pm to 9pm) stands out for its quality and sincerity – no panpipe butchering of *El Cóndor Pasa* here. Save room for dessert, a major focus of dining here. Reserve ahead.

Ukuku's
PERUVIAN $$

(Grau 172, 2nd fl; mains from S20) Crowds of travelers and locals thaw out in this toasty restaurant, which dishes up good local and Andean food (try alpaca steak with baked apples, or the quinoa omelet), as well as pizzas, pastas, Asian-style vegetarian fare and espresso drinks.

IncAbar
CAFE $$

(☑36-8031; Lima 348; mains S30; ☺8:30am-10pm; 🔊) A hipster restaurant fashioned as a gringo magnet. Light breakfasts, curries, veggie stir-fries and pastas are clearly geared to what you're craving, but you won't see one local eating here. There's also a drink menu and happy hour.

Colors   FUSION $$
(📞36-9254; Lima 342; mains S16-28; ⊗7am-11pm; 📶) A couch cafe with free wireless, Colors also caters to travelers with its slick look and fusion food. The menu is so extensive it's hard to root out the specialties, and the staff may not be much help.

Many restaurants don't advertise their *menús* (set meals), which are cheaper than ordering à la carte. Locals eat *pollo a la brasa* (roast chicken) and economical *menús* on Jirón Tacna between Calles Deustua and Libertad.

For a cheap snack, try *api* (hot, sweet corn juice) – a serious comfort food found in several places on Calle Oquendo between Parque Pino and the supermercado. Order it with a paper-thin, wickedly delicious envelope of deep-fried dough.

If you're feeling MSG-deprived, head to Calle Arbulú to fill up at a cheap and cheerful *chifa* (Chinese restaurant). For self-catering, head to Supermercado Central (Oquendo s/n; ⊗8am-10pm), but be wary of pickpockets.

🍷 Drinking

Central Puno's nightlife is geared toward tourists, with lively bars scattered around the bright lights on Jirón Lima (where touts hand out free-drink coupons) and next to the plaza on Jirón Puno.

Kamizaraky Rock Pub   PUB
(Grau 158) With a classic-rock soundtrack, unbelievably cool bartenders and liquor-infused coffee drinks essential for staying warm during Puno's bone-chilling nights, it may be a hard place to leave.

☆ Entertainment

Ekeko's   CLUB
(Lima 355, 2nd fl) Travelers and locals alike gravitate to this tiny, ultraviolet dance floor splashed with psychedelic murals. It moves to a thumping mixture of modern beats and old favorites, from salsa to techno trance, which can be heard several blocks away.

🛍 Shopping

Artesanías (handicrafts, from musical instruments and jewelry to scale models of reed islands), wool and alpaca sweaters, and other typical tourist goods are sold in every second shop in the town center. For household goods and clothes, head to Mercado Bellavista (Av El Sol) and watch out for pickpockets.

ℹ Information

Dangers & Annoyances

There are scenic lookouts on the hills above town, but as assaults and robberies have been reported (even by groups), it's not recommended to visit them unless there is a drastic improvement in security.

Emergency

Policía de Turismo (Tourist Police; 📞35-3988; Deustua 558; ⊗24hr) There is also a police officer on duty in the *terminal terrestre* (24 hours) – ask around if you need assistance.

Immigration

Bolivian Consulate (📞35-1251; Arequipa 136, 2nd fl; ⊗8am-2pm Mon-Fri)

Oficina de Migraciónes (Immigration Office; 📞35-7103; Ayacucho 270-280; ⊗8am-1pm & 2-4:15pm Mon-Fri) May help with student and business visas; doesn't give tourist-card extensions.

Medical Services

Botica Fasa (📞36-6862; Arequipa 314; ⊗24hr) A well-stocked pharmacy that's

LAKE TITICACA PUNO

🛈 STAYING HEALTHY AT ALTITUDE

Ascend to nearly 4000 meters direct from the coast and you run a real risk of getting *soroche* (altitude sickness; see p552). Plan on spending some time in elevation stops like Arequipa (2350m) or Cuzco (3326m) first to acclimatize, or take it very easy after arriving in Puno. Higher-end hotels (and even some buses) offer oxygen, but this is a temporary fix; your body still needs to acclimatize at its own pace.

High altitude makes for extreme weather conditions. Nights get especially cold, so check if your hotel provides heating. During the winter months of June to August (the tourist high season), temperatures can drop well below freezing. Meanwhile, days are very hot and sunburn is a common problem.

attended 24 hours, though you may have to pound on the door late at night.

Medicentro Tourist's Health Clinic (☑36-5909, 951-62-0937; Moquegua 191; ☺24hr) English & French spoken; will also come to your hotel.

Money

Bolivianos can be exchanged in Puno or at the border. You'll find an ATM inside the *terminal terrestre* that accepts most bank cards and dispenses US dollars and soles. **Scotiabank** (Jirón Lima 458), **Interbank** (Lima at Libertad) and **Banco Continental** (Lima at Grau) all have branches and ATMs on Jirón Lima; there's another Banco Continental at Libertad. There's a Moneygram branch on Jirón Puno, just down from the Plaza.

Post

Serpost (Moquegua 267; ☺8am-8pm Mon-Sat)

Tourist Information

iPerú (☑36-5088; Plaza de Armas, cnr Lima & Deustua; ☺9am-6pm Mon-Sat, 9am-1pm Sun) Puno's helpful and well-informed tourist office; also runs Indecopi, the tourist-protection agency, which registers complaints about travel agencies and hotels.

 Getting There & Away

Air

The nearest airport is in Juliaca, about an hour away. See p169 for more information on flights. Hotels can book you a shuttle bus for around S15. Airlines with offices in Puno include **LAN** (☑36-7227; Tacna 299) and **Star Perú** (Lima 154).

Boat

There are no passenger ferries across the lake from Puno to Bolivia, but you can get to La Paz via the lake in one or two days on high-class tours that visit Isla del Sol and other sites along the way. **Transturin** (☑35-2771; www.transturin.com; Ayacucho 148; 2-day tour US$241) has a bus/catamaran/bus combination, departing at 6:30am from Puno and arriving in La Paz at 7:30pm, or the following day at noon, with an overnight onboard. From Puno, **Crillon Tours** (☑35-2771; www.titicaca.com; Ayacucho 148) also visits Isla del Sol (p190) on the way to La Paz using hydrofoil boats. In total it's a 13-hour trip. Leon Tours is their Puno operator.

Bus

The **terminal terrestre** (☑36-4737; Primero de Mayo 703), three blocks down Ricardo Palma from Av El Sol, houses Puno's long-distance bus companies. The terminal has an ATM and charges a departure tax of S1.

Buses leave for Cuzco every hour from 4am to 10pm, and for Arequipa every hour from 2am to 10pm. **Ormeño** (☑36-8176; www.grupo-ormeno.com.pe) is the safest, with the newest, fastest buses. **Cruz del Sur** (☑in Lima 01-311-5050; www.cruzdelsur.com.pe) has service to Arequipa. **Civa** (☑365-882; www.civa.com.pe) goes to Lima. **Tour Peru** (☑35-2991; www.tourperu.com.pe) goes to Cuzco and also crosses to La Paz, Bolivia, via Copacabana, daily at 7:30am.

The most enjoyable way to get to Cuzco is via **Inka Express** (☑36-5654; www.inkaexpress.com; Tacna 346), whose luxury buses with panoramic windows depart every morning at 8am. Buffet lunch is included, along with an English-speaking tour guide and oxygen. The sites briefly visited en route include Andahuaylillas, Raqchi, Abra la Raya and Pucará. The trip takes about eight hours and costs S143 from Inka Express.

Local *combis* to Chuquito, Juli, Pomata and the Bolivian border leave from **terminal zonál** (Simón Bolívar s/n), a few blocks northwest of *terminal terrestre*. Head out along Av El Sol until you see the hospital on your right, then turn left and you'll hit the *terminal zonál* (regional terminal) after two long blocks.

To get to Capachica (1¼ hours, S4), catch a *combi* from Jirón Talara, just off El Sol opposite the Mercado Bellavista. They leave once an hour from about 6am to 2pm. *Combis* to Luquina leave from opposite the Brahma Beer distributor on Manchero Rossi, about 1.5km south of town, every hour or so in the morning.

Train

The train ride from Puno to Cuzco retains a certain renown from the days – now long gone – when the road wasn't paved and the bus journey was a nightmare. Train fares have skyrocketed in recent years and most travelers now take the bus. The fancy Andean Explorer train, which includes a glass-walled observation car and complimentary lunch, costs US$150; there's no cheaper option. This one's for train buffs, since it's only marginally more comfortable than the better buses, and the tracks run next to the road for much of the way, so the scenery is comparable to a much cheaper bus ride.

Trains depart from Puno's **train station** (☑36-9179; www.perurail.com; Av La Torre 224; ☺7am-12pm & 3-6pm Mon-Fri, 7am-3pm Sat) at 8am, arriving at Cuzco around 6pm. Services run on Monday, Wednesday and Saturday from November to March, with an extra departure on Friday from April to October. Tickets can be purchased online.

 Getting Around

A short taxi ride anywhere in town (and as far as the transport terminals) costs S4. *Mototaxis* are

PUNO BUSES

DESTINATION	COST* (SOLES)	DURATION (HRS)
Arequipa	56/72	5
Cuzco	20/40	6-7
Juliaca	3.50	1
Lima	140/170	18-21
Copacabana, Bolivia	25	3-4
La Paz, Bolivia	30	6

* Prices are general estimates for normal/luxury buses

a bit cheaper at S2, and *triciclos* cheapest of all at S1.50 – but it's an uphill ride, so you may find yourself wanting to tip the driver more than the cost of the fare!

Around Puno

SILLUSTANI

Sitting on rolling hills on the Lake Umayo peninsula, the funerary towers of **Sillustani** (admission S10; ⊙8am-5pm) stand out for miles against the desolate altiplano landscape.

The ancient Colla people who once dominated the Lake Titicaca area were a warlike, Aymara-speaking tribe, who later became the southeastern group of the Incas. They buried their nobility in *chullpas* (funerary towers), which can be seen scattered widely around the hilltops of the region.

The most impressive of these towers are at Sillustani, where the tallest reaches a height of 12m. The cylindrical structures housed the remains of complete family groups, along with plenty of food and belongings for their journey into the next world. Their only opening was a small hole facing east, just large enough for a person to crawl through, which would be sealed immediately after a burial. Nowadays, nothing remains of the burials, but the *chullpas* are well preserved. The afternoon light is the best for photography, though the site can get busy at this time.

The walls of the towers are made from massive coursed blocks reminiscent of Inca stonework, but are considered to be even more complicated. Carved but unplaced blocks and a ramp used to raise them are among the site's points of interest, and you can also see the makeshift quarry. A few of the blocks are decorated, including a well-known carving of a lizard on one of the *chullpas* closest to the parking lot.

Sillustani is partially encircled by the sparkling Lago Umayo (3890m), which is home to a wide variety of plants and Andean water birds, plus a small island with vicuñas (threatened, wild relatives of llamas). Birders take note: this is one of the best sites in the area.

Tours to Sillustani leave Puno at around 2:30pm daily and cost from S35. The round-trip takes about 3½ hours and allows you about 1½ hours at the ruins. If you'd prefer more time at the site, hire a private taxi for S70 with one hour waiting time. To save money, catch any bus to Juliaca and ask to be let off where the road splits (S3, 25 minutes). From there, occasional *combis* (S2, 20 minutes) go to the ruins.

For longer stays, **Atun Colla** (📞365-808, 951-50-2390; www.turismoatuncolla.com) offers *turismo vivencia* (homestays). You can help your host family with farming, hike to lookouts and lesser-known archaeological sites, visit the tiny museum and eat dirt – this area is known for its edible *arcilla* (clay). Served up as a sauce on boiled potato, it goes down surprisingly well.

CUTIMBO

Just over 20km from Puno, this dramatic **site** (admission S6; ⊙8am-5pm) has an extraordinary position atop a table-topped volcanic hill surrounded by a fertile plain. Its modest number of well-preserved *chullpas,* built by the Colla, Lupaca and Inca cultures, come in both square and cylindrical shapes. You can still see the ramps used to build them. Look closely to find several monkeys, pumas and snakes carved into the structures.

This remote place receives few visitors, which makes it both enticing and

BORDER CROSSING: BOLIVIA

There are two viable routes from Puno to Bolivia. The north-shore route is very much off the beaten track and rarely used. There are two ways to go via the south shore: through either Yunguyo or Desaguadero. The only reason to go via Desaguadero is if you're pressed for time. The Yunguyo route is safer, prettier and far more popular; it passes through the chilled-out Bolivian lakeshore town of Copacabana, from where Isla del Sol – arguably the most significant site in Andean mythology – can be visited.

US citizens have to pay US$135 cash in US dollars for a tourist visa to enter Bolivia. This can be done at the border. Also, there's a Bolivian consulate in Puno (p177).

Note that Peruvian time is one hour behind Bolivian time, and Bolivian border agents often charge an unofficial B$30 (collaboration fee) to use the border. Always keep your backpack with you when crossing the border.

Via Yunguyo toward Copacabana

There are two ways to do this.

The quickest and easiest way is with a cross-border bus company such as Perú Tour or **Ormeño** (☑36-8176; www.grupo-ormeno.com.pe). Purchase tickets at the terminal at least one day in advance. The service stops at a *casa de cambio* (exchange bureau) at the border and waits for passengers to check through before continuing to Copacabana (S25, three to four hours). Here, another bus that's waiting can take you straight to La Paz (B$30, 3½ hours).

The other alternative is catching local transport – *micros* – from the *terminal zonál*. This slow method of transport is only recommended if you want to stop at some or all of the south-shore towns (see p186). Leave early (as early as 8am) to allow enough time. Between towns, *micros* are regular, especially on Sunday, the market day in both Juli and Yunguyo. It's a great way to get off the beaten track and rub shoulders with locals.

Yunguyo is the end of the line. Catch a *triciclo* to Kasani or cross on foot – it's a pleasant 2km along Av Ejército. The *casas de cambio* here offer a better exchange rate than their Bolivian counterparts.

First visit the Peruvian police, followed by Control Migratorio (Immigration Office) on the left. Walk to the arch and the 'Welcome to Bolivia' sign for Bolivian immigration services.

A *combi* to Copacabana is B$3. *Combis* leave more frequently on Sunday; on weekdays you may have to wait up to an hour. If you are inclined to walk the 8km, it's a straightforward stroll around the lake.

The border is open from 7:30am until 6pm, Peruvian time.

Via Desaguadero toward La Paz

If you're going straight from Puno to La Paz, unsavory Desaguadero is faster, slightly cheaper and more direct than Yunguyo. It's also less scenic and less safe. Avoid spending the night in Desaguadero.

Combis leave Puno's *terminal zonal* for Desaguadero (S8, 2½ hours) throughout the day.

In Desaguadero, visit the Peruvian Dirección General de Migraciones y Naturalización to get stamped out of Peru. Then head to the building that says 'Migraciones Desaguadero,' to the left of the bridge, to complete Bolivian formalities.

Catch a *triciclo* to the Bolivian-side transport terminal, from where you can get to La Paz in 3½ hours either by *combi* or *colectivo* (shared transportation; B$30).

The border is open from 8:30am to 8:30pm Bolivian time.

Note: the Peruvian police have a bad reputation here, sometimes demanding a non-existent 'exit tax.' You are not required to visit the Peruvian police station before leaving the country, so if anyone asks you to accompany them there, politely but firmly refuse. There are no ATMs in Desaguadero, so bring cash from Puno if your nationality requires a tourist visa.

potentially dangerous for independent travelers, especially women. Go in a group and keep an eye out for muggers. People are known to hide behind rocks at the top of the 2km trail that leads steeply uphill from the road.

Combis en route to Laraqueri leave the cemetery by Parque Amista, 1km from the center of Puno (S3, one hour). You can't miss the signposted site, which is on the left-hand side of the road – just ask the driver where to get off. The high cost of a taxi (approximately S30 one way) may make a taking package tour (S94) from Puno worth it.

Lake Titicaca Islands

Lake Titicaca's islands are world famous for their peaceful beauty and the living tradition of their agrarian cultures, which date to pre-Columbian times. A homestay here offers a privileged glimpse of another way of life.

Be aware that not all islanders welcome tourism, which only stands to reason since not all benefit from tourism and may see the frequent intrusions into their daily life as disruptive. It's important to respect the privacy of islanders and show courtesy. See the boxed text (p183) for more tips about responsible tourism on Lake Titicaca's islands.

All travel agencies in Puno offer one- and two-day tours to Uros, Taquile and Amantaní. Travelers often complain that the guided island-hopping tours offer only a superficial view of the islands and their cultures. For more insight into the culture, it's recommended to travel independently if you have the time. All ferry tickets are valid for 15 days, so you can island-hop at will.

ISLAS UROS

Just 7km east of Puno, these unique **floating islands** (admission S5) are Lake Titicaca's top attraction. Their uniqueness is due to their construction. They have been created from nothing; built entirely with the buoyant *totora* reeds that grow abundantly in the shallows of the lake. The lives of the Uros people are interwoven with these reeds. Partially edible (tasting like hearts of palm), the reeds are also used to build homes, boats and crafts. The islands are constructed from many layers of the *totora*, which are constantly replenished from the top as they rot from the bottom, so the ground is always soft and springy.

Some islands also have elaborately designed versions of traditional tightly bundled reed boats on hand and other whimsical reed creations, like archways and even swing sets. Be prepared to pay for a boat ride or to take photographs.

Intermarriage with the Aymara-speaking indigenous people has seen the demise of the pure-blooded Uros, who nowadays all speak Aymara. Always a small tribe, the Uros began their unusual floating existence centuries ago in an effort to isolate themselves from the aggressive Collas and Incas.

The popularity of the islands has led to aggressive commercialization in some cases. The most traditional reed islands are located further from Puno through a maze of small channels, only visited by private boat. Islanders there continue to live in a relatively traditional fashion and prefer not to be photographed.

Getting to the Uros is easy – there's no need to go with an organized tour. Ferries leave from the port for Uros (return trip S12) at least once an hour from 6am to 4pm. The community-owned ferry service visits two islands, on a rotation basis. Ferries to Taquile and Amantaní can also drop you off in the Uros.

An outstanding option is staying in the reed huts of Isla Khantati with boundless personality Cristina Suaña (☎951-69-5121,

---

ⓘ BOAT TRAVEL ON LAGO TITICACA

Water transport experiences on Titicaca are sometimes endurance events, so inquire ahead about the boat you will be taking, and bring warm layers to stay out on deck. Three types of boats ply these waters. High-speed boats (*veloz*) take large groups of 30 to 40 people. *Lancha rápida*, the most common option, is slightly slower. The slowest form of travel are *embarcaciones artesenales*, which take twice as long as the speed boats. Ferries sometimes have truck motors and carry a lot of cargo – guaranteeing a slow ride. It's common to get woozy or sea sick on boats that have in-cabin motors which produce odor, particularly if you're confined in-cabin because of the cold or high seas.

951-47-2355; uroskhantati@hotmail.com; per person full board S165), an Uros native whose entrepreneurship earned her international accolades. Over a number of years, her family have built a number of impeccable semi-traditional huts (with solar power and outhouses) that occupy half the tiny island, along with shady decks, cats and the occasional flamingo. The rates include transfers from Puno, fresh and varied meals, fishing, some cultural explanations, and the pleasure of the company of the effervescent Cristina. The hyper-relaxed pace means a visit here is not ideal for those with little time on their hands.

ISLA TAQUILE

Inhabited for thousands of years, Taquile Island (admission S5), 35km east of Puno, is a tiny 7-sq-km island with a population of about 2200 people. Taquile's lovely scenery is reminiscent of the Mediterranean. In the strong island sunlight, the deep, red-colored soil contrasts with the intense blue of the lake and the glistening backdrop of Bolivia's snowy Cordillera Real on the far side of the lake. Several hills boast Inca terracing on their sides and small ruins on top.

The natural beauty of the island makes it stand out. Quechua-speaking islanders are distinct from most of the surrounding Aymara-speaking island communities and maintain a strong sense of group identity. They rarely marry non-Taquile people.

Taquile has a fascinating tradition of handicrafts, and the islanders' creations are made according to a system of deeply ingrained social customs. Men wear tightly woven woolen hats that resemble floppy nightcaps, which they knit themselves. These hats are closely bound up with social symbolism: men wear red hats if they are married and red and white hats if they are single, and different colors can denote a man's current or past social position.

Taquile women weave thick, colorful waistbands for their husbands, which are worn with roughly spun white shirts and thick, calf-length black pants. Women wear eye-catching outfits comprising multi-layered skirts and delicately embroidered blouses. These fine garments are considered some of the most well-made traditional clothes in Peru, and can be bought in the cooperative store on the island's main plaza.

Make sure you already have lots of small bills in local currency, because change is limited and there's nowhere to exchange dollars. You may want to bring extra money to buy some of the exquisite crafts sold in the cooperative store. A limited electricity supply was introduced to the island in the 1990s but it is not always available, so remember to bring a flashlight for an overnight stay.

● Sights & Activities

Visitors are free to wander around, explore the ruins and enjoy the tranquility. The island is a wonderful place to catch a sunset and gaze at the moon, which looks twice as bright in the crystalline air, rising over the breathtaking peaks of the Cordillera Real. Take in the lay of the land while it's still light – with no roads, streetlights or big buildings to use as landmarks, travelers have been known to get so lost in the dark that they end up roughing it for the night.

A stairway of more than 500 steps leads from the dock to the center of the island. The climb takes a breathless 20 minutes if you're acclimatized – more if you're not.

✯✯ Festivals & Events

The Fiesta de San Diego (Feast of St James; July 25) is a big feast day on Taquile. Dancing, music and general carousing go on for several days until the start of August, when islanders make traditional offerings to Pachamama (Mother Earth). Easter and New Year's Day are also festive and rowdy. Many islanders go to Puno for La Virgen de Candelaria and Puno Week, when the island becomes somewhat deserted.

⌆ Sleeping & Eating

The *hospedajes* (small, family-owned inns) on Taquile offer basic accommodation for around S20 a night. Meals are additional (S10 to S15 for breakfast, S20 for lunch). Options range from a room in a family house to small guesthouses. Most offer indoor toilets and showers with electric showers. Lodgings can either be booked with a tour operator or on your own once you arrive. As the community rotates visitors to lodgings, there is little room for choosing.

Restaurants all offer the same fare of *sopa de quinua* (quinoa soup – absolutely delicious everywhere on Lake Titicaca) and lake trout; dishes start at S20. Consider eating in the Restaurante Comunál, Taquile's only community-run food outlet.

● Getting There & Away

Ferries (round-trip S20; admission to island S5) leave from the Puno port for Taquile from 6:45am. If the ferry stops in Islas Uros, you will

ETHICAL COMMUNITY TOURISM

After Cuzco, Puno is Peru's most touristed town, as it's a base for excursions on and around Lake Titicaca. Archaeology and mythology draw tourists here, sure, but what makes us stay is the chance to spend time in a rich and fascinating culture. Since *turismo vivencial* (homestay tourism) took off around Puno, it has become the basis of the local tourism industry.

There are dozens of tour agencies, in many cases offering the same thing at wildly different prices. The main difference for this discrepancy is the amount of money the agency pays to the host families. Nearly all of the cheaper agencies (and some of the more expensive ones) pay little more than the cost of the visitors' meals. While it's difficult to find out for certain which agencies fairly compensate the host families, the following tips can help you contribute to a better experience.

» Use one of the agencies listed here or one recommended by fellow travelers.

» Check that your guide rotates both homestays and floating island visits.

» Insist on handing payment for your lodging to the family yourself.

» Expect to pay well for your homestay. Visitors must pay at least US$50 for a typical two-day island excursion for the host family to make a profit from your stay.

» Travel to the islands independently – it's easy.

» Carry out your trash – islanders have no way of disposing of it.

» Bring gifts of things the islanders can't grow, such as fresh fruit or school supplies (pens, pencils, notebooks).

» Don't give candy or money to kids, so they don't learn to beg.

» Support communal enterprises, which benefit all. On Taquile, families take turns to run the Restaurante Comunál, which gives many people their only opportunity to benefit from the tidal wave of tourism that hits their island daily. Luquina Chico and Isla Ticonata run their tourism communally, through rotation of accommodation, profit sharing, and shared work providing food, transport, guiding and activities.

» Consider visiting one of the communities around the lake. They're harder to get to than the islands but are far more peaceful and less touristed – here you'll see a living, agrarian community.

also have to pay the admission there. There's a ferry from Amantaní to Taquile every morning; it's also possible to get here by ferry from Llachón.

ISLA AMANTANÍ

The more remote Amantaní Island (admission S5), population 4000, is a few kilometers north of the smaller Taquile. Almost all trips to Amantaní involve an overnight stay with islanders. Guests help cook on open fires in dirt-floored kitchens. Witnessing the different aspects of rural life can create engaging and memorable experiences.

The villagers sometimes organize rousing traditional dances, letting travelers dress in their traditional party gear to dance the night away. Of course, your hiking boots might give you away. Don't forget to look up at the incredibly starry night sky as you stagger home.

The island is very quiet (no dogs allowed!), boasts great views and has no roads or vehicles. Several hills are topped by ruins, among the highest and best-known of which are Pachamama (Mother Earth) and Pachatata (Father Earth). These date to the Tiwanaku culture, a largely Bolivian culture that appeared around Lake Titicaca and expanded rapidly between 200 BC and AD 1000.

As with Taquile, the islanders speak Quechua, but their culture is more heavily influenced by the Aymara.

🛏 Sleeping & Eating

When you arrive, Amantani Community Lodging (☑36-9714), basically the island families, will allocate you to your accommodation according to a rotating system. Please respect this process, even if you are with a guided group. There's no problem with asking for families or friends to be together. A bed and full board starts at S30 per person per night.

❶ Getting There & Away

Ferries (round-trip S30; admission to island S5) leave from the Puno port for Amantaní at 8am every day. There are departures from Amantani to Taquile and Puno around 4pm every day – check, though, as times vary – and sometimes from Amantani to Puno around 8am, depending on demand.

ISLA SUASI

On the northeastern part of the lake, this beautiful solar-powered island offers a total retreat into nature. The only privately owned island on Titicaca, it has been leased long term by a luxury hotel. Remote ecolodge **Casa Andina Isla Suasi** (☑1-213-9739; www. casa-andina.com; per person all-inclusive 2-days/1-night S1090) is as exclusive as resorts get. Terraced rooms are well-appointed, with down duvets, fireplaces, peaked ceilings and lake views. With lush flower gardens, trails, wild vicuña (relatives of llamas) and spots for swimming (yes, people do swim here!), it's unique in the region for presenting more of a nature experience than a cultural one. Spa treatments and steam saunas with eucalyptus leaves provide a little pampering. With games, canoes and guide-led activities, it's also a great destination for families. The island is a five-hour boat trip from Puno or over a three-hour drive on dirt roads, with a short boat transfer from Cambria. A US$12 entry fee (included in lodging fees) helps local conservation projects.

The hotel provides daily transfers at 7:30am for guests from the pier in Puno, with stops to visit the Uros Islands and Isla Taquile.

Capachica Peninsula & Around

Poking far out into the northwestern part of the lake, midway between Juliaca and Puno, the Capachica Peninsula has the same beauty as the lake islands but without the crowds and commercial bent. Each *pueblito* (tiny town) boasts its own glorious scenery, ranging from pastoral and pretty to coweringly majestic. A few days here among the local people – handsome, dignified men in vests and black hats, and shy, smiling women in intricate headgear – with nothing to do but eat well, climb hills and trees, and stare at the lake, can provide a real retreat. Home-stay is the only accommodation on offer and a major element of the fun.

Strung along the peninsula between the towns of Capachica and Llachón, the villages of Ccotos and Chifrón are linked by deserted, eminently walkable dirt roads and lackadaisical bus services (it's generally quicker to walk over the hill than drive around by the road). Escallani is further north, slightly off the peninsula proper, not far from Juliaca. Locals get to the mainland by *lancha* (small motorboat), which they are happy to hire out.

There is no internet reception on the peninsula, but cell phones work. There are no banks or ATMs and, as elsewhere in Peru, breaking big notes can be very difficult. Bring all the money you need, in bills of S20 or smaller if possible.

Travel agencies in Puno (p171) can get you to any of the peninsula's communities. **Cedesos** (☑36-7915; www.cedesos.org; 3rd fl, Moquegua 348, Puno) offers fully guided, standard and tailored trips to these communities and others in the area. This NGO works to improve local income and standards of living through tourism. It offers villagers training and cheap credit to ready themselves to receive tourists. Tours are not cheap, but they're well organized and come highly recommended by readers.

All of the communities listed below offer the same deal on food and accommodation, similar to that encountered on Isla Amantaní. Families have constructed or adapted basic rooms for tourists in their homes, and charge around S25 per person per night for a bed, or about S70 for full board. Full board is recommended – each town has at least one shop, but supplies are limited and the meals provided by the families are healthy and tasty. Apart from trout, the diet is vegetarian, with emphasis on quinoa, potatoes and locally grown *habas* (broad beans).

Llachón and, to a lesser extent, Escallani are set up for travelers just turning up. For other communities, it's very important to arrange accommodation in advance, as hosts need to buy supplies and prepare. It's preferable to call rather than email. Generally, only Spanish is spoken.

CAPACHICA

The peninsula's blisteringly forgettable commercial center has a couple of very basic restaurants and *hospedajes,* as well as a pretty church and an astonishingly oversized sports coliseum, all of which you can see from the bus. There's no reason to stop here unless you need to switch buses, use the internet or a public telephone (there are a couple around the plaza); these services are unavailable elsewhere on the peninsula.

LLACHÓN

Almost 75km northeast of Puno, this pretty little village community near the peninsula's southern tip offers fantastic views and short hikes to surrounding pre-Inca sites. The most developed of the peninsula's communities, thanks to locally managed tourism, it nevertheless feels far from the bright lights of modern Peru. With few cars and no dogs, it's an incredibly peaceful place to sit and enjoy stunning views of Lake Titicaca, while sheep, cows, pigs, llamas and kids wander by. From January to March, native birds are also a feature.

Some accommodation recommendations are given below, but it's possible to simply turn up in town and ask around.

Community leader **Félix Turpo** (☎951-66-4828; hospedajesamary@hotmail.com) has a gorgeous garden and the Capachica Peninsula's most spectacular view, overlooking Isla Taquile. It's also the spot to enjoy a rare hot shower, consisting of a black rubber pipe on a warm rock (it's recommended to shower during daylight hours).

Magno Cahui (☎951-82-5316; hospedaje tikawasi@yahoo.es), his wife and their very cute children have cozy cabins built around his grandfather's stone altar, and another incredible view of Lake Titicaca.

Local legend **Valentín Quispe** (☎951-82-1392; llachon@yahoo.com) and his wife Lucila have a charming guesthouse hidden down a stone path, by an enchanting overgrown cemetery. They also rent out kayaks.

Richard Cahui Flores (☎951-63-7382; hos pedajesamary@hotmail.com) works with lots of families and is the best point of contact for advance bookings as he will set you up with somebody else if he doesn't have space in his tranquil farmhouse.

CHIFRÓN

If you found Llachón a bit too built-up, tiny somnolent Chifrón (population 24), off the main road in the northeast corner of the peninsula, is for you. Drowsing in rustling eucalypts above a deserted beach, three families offer very basic accommodation for a maximum of 15 people. This is truly a chance to experience another world. Con-

tact **Emiliano** (☎951-91-9252/9652; playachi fron_01@hotmail.com) to arrange a stay.

CCOTOS & ISLA TICONATA

You can't get much further off the beaten track than Ccotos, two-thirds of the way down the peninsula's east coast. Nothing ever happens here except the annual Miss Playa (Miss Beach) competition, in which the donning of bathing suits stirs much controversy. Stay with the engaging **Alfonso Quispe** (☎951-85-6462; incasamanatours@ yahoo.es) and his family, right on the edge of the lake. Catch your own fish for breakfast, bird-watch, hike to the lookout and some overgrown ruins, and relax on the beach, which is arguably Capachica's most beautiful (but it's a tough call).

A couple of hundred meters off Ccotos, Isla Ticonata is home to a fiercely united community and some significant mummies, fossils and archaeological sites. Isla Ticonata is only accessible by organized tour, and is a rare example of Lake Titicaca's local communities calling the shots on tour agencies, to the benefit of all. Tours can be booked in Puno at short notice through Cedesos or the travel agencies. Activities include fishing, dancing, cooking and helping till the family *chakras* (fields).

ESCALLANI

You could spend days ogling the majestic views of reed beds, patchwork fields, craggy rocks and the perennially snowcapped Illimani (Bolivia's highest mountain). The lake takes on a completely different aspect from the settlement of Escallani, located off the peninsula and on the way to Juliaca. **Rufino** (☎951-64-5325, Spanish only) and his large family have built a rambling complex of more than a dozen rustic, straw-thatched cabins high above the town. Rufino doesn't have telephone service; to reserve a spot, call his relatives in Juliaca well in advance. This area is a little more ready than other communities to receive guests unannounced – ask around at the plaza to find his place. There are also rumors of rock-climbing areas.

The trip from Juliaca to Escallani via Pusi by local *micro* is highly recommended for hardy travelers. The scenery on this unpaved, little-traveled road is unparalleled – sit on the left side of the bus if you're heading from Juliaca to Escallani so that you can see the lake.

TITILAKA

Secluded on the rugged shoreline of Lake Titicaca, luxury hotel **Titilaka** (in Lima
☎1-700-5105; www.titilaka.com; Lake Titicaca; s/d with full board from US$301/530; @🖥) is a
destination in itself. The look is whimsical Euro-Andino, with a palette that ranges from
neutral to flirty (think blushing rose and purples). Touches of exquisite folk art combine
with the sculptures and black and white photography of well-known Peruvian artists.
Huge picture windows drink in the serene landscapes in every direction. Rooms sport
king-sized beds warmed by hot water bottles, deep tubs, iPod docks and window ledge
seating. There are games for kids, a spa and gourmet restaurant. The staff is groomed
to please. Private guided tours give guests an intimate view of the islands. While most
guests go for the three-day packages, the nightly rate includes full board and local excursions like walks and kayaking. It's one hour south of Puno.

❶ Getting There & Around

From Puno, catch a *combi* advertising either
Capachica or Llachón from outside the Mercado Bellavista. All will stop in Capachica (S4,
80 minutes). From the plaza here continue to
Llachón (S2, 45 minutes) or other destinations.

For Ccotos (S1.50, 35 minutes) or Escallani
(S2.50, 45 minutes), *combis* leave the plaza of
Capachica only on Sundays from 8am to 2pm.
You could also take a taxi (S15) or *mototaxi* (S10)
to Ccotos; it's a bit steeper for Escallani (S40).

For Chifrón, there is no public transport.
Take a taxi from Capachica (S10) or *mototaxi*
(S7). Alternately, you can hike over the hill from
Llachón, or walk the 3km from Capachica.

Llachón is also accessible via the Taquile ferry.
The easiest way to combine the two is to arrive
by road, then have your host family in Llachón
show you where to catch the ferry to Taquile.

South-Shore Towns

The road to Bolivia via Lake Titicaca's southern shore passes through bucolic villages
noted for their colonial churches and beautiful views. Traveling this route is an easy way
to get a relatively untouristed peek at the
region's traditional culture. If you can coor-
dinate the transportation connections, you
can visit a few of the following towns in a
daytrip from Puno or continue on to Bolivia.

For public transport to any south-shore
town, go to Puno's *terminal zonál*. *Combis*
leave when full. The route includes Ichu
(S1, 15 minutes), Chucuito (S1.50, 30 minutes), Juli (S4, one hour), Pomata (S6, 1½
hours) and the Bolivian border at Yunguyo
(S6.50, 2¼ hours) or Desaguadero (S7.50, 2½
hours). Direct transport to the towns closer
to Puno are more frequent, but *combis* to
most towns leave at least hourly – more often for closer destinations.

ICHU

Ten kilometers out of Puno, this rural community spread across a gorgeous green
valley is home to a little-known ruin with
superb views. It's a great place for a hike.

Leave the Panamericana at Ichu's second exit (after the service station) and head
inland past the house marked 'Villa Lago
1960.' Walk 2km, bearing left at the junction,
aiming for the two small, terraced hills you
can see in the left of the valley. After bearing left at a second junction (you'll pass the
school if you miss it), the road takes you between the two hills. Turn left again and head
straight up the first one. Fifteen minutes of
stiff climbing brings you to the top, where
you'll be rewarded with the remains of a
multilayered temple complex, and breathtaking 360-degree views.

This can be done as an easy half-day trip
from Puno. Take plenty of water and food as
there's no store.

CHUCUITO

☎051 / POP 1100

Quiet Chucuito's principal attraction is the
outlandish **Templo de la Fertilidad** (Inca Uyu;
admission S5; ⊗8am-5pm). Its dusty grounds are
scattered with large stone phalluses, some up
to 1.2m in length. Local guides tell various entertaining stories about the carvings, including tales of maidens sitting atop the stony
joysticks to increase their fertility. Further
uphill from the main road is the main plaza,
which has two attractive colonial churches,
Santo Domingo and **Nuestra Señora de la
Asunción**. You'll have to track down the elusive caretakers to get a glimpse inside.

🍴 Sleeping & Eating

There are a couple of very basic places to eat
near the plaza. Both lodgings have upscale
restaurants with touristy menus.

Taypikala Lago
HOTEL $$$

(☎79-2266; www.taypikala.com; Calle Sandia s/n; s/d/tr S$201/254/320) Across the highway, the swanky new sister hotel of the original Tapikala offers even better views, with understated luxury and subtle architecture.

Taypikala Hotel
HOTEL $$

(☎79-2252; www.taypikala.com; Km18 Panamericana Sur) It would be hard to miss the bumpy lavalike exterior of the Taypikala Hotel, a new-age confusion of model condors and artificial rocks worthy of an amusement park. Rooms have lake and garden views, and are decorated with copies of local rock art. At the time of research it was closed, but it may reopen.

Albergue Las Cabañas
CABINS $$

(☎36-8494; www.chucuito.com; Tarapacá 153; s/d/tr S64/96/126) This lodging near the main plaza has a charming, overgrown garden, rustic stone cabins and family bungalows complete with wood-burning fires.

LUQUINA CHICO

This tiny community, 53km east of Puno on the Chucuito Peninsula, is stunning. If your thought is to relax in a rural community, it also boasts the best standard of homestay accommodation of any community around the lake. The community is making economic strides thanks to tourism.

Sweeping views of Puno, Juliaca and all the islands of the lake can be taken in from both the headland's heights or the fertile flats by the lake. In the wet season, a lagoon forms which attracts migrating wetland birds.

Chullpitas (miniature burial towers) are scattered all around this part of the peninsula. They are said to house the bodies of *gentiles,* little people who lived here in ancient times, before the sun was born and sent them underground.

Homestays (from S20) offer full board (SS28). To get here, catch a *combi* labeled 'Luquina Chico' (S2.50, 1½ hours) from Puno, or take the ferry to or from Taquile and ask the driver to drop you off. Ask around about renting kayaks. Edgar Adventures (p171) can also get you here on a mountain bike, a somewhat grueling but extremely scenic three-hour ride along the peninsula.

JULI
☎051 / POP 8000

Past Chucuito, the road curves southeast away from the lake and through the commercial center of Ilave, best known for its livestock market and a lively sense of community justice, manifested most famously with the lynching of the town mayor in 2004. Ilave is best avoided in times of civil strife. Sleepy, friendly Juli is a more tourist-friendly stop. It's called Peru's *pequeña Roma* (little Rome) on account of its four colonial churches from the 16th and 17th centuries, which are slowly being restored. Churches are most likely to be open on Sundays, though opening hours here should not be taken as gospel. It's worth hammering on the door if one seems closed.

Dating from 1570, the adobe baroque church of San Juan de Letrán (admission S6; ◷8:30am-5pm Tue-Sun) contains richly framed *escuela cuzqueña* (Cuzco School) paintings that depict the lives of saints. The imposing 1557 church of Nuestra Señora de la Asunción (admission S6; ◷8:30am-5pm Tue-Sun) has an expansive courtyard approach that may awaken urges to oratory. Its interior is airy, and the pulpit is covered in gold leaf. The church of Santa Cruz has lost half its roof and remains closed for the foreseeable future. The 1560 stone church of San Pedro, on the main plaza, is in the best condition, with carved ceilings and a marble baptismal font. Mass is celebrated here every Sunday at 8am.

Sunday is also the day of Juli's market, the region's largest. Wednesday is a secondary market day.

Micros (S4, one hour) from the *terminal zonal* in Puno drop you off near the market, 10 minutes' walk downhill from the center, but leave from Jirón Lima, two blocks up from the plaza. Internet cafes and basic guesthouses can be found around here.

POMATA
☎051 / POP 1800

Beyond Juli, the road continues southeast to Pomata, 105km from Puno. As you arrive, you'll see Dominican church Templo de Pomata Santiago Apóstolo (admission S2) – totally out of proportion with the town it dominates, in terms of both size and splendor – dramatically located on top of a small hill. Founded in 1700, it is known for its windows made of translucent alabaster and its intricately carved baroque sandstone facade. Look for the puma carvings – the town's name means 'place of the puma' in Aymara.

Just out of Pomata, the road forks. The main road continues southeast through Zepita to the unsavory border town of

LAKE TITICACA SOUTH-SHORE TOWNS

Desaguadero. The left fork hugs the shore of Lake Titicaca and leads to another, more pleasant border crossing at Yunguyo. If you're going this way, consider stopping off at the **Mirador Natural de Asiru Patjata** lookout, a few kilometers from Yunguyo. Here, a 5000m-long rock formation resembles a *culebra* (snake), whose head is a viewpoint looking over to Isla del Sol. The area around here is known for its isolated villages and shamans.

Colectivos from the Terminal Zonal in Puno stop here (S6, 1½ hours); they are marked with signs for Yunguyo or Desgaguadero.

Bolivian Shore

If you are drawn to the idea of staying longer in Bolivia, Lonely Planet's *Bolivia* guidebook has more comprehensive information.

COPACABANA

📱591-02 / POP 54,300 / ELEV 3808M

Just across the border from Yunguyo, Copacabana is a restful Bolivian town on Lake Titicaca's south shore. For centuries it has been the site of religious pilgrimages, and today local and international pilgrims flock to its fiestas. Small and bright, it makes a handy base for visiting the famous Islas del Sol y de la Luna. On the weekend it's full of visitors from La Paz; during the week, it snoozes.

In the 16th century the town was presented with an image of the Virgen de la Candelaria (now Bolivia's patron saint), sparking a slew of miracles. Copacabana's Moorish cathedral, where the Virgen is housed in a mystifyingly insalubrious chapel, is still a pilgrimage site.

Be prepared for heavy rains, especially during December and January, and chilly nights year-round.

⊙ Sights & Activities

Much of the action in Copa centers around Plaza 2 de Febrero and 6 de Agosto, the main commercial drag, which runs east to west. The transportation hub is in Plaza Sucre. At its western end is the lake and a walkway (Costañera), which traces the lakeshore.

Cathedral   CHURCH
The sparkling white *mudéjar* cathedral, with its domes and colorful *azulejos* (blue Portuguese-style ceramic tiles), dominates the town.

The cathedral's black **Camarín de la Virgen de Candelaria statue**, carved by Inca Tupac Yupanqui's grandson, Francisco Yupanqui, is encased above the altar upstairs in the niche *(camarín);* note, visiting hours can be unreliable. The statue is never moved from the cathedral, as superstition suggests that its disturbance would precipitate a devastating flood of Lake Titicaca.

The cathedral is a repository for both European and local religious art and the **Museo de la Catedral** (per person B$10; ☉all day) contains some interesting articles – offerings from hopeful individuals. Unfortunately, the museum is open only to groups of four or more (unless, of course, you're happy to pay) and you'll most probably need to chase down a sister to arrange your visit.

Cerro Calvario   LOOKOUT
The summit of Cerro Calvario can be reached in half an hour and is well worth the climb, especially in the late afternoon to watch the sunset over the lake. The trail to the summit begins near the **church** at the end of Calle Destacamento and climbs past the 14 stations of the cross.

FREE Museo Taypi   MUSEUM
(Hotel Rosario del Lago) Museo Taypi is a small, private cultural museum within the grounds of Hotel Rosario. It features a small, lovely collection of antiquities and cultural displays on the region. Here, too, is Jalsuri, a fair-trade craft shop selling quality *artesanía*.

✦ Festivals & Events

Alasitas Festival   FESTIVAL
Held on January 24.

Fiesta de la Virgen de Candelaria   FESTIVAL
A bash honoring the patron saint of Copacabana and all Bolivia, with much music, traditional Aymará dancing, drinking and feasting. Celebrations culminate with the corralling of 100 bulls. From February 2 to 5.

Semana Santa   RELIGIOUS HOLIDAY
As part of the Holy Week celebrations, the town fills with pilgrims on Good Friday, with processions.

Bolivian Independence Day   NATIONAL HOLIDAY
Copacabana stages its biggest event during the first week in August. It's characterized by round-the-clock music, parades, brass bands, fireworks and amazing alcohol consumption. This coincides with a traditional

pilgrimage that brings thousands of Peruvians into the town to visit the Virgin.

👉 Tours

To visit Islas del Sol y de la Luna, you can either take a ferry (p190), or go the luxury route with a La Paz–based tour operator for a guided excursion (definitely adding a night or two in their hotels on Isla del Sol).

🛏 Sleeping

Hotels (many shoddy) are springing up like reeds in Copacabana. A host of budget options abound charging around B$30 per person (significantly more in high season and festivals), especially along Calle Jáuregui.

🏨 Las Olas   BOUTIQUE HOTEL $$

(☑7-250-8668; www.hostallasolas.com; Michel Pérez 1-3; s B$210-224, d B$266-294; @🛜) Creative and stylish with million-dollar vistas, this is a once-in-a-lifetime experience and well worth the splurge. There are kitchens, private terraces with hammocks, and a solar-powered Jacuzzi. Reserve ahead.

Hotel La Cúpula   HOTEL $$

(☑862-2029; www.hotelcupula.com; Michel Pérez 1-3; s/d/ste B$133/210/266; 🛜) An inviting oasis on the slopes of Cerro Calvario. Rooms are pretty basic (and beds will be too soft for some), but we love the gardens, hammocks, shared kitchen and friendly atmosphere. The helpful staff speak several languages. Best to reserve ahead.

Hostal Flores del Lago   HOTEL $

(☑862-2117; www.taypibolivia.com; Jauregui; s/d/tr B$80/120/180; 🛜) Another top-tier budget buy is this large four-story option on the north side of the harbor. The clean rooms are slightly damp, but you'll love the views and the friendly lobby area.

🏨 Ecolodge del Lago   LODGE $$

(☑862-2500; www.ecocopacabana.com; s/d/tr B$180/320/480) Situated 20 minutes on foot along the Costañera (or a quick taxi ride), this ecofriendly place is right on the lake in a wonderful natural paradise. Quirky adobe rooms and self-equipped apartments are self-heated thanks to the mud bricks, and have solar-powered water. A garden of dahlias and gladioli affords great views of the lake.

Hostel Leyenda   HOTEL $

(☑7-067-4097; hostel.leyenda@gmail.com; cnr Av Busch & Constanera; s/d B$80/120 incl breakfast; 🛜) A solid bet for budgeters, with views of the water, a lush garden and 'Bolivian Boutique' rooms. The corner rooms have lots of space for the same price, and the top-story suite (also the same price) has a totora raft and its own terrace.

Hostal Sonia   HOTEL $

(☑862-2019; hostalsoniacopacabana@gmail.com; Murillo 256; s/d B$40/70; @🛜) This lively spot has bright and cheery rooms, great views from the upstairs rooms and a top-floor terrace, making it one of the top budget bets in town.

🍴 Eating & Drinking

Tourist-focused restaurants line the bottom block of Calle 6 de Agosto, but varied and exciting food is not a feature of Copacabana. The local specialty is *trucha* (trout) farmed on Lake Titicaca. Competitive stalls along the beachfront serve it in every style. On a cold morning, head to the market for a cup of *api* – a hot, sweet, purple-corn drink.

La Orilla   INTERNATIONAL $$

(☑862 2267; 6 de Agosto; mains B$25-45; ⏱4pm-9:30pm Mon-Sat; 🍴) A cozy maritime-themed restaurant with fresh, crunchy, from-the-vine vegetables, crispy and super savory pizzas, and interesting trout creations that incorporate spinach and bacon (mmm, bacon).

La Cúpula Restaurant   INTERNATIONAL $$

(www.hotelcupula.com; Michel Pérez 1-3; mains B$20-50; ⏱closed lunch Tue; 🍴) The inventive use of local ingredients includes tasty vegetarian lasagna, and there's plenty for carnivores, too. Cheese fondue with authentic Gruyère cheese is to die for. The glassy surroundings maximize the fabulous view of the lake.

Kota Kahuaña   INTERNATIONAL $$

(☑862-2141; Paredes at Costañera; mains B$25-55) This hotel restaurant has excellent views, great service and well-prepared international dishes. Stuffed trout, an excellent salad bar, satisfying main courses and Bolivian wines ensure a fine-dining experience.

Pueblo El Viejo   INTERNATIONAL $$

(6 de Agosto 684; mains B$35-50) Readers love this rustic, cozy and chilled cafe-bar, with its ethnic decor and laid-back atmosphere. It serves up a good burger and pizza and is open until late. Service can be quite slow, plan on being here awhile.

Pensión Aransaya   BOLIVIAN $

(6 de Agosto 121; almuerzo B$15, mains B$25-40; ⏱lunch) Friendly local favorite for a cold

beer and trout with all the trimmings. It's very traditional and popular with the locals.

Waykys   BAR
(16 de Julio, at Busch) A warm den with cozy corners, graffiti-covered walls and ceilings (add yours), a billiards table, book exchange and a varying range of music.

Nemos Bar   BAR
(6 de Agosto 684) This dimly lit, late-night hangout is a popular place for a tipple.

❶ Information

DANGERS & ANNOYANCES

Beware illegal minibuses and taxis offering service between Copacabana and La Paz: express kidnappings have been reported. Travelers are encouraged to take the formal tourist buses (or the larger buses) and travel by day.

During festivals stand far back from fireworks displays and be wary of light-fingered revelers.

MEDICAL SERVICES

There is a basic hospital on the southern outskirts of town. For serious situations head straight to La Paz.

MONEY

Shops on Calle 6 de Agosto exchange foreign currency (dollars preferred). **Banco Bisa ATM** (6 de Agosto & Pando) works only sometimes.

POST

Post office (☉8:30am-noon & 2:30-4pm Tue-Sun) On the north side of Plaza 2 de Febrero, but often closed or unattended.

TELEPHONE

Offices are dotted along 6 de Agosto and around town.

TOURIST INFORMATION

Centro de Información Turística (16 de Julio, nr Plaza Sucre; ☉9am-1pm, 2-6pm Wed-Sun) There is a helpful English-speaking attendant, although only rudimentary information is available.
Copacabana Community Tourism Site (www.copacabana-bolivia.com) Has a good events calendar and updated info on community tourism projects.

❶ Getting There & Away

BUS

Most buses leave from near Plazas 2 de Febrero or Sucre. The more comfortable nonstop tour buses from La Paz to Copacabana – including Milton Tours and Combi Tours – cost from around B$25 to B$30 and leave Copacabana at 1:30pm (3½ hours). Tickets can be purchased from tour agencies. You will need to exit your

bus at the Estrecho de Tiquina to cross via **ferry** (B$1.50 per person, B$35-40 per car; ☉5am-9pm) between the towns of San Pedro de Tiquina (tourist info office on the main plaza) to San Pablo de Tiquina.

Buses to Peru, including Arequipa, Cuzco and Puno, depart and arrive in Copacabana from Av 6 de Agosto. You can also get to Puno by catching a public minibus from Plaza Sucre to the border at Kasani (B$3, 15 minutes).

BOAT

Buy your tickets for boat tours to Isla de la Luna and Isla del Sol from agencies on 6 de Agosto or from beach-front kiosks. Separate return service is available from both islands.

Asociación Unión Marines (Costanera; ☉departing Copacabana 8:30am & 1:30pm; B$20 one-way, B$25 round-trip) Ferry service to the north and south of Isla del Sol, with a stop on the return at a floating island.

Titicaca Tours (Costanera; ☉departing Copacabana 8:30am, B$35 round-trip) Offers a round-trip boat tour that stops in Isla de la Luna for an hour, continuing to the southern end of Isla del Sol for a two-hour stop before heading back to Copacabana.

ISLAS DEL SOL Y DE LA LUNA

The most famous island on Lake Titicaca is Isla del Sol (Island of the Sun), the legendary birthplace of Manco Cápac and his sister-wife Mama Ocllo, and indeed the sun itself. Both Isla del Sol and Isla de la Luna (Island of the Moon) have Inca ruins, reached by delightful walking trails through spectacular scenery dotted with traditional villages – there are no cars on the islands. Sunshine and altitude can take their toll, so bring extra water, food and sun block. You can visit the main sights in a day, but staying overnight is far more rejuvenating.

Water is a precious commodity. The island does not yet have access to water mains and supplies are carried by person or donkey. Please bear this in mind; think twice before taking showers (after all, we're all in – and on! – the same boat).

Note: in high season (June to August and also during festivals) prices listed here may double.

◉ Sights & Activities

Isla del Sol's Inca remains include the Chincana labyrinth complex in the north, and fortresslike Pilkokayna and the verdant, gorgeous Inca Stairway in the south. The Chincana is the site of the sacred Titi Khar'ka (Rock of the Puma), which features in the Inca creation legend and gave the lake its name. The largest villages are Yumani to the south and Ch'allapampa in the north.

Far less touristed, quiet Isla de la Luna boasts the partially rebuilt ruins of the convent that housed virgins of the sun – women chosen at a young age to serve as nuns to the sun god Inti.

Sleeping & Eating

Basic hostels in restful beachside Ch'allapampa charge B$25 to B$35 per person for accommodation. There are a handful of basic restaurants and shops.

The most scenic spot to stay is Yumani, at the other end of the island. Far more developed, dozens of accommodations range from B$25 to B$90 per person, and there are relatively sophisticated dining options (pizza and vegetarian fare) on offer.

On Isla de la Luna, there are three hostels in the main settlement on the east side of the island, with ultra-basic rooms going for about B$15 to B$25 per person. Food in town will cost about B$25 to B$30 a meal. Ask around. The hotel on the east-side tourist dock costs B$20 per person, but you miss out on being in the main community.

If camping, it's best to ask permission from the local authority and then set up away from villages, avoiding cultivated land (a nominal payment of B$10 should be offered).

🛈 Getting There & Around

BOAT

To Isla de la Luna, travel by ferry from either Copacabana or Yampupata, or with a guided tour.

Tickets may be purchased at the ticket kiosks on the beach or from Copacabana agencies. Boats to the northern end of the island land at Cha'llapampa, while those going to the southern end land at either Pilko Kaina or the Escalera del Inca (Yumani).

Launches embark from Copacabana beach around 8:30am and 1:30pm daily. Depending on the season and the company, they may drop you off at a choice of the island's north or south (check with the agency). Return trips leave Yampupata at 10:30am and 4pm (B$20 one-way), and Cha'llapampa at 1pm (B$20).

Most full-day trips go directly north to Cha'llapampa (two to 2½ hours). Boats anchor for 1½ hours only – you'll have just enough time to hike up to the Chincana ruins, and return again to catch the boat at 1pm to the Escalera del Inca and Pilko Kaina in the island's south. Here, you'll spend around two hours before departing for Copa.

Half-day trips generally go to the south of Isla del Sol only.

Those who wish to hike the length of the island can get off at Cha'llapampa in the morning and walk south to the Escalera del Inca (Yumani) for the return boat in the afternoon.

Alternatively, you can opt to stay overnight or longer on the island (highly recommended), then buy a one-way ticket to Copacabana with any of the boat companies. See p190.

Cuzco & the Sacred Valley

Places to Eat

» Cicciolina (p221)

» La Bodega 138 (p221)

» Huacatay (p240)

» Indio Feliz (p249)

» Chicha (p221)

Best Places to Stay

» Machu Picchu Pueblo Lodge (p247)

» Greenhouse (p238)

» Ecopackers (p214)

» Niños Hotel (p214)

» Inkaterra La Casona (p214)

Why Go?

Incas deemed this spot the belly button of the world. Sure enough, a visit to Cuzco tumbles you back into the cosmic realm of ancient Andean culture – one that was knocked down and fused with the finest colonial and religious splendors of Spanish conquest, only to be repackaged as a thriving tourist trap. Welcome to a mystical and whimsical world of paradox. But Cuzco is only the gateway. Beyond lies the Sacred Valley, Andean countryside dotted with villages, high altitude hamlets and ruins linked by trail and solitary railway tracks to the country's biggest draw – Machu Picchu.

Old ways are not forgotten. Colorful textiles link to the past, as do the wild fiestas and carnivals with the fiber of pagan tradition in solemn Catholic rituals. Just as dynamic is a landscape that careens from Andean peaks to orchid-rich cloud forests and Amazon lowlands. Explore it on foot or by fat tire, rafting wild rivers or simply braving the local buses to the remote and dust-worn corners of this far-reaching department.

When to Go

Cuzco

Jun–Aug High season for tourism, events and festivals, days are sunny and nights cold.	**Late Jun** Celebrate the solstice at Inti Raymi, the largest festival of the year.	**Sep–Oct** Shoulder season for tourism, with fewer crowds in Machu Picchu.

Regional Cuisine

Sunday lunch with a country stroll is a Cuzco ritual. Locals head to the villages south of town: **Tipón** is *the* place to eat *cuy* (guinea pig), **Saylla** is the home of *chicharrón* (deep-fried pork) and **Lucre** is renowned for duck.

Look for the following foods in local restaurants, on the street and at festivals:

Anticucho Beef heart on a stick, punctuated by a potato, is the perfect evening street snack.

Caldo de gallina Healthy, hearty chicken soup is the local favorite to kick a hangover.

Chicharrones Definitely more than the sum of its parts: deep-fried pork served with corn, mint leaves, fried potato and onion.

Choclo con queso Huge, pale cobs of corn are served with a teeth-squeaking chunk of cheese in the Sacred Valley.

Cuy Raised on grains at home, what could be more organic? The faint of heart can ask for it served as a filet (without the head and paws).

Lechón Suckling pig with plenty of crackling, served with tamales (corn cakes).

DON'T MISS

The Corpus Christi parade on Cuzco's Plaza de Armas dusts off the saints for a spin through the ecstatic crowds in early June.

Boleto Turístico & Boleto Religioso

To visit most sites in the region, you will need Cuzco's official **boleto turístico** (tourist ticket; adult/student under 26 with ISIC card S130/70), valid for 10 days. Among the 17 sites included are: Sacsaywamán, Q'enqo, Pukapukara, Tambomachay, Pisac, Ollantaytambo, Chinchero and Moray, as well as an evening performance of Andean dances and live music at the Centro Qosqo de Arte Nativo. While some inclusions are admitted duds, you can't visit any of them without it.

Three partial *boletos* (adult/student S70/35) cover the ruins immediately outside Cuzco, the museums in Cuzco, and the Sacred Valley ruins. They are valid for one day, except for the Sacred Valley option, which is valid for two.

Purchase *boletos turísticos* from **Dircetur/Cosituc** (261-465; www.boletoturisticocusco.com; La Municipalidad, office 102, Av El Sol 103; 8am-6pm Mon-Fri) or at the sites themselves, except for the Centro Qosqo de Arte Nativo. Students must show valid ID.

The **boleto religioso** (religious tourist ticket; adult/student S50/25), valid for 10 days, secures entry to Cuzco's churches, the Museo de Arte Religioso and Cuzco's most significant display of contemporary art at Museo Quijote. It's available at any of the sites.

MAIN POINTS OF ENTRY

National flights arrive at Cuzco's Aeropuerto Internacional Alejandro Velazco Astete but plans are pending to build an airport in the Sacred Valley near Chinchero. Buses (including international routes) go to the Terminal Terrestre in Cuzco.

Need to Know

» Those arriving from lower altitudes may experience altitude sickness. Take it easy the first few days of your visit or start in the slightly lower Sacred Valley.

Top Tip

» Since Machu Picchu tickets can no longer be purchased online, get this business done early with an authorized agent listed at www.machupicchu.gob.pe or in person at Cuzco's Dirección Regional de Cultura. To add entry to the coveted Wayna Picchu hike, purchase even earlier.

Resources

» www.lonelyplanet.com /peru/cuzco

» www.machupicchu .gob.pe

» www.peru.travel

» www.saexplorers.org

CUZCO

084 / POP 350,000 / ELEV 3326M

Cosmopolitan Inca capital, Cuzco (also Cusco, or Qosq'o in Quechua) today thrives with a measure of contradiction. Ornate cathedrals squat over Inca temples, massage hawkers ply the narrow cobblestone streets, a woman in traditional skirt and bowler offers bottled water to a pet llama while the finest boutiques hawk alpaca knits for small fortunes. The foremost city of the Inca Empire is now the undisputed archaeological capital of the Americas, as well as the continent's oldest continuously inhabited city. Few travelers to Peru will skip visiting this

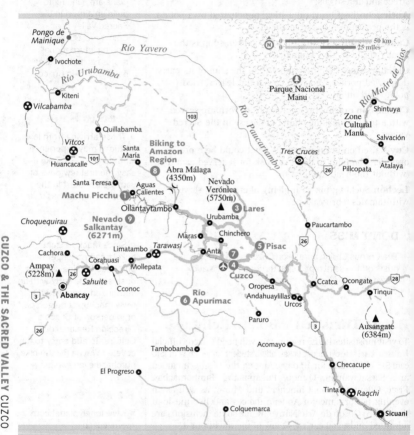

Cuzco & the Sacred Valley Highlights

❶ Drink in the sublime grandeur of **Machu Picchu** (p246)

❷ Get swept into the colorful frenzy of a traditional **festival** (p213)

❸ Hike through traditional villages and terraced agriculture on the spectacular **Lares trek** (p38)

❹ Explore the narrow streets and shops of bohemian **San Blas** (p205)

❺ Wander ancient ruins in stunning settings throughout the **Sacred Valley** (p233)

❻ Take on the wild Apurímac or Tampobata Rivers on a **whitewater rafting trip** (p208)

❼ Dine on haute cuisine or *cuy*: **Cuzco restaurants** (p221) can cater to any whim

❽ Barrel from the high Andes down into the Amazon on a **mountain bike** (p209)

❾ Trek your way up from the tropics on the **Salkantay route** (p39) to Machu Picchu

premier South American destination, also the gateway to Machu Picchu.

Visitors to Cuzco get a glimpse of the richest heritage of any South American city. Married to 21st century hustle, at times it's a bit disconcerting (note the KFC and McDonalds behind the Inca stones). As rent soars on the Plaza de Armas and in trendy San Blas, locals are increasingly pushed to the margins. Foreign guests undoubtedly have the run of the roost, showing respect toward today's incarnation of this powerhouse culture is imperative.

History

Legend tells that in the 12th century, the first *inca* (king), Manco Capac, was ordered by the ancestral sun god Inti to find the spot where he could plunge a golden rod into the ground until it disappeared. At this spot – deemed the navel of the earth (*qosq'o* in the Quechua language) – he founded Cuzco, the city that would become the thriving capital of the Americas' greatest empire.

The Inca empire's main expansion occurred in the hundred years prior to the arrival of the conquistadors in 1532. The ninth *inca,* Pachacutec, gave the empire its first bloody taste of conquest, with unexpected victory against the more dominant Chanka tribe in 1438. His was the first wave of expansion that would create the Inca empire.

Pachacutec also proved himself a sophisticated urban developer, devising Cuzco's famous puma shape and diverting rivers to cross the city. He built fine buildings, including the famous Qorikancha temple and a palace on a corner of what is now the Plaza de Armas. Among the monuments he built in honor of Inca victories are Sacsaywamán, the temple-fortress at Ollantaytambo and possibly even Machu Picchu.

Expansion continued under following generations until Europeans discovered the New World; at that point, the empire ranged from Quito, in Ecuador, to the area south of Santiago in Chile. Shortly before the arrival of the Europeans, Huayna Cápac had divided his empire, giving the northern part to Atahualpa and the southern Cuzco area to another son, Huascar. The brothers fought bitterly for the kingdom. As a pure-blooded native *cuzqueño* (inhabitant of Cuzco), Huascar had the people's support, but Atahualpa had the backing of the battle-hardened northern army. In early 1532 they won a key battle, capturing Huascar outside Cuzco.

Meanwhile, Francisco Pizarro landed in northern Peru and marched southward. Atahualpa himself had been too busy fighting the civil war to worry about a small band of foreigners, but by 1532 a fateful meeting had been arranged with the Spaniard in Cajamarca. It was a meeting that would radically change the course of South American history: Atahualpa was ambushed by a few dozen armed conquistadors, who succeeded in capturing him, killing thousands of indigenous tribespeople and routing tens of thousands more.

In an attempt to regain his freedom, the *inca* offered a ransom of a roomful of gold and two rooms of silver, including gold stripped from the temple walls of Qorikancha. But after holding Atahualpa prisoner for a number of months, Pizarro murdered him anyway, and soon marched on to Cuzco. Mounted on horseback, protected by armor and swinging steel swords, the Spanish cavalry was virtually unstoppable.

Pizarro entered Cuzco on November 8, 1533, by which time he had appointed Manco, a half-brother of Huascar and Atahualpa, as the new puppet leader. After a few years of keeping to heel, however, the docile puppet rebelled. In 1536, Manco Inca set out to drive the Spaniards from his empire, laying siege to Cuzco with an army estimated at well over a hundred thousand people. Indeed, it was only a desperate last-ditch breakout and violent battle at Sacsaywamán that saved the Spanish from complete annihilation.

Manco Inca was forced to retreat to Ollantaytambo and then into the jungle at Vilcabamba. After Cuzco was safely recaptured, looted and settled, the seafaring Spaniards turned their attentions to the newly founded colonial capital, Lima. Cuzco's importance quickly waned, and it became just another colonial backwater. All the gold and silver was gone, and many Inca buildings were pulled down to accommodate churches and colonial houses.

The Spanish kept chronicles in Cuzco, including Inca history as related by the Incas themselves. The most famous of these accounts is *The Royal Commentaries of the Incas,* written by Garcilaso de la Vega, the son of an Inca princess and a Spanish military captain.

⊙ Sights

While the city is sprawling, areas of interest to visitors are generally within walking distance,

DON'T MISS

STARGAZING WITH THE ANCIENTS

The Incas were the only culture in the world to define constellations of darkness as well as light. Astronomy wasn't taken lightly: some of Cuzco's main streets are designed to align with the stars at certain times of the year. Understanding their interest is a cool way to learn more about the Inca worldview. We recommend a visit to the Cuzco Planetarium (www.planetariumcusco.com; per person around S30) before you head out trekking and watching the night sky on your own. Think of how clever you'll feel pointing out the Black Llama to your fellow hikers. Reservations are essential. Price varies with group size and includes pickup and drop-off.

with some steep hills in between. The center of the city is the Plaza de Armas, while traffic-choked Av El Sol nearby is the main business thoroughfare. Walking just a few blocks north or east of the plaza will lead you onto steep, twisting cobblestone streets, little changed for centuries. The flatter areas to the south and west are the commercial center.

The alley heading away from the northwest side of the Plaza de Armas is Procuradores (Tax Collectors), nicknamed 'Gringo Alley' for its tourist restaurants, tour agents and other services. Watch out for predatory touts. Beside the hulking cathedral on the Plaza de Armas, narrow Calle Triunfo leads steeply uphill toward Plaza San Blas, the heart of Cuzco's eclectic, artistic *barrio* (neighborhood).

A resurgence of indigenous pride means many streets have been signposted with new Quechua names, although they are still commonly referred to by their Spanish names. The most prominent example is Calle Triunfo, which is signposted as Sunturwasi.

At tourist sites, freelance guides speak a varying amount of English or other foreign languages. For more extensive tours at major sites, such as Qorikancha or the cathedral, you should always agree to a fair price in advance. Otherwise, a respectable minimum tip for a short tour is S5 per person in a small group, and a little more for individuals.

Opening hours are erratic and can change for any reason – from Catholic feast days to the caretaker slipping off for a beer with his mates. A good time to visit Cuzco's well-preserved colonial churches is in the early morning (from 6am to 8am), when they are open for Mass. Officially, they are closed to tourists at these times, but if you go in quietly and respectfully as a member of the congregation, you can see the church as it should be seen. Flash photography is not allowed inside churches or museums.

CENTRAL CUZCO

Plaza de Armas   PLAZA
In Inca times, the plaza, called Huacaypata or Aucaypata, was the heart of the capital. Today it's the nerve center of the modern city. Two flags usually fly here – the red-and-white Peruvian flag and the rainbow-colored flag of Tahuantinsuyo. Easily mistaken for an international gay-pride banner, it represents the four quarters of the Inca empire.

Colonial arcades surround the plaza, which in ancient times was twice as large, also encompassing the area now called the Plaza Regocijo. On the plaza's northeastern side is the imposing cathedral, fronted by a large flight of stairs and flanked by the churches of Jesús María and El Triunfo. On the southeastern side is the strikingly ornate church of La Compañía de Jesús. The quiet pedestrian alleyway of Loreto, which has Inca walls, is a historic means of access to the plaza.

It's worth visiting the plaza at least twice – by day and by night – as it takes on a strikingly different look after dark, all lit up.

La Catedral   CHURCH
(Map p198; Plaza de Armas; admission S25 or with boleto religioso; ◷10am-5:45pm) A squatter on the site of Viracocha Inca's palace, the cathedral was built using blocks pilfered from the nearby Inca site of Sacsaywamán. Its construction started in 1559 and took almost a century. It is joined by Iglesia del Triunfo (1536) to its right and Iglesia de Jesús María (1733) to the left.

El Triunfo, Cuzco's oldest church, houses a vault containing the remains of the famous Inca chronicler Garcilaso de la Vega, who was born in Cuzco in 1539 and died in Córdoba, Spain, in 1616. His remains were returned in 1978 by King Juan Carlos of Spain.

The cathedral is one of the city's greatest repositories of colonial art, especially for works from the *escuela cuzqueña* (Cuzco school), noted for its decorative combination of 17th-century European devotional painting styles with the color palette and iconography of indigenous Andean artists. A classic example is the frequent portrayal of the Virgin Mary wearing a mountain-shaped skirt with a river running around its hem, identifying her with Pachamama (Mother Earth).

One of the most famous paintings of the *escuela cuzqueña* is *The Last Supper* by Quechua artist Marcos Zapata. Found in the northeast corner of the cathedral, it depicts one of the most solemn occasions in the Christian faith, but graces it with a small feast of Andean ceremonial food; look for the plump and juicy-looking roast *cuy* (guinea pig) stealing the show with its feet held plaintively in the air.

Also look for the oldest surviving painting in Cuzco, showing the entire city during the great earthquake of 1650. The inhabitants can be seen parading around the plaza with a crucifix, praying for the earthquake to stop, which it miraculously did. This precious crucifix, called **El Señor de los Temblores** (The Lord of the Earthquakes), can still be seen in the alcove to the right of the door leading into El Triunfo. Every year on Holy Monday, the Señor is taken out on parade and devotees throw *ñucchu* flowers at him – these resemble droplets of blood and represent the wounds of crucifixion. The flowers leave a sticky residue that collects smoke from votive candles lit beneath the statue: this is why he's now black. Legend has it that under his skirt, he's lily white.

The **sacristy** of the cathedral is covered with paintings of Cuzco's bishops, starting with Vicente de Valverde, the friar who accompanied Pizarro during the conquest. The crucifixion at the back of the sacristy is attributed to the Flemish painter Anthony van Dyck, though some guides claim it to be the work of the 17th-century Spaniard Alonso Cano. The original wooden **altar** is at the very back of the cathedral, behind the present silver altar, and opposite both is the magnificently carved **choir**, dating from the 17th century. There are also many glitzy silver and gold **side chapels** with elaborate platforms and altars that contrast with the austerity of the cathedral's stonework.

The huge main doors of the cathedral are open to genuine worshippers between 6am and 10am. Religious festivals are a superb time to see the cathedral. During the feast of Corpus Christi (p213), for example, it is filled with pedestals supporting larger-than-life statues of saints, surrounded by thousands of candles and bands of musicians honoring them with mournful Andean tunes.

Iglesia de La Compañía de Jesús CHURCH

(Map p198; Plaza de Armas; admission S15 or with boleto religioso; ⏲9-11:30am & 1-5:30pm) Built upon the palace of Huayna Cápac, the last Inca to rule an undivided, unconquered empire, the church was built by the Jesuits in 1571 and reconstructed after the 1650 earthquake.

The Jesuits planned to make it the most magnificent of Cuzco's churches. The archbishop of Cuzco, however, complained that its splendor should not rival that of the cathedral, and the squabble grew to a point where Pope Paul III was called upon to arbitrate. His decision was in favor of the cathedral, but by the time word had reached Cuzco, La Compañía de Jesús was just about finished, complete with an incredible baroque facade and Peru's biggest altar, all crowned by a soaring dome.

Two large canvases near the main door show early marriages in Cuzco and are worth examining for their wealth of period detail. Local student guides are available to show you around the church, as well as the grand view from the choir on the 2nd floor, reached via rickety steps. Tips are gratefully accepted.

Choco Museo MUSEUM

(Map p198; ☎24-4765; Calle Garcilaso 210; www.chocomuseo.com; admission S2; ⏲10:30am-6:30pm) The wafting aromas of bubbling chocolate will mesmerize you from the start. While the museum is frankly lite, the best part of this French-owned enterprise are the organic chocolate-making workshops (S70 per person). You can also come for fondue or a fresh cup of fair-trade hot cocoa. It organizes chocolate farm tours close to Santa María. It's multi-lingual and kid-friendly.

Museo de Plantas Sagradas, Mágicas y Medicinales MUSEUM

(Map p198; ☎22-2214; Calle Santa Teresa 351; admission S15; ⏲10am-7pm Mon-Sat, 12-6pm Sun) This fascinating new museum leaves no leaf unturned, exploring the history and workings of Peruvian medicinal plants, sacred plants and hallucinogenics. Highlights include displays on biopiracy, coca's 8000 years of cultivation, and trippy multi-layered visuals that emulate the *ayahuasca* experience. Unfortunately, all of the dioramas are in Spanish. It's

Central Cuzco

Sacsaywamán

To Q'enqo (3km);
Pukapukara (7km);
Tambomachay (7km)

Iglesia de
San Cristóbal

Iglesia de
Santa Teresa

To Transport to
Limatambo (700m)

Plaza de
Armas

La Catedral

Plaza del
Tricentenario

Plazoleta
Nazarenas

Triunfo
(Sunturwasi)

Santa
Catalina
Angosta

Plaza
Regocijo

Plazoleta
Espinar

Plaza
San
Francisco

Choquechaka

Pumacurco

Arco

Ese

Iris

Kiskapata

Resbalosa

Suecia

Coricalle

Amargura

Tecsecocha

Saphi

Tigre

Tambo de
Montero

Siete Cuartones

Teatro

Santa Teresa

Granada

Tordo

San Juan de Dios

Garcilaso

Heladeros

Calle del Medio

Espinar

Mantas

Marquez

San Bernardo

Mesón de la Estrella

Santa Clara

Quera

San Andrés

Ayacucho

Maruri

Loreto

Av El Sol

Almagro

Huaynapata

Purgatorio

Atalda

Procuradores

Platos

Ladrillos

Tucumán

Steps

Plaza

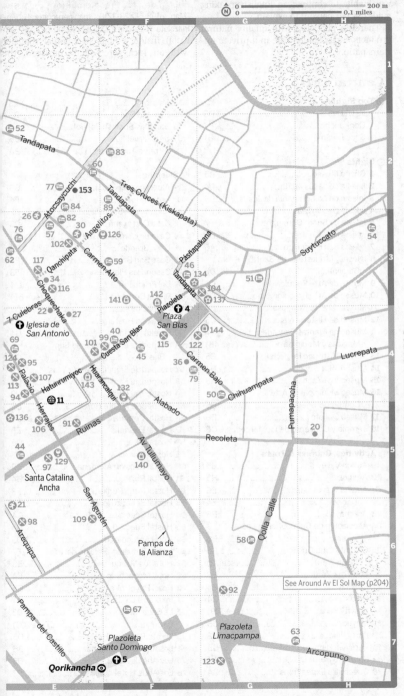

0 — 200 m
0 — 0.1 miles

E F G H

Tandapata

52

83

60

77 Atocsaycuchi 153

Tres Cruces (Kiskapata)

84 Tandapata

26 82 89

76 57 30 Angelitos 126

102 Carmen Alto

62

117 Qanchipata 59 Pastapakana

34 46 134

116 Tandapata

141 104

7 Culebras 22 27 142 137

Iglesia de Plazoleta 4 144

San Antonio Plaza Lucrepata

69 40 San Blas

124 95 101 99 Cuesta San Blas 115 122

107 45 Carmen Bajo

113 Palacio Hatunrumiyoc 143 132 36 Chihuampata

94 Huaracalqui 79

136 Herrajes Alabado 50

106 91 Ruinas

44 Recoleta

97 129 Av Tullumayo 140 20

Santa Catalina
Ancha

21

98 109

San Agustin

Pampa de
la Alianza

58

Qolla Calle

See Around Av El Sol Map (p204)

92

67

Plazoleta
Limacpampa

63

Pampa del Castillo Plazoleta Arcopunco

Santo Domingo

Qorikancha 5 123

Suytuccato

54

51

11

Arequipa

Pumapacha

worthwhile to contract an English-speaking guide (S4 per person) to explain.

There's a gift shop with quality natural products and a lauded cafe in a private upstairs patio.

Museo de Arte Precolombino MUSEUM
(Map p198; ☑23-3210; map.perucultural.org.pe; Plazoleta Nazarenas 231; admission S22; ☺9am-10pm) Inside a Spanish colonial mansion with an Inca ceremonial courtyard, this

dramatically curated pre-Columbian art museum showcases a stunningly varied, if selectively small, collection of archaeological artifacts previously buried in the vast storerooms of Lima's Museo Larco. Dating from between 1250 BC and AD 1532, the artifacts show off the artistic and cultural achievements of many of Peru's ancient cultures, with exhibits labeled in Spanish, English and French.

CUZCO & THE SACRED VALLEY IN...

Two Days

Spend one day exploring the city of Cuzco, starting with an early *jugo* (fruit juice) in **Mercado San Pedro**, then getting cultural with some of the city's many museums. **Museo Quijote** and the **Museo Histórico Regional** are highly recommended for fine art; **El Museo de Arte Popular** and **Museo Irq'i Yachay** for folksy art; and the **Museo Inka** for preconquest Peruvian artifacts. After lunch, see the most imposing relics left by the Incas and the Spanish conquistadors, respectively, at **Qorikancha** and **La Catedral**. At 6:45pm check out the nightly music and dance show at the **Centro Qosqo de Arte Nativo**. The next day, get up early and board a train to **Machu Picchu**, Peru's most renowned ancient site.

Four Days

Follow the Cuzco day of the two-day itinerary. On the second day enjoy a decadent breakfast and explore **Sacsaywamán** in the morning. Then bus to ancient, cobbled **Ollantaytambo** and use the afternoon to hike through the ruins above town. Take an early morning train to **Aguas Calientes** and hop on a bus to **Machu Picchu**. Wander through the marvels of Machu Picchu all day; get a guide for the inside story. Return to Ollantaytambo. There's still time to take local buses to the spectacular salt pans of **Salinas** on the way back to Cuzco.

One Week

Follow the Cuzco day of the two-day itinerary. On the second day, follow the **walking tour** up through arty San Blas to the impressive fortress of **Sacsaywamán**. Flag down local buses to the nearby ruins of **Tambomachay**, **Q'enqo** and **Pukapukara**. On the third day, start trekking the spectacular, rugged **Salkantay trail** to **Machu Picchu**.

Highlights include the Nazca and Moche galleries of multicolored ceramics, *queros* (ceremonial Inca wooden drinking vessels) and dazzling displays of jewelry made with intricate gold- and silverwork.

Museo Inka   MUSEUM
(Map p198; ☎23-7380; Tucumán at Ataúd; admission S10; ⊗8am-6pm Mon-Fri, 9am-4pm Sat) The charmingly modest Museo Inka, a steep block northeast of the Plaza de Armas, is the best museum in town for those interested in the Incas. The restored interior is jam packed with a fine collection of metal- and goldwork, jewelry, pottery, textiles, mummies, models and the world's largest collection of *queros*. There's excellent interpretive information in Spanish and English-speaking guides are usually available for a small fee.

The museum building, which rests on Inca foundations, is also known as the Admiral's House, after the first owner, Admiral Francisco Aldrete Maldonado. It was badly damaged in the 1650 earthquake and rebuilt by Pedro Peralta de los Ríos, the count of Laguna, whose crest is above the porch. Further damage from the 1950 earthquake has

now been fully repaired, restoring the building to its position among Cuzco's finest colonial houses. Look for the massive stairway guarded by sculptures of mythical creatures, and the corner window column that from the inside looks like a statue of a bearded man but from the outside appears to be a naked woman. The ceilings are ornate, and the windows give good views straight out across the Plaza de Armas.

Downstairs in the sunny courtyard, highland Andean weavers demonstrate their craft and sell traditional textiles directly to the public.

Museo de Historia Natural   MUSEUM
(Map p198; Plaza de Armas; admission S2; ⊗9am-5pm Mon-Fri) The university-run natural history museum houses a somewhat motley collection of stuffed local animals and birds and over 150 snakes from the Amazon. The entrance is hidden off the Plaza de Armas, to the right of Iglesia de la Compañía de Jesús.

Iglesia y Monasterio de Santa Catalina   CHURCH
(Map p198; Arequipa s/n; admission S8; ⊗8:30am-5:30pm Mon-Sat) This convent houses many

colonial paintings of the *escuela cuzqueña*, as well as an impressive collection of vestments and other intricate embroidery. The baroque side chapel features dramatic friezes, and many life-sized (and sometimes startling) models of nuns praying, sewing and going about their lives. The convent also houses 13 real, live contemplative nuns.

FREE **Museo Irq'i Yachay** MUSEUM
(Map p198; ☏24-1416; www.aylluyupaychay.org; Teatro 344; ⊙10am-1pm & 2-5pm Mon-Fri) More than a museum, Museo Irq'i Yachay is the fascinating by-product of an NGO that seeks to give opportunities for cognitive development to kids in remote communities. Since the most isolated and neglected communities are also guardians of traditional culture, the result is an engrossing glimpse of Andean culture.

The kids paint what they know – animals, mountains, rivers, people – and incorporate the symbols of the weavings that surround them from birth: north is hope and future, red is love and revenge. Along with the art itself, there's an impressive display of textiles. Accompanying interpretive information in Spanish and English explains this symbology in detail and makes this museum a must for textile fans.

Templo y Convento de La Merced CHURCH
(Map p198; ☏23-1821; Mantas 121; admission S6; ⊙8am-noon & 2-5pm Mon-Sat) Cuzco's third most important colonial church, La Merced was destroyed in the 1650 earthquake, but was quickly rebuilt. To the left of the church, at the back of a small courtyard, is the entrance to the monastery and museum. Paintings based on the life of San Pedro Nolasco, who founded the order of La Merced in Barcelona in 1218, hang on the walls of the beautiful colonial cloister.

The church on the far side of the **cloister** (⊙8-11am) contains the tombs of two of the most famous conquistadors: Diego de Almagro and Gonzalo Pizarro (brother of Francisco). Also on the far side of the cloister is a small religious museum that houses vestments rumored to have belonged to conquistador and friar Vicente de Valverde. The museum's most famous possession is a priceless solid-gold monstrance, 1.2m high and covered with rubies, emeralds and no fewer than 1500 diamonds and 600 pearls. Ask to see it if the display room is locked.

Museo Histórico Regional MUSEUM
(Map p198; Calle Garcilaso at Heladeros; entry with boleto turístico; ⊙8am-5pm Tue-Sun) This eclectic museum is housed in the colonial Casa Garcilaso de la Vega, the house of the Inca-Spanish chronicler who now lies buried in the cathedral. The chronologically arranged collection begins with arrowheads from the Preceramic Period and continues with ceramics and jewelry of the Wari, Pukara and Inca cultures.

There is also a Nazca mummy, a few Inca weavings, some small gold ornaments and a strangely sinister scale model of the Plaza de Armas. A big, helpful chart in the courtyard outlines the timeline and characters of the *escuela cuzqueña*.

Museo Municipal de Arte Contemporáneo MUSEUM
(Map p198; Plaza Regocijo; entry with boleto turístico; ⊙9am-6pm Mon-Sat) The small collection of contemporary Andean art on display at this museum in the municipality building is really one for the fans. Museo Quijote has a much better collection, putting a representative range of Peru's contemporary artists on show, with interpretive information that puts art in context with history.

FREE **Iglesia San Francisco** CHURCH
(Map p198; Plaza San Francisco; ⊙6:30-8am & 5:30-8pm Mon-Sat, 6:30am-noon & 6:30-8pm Sun) More austere than many of Cuzco's other churches, Iglesia San Francisco dates from the 16th and 17th centuries and is one of the few that didn't need to be completely reconstructed after the 1650 earthquake. It has a large collection of colonial religious paintings and a beautifully-carved cedar choir.

The attached **museum** (admission S8; ⊙9am-noon & 3-5pm Mon-Fri, 9am-noon Sat) houses supposedly the largest painting in South America, which measures 9m by 12m and shows the family tree of St Francis of Assisi, the founder of the order. Also of macabre interest are the two crypts, which are not totally underground. Inside are human bones, some of which have been carefully arranged in designs meant to remind visitors of the transitory nature of life.

Museo de Arte Religioso MUSEUM
(Map p198; cnr Hatunrumiyoc & Herrajes; admission S15 or with boleto religioso; ⊙8-11am & 3-6pm Mon-Sat) Originally the palace of Inca Roca, the foundations of this museum were converted

Around Av El Sol

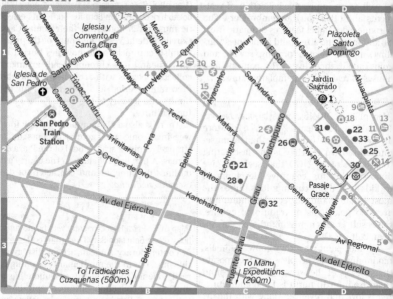

Around Av El Sol

See Central Cuzco
Map (p198)

from a deadly disease and subsequently dedicated his life to carving this pulpit for the church. Supposedly, his skull is nestled in the topmost part of the carving. In reality, no one is certain of the identity of either the skull or the woodcarver.

AVENIDA EL SOL & DOWNHILL

Museo de Arte Popular   MUSEUM
(Map p198; Basement, Av El Sol 103; admission with boleto turístico; ⊙9am-6pm Mon-Sat, 8am-1pm Sun) Winning entries in Cuzco's annual Popular Art Competition are displayed in this engaging museum. This is where the artisans and artists of San Blas showcase their talents in styles ranging from high art to cheeky, offering a fascinating, humorous take on ordinary life amid the pomp and circumstance of a once-grandiose culture.

Small-scale ceramic models depict drunken debauchery in the *picantería* (local restaurant), torture in the dentist's chair, carnage in the butcher shop, and even a caesarean section. There's also a display of photographs, many by renowned local photographer Martín Chambi, of Cuzco from the 1900s to the 1950s, including striking images of the aftermath of the 1950 earthquake in familiar streets.

Qorikancha   RUIN
(Map p198; Plazoleta Santo Domingo, admission S10; ⊙8:30am-5:30pm Mon-Sat, 2-5pm Sun) If you visit only one site in Cuzco, make it these Inca ruins, which form the base of the colonial church and convent of Santo Domingo. Qorikancha was once the richest temple in the Inca empire; all that remains today is the masterful stonework.

In Inca times, Qorikancha (Quechua for 'Golden Courtyard') was literally covered with gold. The temple walls were lined with some 700 solid-gold sheets, each weighing about 2kg. There were life-sized gold and silver replicas of corn, which were ceremonially 'planted' in agricultural rituals. Also reported were solid-gold treasures such as altars, llamas and babies, as well as a replica of the sun, which was lost. But within months of the arrival of the first conquistadors, this incredible wealth had all been looted and melted down.

Various other religious rites took place in the temple. It is said that the mummified bodies of several previous *incas* (kings) were kept here, brought out into the sunlight each day and offered food and drink, which was then ritually burnt. Qorikancha

into a grand colonial residence and later became the archbishop's palace. The beautiful mansion is now home to a religious-art collection notable for the accuracy of its period detail, and especially its insight into the interaction of indigenous peoples with the Spanish conquistadors.

There are also some impressive ceilings and colonial-style tile work that's not original, having been replaced during the 1940s.

SAN BLAS
Known as the artists' neighborhood, San Blas is nestled on a steep hillside next to the center. With classic architecture, its signature blue doors and narrow passageways without cars, it has become a hip part of town. As a result, it is full of restaurants, watering holes and shops.

Iglesia de San Blas   CHURCH
(Map p198; Plaza San Blas; admission S15 or with boleto religioso; ⊙10am-6pm Mon-Sat, 2-6pm Sun) This simple adobe church is comparatively small, but you can't help but be awed by the baroque, gold-leaf principal altar. The exquisitely carved pulpit, made from a single tree trunk, has been called the finest example of colonial wood carving in the Americas.

Legend claims that its creator was an indigenous man who miraculously recovered

---

ℹ️ **COOL FOR KIDS: THE CHIQUITY CLUB**

This excellent children's **activity center** (Map p198; 📞23-3344; www. chiquityclubcusco.com; Marquez 259; child with parents S15; ⏰9am-8pm Thu-Tue; 📶) offers a great way for young families to decompress. The brainchild of a bilingual Waldorf-trained teacher, this multifaceted space includes covered play areas, a climbing wall and sandbox of 'fossils.' There's also a library with English language books, an art room, a dress-up theatre and a rockin' dark mini-discoteca, pulsing strobes and fun tunes. The ideal age for visitors is one to nine years old. It also offers baby-sitting services and activity kits to go.

---

was also an observatory from which high priests monitored celestial activities. Most of this is left to the imagination of the modern visitor, but the remaining stonework ranks with the finest Inca architecture in Peru. A curved, perfectly fitted 6m-high wall can be seen from both inside and outside the site. This wall has withstood all of the violent earthquakes that leveled most of Cuzco's colonial buildings.

Once inside the site, the visitor enters a courtyard. The octagonal font in the middle was originally covered with 55kg of solid gold. Inca chambers lie to either side of the courtyard. The largest, to the right, were said to be temples to the moon and the stars, and were covered with sheets of solid silver. The walls are perfectly tapered upward and, with their niches and doorways, are excellent examples of Inca trapezoidal architecture. The fitting of the individual blocks is so precise that in some places you can't tell where one block ends and the next begins.

Opposite these chambers, on the other side of the courtyard, are smaller temples dedicated to thunder and the rainbow. Three holes have been carved through the walls of this section to the street outside, which scholars think were drains, either for sacrificial *chicha* (fermented corn beer), blood or, more mundanely, rainwater. Alternatively, they may have been speaking tubes connecting the inner temple with the outside. Another feature of this side of the complex is the floor in front of the chambers: it

dates from Inca times and is carefully cobbled with pebbles.

The temple was built in the mid-15th century during the reign of the 10th *inca*, Túpac Yupanqui. After the conquest, Francisco Pizarro gave it to his brother Juan, but he was not able to enjoy it for long – Juan died in the battle at Sacsaywamán in 1536. In his will, he bequeathed Qorikancha to the Dominicans, in whose possession it has remained ever since. Today's site is a bizarre combination of Inca and colonial architecture, topped with a roof of glass and metal.

Colonial paintings around the outside of the courtyard depict the life of St Dominic, which contain several representations of dogs holding torches in their jaws. These are God's guard dogs (*dominicanus* in Latin), hence the name of this religious order.

Iglesia de Santo Domingo   CHURCH

The church of Santo Domingo is next door to Qorikancha. Less baroque and ornate than many of Cuzco's churches, it is notable for its charming paintings of archangels depicted as Andean children in jeans and T-shirts. Opening hours are erratic.

Museo del Sitio de Qorikancha   MUSEUM

(Map p204; Av El Son s/n; admission with boleto turístico; ⏰9am-6pm Mon-Sat, 8am-1pm Sun) There are sundry moth-bitten archaeological displays interpreting Inca and pre-Inca cultures at this small, mangy, underground archaeological museum, which is accessed off Av El Sol.

Museo Quijote   MUSEUM

(Map p198; www.museoelquijote.com; Galería Banco la Nacion, Calle Almagro s/n; entry S10 or with boleto religioso; ⏰9am-6pm Mom-Fri, 9am-1pm Sun) In a new location housed inside a bank, this privately owned museum of contemporary art houses a diverse, thoughtful collection of painting and sculpture ranging from the folksy to the macabre. There's good interpretive information about 20th-century Peruvian art history, some of it translated into English.

Activities

Scores of outdoor outfitters in Cuzco offer trekking, rafting and mountain-biking adventures, as well as mountaineering, horseback riding and paragliding. Price wars can lead to bad feelings among locals, with underpaid guides and overcrowded vehicles. The cheaper tours are liable to be the most crowded, multilingual affairs. Due to tax exemptions for new agencies, cheaper outfits also regularly change names and offices, so ask other foreign tourists for the most recent recommendations.

No company can ever be 100% recommended, but those listed in the following sections are reputable outfits that have received mostly positive feedback from readers.

Trekking

The department of Cuzco is a hiker's paradise. Ecosystems range from rainforest to high alpine environments in these enormous mountain ranges. Trekkers may come upon isolated villages and ruins lost in the undergrowth. Since altitudes vary widely, it is essential to properly acclimatize before undertaking any trek.

Of course, most come to hike the famed Inca Trail to Machu Picchu. Be aware that it's not the only 'Inca trail.' What savvy tourism officials and tour operators have christened the Inca Trail is just one of dozens of footpaths that the Incas built to reach Machu Picchu, out of thousands that crisscrossed the Inca empire. Some of these overland routes are still being dug out of the jungle by archaeologists. Many more have been developed for tourism, and an ever-increasing number of trekkers are choosing them.

For more detailed hiking information, purchase an *Alternative Inca Trails Information Packet* from the South American Explorers Club. Closer to Cuzco, imaginative operators have developed multiday Sacred Valley trekking itineraries that go well off the beaten track to little-visited villages and ruins.

For full coverage of the Inca Trail and alternative trekking routes to Machu Picchu, see p38. Other recommended treks to archaeological sites include Choquequirau (p265) and Vilcabamba (263).

Other highly recommended treks include Lares (p213) and Ausangate (p264).

The following companies are Cuzco-based trekking specialists often recommended by readers. For international outfitters and those offering Peru-wide treks, see p36.

Andina Travel HIKING
(Map p198; 25-1892; www.andinatravel.com; Plazoleta Santa Catalina 219)

Apu's Peru HIKING
(Map p204; 23-3691; www.apus-peru.com; Cuichipunco 366)

Eco Trek Peru HIKING
(Map p198; 24-7286; www.ecotrekperu.com; Atocsaycuchi 599)

X-treme Tourbulencia HIKING
(Map p198; 22-5872; www.x-tremetourbulencia.com; Plateros 358)

Peru Treks HIKING
(Map p204; 22-2722; www.perutreks.com; Av Pardo 540)

Peruvian Highland Trek HIKING
(Map p198; 24-2480; www.peruvianhighlandtrek.com; Calle del Medio 139)

Quechua's Expeditions HIKING
(Map p198; 23-7994; www.quechuasexpeditions.com; Suecia 344)

WHEN TO GO

The best time to go trekking in the Andes or the Amazon is during the colder dry season, which lasts roughly from May until September. Make reservations for treks during high seasons several months in advance, and up to a year in advance for the Inca Trail. In the wettest months of January to March, trails have a tendency to turn into muddy slogs, and views disappear under a blanket of clouds. Note that the Inca Trail is completely closed during the month of February for its annual cleanup. The high jungle Vilcabamba trek is not recommended outside June to August due to heavy rainfall. Temperatures can drop below freezing year-round on all the other, higher-altitude treks, and it occasionally rains even during the dry season.

WHAT TO BRING

Modern internal-framed backpacks, tents, sleeping bags and stoves can all be rented in various places in Calle Plateros from around S15 to S20 per item per day. Check all equipment carefully before you agree to rent it, as some is pretty shoddy, and most isn't modern or lightweight.

Also take water-purification tablets or a purification system from home. Once you're trekking, there is usually nowhere to buy food, and the small villages where treks begin have very limited supplies, so shop in advance in Cuzco. If you're on a guided trek, take a stash of cash for tipping the guide and the *arrieros* (mule drivers). About US$10 per day per trekker is the minimum decent tip to a guide; a similar amount to divide between *arrieros* is appropriate.

For more tips on appropriate trekking gear, see p38.

River Running

Rafting isn't regulated in Peru – literally anyone can start a rafting company. On top of this, aggressive bargaining has led to lax safety by many cheaper rafting operators. The degree of risk cannot be stressed enough: there are deaths every year. Rafting companies that take advance bookings online are generally more safety conscious (and more expensive) than those just operating out of storefronts in Cuzco.

When choosing an outfitter, it's wise to ask about safety gear and guide training, ask about the quality of the equipment used (ie how old are the flotation devices) and check other traveler comments. Be wary of new agencies without a known track record.

The following rafting companies have the best reputations for safety:

Amazonas Explorer   BOATING
(☑25-2846; www.amazonas-explorer.com; Av Collasuyu 910, Miravalle) A professional international operator with top-quality equipment and guides, offering rafting trips on the Ríos Apurimac and Tambopata.

Apumayo   BOATING
(Map p198; ☑24-6018; www.apumayo.com; Jirón Ricardo Palma Ñ-11, Urb. Santa Monica) Another professional outfitter that takes advance international bookings for Río Tambopata trips. Also equipped to take travelers with disabilities.

Mayuc   BOATING
(Map p198; ☑24-2824; www.mayuc.com; Portal Confiturías 211) This monster operator, very popular with bargain hunters, dwarfs the competition.

River Explorers   BOATING
(☑26-0926; www.riverexplorers.com; Urb. Kennedy A, B-15) Runs all sorts of sections, including trips of up to six days on Río Apurímac.

RÍO URUBAMBA

Rafting the Río Urubamba through the Sacred Valley could offer the best rafting day trip in South America, but Cuzco and all the villages along its course dispose of raw sewage in the river, making for a smelly and polluted trip. Seriously – close your mouth if you fall in.

Despite its unsavory aspects, the **Ollantaytambo to Chilca** (class II to III) section is surprisingly popular, offering 1½ hours of gentle rafting with only two rapids of note. **Huarán** and **Huambutio to Pisac** are other pollution-affected sections.

There are a variety of cleaner sections south of Cuzco on the upper Urubamba (also known as the Vilcanota), including the popular **Chuquicahuana** run (class III to IV+; class V+ in the rainy season). Another less-frenetic section is the fun and scenic **Cusipata to Quiquihana** (mainly class II to III). In the rainy season, these two sections are often combined. Closer to Cuzco, **Pampa to Huambutio** (class I to II) is a beautiful section, ideal for small children (three years and over) as an introduction to rafting.

RÍO SANTA TERESA

Río Santa Teresa offers spectacular rafting in the gorge between the towns of Santa Teresa and Santa María, and downstream as far as Quillabamba. One word of warning: the section from Cocalmayo Hot Springs to Santa María consists of almost nonstop class IV to V rapids in a deep, inaccessible canyon. It should only be run with highly reputable operators, such as local experts Cola de Mono (p260). Be very aware, if considering a trip here, that guiding this section safely is beyond the powers of inexperienced (cheaper) rafting guides. This is not the place to economize. It's not a bad idea to raft another section in the area with your chosen operator before even considering it.

OTHER RIVERS

Run from May to November, the **Río Apurímac** offers three- to 10-day trips through deep gorges and protected rainforest. Apurímac features exhilarating rapids (classes IV and V) and wild, remote scenery with deep gorges. Sightings of condors and even pumas have been recorded. Four-day trips are the most relaxed and avoid the busier campsites, although three-day trips are more commonly offered. Camping is on sandy beaches, which have become increasingly overused. Sand flies can be a nuisance. Make sure your outfitter cleans up the campsite and practices a leave-no-trace ethic.

An even wilder expedition, the 10- to 12-day trip along the demanding **Río Tambopata** can only be run from May to October. The trip starts in the Andes, north of Lake Titicaca, and descends through the heart of the Parque Nacional Bahuaje-Sonene deep in the Amazon jungle. Just getting to the put-in from Cuzco is a two-day drive. The first days on the river are full of technically demanding rapids (classes III and IV) in wild Andean scenery, and the trip finishes with a couple of gentle floating days n the rainforest. Tapirs, capybara, caiman, giant otters and jaguars have all been seen by keen-eyed boaters.

Rivers further from Cuzco are days away from help in the event of illness or accident. t's essential to book a top-notch outfitter employing highly experienced rafting guides with first aid certification and knowledge of swift-water rescue techniques.

Mountain Biking

Mountain-biking tours are a growing industry in Cuzco, and the local terrain is superb. Rental bikes are poor quality and it is most common to find *rígida* (single suspension) models, which can make for bone-chattering downhills. Good new or second-hand bikes are not easy to buy in Cuzco either. If you're a serious mountain biker, consider bringing your own bike from home. Selling it in Cuzco is eminently viable.

If you're an experienced rider, some awesome rides are quickly and easily accessible by public transport. Take the Pisac bus (stash your bike on top) and ask to be let off at **Abra de Ccorao**. From here, you can turn right and make your way back to Cuzco via a series of cart tracks and single track; halfway down is a jump park constructed by local aficionados. This section has many variations and is known as **Yuncaypata**. Eventually, whichever way you go, you'll end up in Cuzco's southern suburbs, from where you can easily flag down a taxi to get you home.

If you head off the other side of the pass, to the left of the road, you'll find fast-flowing single track through a narrow valley, which makes it difficult to get lost. It brings you out on the highway in Ccorao. From here, follow the road through a flat section then a series of bends. Just as the valley widens out, turn left past a farmhouse steeply downhill to your left and into challenging single track through a narrow valley, including a hairy river crossing and some tricky, steep, rocky, loose descents at the end, reaching the village of Taray. From here it's a 10-minute ride along the river to Pisac, where you can catch a bus back to Cuzco.

Many longer trips are possible, but a professionally qualified guide and a support vehicle are necessary. The partly paved road down from **Abra Málaga to Santa María**, though not at all technical, is a must for any cyclist. It is part of the Inca Jungle Trail (see p38), offered by many Cuzco operators. **Maras to Salinas** is a great little mission. The **Lares Valley** offers challenging single track,

which can be accessed from Cuzco in a long day. If heading to Manu in the Amazon Basin, you can break up the long bus journey by biking from **Tres Cruces to La Unión** – a beautiful, breathtaking downhill ride – or you could go all the way down by bike. The outfitters of Manu trips can arrange bicycle rental and guides. The descent to the **Río Apurímac** makes a great burn, as does the journey to **Río Tambopata**, which boasts a descent of 3500m in five hours. A few bikers attempt the 500km-plus trip all the way to Puerto Maldonado, a great hot and sweaty challenge.

The following bike operators are recommended:

Amazonas Explorer   ADVENTURE TOUR
(☑25-2846; www.amazonas-explorer.com) Offers excellent two- to 10-day mountain-biking adventures; great for families, with kids' bikes available.

Cusco Aventuras   ADVENTURE TOUR
(☑984-13-7403; cuscoaventura@hotmail.com) Local legend of loconess Luchín will give you the ride of your life.

Party Bike   ADVENTURE TOUR
(Map p198; ☑24-0399; www.partybiketravel.com; Carmen Alto 246) Traveler recommended, with downhills, tours to the valley and through Cusco.

Gravity Peru   ADVENTURE TOUR
(☑22-8032; www.gravityperu.com; Santa Catalina Ancha 398) Allied with well-known Gravity Bolivia, this professionally run operator is the only one offering double-suspension bikes for day trips. Highly recommended.

Horseback Riding

Most agencies can arrange a morning or afternoon's riding. Alternatively, you can walk to Sacsaywamán, where many ranches are located, and negotiate your own terms. Choose carefully, however, as horses may be in a sorry state.

Select agencies will offer multiday trips to the area around Limatambo, and there are some first-rate ranches with highly trained, high-stepping thoroughbred Peruvian *paso* horses in Urubamba (see p238).

Bird-Watching

Serious birders should definitely get a hold of *Birds of the High Andes,* by Jon Fjeldså and Niels Krabbe. One of the best birding trips is from Ollantaytambo to Santa Teresa or Quillabamba, over Abra Málaga. This provides a fine cross section of habitats from 4600m to below 1000m. Englishman Barry Walker is a self-confessed 'birding bum' and the best resident ornithologist to give serious birders plenty of enthusiastic advice. He has written a field guide, *The Birds of Machu Picchu*, and runs tour agency **Birding in Peru** (☎22-5990; www.birding-in-peru.com) with bird-watching trips throughout Peru, Bolivia and Chile.

Other Activities

For a post-trek splurge, a number of spas offer massage services, including the highly professional **Siluet Sauna & Spa** (Map p204; ☎23-1504; Quera 253; ☺10am-10pm) and the luxurious **Samana Spa** (Map p198; ☎23-3721; www. samana-spa.com; Tecsecocha 536; ☺10am-7pm Mon-Sat). Beware of cheap massages touted in the street; most practitioners lack formal training and there are reports of massages getting much more *intimate* than expected.

Sacred Valley Via Ferrata　ADVENTURE SPORTS
(☎984-11-2732; www.naturavive.com; per person S160) 'Iron Way' in Italian, this climb features a series of ladders, holds and bridges built into a sheer rock face. First developed in the Italian Alps in WWII, it's a way for reasonably fit non-rock climbers to have some adrenaline-pumping fun. It was constructed and is operated by rock-climbing and high-mountain professionals. In a stunning setting in the Sacred Valley, it features a 300m vertical ascent, a heart-hammering hanging bridge 200m above the valley floor and a 100m rappel. There is also a zip line (S160) accessed by a 40-minute hike. Each activity takes three to four hours and the price includes pickup and drop-off in Cuzco or Urubamba, climbing and lunch.

Action Valley　ADVENTURE SPORTS
(Map p198; ☎24-0835; www.actionvalley.com; Santa Teresa 325; ☺9am-5pm Sun-Fri, closed mid-Jan to mid-Feb) Adventure park extraordinaire, this place is a terror for acrophobes and a blast for kids and juvenile adults. Offerings include paintball (S75), a 10-meter climbing wall (S36), a 122m bungee jump (S230) and a bungee slingshot (S230). It's also possible to go paragliding (S315) from the *mirador* of Racchi. The park is 11km outside Cuzco on the road to Poroy.

🏊 Courses

Cuzco is one of the best places in South America to study Spanish. Shop around – competition is fierce and students benefit

with free cultural and social activities. Salsa lessons and cooking nights are more or less ubiquitous.

The standard deal is 20 hours of classes per week, either individual or in groups of up to four people. Most schools will also let you pay by the hour or study more or less intensively. Rates usually run at around S16 per hour for group lessons and S23 per hour for private lessons.

Visit your school on a Friday to get tested and assigned to a group for a Monday start or show up any time to start individual lessons. All schools can arrange family homestays and volunteer opportunities.

Amigos　LANGUAGE COURSE
(Map p198; ☎24-2292; www.spanishcusco.com; Zaguan del Cielo B-23) A long-established nonprofit school with an admirable public service record.

Excel Language Center　LANGUAGE COURSE
(Map p204; ☎23-5298; www.excel-spanishlanguageprograms-peru.org; Cruz Verde 336) Highly recommended for its professionalism.

Fairplay　LANGUAGE COURSE
(Map p198; ☎984-78-9252; www.fairplay-peru.org; Choquechaca 188) A unique nonprofit NGO, Fairplay trains Peruvian single mothers to provide Spanish lessons and homestays. Students pay two-thirds of their class fees directly to their teachers. Individual classes only, priced according to the teacher's level of experience.

Proyecto Peru　LANGUAGE COURSE
(Map p198; ☎24-0278, 984-68-3016; http://proyectoperucentre.org; Calle Seite Cuartones 290) Also offers Quechua and business or medical Spanish. In a new downtown location.

San Blas Spanish School　LANGUAGE COURSE
(Map p198; ☎24-7898; www.spanishschoolperu. com; Carmen Bajo 224) Students enjoy the informal teaching here, in tune with the school's location in the heart of bohemian San Blas.

👉 Tours & Guides

There are hundreds of registered travel agencies in Cuzco, but things change quickly, so ask other travelers for recommendations. Be aware that many of the small travel agencies clustered around Procuradores and Plateros earn commissions selling trips run by other outfitters, and this can lead to organizational mix-ups. If the travel agency

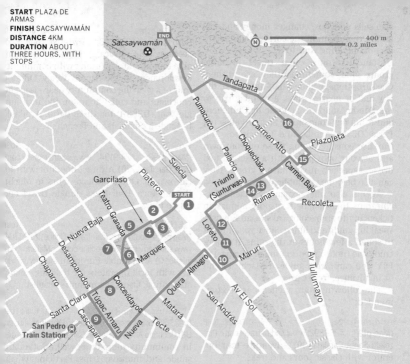

START PLAZA DE ARMAS
FINISH SACSAYWAMÁN
DISTANCE 4KM
DURATION ABOUT THREE HOURS, WITH STOPS

Walking Tour
Cuzco

Start from the middle of the **1** **Plaza de Armas**, one of the most stunning public spaces in South America. Stroll up Calle del Medio and head southwest across **2** **Plaza Regocijo**. On your left, a beautiful **3** **building**, once a hotel, is now home to restaurants and chic boutiques. Head up Calle Garcilaso, named for the Inca chronicler Garcilaso de la Vega, whose childhood home now houses the **4** **Museo Histórico Regional**. It sits amidst colonial mansions, **5** **Hotel los Marqueses** is particularly stunning.

On Sundays, Quechua-speaking *campesinos* (country folk) meet in **6** **Plaza San Francisco**. Drop in to the **7** **church and museum of San Francisco** if you're so inclined. Past the colonial archway is the **8** **church and convent of Santa Clara**. If it's open, peek inside at the mirrors, used in colonial times to entice curious indigenous people into the church for worship.

Just beyond, the bustle of **9** **Mercado San Pedro** spills out onto the pavement. Fuel up at one of the many stalls, then step out onto Calle Nueva and follow to Avenida El Sol

opposite the **10** **Palacio de Justicia**, a big white building with a pair of lawn-mowing llamas in the back garden. Head up Maruri and take a left into **11** **Loreto**, a walkway with Inca walls on both sides. The west wall belongs to Amaruqancha (Courtyard of the Serpents). The east wall is one of the best and oldest in Cuzco, belonging to the Acllahuasi (House of the Chosen Women). Post conquest, it became part of the **12** **closed convent of Santa Catalina**.

Loreto returns you to the Plaza de Armas. Turn right up Triunfo (signposted as Sunturwasi) and across Palacio into Hatunrumiyoc, another alley named after the **13** **12-sided stone**. This belongs to a wall of the palace of the sixth *inca*, Inca Roca, which now houses the **14** **Museo de Arte Religioso**.

Hatunrumiyoc ends at Choquechaca. From here it's only a short puff up to **15** **Plaza San Blas**, Cuzco's bohemian HQ. Head left along **16** **Tandapata** for the classic cobblestone experience. Inca irrigation channels run down ancient stairways, and rock carvings adorn walls and stones in the path.

If you wish, forge uphill to Sacsaywamán.

also sells ponchos, changes money and has an internet cabin in the corner, chances are it's not operating your tour.

Standard tours often travel in large groups and sometimes they are rushed. Classic options include a half-day tour of the city and/or nearby ruins, a half-day trip to the Sunday markets at Pisac or Chinchero and a full-day tour of the Sacred Valley (eg Pisac, Ollantaytambo and Chinchero). You can also consider doing these on your own and at your own pace with a licensed taxi driver, especially if you have a group. They can also be done via public transport.

Agents also offer expensive Machu Picchu tours that include transport, admission tickets to the archaeological site, an English-speaking guide and lunch. Since you only get to spend a few hours at the ruins, it's more enjoyable (not to mention much cheaper) to DIY. You can hire a guide at Machu Picchu or in advance, from Cuzco.

The following tour agencies are recommended:

Andina Travel
ADVENTURE TOUR
(Map p198; ☎25-1892; www.andinatravel.com; Plazoleta Santa Catalina 219) Adventure tour operator with classic tours and treks.

Antipode
ADVENTURE TOUR
(Map p198; ☎970-440-448; www.antipode-travel.com; Choquechaca 229) An attentive, French-run outfit offering classic tours, treks and shorter local adventure outings.

🌱 Chaski Ventura
CULTURAL TOUR
(Map p204; ☎23-3952; www.chaskiventura.com; Manco Cápac 517) Pioneer of alternative and community tourism, with quality itineraries and guides, also involved in community development. Offers package trips to the jungle, overnights in Sacred Valley communities and Machu Picchu. French, English and Spanish spoken.

Fertur
TOUR
(Map p198; ☎22-1304; www.fertur-travel.com; San Agustín 317) Local office of long-established, very reliable agency for flights and all conventional tours.

Milla Turismo
TOUR
(Map p204; ☎23-1710; www.millaturismo.com; Av Pardo 800) Reputable conventional tour operator with travel agency services and recommended private tours with knowledgeable drivers.

🌱 Respons
CULTURAL TOUR
(Map p198; ☎23-3903; www.respons.org; Choquechaca 216-C, staircase) High-end sustainable tour operator working with community development in the Sacred Valley. Offers a tour of a weaving community near Pisac and chocolate and coffee tours on the Inca jungle trail (US$370 for three days). Available in English, Spanish and French.

SAS Travel
TOUR
(Map p198; ☎24-9194; www.sastravelperu.com; Calle Garcilaso 270) A direct operator with local owners. Offers package tours to Machu Picchu, Inca Trail treks, jungle travel and Cusco tours.

SATO
TOUR
(Map p204; South American Travels Online ☎22-1304 www.southamericatravelsonline.com; Matara 437 interior-G) A reputable European agency working with local operators for trekking, hiking and rafting, also a last-minute specialist.

🌱 Turismo Caith
CULTURAL TOUR
(☎23-3595; www.caith.org; Centro Yanapanakusun Urb Ucchullo Alto, N4, Pasaje Santo Toribio) Leader in community tourism as well as standard single and multiday trips. Participants can help with educational projects.

The following operators also go into the jungle. For more options, see p454.

Manu Expeditions
ADVENTURE TOUR
(off Map p204; ☎22-5990, 22-4235; www.manu expeditions.com; Clorinda Matto de Turner 330 Urb Magisterial) Destinations include Manu Biosphere Reserve and horseback riding around Sacred Valley.

Manu Nature Tours
ADVENTURE TOUR
(Map p204; ☎25 2721; www.manuperu.com; Pardo 1046) Reputable outfitter with its own rainforest lodges in Manu.

Guides
The following guides for Machu Picchu and around Cuzco are recommended:

Asociación de Guías Oficiales de Turismo
GUIDED TOUR
(Map p198; Agotur; ☎24-9758; www.agoturcusco.org.pe; Heladeros 157) A good way to contact guides.

Adam Weintraub
GUIDED TOUR
(☎962-859-000; www.photoexperience.net) A native of Seattle, Adam has many years' experience in Peru and guides custom high-end

YOUR SACRED VISION FOR SALE

Shamanic ceremonies may be native to the Amazon, but they have become a hot commodity in Cuzco and the Sacred Valley. The psychedelic properties of the San Pedro and *ayahuasca* plants have earned them fame and piqued public curiosity and the interest of psychonauts who travel in search of these experiences. Extremely powerful drugs, they can be highly toxic in the wrong hands.

Yet they are ubiquitous. In Cuzco, San Pedro is offered alongside massages by street hawkers; *ayahuasca* ceremonies are advertised in hostels. Of course, travelers can decide what is right and wrong for them. It's important to note that these are not recreational drugs. A real shaman knows the long list of dos and don'ts for practitioners, and they screen participants. Ceremonies can require multiple days for preparation, fasting and extended rituals.

It is hard not to be skeptical about a store-bought spiritual experience. Many *cuzqueños* believe that it's a mockery to make these sacred ceremonies into moneymakers. Still, participating in a 'guided ceremony' can be a lot safer than scarfing down a powerful narcotic by yourself, as long as you trust the practitioners (in some cases, female guests have been attacked while under the influence). Avoid casual opportunities. Serious operations often use a medical questionnaire. It's also advisable to look into ceremonies and ask previous participants about their experience before signing up.

A good place to learn more about rituals of *ayahuasca* and San Pedro is the new Museo de Plantas Sagradas, Mágicas y Medicinales in Cuzco.

photography tours and workshops over all of Peru, as well as shorter trips out of Cuzco.

Alain Machaca Cruz   GUIDED TOUR
(☑984-056-635, 973-220-893; alain_313@hotmail.com) Recommended for interesting alternative city tours where you can make *chicha* or see *cuy* farms, and hikes and visits to surrounding communities. Quechua and English spoken.

Leo Garcia   GUIDED TOUR
(☑984-70-2933, 984-75-4022; leogacia@hotmail.com) Personable, passionate and supremely knowledgeable about all things Inca.

Raul Castelo   GUIDED TOUR
(☑24-3234, 984-31-6345; raulcastelo10@hotmail.com) Has his own transport and specializes in customized tours to Sacred Valley, Machu Picchu, Cuzco, Cuzco–Puno and Lares.

✸ Festivals & Events

Cuzco and the surrounding highlands celebrate many lively fiestas and holidays. In addition to national holidays (p534), the following are the most crowded times, when you should book all accommodations well in advance:

El Señor de los Temblores   FESTIVAL
(The Lord of the Earthquakes) This procession on the Monday before Easter dates to the earthquake of 1650.

Crucifix Vigil   FESTIVAL
On May 2 to 3, a Crucifix Vigil is held on all hillsides with crosses atop them.

Q'oyoriti   FESTIVAL
Less well-known than the spectacular Inti Raymi are the more traditional Andean rites of this festival (see the boxed text, p266), which is held at the foot of Ausangate the Tuesday before Corpus Christi, in late May or early June.

Corpus Christi   RELIGIOUS
Held on the ninth Thursday after Easter, Corpus Christi usually occurs in early June and features fantastic religious processions and celebrations in the cathedral.

Inti Raymi   FESTIVAL
Cuzco's most important festival, the 'Festival of the Sun' is held on June 24. It attracts tourists from all over Peru and the world, and the whole city celebrates in the streets. The festival culminates in a re-enactment of the Inca winter-solstice festival at Sacsaywamán. Despite its commercialization, it's still worth seeing the street dances and parades, as well as the pageantry at Sacsaywamán.

Santuranticuy Artisan Crafts Fair   FESTIVAL
A crafts fair is held in the Plaza de Armas on December 24 (Christmas Eve).

🛏 Sleeping

Cuzco has hundreds of hotels of all types, and just about the only thing they have in common is that they charge some of the highest room rates in Peru. Cuzco fills to bursting between June and August, especially during the 10 days before Inti Raymi on June 24 and during Fiestas Patrias (Independence Days) on July 28 and 29. Book in advance for these dates.

Prices are market driven and vary dramatically according to the season and demand. Rates quoted here are for high season.

Though the Plaza de Armas is the most central area, you won't find any bargains there, and accommodations along Av El Sol tend to be bland, expensive and set up for tour groups. As Cuzco is such a compact city, it's just as convenient to stay in another neighborhood nearby. Hilly San Blas has the best views and is deservedly popular. There are also many options west of the Plaza de Armas around Plaza Regocijo, in the commercial area towards the Mercado Central, and downhill from the center in the streets northeast of Av El Sol.

Many of Cuzco's guesthouses and hotels are located in charming colonial buildings with interior courtyards, which can echo resoundingly with noise from other guests or the street outside. Many places that offer breakfast start serving as early as 5am to accommodate Inca Trail trekkers and Machu Picchu day-trippers. For this reason, early check-ins and check-outs are the rule.

With advance notice, most midrange and top-end places will pick you up for free at the airport, the train station or the bus terminal.

Inquire about hot water for showers before committing yourself to a hotel. It's often sporadic, even in midrange accommodations, and there's nothing worse after a multiday trek than a lukewarm shower! In some hotels the hot water is more reliable on some floors than others. It helps to avoid showering at peak times of day, and it's always worth telling reception if you're having trouble – they may simply need to flick a switch or hook up a new gas canister.

All places listed claim to offer 24-hour hot-water showers, and unless otherwise noted, midrange and above places include cable TV and internet access. The top hotels all feature rooms with heating and telephone; exceptions are noted in the review.

All top-end and some midrange hotels have oxygen tanks available, at a price, for altitude sufferers.

Cuzco's swanky top-end hotels are usually booked solid during high season. Reserving through a travel agency or via the hotel's website may result in better rates.

CENTRAL CUZCO

Many of the side streets that climb northwest away from the Plaza towards Sacsaywamán (especially Tigre, Tecsecocha, Suecia, Kiskapata, Resbalosa and 7 Culebras) are bursting with cheap crash pads. High-end hotels on the plaza are often overpriced.

TOP CHOICE **Ecopackers** HOSTEL $
(Map p198; ☑23-1800; www.ecopackersperu.com; Santa Teresa 375; dm S25-41, d/ste S120/135; @🖧) Thought has been put into this big backpacker haven that's a stone's throw from Plaza Regocijo. One of the all-inclusives (with bar, pool room and sunbathing), it ups the ante by being clean, friendly and service-minded. There's lovely wicker lounges in the courtyard and the sturdy beds are extra-long. There's also 24-hour security.

TOP CHOICE **Inkaterra La Casona** BOUTIQUE HOTEL $$$
(Map p198; ☑23-5873; www.lacasona.info; Atocsaycuchi 616; suites incl breakfast from US$410; @🖧) Hitting the perfect balance of cozy and high style, this renovated grand colonial in tiny Plazoleta Nazarenas is simply debonair. Rustic meets majestic with original features like oversized carved doors, rough-hewn beams and stone fireplaces are enhanced with radiant floors, glittering candelabras, plush divans and gorgeous Andean textiles.

Even though the telly is tucked away, tech isn't far with laptop loans and iPod docks. Service is impeccable and highly personal.

Niños Hotel HOTEL $$
(☑23-1424, 25-4611; www.ninoshotel.com; Meloc 442; s/d without bathroom S63/126, d/tr incl breakfast S137/200; @🖧) Long beloved and highly recommended, these hotels are run by a Dutch-founded nonprofit foundation that serves underprivileged children in Cuzco. Both are in rambling colonials with sunny courtyards. Refurbished rooms are bordered with bright trim and feature plaid throws and portable heaters. In the coldest months there's hot water bottles to tuck in bed.

The public cafeteria features homemade cakes and breads as well as box lunches.

Breakfast is not included. The other branch is at Fierro 476.

La Lune
BOUTIQUE HOTEL $$$

(Map p198; 24-0543; www.onesuitehotelcusco.com; San Agustín 275; d incl breakfast US$450-550; @🛜) Christened the anti-hotel, it's hard to get more exclusive than this: a two-suite hotel with 24-hour concierge service from its French owner, Artur. He wants you to relax. So stays also include drinks from a full bar and a professional massage under a stained glass window. So far, it has been a hit with visiting celebrities and diplomats.

Suites are luxuriant, with tasteful modern decor, organic Cacharel bedding and an optional bed for Fido. Each suite takes two guests maximum, the pricier option comes with Jacuzzi (filled with rose petals at your bidding).

Casa Cartagena
BOUTIQUE HOTEL $$$

(Map p198; in Lima 01-242-3147; www.casacartagena.com; Pumacurco 336; suites from US$450; @🛜⛲) Fusing modern with colonial, this Italian-owned boutique hotel is dripping in style. Its sixteen suites feature walls with oversized stripes, king-sized beds, iPod docks, bouquets of long-stemmed roses and enormous bathtubs lit by candles. Management boasts that both Neruda and Che Guevara bedded down in this historic mansion, actually a modest pension half a century ago: no word on how their politics fit in now. There's a lovely onsite spa and room service is free.

Hotel Arqueólogo
BOUTIQUE HOTEL $$$

(Map p198; 23-2569; www.hotelarqueologo.com; Pumacurco 408; d/superior incl breakfast S384/451; @🛜) Feeling luxurious but also lived-in, this antique French-owned guesthouse gives a real feel for Cuzco, down to the Inca stonework. Tasteful rooms with original murals and tapestries overlook a vast courtyard paved in river stones. Relax on the lawn out back, pet the three-legged dog or sip a complimentary pisco sour in the fireplace lounge.

The sale of local weavings helps fund public libraries. French, English and German are spoken.

Hotel Monasterio
LUXURY HOTEL $$$

(Map p198; 60-4000; www.monasterio.orient-express.com; Calle Palacio 136; d from US$700, ste S2150-5952; @🛜) Arranged around graceful 16th-century cloisters, the five-star Monasterio has long been Cuzco's jewel, with majestic public areas and over 100 rooms surrounding genteel courtyards. Jesuit roots show in the irregular floor plans, though some of the renovation touches (ie a plasma TV that emerges from the foot of the bed) seem a little gauche.

In addition to two high-end restaurants, don't miss the chapel with its original gold-leaf paintings.

Midori
HOTEL $$$

(Map p198; 24-8144; www.midori-cusco.com; Ataúd 204; s/d incl breakfast S221/280; @🛜) Popular with small tour groups, this small hotel is classic and comfortable. Enormous rooms feature a living area, brocade fabrics and firm beds. Locally recommended.

Pariwana
HOSTEL $

(Map p198; 23-3751; www.pariwana-hostel.com; Mesón de la Estrella 136; dm S24-36, d with/without bathroom S98/85; @🛜) Resembling spring break, this notably clean, newer hostel is filled with uni-types lounging on poufs and playing ping-pong in the courtyard of a huge colonial. Wi-fi connection comes in the common areas. Beds in newish dorms are well-spaced and the penthouse suite is well worth the splurge. The chic bar is invite-only.

Tierra Viva
HOTEL $$$

(Map p198; 60-1317; www.tierravivahoteles.com; Saphi 766; s/d/tr incl breakfast S300/330/360; @🛜) With modern stylings and notable service, this new Peruvian hotel chain offers two comfortable midrange options in downtown Cuzco. The **Plaza de Armas option** (Suecia 345) is more spacious, with an interior courtyard. Doubles sport hardwood floors or Berber carpets, white linens and colorful throws. Buffet breakfast is available from 5am on.

The Point
HOSTEL $

(Map p198; 25-2266; www.thepointhostels.com; Mesón de la Estrella 172; dm S22-30, s/d without bathroom S50/80; @🛜) An industrial-sized party palace, with daily events, on-site bar The Horny Llama, foosball and a grassy backyard with hammocks. Another good choice for the socially inclined. Hosts electronic music parties of some note.

Hostal Suecia I
HOTEL $

(Map p198; 23-3282; www.hostalsuecial.com; Suecia 332; s/d incl breakfast S60/90; 🛜) Most rooms in this pint-sized guesthouse are very basic, but location and staff are fabulous and there's a sociable, stony, indoor courtyard.

The two newer doubles on the top floor (311 and 312) are a good value.

Hostal Rojas
GUESTHOUSE **$$**

(☎22-8184; Tigre 129; s/d incl breakfast S60/100; @🖙) Very friendly, clean and stuffed with bric-a-brac, this family-run hostel is notably cheap for solo travelers. A three-minute walk from the Plaza de Armas.

Loreto Boutique Hotel
HOTEL **$$**

(Map p198; ☎22-6352; www.loretoboutique hotel.com; Loreto 115; s/d/tr incl breakfast S199/252/305) Maybe you're paying for the plaza location, since 'boutique' is an overstatement here. Dimly-lit in daytime, Loreto has well-heeled, snug rooms bathed in neutrals. The best feature are the four rooms with surviving Inca walls.

El Balcón Hostal
HOTEL **$$**

(☎23-6738; www.balconcusco.com; Tambo de Montero 222; s/d/tr incl breakfast S160/220/270; @🖙) This renovated building dating from 1630 has just 16 basic rooms, all with balconies, phone and TV. The garden blooms with fuchsias and offers great views over Cuzco. There's also a sauna.

Hotel los Marqueses
HOTEL **$$**

(Map p198; ☎26-4249; www.hotelmarqueses. com; Calle Garcilaso 256; s/d/tr incl breakfast from S196/252/308; 🖙) Romance pervades this colonial villa, built in the 16th century by Spanish conquistadors. Classic features include *escuela cuzqueña* paintings, courtyard fountains and balconies looking out on the cathedral on the Plaza de Armas. Rooms are large and airy, with some brass beds and carved wooden doors. Some have split-level sleeping areas and skylights. Most guests come on package tours. Wi-fi is available only on the patio.

Andenes de Saphi
HOTEL **$$**

(Map p198; ☎22-7561; www.andenesdesaphi.com; Saphi 848; s/d/tr S146/164/190; 🖙) At the far end of Saphi, where the city starts to become more rural, this dependable, modern hotel has a rustic wooden construction with skylights and murals in every room.

Hotel Royal Inca I
HOTEL **$$$**

(Map p198; ☎23-1067; www.royalinkahotel.com; Plaza Regocijo 299; s/d incl breakfast S205/269; @🖙) Quiet as a mausoleum, this central hotel features good-quality rooms. Those in the colonial building are a bit dated but comfortable and luxurious, while the modern ones are big, bright and cheery. The oddest feature might be the mix of kitsch in the public areas, including gold masks and an oversized wall mural with an indigenous nature scene bordering on soft porn.

Renacimiento
APARTMENT **$$**

(☎22-1596; www.cuscoapart.com; Ceniza 331 s/d S100/160; 🖙) An unsigned treasure, this colonial mansion has been converted into 12 stylish one- and two-bedroom apartments sleeping one to six people, each unique in design and furnishing. Cozy and comfortable, it's fabulous for families.

Mama Simona
HOSTEL **$**

(☎26-0408; www.mamasimona.com; Calle Ceniza 364; dm S25-33; @🖙) A new player in town this hostel is styled for hipsters, with a crushed velvet sofa and oddball decor. Beds have nice down covers and the shared kitchen with picnic tables is undoubtedly cute but we wish it were a little cleaner. It's two blocks northeast of Plaza San Francisco.

Hospedaje Familiar
Munay Wasi
GUESTHOUSE **$**

(Map p198; ☎22-3661; Huaynapata 253; s/d/tr/c S40/50/90/100; @) This friendly, homey family inn is housed in a ramshackle adobe building without a single right angle to its name. Room 201, which has huge windows, minibalconies and a magic view of downtown Cuzco, is understandably popular with families. The reception is on the second floor of the interior courtyard.

Loki Hostel
HOSTEL **$**

(☎24-3705; www.lokihostel.com; Cuesta Santa Ana 601; dm S23-30, d/tr incl breakfast S85/110; @🖙) This 450-year-old national monument is a great place to eat, drink and be merry – sleeping, not so much. If it feels like a village, that's because it practically is: its capacity of 280 guests is among Cuzco's highest. On weekends the on-site bar features local bands and DJs.

WalkOn Inn
HOSTEL **$**

(Map p198; ☎23-5065; www.walkoninn.com; Suecia 504; dm/s/d S25/65/75; @🖙) A five-minute puff up from the Plaza de Armas, this quieter hostel has views but rather indifferent service. Breakfast is not included.

Del Prado Inn
HOTEL **$$$**

(Map p198; ☎22-442; www.delpradoinn.com; Suecia 310; s/d/tr incl buffet breakfast S225/390/435; @🖙) Del Prado is a solid option, with efficient staff and just over a dozen snug rooms reached by elevator. Some have tiny balconies with corner views of the plaza. Check out the original Inca walls in the dining room.

Los Andes de America HOTEL $$$

(Map p198; ☑60-6060; www.cuscoandes.com; Calle Garcilaso 150; s/d incl breakfast S347/410) A Best Western hotel noted for its buffet breakfast, which includes regional specialties such as *mote con queso* (cheese and corn) and *papa helada* (frozen potato). Rooms are warm and comfortable, bathrooms are big and relatively luxurious, and the atrium features a scale model of Machu Picchu.

Hostal Suecia II HOTEL $

(Map p198; ☑23-9757; Tecsecocha 465; s/d/tr S40/60/80, s/d/tr without bathroom S30/40/60) This long-standing backpacker favorite continues to offer excellent value with central location, friendly owners, a light, bright, flowery patio, decent rooms and a book-lending library. Its hostess, Señora Yolanda, has been here 20 years.

Hostal Corihuasi GUESTHOUSE $$

(Map p198; ☑23-2233; www.corihuasi.com; Suecia 561; s/d/tr incl breakfast S119/149/178) A brisk walk uphill from the main plaza, this family-feel guesthouse inhabits a mazelike colonial building with postcard views. Amply sized rooms are outfitted in a warm, rustic style with alpaca-wool blankets, hand-woven rugs and solid wooden furnishings. Room 1 is the most in demand for its wraparound windows, ideal for soaking up panoramic sunsets. Airport transfer included.

Casa Grande HOTEL $$

(Map p198; ☑24-5871; www.casagrandelodging.com.pe; Santa Catalina Ancha 353; s/d/tr incl breakfast S110/140/170; @🛜) Location trumps quality in this colonial hotel. The rickety balcony wrapped around a charming patio is the best of this place. Rooms are basic, but all have cable TV and, unusually, separate shower and toilet.

Hospedaje Monte Horeb GUESTHOUSE $$

(Map p198; ☑23-6775; montehoreb cusco@yahoo.com; San Juan de Dios 260, 2nd fl; s/d incl breakfast S84/112) With an inner-courtyard entry, this serene and well-cared for option has big, old-fashioned rooms, an inviting balcony and a curious mix of furnishings.

Piccola Locanda GUESTHOUSE $$

(Map p198; ☑23-6775; www.piccolalocanda.com; Kiskapata 215; d with/without bathroom S140/126; 🛜) While it's pretty pricey for what you get, this colorful Italian-owned lodging is snug, with quixotic, bright rooms and a cave-like cushioned lounge. Has an in-house responsible-travel operator, and sponsors community projects. Entrance is on Resbalosa.

Teatro Inka B&B GUESTHOUSE $$

(Map p198; ☑24-7372, in Lima 01-976-0523; www.teatroinka.com; Teatro 391; s/d/tr incl breakfast S66/98/119; @🛜) An array of dark but decent doubles sit around an interior courtyard. All rooms are good value, and the penthouse suite is well worth splashing out on.

Albergue Municipal HOSTEL $

(Map p198; ☑25-2506; albergue@municusco.gob.pe; Kiskapata 240; dm/d S17/40; @) The Cuzco answer to the YMCA, it's a good choice for the tight of budget, with plenty of space, great views, kitchen access (breakfast only) and laundry facilities. All rooms have shared bathrooms.

Los Angeles B&B HOTEL $$

(Map p198; ☑26-1101; www.losangelescusco.com; Tecsecocha 474; s/d incl breakfast S117/140; @🛜) This old colonial sports worn rooms with gold bedspreads and dark, carved furniture around a central courtyard.

Hostal Andrea GUESTHOUSE $

(☑23-6713; andreahostal@hotmail.com; Cuesta Santa Ana 514; s/d S40/45, s/d without bathroom S10/20; @🛜) Cuzco's cheapest, this place is practically falling apart, but the kind, unassuming staff make it a reader favorite. Wi-fi is available only in the living room.

SAN BLAS

Second Home Cusco BOUTIQUE HOTEL $$$

(Map p198; ☑23-5873; www.secondhome cusco.com; Atocsaycuchi 616; d/tr incl breakfast S318/384; @🛜) A cozy boutique lodging with three chic suites, featuring original artwork, adobe walls and skylights. Carlos Delfin, the affable and cosmopolitan English-speaking owner, orchestrates free airport pickups and even private tours; he has even hunted down the best baguettes in town to serve at breakfast. Longer stays are discounted.

La Encantada BOUTIQUE HOTEL $$$

(Map p198; ☑24-2206; www.encantadaperu.com; Tandapata 354; s/d incl breakfast S212/265; @🛜) Bright and cheerful, this modern boutique hotel features terraced gardens and immense views from iron-rail balconies. A circular staircase leads to small, tasteful rooms

THE GUINEA PIG'S CULINARY RISE

Love it or loathe it, *cuy*, or guinea pig (or *Cavia porcellus* if you really must know), is an Andean favorite that's been part of the local culinary repertoire since pre-Inca times. And before you dredge up childhood memories of cuddly mascots in protest, know that these rascally rodents were gracing Andean dinner plates long before anyone in the West considered them worthy pet material.

Pinpointing the gastronomic history of the *cuy*, a native of the New World, is harder than trying to catch one with your bare hands. It's believed that *cuy* may have been domesticated as early as 7000 years ago in the mountains of southern Peru, where wild populations of *cuy* still roam today. Direct evidence from Chavín de Huántar shows that they were certainly cultivated across the Andes by 900 BC. Arrival of the Spanish in the 18th century led to the European debut of *cuy*, where they rode a wave of popularity as the must-have exotic pet of the season (Queen Elizabeth I of England supposedly kept one).

How they earned the name guinea pig is also in doubt. Guinea may be a corruption of the South American colony of Guiana, or it may refer to Guinea, the African country that *cuy* would have passed through on their voyage to Europe. Their squeals probably account for the latter half of their name.

Cuy are practical animals to raise and have adapted well over the centuries to survive in environments ranging from the high Andean plains to the barren coastal deserts. Many Andean households today raise *cuy* as part of their animal stock and you'll often see them scampering around the kitchen in true free-range style. *Cuy* are the ideal livestock alternative: they're high in protein, feed on kitchen scraps, breed profusely and require much less room and maintenance than traditional domesticated animals.

Cuy is seen as a true delicacy, so much so that in many indigenous interpretations of *The Last Supper*, Jesus and his disciples are sitting down to a hearty final feast of roast *cuy*.

An integral part of Andean culture, even beyond the kitchen table, *cuy* are also used by *curanderos* (healers) in ceremonial healing rituals. *Cuy* can be passed over a patient's body and used to sense out a source of illness and *cuy* meat is sometimes ingested in place of hallucinogenic plants during shamanistic ceremonies.

If you can overcome your sentimental inhibitions, sample this furry treat. The rich flavors are a cross between rabbit and quail, and correctly prepared *cuy* can be an exceptional feast with thousands of years of history.

with soft linens and king-sized beds. The onsite spa helps hikers work out the aches and kinks. Be aware that checkout is at 9am.

Hostal Pensión Alemana HOTEL $$
(Map p198; ☎22-6861; www.cuzco-stay.de; Tandapata 260; s/d/tr incl breakfast S154/184/232; @🖥) Attentive and lovely, this polished Swiss-German lodge wouldn't look out of place in the Alps. Nice touches include air purifiers and complimentary tea and fruit. Couples should note there are very few matrimonial beds. Enjoy the tiled garden – rare in Cuzco – and the terraces with sweeping views.

Madre Tierra B&B $$
(Map p198; ☎24-8452; www.hostalmadretierra. com; Atocsaycuchi 647; d/tr S130/207; @🖥) Warm and super cozy, with plenty of B&B-style luxury comfort touches, Madre Tierra

is a vine-entwined, slightly claustrophobic little jewel box. Rooms have skylights and funky dimensions. Good value for money.

Amaru Hostal HOTEL $$
(Map p198; ☎22-5933; www.cusco.net/amaru Cuesta San Blas 541; s/d/tr incl breakfast S105/135/189; @🖥) In a characterful old building in a prime location, Amaru is deservedly popular. Flowerpots sit outside well-kept rooms with styles that are a little dated. Some feature rocking chairs from which to admire the rooftop view. Rooms in the outer courtyard are noisy, and those at the back are newest.

Hostal Marani HOTEL $$
(Map p198; ☎24-9462; www.hostalmarani com; Carmen Alto 194; s/d/tr incl breakfast S109/173/227; 🖥) Recommended, this airy

oasis is friendly and lovely. The Spanish-tile courtyard is surrounded by modest rooms that vary in size and shape. A few upstairs have vaulted ceilings, skylights and city views.

Tika Wasi
HOTEL **$$**
(Map p198; ☏23-1609; www.tikawasi.com; Tandapata 491; s/d/tr incl breakfast S89/122/155, superior s/d/tr S89/166/199; ☏) Behind a tall wall, this modern inn offers a personable option. Rooms are bright and airy, overlooking small, sunny decks to hang out on. Breakfast is buffet. Non-nationals should be sure to get the tax subtracted from the room price.

Samay Wasi
HOSTEL **$**
(Map p198; ☏25-3108; www.samaywasiperu.com; Atocsaycuchi 416; dm S30, s/d/tr incl breakfast S64/68/90; @☏) A friendly, rambling hostel clinging precariously to the hillside, hidden up a flight of stairs teetering way above town. There's a proper kitchen and shipshape rooms. Some are a bit musty so ask to see a few. With major city views. Accepts credit cards.

Hospedaje el Artesano de San Blas
GUESTHOUSE **$**
(Map p198; ☏26-3968; hospedajeartesano790@hotmail.com; Suytuccato 790; s/d S30/50; ☏) If you're wondering why it's such a deal, just try walking here with a full pack. Still, this peaceful and falling-down-charming colonial house has large rooms and a sunny patio with wi-fi reception. Kitchen available.

Hostal Rumi Punku
HOTEL **$$$**
(Map p198; ☏22-1102; www.rumipunku.com; Choquechaca 339; s/d incl breakfast S223/279; @☏) Recognizable by the monumental Inca stonework around the entrance, Rumi Punku (Stone Door) is a stylish complex of old colonial houses, gardens and terraces. The rooftop terraces and other outdoor areas are utterly charming. Rooms ooze comfort and class, with central heating, wooden floors and European bedding. It's probably not worth the upgrade to a superior room unless you want a bigger bed. Sauna and Jacuzzi are available for a minimal charge.

Casona Les Pleiades
B&B **$$**
(Map p198; ☏50-6430; www.casona-pleiades.com; Tandapata 116; d/tr incl breakfast S165/210; @☏) A pleasant French-run B&B with a sunny courtyard featuring fresh flowers and balcony seating. The buffet breakfast is served

in cozy booths. Heaters and lockboxes are supplied in rooms.

Casa San Blas
BOUTIQUE HOTEL **$$$**
(☏23-7900; www.casasanblas.com; Tocuyeros 566; s/d/ste incl breakfast S330/360/528; @☏) Down a short passageway, this revamped colonial features smart, spare rooms with nice bedding, hardwood floors and Andean textiles. It has a cozy feel, though service is somewhat impersonal.

Casa de Campo Hostal
HOTEL **$$**
(Map p198; ☏24-4404; www.hotelcasadecampo.com; Tandapata 298; s/d/tr incl breakfast S119/145/172; @☏) The steep climb here (and to your room) might leave you on your knees, but the views astound. With a warm and friendly vibe, this hillside inn is almost perfect but installations are aging. Some rooms don't even have working electrical outlets (and most have just one), so check before settling in. Breakfast includes a sprawling buffet that includes fresh fruit and cereal. Heaters cost extra.

Pisko & Soul
HOSTEL **$**
(Map p198; ☏22-1998; info@piskoandsoul.com; Carmen Alto 294; dm/d incl breakfast S27/108; @☏) This Peruvian hostel goes for the Spanish language school formula, with free lessons, evening events and barbecues. Small dorms have snug down covers but the bathrooms could use some bleach.

Hospedaje Familiar Kuntur Wasi
HOTEL **$**
(Map p198; ☏22-7570; Tandapata 352A; r per person with/without bathroom S60/35) Quiet and economical, this simple hotel features shipshape rooms and free buffet breakfast. Interior rooms lack natural light, and there have been mixed reviews about the management, but it's a hard bargain to beat.

Los Apus Hotel & Mirador
HOTEL **$$$**
(Map p198; ☏26-4243; www.losapushotel.com; Atocsaycuchi 515; s/d incl breakfast S260/315; ☀@☏) With understated class, this longtime Swiss-run hotel features central heating, large bedrooms with down duvets and colonial *cuzqueño*-style art. It may seem overpriced, but you are also paying for the high-tech alarm system and an emergency water supply. A wheelchair-accessible room for travelers with disabilities is available.

Eureka Hostal
HOTEL **$$**
(Map p198; ☏23-3505; www.peru-eureka.com; Chihuampata 591; s/d/tr S198/231/297; @☏) A

funky blend of old and new, Eureka's stylish lobby and sun-soaked cafeteria invite further acquaintance. Rooms are comfortable but a little odd, with a child-like take on traditional motifs. Orthopedic mattresses and down quilts make them as comfortable as they are cool. Flexible tarifs can make it an even better deal.

Hostal el Grial HOTEL $$
(Map p198; 22-3012; www.hotelelgrial.com; Carmen Alto 112; s/d/tr S80/119/170) A good value in a rickety old wood-floored building; all rooms have orthopedic mattresses and some have views.

Pantastico GUESTHOUSE $
(Map p198; 954-387; www.hotelpantastico.com; Carmen Bajo 226; s/d S65/90, dm/s/d/tr without bathroom S30/45/70/90; @🛜) This newish bed and bakery features fresh bread daily at 5am. From the looks of it, few of the guests have theirs hot (though breakfast is included). There's also good water pressure and a hardcore hippie groove: if you want to shop for San Pedro experiences or make organic pizza, it's your spot.

Hospedaje Inka GUESTHOUSE $
(Map p198; 23-1995; http://hospedajeinka.weebly.com; Suytuccato 848; dm/s/d incl breakfast S20/25/40; 🛜) This scruffy but charming converted hillside farmhouse high above the Plaza San Blas affords some great views. There's erratic hot water, private bathrooms and a large farm kitchen available for cooking your own meals. Taxis can't climb the final uphill stretch, so be prepared for a stiff walk.

AVENIDA EL SOL & DOWNHILL
Hostal San Juan Masías GUESTHOUSE $
(Map p204; 43-1563; hostalsanjuanmasias@yahoo.es; Ahuacpinta 600; s/d/tr S50/80/120, s/d/tr without bathroom S35/60/90; @) An excellent alternative guesthouse run by Dominican nuns on the grounds of the busy Colegio Martín de Porres, this place is clean, safe and friendly, and overlooks frequent volleyball matches on the courtyard. Simple, spotless rooms with heat are arranged off a long, sunny hallway. Continental breakfast is included.

Hotel Libertador Palacio del Inka LUXURY HOTEL $$
(Map p198; 23-1961; www.libertador.com.pe; Plazoleta Santo Domingo 259; d/ste US$210/260; ✳@🛜) Opulence bedecks this colonial mansion. It's built over Inca foundations, with parts of the building dating back to the

16th century, when Francisco Pizarro was an occupant. It's as luxurious and beautiful as you'd expect, with a fine interior courtyard and ample rooms that were recently renovated. It also features a Peruvian restaurant bar and business center.

Yanantin Guest House GUESTHOUSE $$
(Map p204; 25-4205; www.yanantin.com Ahuacpinta 775; s/d incl breakfast S95/108; 🛜) This small guesthouse has an assortment of well-heeled rooms large enough for desks and coffee tables. Organic toiletries are offered and the comfy beds feature cotton sheets and down bedding. A good value.

Mirador Hostal GUESTHOUSE $
(Map p204; 24-8986; soldelimperiocusco@yahoo.es; Ahuacpinta s/n; s/d/tr incl breakfast S45/65/90; @🛜) A cheery, rambling concrete jungle overlooking a main road. Rooms are basic and somewhat run-down but clean. Friendly, helpful staff make it a favorite. Rates include breakfast.

Hostal Inkarri HOTEL $$
(Map p198; 24-2692; www.inkarrihostal.com Qolla Calle 204; s/d/tr incl breakfast S106/133/180; @🛜) A roomy place with a pleasant stone courtyard, well-kept colonial terraces and whimsical collections of old sewing machines, phones and typewriters. A very good value, but watch for rooms on the musty side.

Los Aticos HOTEL $$
(Map p204; 23-1710; www.losaticos.com; Quera 253, Pasaje Hurtado Álvarez; d/apt incl breakfast S132/172; @🛜) Hidden in a small passageway, this sleepy spot is off the radar but well worth snagging. Rooms have comfy beds with down duvets and parquet floors. There's also self-service laundry and a full guest kitchen. The three mini-apartments sleep up to four and are good value for self-catering groups or families.

Picol Hostal HOTEL $$
(Map p204; 24-9191; picolhostal@gmail.com; Quera 253, Pasaje Hurtado Álvarez; s/d/tr incl breakfast S60/90/110; 🛜) In a bustling commercial district, this small hotel has agreeable staff and tiny, well-kept and airy doubles. The triples are a little too tight.

GREATER CUZCO
Hospedaje Turismo Caith GUESTHOUSE $
(23-3595; www.caith.org; Urb Ucchullo Alto, Pasaje Sto Toribio N4; r per person incl breakfast S70; 🛜) This rambling farmhouse-style hostel also

runs an onsite girls foundation. Huge picture windows and various balconies and patios look toward the Plaza de Armas, a 20-minute walk or a five-minute taxi ride away. It's great for families – big rooms and cots are available, and the rambling, grassy garden is a perfect place for kids to run around.

Torre Dorada Residencial GUESTHOUSE **$$**
(☎24-1698; www.torredorada.com; Los Cipreses N-5, Residencial Huancaro; s/d incl breakfast S252/292; @) With lovely and original decor in bright colors, Torre Dorada is a modern, family-run hotel in a quiet residential district close to the bus terminal. Though it isn't close to the action, guests rave about the high quality of service. It offers free shuttles to the airport, train stations and the town center. Fluent English is spoken.

Hostal San Juan de Dios GUESTHOUSE **$$**
(☎24-0135; www.hostalsanjuandedios.com; Manzanares 264, Urb Manuel Prado; s/d incl breakfast S93/119; @) With a wonderful staff, this spotless guesthouse is part of a nonprofit enterprise that supports a hospital clinic and also provides job opportunities for young people with disabilities. The quiet, carpeted rooms have large windows; most have twin beds, though there's one matrimonial double. Staff help with everything from laundry services to making international phone calls.

It's a 30-minute walk or S6 taxi ride from the city center, near shops and amenities.

✖ Eating

Cuzco's location, nearly dropping off the eastern edge of the Andes, gives it access to an unbelievable range of crops from highland potatoes and quinoa to avocados and *ají picante* (hot chili).

CENTRAL CUZCO

TOP CHOICE **Cicciolina** INTERNATIONAL **$$$**
(Map p198; ☎23-9510; Triunfo 393, 2nd fl; mains S30-55; ☺8am-late) On the 2nd floor of a lofty colonial courtyard mansion, Cicciolina has long held its position as Cuzco's best restaurant. The eclectic, sophisticated food is divine, starting with house-marinated olives, continuing with crisp polenta squares with cured rabbit, huge green salads, charred octopus and satisfying mains like squid-ink pasta and tender lamb.

The service is impeccable, and the warmly-lit seating will make any laid-back globetrotter feel at home. Highly recommended.

CHEAP EATS

You might be sharing a table with office workers on break at these popular lunch spots. Often not advertised, a lunchtime *menú* (set meal) includes soup, a main course, a drink and sometimes dessert.

Restaurante Egos (Arequipa 248; menú S8)

Restaurante Chihuanhuay (Cuesta el Almirante facing Museo Inka; menú S7)

Kukuly (Huaynapata 318; menú S7)

Q'ori Sara (Calle Garcilaso 290; menú S8)

TOP CHOICE **La Bodega 138** PIZZERIA **$$**
(Map p198; ☎26-0272; Herrajes 138; mains S18-35; ☺6:30-11pm Mon-Sat) Sometimes you are homesick for good atmosphere and uncomplicated menus. In comes La Bodega, a fantastic laid-back enterprise run by a family in what used to be their home. Thin crust pizzas are fired up in the adobe oven, organic salads are fresh and abundant and the prices are reasonable. A true find.

Chicha NOVOANDINA **$$$**
(Map p198; ☎24-0520; Regocijo 261, 2nd fl; mains S24-50) A Gastón Acurio venture serving up haute versions of *cuzqueño* classics. Their riff on *anticuchos* (beef skewers) is a delectable barbecued octopus, grilled on skewers with crisp herbed potato wedges. Other contenders include *rocoto relleno*, the wonton-style *sopa de gallina* and *chairo* (beef soup) served in a clay pot. The *chicha morada* is beyond fresh.

Naturally, debate rages as to whether it's worth the price (and pretension): our vote is yes.

Limo PERUVIAN **$$$**
(Map p198; ☎24-068; Portal de Carnes 236, 2nd fl; mains S24-60; ☺11am-11pm Mon-Sat) Start with a tart pisco sour, it's the perfect compliment to the fresh Peruvian-Asian seafood creations. For starters, a basket of native potatoes, served with sauces, is a fun change from bread on the table. *Tiraditos,* strips of raw fish in a fragrant sauce, simply melt on the tongue. Other hits are the creamy *causas* (potato dish) and *sudadito,* a mix of greens, corn and seared scallops. Elegant ambience and attentive service.

El Hada
ICE CREAM $

(Map p198; Arequipa 167; ice cream from S6; ⊙11am-8pm Mon-Sat) Served in fresh-made cones with a hint of vanilla or lemon peel, these exotic ice creams are ecstasy. Flavors like Indonesian cinnamon, bitter chocolate or roasted apples do not disappoint. Cap it off with an *espress* – Café Bisetti, Peru's best roaster, is offered.

Le Soleil
FRENCH $$$

(Map p198; ✍24-0543, San Agustín 275; mains S39-65; ⊙12:30-3pm Mon-Fri, 7-10:30pm Sat) Cuzco's go-to spot for traditional French cooking, this romantic white-linen restaurant does not disappoint. The menu features staples like brandied trout, baked ratatouille with goat cheese and herbs, and duck à l'orange. You can also go for an eight-course tasting menu or the three-course *menú del día* (S69). Ingredients like fish stock may be in non-meat dishes, so vegetarians should order carefully.

🍃 Green's Organic
CAFE $$

(Map p198; ✍24-3399; Santa Catalina Angosta 235, 2nd fl; mains S21-44; ⊙11am-10pm; 🛜✍) With all-organic food and a bright farmhouse feel, Green's Organic oozes health. Inventive salads with options like roasted fennel, goat cheese, beets and spring greens are a welcome change of pace and the heartier fare includes pastas and alpaca dishes. Come early (or late) as it fills up fast and service is notably slow.

Deli Monasterio
BAKERY $$

(Map p198; Calle Palacio 140; sandwiches S14; ⊙8am-6pm) Crusty, authentic baguettes are the highlight here (come early) but you can also get nice lunchboxes (perfect for day excursions) with gourmet and veggie options. The mini *pain au chocolat* and passion fruit cookies aren't bad either.

Trujillo Restaurant
PERUVIAN $

(✍23-3465; Av Tullumayo 542 at Plaza Limacpampa; mains S15-28; ⊙8am-8pm Mon-Sat, noon-6pm Sun) Run by a northern Peruvian family, this simple dining hall by Qorikancha nails northern classics such as *seco de cabrito* (goat stewed in beer and cilantro) and a variety of ceviches. The *aji de gallina* (a creamy chicken stew served with rice and potatoes) is the best in all of Cuzco.

CBC Bakery
BAKERY $

(Map p198; ✍23-4035; qosqomaki.org/tallerpanaderia; Tullumayo 465; pastries S3; ⊙7:30am-8pm Mon-Sat) The best chocolate croissants in town, plus other scrumptious baked goods are made in this charitable foundation that capacitates local at-risk youth as bakers.

La Justina
PIZZERIA

(Map p198; ✍25-5474; Calle Palacio 110; pizza S19-30; ⊙6-11pm Mon-Sat) Traipse through an uneven stone courtyard to this little gem, a pizza joint with wooden tables and gorgeous wood-fired pies. Original toppings include tomato, bacon and basil or spinach and garlic.

Uchu Peruvian Steakhouse
PERUVIAN $$

(Map p198; ✍24-6598; Calle Palacio 135; mains S22-48; ⊙12:30-11pm) With a cozy, cavernous ambience of low-lit adobe, dark tables and bright turquoise walls, this chic eatery has a simple menu of meat (steak, alpaca or chicken) and fish cooked on hot volcanic stones at your table and served with delicious sauces. The staff is knowledgeable and quick to serve, a real treat.

Kintaro
JAPANESE $

(Map p198; Plateros 326, 2nd fl; menu S15, rolls S10-38; ⊙12-3:30pm & 6:30-10pm Mon-Sat) Local expats rave about the noodle bowls. The set lunch proves a good deal and provides a welcome change from local flavors. Also serves sushi and sake.

A Mi Manera
PERUVIAN $$

(Map p198; ✍22-2219; www.amimaneraperu.com; Triunfo 392, 2nd fl; mains S22-42; ⊙10am-10pm) For a reasonably priced night out, this romantic restaurant serves up traditional Peruvian cuisine and pasta. Offerings like steak in port sauce, spicy yucca or mashed muña potatoes comfort and satisfy.

Los Perros
FUSION $

(Map p198; Tecsecocha 436; mains S17-24) This Australian-founded gathering spot serves Asian-slanted bar food at good prices in an intimate couch bar. Try the sesame chicken sandwich – tender with a side of guacamole and big enough for two.

Aldea Yanapay
CAFE $

(Map p198; ✍25-5134; Ruinas 415, 2nd fl; menú S15, mains from S22; ⊙9am-11:30pm; ✍) The stuffed animals, board games and decor perfectly evoke the circus you dreamed of running away with as a child. Aldea Yanapay is pitched at families but will appeal to anyone with a taste for the quixotic. Food includes burritos, falafel and tasty little fried things o pick at, and there's a whole separate menu for vegetarians.

Profits go to projects helping abandoned children. Highly recommended.

Divina Comedia
INTERNATIONAL $$

23-2522; www.hotelarqueologo.com; Pumacurco 408; mains S25-35; 12-3pm & 6-11pm Mon-Sat) With sopranos singing live arias, this unusual upscale eatery fills a small niche of romantic dining with entertainment. The food combines Peruvian ingredients with Mediterranean influences; start with tapas, a notable specialty is duck, slow-cooked to utter tenderness, or maybe that's what you're feeling just before the music stops.

El Encuentro
VEGETARIAN $

Map p198; Santa Catalina Ancha 384; menu S8; 6:30am-10pm;) Incredibly economical, this vegetarian restaurant offers set lunch with a salad bar starter, rib-sticking barley soup and mains like tofu and wilted veggies with rice. What it lacks in subtlety, it makes up for in abundance. There's a second location with more limited hours at Choquechaca 136.

El Ayllu
CAFE $

(Map p198; Marquez 263; mains S10; 6:30am-10pm) This old-fashioned cafe is beloved by Peruvians. Longtime staff chat up clients and serve traditional pastries like lengua de suegra and pork sandwiches. Traditional breakfasts are worth trying and coffee is roasted the traditional local way – with orange, sugar and onion peels.

Marcelo Batata
PERUVIAN $$

(Map p198; Calle Palacio 121; mains S21-38; 2-11pm) A sure bet for Peruvian food, often with an added twist. The chicken soup with hierba Luisa, a local herb, is exquisite, and that's only the start of an eclectic fusion menu. You might also want to sample their daring array of cocktails from the rooftop deck – the city views make it the best outdoor venue in Cuzco.

Los Toldos
PERUVIAN $

(Map p198; cnr Almagro & San Andrés; mains S12-20; lunch & dinner Mon-Sat) A local favorite for abundant cheap eats, this rotisserie restaurant features a worthwhile salad bar (try the black olive sauce). Most people can't go past the Peruvian classic cuarto de pollo (quarter of a chicken), done here to perfection.

Real McCoy
PUB $$

(Map p198; 26-1111; Plateros 326, 2nd fl; mains from S14; 7:30am-late;) Tempts the homesick Brit with chips and gravy, real baked beans and roast dinners with Yorkshire pudding. Inviting and chilled out, the Real McCoy welcomes guests with comfy couches, beanbags and sports on TV. Happy hour is 5pm to 8pm.

Victor Victoria
PERUVIAN $$

(Map p198; 25-2854; Tecsecocha 466; mains from S15; 7am-10pm) Serving princely portions of primarily Peruvian food, this central restaurant has a stout following of backpackers. Quinoa laced with cheese is deliriously good and cuy (guinea pig) – served with stuffed rocoto peppers, corn and potatoes – is notably authentic (order ahead).

Self-Catering

Small, overpriced grocery shops near the Plaza de Armas include **Gato's Market** (Map p198; Santa Catalina Ancha 377; 9am-11pm) and **Market** (Map p198; Mantas 119; 8am-11pm). For a more serious stock-up head to supermarket **Mega** (Map p204; cnr Matará & Ayacucho; 10am-8pm Mon-Sat, to 6pm Sun).

SAN BLAS

Jack's Café
CAFE $

(Map p198; 25-4606; Choquechaca 509; mains S12-20; 7:30am-11:30pm) A line often snakes out the door at this Western-style, Australian-run eatery. With fresh juices blended with mint or ginger, strong coffee and eggs heaped with smoked salmon or roasted tomatoes, it's easy to get out of bed. Also has nice cafe food, soups and good service.

Granja Heidi
CAFE $$

(Map p198; 23-8383; Cuesta San Blas 525, 2nd fl; mains S18-38; 11:30am-9:30pm Mon-Sat) A cozy Alpine cafe serving healthy fare, some of it provided from the small farm of the German owner. In addition to Peruvian fare (rocoto relleno is served vegetarian, with stuffed chili and peanuts), there are crepes and huge bowls of soups and salads. Save room for dessert.

The Meeting Place
CAFE $

(Map p198; 24-0465; Plazoleta San Blas; mains S15-21; 8:30am-4pm Mon-Sat;) Owned by Idaho natives, this cafe nails gringo breakfast. Start with organic coffee or nice loose-leaf teas, oversized waffles and egg combinations. We hear the half-pound bacon cheeseburgers merit a lunchtime visit. Service is swift and friendly. All proceeds go to support community projects.

Prasada
VEGETARIAN $

(Map p198; ✆25-3644; Canchipata 269; mains S6; ⊙8am-6pm; ☏) The best bang for your pesos, serving tacos, tortilla soup and lentil burgers with fresh toppings and generous servings. Pair with a jar of fresh-squeezed juice and you're ready for the hike up to Sacsaywamán. There is a second takeout-only location (with one stool) at Choquechaca 152.

La Quinta Eulalia
PERUVIAN $$

(Map p198; ✆22-4951; Choquechaca 384; mains S25-50) This Cuzco classic has been in business for over half a century and its courtyard patio is a score on a sunny day. The chalkboard menu features the tenderest roast lamb, alpaca and traditional sides like the phenomenal *rocotto relleno*, spicy peppers stuffed with beef, peas and carrots topped with dribbling cheese. It is one of the best places to order *cuy*.

Juanito's
SANDWICHES $

(Map p198; Qanchipata 596; sandwiches S15; ⊙8am-8pm) With the griddle hopping, this sandwich shop churns out made-to-order numbers. Vegetarians get big fried-egg sandwiches and new combos like chicken and walnuts prove tasty.

Pacha Papa
PERUVIAN $$

(Map p198; ✆24-1318; Plazoleta Plaza San Blas 120; mains S12-30; ⊙11am-11pm) Invoking a rustic highland ambience, this open courtyard with wooden tables serves up well-prepared Peruvian classics, cooked over a wood fire or in clay pots. It's also livened by a harpist on weekends. It's a good spot to try buttered corn in herbs, *aji de gallina* or oven-fired trout. *Cuy* should be ordered in advance.

Korma Sutra
INDIAN $$

(Map p198; ✆23 3023; Tandapata 909; mains S25; ⊙1-10pm Mon-Sat; ☏) If you are craving spice, this London-style curry house will do the trick, with its garlicky naan, lassies and a variety of creamy kormas and curries. It's relaxing in the evening, with low-lit violet walls and cushioned booths.

Picantería María Angola
PERUVIAN $$

(Map p198; Choquechaca 292; mains S15-25; ⊙11am-7pm) A good place to try local foods such as *ubre* (breaded udder), *tripa* (tripe) or *panza apanada* (stomach lining), or more appetizing *chicharrones* and *costillares* (ribs). Turn right and head up the stairs when you walk in.

AVENIDA EL SOL & DOWNHILL

Pampa de Castillo is the street near Qorikancha where local workers lunch on Cuzco classics. Expect lots of *caldo de gallina* (chicken soup) and *chicharrones,* deep-fried pork chunks with corn, mint and, of course potato, in a range of restaurants.

Don Estéban and Don Pancho
CAFE $$

(Map p204; ✆25-2526; Av El Sol 765A; snacks S5-15; ⊙8am-10pm) A longtime local favorite for empanadas; the *empanada de ají de gallina* is especially scrumptious. They also serve *cuzqueño* breakfasts.

GREATER CUZCO

Most popular local restaurants are outside the historic center and focus on lunch; few open for dinner. Don't expect to encounter any language other than Spanish in these places, but the food is worth the effort!

Tradiciones Cusqueñas
PERUVIAN $$

(off Map p204; ✆23-1988; Belén 835; mains S20-40; ⊙11am-10pm) The home of a good Sunday lunch, Cuzco-style. It features jolly, utilitarian decor, huge piles of meat and potatoes, and delicious homemade *limonada* (lemonade). Come hungry!

Olas Bravas
CEVICHE $$

(✆43-9328; Mariscal Gamarra 11A; ceviche S22; ⊙9am-5pm) Most *cuzqueños* think Olas Bravas offers the best ceviche in town, so it's often packed. Even if ceviche isn't your thing, this is a great place to try other *criollo* (coastal) dishes, such as *causas* and *seco a la norteña* (goat stew). Check out the hammocks and the mural of the surfer.

Señor Carbón
BARBECUE $$

(✆24-4426; Urb Magisterio Segunda Etapa H5; buffet S40; ⊙lunch & dinner) Cuzco's only Rodizio-style grill. The buffet is a carnivore's dream – all the meat you can eat, cooked to your liking, plus salad bar. If you can still fit it in, there's a scoop of ice cream for dessert.

🍷 Drinking

The European pubs are good places to track down those all-important soccer matches, with satellite TVs more or less permanently tuned in to sports.

7 Angelitos
BAR

(Map p198; Siete Angelitos 638; ⊙6pm-late Mon-Sat) This tiny hillside haunt is the city's unof-

THE LUCKY TOAD

Ever wondered what *cuzqueños* do to relax instead of whiling away the hours over a game of darts or pool in the local bar? Well, next time you're in a *picantería* (local restaurant) or *quinta* (house serving typical Andean food), look out for a strange metal *sapo* (frog or toad) mounted on a large box and surrounded by various holes and slots. Men will often spend the whole afternoon drinking *chicha* (fermented corn beer) and beer while competing at this old test of skill in which players toss metal disks as close to the toad as possible. Top points are scored for landing one smack in the mouth. Legend has it that the game originated with Inca royals, who used to toss gold coins into Lake Titicaca in the hopes of attracting a *sapo*, believed to possess magical healing powers and to have the ability to grant wishes.

ficial hipster lounge and late-night backup: when everything else has closed and the sun has come up, knock on the door. Happy hours are 7:30pm to 9:30pm and 11pm to 11:30pm.

Fallen Angel COCKTAIL BAR
(Map p198; 25-8184; Plazoleta Nazarenas 221; 6pm-late) This ultrafunky lounge redefines kitsch with glitter balls, fake fur and even bathtub-cum-aquarium tables complete with live goldfish. It isn't cheap, but the decor really is worth seeing and the occasional theme parties held here are legendary.

Norton Rats PUB
(Map p198; cnr Santa Catalina Angosta & Plaza de Armas, 2nd fl; 7am-late) Run by a motorcycle enthusiast, this unassuming expat-style bar overlooks the Plaza de Armas. It's a boon for people watching, if you can get a balcony seat. Though known for delicious 200g burgers, it's also got TVs, darts and billiards to help you work up a thirst. Avoid the burritos. Happy hour is 7pm to 9pm.

Cross Keys PUB
(Map p198; Triunfo 350; 10am-late;) If you are thirsty for an Old Speckled Hen, visit the most established expat and traveler watering hole in town. This typical British pub has all the trappings, with leather barstools and dark wood. As well as a long list of imported beer, it offers good-value comfort food.

The Frogs PUB
(Map p198; Huarancalqui 185) Gloriously glamorous and run by high-profile hipsters, the Frogs offers a bit of everything. There's cafe service from breakfast until 11pm, nightly live music (ranging from acoustic to reggae and funk), billiards, beanbags, fairy lights and hookah pipes. Open early till late.

Piscuo COCKTAIL BAR
(Map p198; 231-782; Portal Belén 115, second fl) This low-lit, minimalist bar is in with local professionals who sit at the wraparound bar ordering the rainbow selection of mixed drinks. With live bands on Friday and Saturday.

Paddy Flaherty's PUB
(Map p198; 24-7719; Triunfo 124; 11am-late) This cramped little Irish pub is packed with random memorabilia, TVs, a working train set and homesick European travelers eating excellent-value hot sandwiches. Happy hours are from 7pm to 8pm and 10pm to 10:30pm.

☆ Entertainment

Clubs open early, but crank up a few notches after about 11pm. Happy hour is ubiquitous and generally entails two-for-one on beer or certain mixed drinks.

In popular *discotecas* (beware the word 'nightclub' – it is often used in Peru to indicate a brothel), especially right on the Plaza de Armas, both sexes should beware of drinks being spiked. The tried-and-true stops on the big night out in Cuzco are *discotecas* Inka Team, Roots and Ukuku's.

TOP CHOICE **Ukuku's** LIVE MUSIC
(24-2951; Plateros 316; 8pm-late) The most consistently popular nightspot in town, Ukuku's plays a winning combination of crowd pleasers – Latin and Western rock, reggae and *reggaetón* (a blend of Puerto Rican *bomba*, dancehall and hip-hop), salsa, hip-hop etc – and often hosts live bands. Usually full to bursting after midnight with as many Peruvians as foreign tourists, it's good, sweaty, dance-a-thon fun. Happy hour is 8pm to 10:30pm.

CUZCO & THE SACRED VALLEY CUZCO

MUSEO DEL PISCO

When you have had your fill of colonial religious art, you may want to investigate the new **pisco museum** (Map p198; ☑26-2709; museodelpisco.org; Santa Catalina Ancha 398; ⊙11am-1am), where the wonders of the national drink are extolled, exalted and – of course – sampled. Opened recently by an enthusiastic expat, this museum-bar is Pisco 101, combined with a tapas and sushi lounge. Ambitions go far beyond the standard pisco sour, although those do border on perfection. Then there's the mixologist whipping up original cocktails like *valicha*, pisco with jungle fruit kion, spearmint and tart apple. Tapas like delicious alpaca miniburgers on sesame buns and *tiradito* marinated in cumin-*chile* sate your hunger. Look for special tastings and master distiller classes announced on the Facebook page.

Muse, Too   LIVE MUSIC
(Map p198; ☑984-76-2602; Tandapata 710; ⊙8am-late) A good option for live entertainment, it's the laid-back San Blas version of the center's iconic cafe-bar. Muse, Too serves up fresh, funky food through the day, big-screen sport and movies in the afternoon, and live music and cocktails at night.

**Centro Qosqo de
Arte Nativo**   PERFORMING ARTS
(Map p204; ☑22-7901; Av El Sol 604; admission with boleto turístico) Has live nightly performances of Andean music and dance at 6:45pm.

Km 0   LIVE MUSIC
(Map p198; ☑23-6009; Tandapata 100; ⊙11am-late Tue-Sat, 5pm-late Sun & Mon) This convivial bar just off Plaza San Blas has a bit of everything. It serves good Thai food in the evening, and there's live music late every night – local musicians come here to jam after their regular gigs. Happy hour is 9pm to midnight.

Muse   LIVE MUSIC
(Map p198; ☑25-3631, 984-23-1717; Triunfo 338, 2nd fl; 🛜) Known as a good place to start your night out, this restaurant lounge, a longtime Cuzco hangout, has very cool staff and live music in the evenings. Food includes good vegetarian options.

Inka Team   CLUB
(Map p198; Portal de Carnes 298; ⊙8pm-late) Though it may change names, this place usually has the most up-to-the-minute electronic music collection, with trance, house and hip-hop mixed in with mainstream. There are chill-out sofas upstairs but this isn't the place for chat. A good mix of locals and tourists hang out here. Happy hour is 9pm to midnight.

Mama Africa   CLUB
(Map p198; Portal Harinas 191, 2nd fl; ⊙7pm-late) A favorite with Israelis, Mama Africa is the classic backpackers' hangout, usually packed with people sprawled across cushions or swaying to rock and reggae rhythms. Happy hour is 8:30pm to 11pm.

🛍 Shopping

San Blas – the plaza itself, Cuesta San Blas, Carmen Alto, and Tandapata east of the plaza – offers Cuzco's best shopping. It's the artisan quarter, packed with the workshops and showrooms of local craftspeople. Some offer the chance to watch artisans at work and see the interiors of colonial buildings while hunting down that perfect souvenir. Prices and quality vary greatly, so shop around and expect to bargain, except in the most expensive stores, where prices are often fixed. Some of the best-known include **Taller Olave** (Map p198; ☑23-1835; Plaza San Blas 651), which sells reproductions of colonial sculptures and pre-colonial ceramics. **Taller Mendivil** (☑23-3247; San Blas (Map p198; Cuesta de San Blas, Plaza San Blas); city center (Map p198; cnr Hatunrumiyoc & Choquechaca) is nationally famous for its giraffe-necked religious figures and sun-shaped mirrors, and **Taller and Museo Mérida** (Map p198; ☑22-1714; Carmen Alto 133) offers striking earthenware statues that straddle the border between craft and art.

The same area is also home to an ever-evolving sprinkling of jewelry stores and quirky, one-off designer-clothes stores – a refreshing reminder that the local aesthetic is not confined to stridently colored ponchos and sheepskin-rug depictions of Machu Picchu. These and other mass-produced tourist tat from textiles to teapots are sold from pretty much every hole-in-the-wall in the historic center, and at the vast **Centro**

Artesenal Cuzco (Map p204; cnr Avs El Sol & Tullumayo; ⊙9am-10pm).

If you're the type who likes to get your souvenir shopping done fast, **Aymi Wasi** (Nueva Alta s/n) is for you. It's got *everything* – clothes, ornaments, toys, candles, jewelry, art, ceramics, handbags... Your friends and family will never suspect you bought all their gifts in one place! And it's all hand-made and fair trade.

Cuzco is not known for its clothes-shopping, though there are a few cool stores hidden away in the **Centro Comercial de Cuzco** (Map p198; cnr Ayacucho & San Andrés; ⊙11am-10pm).

Tatoo (Map p198; ☎25-4211; Calle del Medio 130; ⊙9am-9:30pm) has brand-name outdoor clothing and technical gear at high prices. Many shops in Calle Plateros and Mercado El Molino have a good range of lower-quality, much cheaper gear.

Textiles

Centro de Textiles Tradicionales del Cuzco   HANDICRAFTS
(Map p204; ☎22-8117; www.textilescusco.org; Av El Sol 603A; ⊙7:30am-8:30pm Mon-Sat, 8:30am-8:30pm Sun) This nonprofit organization, founded in 1996, promotes the survival of traditional weaving. You may be able to catch a shop-floor demonstration illustrating different weaving techniques in all their finger-twisting complexity. Products for sale are high end.

Inkakunaq Ruwaynin   HANDICRAFTS
(Map p198; ☎26-0942; www.tejidosandinos.com; inside CBC, Tullumayo 274; ⊙9am-7pm) This weaving cooperative with quality goods is run by 12 mountain communities from Cuzco and Apurimac; it's at the far end of the inner courtyard. There's also an online catalog.

Casa Ecológica   HANDICRAFTS
(Map p198; ☎25-5646; www.casaecologicacusco.com; Triunfo 393; ⊙9am-9pm Mon-Sun) Hand-made textiles from 29 communities as far away as Ausangate, plus homemade jams and essential oils.

Markets

Mercado San Pedro   MARKET
(Map p204; Plazoleta San Pedro) Cuzco's central market is a must-see. Pig heads for *caldo* (soup), frogs (to enhance sexual performance), vats of fruit juice, roast *lechón* (suckling pig) and tamales are just a few of the foods on offer. Around the edges are typical clothes, spells, incense and other random products to keep you entertained for hours.

Mercado Modelo de Huanchac   MARKET
(Map p204; cnr Avs Garcilaso & Huascar). Less touristy and just as interesting, Huanchac is the local destination of choice for breakfast the morning after, specializing in the two hangover staples – jolting acid ceviche and greasy *chicharrones*.

El Molino   MARKET
(off Map p204; Urbanizacion Ttio) Just beyond the *terminal terrestre,* this market is Cuzco's answer to the department store. Even more congested than San Pedro, it's a bargain hunter's paradise for clothes, housewares, bulk food and alcohol, *electrodomésticos* (electronic goods), camping gear, and pirated CDs and DVDs.

❶ Information

Bookstores
Many guesthouses, cafes and pubs have book exchanges. The best source of historical and archaeological information about the city and the surrounding area is the pocket-sized *Exploring Cuzco* by Peter Frost.

Recommended bookstores include the following:

Bookstore Kiosk (Map p198; Mantas 113; ⊙9am-2pm & 4-9pm Mon-Sat) Novels and magazines in English and German. Located just inside the door of Centro Comercial.

Jerusalén (Map p198; Heladeros 143; ⊙10am-2pm & 4-8pm Mon-Sat) Cuzco's most extensive public book exchange (two used books, or one plus S8, will get you one book) plus used guidebooks, new titles and music CDs for sale.

SBS Bookshop (Map p204; Av El Sol 781A; ⊙9am-9pm Mon-Sat) Small, but specializes in foreign-language books, especially in English.

Dangers & Annoyances
Most travelers will experience few problems in Cuzco. Most crimes reported are bags stolen from the backs of chairs in public places, or from overhead shelves in overnight buses. Walk around with a minimum of cash and belongings. If you keep your bag in your lap and watch out for pickpockets in crowded streets, transport terminals and markets, you are highly unlikely to be a victim of crime in Cuzco.

Robberies and even rapes in cabs have been reported. Use only official taxis, especially at night. (Look for the company's lit telephone number on top of the car.) Lock your doors from the inside, and never allow the driver to admit a second passenger.

Avoid walking by yourself late at night or very early in the morning. Revelers returning late from bars or setting off for the Inca Trail before sunrise are particularly vulnerable to 'choke and grab' attacks. For tips on avoiding theft and other common scams, see p537.

Don't buy drugs. Dealers and police often work together and Procuradores is one of several areas in which you can make a drug deal and get busted all within a couple of minutes. Drink spiking has been reported. Women especially should try not to let go of their glass or accept drinks from strangers.

Take care not to overexert yourself during your first few days if you've flown in from lower elevations, such as Lima. You may find yourself quickly becoming winded while traipsing up and down Cuzco's narrow streets. For more advice on altitude sickness, see p552.

Embassies & Consulates

Most foreign embassies and consulates are located in Lima (p532). The following are honorary consul representatives in Cuzco:

Belgium (☎25-1278)
France (☎23-3610)
Germany (☎23-5459)
Italy (☎22-4398)
UK (☎23-9974)
USA (☎984-62-369)

Emergency

Policía de Turismo (PolTur, Tourist Police; ☎23-5123; Plaza Túpac Amaru s/n; ☼24hr) If you have something stolen, you'll need to see these guys to get an official police report for insurance claims.

Immigration

Oficina de Migraciónes (Immigration Office; Map p204; ☎22-2741; www.digemin.com.pe; Av El Sol 612; ☼8am-4:30pm Mon-Fri) Can renew tourist visas and replace a lost Tarjeta Andina (tourist card) – be prepared for a lot of red tape.

Internet Access

Internet cafes are found on almost every street corner. Many hotels and cafes offer free wireless.

Internet Resources

Andean Travel Web (www.andeantravelweb.com) More than 1000 pages of information and recommendations.

Diario del Cusco (www.diariodelcusco.com) Online edition of the local newspaper (Spanish-language).

Municipalidad del Cusco (www.municusco.gob.pe) The city's official website.

Jack's Guide (www.jacksguide.com) Good bilingual information for visitors and calendar of events.

Laundry

Lavanderías (laundries) will wash, dry and fold your clothes from around S3 per kg. They're everywhere, but cluster just off the Plaza de Armas on Suecia, Procuradores and Plateros, and on Carmen Bajo in San Blas. The further you get from the Plaza de Armas, the cheaper they get.

Left Luggage

If you're going trekking for a few days or even just on an overnight excursion, any hostel will store your bags for free. Always get a receipt, and lock your bags. The bags should have identifying tags showing your name and the drop-off and expected pickup dates. For soft-sided bags, we recommend placing them inside a larger plastic bag and sealing them shut with tape. Then sign your name across the seal, so that you can tell if your bag has been opened while you were away. It's best to keep all valuables (eg passport, credit cards, money) on your person. Trekkers are required to carry their passport with them on the Inca Trail.

Medical Services

Pharmacies abound along Av El Sol. Cuzco's medical facilities are limited; head to Lima for serious procedures.

Clinica Pardo (☎24-0997; Av de la Cultura 710; ☼24hr) Well equipped and expensive – perfect if you're covered by travel insurance.

Clínica Paredes (Map p204; ☎22-5265; Lechugal 405; ☼24hr) Consultations S60.

Hospital Regional (☎23-9792, emergencies ☎22-3691; Av de la Cultura s/n; ☼24hr) Public and free, but wait times can be long and good care is not guaranteed.

Traveler's Clinic Cusco (☎22-1213; Puputi 148; ☼24hr) A private clinic with swift bilingual service and on-call doctor, deals mostly with altitude sickness patients and travelers' illnesses. It's a 10 minute walk from San Blas.

Money

ATMs abound in and around the Plaza de Armas, and are also available at the airport, Huanchaq train station and the bus terminal. All accept Visa, most accept MasterCard, and many will even allow you to withdraw from a foreign debit account. There are several big bank branches on Av El Sol; go inside for cash advances above daily ATM limits. *Casas de cambio* (foreign-exchange bureaus) give better exchange rates than banks, and are scattered around the main plazas and especially along Av El Sol. Moneychangers can be found outside banks, but their rates aren't much better than *casas de cambio* and rip-offs are common.

Banco Continental (Map p198; Av El Sol 368; ☼9:15am-6:30pm Mon-Fri, 9:30am-12:30pm Sat)

BCP (Map p198; Av El Sol 189; ☼9am-6:30pm Mon-Thu, to 7:30pm Fri, to 1pm Sat)

Interbank (Map p198; Av El Sol 380; ⊙9am-5:30pm Mon-Fri, 9:15am-12:30pm Sat)

Post

DHL (Map p204; 📱24-4167; Av El Sol 608; ⊙8:30am-7pm Mon-Fri, 9am-1pm Sat) International express mail and package courier services.

Main post office (Map p204; 📱22-4212; Av El Sol 800; ⊙8am-8pm Mon-Sat) General delivery (poste restante) mail is held here at the main post office; bring proof of identity.

Tourist Information

Travel agencies are all too willing to help out with travel arrangements – for a hefty commission, of course. The following independent tourist information centers are recommended:

DIRCETUR (Map p198; 📱22-3701; www.dirceturcusco.gob.pe; Mantas 117; ⊙8am-8pm Mon-Sat, 9am-2pm Sun) The official provider of Cuzco tourism information. Well meaning but motley and sporadic; iPerú is more informative.

Dirección Regional de Cultura Cusco (Map p204; 📱58-2030; www.drc-cusco.gob.pe; Av de la Cultura 238; ⊙7:15am-6:30pm Mon-Sat) The place in Cuzco to purchase Machu Picchu entry tickets; closed on holidays.

iPerú (www.peru.travel) airport (📱23-7364; Aeropuerto, Main Hall; ⊙6am-4pm); city center (Map p198; 📱25-2974; Portal de Harinas 177, Plaza de Armas; ⊙8am-8pm) Excellent source for tourist information for both the region and entire country. Also has adjoining section of guarded ATMs at plaza location.

South American Explorers Club (Map p198; 📱24-5484; www.saexplorers.org; Atocsaycuchi 670; ⊙9:30am-5pm Mon-Fri, to 1pm Sat) Gives unbiased advice and sells information booklets, including alternatives to the Inca Trail and Amazon jungle adventures. SAE's Cuzco clubhouse has good-quality maps, books and brochures for sale, a huge stock of travel information and recommendations, wi-fi access, a book exchange and rooms for rent. Weekly events and limited volunteer information are available to nonmembers.

🅰 Getting There & Away

Air

Most flights from Cuzco's **Aeropuerto Internacional Alejandro Velasco Astete** (CUZ; 📱22-2611) are in the morning, because climatic conditions in the afternoon typically make landings and takeoffs more difficult. If you have a tight connection, it's best to reserve the earliest flight available, as later ones are more likely to be delayed or canceled.

Several airlines offer daily flights to and from Lima, Juliaca, Puerto Maldonado and Arequipa. Check in at least two hours before your flight – even people with confirmed seats and boarding passes have been denied boarding because of overbooking errors. During the rainy season, flights in and out of Puerto Maldonado are often seriously delayed. Departure taxes are included in ticket prices.

Official taxis from the airport to addresses near the city center cost S12 to S25.

The following airlines serve Cuzco:

LAN (Map p204; 📱25-5555; www.lan.com; Av El Sol 627B; ⊙8:30am-7pm Mon-Sat, to 1pm Sun)

Peruvian Airlines (Map p198; 📱25-4890; www.peruvianairlines.pe; Calle del Medio 117; ⊙9am-7pm Mon-Sat, 9am-12pm Sun)

Star Perú (Map p204; 📱01-705-9000; www.starperu.com; Av El Sol 679; ⊙9am-1pm & 3-6:30pm Mon-Sat, 9am-12:30pm Sun)

TACA (Map p204; 📱0800-18-2222; www.taca.com; Av El Sol 602; ⊙9am-6pm)

Bus & Taxi

The journey times given here are only approximate and apply only if road conditions are good. Long delays are likely during the rainy season, particularly going to Puerto Maldonado or towards Lima via Abancay. This road is now all paved, but landslides can block the road in the rainy season.

INTERNATIONAL

All international services depart from the **terminal terrestre** (off Map p204; 📱22-4471, Vía de Evitamiento 429), about 2km out of town towards the airport. Take a taxi (S3). To get there on foot, take Av El Sol. After it turns into Alameda Pachacutec there is a pedestrian lane in the middle of the road. Straight after the tower and statue of Pachacutec, turn right, following the railway lines into a side street, which reaches the terminal in five minutes.

To get to Bolivia, catch **Trans Salvador** (📱23-3680), **Littoral** (📱24-8989), **Real Turismo** (📱24-3540), or **San Luis** (📱22-3647) to La Paz via Copacabana; all depart at 10pm. **Tour Peru** (📱24-9977, www.tourperu.com.pe) offers the best value service to Copacabana, departing at 8am daily. **CIAL** (📱in Lima 01-330-4225) departs at 10:30pm for La Paz via Desaguadero (S70, 12 hours). This is the quickest way to get to La Paz.

Ormeño (📱26-1704; www.grupo-ormeno.com.pe) travels to most South American capitals.

LONG DISTANCE

Buses to major cities leave from the *terminal terrestre*. Buses for more unusual destinations leave from elsewhere, so check carefully in advance.

Ormeño (📱26-1704; www.grupo-ormeno.com.pe) and **Cruz del Sur** (📱24-3621;

CUZCO BUSES

DESTINATION	COST* (SOLES)	DURATION (HRS)
Abancay	15-20	5
Arequipa	25/126	9-11
Ayacucho	65/95	14-16
Copacabana (Bolivia)	50/70	15
Ica	90/176	14-15
Juliaca	20-35	5-6
La Paz (Bolivia)	60/80	12
Lima	90/176	18-22
Nazca	90/180	14
Puerto Maldonado	50/70	11
Puno	20-40	6-7
Quillabamba	25-35	6-7
Tacna	60/125	17

*Prices are general estimates for normal/luxury buses

www.cruzdelsur.com.pe) have the safest and most comfortable buses across the board. Of the cheaper companies, **Wari** (☏22-2694) and especially Tour Peru have the best buses.

There are departures to Juliaca and Puno every hour from 4am to 11pm, and at random hours through the day. Cheap, slow options include **Power** (☏22-7777) and **Libertad** (☏950-018-836); these stop to let passengers on and off along the way, so you can use them to access towns along the route. Midrange-priced **Littoral** (☏23-1155) and **CIAL** (☏965-401-414) are faster and more comfortable.

The most enjoyable way to get to Puno is via **Inka Express** (☏24-7887; www.inkaexpress. com; Av La Paz C32, El Óvalo) or **Turismo Mer** (☏24-5171; www.turismomer.com; Av La Paz A3, El Óvalo), which run luxury buses every morning. The service includes lunch and an English-speaking tour guide, who talks about the four sites that are briefly visited along the way: Andahuaylllas, Raqchi, Abra la Raya and Pucará. The trip takes about eight hours and costs around S143.

Departures to Arequipa (S25 to S30, nine hours) cluster around 6am to 7am and 7pm to 9:30pm. Ormeño offers a deluxe service at 9am.

Cruz del Sur, **CIVA** (☏24-9961; www.civa. com.pe) and **Celtur** (☏23-6075) offer relatively painless services to Lima. Wari is the best of the cheaper options. Most buses to Lima stop in Nazca (12 hours) and Ica (14 hours). These buses go via Abancay and can suffer holdups in rainy season. Between January and April, it may

be worth going via Arequipa (25 to 27 hours) instead.

Buses depart every couple of hours through the day for Abancay and Andahuaylas (S45, six to eight hours). Celtur has slightly nicer buses than other companies on this route. Change at Andahuaylas to get to Ayacucho via rough roads that get very cold at night. If you're going to Ayacucho by bus, wear all of your warm clothes and if you have a sleeping bag, bring it onboard the bus.

San Martín (☏984-61-2520) and **Expreso Sagitário** (☏22-9757) offer direct buses to Tacna (S70, 17 hours). Expreso Sagitário also goes to Arequipa, Lima and Puno, and may be more open to bargaining than other companies.

Various companies depart for Puerto Maldonado between 3pm and 4:30pm; CIVA is probably the best option.

Buses to Quillabamba via Santa María leave from the Santiago terminal, a brisk 20-minute walk from the center. Around the corner in Calle Antonio Lorena, many more companies offer air-conditioned, speedy comfort in the form of modern minivans that cost twice as much and cut a couple of hours off the trip. There are departures of both types of service at 8am, 10am, 1pm and 8pm. Change at Santa María to get to Santa Teresa.

Transportes Siwar (off Map p204; Av Tito Condemayta 1613) has buses to Ocongate and Tinqui (S9, three hours), the start of the Ausangante trek, leaving from behind the Coliseo Cerrado several times a day.

Transportes Gallito de las Rocas (☑22-895; Diagonal Angamos) buses depart to Pauartambo (S9, three hours) daily and to Pilcopaa (S20, 10 to 12 hours) Monday, Wednesday and riday at 5am. The office is on the first block off v de la Cultura; look for 'Paucartambo' painted n a lamp post between auto shops.

REGIONAL SERVICES

n 2014, the government will restrict the use of ld colectivos; note that some of these services nay be cut or reduced in the future.

Minibuses to Calca (S6, 1½ hours) via Pisac S2.50, one hour) leave frequently from the erminal at Tullumayo 207.

Minibuses to Urubamba (S8, 1½ hours) via Pisac (S2.50, one hour) leave frequently from he terminal in Puputi, just north of Av de la Cultura.

Minibuses to Urubamba (S6, 1½ hrs) and Olantaytambo (S12, two hours) via Chinchero (S4, one hour) leave from near the Puente Grau. Just around the corner on Pavitos, faster colectivos eave when full for Urubamba (S7, one hour) and Ollantaytambo (S10-15, 1½ hours) via Chinchero.

Colectivos to Urcos (S5) via Tipón (S5), Piquilacta (S5) and Andahuaylillas (S5) leave from the middle of the street outside Tullumayo 207. For S80 they'll drive you into the ruins at Tipón and Piquillacta, wait and bring you back.

You can also get to the these destinations, and Saylla, by catching a minibus headed for Urcos (S5) from a terminal just off Av de la Cultura opposite the regional hospital. Shared taxis to Lucre (S2.50, one hour) depart from Huascar, between Av Garcilaso and Manco Capac, between 7am and 7pm.

Minibuses for Limatambo (S12, two hours) and Curahuasi (S15, four hours) leave Arcopata when full, a couple of blocks west of Meloc, until about 3pm.

Unless otherwise stated, these services run from at least 5am until 7pm. Early and late services may charge more.

Car & Motorcycle

Given all the headaches and potential hazards of driving yourself around, consider hiring a taxi for the day – it's cheaper than renting a car. If you must, you'll find a couple of car-rental agencies in the bottom block of Av El Sol. Motorcycle rentals are offered by a couple of agencies in the first block of Saphi heading away from the Plaza de Armas.

Train

Cuzco has two train stations. **Estación Huanchac** (☑58-1414; ⊙7am-5pm Mon-Fri, to midnight Sat & Sun), near the end of Av El Sol, serves Juliaca and Puno on Lake Titicaca. **Estación Poroy**, east of town, serves Ollan-

taytambo and Machu Picchu. The two stations are unconnected, so it's impossible to travel directly from Puno to Machu Picchu. (Downtown Estación San Pedro is used only for local trains, which foreigners cannot board.)

You can take a taxi to Poroy (S30) or the station in Ollantaytambo (S80) from Cuzco. Return trips are slightly more expensive.

You can buy tickets at Huanchac station, and there are ATMs in the station, but the easiest way is directly through the train companies.

TO OLLANTAYTAMBO AND MACHU PICCHU

The only way to reach Aguas Calientes (and access Machu Picchu) is via train. It takes about three hours. Three companies currently offer the service, the latter two only from Ollantaytambo:

» **Peru Rail** (www.perurail.com; ticket office: Portal de Panes 214, Plaza de Armas; ⊙8am-10pm) Formerly the only service to Aguas Calientes, with multiple departures daily from Estación Poroy, 20 minutes outside of Cuzco. There are three levels of service: Expedition (from US$144 roundtrip), Vistadome (from US$160 roundtrip) and the luxurious Hiriam Bingham (from US$700 roundtrip). The Hiram Bingham includes brunch, afternoon tea, entrance to Machu Picchu and a guided tour. It runs daily except Sunday.

» **Inca Rail** (☑23-3030; www.incarail.com; Cuzco ticket office: Portal de Panes 105, Plaza de Armas) New company with three departures daily from Ollantaytambo and four levels of service (roundtrip US$82-180). Children get a significant discount. An environmentally sustainable practice business.

» **Machu Picchu Train** (Map p204; ☑22-1199; www.machupicchutrain.com; Cuzco ticket office: Av El Sol 576; ⊙7am-5pm Mon-Fri, 7am-12pm Sat) New service of panoramic-view trains, traveling only from Ollantaytambo to Aguas Calientes (roundtrip adult/child from US$100/70) three times daily in high season. Breakfast or snacks may be served.

Fares may vary according to departure hours: more desirable times are usually more expensive. It is common for trains to sell out, especially at peak hours, so buy your ticket as far ahead of time as possible.

The quickest 'cheaper' way to get from Cuzco to Aguas Calientes is to take a combi to Ollantaytambo and catch the train from there.

TO PUNO

Peru Rail (www.perurail.com; Estación Huanchac; ticket US$150; ⊙7am-5pm Mon-Fri, 7am-12pm Sat) Andean Explorer, a luxury train with a glass-walled observation car, goes to Puno. Trains depart from Estación Huanchac at 8am, arriving at Puno around 6pm, on Monday,

Wednesday and Saturday from November to March, with an extra departure on Friday from April to October. Lunch is included. For more information, see p178.

❶ Getting Around

To/From the Airport

The airport is about 6km south of the city center. The *combi* lines Imperial and C4M (S0.60, 20 minutes) run from Av El Sol to just outside the airport. A taxi to or from the city center to the airport costs S10. An official radio taxi from within the airport costs S12 to S25. With advance reservations, many hotels offer free pickup.

Bus

Local rides on public transportation cost only S0.60, though it's easier to walk or just take a taxi than to figure out where any given *combi* is headed.

Taxi

There are no meters in taxis, but there are set rates. At the time of research, trips within the city center cost S4, and to destinations further afield, such as El Molino, were S8. Check with your hotel whether this is still correct, and rather than negotiate, simply hand the correct amount to your driver at the end of your ride; he is unlikely to argue if you seem to know what you're doing. Official taxis, identified by a lit company telephone number on the roof, are more expensive than taxis flagged down on the street, but they are safer.

Unofficial 'pirate' taxis, which only have a taxi sticker in the window, have been complicit in muggings, violent assaults and kidnappings of tourists. Before getting into any taxi, do as savvy locals do and take conspicuous note of the registration number.

AloCusco (☎22-2222) is a reliable company to call.

Tram

The Tranvia is a free-rolling tourist tram that conducts a 1½ hour hop-on, hop-off city tour (S15). It leaves at 8:30am, 10am, 11:30am, 2pm, 3:30pm, 5pm and 6:30pm from the Plaza de Armas.

AROUND CUZCO

The four ruins closest to Cuzco are Sacsaywamán, Q'enqo, Pukapukara and Tambomachay. They can all be visited in a day – far less if you're whisked through on a guided tour. If you only have time to visit one site, Sacsaywamán is the most important, and less than a 2km trek uphill from the Plaza de Armas in central Cuzco.

The cheapest way to visit the sites is to take a bus bound for Pisac and ask the driver to stop at Tambomachay, the furthest si from Cuzco (at 3700m, it's also the highest It's an 8km walk back to Cuzco, visiting a four ruins along the way. Alternatively, a ta will charge roughly S40 to visit all four site

Each site can only be entered with the *be leto turístico*. They're open daily from 7a to 6pm. Local guides hang around offerin their services, sometimes quite persistentl Agree on a price before beginning any tour

Robberies at these sites are uncommo but not unheard of. Cuzco's tourist polic recommend visiting between 9am and 5pm

Sacsaywamán

This immense ruin of both religious an military significance is the most impressiv in the immediate area around Cuzco. Th long Quechua name means 'Satisfied Falcon though tourists will inevitably remembe it by the mnemonic 'sexy woman.' Sacsay wamán feels huge, but what today's visito sees is only about 20% of the original struc ture. Soon after the conquest, the Spaniard tore down many walls and used the blocks t build their own houses in Cuzco, leaving th largest and most impressive rocks, especiall those forming the main battlements.

In 1536 the fort was the site of one of th most bitter battles of the Spanish conquest More than two years after Pizarro's entr into Cuzco, the rebellious Manco Inca recap tured the lightly guarded Sacsaywamán an used it as a base to lay siege to the conquis tadors in Cuzco. Manco was on the brink o defeating the Spaniards when a desperate last-ditch attack by 50 Spanish cavalry led b Juan Pizarro, Francisco's brother, succeeded in retaking Sacsaywamán and putting an end to the rebellion. Manco Inca survived and re treated to the fortress of Ollantaytambo, bu most of his forces were killed. Thousands o dead littered the site after the Incas' defeat attracting swarms of carrion-eating Andean condors. The tragedy was memorialized by the inclusion of eight condors in Cuzco's coat of arms.

The site is composed of three different areas, the most striking being the magnifi cent three-tiered zigzag fortifications. One stone, incredibly, weighs more than 300 tons. It was the ninth *inca*, Pachacutec, who envisioned Cuzco in the shape of a puma, with Sacsaywamán as the head, and these 22 zigzagged walls as the teeth of the puma. The walls also formed an extremely effective de

MORE RUINS TO EXPLORE

Take any Pisac-bound transportation to reach these ruins, located just outside of Cuzco. Entry is included in the *boleto turístico* or the partial *boleto*; open daily 7am to 6pm.

Q'enqo

The name of this small but fascinating ruin means 'zigzag.' A large limestone rock, it's riddled with niches, steps and extraordinary symbolic carvings, including the zigzagging channels that probably gave the site its name. Scramble up to the top to find a flat surface used for ceremonies: look carefully to see laboriously etched representations of a puma, a condor and a llama. Back below, you can explore a mysterious subterranean cave with altars hewn into the rock. Q'enqo is about 4km northeast of Cuzco, on the left of the road as you descend from Tambomachay.

Pukapukara

Just across the main road from Tambomachay, this commanding structure looks down on the Cuzco valley. In some lights the rock looks pink, and the name literally means 'Red Fort,' though it is more likely to have been a hunting lodge, a guard post and a stopping point for travelers. It is composed of several lower residential chambers, storerooms and an upper esplanade with panoramic views.

Tambomachay

In a sheltered spot about 300m from the main road, this site consists of a beautifully wrought ceremonial stone bath channeling crystalline spring water through fountains that still function today. It is thus popularly known as El Baño del Inca (The Bath of the Inca), and theories connect the site to an Inca water cult. It's 8km northeast of Cuzco.

ensive mechanism that forced attackers to expose their flanks when attacking.

Opposite is the hill called **Rodadero**, with retaining walls, polished rocks and a finely carved series of stone benches known as the Inca's Throne. Three towers once stood above these walls. Only the foundations remain, but the 22m diameter of the largest, Muyuc Marca, gives an indication of how big they must have been. With its perfectly fitted stone conduits, this tower was probably used as a huge water tank for the garrison. Other buildings within the ramparts provided food and shelter for an estimated 5000 warriors. Most of these structures were torn down by the Spaniards and later inhabitants of Cuzco.

Between the zigzag ramparts and the hill lies a large, flat parade ground that is used for the colorful tourist spectacle of **Inti Raymi**, held every June 24.

To walk up to the site from the Plaza de Armas takes 30 to 50 minutes, so make sure you're acclimatized before attempting it. Arriving at dawn will let you have the site almost to yourself, though solo travelers shouldn't come alone at this time of day.

Another option is to take a taxi tour which also includes Q'enko, Pukapukara and Tambomachay (S55).

THE SACRED VALLEY

Tucked under the tawny skirts of formidable foothills, the beautiful Río Urubamba Valley, known as El Valle Sagrado (The Sacred Valley), is about 15km north of Cuzco as the condor flies, via a narrow road of hairpin turns. Long the home of attractive colonial towns and isolated weaving villages, in recent years it has become a destination in its own right. Star attractions are the markets and the lofty Inca citadels of Pisac and Ollantaytambo, but the valley is also packed with other Inca sites. Trekking routes are deservedly gaining in popularity. Adrenaline activities range from rafting to rock climbing. Most activities can be organized in Cuzco or at some hotels in Urubamba.

A multitude of travel agencies in Cuzco offer whirlwind tours of the Sacred Valley, stopping at markets and the most significant archaeological sites. If you have a day or two to spare, spend it exploring this peaceful, fetching corner of the Andes at

The Sacred Valley

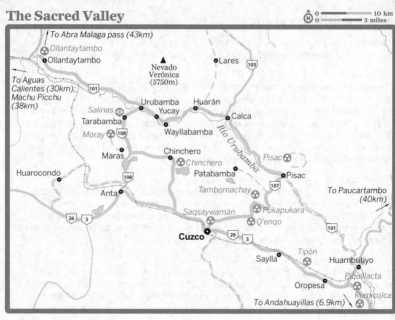

your own leisure. The archaeological sites of Pisac, Ollantaytambo and Chinchero can be visited with a *boleto turístico,* which can be bought directly onsite.

Pisac

📞 084 / POP 900 / ELEV 2715M

It's not hard to succumb to the charms of sunny Pisac, a bustling colonial village at the base of a spectacular Inca fortress perched on a mountain spur. Its pull is universal and recent years have seen an influx of expats and new age followers in search of an Andean Shangri-la. Located just 33km northeast of Cuzco by a paved road, it's the most convenient starting point to the Sacred Valley.

👁 Sights & Activities

Mercado de Artesania   MARKET

Pisac is known far and wide for its market, by far the biggest and most touristy in the region. Official market days are Tuesday, Thursday and Sunday, when tourist buses descend on the town in droves. However, the market has taken over Pisac to such an extent that it fills the Plaza de Armas and surrounding streets every day; visit on Monday, Wednesday, Friday or Saturday if you want to avoid the worst of the crowds.

Pisac Ruins   RUINS

(admission with boleto turístico; ⊙dawn-dusk) This hilltop Inca citadel lies high above the village on a triangular plateau with a plunging gorge on either side. Though it's a truly awesome site, it gets relatively few tourists except midmorning on Sunday, Tuesday and Thursday, when tour groups flood in.

The most impressive feature is the agricultural **terracing**, which sweeps around the south and east flanks of the mountain in huge and graceful curves, almost entirely unbroken by steps (which require greater maintenance and promote erosion). Instead the terracing is joined by diagonal flights of stairs made of flagstones set into the terrace walls. Above the terraces are cliff-hugging footpaths, watched over by caracara falcons and well defended by massive stone doorways, steep stairs and a short tunnel carved out of the rock. Vendors sell drinks at the top.

This dominating site guards not only the Urubamba Valley below, but also a pass leading into the jungle to the northeast. Topping the terraces is the site's **ceremonial center**, with an *intihuatana* (literally 'hitching post of the sun'; an Inca astronomical tool), several working water channels, and some painstakingly neat masonry in the well-preerved **temples**. A path leads up the hillside to a series of ceremonial baths and around to the military area. Looking across the Kitamayo Gorge from the back of the site, you'll also see hundreds of holes honeycombing the cliff wall. These are **Inca tombs** that were plundered by *huaqueros* (grave robbers), and are now completely off-limits to tourists.

The site is large and warrants several hours of your time. To walk there from town, take the steep but spectacular 4km trail. It's about two hours up and 1½ hours back. It's highly worthwhile, but undeniably grueling: recommended training for the Inca Trail! Taking a taxi up and walking back is a good option.

The footpath to the site starts from above the west side of the church. There are many crisscrossing trails, but if you keep heading upward toward the terracing, you won't get lost. To the west, or the left of the hill as you climb up on the footpath, is the Río Kitamayo Gorge; to the east, or right, is the Río Chongo Valley.

Horno Colonial San Francisco LANDMARK
(Mariscal Castilla s/n; snacks S2.50; ⏱6am-6pm) Huge clay ovens for baking empanadas and other goodies and *castillos de cuyes* (miniature castles inhabited by guinea pigs) are found in many nooks and crannies, particularly in Mariscál Castilla. But this is the town's most authentic – a colonial oven dating back to 1830. Stop in for hot cheese and oregano empanadas with *chicha morada*.

ℹ️ **TAXI TOURS**

If you are short on time to see the sights outside Cuzco, consider taking a taxi tour. Particularly if you have two or more people, they can be a good deal, and also allow you to take your time (or not) visiting various ruins and markets. From Cuzco, a tour of the Sacred Valley (possibly including Pisac, Ollantaytambo, Chinchero, Maras and Moray) runs S120 to S150 (for the whole car); to the Southern Valley (with options to Tipón, Pikillacta and Raqcchi) costs around S90 to S170.

One reliable option is **Virgin Estrella Taxi Tours** (📞973-195-551, 974-955-374) in Cuzco.

If, for some strange reason, you only have five minutes in Pisac, spend it here – you'll get a pretty good feel for the place.

Jardín Botanico GARDENS
(📞63-5563; Grau, cuadra 4; admission S6; ⏱8am-4:30pm) While you are wandering town, it's worth popping in to the botanical garden, a private enterprise with a huge courtyard full of beautiful specimens and a resident cat.

Club Royal Inka SWIMMING
(admission S10; ⏱8am-4pm) Ideal for families, this private recreation area is a fabulous place to while away an afternoon. A day pass allows access to an Olympic-sized indoor pool that's decked with fountains, grassy areas and an ornamental duck pond. There's also a restaurant, a trout pond and facilities for barbecues, billiards, table tennis, volleyball, tennis and *sapo* (see p225).

It's about 1.5km out of town.

La Capilla CHURCH
In recent times, the INC (Instituto Nacional de Cultura), in a characteristically controversial move, demolished the church in the main square in order to reconstruct it in colonial style. Masses, which have moved to a nearby chapel, are worth visiting. On Sunday, a Quechua-language mass is held at 11am.

Traditionally dressed locals descend from the hills to attend, including men in traditional highland dress blowing horns and *varayocs* (local authorities) with silver staffs of office.

Amaru VILLAGE
If you are interested in textiles, it's worth visiting this weaving community that's a 40-minute trip by taxi.

🎭 **Festivals & Events**

La Virgen del Carmen FESTIVAL
Street processions and masked dancing mark the celebration of 'Mamacha Carmen' who defeats demons climbing on rooftops and balconies. This renowned celebration of the Virgin of Carmen takes place from around July 15 to July 18.

🛏️ **Sleeping**

Pisac had become a new-age hub of sorts. Foreign-run mystical and spiritual retreats on the outskirts of town offer packages with shamanic ceremonies; some are vastly more commercial than others.

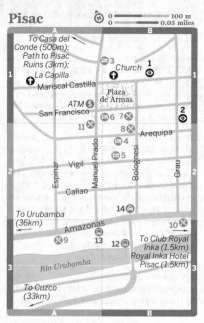

Pisac

TOP CHOICE Hotel Pisac Inca GUESTHOUSE $
(☑43-6921; www.hotelpisacinca.com; Vigil 242; s/d S35/70, s/d/tr without bathroom S25/50/75; @🛜) Sisters Tatiana and Claudia run this small, cheerful lodging with a handful of colorful rooms around a tiny courtyard. Kitchen use is extra but it's a steal.

Pisac Inn INN $$
(☑20-3062; www.pisacinn.com; Plaza de Armas; d incl breakfast from S146; @🛜) This lovely plaza hotel features an inviting courtyard and romantic rooms with goose down bedding, dark blue walls and Andean decor. Rooms with king-sized beds are a slight upgrade. The location means it may get noisy early when merchants are setting up outside. German, English and French are spoken.

La Casa del Conde GUESTHOUSE $$
(☑78-7818; www.cuzcovalle.com; s/d S50/70, s/d/tr incl breakfast S119/159/212; 🛜) Guests rave about this lovely country house, nestled into the foothills with blooming flower patches. Family-run and brimming with personality, its lovely rooms feature down duvets, heat and cable TV. There's no car access. It's a 10-minute walk uphill from the plaza, but a mototaxi can leave you at the chapel that's five minutes away.

Hospedaje Kinsa Ccocha HOTEL
(☑20-3101; Arequipa 307A; s/d S50/70, s/d without bathroom S25/50) With a fertile fig tree in its stony patio, this simple lodging has a nice vibe and thoughtful touches, such as plenty of power plugs, good towels and strong, hot showers. Breakfast is not offered.

Royal Inka Hotel Pisac HOTEL $$
(☑20-3064, 20-3066; www.royalinkahotel.com s/d incl breakfast S154/212; 🛜🏊) Once a large hacienda, this hotel is surprisingly unpretentious. Rooms are generous, many with views of the ruins, surrounded by well-tended flower gardens and conservatories. Guests can access the facilities of Club Royal Inka across the road, plus the on-site spa and Jacuzzi. The wi-fi only works in some areas.

A highly worthwhile splurge, located about 1.5km from the plaza up the road to the ruins.

Hospedaje Beho GUESTHOUSE $
(☑20-3001; artesaniasbeho@yahoo.es; Intihuatana 113; s/d/tr S35/70/105, s/d without bathroom S20/40) On the path to the ruins, this family-run handicrafts shop offers no-frills lodging with warm showers. The raggedy, rambling garden is a tranquil haven from the madness of the market streets just outside.

Club Royal Inka CAMPGROUND $
(☑20-3064, 20-3066; camping per person S20; 🏊) Camping doesn't get any better than this.

COMMUNITY TOURISM IN THE SACRED VALLEY

In recent times, rural communities of the valley have become far more accessible to visitors. While usually hospitable to passersby, they feature little infrastructure for visitors, so it's best to organize a visit in advance. Some great options include:

La Tierra de los Yachaqs (☏971-502-223; www.yachaqs.com) A rural tourism network. Guests visit Andean communities, trek to highland lakes and learn about natural medicine and artisan traditions.

Parque de la Papa (☏084-24-5021; www.parquedelapapa.org; Pisac) Day treks and cooking workshops are some of the offerings of this new nonprofit which promotes potato diversity and communal farming.

For a guided trip to visit traditional communities, check out these recommended operators: **Journey Experience** (www.thejoex.com), **Chaski Ventura** (www.chaskiventura.com) and **Respons** (www.respons.org).

for S20, you get to pitch a tent in your own designated, fenced-off site with a fireplace, a light and a power plug, and enjoy all the amenities of the club, including the Olympic-size pool. There is also a playground for kids.

🍴 Eating

Ulrike's Café   CAFE $
(☏20-3195; Manuel Prado s/s; veg/meat menú S17/20, mains from S11; ⊙9am-9pm; 🛜🍷) This sunny cafe serves up a great vegetarian *menú,* plus homemade pasta and melt-in-the-mouth cheesecake and brownies. There's a book exchange, DVDs and special events such as yoga classes. English, French and German are spoken.

Mullu   FUSION $$
(☏20-3073; www.mullu.pe; San Francisco s/n, 2nd fl; mains S14-44; ⊙9am-9pm) Josip welcomes his guests with high-octane hospitality and a menu of wanderlust (think Thai meets Amazonian and flirts with highland Peruvian). Chill and very welcoming, the traditional lamb is tender to falling-off-the-bone, soups and fusion spring rolls also satisfy.

Restaurante Cuchara de Palo   INTERNATIONAL $$
(☏20-3062; Plaza de Armas; mains S15-38; ⊙7:30-9:30am & noon-8pm) Inside Pisac Inn, this fine-dining restaurant offers organic salads and original dishes like pumpkin ravioli drizzled with corn and cream. It doesn't always hit the mark but it has great ambience.

Prasada   VEGETARIAN $
(Arequipa 306; mains S7-12; ⊙11am-5pm Tue-Sun; 🍷) This humble cafe serves quick, healthy bites like tacos and oversized lentil burgers – a good bang for the buck.

Restaurante Yoly   PERUVIAN $
(☏20-3114; Amazonas s/n; menú S4; ⊙6am-8:30pm) Popular with locals, this bare-bones restaurant offers home cooking in set meals with soup and drink included.

Restaurante Valle Sagrado   PERUVIAN $
(☏20-3009; Amazonas s/n; menú S6-15; ⊙8am-9pm) The *menú turístico* here is somewhat fancier; if you want to eat what the locals are eating (and pay only what they are paying), order the basic *menú.*

ℹ Information

There's an ATM in the Plaza de Armas. There are slow cybercafes around the plaza and a mini-supermarket on Bolognesi.

ℹ Getting There & Away

Buses to Urubamba (S2.50, one hour) leave frequently from the downtown bridge between 6am and 8pm. Minibuses to Cuzco (S3.50, one hour) leave from Calle Amazonas when full. Many travel agencies in Cuzco also operate tour buses to Pisac, especially on market days.

For the Pisac ruins, minivans (S25-30 per van) near the plaza leave regularly or hire a taxi from near the bridge into town to drive you up the 7.5km paved road.

Pisac to Urubamba

Between Pisac and Urubamba is a series of pretty villages (as well as the nontouristy but fairly uninteresting town of Calca), which can easily be explored in a day. **Yucay** and **Huarán** offer boutique accommodation

GREENHOUSE

For a stint of serious relaxation, stay at this recommended **country inn** (☑984-770-130; www.thegreenhouseperu.com; Km 60.2 Carretera Pisac–Ollantaytambo, Huarán; s/d/tr S165/210/335; @☎), replete with dogs lounging on their pillows and hammocks in the lush garden. Large rooms are well-appointed and afford complete privacy. The social area is an open living-dining room with a glass wall on the garden. As green as its name, it features solar panels, composting and recycling, uses recycled river water for gardening and offers guests water refills. Gabriel and Bryan play the ultimate hosts: recommending local hikes, turning off the internet during daytime hours to increase your unplugged time, and creating fabulous family dinners (S45) that gather guests around a common table.

and food options, and make excellent bases for leisurely exploration of the safe, scenic Sacred Valley and its many intriguing side valleys.

A visit to the community of **Patabamba** offers a fascinating participative demonstration of the weaving process, all the way from picking the plants to making dyes, to shearing sheep and setting up a loom – with explanations of the meanings of colors and patterns. There are also excellent trekking options. Campsites and homestays are available with advance notice. Prices vary wildly, depending on group size and transport needed. Both **Journey Experience** (☑084-60-1203; www.thejoex.com) and **Chaski Ventura** (☑23-3952; www.chaskiventura.com; Manco Cápac 517; overnight with 3 meals S156 per person) offer visits.

In Huarán, adventure tour operator **Munaycha** (☑984-770-381; www.munaycha.com; Km 60.2 Carretera Pisac–Ollantaytambo, Huarán) comes highly recommended. Among other trips, it guides Lares treks, as well as more local options, and a variety of mountain bike trips. We have heard rave reviews about trek-bike combinations to Huaipo Lake near Chinchero.

Buses running between Pisac and Urubamba pass regularly.

Urubamba

☑084 / POP 2700 / ELEV 2870M

A busy and unadorned urban center, Urubamba is a transport hub surrounded by bucolic foothills and snowy peaks. The advantages of its lower altitude and relative proximity to Machu Picchu make it popular with both high-end hotels and package tours. While there is little of historical interest, nice countryside and great weather make it a convenient base from which to explore the extraordinary salt flats of Salinas and the terracing of Moray.

Since Urubamba is quite spread out, the mode of transport of choice are *mototaxis* (three-wheeled motorcycle rickshaw taxis). The Plaza de Armas is five blocks east and four blocks north of the terminal, bounded by Calle Comercio and Jirón Grau.

◉ Sights & Activities

Many outdoor activities that are organized from Cuzco (see p210) take place near here, including horseback riding, rock climbing, mountain biking, paragliding and hot-air balloon trips.

Perol Chico HORSE RIDING
(☑984-62-4475; www.perolchico.com; overnight packages from US$510) This place is run by Dutch-Peruvian Eduard van Brunschot Vega, with an excellent ranch outside Urubamba with Peruvian *paso* horses. Eduard organizes horseback-riding tours that last up to two weeks. An overnight in the Sacred Valley with rides to Salinas, Maras and Moray includes all meals and luxury accommodations. Advance bookings are required.

Cusco for You HORSE RIDING
(☑79-5301, 987-841-000; www.cuscoforyou.com; day trip US$165) Highly recommended for horseback-riding and trekking trips from one to eight days long. Horseback riding day trips go to Moray and Salinas. Ask about special rates for families and groups.

⎙ Sleeping

A new hub of luxury hotels, Urubamaba has surprisingly few mid-to-low end offerings. Most hotels are lined up along the highway, west of town and the bus terminal, on the way to Ollantaytambo.

Las Chullpas
TOP CHOICE   CABINS $$

(20-1568; www.chullpas.pe; Pumahuanca Valley; s/d/tr/q S120/150/180/220; @♠) Hidden 3km above town, these rustic woodland cottages make for the perfect getaway. Rooms feature comfortable beds and fireplaces. The site, nestled among thick eucalyptus trees, is spread out with inviting pathways and lounge areas with hammocks. There is also an open kitchen serving vegetarian food, holistic treatments and a sweat lodge (available on request).

Much of the food is grown organically on site, and efforts are made towards composting and recycling. The affable Chilean owner also guides treks, especially to the Lares Valley. Highly recommended. Come with good directions, the roads are unmarked and not all taxi drivers know it.

Río Sagrado Hotel
LUXURY HOTEL $$$

(20-1631; www.riosagradohotel.com; d incl breakfast from S1311; @♠) A design haven of cottage-style rooms with rough-hewn beams and exquisite accents of Ayacucho embroidery, this Orient Express property is the epitome of understated luxury. The steep hillside location affords privacy for rooms set on terraced pathways perfumed with jasmine blooms. Or enjoy the river view from hammocks set amidst cascading waterfalls. Service is smooth and top-notch.

Facilities include a spa, hot tubs, a sauna, restaurant, and breakfast in a hot-air balloon suspended above the lawn.

K'uychi Rumi
BUNGALOW $$$

(20-1169; www.urubamba.com; d/q S470/810; @♠) 'Rainbow Stone' in Quechua, this walled compound of two-story cottages tucked into gardens offers a lost retreat. It's family-friendly and popular among European travelers. There are various configurations, but most are two-bedroom with kitchenette, fireplace and terrace balcony, linked by a labyrinthine trail with hummingbirds zipping around and very friendly dogs that guard the property. It's between Km 74 and Km 75 on the main highway, more than 2km west of town.

Sol y Luna
BOUTIQUE HOTEL $$$

(20-1620; www.hotelsolyluna.com; Fundo Huincho lote A-5; @♠☰) A bit of a living fairytale, this luxury property runs wild with whimsy. Fans of folk art will be overwhelmed – its 43 casitas feature original murals and comic, oversized sculptures by noted Peruvian artist Federico Bauer. The playful feel spills over to bold tropical hues and a decor of carved wooden beds, freestanding tubs and dainty rod-iron chandeliers.

French-Swiss owned, it all conspires to charm you. Avant-garde circus productions with former Cirque de Soleil artists provide evening entertainment. For daytime fun, Peruvian *paso* horses can be ridden on the fifteen hectares and beyond. With eccentric atmosphere, its acclaimed restaurant Wayra is the creation of Lima's Malabar-famed chef, there's also a more casual open-air offering featuring food tours and chef visits.

Tambo del Inka
LUXURY HOTEL $$$

(58-1777; www.libertador.com.pe; d from US$689; @♠☰) Just like Hogwarts, Tambo del Inca features its own train station – handy in this case for a morning jaunt to Machu Picchu. Stark and commanding, this Leed-certified hotel (with its own water treatment plant and UV air filters) occupies an immense riverside spread dotted with giant eucalyptus trees.

The resource does not go unnoticed: eucalyptus is a staple of interior decor and even spa treatments. The hotel's best features: the chromo-therapeutic indoor-outdoor pool which changes colors at night, and a hipster lounge with round tables with leather armchairs, backlit by an immense mural of fractured onyx. Rooms are appealing and comfortable, but it seems a little cheeky that standards like breakfast and wi-fi cost extra.

Los Jardines
HOTEL $

(20-1331; www.los-jardines-urubamba.com; Jr Convención 459; s/d S56/80) Noted for its very accommodating service, this reader-recommended family hotel occupies a large adobe home surrounded by flower gardens. Rooms are basic but clean, some feature large picture windows. The buffet breakfast served in the garden is extra. It's within walking distance of the plaza.

Hostal los Perales
GUESTHOUSE $

(20-1151; ecolodgeurubamba.com; Pasaje Arenales 102; r per person S25) Tucked down a hidden country lane, this welcoming family-run guesthouse offers good-value, basic rooms around lovely overgrown gardens. Its elderly owners are sweet, serving banana pancakes and sacha tomato jam from their own tree for breakfast. It's easy to get lost, so take a mototaxi (S1) from the terminal.

Casa Andina LUXURY HOTEL **$$$**
(☑in Lima 1-213-9739; www.casa-andina.com; d incl breakfast S555; @☎) In a lovely countryside setting, this Peruvian chain has 92 rooms in townhouse-style buildings on manicured lawns. The main lobby and restaurant occupies an inviting high-ceiling glass lodge. Classic rooms offer standard amenities and plasma TVs. Among activities are riding, biking and visits to Maras and Moray.

Los Cedros CAMPGROUND **$**
(☑20-1416; campsites per person S8, house from S265) A pastoral campground around 4km above the city on winding country roads. Breakfast (S14) is available. There's also a fully furnished two-story house for hire in the grassy grounds, the site of open-air Full Moon parties.

✖ Eating & Drinking
High-end hotels have good restaurants open to the public. There are a few touristic *quintas* (houses serving typical Andean food) along the highway east of the *grifo*.

[TOP CHOICE] Huacatay PERUVIAN **$$**
(☑20-1790; Arica 620; mains S28-42; ☺1-9:30pm Mon-Sat) In a little house tucked down a narrow side street, Huacatay is worth hunting down. The tender alpaca steak, served in a port reduction sauce with creamy quinoa risotto and topped with a spiral potato chip, is the very stuff memories are made of. But not every dish is a hit – the trout is on the dry side. Still, it makes a lovely night out. Staff aim to please and there's warm ambience.

Tres Keros Restaurant Grill & Bar NOVOANDINA **$$**
(☑20-1701; cnr hwy & Señor de Torrechayoc; mains from S26; ☺lunch & dinner) Garrulous chef Ricardo Behar dishes up tasty gourmet fare, smokes his own trout and imports steak from Argentina. Food is taken seriously here, and enjoyed accordingly. It's 500m west of town.

🔒 Shopping

Seminario Cerámicas CERAMICS
(☑20-1002; www.ceramicaseminario.com; Berriozabal 405; ☺8am-7pm) The internationally known local potter Pablo Seminario creates original work with a pre-conquest influence. His workshop – actually a small factory – is open to the public and offers a well-organized tour through the entire ceramics process.

ℹ Information
Banco de la Nación (Mariscal Castilla s/n) changes US dollars. There are ATMs at the *grifo* (gas station) on the corner of the highway and the main street, Mariscal Castilla, and along the highway to its east. **Clínica Pardo** (☑984-10-8948), on the highway a couple of blocks west o the *grifo*, offers medical attention.

ℹ Getting There & Away
Urubamba serves as the valley's principal transportation hub. The bus terminal is about 1km west of town on the highway. Buses leave every 15 minutes for Cuzco (S4, two hours) via Pisac (S2.50, one hour) or Chinchero (S3, 50 minutes). Buses (S1.50, 30 minutes) and *colectivos* (S2.50, 25 minutes) to Ollantaytambo leave often.

Colectivos to Quillabamba (S35, 5 hours) leave from the *grifo*.

A standard *mototaxi* ride around town costs S1

Salinas
Salinas is among the most spectacular sight in the whole Cuzco area, with thousands o salt pans that have been used for salt extraction since Inca times. A hot spring at the top of the valley discharges a small stream of heavily salt-laden water, which is diverted into salt pans and evaporated to produce a salt used for cattle licks. It all sounds very pedestrian but the overall effect is beautifu and surreal.

To get here, cross the Río Urubamba over the bridge in Tarabamba, about 4km down the valley from Urubamba, turn right and follow a footpath along the south bank to a small cemetery, where you turn left and climb up a valley to the **salt pans** (admission S5; ☺9am-4:30pm) of Salinas. It's about a 500m uphill hike. A rough dirt road that can be navigated by taxi enters Salinas from above, giving spectacular views. Tour groups visit via this route most days. A taxi from Urubamba to visit Salinas and the nearby Moray costs around S80. You can also walk or bike here from Maras. If it's hot, walk the downhill route from Maras and arrange ahead a taxi pickup.

Chinchero
☑084 / POP 900 / ELEV 3762M
Known to the Incas as the birthplace of the rainbow, this typical Andean village combines Inca ruins with a colonial church,

ome wonderful mountain views and a olorful Sunday market. On a high plain vith sweeping views to snow-laden peaks, t's quite beautiful. Since it is very high, t's unwise to spend the night until you're omewhat acclimated. Entry to the historic precinct, where the ruins, the church and he museum are all found, requires a *boleto urístico*.

Sights & Activities

Iglesia Colonial de Chinchero CHURCH
(8am-5:30pm; admission with boleto turístico) Among the most beautiful churches in the valley, this colonial church is built on Inca foundations. The interior, decked out in merry floral and religious designs, is well worth seeing.

Mercado de Chinchero MARKET
The Chinchero market, held on Tuesday, Thursday and especially Sunday, is less toursty than its counterpart in Pisac and well worth a special trip. On Sunday, traditionally dressed locals descend from the hills for he produce market, where the ancient practice of *trueco* (bartering) still takes place; his is a rare opportunity to observe genuine bartering.

Wayllabamba HIKING
On the opposite side of the valley, a clear trail climbs upward before heading north and down to the Río Urubamba Valley about four hours away. At the river, the trail turns left and continues to a bridge at Wayllabamba, where you can cross. From here, the Sacred Valley road will take you to Calca (turn right, about 13km) or Urubamba (turn left, about 9km). You can flag down any passing bus until midafternoon, or continue walking to **Yucay**, where the trail officially ends. In Yucay you'll find a colonial church, an Inca ruin, and more than one charming accommodation option.

Centro de Textiles Tradicionales HANDICRAFTS
(Manzanares s/n) The best artisan workshop in town, though they're found on every street.

Ruinas Inca RUINS
The most extensive ruins here consist of terracing. If you start walking away from the village through the terraces on the right-hand side of the valley, you'll also find various rocks carved into seats and staircases.

Museo del Sitio MUSEUM
(22-3345; admission S7; 8am-5pm Tue-Sun) A small archaeological museum opposite the church houses a collection heavy on broken pots – not worth the extra admission.

Sleeping & Eating
Both lodgings feature good restaurants; there's little other selection in town.

La Casa de Barro INN $$
(30-6031; www.lacasadebarro.com; cnr hwy & Miraflores; s/d/tr incl breakfast S133/186/225) A wonderful retreat for couples or families, with curvy, rambling stairways and nooks, an overgrown garden, and tasteful rooms with snug quilts. The colorful adobe house is architect-designed with Italian influence. It is also well set up for children, with a playroom and swings. They can arrange excursions around the region. A set menu in the restaurant is S50.

Hospedaje Mi Piuray GUESTHOUSE $
(30-6029; www.hospedajemipiuraycusco.com; Garcilaso 187; s/d/tr/q incl breakfast S40/70/80/90) A welcoming family hostelry with large, neat rooms with pastel accents and a sunny courtyard. There's also an onsite restaurant and bar.

Getting There & Away
Combis and *colectivos* traveling between Cuzco (S4/S6, one hour) and Urubamba (S3/S6, 30 minutes) stop on the corner of the highway and Calle Manco Capac II; just flag down whatever comes along. They will also drop you off at intermediate points such as the turnoff to Maras.

Moray & Maras
The impressively deep amphitheater-like terracing of **Moray** (admission S10; dawn to dusk), reached via the small town of **Maras** (admission S5), is a fascinating spectacle. Different levels of concentric terraces are carved into a huge earthen bowl, each layer of which has its own microclimate, according to depth. Some theorize that the Incas used the terraces as a kind of laboratory to determine the optimal conditions for growing crops of each species. There are three bowls, one of which has been planted with various crops as a kind of living museum.

Though refreshingly off the beaten path, this site is not challenging to reach. Take any transportation bound between Urubamba and Cuzco via Chinchero and ask to be let off at the Maras/Moray turnoff. Taxis usually wait at this turnoff to take tourists to Moray and back for around S30, or both Moray and Salinas and back to the turnoff for around S50. If you're coming in the depths of low season, it's worth calling the **Maras taxi company** (☏75-5454, 984-95-6063) to ensure that a taxi is waiting for you at the turnoff. A taxi from Urubamba to visit both Salinas and Moray costs around S80.

You could also tackle the 4km walk to the village of Maras yourself. From there, follow the road another 9km to Moray.

From Maras, you can walk or bike to Salinas, about 6km away. The trail starts behind the church. The Maras taxi company rents out bikes for this purpose – this is a fun, fast, single-track ride.

Ollantaytambo

☏084 / POP 700 / ELEV 2800M

Dominated by two massive Inca ruins, the quaint village of Ollantaytambo (known to locals and visitors alike as Ollanta) is the best surviving example of Inca city planning, with narrow cobblestone streets that have been continuously inhabited since the 13th century. After the hordes passing through on their way to Machu Picchu die down around late morning, Ollanta is a lovely place to be. It's perfect for wandering the mazy, narrow byways, past stone buildings and babbling irrigation channels, pretending you've stepped back in time. It also offers access to excellent hiking and biking.

Currently, Ollantaytambo suffers for being a thoroughfare between Cuzco and the jungle. Since there are no alternate roads, huge semi trucks and buses barrel through the narrow main street (barely missing pedestrians). Locals question the disruption of town life, along with the effect of excessive exhaust on the ruins, but talk of an alternative road has not materialized in any immediate plans.

There are a couple of internet cafes and ATMs in and around Plaza de Armas. There are no banks, but several places change money.

⊙ Sights & Activities

Ollantaytambo Ruins   RUINS
(admission with boleto turístico; ⊙7am-5pm) The huge, steep terraces that guard Ollantaytambo's spectacular Inca ruins mark one of the few places where the Spanish conquistador lost a major battle.

The rebellious Manco Inca had retreated to this fortress after his defeat at Sacsaywamán. In 1536, Hernando Pizarro, Francisco's younger half-brother, led a force of 70 cavalrymen to Ollantaytambo, supported by large numbers of indigenous and Spanish foot soldiers, in an attempt to capture Manco Inca.

The conquistadors, showered with arrows, spears and boulders from atop the steep terracing, were unable to climb to the fortress. In a brilliant move, Manco Inca flooded the plain below the fortress through previously prepared channels. With Spaniards' horses bogged down in the water, Pizarro ordered a hasty retreat, chased down by thousands of Manco Inca's victorious soldiers.

Yet the Inca victory would be short lived. Spanish forces soon returned with a quadrupled cavalry force and Manco fled to his jungle stronghold in Vilcabamba.

Though Ollantaytambo was a highly effective fortress, it also served as a temple. A finely worked **ceremonial center** is at the top of the terracing. Some extremely well built walls were under construction at the time of the conquest and have never been completed. The stone was quarried from the mountainside 6km away, high above the opposite bank of the Río Urubamba. Transporting the huge stone blocks to the site was a stupendous feat. The Incas' crafty technique to move massive blocks across the river meant carting the blocks to the riverside then diverting the entire river channel around them.

The 6km hike to the **Inca quarry** on the opposite side of the river is a good walk from Ollantaytambo. The trail starts from the Inca bridge by the entrance to the village. It takes a few hours to reach the site, passing several abandoned blocks known as *piedras cansadas* – tired stones. Looking back towards Ollantaytambo, you can see the enigmatic optical illusion of a pyramid in the fields and walls in front of the fortress. A few scholars believe this marks the legendary place where the original Incas first emerged from the earth.

KB Tambo   MOUNTAIN BIKING
(☏20-4091; www.kbperu.com; Ventiderio s/n) Considered the best tour operator in town for mountain biking and recommended for families. Also offers treks.

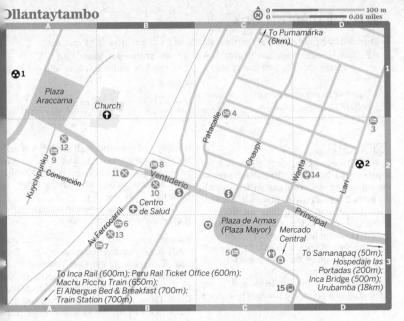

Ollantaytambo

Sota Adventure   ADVENTURE SPORTS

(63-4003; www.sotaadventure.com) Sota Adventure comes highly recommended by readers, particularly for horseback riding. The family-run business also offers mountain biking and multiday hikes.

🎪 Festivals & Events

Día de los Reyes Magos   FESTIVAL

Epiphany is celebrated on January 5 to 8, when residents of surrounding communities arrive on foot to Ollanta to celebrate the arrival of the three kings. Following a procession, there are traditional dances and a bullfight.

Señor de Choquechilca   FESTIVAL

Occurring during Pentecost in late May or early June, the town's most important annual event commemorates the local miracle of the Christ of Choquechilca, when a wooden cross appeared by the Incan bridge. It's celebrated with music, dancing and colorful processions.

🛏 Sleeping

There are lots of budget and midrange accommodations in the streets east of the Plaza de Armas.

EXPLORE MORE OLLANTA

Charmed by this small town? There's plenty to do if you want to extend your stay:

» Explore Pinkulluna ruins, with great views of town (and they're free!). Take the entry on Calle Lari. The trail is very steep, so hike carefully and wear boots with good traction.

» Day hike to Intipunku, an old Inca lookout.

» Hike or mountain bike to Pumamarka, a nearly forgotten Inca ruin, a half-day trip.

TOP CHOICE Apu Lodge INN $$

(☏79-7162; www.apulodge.com; Lari s/n; s/d/q incl breakfast S140/160/240; @☎) Backed against the ruins, this modern lodge with a sprawling lawn is a real retreat, thanks to the welcoming staff and the helpful attention of its Scottish owner. The ample, cozy rooms feature powerful hot showers that melt your muscle aches. Wi-fi is available in the common area. Breakfast includes yogurt, cereal, fresh fruit and eggs.

In addition to guided treks and horse rides, staff can point you towards a number of worthwhile DIY hikes.

Casa de Wow HOSTEL $

(☏20-4010; www.casadewow.com; Patacalle s/n; S110, dm/s/d without bathroom S40/55/90; @☎) A cozy little home away from home, thanks to the caring attention of Winn, a North Carolina native, and her partner Wow, a local artist. Bunks are snug and couples have a shot at the fantastic handmade Inca royalty bed (though unlike the original, these raw beams are held together with rope, not llama innards).

El Albergue Bed & Breakfast B&B $$$

(☏20-4014; www.elalbergue.com; Estación de Tren; d/tr incl breakfast S204/259, d superior S303; @☎) On the train platform, this romantic pit stop exudes Andean charm. Surrounded by green lawns with lush flowerbeds, tasteful tile rooms feature dark hardwood trim, tapestries and quality linens in an early 20th century building. There's portable heaters, games for kids and sauna access. It's 800m (all uphill) from the village center but there's an excellent on-site restaurant.

KB Tambo Hostal GUESTHOUSE $

(☏20-4091; www.kbperu.com; Ventiderio s/n; per person regular/superior incl breakfast S58/77; @☎) Travelers who enjoy a laid-back vibe suck this place up like a pisco sour after a dusty day. With comfortable doubles, this homey American-owned guesthouse is friendly and generous with local tips. It may be hard to get a room as a walk-in, particularly a single. KB also runs mountain-bike trips featuring the best quality bikes in Ollanta.

The website has a wealth of good information on traveling the region.

Samanapaq INN $$

(☏20-4042; www.samanapaq.com; cnr Principal & Alameda de las Cien Ventanas; s/d/t S199/244/318) Recommended entirely for the tireless charm of Don Jaime and his mellow Great Dane Venus, this sprawling complex features lawns for the kids to run on, comfortable shared spaces and 20 motel-style rooms with massage-jet showers. There's a pottery workshop onsite. Wi-fi should be available shortly.

Chaska Wasi HOSTEL $

(☏20-4045; www.hostalchaskawasi.com; Plaza de Armas s/n; dm S35, d with/without bathroom S50/40; @☎) Backpackers flock here to enjoy the company of the lovely, helpful Katy and her tribe of cats. Cheerful basic rooms with electric showers are excellent value, shared spaces are chilled out and perfect for meeting people, and there are bicycles for rent and a DVD library.

Hotel Muñay Tika HOTEL $$

(☏20-4111; www.munaytika.com; Av Ferrocarril s/n; s/d/tr incl breakfast S107/133/170; @☎) Though the native corn drying in the courtyard might say otherwise, this hotel is modern and spacious. Rooms with tinted windows feature parquet floors and down duvets. The garden is a nice area to hang out in.

K'uychi Punku Hostal HOTEL $$

(☏20-4175; www.kuychipunku.com; Kuyuchipunku s/n; s/d/tr incl breakfast S75/105/135; ☎) Run by the wonderful Bejar-Mejía family, this recommended hotel may be open to bargaining. Lodgings are in an Inca building with 2m-thick walls and a modern section with less personality. A breakfast including ggs and fresh juice is served in Ollanta's most photographed outdoor dining room. Recommended.

Hostal las Orquídeas
HOTEL $$

20-4032; www.hotellasorquideasllantaytambo. om; Av Ferrocarril s/n; s/d incl breakfast S85/125) Has a small, grassy courtyard and rooms with parquet floors, down bedding and TVs.

Hospedaje las Portadas
GUESTHOUSE $

20-4008; Principal s/n; dm/s/d/tr 15/30/50/75) Although all of the tourist and local buses pass by outside, this family-run place still manages to achieve tranquility. It has a flowery courtyard, a grassy lawn and a rooftop terrace made for star-gazing. Camping is allowed for S10 per person.

✖ Eating

TOP CHOICE El Albergue Restaurante
INTERNATIONAL $$

20-4014; Estación de Tren; mains S19-45; 5am-9pm) Inside El Albergue, this whistle stop cafe serves elegant dinners of well-priced, classic Peruvian fare. Foremost, it's inviting, with an open kitchen bordered by heaping fruit bowls and candles adorning each linen-topped table. For starters, try the causas or organic greens from the garden. Lamb medallions with chimichurri (herb sauce) are a standout, as well as the molle pepper steak – the spice comes from the tree outside. Those less hungry can order homemade pasta in half-portions. For train passengers, it may be worth stopping by the patio option Café Mayu for an espresso or homemade aguantamayo cheesecake.

Puka Rumi
CAFE $$

20-4091; Ventiderio s/n; mains S5-32; 7:30am-10pm) A tiny locale where locals rave about the steaks, travelers melt over the breakfasts, and everyone enjoys the fresh but nontraditional burritos, which could feed two with pancake-like tortillas and a wide array of ingredients presented fajita-style in separate bowls.

Tutti Amore
ICE CREAM $

(Av Ferrocarril s/n; ice cream S5; 8:30am-7pm) Andres from Rosario, Argentina, serves up homemade gelato-style ice cream. Classics like dulce de leche and banana split are present, but the jungle fruit flavors are worth a try. It's halfway down the hill to the train station.

Hearts Café
CAFE $

(20-4078; cnr Ventiderio & Av Ferrocarril; menú S18, sandwiches S10-14 7am-9pm;) Serving healthy and hearty food, beer and wine and fabulous coffee, Hearts is a longtime local favorite, with some organic produce and box lunches for excursions. Breakfasts like huevos rancheros target the gringo palette perfectly, and the corner spot with outdoor tables was made for people watching.

Long run by a renowned NGO, it is set to change hands, which probably means it will lose the charitable aspect.

Mayu Pata
PERUVIAN $$

(mains S12-34; 10am-10pm) Tucked away by the riverside, this bright restaurant, run by the owner of Puka Rumi, offers enormous salads, adobe oven-fired pizzas and trout.

🍷 Drinking

Ganso
BAR

(984-30-8499; Waqta s/n; 2pm-late) Treehouse meets circus meets Batman! The hallucinatory decor in tiny, friendly Ganso is enough to drive anyone to drink. The firemen's pole and swing seats are the icing on the cake.

ⓘ Getting There & Away

Bus & Taxi

Frequent combis and colectivos shuttle between Urubamba and Ollantaytambo (S1.50/2.50, 30 minutes), from 6am to around 5pm. To get to Cuzco, it's easiest to change in Urubamba, though there are occasional departures direct from the train station in Ollantaytambo to Cuzco's Puente Grau (combis S10, two hours, colectivos S12, 1½ hours).

Even though Ollantaytambo is closer to Santa María (for those traveling on to Santa Teresa) and Quillabamba, those buses pass through here already full. It's best to backtrack to Urubamba's bus terminal to get a seat.

Train

Ollantaytambo is a transport hub between Cuzco and Machu Picchu: the cheapest and quickest way to travel between Cuzco and Machu Picchu is to catch a combi between Cuzco and Ollantaytambo (two hours), and then the train between Ollantaytambo and Aguas Calientes (two hours). Three companies currently offer the service:

Peru Rail (www.perurail.com; Av Ferrocarril s/n; 5am-9pm) Formerly the only service to Aguas Calientes, with multiple departures daily. There are three levels of service: Expedition (from US$98 roundtrip), Vistadome (from

US$146 roundtrip) and the luxurious special service (from US$540 roundtrip).

⚓**Inca Rail** (☎43-6732; www.incarail.com; Av Ferrocarril s/n) New company with three departures daily from Ollantaytambo and four levels of service (roundtrip US$82-180). Children get a significant discount. An environmentally sustainable practice business.

Machu Picchu Train (www.machupicchutrain.com; Av Ferrocarril s/n) A new service of panoramic view trains, travels only from Ollantaytambo to Aguas Calientes (roundtrip adult/child from US$100/70) three times daily in high season. Breakfast or snacks may be served.

Show up at least one day beforehand to buy tickets; during high season, make reservations as far in advance as possible. Buy a return ticket. Trains leaving Aguas Calientes usually fill up since the vast number of people who hike to Machu Picchu return to Cuzco by train.

MACHU PICCHU & THE INCA TRAIL

Shrouded by mist and surrounded by lush vegetation and steep escarpments, the sprawling Inca citadel of Machu Picchu is one icon that lives up to every expectation. Like the Mona Lisa, the pyramids and San Francisco's Golden Gate Bridge, this icon has been seared into our collective consciousness, though nothing can diminish the thrill of being there. If you have the time and the interest, hiking to Machu Picchu via the scenic Inca Trail, as its ancient inhabitants once did, offers a full-immersion experience. But no pilgrimage is without its challenges. All visitors must pass through the gateway to Machu Picchu, Aguas Calientes. Part tourist trap, part Wild West, this shabby town is isolated from the rest of the region and only accessible by railway.

Aguas Calientes

☎084 / POP 1000 / ELEV 2410M

Also known as Machu Picchu Pueblo, this town lies in a deep gorge below the ruins. A virtual island, it's cut off from all roads and enclosed by stone cliffs, towering cloud forest, and two rushing rivers. Despite its gorgeous location, Aguas Calientes has always been a bit of a no-man's land, with a large itinerant population, slack services that count on one-time customers and an architectural tradition of rebar and unfinished

cement. With merchants pushing the hard sell, it's hard not to feel overwhelmed. Your best bet is to go without expectations.

Yet spending the night offers one distinct advantage: early access to Machu Picchu which turns out to be a pretty good reason to stay.

Note that the footpath from the train station to the Machu Picchu bus stop is stepped. Wheelchairs should be directed across the small bridge to Sinchi Roca and through the center of town.

◉ Sights & Activities

Museo de Sitio Manuel Chávez Ballón   MUSEUM

(admission S22; ⊙9am-5pm) This museum has superb information in Spanish and English on the archaeological excavations of Machu Picchu and Inca building methods. Stop here before or after the ruins to get a sense of context (and to enjoy the air-conditioning and soothing music if you're walking back from the ruins after hours in the sun!)

There's a small botanical garden outside down a nifty, nerve-testing set of Inca stairs. It's by Puente Ruinas, at the base of the footpath to Machu Picchu.

Las Termas   HOT SPRINGS

(admission S10; ⊙5am-8:30pm) Weary trekkers soak away their aches and pains in the town's hot springs, 10 minutes' walk up Pachacutec from the train tracks. These tiny, natural thermal springs, from which Aguas Calientes derives its name, are nice enough but far from the best in the area (that would be Santa Teresa's Cocalmayo), and get scummy by late morning. Towels can be rented cheaply outside the entrance.

Putucusi   MOUNTAIN

For those who still have energy left for trekking, the steep hike up this toothy minimountain, directly opposite Machu Picchu, is highly recommended. Follow the railway tracks about 250m west of town and you'll see a set of stairs; this is the start of a well-marked trail. Parts of the walk are up ladders, which get slippery in the wet season, but the view across to Machu Picchu is worth the trek. Allow three hours.

🛏 Sleeping

Lodgings here are consistently overpriced – probably costing two-thirds more than similar counterparts in less-exclusive locations. Bargain *hospedajes* can be found in the area uphill of the souvenir market; few are cheaper than Hospedaje los Caminantes and Iostal John.

Machu Picchu Pueblo Hotel   LODGE $$$

(in Lima 01-610-0400; www.inkaterra.com; d casitas from S1640, villas from S2532; ✳@🛜🛁) Luxuriant and set amid tropical gardens, these chic Andean-style cottages (many with their own private pool) connected by stone pathways are pure indulgence. The devil is in the details: iPod docks, subtle, classy decor, and showers with glass walls looking out onto lush vegetation. The onsite spa features a bamboo-eucalyptus sauna, but the best feature are the guided excursions included in your stay.

Choose from bilingual tours for bird watching, tea plantation visits and orchid walks, or take a trip to the hotel's conservation site protecting the rare Andean spectacled bear. Rates include half-board and kids under 12 stay for free.

El Mapi   DESIGN HOTEL $$$

(21-1011; www.elmapihotel.com; Pachacutec 109; d casitas from S1640, villas from S2532; ✳@🛜) Spare and ultra-modern, this new design hotel occupies a central spot in the middle of town. Lofty ceilings, burnished steel and oversized nature photos create a cool, stripped down atmosphere, though the stark, all-white rooms take it a little too far. Perks include enjoying a welcome pisco sour at the stylish bar and the enormous buffet breakfast which provides ample fuel for a day in the ruins. There's also a warm landscaped pond for dips, a full-service restaurant and an onsite boutique.

Rupa Wasi   HOTEL $$$

(21-1101; www.rupawasi.net; Huanacaure s/n; d incl breakfast S472; 🛜) Hidden away up a steep flight of stairs, Rupa Wasi clings to the hillside with wooden stairways and moss-strewn stone pathways. It's quaint and a little wild, but the price only reflects its proximity to Machu Picchu. Cabin-style rooms feature down duvets and views; a nice American breakfast is served in the Tree House cafe.

Gringo Bill's   HOTEL $$$

(21-1046; www.gringobills.com; Colla Raymi 104; d/tr/ste incl breakfast S199/278/358; @🛜🛁) One of the original Aguas Calientes lodgings, friendly Bill's features well-heeled rooms in a multi-tiered construction. Rooms

are smart, with beds covered in thick cotton quilts and large bathrooms. Suites feature massage jet tubs and TVs. The mini pool only has space for two. Larger suites easily accommodate families.

Hospedaje los Caminantes   GUESTHOUSE $

(21-1007; los-caminantes@hotmail.com; Av Imperio de los Incas 140; per person with/without bathroom S35/20; 🛜) The best bargain digs are in this big, multistory guesthouse. Dated but clean rooms with laminate floors feature reliable hot water and a few balconies. The train whistling directly outside your window at 7am is an unmistakable wake-up call. Breakfast isn't included but available (S8 to S10) below at the strangely upscale in-house cafe.

La Cabaña Hotel   HOTEL $$$

(21-1048; www.lacabanamachupicchu.com; Pachacutec s/n; s/d incl breakfast S336/392; @🛜) Further uphill than most of the hotels, this popular spot features woody, cozy rooms, in part thanks to down duvets and heaters. In addition to buffet breakfast, there's complimentary tea and fruit round the clock.

Wiracocha Inn   HOTEL $$

(21-1088; wiracochainn.com; Wiracocha s/n; s/d incl breakfast S172/225) On a side street crowded with midrange hotels, this newer option has well-kept and polished rooms, amiable service and a sheltered patio area near the river. Rooms feature down bedding and TVs.

Hotel Presidente   HOTEL $$

(21-1065; reservas@siahotels.com; Av Imperio de los Incas s/n; d with view S210, s/d/tr incl breakfast S159/199/225; 🛜) A solid and very secure option featuring small double beds and flat screen TVs. It's worth paying the extra for a room with a view, not just for the outlook over the river but to get as far from the train tracks as possible.

Sumaq Machu Picchu Hotel   HOTEL $$$

(21-1059; www.sumaqhotelperu.com; Hermanos Ayar s/n; s/d with some meals from S1312/1594; ✳@🛜) Ungainly on the outside, this high-end hotel has a soothing interior. Light-flooded, white-walled spaces with splashes of bold color give it a modern feel that's luxurious without being pompous. Rooms boast views of either river and mountains, or a hillside with manmade water cascades. There are multiple eating and drinking areas, and a full spa with sauna and Jacuzzi.

Aguas Calientes

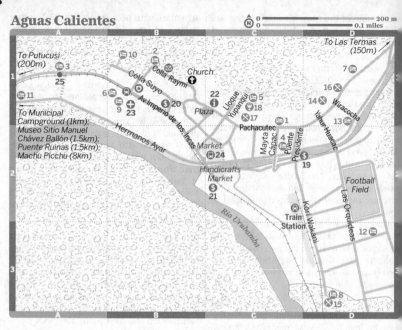

Room rates include buffet breakfast, afternoon tea and either lunch or dinner.

Hostal Muyurina HOTEL **$$**
(☎21-1339; www.hostalmuyurina.com; Lloque Yupanqui s/n; s/d/tr incl breakfast S199/239/292; ☎) Sparkling new and keen to please, Mayu-

rina is a friendly option. Rooms have phones and TV.

Supertramp Hostel HOSTEL **$**
(☎79-1224; supertramphostel@hotmail.com; Calle Chaskatika s/n; dm incl breakfast from S26; ☎) Pancakes at 5am will brighten anyone's day, so it matters less that the hot water is on-

nd-off and rooms are a little cramped. It's he only real hostel in town, with good staff, kitchen access and a small store with provisions nearby. Train station pick-up available.

Machupicchu Hostal　　　　HOTEL **$$**
(✆21-1212; reservas@siahotels.com; Av Imperio de os Incas s/n; s/d/tr incl breakfast S120/135/180; @🛜) One of the tidy midrange inns right next to the train tracks, this place has buffet breakfasts and a small flower-festooned nterior courtyard. Small, dark rooms echo with sounds of the guesthouse, and you will certainly hear every train that goes by.

Hostal John　　　　HOTEL **$**
(✆21-1022; jtrujillo3@hotmail.com; Mayta Cápac 05; per person S20) Uphill from the plaza, this friendly spot offers bare, cell-like rooms that night mean incarceration elsewhere, but offer unbeatable value in Aguas Calientes. The related Hotel Joe across the street is similar but less appealing.

Municipal Campground　　　　CAMPGROUND **$**
camping per tent S15) This small, charming campground has toilets, showers and kitchen facilities for rent. It's a 20-minute walk downhill from the center of town on the road to Machu Picchu, before the bridge.

🍴 Eating

Touts standing in the street will try to herd you into their restaurant, but take your time making a selection. Standards are not very high in most restaurants – if you go to one off this list, snoop around to check the hygiene first.

TOP CHOICE Indio Feliz　　　　FRENCH **$$$**
(✆21-1090; Lloque Yupanqui 4; menú S55, mains from S38; ⊙11am-10pm) It's hard to overstate the pleasure that can be derived from this multi-award-winning restaurant. Of course, hospitality is the strong suit of French cook Patrik, but the food does not disappoint. Start with *sopa criolla,* a potent and flavorful broth, served with hot bread, homemade butter and optional chilis. There are also nods to traditional French cooking – like Provençal tomatoes, crispy-perfect garlic potatoes and a melt-in-your-mouth *tarte aux pommes.*

The candlelit decor shows the imagination of a long-lost castaway with imitation Gauguin panels, a carved figurehead damsels, colonial benches and vintage objects. The S50 *menú* is an extremely good value

for a decadent dinner. Indio Feliz has good wheelchair access and is in the process of adding an upstairs bar and terrace, which provides another reason not to leave here.

Café Inkaterra　　　　PERUVIAN **$$$**
(✆21-1122; Machu Picchu Pueblo Hotel; mains S25-60; ⊙11am-9pm) Second to none for ambience, this tucked-away riverside restaurant is housed in elongated thatched rooms with views of water tumbling over the boulders. With quite reasonable prices, try the perfectly executed *lomo saltado* with flavorful sauce and crisp red onions. Look carefully, it's hidden behind the train station.

Tree House　　　　FUSION **$$$**
(✆21-1101; Huanacaure s/n; S32-59; ⊙4:30am-10pm) With just a few tables, the rustic ambience of Tree House provides a cozy setting for its inviting fusion menu. Dishes like chicken soup with wontons and ginger, red quinoa risotto and crispy trout are lovingly prepared. For dessert, order the lip-smacking fruit crumble. Reserve ahead. It's part of the hotel Rupa Wasi.

Café de Paris　　　　BAKERY **$**
(Plaza Wiyawaina s/n; pastries S1-4; ⊙7am-9pm) We don't know how these Frenchmen got here, we're just thankful. This open-air stand sells *pain au chocolat,* fresh croissants and desserts. The upstairs bakery offers community classes, which should leave an interesting cultural imprint on the rural Andean baking.

Govinda　　　　VEGETARIAN **$$**
(Pachacutec s/n; menú S15-30; ⊙10:30am-9pm; 🌿) A trusty Hare Krishna vegetarian standby serving chapati bread and meatless interpretations of Peruvian classics. Be warned, hours may be sporadic.

🍷 Drinking

There isn't much nightlife in Aguas Calientes. Desperate restaurants offer a four-for-one happy hour (probably not the best way to prepare for running up Wayna Picchu). **Wasicha** (✆21-1282; Lloque Yupanqui s/n) is a popular *discoteca* with dancing till the wee hours. At the time of writing, the Indio Feliz restaurant was adding a rooftop bar geared towards grown-ups.

ℹ Information

There's a helpful branch of **iPerú** (✆21-1104; Pachacutec, cuadra 1; ⊙9am-1pm & 2-6pm) near the **Machu Picchu ticket office**

(⏱5:20am-8:45pm). If the ATM at **BCP** (Av Imperio de los Incas s/n) runs out of money, there are four others in town, including one on Av Imperio de los Incas. Currency and traveler's checks can be exchanged in various places at highly unfavorable rates, so it's best to bring plenty of Peruvian currency with you from Cuzco. Pay phones and cybercafes are scattered around the town, and there's a small **post office** (Colla Raymi s/n). There's a **medical center** (☑21-1005; Av Imperio de los Incas s/n; ⏱emergencies 24hr) by the train tracks.

ℹ Getting There & Away

There are only three options to get to Aguas Calientes, and hence to Machu Picchu: trek it, catch the train via Cuzco and the Sacred Valley, or travel by road and train via Santa Teresa.

Train

Buy a return ticket to avoid getting stranded in Aguas Calientes – outbound trains sell out much quicker than their inbound counterparts. All train companies have ticket offices in the train station, but you can check their websites for up-to-date schedules and ticket purchases. For more information, see p231.

To Cuzco (three hours), **PeruRail** (www.perurail.com) has service to Poroy and taxis connect to the city, another 20 minutes away.

To Ollantaytambo (two hours), all three companies provide service: Peru Rail, **Inca Rail** (☑in Cuzco 23-3030; www.incarail.com) and **Machu Picchu Train** (☑in Cuzco 22-1199; www.machupicchutrain.com).

To Santa Teresa (45 minutes), Peru Rail travels at 6:44am, 12:35pm and 1:30pm daily. Tickets (US$12) can only be bought from Aguas Calientes train station on the day of departure, but trains actually leave from the west end of town, outside the police station. You can also do this route as a guided multisport tour (see p38).

Bus

There is no road access to Aguas Calientes. The only buses go up the hill to Machu Picchu (round-trip S50, 25 minutes) from 5:30am to 2:30pm; buses return until 5:45pm.

Machu Picchu

For many visitors to Peru and even South America, a visit to the Inca city of Machu Picchu is the long-anticipated highpoint of their trip. In a spectacular location, it's the best-known archaeological site on the continent. This awe-inspiring ancient city was never revealed to the conquering Spaniards and was virtually forgotten until the early part of the 20th century. In the high season,

from late May until early September, 2500 people arrive daily. Despite this great tourist influx, the site manages to retain an air of grandeur and mystery, and is a must for all visitors to Peru.

The site is most heavily visited between 10am and 2pm. June through August are the busiest months.

History

Machu Picchu is not mentioned in any of the chronicles of the Spanish conquistadors. Apart from a couple of German adventurers in the 1860s, who apparently looted the site with the Peruvian government's permission, nobody apart from local Quechua people knew of Machu Picchu's existence until American historian Hiram Bingham was guided to it by locals in 1911. You can read Bingham's own account of his 'discovery' in the classic book *Inca Land: Explorations in the Highlands of Peru,* first published in 1922 and now available as a free download from Project Gutenberg (www.gutenberg.org).

Bingham was searching for the lost city of Vilcabamba, the last stronghold of the Incas, and he thought he had found it at Machu Picchu. We now know that the remote ruins at Espíritu Pampa, much deeper in the jungle, are actually the remains of Vilcabamba. The Machu Picchu site was initially overgrown with thick vegetation, forcing Bingham's team to be content with roughly mapping the site. Bingham returned in 1912 and 1915 to carry out the difficult task of clearing the thick forest, when he also discovered some of the ruins on the so-called Inca Trail. (Over the course of his various journeys, Bingham took thousands of artifacts back to the USA with him; see p490 to learn about the fight for their return to Peru.) Peruvian archaeologist Luis E Valcárcel undertook further studies in 1934, as did a Peruvian-American expedition under Paul Fejos in 1940 and 1941.

Despite scores of more recent studies, knowledge of Machu Picchu remains sketchy. Even today archaeologists are forced to rely heavily on speculation and educated guesswork as to its function. Some believe the citadel was founded in the waning years of the last Incas as an attempt to preserve Inca culture or rekindle their predominance, while others think that it may have already become an uninhabited, forgotten city at the time of the conquest. A more recent theory suggests that the site

READ UP ON THE RUINS

If you are wondering what it's like to hike the Inca Trail, or its lesser-known alternatives, pick up Mark Adams' *Turn Right at Machu Picchu* (2010). Not a hero's tale, the humorous travelogue is a first-person account of one adventure editor bumbling out into the wild. On the way, it provides an entertaining layman's look at Inca history and the striving explorations of Hiram Bingham.

was a royal retreat or the country palace of Pachacutec, abandoned at the time of the Spanish invasion. The site's director believes that it was a city, a political, religious and administrative center. Its location, and the fact that at least eight access routes have been discovered, suggests that it was a trade nexus between Amazonia and the highlands.

It seems clear from the exceptionally high quality of the stonework and the abundance of ornamental work that Machu Picchu was once vitally important as a ceremonial center. Indeed, to some extent, it still is: Alejandro Toledo, the country's first indigenous Andean president, impressively staged his inauguration here in 2001.

⊙ Sights & Activities

Don't miss the Museo de Sitio Manuel Chávez Ballón (see p246) by Puente Ruinas at the base of the climb to Machu Picchu. Buses headed back from the ruins to Aguas Calientes will stop upon request at the bridge. From here it's under a half-hour walk back to town.

INSIDE THE COMPLEX

Unless you arrive via the Inca Trail, you'll officially enter the ruins through a ticket gate on the south side of Machu Picchu. About 100m of footpath brings you to the maze-like main entrance of Machu Picchu proper, where the ruins lie stretched out before you, roughly divided into two areas separated by a series of plazas.

Note that the names of individual ruins speculate their use – in reality, much is unknown. To get a visual fix of the whole site and snap the classic postcard photograph, climb the zigzagging staircase on the left immediately after entering the complex, which leads to the Hut of the Caretaker.

Hut of the Caretaker of the Funerary Rock   RUIN

An excellent viewpoint to take in the whole site. It's one of a few buildings that has been restored with a thatched roof, making it a good shelter in the case of rain. The Inca Trail enters the city just below this hut. The carved rock behind the hut may have been used to mummify the nobility, hence the hut's name.

Ceremonial Baths   RUIN

If you continue straight into the ruins instead of climbing to the hut, you pass through extensive terracing to a beautiful series of 16 connected ceremonial baths that cascade across the ruins, accompanied by a flight of stairs.

Temple of the Sun   RUIN

Just above and to the left of the baths is Machu Picchu's only round building, a curved and tapering tower of exceptional stonework.

Royal Tomb   RUIN

Below the Temple of the Sun, this almost hidden, natural rock cave was carefully carved by Inca stonemasons. Its use is highly debated; though known as the Royal Tomb, no mummies were actually ever found here.

Sacred Plaza   PLAZA

Climbing the stairs above the ceremonial baths, there is a flat area of jumbled rocks, once used as a quarry. Turn right at the top of the stairs and walk across the quarry on a short path leading to the four-sided Sacred Plaza. The far side contains a small viewing platform with a curved wall, which offers a view of the snowy Cordillera Vilcabamba in the far distance and the Río Urubamba below.

Temple of the Three Windows   RUIN

Important buildings flank the remaining three sides of the Sacred Plaza. The Temple of the Three Windows features huge trapezoidal windows that give the building its name.

Principal Temple   RUIN

The 'temple' derives its name from the massive solidity and perfection of its construction. The damage to the rear right corner is the result of the ground settling below this corner rather than any inherent weakness in the masonry itself.

Machu Picchu

This great 15th century Inca citadel sits at 2430m on a narrow ridge top above the Río Urubamba. Traditionally considered a political, religious and administrative center, new theories suggest that it was a royal estate designed by Pachacutec, the Inca ruler whose military conquests transformed the empire. Trails linked it to the Inca capital of Cuzco and important sites in the jungle. As invading Spaniards never discovered it, experts still dispute when the site was abandoned and why.

At its peak, Machu Picchu was thought to have some 500 inhabitants. An engineering marvel, its famous Inca walls have polished stone fitted to stone, with no mortar in between. The citadel took thousands of laborers 50 years to build – today its cost of construction would exceed a billion US dollars.

Making it inhabitable required leveling the site, channeling water from high mountain streams through stone canals and building vertical contention walls that became agricultural terraces for corn, potatoes and coca. The drainage system also helped combat heavy rains (diverting them for irrigation), while east-facing rooftops and farming terraces took advantage of maximum sun exposure.

The site is a magnet to mystics, adventurers and students of history alike. While its function remains hotly debated, the essential grandeur of Machu Picchu is indisputable.

CAROLYN MCCARTHY

Intihuatana
'Hitching Post of the Sun', this exquisitely carved rock was likely used by Inca astronomers to predict solstice It's a rare survivor since invading Spaniards destroyed *intihuatanas* throughout the kingdom to eradicate paga blasphemy.

Western Agricultural Terraces

Sacr

To Hut of the Caretaker of the Funerary Rock

←

Temple of the Three Windows
Enjoy the commanding views of the plaza below through the huge trapezoidal windows framed by three-ton linte Rare in Inca architecture, the presence of three window may indicate special significance.

CAROLYN MCCARTHY

TOP TIPS

» **Visit** before mid-morning crowds
» **Allow** at least three hours to visit
» **Wear** walking shoes and a hat
» **Bring** drinking water
» **Gain** perspective walking the lead-in trails

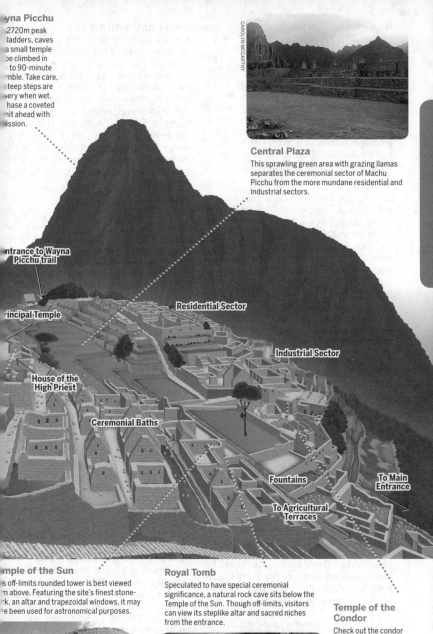

yna Picchu

2720m peak
ladders, caves
a small temple
be climbed in
to 90-minute
mble. Take care,
steep steps are
very when wet.
hase a coveted
nit ahead with
ission.

Central Plaza

This sprawling green area with grazing llamas
separates the ceremonial sector of Machu
Picchu from the more mundane residential and
industrial sectors.

**ntrance to Wayna
Picchu trail**

rincipal Temple

Residential Sector

Industrial Sector

**House of the
High Priest**

Ceremonial Baths

Fountains

**To Main
Entrance**

**To Agricultural
Terraces**

CAROLYN MCCARTHY

mple of the Sun

s off-limits rounded tower is best viewed
m above. Featuring the site's finest stone-
k, an altar and trapezoidal windows, it may
e been used for astronomical purposes.

Royal Tomb

Speculated to have special ceremonial
significance, a natural rock cave sits below the
Temple of the Sun. Though off-limits, visitors
can view its steplike altar and sacred niches
from the entrance.

CAROLYN MCCARTHY

Temple of the
Condor

Check out the condor
head carving with
rock outcrops that
resemble outstretched
wings. Behind, an off-
limits cavity reaches
a tiny underground
cell that may only be
entered by bending
double.

House of the High Priest
RUIN

Opposite the Principal Temple.

Sacristy
RUIN

Behind and connected to the Principal Temple lies this famous small building. It has many well-carved niches, perhaps used for the storage of ceremonial objects, as well as a carved stone bench. The Sacristy is especially known for the two rocks flanking its entrance; each is said to contain 32 angles, but it's easy to come up with a different number whenever you count them.

Intihuatana
RUIN

This Quechua word loosely translates as the 'Hitching Post of the Sun' and refers to the carved rock pillar, often mistakenly called a sundial, which stands at the top of the Intihuatana hill. The Inca astronomers were able to predict the solstices using the angles of this pillar. Thus, they were able to claim control over the return of the lengthening summer days. Exactly how the pillar was used for these astronomical purposes remains unclear, but its elegant simplicity and high craftwork make it a highlight of the complex.

Central Plaza
PLAZA

At the back of the Intihuatana another staircase descends to the Central Plaza.

Prison Group
RUIN

At the lower end of this latter area is the Prison Group, a labyrinthine complex of cells, niches and passageways, positioned both under and above the ground.

Temple of the Condor
RUIN

The centerpiece of the Prison Group is this 'temple' named for a carving of the head of a condor with outstretched wings.

INTIPUNKU

The Inca Trail ends after its final descent from the notch in the horizon called Intipunku (Sun Gate). Looking at the hill behind you as you enter the ruins, you can see both the trail and Intipunku. This hill, called Machu Picchu (Old Peak) gives the site its name. It takes about an hour to reach Intipunku, and if you can spare at least half a day for the round trip, it may be possible to continue as far as Wiñay Wayna. Expect to pay S15 or more as an unofficial reduced-charge admission fee to the Inca Trail, and be sure to return before 3pm, which is when the checkpoint typically closes.

INCA DRAWBRIDGE

A scenic but level walk from the Hut of the Caretaker of the Funerary Rock takes you right past the top of the terraces and out along a narrow, cliff-clinging trail to the Inca drawbridge. In under a half-hour walk, the trail gives you a good look at cloud-forest vegetation and an entirely different view of Machu Picchu. This walk is recommended, though you'll have to be content with photographing the bridge from a distance, as someone crossed the bridge some years ago and tragically fell to their death.

CERRO MACHU PICCHU

A 1½- to two-hour climb brings you to the top of Machu Picchu mountain, to be rewarded with the site's most extensive view along the Inca Trail to Wiñay Wayna and Phuyupatamarka, down to the valley floor and the impressive terracing near Km 104 (where the two-day Inca Trail begins) and across the site of Machu Picchu itself. This walk is more spectacular than Wayna Picchu, and less crowded. Allow yourself plenty of time to enjoy the scenery (and catch your breath!). Recommended.

WAYNA PICCHU

Wayna Picchu is the small, steep mountain at the back of the ruins. Wayna Picchu is normally translated as 'Young Peak,' but the word *picchu*, with the correct glottal pronunciation, refers to the wad in the cheek of a coca-leaf chewer. Access to Wayna Picchu is limited to 400 people per day – the first 200 in line are let in at 7am, and another 200 at 10am. A ticket (S24) may only be obtained when you purchase your entrance ticket. These spots sell out a week in advance in low season and sooner in high season, so plan accordingly.

At first glance, it would appear that Wayna Picchu is a difficult climb but, although the ascent is steep, it's not technically difficult. However, it is not recommended if you suffer from vertigo. Hikers must sign in and out at a registration booth located beyond the central plaza between two thatched buildings. The 45- to 90-minute scramble up a steep footpath takes you through a short section of Inca tunnel.

Take care in wet weather as the steps get dangerously slippery. The trail is easy to follow, but involves steep sections, a ladder and an overhanging cave, where you have to end over to get by. Part way up Wayna Picchu, a marked path plunges down to your left, continuing down the rear of Wayna Picchu to the small **Temple of the Moon**. From the temple, another cleared path leads up behind the ruin and steeply onward up the back side of Wayna Picchu.

The descent takes about an hour, and the ascent back to the main Wayna Picchu trail longer. The spectacular trail drops and climbs steeply as it hugs the sides of Wayna Picchu before plunging into the cloud forest. Suddenly, you reach a cleared area where the small, very well-made ruins are found.

Cerro Machu Picchu is a very good alternative if you miss out.

🛏 Sleeping & Eating

Most people either arrive on day trips from Cuzco or stay in Aguas Calientes.

Machu Picchu Sanctuary Lodge   **$$$**
☑984-81-6956;   www.sanctuarylodgehotel.com;
standard/mountain view/ste US$975/1400/1750)
Now run by Orient Express, this exclusive hotel has one feature no one else can match: location. It's the only place to stay at Machu Picchu, though the advantage is not so great, since buses start running early to the ruins and the early closing time means no one will get that cherished sunset photo.

As would be expected, staff attention is impeccable and rooms are comfortable, with sober decor, docking stations and eat-in options. There is also a spa, manicured gardens and personalized guide service for the ruins. It's often full, so book at least three months ahead. Two restaurants serve meals, and a popular **lunch buffet** (S97; ⊙11:30am-3pm) is open to the public and includes non-alcoholic drinks.

ℹ Information

Machu Picchu Historical Sanctuary (www.machupicchu.gob.org; adult/student S128/65; ⊙6am-4pm) Entrance tickets often sell out: buy them in advance in Cuzco. Guests can only enter until 4pm though those inside are not expelled until 5pm. Check for changes in online purchasing: it was possible to use Verified by Visa, but rampant fraud had the feature close down mid-2012.

The ruins are most heavily visited between 10am and 2pm, and June to August are the busiest months. Plan your visit early or late in the day to avoid the worst of the crowds. A visit early in the morning midweek during the rainy

season guarantees you more room to breathe, especially during February, when the Inca Trail is closed.

Walking sticks or backpacks over 20L are not allowed into the ruins. There are baggage check offices outside the entrance gate (S5 per item; ⊙6am-4pm) and inside the complex (S3 per item; ⊙6am-5pm).

Local guides (per person S100-150, in groups of 6-10 S20) are readily available for hire at the entrance. Their expertise varies, look for one wearing an official guide ID from DIRCETUR. Agree on a price in advance, clarify whether the fee is per person or group, and agree on the tour length and maximum group size.

The information and illustration provided in this book should be enough for a self-guided tour. For really in-depth explorations, take along a copy of *Exploring Cuzco* by Peter Frost.

Dangers & Annoyances

Inside the ruins, do not walk on any of the walls – this loosens the stonework and prompts a cacophony of whistle blowing from the guards. Overnighting here is also illegal: guards do a thorough check of the site before it closes. Disposable plastic bottles and food are not allowed in the site, though vigilance is a bit lax. It's best to eat outside the gate, use camping-type drink bottles and pack out all trash, even organic waste. Water is sold at the cafe just outside the entrance, but only in glass bottles.

Use of the only toilet facilities, just below the cafe, will set you back S1.

Tiny sand fly–like bugs abound. You won't notice them biting, but you may be itching for a week. Use insect repellent.

The weather at Machu Picchu seems to have only two settings: heavy rain or bright, burning sunlight. Don't forget rain gear and sun block.

ℹ Getting There & Around

From Aguas Calientes, frequent buses for Machu Picchu (S50 round-trip, 25 minutes) depart from a ticket office along the main road from 5:30am to 2:30pm. Buses return from the ruins when full, with the last departure at 5:45pm.

Otherwise, it's a steep walk (8km, 1.5 hours) up a tightly winding mountain road. First there's a flat 20-minute walk from Aguas Calientes to Puente Ruinas, where the road to the ruins crosses the Río Urubamba, near the museum. A breathtakingly steep but well-marked trail climbs another 2km up to Machu Picchu, taking about an hour to hike (but less coming down!)

For information about getting to Aguas Calientes, see p231.

The Inca Trail

The most famous hike in South America, the four-day Inca Trail, is walked by thousands every year. Although the total distance is only about 24 miles, the ancient trail laid by the Incas from the Sacred Valley to Machu Picchu winds its way up and down and around the mountains, snaking over three high Andean passes en route, which have collectively led to the route being dubbed 'the Inca Trial.' The views of snowy mountain peaks, distant rivers and ranges, and cloud forests flush with orchids are stupendous – and walking from one cliff-hugging pre-Columbian ruin to the next is a mystical and unforgettable experience.

For information on trekking an alternative route, see p38.

The Hike

Most trekking agencies run buses to th start of the trail, also known as Piscacuch or Km 82 on the railway to Aguas Calientes

After crossing the Río Urubamb (2600m) and taking care of registration for malities, you'll climb gently alongside th river to the trail's first archaeological site **Llactapata** (town on top of terraces), befor heading south down a side valley of the Rí Cusichaca. (If you start from Km 88, turn west after crossing the river to see the little visited site of **Q'ente** (Hummingbird), abou 1km away, then return east to Llactapata on the main trail.)

The trail leads 7km south to the hamle of **Wayllabamba** (Grassy Plain; 3000m) near which many tour groups will camp fo the first night. You can buy bottled drink and high-calorie snacks here, and take a breather to look over your shoulder fo

Inca Trail

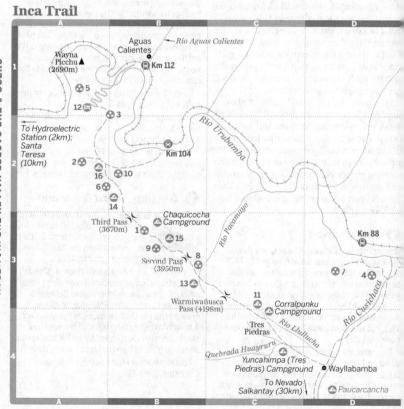

iews of the snowcapped **Nevado Verónica** 5750m).

Wayllabamba is situated near the fork of Ríos Llullucha and Cusichaca. The trail crosses the Río Llullucha, then climbs steeply up along the river. This area is known as **Tres Piedras** (Three White Stones/3300m), though these boulders are no longer visible. From here it is a long, very steep 3km climb through humid woodlands.

The trail eventually emerges on the high, bare mountainside of **Llulluchupampa** 3750m), where water is available and the flats are dotted with campsites, which get very cold at night. This is as far as you can reasonably expect to get on your first day, though many groups will actually spend their second night here.

From Llulluchupampa, a good path up the left-hand side of the valley climbs for a two- to three-hour ascent to the pass of **Warmiwañusca**, also colorfully known as

'Dead Woman's Pass.' At 4200m above sea level, this is the highest point of the trek, and leaves many a seasoned hiker gasping. From Warmiwañusca, you can see the Río Pacamayo (Río Escondido) far below, as well as the ruin of Runkurakay halfway up the next hill, above the river.

The trail continues down a long and knee-jarringly steep descent to the river, where there are large campsites at **Paq'amayo**. At an altitude of about 3600m, the trail crosses the river over a small footbridge and climbs toward **Runkurakay** (3750m; Egg-Shaped Building), a round ruin with superb views. It's about an hour's walk away.

Above Runkurakay, the trail climbs to a false summit before continuing past two small lakes to the top of the second pass at 3950m, which has views of the snow-laden Cordillera Vilcabamba. You'll notice a change in ecology as you descend from this pass – you're now on the eastern, Amazon slope of the Andes and things immediately get greener. The trail descends to the ruin of **Sayaqmarka** (Dominant Town), a tightly constructed complex perched on a small mountain spur, which offers incredible views. The trail continues downward and crosses an upper tributary of the Río Aobamba (Wavy Plain).

The trail then leads on across an Inca causeway and up a gentle climb through some beautiful cloud forest and an Inca

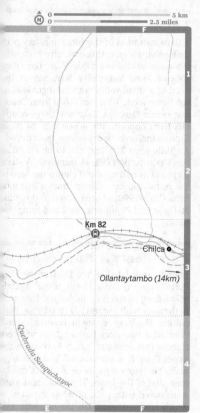

Inca Trail

◎ Sights

◎ Sleeping

tunnel carved from the rock. This is a relatively flat section and you'll soon arrive at the third pass at almost 3600m, which has grand views of the Río Urubamba Valley, and campsites where some groups spend their final night, with the advantage of watching the sun set over a truly spectacular view, but with the disadvantage of having to leave at 3am in the race to reach the Sun Gate in time for sunrise. If you are camping here, be careful in the early morning as the steep incline makes the following steps slippery.

Just below the pass is the beautiful and well-restored ruin of Phuyupatamarka (City Above the Clouds), about 3570m above sea level. The site contains six beautiful ceremonial baths with water running through them. From Phuyupatamarka, the trail makes a dizzying dive into the cloud forest below, following an incredibly well-engineered flight of many hundreds of Inca steps (it's nerve-racking in the early hours, use a headlamp). After two or three hours, the trail eventually zigzags its way down to a collapsed red-roofed white building that marks the final night's campsite.

A 500m trail behind the old, out of use, pub leads to the exquisite little Inca site of Wiñay Wayna (also spelled Huiñay Huayna), which is variously translated as 'Forever Young,' 'To Plant the Earth Young' and 'Growing Young' (as opposed to 'growing old'). Peter Frost writes that the Quechua name refers to an orchid (*Epidendrum secundum*) that blooms here year-round. The semitropical campsite at Wiñay Wayna boasts one of the most stunning views on the whole trail, especially at sunrise. For better or worse, the famous pub located here is now deteriorated and no longer functioning. A rough trail leads from this site to another spectacular terraced ruin, called Intipata, best visited on the day you arrive to Wiñay Wayna, consider coordinating it with your guide if you are interested.

From the Wiñay Wayna guard post, the trail winds without much change in elevation through the cliff-hanging cloud forest for about two hours to reach Intipunku (Sun Gate) – the penultimate site on the trail, where it's tradition to enjoy your first glimpse of majestic Machu Picchu while waiting for the sun to rise over the surrounding mountains.

The final triumphant descent takes almost an hour. Trekkers generally arrive long before the morning trainloads of tourists, and can enjoy the exhausted exhilaration of reaching their goal without having to pus past enormous groups of tourists fresh o the first train from Cuzco.

CUZCO TO PUNO

The rickety railway and the paved road t Lake Titicaca shadow each other as the both head southeast from Cuzco. En rout you can investigate ancient ruins and pas toral Andean towns that are great detour for intrepid travelers who want to leave th Gringo Trail far behind. Most of the follow ing destinations can be reached on day trip from Cuzco; for points of interest closer t Puno, see p170. Inka Express and Turism Mer run luxury bus tours (see p229) betwee Cuzco and Puno that visit some but not all c these places. Local and long-distance high way buses run more frequently along thi route and are less expensive.

Tipón

A demonstration of the Incas' mastery ove their environment, this extensive Inca sit (admission with boleto turístico; ◷7am-6pm) con sists of some impressive terracing at th head of a small valley with an ingenious ir rigation system. It's about 30km from Cuzcc just before Oropesa. Take any Urcos-boun bus from opposite the hospital in Av de 1 Cultura in Cuzco, or a *colectivo* from outsid Av Tullumayo 207, and ask to be let off a the Tipón turnoff (S3, 45 minutes). A stee dirt road from the turnoff climbs the 4km t the ruins. You can also contract a taxi tou from Cuzco (S90) to drive you into the ruin at Tipón and Piquillacta, wait and bring yo back.

Piquillacta & Rumicolca

Literally translated as 'the Place of the Flea Piquillacta (admission with boleto turístico ◷7am-6pm) is the only major pre-Inca rui in the area, built around AD 1100 by the War culture. The large ceremonial center feature crumbling two-story buildings, all with en trances that are strategically located on th upper floor. It is surrounded by a defensiv wall. The stonework here is much crude than that of the Incas. The floors and wall were paved with slabs of white gypsum, c which traces remain. On the opposite side of the road about 1km further east, the hug nca gate of **Rumicolca** is built on Wari foundations. The cruder Wari stonework contrasts with the Inca blocks. It's interesting to see indigenous people working with the mud that surrounds the area's swampy lakes – the manufacture of adobe (mud bricks) is one of the main industries of this area.

Urcos-bound buses from Cuzco pass by both sites.

Andahuaylillas

084 / POP 840 / ELEV 3123M

Don't confuse this place with Andahuaylas, west of Cuzco. Andahuaylillas is more than 35km southeast of Cuzco, about 7km before the road splits at Urcos. This pretty Andean village is most famous for its lavishly decorated **Iglesia de San Pedro** (admission S10; 7am-5:30pm), which is almost oppressive in its baroque embellishments. The church dates from the 17th century and houses many carvings and paintings, including a canvas of the Immaculate Conception attributed to Esteban Murillo. There are reportedly many gold and silver treasures locked in the church, and the villagers are all involved in taking turns guarding it 24 hours a day. Is the rumor true or not? All we can tell you is that the guards take their job *very* seriously.

Near the church are the shop of the **Ñewar Project**, a women's cooperative that makes distinctive dolls clad in traditional costumes, and the eclectic **Museo Ritos Andinos** (admission by donation; 7am-6pm), whose somewhat random displays include a mummified child and an impressive number of deformed craniums.

To reach Andahuaylillas (S7, one hour), take any Urcos-bound bus from the terminal just off Av de la Cultura in Cuzco.

Raqchi

084 / POP 320 / ELEV 3480M

The little village of **Raqchi**, 125km southeast of Cuzco, is wrapped around an **Inca ruin** (admission S10) that looks from the road like a strange alien aqueduct. These are the remains of the Temple of Viracocha, which was once one of the holiest shrines in the Inca empire. Twenty-two columns made of stone blocks helped support the largest-known Inca roof; most were destroyed by the Spanish, but their foundations are clearly seen. The remains of many houses and storage buildings are also visible, and reconstruction is an ongoing process.

The people of Raqchi are charming and environmentally conscious, working periodically to eradicate litter left by visitors. And they are famous potters – many of the ceramics on sale in the markets of Pisac and Chinchero come from here.

You can experience life in Raqchi by organizing a homestay (984-82-0598, 984-67-9466; raqchitours55@hotmail.com; package per person S93). Thirteen families offer accommodation in basic but comfortable guestrooms, with private bathrooms and showers. The point of contact is Humberto Rodriguez. Packages include all meals, a night-time fiesta and a highly recommended day of guided activities. These include a visit to the ruins (admission not included), a heart-pumping hike up to the local *mirador* (lookout) and a ceramics workshop.

On the third Sunday in June, Raqchi is the site of a colorful fiesta with much traditional music and dancing.

Raqchi to Abra La Raya

About 25km past Raqchi is bustling Sicuani, a market town of 12,000 people, halfway from Cuzco to Puno. There's no real reason to stop here except to break the journey. A few economical places to stay are located near the bus terminal.

Twenty minutes past Sicuani – just before Abra la Raya, the high pass that marks the boundary between the Cuzco and Puno departments – are the **Aguas Calientes de Marangani** (admission S5; daylight hr). This complex of five fabulously hot thermal pools is linked by rustic bridges over unfenced, boiling tributaries. Quite a sight, it isn't odd to see locals washing themselves, their kids and their clothes in the pools. Consider it an accessible, off-the-beaten-track experience.

You can count on local transport to hop between Cuzco, Andahuaylillas, Raqchi, Sicuani and the baths from early morning until at least 3pm. For points of interest south of here, see p170.

CUZCO TO THE JUNGLE

There are three overland routes from Cuzco to the jungle. The least-developed, cheapest and quickest goes northwest from Ollantaytambo over the Abra Málaga Pass, to the secondary jungle around Quillabamba and into little-visited Ivochote and Pongo de Mainique beyond.

The other two routes are more popular but are rarely accessed by road. You can get to the area around Parque Nacional Manu through Paucartambo, Tres Cruces and Shintuya, or to Puerto Maldonado via Ocongate and Quince Mil. To get deep into these areas, most people go on organized tours which include light-plane flights in and out, or in some cases, 4WD road transport.

Some of these roads are muddy, slow and dangerous. Think twice before deciding to travel overland, and don't even contemplate it in the wettest months (January to April). An invaluable resource for independent travelers is the *Peruvian Jungle Information Packet,* sold by the South American Explorers Club (084-24-5484; www.saexplorers.org; Atocsaycuchi 670, Cuzco; 9:30am-5pm Mon-Fri, to 1pm Sat).

Cuzco to Ivochote

Soon after Ollantaytambo, the road leaves the narrowing Sacred Valley and climbs steeply over the 4350m Abra Málaga. From here it's a dizzying, scenic, mostly unpaved descent straight into Amazonia. Dusty Santa María has bus company offices and a couple of very basic *hospedajes* and restaurants. It marks the junction where you turn off for Santa Teresa and the backdoor route to Machu Picchu, or continue down to Quillabamba.

SANTA TERESA
084 / POP 460 / ELEV 1900M
The makeshift feel of Santa Teresa persists even some years after the flooding that took place in 2010, 1998 and a decade before. In its tiny center, most buildings are prefabricated emergency-relief shells and, strangely, the most permanent construction is the puzzling Plaza de Armas statue. Yet as more and more backpackers come seeking a cheaper access point to Machu Picchu, services are slowly starting to grow. The real attractions are a few kilometers outside town – the Cocalmayo hot springs and the Cola de Mono zipline are both worth the time and effort required to get to them.

◉ Sights & Activities
For information on hiking the alternate route to Machu Picchu, see p38.

Cola de Mono ADVENTURE SPORT
(79-2413, 959-743-060; www.canopyperu.com zipline US$60) South America's highest zipline is a must for thrill seekers. A total 2500m of cables with six separate section whiz high above the spectacular scenery the Sacsara Valley. Allow two hours.

The owners of Cola de Mono, river guide from way back, also run rafting on the spectacular, and so far little-exploited, Sant Teresa river (see p208 for more information and camping on their extensive grounds.

To get there, it's a pleasant 2km (half hour) stroll east – just follow the road out town or take a taxi (S10).

Llactapata HIKIN
You can hike to the hydroelectric station vi Llactapata, a six-hour walk up and over hill on the well-marked Inca Trail, affordin views of Machu Picchu and access to a hal cleared ruin. The trail is well-marked an can be done without a guide, though the are helpful to indicate ruins, as well as th flora and fauna. Start early as it gets hot o the trail. Hire a taxi (S35, 30 minutes) to dro you off at the start in Lucmabamba. You ca take a *colectivo* back from the Hydroelectr ca, or continue on to Machu Picchu.

Baños Termales Cocalmayo HOT SPRING
(admission S5; 24 hr) These stunningl landscaped, council-owned natural ho springs are truly a world-class attractio Pools washed out in the river flooding 2010 have been rebuilt, though camping a eas have not. As if huge, warm pools and natural shower straight out of a jungle fan tasy weren't enough, you can buy beer an snacks.

It's 4km from town. You can reliably catc a *colectivo* from Santa Teresa to Cocalmay at around 3pm, when vehicles head dow to collect Inca Jungle Trail walkers arrivin from Santa María. Otherwise, you may hav to brave the unshaded, dusty walk (with car driving too fast) or pay a taxi around S3 round-trip.

Tour de Cafe TOU
(per person S25) Run by Eco Quechua, thi 2½-hour tour visits a family coffee farr steeped in local tradition (see the *cuys* be ing raised in the kitchen!). You can also pic tropical fruit and see a fish farm in actio Not a modern operation, this is old-styl cultivation in transition, in the process o introducing new techniques to improve pro

YELLOW RIVER LODGE

A cozy, lazy option on the alternative route to Machu Picchu, this welcoming family **homestay** (☑63-0209; www.quellomayo.com; r per person with half-board S60, camping per person S10) is an organic farm harvesting Arabica bean coffee, chocolate and tropical fruit. Simple rooms have comfortable beds and colorful walls, but you are likely to spend most of your time exploring the lush surroundings. Home cooked meals (S15 to S20) are available at the restaurant. If you want to learn more about coffee, there are roasting workshops onsite.

The riverside campsite includes a shower, grill and adobe oven. It's located in Quellomayo, 25 minutes outside of Santa María on the way to Santa Teresa. To get there, take a bus from Cuzco to Santa María and grab a taxi (S25 to S50) from there or trek via an old Inca trail – the website has details.

---

ductivity. It's an interesting visit and 50% of visitor fees goes to help local farmers.

🛏 Sleeping & Eating

A handful of *hospedajes* in the center offers bare-bones accommodation. At the time of research, there were no recommendable restaurants in town. Hot meals are available at the market and the rotisserie chicken restaurants on the plaza – choose based on cleanliness.

TOP CHOICE Eco Quechua   LODGE **$**
☑63-0877, 984-756-855; www.ecoquechua.com; Sauce Pampa; per person with half-board S75, camping per tent S12) Run by Juan Carlos and Janet, a wonderful and energetic young couple, this funky thatched lodge lets you sample jungle living right outside of Santa Teresa. The open-air living room is cloaked in thick vegetation. Rooms feature mosquito nets, but it's still a good idea to use repellant.

With outdoor stall bathrooms, it's a little rustic, but undoubtedly the most ambient spot in Santa Teresa and a fun place for groups to congregate. The owner is also a guide knowledgeable about local hikes and tours. At the time of research, the shorter route from town was under reparation and it was a S30 taxi ride.

Albergue Municipal   HOSTEL **$**
☑984-145-049; dm/d S20/60) Next to the football field, this gated circular compound is one of the best options in town. It has a manicured lawn and cool, spacious rooms. Doubles feature tile floors and mini-fridges. The one dorm holds up to 11 people. Book ahead via the municipality. If the gate is closed, the caretaker may be out.

Hotel El Sol   HOTEL **$**
(☑63-7158; Av Calixto Sanchez G-6; s/d S40/60) This partially finished cement multistory is one of the best deals in town, though prices may go up as the building does! Friendly, it features nice, clean rooms with bright sheet sets, hot water bathrooms and cable TV.

❶ Information

There are no banks or ATMs in Santa Teresa – you must bring all the cash you need. You may be able to change dollars at an extremely unfavorable rate. Internet access is poor, but available in a few cafes.

Cusco Medical Assistance in Carrión provides 24-hour medical attention.

❶ Getting There & Away

To get to Santa Teresa from Cuzco, take a bus headed for Quillabamba from the Santiago terminal, get off in Santa María, and catch a local *combi* or *colectivo* (S10, one hour) to Santa Teresa. These shared vans and wagons take on the winding, dirt road to Santa Teresa like Formula One competitors – try to chose one who seems more conservative, it's a lot to stomach.

To get to Machu Picchu, train tickets on this route are sold only at the Peru Rail ticket office. Daily trains (one-way/return US$18/30) leave from the hydroelectric station, about 8km from Santa Teresa, at 7:54am, 3pm, and 4:35pm. Be at the bus terminal an hour prior to your train to catch a *combi* (S3, 25 minutes). The 13km train ride to Aguas Calientes takes 45 minutes. Some choose to walk by the railway tracks instead, an outstandingly cheap way to get to Machu Picchu; it takes around four very dusty and sweaty hours.

You can also do this route as part of one of the guided multisport tours on offer (see p38).

Combis going directly to Quillabamba (S10, two hours) depart from Santa María's Plaza de Armas every 15 minutes. *Colectivos* to Santa María leave often from the bus terminal. From

Santa María you can connect to Cuzco (S25-50, five to six hours).

QUILLABAMBA
📞 084 / POP 8800 / ELEV 1050M

Welcome to the jungle! Quillabamba's tropical vibe is palpable, with heat that becomes oppressive by 9am, music that blares all night, and the land-that-time-forgot feel to most hotels and restaurants.

Quillabamba itself has few attractions and sees little tourism, but there are some outstanding, watery natural attractions nearby. The streets north and south of the Mercado Central, rather than the eternally somnolent Plaza de Armas, are Quillabamba's commercial center.

👁 Sights & Activities

Locals are justifiably proud of **Sanbaray** (admission S5; ⏱8am-late), a delightful complex of swimming pools, lawns, bars and a decent trout restaurant. It's a 10-minute *mototaxi* ride (S3) from the center.

La Balsa, hidden far down a dire dirt track, is a bend in the Río Urubamba that's perfect for swimming and river tubing. Enterprising locals sell beer and food here on weekends.

Mandor, **Siete Tinajas** and **Pacchac** are beautiful waterfalls where you can swim, climb and eat jungle fruit straight off the tree. Siete Tinajas and Pacchac are accessible via public transport for a few soles each to Charate; taxi transport to Mandor with waiting time will set you back S25.

👉 Tours & Guides

Eco Trek Peru   ADVENTURE TOUR
(📞in Cuzco 24-7286; www.ecotrekperu.com) This agency has passionate specialists in multiday trips in this part of the world.

Bici Aventura   BIKING
(Calle 2 de Mayo 423) Provides information, bikes and guides for road and single-track missions.

Roger Jara   GUIDED TOUR
(rogerjaraalmiron@hotmail.com) Guided trips to all of the attractions listed above, as well as remnant virgin jungle near Quillabamba. Roger can also guide you through the area's big draws, Pongo de Mainique and Vilcabamba. He speaks some English.

🛏 Sleeping

There are many cheap, cold-water hostels around the Plaza de Armas and the Mercado.

Hostal Don Carlos   HOTEL $$
(📞28-1150; www.hostaldoncarlosquillabamba.com Jirón Libertad 556; s/d/tr S75/110/120; @) With an onsite cafe, this colonial-style hotel features bright, ample rooms around a sunny interior courtyard. Rooms have hot showers and frigobars. It's half a block from the Plaza de Armas.

Hostal Alto Urubamba   HOTEL $
(📞28-1131; altourubamba@gmail.com; 2 de Mayo 333; s/d/tr S45/75/85, s/d/tr without bathroom S20/30/40) Clean, comfortable-enough rooms with fans encircle a sunny courtyard in this demently noisy, long-established traveler favorite.

🍴 Eating & Drinking

Looking at the *heladerías* (ice-cream shops) on every corner, you could be forgiven for assuming that locals subsist on ice cream. Given the shortage of alternatives, you could be forgiven for doing the same.

Pizzería Alamos   PIZZERIA $
(Espinar s/n; pizzas from S10; ⏱7am-11pm Mon-Sat, 3-11pm Sun) No other place in town is quite so kind to foreign tourists. Staffed by enthusiastic youth, this restaurant fires up pizzas that are big enough to feed an army of Inca warriors, and the open-air courtyard bar is a local hangout after dark.

Heladería la Esquina   ICE CREAM $
(cnr Espinar & Libertad; sandwiches from S3 ⏱8am-11pm Mon-Sat) This retro cafe serves up delicious juices, cakes, ice cream and fast-food snacks. Service is grouchy, but the 1950s-diner decor makes up for that.

Niko's   BAR
(Pio Concha s/n) For a drink, try Niko's.

ℹ Information

BCP (Libertad 549) and Banco Continental on Bolognesi near the corner of Grau have ATMs and change US dollars. There's arm-chewingly slow internet access at a few places around the Plaza de Armas. Limited tourist information is available on the 3rd floor of the Municipalidad.

ℹ Getting There & Away

Walk south along Torre four blocks past Plaza Grau, to Plaza de Banderas, to find transport to Huancacalle. Turn right at the end of Plaza de Banderas to find minivans (S35, five to seven hours) to Cuzco in the first block, and the *terminal terrestre* a block later. Buses for Cuzco (S25) leave from here several times a day before 8am and between 1:30pm and 9:30pm. Minivans leave early in the morning and in the evening. All

BE SAFE IN THE JUNGLE

In recent times, the increased activity of narcotraffickers and Shining Path guerillas in specific jungle areas may alter advisable routes for travel and trekking. At the time of writing, the government was increasing military presence in these areas for security. However, it is always wise to consult with knowledgeable guides and tour operators, or an unaffiliated organization like South American Explorers (p260), before heading out. It is important to use good, responsible local guides and never go on your own. Currently, it is unadvisable to visit Vilcabamba, Ivochote, Kiteni and beyond, but we have included information on these areas as the situation is subject to change.

top at Ollantaytambo and Urubamba en route, but charge full fare wherever you get off.

Minivans leave from Quillabamba's market area for Kiteni (three to six hours) and Ivochote (six to eight hours), further into the jungle.

ℹ Getting Around
The basic *mototaxi* fare around town is S2.

HUANCACALLE
☏ 084 / POP 300 / ELEV 3200M

Peaceful, pretty Huancacalle is best known as the jumping-off point for treks to Vilcabamba, but many more hikes from three to 10 days long are possible from here, including to Puncuyo, Inca Tambo, Choquequirau and Machu Picchu. The town's biggest building is Hostal Manco Sixpac (☏ 84-6006, 84-005, relative in Cuzco 974-922-484; per person without bathroom S20), run by the Cobos family of local guides. It's the only lodging with hot water. You can organize mules and guides here.

Manco Inca's huge palace fortress of Vitcos (also known as Rosaspata) is an hour's walk up the hill, and from there you can continue to the amazing, sacred white rock of Yurac Rumi. The whole easy-to-follow circuit, which starts just over the bridge at the end of the road, takes a leisurely three hours, including plenty of time for photos and admiration of both scenery and ruins.

VILCABAMBA
The real 'lost city of the Incas,' Vilcabamba – also known as Espíritu Pampa – is what Hiram Bingham was looking for when he stumbled on Machu Picchu. The beleaguered Manco Inca and his followers fled to this jungle retreat after being defeated by the Spaniards at Ollantaytambo in 1536. The long, low-altitude trek, which takes four to nine days, is very rugged, with many steep ascents and descents before reaching Vilcabamba, 1000m above sea level. You can start at either Huancacalle or Kiteni. This area may be insecure, see the boxed text.

IVOCHOTE & BEYOND
At the time of writing, this area was considered unsafe for travelers, given activity of guerilla groups and narcotraffickers. Since the government has engaged in an active campaign to curb illicit activity, this may change by the time you read this. Regardless, it is wise to ask outfitters knowledgeable about the area about current conditions before traveling.

A long eight-hour-plus bus journey from Quillabamba takes you through the oil town of Kiteni and on to the more remote Ivochote, a small jungle village with a few basic accommodations. This base connects further into Amazonia by river.

The first major landmark past Ivochote is the Pongo de Mainique, a steep-walled canyon carved by cascading waterfalls on the lower Río Urubamba, which marks the border between Amazonia's high and lowland cloud forest. Prolific bird life here includes military macaws and quetzals; there are also spider monkeys and many orchid varieties. Between June and November, boats can be found in Ivochote to take you there and back – the trip takes the best part of a day. You'll pay anything from S60 to S450 per person; group size is a big factor.

Past the Pongo, at the indigenous Matsiguenka (or Machigengua) community of Timpía, you can find local guides and transport for Santuario Nacional Megantoni. Accommodation is available at Sabeti Lodge (☏ 84-81-2555, 84-81-3885; www.sabetilodge.com; s/d with full board US$105/160), owned by the community. There's fishing and wildlife watching. You can also camp on the riverside. Given that instructions are needed to arrive, it's best to reserve ahead.

Cuzco to Manu

PAUCARTAMBO

POP 1300 / ELEV 3200M

This small village lies on the eastern slopes of the Andes, about 115km and three hours northeast of Cuzco along a cliff-hanging road, paved only until Huancarán.

Paucartambo is famous for its riotously colorful celebration in honor of the **Virgen del Carmen**, a festival held annually from July 15 to 18, with hypnotic street dancing, wonderful processions and all manner of weird costumes. The highly symbolic dances are inspired by everything from fever-ridden malaria sufferers to the homosexual practices of the Spanish conquistadors.

Accommodation for the festival needs to be organized in advance; you either have to find a room in one of a few basic hotels or hope a local will give you some floor space. Many tourist agencies in Cuzco run buses specifically for the fiesta and can help arrange accommodations with local families.

Transportes Gallito de las Rocas (☑084-22-6895; Diagonal Angamos, 1st block off Av de la Cultura, Cuzco) buses depart Cuzco to Paucartambo (S9, three hours) daily and to Pilcopata (S20, 10 to 12 hours) on Monday, Wednesday and Friday. Look for 'Paucartambo' painted on a lamp post between auto shops to find the office.

TRES CRUCES

About two hours beyond Paucartambo is the extraordinary jungle view at Tres Cruces, a lookout off the Paucartambo–Shintuya road. The sight of the mountains dropping away into the Amazon Basin is gorgeous in itself, but is made all the more magical by the sunrise phenomenon that occurs from May to July (other months are cloudy), especially around the time of the winter solstice on June 21. The sunrise here gets optically distorted, causing double images, halos and an incredible multicolored light show. At this time of year, many travel agencies and outdoor adventure outfitters run sunrise-watching trips from Cuzco.

During Paucartambo's Fiesta de la Virgen del Carmen, minibuses run back and forth between Paucartambo and Tres Cruces all night long. You can also take a truck en route to Pillcopata and ask to be let off at the turnoff to Tres Cruces (a further 13km walk). Alternatively, ask around in Paucartambo to hire a truck. Make sure you leave in the middle of the night to catch the dawn, and take plenty of warm clothing. Camping is possible but take all your own supplies.

Tres Cruces is within Parque Nacional Manu. For details of the onward trip to Shintuya and the Manu area, see p455.

Cuzco to Puerto Maldonado

Almost 500km long, this road takes a day to travel in the dry season. Most travelers choose to fly from Cuzco to Puerto Maldonado. Now paved, this route is part of the Interoceánica, a highway that unites the east and west coasts of South America for the first time.

Various companies depart from Cuzco's *terminal terrestre* for Puerto Maldonado between 3pm and 4.30pm daily. CIVA (S60, 17 hours, departs 4pm) is probably the best option. If you want to split up the journey, the best places to stop are Ocongate and Quince Mil, which have basic accommodations.

The route heads toward Puno until soon after Urcos, where the road to Puerto Maldonado begins. About 75km and 2½ hours from Cuzco, you come to the highland town of **Ocongate**, which has a couple of basic hotels around the plaza.

From here, trucks go to the village of **Tinqui**, an hour's drive beyond Ocongate, which is the starting point for the spectacular seven-day trek encircling Ausangate (6384m), the highest mountain in southern Peru.

After Tinqui, the road drops steadily to **Quince Mil**, 240km from Cuzco, less than 1000m above sea level, and the halfway point of the journey. The area is a gold-mining center, and the hotel here is often full. After another 100km, the road into the jungle reaches the flatlands, where it levels out for the last 140km into Puerto Maldonado.

AUSANGATE

Snowcapped Ausangate (6384m), the highest mountain in southern Peru, can be seen from Cuzco on a clear day. Hiking a circuit around its skirts is the most challenging alpine hike in the region. It takes five to six days and crosses four high passes (two over 5000m). The route begins in the rolling brown *puna* (grasslands of the Andean plateau) and features stunningly varied scenery, including fluted icy peaks, tumbling glaciers, turquoise lakes and green marshy valleys. Along the way you'll stumle across huge herds of alpacas and tiny amlets unchanged in centuries. The walk tarts and finishes at Tinqui, where there re warm mineral springs and a basic hotel, and mules and *arrieros* (horsemen) are vailable for about S30 per day each. Average price is US$500 for an organized, tent-based trek with operators such as Apus Peru (🖋23-2691; www.apus-peru.com) or specialist guides.

For a luxurious, lodge-based experience f Ausangate, check out Andean Lodges (🖋22-4613; www.andeanlodges.com; from S$610). Ecofriendly technologies are used n bathrooms and restaurants.

CUZCO TO THE CENTRAL IGHLANDS

Traveling by bus from Cuzco to Lima via Abancay and Nazca takes you along a remote route closed from the late 1980s until the late 1990s due to guerilla activity and banditry. It is now much safer, and paved. You should still check recent news reports before heading out this way as rainy season landslides can really slow a trip. Going west from Abancay to Andahuaylas and Ayacucho is a tough ride on a rough road rarely used except by the most hardcore travelers.

Cuzco to Abancay

There are several worthwhile stops along this four-hour, 200km ride. It's possible to make a day out of visiting one or two, bus hopping your way to Abancay. Start by catching a *colectivo* to Limatambo (S12, two hours) from Arcopata in Cuzco.

Limatambo, 80km west of Cuzco, is named after the Inca site of Rimactambo, also popularly known as Tarawasi (admission S10), which is situated beside the road, about 2km west of town. The site was used as a ceremonial center, as well as a resting place for the Inca *chasquis* (Inca runners who delivered messages over long distances). The exceptional polygonal retaining wall, noteworthy for its 28 human-sized niches, is in itself worth the trip from Cuzco. On the wall below it, look for flower shapes and a nine-sided heart amid the patchwork of perfectly interlocking stones. There is basic, hard-to-find accommodation in Limatambo.

The natural thermal baths of Cconoc (admission S3) are a 3km walk downhill from a turnoff 10km east of minor transport hub Corahuasi, 1½ hours east of Abancay. They have a restaurant, a bar, taxis and a basic hotel.

The Inca site of Saihuite (admission S10), 45km east of Abancay, has a sizable, intricately carved boulder called the Stone of Saihuite, which is similar to the famous sculpted rock at Q'enqo, near Cuzco, though it's smaller and more elaborate. The carvings of animals are particularly intricate. Ask to be let off at the turnoff to the ruins, from where it is a 1km walk downhill.

Cachora, 15km from the highway from the same turnoff as Saihuite, is the most common starting point for the hike to Choquequirau. There are a few guesthouses, a campground and local guides and mules for hire.

Choquequirau

Remote, spectacular, and still not entirely cleared, the ruins of Choquequirau are often described as a mini-Machu Picchu. This breathtaking site at the junction of three rivers – and the fairly challenging four-day hike required to get there and back – has been firmly positioned as 'the next big thing' for the last few years.

It seems inevitable that controls and permits will be introduced in time. In theory, travelers can organize this walk on their own easily, but at the time of research, essential footbridges were out and it was not possible to make the hike. Inquire with operators first, even if you plan on going on your own.

A guided version costs US$380 on average. Apus Peru (🖋84-23-2691; www.apus-peru.com) joins this trek up with the Inca Trail, for a total of nine days of spectacular scenery and an ever-more-impressive parade of Inca ruins culminating in Machu Picchu.

Abancay

🖋083 / POP 13,800 / ELEV 2378M

This sleepy rural town is the capital of the department of Apurímac, one of the least-explored regions in the Peruvian Andes. Travelers may opt to use it as a rest stop on the long, tiring bus journey between Cuzco and Ayacucho.

Jirón Arequipa, with banks, is the main commercial street; its continuation, Av las Arenas, has restaurants and entertainment.

THE Q'OYORITI PILGRIMAGE

Important geographical features such as rivers and mountains are *apus* (sacred deities) for the Andean people, and are possessed of *kamaq* (vital force). At 6384m, Ausangate is the Cuzco department's highest mountain and the most important *apu* in the area – the subject of countless legends. It is considered the *pakarina* (mythical place of sacred origin) of llamas and alpacas, and controls the health and fertility of these animals. Its freezing heights are also where condemned souls are doomed to wander as punishment for their sins.

Ausangate is the site of the traditional festival of Q'oyoriti (Star of the Snow), held in late May or early June between the Christian feasts of the Ascension and Corpus Christi. Despite its overtly Catholic aspect – it's officially all about the icy image of Christ that appeared here in 1783 – the festival remains primarily and obviously a celebration and appeasement of the *apu,* consisting of four or more days of literally nonstop music and dance. Incredibly elaborate costumes and dances – featuring, at the more extreme end, llama fetuses and mutual whipping – repetitive brass-band music, fireworks, and much throwing of holy water all contribute to a dizzy, delirious spectacle. Highly unusual: no alcohol is allowed. Offenders are whipped by anonymous men dressed as *ukukus* (mountain spirits) with white masks that hide their features, who maintain law and order.

It's a belief fervently held by many *cuzqueños* (inhabitants of Cuzco) that if you attend Q'oyoriti three times, you'll get your heart's desire. The traditional way to go about this is to buy an *alacita* (miniature scale model) of your desire. Houses, cars, trucks, petrol stations, university degrees, driver's licenses, money: the usual human desires are on offer for a few soles at stalls lining the pilgrimage pathway. You then line up in the church to have it blessed by a priest. Repeat three years in a row and see what happens.

Q'oyoriti is a pilgrimage – the only way in is by trekking three or more hours up a mountain, traditionally in the wee small hours to arrive around dawn. The sight of a solid, endless line of people quietly wending their way up or down the track and disappearing around a bend in the mountain is unforgettable, as is Q'oyoriti's eerie, other-worldly feel. The fact that everyone's sober at a party gives it an unusual vibe. The majority of attendees are traditionally dressed *campesinos* for whom seeing a foreigner may be a novelty (they may even point you out).

Discomfort is another aspect of the pilgrimage. Q'oyoriti takes place at an altitude of 4750m, where glaciers flow down into the Sinakara Valley. It's brutally cold, and there's no infrastructure, no town here, just one big elaborate church (complete with flashing lights around the altar) built to house the image of El Señor de Q'oyoriti (The Christ of Q'oyoriti). The temporary toilets are a major ordeal. The blue plastic sea of restaurants, stalls and tents is all carried in, on foot or donkey. The whole thing is monumentally striking: a temporary tent city at the foot of a glacier, created and dismantled yearly to honor two mutually contradictory yet coexisting religions in a festival with dance and costumes whose origins no one can remember.

◎ Sights & Activities

During the dry season (late May to September), hikers and climbers may want to take advantage of the best weather to head for the sometimes snowcapped peak of Ampay (5228m), about 10km north-northwest of town. The mountain is also the center of the 3635-hectare Santuario Nacional Ampay, where camping and birding are good.

✲ Festivals & Events

Abancay has a particularly colorful Carnaval held in the week before Lent, which is a chance to see festival celebrations unaffected by tourism. It includes a nationally acclaimed folk-dancing competition. Book ahead or arrive before the festivities start. Abancay Day, the anniversary of the town's founding, happens on November 3.

🛏 Sleeping & Eating

Accommodations are geared more toward business travelers than tourists. There are plenty of restaurants and cafes on Arenas, with a fair share of rotisserie joints and *chifas*. Abancay's nightlife centers on Arenas and Pasaje Valdivia just off it.

Hotel Turistas HISTORIC HOTEL $$
(☑32-1017; www.turismoapurimac.com; Díaz Bárenas 500; s S62-98, d S107-148; @🛜) A colonial mansion with a whiff of former grandeur, it's nonetheless a city landmark. Rooms are plain for what you might imagine, but comfortable, with phones and TVs. Breakfast is included but the coffee is not recommended. Be sure to ask for the 18% tax to be discounted.

Hotel Saywa HOTEL $
(☑32-4876; www.hotelsaywa.com; Arenas 302; d/tr incl breakfast S60/75/120; 🛜) A friendly spot with good options for solo travelers. Attractive rooms have parquet floors and TV, there's also an onsite tour agency.

Villa Venecia PERUVIAN $$
(☑50-4662; Av Bella Abanquina; mains from S15; ⏱11am-4pm) Worth the short taxi ride (it's behind the stadium), Villa Venecia is Abanay's most noteworthy restaurant. Serving up every local food imaginable, it's the living embodiment of the Peruvian mantra '*bueno, barato y bastante*' – 'good, cheap and plentiful.' The *tallarines* (spaghetti) are an Abanay specialty.

❶ Getting There & Away

Colectivos to Corahuasi via Saihuite (S10, 1½ hours) leave from Jirón Huancavelica, two blocks uphill from Arenas. Vehicles to Cachora leave from one block further uphill. Buses towards Cuzco, Andahuaylas and Lima leave from the *terminal terrestre*.

At least seven companies run buses to Cuzco (S15, five hours), clustered around 6am, 11am and 11pm. Dozens of buses depart to Lima (S60 to S170, 14 to 18 hours) every day, mostly in the afternoon and between 10:30pm and midnight. Departures to Andahuaylas (S10, five hours) cluster around 11:30am and 11:30pm. The faster, more comfortable minibuses to Andahuaylas (S20, four hours) are a little bit reckless.

Terminal departure tax is S1. Taxis go to the center (S3).

Andahuaylas
☑083 / POP 6800 / ELEV 2980M

Andahuaylas, 135km west of Abancay on the way to Ayacucho, is the second-most important town in the department of Apurímac, and a convenient halfway stop on the rough but scenic route between Cuzco and Ayacucho.

◉ Sights & Activities

Andahuaylas' main attraction, the beautiful Laguna de Pacucha, is 17km from town and accessible by bus or taxi. About 15km past the end of the lake is the imposing hilltop site of Sondor, built by the Chanka culture. The Chankas were traditional enemies of the Incas, but evidently shared their appreciation of a good view. You can easily access both the lake and the ruin by catching a microbus to Sondor (S3, one hour) from the corner of Av Martinelli and Av Casafranca. Go in the morning – transport peters out by 4pm. You can also take a taxi.

Both Andahuaylas and Pacucha have Sunday markets that are worth perusing.

✵✵ Festivals & Events

The annual Fiesta de Yahuar (Blood Feast) is on July 28, when traditional dances and music are performed. In the village of Pacucha, the festival includes lashing a condor to the back of a bull and allowing the two to fight in a representation of the highland people's struggle against the Spanish conquistadors.

🛏 Sleeping

You can't always expect a hot shower in an Andahuaylas hotel, but you can undoubtedly count on cable TV. Go figure.

Sol de Oro HOTEL $
(☑42-1152; soldeorohotel@hotmail.com; Jr Trelles 164; s/d incl breakfast S70/80; @🛜) The best Andahuaylas has to offer, this remodeled hotel has comfortable beds and hot showers and receives happy reviews from guests.

El Encanto de Oro Hotel HOTEL $
(☑42-3066; www.hotelandahuaylas.com; Av Casafranca 424; s/d/tr incl breakfast S50/80/100; 🛜) Features spotlessly clean rooms of varying shapes and sizes, all with frilly curtains and phones. Friendly and caring, near the market and the Pachuco bus stop.

Imperio Chanka HOTEL $$
(☑42-3065; www.imperiochankahotel.com; Vallejo 384; s/d incl breakfast S80/100) With a modern look, this multi-story cement building features good, clean rooms that are well looked after. There's also an onsite restaurant.

Hostal Cruz del Sur HOTEL $
(☑42-1571; Andahuaylas 117; d S45, s/d/tr without bathroom S20/30/45) This is the best cheap

choice in town, with spacious rooms off outdoor balconies around a flowery patio.

✕ Eating & Drinking

El Cappuccino
CAFE $

(☑42-1790; Cáceres Tresierra 321; mains from S9; ⊙9am-11pm Mon-Sat; @) This cheery, breezy, French-run place is a haven of Western home comforts: yummy crepes, waffles and sandwiches, loads of vegetarian options, Andahuaylas' best coffee, plus books, magazines and games. A deservedly popular hangout with both locals and travelers.

Chifa El Dragón
CHINESE $

(☑42-1749; cnr Ramos & Trelles; menú from S8; ⊙7am-10pm) El Dragón is a smart restaurant serving Chinese dishes with a touch of *criollo* influence.

ⓘ Information

BCP (Ramón Castilla s/n) has an ATM and changes US dollars. There's a Western Union office and several *casas de cambio* on Ramón Castilla. There are plenty of internet cafes, some fast – look for the Speedy sign. **Clínica Señor de Huanca** (☑42-1418; Andahuaylas 108) provides 24-hour emergency medical attention.

ⓘ Getting There & Away
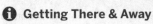

Air

LC Peru (☑in Lima 1-204-1313; www.lcperu.pe) flies daily to Lima (S292). **Explora Apurímac** (☑42-2877; Plaza de Armas s/n; ⊙8am-1pm & 3-8pm) travel agency books tickets. A taxi to the airport will cost about S25.

Bus

Heading east, **Celtur** (☑42-2337; cnr Vallejo & Ugarte), **Señor de Huanca** (☑42-1218; Martinelli 170), **Expreso los Chankas** (☑42-2441; Malecón Grau s/n) and **Molina Union** (☑42-1248; Av los Sauces s/n) run daily to Cuzco (S25, nine hours) via Abancay (S10, five hours) throughout the day.

Several companies run faster, more comfortable and expensive minibuses to Abancay (S20, four hours).

Heading west, Celtur and Los Chankas have daily services to Ayacucho around 7am and 7pm (S35, six to seven hours). Direct buses to Lima (S70, 20 to 22 hours) are run by **Wari** (☑42-1936; Malecón Grau s/n) at 6am, 11am, 2pm and 5pm, and Molina Union at 10am and 4pm.

Bus companies leave from the *terminal terrestre* but arrive to their offices, except Expreso Molino and Wari, which only use their own offices. Minibus companies all operate out of the terminal. Terminal departure tax is S1.

Central Highlands

Best Places to Eat

- Huancahuasi (p282)
- Via Via (p296)
- Café Coqui (p282)
- Pollos y Parrilladas el Centro (p288)

Best Places to Stay

- Hacienda la Florida (p274)
- Villa Jennifer (p306)
- La Casa de la Abuela (p281)
- Hotel Sevilla (p294)

Why Go?

If it's breathtaking ancient ruins or immersion in uninterrupted wilderness that you crave during your Peruvian voyage, listen up. The rocky, remote central highlands can match the country's better-known destinations for these things and more: with the almost absolute absence of other travelers.

This sector of the Andes is Peru at its most Peruvian: at its zenith from Easter to July for the greatest of its myriad fiestas. Travel here is not for the faint-hearted. But adventure-spirited souls will discover better insights into local life than are possible elsewhere: bonding with locals on bumpy buses, perhaps, or hiking into high hills to little-known Inca palaces.

Life in this starkly beautiful region is lived largely off the land: donkeys ply roads more than cars and bright indigenous dress predominates in communities secreting Peru's best handicrafts. The region's rearing, lake-studded mountains, it often seems, shield the central highlands from the 21st century.

When to Go
Ayacucho

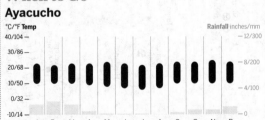

Jan Hot but rain-prone summer weather as Huancayo celebrates New Year with particularly quirky *Año Nuevo* festivities.

Mar/Apr Peru's biggest and best Easter party unfolds during Ayacucho's Semana Santa.

Jul & Aug Dry weather with chilly, star-heavy nights conducive to toddies and thermal bath relaxation in Huancavelica.

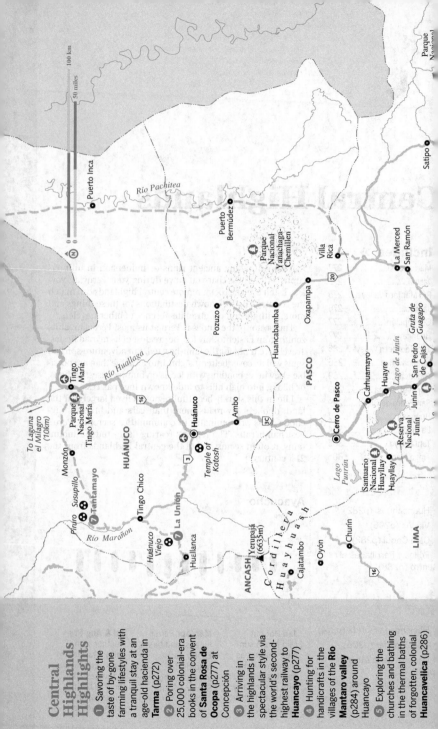

Central Highlands Highlights

1 Savoring the taste of by-gone farming lifestyles with a tranquil stay at an age-old hacienda in **Tarma** (p272)

2 Poring over 25,000 colonial-era books in the convent of **Santa Rosa de Ocopa** (p277) at Concepción

3 Arriving in the highlands in spectacular style via the world's second-highest railway to **Huancayo** (p277)

4 Hunting for handicrafts in the villages of the **Río Mantaro valley** (p284) around Huancayo

5 Exploring the churches and bathing in the thermal baths of forgotten, colonial **Huancavelica** (p286)

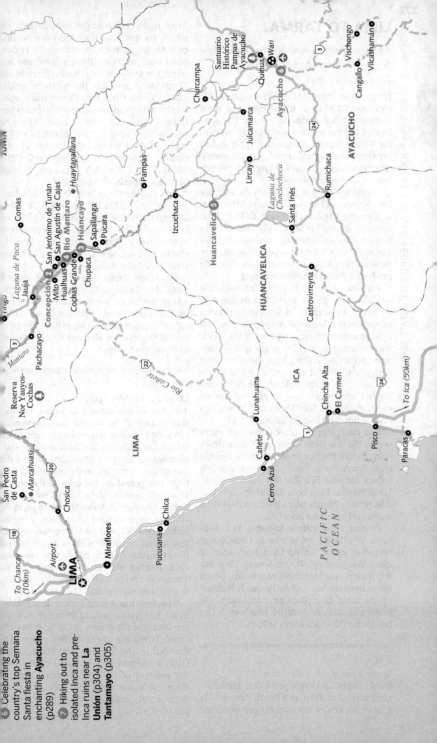

6 Celebrating the country's top Semana Santa fiesta in enchanting **Ayacucho** (p289)

7 Hiking out to isolated Inca and pre-Inca ruins near **La Unión** (p304) and **Tantamayo** (p305)

LIMA TO TARMA

San Pedro de Casta & Marcahuasi

Isolated San Pedro de Casta (population 500, elevation 3200m) is the perfect precursor to your Central Andes adventure. The road from Chosica twists spectacularly upward for 40km around a sheer-sided valley before arriving at this mountainside town clustered around a ridge and resounding with the bellows of *burros* (donkeys).

People come here principally to visit the little-known archaeological site of Marcahuasi, a nearby 4-sq-km plateau at 4100m. Marcahuasi is famed for its weirdly eroded rocks shaped into animals such as camels, turtles and seals, which have a mystical significance for some people (who claim they are signs of a pre-Inca culture or energy vortices).

Because of the altitude, it's not advisable to go to Marcahuasi from Lima in one day; acclimatize overnight in San Pedro. It takes two hours to hike the 2km up to the site; you can sometimes catch a bus part of the way if it's not engaged on other municipality business (departing 7:30am from the plaza most days), then hike for 45 minutes. A Centro de Información (Plaza de Armas, San Pedro) has limited information and maps; staff can arrange guides for S10. Mules and horses can also be hired for similar prices.

You can camp at Marcahuasi but carry water: the few lakes there aren't fit to drink from. In San Pedro, accommodations include basic Gran Hotel Turístico Municipal (s/d without bathroom S10/20), just off the plaza. Local families have beds (ask at the information center). Simple plaza restaurants serve a *menú* (set meal) for about S5.

Getting there entails taking a bus from Lima to Chosica; minibuses to Chosica can be picked up in Central Lima from Arica at Plaza Bolognesi (S3.50, two hours). Then ask for Transportes Municipal San Pedro, which leaves from the bus yard by Parque Echenique on the main drag (the Carretera Central) in Chosica at 9am and 3pm (S6, four hours). The bus back to Choisica leaves at 2pm.

La Oroya

☑ 064 / POP 35,000 / ELEV 3731M

Bleak, chilly La Oroya, self-titled 'metallurgical capital of Peru and South America,' is a smelting center for mineral ore extracted from the Central Andes (see boxed text, p300). Tourism-wise it's worthy of a mention only for its position on one of the region's main road junctions. Routes from here lead north towards Cerro de Pasco, Huánuco and Tingo María (and into the northern jungle), east to Tarma (then into the central jungle), south to Huancayo and Ayacucho (and eventually Cuzco) and west to Lima. There are two parts to town: a vast industrial swath south of the river and the old town (more convenient for onward bus connections) to the northeast. Be wary going out at night here: even locals advise against it.

Few travelers stop here. If stranded, basic Hostal Inti (☑39-1098; Arequipa 117; d without bathroom S18) has hot showers. In the old town, other uninspiring but safe-enough options can be found along Darío León for similar prices. Don't bank on hot water, even if the hotel advertises it.

Huancayo buses pass through the old town. For Tarma (S15, change at El Cruce where the Tarma road branches off), Cerro de Pasco (S20) and Huánuco, buses and/or *colectivo* (shared) taxis leave from the other side of the river on Horacio Zevallos Gomez in the west of town.

Tarma

☑ 064 / POP 60,500 / ELEV 3050M

Travelers seldom make it to Tarma, but they should. One of the region's most welcoming cities with a balmy climate by altiplano (highlands) standards, this is a great stopover – surrounded on all sides by scrubby, brown dirt mountains secreting some intriguing day trips, but poised on the cusp of the *ceja de la selva* (eyebrow of the jungle) with a road linking the central Andes to the Amazon Basin and its associated attractions. *Limeños* (inhabitants of Lima) come here to experience the nearest accessible tract of jungle to their desert capital and the city is now cottoning on to tourism with facilities ever-improving. Tarma can also be used as a base for exploring *la selva central* (Central Amazon; see p459).

The area has a long history too. Hidden in the mountains around town are Inca and pre-Inca ruins that have yet to be fully excavated. Tarma was one of the first places to be founded by the Spanish after the conquest (1538 is the generally accepted date). Nothing remains of the early colonial era, but there are many attractive 19th- and early 20th-century houses with white walls and red-tiled roofs.

◉ Sights

ocal excursions include visits to one of eru's key pilgrimage sites, El Señor de Iuruhuay (the Christ of Muruhuay) near cobamba (9km from Tarma; p299) and San edro de Cajas (41km away; p299).

stronomical Observatory   OBSERVATORY
🕾 32-2625; Huánuco 614; admission S5; ⊗ 8-10pm ri) Tarma is high in the mountains and he clear nights of June, July and August rovide ideal opportunities for stargaz-1g, though the surrounding mountains do mit the amount of observable heavens. A mall astronomical observatory is run by the wners of Hospedaje Central: admission in-ludes a talk (in Spanish) on constellations nd a peek at some stars.

Cathedral   CHURCH
(Plaza de Armas) The town's cathedral is mod-ern (1965), and it contains the remains of Tarma's most famous son, Peruvian presi-dent Manuel Odría (1897–1974). He organ-ized construction of the cathedral during his presidency. The old clock in the cathedral tower dates from 1862.

Tarmatambo   ARCHAEOLOGICAL SITE
Of the myriad archaeological ruins near Tar-ma, best known is Tarmatambo, 6km south. Former capital of the Tarama culture and later a major Inca administrative center, the fairly extensive remains include storehouses, palaces and an impressive, still-used aque-duct system. Ask at the tourist office about guides to take you there and to other sites: going solo, these ruins are difficult to find.

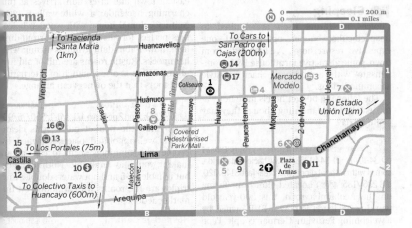

✲✿ Festivals & Events

The big annual attraction is undoubtedly Easter. For good information on this and other regional festivities (in Spanish) visit www.tarma.info.

Semana Santa   REGLIGIOUS
(Holy Week) Many processions are held, including several by candlelight after dark. They culminate on the morning of Easter Sunday with a marvelous procession to the cathedral along an 11-block route entirely carpeted with flower petals, attracting thousands of Peruvian visitors. Hotels fill fast and increase prices by up to 50% at these times.

Tarma Tourism Week   FESTIVAL
Another fiesta, held near the end of July, featuring dress-up parades, music, dancing and much raucous merriment.

🛏 Sleeping

Choices in Tarma itself are limited to unspectacular budget options and one expensive resort hotel. A short ride from town, some attractive farmhouse B&Bs compensate with atmospheric hacienda-style accommodations.

The following budget hotels have hot water, usually in the morning, though they may claim all day.

TOP CHOICE Hacienda La Florida   HACIENDA $$
(☑34-1041, 01-344-1358; www.haciendalaflorida.com; s with/without dinner incl breakfast S140/120, d S 236 /186; 🐕❄) Located 6km from Tarma on the Acobamba road, this 300-year-old working hacienda is now a B&B owned by a welcoming Peruvian–German couple, Pepe and Inge. Rooms boast wooden parquet floors and private bathrooms, there is attractive space for campers (per person S14) and the filling breakfasts have a delectable German slant. Visitors can partake in farm life, or in various two-day workshops (minimum of six people) on relaxation techniques and cooking classes. El Señor de Muruhuay sanctuary is a one-hour hike away and local tours start from S26.50.

Los Portales   HOTEL $$$
(☑32-1411; www.losportaleshoteles.com.pe; Castilla 512; s/d/ste incl breakfast S220/320/670; @🐕❄) Set in secluded gardens in the west of town, this hotel features a children's playground and 45 standard hotel rooms with cable TV and wi-fi internet access. Rates include continental breakfast and the restaurant

provides room service. The two suites have Jacuzzis. This is the best choice for accommodation in Tarma city itself. The town's best disco, Kimera, is also here along with Pollo Stop (a popular chicken restaurant).

Hospedaje El Dorado   GUESTHOUSE
(☑32-1914; fax 32-1634; Huánuco 488; s with/without bathroom S30/20, d S50) Sizable, clean, occasionally worn rooms face a leafy internal courtyard and come with cable TV and hot showers. Friendly staff and an in-house cafeteria help make this central Tarma's most mochilero-friendly (backpacker) sleeping option.

Hacienda Santa María   HACIENDA $
(☑32-1232; www.haciendasantamaria.com; Vista Alegre 1249; s/d incl breakfast S125/210) Calle Vienrich becomes Vista Alegre to the north east of town and after 1km arrives at this charming hacienda: a white-walled, 18th century colonial house with wooden balconies perfect for surveying the surrounding lush, flower-abundant grounds strung with hammocks. Rustic rooms are full of old furniture. There is also a clutch of alternative local tours that the owners can arrange.

El Vuelo del Condor   GUESTHOUSE $
(☑32-2399; Jirón 2 de Mayo 471; s/d/tr S50/75/90; ❄🐕) Amid the market bustle, this clean, secure, well-appointed place is owned by people who genuinely seem to care about making your stay enjoyable. Nothing fancy but reliable wi-fi and hot water; doubles and triples are the rooms with windows on the market action.

Hospedaje Central   GUESTHOUSE $
(☑32-2625; Huánuco 614; s with/without bathroom S30/20, d S55) Aged hotel with an astronomical observatory, dark, simple-but-adequate rooms, friendly staff and ample tourist information.

🍴 Eating & Drinking

Following the closure of the city's best eatery, there are disappointingly few good restaurants.

Restaurant Chavín de Grima   PERUVIAN $
(Lima 270; meals S10-15; ☉7am-10pm) For breakfasts and cheap set lunches on the Plaza de Armas you won't go far wrong by heading to this popular place. A wholesome two-course menú del dia (set menu of the day) is a mere S4.50.

Restaurant Señorial/
El Braserito   PERUVIAN $
Huánuco 138/140; mains S12-24; ⊙8am-3pm &
6-11pm) Two restaurants rolled into one (just
one side is opened if it's slow), this is the local favorite. It's seen better days than these
but there's something inexplicably appealing about the array of meaty options complemented by the nonstop *telenovelas* and
inane reality shows blaring from the TV. The
wholesome menu features the usual Peruvian standards, including *cuy* (guinea pig)
and *trucha* (trout).

El Che Parrillas   PARRILLA $
Lima 558; mains S15; ⊙11am-midnight) The *parrillas* (grilled meats) at this 2nd-floor restaurant are sublime.

La Colonia 'H'   BAR
Callao 822; ⊙until 2am) The best place for a
beer or three.

ⓘ Information

Casas de cambio (foreign-exchange bureaus) are at the western end of Lima.

BCP (☎32-2149; Lima at Paucartambo) You
can change money here; it also has an ATM.

Locutorio Telefónica (Lima 288) Internet for
S1.50 per hour.

Tourist office (☎32-1010, ext 20; fax 32-3483;
Jirón 2 de Mayo 775; ⊙8am-1pm & 3-6pm Mon-
Fri) On the Plaza de Armas, offering information about local tours, in Spanish. Day tours
of Tarmatambo, San Pedro de Cajas, Gruta de
Huagapo and some of the nearer jungle sights
are around S45.

ⓘ Getting There & Around

Most transport to and from Lima arrives about
800m to the west of the Plaza de Armas, near
the óvalo (main roundabout) at the arched entrance to central Tarma. This is where you'll find
the forlorn (but official) *terminal terrestre* (bus
station) with daily buses to Lima (S20/30, six
hours) at 11.30am, 1.30pm and several services
between 11am and midnight. The higher tariffs
are for fully reclining seats, usually on the bottom deck. La Merced–bound buses depart at
3pm and 6pm.

Bus

Bus companies often have their own terminals
in Tarma.

Los Angelitos (Vienrich 573) Minivans to La
Merced at 12.30pm, 3.30pm and 7pm (S10,
two hours).

Los Canarios (☎32-3357; Amazonas 694) Has
small buses to Huancayo (S10, three hours)

via Jauja (S7, two hours) leaving almost hourly
from 5am to 6pm.

Transportes Chanchamayo (☎32-1882;
Callao 1002) Has 9am, 2pm and 11pm departures to Lima (S20). A La Merced bus departs
at 2.30pm.

Transportes Junín (☎53-2333; Amazonas
669) Has eight daily services to Lima (almost
hourly until 1pm, then none until 11pm) including *bus-camas* (bed buses) at 11:30am and also
11:45pm (S20 to S30). It also has 5:30am and
1pm departures for Cerro de Pasco (S12, two to
three hours).

Other Transport

By the gas station opposite the *terminal terrestre*, *colectivo* taxis take up to four passengers
to Lima (S30 each) or local destinations such
as Junín or La Oroya (S15). If you want to go
to Cerro de Pasco or Huánuco, you can take
colectivos from here, too, though you will have to
change at El Cruce (the crossroads of the Tarma
and La Oroya-Cerro de Pasco roads). Fast *colectivo* taxis to Huancayo (S20) leave from Jauja,
about 600m south of the *terminal terrestre*.

Amazon-bound vehicles also leave from the
northeastern end of town near Estadio Unión
Tarma (a *mototaxi* – motorcycle taxi – here costs
S2) including *colectivos* to La Merced (S15 to
S20, 1½ hours) via Acobamba (S2, 10 minutes).
The journey to La Merced is spectacular, dropping about 2.5km vertically to the jungle in the
space of just over an hour. For destinations
beyond La Merced, change at the convenient
Transportes San Juan La Merced bus terminal.
Ask around the stadium area for other destinations. A bus opposite the Estadio Unión has minibuses to Acobamba and Palcamayo. Cars for
San Pedro de Cajas (S5) leave from the northern
end of Moquegua. The tourist office can help
with transport-related queries.

RÍO MANTARO VALLEY

Southeast of Tarma, the wide fertile agricultural plain of the Río Mantaro valley opens
up to reveal a gentler side to the mostly-
rugged highlands: undulating pastoral
panoramas, the sophisticated modern city of
Huancayo and, dotted in-between, a number
of villages internationally renowned for the
quality of their handicrafts. For those who
still crave remoter adventures, there is the
wild Reserva Nor Yauyos-Cochas, a number
of high-altitude hikes and even kayaking opportunities right down the valley.

Festivals are a way of life here. Residents
say that there is a festival occurring each
day of the year, and chancing upon some

colorful celebration is highly likely. The valley, split by the Río Mantaro throughout its length, runs northwest–southeast between Jauja and Huancayo. South of Jauja, the road branches to follow both the west and east sides of the Río Mantaro valley to Huancayo. Local bus drivers refer to these as *derecha* (right, or west) and *izquierda* (left, or east).

From Huancayo, some classic Andean travel routes connect through the hardgoing but delightfully scenic valleys south to Ayacucho, and eventually on to Cuzco.

Jauja

📞 064 / POP 25,000 / ELEV 3250M

Coming from Lima, the first place you pass along this route is Jauja, a small, bustling colonial town of narrow traffic-swamped streets about 60km southeast of Tarma and 50km north of Huancayo. It offers some decent accommodations, which can be used as a base for sampling attractions including a lakeside resort and several interesting hikes to archaeological ruins.

Sights & Activities

Jauja was Francisco Pizarro's first capital in Peru, though this honor was short-lived. Some finely carved wooden altars in the main church are all that remain of the early colonial days. Before the Incas, this area was home to an important Huanca indigenous community, and Huanca ruins can be seen on a hill about 3km southeast of town. A brisk walk or *mototaxi* will get you there.

About 4km from Jauja is Laguna de Paca, a small lakeside resort offering restaurants, rowboats and fishing. A boat ride around the lake will cost about S3 per passenger (five-person minimum). There are ducks and gulls, and you can stop at Isla del Amor – a tiny artificial island. A *mototaxi* here costs S3.

A well-preserved Camino del Inca (Inca road) runs from Jauja to Tarma. The most spectacular section is from Tingo (30 minutes from Jauja by taxi) to Inkapatakuna (30 minutes from Tarma), a scenic six- to eight-hour hike.

Half an hour west of Jauja on the Lima road, is Pachacayo, gateway to the remote Reserva Nor Yauyos-Cochas, an iconic Andean smorgasbord of glimmering blue-green mountain lakes nestled within towering peaks and home to the Pariacaca

Glacier. You'll need your own 4WD vehicle (hire one in Lima or Huancayo) to get there; otherwise contact the folks at Hostal Manco Cápac who may be able to help with arrangements.

There is a colorful market in the town center every Wednesday morning. Some good general information can be found at www.jaujamiperu.com (Spanish).

Sleeping

Many visitors stay in Huancayo and travel to Jauja by minibus or *colectivo* taxi.

Hostal Manco Cápac
GUESTHOUSE $
(☎36-1620; www.hostal-mancocapac.com; Manco Cápac 575; without bathroom incl breakfast s S35/50, d S80) By far the best choice in Jauja is this secure, peaceful house with huge rooms abutting two courtyard gardens. Bathrooms are clean and showers hot: each room is allotted its own exclusive bathroom. It's three blocks north of the Plaza de Armas and rates include a continental breakfast with freshly brewed coffee. The owners are great sources of local information, but book in advance as they are not always there.

Hostal María Nieves
GUESTHOUSE $
(☎36-2543; Gálvez 491; s with/without bathroom S40/35, d S50/40) This place also comes recommended: the friendly owner is accustomed to hosting the odd stray gringo and offers nine homely rooms of which three have private bathrooms. Breakfast is available on request.

Eating

Out by Laguna de Paca, a string of lakeshore restaurants attempt to entice diners with shrill, piped Andean music. Music aside, the lakeside tables are pleasant enough to sit at. There is little to choose between the bunch, though most offer a creditable plate of *pachamanca* (meat, potatoes and vegetables cooked in an earthen 'oven' of hot rocks). Another specialty here is clay-baked *trucha* seasoned with chilies, garlic and lemon, wrapped in banana leaves and baked in Laguna mud: delicious. Jauja also has several simple, central restaurants.

El Paraíso
PERUVIAN $
(Ayacucho 917; mains S12-14; ⊙lunch & dinner) The best eatery in town is this vast plant-filled restaurant popular with locals who are attracted by bargain specialties such as *trucha* (from Laguna de Paca) or *picante de*

uy (roast guinea pig in a spicy sauce). It's ιst south of the main plaza.

🌀 Getting There & Away

auja has the regional airport (currently under xpansion to allow bigger planes to land), with aily flights to/from Lima courtesy of **LC Peru** www.lcperu.pe). The airport is south of town on e Huancayo road.

Buses, minibuses and taxis all congregate at e south side of town by the bus yard at the tersection of Ricardo Palma with 28 de Julio bout 800m from the Plaza de Armas. During e day, frequent, inexpensive minibuses (S3) nd *colectivos* (S5) leave from here for Huan-ayo (50 minutes). Minibuses also leave for arma (S7, 1½ hours) and La Oroya (two hours). *olectivos* will also leave to these destinations if ere is demand: they normally only leave when ey have five passengers (that means two in the ont seat).

❶ Getting Around

lototaxis run anywhere in town for around 1.50. Take a *mototaxi* to get to Laguna de aca (S3).

Jauja is one of the few towns in the central ighlands that sells bicycles. Shops on Junín rovide fairly reliable mountain bikes if you plan n staying a while.

Concepción

📞 064 / ELEV 3283M

'rom Concepción, a village halfway between auja and Huancayo on the *izquierda* side, ou can travel to charming Ocopa village, ome to the famous convent of Santa Rosa le Ocopa (admission S5; ⊗9am-noon & 3-6pm Ved-Mon).Admission is by 45-minute guided our every hour or once groups are large nough (seven person minimum). There is 50% student discount. The building, set round beautiful gardens and cloistered in-ernal courtyards, was built by the Francis-cans in the early 18th century as a center for nissionaries heading into the jungle. During he years of missionary work, the friars built ıp an impressive collection of indigenous ırtifacts and stuffed jungle wildlife, now lisplayed in the convent's museum. There s a large collection of colonial religious art mainly in the *escuela cuzqueña* – Cuzco School – style, a combination of Spanish ınd Andean artistic styles). The highlight, nowever, is the fantastic 2nd-floor library of some 25,000 volumes – many dating back to he 15th century.

Frequent *colectivos* (Monday to Satur-day) leave from the plaza in Concepción for Ocopa, about 5km away. *Mototaxis* charge S15 for the return trip, inclusive of an hour's wait. Concepción is easily visited by taking a Huancayo–Jauja *izquierda* bus.

Huancayo

📞 064 / POP 323,050 / ELEV 3244M

The central altiplano's megametropolis, bustling Huancayo mixes its modern facade with a strong underlying sense of tradition. For many travelers this self-confident, cos-mopolitan city will be their first experience of the Peruvian highlands – it stands within a lush, visually arresting valley on an excit-ing overland mountain route to Cuzco – and while its charms are less obvious than those of other Andean locales, Huancayo does not disappoint.

Some of Peru's finest dining outside of Lima and Cuzco lies within the teeming streets, yet once you've sipped your espresso and sampled the region's renowned cuisine in well-appointed restaurants, prepare your-self for Peru's most interesting handicrafts – sold in the markets here and in the valley beyond – and vibrant and varied fiestas that take place almost daily.

There are, too, opportunities to learn Spanish or Quechua, to master musical in-struments or to dabble in Andean cooking. For the adventurous, the dusty nearby hills hide weird rock formations and spectacu-lar lakes while further afield, Andes trek-king, extreme mountain biking and jungle tramping await. To top it all, Huancayo is the terminus for two of Peru's (and South America's) best railway journeys, including the world's second-highest railway over the Andes to/from Lima.

👁 Sights

Huancayo is a sizeable town; you'll end up doing a lot of walking. Most attractions lie outside the center. In the city itself, the most notable sight is the Iglesia de La Merced, on the first block of Real, where the Peru-vian Constitution of 1839 was approved.

Museo Salesiano MUSEUM
(📞24-7763; Santa Rosa 299; admission S5; ⊗8am-noon & 2-6pm Mon-Fri) The museum can be entered from the Salesian school, and has Amazon fauna, pottery and archaeology ex-hibits. Hours vary.

Huancayo

To El Tambo
district (1km);
Huancahusi
(1.5km)

To Terminal Los
Andes (200m);
Colectivo taxis to
Tarma, La Oroya &
the north (200m)

Arequipa

Mariscal Castilla

Psje
Salesiano

Rio Shulcas

Santa Rosa

2

Pasaje
Verand

10

47

41

Centenario

16

21

Omar Yali

Ayacucho

1

Ancash

19

6

15

4

7

43

Amazonas

Cuzco

Cathedral

18

Plaza de la
Constitución

Giráldez

17

22

Plaza
Amazonas

Huancavelica

Puno

Arequipa

14

34

33

28

Real

8

5

30

38

Marañón

Liberdad

Moquegua

Breña

44

27

32

25

24

Sunday
Craft Market

Junin

Lima

40

Centro
Civico

11

Loreto

Ica

Piura

13

31

Municipalidad

Piura

Piura

Cajamarca

29

Huánuco

20

23

Moquegua

Tarapaca

Arequipa

Junin

Huancavelica

Libertad

Angaraes

Cerro de la Libertad VIEWPOINT

(cnr Giráldez & Torre Tagle; admission free; ◷dawn-dusk) Head northeast on Giráldez for a great view of the city. About 2km from the town center is a popular recreational and dining locale where, apart from the city view, there are artwork stalls and a playground.

Parque de la Identidad Huanca PARK

(cnr Santa Felicita & San Maros; admission free; ◷dawn-dusk) In the suburb of San Antonio, this is a fanciful park full of stone statues and miniature buildings representing the area's culture.

🏃 Activities

Incas del Perú ADVENTURE TOUR

(☐22-3303; www.incasdelperu.org; Giráldez 652) Ever-active Lucho Hurtado of Incas del Perú, in the same building as the restaurant La Cabaña, organizes most activities. Lucho is a local who speaks English and knows the surrounding area well. He arranges demanding, multiday mountain-bike tours and Andean mountain-trekking expeditions to the lake and glacier of Huaytapallana; the cost for trekking per one/two people is around S1000/1700 for a three-day excursion.

Tours are arranged by Lucho, who guides treks down the eastern slopes of the Andes and into high jungle on foot, horseback or public transport. It isn't luxurious, but it's a good chance to experience something of the real rural Peru: you can stay on Lucho's father's ranch in the middle of nowhere. Four-day/three-night trips are S400 per person including food. Accommodations are rustic and trips can involve camping.

On a less-physically demanding note, the same company arranges Spanish and Quechua lessons, including meals and accommodations with a local family (if you wish), from about S400 to S600 per week. Lessons can be modified to fit your interests. You can also learn to cook local dishes, engage in the local handicraft of gourd carving or discover how to play Andean panpipes.

Torre Torre HIKING

The eroded geological formations known as Torre Torre (*torre* means 'tower' and some of the outcrops here are thus shaped) lie 2km further up in the hills beyond Cerro de la Libertad. There is a sign and a fairly obvious path. To make a longer route, continue along the ridge keeping Huancayo to your left (west). You'll eventually come to another

Huancayo

rock formation, known as Corona del Fraile (crown of the monk, or monk's head), a round-topped rock surrounded by a crown of eucalyptus trees, below which are several waterfalls. You can return to Huancayo from this end of the ridge. While safe enough during daylight hours, look out for packs of stray dogs, particularly in the houses below Torre Torre.

✨ Festivals & Events

There are hundreds of fiestas in Huancayo and surrounding villages – supposedly almost every day somewhere in the Río Mantaro valley. Ask at the tourist office.

Año Nuevo   TRADITIONAL DANCE
(January 1–6) New Year festivities in Huancayo are some of Peru's most unusual. Dances

performed include the *huaconada,* in which revelers dress up to look like quirky old men with big noses, representing village elders who, in times past, would drop by the houses of lazy or mischief-making villagers and whip them into behaving for the coming year. Plenty of butt-whipping takes place Mito, an hour north of Huancayo, also has vivid celebrations.

Semana Santa   RELIGIOUS
(Holy Week) One of the biggest events in Huancayo, with big religious processions attracting people from all over Peru at Easter.

Fiestas Patrias   FESTIVAL
(July 28 & 29) Peru's Independence Days are celebrated by processions by the military

nd schools. Hotels fill up and raise their ·rices during these times.

🛏 Sleeping

TOP CHOICE **Casa de la Abuela** HOSTEL $

(☑23-4383; www.incasdelperu.com; cnr Cuzco . José Galvez; dm/s/d with shared bathroom incl reakfast S30/40/70; @🛜) Now in a differ-nt location a 20-minute walk from cen-ral Huancayo, La Casa de la Abuela is run y Incas del Peru and makes every effort o welcome tired travelers. This brightly ·ainted house is clean and friendly, with nviting chill-out areas, kitchen facilities, ·ing-pong, cable TV and DVD. It's popular vith backpackers, who can chose from ame-·able dorms or compact rooms with shared ·athrooms. Camping space in the garden is ·15 per person. Rates include continental ·reakfast with homemade bread and jam nd real, freshly brewed coffee. Good tourist nformation is available too. It's worth being urther from the center to be here.

·eru Andino GUESTHOUSE $

(☑22-3956; www.peruandino.com; Psje San Anto-io 113; s with/without bathroom S40/35, d with/ vithout bathroom S90/80, all incl breakfast) A ·ackpacker favorite, this quiet, secure resi-dential house is near Parque Túpac Amaru ·· few blocks northeast of the map. You ·ouldn't be in better hands than those of he couple running the place and there is ·· self-catering kitchen, laundry facilities, ·ot showers, some tour information and ·ree bus/train station pick-up with advance ·otice.

·lotel los Balcones HOTEL $

(☑21-1041; Puno 282; s/d/tr S45/55/75; @🛜) Sporting plenty of namesake hard-to-miss, ·alconies, this is an attractive, modern, airy and spacious new-style hotel. Tastefully fur-nished rooms come with cable TV, phone, alarm clock and reading lights: there's com-plimentary internet access and a busy in-house restaurant too. Look no further for reasonably priced city-center comfort.

Hotel Sauna Blub HOTEL $$

(☑22-1692; www.hotelblubperu.com; Psje Verand 187; s/d incl breakfast S110/130; 🛜) A little west of the center overlooking the river (or its bone-dry bed), the tucked-away Blub has well-appointed, inviting rooms with ca-ble TV, telephones, minifridges and, as the name implies, a sauna.

Hostal El Marquez HOTEL $$

(☑21-9026; www.elmarquezhuancayo.com; Puno 294; s/d/ste incl breakfast S150/190/220; @🛜) This comfortable hotel is better than most, though is somewhat lacking in character and certainly not worth what you pay. Re-cently done-up, carpeted rooms get the usual direct-dial phones and cable TV, while three suites feature a large bathroom with Jacuzzi tub, king-sized bed and minibar. A small cafe offers room service, and continen-tal breakfast is included.

Hotel Turismo HOTEL $$

(☑23-1072; www.hoteles-del-centro.com; Ancash 729; s/d S195/215; 🛜) This pleasant-looking old building has wooden balconies, public areas with a certain faded grandeur and good views of the shoe-shines at work out-side the Centro Civico. Rooms vary in size and quality but all have bathrooms. The hotel has a restaurant and bar and is part of the same organization as the Hotel Presi-dente, meaning both are identically priced. Given that, our preference is for this one (more character).

Casa de la Abuela VIP GUESTHOUSE $$

(☑23-4383; Huancas 381; www.incasdelperu.com; s/d S80/120; 🛜) Incas del Peru's latest venture is a step up from backpacker accommoda-tions with private bathrooms and even a suite (S150) alongside a delicious breakfast that includes real coffee.

Susan's Hotel HOTEL $$

(☑20-2251; www.susanshotel.com; Real 851; s/d S70/90; 🛜) This spotless, cheerful hotel has rooms with good-sized bathrooms, cable TV, writing desks and firm mattresses. However, Susan's follows the pattern of Huancayo hotels that attain reasonable standards, then develop a somewhat condescending at-titude. Rooms are dark and overpriced for what they are; get one at the rear for peace and quiet. The 5th-floor restaurant has cracking views.

Hotel Olímpico HOTEL $

(☑21-4555; Ancash 408; s/d S70/80; 🛜) If you insist on *actual* plaza views this is the best of the somewhat ailing trio on the south side of Plaza de la Constitución. Guests re-port the service as decent overall, and it's not much of a hike to the restaurant of the same name underneath. There is cable TV in all the ample, but often gloomy, rooms.

Hotel Villa Rica
HOTEL $

(☏21-7040; Real 1291; s/d S13/22) Conveniently located for the bus stations at the south end of Real, this is a secure hotel (no way anyone's getting through the grills on those doors) and the best of the budget bunch in the vicinity. There is hot water in the evenings and rooms are clean.

Hotel Santa Felicita
HOTEL $

(☏23-5476; irmaleguia@hotmail.com; Giráldez 145; s/d S50/70; @) Large rooms at this attentive hotel get plaza views, sizable hot showers, cable TV and phone.

Hotel Confort
HOTEL $

(☏23-3601; Ancash 237; s/d S30/40) Don't get alarmed by the name – these are about the cheapest half-decent accommodations in the city center. And the Confort has been around a long time. Experience counts, right?

Hotel Presidente
HOTEL $$

(☏23-5419, 23-1736; www.hoteles-del-centro.com; Real 1138; s/d incl breakfast S195/215; @🛜) This good modern hotel includes breakfast in the price, and has ample, nicely carpeted rooms and spacious bathrooms.

✖ Eating

Good news for snack lovers: the blocks of Real south of the Plaza abound in cake shops and snack stalls selling strips of grilled *pollo* (chicken) and *lomo* (beef), often in kebab format. Huancayo has some fabulous restaurants: regional specialties include *papas a la huancaína* (boiled potato in a creamy sauce of cheese, oil, hot pepper, lemon and egg yolk, served with boiled egg and olives). The city is also known for its trout, reared in nearby lakes.

Try **Supermercado Día** (Giráldez) for self-catering.

TOP CHOICE Café Coqui
BAKERY $

(Puno 298; snacks from S3; ☉7am-10.30pm) This modern bakery–coffee shop is a contender for the best breakfast stop in the Central Andes, serving tasty sandwiches, pastries, empanadas, real espresso and other coffees. It's lively from morning until evening and now even does a line in pizzas and other more substantial fare. There's live music sometimes from the upstairs balcony.

TOP CHOICE Huancahuasi
PERUVIAN $$

(☏24-4826; Mariscal Castilla 222; mains S16.50-29.50; ☉8am-7pm Sun-Thu, to 2am Fri & Sat)

Northwest of town, Real becomes Mariscal Castilla in El Tambo district. The local eatery of choice is this classy establishment. A flower-filled courtyard and walls decorated with San Pedro de Cajas tapestries and poems set the ambience for tucking into regional goodies such as *pachamanca, papas a la huancaína* and *ceviche de trucha* (river trout ceviche). It's all well presented and the service comes with a smile. A taxi ride from the center is S3.

Sofa Café Paris
CAFE

(Puno 254; snacks from S3, meals S12; ☉4-11pm) With just the comfortable, chilled vibe you'd hope from the name, Sofa Café Paris is in a new venue: bigger, better, livelier than before and with a wrap-around mezzanine level to oversee the action below. It favors Nirvana over Andean music and is frequented by trendy young *huancaínos* (Huancayo residents). It does elaborate coffees (it has what must be Huancayo's second coffee machine) and cakes, alongside other more substantial Peruvian fare.

Detrás de la Catedral
PERUVIAN $

(Ancash 335; mains S15-22; ☉11am-11pm) This well-run, attractively presented place exudes a woody, warm feeling and has garnered plenty of regular patrons with its broad menu selection – helped by a user-friendly picture menu decoder. Enjoy filling burgers (veggie or carnie), specials such as *asado catedra* (barbecued meats done in house style) and tasty desserts such as chocolate-drenched *pionono helado* (pastry with caramel filling). Surrealist paintings grace the walls.

La Italia
ITALIAN $

(Torres 441; large pizza S26-31, pastas S18-24; ☉6-11pm Mon-Sat) One of a growing group of quality eateries around Parque Túpac Amaru, this has the best Italian food for many many miles around. It's owned by an Italian, let no more be said.

Leopardo
PERUVIAN $

(Cnr Libertad & Huánuco; mains S14-23; ☉6:30am-7:30pm) This joint is *so* Huancayo, right down to the model train in the central dining area, effortlessly combining common people's cafeteria with upscale restaurant. Go for Andean (a mondongo *especial*, a tripe, maize and vegetable broth) or coast (Tacu Tacu, a concoction of beans, rice and chili fried golden-brown and served with steak). It's so popular it opened an identical restaurant: right across the street.

hicharronería Cuzco
LATIN AMERICAN $

Cuzco 173; mains S5-10) Traditional plates of *chicharrones* (deep-fried pork chunks) at his carnivore-dedicated hole in the wall are about S7.

a Cabaña
INTERNATIONAL $

Giráldez 652; mains around S15; ⊙5-11pm) This haunt is popular with locals and travelers alike for its relaxed ambience, hearty food and tasty pisco sours. When you're suitably mellow order a scrumptious pizza or graze on trout, juicy grills and al dente pastas, among other less-filling appetizers. Live *folklórica* bands play Thursday to Saturday. Next door, El Otro Lado is open for lunch from April to October.

ntojitos
INTERNATIONAL $$

Puno 599; S15-25; ⊙5pm-late Mon-Sat) This restaurant-cum-bar, housed in an antique-filled, wood-beamed, two-story building with the obligatory Lennon and Santana posters, brings in vociferous crowds of upscale locals bent on having roaring conversations over the sounds of anything from *cumbia* (a salsalike Colombian musical style) to Pink Floyd. The well-prepared bar food consists of burgers, pizzas and grills.

Restaurant Olímpico
PERUVIAN $$

Giráldez 199; mains S16.50-28) Here for more than six decades, this is Huancayo's oldest (though modernized) restaurant. It features a large open kitchen where you can see the traditional Peruvian dishes prepared. It's classy, in a really retro way.

Chifa Centro
CHINESE $

Giráldez 245; www.chifacentro.com.pe; meals S10-20) Serves up Huancayo's tastiest Chinese food in huge portions.

Govinda
VEGETARIAN $

Cuzco 289; mains S6-10; ⊙8:30am-8:30pm Mon-Fri, 9am-5pm Sat) One of Huancayo's better vegetarian restaurants, with English spoken.

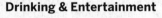

Drinking & Entertainment

There are no stand-out nightclubs: at the time of writing, the best were **Galileo Disco-Pub** (Breña 378) and flashier **Discoteca Taj Mahal** (Huancavelica 1052). Take a taxi back late at night.

Antojitos
LIVE MUSIC

(Puno 599; ⊙5pm-late Mon-Sat) Local bands perform at this bar-restaurant most nights from 9pm.

La Cabaña
TRADITIONAL MUSIC

(Giráldez 652; ⊙5-11pm) This popular eatery has live *folklórica* music and dancing on the weekends.

Peña Restaurant Turisticoa Wanka Wanka
TRADITIONAL MUSIC

(Jirón Parra del Riego 820) In El Tambo, this *peña* (bar or club featuring live folkloric music) attracts local bands such as Kjantu and has good *cumbia* and folk music. Take a taxi here (S3).

 ## Shopping

Huancayo is the central altiplano's best shopping center by a distance, whether you desire traditional markets (there are two main markets here), souvenirs or American-brand jeans.

Mercado Mayorista
MARKET

The colorful daily produce market spills out from Mercado Mayorista (which is covered) east along the railway tracks. In the meat section you can buy Andean delicacies such as fresh and dried frogs, guinea pigs and chickens, while an incredible variety of fruits and vegetables you won't be able to pronounce the names of also beckon. Don't miss trying the *tokuc* (rotten potato drink). Stallholders are friendly and let you try before you buy. Wandering through the different sections, the smells of different products rise up to hit you: it's like a sensory crash course in the ingredients of classic Peruvian dishes. It's one of Peru's most interesting city markets, without doubt. The most important day is Sunday, coinciding with Huancayo's weekly craft market.

Feria Dominical
HANDICRAFTS

(Huancavelica) This Sunday craft market occupies numerous blocks along Huancavelica to the northwest of Piura, offering weavings, textiles, embroidered items, ceramics and wood carvings. *Mates burilados* (carved gourds) and many other items from various villages in the Río Mantaro valley are sold here – handy if you don't have time to make the trek out to the villages yourself. Keep an eye on your valuables though.

Casa del Artesano
SOUVENIRS

(Plaza de la Constitución) Handy Casa del Artesano on the south corner of the plaza, has a wide range of art souvenirs for sale in a somewhat more secure environment.

ℹ Information

BCP, Interbank, Banco Continental and other banks and *casas de cambio* are on Real. Most banks open on Saturday morning and have ATMs. You'll need to walk less than a block along Real to find some of the city center's abundant internet cafes; S1.50 seems the going hourly rate and most do international phone calls.

Clínica Ortega (☎23-5430; Carrín 1124; ☺24hr) English is spoken. Southwest of the center.

Dr Luis Mendoza (☎23-9133; Real 968) For a dentist, try here.

Incas del Perú (☎22-3303; www.incasdelperu. org; Giráldez 658) A recommended source for information on just about anything in the area.

Lavandería Chic (Breña 154; ☺8am-10pm Mon-Sat, 10am-6pm Sun) Offers both self-service (S10 per load, wash and dry, soap included) and drop-off laundry (S12 per load).

Main post office (Centro Cívico)

Policía de Turismo (☎23-4714, 21-9851; Ferrocarril 580) Can help with tourist information, as well as with emergencies.

Tourist office (Casa del Artesano, Real 481; ☺10am-1:30pm & 4-7:30pm Mon-Fri) Located upstairs in the indoor crafts market with limited information.

ℹ Getting There & Away

Bus

Huancayo is slowly organizing its bus terminals, with **Terminal Los Andes** at the northern end of Av Ferrocarril handling most bus departures north to Tarma and *la selva central*. For Lima (west) and destinations in the southern valleys such as Huancavelica and Ayacucho, bus companies still have their own offices and departure points scattered around town. In this section, we do not list all companies; those listed here are either the better options or the only options.

From Terminal Los Andes, an S3 taxi ride from central Huancayo, there are departures at least hourly for Satipo (S22, six to seven hours) via Tarma (S10, two hours), San Ramón (S16, 4¼ hours) and La Merced (S16, 4½ hours). Many services continue as far as Mazamari (S25, 7½ hours). **Selva Tours** (☎21-8427) are a recommended company with hourly departures to Satipo and several to Mazamari.

For Lima, one-way ticket prices range from S30 to S60. For S45 to S60 you get a bed seat on a *bus-cama;* for S30 you get an ordinary seat. Travel time is seven hours. There are other levels of comfort in between the two. The best company for comfort is **Cruz del Sur** (☎24-5650; Ayacucho 281-287), followed by **Etucsa** (☎22-6524; Puno 220), which has somewhat more frequent departures (*bus-cama* services are 11.45pm and midnight). Check each company's buses, or at least brochures, before deciding. If you are in a hurry, **Comité 12** (Loreto 421) has speedy *colectivo* taxis to Lima (S50, five hours).

For Ayacucho (S30, eight to nine hours) the recommended service is **Expreso Molina** (☎22-4501; Angaraes 334), with morning and night departures on a mostly rough, unpaved road.

RÍO MANTARO VALLEY VILLAGES

Two main road systems link Huancayo with the villages of the Río Mantaro valley: *izquierda* (left) is the east and *derecha* (right) is the west side of the river, as you head into Huancayo from the north. It is best to confine your sightseeing on any given day to one side or the other; few bridges link the two sides.

Perhaps the most interesting excursion on the east side is a visit to the twin villages of **Cochas Grande** and **Cochas Chico**, about 11km from Huancayo. These villages are the major production centers for the incised gourds that have made the district famous. Oddly enough, the gourds are grown mainly on the coast, in the Chiclayo and Ica areas. Once transported into the highlands, they are dried and scorched, then decorated using woodworking tools. Gourd carving can be seen at various houses in the village.

On the west side, the town of **Chupaca** has an interesting livestock market. Starting early, you can visit and continue by bus to **Ahuac**, then hike a further 1km up to **Laguna Ñahuimpuquio**, which offers restaurants, boat rides and a cave to explore. From the east shore a path climbs to a ridge for great valley views and the ruins of **Arwaturo**, constructed to maximize illumination by the sun's rays.

Other villages known for their handicrafts include: **San Agustín de Cajas** (wicker furniture); **Hualhuas** (wool products, including ponchos and weavings); and **San Jerónimo de Tunán** (filigree silverwork).

While most trading is done in Huancayo, the villages are easily visited from the city. They have few facilities but there is no substitute for the experience of seeing the crafts in the villages themselves. The key is an ability to speak some Spanish and make friends with the locals.

There's also a service via the longer but safer route via Rumichaca (S40, 10 hours).

Huancavelica (S13, three to four hours) is served most frequently by **Transportes Ticllas** (954-175-420; Ferrocarril 1590) with almost hourly buses.

Los Canarios (21-5149; Puno 739) serves Tarma almost hourly (S10, three hours) and will stop at Jauja and Concepción.

Turismo Central (22-3128; Ayacucho 274) has buses north to Huánuco (S36, seven hours), Tingo María (S36, 10 hours) and Pucallpa (S51, 22 hours). It also has an office located in Terminal Los Andes.

Inexpensive minibuses (S3) and *colectivos* (S5) for Jauja (about 50 minutes) and Concepción (S2, 30 minutes) leave from around Plaza Amazonas in central Huancayo, going via many of the Río Mantaro valley handicrafts centers such as San Jerónimo de Tunán.

Taxi

Colectivo taxis for Huancavelica (S25, 2½ hours) leave when full (four-passenger minimum) from, among other places, Angares opposite the Expresso Molina bus terminal. *Colectivo* taxis for Andean destinations to the north including Tarma (S15) and La Oroya (S18) now leave from a convenient location outside Terminal Los Andes.

Train

Huancayo has two unconnected train stations in different parts of town.

A special tourist train, the **Ferrocarril Central Andino** (226-6363; www.ferrocarrilcentral.com.pe), runs fortnightly up from Lima between mid-April and October for S120/195 one-way/round-trip (S85/130 for children). There are more expensive *turístico* services that include accommodations in Huancayo. The 12-hour trip leaves Lima at 7am Friday and departs Huancayo for the return trip at the rather inconvenient time of 6pm Sunday. For this return night leg bring along warm clothes and perhaps a blanket.

It's a fabulous run, reaching 4829m and passing La Galera which clocks in as one of the world's highest passenger railway stations (the Tibetans are the record holders, followed by the Bolivians). It operates on a single-gauge track and is popular with train enthusiasts the world over. The best ways to book are either to visit the Incas del Perú website (www.incasdelperu.org), where there is an online booking form, or the train's official website. Trains leave from the Central Train Station.

The **Chilca train station** (21-6662; Prado cuadra 17 s/n) for Huancavelica is at the southern end of town and, as of 2011, the *Tren Macho* is once again running following track improvements. It leaves Huancayo at 6.30am on Monday,

MARKET DAYS AROUND HUANCAYO

Each village and town in the Río Mantaro valley has its own *feria* (market day).

Monday San Agustín de Cajas, Huayucachi.

Tuesday Hualhuas, Pucara.

Wednesday San Jerónimo de Tunán, Jauja.

Thursday El Tambo, Sapallanga.

Friday Cochas.

Saturday Matahuasi, Chupaca, Marco.

Sunday Huancayo, Jauja, Mito, Comas.

Wednesday and Friday, returning at the same time from Huancavelica on Tuesday, Thursday and Saturday. Tickets are S9/13 1st/buffet class. Buffet class is comfortable, with padded seats and guaranteed seating; 1st class has reserved seats with less padding. The real draw of this train is that it is one used by locals (as opposed to just tourists) and so has plenty of color: umpteen food vendors and even a blind violinist plays for tips. This service notoriously chops and changes: for the latest updates, contact Lucho Hurtado of Incas del Perú (p284) who is passionate (and pretty confident) about keeping the line working.

The ticket office is open from 6am until noon; the station is a fair hike from town so take a taxi.

ℹ Getting Around

Local buses to nearby villages leave from the street intersections shown on the map. Just show up and wait until a bus appears: most routes have buses every few minutes. Cochas buses (from Giráldez and Huancas) are cream-brown and come every 15 minutes. Ask other passengers if you're unsure. The tourist office is a good source of local bus information.

THE SOUTHERN VALLEYS

The roads get rougher and are often blocked by impromptu fiestas, the valleys get sheerer and lonelier and, like strange treasures in a chest with the lid only just lifted, the colonial architecture gleams in the sharp mountain light. You have arrived in the most quintessentially Andean swathe of the central highlands. The two outstanding jewels are the cities of Huancavelica and Ayacucho, both developing in magnificent opulence on the back of silver mines discovered in the nearby hills in the 16th and 17th centuries. The region has a sadder chapter to its history, too, as the stronghold of the Sendero Luminoso (Shining Path) revolutionary group that terrorized Peru in the 1980s and made this entire area off limits for travelers. Today these valleys are some of the poorest parts of Peru, but they know how to have a party like no one else: Ayacucho's Semana Santa is the country's best fiesta.

Huancavelica

📞 067 / POP 41,350 / ELEV 3690M

It's a mystery why more travelers don't visit this pretty colonial city. It's bursting with beautiful churches, charming plazas and mineral springs and lies picturesquely nestled within craggy peaks. These days, it's even easily accessible, with a good road connecting it to Huancayo 147km to the north. Still, few people make it here and therein lies another attraction: Huancavelica is a safe, serene spot to take a break from the Gringo Trail and soak up life as locals live it. This entails partying at one of the frequent fiestas, browsing the markets or, for the most part, just watching the colorful cross-section of society pass by.

Huancavelica was a strategic Inca center and shortly after the conquest the Spanish discovered its mineral wealth. By 1564 the Spaniards were sending indigenous Peruvian slaves to Huancavelica to work in the mercury and silver mines. The present town was founded in 1571 under the name of Villa Rica de Oropesa (Rich Town of the Lord), somewhat ironic given that Huancavelica is today the poorest city in Peru. Bear in mind the city suffers from frequent bone-chilling winds and icy temperatures at night.

⊙ Sights & Activities

FREE **Instituto Nacional de Cultura** MUSEUM
(INC; 📞45-3420; Raimondi 205; ⊙10am-1pm & 3-6pm Tue-Sun) The INC, in a colonial building on Plaza San Juan de Dios, has information and displays about the area; ask the helpful director if you have any questions. A small museum features Inca artifacts, fossils, displays of local costumes and paintings by Peruvian impressionist artists. You can even take a class in *folklórico* dancing here.

Laguna de Choclococha LAK
One of many lakes adorning the Rumichaca road, this body of water, 70km south of Huancavelica, can be visited by taking the Rumichaca-bound bus at 4:30am. It's about two hours to Choclococha 'town' (then a 10-minute walk); the same bus can pick you up again on its return to Huancavelica at 2pm (check with the driver). This lake at 4700m is dazzling on a sunny day when the surrounding mountains are mirrored in its waters. Birdlife at the lake includes condors. There is good hiking, fishing and lakeside restaurants.

Thermal Baths

San Cristóbal Mineral Springs BATHHOUSE
(pool/private shower S1.50/3; ⊙8am-5pm) These mineral springs are fed into two large, slightly murky swimming pools. The lukewarm water supposedly has curative properties. You can rent a towel, soap and a bathing suit if you've forgotten yours (though the selection is limited and unlovely). You can reach the springs via a steep flight of stairs – enjoy the view of the city as you climb. Baths are often closed on Thursdays for cleaning.

Saccsachaca SPRINGS
(admission S1; ⊙8am-5pm) Some 2km east of the center are these infinitely more scenic springs, accessed via the bridge at the end of Javier Heraud off Donovan. On the other side, follow the rough road that climbs above the river via the first of the two pools (Los Incas) and continue to the best, Tres Boas. Here a spread of natural pools and waterfalls tumble invitingly down the valley side above the river. Water is not hot, however, and you should bring your own swimming things.

Churches

Huancavelica churches are noted for their silver-plated altars, unlike the altars in the rest of Peru's colonial churches, which are usually gold-plated. There are several churches of note here, although they are generally closed to tourism. However, you can go as a member of the congregation when they are open for services, usually early in the morning on weekdays, with longer morning hours on Sunday. The oldest church in Huancavelica is **Iglesia de Santa Ana**, founded in the 16th century. Dating from the 17th-century are **Iglesia de San Francisco**, renowned for its 11 intricately worked altars; **Iglesia de Santo Domingo**, with famous statues of Santo Domingo and

Huancavelica

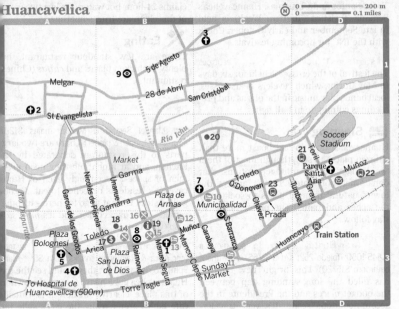

N | 0 ——— 200 m
0 ——— 0.1 miles

Huancavelica

◉ Sights

1 Cathedral B3
2 Iglesia de La Ascensión A1
3 Iglesia de San Cristóbal C1
4 Iglesia de San Francisco A3
5 Iglesia de San Sebastián A3
6 Iglesia de Santa Ana D2
7 Iglesia de Santo Domingo C2
8 Instituto Nacional de Cultura B3
9 San Cristóbal Mineral Springs B1

🛏 Sleeping

10 Gran Hostal La Portada C2
11 Hospedaje San José C3
12 Hotel Ascensión B3
13 Hotel Presidente
    Huancavelica B3

🍴 Eating

14 Bistro Constanza B3
15 Pollos y Parrilladas El Centro B3
16 Restaurant Joy B3

ℹ Information

17 BCP B3
18 Lavandería Sam B3
19 Tourist Office B3

ℹ Transport

20 Combi/Colectivo Terminal
    (Colectivos to Huancayo) C2
21 Expreso Lobato D2
22 Expreso Molina D2
23 Transportes Ticllas C2

La Virgen del Rosario, which were made in Italy; **Iglesia de San Sebastián**, which has been well restored; **Iglesia de San Cristóbal**; and **Iglesia de La Ascensión**.

Cathedral   CHURCH
Built in 1673, Huancavelica's most spectacular religious building has been restored and contains what some say is the best colonial altar in Peru, with ornate cedar woodwork, as well as *escuela cuzqueña* paintings.

🎊 Festivals & Events

Huancavelica's vibrant fiestas are renowned and, due to the mostly indigenous population, feel particularly authentic. Colorful traditional festivities occur on major Peruvian holidays, such as Carnaval, Semana Santa,

Todos Santos and Christmas. Huancavelica's Semana Turística (Tourism Week) is held in late September and early October. Check with the INC for upcoming festivals.

Fiesta de las Cruces
RELIGIOUS

The festival of the crosses is held for six days in May during which revelers bear crosses, local bands play music in the plazas and proceedings culminate in bull fights.

🛏 Sleeping

Huancavelica does in fact boast more than a dozen places to stay, though most of them are budget to superbudget options that don't offer hot water. There's always the town's natural mineral baths to soak away the aches and pains. The better places to stay follow.

TOP CHOICE Gran Hostal La Portada
GUESTHOUSE $

(☑45-1050; Toledo 252; s/d S40/65, s/d without bathroom S15/20) This bright new offering has filled the long-standing gap between the budget places and the Presidente in the accommodations scene. It's very traveler-friendly: cozy (and spotless) rooms are done up in welcoming orange, have cable TV and hot water and center on a quiet courtyard.

Hotel Presidente Huancavelica
HOTEL $$

(☑/fax 45-2760; Plaza de Armas; s/d inc breakfast S195/215, backpacker rooms s/d S50/70; 🕾) Presentable old Hotel Presidente Huancavelica is, truth be told, a bit pricey for what you actually get, although the location couldn't be better. Rooms are plain but do benefit from guaranteed hot showers, telephone, cable TV and a laundry service – not to forget a handy restaurant. It's also shown their powers of adaptability by offering some of its rooms out to backpackers at discounted prices. These are clean, decent lodgings, but breakfast isn't included.

Hospedaje San José
GUESTHOUSE $

(☑45-1014; Huancayo s/n; s/d S35/45, without bathroom S15/30) At the southern end of Baranca by the market, a cluttered entrance leads up to surprisingly large rooms with comfortable beds and hot water. Many rooms get good views over town.

Hotel Ascensión
HOTEL $

(☑45-3103; Manco Cápac 481; s/d S35/50) On the Plaza de Armas, this hotel has larger but considerably darker and mustier rooms than its posher neighbor the Presidente. It

claims 24-hour hot water: the last two words of this claim are true, sometimes.

🍴 Eating

There are few standout restaurant, but plenty of chicken places and *chifas* (Chinese restaurants).

TOP CHOICE Pollos y Parrilladas
El Centro
PARRILLA

(cnr Manuel Segura & Muñoz; mains S12-17; ⊗breakfast, lunch & dinner) There are two large parts to this restaurant separated by the kitchen, and at lunchtime they need every inch of space as seemingly each of Huancavelica's residents descends to eat. A good grilled steak is what to go for here – it comes served on its own cooker and it's *muy sabroso* (very tasty).

Bistro Constanza
BISTRO $

(cnr Arica & Raimondi; snacks from S5; ⊗8am-9pm) No one thought they would see the day Huancavelica got a bistro (except the owners of this place, clearly) but here it is. Outside cafe tables aren't really the city's style but who knows: Plaza San Juan de Dios could become the next St Mark's Sq. Stranger things have happened, and the sandwiches are good, as well as the pisco sours.

Restaurant Joy
PERUVIAN $

(Toledo 230; mains S10-15; ⊗9am-2pm & 5-10pm) Been around ages, this place: they must be doing something right, and it's unlikely to be the Beetles paraphernalia alone. Good grilled trout.

🛍 Shopping

There are small daily markets, but Sunday is market day, and the best day to see locals in traditional dress. The main market snakes up Barranca then continues along Torre Tagle behind the cathedral. Handicrafts are sold almost every day on the north side of the Plaza de Armas and also by the Municipalidad. Colorful wool leggings are especially popular.

ℹ Information

More than a dozen central places provide internet access.

BCP (Toledo 384) Has a Visa ATM and changes money.

Cielo Azul (www.turismocieloazul.com) Run by the tourist office; offers tours to surrounding sites including the mines for a reasonable S20.

Hospital de Huancavelica (☎45-3369; Av Andrés Cáceres)

Lavandería Sam (Toledo 346) A reasonably modern place to get your gear washed.

Main post office (Pasaje Ferrua 105) Near Iglesia de Santa Ana.

Tourist office (☎98-004-2093; Manuel Segura 140; ☺9am-1pm & 2-7pm Mon) Provides good directions (in Spanish) for local hikes such as the 6km hike to the ghostly deserted mine of Santa Barbara, as well as transport information.

❶ Getting There & Away

Huancavelica now sports a paved road connecting it to Huancayo (the easiest means of approach). This is a beautiful route that ascends on mountain contours then loops down to a narrow river valley and Izcuchaca before opening out again into lush alpine meadowland with thatched-roof settlements (some prettily painted) and wandering herds of llamas. You can also reach Huancavelica directly from Pisco via a 4850m pass and from Ayacucho via Rumichaca. Buses ply all these routes but are of the ponderous local variety – filled with locals and their goods.

The most interesting way to Huancavelica, however, is by train from Huancayo (albeit slightly slower than the buses and taking a route along the valley bottom).

If you are in a hurry, from Huancayo it's a good idea to take a *colectivo* taxi: these take 2½ hours via the scenic alpine route.

Bus

All major buses usually depart from the *terminal terrestre,* inconveniently located about 2km to the west of the town center. A taxi here costs S3. Buy your bus tickets in the downtown offices, and ask about where the buses depart from.

Companies serving Huancayo (S13, three hours) include **Transportes Ticllas** (☎95-417-5420; Muñoz 7) with almost hourly daily departures. Other companies go less often or at night, or may go via Huancayo en route to Lima.

For Lima (S30 to S40, 10 to 13 hours) companies go via Huancayo or via Pisco. The higher price tag is for more luxurious *bus-camas.* Via Huancayo is usually a little faster but it depends on road conditions. The Pisco route is freezing at night: bring warm clothes. Several companies clustering around Parque Santa Ana offer Lima services including **Expreso Lobato** (O'Donovan 519), which has comfortable overnight buses via Huancayo.

For Ayacucho, buses now run via Rumichaca nightly (S40, seven to eight hours). **Expreso Molina** (☎45-4244; Muñoz 608) leaves at 11:30pm. If you really don't want to travel at night, the 'easiest' option is taking a 4:30am (!) minibus to Rumichaca. In the west of Huancavelica from Plaza Tupac Amaru, **San Juan Bautista** minibuses depart daily (S10, six hours). Then wait for an Ayacucho-bound bus coming from the coast. Most days buses from Lima don't get to Rumichaca until about 2pm so you might want to try your hitchhiking skills rather than waiting for several hours in this rather bleak spot. Ensure, however, that there are at least two of you, and remember that hitchhiking can always be risky. You can also (laboriously) get to Ayacucho via minibus, changing at Lircay and Julcamarca.

Taxi

Colectivo taxis for Huancayo (S25, 2½ hours) leave when full (four-passenger minimum). They leave from the combi/*colectivo* terminal on Garma by the river.

Train

Trains currently leave for Huancayo at 6:30am on Tuesday, Thursday and Saturday. See p285 for more details.

Ayacucho

☎066 / POP 151,000 / ELEV 2750M

The name of this mesmerizing colonial city, originating from the Quechua *aya* (death, or soul) and *cuchu* (outback), offers a telling insight into its past. Ayacucho's status as isolated capital of a traditionally poor department provided the perfect breeding ground for Professor Abimael Guzmán to nurture the Sendero Luminoso (Shining Path) Maoist revolutionary movement bent on overthrowing the government and causing thousands of deaths in the region during the 1980s and '90s (for more on this history, see the boxed text, p292). Yet the city's historically poor links with the outside world have also helped foster a fiercely proud, independent spirit evident in everything from the unique festivals to the booming cultural self-sufficiency.

The shadow of Ayacucho's dark past has long been lifted but travelers are only just rediscovering its treasures. Richly decorated churches dominate the vivid cityscape alongside peach- and pastel-colored colonial buildings hung with wooden balconies. Among numerous city festivities, Ayacucho boasts Peru's premier Semana Santa celebrations, while in the surrounding mountains lie some of the country's most significant archaeological attractions.

Perhaps Ayacucho's greatest allure is the authenticity with which it pulls off its

Ayacucho

0 — 200 m
0 — 0.1 miles

To Museo de
la Memoria (500m)

To Clínica de la Esperanza (1km);
Museo Arqueológico
Hipólito Unanue (1km);
Terminal Terrestre (3.5km)

Quinua

33

Psje Próceres

25

42

41

46

Manco Cápac

Calle de la Vega

Libertad

9 de Diciembre

Asamblea Independencia

43

Los Andes

To Buses to
Wari Ruins &
Quinua (200m)

40

Cáceres

30

31

12

Río Totora

32
26 6
27

Bellido

38 36

29 15

18

21

Callao

44

Portal
Unión

45

34

Iglesia de
San Agustín

28

Cuzco

14

F Pizarro

9

24

Iglesia de
San Francisco
de Paula

Plaza
de Armas

22

37

Lima

11 23

20 39

Portal
Constitución

Museo
de Arte
Popular

Cathedral
Portal Municipal

Arequipa

19

Sol

Iglesia de La Compañía

Portal
Independencia

Tres Máscaras

1

San Martín

2

16

F Pizarro

35

8

17

Nazareno

Mercado

4

Grau

28 de Julio

3

M Castilla

To Terminal
Terrestre Zona Sur
(2km); Airport (4km)

Vivanco

Londres

2 de Mayo

Underground River

Iglesia de
San Juan
de Dios

Itana

Chorro

7

San Blas

Río Alameda

Bolognesi

5 10

BARRIO SANTA
ANA

13

291

Ayacucho

CENTRAL HIGHLANDS AYACUCHO

Ayacucho

charms. Its development has been tasteful, its commercialization blissfully limited and, if you take to the pedestrianized, cobbled city central streets early enough, it is easy to imagine yourself transported back several centuries to its colonial heyday. That said, these days designer-clad students and businesspeople are increasingly in evidence and behind many colonial facades are plenty of sumptuous accommodations and suave restaurants. What is clear is that Peru's most enticing Andean city after Cuzco is experiencing a resurgence – one that is well worth witnessing.

History

Some of Peru's first signs of human habitation were allegedly discovered in the Pikimachay caves, near Ayacucho (today there is nothing of interest to be seen there).

Five hundred years before the rise of the Incas, the Wari dominated the Peruvian highlands and established their capital 22km northeast of Ayacucho (see the boxed text, p296). The city's original name was San Juan de la Frontera de Huamanga (locals still call it Huamanga) and it grew rapidly after its founding in 1540 as the Spanish sought to defend it against attack from Manco Inca. Ayacucho played a major part in the battles for Peruvian independence, commemorated by an impressive nearby monument (see the boxed text, p298).

Ayacucho's first paved road connection with the outside world (to Lima) came only

THE SHINING PATH: AN ONGOING CONFLICT

The Sendero Luminoso's (Shining Path's) activities in the 1980s focused on deadly political, economic and social upheaval. They caused violent disruption, particularly across the Central Highlands and Amazon jungle, which were almost completely off-limits to travelers at the time (for more on Peru's Internal Conflict see p500). Things finally changed when the Sendero Luminoso's founder, Guzmán, a former Ayacucho university professor, was captured and imprisoned for life in 1992. Guzmán was followed quickly by his top lieutenants. This led to a lull in activities, as Guzmán had not had time to prepare a direct successor for the cause.

But fragmented groups of Sendero Luminoso revolutionaries carried on in far re-moter areas of Peru, albeit sporadically and with vastly reduced numbers. These groups largely split from the original Maoist philosophy of Guzmán, and in recent years their most notable activity has been drug trafficking (the US State Department confirms the group's links with the drugs trade).

The last major clash in the Ayacucho region was in April 2009, when Shining Path rebels killed 13 army officers. A high-profile incident in August 2011 saw tourists on a high-end tour to Choquequirao, a major Inca site in the Cuzco region, politely asked to hand over valuables to help the cause of the revolution.

This sparked media reports of a Sendero Luminoso re-emergence, which proved to be an exaggeration, particularly when its last remaining high-profile leader, Florindo Flores Hala (aka 'Artemio') was captured in February 2012. But, perhaps to make a statement of their continued relevance, the Sendero Luminoso pulled off their most drastic action in over a decade in April 2012 when they captured and held hostage 40 workers in a remote trans-Andean gas pipeline. No one was hurt and the hostages were released after several days.

Today the number of remaining Sendero Luminoso members is, according to the *Wall Street Journal*, only around 500. Activity is mostly in remote Amazon valleys such as the Upper Huallaga valley north of Tingo María which, not by coincidence, contain significant cocaine production areas and which are not safe for tourists to visit. Outside such areas, the threat to tourists remains minor, and all of the listings in this chapter can be visited as safely as anywhere else in Peru. The overwhelming majority of Peruvians, it should be emphasized, have no allegiance to any faction of the Sendero Luminoso, or to the military searching for the remainder of them.

in 1999, which conveys how isolated the city previously was. But it's turned to face the 21st century and, following Guzmán's capture in 1992, is again a safe place to visit. The populace doesn't discuss the dark days of the 1980s much and welcomes travelers with good cheer.

◉ Sights

Sights in Ayacucho consist primarily of churches and museums. While the listed museums have posted (frequently altering) opening times, churches are a law unto themselves. Some list their visiting times on the doors; with others you will have to take potluck. During Semana Santa churches are open for most of the day; at other times ask at the tourist office, which publishes the guide *Circuito religioso* with information on opening hours. Joining the congregation for mass (usually 6am to 8am Monday to Saturday) is an interesting way of seeing inside the churches.

The **Plaza de Armas** (also known as Plaza Mayor de Huamanga) is one of Peru's most beautiful plazas and should be a starting point for city explorations. The four sides of the plaza, clockwise from the east are Portal Municipal, Portal Independencia, Portal Constitución and Portal Unión. Around here are many gorgeous colonial mansions, including the offices of the department of Ayacucho (the **Prefectura**). Ask at the tourist office for details on how to visit these buildings, which are often open during office hours.

Cathedral   CHURCH
(Portal Municipal) This spectacular 17th-century cathedral on the Plaza de Armas has a religious-art museum. The moody facade doesn't quite prepare you for the intricacy

the interior, with its elaborate gold-leaf altar being one of the best examples of the Baroque-Churrigueresque style (in which cornices and other intricate, Spanish-influenced workmanship mingled with Andean influences, often evinced by the wildlife depicted). Several other churches in Ayacucho also exhibit Churrigueresque design. See the boxed text (p294) for more on Ayacucho's other churches.

Museo de la Memoria
MUSEUM

(Prolongación Libertad 1229; admission S2; ☺9am-1pm & 3-5pm) In an unlikely location 1.5km northwest of the center is Ayacucho's most haunting museum, remembering the impact the Sendero Luminoso had on Peru in the city that was most deeply affected by the conflict. Its simple displays (in Spanish) are nonetheless moving: there are eyewitness accounts of the horrors that went on and a particularly poignant montage of photos of mothers who had children killed in the fighting.

Museo de Arte Popular
MUSEUM

(Portal Independencia 72; admission free; ☺8am-1pm & 1.30-3.15pm Mon-Fri) The popular art here covers the *ayacucheño* (natives of Ayacucho) spectrum – silverwork, rug- and tapestry-weaving, stone and woodcarvings, ceramics (model churches are especially popular) and the famous **retablos** (ornamental religious dioramas). These are colorful wooden boxes varying in size and containing intricate papier-mâché models: Peruvian rural scenes or the nativity are favourites, but interesting ones with political or social commentary can be seen here. Photographs show how Ayacucho changed during the 20th century. Opening hours here change frequently.

Museo Andrés Avelino Cáceres
MUSEUM

(Jirón 28 de Julio 508-512; admission S4; ☺8am-noon or 9am-1pm & 3-5pm Mon-Fri, 9am-1pm Sat) Housed in the Casona Vivanco, a gorgeous 16th-century mansion. Cáceres was a local man who commanded Peruvian troops during the War of the Pacific (1879–83) against Chile. Accordingly, the museum houses maps and military paraphernalia from that period, as well as colonial art: check the painting of the Last Supper – with *cuy*!

Museo Arqueológico Hipólito Unanue
MUSEUM

(admission S4; ☺9am-1pm & 3-5pm Tue-Sun) In the Centro Cultural Simón Bolívar at the university, located more than 1km north from the city center along Independencia – you can't miss it. Wari ceramics make up most of the small exhibition, along with relics from the region's other various civilizations. While there, visit the university library for a free exhibition of mummies, skulls and other niceties. The buildings are set in a botanical garden. The best time to visit the museum is in the morning: afternoon hours sometimes aren't adhered to.

Mirador de Carmen Alto
VIEWPOINT

This *mirador* offers fabulous views of Ayacucho, as well as decent restaurants. Taxis here charge S5, otherwise catch a bus from the Mercado Central or walk (one hour).

Centro Turístico Cultural San Cristóbal
SQUARE

(Jirón 28 de Julio 178) This is a remodeled colonial building with the courtyard transformed into a hip little mall. Here you'll find bars, restaurants and coffee shops, along with art galleries, craft stores and flower stands. A nice place to hang during the day.

Plaza Moré
SQUARE

(Jirón 28 de Julio 262) Similar to Centro Turístico Cultural San Cristóbal, only better in terms of quality and quantity for restaurants and shops.

Courses

Via Via
COOKING COURSE

(☎31-2834; www.viaviacafe.com; Portal Constitución 4) Runs Quechua courses (S30 per two hours) and cooking courses geared towards Ayacucho specialties (S50 per four hours) Fees are per lesson for private tuition, and significantly less for groups.

Tours

Several agencies arrange local tours; most cater to Peruvian tourists and guides mainly speak Spanish. Ask about tours in other languages.

Wari Tours
ADVENTURE TOUR

(☎31-1415; Lima 138) Experience-rich multilingual tours to regional destinations. Half-day tours cost around S40.

Festivals & Events

The tourist office here is a good source of information about the many minor fiestas held throughout the department.

AYACUCHO'S CHURCHES

Ayacucho, the 'Ciudad de las Iglesias' (City of Churches) boasts more than 30 churches and temples. In the likely event that you don't have time to visit each one, here is a crash course in the most significant.

Templo de San Cristóbal (Jirón 28 de Julio, cuadra 6) The oldest city church, dating from 1540.

Iglesia de Santa Clara (Grau at Nazareno) Attracts thousands of pilgrims annually for the image of Jesus of Nazareth supposedly inside.

Iglesia de Santo Domingo (Jirón 9 de Diciembre at Bellido) One of the most photogenic churches, dating from 1548. Allegedly built with the stone of a former Inca fortress, it contains some superb examples of Churrigueresque-style painting.

Iglesia de La Merced (Jirón 2 de Mayo at San Martín) Dating from 1550, full of colonial art and with one of Peru's oldest convents (1540) attached.

Iglesia de Santa Teresa (Jirón 28 de Julio) Gorgeous church-cum-monastery with an altar studded in seashells.

Iglesia de San Francisco de Asis (Jirón 28 de Julio) Visually striking stone church containing *retablos* (ornamental religious dioramas) and an attractive 17th-century adjoining convent. It's opposite the market.

Semana Santa   RELIGIOUS
Held the week before Easter, this is Peru's finest religious festival and attracts visitors from all over the country. Rooms in most hotels fill well in advances so book well ahead. The tourist office has lists of local families who provide accommodations for the overflow.

Each year, iPerú prints a free brochure describing the Semana Santa events with street maps showing the main processions. Celebrations begin on the Friday before Palm Sunday and continue for 10 days until Easter Sunday. The Friday before Palm Sunday is marked by a procession in honor of La Virgen de los Dolores (Our Lady of Sorrows), during which it is customary to inflict 'sorrows' on bystanders by firing pebbles out of slingshots. Gringos have been recent targets, so be warned.

Each succeeding day sees solemn yet colorful processions and religious rites, which reach a fever pitch of Catholic tradition. They culminate on the Saturday before Easter Sunday with a huge all-night party including dawn fireworks to celebrate the resurrection of Christ. If you want to party too, stay on your guard, as proceedings are notoriously wild. Crime in the city escalates dramatically during festivities: robbery and rape are not unheard of.

In addition to the religious services, Ayacucho's Semana Santa celebrations include art shows, folk-dancing competitions, local music concerts, street events, sporting events (especially equestrian ones), agri cultural fairs and the loving preparation o traditional meals.

🛏 Sleeping

Ayacucho isn't short of accommodation these days, but in addition to the myria small hotels and *hospedajes* (small, fami ly-owned inns) with generally limited fa cilities, there is an ever-growing numbe of plusher (yet still reasonably priced) op tions with creature comforts such as round the-clock hot water. During Semana Sant prices rise markedly – by 25% to even 75%

TOP CHOICE **Hotel Sevilla**   HOTEL $$
(📞31-4388; www.hotelsevillaperu.com; Jirón Liber tad 635; s/d incl breakfast S60/95; 🛜) The Sevilla is new on the scene and one of the nicest brightest, best-value hotels in Ayacucho Cozy rooms get desks, minifridges and micro waves. Accommodations are set back across a courtyard from the street. Crucially, the own ers know how to take care of their guests. A restaurant is currently under construction.

TOP CHOICE **Via Via**   HOTEL $$
(📞31-2834; www.viaviacafe.com; Portal Con stitución 4; s/d/ste S90/120/130; 🛜) The most imaginative sleeping option is new-kid-on-the-block Via Via, with an enviable plaza location and cool, vibrantly decorated rooms

emed around different continents. Travelers will feel like they've landed in a veritable oasis: there is a sun-roof and hammock room and it's all centered on a plant-filled courtyard. English and Dutch are spoken.

ostal Tres Máscaras GUESTHOUSE $

(31-2921; Tres Máscaras 194; s/d S40/50, s/d without bathroom S18/30) The pleasing walled garden and friendly staff make this an enjoyable place to stay. Hot water is on in the morning and later on request. A room with TV is S5 extra. Continental/American breakfast is available for S6/7.

otel Santa Rosa HOTEL $$

(31-4614; Lima 166; www.hotel-santarosa.com; s/d incl breakfast S85/125; 🛜) Less than a block from the Plaza de Armas, this capacious hotel with its twin courtyards has spacious, airy and cosily furnished rooms. Some come with a fridge (a luxury in the Central Andes) and all have TV, DVD player and phone. The bathrooms are large and the showers have oodles of hot water. There's also a decent and well-priced on-site restaurant for meals.

ostal El Marqués de Valdelirios GUESTHOUSE $

(31-7040; Bolognesi 720; s/d S50/70) This lovely, unsignposted colonial building is about 700m from the center. While it is in a quiet location, the walk back at night involves passing through some dark neighborhoods. There is a grassy garden where food can be served. Rooms vary in size and in amenities (views, balconies, telephone) but all have beautiful furniture, cable TV and hot showers.

lotel Sierra Dorada HOTEL $$

(31-9639; www.sierradorada.com.pe; Parque del Colegio de Ingenieros; s/d incl breakfast S90/140; 🛜) Business-oriented hotel in a bright yellow building situated in a quiet residential area 2km north of the plaza. Rooms won't blow your mind but they're *muy comodo* (very comfortable).

ostal Florida GUESTHOUSE $

(31-2565; fax 31-6029; Cuzco 310; s/d S35/50) This traveler-friendly *hostal* (guesthouse) has a relaxing courtyard garden and clean rooms (those on the upper level are better) with bathrooms and TV, hot water in the morning and later on request. There is a basic cafeteria too.

Hotel San Francisco de Paula HOTEL $$

(31-2353; www.hotelsanfranciscodepaula.com; Callao 290; s/d incl breakfast S70/90; 🛜) This rather rambling, oldish hotel isn't flash, but it is presentable, with public areas decorated with bizarre indigenous art. It has a restaurant and bar and decent-sized, tiled rooms get the usual midrange facilities. Outside doubles are better as the inside singles can be very poky.

Hotel La Crillonesa HOTEL $

(31-2350; Nazareno 165; s/d S30/40) A popular and helpful hotel, it offers a rooftop terrace with photogenic views, a TV room, tour information and 24-hour hot water. Its rather small, clean rooms have comfy beds and generally functioning cable TV. The best rooms are right at the top.

La Colmena Hotel HOTEL $

(31-1318; Cuzco 140; s/d S40/60) This popular hotel is often full by early afternoon, partly because it's one of the longest-standing places in town and partly because it's only steps from the plaza. It's a great building that has spruced itself up significantly of late. It also has a locally popular restaurant and an agreeable courtyard.

Hostal Ayacuchano HOTEL $

(31-9891; Tres Máscaras 588; s/d S15/30) Amply sized, inoffensively decorated well-furnished rooms get cable TV and, in some cases, even balconies. Not all singles have private bathrooms, but the bathrooms in some of the doubles are the sanitary surprises of Ayacucho: spacious, with actual baths and hot water to boot.

Hotel Santa María HOTEL $$

(/fax 31-4988; Arequipa 320; s/d S95/125; 🛜) Of the places opened during the hotel rush of the late '90s, this one seems to have got it right. It looks impressive from the outside and, despite a slightly sterile interior, the rooms are very comfortable, quite spacious and tastefully decorated.

Hostal Marcos GUESTHOUSE $

(31-6867; Jirón 9 de Diciembre 143; s/d incl breakfast S40/80) Twelve spotless rooms in a little place somewhat sequestered away at the end of an alley, which is clearly signposted off Jirón 9 de Diciembre. Rooms offer 24-hour hot water and cable TV.

✕ Eating

Regional specialties include *puca picante,* a potato and beef stew in a spicy red peanut and pepper sauce, served over rice; *patachi,* a wheat soup with various beans, drie

THE WARI

Before the Incas ruled the roost in the Peruvian Highlands, the Wari were top dogs. Their empire extended north beyond Chiclayo and south as far Lake Titicaca, with its capital on the pampa above Ayacucho. The heyday was from AD 600 to AD 1100, during which time the Wari took control over many settlements previously occupied by the Moche people in northern Peru, had dealings with the Tiwanaku culture to the south and established a power base in Cuzco.

The Wari rose to dominance through developing a series of key administrative centers in topographically contrasting regions: Moquegua on Peru's southern coast, Piquillacta near Cuzco and Viracochapampa in the northern highlands. This maximized trade in resources including coca, cotton and corn. At its zenith, the empire enjoyed wealth then-unprecedented in Peruvian civilizations.

The capital, now a swathe of ruins 22km northeast of Ayacucho, once housed some 50,000 people and was well-organized into sectors for agriculture, workshops and a grandiose area reserved for burial of dignitaries (the Cheqowasi sector of the site shows this). The Wari certainly had grand plans. Their architectural style placed an emphasis on a display of power with public spaces, possibly for nobles to interact in, and platforms to promote rank seniority. They also excelled in producing weaving, as well as distinctive ceramics which indicate sophisticated trade interaction with neighboring cultures such as the Tiwanaku.

However, by AD 1000, for unknown reasons, the empire had entered a period of decline. It has been speculated that because defense had never been a priority, Wari buildings were vulnerable to attack. Significantly, however, the civilization left behind a legacy of roads and settlements so important that they were still in use by the Inca empire almost 500 years later.

---

potatoes and lamb or beef; and *mondongo,* a corn soup cooked with pork or beef, red peppers and fresh mint. *Chicharrones* and *cuy* are also popular. Vegetarians may accordingly be challenged to find meatless fare: *chifas* are often the best bet. Within the Centro Turístico San Cristóbal, some upbeat eats provide quality food and atmospheric, if slightly touristy, dining, while Plaza Moré further down has gone one step further and offers eateries which are positively gourmet: an indication of the changing face of Ayacucho, perhaps. After all, how many towns in the Andes can boast a *Barrio Gastronómico* (gastronomic neighborhood)?

TOP CHOICE Via Via INTERNATIONAL $$

(☑31-2834; Portal Constitución 4; mains S14-24; ☺10am-10pm Mon-Thu, to midnight Fri & Sat) With its upstairs plaza-facing balcony, Via Via has the best views (and steepest prices) with which to accompany your meal in Ayacucho. It's ethically sourced, organic food – the spicy *albondigas* (meatballs) are tempting – but this is Peruvian-European fusion cuisine, so you'll find something to sate you (like *quinnoto,* a risotto with quinoa, or *salteado de alpaca,* a lomo saltado

using alpaca meat instead of beef), and crisp South American wine (from S30) to wash it down.

TOP CHOICE Mamma Mia ITALIAN $

(Jirón 28 de Julio 262; pizzas S18-25; ☺4pm-midnight) Don't pay attention to the myriad signs offering pizza around Ayacucho these days (they're taking a leaf out of Cuzco's book) this is the only place worth coming to. The Ukrainian owner has pooled his extensive catering experience and come up with an atmospheric place where you can laze away the late afternoon with real coffee and great cakes, or come later for delicious pizza and pasta. Round off your meal with a Mamma Mia cocktail: vodka, coconut rum, peach schnapps and melon.

Café Miel CAFE $

(Portal Constitución 4; snacks from S2; ☺10am-10pm) Breakfast is the best time to visit this reader-recommended place with its chirpy atmosphere and checkered tablecloths – we're talking great fruit salads and some of Ayacucho's best (freshly brewed) coffee. It serves hearty lunches and great chocolate cake too.

Niño
PARRILLA $

Jirón 9 de Diciembre 205; mains S10-20; ⊘11am-
⊙m & 5-11pm) In a colonial mansion with a
sheltered patio containing tables overlook-
ng a garden, El Niño specializes in grills
et dishes up a variety of Peruvian food. The
ndividual *parrillada* is good, although in
ractice sufficient for two modest eaters.
his is one of the city's best restaurants.

a Casona
PERUVIAN $

Bellido 463; mains S12-22; ⊘7am-10:30pm) This
opular, ambient courtyard restaurant has
een recommended by several travelers for
s big portions. It focuses on Peruvian food
uch as the excellent *lomo saltado* and of-
en has regional specialties. Service has im-
roved markedly since our last visit.

ecreo Las Flores
PERUVIAN $

Jirón José Olaya 106; meals S12-21.50; ⊘8am-
om) *Cuy, cuy* and more *cuy* (guinea pig):
ometimes it's refreshing to have less
hoice on the menu (giving you more time
or eating) and this is where this *recreo*
country-style restaurant) comes in. Inside
: resembles a vast communist-style cafete-
ia but over by the windows that feeling is
ess apparent. This and several other places
earby form 'Barrio Gastronómico' in Con-
hapata district south of center.

reamz
ICE CREAM $

Psje Proceres 114; ice cream S8; ⊘10am-9pm) Fla-
ors at this ice-cream parlor include Belgian
hocolate, *chicha morada* (an iconically
eruvian, sweet, unfermented, purple corn
rink) and Baileys: there's real machine-
ade coffee too.

estaurant Los Alamos
PERUVIAN $

Cuzco 215; mains S12-20; ⊘7am-10pm) In an at-
ractive patio within the hotel of the same
ame, this restaurant has good service, a
ong menu of Peruvian selections and a few
egetarian plates; it may have musicians in
he evening.

Vallpa Sua
FAST FOOD $

Calle de la Vega 240; mains S8-20; ⊘6-11pm Mon-
Sat) This is an upscale, locally popular and
usy chicken restaurant, with a quarter-
hicken and fries starting at S8.

Drinking & Entertainment

This is an important university city, so you'll
ind a few bar-clubs to dance or hang out in,
nostly favored by students. Ask at the tour-
st office about the latest *peña* (bar or club

featuring live folkloric music) scene: at last
report there were no stand-out choices.

Taberna Magía Negra
BAR

(Jirón 9 de Diciembre 293; ⊘4pm-midnight Mon-
Sat) It's been around longer than most and
the youth of today prefer the newer venues
but this bar-gallery has local art, beer, pizza
and great music.

The Rock
CLUB

(Cáceres 1035; ⊘to 2am Wed-Sat) The liveliest
local disco, known locally as Maxxo, where
gringos, as well as locals, go to strut their
stuff. There is another disco on the same
block playing mostly salsa.

Tupana Wasi
LIVE MUSIC

(Jirón 9 de Deciembre 206, 2nd fl; ⊘7pm-late Mon-
Sat) Good live bands, from folkloric to rock,
perform here.

🛍 Shopping

Ayacucho is a renowned handicraft center: a
visit to the Museo de Arte Popular will give
you an idea of local products. The tourist office can recommend local artisans who will
welcome you to their workshops. The Santa
Ana *barrio* (neighborhood) is particularly
well known for its crafts: there are various
workshops around Plazuela Santa Ana. A
craft market (Independencia & Quinua) is open
during the day.

Edwin Pizarro
HANDICRAFTS

(☎96-618-0666) For *retablos*, the workshop of
Edwin Pizarro's in Barrio Belén is highly recommended. He's renowned locally as one of
the best artisans in the business, and will per-
sonalize his lovingly made creations by adding figures appropriate to the customer. The
workshop is a tough 15-minute walk above
central Ayacucho (opposite Templo de Belén)
and can be hard to find: a taxi's not a bad idea.

ℹ Information

Internet cafes are on almost every block, particularly along the pedestrianized section of
Jirón 9 de Deciembre. Almost every hotel now
offers wi-fi.

BCP (Portal Unión 28) Visa ATM.

Clínica de La Esperanza (☎31-7436; Independencia 355; ⊘8am-8pm) English is spoken.

Inka Farma (Jirón 28 de Julio 250; ⊘7am-
10:30pm) Pharmacy.

Interbank (Jirón 9 de Diciembre 183)

iPerú (☎31-8305; iperuayacucho@promperu.
gob.pe; Plaza Mayor, Portal Municipal 45, Municipalidad Huamanga; ⊘9am-6pm Mon-Sat,

to 1pm Sun) One of Peru's best tourist offices. Helpful advice; English spoken.

Police (Jirón 28 de Julio 325; ☺24hr)

Lavandería Arco Iris (Bellido 322) Provides both wash-and-dry and dry-cleaning services.

Money changers (Portal Constitución) On the southwest corner of the Plaza de Armas.

Policía de Turismo (☎31-7846; Jirón 2 de Mayo 100; ☺7:30am-8pm)

Post office (Asamblea 293; ☺8am-8pm Mon-Sat) It's 150m from the Plaza de Armas.

ⓘ Getting There & Around

Air

The airport is 4km from the town center. Taxis charge about S10. Flight times and airlines can change without warning, so check airline websites for latest schedules. Daily flights to Lima are with **Star Perú** (☎31-3660; Jirón 9 de Diciembre 127) at 6:50am and with **LC Peru** (☎31-6012; Jirón 9 de Diciembre 160) at 5pm.

Bus

Most buses (to long-distance north- and south-bound destinations) arrive and depart from the snazzy new *terminal terrestre* to the north of the city center, although you can still buy tickets at the downtown offices (it's best to ask when buying your ticket where your bus departs from). A taxi here costs S8. *Terminal terrestre zona sur* handles departures to regional destinations south of Ayacucho.

Transport connections with Lima are via the relatively fast and spectacular Hwy 24 that traverses the Andes via Rumichaca to Pisco. Night departures outnumber day departures, but day trips are naturally more interesting for the wild scenery en route. Choose your bus and company carefully. Ticket prices to/from Lima range from S30 for a regular seat to S60 for a reclining armchair that you can sleep in. The trip takes around nine hours. Take warm clothing if traveling by night. For the below, departures are all from the *terminal terrestre* unless otherwise stated.

For Lima, **Expreso Molina** (☎31-9989; Jirón 9 de Diciembre 459-73) is a good option. There are two daily departures and no less than seven night departures with the 'special' *cama* service being best for comfort. **Expreso Internacional Palomino** (☎31-3899; Manco Cápac 255) also offers an evening *cama* service. Another reliable cheap option is **Turismo Libertadores** (☎31-3614; Manco Cápac 295).

There is an exception to every rule, of course, and **Cruz del Sur** (☎31-2813; Cáceres 1264), the fanciest Lima service of all, leaves from its own terminal. It charges its own brand of prices too:

AROUND AYACUCHO

Ayacucho has several interesting excursions in the vicinity: running the gamut of regional history from the pre-Inca to Peruvian independence. See p298 for information on how to reach the below destinations. You can reach them via day tours with agencies in Ayacucho for about S60 per person.

The extensive **Wari Ruins** (admission incl small museum S3; ☺8am-5:30pm), 20km above Ayacucho on the road to Quinua, are some of the most significant surviving remains of the Wari culture (see boxed text, p296), scattered among fields of bizarre opuntia cacti: a moody spot to contemplate this once powerful civilization. Information is in Spanish only. Don't leave the site too late to look for return transport – vehicles get hopelessly full in the afternoon.

A further 17km beyond the Wari ruins is the pretty village of **Quinua**, with a **museum** (admission S5) with erratic hours displaying various relics from the major independence battle fought in this area. Beside the museum is the room where the Spanish royalist troops signed their surrender, leading to the end of colonialism in Peru. The 40m-high white **obelisk** (admission S1), intermittently visible for several kilometers as you approach Quinua, is 15 minutes' walk above town via Jirón Sucre and commemorates the Battle of Ayacucho, the decisive conflict in the war of Peruvian independence. From here, you can elect to go **horse-riding** on rather scrawny-looking steeds to waterfalls where swimming is possible. The whole area is protected as the 300-hectare **Santuario Histórico Pampas de Ayacucho**.

The ruins of **Vilcashuamán**, a former Inca stronghold (considered the geographical center of the Inca empire), lie some 115km south of Ayacucho. Little remains of the city's early magnificence but an intact five-tier pyramid called an *usnu* survives, topped by a huge stone-carved double throne. From the Vilcashuamán turn-off it's only 2km to **Vischongo**, where you can base yourself overnight (basic accommodations). You can also take a 1½-hour hike to a **Puya raimondii forest** (see p526).

57 above or S97 below for semireclining/fully-
clining seats.

Traveling south or north to other Andean
wns presents challenges. Many roads are
npaved and subject to washouts in the rainy
eason. Destinations in this category include
ndahuaylas, Abancay and Cuzco to the south-
ast and Huancayo to the north. Be prepared
r delays. That said, the road to Andahuaylas/
bancay/Cuzco is now fast-improving and paved
parts. For Cuzco (S65, 14 to 16 hours) and
ndahuaylas (S35, six to seven hours), seek out
xpreso Turismo Los Chankas (Manco Cápac
50), which has four departures daily. It's a long,
ugh trip: the journey can be broken at Anda-
uaylas. Departures are from the city center
ffice. Be advised that robberies occasionally
ccur on the night bus: traveling during the day
recommended.

For Huancayo (S30 to S40, nine to 12 hours),
xpreso Molina is again the preferred choice, with
ne daily and five night departures. The more
xpensive (and longer) services are for the safer
ute via Rumichaca. Take note: the cheaper serv-
e, which includes the one daytime departure, is
tough (albeit spectacular) 250km trip and not
r the faint-hearted. Around 200 of those kilom-
ters take you along a narrow, potholed, unpaved
ad between Huanta and Mariscal Cáceres
rough the wild Río Mantaro valley. The road
uns at times high along unguarded cliff faces
ith nothing but space between your bus window
nd the foaming river below. Sit on the right side
f the bus if you don't like vertiginous drops.

Change in Huancayo for onward services to
uánuco, Tingo María, Pucallpa and Satipo.

For Huancavelica, Expreso Molina has nightly
epartures. For daytime travel, you'll need
o take a minibus to Julcamarca, from where
urther minibuses can be found to Lircay and
hen Huancavelica. This will be a colorful but
ramped and uncomfortable trip.

The new *terminal terrestre zona sur* has at
east brought order to regional south-bound de-
artures. Buses to Vischongo (S10, four hours)
eave from here. Departures are normally in the
norning. There are also buses to Vilcashuamán
S14, five hours) about hourly from 5am to 9am.
taxi to the terminal costs S4.

Pickup trucks and buses go to many local
illages, including Quinua (S3, one hour), and to
he Wari ruins (also S3, 40 minutes), departing
rom the Paradero Magdalena at the traffic circle
t the east end of Cáceres.

NORTH OF TARMA

North of Tarma the highway passes through
ome of the more visually stark and tropi-
ally lush scenery in Peru in relatively short
succession. Climbing high on to the altiplano, you pass through Junín, perched on
the southern edge of the eponymous lake,
before lurching upwards to Peru's highest
town, breath-sapping mining town Cerro de
Pasco. The road then plunges downwards
toward Huánuco, jumping-off point for
some fabulous archaeological excursions,
before dipping down again to the *ceja de la
selva* in tropical Tingo María.

Acobamba

☑ 064 / ELEV 2950M

Colorful Acobamba, about 9km from Tarma,
has profited substantially from and is famous for the religious sanctuary of **El Señor
de Muruhuay**, a white shrine visible on a
hill 1.5km away.

The sanctuary, one of Peru's top pilgrimage sites, is built around a rock etching of
Christ crucified. The image supposedly
appeared to smallpox sufferers during a
regional epidemic, healing them when authorities had left them for dead. Historians
claim it was carved with a sword by a royalist officer who was one of the few survivors
after losing the major independence Battle
of Junín but this story has less cachet and
legends relating to the image's miraculous
appearance persist. A small chapel replaced
the previous roughly thatched hut at the
site in 1835 and the present sanctuary, inaugurated in 1972, is a modern building with
an electronically controlled bell tower and
is decorated with huge weavings from San
Pedro de Cajas.

The feast of El Señor de Muruhuay, held
throughout May, has been celebrated annually since 1835. There are religious services, processions, dances, fireworks, ample
opportunities to sample local produce and
even a few gringos. Stalls sell *chicha* (corn
beer) and *cuy,* but be wary unless your
stomach is travel-hardened. Visitors usually
stay in nearby Tarma, although Acobamba
has accommodations.

San Pedro de Cajas

☑ 064

Forty kilometers up in the hills from Tarma,
peaceful San Pedro is the production center
for the country's finest *tapices* (tapestries).
Most of the village is involved in making
these high-quality woven wall hangings, depicting moving scenes from rural Peruvian

MINING OR UNDERMINING? THE ISSUES WITH THE ALTIPLANO'S MINERAL WEALTH

Mining is Peru's *numero uno* source of income, and the Central Highlands accounts for a sizable chunk of it. But with the affluence that the extraction of zinc, lead, silver, copper and gold brings (Peru ranks within the world's top four exporters for each) questions, concerning the distribution of that wealth, and the detriment that extraction brings to the environment, are raised. And Peru's major mining centers are some of the poorest and most polluted places in the country, if not the continent. Mining or mineral processing is the economic lifeblood of Cerro de Pasco (one of South America's main zinc and lead mines) and La Oroya (the Highlands' main ore smelting center).

Yet it could also be the ruination of these cities. Contamination rates are high: La Oroya recently featured in a Blacksmith Institute list of the world's worst polluted places. While Doe Run, the company which own the La Oroya smelter, shut down production after this list was compiled, there have since been clamors to restart operations from residents despite their awareness of the risks.

Huelgas (strikes) over working and living conditions are also regularly reported, but as poignantly in evidence are the conditions people are prepared to endure to keep their jobs in this industry. Nowhere is this more evident than Cerro de Pasco, where the pit owned by Volcan Compañia Minera is in the middle of the city (it is ironically referred to as Peru's biggest Plaza de Armas). Not only do nine out of 10 children have above-average levels of minerals in their blood (according to research by the US-based Centers for Disease Control) but, with the majority of available water supplying the mine, running tap water is only available for limited hours. A significant percentage of the city's population lives in poverty. But there is a more imminent danger. Houses cluster around the rim, and subsidence from the ever-present hole outside the properties is a problem. In 2008, Volcan was allowed to buy a portion of the historic city center. With the pit now poised to eat up the heart of Cerro de Pasco, Peruvian congress passed a bill proposing an audacious and costly solution to the problem: relocating the entire city some 20km away. But this, officials estimate, could take US$500 million and over a decade to execute. And time, for many residents, is running out. Watch the space. Soon, Cerro de Pasco might not be there at all: a victim, like many Peruvian mining towns, of its own success.

life. You can watch locals weaving in workshops round the Plaza de Armas: it's one of Peru's best opportunities for witnessing handicraft production – and purchasing the results.

The **Casa del Artesano** (Plaza de Armas; ◷9am-7pm) is one of the largest workshops. On the same street, down from the plaza, basic *hospedajes* offer rooms. *Colectivo* taxis from Tarma (S5, one hour) serve San Pedro regularly.

About 28km up on the way to San Pedro (just passed the village of Palcomayo) you'll pass the **Gruta de Huagapo**, a huge limestone cave that ranks among Peru's largest subterranean systems. A proper descent into the Gruta de Huagapo requires caving equipment and experience: tourist facilities consist only of a few ropes. The cave contains waterfalls, squeezes and underwater sections (scuba equipment required). It is possible to enter the cave for a short distance but you soon need technical gear.

Junín & Around
☑ 064 / ELEV 4125M

An important independence battle wa fought at the pampa of Junín, 55km du north of La Oroya. This is now preserved a the 25-sq-km **Santuario Histórico Chaca marca**, where there is a monument 1.5km off the main road.

In Junín village, basic cold-water *hos pedajes* charge around S15 for basic rooms.

About 10km beyond the village is the in teresting **Lago de Junín**, which, at abou 30km long and 14km wide, is Peru's larges lake after Titicaca. More than 4000m abov sea level, it is the highest lake of its size i the Americas and is known for its birdlife Some authorities claim one million bird live on and around the lake at any one time These include one of the western world' rarest species, the Junín Grebe and, amon the nonwinged inhabitants, wild *cuy*. It' a little-visited area and recommended fo nyone interested in seeing water and norebirds of the high Andes. The lake and s immediate surroundings are part of the 3-sq-km **Reserva Nacional Junín**. Visit by aking a *colectivo* 5km north from Junín to ne hamlet of **Huayre**, from where a 1.5km ath leads to the lake. Otherwise it can be uite hard to actually visit or even see the ake as it is mostly surrounded by swampy narshlands.

The wide, high plain in this area is bleak, vindswept and very cold: bring warm, vindproof clothing. Buses ply the route via unín quite often: watch for intermittent erds of llama, alpaca and sheep.

Cerro de Pasco (Cerro)

063 / POP 66,860 / ELEV 4333M

Vith its altitude-sickness-inducing height bove sea level and its icy, rain-prone clinate, this dizzyingly high altiplano mining ettlement is never going to be a favorite raveler destination. First impressions however are still striking: houses and streets pread haphazardly around a gaping artificial hole in the bare hills several kilometers vide. The Spanish discovered silver here n the 17th century and this, along with ther mineral wealth (see the boxed text), nas made Cerro a lucrative Peruvian asset. t has also worked hard at image improvement recently and boasts decent hotels to ake your mind off the cold and industrial elamor. Besides being the highest place of ts size in the world, Cerro attracts the odd raveler as a springboard for visiting some of Peru's most spectacular rock formations. f you are traveling by *colectivo* taxi around the altiplano it is also handy for picking up a connecting ride. The high, oxygen-poor altitude makes the town bitterly cold at night.

Change your money at **BCP** (Arenales 162), which has an ATM. It's below Hotel Arenales, near the bus station. Emergency health care is available at **Clínica Gonzales** (42-1515; Carrión 99).

Uphill from the bus station on Plaza Daniel Carrión, **Hostal Santa Rosa** (42-2120; Libertad 269; s/d without bathroom S14/20) has basic, spacious rooms sharing three bathrooms and one highly prized hot shower. The owner is a guide, with information on how to visit the rock formations at Santuario Nacional Huayllay (see the boxed text below). On the opposite side of the plaza is the chirpy new **Plaza Apart Hotel** (42-3391; Prado 118; s/d S80/100) with big, well-appointed, welcoming rooms and cable TV and, attached, Cerro's best place to grab a bite to eat.

The bus terminal five blocks south of the Plaza de Armas has buses to Huánuco (S10, three hours), Huancayo (S15, four hours), Lima (S25 to S40, eight hours), La Oroya (S10, 2½ hours) and Tarma. There are also minibuses to Tarma (S6, three hours). Faster *colectivos* from the bus terminal charge S20 to either Huánuco or Tarma: for the latter you will likely have to change at El Cruce where the Tarma road branches off.

Huánuco

062 / POP 170,000 / ELEV 1894M

Huánuco lay on the important Inca route from Cuzco to Cajamarca, the key settlement in the north of the empire, and developed as a major way station accordingly. The Incas

---

WORTH A TRIP

SANCTUARIO NACIONAL HUAYLLAY

An infrequently used road runs southwest of Cerro de Pasco to Lima, passing close to Huayllay, a village near the 6.8-sq-km **Santuario Nacional Huayllay** or *bosque de piedras* (forest of stones). It's the world's largest and highest rock forest with rock formations looming out of the desolate pampa in such shapes as an elephant, a king's crown and an uncannily lifelike grazing alpaca. The area is highly rated for rock-climbing. The sanctuary also has thermal baths and prehistoric cave paintings: you might need a guide to find these. Señor Raul Rojas of Hostal Santa Rosa in Cerro de Pasco is a recommended guide and charges S40 per person for day trips here. You can get here independently (the sanctuary entrance is just before Huayllay village, a 25km run from the Cerro–Lima road) by taking a *colectivo* from Parque Minero in Cerro de Pasco, near the bus terminal (S6, 30 to 40 minutes). DIY trip: the intrepid can choose to forge on to Lima from here, via the lushly rolling Chillón valley and the towns of **Obrajillo** and **Canta** where there are spectacular waterfalls, as well as good horse-riding and hiking.

chose Huánuco Viejo, 150km west, as their regional stronghold but the exposed location prompted the Spanish to move the city to its current scenic setting on the banks of the Río Huallaga in 1541. Little is left of its colonial past but the profusion of archaeological remains in the surrounding mountains is the main reason to linger in this busy little place. Locals also boast Huánuco's perfect

elevation gives it the best climate in Per indeed, after the wild climes of the altiplan it seems positively balmy. It certainly make for a convenient and tempting stopover o the Lima–Pucallpa jungle route. Nearby one of Peru's oldest Andean archaeologica sites, the Temple of Kotosh (aka the Temp of the Crossed Hands), while further up i

Huánuco

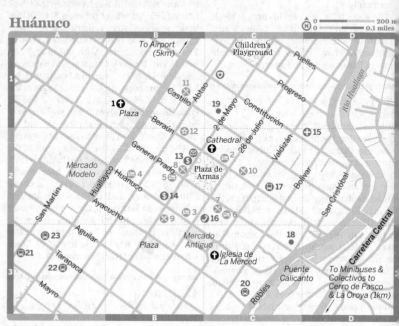

Huánuco

◎ Sights
1 Iglesia San Francisco B1

🛏 Sleeping
2 Grand Hotel Huánuco C2
3 Hostal Huánuco...................................B2
4 Hotel Imperial.....................................B2
5 Hotel Trapiche
   Suites..B2
6 Sosa Hotel C2

🍴 Eating
7 Chifa Khon Wa.....................................C2
8 Hotel Real Cafe....................................B2
9 Huapri..B2
10 La Piazzetta...C2
11 Lookcos Burger
   Grill..B1

✦ Entertainment
12 Anambique...B2

ℹ Information
13 Banco Continental B2
14 BCP B2
15 Hospital Nacional Hermillo
   Valdizán D2
16 Locutorio Público.................................C2

🚍 Transport
17 Bahía Continental C2
18 Comité Autos No 5 ....C3
19 LC Peru C1
20 León de Huánuco..................................C3
21 Marañon Express A3
22 Turismo Central A3
23 Turismo Unión A3

he hills lie the still more impressive ancient ruins of Huánuco Viejo and Tantamayo.

◎ Sights

ights in the city itself are thin on the ground: you might try seeing if **Iglesia San Francisco** (cnr Huallayco & Beraún) is open – 's Huánuco's most appealing church with avish baroque-style altars and interesting *escuela cuzqueña* paintings – but don't hold our breath.

emple of Kotosh   RUINS
admission incl guided tour S5; ⊙8am-6pm) This slightly dilapidated temple ruin is also known as the Temple of the Crossed Hands because of the life-sized mud molding of , pair of crossed hands, which is the site's ighlight. The molding dates to about 2000 BC and is now at Lima's Museo Nacional le Antropología, Arqueología e Historía del Perú; a replica remains. Little is known bout Kotosh, one of the most ancient of Andean cultures. The temple site is easily visted by taxi (S12, including a 30-minute wait and return). In the hills 2km above the site, Quillaromi cave has impressive prehistoric aintings. Kotosh is about 5km west of town off La Unión road.

✰✰ Festivals & Events

Dance of the Blacks   TRADITIONAL DANCE
Huánuco's most intriguing festival sees revelers remember the slaves brought to work in the area's mines by donning black masks, dressing up brightly and drinking until the early hours. It's held January 1st, 6th and 18th.

🛏 Sleeping

On the southeast side of the plaza is a glut of uninspiring options offering basic accommodations with a plaza price tag.

TOP CHOICE Hostal Huánuco   GUESTHOUSE $
(☑51-2050; Huánuco 777; s/d S35/40, s without bathroom S15) This traditional mansion simply exudes character, with old-fashioned tiled floors, a 2nd-floor terrace overlooking a garden and hall walls covered with art and old newspaper clippings. Delightful rooms contain characterful old furniture and have comfortable beds. Showers are hot but can take an age to warm up, so ask in advance.

Sosa Hotel   HOTEL $
(☑51-5803; hotelsosa@hotmail.com; General Prado 872; s/d S30/60) The main draw at this new five-story hotel are the huge, tiled hot-water bath/showers that most of the clean, tastefully decorated rooms come with. One room has a Jacuzzi; there's a small restaurant below.

Hotel Imperial   HOTEL $
(☑51-4758; hotelimperial_hco@hotmail.com; Huánuco 581; s/d S35/60; ☎) Near the market, this offers little out of the ordinary but has decent-sized pastel-colored rooms, dependable hot water, cable TV and a pleasing cafe, all within clean, secure environs.

Hotel Trapiche Suites   BOUTIQUE HOTEL $$
(☑51-7091; hoteltrapichehuanuco@hotmail.com; General Prado 636; s/d S87/114; ☎) It's official: boutique hotels have reached Huánuco. Rooms at this snazzy spot have funky artwork on the walls; huge, comfy, colorful beds; copiously stocked minifridges; and telephones. It's clearly aiming at well-to-do business types (who, if they exist in the city right now are keeping a low profile) and offers a viable luxury alternative to the city's other more staid top hotels.

Grand Hotel Huánuco   HOTEL $$
(☑51-4222; www.grandhotelhuanuco.com; Beraún 775; s/d S135/189; ☎⊠) On the Plaza de Armas is this grande dame of Huánuco hotels. Its public areas are airy and pleasant, highceilinged rooms have solid parquet floors as well as a phone and a fuzzy, mainly Spanishlanguage cable-TV service. A sauna, billiard room, Jacuzzi, pretty good restaurant and bar are on the premises.

🍴 Eating

The 24-hour cafe at the Hotel Real is an excellent choice for midnight munchies or predawn breakfasts. For more formal dining try the stately dining room at the Grand Hotel Huánuco.

TOP CHOICE Huapri   FAST FOOD $
(Cnr jirón 2 de Mayo & Huánuco; menú S6; ⊙lunch & dinner) The only place in town where you have to queue to get through the door. You pay first (a fixed fee for as much as you like of whatever's on). *Salchipapas* (sausages and fries) with eggs is popular.

Lookcos Burger Grill   BURGERS $
(Castillo 471; meals S7.50-15; ⊙6pm-midnight) This large, squeaky-clean restaurant serves mean burgers and sandwiches. Popular with a young student crowd, the upstairs sports a balcony, and a bar blares out Peruvian rock (and sometimes karaoke) come nightfall.

Chifa Khon Wa
CHINESE **$**

(www.khonwa.pe; General Prado 820; mains S10-15; ⊙10:30am-11pm) Khon Wa is the largest and most popular Chinese eatery in town: on the back of its success the owners opened a decent hotel above the restaurant. With two cooking areas, a children's play park and fast, attentive service, dining here is a pleasure. The chicken fried rice (with very hot chilies) is a good option at lunchtime.

La Piazzetta
PIZZA **$$**

(Beraún 845-847; medium/large pizza S19/26; ⊙6-11pm Mon-Sat) This upscale restaurant does quality Italian food including tasty pizzas: service is prompt and there is a good range of Chilean and Argentine wines.

☆ Entertainment

Anambique
BAR

(Beraún 635; ⊙6pm-late) A suave, mellow kind of place with a small dance floor downstairs and a cozy upstairs area for drinks: the house sangria is what most of the clientele choose to knock back.

ⓘ Information

Almost identical sets of internet *cabinas* grace most blocks. Huánuco's tourist office was indefinitely closed at the time of research. The best online resource about Huánuco is www.huanuco.com.

Banco Continental (Jirón 2 de Mayo 1137) Has a pair of ATMs.

BCP (Jirón 2 de Mayo 1005) With a Visa ATM.

Hospital Nacional Hermillo Valdizán (☑51-3370, 51-2400; Hermillo Valdizán 950) Central.

Locutorio Público (Jirón 28 de Julio 810) Make cheap overseas phone calls here.

ⓘ Getting There & Away

Air

LC Peru (☑51-8113; www.lcperu.pe; Jirón 2 de Mayo 1321) flies to and from Lima daily. The airport is 5km north of town. Take a cab (S10) to get there.

Bus & Taxi

Buses go to Lima (S20 to S30, eight hours), Pucallpa (S30, 11 hours), La Merced (S20, six hours), Huancayo (S20, six hours) and La Unión (S15, five hours), with companies all over town. The following are among the best:

Bahía Continental (☑51-9999; Valdizán 718) One of the more luxury options. Regular bus to Lima at 10am plus *bus-camas* at 10pm and 10:15pm.

León de Huánuco (☑51-1489; Robles 821) Lima at 10am, 8:30pm and 9:30pm; La Merced at 8pm; Pucallpa at 7pm.

Marañon Express (San Martin 520) Tantamay at 2am and 10am/1pm.

Turismo Central (☑51-1806; Tarapaca 552) Pucallpa 7pm and 8pm, Huancayo 9.30pm.

Turismo Unión (☑52-6308; Tarapaca 449) La Unión at 7:15am (S15). Other companies near Turismo Unión also go west toward villages on the eastern side of the Cordillera Blanca: rough roads, poor buses.

For Tingo María (S10, 3½ hours), take a Pucallpa-bound bus or a *colectivo* taxi (S18, two hours) with **Comité Autos No 5** (General Prado 1085) near the river. There are more *colectivo* taxis for Tingo María nearby.

For Cerro de Pasco, minibuses (S10, three hours) or *colectivo* taxis (S20, two hours) leave from Paradero de Cayhuayna, a 1km *mototaxi* ride from the center, as do *colectivos* to La Oroya and the Tarma turn-off (S40, 3½ hours).

La Unión

ELEV 3200M

This tiny town is the first significant community on the rocky road from Huánuco to Huaraz: an exciting way to connect the Central Highlands and the Cordillera Blanca. From here you can hike to the extensive Inca ruins of Huánuco Viejo (admission S4; ⊙8am-6pm) on a swathe of barren pampa at 3700m. It's a two-hour trek on a steep path from behind the market heading toward a cross on a hill. Minivans leaving from the market at 5am, as well as other vehicles, can take you to within a 30-minute walk of the site. There are 2 sq km of ruins and supposedly more than 1000 buildings and storehouses in total here. Most impressive is the *usnu*, a huge 4m-high ceremonial platform with engravings of animals (monkeys with lion faces) adorning the entrance. A key figure in the Inca resistance against the Spanish, Illa Tupac, defended Huánuco Viejo until 1543 significantly after many Inca settlements had fallen. Looking at the site's defensive advantages today, it's easy to see how.

La Unión has public but no listed phones and a handy Banco de la Nación (Jirón 2 de Mayo 798) with what is surely Peru's remotest Visa ATM. Just a block from here you'll also find Hostal Picaflor (Jirón 2 de Mayo 840; s/d without bathroom S15/25). Basic but agreeable rooms cluster around a bright courtyard. Basic eateries include Restaurant Recreo rón 2 de Mayo 971; mains S10-15), with relaxed ourtyard dining.

All transport arrives/departs from the ell-ordered bus terminal on Commercio the west end of town. Companies leave ound 6pm for Lima (S20, 10 hours) while o or three buses daily ply the route east to uánuco (S15, five hours), as well as to Tanmayo (three hours). **La Unión Huánuco** is a service to Huaraz that departs at the godly hour of 3:45am, taking five hours.

antamayo

EV 3400M

ntamayo is connected only by a rough ack to the outside world. The first sign ou are approaching is the green-brown atchwork of fields standing out from the ark, precipitous sides of the Upper Mañon valley. From this serene, chilly village ws a river that will, hundreds of kilomers downstream, morph into the Amazon self. Tantamayo was capital of the olumbian Yarowilca culture, remains of hich are scattered throughout the nearby lls. The most impressive ruins are : **Piruro** and **Susupillo**. This culture was ne of the oldest known in Peru and very rchitecturally advanced. Buildings were onstructed with up to six floors connected ia internal spiral staircases, giving them a ifferent appearance to the constructions of ie Incas, whom many believe were unable emulate Yarowilca style.

Piruro is easiest to visit: it's a 1½-hour alk down from Tantamayo village and up le other side of the valley. The path is hard find: be sure to ask. For Susupillo, vehiles can take you to the village of Florida, 20-minute drive from Tantamayo, from here you can hike to the site.

The basic lodgings in Tantamayo inlude hospitable **Albergue Ocaña Althuas** Capitán Espinosa s/n; s/d without bathroom 10/20) beyond the plaza on the main street nto town. The folks here provide meals. antamayo has public phones (these can't ial internationally) but no listed ones, no ell phone reception and no banks. *Colecivo* taxis, minibuses and buses from Huáuco make the journey in anything from six o eight hours (bus S20, *colectivo* taxi S40). antamayo is also connected to La Unión three hours) from where you can catch onvard buses to Lima.

Tingo María

062 / POP 55,000 / ELEV 649M

This languid, humid university and market town lies in the *ceja de la selva:* its back may rest against the mountains – as the conical, forested hills that flank it testify – but its feet are firmly fixed in the lush vegetation of the Amazonas region and its sticky, tropical embrace. Tingo María, or Tingo for short, is a popular weekend destination for holidaying *limeños,* while travelers pause here en route to the Amazon.

The main attraction is Parque Nacional Tingo María: a lush forested wilderness with caves and great bathing spots. Sadly, this adventure comes with its dangers (see below).

⊙ Sights & Activities

Parque Nacional Tingo María   PARK
This 180-sq-km park lies on the south side of town, around the mouth of the Río Monzón, a tributary of the Río Huallaga. The most distinguishing feature is the **Bella Durmiente** (Sleeping Beauty), a hill overlooking the town, which, from some angles, looks like a recumbent woman wearing an Inca crown.

Also in the park is **La Cueva de las Lechuzas** (the Cave of the Owls), which, despite its name, is known for the colony of oilbirds that lives inside. In addition, there are stalactites and stalagmites, bats, parrots and other birds around the cave entrance, but the oilbirds are the main attraction.

The caves are about 6km away from Tingo María; taxis can take you there. There is a S5 national-park fee and guides can show you around. The best times to visit the park are in the morning, when sunlight shines into the cave mouth, or dusk, when the oilbirds emerge. Don't be tempted to use your flashlight to see the birds, as it disturbs their sleeping and breeding patterns.

There are myriad great **bathing spots** in and around the park. Recommended are the **San Jacintillo Medicinal Springs**, 1km before the Cave of the Owls; **Velo de las Ninfas** and **Cueva de los Tambos**, 9km south of Tingo; and the **Laguna el Milagro**, 35km north of town. There is a nominal entrance fee of S3 to S5 at each spot.

For information on the dangers and annoyances unfortunately associated with the park, please see p306. The Cave of the Owls has police protection, but the road there is still risky, as are more remote destinations.

🛏 Sleeping & Eating

TOP CHOICE **Villa Jennifer** LODGE $$
(☎96-260-3509, 79-4714; www.villajennifer.net; Castillo Grande Km 3.4; dm S50, s/d S100/120; 🔊🏊) Located north of the airport is this peaceful tropical hacienda and lodge, run by a Danish-Peruvian couple. They have done wonders out of a lush expanse of tropical bushland bounded by rivers on two sides. Suave rustic accommodations range from simple rooms with shared bathrooms to airy minihomes that can sleep up to 10 people. You can also play table tennis, darts or table soccer, catch a movie in the DVD lounge or go see the resident animals, including crocodiles, tortoises, a sloth and some monkeys. There's also camping space (per person S20) and backpackers rooms (per person S50, two-person minimum): a cut above your average dorm. In the excellent **restaurant** (☉10:30am-6pm), be sure to try the local fruit *anonas* – or custard apples – which are delectable. There are also two swimming pools and minigolf.

Hostal Palacio GUESTHOUSE $
(☎56-2319; www.hostal-palacio.com; Raimondi 158; s/d S20/30) A good budget option in the center of town, with four floors of rooms around a plant-filled courtyard. Cable TV is S5 extra per night, but all rooms have telephones, which can dial internationally!

ℹ Information

There have been reports of travelers being robbed and raped at gunpoint en route to destinations within Parque Nacional Tingo María. It is strongly recommended that you do not venture into the countryside around Tingo without a guide and ensure you return well before dark. Increased police protection at key park attractions has improved security somewhat, but remember that this is a remote area. Furthermore, the Huallaga valley that runs north of Tingo to Tarapoto is a cocaine production area and also one of the last bastions of the Sendero Luminoso (Shining Path; see the boxed text, p292). Risk to tourists from drugs traffickers and the Sendero Luminoso is very low but care should still be taken.

BCP (Raimondi 249) Also changes US cash. It has a Visa ATM and may change traveler's checks.

Main post office (Plaza Leoncio Prado)

Tourist office (☎56-2058, 56-2351, ext 116; Alameda Perú 525) On Plaza Leoncio Prado. Publishes useful information on sights in Parque Nacional Tingo María.

ℹ Getting There & Away

Air

Flights from Tingo María are not currently operating: Huánuco has the nearest airport.

Bus & Taxi

Transport here mostly serves Lima and destinations in between such as Huánuco, as well as local villages and Pucallpa. The road between Tingo and Pucallpa can be risky; see p306.

Buses to Lima (S40 to S60, 12 hours) are operated, among others, by **Transportes León de Huánuco** (☎56-2030, 962-56-2030; Pimentel 164). Buses usually leave at 7am or 7pm. Some operators go to Pucallpa (S20, nine hours). Faster service to Pucallpa is with **Turismo Ucayali** (cnr Tito Jaime Fernández s/n, cuadra 2), which has *colectivo* taxis (S45, 4½ hours).

From around the gas station on Av Raimondi near the León de Huánuco bus terminal, *colectivos* depart to Huánuco (S18, two hours) and other destinations.

Selva Tours (☎56-1137; Raimondi 205-207) has cars to Tocache (S40, three to four hours) and eventually Tarapoto (S95, nine hours). Tarapoto vehicles go direct if there's the demand but normally you'll have to change at Tocache or Janjui or both.

Transportes Cueva del Pavos is a signed stop with *mototaxis* to the Cave of the Owls in Parque Nacional Tingo María. It's about S20 for the round-trip, including a wait at the cave.

North Coast

Why Go?

The apocalyptic dune desertscape that makes up Peru's unruly north coast is a startling clash of sun and sand that refuses to relinquish the horizon for some 1300km from Lima to the Ecuadorian border. Cerulean waters settling in on Peru's best beaches bounce off the seemingly barren desert, but scattered about this heaving coastline are enough antediluvian ruins to send archaeologists into a head-spinning frenzy of Raiders of the Lost Ark proportions.

Travelers drool at the gold-laden million-dollar once-buried treasures at Sipán; they marvel at the largest pre-Columbian city in the Americas at Chan Chan; they scratch their heads in wonder at the remnants of the continent's oldest civilization at Caral. Meanwhile, graceful surf, enduring sunny months and frisky seaside resorts beckon modern-day sun worshippers down from the Andes, a white-knuckle, jaw-dropping adventure in itself.

Best Places to Eat

- La Sirena d'Juan (p353)
- Mar Picante (p319)
- Fiesta Chiclayo Gourmet (p335)
- Capuccino (p347)
- Big Ben (p329)

Best Places to Stay

- Sunset Hotel (p351)
- Loki del Mar (p351)
- Chaparrí Ecolodge (p341)
- Playa Colán Lodge (p344)
- Hostal Colonial (p318)

When to Go

Trujillo

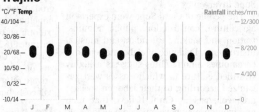

Mar Summer's sizzling sun remains, but prices smolder back down to earth.	**Apr–Nov** The further north you go, the shinier the sun and fewer the people.	**Nov–Feb** Surf's up in Máncora, Huanchaco and Puerto Chicama.

Barranca

 01 / POP 54,000

Barranca, located 195km north of Lima, has a relaxed, fountain-spouting plaza and a cacophonous stream of traffic passing through on the Carretera Panamericana, which bisects the town. Neighboring Pativilca, located 10km further north, is where the road branches off to Huaraz and the Cordillera Blanca. This spectacular route climbs inland through cactus-laden cliff faces; watch the cathedrals of sheer rock slowly turn into a carpet of greenery as the road climbs up to Huaraz.

◉ Sights

Caral   RUIN

(adult S11; ◷9am-4pm) About 25km inland from Barranca lie the monumental ruins of the urban settlement of Caral, which confounded Peruvian archaeologists when they proved to be part of the oldest civilization in all of South America. Before Caral's discovery, the city of Chavín de Huántar near Huaraz, built around 900 BC, held that particular title. Caral culture arose in the Supe Valley some 4500 to 5000 years ago, making it one of the world's earliest large cities, alongside those in Mesopotamia, Egypt, India and China. This ancient culture was a conglomeration of 18 city-states and controlled the three valleys of Supe, Pativilca and Fortaleza, with the main seat of government at Caral. At the site, six stone-built pyramids (most of which have been excavated) were found alongside amphitheaters, ceremonial rooms, altars, adobe complexes and several sunken circular plazas. Most of the pyramids have stairways leading to their peaks, where offerings were once made; the stairs can be climbed for great views of the lush Supe River valley.

The people of Caral-Supe were experts in agriculture, construction, public administration and making calendars and musical instruments. Evidence of elaborate religious ceremonies among elites suggests a highly stratified culture in which classes were organized according to their labor in society; archaeologists at Caral believe that men and women may have enjoyed considerable equality. Among the many artifacts you'll see at the site are millennia-old bone flutes and Peru's oldest *quipus* (a system among Andean cultures of tying cords in knots to convey information). A large geoglyph – a design carved into earth – called Chupaci-garo attests to the Caral people's sophisticated measurements of the movements of the stars. Unesco declared the Sacred City of Caral a World Heritage site in 2009.

Considering how few people visit Caral, the site is well set out for visitors. There are plaques in both Spanish and English illustrating points of interest. **Proyecto Especial Arqueológico Caral** (www.caralperu.gob.pe) is in charge here, and its **Lima office** (☎01-205-2500; Av Las Lomas de La Molina 32, Lima 12) has tonnes of information and also offers informative full-day tours – often including Chupacigaro – on weekends for S9 per person (see the website for a calendar). Weekends are a great time to visit because handicrafts and local food are for sale at the site. **Lima Tours** (☎01-619-6900; www.limatours.com.pe; Jr de la Unión 1040, Central Lima) in Lima arranges expensive private tours to Caral and Paramonga on request. *Colectivo* (shared transportation) taxis depart from Calle Berenice Davila in Barranca to the nearby hamlet of Caral fairly regularly for S10 (two hours). Alternatively, elusive private taxis will cost S70 for the return journey (including waiting time); some charge S2 per hour for the same route.

The road out here is rough and may be impassable during the December to March wet season. Spanish-speaking local guides are also available at the site for S29 per group (up to 29 people).

Paramonga   RUIN

(admission S4; ◷closed Mon) The adobe temple of Paramonga is situated 4km beyond the turnoff for the Huaraz road and was built by the Chimú culture, which was the ruling power on the north coast before it was conquered by the Incas (see p515). The finer details of the massive temple have long been eroded, yet the multi-tiered construction is nonetheless impressive and affords fantastic panoramas of the lush valley. *Colectivos* from Barranca (S2.50, 25 minutes) leave from the corner of Ugarte and Lima and will drop you off at a spot 3km from the entrance. A private return taxi here, including wait time, will cost about S40 but are hard to come by.

🛏 Sleeping & Eating

Most hotels are along Barranca's main street.

Hotel Chavín   HOTEL $

(☎235-2253; www.hotelchavin.com.pe; Gálvez 222; s/d/tr S80/145/180; 🛜🅿) Barranca's big show

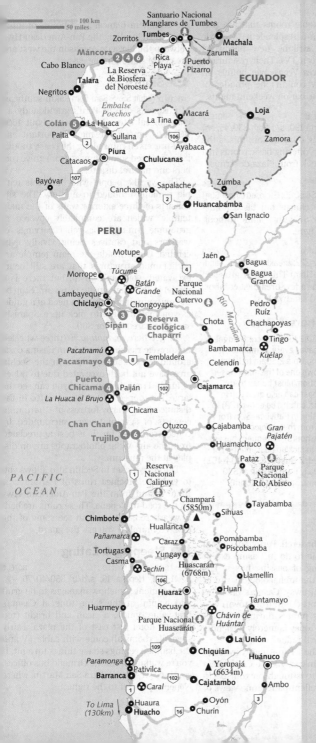

North Coast Highlights

1 Wander the ginormous ruins of **Chan Chan** (p323), the largest pre-Columbian city in the Americas

2 Indulge in sun, surf and sand at **Máncora** (p350), Peru's premier beachside hot spot

3 Ogle the vast wealth of once-buried booty at the **Museo Tumbas Reales de Sipán** (p340) outside Chiclayo

4 Drag your board up the coast in search of that elusive perfect swell at **Huanchaco** (p326), **Puerto Chicama** (p331), **Pacasmayo** (p331) and **Máncora** (p350)

5 Hide yourself away in the (nearly) undiscovered sands at **Colán** (p344)

6 Find ceviche salvation in the coastal desert at **Mar Picante** (p319), **Big Ben** (p329) and **Las Gemelitas** (p353)

7 Settle in on a search for the elusive South American spectacled bear at the rustic **Reserva Ecológica Chaparrí** (p341)

hotel has comfortable rooms that are perfectly preserved in a resplendent '70s style contrasting with striking new hardwood floors and flat-screen TVs. Their restaurant, El Liberador, serves Vegas-style buffets on Sundays and they couldn't be prouder of their karaoke in the bar on weekend nights.

Hostal Continental
HOTEL $

(☎235-2458; A Ugarte 190; s/d from S30/45; ☎) Though still oozing dilapidation, this is the best budget choice, offering basic rooms in a solid location a block from Plaza de Armas.

Seichi
CAFE $

(A Ugarte 184; mains S8.50-15; ☺closed dinner Sun) This modern cafe churns out tasty, home-cooked *menús* for S7 with a smile to boot. Hard to find fault here.

Cafetería El Parador
CAFE $

(Hotel Chavín, Gálvez 222; breakfasts S9-15, sandwiches S6-12; ☺7am-11pm) This diner attached to Hotel Chavín has a few breakfast combos, passable coffee and sandwiches.

ⓘ Getting There & Away

Turismo Barranca (☎235-3549; cnr Bolognesi & Plaza de Armas) leaves every 10 minutes for Lima (S15, four hours) from 2:30am to 10pm. Alternatively, flag down one of the many buses heading in that direction. Most buses from Lima going up the coast can also drop you in Barranca. For Huaraz, catch a *colectivo* (S2) to the Pecsa petrol station in Pativilca, 3km from the Huaraz turnoff. From there, *colectivos* leave when full (S30, three hours); infrequent buses from Lima also stop to pick up passengers. For something more fixed, **Z Buss** (☎964-404-463) departs four times daily from Pativilca (S20, four hours, 11am, noon, 3pm and 5:30pm).

Casma

☎043 / POP 24,700

A small and unflustered Peruvian coastal town; there is little to do in Casma except watch the whirring of passing buses. The big draw here is the archaeological site of Sechín, about 5km away. Casma's once-important colonial port (11km from town) was sacked by various pirates during the 17th century; the town today is merely a friendly blip on the historical radar.

From here, the Pan-American Hwy branches off for Huaraz via the Callán Pass (4225m). This route is tough on your backside but offers excellent panoramic views of the Cordillera Blanca. Most points of interest in town lie along the Pan-American Hwy between the Plaza de Armas in the west and the petrol station in the east.

◉ Sights

Sechín (adult S5; ☺8am-6pm), 5km southeast of Casma, is one of Peru's granddaddy archaeological sites, dating from about 1600 BC. It is among the more important and well-preserved ruins along the coast, though it has suffered some damage from grave robbers and natural disasters.

The warlike people who built this temple remain shrouded in mystery. The site consists of three exterior walls of the main temple, which are completely covered in gruesome 4m-high bas-relief carvings of warriors and captives being vividly eviscerated. Ouch. Inside the main temple are earlier mud structures that are still being excavated: you can't go in, but there is a model in the small onsite museum. Stop by the museum first if you're in need of a guide, as you may be able to pick up a Spanish-speaking caretaker for S30.

To get here, a *mototaxi* (three-wheeled motorcycle rickshaw taxi) from Casma costs around S6. Other early sites in the Sechín area have not been excavated due to a lack of funds. From the museum, you can see the large, flat-topped hill of Sechín Alto in the distance. The nearby fortress of Chanquillo consists of several towers surrounded by concentric walls, but it is best appreciated from the air. Aerial photographs are on display at the museum.

The entry ticket to Sechín also allows you to visit the Mochica ruins of Pañamarca, 10km inland from the Pan-American Hwy on the road to Nepeña. These ruins are badly weathered, but you can see some of the covered murals if you ask the guard.

🛏 Sleeping & Eating

Hostal Monte Carlo
HOTEL $

(☎41-1421; Nepeña 16; s/d/tr S30/40/70; ☎) Management somehow manages to be gruff and helpful at the same time at Casma's best-value option, a clean and bright (too bright!) hotel just east of the plaza. Fairly spacious rooms all come with cable TV and the bamboo ceilings shake things up a bit. If you're walking from the Ormeño bus offices, continue west until Plaza San Martín, where Nepeña splits off to the right.

ostal Gregori · HOTEL $

9-631-4291; Ormeño 579; s/d S35/55; 🛜) This
nce funky white hotel with random potted
ants in specially designed crevices and
rchitecturally rakish wall angles is a little
ore off white these days. But there's hot
ater and cable TV in the spacious rooms
nd a few angled wooden chaise longues to
ick back in.

otel El Farol · HOTEL $$

41-1064; Túpac Amaru 450; s/d incl breakfast
85/120; 🛜❄) One of the (brace yourself for
oetic license) *fanciest* places to bed down
n Casma, El Farol curves around a fetch-
ng garden, complete with a dainty gazebo,
amboo-lined restaurant/bar and seasonal
ool (November to March). Though a little
vorse for wear, the walled-in compound
upplies an oasis of calm from the street
lamor and there's a faded seaside glory
bout the place.

otel Los Poncianas · RESORT $$

41-1599; www.lasponcianashotel.com; Panamer-
cana Norte Km 376; s/d incl breakfast S125/175;
❄🛜❄) Just a block off the main highway
nd six blocks from the Plaza de Armas, this
ranquil place is in a hushed spot and boasts
everal pools (including one for the kiddies).
t's very popular with Peruvian families and
ffers throwback '70s resort luxury that may
r may not hold nostalgic value depending
n your perspective.

l Tío Sam · PERUVIAN,CHINESE $

71-1447; Huarmey 138; mains S14-20) Part
chifa (Chinese restaurant), part regional
uisine, this is your best bet in Casma, bipo-
arity notwithstanding. In fact, their ceviche,
which outclasses the town, was Ancash's
est in 2010. There are also lots of fried
things, too, along with good-looking steaks
nd seafood.

La Careta · STEAKHOUSE $

(Peru 885; mains S9.50-34.50; ⏰from 6pm, closed
Tue) This popular, orange-tableclothed meat-
ery serves sizzling grills nightly amid an odd
decorative duo of bullfighting paintings and
model cars. All plates come with fries and
a salad – not bad – though the indoor potted plants are the most impressive 'greens'
in the house.

Walter's · PERUVIAN $

(Bolivar s/n; mains S4.50-18) Along a line of
worthy options one half-block south of Plaza
de Armas, Walter's is a decent breakfast spot
if its popularity with the Policía Nacional
is any indication. There are a few combos,
which you can switch up with scrambled
eggs if you wish.

ℹ️ Information

There's a branch of **BCP** (🛜71 1314, 71 1471;
Bolívar 111) here. Several internet cafes line the
plaza.

ℹ️ Getting There & Away

Colectivo taxis to Chimbote leave frequently
from the **ETACSA/Las Casmeños** (🛜46-5083;
Nepeña s/n) office a half block east of Plaza de
Armas.

Most bus companies are on Ormeño in front
of the petrol station at the eastern end of town.
Many buses stop here to pick up extra passengers. **Cruz del Norte/Transportes Huandoy**
(🛜41-1633; Ormeño 121) offer frequent services
to Lima and three daily departures for Huaraz
at 9am, 2pm and 9pm (the latter, along with
Yungay Express, has buses that take the scenic
route via the Callán Pass). Faster minivans to
Huaraz also leave from in front of this office
when full.

Tepsa (🛜41-2275; Huamay 356) has comfortable buses to Lima departing at 12:30am daily.
Erick El Rojo (🛜41-1571; Ormeño 145) has five
daily departures to Trujillo and one 7:30pm
departure to Tumbes. **Etta** (Ormeño s/n), below

CASMA BUSES

DESTINATION	COST (S)	DURATION (HR)
Chimbote	6	1
Huaraz	20-25	2½-3
Lima	20-50	5½
Máncora	50-60	11
Trujillo	10	3
Tumbes	50-60	12-13

Hostal Gregori, hits all coastal cities north, including Máncora and Tumbes, departing at 8:30am and 9pm daily.

For Sechín, *mototaxis* (S6) make the run. They are all around town, but there's an honest cluster operating as Motocars Virgen de Fatima on Plaza San Martín.

Sample travel times and costs from Casma are shown in the table, p311 (prices fluctuate with the quality of the bus/classes).

Chimbote

Chimbote is Peru's largest fishing port: with fish-processing factories lining the roads in and out of town, you'll probably smell it before you see it. The odor of fermenting fish may take a while to get used to, but the quiet, open plaza in the town's heart is less overwhelming. The fishing industry has declined from its 1960s glory days due to overfishing, but you'll still see flotillas moored offshore every evening. This roguish port town is a transit hub, not a tourist destination, but you may have to stay overnight if you're catching an early morning bus to Huaraz via the hair-raising Cañón del Pato route.

🛏 Sleeping

There are lots of hotels in Chimbote, though nothing in the top-end range.

Hotel San Felipe HOTEL $$
(☑32-3401; hsanfelipe@hotmail.com; Pardo 514; s/d incl breakfast S75/115; @☏) The town's best option is family run with a helpful smile. Equipped with elevators, it offers clean rooms with strong hot showers and cable TV. Be sure to take your continental breakfast on the 5th-floor terrace with plaza views. A glitzy downstairs casino will

help you live out your Las Vegas card-shar fantasies.

Hostal Chifa Canton HOTEL $
(☑34-4388; Bolognesi 498; s/d with breakfas S95/120; @☏) Hostal Chifa Canton ha large, carpeted rooms with modern amen ties. Some rooms look out over the sea. has a great *chifa* where portions are bi enough to serve two. It also has a pool ha for guests.

Hospedaje Chimbote HOTEL
(☑51-5006; Pardo 205; s/d S30/40, without bath room S20/30) A team of seven siblings own this lovely budget option, which has been i the family since opening in 1959. Cell-lik rooms here have windows onto the corrido which is a bright, freshly-painted joy fo these prices. Hot water comes with en-suit rooms only.

🍴 Eating

The *chifa* at **Hostal Chifa Canton** (Bolognes 498; mains S8.50-35.50) is superb. For espress and higher-end Peruvian fusion, try **Capuc cino Café** (Villavicencio 455; mains S20-30` There are plenty of good spots along Bolog nesi and Pardo in the vicinity of Plaza d Armas as well.

❶ Getting There & Away

Bus

For Casma (S6, 45 minutes), *colectivos* depart from the corner of Pardo and Balta.

All long-distance buses leave from the Terminal Terrestre, about 5km east of town (S6 taxi ride or catch *colectivo* 25 on Pardo for S1.50). **America Express** (☑35-1911) has buses leaving for Trujillo every 15 minutes from 5:25am to 9:30pm. Dozens of companies run mostly overnight buses to Lima, leaving between 10pm

CHIMBOTE BUSES

DESTINATION	COST (S)	DURATION (HR)
Caraz	25	6-7
Chiclayo	15-20	6
Huaraz	25-60	5-8
Lima	25-85	6-7
Máncora	90-120	11
Piura	50-80	8
Trujillo	8	2
Tumbes	40-120	12

nd midnight, though a few depart in daylight. eputable companies, several of which also have ffices lined up along Bolognesi with the banks, clude **Oltursa** (☑35-3585; www.oltursa.pe), **inea** (☑35-4000; www.linea.pe), **Civa** (☑35-308; www.turismociva.com) and **Cruz Del ur** (☑35-2665; www.cruzdelsur.com.pe). The tter has the most frequent and most comfortble departures at 11am, 2:30pm, 11:15pm and :30pm.

Buses to Huaraz and the Cordillera Blanca run long one of three routes: via the dazzling yet ugh road through the Cañón del Pato (p391), a an equally rough road that climbs through ne mountains from Casma, or via the longer, omfortably paved route through Pativilca. ravel times on these routes range from seven nine hours. **Yungay Express** (☑35-0855) as an 8:30am bus to Caraz and Huaraz through ne Cañón del Pato and 1pm and 10pm buses via asma. **Movil Tours** (☑35-3616; www.movil urs.com.pe) has 12:30pm, 11:10pm, 11:50pm nd 12:30am departures to Huaraz via Casma nat also stop in Caraz. It pays to book Huaraz uses a day in advance.

Sample travel times and costs from Chimbote re shown in the table (prices fluctuate with the uality of the bus/classes).

Trujillo

☑044 / POP 291,400

tand in the right spot and the glamor-usly colonial streets of old Trujillo look ike they've barely changed in hundreds of ears. Well, there are more honking taxis low – but the city still manages to put on a lashing show with its flamboyant buildings nd profusion of churches. Francisco Pizarro ounded Trujillo in 1534, and he thought so ighly of this patch of desert he named it fter his birthplace in Spain's Estremadura. Spoiled by the fruits of the fertile Moche Valley, Trujillo never had to worry about noney – wealth came easily. With life's es-sentials taken care of, thoughts turned to olitics and life's grander schemes; the city has a reputation for being a hotbed of re-volt. The town was besieged during the nca rebellion of 1536 and in 1820 was the irst Peruvian city to declare independence rom Spain. The tradition continued into he 20th century, as bohemians flocked, po-ets put pen to paper (including Peru's best poet, César Vallejo), and rebels raised their ists defiantly in the air. It was here that he Alianza Popular Revolution Americana APRA) workers' party was formed – and nany of its members were later massacred.

The behemoth Chimú capital of Chan Chan is nearby, though little remains of what was once the largest adobe city in the world. Other Chimú sites bake in the surrounding desert, among them the immense and suitably impressive Moche Huacas del Sol y de la Luna (Temples of the Sun and Moon), which date back 1500 years. When you get yourself ancient-cultured out, the village of Huanchaco beckons with its sandy beach, respectable surf and a more contemporary interpretation of sun worship.

◉ Sights

Trujillo's colonial mansions and churches, most of which are near the Plaza de Armas, are worth seeing, though they don't keep very regular opening hours.

Hiring a good local guide is recommended if you are seriously interested in history. The churches are often open for early morning and evening masses, but visitors at those times should respect worshippers and not wander around.

The creamy pastel shades and beautiful wrought-iron grillwork fronting almost every colonial building are unique Trujillo touches.

PLAZA DE ARMAS

Trujillo's spacious and spit-shined main square, surely the cleanest in the Americas and definitely one of the prettiest, hosts a colorful assembly of preserved colonial buildings and an impressive statue dedicated to work, the arts and liberty. Elegant mansions abound, including **Hotel Libertador** (Independencia 485).

At 9am on Sundays there is a **flag-raising ceremony** on the Plaza de Armas, complete on special occasions with a parade, *caballos de paso* (pacing horses) and performances of the *marinera* (a typical coastal Peruvian dance involving much romantic waving of handkerchiefs).

FREE **Casa de Urquiaga**   HISTORIC BUILDING (Pizarro 446; ◉9:15am-3:15pm Mon-Fri, 10am-1pm Sat) Owned and maintained by Banco Central de la Reserva del Perú since 1972, this beautiful colonial mansion's history dates to 1604, though the original house was completely destroyed in the earthquake of 1619. Rebuilt and dramatically preserved since, it now houses exquisite period furniture, including a striking writer's desk once used by Simón Bolívar, who organized much of

Trujillo

Comercio

Old City Wall

De la Torre

Chavez

Mansiche

44

Estadio Mansiche

Industrial

Zepita

25

36

San Martín

30

España

Carrión

Salaverry

47

Independencia

Colón

19

27

9

Zepita

8

Iglesia de San Francisco

28

Junín

Casa Ganoza Chopitea

32

Pizarro

18

33

26

Juan Pablo II

San Martín

17

34

Gamarra

46

Palacio Iturregui

49

22

1

37

Casa de la Emancipación

35

15

Orbegoso

6

38

13

14

Independencia

Plaza de Armas

Pizarro

3

39

Mercado Central

5

40

Almagro

Casa de Urquiaga

31

7

48

Bolívar

Independencia

Bolognesi

29

Ayacucho

Ugarte

10

2

23

Pizarro

Corne

España

Bolívar

4

20

Ayacucho

29 de Diciembre

Moche

To Mar Picante (200m);
Movil Tours (1.5km);
Oficina de Migraciones (2.5km);
Transportes Horna (5km)

Larco

To America Express (1.5km); Linea Terminal (1.5km)

his final campaign to liberate Peru from the Spanish empire from Trujillo in 1824. There is also a small collection of Moche, Nazca, Chimu and Vicús pottery. It's a working bank, so security is high for a free attraction.

FREE **Basílica Menor Catedral** CHURCH
(☉10-11am) Known simply as 'catedral,' this bright, *ají de gallina*–colored (yellow) church fronting the plaza was begun in 1647, destroyed in 1759, and rebuilt soon afterward. The cathedral has a famous basilica (but unless you are attending mass, you have a one-hour window each day to pop in) and a **museum** (Admission S4; ☉9am-1pm & 4-7pm Mon-Fri, 9am-noon Sat) of religious and colonial art that is pricier than it is worth, though there are intriguing frescos in the downstairs basement (along with a few bats).

EAST OF PLAZA DE ARMAS

TOP CHOICE **Palacio Iturregui** HISTORIC BUILDING
(Pizarro 688; adult S5; ☉8-10am Mon-Sat) This canary yellow 19th-century mansion is unmistakable and impossible to ignore unless you're color blind. Built in neoclassical style, it has beautiful window gratings, 36 slender interior columns and gold moldings on the ceilings. General Juan Manuel Iturregui lived here after he famously proclaimed independence. Today, it's a private social club, so visits are restricted. You can pop into the interior courtyard any time of day but visiting the ornate rooms is restricted to the listed opening hours.

Museo de Arqueología MUSEUM
(Junín 682; adult/child S5/1; ☉9am-5pm Mon-Sat, to 1pm Sun) This well-curated museum features a rundown of Peruvian history from 12,000 BC to the present day, with an emphasis on Moche, Chimu and Inca civilizations as well as the lesser-known Cupisnique and Salinar cultures. But it's also worth popping in for the house itself, a restored 17th-century mansion known as La Casa Risco which features striking cedar pillars and gorgeous painted courtyard walls.

FREE **Casa de la Emancipación** HISTORIC BUILDING
(Pizarro 620; ☉9am-1pm & 4-8pm Mon-Sat) Now the Banco Continental building, this hodgepodge of colonial and Republican styles is where Trujillo's independence from colonial rule was formally declared on December 29, 1820. Check out the unique cubic

NORTH COAST TRUJILLO

Trujillo

Cajabamba marble stone flooring; there are also galleries dedicated to revolving art exhibitions, Peruvian poet César Vallejo and period furniture. It hosts live music events as well – look for posters around town on your visit.

Casona Orbegoso   HISTORIC BUILDING
(Orbegoso 553) Named after a former president of Peru, this beautiful 18th-century corner manor is home to a collection of well-worn art and period furnishings, but its stuck-in-time feel is being increasingly insured by its ongoing closure for renova-

tions. There was no estimated reopening date when we came through.

Other Historic Buildings   ARCHITECTURE
Additional buildings worth a flyby are the 17th-century **Iglesia de la Merced** (Pizarro) which has a striking organ and cupola. Uniquely, an altar here is painted on the wall, an economical shortcut when funds ran out for a more traditional gold or carved-wood alternative. **Iglesia del Carmen** (cnr Colón & Bolívar) is home to an impressive Carmelite museum. Unfortunately, neither were open for visitors at time of research.

On the opposite side of Bolívar, Iglesia de
an Agustín (cnr Orbegoso & Bolívar; ⊙9am-
›on & 4-7:30pm) has a finely gilded high altar
nd dates from 1558. Further southeast is
;lesia de Belén; north of here is another
nansion, the 1709 Casa de Mayorazgo de
acala (Pizarro 314; ⊙9:30am-1pm & 4-7pm Mon-
i), which houses Scotiabank.

ORTH & WEST OF PLAZA DE ARMAS

Casa Ganoza
hopitea
HISTORIC BUILDING
ndependencia 630) Northeast of the cathe-
ral, this c 1735 mansion, also known as
'asa de los Léones, is considered to be the
est preserved mansion of the colonial pe-
iod in Trujillo. The details are stunning,
:om the elaborate gateway at the entrance
› 300-year-old frescos, Oregon pine pillars
nd rustic ceilings inside, some tied together
vith sheepskin.

Take note of the 'JHS' insignia above the
ntrance between the male and female lions
‹from which one of the building's names de-
ives). It stands for 'Jesus,' 'Hombre' (Man),
;alvador' (Savior) and stems from the build-
ng's time as a convent (as does the lazy Su-
an by the bathrooms). Best of all, perhaps,
; that it now houses the wonderful Casona
Deza cafe (p319).

Museo Cassinelli
MUSEUM
N de Piérola 607; admission S7; ⊙9am-1pm &
3-6pm Mon-Sat) This private archaeological
:ollection housed in the basement of a Rep-
ol gas station (the one on the west side of
he intersection, not the east side) is fascinating, with some 2000 ceramic pieces on
display (curated from a collection owned by
Italian immigrants) that certainly don't be-
ong under a gritty petrol dispensary.

Have a look at the bird-shaped whistling
pots, which produce clear notes when air is
plown into them (ask the curator to show
you). Superficially the pots are very similar,
but when they are blown each produces a
completely different note that corresponds
to the calls of the male and female birds. The
mummified eight-month-old female fetus,
born premature, is estimated to date from
AD 250 and will blow your mind as well.

Museo de Zoología
MUSEUM
(San Martín 368; admission S2; ⊙9am-6pm) This
museum is mainly a taxidermic collection
of Peruvian animals (many so artificially

stuffed they look like nightmarish carica-
tures of their former selves).

Churches
ARCHITECTURE
There are several other interesting churches
near the Plaza de Armas, though most are
usually closed up: Iglesia de la Compañía
(Independencia), now part of the Universidad
Nacional de Trujillo, Iglesia de Santa Ana
(cnr Mansiche & Zepita), Iglesia de Santo Do-
mingo (cnr Pizarro & Bolognesi) and Iglesia de
Santa Clara (cnr Junín & Independencia).

☞ Tours & Guides

There are dozens of tour agencies in Trujillo. Some agencies supply guides who
speak English but don't know much about
the area; some supply guides who are well
informed but don't speak English. Entrance
fees are *not* included in the tours prices listed below. If you prefer your own guide, it's
best to go with a certified official guide who
knows the area well. Ask at iPerú for a list of
certified guides and contact details.

Trujillo Tours
CULTURAL TOUR
(☎23-3091; www.trujillotours.com; Almagro 301;
⊙7:30am-1pm & 4-8pm) Friendly and recommended Trujillo Tours has three- to four-hour
tours to Chan Chan and Huanchaco (S64),
Moche Huacas del Sol y de la Luna (S66), as
well as city tours (S53). Tours are available in
English, French, Portuguese and German.

Chan Chan Tours
CULTURAL TOUR
(☎24-3016; chanchantourstrujillo@hotmail.com;
Independencia 431; ⊙8am-1pm & 3-8pm) Right
on the square, this established agency organizes trips to Chan Chan and Moche Huacas
Sol y de la Luna for S15 to S20 per person
(two-person minimum) as well as trips further afield. The guides speak some English.

✷ Festivals & Events

Fiesta de la Marinera
DANCE
This is the national *marinera* contest; held
in the last week in January.

El Festival Internacional
de la Primavera
FESTIVAL
(International Spring Festival) Trujillo's major
festival is celebrated with parades, national
dancing competitions (including, of course,
the *marinera*), *caballos de paso* displays,
sports, international beauty contests and
other cultural activities. It all happens in the
last week in September and better hotels are
booked out well in advance.

🛏 Sleeping

Decent budget places are thin on the ground in Trujillo, but pay a little extra and you'll be soaking up colonial ambience. Some travelers prefer to stay in the nearby beach town of Huanchaco. Many midrange hotels can be noisy if you get the streetside rooms. For a city of its size and history, Trujillo lags way behind when it comes to design and boutique hotels (OK, there are none). It pays to inquire about environmental policies at hotels here – some have been accused of burning carbon mineral bricks at night as a source for heating water, an environmentally damaging (but cheap) practice that is prohibited in Peru depending on emission levels.

TOP CHOICE Hostal Colonial   HISTORIC HOTEL $$

(☑25-8261; www.hostalcolonial.com.pe; Independencia 618; s/d/tr S60/90/120; ☎) This tastefully renovated, rose-colored colonial mansion (now HI-affiliated, though not a hostel) has a great location just a block from the Plaza de Armas. Chatty and helpful staff, a tour desk, popular cafe (with room service), gorgeous courtyards, open spaces and a garden synergistically come together to keep attracting travelers. Some of the cozy rooms have balconies and great views of Iglesia de San Francisco opposite.

Hotel Libertador   HISTORIC HOTEL $$$

(☑23-2441; www.libertador.com.pe; Independencia 485; s/d S475/510, ste from S668.80, prices incl breakfast; ☀@☎☲) The classy dame of the city's hotels, the 79-room Libertador is in a beautiful building that's the Audrey Hepburn of Trujillo – it wears its age with refined grace. It earns its four stars with a beautiful and lush courtyard pool, archways aplenty and comfortable rooms with all expected amenities. Rooms are centered around a bright atrium that encompasses the three floors, but try to avoid the streetside rooms unless you want to watch the goings-on, as they tend to be noisy.

Residencial Munay Wasi   GUESTHOUSE $

(☑23-1462; www.munaywasihostel.com; Colón 250; dm S30, s/d/tr incl breakfast S45/70/100; @☎) A pleasant, family-run budget option that woos travelers with a nice garage/courtyard (better than it sounds), eight rooms with hot water (three have international cable TV, as well as a small communal lounge), a guest kitchen and a wholly different atmosphere than most spots in Trujillo. You are sleeping in someone's home – and your experience follows suit.

Hospedaje el Conde de Arce   GUESTHOUSE

(☑29-5117; elcondedearce@hotmail.com; Independencia 577; dm S20, s/d S45/60; ☎) With giant, cluttered patio, this is a simple, safe budget lodging right in the center of town. The rooms are weathered but spacious, emptying out onto a bright cement courtyard. It's all overseen by the young, friendly and English-speaking Nathaly, the daughter of the longtime owner, and her adorable but timid dog, Tommy. It's not a bad deal by Trujillo standards.

Pullman Hotel   HOTEL $$

(☑47-1645; Pizarro 879; s/d S74/92; ☀@☎) The modern lobby here faces a pedestrian street near the Plazuela el Recreo and therefore doesn't suffer from much street noise. Neat and spotless, the parquet- or tile-floored rooms feature modern amenities; newly renovated rooms have whimsical, purple polka-dotted bathrooms that are a nice change of pace for Trujillo and LCD TVs. The front desk couldn't be friendlier, the pottery-walled atrium is pleasant and it's a five-minute walk to some northern bus stations.

Los Conquistadores Hotel   HOTEL $

(☑48-1650; www.losconquistadoreshotel.com; Almagro 586; s/d incl breakfast S200/240; ☀@☎) A few steps away from the Plaza de Armas, this discerning, 54-room choice got a modern makeover in 2012. New rooms ooze contemporary elegance, dressed up in soft creams and whites, and now rival any in Trujillo. The lobby beckons with Sipán gold replicas and there's a classic hotel bar for a pisco sour nightcap, room service (7am to 11pm) from the downstairs restaurant and open-ended hallways that catch a breeze.

Hostal Solari   HOTEL $$

(☑24-3909; www.hostalsolari.com.pe; Almagro 715; s/d with breakfast S80/130; @☎) A borderline contemporary spot, this place has massive, sensibly decorated rooms, which feature polished floorboards, a separate sitting/luggage storage area, fine mattresses, Aquos LCD TVs and minifridges. A cafe provides room service and the friendly front-desk staff will arrange tours and confirm airline tickets.

Gran Hotel Turismo   HOTEL $$

(☑24-4181; hotelturismo@speedy.com.pe; Gamarra 747; s/d incl breakfast s/d/tr S55/80/120; ☀☎)

ep back in time at this retro hotel, which n't the result of savvy trend following, it rather a likely lack of refurbishment nce the swinging '60s. Original hip decor cludes an ancient phone switch box that ould leave anyone under 20 totally aghast. ie hallways are the length of football elds – you can play a mean game of (take ur pick) shuffleboard, curling, bowling ere. Cozy rooms do have colorful new bed-reads that scream *Austin Powers,* but eve-thing else seems to have been untouched r decades. Groovy.

aint Germain Hotel
HOTEL **$$**

25-0574; www.saintgermainhotel.net; Junín 585; d incl breakfast S89/140; @🖂) The modern-sque Saint Germain has great rooms to get mfortable in and the usual slew of mod-n conveniences, as well as immaculate athrooms. The rooms facing inward are uieter than most and have windows onto a right light well. There's a bar and cafe here.

ostal el Ensueño
GUESTHOUSE **$**

24-2583; Junín 336; s S20-40, d S40-50; 🖂) he hallways here are dark and narrow, but ie rooms are perfectly acceptable and come ith decent bathrooms. They sometimes llow couples to squeeze into the single ooms, where you'll be spooning out of ne-essity but smiling about the extra *céntimos* 1 your pockets. The owners also run three ther guesthouses in the vicinity if you turn p and it's full.

otel El Brujo
HOTEL **$$$**

47-4545; www.elbrujohotel.com; Independen-ia 978; s/d incl breakfast S192/256; ✷@🖂) A omplete revamp of this hotel means a new ame and higher prices, but it's a clean, leasant and quiet option very close to sev-ral northern bus stations. It's very business-ike, with modern, carpeted rooms and all he requisite amenities (minibar, cable TV nd writing desk). There's 24-hour room ervice and a great new terrace with city iews. Foreign passport holders get a S81 iscount on listed prices.

✕ Eating

The 700 *cuadra* of Pizarro is where Trujillo's ower brokers hang out and families con-erge, and they're kept well fed by a row of rendy yet reasonably priced cafes and res-aurants. Some of the best eateries in Trujillo re found a short taxi ride outside the town enter.

⌜TOP⌟choice Mar Picante
PERUVIAN, SEAFOOD **$$**

(www.marpicante.com; Húsares de Junín 412; mains S18-30; 🖂10am-5pm) If you come to Trujillo without sampling this bamboo-lined sea-food palace's *ceviche mixto* ordered with a side of something spicy, you haven't lived life on the edge. You'll get raw shrimp, fish, crab, scallops and onions, marinated as usual in lime juice, piled on top of yucca and sweet potato with a side of toasted corn *(chancha)* and corn on the cob, along with a shot of *ro-coto*-fired juice that will jolt your taste buds into submission when you pour it on. This is the North Coast's best! Service is swift and friendly as well, no small feat consider-ing it's always packed. Take a taxi (S3.50) or leg it southwest on Larco from the center. Húsares de Junín splits off to the southeast 200m south of España.

⌜ Casona Deza
CAFE **$**

(Independencia 630; mains S10-25; 🖂) This spa-cious, atmospheric cafe occupies one of the city's most fiercely preserved colonial homes: the Casa Ganoza Chopitea mansion (c 1735), resurrected via auction by a local team of brothers passionate about Trujillo. As far as the cafe is concerned, expect ex-cellent espresso, house-made desserts and tasty pizzas and sandwiches, often sourced organically, that go down brilliantly in the airy courtyard or in one of the several rooms lined tastefully with antique furniture. Whether you're here for coffee, wine, suste-nance or architectural oohing and aahing, it's an addictive spot.

Juguería San Agustín
JUICE BAR **$**

(Bolívar 526; juice S2-5; 🖂8:30am-1pm & 4-8pm Mon-Sat, 9am-1pm Sun) You can spot this place by the near-constant lines snaking around the corner in summer as locals queue for the drool-inducing juices, but don't leave it at that. The chicken (S6) and *lechon* (suck-ling pig; S7) sandwiches, slathered with all the fixings, are what you'll be telling friends back home about on a postcard.

Restaurant Demarco
PERUVIAN **$$**

(Pizarro 725; mains S10-45; 🖂7:30am-11pm; 🖂) An elegant choice with veteran cummer-bund-bound waiters who fawn over you like in the '40s, this tableclothed classic offers a long list of sophisticated meat and seafood dishes along with good-value lunch specials (S14.50) and pizzas. They have mouthwater-ing *chupe de camarones,* a seafood stew of jumbo shrimp simmering in a buttery broth with hints of garlic, cumin and oregano, and the desserts are excellent, from classic tiramisu to mile-high *tres leches* (a spongy cake made with evaporated milk).

Chifa Heng Lung
CHINESE **$$**
(Pizarro 352; mains S10.50-42.50; ⊙to 11:30pm) Owned by a Chinese family of veteran chefs, this vaguely upscale, tasty option packs a wallop of flavorful infusion for Peruvinized palettes. The menu is a predictable list of Cantonese dishes, but very long on options and flavors.

Café Bar Museo
CAFE **$**
(cnr Junín & Independencia; mains S6-15, cocktails S18-22; ⊙closed Sun) This locals' favorite shouldn't be a secret. The tall, wood-paneled walls covered in artsy posters and the classic marble-top bar feels like a cross between an English pub and a Left Bank cafe.

Oviedo
BREAKFAST, CAFE **$**
(Pizarro 758; breakfast & sandwiches S6-14; ⊙8am-midnight) If you're sick of the tiny plate of eggs your hotel is throwing at you in the morning, check out Oviedo's long list of breakfasts – from a simple continental to a hearty *criollo* (spicy Peruvian fare with Spanish and African influences) that comes with a pork chop.

El Sol Restaurante Vegetariano
VEGETARIAN **$**
(Zepita 704; meals S3-8; ⊙8:30am-6pm Mon-Sat, to 4pm Sun) The tiny corner spot known as 'The Sun' maintains a short but surprising list of imitation meat dishes and always has a daily lunch *menú* for about S5. Plenty of nonvegetarians eat here, attesting to its hearty and delicious offerings, and there are macrobiotic options to boot.

Supermercado Metro
SELF-CATERING **$**
(Pizarro 700) For self-caterers.

Drinking & Entertainment

Trujillo's local newspaper La Industria (www.laindustria.pe) is the best source for information about local entertainment, cultural exhibitions and other events.

TOP CHOICE El Celler de Cler
BAR
(cnr Gamarra & Independencia; mains S12-24, cocktails S12-18; ⊙6pm-1am) This atmospheric spot is the only spot in Trujillo to enjoy a cocktail on a 2nd-floor colonial balcony. The wrap-around number here dates to the early 1800s, but the coup doesn't stop there: antiques fuel the decor, from a '50s-era American cash register to an extraordinary Industrial Revolution pulley lamp from the UK.

The food is upscale pasta and grills (great meat, typically disappointing fries), but it's the creative cocktails that shine, like the classic *chilcano* (pisco, ginger ale and lime juice), souped up here with any number of twists (*rocoto, ají limo, maracuya* etc). Try to go after rush hour or on a weekend as ambience notwithstanding, the streets below are noisy.

Picasso Lounge
CAFE, BAR
(www.picassocafelounge.com; Bolívar 762) This shotgun-style cafe and bar approaches Trujillo's trendiness tipping point and is a great place to check out some contemporary local art. Exhibitions change every two months. When the bartender is on (Thursday to Saturday from 8pm), there's a well-rounded cocktail list with some creative pisco concoctions.

Restaurante Turístico Canana
LIVE MUSIC
(♪San Martín 791; admission S20; ⊙from 11pm Thu-Sat) Although this place serves good Peruvian coastal food, late Thursday to Saturday is the time to go. Local musicians and dancers perform, starting at around 11pm, and you just might find yourself joining in. Better start drinking now.

Information

Dangers & Annoyances

Single women tend to receive a lot of attention from males in Trujillo – to exasperating, even harassing, levels. If untoward advances are made, firmly state that you aren't interested. Inventing a boyfriend or husband sometimes helps get the message across. See p541 for more advice for women travelers.

Like many other cities, the noise pollution levels in Trujillo are high. Civic groups have attempted to protest the constant bleating of taxi horns.

Emergency
Policía de Turismo (Tourist Police, Poltur; ♪29-1770; Independencia 572) Shockingly helpful. Tourist police wear white shirts around town and some deputies speak English, Italian and/or French.

Immigration
Oficina de Migraciónes (♪28-2217; www.digemin.gob.pe; Larco, cuadra 12; ⊙8am-4:15pm Mon-Fri, 9am-1pm Sat) Handles visas for foreign residents and tourist visa extensions.

Medical Services

Clínica Americano-Peruano (☎24-5181; Mansiche 810) The best general medical care in town, with English-speaking doctors. It charges according to your means, so let the clinic know if you don't have medical insurance.

Money

Changing money in Trujillo is a distinct pleasure; some of the banks are housed in well-preserved colonial buildings and all have ATMs that accept Visa and MasterCard. If lines are long, visit the casas de cambio (foreign-exchange bureaus) near Gamarra and Bolívar, which give good rates for cash.

Banco Continental (Pizarro 620) Housed in the handsome Casa de la Emancipación. Good rates for cash.

BCP (Gamarra 562) Has the lowest commission for changing traveler's checks.

HSBC (Gamarra 574) Fee-less ATM.

Post

Serpost (Independencia 286) Postal services.

Tourist Information

Local tour companies can also provide you with some basic information on the area.

iPerú (☎29-4561; cnr Almagro 420; ⊙9am-6pm Mon-Sat, 10am-2pm Sun) Provides tourist information and a list of certified guides and travel agencies.

ⓘ Getting There & Away

Air

The airport (TRU) is 10km northwest of town. **LAN** (☎22-1469; www.lan.com; Almagro 490) has three daily flights leaving Lima for Trujillo – at 6:05am, 4:50pm and 8:15pm – and returning from Trujillo to Lima at 7:45am, 6:45pm and 10pm. On average, fares range from S343 to S486. **Taca** (☎0-800-1-8222; www.taca.com; César Vallejo Oeste 1345, Real Plaza) flies the same route twice per day for as low as S142, leaving Lima at 1:05pm and 9pm, and returning from Trujillo at 2:50pm and 10:45pm.

Bus

Buses often leave Trujillo full, so booking a little earlier is advised. Several companies that go to southern destinations have terminals on the Panamericana Sur, the southern extension of Moche, and Ejército; check where your bus actually leaves from when buying a ticket.

Línea has services to most destinations of interest to travelers and is one of the more comfortable bus lines.

There's an enclave of bus companies around España and Amazonas offering Lima-bound night buses (eight hours).

If you want to travel to Huaraz by day, you'll need to go to Chimbote and catch a bus from there. For more frequent buses to Cajamarca and the northern Highlands, head to Chiclayo.

For Otuzco, combis depart between the 17th and 18th cuadras of Prolongacíon Unión northeast of town. **Tours Pacifico** (☎42-7137; Prolongacíon Unión, cuadra 22) heads up the mountain six times per day in buses.

America Express (☎26-1906; La Marina 315) A S5 taxi ride south of town, with buses to Chimbote every 20 minutes between 4am and 10:30pm.

Cial (☎20-1760; www.expresocial.com; Ejército & Amazonas 395) A 10pm bus to Lima.

Civa (☎25-1402; www.civa.com.pe; Ejército 285) A 10pm bus to Lima.

Cruz del Sur (☎26-1801; www.cruzdelsur.com.pe; Amazonas 437) One of the biggest and priciest bus companies in Peru. It goes to Lima five times a day and Guayaquil at 11:45pm on Sunday, Wednesday and Friday. They also have a **booking office** (Gamarra 439; ⊙9am-9pm Mon-Sat) in the centre.

El Dorado (☎24-4150; www.transporteseldorado.com.pe; N de Piérola 1070) Has rudimentary buses to Piura five times daily (12:30pm, 8pm, 8:30pm, 10:20pm, 11pm) and four to Máncora and Tumbes (12:30pm, 8pm, 8:30pm, 9pm).

Ittsa (☎25-1415; www.ittsabus.com; Mansiche 143) Has buses for Piura (9am, 1:30pm, 11:15pm, 11:30pm, 11:45pm), as well as 11 Lima-bound departures from 9am to 11:15pm.

Línea The company's **booking office** (☎24-5181; www.linea.pe; cnr San Martín & Orbegoso; ⊙9am-9pm Mon-Fri, 9am-7pm Sat) is conveniently located in the historical center, although all buses leave from the **terminal** (☎29-9666; Panamericana Sur 2855) on Panamericana Sur, a S5 taxi ride away. Línea goes to Lima nine times daily between 8:30am and 10:45pm; to Piura at 1:30pm and 11pm, to Cajamarca at 10:30am, 1pm, 10pm and 10:30pm; to Chiclayo six times between 6am and 7pm, stopping at Pacasmayo and Guadalupe; to Chimbote four times a day (5:30am, 11am, 2pm and 7pm); and to Huaraz at 9pm and 9:15pm.

Movil Tours (☎28-6538; www.moviltours.com.pe; America Sur 3959, Ovalo Larco) Specializes in very comfortable long-haul tourist services. It has a 10pm service to Lima; 10am, 9:40pm and 10:20pm departures to Huaraz, the former two continuing on to Caraz; a bus at 4:45pm to Chachapoyas; and a 3pm bus to Tarapoto. A taxi to the station is S5 or catch a red-signed A combi (California/Esperanza) on Av España and hop off at Ovalo Larco.

Oltursa (☎26-3055; www.oltursa.pe; Ejército 342) Offers three daily departures at noon, 10pm and 11pm. Oltursa shares an authorized

TRUJILLO BUSES

DESTINATION	COST (S)	DURATION (HR)
Bogotá	495	56
Cajabamba	25-35	12
Cajamarca	16-135	6-7
Caraz	45-60	8
Chachapoyas	60-75	15
Chiclayo	14-30	3-4
Chimbote	8-57	2
Guayaquil (Ec)	137.50-201	18
Huaraz	35-60	5-9
Lima	25-100	8-9
Máncora	27-70	8-9
Otuzco	6-10	2
Piura	25-45	6
Quito (Ec)	233.80	32
Tarapoto	85-105	18
Tumbes	27-80	9-12

booking agency with Ittsa on Plaza de Armas, but this office sometimes charges commissions.

Ormeño (📞25-9782; www.grupo-ormeno.com. pe; Ejército 233) Has two night buses to Lima leaving at 7pm and 10pm, as well as one night bus (9pm) to Máncora and Tumbes, continuing on to Guayaquil, on the Ecuadorean coast. Additionally, they have a Monday and Friday departure (10pm) to Quito, continuing on to Bogotá in Colombia.

Transportes Horna (📞24-3514; America Sur 1368) Has seven daily departures to Huamachuco and three buses to Cajamarca (1:30pm, 8pm, 11:30pm).

Turismo Días (📞20-1237; www.turdias.com; N de Piérola 1079) Opposite El Dorado, has four departures to Cajamarca (10am, 1:15pm, 10:30pm, 11pm) and two to Cajabamba (8pm, 9pm).

AROUND TRUJILLO

Green-signed B combis to Huaca Esmeralda (S1), Chan Chan (S1) and Huanchaco (S1.50) pass the corners of España and Ejército, and España and Industrial every few minutes. Buses for La Esperanza go northwest along the Panamericana and can drop you off at La Huaca Arco Iris. For Huacas del Sol y de la Luna, take a taxi (S4) to the Primax petrol station at Ovalo Grau southeast of the centre, where combis (S1.50) pass every 15 minutes or so. Note that these buses are worked by professional thieves; keep valuables hidden and watch your bags carefully. A taxi to most of these sites will cost S10 to S15.

El Complejo Arqueológico la Huaca el Brujo, about 60km northwest of Trujillo, is harder to reach. The safest route is catching a bus in Trujillo, bound for Chocope (S3.50, 1½ hours) from Ovalo del Papa southwest of town. Switch for a colectivo to Magdalena de Cao (S2.50, 20 minutes), where you'll need to negotiate with a mototaxi to take you to and from the site with waiting time (S5 each way plus something for waiting is about right; few tourists visit this site so options are slim – do not bank on randomly grabbing something after your visit). There are also Chocope-bound buses from the Provincial Bus Terminal Interurbano southeast of central Trujillo, but this neighborhood is best avoided by tourists.

❶ Getting Around

The **airport** (📞46-4013), 10km northwest of Trujillo, is reached cheaply on the Huanchaco combi, though you'll have to walk the last kilometer. It takes around 30 minutes. A taxi from the city center costs S15.

A short taxi ride around town costs about S3.50. For sightseeing, taxis charge about S20 (in town) to S25 (out of town) per hour.

Around Trujillo

The Moche and Chimú cultures left the greatest marks on the Trujillo area, but they were by no means the only cultures the region. In a March 1973 *National Geographic* article, Drs ME Moseley and CJ Mackey claimed knowledge of more than 000 sites in the Río Moche valley and many nore have been discovered since.

Five major archaeological sites can be asily reached from Trujillo by local bus or axi. Two of these are principally Moche, ating from about 200 BC to AD 850. The ther three, from the Chimú culture, date rom about AD 850 to 1500. The recently xcavated Moche ruin of La Huaca el Brujo 60km from Trujillo) can also be visited, but 's not as convenient.

Joining a tour to the archaeological sites sn't a bad idea, even for budget travelers. he ruins will be more interesting and neaningful with a good guide. Alternately, ou could hire an onsite guide.

The entrance ticket for Chan Chan is also alid for the Chimú sites of La Huaca Esneralda and La Huaca Arco Iris, as well as he Chan Chan museum, but it must be used vithin two days. All sites are open from 9am o 4:30pm and tickets are sold at every site, xcept La Huaca Esmeralda.

🎯 Sights

Chan Chan RUIN
adult S11; ⊙9am-4:30pm) Built around AD 300 and covering 20 sq km, Chan Chan is he largest pre-Columbian city in the Ameri-as, and the largest adobe city in the world. At the height of the Chimú empire, it housed in estimated 60,000 inhabitants and con-ained a vast wealth of gold, silver and ce-amics. The wealth remained more or less indisturbed after the Incas conquered the ity, but once the Spaniards hit the stage, the

looting began. Within a few decades little but gold dust remained. Remnants of what was found can be seen in museums nearby. Although Chan Chan must have been a daz-zling sight at one time, devastating El Niño floods and heavy rainfall have severely erod-ed the mud walls of the city. Today the most impressive aspect of the site is its sheer size; you'll need an active imagination to fill in the details.

The Chimú capital consisted of 10 walled citadels, also called royal compounds. Each contained a royal burial mound filled with vast quantities of funerary offerings, in-cluding dozens of sacrificed young women and chambers full of ceramics, weavings and jewelry. The Tschudi Complex, named after a Swiss naturalist, is the only section of Chan Chan that's partially restored. It is possible that other areas will open in the fu-ture, but until they are properly policed and signed, you run the risk of being mugged if you visit them.

At the Tschudi Complex you'll find an en-trance area with tickets, snacks, souvenirs, bathrooms, the small **Museo de Sitio Chan Chan** (admission free with Chan Chan ticket) with information in English and Spanish, and guides (S20). The complex is well marked by fish-shaped pointers, so you can see eve-rything without a guide if you prefer. Your entry ticket for Chan Chan is also valid for the Chimú sites of La Huaca Esmeralda and La Huaca Arco Iris.

Combis to Chan Chan leave Trujillo every few minutes, passing the corners of España and Ejército, and España and Industrial. A taxi from Trujillo runs S10.

Around Trujillo

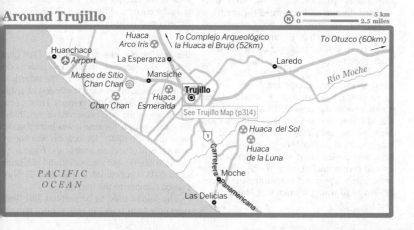

See Trujillo Map (p314)

Tschudi Complex

Also called the Palacio Nik-An, the complex's centerpiece is a massive, restored **Ceremonial Courtyard**, whose 4m-thick interior walls are mostly decorated with re-created geometric designs. The ground-level designs closest to the door, representing three or four sea otters, are the only originals left and are slightly rougher looking than the modern work. A ramp at the far side of the high-walled plaza enters the 2nd level (early wheelchair access?). Though all the Chan Chan walls have crumbled with time, parts of Tschudi's walls once stood more than 10m high.

Head out of the Ceremonial Courtyard and walk along the **outside wall**, one of the most highly decorated and best re-stored of Tschudi's walls. The adobe friezes show waves of fish rippling along the entire length of the wall above a line of seabirds. Despite their time-worn appearance, the few rougher-looking originals retain a fluidity and character somehow lacking in the contemporary version.

At the end of this wall, the marked path goes through the labyrinthine **Audience Rooms**. Their function is unclear, but their importance is evident in both the quantity and quality of the decorations – the rooms have the most interesting friezes in Tschudi. Living so close to the ocean, the Chimú based much of their diet on seafood, and the importance of the sea reached venerable proportions. Fish, waves, seabirds and sea mammals are represented throughout the city, and in the Audience Rooms you'll find all of them in the one place. For the Chimú, both the moon and the sea were of religious importance (unlike the Incas, who worshipped the sun and venerated the earth).

Further on, the **Second Ceremonial Courtyard** also has a ramp to the 2nd level. From behind this plaza, you can see a huge rectangular depression that was once a **walk-in well** supplying the daily water needs of the royal compound.

To the left is an area of several dozen small, crumbling cells that has been called the **Military Sector**. Perhaps soldiers lived here, or the cells may have been used for storage. Next is the **Mausoleum**, where a king was buried along with human sacrifices and ceremonial objects. To the left of the main tomb, a pyramid containing the bodies of dozens of young women was found.

The final area is the **Assembly Room**. This large rectangular room has 24 seats set into niches in the walls, and its amazing acoustic properties are such that speakers sitting in any one of the niches can be clearly heard all over the room.

Museo de Sitio Chan Chan

The site museum contains exhibits explaining Chan Chan and the Chimú culture. It is on the main road, about 500m before the Chan Chan turnoff. The museum has a few signs in Spanish and English but a guide is still useful. A sound-and-light show plays in Spanish every 30 minutes. The aerial photos and maps showing the huge extension of Chan Chan are fascinating, as tourists can only visit a tiny portion of the site.

Complejo Arqueológico RUI

Huaca Esmeralda

(admission free with Chan Chan ticket) Halfway between Trujillo and Chan Chan, this Chimú temple is to the south of the main road, four blocks behind the Mansiche Church. Thieves reportedly prey on unwary tourists wandering around, so go with a large group or a guide and keep your eyes open.

Huaca Esmeralda was buried by sand and was accidentally discovered by a local landowner in 1923. He attempted to uncover the ruins, but El Niño of 1925 began the process of erosion, which was exacerbated by the floods and rains of 1983. Although little restoration work has been done on the adobe friezes, it is still possible to make out the characteristic Chimú designs of fish, seabirds, waves and fishing nets.

Green-signed B *combis* to Huaca Esmeralda leave Trujillo every few minutes; they pass the corners of España and Ejército, and España and Industrial.

Huaca Arco Iris

(Rainbow Temple; admission free with Chan Chan ticket) Also known locally as Huaca del Dragón, Huaca Arco Iris is in the suburb of La Esperanza, about 4km northwest of Trujillo. Dating from the 12th century, Huaca Arco Iris is one of the best preserved of the Chimú temples – simply because it was buried under sand until the 1960s. Its location was known to a handful of archaeologists and *huaqueros* (grave robbers), but excavation did not begin until 1963. Unfortunately, the 1983 El Niño caused damage to the friezes.

The *huaca* used to be painted, but these days only faint traces of yellow hues remain

consists of a defensive wall more than
n thick enclosing an area of about 3000
meters, which houses the temple itself.
ne building covers about 800 sq meters in
o levels, with a combined height of about
m. The walls are slightly pyramidal and
overed with repeated rainbow designs,
ost of which have been restored. Ramps
ad the visitor to the very top of the temple,
om where a series of large bins, found to
ontain the bones of infants – possibly hu-
an sacrifices – can be seen. This may have
en a fertility temple since in many ancient
lltures the rainbow represents rain, con-
dered to be the bringer of life.

There is a tiny onsite museum, and local
uides are available to show you around.

Buses for La Esperanza go northwest
ong the Panamericana and can drop you
f at Huaca Arco Iris.

uacas del Sol y de la Luna   RUIN

www.huacasdemoche.pe; adult S11; ⊘9am-
30pm) The Temples of the Sun and the
Moon are more than 700 years older than
han Chan and are attributed to the Moche
eriod. They are on the south bank of the
ío Moche, about 10km southeast of Trujillo
y a rough road. The entrance price includes
guide.

The Huaca del Sol is the largest single
re-Columbian structure in Peru, although
bout a third of it has been washed away.
he structure was built with an estimated
10 million adobe bricks, many of them
arked with symbols representing the
orkers who made them.

At one time the pyramid consisted of sev-
ral different levels connected by steep flights
f stairs, huge ramps and walls sloping at 77
egrees. The last 1500 years have wrought
heir inevitable damage, and today the pyr-
mid looks like a giant pile of crude bricks
artially covered with sand. The few graves
ithin the structure suggest it may have been
huge ceremonial site. Certainly, its size
lone makes the pyramid an awesome sight,
nd the views from the top are excellent.

Size isn't everything, however. The
maller but more interesting Huaca de la
una is about 500m away across the open
esert. This structure is riddled with rooms
hat contain ceramics, precious metals and
ome of the beautiful polychrome friezes for
vhich the Moche were famous. The *huaca*
tomb or grave) was built over six centuries
o AD 600, with six succeeding generations
xpanding on it and completely covering

the previous structure. Archaeologists are
currently onion-skinning selected parts of
the *huaca* and have discovered that there
are friezes of stylized figures on every level,
some of which have been perfectly preserved
by the later levels built around them. It's
well worth a visit; you'll see newly excavated
friezes every year and the new and excellent
Museo Huacas de Moche (Admission S3;
⊘9am-4:30pm) is a long-time-coming permanent home for numerous objects excavated
from the site. There's a research center and
theater as well.

As you leave, check out the souvenir
stands, some of which sell pots made using
the original molds found at the site. Also
look around for *biringos,* the native Peruvian hairless dogs that hang out here. Their
body temperature is higher than the normal
dog and they have traditionally been used as
body warmers for people with arthritis.

Combis for the Huacas del Sol y de la
Luna pass Ovalo Grau in Trujillo every 15
minutes or so. It's also possible to take a
taxi (S15).

Complejo Arqueológico
la Huaca el Brujo   RUIN

(adult S11; ⊘9am-4pm) This archaeological
complex consists of the Huaca Prieta site,
the recently excavated Moche site of Huaca
Cao Viejo with its brilliant mural reliefs, and
Huaca el Brujo, which is only starting to be
excavated. The complex is 60km from Trujillo on the coast and is hard to find without a guide. It's technically not open to the
public as there is little to see so far, but tour
agencies in Trujillo can arrange a visit to the
area on request.

Reaching the complex on your own is
complicated. The safest route is catching a
bus in Trujillo bound for Chocope (S3.50,
1½ hours) from Ovalo del Papa southwest of
town. Switch for a *colectivo* to Magdalena de
Cao (S2.50, 20 minutes), where you'll need
to negotiate with a *mototaxi* to take you to
and from the site with waiting time. There
is very little public transport out this way.

Huaca Cao Viejo   RUIN

The main section of Huaca Cao Viejo is a 27m
truncated pyramid with some of the best
friezes in the area. They show magnificently
multicolored reliefs – much more color than
you see at the *huacas* closer to Chiclayo
– with stylized life-sized warriors, prison-
ers, priests and human sacrifices. There are
also many burial sites from the Lambayeque

culture, which followed the Moche. The people who live near this *huaca* insist that it has positive energy and ceremonies are occasionally performed here when someone needs to soak up a bit of the good vibes.

Huaca Prieta   RUIN

Huaca Prieta has been one of the most intensively studied early Peruvian sites. However, for nonarchaeologists, it's generally more interesting to read about than to tour. Although it's simply a prehistoric pile of refuse, it does afford extensive vistas over the coastal area and can be visited along with the other *huacas* in the archaeological comple

Huanchaco

☎ 044 / POP 41,900

This once-tranquil fishing hamlet, 12k outside Trujillo, woke up one morning find itself a brightly highlighted paragra on Peru's Gringo Trail. Though you ca almost picture Huanchaco on postcar of days gone by, the beach is distinct

---

PRE-COLUMBIAN PEOPLES OF THE NORTH COAST

Northern Peru has played host to a series of civilizations stretching as far back as 5000 years. Listed below are the major cultures that waxed and waned in Peru's coastal desert areas over the millennia.

Huaca Prieta

One of first peoples on the desert scene, the Huaca Prieta lived at the site of the same name (p324) from around 3500 BC to 2300 BC. These hunters and gatherers grew cotton and varieties of beans and peppers and subsisted mainly on seafood. They were pre-ceramic people who had developed netting and weaving, but didn't use jewelry. At their most artistic, they decorated dried gourds with simple carvings. Homes were single-room shacks half buried in the ground; most of what is known about these people has been deduced from their middens.

Chavín

Based around Huaraz in Peru's central Andes, the Chavín also had a significant cultural an artistic influence on coastal Peru, particularly between the years 800 BC and 400 BC. For more information on the Chavín culture, see p397.

Moche

Evolving from around AD 100 to AD 800, the Moche created ceramics, textiles and metalwork, developed the architectural skills to construct massive pyramids and still had enoug time for art and a highly organized religion.

Among all their expert productions, it's the ceramics that earn the Moche a ranking in Peru's pre-Inca civilization hall of fame. Considered the most artistically sensitive and technically developed of any ceramics found in Peru, Moche pots are realistically decorate with figures and scenes that leave us with a very descriptive look at everyday life. Pots wer modeled into lifelike representations of people, crops, domestic and wild animals, marine life and monumental architecture. Other pots were painted with scenes of ceremonial activities and everyday objects.

Some facets of Moche life illustrated on pots include punishments, surgical procedures (such as amputation and the setting of broken limbs) and copulation. One room in Lima's Museo Larco (p65) is devoted to pots depicting a cornucopia of sexual practices, some the products of very fertile imaginations. Museo Cassinelli in Trujillo (p317) also has a fine collection.

A few kilometers south of Trujillo, there are two main Moche sites: Huaca del Sol and Huaca de la Luna (p325).

The Moche period declined around AD 700, and the next few centuries are somewhat confusing. The Wari culture, based in the Ayacucho area of the central Peruvian Andes, began to expand after this time, and its influence was reflected in both the Sicán and Chim cultures.

verage. Nevertheless, the slow pace of life attracts a certain type of beach bum and the town has managed to retain much of its villagey appeal. Today, Huanchaco is happy to dish up a long menu of accommodations and dining options to tourists and great waves for budding surfers. Come summertime, legions of local and foreign tourists descend on its lapping shores, and this fast-growing resort town makes a great alternative base for exploring the ruins surrounding Trujillo.

Huanchaco's defining characteristic is that local fishermen are still using the very same narrow reed boats depicted on 2000-year-old Moche pottery. The fishermen paddle and surf these neatly crafted boats like seafaring cowboys, with their legs dangling on either side – which explains the nickname given to these elegantly curving steeds, *caballitos de tortora* (little horses). The inhabitants of Huanchaco are among the few remaining people on the coast who remember how to construct and use the boats, each one only

Sicán

The Sicán were probably descendants of the Moche and flourished in the same region from about AD 750 to 1375. Avid agriculturalists, the Sicán were also infatuated with metallurgy and all that glitters. The Sicán are known to many archaeologists for their lost-wax (mold-cast) gold ornaments and the manufacture of arsenical copper, which is the closest material to bronze found in pre-Columbian New World archaeology. These great smiths produced alloys of gold, silver and arsenic copper in vast quantities, using little more than hearths fired by *algarrobo* (carob tree) wood and pipe-blown air to achieve the incredible 1,000°C temperatures needed for such work.

Artifacts found at Sicán archaeological sites suggest that this culture loved to shop, or at least trade. They were actively engaged in long-distance trade with peoples along the length and breadth of the continent, acquiring shells and snails from Ecuador, emeralds and diamonds from Colombia, bluestone from Chile and gold from the Peruvian highlands.

With a structured and religiously controlled social organization, the Sicán engaged in bizarre and elaborate funerary practices, examples of which can be seen at the Museo Nacional Sicán in Ferreñafe (p341).

Unfortunately, as was the case with many pre-Inca societies, the weather was the ultimate undoing of the Sicán. Originally building their main city at Batán Grande (p342), northeast of Trujillo, they were forced to move to Túcume (p341) when El Niño rains devastated the area in the 13th century.

Chimú

The Chimú were contemporaries of the Sicán and were active from about AD 850 to 1470. They were responsible for the huge capital at Chan Chan (p323), just north of Trujillo. The artwork of the Chimú was less exciting than that of the Moche, tending more to functional mass production than artistic achievement. Gone, for the most part, was the technique of painting pots. Instead, they were fired by a simpler method than that used by the Moche, producing the typical blackware seen in many Chimú pottery collections. While the quality of the ceramics declined, skills in metallurgy developed, with gold and various alloys being worked.

The Chimú are best remembered as an urban society. Their huge capital contained about 10,000 dwellings of varying quality and importance. Buildings were decorated with friezes, the designs molded into mud walls, and important areas were layered with precious metals. There were storage bins for food and other products from across the empire, which stretched along the coast from Chancay to the Gulf of Guayaquil (southern Ecuador). There were huge walk-in wells, canals, workshops and temples. The royal dead were buried in mounds with a wealth of offerings.

The Chimú were conquered by the Incas in 1471 and heavy rainfall has severely damaged the adobe moldings of this once vast metropolis.

lasting a few months before becoming water-logged. You'll see rows of these iconic craft extending their long fingers to the sun as they dry along the beach – the postcard view of Huanchaco today.

⊙ Sights

The curving, gray-sand beach here is fine for swimming during the December to April summer, but expect serious teeth chatter during the rest of the year. The good surf here, perfect for beginners, draws its fair share of followers and you'll see armies of bleached-blond surfer types ambling the streets with boards in hand.

There is a S0.50 charge between 10:30am and 6:30pm to enter the town pier.

 Santuario de la Virgen del Socorro CHURCH
(⊙9am-12:30pm & 4-7pm) This church above town is worth a visit. Built between 1535 and 1540, it is said to be the second-oldest church in Peru. There are sweeping views from the restored belfry.

🏃 Activities

You can rent surfing gear (S15 to S30 per day for a wetsuit and surfboard) from several places along the main drag.

Muchik SURFING
(☑63-4503; www.escueladetablamuchik.com; Larco 650) Huanchaco's longest-running surf school and said to be the most reliable. Two-hour lessons run S45 and board/wetsuit rental is S15 per day.

Un Lugar SURFING
(☑94-957-7170; www.unlugarsurfschoolperu.com; Atahualpa 225) Two blocks back from the main beach road. This rustic surf school/guesthouse is run by highly skilled Juan Carlos and provides private two-hour lessons for S45. It also rents boards and suits, and organizes surfing safaris to Puerto Chicama and other iconic Peruvian surf spots. Barebones bamboo treehouse-style rooms are also available for S15 per person.

Wave SURFING
(Larco 850) Surf school that rents surfing gear.

🌟 Festivals & Events

Carnaval FESTIVAL, RELIGIOUS
A big event in Huanchaco; in February/March.

Festival del Mar CULTUR
This festival re-enacts the legendary arriv of Takaynamo, founder of Chan Chan. E pect surfing and dance competitions, cu tural conferences, food, music and mu merrymaking. Held every other year (eve years) during the first week in May.

🛏 Sleeping

You can find Naylamp in the northern pa of Huanchaco, while at the southern en of town there are a few guesthouses in th small streets running perpendicular to th beach. All the options here have hot show ers; most have cable TV. You can get di counts of up to 50% outside festival an holiday times, so be sure to ask.

TOP CHOICE Naylamp GUESTHOUSE
(☑46-1022; www.hostalnaylamp.com; Larco 142 campsites with/without tent S13/10, s/d/ S35/50/80; @🛜) Top of the pops in th budget stakes, Naylamp has one building o the waterfront and a second, larger buil ing behind the hotel. Great budget room share a spacious sea-view patio, and th lush camping area has perfect sunset view Kitchen, laundry service and a cafe are a thrown in. The only thing missing is wate in the pool.

Hospedaje Oceano GUESTHOUSE
(☑46-1653; www.hospedajeoceano.com; Los Cerez es 105; r/tr from S40/60; @🛜) Ideally locate between one of the town's most lush an pleasant *plazoletas* and the ocean, this su perbly welcoming family-run spot will hav you feeling like kin within minutes of ar rival. From the outside, it's indistinguishabl from any number of dismissible Peruvia guesthouses, but the great Mediterranean tilted rooms offer a pleasant surprise upor popping your bags down.

Best of all? The family makes addictive homemade *cremoladas* (Italian ices; S2) which are listed on the daily-changing men complete with their requisite health benefit (cappuccino and coconut are extraordinary)

Hostal Caballito de Totora BOUTIQUE HOTEL $
(☑46-1154; www.hotelcaballitodetotora.com.pe; La Rivera 348; s S35, d from S90, ste from S360, all inc breakfast; ✳@🛜⛱) Although regular rooms can be a little stuffy, the suites here are the best single rooms in Huanchaco, decked in modern motifs that even outdo Trujillo for trendiness (not hard to do, but these wouldn't be out of place in Miami). They

fer perfect sea views, wide, circular tubs
d private patios to boot.

A cozy bar and a lobby pier photo add to
e ambience. It's the one hotel in Huan-
aco that feels truly boutique.

Casa Suiza GUESTHOUSE **$**

46-1285; www.casasuiza.com; Los Pinos 308;
n/s S20/25, d with/without bathroom S65/40;
) The Swiss House's spacious rooms
ve Peru-themed, airbrushed murals. The
tle cafe downstairs prepares crunchy crust
zzas, and the patio upstairs hosts a nice
ew and the occasional barbecue. Good-
ality bikes are also available for rent
er half-day S15). French-American owner
ilippe Faucon cultivates a pleasant vibe
hen he is in town; otherwise, the welcome
at slips a little and the front desk can be
allenging.

urf Hostal Meri HOSTEL **$**

46-2264; hostel.meri@gmail.com; La Rivera
0; dm S20, s/d without bathroom S30/50, tr
75; @) Full of tattered antique furniture,
is rustic beddown across the street from
e beach is vaguely hippie-esque with a
od communal hostel vibe. The Finnish-
eruvian owners are big surfers (it doubles
s a school) and there are ample public
ang spaces, including a couple of great
ammocks and sun-drenched sea-view
ecks.

otel Bracamonte HOTEL **$$**

46-1162; www.hotelbracamonte.com.pe; Los Ol-
os 160; s/d/tr incl breakfast from S124/150/197;
) Popular, friendly, welcoming and
ecure behind high walls and a locked gate,
he Bracamonte is one of the oldest of Huan-
haco's nicer hotels and it remains one of
he top choices. Nice gardens, a games room,
arbecue, restaurant, bar and toddlers' play-
round make it great for families; the execu-
ive rooms are probably the best maintained
n Huanchaco.

Overall, it's the most equipped and near
esortlike choice.

luanchaco Hostal HOTEL **$**

46-1272; www.huanchacohostal.com; Plaza de
rmas; s/d/tr S75/120/145;) On the town's
mall Plaza de Armas, this cozy little place
as spartan rooms and a handsome back-
/ard concealing a secluded pool and garden.
There are plenty of arty touches to make it
eel homey.

McCallum Lodging House GUESTHOUSE **$**

(46-2350; mccallum-lodging-house@hotmail.com;
Los Ficos 305; dm/s/d/tr S15/25/45/60;) This
family-run guesthouse levels the playing field
of its crude construction with friendliness
and camaraderie – travelers gather around
the nice communal kitchen and hammock-
strewn concrete garden and discuss the day's
waves. Rooms are basic but clean with 24-
hour hot water and a matriarch (Patricia),
who will fawn over you like her own.

My Friend Hospedaje GUESTHOUSE **$**

(46-1080; www.myfriendsurfhostal.com; Los
Pinos 158; dm/d/tr S10/20/30;) This hole-
in-the-wall attracts droves of backpackers
and surfers with only a few *nuevo soles* left
in their pockets. The little cafe downstairs
serves breakfast, there are electric hot-water
showers, and it moonlights as a surf school.
Not a bad deal.

✖ Eating & Drinking

Not surprisingly, Huanchaco has oodles of
seafood restaurants, especially near the *ca-
ballitos de tortora* stacked at the north end
of the beach. Entertainment is of the reggae
and beer variety – try Mamacocha on Los
Pinos. On weekends, *trujillanos* descend on
the town and things are a little more lively.

TOP CHOICE Restaurant

Big Ben PERUVIAN, SEAFOOD **$$**

(www.bigbenhuanchaco.com; Larco 836; mains
S17-40; 11:30am-5:30pm;) This sophisticated seafooder at the far north end of town
specializes in lunchtime ceviches (S39 to
S46) and is the best in town for top-notch
seafood. Though ceviche is the main draw,
the menu is also heavy on fresh fish, *sudados* (seafood stews) and prawn dishes, all of
which go down even better on the umbrella-
dotted 3rd-floor patio with views.

Otra Cosa VEGETARIAN **$**

(Larco 921; dishes S6-13; from 8am;) This
Dutch-Peruvian beachside pad is Huanchaco's requisite traveler's hub, serving
up yummy vegetarian victuals like falafel,
crepes, Spanish tortillas, Dutch apple pie and
tasty curry-laced burritos (one of which is *almost* a breakfast burrito!). Coffee is organic
as well. Half of the tips are donated to char-
ity, and local organizations like Skip (www.
skipperu.org) and MySmallHelp Peru (www.
mysmallhelp.org) are supported through a
small clothing and jewelry shop.

OTUZCO: PERU'S FAITH CAPITAL

The small provincial mountain town of Otuzco is only two hours away from Trujillo, making it the only place in Peru where you can go coast-to-Andean peaks in such a short amount of time. The cobblestone streets, cool weather and relaxed pace of life make this a great day trip or stopover on the mountain route to Cajamarca. The modern church here dramatically houses the Virgen de la Puerta (Virgin of the Door) outside its walls on the 2nd floor balcony of the town cathedral. This patron saint is the impetus behind the popular Peruvian pilgrimage on December 15 (one of South America's most important), when pilgrims of all ages leg it the 73km from Trujillo as a test to their faith. What? Not impressed? Let's not forget Trujillo is at sea level and Otuzco sits at a cool 2641m. The town's conviction has earned it the title of Peru's Capital de la Fe (Capital of Faith).

The trip itself is worthwhile (we mean the drive, of course), as you'll be greeted by excellent mountain scenery through coastal subtropical crops and into the highland agricultural regions.

There are some modest places to stay, the best being the cheap **Hostal Los Portales** (hotellosportalesdeotuzco@hotmail.com; Santa Rosa 680; s with/without bathroom S30/15, d with/without bathroom S45/30, tr with/without bathroom S60/30). A few inexpensive restaurants serve Peruvian food – **Restaurante Otuzco** (Tacna 451; menús S4-5) has a good reputation with locals.

Tours Pacifico (☎43-6138; Progreso 301) heads to Trujillo (S6 to S8, 1½ hours) six times daily. You can pick up a *colectivo* to Huamachuco (S10, 3½ hours) at the crossroads 3.5km south of town. They pass at 10am, 2:30pm and 8pm. A taxi to the crossroads is S1.

Mococho

PERUVIAN, SEAFOOD $$

(☎Bolognesi 535; 3-course meal S45; ⏰1-3pm, closed Mon) This tiny place sits secluded in a walled garden where the legend of chef Don Victor is carried on by his widow and son, Wen. Local fisherman knock on the door here every morning shouting, 'Hey Chinese! The catch of the day is ...' and Wen, the only Chinese-Peruvian restaurateur in town, serves up just two dishes with whatever's fresh that day: a ceviche appetizer and a steamed whole fish (filets for solo diners) in a sharply colored, wildly flavorful *criollo* sauce. It's not cheap, but it's fresh and excellent, despite the Halls served as an after-meal mint.

El Caribe

PERUVIAN, SEAFOOD $$

(Atahualpa 150; mains S20-25; ⏰10am-5pm) This is a local favorite for the reasonably priced seafood and *comida criolla* (local cuisine). Ceviche here is half the price of the expensive options and double the price of the cheapies, but do you really want to eat raw fish for under S10?

Jungle Bar Bily

BAR, SEAFOOD

(Larco 420; cocktails S12-18; closed Mon; ☎) Travelers gravitate to this quasi-Polynesian-themed bar due to location (across from the pier), good music (U2, R.E.M.) and a popular S15 ceviche, among other good-value sea food. Happy hour (6pm to 10pm) nets a 50% discount on selected cocktails.

ℹ Information

Most services are in Trujillo, a short ride away. See www.huanchacovivo.com for useful tourist info. Next to the *municipalidad* (town hall) are three ATMs that accept MasterCard and Visa cards.

Dangers & Annoyances

Be careful walking the streets late at night, as robberies are not uncommon.

Internet

Internet K.M.E.K (La Riviera 735; per hr S1; ⏰3-10pm) Also can change US dollars.

Post

Serpost (Manco Cápac 360)

ℹ Getting There & Away

Some bus companies (Línea, for example) keep a ticket office in Huanchaco, but buses depart from Trujillo. *Combis* to Huanchaco frequently leave from Trujillo (S1.50). To return, just wait on the beachfront road for the bus as it returns from the north end. A taxi to or from Trujillo should cost S12.

uerto Chicama (Puerto Ialabrigo)

044

ιe small fishing outpost of Puerto Chi-
ma might not look like much, but it's
ε offshore action that draws a dedicated
.lowing. Puerto Chicama, also known as
ιerto Malabrigo, lays claim to one of the
ngest left-hand point breaks in the world.
riginally a busy port for the sugar and cot-
n grown on nearby haciendas, Puerto Chi-
ma now draws adrenaline-seeking surfers
ιho try their luck catching that rare, long
le. Peru's national surfing championships
ε usually held here in April.

The lengthy break is caused by a shallow,
ιt beach and on the right wave on the right
ιy at the right time, it's possible to hitch a
2km ride here on a 2m wave! Good waves
ιn be found year-round, but the marathon
ιreaks only come about when the condi-
ions are just so, usually between March and
ιne. There is some gear available for hire
: El Hombre, though it's best to bring your
ιwn. The water is very cold for much of the
ιar, except for December through March.

The French-owned El Inti (☑57-6138; www.
tisurfcamp.com; s/d S45/80, ste S150; @ 🛜) has
sea-view terrace restaurant where friendly
ιwner Nicholas, a former Chamonix–Mont-
ϊlanc chef, churns out impressive gourmet
ιeals year-round (S20 to S35; call ahead in
ιff season). There are a few garden bamboo
ιungalows here and an outstanding new
ιnd-floor suite that outclasses the town with
ιmazing sea views from the deep Jacuzzi
ιb. Next door, El Hombre (☑57-6077; hos-
εdaje-restaurant-elhombre@hotmail.com; s/d
ιithout bathroom S20/40, with bathroom S40/80)
ι the original surfers' hostel and is run by
ιhe daughter of local legend 'El Hombre,' a
ιurfer guru who's been at it for more than
ι0 years. Facing the ocean, the hostel has
ιlead simple rooms, great communal bath-
ιooms, good simple meals (S10 to S14) and
ι communal TV often seen flickering with
ιurf videos.

Some surf shops in Huanchaco, includ-
ng Un Lugar and The Wave (p328), arrange
ιurfing safaris to Puerto Chicama. The
ιasiest independent route is catching an El
Ɔorado (☑24-4150; www.transporteseldorado.
om.pe; N de Piérola 1070, Trujillo) bus to Puerto
Malabrigo (S6, two hours). A faster route
ι a colectivo to the town of Paiján, 40km
ιurther north on the Panamericana (S7, 1½

hours). From here you can catch *colectivos*
for the 16km to Puerto Chicama (S2, 20
minutes).

Pacasmayo

☑044 / POP 25,700

This lively, mostly forgotten beach town is
crammed with colonial buildings in various
states of disrepair and blessed with a pretty
stretch of beach. Dedicated surfers often drop
in, particularly from May to August, when
there is a decent offshore break. It's also a
great place to spend some time away from
the more popular resort towns and get swept
up in the ageing nostalgia of the whole place.

⊙ Sights & Activities

A few kilometers north, just before the village of Guadalupe, a track leads toward the
ocean and the little-visited ruins of Pacat-
namú, a large site that was inhabited by the
Gallinazo, Moche and Chimú cultures and
is regarded by archaeologists as one of the
coast's most impressive.

Muelle Pacasmayo   PIER

(admission S1) What's said to be the longest
pier in Peru has a storied history. Originally constructed between 1870 and 1874, it
initially clocked in at a whopping 743.4m.
Today, it stands at 544m after a chunk was
swept out to sea in 1924. In the '40s, two
overloaded train cars fell into the sea from
the pier as well.

Balin Surf Shop   SURFING

(Junín 84) Rents boards and does repairs.

🛏 Sleeping & Eating

There are several cheap, basic-but-clean
hotels in town and some swisher converted
colonial mansions and new constructions
along the beach.

Hospedaje El Mirador   HOTEL $

(☑52-1883; www.pacasmayoperu.com; Aurelio Her-
rera 10; s/d/tr from S40/60/90; @🛜) All tiles,
bricks and Brazilians, this surfers' hangpad
has good rooms varying from *económico*
(basic) to *de lujo* (luxury); all have hot water,
communal balconies and wall-mounted flat-
screen TVs with international channels; the
nicest rooms have kitchens and DVD players.

Hotel Pakatnamú   HOTEL $

(☑52-2368; www.actiweb.es/hotelpakatnamu;
Malecón Grau 103; s/d/tr S75/105/125; ❅@🛜)
This freshly painted bright yellow colonial

building along the waterfront has more storied character than others, despite abrupt color changes from one hallway to the next. The plush rooms here come with TV and fridge, there's a cozy bar/restaurant and the open-ended hallways spill out onto a wonderful sea-view terrace.

La Estación Gran Hotel HOTEL $
(☎52-1515; www.hotellaestacion.com.pe; Malecón Grau 69; s/d S90/135, ste from S165, all incl breakfast; @🛜❄) The majestic, restored Republican-era facade doesn't carry over to the interiors, but there is a great rooftop terrace, small pool and ground-floor bar/restaurant (mains S20 to S30). Its sea soundtrack is the best eats in town, notably the fabulous fish *a lo macho* (creamy shellfish sauce with *ají* and garlic).

❶ Information

There are **BCP** (Ayacucho 20), **BBVA** (2 de Mayo 9) and **Banco de la Nación** (8 de Julio & Lima) ATMs in town, though BCP is the most convenient on Plaza de Armas. Internet is ubiquitous.

❶ Getting There & Away

Emtrafesa (www.emtrafesa.com.pe; 28 de Julio 104) has frequent buses to Trujillo (S8, 1¾ hours), Chiclayo (S9, 1¾ hours), Cajamarca (S20 to S30, 4½ hours, 2pm and 11:30pm) as well as points further north.

Chiclayo

📋074 / POP 256,900

Spanish missionaries founded a small rural community on this site in the 16th century. Either by chance or through help from above, Chiclayo has prospered ever since. In one of the first sharp moves in Peruvian real estate, the missionaries chose a spot that sits at the hub of vital trade routes connecting the coast, the highlands and the deep jungle. Chiclayo's role as the commercial heart of the district has allowed it to overtake other once-vital organs of the region, such as the nearby city of Lambayeque, and this bustling metropolis shows few signs of slowing down.

La Ciudad de la Amistad (the City of Friendship) holds a friendly, outstretched hand to the wayward venturer. While it's shaking hands hello, it will probably slip in a bold mix of unique regional dishes to tickle your taste buds. Known for its *brujos* (witch doctors), the fascinating market here

is a Wal-Mart of shamanistic herbs, elixir and other sagely curiosities. While the town itself is pretty light on tourist attraction the dozens of tombs with Moche and Chimú archaeological booty surrounding the area should not be missed.

◉ Sights & Activities

In 1987 a royal Moche tomb at **Sipán**, 30km southeast of Chiclayo, was located by researchers. This find proved to be extraordinary, as archaeologists recovered hundreds of dazzling and priceless artifacts from the site. Excavation continues. Partly because of the rare treasures, the Chiclayo area has single-handedly cornered the Peruvian market for exceptionally well-designed museums a case in point is the excellent museum in **Lambayeque**, 11km north of Chiclayo. Other sites worth visiting are the ruins at **Túcume** another great museum in **Ferreñafe**, as well as a number of coastal villages.

The **Plaza de Armas** is a great place to amble as it fills nightly with sauntering couples, evangelical preachers and an army of underemployed shoe shiners.

Mercado Modelo MARKET
(Arica btwn Balta & Cugilevan; ☉7am-8pm Mon-Sat, to 2pm Sun) This is one of Peru's most interesting markets, sprawling over several blocks. Most notable for tourists is the *mercado de brujos* (witch doctors' market) in the southwest corner. This area is a one-stop shop for medicine men and has everything you might need for a potent brew: whale bones, amulets, snake skins, vials of indeterminate tonics, hallucinogenic cacti and piles of aromatic herbs.

If you'd like to make contact with a *brujo* for a healing session, this is a good place to start, but be wary of sham shamans. It's best to go with a reliable recommendation (see also p346).

Cathedral CHURCH
This cathedral was built in the late 19th century. In contrast, the Plaza de Armas (Parque Principal) wasn't inaugurated until 1916 which gives an idea of how new the city is by Peruvian standards.

Paseo de las Musas PARK
This pleasant, narrow city park showcases classical-style statues of mythological figures.

Travelers with kids might want to check out the **children's playground** at the west end of Aguirre.

🍴 Tours & Guides

gencies offer frequent inexpensive tours Sipán, Túcume, Ferreñafe, Batán Grande, mental/Santa Rosa and Reserva Ecológica haparrí, and the museums in Lambayeque. ours cost between S50 and S130, depending on whether entrance fees to museums re included.

loche Tours   CULTURAL TOURS

(🍴23-4637; www.mochetourschiclayo.com.pe; alle 7 de Enero 638; ⊙8am-8pm Mon-Sat, to noon un) Highly recommended for cheap daily ours with Spanish- or English-speaking uides.

ipán Tours   CULTURAL TOURS

(🍴22-9053; www.sipantours.com; Calle 7 de Enro 772; ⊙8:30am-1:30pm & 4:30-8:30pm) Offers uided tours in Spanish.

🛏 Sleeping

lotel Mochiks   BOUTIQUE HOTEL $$

(🍴20-6620; www.hotelmochiks.com; Tacna 615; s/d ncl breakfast S135/180; ❄@🌐) This newcomer nade an immediate impression on the hotel cene in the city, owing much of its success to sense of style that was previously MIA. Tall nd narrow, the lobby, cafe and 2nd-floor bar re decked out in chromes and moody reds, vhich contrast perfectly with the smallish ut soothing beige-toned rooms.

Everything is new and well-maintained; he trendiness is held in check with small ndigenous Moche touches here and there. At 25 rooms, it's the perfect size.

TOP CHOICE ⭐ Hotel Embajador   HOTEL $

(🍴20-4729; www.hotelembajadorchiclayo.com; Calle 7 de Enero 1368; s/d/tr incl breakfast S80/120/140; @🌐) This fab 23-room choice makes no bones about it: lime and tangerine are its favorite colors and you will be pummeled with chem at every turn. It makes for a fun and festive choice that's toploaded with value and personality: a minimalist cafe, trapezoidal bathroom mirrors, suite Jacuzzi tubs, included airport transfers and a lovely front desk staff. Everything is clean, freshly painted, cheery and shrouded in ample natural light. Hop aboard the citrus spectacular!

Hotel Paraíso   HOTEL $

(🍴22-8161; www.hotelesparaiso.com.pe; Ruíz 1064; s/d incl breakfast S80/100; ❄@🌐) Brighter and cheerier than its immediate neighbors, the value equation falls in Hotel Paraíso's favor, boasting all the mod cons of far fancier hotels for a fraction of the price. Spotless and modern tiled rooms boast decent furniture, hot showers and cable TV. Breakfast is available in its 24-hour cafe. It's the cheapest of several hotels on this block, but holds its head up in comparison with anyone in town.

Casa Andina Select Chiclayo   BOUTIQUE HOTEL $$$

(🍴23-4911; www.casa-andina.com; Villarreal 115; r/ ste incl breakfast S616/788; ❄@🌐) The Peruvian boutique chain Casa Andina swooped in and gobbled up this aging relic, formerly the Gran Hotel Chiclayo. A 100% makeover was under way during our visit (expected completion 2014). Presume superswankiness (for Chiclayo) across the board, including room service, spa, cappuccino bar, casino, fitness center, free parking and the namesake Plaza sports bar, all churned out in the company's tasteful modern decor. Airport transfer included.

Hotel Kalu   HOTEL $$

(🍴22-9293; www.hotelkalu.com; Ruíz 1038; s/d S100/120; 🌐) These quarters on a rambunctious commercial street are dressed with stylish '80s pizzazz. With dazzling colors, an attentive doorman and a willingness to knock S30 off the price if you're staying any length of time, it's a great option all-round, though street noise is an issue (try to go for something in the middle of the building).

Whether it may have once been a love motel remains debatable, but, for the record, our reception-advertised adult channels did *not* work.

Costa Del Sol   BUSINESS HOTEL $$$

(🍴22-7272; www.costadelsolperu.com; Balta 399; s/d incl breakfast S285/350; ❄@🌐) Part of a northern Peru chain, this fully loaded business hotel is one of Chiclayo's best, though reviews have been mixed. It must now answer to a higher multinational power in the form of Ramada, who took the reins in 2012. All the creature comforts are here, including pool, gym, sauna and massage rooms.

We aren't chain hotel fans, mind you, but this is Chiclayo.

Hostal Sicán   HOTEL $

(🍴20-8741; hsican@hotmail.com; Izaga 356; s/d/ tr incl breakfast S40/55/75; @) This appealing pick has lots of polished wood and wrought iron creating an illusion of grandeur. The rooms are small, comfortable and cool. All feature wood paneling, as well as tasteful bits of art and a TV. A great choice, it sits on

Chiclayo

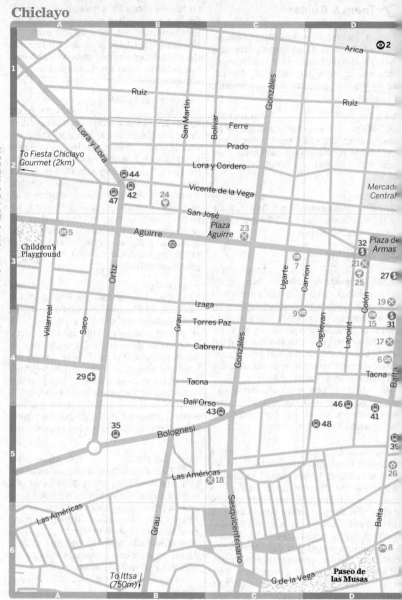

To Fiesta Chiclayo
Gourmet (2km)

Children's
Playground

Arica

Ruíz

San Martín
Bolívar
Ferre
Prado
Lora y Cordero
Vicente de la Vega

Ruíz

Gonzáles

Mercado
Central

Aguirre

San José

Plaza
Aguirre

24

23

32 Plaza de
Armas

7

Ugarte
Carrion

21
25

27

Izaga

Torres Paz

Cabrera

9

Ongifievan
Lapoint

Colón

19

15
31

17

Grau

Saco

Ortiz

Villarreal

29

Tacna

Dall'Orso

43

Tacna

Balta

6

46

41

35

Bolognesi

48

39

Las Américas

18

26

Las Américas

Sesquicentenario

Grau

Balta

8

G de la Vega

Paseo de
las Musas

To Ittsa
(750m)

one of Chiclayo's most charming brick-lined streets.

Hostal Victoria HOTEL $
(☎ 22-5642; victoriastar2008@hotmail.com; Izaga 933; s/d/tr S30/50/60; ☎) This is a great find

just east of the main plaza. It's quiet, sanitary and has colorful rooms spruced up by tiny ceramics and textiles here and there. There's a friendly family vibe to the whole place. Prices listed here are for foreigners;

Peruvians pay a bit more, perhaps to make up for the lopsided Machu Picchu prices!

Hostal Colibrí HOTEL $

(☑22-1918; hostalcolibri@gmail.com; Balta 010-A; s/d/tr incl breakfast S55/80/90; �) Overlooking the leafy Paseo de las Musas, the newish Colibrí is a longish walk from the center but is top value. Brightly lit and brightly painted, it's a modern choice, with a friendly front desk, a burger joint in the bottom and a 2nd floor coffee/cocktail bar with patio views of the park. Funky bathrooms, too.

Pirámide Real HOTEL $

(☑22-4036; piramidereal@hotmail.com; Izaga 726; s/d S30/40; ☎) Blink and you'll miss the tiny entrance to this place. Things don't get any bigger inside, but if you're willing to forgo space, there's clean and tidy rooms with writing desks, hot water and cable TV – a reasonably good deal at this price range. There are only matrimonial rooms, though (no doubles), so it's suitable for couples, not so much for buds.

Latinos Hostal HOTEL $$

(☑23-5437; latinohotelsac@hotmail.com; Izaga 600; s/d S90/140; ✳@☎) An excellent choice, this hotel is thoroughly maintained with perfect little rooms. Some of the corner rooms have giant curving floor-to-ceiling windows for great street views and plenty of light. The staff is very helpful.

Hospedaje San Lucas GUESTHOUSE $

(☑99-328-4301; pamelacalambrogio@hotmail.com; Aguirre 412; s/d S20/35; @☎) Elementary but trim and tidy, this shoestringer steps up successfully to its 'Welcome Backpackers' motto. There's a nice city view from the top floor, electric hot showers and some locally made laurel wood furniture to give it some flare.

✕ Eating

Chiclayo is one of the best places to eat on the North Coast. *Arroz con pato a la chiclayana* (duck and rice cooked in cilantro and beer) and *tortilla de manta raya* (Spanish omelet made from stingray) are endless sources of culinary pride. For dessert, try the local street sweet called a King Kong, a large cookie filled with a sweet caramel cream made of milk and sugar; it's available everywhere. If you are aching for a coffee that didn't come from a tin of Nescafe, there's a Starbucks at C.C. Real Plaza.

TOP CHOICE Fiesta Chiclayo Gourmet REGIONAL $$$

(☑20-1970; www.restaurantfiestagourmet.com; Salaverry 1820; mains S35-49) Few things are as satisfying as scraping those last bits of slightly charred rice off the bottom of an iron-clad pan and savoring all that's great

Chiclayo

about a rice dish like *arroz con pato a la chiclayana,* made here with farm-raised duck that must be a black-feathered quacker not a day over three months old.

Blindsiding your palette with a wholly unexpected delight is *ceviche a la brasa,* traditional raw fish served *warm* in cornhusks after an 11th-hour searing. The pisco sours are constructed tableside, service is exquisite, and the best of this region's world-famous cuisine is outrageously great. Call for a reservation here or visit a sister restaurant in Lima (p85), Trujillo or Tacna. A S5 taxi ride covers the 2km from the centre.

El Pescador   SEAFOOD, PERUVIAN **$**
(San José 1236; mains S10-20; ⏰11am-6pm) This little local's secret packs in the droves for

outstanding seafood and regional dishes at laughable prices. The ceviches here (S10 to S12) are every bit as good as places charging double or even triple the price; and weekend specials like *cabrito con frijoles* (goat with beans; Saturday) and *arroz con pato* (duck with rice; Sunday) are steals at under S14.

Owner Oscar and his brother (the chef) work their tails off to make sure you're happy.

El Ferrocol   SEAFOOD, PERUVIAN **$**
(Las Américas 168; mains S13-27; ⏰9am-7pm) This brash hole-in-the-wall, a little out of the center, is well worth the trip, but not for the service or atmosphere. Chef Lucho prepares some of the best ceviche in all of Chiclayo, served here with lovely fried *tortitas de*

cla (fried corn patties). There's eight to ~~oose~~ from along with the usual standards.

~staurant Romana~ PERUVIAN $$

~lta~ 512; mains S13-25; ⊙7am-1am; ☎) This ~pular~ place serves a bunch of different ~shes~, all of them local favorites. If you're ~eling~ brave, try the *chirimpico* for break-~st~: it's stewed goat tripe and organs and ~guaranteed~ to either cure a hangover or ~e~ you one. If not, the *humitas* (steamed ~ugh~ with corn and cheese wrapped in ~rn~ husks) are a tasty, can't beat treat at ~.50~ and there's an extensive egg menu.

For other meals, there's pasta, steaks, sea-~od~, chicken or pork *chicharrones* (bread-~and~ fried) with yucca – you name it.

~ez~ Maggy PIZZERIA $

~lta~ 413; pizzas S12-31; ⊙6-11pm) It's not how ~pa~ Giuseppe used to make it, but the ~od-fired~ pizzas at this restaurant have a ~etty~ darn good crust and fresh toppings. ~ey~ have convenient personal-size pizzas ~r~ solo diners.

~Tia~ PERUVIAN, BURGERS $

~guirre~ 662; burgers S1-6) Lines run very deep ~this~ no-frills Peruvian haunt, whose burg-~stand~ draws legions of *céntimo* pushers ~r~ burgers (loaded with fries!) that are prac-~cally~ free if you take them away (S1 to S4). ~side~, they're pricier (S2 to S6), along with ~long~ list of country staples served by smil-~g~ staff.

They do an S3 *suspiro de limeña* (milk ~aramel~ and meringue) that's just big ~nough~ that you don't feel guilty.

~eladaría~ Hoppy DESSERTS $

~www.heladoshoppychiclayo.blogspot.com~; Haya de Torre, C.C. Open Plaza; scoops S3-7) If you're ~nesin'~ for something other than industrial-~ed~ ice cream, they do a decent job here with ~e~ homemade stuff, especially considering ~l~ the Italians went to Brazil and Argentina. ~ood~ flavors include pisco sour and lucuma; ~ere~ are milkshakes and snacks as well.

~ebron~ PERUVIAN $$

~www.hebron.com.pe~; Balta 605; mains from S16; ~24hr~; ☎) This flashy, contemporary and ~right~ two-story restaurant is a luxury ~ollería~ (restaurant specializing in roast ~hicken~) but color us as unimpressed with ~e~ main attraction as the walls are orange. ~till~, people flock here, especially families ~r~ the giant children's playground. A Sun-~ay~ all-you-can-eat lunch buffet runs S27.

HUAQUEROS

The word *huaquero* is heard frequently on the north coast of Peru and literally means 'robber of *huacas*.' *Huacas* are pyramids, temples, shrines and burial sites of archaeological significance.

Since the Spanish conquest, *huaqueros* have worked the ancient graves of Peru, selling valuables to anybody prepared to pay. To a certain extent, one can sympathize with a poor *campesino* (peasant) hoping to strike it rich, but the *huaquero* is one of the archaeologist's greatest enemies. The *huaqueros'* efforts have been so thorough that archaeologists rarely find an unplundered grave.

Supermercado Metro SELF-CATERING $

(cnr Gonzáles & Aguirre; ⊙8am-10pm) Solid supermarket.

Drinking

Tribal Lounge BAR, LIVE MUSIC

(Lapoint 682; cocktails S12-22; ⊙closed Mon) An actual living, breathing bar in Chiclayo, this rock-themed spot is run by a local who returned from San Francisco after a decade. Good cocktails as well as live music (acoustic on Thursday, rock on Friday and Saturday from midnight). Great spot for a tipple.

Sabor y Son Cubano BAR, CLUB

(San José 155; cover S10; ⊙closed Sun) This spot gives the over-35 crowd somewhere to shake their rumps on the weekends, with tropical, classic salsa and *merengue* setting the pace.

☆ Entertainment

Premium Boulevard CLUB

(www.premiumboulevard.com; Balta 100; cover S5-10; ⊙closed Sun) This massive club packs in nearly 1500 revelers at capacity, spread between a small karaoke room, a large disco and an absolutely massive convert hall that caters to national and international acts. There's a boisterous vibe fueled typically by salsa, *merengue, cumbia, bachata* and *reggaetón*.

ⓘ Information

Emergency

Policía de Turismo (37-6389; Sáenz Peña 830) Useful for reporting problems.

Immigration

Oficina de Migraciónes (☑20-6838; www.di
gemin.gob.pe; La Plata 30; ☺8:30am-12:30pm
& 2-4pm) Near Paseo de Las Museos; handles
visa issues.

Medical Services

Clínica del Pacífico (www.clinicadelpacifico.
com.pe; Ortiz 420) The best medical assistance in town.

Money

There are several banks on *cuadra* (block) 6 of
Balta as well as a bevy of ATMs convenient to the
bus stations inside Supermarcado Metro, across
from the Emtrafesa station. Moneychangers
outside the banks change cash quickly at good
rates.

Banco Continental (Balta 643)

BCP (Balta 630) Has a 24-hour Visa and
MasterCard ATM.

HSBC (cnr Balta & Izaga) No fee ATM.

Interbank (cnr Colón & Aguirre)

Post

Serpost (Aguirre 140; ☺9am-7pm Mon-Fri, to
1pm Sat) West of Plaza Aguirre.

Tourist Information

Dircetur (☑23-8112; Sáenz Peña 838;
☺7:30am-1pm & 2-4:30pm Mon-Fri) Good
regional tourist info.

iPerú (☑20-5703; Calle 7 de Enero 579; ☺9-
6pm Mon-Sat, 9am-1pm Sun) The best spot for
tourist info in town; with another booth at the
airport.

① Getting There & Away

Air

The airport (CIX) is 1.5km east of town; a taxi
ride there is S5. **LAN** (☑27-4875; www.lan.
com; Izaga 770) departs from Lima to Chiclayo
daily at 4am and 8:10pm, returning to Lima at
5:50am, 6:15pm and 10pm. More economical is

Taca (☑0-800-1-8222; www.taca.com; Cácer
222, C.C. Real Plaza), departing from Lima at
6:10am and 3:30pm and heading back from
Chiclayo at 8:20am and 5:55pm. Prices for the
latter can be as low as S97.

Bus

Cruz del Sur, Movil Tours, Línea, Ittsa and Oltursa usually have the most comfortable buse

Cial (☑20-5587; www.expresocial.com; Bolog
nesi 15) Has a 7:30pm Lima bus.

Civa (☑22-3434; www.civa.com.pe; Bolognes
714) Has the cheapest *comfortable* Lima buse
at 5pm and 8:45pm; also 8pm and 8:30pm;
Jaén buses 9:30am and 9:30pm; Tarapoto
buses at 5:45pm and 6:30pm; and a Chachapoyas bus at 6pm. They are now also serving
Guayaquil at 6:15pm, which is more comfortable and way more convenient than Ormeño.

Cruz del Sur (☑23-7965; www.cruzdelsur.co
pe; Bolognesi 888) Has four departures to Lir
between 7am and 8pm.

Empresa Transcade (☑23-2552; Balta
110) Has buses to Jaén (S14) at 8:30am and
8:30pm.

Emtrefesa (☑22-5538; www.emtrafesa.com;
Balta 110) Has a bus to Jaén (at 10:45pm and
many departures for Trujillo and Pacasmayo.

Ittsa (☑23-3612; www.ittsabus.com; Grau
497) *Bus-cama* to Lima at 8pm.

Línea (☑23-2951; www.linea.pe; Bolognesi
638) Has a comfortable Lima service at 8pm
and regular hourly services to Trujillo and
Piura. Also has buses to Chimbote at 9:15am,
7:30pm and 11pm; buses to Cajamarca at 10ar
11:30am, 10pm and 10:45pm; and buses to
Jaén at 2:15pm and 11pm.

Movil Tours (☑27-1940; www.moviltours.
com.pe; Bolognesi 199) Has two Lima buses a
7:30pm *(bus-cama)* and 8pm; a Tarapoto bus a
6:30pm; and a Chachapoyas bus at 9pm.

Oltursa Terminal (☑22-5611; www.oltursa.
pe; Vicente de la Vega 101); Sales Office (cnr

CHICLAYO REGIONAL MINIBUSES

DESTINATION	COST (S)	DURATION (HR)
Batán Grande	5	¾
Chongoyape	3.50	1½
Ferreñafe	2	½
Lambayeque	1.50	¼
Pimentel	1.60	½
Monsefú	2	¼
Sipán	3	¼
Túcume	2.50	1

CHICLAYO LONG-DISTANCE BUSES

DESTINATION	COST (S)	DURATION (HR)
Bogotá	486	48
Cajamarca	16-40	6
Chachapoyas	30-50	10
Chimbote	20-25	6
Guayaquil (Ec)	81	17
Jaén	20-25	6
Lima	40-125	12-14
Máncora	30-35	6
Pacasmayo	9	2
Piura	12-14	3
Tarapoto	45-120	14
Tumbes	25-50	8
Yurimaguas	65-70	20

lta & Izaga) Four *bus-cama* services to Lima
etween 7pm and 9pm.

rmeño (☏23-4206; www.grupo-ormeno.com.
e; Haya de la Torre 242) The most comfort-
le services to Ecuador and beyond, including
3am departure to Tumbes and Guayaquil as
ell as Bogotá on Tuesdays and Fridays at 1am.

epsa (☏23-6981; www.tepsa.com.pe; Bolog-
esi 504) *Bus-cama* services to Lima at 8:30pm
Monday to Saturday) and 7:30pm (Sunday).

ansportes Chiclayo (☏22-3632; www.trans
orteschiclayo.com; Ortiz 10) Has buses to
ura every half hour from 4:30am to 8:30pm;
nd to Máncora and Tumbes at 10am and
30pm. There is also one Cajamarca departure
: 11pm and one bus to Tarapoto at 6pm.

urismo Dias (☏23-3538; www.turdias.com;
ugilevan 190) Heads to Lima more affordably
: 8pm as well as departures to Cajamarca at
45am, 5pm, 9:45pm and 10:30pm.

epsa's terminal next to its ticketing office hosts
dozen small companies that have at least
x buses throughout the day to Cajamarca,
vo night buses to Tumbes, both departing at
30pm; buses at 8pm, 8:30pm (Monday to
aturday) and 7:30pm (Sunday) to Chachapo-
as; at least six departures daily to Tarapoto; a
0am, 7pm and 10:30pm bus to Yurimaguas and
equent services to Jaén. These times tend to
nange with the setting of each moon, so check
e schedule ahead of time.

The minibus terminal at the corner of San
osé and Lora y Lora has regular buses to Lam-
ayeque and Pimentel.

Buses for Ferreñafe, Sipán, Monsefú and
hongoyape leave frequently from **Terminal

de Microbuses Epsel (Nicolás de Píerola at
Oriente).

Combis to Túcume leave from Leguia 1306
north of the centre.

Around Chiclayo

Given the doubling of guide prices in the last
few years, it hardly makes sense to travel independently to most of the archaeological
sites around Chiclayo – you'll find the organized tours far more convenient.

SIPÁN

The story of Sipán reads like an Indiana Jones movie script: buried treasure,
huaqueros, police, archaeologists and at
least one killing. The archaeological site
(adult S8; ⊙9am-5pm), also known as Huaca
Rayada, was discovered by *huaqueros* from
the nearby hamlet of Sipán. When local archaeologist Dr Walter Alva saw a huge influx of intricate objects on the black market
in early 1987, he realized that an incredible
burial site was being ransacked in the Chiclayo area. Careful questioning led Dr Alva
to the Sipán mounds. To the untrained eye
the mounds look like earthen hills, but in
AD 300 these were huge truncated pyramids
constructed from millions of adobe bricks.

At least one major tomb had already
been pillaged by looters, but fast protective
action by local archaeologists and police
stopped further plundering. Luckily, several other tombs that the grave robbers had

missed were unearthed, including an exceptional royal Moche burial that became known as the Lord of Sipán. One *huaquero* was shot and killed by police in the early, tense days of the struggle over the graves. The Sipán locals were not too happy at losing what they considered their treasure trove. To solve this problem, the locals were invited to train to become excavators, researchers and guards at the site, which now provides steady employment for many. The full story was detailed by Dr Alva in the October 1988 and June 1990 issues of *National Geographic,* and the May 1994 issue of *Natural History.*

The Lord of Sipán turned out to be a major leader of the Moche people, indicated by his elaborate burial in a wooden coffin surrounded by hundreds of gold, ceramic and semiprecious mineral objects, as well as an entourage consisting of his wife, two girls, a boy, a military chief, a flag-bearer, two guards, two dogs and a llama. Another important tomb held the *sacerdote* (priest), who was accompanied into the afterlife with an equally impressive quantity of treasures, as well as a few children, a guardian whose feet were cut off and a headless llama. Archaeologists don't understand why the body parts were removed, but they believe that important members of the Moche upper class took with them in death those who composed their retinues in life.

Some of the tombs have been restored with replicas to show what they looked like just before being closed up more than 1500 years ago. Opposite the entrance is the **Museo de Sitio Sipán** (admission S8, entrance included in site ticket; ☺9am-5pm Mon-Fri), opened in January 2009, which is worth a visit – but note that the most impressive artifacts, such as the Lord of Sipán and the Sacerdote, were placed in the Museo Tumbas Reales de Sipán in Lambayeque, after going on world tour. Spanish- and English-speaking guides can be hired (S30).

Daily guided tours are available from tour agencies in Chiclayo for around S50. Alternately, buses for Sipán (S3, 45 minutes) leave frequently from Chiclayo's Terminal de Microbuses Epsel.

LAMBAYEQUE

♪ 074 / POP 47,900

About 11km north of Chiclayo, Lambayeque was once the main town in the area but now plays second fiddle to Chiclayo.

◉ Sights

The town's museums are its best featu
The two museums in Lambayeque are bo
within a 15-minute walk of the plaza.
Casa de Logia, a block south of the ma
plaza, has a 67m-long, 400-year-old balco
said to be the longest balcony in Peru. Mc
people visit here on an organized tour fro
Chiclayo.

TOP CHOICE Museo Tumbas Reales de Sipán

MUSE

(admission S10; ☺9am-5pm Tue-Sun, last adm sion 4pm) Opened in November 2002, t Museum of the Royal Tombs of Sipán is t pride of northern Peru – as well it should With its burgundy pyramid construction r ing gently out of the earth, it's a world-cla facility specifically designed to showcase t marvelous finds from Sipán. Photography not permitted and all bags must be checke

Visitors are guided through the museu from the top down and are shown some the numerous discoveries from the top in the same order that the archaeologis found them – this small detail alone, rare the museum world, adds a fascinating co text to visits. The first hall contains detaile ceramics representing gods, people, plan llamas and other animals. Descending the 2nd floor there are delicate objects li impossibly fine turquoise-and-gold ear o naments showing ducks, deer and the Lo of Sipán himself. The painstaking and a vanced techniques necessary to create th jewelry place them among the most beaut ful and important objects of pre-Columbia America. Finally, the ground floor feature exact reproductions of how the tombs wei found. Numerous dazzling objects are di played, the most remarkable of which ai the gold pectoral plates representing se creatures such as the octopus and crab. Eve the sandals of the Lord of Sipán were mad of precious metals, as he was carried ever where and never had to walk. Interesting since nobility were seen as part-animal go they used the *nariguera* (a distinctive nos shield) to conceal their very human teeth and the fact that they were no different fron everyone else.

The lighting and layout is exceptiona especially a large, moving diorama of th Lord of Sipán and his retinue, with detail down to the barking Peruvian hairless dog The signage is all in Spanish, but Englisl speaking guides are available for S30.

Bruning Museum
MUSEUM

(adult S8; ⊙9am-5pm) This museum, once a regional archaeological showcase, is now greatly overshadowed by the Museo Tumbas Reales de Sipán; however, it still houses a good collection of artifacts from the Chimú, Moche, Chavín and Vicus cultures. Budding archaeologists will enjoy the displays showing the development of ceramics from different cultures and the exhibits explaining how ceramics and metalwork were made. Architecture and sculpture lovers may find some interest in the Corbusier-inspired building, bronze statues and tile murals adorning the property. Models of several important sites are genuinely valuable for putting the archaeology of the region into perspective. English-speaking guides charge S30.

Getting There & Away
The minibus terminal at the corner of San José and Lora y Lora in Chiclayo has regular buses to Lambayeque (S1.50, 20 minutes), which will drop you off a block from the Bruning Museum.

FERREÑAFE
☏074 / POP 34,500

This old town, 18km northeast of Chiclayo, is worth visiting for the excellent Museo Nacional Sicán (www.sican.perucultural.org.pe; adult S8; ⊙9am-5pm Tue-Sun). Sicán culture arrived in the Lambayeque area between AD 750 and 1375 (see p327), around the same time as the Chimú. The main Sicán site at Batán Grande lies in remote country to the north and is best visited on a tour from Chiclayo (p333) or Pacora (p342). This splendid museum displays replicas of the 12m-deep tombs found there, among the largest tombs found in South America. Enigmatic burials were discovered within – the Lord of Sicán was buried upside down, in a fetal position with his head separated from his body. Beside him were the bodies of two women and two adolescents, as well as a sophisticated security system to ward off grave robbers: the red-colored *sinabrio* dust, which is toxic if inhaled. Another important tomb contained a nobleman sitting in a cross-legged position and wearing a mask and headdress of gold and feathers, surrounded by smaller tombs and niches containing the bodies of one man and 22 young women. The museum is worth the ride out and it's never crowded. Guided tours from Chiclayo to Ferreñafe and Túcume cost around S50 per person, or grab a *colectivo* (S2.50) from Prado just east of Peña. *Combis* for Ferreñafe (S2)

also leave frequently from Chiclayo's Terminal de Microbuses Epsel.

TÚCUME
☏074 / POP 7900

This is a little-known site (adult S8; ⊙8am-4:30pm), which lies around 30km to the north of Lambayeque on the Panamericana. A vast area – with more than 200 hectares of crumbling walls, plazas and no fewer than 26 pyramids – it was the final capital of the Sicán culture (see p327), who moved their city from nearby Batán Grande around AD 1050 after that area was devastated by the effects of El Niño. The pyramids you see today are a composite of structures made by several civilizations; the lower levels belonged to the Sicán while the next two levels, along with the distinctive surrounding walls, were added by the Chimú. While little excavation has been done and no spectacular tombs have been found, it's the sheer size of the site that makes it a memorable visit.

The site can be surveyed from a stunning *mirador* (lookout) atop Cerro Purgatorio (Purgatory Hill). The hill was originally called Cerro la Raya (Stingray Hill), but the name was changed after the Spaniards tried to convert local people to Christianity by dressing as demons atop the hill and throwing nonbelievers to their deaths. There is a small but attractive onsite museum (admission free with site ticket; ⊙closed Mon) with some interesting tidbits. Guides are available for S30.

From Chiclayo (S2.50), *combis* depart from Leguia 1306 north of the centre. You can also catch one from Lambayeque (ask at the Bruning Museum). Guided tours cost around S50 per person (p333).

Reserva Ecológica Chaparrí
WILDLIFE RESERVE

(www.chaparri.org; admission day/overnight S10/30; ⊙7am-5pm) This 34,000-hectare private reserve, located 75km east of Chiclayo, was established in 2000 by the community of Santa Catalina and the famous Peruvian wildlife photographer Heinz Plenge. It offers a completely unique atmosphere for this coast. This is one of the few places in the world where you can spot the rare spectacled bear in its natural habitat; 25 or so have been accounted for (there are also two in rehabilitation captivity). This area is an ornithologist's dream, with more than 237 species of birds, including rare white-winged guans, Andean condors, king vultures and several species of eagle. A large number of threatened species are also found here, including pumas, collared anteaters and Andean weasels. Nearly a third of these vertebrates are not found anywhere else in the world. And there's a friendly fox or two.

You can spend the night in the wonderfully rustic Chaparrí EcoLodge (☏25-5717; www.chaparrilodge.com; s/d incl meals & guide S275/550), where well-appointed adobe and bamboo bungalows await under the looming mountain of the same name. There's solar-heated hot water and solar-powered electricity and each room has its own patio with hammock. It's not fancy, but it's nice enough that you'll be sweetly surprised upon arrival. The food is of the homey Peruvian comfort variety served on a communal table next to a gurgling stream. It's pretty ideal if you are a nature lover.

You can visit the reserve on your own as a day trip by catching a bus from Chiclayo's Terminal de Microbuses Epsel to Chongoyape (S3.50), from where you must contact the local guide association, Acoturc (☏97-889-6377), and arrange a required guide and transport for about S140 for up to three people to tour the reserve. If you can't get through to the association, pop in to the corner shop Fotografía Carrasco (cnr Chiclayo & Olala), where the family can arrange everything as well as set campers up in a *very* rustic campground in a beautiful setting above Chongoyape.

Alternatively, Moche Tours (p333) in Chiclayo arranges day tours, including transportation and guide, for S130 per person (minimum four people).

Batán Grande & Chota

About halfway from Chiclayo to Chongoyape a minor road on your left leads to the Sicán ruins of Batán Grande. This is a major archaeological site where about 50 pyramids have been identified and several burial

Piura

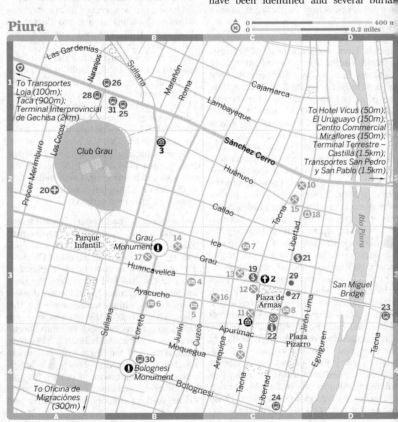

ve been excavated. With the urging of
r Walter Alva, among others, the site was
ansformed into the **Santuario Histórico**
osque de Pomac, but there is no tourist
frastructure. The protected reserve lies
ithin one of the largest dry tropical forests
the world and hosts more than 50 spe-
es of birds; healthy stands of *algarrobo*
arob tree) offer beautiful shade along the
ay. *Combis* to Batán Grande leave from
hiclayo's Terminal de Epsel (S5), but it is
est to go on an organized tour.

One of the best ways to visit this area
on horseback from **Rancho Santana**
97-971-2145; www.cabalgatasperu.com; camp-
g with/without tent rental S10/5, r per person
cl breakfast S35; @) in Pacora, about 45km
ortheast of Chiclayo. Readers rave about
eir experiences riding typical Peruvian
aso horses at this rustic, animal-packed
wiss-owned ranch, which also has a sim-
le but spacious bungalow with hammocks
nd super-sized bathroom; fresh milk and
imple meals are whipped up if needed or
uests may use the kitchen facilities. The
wners are highly knowledgeable of Lam-
ayeque cultures and will pick you up in
hiclayo for half-day to three-day *cabalga-
s* (horse rides) through the Pomac Forest,
atán Grande and the pyramids at Túcume.
he owners care for their horses exception-
lly well and can make even the most inex-

perienced rider feel comfortable. The tours
are a great value at S45 for a half-day to
S300 for three days. You can also camp for
S5 (with cooking and washing facilities) at
the ranch.

A rough but scenic road climbs east from
Chongoyape into the Andes until it reaches
Chota (at an altitude of around 2400m), a
170km journey that takes about eight hours.
Two or three buses a day from Chiclayo travel there, from where a daily bus makes the
rough journey via Bambamarca and Hualgayoc to Cajamarca (five hours).

Piura

📌073 / POP 252,200

After several hours of crossing the vast
emptiness of the Sechura Desert, Piura
materializes like a mirage on the horizon,
enveloped in quivering waves of heat. It's
hard to ignore the sense of physical isolation forced on you by this unforgiving environment; the self-sufficiency imposed
upon early settlers may explain why they
identify as Piuran rather than Peruvian.
Being so far inland, the scorching summer
months will have you honing your radar
for air-conditioning, as you seek out chilled
venues in which to soothe your sweltering
skin. But the lovely narrow cobbled streets

WELCOME TO PIURADISE

If you want to lose a few days in an authentic Peruvian beach town that foreigners haven't yet embraced, look no further than Colán, 15km north of Paita, Piura's main port some 50km west of the city. Paita itself is a dusty, crumbling colonial port town that looks like it sprouted organically from the desert and has a roguish, Wild West feel to it, but as soon as Colán comes into view after you've turned off the main highway, you feel that sense of discovery so often lost in a world of Google Earth and iReports. Not only is Colán home to the oldest colonial church in Peru (it looks like something out of a Cormac McCarthy novel), this white-sand beach is a trendy summer destination for the Peruvian jet set – and is practically deserted the rest of the year. The curving bay has a shallow beach that's excellent for swimming.

Loads of restaurants line the main drag and there are a few great places to plop yourself down for a few days. **Playa Colán Lodge** (☑073-31-3974; www.playacolanlodge.com.pe; 2-/4-/5-person bungalows S178/220/233; ▨) is the best place to stay. Built from a combination of natural materials it has an upmarket Robinson Crusoe feel and hosts cute, pastel-colored bungalows along the beach. There are lots of hammocks, shady palm trees, a tennis court, plus a restaurant and bar. The most Máncora-esque spot is **Luna Nueva** (☑073-66-1761; www.lunanuevadecolan.com; r per person sea-view/pool-view incl breakfast S60/50; ▨▨), where you'll find the best restaurant in town and slightly cramped but well-maintained rooms emptying out onto a shared terrace that is bashed by high tide twice a day. The budget choice is **Hospedaje Frente del Mar** (☑073-70-3117; r S50-80), with a good seaside restaurant, a few rustic rooms at the back and two new and nicer rooms on the street side.

There are buses every 15 minutes to Paita from the Terminal Interprovincial Gechisa in Piura (S4, one hour). *Colectivos* leave from the main **terminal** (cnr Zanjon & Loreto) in Paita, near the market, to Colán (S3, 20 minutes) and Sullana (S6, 1¼ hours).

and charismatic colonial houses of central Piura make up for the fact that there's little else for tourists to do here. Its role as a hub for the spokes of the northern towns means that you'll probably end up spending some time here, sighing in relief at the occasional afternoon breeze.

If so, you have dinner to look forward to: Piura is one of the best towns on the coast for eats.

◉ Sights

Jirón Lima, a block east of the Plaza de Armas, has preserved its colonial character more than most areas in Piura.

FREE **Museo Municipal Vicus** MUSEUM
Huánuco 893; ⊙9am-5pm Tue-Sat, 9am-1pm Sun) This four-story monolith offers a sparse but decent look into Vicus culture, highlighted by the underground **Sala de Oro** (admission S4; ⊙9am-5pm Tue-Fri), where some excellent pieces are displayed, including a gold belt decorated with a life-sized gold cat head that puts today's belt buckles to shame.

FREE **Casa Grau** MUSEU
(Tacna 66; ⊙8am-1pm & 3-6pm Mon-Fri, to noo Sat) This restored colonial home is the birth place of Admiral Miguel Grau, born on Jul 27, 1834. The house was restored by the Pe ruvian navy and is now a naval museum Admiral Grau was a hero of the War of th Pacific against Chile (1879–83), and the cap tain of the British-built warship *Huáscar,* model of which can be seen in the museum

Cathedral CHURC
(Plaza de Armas) Originally constructed i 1588, when Piura was finally built in its cur rent location. The impressive gold-covere side altar of the Virgin of Fatima, built in th early 17th century, was once the main alta in the church. Famed local artist Ignaci Merino painted the canvas of San Martín d Porres in the mid-19th century.

⊨ Sleeping

Hotel Las Arenas HOTEL $$
(☑30-5554; www.hotellasarenas.com.pe; Loret 945; s with/without air-con S110/90, d with/withou air-con S140/120, all incl breakfast; ❀@☎▨) I was a low bar, but this remodeled *casona*

ow offers a smidgeon more character than the other spots in town. It earns its top Piura onors for the small but enchanting pool ith inviting wicker loveseats and copious otted plants, mismatched (depending on the era) but endearing flooring and well-aintained rooms.

There's a small cafe and they'll knock S10 if the price for foreigners.

Mango Verde B&B $$
232-1768; www.mangoverde.com.pe; Country 248; without air-con S100, s/d with air-con S120/160, all cl breakfast; 🌊🏧🛜) About 2km north of Plaza e Armas in a leafy residential area, this mart, 19-room B&B ups the charm ante nd manages to be both industrial and

cozy at the same time (wonderfully inviting common terraces with plush patio furniture next to steel staircases and exposed concrete). Pottery from Catacaos and well-curated art add a bit of color to things and rooms are simple-ish with all the mod cons. It's not mindblowing, but it tries harder than the rest.

Hotel Vicus HOTEL $
(234-3201; www.hotelvicus.com; Guardia Civil B-3; s/d/tr S60/80/105; 🌊🏧🛜⯑) Though upkeep isn't what it should be and the Canadiana illustration reprints from Peter John Strokes' *Old Niagra on the Lake* are out of place, we dig this perfectly reasonable spot. Rooms are spaced out around a drive-in, motel-style

WORTH A TRIP

HANDICRAFT HAVENS: CATACAOS & CHULUCANAS

Catacaos

A bustling small town 12km southwest of Piura, Catacaos is the self-proclaimed capital of *artesanía* (handicrafts) in the region. And justifiably so: its **arts market** (⊙10am-4pm) is the best in northern Peru. Sprawling for several blocks near the Plaza de Armas, here you will find excellent weavings, gold and silver filigree jewelry, wood carvings, ceramics (including lots of pieces from Chulucanas), leather goods and more. The weekends are the best and busiest times to visit.

Not satisfied with the *artesanía* crown, Catacaos is also shooting for the culinary medal, with dozens of *picanterías* (local restaurants) open for lunch daily. You can get local specialties like *chicha, seco de chabelo* (a thick plantain and beef stew), *seco de cabrito* (kid goat), *tamales verdes* (green corn dumplings), *copus* (dried goat heads cured in vinegar and then stewed) and loads of other dishes, not all of them that adventurous. Several good *picanterías* advertising their specialties are located on Jirón Zepita off the Plaza de Armas.

Combis and *colectivos* leave frequently for Catacaos from Av Tacna in Piura (S1.50 to S2, 15 minutes).

Chulucanas

Chulucanas is located about 55km east of Piura, just before the Sechura Desert starts rising into the Andean slopes. It's known Peru-wide for its distinctive ceramics – rounded, glazed, earth-colored pots that depict humans. Chulucanas' ceramics have officially been declared a part of Peru's cultural heritage and are becoming famous outside Peru.

The best place to buy ceramics around here is in La Encantada, a quiet rural outpost just outside of Chulucanas, whose inhabitants work almost exclusively in *artesanía*. La Encantada was home to the late Max Inga, a local legend who studied ceramic artifacts from the ancient Tallan and Vicus cultures and sparked a resurgence in the art form. The friendly artisans are often happy to demonstrate the production process, from the 'harvesting' of the clay to the application of mango-leaf smoke to get that distinctive black-and-white design. The village is reached from Chulucanas by a 30-minute *mototaxi* ride (S10) down a 7km dirt road. A good place to start your hunting is **Ceramica Inge** (Los Ceremistas 591), but a visit to Chulucanas is probably for diehards only (ie you are furnishing your new B&B back home), as lugging this excellent but fragile pottery around Peru with you would be less than ideal.

Civa has frequent buses to Chulucanas from Piura's Terminal Terrestre – Castilla (S4, one hour).

SHOPPING FOR SHAMANS

For the daring adventurer, Huancabamba, deep in the eastern mountains, is well worth the rough 10-hour journey from Piura. This region is famed in Peru for the powerful *brujos* and *curanderos* (healers) who live and work at the nearby lakes of Huaringas. Peruvians from all over the country flock to partake in these ancient healing techniques. Many locals (but few gringos) visit the area, so finding information and guides is not difficult.

The mystical town of Huancabamba is surrounded by mountains shrouded in mist, and lies at the head of the long, narrow Río Huancabamba. The banks of the Huancabamba are unstable and constantly eroding and the town is subject to frequent subsidence and slippage. It has earned itself the nickname La Ciudad que Camina (the Town that Walks). Spooky.

When people from the West think of witchcraft, visions of pointed hats, broomsticks and bubbling brews are rarely far away. In Peru, consulting *brujos* (witch doctors) and *curanderos* (healers) is widely accepted and has a long tradition predating Spanish colonization.

Peruvians from all walks of life visit *brujos* and *curanderos* and often pay sizable amounts of money for their services. These shamans are used to cure an endless list of ailments, from headaches to cancer to chronic bad luck, and are particularly popular in matters of love – whether it's love lost, love found, love desired or love scorned.

The Huaringas lake area near Huancabamba, almost 4000m above sea level, is said to have potent curative powers and attracts a steady stream of visitors from all corners of the continent. The most famous lake in the area is Laguna Shimbe, though the nearby Laguna Negra is the one most frequently used by the *curanderos*.

Ceremonies can last all night and entail hallucinogenic plants (such as the San Pedro cactus), singing, chanting, dancing and a dip in the lakes' painfully freezing waters. Some ceremonies involve more powerful substances like *ayahuasca* (Quechua for 'vine of the soul'), a potent and vile mix of jungle vines used to induce strong hallucinations. Vomiting is a common side effect. For more on the potential dangers of taking *ayahuasca*, see the boxed text, p442. The *curanderos* will also use *ícaros*, which are mystical songs and chants used to direct and influence the spiritual experience. Serious *curanderos* will spend many years studying the art, striving for the hard-earned title of *maestro curandero*.

If you are interested in visiting a *curandero* while in Huancabamba, be warned that this tradition is taken very seriously and gawkers or skeptics will get a hostile reception. *Curanderos* with the best reputation are found closer to the lake district. The small tourist information office (⏰8am-6pm) at the bus station has an elementary map of the area and a list of accredited *brujos* and *curanderos*. In Salala, closer to the lakes, you will be approached by *curanderos* or their 'agents,' but be wary of scam artists – try to get a reference before you arrive. Know also that there are some *brujos* who are said to work *en el lado oscuro* (on the dark side). Expect to pay around S200 for a visit.

If you go, hotels are rudimentary and most share cold-water bathrooms. Hostal El Dorado (☎47-3016; Medina 116; s/d without bathroom S15/28) is on the Plaza de Armas and has a helpful owner.

At the Huancabamba bus terminal, Civa (☎96-971-4205), Turismo Express (☎34-4330), and Transportes San Pedro y San Pablo (☎47-3617) each have a morning service between 7:30am and 8am to Piura (S20, eight hours). Three afternoon buses also depart for Piura between 5pm and 7pm. To visit the lakes, catch the 5am *combi* from this terminal to the town of Salala (S5 to S7, two hours), from where you can arrange treks to the lakes on horseback (S20 to S25).

These days, busy Peruvian professionals can get online and consult savvy, business-minded shamans via instant messenger. Not quite the same thing as midnight chants and icy dunks in the remote lakes of the Andes.

yout with a lush communal patio and have verything you might crave, including three atrimonial rooms with air-con.

It's a nice location just across the bridge om the centre, comparatively quiet, and the est nightlife is a block away. Enough said.

ntiotel   BOUTIQUE HOTEL **$$$**
28-7600; www.intiotel.com; Arequipa 691; s/d cl breakfast S200/260; ❋@☎) Shockingly utting edge for Piura, this modern new-omer is the trendy choice, with industrially terile hallways that lead to spotless rooms ith tasteful art and retro silver minibars, at-screen TVs and nice bathrooms. There's business center and round-the-clock room ervice.

os Portales   HISTORIC HOTEL **$$$**
32-1161; www.losportales.com.pe; Libertad 875; /d incl breakfast from S382/441; ❋@☎❄) Live ut dreams of conquistador grandeur in his beautiful and fully refurbished colonial uilding on the Plaza de Armas. Handsome ublic areas with iron grillwork and black-nd-white checkered floors lead to a pool-ide restaurant and rooms with large cable V, minibar and great beds. It's the nicest op-end choice, but the downstairs bar (clas-ic hotel bar, by the way) blares music on he weekends and there's odd elevator music iped throughout the building at all hours.

Hospedaje San Carlos   GUESTHOUSE **$**
30-6447; Ayacucho 627; s/d/tr S45/60/80; ☎) Vinning the budget stakes by a nose, this ewish little *hospedaje* has immaculate and rim rooms, each with TV. The back rooms re best for light sleepers.

Hospedaje Aruba   GUESTHOUSE **$**
30-3067; Junín 851; s/d without bathroom S25/35, s/d with bathrooms 30/50) All white nd bright, the small, spartan rooms here ulfill the basic crashpad role.

🍴 Eating

To tuck into some regional delicacies, a lunchtime trip to the nearby town of Cata-caos is a must. Vegetarians will be pleased by Piura's wealth of meatless options.

TOP CHOICE Capuccino   CAFE **$$**
(www.capuccino-piura.com; Tacna 786; mains S22-45; ⊘closed Sun; ☎) The real deal. This modern cafe offers gourmet sandwiches and salads (S14 to S22) that are great for lunch (though it's shockingly empty) and there's more sophisticated fare for a fine night out

with a bottle of wine at dinner. Creativity shines here – *lomo saltado* lasagna, *mero* (grouper) in soy and *maracuyá* sauce – and the desserts that you might be missing from home (Toblerone cheesecake, pecan pie) are astonishing.

For caffeine freaks, it's tops in the centre for espressos (S4.50), and these are the best fries you'll have had in weeks. There's no ex-cuse for serving *ají* in packets at this level (even basic restaurants make their own), but the stylish cuisine more than makes up for it.

Chifa Canton   CHINESE **$$**
(cnr Sánchez Cerro & Tacna; mains for 2 S22-32) Peruvian Chinese restaurants almost always guarantee a good meal and this nearly fancy *chifa* is no exception. It's a bummer about the street noise, but the food is fresh and flavorful and the perfect antidote when you tire of ceviche.

Heladería el Chalán   DESSERTS **$**
(Tacna 520; snacks S6.50-19) This fast-food joint has numerous outlets whipping up burgers and sandwiches, but our money's on the ex-cellent selection of juices and the dozens of flavors of cool, cool ice cream. Try *manjar blanco* (milk caramel), try *límon* (lime) – it's all so good, you'll wish the owners canvassed Piura less and spread the love to Chiclayo and Trujillo.

Additional branches at Grau 173 and 453.

Snack Bar Romano   BREAKFAST, PERUVIAN **$**
(Ayacucho 580; menús S6-22, mains S7.50-15; ⊘closed Sun) With an excellent list of sev-eral daily *menús,* this local favorite has been around as long as its middle-aged waiters. It gets the double thumbs-up for ceviches, *sudados* and local specialties.

Don Parce   BREAKFAST, PERUVIAN **$$**
(www.donparce.com; Tacna 642; mains S16-33; ☎) Immensely pleasant spot serving a long list of Peruvian standards as well as daily spe-cials in a convenient, colonial atmosphere off the Plaza de Armas. The best deal is a three-course lunch *menú,* always with a hearty, meaty main dish.

El Uruguayo   STEAKHOUSE **$$$**
(cnr Guardia Civil & Cayeta, Centro Commercial Mi-raflores; steaks S25-70; ⊘from 6:30pm) Beef lov-ers unite at this Uruguayan steakhouse that has fallen out of favor in Trujillo but remains fresh meat, so to speak, in Piura. Cuts range from 200g to 500g and are categorized by

region (Uruguay, Argentina, América) and they do a bang up job with the condiments (*chimichurri,* vinaigrette, *ají*). It's a serious steakhouse, which is scarce in these parts.

Matheo's VEGETARIAN **$**
(Libertad 487; meals S9-14) With two central locations, Matheo's serves as an antidote to the hills of *parrillada* found all over Peru. The all-veggie menu has lots of I-can't-believe-it's-not-meat versions of local dishes. The second branch is at Tacna 532.

Supermercado Multiplaza SELF-CATERING **$**
(Ovalo Grau) For self-caterers.

 Drinking

 Centro Commercial Miraflores BAR
(cnr Guardia Civil & Cayeta) All of Piura's worthwhile nightlife takes place in this small shopping center east of the centre. For a great bar, check out Atiko (cocktails S12 to S22). If you really need to shake your rump, head upstairs to Queens (cover S25 to S30), which gets rowdy on weekends when it fills with gringos and well-heeled Peruvians shakin' their money-makers to an eclectic international music mix. Don't worry – if any of these close, something else will open here.

Shopping

Centro Artesanal Norte HANDICRAFTS
(cnr Huánuco & Libertad; ⊘9:30am-1:30pm & 4-8pm Mon-Fri, to 1:30pm Sun) The *galería de artesanía* is actually a tiny mall of about

a dozen different craft shops featuring regional specialties from baskets to weaving to Chulucanas pottery. With fair and negotiable prices, it's a great stop if you don't have time to go to the outlying craft towns.

ⓘ Information

Internet is ubiquitous and most lodgings offer laundry facilities.

Medical Services
Clínica San Miguel (www.csmpiura.com; Los Cocos 111-153; ⊘24hr) Excellent medical care.

Money
Casas de cambio are at the Ica and Arequipa intersection.
BCP (Grau 133)
HSBC (cnr Libertad & Ica) Fee-less ATM.

Post
Serpost (cnr Ayacucho & Libertad; ⊘9am-7pm Mon-Fri, to 1pm Sat) Also on the plaza.

Tourist information
iPerú (☎32-0249; Ayacucho 377; ⊘9am-6pm Mon-Sat, to 1pm Sun) Has tourist information; the airport also has an iPerú counter.
Oficina de Migraciónes (☎33-5536; www.digemin.gob.pe; cnr Sullana & Integración) Handles visa issues.

ⓘ Getting There & Away
Air
The airport (PIU) is on the southeastern bank of the Río Piura, 2km from the city center. Schedules change often.
    LAN (☎30-2145; www.lan.com; Libertad 875) flies from Lima to Piura at 6:10am, 4:45pm and

---

BORDER CROSSING: ECUADOR VIA LA TINA

The border post of La Tina lacks hotels, but the Ecuadorean town of Macará (3km from the border) has adequate facilities. La Tina is reached by *colectivo* (shared transportation) taxis (S12, 2½ hours) leaving from Sullana, 40km north of Piura, throughout the day. A better option is **Transportes Loja** (☎073-30-5446; www.cooperativaloja.com; Sánchez Cerro Km 1, Piura), which has three daily buses from Piura (9:30am, 1pm and 9pm) that conveniently go straight through here and on to Loja (S28, eight hours).

The border is the international bridge over the Río Calvas and is open 24 hours. Formalities are relaxed as long as your documents are all in order. There are no banks, though you'll find money changers at the border or in Macará. By the time you read this, a new bridge and completely revamped immigration facilities will be in place, with both Peruvian and Ecuadorean immigration offices sharing the same building on the bridge.

Travelers entering Ecuador will find taxis (US$1) and *colectivos* (US$0.50) to take them to Macará. Most nationalities are simply given a T3 tourist card, which must be surrendered when leaving, and granted 90 days' stay in Ecuador. There is a Peruvian **consulate** (☎07-269-4030; www.consuladoperumacara.com; Bolívar 134) in Macará. See Lonely Planet's *Ecuador & the Galápagos Islands* for further information on Ecuador.

PIURA BUSES

DESTINATION	COST (S)	DURATION (HR)
Chiclayo	12-15	3
Chimbote	35	8
Guayaquil (Ec)	50-60	10-12
Huancabamba	25-20	8
Lima	59-135	12-16
Loja (Ec)	28	8
Mancará (Ec)	12	4
Máncora	16-25	3
Trujillo	25-45	6
Tumbes	16-25	5

40pm, returning to Lima at 8:20am, 11:30am, 30pm and 9:50pm. Considerably cheaper is **aca** (0-800-1-8222; www.taca.com; Sánchez erro 234, C.C. Real Plaza), leaving Lima at 50am and 5pm and returning at 8:15am and 50pm, and upstart **Peruvian Airlines** (☑32-206; www.peruvianairlines.pe; Libertad 777), hich departs Lima at 6pm and returns from ura at 8pm.

us

NTERNATIONAL

he standard route to Ecuador goes along the anamericana via Tumbes to Machala. **Civa** (☑34-5451; www.civa.com.pe; cnr Tacna & astilla) is the most comfortable option, depart-g at 9:45pm daily. Alternatively, **Transportes oja** (☑30-5446; www.cooperativaloja.com; ánchez Cerro Km 1) goes via La Tina to Macará S12, four hours) and Loja (S28, eight hours) at :30am, 1pm and 9pm. These buses stop for order formalities, then continue.

OMESTIC

everal companies have offices on the 1100 uadra of Sánchez Cerro, though for Cajamarca nd across the northern Andes, it's best to go to hiclayo and get a connection there.

Civa (☑34-5451; www.excluciva.pe; cnr Tacna Castilla) Has 5pm, 6pm and 6:30pm buses o Lima, frequent buses to Chulucanas and two uses to Huancabamba at 9:30am and 6:30pm, he latter two leaving from Terminal Terrestre – Castilla).

Cruz del Sur (☑32-0473; www.cruzdelsur. com.pe; Bolognesi at Jirón Lima) Has comfortable Lima buses at 3pm, 5:30pm, 6:30pm and :30pm as well as a lone shot to Trujillo at 3pm.

El Dorado (☑32-5855; www.transporteseldo ado.com.pe; Sánchez Cerro 1119) Has 14 buses

for Tumbes between 6:30am and 12:30am that stop in Máncora.

Eppo (☑30-4543; www.eppo.com.pe; Panamericana 243) Offers fast services to Máncora every half hour from its new station behind Real Plaza on the Panamericana.

Ittsa (☑33-3982; www.ittsabus.com; Sánchez Cerro 1142) Has buses to Trujillo (9am, 1:30pm, 11:15pm), Chimbote (11pm), and a *bus-cama* to Lima at 6pm.

Línea (☑30-3894; www.linea.pe; Sánchez Cerro 1215) Hourly buses to Chiclayo between 5am and 8pm, and a 1:30pm and 11pm bus to Trujillo.

Tepsa (☑30-6345; www.tepsa.com.pe; cnr Loreto & Bolognesi) Lima buses at 3pm, 5pm, 6:30pm and 9pm.

Transportes Chiclayo (☑30-8455; www. transporteschiclayo.com; Sánchez Cerro 1121) Hourly buses to Chiclayo.

Transportes San Pedro y San Pablo (☑34-9271; Terminal Terrestre – Castilla) Has a *semicama* for Huancabamba at 6pm.

East of the San Miguel pedestrian bridge, buses and *combis* leave for Catacaos (S1.50 to S2, 15 minutes). Buses to Sullana (S2, 45 minutes) and Paita (S4, one hour) leave from **Terminal Interprovincial de Gechisa** (Prolongación Sánchez Cerro), a S5 taxi ride west of town. Chulucanas and Huancabamba buses leave from **Terminal Terrestre – Castilla** (Panamericana s/n), aka 'El Bosque,' a S3.50 *mototaxi* ride east of town.

Taxi

If you are heading to Máncora, Punta Sal or Tumbes, you can catch much faster *combis* with **Sertur** (☑96-997-6501; www.serturonline. com), which depart hourly between 6:30am and 8:30pm from Terminal Interprovincial de Gechisa (S25, 3½ hours).

Cabo Blanco

☑073

The Pan-American Hwy runs parallel to the ocean north of Talara, with frequent glimpses of the coast. This area is one of Peru's main oil fields, and pumps are often seen scarring both the land and the sea with offshore oil rigs.

About 40km north of Talara is the sleepy town of Cabo Blanco, one of the world's most famous fishing spots. Set on a gently curving bay strewn with rocks, the town has a flotilla of fishing vessels floating offshore where the confluence of warm Humboldt currents and El Niño waters creates a unique microcosm filled with marine life. Ernest Hemingway was supposedly inspired to write his famous tale *The Old Man and the Sea* after fishing here in the early 1950s. The largest fish ever landed on a rod here was a 710kg black marlin, caught in 1953 by Alfred Glassell Jr. The angling is still good, though 20kg tuna are a more likely catch than black marlin, which have declined and are now rarely over 100kg. Fishing competitions are held here and 300kg specimens are still occasionally caught. From November to January, magnificent 3m-high pipeline waves attract hard-core surfers.

Deep-sea fishing boats with high-quality tackle can be rented through Hotel El Merlin and other hotels in the area for S1350 per six-hour day, including drinks and lunch. January, February and September are considered the best fishing months.

Hotel El Merlin (☎25-6188; www.elmerlin. webs.com; s/d with breakfast from S60/100; ❄🛜)

has 14 massive rooms with handsome stor flagged floors, private hot water showe and balconies with ocean views. This ca ernous hotel doesn't get many visitors.

Cabo Blanco is several kilometers down winding road from the Pan-American Hv town of Las Olas. Catch a ride in one of th regular pickup trucks that ply the route (S 20 minutes).

Máncora

☑073 / POP 9700

Peru's worst-kept secret, Máncora is *t* place to see and be seen along the Peruvia coast – in the summer months foreigne flock here to rub sunburned shoulders wi the frothy cream of the Peruvian jet se It's not hard to see why – Peru's best sanc beach stretches for several kilometers in th sunniest region of the country, while doze of plush resorts and their budget-consciou brethren offer up rooms within meters the lapping waves. On shore, a plethora restaurants provides fresh seafood straigl off the boat as fuel for the long, lazy day The consistently good surf draws a su bleached, board-toting bunch and raucou nightlife keeps visitors busy after the su dips into the sea in a ball of fiery flame However, even though it has seen recent e plosive growth, Máncora has somehow mar aged to cling to its fishing community root

Located about halfway between Talar and Tumbes, Máncora has the Pan-Amer can Hwy passing right through its middl within 100m of the surf, where it become Av Piura, which changes to Av Grau hal

---

THE NORTH COAST'S TOP FIVE SURF BREAKS

Dedicated surfers will find plenty of action on Peru's North Coast, from the longest break in the world at Puerto Chicama to consistently good surf at Máncora. Most spots have reliable swell year-round. For the inside scoop on surfing throughout Peru, see p34.

Los Organos (p351) A rocky break with well-formed tubular waves reaching up to 2m; it's for experienced surfers only.

Cabo Blanco (p350) A perfect pipeline ranging between 1m and 3m in height and breaking on rocks; again, experienced surfers only.

Puerto Chicama (p331) On a good day, this is the longest break in the world (up to 2km!); it has good year-round surfing for all skill levels.

Máncora (p350) Popular and easily accessible, with consistently decent surf up to 2m high; it's appropriate for all skill levels.

Huanchaco (p326) Long and well-formed waves with a pipeline; it's suitable for all skill levels.

ty through town. During the December March summer period, the scene can get wdy and accommodation prices tend to uble. But year-round sun means that this one of the few resort towns on the coast at doesn't turn into a ghost town at less pular times.

Activities

here are remote, deserted beaches around áncora; ask your hotel to arrange a taxi or ve you directions by bus and foot, but be repared to walk several kilometers.

urfing & Kitesurfing

urf here is best from November to Febru-y, although good waves are found year-und and always draw dedicated surfers. In ldition to Máncora, Los Organos, Lobitos, lara and Cabo Blanco are popular surfing ots for experienced surfers. You can rent urfboards from several places at the south-rn end of the beach in Máncora (per hour/ ay S10/20) – in front of Del Wawa is the ost convenient. **Máncora Surf Shop** (Piura 52) sells boards, surf clothing and organizes ssons for about S50 per hour. The friendly ilar at **Laguna Camp** (41-1587; www.viva ancora.com/lagunacamp) also does surf les-ons for S50 for 90 minutes of instruction ncluding board rental). For something a ttle more extreme, you can get lessons in itesurfing (per six hours S624); ask at **Del Vawa** (25-8427; www.delwawa.com).

Mud Baths

bout 11km east of town, up the wooded ernández valley, a natural **hot spring** (admis-ion S3) has bubbling water and powder-fine nud – perfect for a face pack. The slightly sul-urous water and mud is said to have curative roperties. The hot spring can be reached by *mototaxi* (S50 including waiting time).

Trekking

o see some of the interior of this desert oast, hire a pickup (around S75, including vaiting time) to take you up the Fernández Valley, past the mud baths and on until the oad ends (about 1½ hours). Continue for wo hours on foot through mixed woodlands vith unique birdlife to reach Los Pilares, vhich has pools ideal for swimming. You an also visit these areas as part of a tour.

Tours & Guides

Úrsula Behr from **Iguana's** (63-2762; www. guanastrips.com; Piura 245) organizes full-day trips to the Los Pilares dry forest, which include wading through sparkling waterfalls, swimming, horseback riding, a soak in the mud baths and lunch for S180 per person. Sea kayaking trips, ideal for bird-spotting, cost S140 per person for the day.

Sleeping

Rates for accommodations in Máncora are seasonal, with the January to mid-March high season commanding prices up to 50% higher than the rest of the year, especially at weekends. During the three major holiday periods (Christmas to New Year, Semana Santa and Fiestas Patrias) accommodations can cost triple the low-season rate, require multinight stays and be very crowded; this time is generally best avoided. High-season rates are given here.

Budget rooms are pricier here than other parts of the coast, but there are cheap beds in *hospedajes* in the center of town and the southern part of the beach. South of town, along Antigua Panamericana, a different Máncora emerges amid multiple tranquil resorts spread out over several kilometers of often desolate beaches, including Las Pocitas and Vichayito Beach. All have restaurants (two of the north's most important restaurants are here) and can be reached by *mototaxi* (S7 to S10). The places further south are the quietest and are more likely to have individual bungalow accommodations.

Sunset Hotel BOUTIQUE HOTEL $$$
(25-8111; www.sunsetmancora.com; Antigua Panamericana 196; s/d incl breakfast S180/250; ❄️ 🛜 ☎️) The intimate, boutique-styled Sunset wouldn't be out of place on the cover of a glossy travel mag. It has beautifully furnished interiors and great aqua-themed rock sculptures, the good-sized rooms supply solid mattresses, hot showers, balconies and views of the seascape. The Argentine owners oversee just five rooms, so you'll never feel your privacy encroached on here.

The pool is tiny and ocean access is rocky, though a short walk brings you to a sandy beach – if you can tear yourself away from the hotel's Italian restaurant, one of the area's best.

TOP CHOICE Loki del Mar HOSTEL $
(25-8484; www.lokihostel.com; dm S28-36, r S86, all incl breakfast; ❄️ @ 🛜 ☎️) Social butterflies flock to this mother of all beach hostels, which is really a self-contained resort masquerading as a backpackers' hangout.

Tucked away in the whitewashed building are spacious dorm rooms with extra wide beds and minimalist privates for those seeking a hostel vibe without the communal snoring.

The party revolves around the massive pool, bar and lounge area, where beer pong rules are clearly laid out and a running board of (mostly) free activities keeps everyone entertained. As far as hostels go, it's punching above its weight class.

Casa de Playa
RESORT **$$**

(☑25-8005; www.casadeplayamancora.net; Antigua Panamericana km 1217; s/d incl breakfast S180/220; ☜☀) This wonderfully friendly place offers up·modern, slick dwellings colored in warm orange and yellow tones and constructed with lots of gently curving lines. Half the room interiors are dressed in smoothed exposed concrete, which contrasts well with the plethora of colorful common areas – all are reached via lush corridors strewn with all manner of vibrant plants.

All the large rooms have hot water, arty bits and a balcony with a hammock and fine sea views. An inviting two-story lounge hangs out over the sea.

Hotelier
HOTEL **$$**

(☑25-8702; www.hotelier.pe; Antigua Panamericana Km 1217; s/d incl breakfast from S150/220; ☀☜☀) If you travel for food, this artsy choice is your resting place. The owner, Javier Ruzo, is the son of one of Peru's most famous chefs, Teresa Ocampo, who spent 30 years at the helm of a Peruvian cooking show on TV (think the Peruvian Julia Childs). Javier, a published chef himself and all-around character, carries on the family tradition at the fabulous restaurant here (p353), but beyond that, he's also an artist and photographer whose work (poems, paintings, photos) gives unique personality to each of the rooms.

Claro de Luna
HOTEL **$$**

(☑25-8080; www.clarodelunamancora.com; Antigua Panamericana Km 1216; s/d incl breakfast S130/220; @☜☀) An English-speaking Argentine family runs this show, which gets rave reviews from travelers for its cozy, down-home atmosphere. Of the nine rooms, five face the sea and four face the small garden. Prices are the same and each is tastefully decorated with subtle art, channeling a vague Santorini aesthetic. Two pools, a movie projection room, kayaks for use and

a lovely ocean-side patio/lounge ensu there's something for everyone (we prefer nice Argentine red on the latter).

DCO Suites
BOUTIQUE HOTEL **$**

(☑25-8171; www.hoteldco.com; ste incl breakfa from S710; ☀@☜) This relative newcom upped the ante for trendsetters into th stratosphere and it remains the discer ing choice of jetsetters, rock stars, hone mooners and other deep-pocketed noma Though the love-it-or-hate-it color scheme a jarring turquoise and white – is serious polarizing, the spacious rooms come wi his and her kimono-style robes, rain-sty showers and lovely curved sandstone wa that fit together like an architectural jigsa puzzle.

Service, privacy and luxury are the trum cards here, whether on the curtained bea cabañas, at the remarkable outdoor spa or the small infinity pool.

Del Wawa
HOTEL

(☑25-8427; www.delwawa.com; 8 de Octubre s/ s/d S50/100; ☀☜) This surfer's mecca is s up right on the beach, and perhaps rid that wave a little too casually at times – lot of chipped paint and dangerously rusty h water heaters in some rooms kill the moo and an aloof front desk doesn't reverse th trend.

But brightly colored adobe rooms fa ing the ocean are hard to beat for locatio as are the newer, warm-colored 2nd floc rooms in a back annex. It has the most idy lic common area on the town beach wit great views of the best breaks from a gagg of comfy, umbrella-shaded beach lounge and there's surfboard rental, kitesurfing in struction, and Christa from Máncora Yog runs classes here every morning. If you ge the right room, you win.

Hostal Las Olas
HOTEL **$**

(☑25-8099; www.lasolasmancora.com; s/d/ incl breakfast from S80/140/220; ☜) This grea couples spot dons a Mediterranean-esqu olive skin tone on the outside and minimal ist white rooms with wood accents on th inside. The small, cozy restaurant looks ont the beach's best breaks and is a surf-spotter' dream.

Newer 2nd- and 3rd-floor rooms are larg er with expansive terraces and ocean views but the cheapest rooms sit under a staircase that sounds like an earthquake when people who've sprung for the best rooms bound up to revel in their better abodes.

Laguna Surf Camp
BUNGALOW $

(☏99-401-5628; www.vivamancora.com/laguna
amp; Veraniego s/n; r per person S40; ☏☀) This
id-back pad is a hidden gem, one block
ack from the beach in its own little rustic
asis. Older Indonesian-style bamboo bun-
alows sit around a pleasant sandy garden
ght near the water and lots of swinging,
ady hammocks will provide days of enter-
ainment. Four newer bungalows are more
pacious and a bargain at S50.

The cheery owner, Pilar, who is also a surf
astructor, is a joy and nailed the essence of
láncora years ago. A pool is in the works.

okopelli
HOSTEL $

(☏25-8091; www.hostelkokopelli.com; Piura 209;
m S30, r S95, all incl breakfast; ☀@☏) This
utch-Peruvian effort is the most intimate
ostel in town, but that doesn't mean it can't
old its own: there's a small pool, cool bar
rea, colorful dorm rooms boasting loads of
xposed brick and three private rooms with
n-room safes, a rarity in Peruvian hostels.
:'s a great alternative if your first choice is
ooked.

Marcilia Beach Bungalows
BUNGALOW $

(☏69-2902; www.marciliadevichayito.com; Antigua
'anamericana Km 1212; r with/without sea-view
140/120, all incl breakfast; @☏) A friendly tri-
ngual Peruvian couple started these rustic
ungalows on Vichayito Beach after years
vorking the cruise ship circuit. Each rustic
ungalow has electric hot water and very
ice bathrooms, but the real coup here is the
ne that sits seaside: book it and you'll feel
ike the entire stretch of beach is your own
rivate paradise.

English, French and Italian are spoken
luently.

🍴 Eating

Seafood rules the culinary roost in Máncora.
Other ingredients tend to be pricier due to
transportation costs. There are several mini-
markets along the strip for self-caterers.

🏆TOP CHOICE La Sirena d'Juan
SEAFOOD, PERUVIAN $$

(☏25-8173; Piura 316; mains S30-35; ☺closed Tue;
☏) Local boy done good, Juan has turned
his intimate little main drag seafooder into
northern Peru's best restaurant. Yellowfin
una fresh from Máncora's waters is the
showstopper here, whether it's prepared as
a *tiradito* (a sort of Peruvian sashimi) in yel-
ow curry or grilled with a mango-*rocoto*-red
pepper chutney.

Also on the menu are creative raviolis
and Peruvian classics given a foodie upgrade
(baby goat in black beer etc). Service in the
small, French farmhouse-style space is per-
sonalized and on point. It's expensive for
Máncora, but you'd probably pay triple this
at home. Reservations are not a bad idea in
high season.

Donde Teresa
SEAFOOD, PERUVIAN $$$

(☏25-8702; Antigue Panamericana Km 1217, Ho-
telier; mains S32-70; ☏) Before Gastón Acurio, there was Teresa Ocampo, Peru's most
recognizable celebrity chef (famous before
Peruvian food was even famous). She lives
in Texas now, but her son, Javier, keeps the
dream alive a short S5 *mototaxi* ride away
on Los Pocitas Beach. Recommended dishes
include a smoked *ají de gallina*, stir-fried
rice with seafood, anything with yellowfin
tuna, and a memorable pisco-dunked bread
pudding.

Javier has lived in France, China and God
knows where else, so his skills are honed
and he even spears his own catches of the
day on occasion! If this restaurant weren't
fabulous, Peruvians would riot. Call ahead in
January, February and July.

Las Gemelitas
SEAFOOD $$

(Bastidas 154; mains S15-20) Three blocks off
the Pan-American Hwy behind the Cruz del
Sur office, this cane-walled restaurant does
great seafood and little else. They do a bang-
up ceviche (emphasize spicy for a nice kick
in the pants) and we have it on good word
that it's one of the few old town Máncora op-
tions using truly fresh catch.

Tao
THAI, CHINESE $$

(Piura 240; mains S12-35; ☺closed Mon) The
aromas of Southeast Asia waft out onto Av
Piura from the interior of this Thai-Chinese
hotspot. Travelers flock here for the taste
bud flip – red, yellow, green and panang
curries, fusion stir-fries and noodles. All
make good use of local tuna, but pork, beef,
chicken and veggies are on the menu as well.
It's upscale, but is always packed with backpackers looking for a culinary upgrade for
the evening.

Green Eggs and Ham
BREAKFAST $

(Grau 503; meals S15 & S18; ☺7:30am-4:30pm)
There's nothing silly about this *Dr Seuss*–
inspired breakfast spot, which counts a
battalion of gringo fans for its homesick-
remedy breakfasts (pancakes, French toast,
hash browns). But the real coup is the

2nd-floor patio – a straight shot through a thatch of tall palms to the crashing waves.

Angela's Place
BREAKFAST, VEGETARIAN $

(Piura 396; breakfasts S6.50-14; mains S5-12; ⊙from 8am) Angela the Austrian bread wizard started selling her delicious sweet potato, yucca and wheat breads from her bicycle years ago. Now you can get them at her cheery cafe on the main drag, along with creative and substantial vegetarian (and vegan!) dishes, energizing breakfast combos and sweet pastries.

La Postrería
DESSERTS $

(Piura 233; desserts S8-12; ⊙closed Wed) This adorable cafe run by an adorable *limeña* knows its way around a latte and is the place to sink your sweet tooth into some great desserts, including *suspiro limeño* (milk caramel and meringue), brownies, cheesecake and the ever-popular apple pie. Cool soundtrack to boot, bouncing from the Cure to Death Cab to Smashing Pumpkins (when they were good).

Beef Grill
BURGERS, STEAKHOUSE $$

(Piura 253; burgers S18-23; ⊙from 5pm) The North Coast's best burgers are an ideal antidote to the seafood blues, but there are more serious slabs of meat coming out of the kitchen too.

Jugería Mi Janett
JUICES $

(Piura 677; juices S3-6) The best juice place in town – come here for massive jugs of your favorite tropical fruit squeeze.

⊙ Information

There is no information office, but the website www.vivamancora.com has tonnes of useful information. There are BCP, BBVA, Globalnet and Banco de la Nación ATMs along the strip, but only the latter is a bank. You'll find scattered internet access on the strip as well.

Banco de la Nación (Piura 625; ⊙8:30am-2:30pm Mon-Fri) Change US dollars here.

Medical Center (www.medicalcentermancora. com; Panamericana s/n; ⊙24hr) If you get stung by a ray or break a bone, head to this full-service clinic at the far northern entrance to town.

⊙ Getting There & Away

Air

Star Perú (⊘01-705-9000; www.starperu.com) flies from Talara, a 40-minute bus ride south of Máncora. The flight leaves the capital at 1:30pm and returns from Talara at 4:50pm. Fares start at S108. It's also an option to fly to Piura with LAN, Taca or Peruvian Airlines (p348) or to Tumbes with LAN (p359) and catch onward road transportation from there.

Bus

Many bus offices are in the center, though most southbound trips originate in Tumbes. *Combis* leave for Tumbes (S10, two hours) regularly; they drive along the main drag until full. *Buscamas* from Máncora go direct to Lima (14 hours); other services can drop you in intermediate cities on the way to Lima (18 hours). Regular minibuses run between Máncora and Punta Sal (S3, 30 minutes).

Cial (⊘96-540-2235; Piura 520) Has a Lima-bound bus at 5:30pm.

Civa (⊘25-8086; Piura 704) Has an economical 3:30pm service to Lima, as well as nicer buses at 5:30pm and 6:30pm; and a midnight bus to Guayaquil.

Cruz del Sur (⊘25-8232; Grau 208) Has a *bus-cama* service to Lima at 5:30pm; buses to Trujillo and Chimbote on Tuesday, Friday and Sunday at 10:30pm; and you can catch its Guayaquil-bound bus from Lima at 9am on Monday, Thursday and Saturday.

MÁNCORA BUSES

DESTINATION	COST (S)	DURATION (HR)
Chiclayo	26-50	6
Chimbote	80	14
Guayaquil (Ec)	60-114	9
Lima	65-165	14-18
Piura	15-30	3½
Sullana	12.50	2½
Trujillo	27-60	9-10
Tumbes	10-15	2

Dorado (📞96-964-2226; Grau 201) Six ...ses a day to Piura between 9:30am and ...30pm; buses for Chiclayo (9:30am, 9:30pm, ...:30pm, midnight) and Trujillo (9:30am, ...30pm, 11pm). A Tumbes-bound bus also ...abs passengers seven times a day.

...ntrafesa (📞41-1324; Grau 193) Heads to Chi-...ayo at 9:30pm and 10pm; Trujillo at 8:30pm, ...30pm and 10pm.

...po (📞25-8140; Piura 679) Fast and regular ...ourly buses to Sullana and Piura between 4am ...d 8pm.

...tursa (📞25-8276; Piura 509) Lima *bus-cama* ...ith wi-fi!) at 5:30pm and 6pm Monday to ...aturday; 4pm and 4:30pm Sunday.

...psa (📞25-8672; Grau 113) Lima bus at 6pm.

...ertur (📞49-6805; Piura 624) Faster *colectivo* ...ns to Piura (departing hourly from 7am to ...pm) and Tumbes (departing hourly from 8am ...6pm).

...unta Sal
📞072 / POP 3300

...he long, curvy bay at Punta Sal, 25km north ...f Máncora, has fine sand and is dotted with ...ocky bits – but it's still great for a dip in the ...cean. The sea here is calm and the lack of ...urfer types means that this tranquil oasis of ...esorts is particularly popular with families.

Off the Pan-American Hwy at Km 1192, ...he seaside **Hotel Punta Sal** (📞59-6700; ...ww.puntasal.com.pe; s/d per person incl full ...oard from S280/479, bungalows for 2 from S582; ...❄@🤖🏊) got a trendy makeover in 2011. It's ...ay nicer than the old Panamericana Punta ...al Club Hotel signs would have you believe ...nd perfect for families. Endless distrac-...ions include minigolf, banana-boat rides, ...vaterskiing, tennis, volleyball, table tennis, ...illiards and a wooden-decked pool. Oh, ...nd a near-life-size replica of a conquista-...or galleon. What else? The seaside drove of ...ainbow-colored bungalows are great, with ...abulous terraces complete with sink-into ...ouches. It also offers deep-sea fishing trips ...or S2183 per day in a boat that will take up ...o six anglers.

The 23 ocean-view rooms at **Hotel Ca-...allito de Mar** (📞54-0048; www.hotelcabal ...todemar.com; s/d per person incl full board from ...95.50/191; ❄@🤖🏊) literally climb up the ...ea cliff and have pretty bamboo accents ...nd private patios. As you climb from the ...sea, prices go down, but views get better. ...Hit the restaurant, bar, Jacuzzi, games room ...nd the gorgeous pool that practically dips ...ts toe into the sea. Activities such as fishing,

boating and waterskiing can be arranged. Air-con is S50 per day extra.

One of the few budget options on this beach, the English-run **Las Terrazas de Pun-ta Sal** (📞50-7701; www.lasterrazasdepuntasal. com.pe; s/d without bathroom S25/50, r from S80; @🤖) has solid rooms inside the main house, as well as some poky small bamboo rooms at the back. The terrace restaurant here has awesome sunset views and wood-fired brick-oven pizza. They were renovating and doing a major cleanup on our visit – expect good beach value for your *soles*.

Regular minibuses run between Máncora and Punta Sal (S3, 30 minutes).

Zorritos
📞072 / POP 9400

About 35km south of Tumbes, Zorritos is the biggest fishing village along this section of coast. While the thin beach here isn't as nice as beaches further south, it is home to interesting coastal **birdlife**. Look for frigate birds, pelicans, egrets and other migratory birds.

At Km 1235 is **Grillo Tres Puntas Eco-hostel** (📞79-4830; campsites S15, r with/without bathroom per person S50/20, all incl breakfast; @🤖🏊), constructed (mainly by volunteers) from natural materials such as bamboo and cane. Everything here, including water, is re-cycled. Breezy, rustic cabins with balconies and hammocks sit on the beach and camp-sites have electricity and a shade roof. There is an artistic elevated patio fashioned from driftwood – great for sunset beers. All rooms share interesting outdoor communal bath-rooms covered in mosaic tiles and seashells. Dog lovers should ask the Spanish owner to show you his 20 Peruvian hairless dogs – he breeds them (there are two hairy dogs here, too, clearly playing second fiddle). Hiking to nearby mud baths can be arranged and they also run popular five-day *hostal*-and-camp-ing tours that take in beaches, trekking, la-goons and mud baths and cost only S550 per person – including everything! It's supreme-ly rustic but pretty idyllic at the same time.

Right in Zorritos, **Puerta del Sol** (📞54-4294; hosppuertadelsol@hotmail.com; Piaggio 109; r per person incl breakfast S40; 🤖) is the skinny little *hospedaje* that could. It has a mini-ature garden bisected by a winding sidewalk and patches of vibrant lawn. The only acces-sory missing is a garden gnome. The rooms

BORDER CROSSING: ECUADOR VIA TUMBES

Shady practices at the border crossing between Ecuador and Peru at Aguas Verdes have earned it the dubious title of 'the worst border crossing in South America.' Whether it deserves to wear that crown is hard to prove empirically, but it pays to be wary.

You are strongly advised to take a direct bus across the border with a major bus company like **Cruz del Sur**, **Civa**, **Ormeño** or **Cifa International** (p359), jump off at immigration to get stamped out and get back on the bus immediately. Scam artists as far back as Máncora rope in travelers by selling them minivan transfers to the border and reminding them they will need to switch buses at the border. With this thought in mind, you think nothing of the minivan stopping short of the border due to a 'road block,' 'transit strike' or 'protest' up ahead (*paro* is the key Spanish word you are looking for). Your minivan passes you off to another car driven by someone who explains the situation ahead and tells you he works for the bus companies who normally operate but only cars can pass. Between the two borders, the car will stop, you will be given a spiel about corrupt immigration officers at the border and asked to help pay them off as well as cover the additional transport measures. Some travelers have paid upwards of US$100 for the privilege. If you must make a connection, however, use only *combis* and *colectivos* and stay out of situations where you are the only passenger, even in a marked taxi. It also goes without saying you should ignore all street touts in Tumbes, who approach foreigners all around town.

Another nugget of wisdom: if you need to change money, avoid doing so at the border as scams and counterfeit bills are rampant here. Many people will offer their services as porters or guides. Most are annoyingly insistent, so unless you really need help, they are best avoided.

Now...on to Ecuador! *Colectivos* (shared transportation taxis; per person S3.50, 25 minutes) and *combis* (minibuses; S2, 40 minutes) for Aguas Verdes on the Peru–Ecuador border leave from several spots around town, most conveniently for travelers from the corner of Puell and Tumbes or Castilla and Feijoo, the latter near the market. It's S15 for the

---

are simple and neat and beach access is available, but there are no views.

Midrange choices include the beachfront **Hotel Los Cocos** (☏9867-1259; www.hotelloscocos.com; Panamericana Km 1242; d incl breakfast S200; ☎❄), with big rooms filled with bamboo furniture, a few arty bits, and sporting balconies with hammocks and sea vistas. The pool has rock features and a separate children's section. There's also a small kids' play area, a trampoline and a beach volleyball court here.

Combis to Zorritos leave regularly from Tumbes (S2.50, about one hour). Coming from the south, just catch any bus heading toward Tumbes.

Tumbes

☏072 / POP 128,600

Only 30km from the Ecuadorean border, Tumbes is in a uniquely green part of coastal Peru, where dry deserts magically turn into mangroves and an expanse of ecological reserves stretches in all directions. It's also the springboard for trips to the excellent and popular beaches of Máncora, two hours further south.

A flashpoint for conflict during the 1940–41 border war between Ecuador and Peru, Tumbes remains a garrison town with strong military presence. It's hot and (depending on the season) dusty or buggy, and most travelers don't stay long. But as far as border towns go, it's not the worst you'll come across – a pleasant plaza, interesting mosaics around town, a cool elevated riverwalk and several pedestrianized streets make for a tolerable evening. The nearby national reserves are distinctive as well and a boon for nature buffs, but most travelers are quick to put Tumbes in their rearview mirror.

◉ Sights

There are several **old houses** dating from the early 19th century on Grau, east of the Plaza de Armas. These rickety abodes are made of split-bamboo and wood and it seems like they are defying gravity through sheer will. The plaza has several outdoor restaurants and is a nice place to relax. The

...ole taxi. Unless you have a real love for loitering at dirty border towns, the Ecuadorian ...rder town of Huaquillas is best avoided. It's far better to take the bus straight through to ...achala or Guayaquil further on in Ecuador.

The Peruvian **immigration office** (El Complejo; [☎]072-56-1178; ⊘24hr) is in the middle ...the desert at Aguas Verdes, about 3km from the border. Travelers leaving Peru obtain ...it stamps here – if you're catching public transportation make sure you stop to complete ...ese border formalities. From the immigration office, *mototaxis* can take you the rest of ...e way to the border (S3).

Aguas Verdes is basically a long, dusty street full of vendors that continues into the ...ar-identical Ecuadorean border town of Huaquillas via the international bridge across the ...o Zarumilla. If you are forced to stay the night at the border, there are a few basic hotels ...Aguas Verdes, but they're all noisy and pretty sketchy. There are some nicer options in ...uaquillas, but really you're better off hanging back in Tumbes for the night or making the ...o-hour bus trip to the city of Machala, where there are much better facilities.

The Ecuadorean immigration office is inside the massive blue-and-white compound ...own as **CEBAF** (Centro Binacional de Atención de Frontera; ⊘24hr), about 4km north of the ...idge. Taxis from the bridge charge US$2.50 and are pretty insistent about being paid ...dollars, not *nuevo soles*. If you find one that will take *soles*, you will overpay like we did ...10). Very few nationalities need a visa for Ecuador, but everyone needs a Tarjeta Andina ...nbarkation card, available for free at the immigration office. You must surrender your Tar-...a Andina when you leave Ecuador. If you lose it, there is no monetary penalty but you will ...t be allowed to re-enter Ecuador for 90 days. Exit tickets out of Ecuador and sufficient ...nds (US$20 per day) are legally required, but rarely asked for. Tourists are allowed only ...0 days per year in Ecuador without officially extending their stay at a consulate – if you ...ave stayed more, you may be fined between US$200 and US$2000 when you leave.

See Lonely Planet's *Ecuador & the Galápagos Islands* for more information.

...edestrian streets north of the plaza (es-...ecially Bolívar) have several large, modern ...onuments and are favorite hangouts for ...oung and old alike.

About 5km south of town, off the Pan-...merican Hwy, is an overgrown archaeo-...gical site that was the home of the Tumpis ...eople and, later, the site of the Inca fort vis-...ed by Pizarro. The story is told in the tiny ...te museum, **Museo de Cabeza de Baca** ...dult S4; ⊘8:30am-4pm Mon-Sat), which also ...isplays some 1500-year-old ceramic vessels ...om all around Tumbes, including Chimú ...nd Inca. One display case is dedicated to ar-...facts seized by customs before they were il-...gally trafficked out of the country. A larger ...useum was under construction when we ...ame through.

🕭 Tours & Guides

...reference Tours ([☎]52-5518; turismomun ...al@hotmail.com; Grau 427; ⊘9am-7:30pm Mon-...ay, to 11am Sun) runs some of the most eco-...omical tours in town if you have a group of ...ree or more and is the preferred (ahem!) ...gency for the nearby parks and reserves.

🛏 Sleeping

Almost all of Tumbes' hotels are in the budget range and most hotels have only cold water, but that's no problem in the heat. Be sure your room has a working fan if you're here in the sweltering summer (December to March). During the wet season and the twice-yearly rice harvests, mosquitoes can be a big problem, and there are frequent water and electricity outages. In the lower end of the budget range, watch your valuables carefully.

TOP CHOICE **Casa César** BOUTIQUE HOTEL **$$**
([☎]52-2883; www.casacesartumbes.com; Huáscar 311; s/d incl breakfast from S110/160; ❋⊕) These former budget digs got the kind of makeover normally reserved for *Queer Eye for the Straight Guy*. It's now a full-on midrange boutique hotel that is professional, friendly and easy on the eyes: sleek, high-design furniture color up the minimalist white aesthetic at play here.

The 20 rooms are named after local fauna and are split between less sleek standards and colorful and bright executives. For Tumbes, it's a step up and the price is right.

Hotel Feijoo   HOTEL $$
(☎52-2126; www.hotelfeijoo.com; Bolognesi 272; s with/without air-con S70/50, d with/without air-con S90/70; ❋☎) The Feijoo, just a block from Plaza de Armas, is one of the cheapest spots for icy air-con, which represents more value than normal in the Tumbes heat. Modern rooms and bathrooms are extra spacious, adding even more value, and look out onto a bright, open-air atrium. There are no front desk smiles that come along with the rooms, but cost-benefit here is palpable.

Hotel Costa del Sol   BUSINESS HOTEL $$$
(☎52-3991; www.costadelsolperu.com; San Martín 275; s/d incl breakfast S285/350; ❋@☎≋) This is the most upscale hotel in town, providing a decent restaurant, a pleasant bar and garden, and a Jacuzzi, swimming pool with a children's section, small casino and gym. The comfortable rooms are decked out in warm, masculine colors and have been upgraded since Ramada grabbed the wheel in 2012 – each features all the ubiquitous mod cons. A cold cocktail is included – and is most welcome.

Hostal Roma   HOTEL $
(☎52-4137; Bolognesi 425; s/d/tr S45/70/95; ☎) Boasting top Plaza de Armas real estate, the Roma is an upper-level budget option and provides guests with clean, comfortable rooms with hot shower, high-octane fan, phone and cable TV. Accustomed to dealing with foreigners, it extends a warm welcome, but can be noisy – there's even an in-house intercom system that's switched on at all hours.

Tilted sinks mean your toiletries don't stay still, but the fact remains that it sits in an ideal price range – above potential stolen laptop, below second mortgage.

Hotel Rizzo Plaza   HOTEL $$
(☎52-3991; www.rizzoplazahotel.com; Bolognesi 216; s/d incl breakfast S98/148; ❋@☎) Just steps from the Plaza de Armas, the ritzy Rizzo gets solid reviews from travelers. With a business center, it leans vaguely suit-and-tie-like, with a professional staff, smallish bathrooms and way too many faux plants.

Hospedaje Lourdes   GUESTHOUSE $
(☎52-2966; Mayor Bodero 118; s/d/tr S40/60/70; ☎) Clean, safe and friendly, the Lourdes offers austere (for Tumbes) rooms with fan, phones, TV and hot showers.

Hospedaje Italia   GUESTHOUS
(☎52-3396; Grau 733; s/d/tr S25/40/50) T Italia is a good deal for double rooms, ea of which has plenty of natural light an space, tiled floors and TVs as standard, b the lack of wi-fi is its downfall.

Hospedaje Amazonas   GUESTHOUS
(☎52-5266; Tumbes 317; s/d/tr S30/45/55) Th place is old, but the coat of paint bein slapped on as we visited signifies some pre ence of maintenance. Big rooms here cut th mustard for a night, with fans, hot wate and TV. Perhaps its best attribute is bein next door to Cruz del Sur.

✗ Eating

There are several bars and restaurants the Plaza de Armas, many with shaded t bles and chairs outside – a real boon hot weather. It's a pleasant place to sit an watch the world go by as you drink a co beer and wait for your bus.

TOP CHOICE ✗ Restaurant
Sí Señor   PERUVIAN, SEAFOOD
(Bolívar 115; mains S15-35) On a quiet corner the plaza with pleasant streetside tables ou side and quixotic, slow-turning fans insic Sí Señor is the long-standing staple doing manner of everything, with a heavy emph sis on fish and seafood. The dizzying men left us indecisive, so the waiter recommen ed a ginger-steamed fish that didn't look lik much upon arrival, but proved to be a mo tasty, healthy dinner. Good stuff.

Moka   CAFÉ
(www.mokatumbes.com; Bolognesi 252; snacks S 10; ☺8am-1pm & 4:30-11pm) This modern ca is so wildly out of place in Tumbes that turns heads. You'll find loads of scrumptioi cakes, flavored *frappuccinos,* juices, mil shakes and not-quite-right espresso (bi from a proper machine nonetheless). Th good menu of *croissantwiches* makes fc a lovely quick bite or breakfast (try chicke salad with avocado).

Don't confuse this with their ice-crear parlor two doors down, unless you're goin for the sweets.

Las Terrazas   SEAFOOD, PERUVIAN $
(Araujo 549; mains S15-30) A little bit out of th town center, this popular place is well wort the S1.50 *mototaxi* ride. Packed with hungr

ners daily, it serves up heaped plates of afood, and will ceviche or cook anything om fish to lobster and octopus. It's all epared in the northern coastal style and ey have music Friday through Monday om 3pm.

It's on a classy 3rd-floor terrace and has owing tablecloths, lots of decorations and festive mood – and completely flips the ript on the rudimentary facade of the ilding itself.

assic Restaurant   SEAFOOD, PERUVIAN **$$**
umbes 185; menú S7, mains S20-27; ⊙8am-5pm)
nall, quiet as a funeral and dignified, Clas-c Restaurant is a wonderful place to escape rrid Tumbes and relax with a long lunch, s many of the town's better-connected lo-ls do. The food is good and mainly coastal, ut secretly we love this place for its air-con. he S7 daily *menú* is a steal.

Information

part from offering tours to local sights, Tumbes ur companies can also provide some tourist formation.

angers & Annoyances
he border crossing has a bad reputation. For etailed warnings, see the boxed text (p357).

mergency
olicía de Turismo (Tourist Police, Poltur; ₂97-288-0013; San Pedro 600, 2nd fl)

nmigration
cuadorean consul (₂52-5949; www.mecua orperu.org.pe; Bolívar 129, 3rd fl; ⊙8am-1pm lon-Fri) On the Plaza de Armas.

ficina de Migraciónes (₂52-3422; www. igemin.gob.pe; Panamericana Km 1275.5)

Along the Pan-American Hwy, 2km north of town. Handles visa issues.

Medical Services
Clinica Feijoo (www.clinicafeijoo.blogspot. com; Castilla 305) One of the better medical clinics in Tumbes.

Money
Banco Continental (Bolívar 129)
BCP (Bolívar 261) Changes traveler's checks and has an ATM.

Post
Serpost (San Martín 208; ⊙9am-7pm Mon-Fri, to 1pm Sat) Postal service on the block south of Plaza Bolognesi.

Tourist Information
iPerú (₂50-6721; Malecón III Milenio, 3rd fl) Provides useful tourist information. Walk south on Bolognesi to the waterfront to find it.

❶ Getting There & Away

Air
The airport (TBP) is 8km north of town. **LAN** (₂52-4481; www.lan.com; Bolognesi 250) has a daily flight from Lima to Tumbes leaving at 5:30pm and returning to Lima at 7:55pm. Fares rise from S379 for foreigners. **Star Perú** (₂50-8548; www.starperu.com; San Martín 275) departs Lima at 1:30pm, returning at 3:45pm on Monday and Friday only.

Bus
You can usually find a bus to Lima within 24 hours of your arrival in Tumbes, but they're sometimes (especially major holidays) sold out a few days in advance. You can take a bus south to another major city and try again from there.

Some companies offer a limited-stop special service, with air-con, bathrooms and very loud

TUMBES BUSES

DESTINATION	COST (S)	DURATION (HR)
Chiclayo	30-50	8
Guayaquil (Ec)	25-118	6
Lima	50-165	16-18
Máncora	7-25	1½-2
Machala (Ec)	12	3
Piura	16-30	4-5
Puerto Pizarro	1.50	¼
Rica Playa	4	1½
Trujillo	27-37	11
Zorritos	2.50	¾

video; some have deluxe, nonstop *bus-cama* services.

Slower services stop at Piura, Chiclayo and Trujillo. If you are heading to Máncora or Piura, much faster *colectivo* minivans are the best way to go.

If you're going to Ecuador, it's easiest to go with Cifa, an Ecuadorean company, or Ormeño. Civa leaves in the middle of the night and Cruz del Sur only departs three days per week. All stop at the border for you to complete passport formalities.

Cial (☑52-6350; www.expresocial.com; Tumbes 958) *Bus-cama* to Lima at 3:30pm.

Cifa (☑52-5026; www.cifainternacional.com; Tumbes 958) Heads to Machala (you must switch in Huaquillas) and Guayaquil six times daily, both in Ecuador, about every two hours from 6am to 5pm.

Civa (☑52-5120; www.excluciva.pe; Tumbes 587) Cheaper *semi-cama* Lima services at 1:30pm and 4:30pm and a *bus-cama* at 3:30pm. A Guayaquil bus departs at 2am.

Cruz del Sur (☑52-6200; www.cruzdelsur. com.pe; Tumbes 319) *Bus-cama* to Lima at 3:30pm and Guayaquil on Monday, Thursday and Saturday at 11am.

El Sol (☑50-9252; Piura 403) Economy buses to Chiclayo (S26) at 8:15am and 9:30am. Also a service to Lima (S55) via Chiclayo (S20) and Trujillo (S28) at 8:20pm.

Oltursa (☑52-2894; www.oltursa.pe; Tumbes 948) *Bus-cama* service to Lima at 3:30pm and 4pm (Monday to Saturday), 2pm and 2:30pm Sunday. Also heads to Trujillo and Chiclayo daily at 8pm.

Ormeño (☑52-2894; www.grupo-ormeno.com. pe; Tumbes 1187) Lima departure at 7:30pm via Chiclayo and Trujillo. Also has a direct bus to Guayaquil at 9:30am.

Sertur (☑94-199-1662; www.serturonline.com; Tumbes 502) Faster minivans to Máncora and Piura every 30 minutes between 5:30am and 8:30pm.

Shaday Adornay (☑61-8672; cnr Tumbes & Piura) Faster minivans to Máncora and Piura hourly between 7am and 10pm.

Tepsa (☑52-2428; www.tepsa.com.pe; Tumbes 199) To Lima at 4pm.

Transportes Chiclayo (☑52-5260; www.trans porteschiclayo.com; Tumbes 570) Daily buses to Chiclayo via Máncora at 12:30pm and 9pm.

Transportes El Dorado (☑52-3480 www. transporteseldorado.com.pe; Tacna 251) Thirteen daily buses to Piura and departures to Chiclayo and Trujillo at 7:30pm, 9pm and 10:30pm.

From around the market area, *colectivos* for Puerto Pizarro leave from the corner of Castilla and Feijoo; for Zorritos, *combis* depart from Castilla near Ugarte; for Rica Playa, *combis* depart from Ugarte 404 near Castilla. Ask locals as the stops aren't marked. For Máncora faster, air-conditioned minivan service offices congregate around the corner of Tumbes and Piura. On the southwest corner of the same intersection, slower, cheaper *combis* also depart regularly. Buses to Casitas leave at 1pm (S10, five hours).

Getting Around

A taxi to the airport is about S20. There are no *combis* to the airport.

Around Tumbes

PUERTO PIZARRO
☑072

About 14km north of Tumbes, the character of the oceanfront changes from the coastal desert, which stretches more than 2000km north from central Chile to northern Peru, to the mangrove swamps that dominate much of the Ecuadorean and Colombian coastlines. There's an explosion of **birdlife** here with up to 200 different migrating species visiting these areas. Boats can be hired to tour the mangroves; one tour goes to a **crocodile sanctuary** where you can see Peru's only crocodiles being nursed back from near extinction. The nearby **Isla de Aves** can be visited (but not landed on) to see the many nesting seabirds, especially between 5pm and 6pm, when huge flocks of birds return to roost for the night. Boats line the waterfront of Puerto Pizarro and cost S30 per hour per boat; you can do a tour of the mangroves and the above-mentioned sites for S40 per boat for up to six people. Two good options are **Turmi** (☑97-298-6199; Grau s/n), the boatman's association, which is your best bet for small groups and independent travelers; or **Manglaris Tours** (☑78-3734; Grau s/n), which has bigger boats and prices as cheap as S5 per person for the standard tour. Both hang out along the walkway to the pier. Tour companies in Tumbes also provide guided tours to the area.

A quick and easy independent day trip from Tumbes is a visit to **Isla Hueso de Ballena**, which has a few lunch restaurants. They are all pretty ramshackle, but **Restaurante Hueso de Ballena** (mains S25-28; ☉9am-6pm) is pretty ideal, right on the sand with a few hammocks as well. It promises an 'orgy of shellfish' and is a good place to try the local specialty, *conchas negras* (black shells) as well as ceviche, seafood rices, *chi*

arrónes and soups, with ingredients all
icked fresh from the water. Boats will take
iu out to the restaurants and back for S25,
:luding wait time.

There are regular *combis* between Puerto
zarro and Tumbes (S1.50, 15 minutes).

ESERVA DE BIOSFERA EL NOROESTE

ie Northwestern Biosphere Reserve con-
ts of four protected areas that cover 2344
km in the department of Tumbes and
rthern Piura. A lack of government fund-
g means that there is little infrastructure
tourist facilities – much of what exists
as funded by organizations such as the
ındación Peruana para la Conservación de
Naturaleza (FPCN; also called ProNatu-
eza), with assistance from international
dies such as the WWF.

Information about the area is available
om the Tumbes office of **Sernanp** (☑072-
-6489; www.sernanp.gob.pe; Panamericana
rte 1739, Tumbes; ⊕8:30am-12:30pm & 3:30-
30pm Mon-Fri), the government department
charge of administering this region. You
ill need to get permission papers to visit
ıy of the protected areas on your own;
ese are free and take minutes to organize,
ough visits are no longer recommended
ıe to safety concerns.

Tour companies in Tumbes can arrange
urs to the two most visited areas, Parque
acional Cerros de Amotape and Santuario
acional los Manglares de Tumbes, as can
rillo 3 Puntos Ecohostel in Zorritos. There
e few roads into these areas and visiting
ıring the wet months of December to April
ın prove very difficult.

arque Nacional Cerros de Amotape

ne tropical dry forest ecosystem of Cerros
e Amotape is protected by this 1515-sq-km
ational park, which makes up the lion's
share of the Biosfera and is home to flora
and fauna including jaguars, condors and
anteaters, though parrots, deer and peccaries are more commonly sighted. Large-scale
logging, illegal hunting and overgrazing are
some of the threats facing this habitat, of
which there is very little left anywhere in
Peru. The best place to spot a wide range
of wild animals is the Zona Reservada de
Tumbes, now encompassed within Amotape
itself. The forest is similar to the tropical
dry forest of other parts of Amotape, but because it lies more on the easterly side of the
hills, it is wetter and has slightly different
flora and fauna, including crocodiles, howler
monkeys and nutria. You can also see various orchids and a wide variety of birds.

Guides are essential for spotting wildlife
and can be arranged in the town of **Rica
Playa**, a small, friendly village located just
within the park. Although there are no hotels here, you can camp and local families
will sell you meals.

Agencies in Tumbes also organize tours
for S230 for up to four people.

Santuario Nacional los Manglares de Tumbes

This national sanctuary was established in
1988 and lies on the coast, separate from the
other three dry-forest areas. Only about 30
sq km in size, it plays an essential role in
conserving Peru's only region of mangroves.

You can travel here by going to Puerto Pizarro and taking a dirt road northeast to the
tiny community of **El Bendito**. From here,
ask around for someone to guide you by canoe. Guided tours are available from Puerto
Pizarro as well, though the mangroves here
are not technically within the protection of
the sanctuary. A visit here is tide-dependent.

Agencies in Tumbes also arrange tours for
S150 for up to four people.

Huaraz & the Cordilleras

Why Go?

Ground zero for outdoor adventure worship in Peru, the Cordilleras are one of the pre-eminent hiking, trekking and backpacking spots in South America. Every which way you throw your gaze, perennially glaciered white peaks razor their way through expansive mantles of lime-green valley. In the recesses of these prodigious giants huddle scores of pristine jade lakes, ice caves and torrid springs. The Cordillera Blanca is the highest mountain range in the world outside the Himalayas, and its 18 ostentatious summits of more than 6000m will not let you forget it for a second.

Huaraz is the fast-beating heart linking the trekking trails and roads that serve as the mountains' arteries. Plans of daring ice climbs, mountain-biking exploits and rock-climbing expeditions are hatched over ice-cold beers in fireplace-warmed bars, often only interrupted by a brief sojourn into the eastern valley to the enigmatic 3000-year-old ruins of Chavín de Huántar.

Best Places to Stay

- » Albergue Churup (p370)
- » Lazy Dog Inn (p370)
- » Llanganuco Mountain Lodge (p389)
- » Hotel San Sebastián (p370)
- » Andes Lodge Peru (p400)

Best Places to Eat

- » Mi Chef Kristof (p372)
- » Café Andino (p372)
- » Chili Heaven (p373)
- » Rinconcito Mineiro (p373)
- » Buongiorno (p399)

When to Go

Huaraz

May–Sep Cordillera's dry season offers the best trekking conditions.

Oct–Dec A relaxed post-season atmosphere in Huaraz; more quality trekking guides available for hire.

Dec–Apr Wet and rainy, but appropriately geared trekkers enjoy the silence.

HUARAZ

043 / POP 48,500 / ELEV 3091M

Huaraz is the restless capital of this Andean adventure kingdom and its rooftops command exhaustive panoramas of the city's dominion: one of the most impressive mountain ranges in the world. Nearly wiped out by the earthquake of 1970, Huaraz isn't going to win any Andean-village beauty contests anytime soon, but it does have personality – and personality goes a long way.

This is first and foremost a trekking metropolis. During the high season the streets

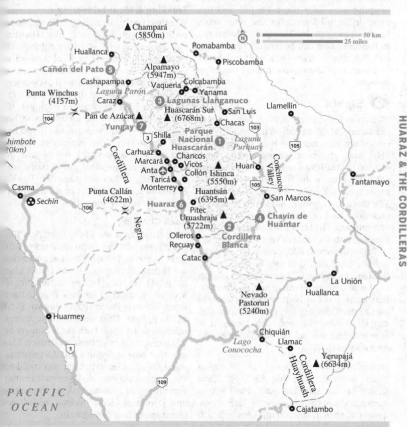

Huaraz & The Cordilleras Highlights

❶ Traipse for weeks around the magnificent peaks of the **Parque Nacional Huascarán** (p379)

❷ Ride the astonishing highway between Huaraz and Chiquián, where postcard-ready panoramas of the **Cordillera Blanca** (p379) and **Cordillera Huayhuash** (p384) lie before you like a painting

❸ See what all this trekking fuss is about at **Lagunas Llanganuco** (p390) and **Laguna 69** (p382), two of the best day trips in the Cordilleras

❹ Journey through mysterious passageways amid the ruins of **Chavín de Huántar** (p396)

❺ Take a white-knuckle ride through the 1000m-high sheer rock walls of the staggering **Cañón del Pato** (p391)

❻ Rest your weary kicks in an idyllic Cordillera mountain lodge like the **Lazy Dog Inn** (p370) or **Llanganuco Mountain Lodge** (p389)

❼ Stroll the solemn grave of a disappeared town at **Yungay** (p389)

buzz with hundreds of backpackers and adventurers freshly returned from arduous hikes or planning their next expedition as they huddle in one of the town's many fine watering holes. Dozens of outfits help plan trips, rent equipment and organize a list of adventure sports as long as your arm. An endless lineup of quality restaurants and hopping bars keep the belly full and the place lively till long after the tents have been put away to dry. Mountain adventures in the off-season can be equally rewarding, but the vibe is more subdued and some places go into hibernation during the rainy season.

◎ Sights

Monumento Nacional Wilkahuaín   RUIN
(admission S5; ☺9am-5pm) This small Wari ruin about 8km north of Huaraz is remarkably well preserved, dating from about AD 600 to 900. It's an imitation of the temple at Chavín done in the Tiwanaku style. Wilkahuaín means 'grandson's house' in Quechua. The three-story temple has seven rooms on each floor, each originally filled with bundles of mummies. The bodies were kept dry using a sophisticated system of ventilation ducts.

Taxis cost about S20, or ask for a *combi* (minibus; around S1) at the bus stops by the Río Quilcay in town. The two-hour walk up to Wilkahuaín is an easy, first acclimatization jaunt and can be a rewarding glimpse into Andean country life, passing farms and simple *pueblos* (villages). Ask locally if it is safe before you set off; see Dangers and Annoyances (p374).

Museo Regional de Ancash   MUSEUM
(Plaza de Armas; adult/child S5/1; ☺8:30am-5:15pm Tue-Sat, 9am-2pm Sun) The Museo Regional de Ancash houses the largest collection of ancient stone sculptures in South America. Small but interesting, it has a few mummies, some trepanned skulls and a garden of stone monoliths from the Recuay culture (400 BC–AD 600) and the Wari culture (AD 600–1100).

Jirón José Olaya   ARCHITECTURE, MARKET
East of town, Jirón José Olaya is on the right-hand side of Raymondi a block beyond Confraternidad. It's the only street that remained intact through the earthquakes and provides a glimpse of what old Huaraz looked like; go on Sunday when a street market sells regional foods.

Mirador de Retaqeñua   LOOK
Mirador de Retaqeñua is about a 45-min walk southeast of the center and has gre views of the city and its mountainous bac drop. It's best to take a S8 taxi here (see Da gers and Annoyances, p374).

🏃 Activities

Trekking & Mountaineering
Whether you're arranging a mountain e pedition or going for a day hike, Huaraz the place to start – it is the epicenter f planning and organizing local Andean a ventures. Numerous outfits can prearran entire trips so that all you need to do is sho up at the right place at the right time. Ma experienced backpackers go camping, hi ing and climbing in the mountains witho any local help and you can too if you ha the experience. Just remember, thou that carrying a backpack full of gear ov a 4800m pass requires much more effo than hiking at low altitudes. See Trekki & Mountaineering (p377) in the Cordiller section for more information.

Rock Climbing
Rock climbing is one of the Cordillera Bla ca's biggest pastimes. Avid climbers will fi some gnarly bolted sport climbs, particular at Chancos, Recuay (p394) and Hatun Mac ay (p394). For some big-wall action that w keep you chalked up for days, head to the f mous Torre de Parón (p390), known local as the Sphinx. Most trekking tour agenci offer climbing trips, both for beginners ar advanced, as part of their repertoire. Ma also rent gear and with a bit of legwork ar some information gathering you could eas ily arrange your own do-it-yourself climbi expedition. In Huaraz, Galaxia Expeditio and Monttrek have indoor *rócodrom* (climbing or bouldering walls).

Ice Climbing
With enough glaciers to sink your ice axe in for the rest of your life, the Cordillera Blanc is a frozen heaven for folks who want to lear ice climbing or attack new peaks and height Since many summits require a degree of tech nical know-how, ice climbing is a big activi in the Cordillera, and many tour and trekkin operators can arrange excursions, equipmer rental and lessons. The best trekking agen cies, listed under Tours & Guides (p367), hav years of experience with ice climbing and sa equipment. In Parque Nacional Huascará (p379) a certified guide is required.

TREMORS & LANDSLIDES

Records of aluviones, a deadly mix of avalanche, waterfall and landslide, date back almost 300 years, but three recent ones have caused particular devastation.

The first occurred in 1941, when an avalanche in the Cojup Valley, west of Huaraz, caused the Laguna Palcacocha to break its banks and flow down onto Huaraz, killing about 5000 inhabitants and flattening the city. Then, in 1962, a huge avalanche from Huascarán roared down its western slopes and destroyed the town of Ranrahirca, killing about 4000 people.

The worst disaster occurred on May 31, 1970, when a massive earthquake, measuring nearly 8.0 on the Richter scale, devastated much of central Peru, killing an estimated 70,000 people. About half of the 30,000 inhabitants of Huaraz died, and only 10% of the city was left standing. The town of Yungay was completely buried by the aluvión caused by the quake and almost its entire population of 25,000 was buried with the city (p389).

Since these disasters, a government agency (Hidrandina) has been formed to control the lake levels by building dams and tunnels, thus minimizing the chance of similar catastrophes. Today, warning systems are in place, although false alarms do occur.

Mountain Biking

Mountain Bike Adventures MOUNTAIN BIKING
(42-4259; www.chakinaniperu.com; Lúcar y Torre 530, 2nd fl; ⊙9am-1pm & 3-8pm) Mountain Bike Adventures has been in business for more than a decade and receives repeated visits by mountain bikers for its decent selection of bikes, knowledgeable and friendly service, and good safety record. The owner is a lifelong resident of Huaraz who speaks English and has spent time mountain biking in the USA – he knows the region's single-track possibilities better than anyone. The company offers bike rentals for independent types (only if you can prove mechanical competency) or guided tours, ranging from an easy five-hour cruise to 12-day circuits around the Cordillera Blanca. Rates start at S100 per day either for rentals or for one-day tours.

Volunteering

For the latest on volunteering opportunities, check out the community notice boards at popular gringo cafes and hangouts around Huaraz.

Seeds of Hope VOLUNTEERING
(94-352-3353; www.peruseeds.org) A recommended aid organization that works with Huaraz' poorest children and provides accommodations to volunteers for a small fee.

Teach Huaraz Peru VOLUNTEERING
(42-5303; www.teachhuarazperu.com) Works primarily with children and can arrange English-teaching and other kinds of experiences for volunteers; homestays with local families are available. Agencies specializing in community and sustainable tourism may also be able to help you arrange different kinds of volunteer activities in the region. It's best to arrange service activities in advance, though agencies sometimes take short-term, walk-in volunteers.

Community Tourism

More than just a buzzword in travel these days, community tourism offers an alternative experience to the traditional low-interaction, look-from-a-distance travel characterized by holidays holed up in resorts or giant tour groups. It brings travelers into close contact with local people, who are major stakeholders and beneficiaries of tourism projects that they design themselves (often with help from outside organizations). Activities range from preparing traditional food to participating in farming and craft production, and in many cases you can combine volunteer activities with a homestay. In addition to the mountain lodges, the following agencies are involved in community tourism and can help you set up trips to learn about traditional weaving, farming, cooking and most other aspects of indigenous life. Almost anything you do with these agencies will benefit local families and contribute to the growing community-tourism movement in the region.

Respons Sustainable Tourism Center CULTURAL TOUR
(42-7949; www.respons.org; Calle 28 de Julio 821; ⊙9am-1pm & 3-7:30pm) Works as a clearinghouse for information about community tourism in the area: arranges homestays,

sells locally made woven goods and shares information free of charge.

Mountain Institute CULTURAL TOUR (☎42-3446; www.mountain.org; Ricardo Palma 100) Arranges excellent trips to the Inca Trail (p383) as well as day trips to the Andean communities of Vicos and Humacchuco the Cordillera Blanca.

Other Activities

Skiers will not find ski lifts in the Cordille Blanca, but there is limited mountain skiin for die-hards who want to climb with sk

Huaraz

k locally for current conditions. **River running** (whitewater rafting) is sometimes offered on the Río Santa, but it's a very polluted river (mine-tailings upstream and raw sewage certainly don't help things) and people have fallen ill doing it. It's not recommended.

HUARAZ & THE CORDILLERAS HUARAZ

Horseback riding is a possibility; although there is no dedicated outfit in Huaraz, horses can be arranged by many travel agencies. The Lazy Dog Inn outside Huaraz has its own horses and does treks to the surrounding mountains. Respons Sustainable Tourism Center offers one-day rides from S160 around the village of Yungar in the Cordillera Negra.

Parapenting (hang gliding) and **parasailing** are increasing in popularity, though you will need to bring all your own equipment. Jangas, 20 minutes north of Huaraz; Wilcacocha, 40 minutes southeast; and Huata near Caraz are popular Cordillera Negra launching spots. Ask at Monttrek for the latest info.

👉 Tours & Guides

Day Tours

Dozens of agencies along Luzuriaga can organize outings to local sites, including several day excursions. One popular tour visits the ruins at Chavín de Huántar (p396); another passes through Yungay to the beautiful Lagunas Llanganuco (p390), where there are superb vistas of Huascarán and other mountains; a third takes you through Caraz to Laguna Parón (p390), which is surrounded by ravishing glaciated peaks; and a fourth travels through Caraz to see the massive *Puya raimondii* plant (p392) and then continues on to Nevado Pastoruri, where you can view ice caves, glaciers and mineral springs.

All of these trips cost between S35 and S45 each; prices may vary depending on the number of people going, but typically include transport (usually in minibuses) and a guide (who often doesn't speak English). Admission fees and lunch are extra. Trips take a full day; bring a packed lunch, warm clothes, drinking water and sunblock. Tours depart daily during the high season, but at other times departures depend on demand. Do not fall for a day trip to Chavín de Huántar on a Monday – the ruins and museum are closed.

Out of the throng of agencies in Huaraz, **Pablo Tours** (📞42-1145; www.pablotours.com; Luzuriaga 501) and **Sechín Tours** (📞42-1419; www.sechintours.com; Morales 602) are popular with travelers.

Trekking & Mountaineering

Mountaineers and trekkers should check out **Casa de Guías** (📞42-1811; www.casadeguias.com.pe; Parque Ginebra 28G; ⊙9am-1pm & 4-8pm Mon-Sat), the headquarters of the

Mountain Guide Association of Peru, for a list of certified guides. All of the agencies below arrange full trekking and climbing expeditions that include guides, equipment, food, cooks, porters and transport. Depending on the number of people, the length of your trip and what's included, expect to pay from under S90 for an easy day out to up to S670 for the most technical mountain per

person per day. Try not to base your sele tion solely on price, as you often get wh you pay for. The list below is by no mea exhaustive; things change, good places bad and bad places get good. One of t best resources for guides in Huaraz is oth travelers who have just come back fro a trek and can recommend (or not reco mend) their guides based on recent expe

Huaraz

ce. The South American Explorers Club
Lima (p96) is also an excellent source of
formation and maps.
Also see p377 and the boxed text, p369.

kyline Adventures TREKKING, MOUNTAINEERING
(42-7097; www.skyline-adventures.com; Pasaje
lustrial 137) Based just outside of Huaraz,
mes highly recommended and provides
ides for treks and mountain climbs.
ads six- and 10-day mountaineering
urses.

ctive Peru TREKKING
(99-648-3655; www.activeperu.com; Gamarra
9) A well-regarded, Belgian-run agency
at also rents gear.

onttrek TREKKING, CLIMBING
(42-1124; www.monttrek.com.pe; Luzuriaga 646,
d fl) A reputable agency that has lots of lo-

cal information, including invaluable topo
maps. Arranges rock climbing, mountain
biking and parapenting trips. Top-end gear
rental as well.

Huascarán TREKKING
(42-2523; www.huascarin-peru.com; Campos
711) Gets repeatedly good reviews from satisfied travelers; also does tours.

Montañero TREKKING, MOUNTAINEERING
(42-6386; Parque Ginebra) This good agency
arranges treks and climbs. It also rents or
sells gear.

Galaxia Expeditions TOURS, TREKKING
(42-5335; www.galaxia-expeditions.com; Parque
Periodista) Peruvian-run agency that uses
good gear but has a hit-or-miss reputation.
Also does local tours, climbing trips and has
an indoor climbing wall.

CHOOSING A TREK OPERATOR

Before you lay out your cold, hard cash for a guided trek make sure you know what you're getting. Ask the company or guide to list the services, products and price they're offering on your contract. In the event that they don't live up to their promises you may or may not be able to do anything about it, but a list ensures that the company understands exactly what you expect.

On your end, it is critical that you are crystal clear with your guides about your experience and fitness level. Also important is that you are properly acclimatized before setting out on a trek. All too often, parties set out for big treks and climbs just after arriving in Huaraz, with the predictable result of altitude sickness and having to turn back. Take the time to adjust in Huaraz, do a couple of acclimatization hikes, and *then* enjoy a trouble-free, multiday trek.

Below are some suggested questions to ask before choosing your guide; keep in mind that the answers will make a difference in the price.

» Can I meet our guide ahead of time? This is an opportunity to meet the person you'll spend a lot of time with for multiple days and nights, and if necessary, to confirm ahead of time that he/she speaks English.

» Will we use public or private transportation?

» Will there be a cook and an *arriero* (mule driver)?

» Will there be a separate cooking tent and a separate bathroom tent?

» How many meals and snacks will we get every day? Many trekkers complain about inadequate breakfasts and too few energizing noshes.

» It is standard to provide food and shelter for the guides, cooks and *arrieros,* which should be discussed beforehand. Remember that prepackaged dehydrated meals are not staples in the Cordillera Blanca. You will almost certainly be eating whole, local foods that weigh more and require more effort to carry.

» How many people will be on our trek? Larger numbers mean lower prices, but make sure you're comfortable trekking with a dozen strangers.

» Can I check the equipment before we set off? If you don't have your own sleeping bag, make sure that the one provided is long enough and warm enough (good to -15°C), and inspect the tents for holes and rain resistance.

HUARAZ & THE CORDILLERAS HUARAZ

MARTES GUERRA

You might want to invest in a water-proof suit or brave the high-altitude chill in your bathing suit if you are in Huaraz on Carnival's Fat Tuesday, a day of intense water fights throughout the city. Known as Martes Guerra (War Tuesday), thousands of kids run around the city with buckets searching for public sources of water and have huge water fights. Women, senior citizens and tourists are prime targets. Police are everywhere, even the military, but none of them can control these wild water bandits. Stay inside your hotel if you don't want to get drenched!

🎊 Festivals & Events

Carnival
RELIGIOUS

Carnival in Huaraz is very busy, with Peruvian tourists flooding to town, many of whom will get soaked on the city's take on **Mardi Gras (Fat Tuesday)**. On **Ash Wednesday** colorful funeral processions for *ño carnavalón* (king of carnival) converge on the Plaza de Armas. Here, his 'will' is read, giving the opportunity for many jabs at local politicians, police and other dignitaries, before the procession continues to the river where the coffin is thrown in. Participants dress in colorful costumes with papier-mâché heads, some of which are recognizable celebrities.

El Señor de la Soledad
RELIGIOUS

Huaraz pays homage to its patron (the Christ of Solitude) beginning May 3. This weeklong festival involves fireworks, music, dancing, elaborately costumed processions and lots of drinking.

Semana de Andinismo
MOUNTAINEERING

Held annually in June, it attracts mountaineers from several countries and competitions and exhibitions are held.

🛏 Sleeping

The prices given here are average high (dry) season rates. Hotel prices can double during holiday periods and rooms become very scarce. Perhaps because Huaraz is seen as a trekking, climbing and backpacking center, budget hotels predominate.

Especially during the high season, locals meet buses from Lima and offer inexpensive accommodations in their houses. Host also employ individuals to meet buses, b beware of scams or overpricing – don't p anybody until you've seen the room.

TOP CHOICE **Albergue Churup** BOUTIQUE HOSTE
(☏42-4200; www.churup.com; Figueroa 1257; S28, s/d incl breakfast S69/99; @🤖) This i mensely popular family-run hostel cont ues to win the top budget-choice accola Immaculate and comfortable rooms sha cushy, colorful lounging areas on eve floor. The building is topped by a massi fireplace-warmed lounge space with ma nificent 180-degree views of the Cord era. If that isn't enough, the affable Quir family, especially the heir to this touris throne, Juan, are consummate hosts and fer a cafe and bar, communal kitchen anc travel office that rents out trekking gear a arranges Spanish lessons. It's so popular new, equally homey annex, Churup II, h opened a block over on Arguedas. Reser tions essential.

TOP CHOICE **Lazy Dog Inn** LODGE
(☏94-378-9330; www.thelazydoginn.com; s/d wi out bathroom S135/210, d inside main house fr S280, cabins S310, all incl breakfast & dinner; @🖨 Run by rugged and proud Canadians Dia and Wayne, this deluxe ecolodge steep in sustainable and community tourism at the mouth of the Quebrada Llaca, 8k east of Huaraz. It's made entirely of ado and built by hand and you can stay in eith comfortable double rooms in the main lod or in fancier private cabins, which have fir places and bathtubs.

Lots of trekking opportunities are ava able here, including numerous day hik right from the lodge as well as day trips horseback. Long and short-term volunte opportunities are also available.

Hotel San Sebastián HOTEL
(☏42-6960; www.sansebastianhuaraz.com; Ita 1124; s/d incl breakfast S170/198; @🤖) A fetc ing white-walled and red-roofed urba sanctuary, this four-story hotel is a neocol nial architectural find. Balconies and arch overlook a grassy garden and inner cour yard with a soothing fountain, and all room have a writing desk, good beds, hot showe and cable TV. Most have balconies as we but if you don't get one, there are plenty communal terraces on various floors.

It's a soothing, tranquil spot to come back after a day on the trails.

eel Guest House
GUESTHOUSE $$

)42-9709; www.steelguest.com; Pasaje Maguina 57; s/d incl breakfast S110/145; @?) The per-ct midrange choice. The rooms at this arming guesthouse are wonderfully styled ith Andean textiles and are white-glove ean right down to the beautiful hardwood oors. The owner tends to dote on her ests, making it feel a little like staying at andma's house. Loads of facilities round t the offerings, including cable TV, out-or hammocks, billiards, steam room and gorgeous roof terrace strewn with potted ants and dead-shot views to Huascarán.

laza's Bed & Breakfast
GUESTHOUSE $$

)42-2529; www.olazas.com; Arguedas 1242; s/d/tr cl breakfast S80/100/140; @?) This smart lit-e hotel has a boutique feel, spacious bath-ooms and comfortable beds, but the best rt is the big lounge area upstairs and assive panoramic terrace. The owner is n established figure in the Huaraz trekking nd tourism scene; he can provide advice no atter where you want to go (so long as he's round). Bus station pickup is included.

otel Colomba
HOTEL $$

)42-1501; www.huarazhotel.com; Francisco de ela 210; s/d incl breakfast from S150/200; @?) he rooms at this wonderfully surpris-ng oasis are speckled around a dense and ompulsively trimmed hedge forest, some pilling out onto a long, relaxing veranda. he sprawling gardens conceal a kids' play-round, making it a great choice for families ooking for secure and enclosed grounds or their kids to safely run amok. It's a little orth of the action, which is another plus for amilies.

ndino Club Hotel
HOTEL $$$

)42-1662; www.hotelandino.com; Pedro Coch-achín 357; s/d from S280/338, d with balcony S433; @?) Because the structure itself feels a little oit too much like a chain hotel, you sacrifice on cozy charm at this 54-room, Swiss-run hotel, but the immaculate rooms all have great views and are packed with the requi-site mod cons. Balcony rooms are worth the splurge for the postcard views to Huascarán peak, wood-burning fireplaces and plant-lined terraces.

The on-site restaurant, Chalet Suisse, serves international and Peruvian food in addition to Swiss specialties.

Familia Meza Lodging
GUESTHOUSE $

(94-369-5908; Lúcar y Torre 538; r per person S20) In the same building as Café Andino (whose wi-fi you can use) and Mountain Bike Adventures, this charming family guesthouse has cheery rooms and is deco-rated throughout with homey, frilly touches. What's more, the owners are friendly and helpful enough to cure the worst bout of homesickness. Bathrooms and hot showers are shared and there's a top-floor communal area with a small kitchen.

If you can snag the top floor single, you'll be dazzled by the views.

Way Inn Lodge
LODGE, RETREAT $$

(99-220-790; www.thewayinn.com; camping S15, dm S35, d without bath with full board S290, bungalows with full board S360-420; @) In a stu-pendous mountainous location between the Cojup and Quilcayhuanca valleys 15km from Huaraz, the Way Inn Lodge's rooms range from bunks in one of their Flintstone-esque 'cave' rooms to deluxe, well-appointed bun-galows with fireplaces. It has evolved into a spiritual retreat center and now concentrates on 10-day *ayahuasca* (hallucinogenic drink) retreats (S1400 deposit plus donation).

It only accepts regular guests during five-day breaks between retreats. Both Chinese medicine and Ayurveda specialists are also on hand and it is working towards becom-ing self-sufficient with a permaculture food forest. As far as *ayahuasca* retreats go, file it under extremely serious and very comfortable.

Jo's Place
GUESTHOUSE $

(42-5505; josplacehuaraz@hotmail.com; Villazón 278; camping S10, dm S15, s/d S30/45, s/d with-out bathroom S25/35; @?) Bright splashes of color and a rambling grassy area mark this informal and slightly chaotic place run by a mumbling Englishman named Jo. Popular with trekkers and climbers (camping is al-lowed and there's plenty of room to dry out your gear), it has four floors linked by spin-dly staircases that lead to a warren of basic rooms, only some with bathrooms (but with hot water).

Jo provides UK newspapers and full Eng-lish breakfasts as well.

Cayesh Guesthouse
GUESTHOUSE $

(42-8821; www.cayesh.net; Morales 867; dm S20, s/d without bathroom S25/40, with bath-room S30/50; ?) The folks at Cayesh take backpackers' delights seriously, offering an extensive DVD library, free kitchen use and luggage storage. The rooms are simple but have comfortable beds from which you can gander at the views of magnificent peaks; fluent English is spoken.

Albergue Benkawasi   GUESTHOUSE $
(☎43-3150; www.huarazbenkawasi.com; Parque Guardia Civil 928; dm S15, s/d/tr S35/60/90; @🛜) With coke-bottle glass windows, plaid bed-spreads and brick walls, the Benkawasi has a kind of '70s mountain chalet feel to it. The owner and his English-speaking Peruvian-Lebanese wife are young and fun and you'll do no better dorm-wise than the S15 four-bed numbers here.

La Casa de Zarela   GUESTHOUSE $$
(☎42-1694; www.lacasadezarela.com; Arguedas 1263; s/d S70/90; 🛜) Zarela's helpfulness is legendary. The 16 rooms here have hot showers and kitchen facilities, as well as lots of neat little patio areas in which to relax with a book. The scenic black-and-white photos of the environs are worth perusing – they offer better views than the small terrace here, which doesn't really face any impressive peaks.

Hostal Schatzi   GUESTHOUSE $$
(☎42-3074; www.schatzihostal.com; Bolívar 419; s/d S75/90; 🛜) Plenty of leafage in the pleasant courtyard here manages to keep the concrete at bay. Charismatic little rooms surround this garden and inside have exposed wood-beam ceilings and great top-floor views (ask for No 6). This is a reliable bet with a bird-chirping soundtrack.

Monte Blanco Hotel   HOTEL $$
(☎42-6384; www.monteblancohotel.com; José de la Mar 620; s/d/tr S60/100/130; 🛜) The friendly Monte Blanco is located on busy Luzuriaga and offers Spartan digs that are clean and shiny with lots of natural light. Big cushioned couches await slumping in the hallways; this is a solid back-up choice.

Hospedaje Raymondi   GUESTHOUSE $
(☎42-1082; Raymondi 820; s/d S40/60, s/d without hot water S20/40; 🛜) If you have an early bus out of town, this is a good budget choice where the hands-on owner will greet you in an immense antique foyer reminiscent of an echoing train station. Inside you'll find dark, austere rooms painted in dizzying, bright patterns. All come with comfy beds and writing desks, and hot showers are provided in

the pricier rooms (the cheaper rooms are little dank – skip them). It has a great sm cafe for early breakfasts. Look for the pur facade with no sign other than 'Hospedaje

Aldo's Guest House   GUESTHOUS
(☎42-5355; Morales 650; s/d/tr S35/50/75; @ Budget travelers love little Aldo's, a chee homey place decorated with bright colo and located right in the center of town. rooms have cable TV and private bathroom with hot showers, and you can use the kitc en or order breakfast and lunches.

B&B My House   GUESTHOUS
(☎42 3375; www.micashuaraz.jimdo.com; Calle de Noviembre 773; s/d incl breakfast S60/80; A small, bright patio and six homey room welcome you to this hospitable B&B. Room have a writing desk and hot shower an there's a cheery communal yard. Englis and French (occasionally) are spoken.

Edward's Inn   GUESTHOUSE
(☎42-2692; www.edwardsinn.com; Bolognesi 12 dm/s/d S25/35/70; @🛜) Rooms in this pop lar place all have hot water, but are otherwis elementary. There is a nice grassy bit and th owner, Edward, speaks excellent English an is a knowledgeable rescue guide.

🍴 Eating

Restaurant hours are flexible in Huaraz with shorter opening times during low season slow spells and longer hours at bus times.

⟨TOP CHOICE⟩ Mi Chef Kristof   PERUVIAN, FUSION $
(Parque del Periodista, 2nd fl; mains S20-29 ⏱closed Sun; 🛜) Belgian chef Kristof is straightshooter who isn't prone to merely letting his Peruvian-European fusion cuisin do the talking. Why eat here? 'In general, it' better than the others,' he says with a grin He's right. Dishes like rich stewed beef ir black beer on a bed of Belgian fries excel, a does the chicken with ratatouille and all his fresh pasta. And Kristof isn't afraid to send out a pisco-laced maracuyá aperitif before plopping down at your table and talking your ear off. Start to finish, it's a culinary carpet ride on the back of a great chef with a larger-than-life personality.

⟨TOP CHOICE⟩ Café Andino   CAFE $
(www.cafeandino.com; Lúcar y Torre 530, 3rd fl; breakfast S8.50-20, mains S7-25; @🛜🖊) This

odern top-floor cafe has space and light in]ades, comfy lounges, art, photos, crackling :eplace, books and groovy tunes – it's the [!]timate South American traveler hangout ld meeting spot. You can get breakfast lytime (Belgian waffles, *huevos ranch-:os*), snacks you miss (nachos!) and the hole scene is the town's best for informa-)n about trekking in the area.

American owner Chris is the go-to java mkie in the Cordilleras and roasts his own :rganic beans here. He was the man respon-ble for first bringing excellent brew to)wn in 1997, after he showed up a year ear-er and had to resort to smashing organic eans brought from Alaska with a rock in le courtyard of Edwards Inn and straining . through a bandanna for his morning jolt. eriously.

:hili Heaven INDIAN, THAI $$

⁾Parque Ginebra; mains $18-35) Whether you end your appetite to India or Thailand, he fiery curries at this English-run hotspot /ill seize your taste buds upon arrival, mer-ilessly shake them up and then spit them •ack out the other side as if you've died and :one to chili heaven (hence the name). They lso bottle their own hot sauces here and •ring in loads of English beers you don't of-en see. Critical *comida peruana* antidote.

:aita PERUVIAN $

:Larrea y Laredo 633, 2nd fl; mains $4.50-15; ⁾10am-3pm) This atmospheric local's haunt s an excellent spot to try *chocho,* the alpine mswer to *ceviche,* with the fish replaced vith *lupine* (an Andean legume). It also loes *ceviche, leche de tigre* (*ceviche* juice) md *chicharrónes,* all served up in a great ipot where the walls are literally covered lead-to-toe in historical photos of beauty jueens, sports teams, school classes and)ther *Huaracino* Kodak moments. Top spot.

Rinconcito Mineiro PERUVIAN $

:Morales 757; menú S7-12; ^P) The is the spot to :uck into homey and cheap Peruvian daily *menús.* The daily blackboard of 10 or so op-:ions includes an excellent *lomo saltado* as well as grilled trout, *tacu-tacu* and the like. It's all served up in a welcoming and clean space tastefully decorated with Andean tex-tiles. It's very, very popular.

California Café BREAKFAST, CAFE $

(www.huaylas.com; Calle 28 de Julio 562; breakfast S10-22; ^P7:30am-6:30pm, to 2pm Sun; ^P) Man-aged by an American from California, this hip traveler magnet does breakfasts at any time, plus light lunches and salads – it's a funky, chilled space to while away many hours. You can spend the day listening to the sublime world music collection or read-ing one of the hundreds of books available for exchange.

La Brasa Roja PERUVIAN $

(Luzuriaga 915; mains S10-26) Hallelujah! Your eternal search for chicken salvation in Peru ends here. This upscale *pollería* (restaurant specializing in roast chicken) is the ultimate budget refueling stop. Not only is the chick-en perfect, but you get five sauces – count 'em, five! – instead of the usual three (black olive and mustard make a surprise appear-ance) as well as a live violinist. No lie.

El Horno PIZZERIA $

(www.elhornopizzeria.com; Parque Periodista; piz-zas S9.50-23.50, mains S12-26; ^Pclosed Sun) If you can cook it on a grill or in a wood-fired oven, El Horno can make it sing. The differ-ent varieties of meat skewers and excellent thin-crust pizzas are the best picks here. The place often fills up with trekking groups, so arrive early.

Pastelería Café
Turmanyé BREAKFAST, CAFE $

(Morales 828; www.arcoiristurmanye.com; sand-wiches S3.50-9, pastries S1.50-5; ^Pfrom 7am, closed Sun) It's slow as dial-up, but excellent *paella,* sandwiches and rich Spanish-style pastries and cakes are a hit at this little eat-ery. It also has the distinction of benefiting the local Arco Iris Foundation, which helps children and young mothers.

Terracota Fusión CHINESE $

(Sal y Rosas 721; mains S6.50-20) This family-run *chifa* seems simple at first but a closer look reveals a tastefully designed room with cutesy Asian-inspired lamps and a welcom-ing, spic-and-span atmosphere. The cuisine isn't too salty – a refreshing about-face – and the wealth of excellent dishes come sized for one (huge) or the whole family (ginormous).

Rossonero DESSERTS $

(Luzuriaga 645, 2nd fl; desserts S3.50-7.50; ^P) This modern den of decadence, billed as a 'sofa-cafe,' is really more of an upscale dessert diner. We're talking numerous variations of *tres leches* and cheesecakes, pecan pie and chocolate cake – you name it – and artisanal house-made ice creams like *manjar blanco* (milk caramel) with cinnamon and port.

Novaplaza
SELF-CATERING $

(cnr Bolivar & Morales; ⊘7am-11:30pm) A good supermarket to pick up goodies for trekking or self-catering.

Drinking

Huaraz is the best place in this part of the Andes to take a load off and get pleasantly inebriated.

TOP CHOICE Sierra Andina
BREWERY

(Centenario 1690; www.sierraandina.com; pint/pitcher S7/30; ⊘3-10pm) The S5 taxi ride to Cascapampa is a small price to pay for the wares afforded at this genuine microbrewery that brought suds salvation to Huaraz when it opened in 2011. Two American beer enthusiasts from Colorado set up shop brewing golden, pale and amber ales as well as a porter to the delight of beer hounds near and far.

The equipment is top notch, while the space is a bit makeshift in a Berlin sort of way (as long as there is alcohol, nobody will notice the second-hand furniture). Good times.

Los 13 Buhos
BAR

(Parque Ginebra; ⊘5pm-late) A supremely cool cafe-bar in newly upgraded Parque Ginebra digs. The owner, Lucho, was the first craft beer brewer in Huaraz and has been known to take out ranting English ads against mass produced Peruvian beers in the paper. He brews and bottles five tasty choices, including red and black ales laced with coca. His new location is chockfull of local art and Spencer Tunick nudes that have turned some Huaraz heads. It's the best bar in town for kicking back on comfy lounge sofas over cold homebrews and liquid-courage inspired conversation.

☆ Entertainment

El Tambo
BAR, CLUB

(José de la Mar 776; ⊘to 4am) If you're hankerin' to shake your groove-thang, this is the most popular disco in town, complete with dance floor trees and loads of nooks and crannies to hide yourself away in. Fashionable with both *extranjeros* (foreigners) and Peruvians, the music swings from techno-*cumbia* to Top 20, salsa and reggae and most things in between.

Shopping

Inexpensive thick woolen sweaters, scarve hats, socks, gloves, ponchos and blanke are available if you need to rug up for th mountains; many of these are sold at stal on the pedestrian alleys off Luzuriaga or the *feria artesanal* (artisans' market) o the Plaza de Armas. A few shops on Parqu Ginebra and several agencies that rer equipment and gear sell quality climbin gear and clothes.

Perú Magico
JEWELRY, HANDICRAF

(José Sucre btwn Farfán & Bolívar; ⊘9am-2pm 3-9pm Mon-Sat) Offers an assortment of jev elry, textiles and pottery from around th country and is the official shop for the mo popular T-shirts in the Andes, Inka Spir (formerly known as Andean Expressions).

Tejidos Turmanyé
CLOTHIN

(José Sucre 883; ⊘8am-5pm) Sells handsom locally made weavings and knit garments t support a foundation that provides occupa tional training to young mothers.

ℹ Information

Dangers & Annoyances

Time to acclimatize is important. The altitude here will make you feel breathless and may give you a headache during your first few days, so don't overexert yourself. The surrounding moun tains will cause altitude sickness if you venture into them without spending a few days acclimatizing in Huaraz first. See p552 for more advice on altitude sickness.

Huaraz is a safe city that experiences little crime; unfortunately, robberies of trekkers and tourists do happen, especially in the area of the Mirador de Retaqeñua and the Wilkahuaín (sometimes also spelled Wilcawain) ruins, and early in the morning when groggy backpackers arrive on overnight buses. In these cases, stay alert and walk with a group or hire a taxi to avoid problems

Emergency

Casa de Guías (☑42-1811; www.casadeguias. com.pe; Parque Ginebra 28G; ⊘9am-1pm & 4-8pm Mon-Sat) Offers safety and rescue courses and will save your life if you get into trouble in the mountains – but only if you're trekking or climbing with one of their guides certified by the Mountain Guide Association (AGM). Ask for a list of guides or see the website. Register here before heading out on a trek or climb.

Policía de Turismo (☑42-1351; Plaza de Armas; ⊘8am-8pm) On the west side of the

aza de Armas. Some officers speak limited
glish.

edical Services

inica San Pablo (www.sanpablo.com.pe;
uaylas 172; ⊙24hr) North of town, this is the
st medical care in Huaraz. Some doctors
eak English.

oney

l of these banks have ATMs and will exchange
S dollars and euros.

CP (Luzuriaga 691)

terbank (José Sucre 687)

cotiabank (José Sucre 760)

ost

erpost (☑42-1031; Luzuriaga 702) Postal
rvices.

ourist Information

he travel agencies mentioned on p367 and
opular meeting points for tourists in Huaraz
an be good sources of local and trekking infor-
ation. The new English newspaper **The Huaraz
elegraph** (www.huaraztelegraph.com) is also a
od source of information.

iPerú (☑42-8812; Plaza de Armas, Pasaje
Atusparia, Oficina 1; ⊙9am-6pm Mon-Sat, to
1pm Sun) Has general tourist information but
little in the way of trekking info.

Parque Nacional Huascarán Office (☑42-
2086; www.sernanp.gob.pe; Sal y Rosas
555;⊙8:30am-1pm & 2:30-6pm Mon-Fri, to
noon Sat) Staff have limited information about
visiting the park.

Getting There & Away

Air

LC Perú (☑42-4734; www.lcperu.pe; Luzuriaga
904) operates flights from Lima to Huaraz
everyday at 8:40am; the return journey leaves
at 10:10am. The Huaraz **airport** (ATA) is actually at Anta, 23km north of town. A taxi will cost
about S20.

Bus

Combis for Caraz, Carhuaz and Yungay leave
every few minutes during the day from a lot just
north of Calle 13 de Diciembre. These will drop
you in any of the towns along the way. Minibuses
south along the Callejón de Huaylas to Recuay,
Catac and other villages leave from the corner

HUARAZ & THE CORDILLERAS HUARAZ

HUARAZ BUSES

DESTINATION	COST (S)	DURATION (HR)
Caraz	6	1½
Carhuaz	3	¾
Casma	23	4-8
Catac	3.50	1
Chacas	25	5
Chavín	12	2½
Chimbote	20-60	5-9
Chiquián	10	4½
Huallanca	12	4
Huari	15	5
La Unión	15	4
Lima	35-100	8
Llamac	25	5
Llamellin	18	8
Monterrey	1	¼
Pomabamba	30	8-9
Recuay	3-10	½-1
San Luis	25	5
Trujillo	35-60	7
Yanama	25	4
Yungay	5	1

terminal at Calle 27 de Noviembre and Confraternidad Internacional Oeste.

A plethora of companies have departures for Lima, so shop around for the price/class/time you prefer. Most depart midmorning or late evening. Some buses begin in Caraz and stop in Huaraz to pick up passengers. During high season it is recommended that you book your seats at least a day in advance.

Two bus routes reach Chimbote on the north coast. The most hair-raising is the bumpy route that follows the Callejón de Huaylas and passes through the narrow, thrilling Cañón del Pato (see p391) before descending to the coast. The most common route crosses the 4225m-high Punta Callán and provides spectacular views of the Cordillera Blanca before plummeting down to Casma and pushing north.

Many small companies with brave, beat-up buses cross the Cordillera to the towns east of Huaraz.

Of the following long-haul companies, Oltursa, Cruz del Sur, Movil Tours and Línea are recommended.

Cial (☑42-9253; www.expresocial.com; Morales 650) Good, midpriced night bus to Lima at 10:30pm.

Cruz del Sur (☑42-8726; www.cruzdelsur.com.pe; Bolívar 491) Has 11am and 10pm luxury nonstop services to Lima.

Línea (☑42-6666; www.linea.pe; Bolívar 450) Has excellent buses at 9:15pm and 9:30pm to Chimbote and Trujillo.

Movil Tours (www.moviltours.com.pe) Ticket Office (Bolívar 452) Terminal (☑42-2555; Confraternidad Internacional Oeste 451) Buses to Lima at 9:30am, 1pm and 2:30pm and four night buses between 10pm and 11pm. Has 9:40pm, 10:20pm and 11:10pm buses to Chimbote via Casma, the first two of which continue on to Trujillo.

Oltursa (☑42-3717; www.oltursa.pe; Raymundi 825) The most comfortable Lima buses at 1:15pm and 10:30pm.

Sandoval Ticket Office (☑42-8069; Cáceres 338) Terminal (cnr Cáceres & Confraternidad) Has eight daily departures to Chavín going on to San Marcos and Huari. Also has buses to Llamellin at 7:30am, 1pm and 7:30pm.

Transportes Alas Peruanas (☑42-2396; Lucar y Torre 444) Buses to Chimbote via Casma at 4am, 8am, 1pm and 8:30pm.

Transportes El Rápido (☑42-2887; Calle 28 de Julio, cuadra 1) Buses leave at 5am and 2pm to Chiquián via Recuay; 6am, 1pm and 3pm to Huallanca; and 6am and 1pm to La Unión.

Transportes El Veloz (☑22-1225; Pasaja Villarán y Loli 143) Buses to Yanama and Pomabamba at 6:15am, 7:15am and 6:30pm as well as Chacas at 8am, 5pm and 11pm.

Transportes Renzo (☑94-360-8607; Raymundi 821) Has a rambling 6:45am and 7pm service to Pomabamba stopping at Piscobamba, Yanama, Colcabamba and Vaqueria Another service leaves at 8pm Monday to Saturday and 3:40pm Sunday for San Luis via Chacas.

Transportes Rodríguez (☑97-112-5201; cnr Calle 27 de Noviembre & Gridilla) Cheaper nigh bus to Lima at 10:30pm.

Turismo Nazario (☑78-6960; Tarapaca 1436) Has a 5am direct bus to Llamac.

Yungay Express (☑42-4377; Raymundi 930) There's a morning bus at 7:15am to Chimbote via Cañón del Pato; and 9am, 2pm and 10pm departures via Casma.

Getting Around

A taxi ride around Huaraz costs about S3. Look for taxis at the bridge on Fitzcarrald or along Luzuriaga.

THE CORDILLERAS

Huaraz lies sandwiched in a valley carvec out by the Río Santa, flanked to the west b the brown Cordillera Negra and to the eas by the frosted Cordillera Blanca. A pavec road runs along the valley, more commonl known as the Callejón de Huaylas, and link a string of settlements while furnishing visi tors with perfect views of lofty elevations.

The Cordillera Negra, though an attrac tive range in its own right, is snowless anc often eclipsed by the stunning, snow-cov ered crown of the Cordillera Blanca.

The Cordillera Blanca, about 20km wide and 180km long, is an elaborate collectior of toothed summits, razor-sharp ridges turquoise-colored lakes and green valley: draped with crawling glaciers. More than 5C peaks of 5700m or higher grace this fairl small area. North America, in contrast, has only three mountains in excess of 5700m and Europe has none. Huascarán, at 6768m is Peru's highest mountain and the high est pinnacle in the tropics anywhere in the world.

South of the Cordillera Blanca is the smaller, more remote, but no less spec tacular Cordillera Huayhuash. It contains Peru's second-highest mountain, the 6634m Yerupajá, and is a more rugged and less fre quently visited range.

Where once pre-Columbian and Inca cul tures used the high valleys as passageways to eastern settlements, backpackers and ountaineers now explore and marvel at ne spectacle of Mother Nature blowing her wn trumpet.

The main trekking areas of the Cordillras include sections of the Cordillera Blani, which is mostly encompassed by Parque acional Huascarán, and the Cordillera uayhuash, to the south of Huaraz. There's mething here for scramblers of all skills nd fitness levels: from short, easy hikes of day or two, to multiweek adventures reuiring technical mountain-climbing skills. oreigners flock here yearly and favorite ikes like the Santa Cruz trek can see a lot f hiking-boot traffic in the high season. Vhile the more remote 10-day Cordillera iuayhuash Circuit doesn't see half as many isitors as the Santa Cruz trek, savvy travelrs are rapidly discovering its rugged beauty nd appreciating the friendly highland culure. Dozens of shorter routes crisscross the ordillera Blanca and can provide an appezing taste of the province's vistas, or can e combined with longer treks to keep you valking in the hills for months on end.

See the boxed text on p369 for advice and nformation about responsible trekking in eru.

Trekking & Mountaineering

When to Go

People hike year-round, but the dry season of mid-May to mid-September is the most popular time to visit, with good weather and the clearest views. It's still advisable to check out the latest weather forecasts, however, as random heavy snowfalls, winds and electrical storms are not uncommon during this period. December to April is the wettest time, when it is often overcast and wet in the afternoons and trails become boggy. With the appropriate gear and some preparation, hiking is still possible and some trekkers find this season more rewarding, as many of the most popular trails are empty. For serious mountaineering, climbers pretty much stick to the dry season.

The management body for Parque Nacional Huascarán, Sernamp (Servicio Nacional de Áreas Naturales Protegidas por el Estado; the government agency administering national parks, reserves, historical sanctuaries and other protected areas under the Ministry of Environment), technically requires the use of local licensed guides for all activity in Parque Nacional Huascarán, including day hikes, trekking and climbing.

Trail Guidebooks & Maps

Lonely Planet's *Trekking in the Central Andes* covers the best hikes in the Cordillera Blanca and the Cordillera Huayhuash. A great resource for the Huayhuash region is the detailed *Climbs and Treks of the Cordillera Huayhuash of Peru* (2005) by Jeremy Frimer, though it's sold out and only available for consultation in Huaraz. The

PICK YOUR PEAK

With 18 glaciated summits over 6000m and more than 50 over 5700m, the Cordillera Blanca is one of the most important ranges in the world for high-altitude climbers. Add to that the sheer multitude of options, generally short approaches and almost no red tape or summit fees (although you have to pay your park fee) and the appeal is obvious. While Huascarán Sur is the undisputed granddaddy and Alpamayo voted 'most beautiful' by climbers and photographers the world over, Pisco is certainly the most popular climb for its straightforward accessibility and moderate technical requirements.

But that may change. Global warming in the Cordillera Blanca has caused glaciers to retreat and undergo significant transformations, and well-plied routes have altered dramatically in recent years.

Here are 10 popular climbs (and major summits) of the Cordillera Blanca, offering everything from relatively easy routes to hard-core ice climbing.

» Huascarán Sur (6768m)

» Chopicalqui (6345m)

» Copa Sur (6188m)

» Quitaraju (6036m)

» Tocllaraju (6034m)

» Alpamayo (5947m)

» Pisco (5752m)

» Ishinca (5550m)

» Urus (5497m)

» Maparaju (5326m)

best overview of climbing in the Cordillera Blanca is Brad Johnson's *Classic Climbs of the Cordillera Blanca Peru* (2003), which got the reprint treatment in 2009.

Felipe Díaz's 1:300,000 *Cordilleras Blanca & Huayhuash* is a popular and excellent map for an overview of the land, with towns, major trails and town plans, though it's not detailed enough for remote treks. He has recently given the same treatment to the Cuzco region. The Alpenvereinskarte (German Alpine Club) produces the most detailed and accurate maps of the region; look for the regularly updated 1:100,000 *Cordillera Blanca Nord* (sheet 0/3a) and *Cordillera Blanca Sur* (sheet 0/3b) maps. For the Cordillera Huayhuash, search for the Alpine Mapping Guild's 1:50,000 *Cordillera Huayhuash* topographic map (though it's sold-out and won't be reprinted). These maps are available in Caraz, Huaraz and at South American Explorers' clubhouses. Also look for Cordillera Blanca and Cordillera Huayhuash topo maps distributed by Skyline Adventures (p369), available at Café Andino (p372) and other fine establishments.

IGN produces six 1:100,000 scale maps covering the Cordilleras, although they're somewhat dated and often use atypical place names.

Tours & Guides

The Casa de Guías and agencies in Huaraz (p367), and Pony Expeditions in Caraz (p392), are good places to start your search for qualified mountain guides, *arrieros* (mule drivers) and cooks. If you wish to put together a support team for your own expedition, trekking agencies can also arrange individual guides, cooks or pack animals.

If your Spanish is up to it and you're not in a great hurry, you can hire *arrieros* (mule drivers) and mules in trailhead villages, particularly Cashapampa, Colcabamba and Vaqueria, among others. Horses, donkeys and mules are used as pack animals, and while llamas are occasionally provided, they cannot carry as much weight. Try to get a reference for a good *arriero* and establish your trekking goals (ie pace, routes) before you depart. Check the state of the pack animals before you hire them – some *arrieros* overwork their beasts of burden or use sick or injured animals.

The Dirección de Turismo and the guides' union generally set prices. Expect to pay around S30 per day for a horse, S20 for a donkey or mule and S40 per day for an *arri-*

ARTESONRAJU'S 15 MINUTES OF FAME

If you think the dramatic peak of Artesonraju (5999m) looks familiar, that's because the mountaintop spent a chunk of the '80s and '90s as the peak featured in Paramount Pictures' live-action logo. The famous view is of its northeast face as seen from Quebrada Arhuaycocha (also known as Mirador Alpamayo).

ero. Official rates for guides are S90 to S1? per day for a trekking guide, S150 to S30 for a climbing guide and S300 to S360 for technical climbing guide.

Qualified guides and *arrieros* are issue with photo identification by the tourism authority – ask for credentials. Even exp rienced mountaineers would do well to ad a local guide, who knows exactly what ha been happening in the mountains, to the group. Prices do not include food and yo may have to provide your *arriero* with tent and pay for their return journey. It customary that you provide food and shelte for any hired staff – confirm what's include before you set off.

Equipment & Rentals

If you lack the experience or equipmer required to mountain it, fear not, as doz ens of 'savoir faire' businesses offer guide gear rental and organize entire adventure for you, right down to the *burros* (donkeys) If you go on a tour, trekking agencies (se p367) will supply everything from tents t ice axes. Some of them also rent out gea independently. Two reliable rental agencie for top-end climbing gear are MountClimb ([☎]42-4322; www.mountclimb.com.pe; Uribe 732 Huaraz) and Monttrek ([☎]42-1124; www.mon trek.com.pe; Luzuriaga 646, 2nd fl, Huaraz).

It often freezes at night, so make sure you have an adequately warm sleeping bag wet-weather gear (needed year-round), an a brimmed hat and sunglasses. Strong sun block and good insect repellent are also a must and can be found easily in Huaraz i you've forgotten them at home.

ℹ Information

To get the lowdown on trekking and the latest conditions, your first port of call should be Casa de Guías (p367), which has information on eather, trail conditions, guides and mule hire. ome IGN and Alpenvereinskarte topographic aps are sold here.

Trekking and equipment-rental agencies are so good sources of local knowledge and can dvise on day hikes. For more impartial advice, e sure to visit popular Huaraz haunts such as afé Andino (p372) and California Café (p373), hose foreign owners keep abreast of local evelopments, sell hiking maps and guides, and eely dole out advice alongside tasty treats.

Cordillera Blanca

ne of the most breathtaking parts of the ontinent, the Cordillera Blanca is the orld's highest tropical mountain range and ncompasses some of South America's high-st mountains. Andean leviathans include he majestic Nevado Alpamayo (5947m), nce termed 'the most beautiful mountain in he world' by the German Alpine Club. Oth-rs include Nevado Huascarán (at 6768m, eru's highest), Pucajirca Oeste (6046m), Jevado Quitaraju (6036m) and Nevado San-a Cruz (Nevado Pucaraju; 6241m).

Situated in the tropical zone, the Cor-illera Blanca stands to be affected greatly s global warming increases; there exists ignificant evidence that the glaciers of the Cordillera Blanca show a measurable de-rease in their volume and that the snow ine has receded in recent decades. Other hreats to the park include litter and high-ltitude grazing on endangered qeñua Polylepis) trees. For more information bout these threats, contact the Mountain Institute in Huaraz.

PARQUE NACIONAL HUASCARÁN

Peruvian mountaineer César Morales Arnao first suggested protecting the flora, fauna and archaeological sites of the Cordillera Blanca in the early 1960s, but it didn't be-come a reality until 1975, when the national park was established. This 3400-sq-km park encompasses practically the entire area of the Cordillera Blanca above 4000m, includ-ing more than 600 glaciers and nearly 300 lakes, and protects such extraordinary and endangered species as the giant *Puya rai-mondii* plant, the spectacled bear and the Andean condor.

Visitors to the park should register (bring your passport) and pay the park fee at the park office in Huaraz. This is S5 per person for a day visit or S65 for a week-long pass (a 21-day pass for the same price was being mulled over at time of research). You can also register and pay your fee at one of the control stations. PNH officials will not sell park permits to trekkers or climbers who are not utilizing the services of a local registered agency or a local licensed guide.

Money from fees is used to help maintain trails, pay park rangers and offset the effects of the legions of visitors to the area. It makes sense that as foreign visitors are among those frequenting the area and causing the greatest change, they should contribute to the financing of the national park with their user fees.

Santa Cruz Trek

This trek ascends the spectacular Quebrada Santa Cruz Valley and crosses the Punta Un-ion Pass (4760m) before tumbling into Que-brada Huarípampa on the other side. Head-turning sights along the way include emer-ald lakes, sensational views of many of the Cordillera's peaks, beds of brightly colored alpine wildflowers and stands of red *qeñua* trees. Another less thrilling sight here, as in many trekking areas, is the constant sight of cow patties dimpling the valleys and mead-ows. Watch your step!

The Santa Cruz is one of the most popular routes in Peru for international trekkers and it is clearly signposted for much of its length. Each day requires about 13km of hiking (be-tween five and eight hours of hiking) and as-cents ranging from 500m to 700m; the third day requires a knee-busting 900m descent.

The first and second days are the tough-est, but probably the most rewarding, as they take you past many small waterfalls and a series of lakes and interconnect-ing marshy areas. The first, smaller lake is Laguna Ichiccocha (also referred to as La-guna Chica), closely followed by the much larger Laguna Jatuncocha (or Laguna Grande). Between here and the camp at Taullipampa (4250m), a 2012 avalanche on the northeast flank of Nevado Artisonraju blew out the ice-and-mud dam holding the small Laguna Arteson Bajo together south

HUARAZ & THE CORDILLERAS CORDILLERA BLANCA

FAST FACTS: SANTA CRUZ

Duration: Four days

Distance: 50km

Difficulty: Easy-moderate

Start: Cashapampa (2900m)

Finish: Vaqueria (3700m)

of the trail, and the lake contents emptied into the valley and washed away a significant portion of the trail. First-time trekkers on this route won't notice a difference, but seasoned Santa Cruzers will note the trail has been altered here and was undergoing repair at time of research. Taullipampa sits in a gorgeous meadow at the foot of the majestic **Nevado Taulliraju** (5830m). The glacial icefall on the flanks of Taulliraju is very active and large chunks regularly break off, especially in the afternoon sun. To the south, Nevado Artesonraju (6025m) and Nevado Parón (5600m) dominate the skyline.

On the third day, trekkers gain major bragging rights as they push over the **Punta Un ión Pass** (4760m), which appears from belo at an angular notch in a seemingly unbroke rocky wall above. The panoramas from bot sides of the pass are captivating. To the we lies **Quebrada Santa Cruz** and its lake while to the southeast, **Quebrada Huarípan pa** plunges steeply down past a scattering lakes. The descent after the notch at the pas spirals tightly down a rocky buttress towar Lagunas Morococha, past thick *qeñua* stand and on to a camp at Paria (3850m).

Day four is rewarded by a quick descer in the hamlet of **Huarípampa** and its tra

Santa Cruz Trek

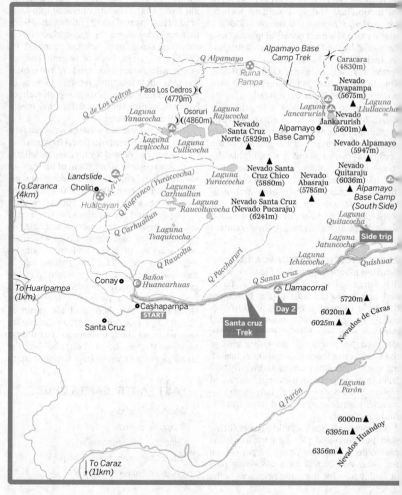

tional thatched-roof Quechua houses. guinea pigs (destined for the dinner table) can often be seen running around in shallow wooden platforms underneath the roofs. and in Vaqueria (3700m), from where you can flag down a *colectivo, camión* (truck) or minibus to Yungay and onto Huaraz.

The completion of a major local transit route to the Lagunas Llanganuco and beyond means that the trek is now shorter and can be completed in three days by acclimatized parties; however, four days allows more scope for viewing alpine flora and exploring side valleys. The 14km side-trip to **Laguna Quitacocha** (day two) and a

spectacular **valley** below Nevado Quitaraju (6036m) takes five to six hours and ascends/descends 800m. The 12km steep hike (seven to eight hours, 700m ascent/descent) to **Alpamayo Base Camp** (South Side), also possible on day two, takes you to the climbers' camp underneath the magnificent **Nevado Alpamayo** (5947m). A 10km side trip at the **Quebrada Paria** (Quebrada Vaqueria) on day three climbs steadily for three hours and 600m in the shadow of **Nevado Chacraraju** (6108m), below its very active glacier and icefall. And an 11km, four- to five-hour side trek to **Quebrada Ranincuray** (day four) that ascends/descends 800m rewards hikers

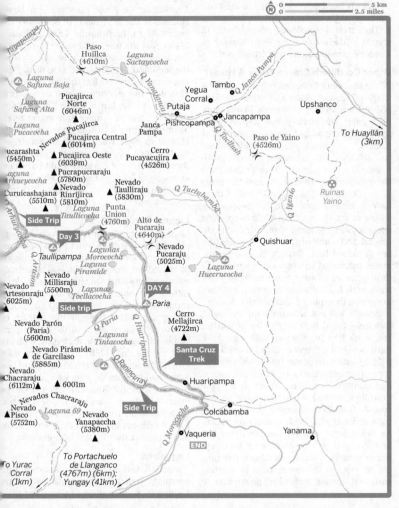

with awesome views, great camping and access to the Lagunas Tintacocha.

The trek can also be extended beyond Vaqueria, following the road out and picking up the walking trail over the Portachuelo de Llanganuco Pass to Quebrada Llanganuco and its jade-green lakes.

Water for cooking and drinking is available from rivers along the way (except on day three, when you'll need to carry water on the approach to the Punta Unión Pass), but be sure to treat or boil it before drinking. You must carry a copy of your passport with you and present it at a checkpoint in Huarípampa.

Colectivo (shared transportation) taxis frequently head out from Caraz to the main trailhead at Cashapampa (S8, 1½ hours).

The trek is just as often done in reverse – daily *colectivos* from Huaraz to Vaqueria provide access to the trailhead.

Other Cordillera Blanca Treks & Hikes

While the Santa Cruz trek attracts the lion's share of visitors, dozens of other trekking possibilities in the Cordillera Blanca supply scenery and vistas just as jaw dropping (minus the crowds). A series of *quebradas* (valleys) – Ishinca, Cojup, Quilcayhuanca, Shallap and Rajucolta (listed north to south) – run parallel to each other from the area around Huaraz up into the heart of the Cordillera Blanca, and most of them have a high-altitude lake (or two) somewhere along the way. Each offers trekking opportunities ranging from one day to several and some of the many possibilities are described here, though there are many more. Interested trekkers can inquire with local agencies about connecting these valley treks with high-altitude traverses, but they are generally explored individually.

Some – but not all – trails on the multiday treks listed here aren't clearly marked yet, so it's best to either go with a guide or have excellent reference maps on hand (see p377). Getting to some trailheads requires travel to nearby towns or along the rugged and beautiful Conchucos Valley (east of the Cordillera Blanca), where a handful of ludicrously friendly indigenous towns provide basic facilities and vivid cultural experiences for the intrepid explorer (see p365). For less ambitious hikers who aren't keen on camping or refuges, consider making a day hike out of some of the longer trips by starting early and turning back with enough time to

transfer back to your hotel. You'll need pay the park entrance (S5) to do these hike

Huaraz–Wilkahuaín–Laguna Ahuac

You can start this relatively easy and we marked day hike (one day) to Laguna Ahu (4560m) in Huaraz or at the Wilkahuaín R ins (p364). From the latter (a S20 taxi rid it takes about four hours and makes an e cellent early acclimatization trip or pleasa day trip; starting in Huaraz adds about tw hours. On the ground you'll notice furry ra bit-like *vizcachas* sniffing around. Looki up, you can't miss the big mountain vie of the southern end of the Cordillera Blanc

Laguna Churup

The hamlet of Pitec (3850m), just abo Huaraz, is the best place to start this si hour hike to the beautiful Laguna Churu (4450m) at the base of Nevado Churup. Yo can select from approaching along eith the left-hand or right-hand side of the va ley; most folks opt for the left approac This day hike is often chosen as an acc matization hike, but note the altitudes ar the 600m ascent – make sure you're read before charging into this one. A taxi fro Huaraz to Pitec will cost about S60; *com bis* for Llupa (S3, 30 minutes) leave Huara from the corner of Raymondi and Luzuriag about every 30 minutes (ask to be droppe off at the path to Pitec); from there it's a tw hour walk to Pitec.

Laguna Parón

Laguna Parón (4200m) was probably mo picturesque before its water levels were low ered from 75m to 15m to prevent a collaps of Huandoy's moraine; still, it is a fantast cally beautiful site with views of Pirámide d Garcilaso (5885m), Huandoy (6395m), Cha raraju (6112m) and several 1000m granit rock walls. Hikers typically hire a truck o taxi to take them 25km to the Electroper station at Laguna Parón and ask the taxi t wait for the day (S180). The walk ramble around the lake on flat terrain for about tw hours and then up the valley for about 4km to a campsite at 4200m. This day hike can b extended into an overnight trip if you wan to step onto the Parón glacier (4900m) at th foot of Artesonraju. See p390 for more infor mation about starting this hike in Caraz.

Laguna 69

Though it is best enjoyed as a beautifu overnight trek past marvelous backdrops Laguna 69 is often done as a long day hike

...e lake is the jewel of the Cordilleras and ...perfect acclimatization walk. The campsite ...the way to the laguna is a true highlight, ...here you can wake up to a crystal morn-...g vision of Chopicalqui (6345m), Huas-...rán Sur (6768m) and Norte (6655m). In ...e morning you scramble up to Laguna ..., which sits right at the base of Chacra-...ju (6112m), and then hike down past the ...mous Lagunas Llanganuco. That's a lot ...' impressive lakes crammed into just two ...ys. The trails to Laguna 69 commence ...ar the Yurac Corral (3800m), on the north-...n tip of a big bend in the Llanganuco road.

...uilcayhuanca Valley

...his three- to four-day hike, also from Pitec, ...only moderately difficult, although you'll ...eed to be well acclimatized to tackle it. It ...inds up the Quilcayhuanca Valley through ...*eñua* trees and grassy meadows until ...eaching the Laguna Cuchillacocha and ...ullpacocha. Along the way, you pass breath-...king views of Nevado Cayesh (5721m), ...laparaju (5326m), Tumarinaraju (5668m) ...nd a half-dozen other peaks over 5700m. ...ecause this trek is not well marked, it's best ...o go with a guide (or have top navigations ...kills and a topo map).

...nca Trail

...his three- to six-day hike along an Inca ...rail, between Huari and the city of Huá-...uco, is just starting to be developed. Hik-...rs cross well-preserved parts of the old Inca ...rail and end up in Huánuco Viejo, which ...vas one of the most important military sites ...f the Incas in northern Peru. This route ...s being organized in conjunction with the ...nka Naani project. It aims to encourage ...ourism that respects the cultural heritage ...f the region and ties together several inde-...endent grassroots tourism initiatives. All ...guides are local (and English-speaking if ...equested) and porters and adobe shelters ...alled *tambos* (the Quechua word for rest-...ng place) are available if you want to sleep ...ut of the elements. Contact the Mountain ...nstitute or Respons Sustainable Tourism ...enter (p365) in Huaraz.

...allejón de Conchucos Treks

...f you're short on time but still want to cross ...he Cordillera and get up close to some icy ...eaks, the relatively easy two- to three-day ...Olleros to Chavín de Huántar trek comes ...o the rescue. You can start the 40km trek ...n either town, though most people start

HUAYHUASH HOGWASH

Some travelers have complained that the community gatekeepers on the Cordillera Huayhuash Circuit some-times purposely write down the wrong date on your receipt in order to fine you later in a random check at the campsite, so keep a keen eye on your transactions and don't head out until all is squared away.

in Olleros (population 1390) in the Calle-jón de Huáylas on the western side of the Cordillera Blanca, where you can arrange llamas as pack animals. Pretty villages and pre-Inca roads with great views of the Uru-ashraju (5722m), Rurec (5700m) and Cashan (5716m) mountains dot the landscape head-ing up to the 4700m Punta Yanashallash Pass. Where you end on the Callejón de Con-chucos side is absolutely gorgeous. Best of all, in Chavín you can soak your weary bones in hot springs and get up early the next day to visit the ruins without the usual throng of tourists. Dedicated riders have mountain-biked this route. To get to Olleros, catch a south-heading *combi* from Huaraz, get off at the Bedoya bridge and hike the 30 minutes up to Olleros. Taxis there cost around S30.

If this trek whets your appetite for am-bling, you can continue on to Huari by bus (see p400) or by walking along the road, and commence the equally impressive **Huari to Chacas trek**, making your way along the eastern flanks of the Cordillera Blanca. Be sure to camp near the Laguna Purhuay – this picturesque spot deserves an overnight visit. The easy two- to three-day route passes several other lakes, reaches its zenith at a 4550m pass and finishes up in the misty high-altitude tropical forests of the Parhua Valley (3500m).

After a rest in the fetching town of Chacas, you can continue on to do the one-to two-day **Chacas to Yanama trek**. This is the shortest of the three hikes and has the lowest pass of the lot, at a 'mere' 4050m. From Chacas you hike through the munici-palities of Sapcha and Potaca and can either finish the trek at Yanama or continue to the Keshu Valley, which has several good places to camp. Colcabamba, a few hours further on from Yanama, is the end of the Santa

Cruz trek and endurance hikers can tag this trek onto the end of their Herculean circuit before returning to Huaraz.

Honda–Ulta

This loop starting at Vicos and ending at the village of Shilla, near Carhuaz, is a moderate trek, with the exception of a couple of difficult high-altitude passes at Laguna Yanayacu (4850m) and Portachuelo Honda (4750m). Along the way, parties can stop at the tiny community of Juitush and the impossibly precious village of Chacas (p401) and linger on views of Yanaragra (5987m), Pucaranra (6156m), Palcaraju (6274m) and two remote lakes. This is a great hike if you want to experience an off-the-beaten-track route and enjoy a few charismatic indigenous villages along the way.

Los Cedros–Alpamayo

This is one of the more dazzling and demanding treks of the Cordillera. The 90km route involves very long ascents to high passes, incredible alpine scenery (including the regal north side of Nevado Alpamayo) and traditional Quechua communities with no road access. Starting in Cashapampa (same as the Santa Cruz trek) or Hualcayan and ending in Pomabamba, it is only recommended for experienced and acclimatized hikers who are familiar with navigation. The route is relatively straightforward, but not signposted. You can treat yourself to well-earned dips in hot mineral spring baths at both ends of this trek.

Cordillera Huayhuash

Often playing second fiddle to Cordillera Blanca, its limelight-stealing cousin, the Huayhuash hosts an equally impressive medley of glaciers, summits and lakes – all packed into a hardy area only 30km across. Increasing numbers of travelers are discovering this rugged and remote territory, where trails skirt around the outer edges of this stirring, peaked range. Several strenuous high-altitude passes of over 4500m throw down a gauntlet to the hardiest of trekkers. The feeling of utter wilderness, particularly along the unspoiled eastern edge, is the big draw and you are more likely to spot the graceful Andean condor here than dozens of *burro*-toting trekking groups.

In the waning moments of 2001, Peru's Ministry of Agriculture declared the Cordillera Huayhuash a 'reserved zone,' giving a transitory measure of protection to near 700 sq km of almost-pristine land. Sin then, the ministry has backed away fro official support as a unique, private- ar community-managed conservation effo has taken root. Several communities who traditional territory lies at the heart of th Huayhuash range are formally recognized 'Private Conservation Areas.' Eight distric along the circuit, Llamac (p395), Pocp Jirishanca, Quishuarcancha, Tupac An aru, Guñog, Huallapa and Pacllón, no charge user fees of S15 to S40, with cos for the entire circuit at S165 at time of wri ing and continuing to rise on a yearly basi Part of the fees goes to improved security fc hikers and part goes to continued conserva tion work. Support this grassroots preserva tion attempt by paying your fees, carryin enough small change and by always askin for an official receipt. Fees are sometime lowered for trekkers without pack animal as part of the calculations are based o 'grazing fees.'

FAST FACTS: CORDILLERA HUAYHUASH

Duration: 10 days

Distance: 115km

Difficulty: Demanding

Start/finish: Llamac

Nearest towns: Chiquián, Llamac and Cajatambo

Cordillera Huayhuash Circuit

Circling a tight cluster of high peaks, includ ing Yerupajá (6617m), the world's second highest tropical mountain, this stunnin, trek crosses multiple high-altitude passe with spine-tingling views. The dramati lakes along the eastern flanks provide grea campsites (and are good for trout fishing and give hikers a wide choice of routes t make this trek as difficult as they want.

Daily ascents range from 500m to 1200m but a couple of days in the middle and a the end of the trek involve major descents which can be just as tough as going uphill The average day involves about 12km on the trail, or anywhere from four to eight hours o hiking, although you may experience at leas one 10- to 12-hour day. Most trekkers take extra rest days along the way, partly because

e length and altitude make the entire cir-
uit very demanding and partly to allow for
e sensational sights to sink in. Others pre-
r a shorter version and can hike for as few
five days along the remote eastern side of
e Huayhuash. Described here is the classic

Huayhuash Circuit trek, but many side trips
and alternate routes along the way can add
a day or two to your trekking time.

The trek starts in Llamac (p395), the last
town for several days as the trail leaves 'civilization,' passing a small pre-Inca platform

Cordillera Huayhuash Circuit

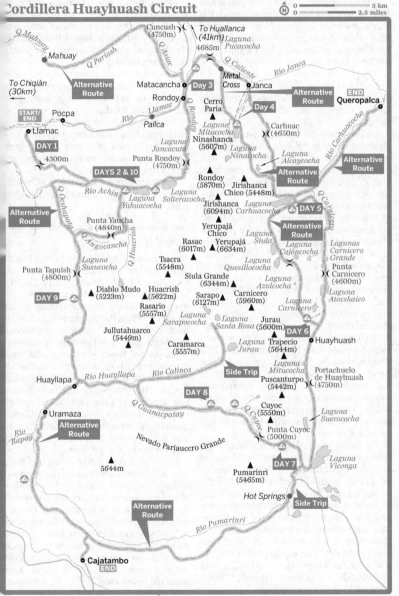

with excellent mountainscapes and 4m-high *cholla* cacti. The Pampa Llamac Pass bursts out on a fabulous view of glaciated peaks: Rondoy (5870m), the double-fanged Jirishanca (6094m), Yerupajá Chico, Yerupajá (6634m) and others – not bad for the first day!

The second and third days take you across three passes over 4500m until you reach the tiny community of Janca (4200m), getting nice views of Laguna Mitacocha (4230m). On day four, southeast of the Carhuac Pass (4650m), you'll see more excellent mountain panoramas and eventually reach a cliff that overlooks Laguna Carhuacocha (4138m) and the glaciated mountains behind Siula Grande (6344m) and Yerupajá looming in the distance.

Midway through the trek, parties hit a short section of paved Inca trail, about 1.5m wide and 50m long, the remnants of an Inca road heading south from the archaeological site of Huánuco Viejo near La Unión. Over the next couple of days work your way toward Laguna Carnicero (4430m), Laguna Mitucocha, the top of Portachuelo de Huayhuash (4750m), and Laguna Viconga (4407m). After several glaciated mountain crowns come into view, including the double-peaked Cuyoc (5550m), you can either camp and continue the main circuit, or you can head southwest along the Río Pumarinri Valley toward Cajatambo, leaving the circuit early. If you keep going, get ready for the challenging 5000m-plus Punta Cuyoc Pass.

On day seven the trail crests a small ridge on Pumarinri (5465m), giving trekkers face-on views of Cuyoc. Look out for the hardy *Stangea henricii,* a grayish-green, flat, rosette-shaped plant of overlapping tongue-like leaves that only grows above 4700m. The highest point on the trek is soon reached, marked by a rather inglorious single pile of stones.

On the eighth day you can continue the direct circuit by hiking past the village of Huayllapa; exit the circuit through Huayllapa and the town of Uramaza to Cajatambo; or make a side trip up the Río Calinca Valley to Lagunas Jurau, Santa Rosa and Sarapococha, where there are some of the best mountain panoramas of the entire trek. The traditional circuit will take you past the glacier-clad pyramid of Jullutahuarco (5449m) and a stupendous 100m-high waterfall. Push on to a small lake near Punta Tapuish (4800m) for good high-altitude camping.

The following day the trail drops gently Laguna Susucocha (4750m) shortly befo a junction (4400m) with Quebrada Ang cancha. The trail skirts boggy meadows ar climbs into rock and scree before reachii Punta Yaucha (4840m), offering wonderf views of the range's major peaks, includii Yerupajá, to the east and many of the n nor glaciated high points to the southea: Go fossil hunting for imprints of ammonit and other creatures that once dwelled und the sea – and imagine the Andes relegated the ocean's bottom.

The last day is short, with an early arriv in Llamac, from where transport to Chi uián and on to Huaraz can be arranged i the middle of the day.

Trekkers should be prepared for aggre sively territorial dogs along the way; ben ing down to pick up a rock usually keep them off – though refrain from throwing unless you absolutely must.

For information on getting to Chiquiá or Llamac for the trailhead, see p394 an p395.

Cordillera Negra

The poor little Cordillera Negra lives literall in the shadows of its big brother range, th Cordillera Blanca, whose towering glaciate peaks to the east block the morning sun an loom dramatically over everything aroun them. The 'Black Range,' which gets its nam from its obvious contrast to the more beauti ful 'White Range,' will probably always loo a bit dressed down – with its arid, muc brown, merely hilly silhouette – against th Cordillera Blanca's stunning icy and cragg profile. Still, the Negra has an importan role to play in the area's ecology as it block warm Pacific winds from hitting the Blanca glaciers and contributing to their thaw. It' also an important agricultural and minin area for the local population.

Although second fiddle to the big-moun tain recreational offerings on the other side of the Callejón de Huaylas, the Cordiller: Negra has some great attractions, especiall for rock climbers, who will find excellen bolted climbs in Recuay and Hatun Mach ay (p394). Mountain-bikers have access to seemingly unlimited kilometers of roads and trails over the rugged landscape; bike-guiding companies (p365) in Huaraz know these old byways well.

Day hikers can also explore these routes. ‸re a truck to take you to Punta Callan 225m) above Huaraz or to Curcuy (4520m) ▸ove Recuay and walk down to town. An‐ her suggested hike is a three-hour ascent the ruins of Quitabamba near Jangas. ‸ke a *colectivo* towards Carhuaz, getting ‸f at La Cruz de la Mina and look for signs the ruins.

The villages over here don't see a lot of ‸urists, and you'll be interacting with in‐ ‸genous people who in many cases live an ‸ntouched, traditional lifestyle.

‸ORTH OF HUARAZ

‸s the Río Santa slices its way north through ‸e Callejón de Huaylas, a road shadows its ‸very curve past several subdued towns to ‸araz and on to the menacingly impressive ‸añón del Pato. The Andean panorama of ‸e Cordillera Blanca looms over the length ‸f the valley like a wall of white-topped sen‐ ‸ies, with the granddaddy of them all, Huas‐ ‸arán, barely 14km away from the road as the ‸ondor flies. Many hiking trailheads are ac‐ ‸essible from towns along this route and two ‸nsealed roads valiantly cross the Cordillera, ‸ne via Carhuaz and another via Yungay.

‸onterrey

☏043 / POP 1100 / ELEV 2800M

‸luddled around a scattered spine of tour‐ ‸st facilities, this tiny *pueblo*, 9km north of ‸luaraz, earns a spot on the map for its natu‐ ‸al **hot springs** (admission S3.50; ⊘6am-5pm). ‸he baths are run by the falling-into-disre‐ ‸air Real Hotel Baños Termales Monterrey ‸ext door. Buses terminate right in front.

The hot springs are divided into two sec‐ ‸ions; the lower pools are more crowded ‸nd, on our visit, far from warm, while the ‸rivate rooms offer the sort of scalding ac‐ ‸ion you're looking for.

Before you wrinkle your nose at the ‸rown color of the water, know that it's due ‸o high iron content rather than question‐ ‸ble hygiene practices. It's best to visit in the ‸morning as the baths are cleaned overnight. ‸he pools get crowded on weekends and ‸holidays.

🛌 Sleeping & Eating

Though there is one great hotel and two ‸great restaurants in Monterrey, it works best as a day trip from Huaraz. On Sun‐ days, many restaurants serve a traditional Peruvian feast called *pachamanca* (*pacha* means 'earth' and *manca* means 'oven' in Quechua), a magnificent bounty of chicken, pork, lamb, guinea pig, corn, potatoes and other vegetables cooked for several hours over hot stones.

El Patio de Monterrey HOTEL $$ (☏42-4965; www.elpatio.com.pe; s/d S189/222; @🛜) The fanciest venture around, this ho‐ tel has colonial-style architecture around a toothsome hacienda, complemented by colonial-style furniture. Most of the ship‐ shape rooms are spacious and have bathtubs, phones and local TV. Some rooms (S376) sleep up to four and a few have a fireplace. Most rooms look out onto a bountiful garden that's strewn with wagon wheels and foun‐ tains; some have a balcony. Meals are avail‐ able in the fireplace-heated restaurant-bar.

El Cortijo PERUVIAN $$$ (Carretera Huaraz; mains S15-60; ⊘8am-7pm) This excellent restaurant grills ostrich (when they can get it in Peru) alongside *cuy* (guin‐ ea pig) and other meats. Outdoor tables are arranged around a fountain (complete with little boy peeing) in a grassy flower-filled garden, with swings for children.

El Ollón de Barro PERUVIAN $$ (Km 7; meals S12-28; ⊘11am-5pm Tue-Sun Jul, 11am-5pm Sat & Sun Aug-Jun) A near-impenetrable wall of hedge guarding a large, enticing gar‐ den with a fronton court, children's swings and trees surrounds this inviting choice. They do a tasty *coca* sour and bang out regional Pe‐ ruvian specialties like *ceviche de pato* (duck ceviche) and *pachamanca* (various meats cooked in an 'oven' of hot stones).

❶ Getting There & Away

Local buses from Huaraz go north along Luzu‐ riaga, west on Calle 28 de Julio, north on Calle 27 de Noviembre, east on Raymondi and north on Fitzcarrald. Try to catch a bus early in the route, as they fill up quickly. The fare for the 20-minute ride is S1. A taxi ride between Huaraz and Monterrey costs about S7.

Carhuaz

☏043 / POP 7100 / ELEV 2638M

Carhuaz, 35km north of Huaraz, lays claim to one of the prettiest plazas in the valley, with a combination of rose gardens and towering palms that make lingering here a pleasure.

The Sunday **market** is a kaleidoscopic treat as *campesinos* (peasants) descend from surrounding villages to sell a medley of fresh fruits, herbs and handicrafts. A road passes over the Cordillera Blanca from Carhuaz, via the beautiful Quebrada Ulta and Punta Olímpica Pass, to Chacas and San Luis.

Carhuaz' annual **La Virgen de La Merced fiesta** is celebrated from September 14 to 24 with processions, fireworks, dancing, bullfights and plenty of drinking – so much that the town is often referred to as *Carhuaz borachera* (drunk Carhuaz)!

You'll find a **Banco de la Nación** with a Visa/Plus ATM on the Plaza de Armas.

🛏 Sleeping & Eating

Don't miss the town's ubiquitous treat, *raspadilla*, a slurpee of Cordillera Blanca glacier ice slathered in fruity syrup.

TOP CHOICE **Hostal El Abuelo**   INN **$$**
(✆39-4456; www.elabuelohostal.com; Calle 9 de Diciembre 257; s/d incl breakfast S105/140; @🛜) The haughtiest place to stay in town is this excellent boutique inn, which has immaculate and charming rooms within a large, older-styled house. All matrimonial rooms feature king-sized beds. A new annex is under construction, which will offer Andean views.

Hotel La Merced   HOTEL **$**
(✆39-4280; Ucayali 724; s/d without bathroom S20/40, r S45) One of the town's oldest running ventures, boasting lots of windows for *cordillera* adulation and plenty of religious posters for internal speculation. Rooms are clean and hot showers.

Alojamiento Cordillera Blanca   GUESTHOUSE **$**
(✆94-389-7678; Aurora 247; s/d S24/45) Forget hospitality, but if you want to arrive Saturday night and wake up in the thick of the market, here are cramped but clean rooms.

Café Arte Andino
El Abuelo   CAFE, PERUVIAN
(Plaza de Armas; breakfast S4-10, sandwiches S 14) This pleasant plaza cafe is owned by l cal architect/cartographer Felipe Díaz (yc probably have his map) and is the best sp to eat as well as shop. Nice ceramics, han woven bags and wall textiles are availab here as well as Díaz' maps and local info mation.

Gerardos Chickens   PERUVIAN
(cnr 2 de Mayo & La Merced) Does better roaste chicken than most for S8 to S15. It's acro from the Huaraz terminal.

🛈 Getting There & Away

The Plaza de Armas is where you can pick up passing minibuses to Yungay (S3, 30 minutes) ar Caraz (S3.50, 45 minutes). *Combis* to Huaraz (S3 50 minutes) leave from a small terminal on the first block of La Merced. Morning and afternoon buses from Huaraz to Chacas and San Luis also pass by the plaza. Buses between Caraz and Lima and Huaraz and Chimbote, pass by here also.

Yungay

☎043 / POP 12,600 / ELEV 2458M

Light on overnight visitors, serene littl Yungay has relatively few tourist services. has the best access for the popular Laguna Llanganuco, via a dirt road that continue over the Cordillera to Yanama and beyonc Surrounded on all sides by lush hills waftin brisk mountain air, it's difficult to believ the heart-wrenching history of this littl junction in the road.

The original village of Yungay is now rubble-strewn zone about 2km south of the new town and marks the site of the singl worst natural disaster in the Andes. Th earthquake of May 31, 1970, loosened 15 mi lion cubic meters of granite and ice fron the west wall of Huascarán Norte. The re

REMOTE RIFUGI

Established by the pioneering Father Ugo de Censi, a priest of the Salesian order, the Italian nonprofit organization Don Bosco, based in Marcará, runs three remote **refuges** (✆44-3061; www.rifugi-omg.org; ⊙May-Sep) deep within the belly of the Cordillera. Each refuge is heated and has a radio, basic medical supplies, 60 beds, and charges S92 per night for bed, breakfast and dinner (S130 with lunch). Profits go to local aid projects. Refuges include Refugio Perú (4765m), a two-hour walk from Llanganuco and a base for climbing Pisco; Refugio Ishinca (4350m), a three-hour walk from Collón village in the Ishinca Valley; and Refugio Huascarán (4670m), a four-hour walk from Musho. Trekkers, mountaineers and sightseers are all welcomed.

DON'T MISS

CAMPO SANTO

On May 31, 1970, when the most of the world was watching the Mexico–Soviet Union FIFA World Cup opening match, a nearly 8.0 magnitude earthquake jolted the Peruvian departments of Ancash and La Libertad. The 45-second shake turned an 83-sq km area into a disaster zone, but it was the loosening of an estimated 50 million cubic meters of rock, ice and snow that broke away from the north face of Mount Huascarán that caused the most cataclysmic disaster in Andean history. The resulting *aluvión* (debris avalanche) barreled 15km down the mountainside at average speeds between 280km/h and 335km/h, burying the entire town of Yungay and nearly all of its inhabitants by the time it came to rest. An entire town, gone in three minutes.

The site of old Yungay (Yungay Viejo), **Campo Santo** (admission S2; ⊘8am-6pm) is overseen by a towering white statue of Christ standing on a knoll above the town's original, Swiss-designed cemetery, from where he overlooks the path of the *aluvión*. Ironically, it was this very cemetery that helped save the lives of 92 of the town's residents, who had just enough time to charge up its steps and elevate themselves out of the path of the *aluvión*. Those, along with some 300 residents attending a circus at the town stadium, were the only survivors out of an estimated 25,000 residents.

Flower-filled gardens follow the solemn pathway of the *aluvión*, with occasional gravestones and monuments commemorating the thousands of people who lie buried beneath the 8m to 12m of soil. At the old Plaza de Armas, you can just see the very top of the cathedral tower, what's left of a crushed Expreso Ancash bus and four palm-tree tips that survived the onslaught (one of them remarkably still alive). A replica of the cathedral's facade has been built in honor of the dead. Nearly every *Yungayano* born before 1955 is buried here in a grave dug by Mother Nature.

Vendors at the entrance draw your attention to a slew of before and after photos, which are well worth a look to gain some context of the absolute destruction of this disaster. The entire site has been declared a national cemetery and excavations of any kind are prohibited.

HUARAZ & THE CORDILLERAS YUNGAY

ulting *aluvión* (debris landslide) dropped over three vertical kilometers on its way to Yungay, 15km away. The town and almost all of its 25,000 inhabitants were buried.

🍴 Sleeping & Eating

Yungay's market, next to the plaza, has several cheap and rustic places to eat.

Hostal Gledel   GUESTHOUSE $
(☑39-3048; Aries Graziani; s/d without bathroom S15/25) The gregarious and generous Señora Gamboa rents out 13 spartan rooms brightened up with colorful bedspreads and new mattresses. Expect at least one hug and a sample of her cooking during your stay. This is both the cheapest and best place to stay in town – it's deservedly popular.

Hostal Sol de Oro   GUESTHOUSE $
(☑39-3116; Santo Domingo 7; s/d/tr S20/30/40) Another acceptable pick, it has bright, clean rooms with solid mattresses and hot showers. Tack on S8 for a TV room.

Restaurant Turístico Alpamayo   PERUVIAN $
(S7-20) Surrounded by gardens just off the main highway at the north end of town, Alpamayo is a pleasant spot, complete with a garden gazebo, to dig into some trout, *cuy* (guinea pig) or *chicharrónes* (breaded and fried).

OUTSIDE OF TOWN

Llanganuco Mountain Lodge   LODGE $$$
(☑94-366-9580; www.llanganucolodge.com; camping S15, dm without/with full board S38/135, s/d with full board from S183/228) About 45 minutes by taxi from Yungay toward the Lagunas Llanganuco, this recommended lodge run by Brit Charlie Good is in a prime position for exploring the lakes area or charging the Santa Cruz trek. Choose camping with hot-water showers and breathtaking views or lodge rooms with down-feather beds and balconies.

Tito, an aspiring chef, handles the excellent food and Shackleton and Dino, two Rhodesian Ridgebacks, handle mascot duties. It sits next to newly excavated Keushu ruins on the shore of an ancient lagoon with views of the three highest peaks in the range. From Yungay, taxis departing in front of the town hospital charge S30 for the ride up and S40 to come back down.

Humacchuco Community Tourism Project GUESTHOUSE **$$**
(☑94-497-6192; www.respons.org; per person incl meals from S190) Six members of the Humacchuco community maintain a comfortable guest house as part of an established sustainable-tourism program. Here visitors can learn about the local culture and natural-resource management, savor a *pachamanca* and go on guided hikes, including a day trip to Laguna 69. You can tailor your own program through Response (p365) in Huaraz.

❶ Getting There & Away

Minibuses run from a small terminal along the highway to Caraz (S2, 15 minutes), Carhuaz (S3.50, 30 minutes) and Huaraz (S5, 1¼ hours). Buses from Caraz to Lima and from Huaraz to Chimbote pick up passengers at the Plaza de Armas.

Departures on beat-up buses from Huaraz to Pomabamba via Lagunas Llanganuco pass by daily.

Lagunas Llanganuco

A dirt road ascends 1350m winding over 28km to the Llanganuco Valley and its two stunning lakes, which are also known as Laguna Chinancocha and Laguna Orconcocha, 28km northeast of Yungay. Nestled in a glacial valley just 1000m below the snow line, these pristine lagoons practically glow under the sun in their bright turquoise and emerald hues. There's a half-hour trail hugging Chinancocha past a jetty and picnic area to where sheer cliffs plunge into the lake. You can take a boat out on the lake for S5, which is a popular day-tripping spot from Huaraz, though count on six hours of travel to and from. Continuing on the road past the lake there's a *mirador* with killer views of the mountain giants of Huascarán (6768m), Chopicalqui (6345m), Chacraraju (6108m), Huandoy (6395m) and others. The road continues over the pass of Portachuelo (4760m) to Yanama on the other side of the Cordillera Blanca; several early-morning vehicles go from Huaraz going to Yanama and beyond.

To reach the Lagunas Llanganuco, yc can take a tour from Huaraz or use buses taxis from Yungay. During the June to A gust high season, frequent minibuses lea from Yungay's small terminal on the ma highway (S15), allowing about two hours the lake area. A national-park admission fr of S5 is charged. During the rest of the yea minibuses do the trip if there's enough d mand. *Colectivo* taxis are available for S per person each way. Go in the early mor ing for the clearest views, especially in th low season.

Caraz

☑043 / POP 13,100 / ELEV 2270M
With an extra helping of superb panorama of the surrounding mountains and a mor kick-back attitude than its rambunctiou brother Huaraz, Caraz makes for a tranqu alternate base of operations. Trekking an hiking trails meander in all directions some are day trips, others are much longe sojourns. One of the few places in the valle spared total destruction by earthquakes c *aluvión,* the town still has a gentle whiff c colonial air. Its lazy Plaza de Armas wouldn be out of place in a much smaller *pueblo.*

Caraz is both the end point of the time honored Llanganuco–Santa Cruz tre (which can also be done in reverse, startin here) and the point of departure for rug ged treks into the remote northern part of the Cordillera Blanca. The north side c Alpamayo (5947m), once enthusiasticall labeled the most beautiful mountain in th world for its knife-edged, perfectly pyrami dal northern silhouette, is easily accessibl from here.

◉ Sights

Laguna Parón LAGOO
This postcard pastel-blue lake (4200m) 25km east of Caraz, is surrounded by spec tacular snow-covered peaks, of which Pirámide de Garcilaso (5885m), at the enc of the lake, looks particularly brilliant. The challenging rock-climbing wall of Torre d Parón, known as the **Sphinx**, is also founc here. The road to the lake goes through a canyon with 1000m-high granite walls – this drive is as spectacular as the better-known Llanganuco trip. Fit and acclimatized hik ers can trek to the lake in one long day, but

's easier to catch local transport to Pueblo arón and hike the remaining four hours.

Organized transport from Caraz runs om S120 return with two hours wait time – ach additional hour is S10.

Cañón del Pato   CANYON

If you continue north from Caraz along the Callejón de Huaylas, you will wind your way through the outstanding Cañón del Pato. It's here that the Cordillera Blanca and the

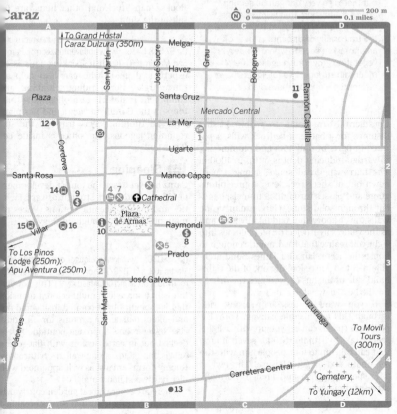

Caraz

HUARAZ & THE CORDILLERAS CARAZ

LAGUNA PARÓN

If you go on your own to Laguna Parón, be aware that you cannot circumnavigate the lake. The north shore is fine, but there is a very dangerous section on the south shore that is impassable due to potential falls up to 100m where the trail briefly disappears in favor of an unmarked section where slippery vegetation grows flush against the mountain surface. Two foreigners have attempted – and two have died.

Cordillera Negra come to within kissing distance for a battle of bedrock wills, separated in parts by only 15m and plummeting to vertigo-inducing depths of up to 1000m. The harrowing road snakes along a path hewn out of sheer rock, over a precipitous gorge and passes through 35 tunnels, handcut through solid stone. Gargantuan, crude walls tower above the road on all sides, and as the valley's hydroelectric plant comes into sight you realize that it's dramatic enough to house the secret lair of a James Bond archvillain. Sit so you're looking out of the right-hand side of the bus (as you face the driver) for the best views along the way.

If you want a less hair-raising ride through this astonishing canyon, Pony Expeditions (p392) can set you up with a sightseeing taxi to Trujillo (S1000, seven hours) that can take up to four people and will stop for photo ops at your leisure. The owner, who speaks English and French, normally drives you himself.

Punta Winchus OUTDOORS

A remote 4157m pass in the Cordillera Negra is the center of a huge stand of 5000 rare *Puya raimondii* plants. This is the biggest-known stand of these 10m-tall members of the pineapple family, which take 100 years to mature and in full bloom flaunt up to 20,000 flowers each! On a clear day you have an astounding 145km panorama from the Cordillera Blanca all the way to the Pacific Ocean. It's 45km west of Caraz and reached by tour vehicles.

🏃 Activities

For detailed trekking information you can visit one of the two main trekking outfits in Caraz.

Pony Expeditions TREKKING, RENTA
(☑39-1642; www.ponyexpeditions.com; José Suc 1266) English- and French-speaking region expert Alberto Cafferata provides equi ment rental (including bicycles), transpo guides, *arrieros* and various excursion Books, maps, fuel and other items are fe sale at the shop.

Apu Aventura TREKKING, CLIMBIN
(☑97-543-6438; www.apuaventura.com; Parq San Martín 103) English-speaking Luis is a experienced guide who can also help a range treks, horse riding, climbing an equipment rental. He also offers quad bik tours in the Cordillera Negra and has plan to begin running kayak trips on the su rounding lagoons. The office is inside Lo Pinos Lodge.

🛏 Sleeping

Caraz has yet to see the tourist developmer of Huaraz and offers straightforward facil ties and budget sleeping options. Prices re main quite stable throughout the year.

Los Pinos Lodge INN
TOP CHOICE
(☑39-1130; www.lospinoslodge.com; Parque Sa Martín 103; s/d S120/140, dm S30, s/d without bath room S35/60, all incl breakfast; @🛜) This popula inn is in a maze-like, multi-colored mansio that is thoughtfully decorated inside and ou and offers outstanding rooms for all budg ets. Newer rooms approach boutique levels decked out in earthy colors with flat-scree televisions and stone-walled bathroom Roomy dorms are just as well-appointed with nice hardwood floors and TVs.

There are several great garden courtyard and a funky restaurant that serves breakfas and snacks. The owner, Luis, organizes trek king and tours of the area.

La Perla de Los Andes HOTEL
(☑39-2007; hostal_perladelosandes@hotmail.com Villar 179; s/d S35/55; 🛜) An excellent-value

DEAD NUN'S CANYON

The Spanish version of the History Channel profiled the Cañón del Pato in its 2012 *Rutas Mortales: Los Andes* TV show, where the perceived-to-be weakly named *Cañón del Pato* (Duck Canyon) was changed to the far more frightening *El Cañón de la Monja Muerta* (Dead Nun's Canyon). Scary!

iendly spot that wears its multiple layers polished wood with pride, La Perla has great location right on Caraz' quiet plaza. ooms are smallish, but they all have cable V, solid mattresses, hot showers and some ive balconies with an ideal plaza view. right, natural light is in excess and the staff helpful.

rand Hostal Caraz Dulzura HOTEL $
⏷39-1523; www.hostalcarazdulzura.com; Sáenz eña 212; s/d/tr incl breakfast S45/70/120; ⏷) bout 10 blocks north of the plaza along ordova, this is a clinically clean and homey ural retreat that provides good bang for our buck. Rooms are bright and have hot nowers and comfortable beds. There's a pa-o backed by a rocky hill and a TV room with few little surprises like cash register lamps.

lostal Chavín HOTEL $
⏷39-1171; chavinhostel@hotmail.com; San Martín 135; s/d/tr/qd S40/60/80/100; ⏷) The owner ere is involved with the local tourism au-nority and can provide information, tours nd local transportation, making this a sen-ible choice. Rooms are simple, but all have V and hot showers and the hotel has a ood location just off the plaza.

Cordillera Blanca Hotel HOTEL $
⏷46-7936; hotelcordillerablanca@hotmail.com; rau 903; s/d S25/40; ⏷) This multistory ho-el opposite the market is decidedly lacking n anything that might resemble character, ut immaculate, brightly-colored rooms Pink! Purple! Green!) and gleaming bath-ooms are good value for money. The res-aurant downstairs, Chifa El Dragón Rojo, offers a Chinese twist on the traditional ollería.

lostal La Casona GUESTHOUSE $
⏷39-1334; Raymondi 319; r per person S15, per person without bathroom S10; @) Although nany of the large rooms here are dark and vindowless, the attractive patio and ani-nated owner makes this place a budget fave.

✖ Eating

Café de Rat BREAKFAST, PIZZERIA $
(José Sucre 1266; breakfast S5-12, pizzas from S15; ⏷7-11am & 5-9pm; ⏷) Don't mind the name, the menu has been cleared of rodents. This atmospheric wood-beamed restaurant and cafe serves sandwiches, pasta, and coffee for breakfast and dinner but is closed for lunch. It also has a book exchange, darts, a bar and music; it's a top spot to hang out,

especially on the upstairs balcony with fire-place and plaza views. Find it above Pony Expeditions.

Café La Terraza BREAKFAST, PERUVIAN $
(José Sucre 1107; menú S7, mains S12-20; ⏷closed Mon) Does some of the best coffee in town and has lots of breakfast options (pan-cakes!), pizzas and pasta – all in an inviting and cheerful art-covered space. Daily menus are good value.

Cafetería El Turista BREAKFAST, PERUVIAN $
(San Martín 1127; breakfast S4-10; ⏷6:30am-noon & 5-8pm) A great place to grab an early break-fast, this tiny little cafe is a one-woman show run by the exuberant Maria. She'll talk your ear off about your travels and hers.

Heladería Caraz Dulzura ICE CREAM $
(Plaza de Armas; ice cream S2-6) This popular ice cream place gets packed on hot days. It also serves some local meals, but the sweet stuff is what it's really all about.

❶ Information

The **Cámara de Turismo** (⏷39-1029; Plaza de Armas; ⏷8am-1pm & 2:30-5pm Mon-Fri), on the Plaza de Armas, has irregular hours and limited tourist information.

Both **BCP** (cnr Villar & Cordova) and **Banco de la Nación** (Raymondi 1051) change cash and traveler's checks and have ATMs. The **Serpost** outlet (San Martín 909) is north of the cathedral.

❶ Getting There & Around

Caraz is often the final destination for buses heading from the coast to the Callejón de Huay-las. Most coastal buses go via Huaraz.

Bus
LONG DISTANCE

Transportes Rodríguez (⏷79-4375; Villar 411) has Lima buses at 8:30pm with economic and *semi-cama* services on alternate days. **Coopera-tiva Ancash** (⏷39-1126; Cordova 139) has serv-ices to Lima at 11am, 7pm and 8pm. **Movil Tours** (⏷39-1184; Pasaje Santa Teresita 334) has the most comfortable Lima *bus-cama* at 9pm as well as good economic services at 7:30am, 1pm and 8:30pm. It also has a *bus-cama* Chimbote bus via Casma at 8:10pm.

Yungay Express (⏷39-1492; Villar 316) has one bus a day to Chimbote via the Cañón del Pato leaving at 9am and two via Casma at noon and 8pm.

CARAZ AREA

Minibuses to Yungay, Carhuaz and Huaraz leave from the station on the Carretera Central.

CARAZ BUSES

DESTINATION	COST (S)	DURATION (HR)
Carhuaz	3.50	¾
Cashapampa	8	1½
Chimbote	25-60	6
Huallanca	7	1
Huaraz	6	1¼
Lima	30-75	8-9
Pueblo Parón	5	1
Yungay	2	¼

Taxi

Colectivo taxis for Cashapampa (S8, 1½ hours) for the northern end of the Llanganuco–Santa Cruz trek leave when full from the corner of Ramón Castilla at Santa Cruz. *Colectivos* to Pueblo Parón (S5, one hour), which is about 9km from the famous Laguna Parón, leave from the same corner. *Colectivos* to Huallanca, for the Cañón del Pato and onwards, leave from the corner of Cordova and La Mar when full.

Mototaxis (S1) trundle around town, but Caraz is easily managed on foot.

SOUTH OF HUARAZ

Covering the southern extent of the Cordillera Blanca and the majestic Cordillera Huayhuash, this part of the Andes refuses to be outdone in the 'breathtaking mountain scenery' stakes. Several peaks here also pass the 6000m mark, huddling to form a near-continuous, saw-toothed ridge of precipitous summits. **Yerupajá** (6617m), Peru's second-highest mountain, is the icing on the Cordillera cake and is followed in height by its second lieutenant **Siulá Grande** (6344m), where climber Joe Simpson fell down into a crevice and lived to tell the tale in the book and movie *Touching the Void*. The rugged and rewarding 10-day Cordillera Huayhuash Circuit (see p384), accessed through the town of Llamac, is the glittering star attraction.

The Puente Bedoya bridge, about 18km south of Huaraz, marks the beginning of a 2km dirt road to the community of **Olleros**, the starting point for the three-day trek across the Cordillera Blanca to Chavín de Huántar (see p396). Respons Sustainable Tourism Center (p365) in Huaraz arranges a colorful day trip (S90 for two people, less per person for larger groups) to the villag of **Huarípampa**, just a few minutes sout of Huaraz, to see two local women dye an weave wool with plants from their own gar dens and on their own hand looms.

Recuay (population 2900), a town 25km from Huaraz, is one of the few municipal ties to have survived the 1970 earthquak largely unscathed. **Catac** (population 2300 10km south of Recuay, is an even smalle hamlet and the starting point for trips to se the remarkable *Puya raimondii* plant.

Further south, about 70km from Huara on the road to Lima and in the vicinity o the village of Pampas Chico, **Hatun Macha** (www.andeankingdom.com/hatunmachay; camp ing S20, dm S30, three-day course incl all meals equipment & transport from Huaraz for two S405 is a rock-climber's paradise. The folks a **Andean Kingdom/Infinite Adventures** (☑42-7304; www.andeankingdom.com; Parque Ginebra, Huaraz) in Huaraz have developed dozens of climbing routes throughout thi 'rock forest' nestled high in the Cordillera Negra. The whole complex, including the climbing routes and a large rustic refuge with kitchen facilities, is at your service for beginning rock-climbing instruction, as wel as hard-core ascents. If that weren't enough two treks around the area take you past ar chaeological remains of rock carvings and a view of the Pacific Ocean (on a clear day) and make for great half-day acclimatization hikes.

Chiquián

☑043 / POP 3700 / ELEV 3400M

A subdued hill town, Chiquián was traditionally the base of operations for folk trekking the Cordillera Huayhuash Circuit. Now,

wever, it can be bypassed using the new
npaved) road that extends to a trailhead
Llamac, though you will be infinitesimally
ore comfortable here. Great views of the
uayhuash come into view as you drive into
e village.

The annual festival in late August is held
honor of Santa Rosa de Lima and cel-
rated with dances, parades, music and
llfights.

Sleeping & Eating

Hotel Los Nogales GUESTHOUSE $
44-7121; www.hotellosnogaleschiquian.com;
omercio 1301; s/d/tr S30/50/70; Colorful,
ean and attractive, this is a great place
bout three blocks from the central plaza.
ooms surround an impossibly charming
lonial-style courtyard garden and meals
re available on request. The owners and
mployees are very friendly and the hot wa-
r, cable TV, wi-fi and room-service coffee
als the deal. If it weren't weird to pick a
otel in Chiquián as one of the top five plac-
s to stay in the region, this would be there.

ran Hotel Huayhuash HOTEL $
44-7049; www.hotelhuayhuash.com; cnr 28 de
lio & Amadeo; s/d S30/50, s/d without bathroom
20/40, all incl breakfast; @) A more contem-
orary choice with very nice rooms, some
ffording good vistas. Hot water and new
at-screen TVs are standard. The restaurant
s one of the nicest in town, but is poorly
un. The hotel owner here is a good source
f information.

Miky PERUVIAN $
2 de Mayo s/n, 2nd fl; menús S4-7; closed Sun)
eing cheap *and* the best often requires
ivine intervention. Well, a light is shining
own on this festive, well-run restaurant
hat's the best spot for your daily *menú* in
own. We searched it down by asking for
he cleanest choice and stumbled upon the
whole town eating here.

Fantastic soups are served as a first
ourse and the juicy *lomo saltado* was the
ne of the best we tried (and we tried way
oo many). Laughably great for S4.

Getting There & Away

f you're interested in heading straight to Chiquián and the Cordillera Huayhuash, you'll find
direct buses from Lima. However, as you'll probably need a few days to acclimatize, note that
Huaraz offers a wider selection of distractions.
Turismo Cavassa (44-7036; Bolognesi 421)

has buses to and from Lima, leaving at 9am daily
from either city (S25, eight hours).

If you're starting the Huayhuash Circuit, catch
the 8am **Turismo Nazario** (78-9699; Comercio 1050) bus to Llamac (S10, 2½ hours), which
is continuing on from its 5am Huaraz (S10, two
hours) departure. **Transportes San Bartolome**
(44-7084; Bolognesi s/n) also goes to Llamac
(S6 to S8) and Quero (S6, 2½ hours) at 8am.
From Quero, you can hike to Mahuay and Mata-
cancha for the trek's alternate start. There is
also a 9am *combi* to Quero (S7). **Transportes
El Rapido** (44-7096; Figueredo 209) goes to
Huaraz at 5am and 2pm (S10).

It's possible to get from Chiquián to Huallanca,
although service is erratic at best. Ask locally.
Huallanca (population 1950) has a basic hotel
and transport continues on from here to La
Unión and Huánuco.

The ride between Huaraz and Chiquián, whether the fogged in morning run from former (sit
on the left) or the afternoon ride back from the
latter (sit on the right), affords some of the most
beautiful scenery you will see in Peru.

Llamac

043 / ELEV 3300M

The ramshackle brick-and-mud village of
Llamac is the traditional starting point for
the Huayhuash Circuit. Though a newly
paved road now allows travelers to bypass
Chiquián and get an early start on the trails,
there is little in the way of services here,
though there's a small Plaza de Armas with
a tumbledown church that still manages to
be draped in bougainvillea. The trailhead
sits behind the Municipalidad on the same
plaza. There is a S15 entry fee to town for
foreigners, the first in the fee circuit.

Trekkers bed down at one of two rudimentary options. **Hostal Los Andenes**
(San Pedro s/n; r per person with/without hot water
S15/10) has utmost basic rooms with shared
bathrooms and warm wool blankets and is
pretty much the town's only spot for a bite to
eat. Travelers congregate in the small room
over set meals for S5 to S12 and pretend to
be entertained by a flat-screen TV showing
loads of DVDs. There is no phone for reservations – you'll need to call the village's public telephone: 83-0785. The other choice
is the even more basic **Hospedaje Santa
Rosa** (94-338-0659; Bolognesi s/n; r per person
S6), with shared baths and a sweet owner
named Igima.

Turismo Nazario (82-4431; Grau s/n)
departs Huaraz for Llamac (S25, 4½ hours)
via Chiquián (S15, two hours) at 5am daily,

returning from Llamac at 11:30am. Transportes San Bartolome (☎83-0827; Bolognesi s/n) heads to Chiquián at the same time in a rougher but cheaper bus (S6 plus S2 for luggage).

CALLEJÓN DE CONCHUCOS

The Conchucos Valley (locally called the Callejón de Conchucos) runs parallel to the Callejón de Huaylas on the eastern side of the Cordillera. Sprinkled liberally with remote and rarely visited gems, this captivating dale is steeped in history and blessed with isolated, postcard-perfect Andean villages so tranquil that they'd fall into comas if they were any sleepier. Interlaced with excellent yet rarely visited hiking trails, this untapped region begs for exploration. Tourist infrastructure is still in its infancy, with a handful of welcoming but modest hotels and erratic transport along rough, unpaved roads that can be impassable in the wet season. If you do make the effort to get here, the highland hospitality of Quechua *campesinos* and awe-inspiring scenery will more than make up for the butt-smacking, time-consuming bumps in the road.

Chavín de Huántar, at the south end of the valley, is the most accessible area of the lot and lays claim to some of the most important and mysterious pre-Inca ruins on the continent. From Huari, just north of Chavín, you can either catch rides on pseudo-regular buses north to Pomabamba, or hike your way north, skirting the eastern peaks of the Cordillera Blanca to Chacas and Yanama (see p400).

Chavín de Huántar

☎043 / POP 2000 / ELEV 3250M

The unhurried town of Chavín abuts the northern end of the ruins and is too often whizzed through by visitors on popular day trips from Huaraz. A shame really, as this attractive Andean township has excellent tourist infrastructure, a slew of nature-centered activities and some of the best-value accommodations in the Cordilleras. If you decide to overnight it here, you get to visit the impressive archaeological site in the early morning and have it all to yourself.

The main drag of Chavín town is Calle 17 de Enero Sur, which leaves the peaceful

Plaza de Armas southbound, passing rows restaurants, internet cafes and the entran to the archaeological site. The Banco de Nación (☺7am-5:30pm Mon-Fri, 9am-1pm Sa on the Plaza de Armas, has a Visa/Plus ATI A small but helpful tourist informatio office (☎45-4235 ext 106; Bolivar s/n; ☺8ar 12:30pm & 2:30-5:30pm) operates out of th Municipalidad building just off the plaza.

◉ Sights

Chavín de Huántar RU

(adult/student S10/5; ☺9am-5pm Tue-Sun)
Unesco World Heritage site since 198 Chavín de Huántar is the quintessential si of the Mid-Late Formative Period (c 120C 500 BC), one of many relatively indepen ent, competitive ceremonial centers sprea throughout the central Andes. It is a st pendous achievement of ancient constru tion, with large temple-like structures abov ground and labyrinthine (now electronicall lit) underground passageways. Althoug squatters built on top of the ruins or carrie away stone artworks, and a huge landslic due to a heavy rainy season in 1945 covere a large portion of the area, this site is still i tact enough to provide a full-bodied glimps into one of Peru's oldest complex societies.

Chavín is a series of older and newer ten ple arrangements built between 1200 B and 500 BC, but most structures visible tc day came from a big building effort betwee 900 and 700 BC. In the middle is a mas sive central square, slightly sunken belov ground level, which like the overall site ha an intricate, extensive and well-engineere system of channels for drainage. From th square, a broad staircase leads up to the por tal in front of the largest and most impor tant building, called the Castillo, which ha withstood some mighty earthquakes ove the years. Built on three different levels o stone-and-mortar masonry (sometimes in corporating cut stone blocks), the walls her were at one time embellished with *tenor* heads (blocks carved to resemble humar heads with animal or perhaps hallucinogen induced characteristics backed by stone spikes for insertion into a wall). Only one o these remains in its original place, althougr the others may be seen in the local museum related to the site.

A series of tunnels underneath the Castillo are an exceptional feat of engineering comprising a maze of complex corridors ducts and chambers. In the heart of this

CHAVÍN PERIOD

Named after the site at Chavín de Huántar, this is considered one of the oldest major cultural periods in Peru, strutting its stuff on the pre-Inca stage from 1200 BC to 500 BC. The Chavín and its contemporaries wielded their influence with great success, particularly between the formative years of 800 BC to 500 BC when they excelled in the agricultural production of potatoes and other highland crops, animal husbandry, ceramic and metal production and engineering of buildings and canals. Chavín archaeologists have formerly referred to this time of political ascendance as the Chavín Horizon, though Early Horizon or late Formative is also used.

The principal Chavín deity was feline (jaguar or puma), although lesser condor, eagle and snake deities were also worshipped. Representations of these deities are highly stylized and cover many Chavín period sites and many extraordinary objects, such the Tello Obelisk in the Museo Nacional de Chavín; the Lanzón, often referred to as the Smiling God, which stands in mystical glory in the tunnels underneath the Chavín site; and the Raimondi Stone at the Museo Nacional de Antropología, Arqueología e Historia del Perú in Lima (p65). The Raimondi Stone (which is currently considered too fragile to move to Chavín) has carvings of a human figure, sometimes called the Staff God, with a jaguar face and large staffs in each hand – an image that has shown up at archaeological sites along the northern and southern coasts of Peru and which suggests the long reach of Chavín interactions. The images on all of these massive stone pillars are believed to indicate a belief in a tripartite universe consisting of the heavens, earth and a netherworld, or as an alternative theory goes, a cosmos consisting of air, earth and water, though these remain elaborate guesses – archaeologists at the site have seen no good evidence to support any of these theories.

As a major ceremonial center, the most powerful players in Chavín were its priests, who seem to have been far more sophisticated than the general population, and dealt primarily with upper ranks of the society, convincing them with formidable rituals of difficult explanation that were occasionally terrifying. One theory says priests relied on sophisticated observation and understanding of seasonal changes, rain and drought cycles, and the movement of the sun, moon, and stars to create calendars that helped the Chavín reign as agriculturalists, though there is as yet no evidence that calendars were created. Others believe that Chavín leaders were getting to the point of being free of system-serving, and heading for authority based on belief rather than for serving an agricultural purpose. Some archaeologists have also argued that women also served as priests and played a powerful role during the Chavín period. Chavín, it seems, remains a rather polarizing mystery.

complex is an exquisitely carved, 4.5m monolith of white granite known as the **Lanzón de Chavín**. In typical terrifying Chavín fashion, the low-relief carvings on the Lanzón represent a person with snakes radiating from his head and a ferocious set of fangs, most likely feline. The Lanzón, almost certainly an object of worship given its prominent, central placement in this ceremonial center, is sometimes referred to as the Smiling God – but its aura feels anything but friendly.

Several beguiling construction quirks, such as the strange positioning of water channels and the use of highly polished mineral mirrors to reflect light, led Stanford archaeologists to believe that the complex was used as an instrument of shock and awe. To instill fear in nonbelievers, priests manipulated sights and sounds. They blew on echoing *Strombus* trumpets, amplified the sounds of water running through specially designed channels and reflected sunlight through ventilation shafts. The disoriented cult novitiates were probably given hallucinogens like San Pedro cactus shortly before entering the darkened maze. These tactics endowed the priests with awe-inspiring power.

The new, outstanding **Museo Nacional de Chavín** (admission free; ☺9am-5pm Tue-Sun), funded jointly by the Peruvian and Japanese governments, houses most of the intricate and horrifyingly carved *tenon* heads, as well as the magnificent Tello Obelisk, another stone object of worship with

LAND OF THE LOST

When the Antamina Mining Company needed a paved road to move mining equipment from Yanacancha to the Conococha crossroads (some 200km east of Huaraz), they simply built it themselves. During the excavation in 2009, they made a startling discovery: over 100 footprints and fossilized remains of at least 12 species of prehistoric animals that paleontologists have dated to the Early Cretaceous Period (about 120 million years ago). Complete skeletons of large marine reptiles known as sauropterygians were found in addition to skeletal remains of other extinct species of crocodiles, flying reptiles called pterosaurs, fish-like reptiles called ichthyosaurs and... dinosaur footprints!

The site, known as **Huellas de los Dinosaurios**, is between Kms 77 and 83 on the highway between San Marcos and Huallanca. At time of writing, the only way to visit was by private car, but ideas were being floated to begin day tours from Chavín de Huántar and Huaraz as early as 2013.

low relief carvings of a caiman and other fierce animals. The obelisk had been moved to a Lima museum long before the 1945 landslide that destroyed much of the original chapel museum, and was only returned to Chavín in 2009.

To get the most from your visit, it's worth hiring a guide to show you around (S30) or go on a guided day trip (including transportation) from Huaraz; this latter option is by far the most budget-friendly way to see these ruins, especially since it can be difficult to get a bus back to Huaraz from Chavín late in the day – you may get stuck in a unlicensed *colectivo* (S25, called *piratas*), or backtracking via San Marcos (S2, 15 minutes) to get an official *combi* (S25, 2½ hours) or *colectivo* (S20 to S25, 2½ hours) back to Huaraz.

Activities

The relaxing sulfur **Quercos thermal baths** (admission S3), a 30-minute walk south of town, house four private baths and one larger pool. Keep your eyes peeled for a small, signed path that leads down to the river. **Horse riding** on Peruvian pacing horses can be arranged through the Cafetería Renato (p399) for S40 per hour (including a guide).

From Chavín you can hike for a few hours into a lofty valley, in the direction of Olleros, to a high pass with stirring views of Huantsán (6395m) – the highest mountain in the southern Cordillera Blanca. If you're interested in longer treks originating here, **Don Donato** (45-4136; Tello Sur 275) of the Asociación de Servicios de Alta Montaña offers a four-day trek (S480) that circles the back side of the Cordillera Blanca, passes by several alpine lakes and exits through the Carhuascancha Valley.

Sleeping & Eating

Chavín has a surprisingly good selection accommodations. Camping by the ruins also possible with permission of the guard

Most of the town's eateries can be found along Calle 17 de Enero Sur and in hotel Restaurants have a reputation for closing soon after sunset, so dig in early.

Hostal Chavín Turístico GUESTHOUSE
(45-4051; soniavalenciapozo@hotmail.co Maytacapac 120; s/d S40/80; @) This ne family-run option is the best place to sta offering well-appointed rooms with cu bedspreads, large bathrooms and – pe haps most refreshingly – no chipped pai or rusty pipes. It's clean as a whistle, wel maintained and closer to the ruins than th plaza options. There's no internet per se, bu the owners have a 3G modem you can us with your laptop or theirs.

La Casona GUESTHOUSE
(45-4116; www.lacasonachavin.com.pe; Plaz de Armas 130; s/d/tr S35/60/90) Nestled i an old house, the well-kept rooms here ar a little on the dark side, but the beautifu courtyard, overflowing with plants, is a excellent place to hang out and soak up th ambience. Some rooms have a TV or a plaz balcony. There's an American manager wh has raised local eyebrows with his San Pedr cultivation and aspirations for a resort over looking the ruins.

Hostal Inca GUESTHOUSE
(45-4021; enrique9541@hotmail.com; Plaza d Armas; s/d S30/60) The reputation of thi

cure, popular place is as solid as its colo-
al foundations and boasts very respectable
oms (though showers are weak and tight).
ere's a small garden tended by the some-
at cranky couple that runs it. Hostal Inca
o houses the lab for the ongoing excava-
n project of the ruins.

Buongiorno   PERUVIAN **$$**
alle 17 de Enero Sur s/n; mains S17-38; ⊙7am–
m) Churning out sophisticated dishes that
tpunch its location's weight class, Buon-
orno is a pleasant surprise in a cordial ur-
n garden setting. The *lomo a la pimienta*,
Peruvian fave of grilled steak in wine,
am and cracked-pepper sauce (S27), is
ree-star Lima quality and the trout *cevi-*
e is also a popular choice.

The cooks here often dart out to the ex-
nsive gardens and grab some fresh organ-
herbs – a nice touch. It's 50m across the
idge from the entrance to the ruins. Atmos-
ere takes a dive at dinner – go for lunch.

afetería Renato   BREAKFAST, PERUVIAN **$**
aza de Armas; breakfast S3-12; ⊙from 7am) On
e casual Plaza de Armas, this cozy place
rves yummy local and international break-
sts alongside homemade yogurt, cheese
d *manjar blanco* (homemade caramel
read). There's a lovely garden you can laze
 while waiting for your bus and the owners
ganize horse trekking from here.

havín Turístico   PERUVIAN **$**
alle 17 de Enero Sur 439; mains S10-20; ⊙to
30pm) A solid option, especially for *trucha*
 ajo (garlic trout) and trout *sudado,* this
ace has a chalkboard of traditional plates
d rickety tables around a tiny courtyard.
he food is tasty and local archaeologists say
's the most reliable choice in town.

Drinking

ama Rawana   BAR
Plaza de Armas 110) It just so happens one of
e few spots in town for a *cold* beer is one
f the Cordilleras' best bars. This cozy joint
 a good time. Belly up to the rustic pine-
ood bar – duck under the low doorway – or
ettle in at one of the few tables. It's reason
one to spend the night here.

ⓘ Getting There & Away

he scenic drive across the Cordillera Blanca via
atac passes the Laguna Querococha at 3980m.
rom here, there are views of the peaks of Pu-
araju (5322m) and Yanamarey (5237m). Along

the way it passes through the Kahuish Tunnel
(4516m above sea level), which cuts through
the Kahuish Pass. As you exit the tunnel and
descend toward Chavín, look out for the massive
statue of Christ built by Italian missionaries and
blessing your journey.

Tour buses make day trips from Huaraz. See
p367 for details of Transportes Sandoval and
other companies that have multiple daily depar-
tures to Chavín (S12, three hours). In Chavín,
Transportes Sandoval (☏99-083-7068; Gran
Terminal Terrestre, Julio Cetello s/n) leaves
from the shiny new bus station south of the
plaza. It serves Huaraz eight times daily between
4am and 9pm (S12, three hours) as well as Huari
(S6, two hours) to the north. **Turismo Andino**
(☏94-498-8425, Gran Terminal Terrestre, Julio
Cetello s/n) has departures to Lima at 6am and
6:30pm (S40, 10 hours).

To continue north along the east side of the
Cordillera Blanca, most of the buses originating
in Huaraz continue on to Huari (S6, two hours),
from where you can catch onward transport on
some of the infrequent buses that pass through
from Lima. *Colectivos* leave frequently from the
Gran Terminal Terrestre to San Marcos (S2, 15
minutes) from where you can catch *colectivos* to
Huari (S6, 45 minutes) and *combis/colectivos* to
Huaraz (S20 to S25, 2½ hours) from the oddly-
named Plaza Chupa, two blocks north of the
quaint Plaza de Armas.

Hikers can walk to Chavín from Olleros in
about three days; it's a popular but uncrowded
hike (see p383).

North of Chavín

The road north of Chavín goes through the
villages of San Marcos (after 8km), Huari
(40km, two hours), San Luis (100km, five
hours), Pomabamba and eventually Sihuas
(population 4000). The further north you
go, the more inconsistent transport be-
comes, and it may stop altogether during
the wet season.

From Sihuas, it is possible to continue on
to Huallanca (at the end of Cañón del Pato)
via Tres Cruces and thus return to the Calle-
jón de Huaylas. This round-trip is scenic, re-
mote and rarely made by travelers.

There are two roads that offer pictur-
esque crossings back to El Callejón de Huay-
las. The road from Chacas to Carhuaz, via
the Punta Olímpica Pass (4890m), is spec-
tacular. A road from Yanama to Yungay
takes passengers over yet another breathtak-
ing pass (4767m) and into the valley made
famous by the Lagunas Llanganuco, with
top views of the towering Huascarán, Chopi-
calqui and Huandoy (6395m) peaks.

HUARI

☎ 043 / POP 4700 / ELEV 3150M

A small Quechua town barely clinging to the mountainside, Huari has nearly 360-degree mountain panoramas from its steep, cobbled streets. Market day here is Sunday, when *campesinos* from surrounding towns descend on Huari to hawk fruits and vegetables. The annual town fiesta, Señora del Rosario, is held in early October and has a strange tradition of cat consumption (residents from Huari are jokingly referred to in Quechua as *Mishikanka,* which literally means 'Deep-Fried Cats' but more figuratively 'Cat Eaters.'). The town has a small and modern Plaza de Armas and a larger Plaza Vigil (known as El Parque) one block away, where you'll find the bus company offices (buses leave from a terminal a few blocks away). There is a Banco de la Nación near the market with a Visa/Plus ATM.

For sweeping panoramas of the valley, keep walking uphill from the El Dorado hotel until you come to a *mirador* (lookout). A good day hike is to Laguna Purhuay, a beautiful lake about 5km away. An excellent two- or three-day backpacking trip continues past the lake to emerge at the village of Chacas. Another three- to four-day trek follows the old Inca highway to Huánuco (see p383).

There are several cheap places to stay in town, but El Dorado (Simón Bolívar 353; r S30, s/d without bathroom S10/20) is the pick of a litter of runts, with the added luxury of no telephone and no toilet seats – yet it remains the most popular spot in town. Hostal Paraíso (☎45-3029; Simón Bolívar 263; s/d S20/30, s/d without bathroom S10/20) is more or less the same. There's modest rooms and a courtyard with some greenery. No hotels in town have internet, but you can connect yourself at Cybershalom (Ancash 773; per hr S1; ⊗7am-11pm).

There's not a lot of choice for food, but Chifa Dragón Andino (Libertad 660; mains S9-15; ⊗from noon, closed Sun) does decent Chinese fare.

Colectivos to San Marcos, for quicker travel to Huaraz, leave from behind the market (S6, 45 minutes). Transportes Sandoval (☎45-7643; Ancash 812, Plaza Vigil) heads to Huaraz six times daily (S15, 4½ hours). From the same office, Chavín Express goes to Lima (S35, 11 hours) once per day at 5:30pm. Turismo Andino (☎99-342-7102; Ancash 836, Plaza Vigil) heads to Lima (S40, 10 hours) at 9am and 5:30pm and Chacas (S15, 2½ hours) at 4am. For Pomabamba (S25, 6½ hours), El Solitario (☎99-342-7102;

Ancash 836, Plaza Vigil) passes by on the ma[in] road around 5pm on Wednesday, Thu[rs]day, Saturday and Sunday only. You'll ha[ve] more options if you got to Huaraz first, b[ut] of course this is well out of the way in t[he] wrong direction. If you want to forge ahea[d] on your own timeframe to San Luis, whe[re] you can catch onward travel to Chacas, Ya[n]ama and Pomabomba, a taxi is anywhe[re] between S200 and S300 depending on yo[ur] negotiation skills. The road is rough a[nd] beautiful.

For Laguna Purhuay you can hire a ta[xi] to take you for about S100 return, includi[ng] waiting time.

YANAMA

☎ 043 / POP 500 / ELEV 3400M

Yanama is a tiny, mountain-enveloped *pu[e]blo,* where the most exciting thing to ha[p]pen in the past decade is a connection to t[he] electricity grid in 2005. The town is abo[ut] 1½ hours' walk (or a 20-minute drive) fro[m] the end of the popular Santa Cruz trek (s[ee] p379) and makes a good stopover point f[or] trekkers and mountain-bikers to refuel a[nd] recharge. The town festival of Santa Ros[a] is held here in August.

A daily morning bus links Yungay wi[th] Yanama, passing the famed Lagunas Llang[a]nuco and traveling within 1km of the villag[e] of Colcabamba (population 360), the star[t]ing point for the Llanganuco–Santa Cru[z] trekking circuit. Facilities are rudimenta[ry] in Yanama and showers can be as fros[ty] as the mountain air. The Municipalida[d] (Plaza de Armas; ⊗8am-1pm & 2-5pm Mon-Fri) ha[s] the only internet connection in town, b[ut] they've generously set aside *one* comput[er] for folks to use for free.

Andes Lodge Peru (☎76-5579; ww[w.] andeslodgeperu.com; Jirón Gran Chavín s/n; s[/d] S70/120, s/d without bathroom S60/100, all in[cl] breakfast) is just a couple of blocks from th[e] Plaza de Armas and one of the best moun[n]tain lodges in the Callejón de Huaylas. Com[]ing back to the home-cooked meals, blazin[g] hot showers, snug beds with down comfor[t]ers and ever-helpful Peruvian owners after [a] day in the mountains is a revelation. All th[e] area excursions can be arranged, includin[g] Laguna 69 and visits to local farmers an[d] weavers. All rooms come with breakfast[;] add S30 per person per day for full board.

A couple of *hospedajes* supply auster[e] rooms for around S15 per person, but th[e] best cheapie in town is Hostal El Pino (☎9[7-] 150-0759; s/d/tr without bathroom S15/25/45[)]

hind the new church with a huge pine
e outside. Exceptionally friendly, it's basic
t has comfortable beds and there are elec-
c showers. Misty views of the mountains
me standard. The same owners run
st restaurant in town on the plaza, **Res-
urant El Pino II** (menús S8-12), where you'll
ed to stop in if you want to sleep at the
esthouse.

In Colcabamba you'll find several home-
ays that offer beds with dinner for S20 to
5 per person.

A few *colectivos* leave for Yungay from
e plaza between noon and 1pm (S15, 3½
urs) or you can catch a Transportes Renzo
Transportes El Veloz bus originating in
Pomabamba, which pass around midday or
10pm. The ride – obviously – is stunning.

POMABAMBA
043 / POP 4400 / ELEV 2950M

Known as the City of Cedars (check out
the specimen on the plaza), Pomabamba is
a great place to spend some time between
trekking trips. Soak in a lung-full of the crisp
mountain troposphere and the small-town
ambience. Several cross-Cordillera treks begin and end at this township and you'd be
forgiven for failing to notice that this is supposed to be the 'largest' settlement north of
Huari.

There are several sets of natural private
hot springs (admission S1) lying in wait for

WORTH A TRIP

CHACAS

This ornate mountain town sits atop a hillcrest at 3360m, surrounded by fertile hills and
with guest appearances by the occasional snow-capped Cordillera peak. The charismatic
main plaza is dominated by a brilliant church built by a religious non-profit Italian aid
organization, Don Bosco, based in Marcará and established by the pioneering Father Ugo
de Censi, a priest of the Salesian order.

White-walled houses around the plaza look idyllic against the mountain backdrop and
many have intricate wooden balconies and brightly colored doors and window shutters
just screaming to have their picture taken. Best of all, the town is whisper-quiet as there's
no traffic to speak of. Look out for the impossibly petite, smiling Andean ladies who sit
meditatively spinning wool on every second corner. This is an excellent place to while
away a few days. The town has few fixed-line phones, yet surprisingly there's **internet**
access (⊗8am-noon & 2-10pm; per hr S2) in the ornate Municipalidad building next to
Banco de la Nación on the plaza (no ATM).

You can do great two- to three-day treks from here to Huari or Yanama, from where
energetic hikers can continue on to do the Santa Cruz trek (p379).

The friendly **Hostal Asunción** (☑79-4482; Bolognesi 370; s/d S25/30, s without bathroom S10) is on the Plaza de Armas – a couple of rooms have windows onto the plaza and
the place manages to scrape together a certain bucolic appeal. A welcoming couple – the
misses spends her day working the wool – runs **Hospedaje Alameda** (☑95-395-5816;
Lima 305; s/d 30/40, s/d without bathroom S15/20), which offers a cute courtyard and
similarly modest rooms (warm beds!) as well as much nicer, newer abodes with private
bathrooms. Both places have hot water. Pilar Ames (the owner of El Cortijo restaurant in
Monterrey, p387) has the most comfortable digs in town at **Hostal Pilar** (☑in Monterrey
42-3813; Ancash 110; d S150), with decent modern facilities. This place is used as part of a
local tour and is open only to those with prior reservations.

Idyllic as it is, the problem with lingering here is food: try **Zazón Andino** (Lima s/n;
menú S5; ⊗closed Sat dinner) on the plaza, which is the best (and only?) choice, managing
to churn out a few edible *menú* choices served by an 11-year-old waitress (just go with it).

Transportes Renzo (☑95-957-1581; Lima 37) and **Transportes El Veloz** (☑78-2836;
Buenos Aires s/n) both go to Huaraz (S23 to S25, 4½ hours), the former at 5pm, the latter
at 1am and 1pm, via Punto Olímpica and Carhuaz. **Transportes Andino** (☑78-2994;
Buenos Aires s/n) has a Lima-bound bus at 4am (S50, 16 hours).

Combis for San Luis (S5, one hour) depart from Bolognesi at Buenos Aires, one block
east of the plaza, from where you can catch passing buses to Pomabamba (Chavin Express, S15, four hours), Huaraz (Transportes El Veloz, S25, five hours) or Lima (Chavin
Express, S45, 12 hours).

weary hikers on the outskirts of town. These may make up for the fact that hot showers aren't ubiquitous in town. It's sometimes possible to arrange trekking guides from here – ask at your hotel. There is a Visa/Plus ATM at Banco de la Nación (Huamachuco, cuadra 5) and internet is available around town.

The next town along toward San Luis or Huari, Piscobamba, has decent views of the mountains and that's about it.

Pomabamba has a better range of accommodations compared to other Cordillera Blanca mountain towns. The best budget spot is Hospedaje Los Begonias (45-1057; lasbegonias_20@yahoo.es; Huamachuco 274; s/d S25/45, s/d/tr without bathroom S20/40/60) in a charming colonial house with a lush entryway and a large hardwood balcony. Rooms follow suit with great hardwood floors and private baths with hot showers; the whole operation is overseen by one of the most hospitable couples in the Cordilleras. They've opened a less atmospheric annex a few doors down, but rooms are just as good. For swankier digs, head up the steep set of steps from the plaza to Hotel Mirador (45-1067; cnr Moquequa & Centenario; s/d S40/70,` s/d without bath S30/50), with cozy, hotel-level rooms, a restaurant and spacious views over the plaza and surrounding mountains. The cheapest is the genial Alojamiento Estrada (50-4615; Huaraz 209; s/d without bathroom S15/30), behind the Plaza de Armas church, with a small courtyard and a hands-on owner who definitely subscribes to the cleanli-ness-is-next-to-godliness theory (she tri… to dust off our road-weary bag before v… entered the room). She'll dote on you wi… grandmotherly curiosity as well, a welcon… turn of events from some of the gruff rece… tions travelers receive outside Huaraz. H… water is available with an hour's notice.

…step up the budget scale but down the hos… tality hierarchy is Hostal Leo (97-144-32… Peru s/n; s/d S25/30), on the plaza itself, wi… good-value rooms boasting gaudy but com… bedspreads and private bathrooms. Odd… hot water is only available in the commun… bathrooms.

Miky's Pollería (Huamachuco 330; ¼ chick… S9) does decent pollo a la brasa (rotisser… chicken) and better fries than most. Davi… David (Huaraz 269; menús S5) has local reg… lars and a respectable daytime menú.

All buses to Huaraz and Lima leave fro… Plaza de Armas or just off it on Huara… Chavin Express (63-1779; Huaraz 452) go… to Lima (S50, 18 hours) twice a day at 5a… and 1pm via Hauri. El Solitario (51-442… Centenario 285) has a 6am Lima bus (S55) vi… Huari (S25) on Sunday, Monday, Thursda… and Friday. Either can drop you in Chav… de Huántar (S30, nine hours). Transporte… Renzo (45-1088; Huaraz 430) heads to Hua… az (S35, eight hours) via Yanama (S10, 3… hours) at 8:45am and 7pm daily. Likewis… Transportes El Veloz (94-303-6951; Per… s/n) does the same route at 8:45am, 6p… and 6:45pm.

Combis go to Sihuas and Piscobamb… daily from the town center.

Northern Highlands

Includes »

Best Places to Eat

- » Magredana (p411)
- » La Patarashca (p433)
- » La Olla de Barro (p429)
- » La Casa de Seizo (p429)
- » El Tejado (p420)

Best Places to Stay

- » Posada del Purhuay (p409)
- » Gocta Andes Lodge (p423)
- » Kentitambo (p426)
- » Estancia Chillo (p424)
- » Pumarinri Amazon Lodge (p432)

Why Go?

Vast tracts of unexplored jungle and mist-shrouded mountain ranges guard the secrets of the northern highlands like a suspicious custodian. Here, Andean peaks and a blanket of luxuriant forests stretch from the coast all the way to the deepest Amazonian jungles. Interspersed with the relics of Inca kings and the jungle-encrusted ruins of cloud-forest-dwelling warriors, connections to these outposts are just emerging from their infancy.

Cajamarca's cobbled streets testify to the beginning of the end of the once-powerful Inca empire, and remnants of the work of these famed Andean masons still remain. The hazy forests of Chachapoyas have only recently revealed their archaeological bounty: the staggering stone fortress of Kuélap, which clings for dear life to a craggy limestone peak. At the jungle gateway of Tarapoto, the Amazon waits patiently on the periphery, as it has for centuries, endowed with a cornucopia of wildlife and exquisite good looks.

When to Go?
Cajamarca

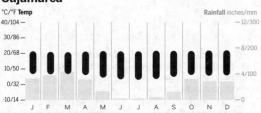

Jan–Apr Rain-soaked but vibrantly lush and full of life with waterfalls in full-gushing glory.

Feb & Mar Let the rowdy mayhem commence: Carnival is on in Cajamarca.

Jun–Oct The rains – and the landslides – are a thing of the past. Enjoy the sunshine.

Cajamarca

📞 076 / POP 146,000 / ELEV 2750M

The most important town in the northern highlands, Cajamarca is a dainty colonial metropolis with a fierce will cradled in a languid valley and stonewalled by brawny mountains in every direction. Descending into the vale by road, Cajamarca's mushroom field of red-tile-roofed abodes surely confesses a secret desire to cling to its village roots. Fertile farmland carpets the entire valley and Cajamarca's streets belong as much to the wide-brimmed-hat-wielding *campesinos* (peasants) bundled in brightly colored scarves, as the young city slickers who frequent the boutique restaurants and bars. In the colonial center, majestic churches border the capacious Plaza de Armas. From here, once-decadent baroque man-sions spread out in concentric circles alo[ng] the cobbled streets, many enclosing ethere[al] hotels and fine restaurants.

Things have changed slowly here. On[ly] recently has the Yanacocha gold mine (s[ee] the boxed text) injected Cajamarca with a[n] avalanche of cash, a steady stream of mo[ney-] eyed engineers and a heaping dose of unru[ly] discontent.

History

In about 1460, the Incas conquered the loc[al] Cajamarca populace and Cajamarca evolve[d] into a major city on the Inca Andean hig[h-] way linking Cuzco and Quito.

After the death of the Inca Huayna Capa[c] in 1525, the remaining Inca empire, whic[h] then stretched from southern Colombia t[o] central Chile, was pragmatically divided be-tween his sons, with Atahualpa ruling th[e] north and Huascar the south. Obviously n[ot]

THERE'S GOLD IN THEM THERE HILLS

The hills outside Cajamarca are laced with gold. Tonnes of it – but don't reach for your shovel and pan just yet, as this gold is not found in the kind of golden nuggets that set prospectors' eyes ablaze. It's 'invisible gold,' vast quantities of minuscule specks that require advanced and noxious mining techniques to be pried out of their earthly ore.

The Yanacocha mine, with a majority stake owned by Denver-based Newmont Mining Corporation, has quarried open pits in the countryside surrounding Cajamarca, becoming one of the most productive gold mines in the world. More than US$7 billion worth of the shiny stuff has been extracted so far. That, combined with plenty of new jobs and an influx of international engineers into Cajamarca, has meant a surge in wealth for the region – but for many locals, all that glitters is not gold.

According to a joint investigation by the *New York Times* and the PBS program *Frontline World* (a US news-magazine on public TV), the history of the mine is clouded by charges of corruption.

In 2000, a large spill of toxic mercury raised doubts about Yanacocha's priorities: gold over safety seemed to be the marching cry. The mine makes its profits by washing vast quantities of mountainside with cyanide solution, a hazardous technique that utilizes masses of water that local farmers also depend on. An internal environmental audit carried out by the company in 2004 verified villagers' observations that water supplies were being contaminated and fish stocks were disappearing.

In the autumn of 2004, disillusioned *campesinos* (peasants) rallied against the opening of a new mine in the area of Quilish, and clashed violently with the police employed to protect the mine's interests. After weeks of conflict, the company eventually gave in and has since re-evaluated its priorities and improved its safety and environmental record.

In an attempt to quell future mining protests, President Ollanta Humala's administration passed the Prior Consultation Law in 2012, which requires mining companies to negotiate with local communities before initiating any new extraction projects. Nevertheless, trouble brewed that same year when Newmont's proposed US$4.8 billion Conga gold and copper mine project set Cajamarca off again. Despite claims from Newmont that the project will create up to 7000 jobs in the region, inject US$50 billion into the local economy and not harm the region's watersheds, locals weren't buying it. Under the slogan 'Conga No Va' (roughly translated as 'No to Conga!'), a far more serious general regional strike that lasted months brought days of daily marches and protests throughout Cajamarca, Celendín and the surrounding region, resulting in at least eight dead; though it officially ended when a two-month State of Emergency was declared in July 2012, thing weren't back to 'normal' until September, and off and on strikes continued at time of writing.

With nearly 50% of Cajamarca's territory concessioned to mining companies, the majority of which encompass many river sources, this is a prominent issue that doesn't look to disappear anytime soon.

veryone was in concord, as civil war soon roke out and in 1532 Atahualpa and his victorious troops marched southward toward uzco to take complete control of the empire. Parked at Cajamarca to rest for a few ays, the Inca emperor was camped at the atural thermal springs, known today as Los años del Inca, when he heard the news that he Spanish were nearby.

Francisco Pizarro and his force of 168 paniards arrived in Cajamarca on November 15, 1532, to a deserted city; most of its 000 inhabitants were with Atahualpa at is hot-springs encampment. The Spaniards

spent an anxious night, fully aware that they were severely outnumbered by the nearby Inca troops, who were estimated to be between 40,000 and 80,000. The Spaniards plotted to entice Atahualpa into the plaza and, at a pre-arranged signal, capture the Inca should the opportunity present itself.

Upon Atahualpa's arrival, he ordered most of his troops to stay outside while he entered the plaza with a retinue of nobles and about 6000 men armed with slings and hand axes. He was met by the Spanish friar Vicente de Valverde, who attempted to explain his position as a man of God and

Cajamarca

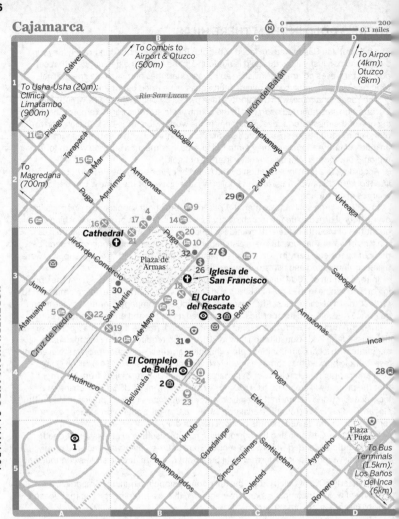

To Combis to
Airport & Otuzco
(500m)

To Airpor
(4km);
Otuzco
(8km)

To Usha-Usha (20m);
Clínica
Limatambo
(900m)

Río San Lucas

To
Magredana
(700m)

Cathedral

Plaza de
Armas

Iglesia de
San Francisco

El Cuarto
del Rescate

El Complejo
de Belén

Plaza
A Puga

To Bus
Terminals
(1.5km);
Los Baños
del Inca
(6km)

presented the Inca with a Bible. Reputedly, Atahualpa angrily threw the book to the ground and Valverde needed little more justification to sound the attack.

Cannons were fired and the Spanish cavalry attacked Atahualpa and his troops. The indigenous people were terrified and bewildered by the fearsome onslaught of never-before-seen cannons and horses. Their small hand axes and slings were no match for the well-armored Spaniards, who swung razor-sharp swords from the advantageous height of horseback to slaughter 7000 indigenous people and capture Atahualpa. The small

band of Spaniards was now literally con quistadors (conquerors).

Atahualpa soon became aware of the Spaniards' lust for gold and offered to fill large room in the town once with gold an twice with silver in return for his freedom The Spanish agreed and slowly the gold an silver began pouring into Cajamarca. Near a year later the ransom was complete about 6000kg of gold and 12,000kg of silve had been melted down into gold and silve bullion. At today's prices, this ransom woul be worth almost S180 million, but the artis tic value of the ornaments and implement

Cajamarca

...at were melted down to create the bullion impossible to estimate.

Atahualpa, suspecting he was not going to e released, sent desperate messages to his llowers in Quito to come to Cajamarca and scue him. The Spaniards, panic-stricken y these messages, sentenced Atahualpa to eath. On July 26, 1533, Atahualpa was led ut to the center of the Cajamarca plaza to e burned at the stake. At the last hour, Ata-ualpa 'accepted' baptism and, as a reward, is sentence was changed to a quicker death y strangulation.

Most of the great stone Inca buildings in ajamarca were torn down and the stones sed in the construction of Spanish homes nd churches. The great plaza where Ata-ualpa was captured and later killed was in oughly the same location as today's Plaza e Armas. The Ransom Chamber, or El 'uarto del Rescate, where Atahualpa was nprisoned, is the only Inca building still tanding.

Sights

Cajamarca's genial Plaza de Armas has a well-kept topiary garden with hedges trimmed into the shape of llamas and other Andean animals. The fine central **fountain** dates from 1692 and commemorates the bicentenary of Columbus' landing in the Americas. Come evening, the town's inhabitants congregate in the plaza to stroll and mull over the important events of the day – a popular pastime in this area of northern Peru.

Two churches face the plaza: the cathedral and the Iglesia de San Francisco. Both are often imaginatively illuminated in the evenings, especially on weekends.

El Complejo de Belén HISTORIC BUILDING
(adult/student S5/2; ⊙9am-1pm & 3-6pm Tue-Sat, 9am-1pm Sun) Construction of this sprawling colonial complex, church and hospital of Belén, made entirely from volcanic rock, occurred between 1627 and 1774. The hospital was run by nuns and 31 tiny, cell-like

bedrooms line the walls of the T-shaped building. The facade here has a fascinating statue of a woman with four breasts – it was carved by local artisans and supposedly represents an affliction (supernumerary nipples, that is) commonly found in one of the nearby towns.

The baroque church next door is one of Cajamarca's finest and has a prominent cupola and a well-carved pulpit. Among several interesting wood carvings, one extremely tired-looking Christ sits cross-legged on his throne, propping up his chin with a double-jointed wrist and looking as though he could do with a pisco sour after a hard day's miracle working. Look out for the oversized cherubs supporting the elaborate centerpiece, which represents the weight of heaven. The outside walls of the church are lavishly decorated. The tourist office is housed in one of the interior complex rooms.

Iglesia de San Francisco
CHURCH, MUSEUM

(admission S3; ⊙9am-noon & 4-6pm Mon-Fri) Iglesia de San Francisco's belfries were finished in the 20th century – too late for the Spanish Crown to collect its tax. Inside are elaborate stone carvings and decadent altars, and at the entrance is an interesting collection of dangling silver sacred hearts. Visit the church's small **Museo de Arte Religioso** (Religious Art Museum) to see 17th-century religious paintings done by indigenous artists and the creepy **catacombs**, where many monks lie buried. The intricately sculpted **Capilla de la Dolorosa** to the right of the nave is considered one of the finest chapels in the city.

El Cuarto del Rescate
RUIN

(⊙9am-1pm & 3-6pm Tue-Sat, 9am-1pm Sun) The Ransom Chamber is the only Inca building still standing in Cajamarca. Although it's called the Ransom Chamber, the room shown to visitors is actually where Atahualpa was imprisoned, not where the ransom was stored. The small room has three trapezoidal doorways and a few similarly shaped niches in the inner walls – signature Inca construction. Although well built, the chamber does not compare with the Inca buildings in the Cuzco area. In the entrance to the site are a couple of modern paintings depicting Atahualpa's capture and imprisonment. The stone of the building is weathered and has only recently been covered by a large protective dome.

The S5 ticket to El Cuarto del Rescate includes El Complejo de Belén and Museo de Etnografía if they are all visited on the same day.

Cathedral
CHUR

(⊙7-8am & 6:30-7:30pm Mon-Sat, 7-8am, ? 11am & 6:30-7:30pm Sun) The Catedral de C jamarca is a squat building that was beg in the late 17th century and only recen finished. Like most of Cajamarca's churche this cathedral has no belfry. This is becau the Spanish Crown levied a tax on finish churches and so the belfries were not bui leaving the church unfinished and there avoiding the tax. Unfortunately, due to 2010 robbery of the crowns of some sain it is no longer open outside mass.

Museo de Arqueológico & Etnografía
MUSE

(⊙9am-1pm & 3-6pm Tue-Sat, 9am-1pm Sun) Th small, sparsely filled museum housed i side the Antigua Hospital de Mujeres, just few meters from El Complejo de Belén, h limited exhibits of local costumes and clot ing, domestic and agricultural implemen musical instruments and crafts made fro wood, bone, leather and stone, as well other examples of Cajamarca culture. Larg scale photographs and modern art inte pretations illustrate traditional lives of th district's farmers.

Cerro Santa Apolonia
LOOKO

(admission S1; ⊙7:30am-6pm) This garde covered viewpoint, overlooking the city fro the southwest, is a prominent Cajamarc landmark. It is easily reached by climbing th stairs at the end of Calle 2 de Mayo and wal ing paths spiral around the whole hilltop. Th pre-Hispanic carved rocks at the summit a mainly from the Inca period, but some a thought to originally date back to the Chaví period. One of the rocks, which is known a the Seat of the Inca, has a shape that sugges a throne, and the Inca (king) is said to hav reviewed his troops from this point.

👉 Tours & Guides

Tour companies provide information an inexpensive guided tours of the city and it surroundings. The companies claim to hav English-speaking guides, but only a few real ly pass muster. Tours to Cumbe Mayo (S20 Los Baños del Inca (S15), Granja Porcó (S20) and Ventanillas de Otuzco (S15) ar the most popular. Tack on an extra S10 pe

CARNAVAL CAJAMARCA

The Peru-wide pageantry of Carnaval is celebrated at the beginning of Lent, usually in February. Not all Carnavals are created equal, however. Ask any Peruvian where the wildest celebrations are at, and Cajamarca will invariably come out trumps.

Preparations begin months in advance; sometimes, no sooner have Carnaval celebrations wound down than planning for the following year begins. Cajamarcans take their celebrations seriously. The festival is nine days of dancing, eating, singing, partying, costumes, parades and general rowdy mayhem. It's also a particularly wet affair and water fights here are worse (or better, depending on your point of view) than you'd encounter elsewhere. Local teenagers don't necessarily limit themselves to soaking one another with water – paint, oil and other unsightly liquids have all been reported.

Hotels fill up weeks beforehand, prices skyrocket and hundreds of people end up sleeping in the plaza. Considering it's one of the most rambunctious festivals in Peru, it certainly seems worth it.

p for an English guide. The companies ll often pool tours. The following agencies e well-regarded by travelers.

larin Tours TOURS
)36-6829; www.clarintours.com; Jirón del Batán 5; ⊙9:30am-noon & 3:30-7pm)

ega Tours TOURS
)34-1876; www.megatours.org; Puga 691; ⊙8am-m)

✦ Festivals & Events

arnaval FESTIVAL
ne Carnaval festivities here are reputed be one of the most popular and rowdy ents in the country (see p409). They're ld in the last few days before Lent.

🛏 Sleeping

otel rates (and other prices) rise during stivals and special events and are also usully slightly higher in the dry season (May to eptember). Prices given here are for May to eptember.

TOP CHOICE Posada del Purhuay HISTORIC HOTEL **$$$**
)46-7028; www.posadapurhuay.com.pe; Km 4.5 arretera Porcón; s/d incl breakfast S240/300; ◉) This luxurious restored 1822 hacinda sitting on 23 hectares off the road to ranja Porcón is a true find. The relaxing rounds are meticulously groomed, leading a lovely colonial hotel offering discerning rvice and a step-back-in-time appeal. Spacious rooms, chock-full of antiquated charm nd period furnishings, surround an impeccable courtyard and fountain. Family getaay? Check. Tuck-yourself-away romantic etreat? Check.

TOP CHOICE Hospedaje Las Jazmines HISTORIC INN **$$**
(36-1812; www.hospedajelosjazmines.com.pe; Amazonas 775; s/d S50/80, without bathroom S40/60; @🤍) In a land of ubiquitous colonial courtyards, this German-run inn is a value standout for its lush version and even more extensive back gardens. Comfy rooms offer hot water and cable TV, some with exposed brick walls. The best thing about it, however, is the in-house Espresso Bar independently run by the folks at Heladería Holanda, which does the best coffee/espresso in town and has become a small traveler hangout and work space. The downside is their lack of mastering reservations or answering emails, but we suspect inevitable change.

Hostal Casona del Inca HISTORIC HOTEL **$$**
(36-7524; www.casonadelincaperu.com; Calle 2 de Mayo 458-460; s/d/tr incl breakfast S100/150/180; @🤍) You might begin questioning your sobriety when you notice that all the brightly painted walls of this plazaside colonial building seem to be on a slight angle. Don't worry – they are. The aged carnival fun-house appearance makes it justifiably popular with gringos and just adds to the charm, however. The rooms follow in the footsteps of this slightly wonky theme and are clean and cozy, some with tiny showers and insufficient shower curtains, so peek around. And don't expect the creaky old floors to afford a sleep in, but that is hardly unique.

El Cabildo HISTORIC HOTEL **$$**
(36-7025; www.cabildo.com; Junín 1062; s/d/tr incl breakfast S100/130; @🤍) One of the town's best-value sleeping options, this huge

historic mansion conceals an eclectic collection of well-maintained and graceful older rooms. Some of the rooms come with split levels and all are filled with plenty of gleaming wood and tasteful decorations. At the mansion's heart, a gorgeous courtyard area is filled with greenery, a fountain and a cacophony of sculptures and statues.

Hotel Cajamarca
HISTORIC HOTEL **$$**

(📞36-2532; www.hotelcajamarca.com.pe; Calle 2 de Mayo 311; s/d incl breakfast S130/180; @🤶) All the rooms in this presentable, spacious hotel in a colonial house have undergone a makeover that includes new, modern bathrooms and cozy new beds. There's a wonderful courtyard and the recommended restaurant occasionally hosts live music. A few rooms in the back have a woodsier feel and fluent English is spoken when the owner's wife is present. The in-house travel agency can arrange all excursions.

El Portal del Marques
HISTORIC HOTEL **$$$**

(📞34-3999; www.portaldelmarques.com; Jirón del Comercio 644; s/d incl breakfast S157/192; @🤶) Set around an immaculately groomed garden, this restored colonial mansion has standard carpeted rooms with flat-screen TVs, minifridges and in-room safes. The mood lighting in the garden makes it a romantic evening hangout.

Los Pinos Inn
HISTORIC HOTEL **$$**

(📞36-5992; www.lospinosinn.com; La Mar 521; s/d incl breakfast S100/140; @🤶) This majestic and drafty colonial building, dripping in marble staircases, intricate tile work and strewn with both period antiques and replicas, looks like a museum yet manages to refrain from being ostentatious. Wide hallways with enormous gilded mirrors lead to a variety of large and varied rooms, all with solid beds. The two-bedroom suite, a fabulous deal for two couples traveling together, offers mountain views and a stately common area.

Hostal Laguna Seca
RESORT **$$$**

(📞58-4300; www.lagunaseca.com.pe; s/d incl breakfast & airport transfer S319/393; ✳@🤶🏊) Situated 6km from Cajamarca near Los Baños del Inca, this Swiss/Peruvian-owned resort is run long-distance from Lima and features rooms boasting large bathrooms with deep tubs for soaking and all the mod cons; much nicer executive rooms (S444) offer king-sized beds. Horseback riding (per hour S30) and bicycle rental (per hour S9) are available and massages and spa health treatments pamper the hedonists amo us. It all falls *just* on the happy side of t cheesy resort teeter-totter.

Hostal Plaza
HISTORIC HOTE

(📞36-2058; Puga 669; s/d/tr S30/50/70, with bathroom S15/30/40; 🤶) This is the top bud choice in a rambling old colonial mansi with two interior courtyards (one with fountain surrounded by commercial esta lishments). The 10 good-value private room are colorfully decorated with kitschy obje and the occasional stuffed animal, cable and offer 24-hour hot water, whereas t flow is only steamy in the communal ba rooms in the mornings and evenings.

Las Americas Hotel
BUSINESS HOTEL

(📞36-3951; www.lasamericashotel.com.pe; Ama nas 622; s/d incl breakfast S155/205; @🤶) Brea ing away from the 'cozy colonial hotel' pac this contemporary property is all busine It has a central atrium filled with plenty plants, a business center, salon and an evator. The 38 rooms are all carpeted a have minifridges, cable TV and excelle mattresses; three of them have Jacuzzi tu and six have balconies, so it pays to che around. A restaurant provides room servi and there's a criminally underused rooft terrace with plaza and church views.

Hotel Casa Blanca
HISTORIC HOTEL

(📞36-2141; www.hotelcasablancaperu.com; Ca 2 de Mayo 446; s/d/tr incl breakfast S100/140/18 @🤶) This dignified old structure on t Plaza de Armas exudes plenty of charact most notably with its trippy stained-gla hovering lobby. Quarters range from po to good-sized and come with cable TV, ren vated bathrooms and minifridge. They kee it oddly dark, though, so try to snag a roo between 205 and 213, which surround open-air rooftop that receives sunlight.

Casa Mirita
HOMESTA

(📞36-9361; www.casa-mirita.blogspot.com; Cáce 1337; s without bathroom S15, r S25; @) This dea simple homestay is a S2 *mototaxi* ride to residential neighborhood southeast of th center. It's an interesting choice for long-sta ers or those looking to be completely off th gringo grid. Two sisters, Mirita, the cook, an Vicki, a tourism official, run the show. Roon are rustic and there's a kitchen for use, meals cost S5. There is an experience to b had here, but it's a hike into an area to whic few (if any!) gringos go.

stal Jusovi
HOTEL $

36-2920; hostaljosuvicajamarca@hotmail.com; nazonas 637; s/d/tr S40/50/60; ☎) Boasting odest rooms that are kept perfectly clean, sovi is a decent budget option. Some oms have cable TV and the rooftop terrace ith views of the cathedral spire is a wel- me addition. Wi-fi in lobby only.

🍴 Eating

OP
HOICE Magredana
FUSION $$

ara Macdougal 140-144; mains S29-40; ⊙closed on, Sun dinner) The most creative menu in e Peruvian Andes comes courtesy of an ish chef who has cooked in 11 countries, ot to mention toured the world with Van Morrison for nearly a decade. The menu eflects this itinerary, with influences from idia, Spain, Thailand and his native Ireland eeping into the eclectic range of sophisti- ited choices. The house chicken – stuffed ith pork, pistachios and herbs, rolled in ba- on and finished with a red wine and tarra- on sauce – is a doozy. The ambience is a bit aphazard, but the food immediately erases nose quirks on arrival. Shaun, the chef, has three-year plan, so get there before 2014.

Heladería Holanda
DESSERTS $

www.heladosholanda.com.pe; Puga 657; ice cream 2-4) Don't miss the tiny entrance on the own's Plaza de Armas; it opens into a large, utch-orange cafe selling what might be the est ice cream in northern Peru. The staff ill shower you with samples of the 20 or o changing flavors, the best of which are ocal, and regional fruits that the Dutch wner buys direct from family farms follow- ng a Fair Trade philosophy. In addition to ne sweets, staff members are single moth- rs and the deaf, an ongoing social project tarted by the owner. It has locations at El Quinde Shopping Center and Los Baños del nca as well.

Querubino
PERUVIAN $$

Puga 589; mains S17-36; ⊙closed Tue) Querubino s a classy spot with real chefs doing upscale ersions of Peruvian classics as well as the occasional creative curveball and season- lly changing specials. The menu is domi- ated by meat and seafood dishes, but try he off menu spaghetti *a la huancaina,* a vondrous invention of fresh pasta doused n *huancaina* sauce (fresh white cheese, *aji imarillo*) with *lomo fino* (tenderloin) – it's reamy, rich and delicious.

Don Paco
PERUVIAN $$

(Puga 726; meals S12-20; ⊙closed Mon) Tucked away near the plaza, Don Paco has a big fol- lowing among both residents and expats. There's something for everyone here, in- cluding typical breakfasts and great rendi- tions of Peruvian favorites, as well as more sophisticated *novocaxamarquino* (new Cajamarcan) fare such as chicken cordon bleu with Andean ham and local cheese in a pomegranate sauce and a recommended duck breast with *sauco* (elderberry) sauce.

Sanguchon.com
FAST FOOD/BAR $

(www.sanguchon.com.pe; Junín 1137; sandwiches S5.90-13.50; ⊙6pm-midnight; ☎) This wildly popular hipster hamburger and sandwich joint features an extensive menu of ridicu- lous handheld drunken eats along with a few veggie choices (with an explanation as to what 'vegetarian' means). The tasty food is very convenient as it is a rowdy bar as well.

Chifa Hong Kong
CHINESE $$

(Jirón del Batán 133; mains S9.50-27) If you're thinking this is a step up from the usual Chi- nese restaurants that abound in Peru, you'd be right – the chef hails from Canton and is working on two decades of experience with stir-fries, noodles and the like. The extensive menu weighs heavily with chicken, beef, pork and duck and everything is damn tasty.

Cascanuez Café Bar
CAFE $

(Puga 554; mains S6-26; ⊙from 7:30am; ☎) A nice cafe for breakfast and light meals but most folks flock here for a decadent means to their sweet tooth ends – nine varieties of *tres leches* cake alone (try chocolate!).

El Marengo
PIZZERIA $

(Junín 1201; pizza S11.50-25.50; ⊙7-11pm) The wood-fired brick oven heats the entirety of this tiny pizzeria and the best pie in town comes out. Squeeze in, get a pitcher of san- gria and call it a night.

El Quinde Shopping Center
SELF-CATERING $

(www.elquinde.com; Av Hoyos Rubio, cuadra 7; ⊙10am-10pm) This shopping center has the closest supermarket to town (Metro), about 2.5km north of the Plaza de Armas.

🍷 Drinking

TOP
CHOICE Usha-Usha
BAR

(Puga 142; admission S5; ⊙closed Sun & Mon) For something a little more intimate, this place is a graffiti-covered, hole-in-the-wall dive bar run by an eccentric local musician Jaime Valera, who has managed to cultivate a heap of charisma in these four walls. He sings his heart out with his musician friends and you walk out with an unforgettable travel memory.

Gruta 100 COCKTAIL BAR
(cnr Santisteban & Belén; ⊘closed Sun & Mon) A cavernous hotspot full of tattered retro furniture and multiple rooms for hiding out with your pisco sours. There's live music on Fridays in an adjacent room with a wraparound balcony.

 Shopping

Small shops selling local and Peruvian crafts line the stairwells along Calle 2 de Mayo south of Junín.

Colors & Creations
(Belén 628; ⊘9am-1pm & 3-7pm Mon-Sat, 10am-1pm & 3-6pm Sun) An artisan-owned-and-run cooperative selling excellent-quality crafts.

 Information

There's internet access practically on every block.

Emergency
Policía de Turismo (Tourist Police, Politur; Jirón del Comercio 1013; ⊘7:45am-1pm & 5-8pm) Special force dealing with crimes against tourists.
Policía Nacional (☑36-2165; cnr Puga & Ayacucho; ⊘24hr) Toward the eastern part of town.

Medical Services
Clínica Limatambo (www.limatambo.com.pe; Puno 265; ⊘24hr) Has the best medical service; west of town.

Money
Interbank (☑36-2460; Calle 2 de Mayo 546) Changes traveler's checks and has an ATM accepting Visa and MasterCard.
Scotiabank (☑Amazonas 750) Changes traveler's checks and has an ATM accepting Visa and MasterCard.

Post
Serpost (Apurimac 626)

Tourist Information
Dirección de Turismo (☑36-2997; www.regioncajamarca.gob.pe; El Complejo de Belén; ⊘7:30am-1pm & 2:30-5pm Mon-Fri) Tourist information and local map for sale (S1.50). It also operates a small **info booth** (⊘8:30am-12:30pm & 3:30-5:30pm Mon-Fri) next to Iglesia de San Francisco.

 Getting There & Away

Air
Schedules are subject to change, as well as occasional cancellations and delays, so reconfirm and arrive early at the airport (CJA), about 4km outside town.
LC Perú (☑36-3115; www.lcperu.pe; Jirón del Comercio 1024) flies this route most economically, with two daily flights leaving Lima for Cajamarca at 5:10am and 3:10pm and returning at 7:15am and 5:15am.
LAN (☑36-7441; www.lan.com; Jirón del Comercio 832) has three flights between Lima and Cajamarca, leaving the capital at 5:40am, 10:30am and 3:30pm, returning from Cajamarca at 7:35am, 12:40pm and 4:50pm.

Bus
Cajamarca continues its ancient role as a crossroads, with buses heading to all four points of the compass. Most bus terminals are close to *cuadra* (block) 3 of Atahualpa, about 1.5km southeast of the center (not to be confused with the Atahualpa in the town center), on the road to Los Baños del Inca.

The major route is westbound to the Panamericana near Pacasmayo on the coast, then north to Chiclayo (eight hours) or south to Trujillo (eight hours) and Lima (14 hours).

The southbound road is the old route to Trujillo (at least 15 hours) via Cajabamba (4½ hours) and Huamachuco (7½ hours). For Huamachuco and on to Trujillo, change at Cajabamba. The trip to Trujillo takes two or three times longer on this rough dirt road than it does along the newer paved road via Pacasmayo, although the old route is only 60km longer. The scenery is prettier on the longer route, but most buses are less comfortable and less frequent beyond Cajabamba.

The rough northbound road to Chota (five hours) passes through wild and attractive countryside via Bambamarca, which has a busy market on Sunday morning. Buses run from Chota to Chiclayo along a rough road.

The staggeringly scenic eastbound road winds to Celendín (p419), then bumps its way across the Andes, past Chachapoyas and down into the Amazon lowlands.

Cial (☑36-8701; www.expresocial.com; Atahualpa 684) Dual economical/*bus-cama* (bed bus) buses to Lima at 6pm (Monday to Saturday) and 5pm (Sunday).
Civa (☑36-1460; www.civa.com.pe; Ayacucho 753) Good buses to Lima at 6:30pm.
Cruz del Sur (☑36-2024; www.cruzdelsur.com.pe; Atahualpa 844) Nice *bus-cama* to Lima at 7pm.
Línea (☑36-6100; Atahualpa 306) The most comfortable Lima-bound *bus-camas* at 6pm and 6:30pm. Chiclayo departures at 10:45am,

CAJAMARCA BUSES

DESTINATION	COST (S)	DURATION (HR)
Bambamarca	15	3½
Cajabamba	10-20	4
Celendín	10	3½
Chachapoyas	50	12-13
Chiclayo	20-45	6
Chota	15-20	4
Huamachuco	20	6
Leimebamba	35	8
Lima	80-130	16
Piura	45	9
Trujillo	20-40	6

:30pm, 10:50pm and 11pm as well as Trujillo : 10:30am, 1pm, 10pm, 10:15pm, 10:30pm and):40pm. It also has a ticket office on the Plaza e Armas.

oyal Palace's (✆34-3063; Reyna Farge 130) ervices to Celendín at 9:30am and 12:30pm; heap buses to Trujillo (10pm) and Lima (6pm, :30pm and 8pm); and Cajabamba at 11pm.

epsa (✆36-3306; www.tepsa.com.pe; Sucre 22) Comfortable *bus-cama* Lima service at pm.

our Atahualpa (✆96-491-6371; Atahualpa 99) Buses to Cajabamba at 2am and 11am, elendín at 4:30am and 1pm, Chota at 10am via ambamarca.

ransportes Chiclayo (✆36-4628; www. ansporteschiclayo.com; Atahualpa 283) Has Chiclayo-bound bus at 11pm which is good for ansferring north to Mancorá or Tumbes.

ransportes Horna (✆36-3218; www.trans orteshorna.pe; Atahualpa 312) Five buses day to Trujillo between 8am and 11pm; two epartures to Cajabamba at 12:30am and :30am; and one daily departure at 2:30am to luamachuco.

ransportes Rojas (✆34-0548; Atahualpa 09) Services to Cajabamba at 2am, 9am, am, 11am, 2pm and 4pm; Celendín at 3pm and hota via Bambamarca at 7pm.

urismo Dias (✆34-4322; www.turdias.com; tahualpa 307) Buses to Trujillo at 10am, :15pm, 10pm and 11pm; Chiclayo at 10:30am, :45pm and 9:45pm; and a direct bus to Piura t 10:30pm, the best option for getting to Mancorá. Buses depart from its terminal at Vía le Evitamiento 1370.

Virgen del Carmen (✆98-391-5869; Atahualpa 33-A) Departs at 4am daily for Chachapoyas ia Celendín and Leimebamba.

Combis for Ventanillas de Otuzco (S1, 20 minutes) leave from the corner of Tayabambo and Los Gladiolos, 500m north along Tarapaca in the market district. These pass the airport (S0.50), though taking a taxi is much faster (S7).

'A' combis (minibuses) for Los Baños del Inca (S1, 25 minutes) leave frequently along Sabogal, near Calle 2 de Mayo.

Around Cajamarca

Places of interest around Cajamarca can be reached by public transportation, on foot, by taxi or with a guided tour. Tour agencies pool their clients to form a group for any trip, although more expensive individual outings can be arranged.

LOS BAÑOS DEL INCA

Atahualpa was camped by these natural **hot springs** (☺5am-8pm) when Pizarro arrived, hence the name. Now you can take a dip in the same pools that an Inca king used to bathe his war wounds – though the pools have probably been cleaned since then. Set around flourishing grounds with sculpted shrubbery, this attractive compound has hot water channeled into private cubicles (S4 to S6 per 30 minutes), some large enough for up to six people at a time. Dip into the public pool (S3), which is cleaned on Monday and Friday; steam rooms and massages are available for S10 and S20 each. This place gets hundreds of visitors daily, so it's best to come in the morning to avoid the rush. There's a **Complejo Recreativo** (admission S1; ☺8am-8pm) opposite the main bath complex that has swimming pools, a children's playground and 'waterslides of the Incas,' which are a big hit with kids, but were indefinitely closed for renovation when we were soaking. The *baños* (baths) are 6km from Cajamarca and have a few hotel possibilities (p409). *Combis* for Los Baños del Inca (S1, 25 minutes) leave from Sabogal in Cajamarca; or take an organized tour from Cajamarca (S15). Bring your own towel as none are provided, though you may purchase one from a few entrepreneurial vendors. Afterwards, pop across the street for a sweet cool down at Heladería Holanda (p411).

CUMBE MAYO

About 20km southwest of Cajamarca, Cumbe Mayo (derived from the Quechua *kumpi mayo*, meaning 'well-made water channel') is an astounding feat of pre-Inca engineering. These perfectly smooth aqueducts were carved around 2000 years ago and zigzag at right angles for 9km, all for a purpose that is as yet unclear, since Cajamarca has an abundant water supply. Other rock formations are carved to look like altars and thrones. Nearby caves contain petroglyphs, including some that resemble wooly mammoths. The countryside is high, windswept and slightly eerie. Superstitious stories are told about the area's eroded rock formations, which look like groups of shrouded mountain climbers.

The site can be reached on foot via a signed road from Cerro Santa Apolonia in Cajamarca. The walk takes about four hours if you take the obvious shortcuts and ask every passerby for directions. Guided bus tours (between S20 and S25) are offered tour companies in Cajamarca; these can be good idea as public transportation to Cumb Mayo is sporadic.

VENTANILLAS DE OTUZCO & COMBAYO

These pre-Inca necropolises have scores funerary niches built into the hillside, hen the name Ventanillas (Windows). Ventan las de Otuzco is in alluring countryside, 8k northeast of Cajamarca, and is easily wal able from either Cajamarca or Los Bañ del Inca (ask for directions). The larger an better-preserved Ventanillas de Combay are 30km away and are best visited on tour from Cajamarca (between S20 an S25). Buses to Ventanillas de Otuzco leav frequently from north of the Plaza de Arma in Cajamarca (S1, 20 minutes).

Cajabamba

076 / POP 14,400 / ELEV 2655M

The old route from Cajamarca to Trujill takes at least 15 hours along 360km of mos ly dirt road via Cajabamba and Huamachu co. Although this route passes through mor interesting scenery and towns than the roa via Pacasmayo, the bus trip is very roug and few tourists come through.

The friendly town of Cajabamba sits on natural ledge overlooking farms and plant tions. Whitewashed houses, red-tiled roo and a striking, bright yellow Plaza de Arma with intricate marble railings lend the plac a colonial aesthetic. The feast of La Virge

---

WORTH A TRIP

MARCAHUAMACHUCO

The massive ruins of the pre-Inca mountain fort of **Marcahuamachuco** (admission free) are situated 10km outside Huamachuco via a track passable only by 4WD or truck. This 2.5km-long site dates from around 400 BC and has tall defensive perimeter walls and interesting circular structures of varying sizes. Marcahuamachuco culture seems to have developed independently of surrounding civilizations of the time. A taxi from Huamachuco can reach within 5km of the site in the dry season (S12), but you'll have to hike along the dirt road the rest of the way. Bring all necessary food and drink with you.

Hostal Colonial (51-1101; Castilla 347; s/d S35/60, tr without bathroom S45;), in a pleasant colonial-style house (no surprises there), is the best place to stay and has a good restaurant downstairs.

Transportes Horna (44-0016; Carrion 1101) has a 4:30pm departure to Cajamarca and multiple daily departures to Trujillo (S25, six hours). **Transportes Los Andes** (44-1555; Pasaje Hospital 109) has 10 departures per day to Cajabamba, where you can switch for additional Cajamarca buses. There are at least three *colectivo* taxis daily to Otuzco, which leave when full from near the plaza (S10, four hours).

el Rosario is celebrated around the first Sunday in October with bullfights, processions, dances and general bucolic carousing, and an interesting cattle market springs up on Mondays. Several sights are within an hour's walk of Cajabamba, including the caverns of **Chivato** and the fetching mountain lagoons of **Ponte** and **Quengococha**. Ask at **Hostal La Casona** (☎35-8285; Bolognesi 720) for information on visiting these sights.

There's a **Banco de la Nación** (Plaza de Armas) here with a Visa/Plus ATM.

Hostal La Casona (☎35-8285; Bolognesi 20; s/d S20/29) gets the ribbon for the top place to stay in town, offering hot showers, cable TV and smallish and cute rooms, several of which have balconies and plaza views.

The food outshines the decor at **Don Lucho** (Prado 227; mains S5-15), just a half block up behind the church. Solid *menús* of the usual Peruvian victuals go for S6 and à la carte dishes are served as well.

Transportes Rojas (☎97-617-1144; Grau 35) has buses to Cajamarca (S10, 4½ hours) at 3am, 5am, 8:30am, 11:30am, 1:30pm and pm. **Transportes Horna** (☎55-1132; Grau 36) has a daily Cajamarca bus (S10, 4½ hours) at 8am as well as 8am and 1:30pm departures to Huamachuco (S10, three hours). **Los Andes** (☎31-5138; Martínez 152) also goes to Huamachuco 10 times a day (S10, 2½ hours).

Celendín

☎076 / POP 16,600 / ELEV 2625M

Easily reached by a partly unpaved road from Cajamarca, Celendín itself is a delightfully sleepy little town that receives few travelers except for those taking the wild and scenic route to Chachapoyas. Celendín is particularly known for high-quality straw hats, which can be bought at its interesting Sunday market. It's an ideal place to observe traditional highland life and interact with local indigenous people, who will certainly take an interest in your unexpected visit.

There's a **Banco de la Nación** (Calle 2 de Mayo 530) here that has a Visa/Plus ATM. The annual fiesta of **La Virgen del Carmen** goes from July 1 to August 6, but the best days for tourists, which include fireworks, procession and bullfighting with matadors from Mexico and Spain in a traditional wooden construction, are from July 28 to August 3.

Hot springs (admission S3) and mud baths will help soothe aching muscles and can be found at Llanguat, reached by a 30-minute drive. You can also take a 7am *combi* from the Plaza de Armas (S5, 45 minutes) on Monday, Wednesday, Friday and Saturday. It returns around noon.

The Dutch-run organization **Proyecto Yannick** (☎77-0590; www.celendinperu.com; Jirón Unión 333) offers volunteer opportunities working with children with Down syndrome, and the English-, German- and Dutch-speaking manager, Susan, also arranges private transportation and tours to the hot springs. Visit the project office for a map and excellent information about hotels, local sites and transport. Susan also rents a **room** (s/d without bathroom S20/25; ☎) in her house just around the corner from the plaza.

Right on the Plaza de Armas, **Hostal Celendín** (☎55-5041; Unión 305; s/d S28.50/43; @☎) has more or less reliable hot water and worn but inviting rooms, a few with balconies and grand plaza views, and a popular restaurant. **Hostal Turistas** (☎55-5047; Gálvez 507; s/d S45/60; ☎) is a new modern choice with nine rooms just around the corner of the plaza.

La Reserva (José Gálvez 420; meals S4-32) is a popular eating choice, with multilevel seating and a warm ambience. **Carbon & Leña** (☎80-5736; Calle 2 de Mayo 416; meals S4-28; ⊙5-11pm) uses, as its name indicates, charcoal and wood fires to roast mainly chicken and pizza but can throw down special meat dishes, such as *chancho con aguaymanto* (pork with Peruvian cherry sauce; S12), with advance notice.

Transportes Rojas (☎55-5108; Pardo 258) has daily buses to Cajamarca (S10, four hours) at 5am and **Royal Palace's** (☎77-6872; Unión 313) also has departures to Cajamarca (S10) at 4am and 2pm. **Virgen del Carmen** (☎79-2918; Cáceres 112), located behind the market, goes to Chachapoyas (S35, nine hours) via Leimebamba (S25, four hours) at 9am and to Cajamarca (S10, 3½ hours) at 3pm.

Chachapoyas

☎041 / POP 22,900 / ELEV 2335 M

Also known as Chachas, Chachapoyas is a laid-back town awash in white and insulated by a buffer of rough unpaved roads and high-altitude cloud forests. The town was an important junction on jungle-coast trade

Chachapoyas

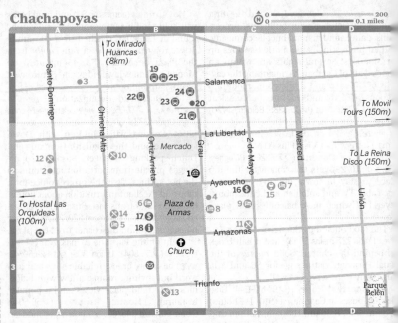

routes until a paved road was built in the 1940s through nearby Pedro Ruíz, bypassing Chachapoyas altogether. The unlikely capital of the department of Amazonas, this pleasant colonial settlement is now a busy market town and makes an excellent base for exploring the awesome ancient ruins left behind by the fierce civilization of the Chachapoyas ('People of the Clouds').

Vast zones of little-explored cloud forest surround the city of Chachapoyas, concealing some of Peru's most fascinating and least-known archaeological treasures. Although the ravages of weather and time, as well as more recent attentions of grave robbers and treasure seekers, have caused damage to many of the ruins, some have survived remarkably well. Kuélap is by far the most famous of these archaeological sites, though dozens of other ruins lie besieged by jungle and make for tempestuous exploration.

History

The Chachapoyas culture was conquered – but never fully subdued – by the Incas a few decades before the Spaniards arrived. When the Europeans showed up, local chief Curaca Huamán supposedly aided them in their conquest to defeat the Inca. Because of the relative lack of Inca influence, the people didn't learn to speak Quechua and today Spanish is spoken almost exclusively. Local historians claim that San Juan de la Frontera de las Chachapoyas was the third town founded by the Spaniards in Peru (after Piura and Lima) and it was, at one time, the seventh-largest town in the country.

Sights

FREE **Instituto Nacional de Cultura**
Museo MUSEUM
(INC; Ayacucho 904; ⊙8am-1pm & 3-5pm Mon-Fri) Houses six mummies and ceramics from several pre-Columbian periods.

Miradors VIEWPOINT
A 10-minute stroll northwest along Salamanca brings you to **Mirador Guayamil**, a lookout with a city panorama. A S30 round-trip taxi ride will take you to **Mirador Huancas** (admission S1; ⊙7:30am-5:30pm), which has soaring views of the Utcubamba valley. It's an easy hike back 1½ hours along the road.

Activities

Trekking

Trekking to the numerous impressive sights and ruins around Chachapoyas is becom

Chachapoyas

ng increasingly popular and is easy to arrange in town. The most popular trek is the four- or five-day Gran Vilaya trek, from Choctámal to the Marañón canyon, through pristine cloud forest and past several ruins and the heavenly Valle de Belén. Another popular adventure heads out to the Laguna de los Cóndores (p426), a three-day trip on foot and horseback from Leimebamba. Both are for walkers in good shape and with stamina. Treks to any of the other ruins in the district can be arranged and tailored to suit your needs.

Tours & Guides

All the tour agencies are found near the Plaza de Armas. Ask around for other travelers' experiences before you choose an agency. Expect to pay S100 to S150 per person for multiday treks (a little more for groups of less than four) and between S50 and S90 for day tours.

Chachapoyas Tours   GUIDED TOUR
(☑94-196-3327; www.kuelapperu.com; Santo Domingo 432) These guys get rave reviews for their day tours of the area. The company also organizes multiday treks and has some English-speaking guides. The office was closed when we came though, due to earthquake damage.

Turismo Explorer   GUIDED TOUR
(☑47-8162; www.turismoexplorerperu.com; Grau 509) This company also has a great reputation and specializes in multiday treks. It has guides who speak excellent English.

🛏 Sleeping

Most places in Chachapoyas fall squarely in the budget category.

TOP CHOICE Hostal Las Orquídeas   GUESTHOUSE $$
(☑47-8271; www.hostallasorquideas.com; Ayacucho 1231; s/d incl breakfast S60/100; @🛜) Long on friendliness and value, this upscale guesthouse offers tile-floor rooms (some bigger than others) that are bright and open and the public area is decorated with cheerful colors and some wood and artsy accents. Renovated rooms offer granite slab bathrooms with design-forward, hot water sinks that approach boutique levels. The staff will help you book travel and arrange excursions, and prices include transfer from the bus station.

Casa Vieja Hostal   BOUTIQUE GUESTHOUSE $$
(☑47-7353; www.casaviejaperu.com; Chincha Alta 569; s/d incl breakfast from S95/145; @🛜) Very comfortable quarters in a classy converted mansion make Casa Vieja Hostal a very special choice. All of the rooms have handcrafted wood accents, decorative or working

THE CHACHAPOYAS

The Chachapoyas, or 'People of the Clouds,' controlled the vast swath of land around present-day Chachapoyas from AD 500 to around 1493, when the Incas conquered the area and ended the Chacha isolation. Very little is known about this civilization, whose inhabitants were thought to be great warriors, powerful shamans and prolific builders who were responsible for one of the most advanced civilizations of Peru's tropical jungles. Today, among the many dozens of cliff tombs and hamlets of circular structures left behind, archaeologists match wits with grave robbers in a race for a deeper understanding of the Chachapoyas.

The Chachapoyas were heavily engaged in trade with other parts of Peru. However, isolated in their cloud-forest realm, they developed independently of these surrounding civilizations. The Chachapoyas speculatively cultivated a fierce warrior cult; depicted trophy heads as well as left human skulls show evidence of trepanation and intentional scalping. The eventual expansion of the Inca empire in the 15th century was met with fierce resistance and sporadic fighting continued well after the initial conquest.

Environmentalists long before Greenpeace members got into rubber dinghies, the Chachapoyas built structures that were in perfect harmony with their surroundings and that took advantage of nature's aesthetic and practical contributions. The Chachapoyas religion is believed to have venerated some of the salient natural features of these territories; the serpent, the condor and the puma were worshipped as powerful representatives of the natural world as were caves, lakes and mountains.

The unique use of circular construction was complemented by intricate masonry friezes, which used zigzags and rhomboids. The buildings were covered by thatch roofs, which were tall and steep to facilitate the runoff of the area's frequent rains. Hundreds of ruins illustrate Chachapoyas architecture, but none stand out as much as the impressive fortified citadel of Kuélap, surrounded by a colossal 20m-high wall and encompassing hundreds of dwellings and temples.

fireplaces and big windows facing onto the verdant garden. A touch of the modern is provided by flat-screen TVs. The included breakfast is taken next door at the endlessly charming Terra Mia Cafe. Discounts up to 30% from October to January.

Casa Andina
HOTEL $$

(96-933-5840; www.casa-andina; Km 39 Carretera Pedro Ruíz; r/ste from S208/281; @♠☀) This well-regarded Peruvian boutique chain's latest offering is in a 21-room colonial-style hacienda in a sublime location down in the Utcubamba valley surrounded by chirimoya plantations off the dirt road to Leimebamba. Rooms are disappointingly simple, but do feature thick mattresses and large bathrooms (avoid the traditional rooms – you'll be happier in the far more spacious superior rooms) but perhaps that blow is eased when you take your breakfast on the riverside veranda. This one is all about location, location, location.

Hotel Revash
GUESTHOUSE $

(47-7391; www.chachapoyaskuelap.com.pe; Grau 517; s S35-60, d S70-150; @♠) The courtyard in this classic mansion is a little more over-grown than endearing, but sleeping here still offers exceptional value and scorching showers. Rooms are colorful and crotchet in a sweet way, with the most expensive one offering loads of space and lavender color schemes. The in-house agency can be pushy but travelers are generally pleased; but confirm the price before setting out.

Hostal La Villa de Paris
HOTEL $

(54-5631; www.hostalvillaparis.com; Prolongación 2 de Mayo, cuadra 5; s/d S85/135, bungalow S295, all incl breakfast; @♠☀) Only 1.5km from the main square, this lovely colonial-style hotel furnished with lots of wood and antiques has the feel of a much more expensive hotel. Large windows and balconies bring in the light. The three-bedroom bungalows with kitchenettes are a great deal if you split it up per couple.

Hostal Belén
GUESTHOUSE $

(47-7830; www.hostalbelen.com; Ortiz Arrieta 540; s/d S45/55; @♠) Also on the plaza in a well-maintained building, Belén has 11 small but tidy rooms, each with one brightly painted wall to cheer up the relative darkness.

ostal Johumaji GUESTHOUSE $
47-7819; hostaljohumajieirl@hotmail.com; Ay-
ucho 711; s/d/tr from S20/30/45; @☎) The
etter of the town's super-cheap hotels,
ohumaji has small, spartan rooms that
re well lit and have electric hot showers,
nough travelers have complained about
reet noise. Regardless, it's a tidy, friendly
noice. Tack on S5 for cable TV.

otel Karajía HOTEL $
31-2606; Calle 2 de Mayo 546; s/d without bath-
om S20/30, s/d S25/45; ☎) The moodiest of

the budget options. Rooms are fine, with hot
water and cable TV and the occasional frilly
touch as is the case with the toilet seat covers and kaleidoscopic bedspreads.

 Eating

Moving east across the Andes, Chachapoyas
is the first place where you begin finding
Amazonian-style dishes, though with local
variations. *Juanes* (steamed rice with fish
or chicken, wrapped in a banana leaf) are
made with yucca instead of rice. *Cecina,* a

THE ROAD TO CHACHAPOYAS: TWO THE HARD WAY

Having sufficiently soaked up both the coastal sun and highland colonial atmosphere in
the mountains, travelers often find themselves itching for a little cloud forest and jungle action. Off to Tarapoto and Chachapoyas you go, right? Not so fast. First, you must
decide: do you have the heart, patience and nerves of steel to brave the astonishingly
scenic but hopelessly nerve-wracking mountain route via Celendín and Leimebamba?
Or would you be more comfortable taking the long way round on the paved route from
Chiclayo? Decisions. Decisions.

Via Celendín

This rough but beautiful road climbs over a 3085m pass before plummeting steeply
to the Río Marañón at the shabby and infernally hot village of **Balsas** (975m), 55km
from Celendín. The road climbs again, through gorgeous cloud forests and countryside
swathed in a lush quilt a million shades of green. It emerges 57km later at **Abra de Barro Negro** (Black Mud Pass; 3678m), which offers the highest viewing point of the drive,
over the Río Marañón, more than 3.5 vertical kilometers below. Ghostly low-level clouds
and mists hug the dispersed communities in this part of the trip and creep eerily among
the hills. The road then drops for 32km to Leimebamba at the head of the Río Utcubamba valley and follows the river as it descends past Tingo and on to Chachapoyas. The final
20km approach into Chachapoyas is freshly paved. Before that, your life teeters precariously on the edge of The End around every corner, your only hope that the driver knows
the nuances of the road more intimately than he does his own wife. Travelers should
carry water and food (and maybe a valium?), as the few restaurants en route are poor.

The road conditions have improved dramatically over the years, but it remains an
accident-prone route and is not without a certain element of risk (thrill?). The good news,
though, is that in 2012 the government signed off on the papers to pave this road, which
should be done 'in a few (Peruvian) years,' as one local put it.

Heading north, the left side of the bus affords the most scenic viewing time, but the
right side is less nauseating for those who fear heights.

Via Chiclayo

Considerably longer and immeasurably less thrilling is the usual route for travelers to
Chachapoyas. From the old Panamericana 100km north of Chiclayo, a paved road heads
east over the Andes via the 2145m Porculla Pass, the lowest Peruvian pass going over
the Andean continental divide. The route then tumbles to the Río Marañón valley. About
190km from the Panamericana turnoff, you reach the town of Jaén, the beginning of a
newly opened route to Ecuador (p420). Continuing east, a short side road reaches the
town of Bagua Chica in a low, enclosed valley (elevation about 500m), which Peruvians
claim is the hottest town in the country. The bus usually goes through Bagua Grande
(population 28,830) on the main road, and follows the Río Utcubamba valley to the
crossroads town of Pedro Ruíz, about 1½ hours from Bagua Grande. From here, a paved
southbound road branches to Chachapoyas, 54km and about 1¼ hours away.

dish made from dehydrated pork in the lowlands, is often made with beef.

TOP CHOICE **El Tejado** PERUVIAN **$$**

(Santo Domingo 426; mains S15-25) This charming little spot doesn't look like much from the outside, but a lovely interior courtyard and dining room awaits. It's a great lunch spot, with *menús* going for S7 Monday to Friday; and the specialty is *tacu-tacu* (an Afro-Peruvian fusion dish of rice, beans and a protein), seen here in nine varieties. The *lomo saltado* version is conversation-stopping good, especially when doused in the seriously tasty house hot pepper sauce.

Café Fusiones CAFE, BREAKFAST **$**

(Chincha Alta 445; breakfast S6-9, snacks S1.50-4.50; ⊘from 7am Mon-Sat; 🛜) The traveler congregation gathers at this artsy cafe that serves organic coffee and espresso, great breakfasts (including regional choices such as *juanes*), muffins doused in *manjar blan-*

co (milk caramel), lentil burgers and the lik Cozy couches included.

La Tushpa STEAKHOUSE, PERUVIAN

(Ortiz Arrieta 753; mains S12-30) Service is i famously slow but always worth the wa at this classic Chachapoyas steak and ch phouse. It doesn't look like much, but th meat-heavy menu is highlighted by th *cuadril* (tri-tip), a succulent beef cut, an interesting creations such as *lomo fino* (si loin) with a spicy pisco sauce. There's a goo deal of pork and chicken to choose from a well, all of which come with delicious hous sauces like *ají* (spicy pepper) and *chim churri* (parsley, garlic, olive oil, oregano an vinegar). A highlight.

Terra Mia Café BREAKFAST, PERUVIAN

(www.terramiacafe.com; Chincha Alta 557; breakfa: S8-13.50; ⊘from 7am; 🛜) The two stylish si: ters that own Casa Vieja opened this sophi: ticated cafe next door to their hotel. It boas: the fanciest espresso machine in town an a wonderful menu of both regional an

---

BORDER CROSSING: ECUADOR VIA JAÉN

If your next port of call is Ecuador, remember that you don't have to spend days on winding roads to get back to the Peruvian coast. From Jaén, a good northbound road heads 107km to San Ignacio (population 10,720) near the Ecuadorian border. Since the peace treaty was signed with Ecuador in late 1998, it has become possible to cross into Ecuador at this remote outpost.

Begin at the fast-growing agricultural center of **Jaén** (population 70,690), which has all of the services of a mid-sized town...along with a reputation for street crime and, judging by the signs, a serous dengue problem (bring repellent). Good hotels include **Prim's Hotel** (☎076-43-1039; www.primshotel.com; Palomino 1353; s without air-con S50, s/d with air-con from S70/90, all incl breakfast; 🌫🛜), a modern facility with a mix of basic and contemporary rooms, friendly staff and a downstairs *chifa;* or the town's best option, **Hotel El Bosque** (☎076-43-1492; hoteleraelbosque@hotmail.com; Muro 632; s/d/tr incl breakfast S100/130/160; 🌫🛜🏊), with bungalows set in gardens around a pool. **Hotel Cancún** (☎076-43-3511; Palomino 1413; s/d S35/45; 🛜) is a solid budget choice, with hot-water showers and cable TV. For a bite, **La Cabaña** (Bolívar 1332; mains S15-20), on Parque Central, does a whole lot of everything for all budgets, including daily lunch specials, sandwiches (S4 to S12), juices, milkshakes and more sophisticated fare.

From Jaén, *autos* (S20, 2½ hours) and *combis* (S12, 2½ hours) leave for **San Ignacio**, where there's a simple hotel and places to eat, from Av Pakumuros in the neighborhood of Pueblo Libre. Change here for another *colectivo* for the rough road to **La Balsa** (S15, two hours) on the Río Blanco dividing Peru from Ecuador. There used to be a *balsa* (ferry) here (hence the name), but there's now a new international bridge linking the countries. Border formalities are straightforward if you have your papers in order, though transiting gringos are rare.

Once in Ecuador, curious yet typical *rancheras* (trucks with rows of wooden seats) await to take you on the uncomfortable and unpredictable (because of the weather) 10km drive to Zumba (US$2, 1½ to 2½ hours). From here, buses go to Loja (US$7.50, six hours) where you can continue on to the famed 'valley of longevity' of Vilcabamba. If you leave Jaén at dawn, you should be able to make it to Vilcabamba in one day.

CHACHAPOYAS BUSES

DESTINATION	COST (S)	DURATION (HR)
Bagua Grande	22	2¼
Cajamarca	55	12
Celendín	35	8
Chiclayo	30-55	9
Leimebamba	10-20	3
Lima	80-135	22
María	15	2½
Pedro Ruíz	5	¾
Tingo Viejo	8	¾
Trujillo	75	12

ternational breakfasts (ahem... waffles!)
d great sandwiches on perfectly soft-
nchy French bread, all served up in a
zy and clean atmosphere with colonial
chways and fashion-forward indigenous
at cushions.

lcería Santa Elena   DESSERTS **$**
mazonas 800-804; mains S1-5) The crotchety
d man here serves the town's best pastries
d cakes; if he likes you, though, he might
row something in for free.

Drinking & Entertainment

achapoyas is famous for its artisan li-
eurs, which come in all sorts of herbal and
uit flavors – working your way through
em all here is a definite good time.

a Reina   BAR, CLUB
yacucho 520; ⊘4pm-2am) An artsy spot to
bricate your mind very cheaply on exotic
uit and Amazonian liqueurs by the shot
2) or the jar (from S16). There's 10 to
oose from, including *mora* (blackberry),
e most popular; *maracuyá* (passion fruit),
e best; and seven *raíces* and *chuchuhuasi*,
vo notorious Amazonian aphrodisiacs. The
me owners run the best disco in town, a
w blocks down at Ayacucho 345 (admis-
on S2).

Information

anco de la Nación (cnr Ayacucho & 2 de
ayo) Has a Visa/MasterCard ATM.

CP (Ortiz Arrieta) Changes US dollars and
aveler's checks and has an ATM.

ternational Language Center (☎47-8807;
ww.ilc-peru.com.pe; Salamanca 1112; ⊘8am-

1pm & 4-7pm) In addition to Spanish lessons
for S30 per hour (and six other languages when
available), the friendly owner here freely doles
out tourist information and often has paid positions for English teachers. It has luggage storage
if you need to stow your bags for a day or two.

iPerú (☎47-7292; Arrieta 582; ⊘8am-7pm)
Excellent maps, transportation information and
recommendations.

Policía Nacional (☎47-7017; Amazonas 1220)

Serpost (Salamanca 945) Postal services.

Getting There & Away

Air

Although Chachapoyas has an airport, at the
time of writing no carriers flew in or out of it.

Bus & Taxi

The frequently traveled route to Chiclayo and
on to Lima starts along the vista-lined route
to Pedro Ruíz along the Río Utcubamba. **Civa**
(☎47-8048; Salamanca 956) has a daily bus
to Chiclayo (6:30pm) and Lima (1pm). The very
comfortable **Movil Tours** (☎47-8545; La Libertad 464) has an express bus to Lima at 1pm, as
well as a 7:30pm bus to Trujillo via Chiclayo and
a Chiclayo direct at 8pm.

Virgen del Carmen (☎79-7707; Salamanca
956) departs for the scenic mountain route
(p419) to Cajamarca via Celendín and Leimebamba daily at 5am, though they are a little
stingy about selling a seat only to Leimebamba.
Transportes Karlita (☎97-502-0813; Salamanca 956) also goes to Leimebamba at noon
and 4pm and you can usually find a more
expensive *colectivo* waiting here alongside the
office to gather up those that couldn't get a seat.
Transportes Hidalgo (☎94-194-0571; cnr Grau
& Pasaje Reina) departs for Leimebamba (S10,
2½ hours) at 12:30pm and 4pm daily. **Poderoso**

Cautivo (☎94-194-0571; Pasaje Reina s/n) goes at noon and 4pm daily.

Getting directly to Kuélap independently is a bit of a pain and requires an early rise. **Transportes Roller** (☎94-174-6658; Grau 300) has one 4am bus that goes to Tingo Viejo, María and on to La Marca, where you'll find the ticket booth and parking lot for Kuélep, returning at 6am. It's a 15-minute walk along a stone sidewalk to the ruins from there. Otherwise, frequent minibuses and *colectivo* taxis for Tingo Viejo and María depart from the 300 cuadra of Grau, from where you'll need to leg an additional two hours (from María) or five to six hours (from Tingo Viejo).

To continue further into the Amazon Basin, **Los Diplimaticos** (☎96-450-9665; Arrieto, cuadra 4) runs *combis* to Pedro Ruíz every 15 minutes between 4am and 6pm. At the crossroads, you can wait for an eastbound bus to continue on to Tarapoto (S35, seven hours), which pass most frequently between 4pm and 11pm. Ask around for trucks and minibuses to other destinations. To reach Jaén and the border route to Ecuador (p420), you'll need to catch a *combi* to Bagua Grande, which also leave frequently from the 300 cuadra of Grau at Pasaje Reina and switch for a *colectivo* to Jaén (S7 to S10, one hour).

If you start early and have plenty of time on your hands, you can see some of the attractions around Chachapoyas by public minibus.

A taxi for the day to Kuélap or to sites around Chachapoyas and Leimebamba costs S150.

Around Chachapoyas

Relics of Chachapoyas and Inca civilizations and daring, rugged scenery speckle the mountains surrounding Chachapoyas. Scores of archaeological sites dot this area, most of them unexcavated and many reclaimed by vivacious jungle. Following is a list of some of the main points of interest, though there are many others – and even more await discovery.

GRAN VILAYA

The name Gran Vilaya refers to the bountiful valleys that spread out west of Chachapoyas, reaching toward the rushing Río Marañón. Abutting the humid Amazon, this region sits in a unique microcosm of perennially moist high-altitude tropics and cloud forests – an ecological anomaly that gave rise to the Chachapoyas culture's moniker, People of the Clouds. The fertility of this lush area was never a big secret – the valley successfully supported the huge populations of the Chachapoyas and Inca cultures, a to date more than 30 archaeological si have been found dotting the mountains. I portant sites like **Pamamarca**, **Pueblo A Pueblo Nuevo** and **Pirquilla** lie connect by winding goat-tracks as they did hundre of years ago, completely unexcavated, a can be visited on multiday hikes. Imma lately constructed Inca roads weave up a around the hills, past many ruined cit camouflaged by centuries of jungle.

The breathtaking, impossibly green a silt-filled **Valle de Belén** lies at the entran of Gran Vilaya. The flat valley floor here dissected by the mouth of the widely m andering Río Huaylla, coiled like a langu serpent. Filled with grazing cattle, hor and surrounded on all sides by mist-cover hills, the vistas here are mesmerizing.

Most travel agencies in Chachapoyas of trekking tours of this region.

KARAJÍA

This extraordinary funerary site hosts s **sarcophagi** perched high up a sheer cl face. Each long-faced tomb is construct from wood, clay and straw and is unique shaped like a stylized forlorn individu The characters stare intently over the va ley below, where a Chachapoyas village on stood; you can see stone ruins scatter among the fields of today. Originally the were eight coupled sarcophagi, but the thi and eighth (from the left) collapsed, ope ing up the adjoining coffins – which we found to contain mummies, plus vario crafts and artifacts related to the decease Look out for scattered bones below the co fins. Only important individuals were buri with such reverence: shamans, warriors an chieftains. The skulls above the tombs a thought to have been trophies of enemies possibly human sacrifices. Locals charge S5 admission fee.

Karajía is a 45-minute walk from th tiny outpost of Cruz Pata, which is tw hours from Chachapoyas. Minibuses fro Chachapoyas travel to Luya (S5.50, 50 mi utes), from where minibuses go to Cruz Pa (S4.50, 50 minutes). All said and done, a da tour from Chachapoyas (S60) is the way t go; the hiking and drive time is a big inves ment to stare up with binoculars for a fe minutes at a set of cliffs 400m away.

REVASH

Near the town of Santo Tomás, Revash an excellent site of several brightly colore

CATARATA DE GOCTA

This 771m **waterfall** (adult/child S5/1; ☉6am-4pm) somehow escaped the notice of the Peruvian government, international explorers and prying satellite images until 2005, when German Stefan Ziemendorff and a group of locals put together an expedition to map the falls and record their height. Various claims ranging from the third-loftiest waterfall on earth to the 15th resulted in an international firestorm in the always-exciting contest to rank the world's highest cascades. Gocta's current measurement is probably correct, give or take a few meters, putting it solidly fifth after Norway's 773m Monge-fossen Falls. Whether you're hung up on numbers or not, the falls are impressive and accessible. It's easier to go with a tour company from Chachapoyas for about S90 – it will provide transportation and a local guide for the two-hour hike to the falls – but it's feasible to catch a *combi* from Chachapoyas to Pedro Ruíz (S5, 45 minutes) and then a *mototaxi* to Cocachimba (S15, 45 minutes) or walk the final 6km from Pedro. The Comunal Tourism Association arranges guides for S30.

The falls are dripping in lore about a mermaid who guards a lost treasure (who knew there were mermaids so far inland?). With luck you might see the bizarre, orange bird called the Andean cock-of-the-rock or, if miracles tend to befall you, the rare and endemic yellow-tailed woolly monkey. In the rainy season, some seven additional drips sprout over the ridge.

The newish **Gocta Andes Lodge** (☎041-63-0552; www.goctalodge.com; s/d S169/209; ☀), in the village of **Cocachimba**, is one of the special spots in the Northern Highlands, sitting on a severely idyllic setting with unimpeded views to the falls, both from the rooms and the small infinity pool. Spacious but simple rooms feature lovely kaleidoscopic textiles, cozy down comforters, vaulted ceilings and balconies which frame the falls like a painting. The grounds are strewn with chickens and hens and llamas (captive?), and offer occasional exotic bird flybys.

If you can't swing the cash, the village itself supports a small cottage tourism industry with several cheaper options, a few restaurants and shops.

nerary buildings tucked into limestone [cl]iff ledges. Looking a bit like attractive-[bu]t-inaccessible summer cottages, these *[p]ullpas* are made of small, mud-set stones [th]at were plastered over and embellished [w]ith red and cream paints. This bright taste [in] decor is still clearly visible today. While [m]uch of the site was looted long ago, the [sk]eletons of 11 adults and one child, along [w]ith a wealth of artifacts such as musical in-[st]ruments and tools made from bones, were [fo]und inside by archaeologists. A number of [p]ictographs decorate the walls of the cliff be-[h]ind the tombs, and a now empty funerary [c]ave, originally containing more than 200 [fu]nerary bundles, lies 1km from the main [se]t of tombs.

The shortest route to the site is to take [a] Leimebamba-bound *combi* and get off in [Y]erbabuena, from where you have a 1½-hour [h]ike or can take a taxi (S40 return). If you're [u]p for the hunt, ask around in Revash for a [m]an who can set you up with horses. A day [to]ur from Chachapoyas is about S90.

LA JALCA (JALCA GRANDE)

This lovely little mountain town, also known as Jalca Grande, is a small, cobblestoned municipality that has managed to retain much of its historical roots, though modernization is slowly creeping its way in. Quechua is still spoken throughout much of the town and traditional, Chachapoyas-influenced round-walled houses with thatch roofs hide around the corners. Look for **Choza Redonda**, a tall-roofed traditional Chachapoyas house that was supposedly continually inhabited until 1964. It is still in excellent condition and was used as a model for the recreation of Chachapoyas houses in Kuélap and Levanto. At the ruins of **Ollape**, a 30-minute walk west of La Jalca, you can see several house platforms and circular balconies decorated with complex designs. To get here, catch a Chachapoyas–Leimebamba bus and ask to be let off at the La Jalca turnoff, from where it's a three-hour walk up a dirt road.

YALAPE

On the road between Chachapoyas and Levanto, these ruins of limestone residential buildings make an easy day trip from Chachas. With good views of Levanto below, Yalape has some decent defense walls with some frieze patterns, all impressed with lots of forest growth. Yalape is four hours' hike from Chachapoyas or half an hour's walk from Levanto. Occasional *combis* head to Levanto between 4:30am and 6am (S6, one hour) from the intersection of Cuarto Centenario and Sosiego, 1km southeast of the plaza in Chachapoyas; they can let you off at Yalape.

Kuélap

ELEV 3100M

Matched in grandeur only by the ruins of Machu Picchu, this fabulous, ruined citadel city in the mountains southwest of Chachapoyas is the best preserved and most accessible of the district's extraordinary archaeological sites. This monumental stone-fortified citadel crowns a craggy limestone mountain and affords exceptional panoramas of a land once inhabited by the Chachapoyas. The site receives remarkably few visitors, but those who make it here get to witness one of the most significant and impressive pre-Columbian ruins in all of South America.

⊙ Sights & Activities

Constructed between AD 500 and 1493, and rediscovered in 1843, Kuélap (adult/student/child S15/8/2; ⊗8am-5pm) is made up of millions of cubic feet of remarkably preserved stone. Juan Crisóstomo Nieto, a judge working in the Chachapoyas area who discovered the ruins, originally said more stone was used in its construction than for the Great Pyramid of Egypt, a comparison that mathematically makes no sense, but nonetheless conveys his intended message: there's a lot of stone here! Though the stonework is not as elaborate as that of the Incas, the 700m-long oval fortress is surrounded by an imposing, near-impenetrable wall that towers on average around 20m high. Entrance into this stronghold is via three deep, lean gates – once believed to be an ingenious security system that forced attacking parties into easily defeated single files – but further speculation has shown that earthquakes, erosion, rain and destroyed mortar might have caused the walls to move from their original positions, creating more narrow passages than originally intended.

Inside are two levels scattered with remnants of more than 400 circular dwellings. Some are decorated with zigzag and rhomboid friezes, and all were once topped by soaring thatched roofs. One dwelling has been reconstructed. In its heyday, Kuélap housed up to 3500 people and, surrounded by wispy cloud, must have been a breathtaking sight. The most impressive and enigmatic structure, named El Tintero (Inkpot), is in the shape of a large inverted cone. Inside, an underground chamber houses the remains of animal sacrifices, leading archaeologists to believe that it was a religious building of some kind. Kuélap Resident Archaeologist Alfredo Narvez has now excavated graves and llama skeletons around El Tintero further support this theory. A 1996 hypothesis by a team from the University of San Diego suggests it may have also been a solar calendar. Another building is a lookout tower with excellent 360-degree vistas. The mountain summit on which the whole citadel sits is surrounded by abundant greenery, towering bromeliad-covered trees and exotic orchids.

☞ Tours & Guides

The guardians at Kuélap are very friendly and helpful; one is almost always on hand to show visitors around and answer questions. Don José Gabriel Portocarrero Chávez runs the ticket booth and has been there for years; he no longer guides but can set you up with a Spanish-speaking guide from the association (S30).

🛏 Sleeping & Eating

Kuélap itself has limited sleeping options, though one extended family operates a few basic options down an often muddy trail from the ruins. Nearby towns provide a good range of accommodations and can be used as a base for exploring the area.

Hospedaje El Bebedero (☎08 978 343; r per person S15) and Hospedaje El Imperio (☎94-173-5833; r per person S10-15) are the best choices just beneath the Kuélap ruins. Neither have electricity but Imperio, run by Teodula Rocha, the friendly wife of the aforementioned Don José, has running water. She has a concession on the snack stand near the ticket booth every other week, so look for her there or inquire with Don José. Bringing your own sleeping bag is recommended. Home-cooked meals at either run S5 to S10. The nearby INC Hostel has free

nping, but the rooms are permanently oc-
pied by the Kuélap excavation team.

The next closest sleeping choices are in
e hamlet of María, a two-hour walk from
élap and connected to Chachapoyas by
ly minibuses. Here you will find a cottage
dustry of half a dozen charming and near-
entical **hospedajes** (r per person S15) – they
go to the same sign-maker for their signs.
offer clean, modest rooms with electric
t water and some will cook up hearty
eals for guests for about S6. **Hospedaje
Torreón** (☑94-170-8040; Av Kuélap s/n;
I S20/30) is your best bet, with perfectly
cent rooms accented with colorful bed-
reads, and hot water. The friendly owner
esn't cook, though, so you'll need to hit a
staurant or buy some of her cakes that she
lls to townsfolk.

In Tingo Vieja, 3km below Tingo Nuevo at
e far base of Kuélap, there's the basic **Hos-
daje León** (☑94-171-5685; s/d S15/25, with-
t bathroom S10/20), with tiny, bucolic rooms,
ectric hot water and run by a friendly older
uple who capitalized on a tourism vision
ars ago. **Estancia Chillo** (☑041-63-0510;
w.estanciachillo.com; r per person incl breakfast
dinner S120), 5km south of Tingo Viejo, is
e of the coolest and quirkiest places to
ay in the area. The beautiful hacienda-style
mpound has rustic and well-designed
oms with the requisite gaudy bedspreads,
unded out by ranch props, wagon wheels,
ightly colored pet parrots wandering the
ounds and dangling bougainvillea. All the
xtures you see were handmade by the own-
r Oscar Arce Cáceres, who let us know he
selling, so things here could change. Call
ead. You can organize guides from here
er day S150) as well as horses (per day S40
 S200) to go out and explore nearby ruins.

🔢 Getting There & Around

9.8km trail climbs from the south end of Tingo
iejo to the ruins, situated about 1200m above
e town. Signposts on the way make the trail
asy to follow, but it is an exhausting, often hot,
imb; allow five to six hours. Remember to bring
ater as none is available along the trail. During
e rainy season (October to April), especially
e latter half, the trail can become very muddy
nd travel can be difficult. You can also hike to
uélap from María in about two hours.

Transportes Roller (Grau 302) has one bus to
uélap (S15, 2½ hours), via Tingo Viejo, Choctá-
nal and María, leaving Chachapoyas at 4am and
eturning from Kuélap at 6am. Alternatively, at
uélap you can ask about getting a ride back to

Chachapoyas with returning private *colectivos*
or *combis*. Frequent *combis* (S8, 50 minutes)
run between Tingo Viejo and Chachapoyas. Tour
agencies arrange day trips from Chachapoyas.

Leimebamba

POP 1100 / ELEV 2050M

This convivial cobblestoned town – often
spelled 'Leymebamba' – lies at the head of
the Río Utcubamba. It has an endearingly
laid-back allure that is maintained by its
relative isolation: the nearest big city is
many hours away by dirt roads. Horses are
still a popular form of transport around
town and the friendliness of the townsfolk
is legendary in the region. Surrounded by a
multitude of archaeological sites from the
Chachapoyas era, this is a great place to base
yourself while exploring the province.

👁 Sights & Activities

**TOP
CHOICE** **Museo Leimebamba** MUSEUM
(www.museoleymebamba.org; adult/student
S15/8; ⊙10am-4:30pm) The mummies found
at Laguna de los Cóndores are now housed
in the Museo Leimebamba, located 3km
south of town. The museum is in a wonderfully constructed complex with multi-
tiered roofs, all generously funded by the
Austrian Archaeological Society. Most of
the mummies are wrapped in bundles and
can be seen in glass cases; some have been
unwrapped for your gruesome viewing
pleasure. Well-presented artifacts on display include ceramics, textiles, wood figures
and photos of Laguna de los Cóndores. A
mototaxi from town costs S5.

La Congona RUIN
The most captivating of the many ancient
ruins strewn around Leimebamba, La
Congona is definitely worth the three-hour
hike needed to get here. The flora-covered
site contains several well-preserved circular
houses, one of which, oddly for Chachapoyas culture, sits on square bases. Inside, the
houses are adorned with intricate niches,
and outside wide circular terraces surround
each house. This archaeological site is renowned for the intricate decoration on the
buildings and particularly for the numerous
sophisticated masonry friezes. A tall tower
can be climbed by a remarkable set of curving steps for wide-angle panoramas of the
surrounding valley.

The site is reached in two hours from Leimebamba along a path beginning at the lower end of Calle 16 de Julio. A guide is recommended; expect to pay around S90 for the complete five-hour circuit.

Laguna de los Cóndores ARCHAEOLOGICAL SITE

This part of Peru hit the spotlight in 1996 when a group of farmers found six *chullpas* (ancient Andean funerary towers) on a ledge 100m above a cloud-forest lake. This burial site was a windfall for archaeologists, and its 219 mummies and more than 2000 artifacts have given researchers a glimpse past the heavy curtain of history that conceals the details of the Chachapoyas civilization. So spectacular was the find that a Discovery Channel film was made about it and a museum was built in Leimebamba to house the mummies and cultural treasures.

Some of the tombs, plastered and painted in white or red-and-yellow ochre, are decorated with signature Chachapoyas zigzag friezes. All lie huddled against the cliff on a natural ledge overlooking the stunning Laguna de los Cóndores. Don't get too excited about spotting any of the wide-winged Andean wonders though – this lake was renamed after the find to make it more 'tourist friendly.'

The only way to get to the laguna is by a strenuous 10- to 12-hour hike on foot and horseback from Leimebamba. The standard tour is three days: one day to hike in, a day of sightseeing and an eight- to nine-hour return journey. Horses and guides can be arranged either in Leimebamba or at travel agencies in Chachapoyas. Guides are around S450 for the three-day circuit.

Tours & Guides

Local guides (inquire at the museums) will arrange trips to the tombs and various other sites; some are easily visited on a day trip, while others require several days. Homer Ulllen, the son of the owner of the Albergue Turístico de la Laguna de los Cóndores (Amazonas 320), can guide you to sites near their land. Expect to pay around S50 per day for a Spanish guide, S120 for English (not including food) and S30 for horses. Wira Wira Tours (☎94-185-6029; bifar952@yahoo.com; Próspero, cuadra 3) also comes highly recommended.

Sleeping & Eating

Unfortunately, all the good spots to eat are by the museum. There are a handful of *pollerías* and simple spots in town but N╴ workers who spend considerable time in ╴ area won't vouch for any of them. In to╴ eat at La Casona.

TOP CHOICE **Kentitambo** BOUTIQUE GUESTHOUS╴

(☎97-111-8259; info@vilayatours.com; s/d ╴ breakfast S300/450; ☎) Owned by a mu╴ lingual gringa/Incan historian who w╴ a member of the original team who bu╴ the Museo Leimebamba, this wonderfu╴ romantic, two-room guesthouse is an ╴ clusive design-forward getaway for d╴ cerning nature lovers. King-sized beds a╴ filtered rainwater showers are highligl╴ of the colorful, rustic bungalows built ╴ earthquake-proof *quincho* style, but t╴ real coup is the spacious front porch╴ with hammocks that reach out into the s╴ rounding nature – perfect for ogling t╴ exotic birdlife that congregates on the pro╴ erty. It's next door to KentiKafé.

TOP CHOICE **La Casona** GUESTHOUSE

(☎83-0106; www.casonadeleymebamba.com; An╴ zonas 221; s/d incl breakfast S95/160; ☎) Th╴ friendly, rambling guesthouse run by ╴ brother-sister team is chock-full of an╴ quated character and homespun char╴ Old rooms feature polished hardwood floo╴ while all rooms feature new bathrooms wi╴ hot water. Breakfast is a real treat, with ╴ espresso machine along with homema╴ cheese, butter and milk from their ow╴ cows. Some rooms have little balconies loo╴ ing onto the quiet street below, others ha╴ views over the town's tiled roofs and su╴ rounding mountains. Nelly, the matriarc╴ here, runs a mean kitchen for guests; outsi╴ ers are welcome with advance notice.

Albergue Turístico de la

Laguna de los Cóndores GUESTHOUS╴

(☎79-7908; www.loscondoreshostal.com; Amaz╴ nas 320; s/d without bathroom S15/30, incl brea╴ fast S50/100) Located half a block from th╴ plaza, this is a family-run affair with a ve╴ dant courtyard and lots of comfortable si╴ ting areas draped in thick, colorful blanket╴ It has hot showers, cozy rooms and tours ╴ the area can be arranged from here. On th╴ budget end, the shared bathrooms here ge╴ you the most character for the *sole*.

TOP CHOICE **KentiKafé** CAFE

(www.museoleymebamba.org/kentikafe.htm╴ snacks S2.50-5; ☺8:30am-5:30pm; ☎) Just ╴

STRICTLY FOR THE BIRDS...& THE MONKEYS

The 2960-hectare **Abra Patricia-Alto Nieva Private Conservation Area** (☎084-24-5256; www.ecoanperu.org; admission S40; s/d S318/530, without bathroom S265/477, all incl meals & admission), about 40 minutes east of Pedro Ruíz on the road to Moyobamba (reachable by S35 *colectivo* from Nuevo Cajamarca), is a bird-watcher's paradise managed by the Association of Andean Ecosystems (ECOAN). More than 300 species call this area home, 23 of which are considered globally threatened. ECOAN's **Owlet Lodge** offers large and exceptionally clean, quiet rooms for nature lovers and anyone who just wants to get away from the noise of civilization. The gourmet meals are served in a dining room with views of mountainous forest that has never seen the swipe of a chainsaw. Although an obvious favorite of bird-watching tour groups – who come to see such endemic species as yellow-scarved tanager, Lulu's tody-tyrant and the extremely rare long-whiskered owlet – it's also the best place to see the critically endangered yellow-tailed woolly monkey.

ort stroll across the street and up the hill om Museo Leimebamba and perched on hill with views of the museum and valley low, KentiKafé maintains about a dozen eders visited by the Marvelous Spatuletail ummingbird (p428) and 16 other humngbird species – they drink some 5kg sugar per day! You can lie in wait for mpses of the Spatuletail while sipping per-fresh gourmet coffee, and feasting on memade cakes and wonderful sandwich-such as chicken and avocado; or pay S10 visit the feeders further afield in a quieter ea away from espresso cup clanking.

Mishqui PERUVIAN **$**
]95-355-2111; Austria s/n; menús S15-18; ☺7am-pm) The cute cook here, Doris, takes her le as a chef seriously, donning the hat and l. You'll need to call in advance, but she hips up clean, downhome *menús* from e front of her home, complete with fancy blecloths and cutlery. It's across the street om the museum.

Shopping

MAL HANDICRAFTS
an Augustín 429; ☺9am-6pm) Located on the aza, AMAL is a women's artisan coopera-ve selling top-grade handicrafts and local eavings. Better than the shop, however, is eading up to their small workshop about a ve-minute walk along the road to the mu-eum. Here, you can see them in action as ell as pick out your own material to cus-om design anything from backpacks and ecorative computer cases to purses and blecloths.

ℹ Information

There is a police station on the plaza and an internet spot across from Transportes Karlita. Leimebamba doesn't have an ATM; bring cash.

ℹ Getting There & Away

Hidalgo Tours (☎94-194-0571; Bolívar 608) departs for Chachapoyas (S10, 2½ hours) at 5am and 6:30am daily. **Poderoso Cautivo** (☎94-194-0571; San Agustín 314) goes at 5am and 7am daily for the same price. **Transportes Karlita** (☎97-194-3024; cnr Amazonas & 16 de Julio) is the early bird, heading out at 4am and 5am. Reserve a seat the night before. A taxi to Chachapoyas costs between S100 and S120. **Virgin del Carmen** (☎96-483-3033; Plaza de Armas) has a daily bus to Chachapoyas (S10, 2½ hours) from Celendín that passes through at about 3pm. In the reverse direction, heading toward Celendín (S25, five hours) and Cajamarca (S30, eight hours), they pass at about 8am. Occasional trucks and private vehicles pick up paying passengers to Chachapoyas and Celendín.

Pedro Ruíz

This dusty transit town sits at the junction of the Chiclayo–Tarapoto road and the turnoff to Chachapoyas. When traveling from Chachapoyas, you can board east or west bound buses here. The journey east from Pedro Ruíz is spectacular, climbing over two high passes, traveling by a beautiful lake, and dropping into fantastic high-jungle vegetation in between.

Pedro has a Visa/MasterCard ATM on Marginal across from the PetrolPeru gas station.

DAHLING, YOU LOOK MARVELOUS!

You don't have to be a big-time birdwatcher to get turned on by the Marvelous Spatuletail (*Loddigesia mirabilis*), a rare and exquisitely beautiful hummingbird that lives in limited habitats of scrubby forest between 2000m and 2900m in northern Peru's Utcubamba valley. As with most bird species, the males get the prize in the looks category, and the Marvelous male is no exception, with his shimmering blue crown and green throat and a sexy set of curved and freakishly long quills that splay out from his backside and end in wide, feather 'rackets' or 'spatules.' He can independently maneuver these long plumes into extravagant mating displays, crossing the two spatuletail feathers over each other or swinging them in front of his head as he hovers in front of a female.

According to some Peruvians in the Utcubamba valley, the spatuletail's most spectacular anatomical feature is its heart, which is considered an aphrodisiac when eaten. The hunting of the birds for this purpose has probably contributed to keeping its numbers low – perhaps less than 1000 pairs remain – although conservation efforts in the region have led to increased awareness about the precarious status of the bird, whose habitat is quickly diminishing due to deforestation and agricultural development, and the need to protect it. Some conservation centers like KentiKafé (p426) in Leimebamba as well as the **Marvelous Spatule Tail Interpretation Center** (admission S26.50; r per person incl breakfast S120; ⊙6am-6pm), known colloquially as Heumbo, 15 minutes west of Pomacochas on the road to Pedro Ruíz. Here you'll find spectacular chances to see the Marvelous Spatuletail in all its glory – at time of writing there were four males, three females and four babies hovering around. The latter maintains feeders on a 12-hectare private reserve that attracts this and many other hummingbirds; the views over the valley and the plunging road from here are also spectacular. You can spend the night at the interpretation center as well. Grab a *colectivo* from Pedro Ruíz (S15, 15 minutes).

🛏 Sleeping & Eating

The main avenues, Cahuide and Marginal, are lined with local restaurants. Virgin de Chuquichaca (mains S7 to S15) is purportedly the cleanest and the *lomo saltado* worked out for us.

Casablanca Hotel HOTEL $
(☑83-0171; Marginal 122; s/d/tr S25/45/65) The pick of the sorry hotels in Pedro Ruíz is by the road junction, but try to get a room away from the noisy highway. Rooms are basic but perfectly decent with cable TV and hot water.

ⓘ Getting There & Away

Buses from the coast pick up passengers heading to Rioja or Moyobamba (S25 to S30, five hours) and Tarapoto (S30 to S35, seven hours) and in the opposite direction to Chiclayo (S30, seven hours) and Lima (S65 to S135, 18 to 22 hours). The most comfortable choice is **Movil Tours** (☑83-0085; Cahuide 653), which departs east at 6am and 11am and west for Lima at 2pm, 2:30pm and 7:30pm. **Civa** (☑94-172-7323; Marginal s/n) heads east at 3pm and 1am; and west to Chiclayo and Lima at 2pm and 8pm. More economical choices include **GH Bus** (☑79-4314; Cahuide 841) heading east

at 1pm and to Lima at 11am and 12:30pm; and **TSP** (☑99-845-5075; Cahuide 890), heading to Tarapoto at 4pm, 7pm and 10:30pm and Lima at 5pm and 8pm. There are several other options as well.

If coming from Tarapoto, Los Diplomaticos (☑96-450-9774; Marginal s/n), next to the PetrolPeru gas station, runs *combis* to Chachapoyas (S5) every 30 minutes or so.

Moyobamba

☑042 / POP 41,800 / ELEV 860M
Moyobamba, the capital of the department of San Martín, was founded in 1542, but earthquakes (most recently in 1990 and 1991) have contributed to the demise of any historic buildings. Nevertheless, Moyobamba is a pleasant enough town to spend a few days in and local tourist authorities are slowly drumming up sites of interest to visit. The region is famed for its orchids; there's an orchid festival held in October and a giant orchid statue guards the town's entrance.

The pretty town *malecón* (water promenade), seven blocks northeast of the plaza, hosts a Spring Breaky lineup of bars and discos with extreme views of the verdant river valley below.

⊃ Sights & Activities

años Termales de San Mateo HOT SPRINGS
dmission S1.50; ⊙5am-9pm) The well-main-
ined hot springs with temperatures of
ound 40°C are 5km south of town. *Mo-
taxis* cost S5. On weekends the baths get
owded with locals.

aqanki Orchid Center GARDENS
ww.waqanki.com; Carretera a Los Baños Termales
e San Mateo; admission S0.50; ⊙8am-6pm)
bout 3km outside of town, here you'll find
me 150 species of orchids growing along
o-, four- and six-hour trail circuits wind-
g through beautiful forest.

⹓ Tours & Guides

ingana Magic ECOTOUR
56-3163; www.tinganaperu.com; Reyes Guerra
22; ⊙8am-1pm & 2-5pm Mon-Fri) Can arrange
urs around the area to Cascadas Paccha
nd Lahuarpía, two impressive waterfalls,
ach 30 minutes away by car; plus caves and
cological reserves.

⛺ Sleeping & Eating

TOP
CHOICE **La Casa de Seizo** BUNGALOW $
79-4766; rumipata@hotmail.com; Carretera
Los Baños Termales de San Mateo; s/d/tr
35/60/90; ❄) A five-minute walk from the
an Mateo hot springs and Waqanki Orchid
Center, La Casa de Seizo (formerly Hospeda-
e Rumipata) is situated in a verdant and
dyllic setting outside of Moyobamba. The
apanese-Peruvian/Venezuelan couple run-
ing the show couldn't be sweeter or better
ooks: whether Seizo plucks a tilapia from
heir own pond and sashimis it before your
yes, whips up his soy-garlic-ginger fish or
eeds you his cafe-smoked chicken, you are
n for a real treat. Well-appointed exposed
rick rooms in the main house and a series
f thatched-roof bungalows, which were be-
ng relocated deeper into the forest on our
visit, are where you'll sleep off the food.
Meals are S10 to S20 but the experience is
priceless.

El Portón GUESTHOUSE $
86-6121; casahospedajeelporton@hotmail.com;
San Martín 449; s/d S50/80; ❄) This tranquil
choice offers rooms surrounding a well-
manicured garden where you'll also find a
few strewn hammocks and a pleasant breakfast nook. Rooms are small, but everything
is new and shiny and little touches of knick-

knack charm here and there and a homespun vibe give it a leg up on the competition.

Hospedaje Bet-El GUESTHOUSE $
(56-2796; www.moyobambabetel.com; Callao
517-537; s/d/tr incl breakfast S41/57/85) You'll
have to suck up the Christian imagery, but
if that's not an issue, this is a solid choice
with rooms emptying out onto an interior
atrium that a very funky tree calls home.
There's oddly no hot water (purportedly on
the way) but the espresso served in the attached cafe is scalding – perhaps the best
reason to choose here.

Hospedaje Santa Rosa GUESTHOUSE $
(50-9890; Canga 478; s/d from S15/30; @❄) A
great shoestring pick with a few rudimentary, cold water rooms set around a brick
patio. The occasional potted plant helps
liven up the concrete-jungle feel. Ask for
one with a toilet seat unless you prefer sitting on the rim.

TOP
CHOICE **La Olla de Barro** AMAZONIAN, REGIONAL $$
(www.laolladebarro.com; Canga at Filomeno; mains
S6-18; ⊙closed dinner Sun) Double dare your
friends to go for the fried ants or alligator at
this local institution set up tiki lounge-style,
all while you savor the phenomenal *inchi-
capi* (chicken soup with peanuts, cilantro
and yucca). This is the best place in town to
sample local jungle dishes and besides the
aforementioned best soup ever, you'll find
loads of river fish (avoid endangered wild
paiche from October to February, when its
commercial fishing is prohibited due to near
commercial extinction) and exotic regional
fruit sours like *camu-camu* and *cocona* to
chase it all down with. Don't miss it.

El Matador STEAKHOUSE $
(Puno C-2; mains S15-20; ⊙from 6pm Mon-Sat)
Great little upscale (for Moyobamba) steak-
house serving chicken and just five slabs of
carne on the *parilla:* sirloin, tri-tip, beef-
steak, pork chop and barbecue ribs. There
are a few more reds on the wine list than
average, but that inviting patio is perfect for
a cold, cold Cusqueña.

ⓘ Information

BCP (Calle de Alvarado 903) Changes money
and has an ATM.

Directur (56-2043; San Martín 301;
⊙7:30am-1pm & 2:30-5:30pm Mon-Fri) Help-
ful, but quite limited regional tourism informa-
tion for travelers.

Oficina de Información Turística (☑56-2191 ext 542; www.turismosanmartin.com; Canga 262; ☻8am-1pm & 2:30-5:15pm Mon-Fri) The municipality tourism office is a good place to pick up maps and info.

❶ Getting There & Away

Colectivos to Rioja (S4, 30 minutes) and Tarapoto (S20, two hours) leave frequently from Terminal Cajamarca on the corner of Benavides and Filomeno, three blocks east of the Plaza de Armas; and the 200 cuadra of Benavides.

The bus terminal is on Grau, about 1km from the center. Most buses between Tarapoto and Chiclayo stop here to pick up passengers.

Tarapoto

☑042 / POP 65,900 / ELEV 356M

Tarapoto, the largest and busiest town in the department of San Martín, straddles the base of the Andean foothills and the edge of the vast jungles of eastern Peru. A sweltering rainforest metropolis, it dips its toe into the Amazon Basin while managing to cling to the rest of Peru by the umbilical cord of a long paved road back to civilization. From here you can take the plunge deeper into the Amazon, or just enjoy the easily accessible jungle lite, with plenty of places to stay and eat and reliable connections to the coast.

There's a bunch of natural sights to explo nearby, from waterfalls to lagoons, a river-running opportunities will enterta the adventure-seeking contingent.

◉ Sights

Tarapoto itself has little to do, apart fro just hanging out in the town's Plaza Mayo but you can make several excursions nearby towns, waterfalls and lakes. There a small regional museum run by the unive sity on Maynas.

Laguna Azul LA
Also called Laguna de Sauce, this popula local spot is reached by crossing the R Huallaga, 45km away, on a vehicle raft fer and continuing by car for another 45 mi utes. Day tours (S85 per person, minimu two people) and overnight excursions ar available. You'll find good swimming, boa ing and fishing here, and accommodation ranging from camping to upscale bunga lows, are available. Several *combis* a da go to nearby Sauce from a bus stop in th Banda de Shilcayo district, east of the tow Taxi drivers know it.

Cataratas de Ahuashiyacu WATERFAL
This 40m waterfall is about 45 minute from Tarapoto toward Yurimaguas. There

Tarapoto

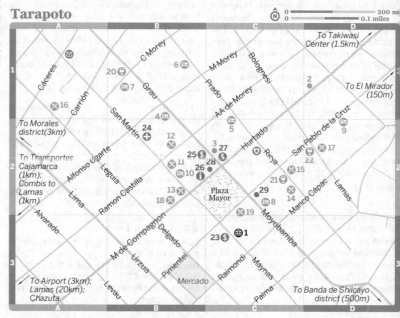

small restaurant nearby and a locally fa-
red swimming spot. Five-hour tours cost
8 to S65 per person. Also popular is a
milarly priced trip to the **Cataratas de**
uacamaillo, which involves two hours of
king and wading across the river several
mes. These places can be reached by public
ansportation and then on foot, but go with
guide or get detailed information to avoid
tting lost.

hazuta VILLAGE

two-hour drive will find the impressive
0m, three-level **Tununtunumba** waterfalls,
nother small museum showcasing pre-Inca
nerary urns, artisanal crafts and a port on
e Río Huallaga with great fishing. Agen-
es in Tarapoto are starting to promote
nystical tourism' here, where trips include
visit to local *brujos* (witch doctors). Day
urs to Chazuta (S70 to S125) are road con-
ition dependent. *Combis* leave from Jirón
laya four times a day.

amas VILLAGE

. small indigenous village that unfortu-
ately lost many of its colonial buildings in
2005 earthquake; however, it's a standard
ur destination for its small museum and
rafts. The large indigenous population here
as an annual **Feast of Santa Rosa de**
.ima in the last week of August. Although
ninibuses and *colectivos* go to Lamas from

the 10th cuadra of Jirón Urgarte, it's easiest
to visit with a guided tour (S28 to S55 per
person, four to six hours), which usually includes a visit to Ahuashiyacu waterfalls.

🏃 Activities

Rafting

The local river-running specialists run
whitewater rafting trips on the Río Mayo,
30km from Tarapoto, and on the lower Río
Huallaga, offered from June to November.
The shorter trips (half-day trips, from S70
per person) are mainly class II and III whitewater, while longer trips (up to six days,
from July to October only) ride out class III
and class IV rapids. Rafting trips to the class
III rapids of the upper Mayo, 100km from
Tarapoto, are possible. Inflatable kayaks are
available for rent with mandatory guide for
S100 for a half-day. Try safety-first **Ecoru-**
tas (☏52-3082; www.ecorutas.pe; Hurtado 435)
whose owner, Julio, speaks a bit of English;
or **Kuriyacu** (☏94-279-3388; www.kuriyacu.
com), who can arrange guides in English and
French.

Rehabilitation/Ayahuasca

Brujos play a pivotal role in the pueblos of
the jungle. A few kilometers north of Tarapoto, you'll find the **Takiwasi Center** (☏52-
2818; www.takiwasi.com; Prologación Alerta 466),
a rehabilitation and detox center started in

Tarapoto

the early 1990s by French physician Jacques Mabit. The center combines traditional Amazonian medicines and plants, as used by *brujos* or *curanderos* (healers), with a combination of psychotherapy. This treatment is not for the fainthearted: intense 'vomit therapy' and *ayahuasca* (hallucinogenic brew made from jungle vines) are used as part of the healing process. Rehabilitation programs for all kinds of ailments cost around S3000 per month, though no one is turned away for lack of funds. Information and introductory sessions can be organized.

Tours & Guides

All of these licensed agencies have several years' experience in local tourism.

Martín Zamora Tours
GUIDED TOURS

(☑52-5148; www.martinzamoratarapoto.com; Grau 233) Tarapoto's go-to operator for day tours and longer excursions to local lakes and waterfalls and cultural trips.

Quiquiriqui Tours
GUIDED TOURS

(☑52-4016; www.qtperu.com; San Martín 373-377) A full-service travel and tour agency that books flights, offers information on and arranges higher-end tours to local sites.

Sleeping

TOP CHOICE Pumarinri Amazon Lodge
JUNGLE LODGE $$$

(☑042-52-6694; www.pumarinri.com; Carretera Chazuta Km 16; s/d/ste incl breakfast S159/209/309; ✳☒) Located 30km east of Tarapoto on the banks of the Río Huallaga and surrounded by transitional mountain rainforest, this thatched-roof retreat is a perfect escape from the *mototaxi* blues. Most rooms are upscale-basic but very comfortable with expansive river view terraces while the newer annex adds flat-screen satellite TVs, air-con and concrete Jacuzzi soaking tubs big enough for three. Excursions from the tranquil setting include nearby waterfalls, treks to spot the poison dart frog, boat tours and bird-spotting some 260 recorded species within a 16km radius. Upon return, the Lima-trained kitchen fishes your *gamitana* straight from their own breeding pond. Three-day, two-night packages (S450) including all meals, excursions and transfers are perfect value.

La Patarashca Hospedaje
GUESTHOUSE $

(☑52-3899, 52-7554; www.lapatarashca.com; Lamas 261; s without/with air-con S50/70, d with-

out/with air-con S90/135, tr without air-con S12 all incl breakfast; ✳☒) It's not without issue but a pregnant cat didn't come crashing through the ceiling of our room this tin around, so things are on the up and u Tucked away on sprawling grounds flus with jungly fauna, the varied rooms he all have hot-water electric showers (son squeezed into rather cramped bathroom and cable TVs, while nice bits of furnitu and crafty lamps make them feel home and welcoming. A few ornery macaws dri home a sense of place; as does the best r gional restaurant in town, attached by small walkway.

Tucan Suites
APART-HOTEL $$

(☑52-8383;TK; www.tucansuites.com; 1st de Ab 315; s/d S209/249, apt from S369; ✳@☒) Th brand-spanking new apart-hotel in the *ba rio* (neighborhood) of Banda de Shilcayo Tarapoto's first four-star hotel. Spacious one and two-bedroom suites feature chrome-tile kitchenettes and soundproof glass, anothe city first (and wholly welcomed). Eight of th duplex rooms have open-air kitchenettes an the restaurant drops out onto a tri-level po terrace. You'll sleep no sounder in town.

El Mirador
GUESTHOUSE

(☑52-2177; www.elmiradorentarapoto.blogspot com; San Pablo de la Cruz 517; s/d/tr incl breakfas S60/85/95; ✳☒) Travelers swoon over thi friendly choice, probably because the matri arch here showers them with grandmoth erly love; or perhaps it's the excellent break fast on the small terrace with hammock and jungle views? Rooms in the main hous are nothing beyond basic, with fans, ho showers and cable TV; a new annex prom ises air-con, larger rooms and shockingl bright yellow bathrooms. Being a few blocks away from the center cuts down most o the *mototaxi* noise. Rates include airpor transfers.

Casa de Palos
GUESTHOUSE $

(☑94-031-7681; www.casadepalos.pe; Prado 155 s/d with fan S60/90, with air-con S80/100, all inc breakfast; ✳☒) This small, nine-room guest house boasts 'boutiquey' rooms with unfin ished concrete flooring and rustic woven headboards, giving it a smidgeon more char acter for this price range. Rooms surround a jungly makeshift courtyard full of chirping canaries and tiny gawking monkeys (though all are caged). There's an expansive 2nd-floor open-air terrace for breakfast.

Posada Inn   GUESTHOUSE $$

52-2234; laposada_inn@latinmail.com; San
tín 146; s/d incl breakfast S55/110, with air-con
/120; ▣⑤) This quaint hotel has beamed
lings and an inviting wooden staircase.
e classy rooms are an eclectic mix: some
ve balconies, some have air-con and some
ed new flooring. Even though it's right in
e town center, La Posada manages to re-
ain quiet.

tel Monte Azul   HOTEL $$

52-2443; www.hotelmonteazul.com.pe; Morey
; s/d S75/109, with air-con S109/159, all incl
akfast; ▣@⑤) Adorned with some nice
pping areas, it's cozy, orderly and bright
d at this price is pretty good bang for
ur buck. The staff is always switched on
d friendly, and the rooms all have quality
attresses and minifridges. Prices include
port pickup.

ojamiento Grau   GUESTHOUSE $

)52-3777; Grau 243; s/d/tr S25/50/75; ⑤) Fam-
run and friendly, this place has quiet,
an, elementary rooms with cold water
owers, all with exposed brick walls and
ndows to the inside. A very solid budget
tion.

ospedaje Misti   GUESTHOUSE $

)52-2439; Prado 341; s/d/tr from S25/45/50)
e skinny, leafy courtyard that frames the
oms redeems the typically modest dwell-
g here. Tiny bathrooms with cold water
ave little maneuvering room, but you get a
/ and ceiling fan – good shoestring value.
o extra charge for the kitschy '80s office
rniture.

otel Nilas   HOTEL $$

)52-7331/2; www.hotelnilas.com; Moyobamba
3; s/d incl breakfast S130/180; ▣@⑤☀) This
tschy lower midrange choice has a palm-
inged 3rd-floor and inviting pool that
ves it an edge in this price range, though
e spacious rooms are nothing special and
uth be told, could do with a visit from the
shion police. Amenities include a gym, res-
urant and conference center tucked away
nong the maze of cheery floors.

🍴 Eating

on't leave Tarapoto without trying *inchi-
api* (chicken soup with peanuts, cilantro
nd yucca) or *juanes* (steamed rice with fish
r chicken, wrapped in a banana leaf).

TOP
CHOICE **La Patarashca**   AMAZONIAN/REGIONAL $$

(www.lapatarashca.com; San Pablo de la Cruz 362;
mains S13-32; ⑤) Outstanding regional Amazon cuisine is on tap in Patarashca's casual
2nd-floor dining room. Don't miss the salad
made of *chonta,* thin strips of a local hearts
of palm, with avocados doused in vinaigrette; or the namesake *patarashcas,* heaping platters of giant shrimp or fish served
soaking in a warm bath of tomatoes, sweet
peppers, onions, garlic and *sacha culantro*
(a type of cilantro) wrapped in a *bijao* leaf.
Avoid wild *paiche* from October to February,
which its commercial fishing is prohibited
due to near commercial extinction.

Tío Sergio Fast Food Amazonico   PERUVIAN $

(San Pablo de la Cruz 244; mains S7-20; ◷24hr; ⑤)
This interesting newcomer is on to something: great food from an open professional
kitchen in a trendy atmosphere at pauper
prices. The owners were already famous
around town from their regional smoked
pork and chorizo business, so those feature
prominently on the menu of burgers, house-
made pastas and sandwiches (there's even
a kid's menu). The umbrella-strewn back
patio is very pleasant and it never closes.
Gold mine.

Café d' Mundo   ITALIAN $$

(Calle de Morey 157; mains S8-32, pizza S15-32;
◷6pm-midnight) A dark and sexy establish-
ment illuminated nightly by moody can-
dlelight, this hip restaurant and bar has
outdoor seating and snug indoor lounges.
Good pizzas are the mainstay (try the cap-
rese with avocado) but some interesting re-
gionalized lasagnas and other pastas adorn
a small menu and a full bar will help you
pass the rest of the evening away comfort-
ably. Service definitely plays second fiddle
here to food and atmosphere.

Chifa Tai Pai   CHINESE $

(Rioja 252; mains S13-27; ◷11:30am-2pm &
5-11pm) If you haven't taken to jungle cuisine,
this is the yin to its yang, an excellent *chifa*
dishing out vibrant, hugely portioned Chi-
nese-Peruvian fusion. The namesake plate,
Tai Pai a la plancha, is a heaping kitchen
sink dish of chicken, pork, duck and shrimp
served on a sizzling hot plate. Portions can
easily serve two.

El Brassero   STEAKHOUSE $

(San Pablo de la Cruz 254; mains S13-22; ◷closed
Sun) Pork ribs are the specialty at this great
grill, served up simple, *a la piemienta,* with

oregano or sweet and sour, but they rake everything over the coals, including burgers, chicken and chorizo. And even though they tried to pull one over on us (slipping us pork when we ordered beef), it was still tasty so we weren't mad. Stop by for lunch for good-value S8 *menús*.

Café Plaza CAFE $
(San Martín 109; snacks S7-10, breakfast S12-20;) This modern corner cafe is the spot to double-down on serious espresso and people watching. Light snacks and desserts or a quick regional breakfast of softball-sized *juanes* are served as well. It's very popular with gringos and caffeine aficionados.

El Rincón Sureño STEAKHOUSE $$$
(Leguia 458; steaks S20-63) The nicest restaurant in town is a swish-looking establishment with intimate wood-lined rooms, rounded out by myriad archways, farmstead paraphernalia and cummerbund-bound waiters. Locals swear the meat is top notch, but we were sorely disappointed with our S25 *bife a la pimienta*. Maybe you have to splash out for the S65 *bife de chorizo*, a superior cut of Peruvian beef prepared Argentine style? For Tarapoto, the wine list is impressive.

Banana's Burgers BURGERS $
(Calle de Morey 102; burgers S5-14; to 4am) Bar stool burger bar and regional juices.

Supermercado la Inmaculada SELF-CATERING $
(Calle de Compagnon 126; 8:30am-10pm) This supermarket has everything you might need for self-catering.

Drinking

La Alternativa BAR
(Grau 401; 9am-8pm) Like drinking in a medieval pharmacy or maybe a Taratino film, a night out here harkens to a time when alcohol was literally medicine (like, for ailments, not for your emotional problems); and your local apothecary was the place to get sauced on God knows what elixir happened upon the inside of a bottle. Shelves here are stacked pharmaceutical-style with dusty bottles containing *uvachado* and other 15 other homemade natural concoctions based on soaking roots, vines etc in cane liquor. The moody lighting and roaming acoustic guitar-wielding songster are bonuses.

Stonewasi Taberna
(Lamas 218; cocktails S6-18) Stonewasi is a years in now and still the northern hi lands' best bar – and the place to see a be seen in Tarapoto. Recycled sewing tab street side are chock-full of punters, *mo taxi* drivers and the town's bold and bea tiful thronging to a theme of internatio rock and house music.

La Fruta Madre JUICE
(Rioja 240; juices S5.50-6.50; closed Sun) P ticularly inviting juice bar; hilarious nam

Information
BCP (Maynas 130) Cashes traveler's checks and has an ATM.
Clínica San Martín (San Martín 274; 24hr) The best medical care in town.
Interbank (Grau 119) ATM.
Oficina de Información Turistica (52-618 Hurtado s/n; 8am-8pm Mon-Sat, to 1pm Su The *municipalidad's* tourist info on Plaza May
Policía Nacional (52-2141; cnr Rioja & Hurtado)
Scotiabank (Hurtado 215) Cashes traveler's checks and has an ATM.
Serpost (San Martín 482) Postal services.

Getting There & Away
Air
The **airport** (TTP) is 3km southwest of the center, a S4 *mototaxi* ride.

LAN (52-9318; www.lan.com; Hurtado 183 has two scheduled flights per day leaving Lima at 9:20am and 8:20pm, returning to Lima at 11am and 10pm. A third flight in between depar at various hours depending on the day of the week. Flights start at S372.

Star Perú (52-8765; www.starperu.com; San Pablo de la Cruz 100) has two daily flights from Lima to Tarapoto and vice versa at varying hours depending on the day from S258.50. It also departs from Tarapoto to Pucallpa at

ROAD TIP

The southbound journey via Bellavista to Juanjuí (145km) and on to Tocache Nuevo, Tingo María (485km) and Pucallpa (674km) is safe during the day only. At time of research, the road was paved to Juanhuí and from Tocache Nuevo to Tingo María with works in progress in between. If you go, avoid traveling at night.

TARAPOTO BUSES

DESTINATION	COST (S)	DURATION (HR)
Chazuta	8	½
Chiclayo	40-80	14
Jaén	40	9-12
Juanjuí	15	3
Lamas	5	¾
Lima	100-165	26-30
Moyobamba	20	2
Pedro Ruíz	40-45	7
Piura	60	16-17
Pucallpa	100	16-18
Sauce	15	4
Tingo María	80	13
Tocache Nuevo	50	8
Trujillo	65-150	15-18
Yurimaguas	15-20	2½

30pm on Tuesday and Saturday, returning to rapoto on Monday and Thursday at 6:45pm. res for this route start at S291.90. You can so fly to Iquitos, departing Tarapoto at 3:15pm ery day except Monday and Wednesday, when e flight departs at 1:45pm. It returns from uitos at 5pm every day except Monday and ednesday when it returns at 3:30pm. Fares art at S283.

Taca (0-800-1-8222; www.taca.com; Plaza ayor 182) flies from Lima to Tarapoto at 8pm, turning at 10pm daily from S167.20.

us & Taxi

everal companies head west on the paved road Lima via Moyobamba, Chiclayo and Trujillo, enerally leaving between 8am and 4pm. All ese companies can be found along the same adra of Salaverry and its cross streets in the orales district, an S2 mototaxi ride from the wn center. If you're heading to Chachapoyas, u'll need to change in Pedro Ruíz.

iva (52-2269; www.civa.com.pe; Salaverry 40) Has a comfortable 2:45pm bus to Lima topping at Chiclayo and Trujillo.

jetur (52-6827; Salaverry 810) Has the ost frequent departures to Chiclayo and Tru-lo at 8am, 9:30am, noon, 1:30pm and 4pm.

Gran Pajatén (50-3035; Olaya 1278) ombis to Chazuta at 10:30am, 12:30pm, 30pm and 6pm.

Expreso Huamanga (94202-6486; Salaverry 655) Slower, cheaper buses to Chiclayo via Jaén for the alternative Ecuador border crossing (see p420) at noon and 4:30pm.

Movil Tours (52-9193; www.moviltours.com.pe; Salaverry 880) Top-end express buses to Lima leave at 8am and 1pm, with a 3pm departure to Trujillo and a 4pm bus to Chiclayo.

Transmar Express (53-2392; Moraca 117) Departs at 8am on Monday, Wednesday and Friday for the ride to Pucallpa via Juanjuí, Tocache Nuevo and Tingo María.

Transportes Cajamarca (59-9122; Ugarte 1438) Runs colectivos to Yurimaguas and Moyobamba throughout the day.

Transportes Chiclayo (94-952-1716; www.transporteschiclayo.com; Pasaje Menendez 104) Comfortable 4pm bus-cama to Chiclayo.

Transportes Gilmer (53-0749; Ugarte 1346) Plies the newly paved road to Yurimaguas every two hours from 5am to 7pm.

TSP (97-963-9716; Aviación 100) Has a direct Piura bus at noon, a good choice for transferring on to Mancorá.

ⓘ Getting Around

Mototaxis cruise the streets like circling sharks. A short ride in town is around S1.50, to the bus stations S2 to S3.

Amazon Basin

Best Places to Eat

» Frio y Fuego (p477)
» Burgos's House (p444)
» Das Tee Haus (p462)
» Amazon Bistro (p477)
» Belén Mercado (p474)

Best Places to Stay

» Casa Morey (p475)
» Hacienda Concepción (p447)
» La Casa Fitzcarraldo (p475)
» Ceiba Tops (p485)
» Manu Paradise Lodge (p456)

Why Go?

The best-protected tract of the world's most biodiver forest, the strange, sweltering, seductive country-within country that is Peru's Amazon Basin, is changing. Its she vastness and impenetrability has long protected its indi enous communities and diverse wildlife from external ey Tribes still exist here that have never had contact with o side civilization. More plant types flourish in one rainf est hectare than in any European country, and fauna is fantastic it defies the most imaginative western sci-fi com

But as the 21st century slowly dawns on this entici expanse of arboreal wilderness, exploitation of the rainf est's abundant natural resources threatens to irreversib damage it. The lush Peruvian Amazon offers phenomen wildlife-spotting, forays into untamed forest from the ju gle's best selection of lodges and raucous city life. But it al begs for protection. Remember that as, forging through by rough road and raging river, you'll feel like the explore who first brought international attention to this region.

When to Go
Iquitos

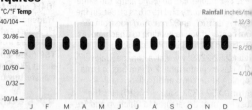

Jan Rising temperatures and water levels; a perfect time to visit the waterfalls near La Merced-

Apr & May Rains subside, heralding courtship season for many birds

Jun The rainy season ends: cue the jungle's best parties, like debauched San Juan in Iquitos

Need to Know

Allow plenty of time for your Amazon adventure: erratic weather causes delays, in forms such as landslides, broken boats and cancelled flights. Even on a good day, road and river transport is prone to overcrowding and severe hold-ups.

SELVÁMANOS

The jungle's new music festival, Selvámanos (p462) near Oxapampa, has a spectacular national park setting worth the trip out alone. Add to that a line-up from electronica to cumbia to reggae and a cultural festival that runs simultaneously and you have another can't-miss date in your Peruvian fiesta diary each June.

Jungle Checklist

this is your first jungle voyage, you'll find things far more relaxing than the movies make out. The jungle, you'll see, has largely been packaged to protect delicate tourists. With lodge facilities and the below kit list, you should be ready for most eventualities.

» Two pairs of shoes, one for jungle traipsing, one for camp.

» Spare clothes – in this humidity clothes get wet quickly; take a spare towel, too.

» Binoculars and a zoom lens camera, for wildlife in close-up.

» Flashlight for night walks.

» Mosquito repellent with DEET – bugs are everywhere.

» Sunblock and sunglasses – despite that foliage, you'll often be in direct sun.

» First-aid kit for basics such as bites, stings or diarrhea.

» Plastic bags to waterproof gear and pack nonbiodegradable litter to take back with you.

» Lightweight rainproof jacket.

» Sleeping bag, mat or hammock if sleeping outside.

» Books – cell phones rarely work and neither do TVs; electricity is limited to several hours daily.

For tips on viewing wildlife, see p524.

MAIN POINTS OF ENTRY

» Puerto Maldonado (South Amazon): connected by road, river and air.

» La Merced/San Ramon: connected by road.

» Pucallpa (Central Amazon): connected by road, river and air.

» Iquitos (Northern Amazon): connected by river and air.

Fast Facts

» Elevation: 0-1800m

» Percentage of country covered: 60%

» Main City: Iquitos

» Major Industries: tourism, coffee, agriculture, fishing, cocaine processing

» Yearly Rainfall: 3000-3500mm

Resources

One of the best independent resources is in one of the South American Explorer offices (www.saexplorers.org) in Lima or Cuzco; otherwise see lodge websites like www.manuexpeditions.com (Manu) or www.inkaterra.com (southern Amazon).

Must-try Foods

» *Juane*: Steamed rice with rice or chicken, wrapped in a jungle leaf

» Ceviche: The Amazon version, with freshwater fish

» *Parrilladas de la selva*: Jungle barbecue, with meat marinaded in Brazil-nut sauce

AMAZON BASIN

SOUTHERN AMAZON

Abutting the neighboring nations of Bolivia and Brazil, the vast tract of the southern Amazon Basin is one of the Peru's remotest territories: comparatively little of it is either inhabited or explored. That said, this is changing almost as fast as a Peruvian bus timetable, thanks to the Trans-Oceanic Highway (see boxed text, p441) transecting much of the region. Yet with well-developed facilities for ecotravelers, the benefits of travel here are clear: visitors will, with relatively little effort, be rewarded with a treasure trove of unforgettable close encounters of the wild kind.

Puerto Maldonado

♪082 / POP 56,000 / ELEV 250M

At first sight a mayhem of mud streets and manically tooting *mototaxis* (three-wheeled motorcycle rickshaw taxis), Puerto Maldonado soon endears itself to you. Its money-spinning proximity to some of the most easily visited animal-rich jungle in the entire Amazon Basin is its blessing but also its curse: travelers arrive, yet all too quickly leave again en route to the lodges and wildlife on the nearby rivers.

Yet the town's languid, laid-back ambience invites you to linger. Whether you arrive by air or by road, Puerto Maldonado will certainly be a shock to the system. Unlike Peru's larger Amazon cities further north, this is a rawer, untidier jungle town (although it's rapidly becoming more well-heeled) with a mercilessly sweltering climate and a fair quantity of mosquitoes. But its beautiful plaza and burgeoning accommodation options will, together with a lively nightlife, provide plenty of reason to hang around here for a couple of days.

The town itself has been important over the years for rubber, logging, gold and oil prospecting, and its commercial role has taken on greater dimensions as a port of call on the Transoceanic Highway (see boxed text, p441). It's of foremost importance to travelers, however, as the jumping-off point for a voyage on the Ríos Tambopata and Madre de Dios, converging here. These watery wonderlands offer the most accessible primary jungle locales in the country, yet are served by excellent accommodation options for those craving that touch of luxury. Undisputedly, Puerto Maldonado offers travelers more chance to see, feel and he the Amazonian jungle than anywhere el in Peru.

⊙ Sights & Activities

You'll wind up needing wheels to naviga Puerto Maldonado: while the city center compact the two main ports (the Río Mad de Dios and Tambopata ferry docks) an sights like the obelisco are spread-eagled its edges. This is a good opportunity to tak a *mototaxi:* one of the city's memorable e periences in any case.

Obelisco
TOWE
(cnr Fitzcarrald & Madre de Dios; admission S. ⊙10am-4pm) Although this strangley cosmi blue building was designed as a modern *m rador* (lookout tower), its 30m height un fortunately does not rise high enough abov the city for viewers to glimpse the river The view is still fantastic: a distant glimme of jungle and plenty of corrugated-meta roofs can be admired! Photos displayed o the way up document such historic mo ments as when the first *mototaxi* arrive in town.

Butterfly Farm
FAR
(Av Aeropuerto km6; admission S20) Peru boast the greatest number of butterfly specie in the world (some 3700) and you can se many of them here at this well-run butter fly conservation project, initiated in 1996 There are also displays on rainforest conser vation. This is a welcome center for traveler en route to one of Inkaterra's jungle lodge and if you're in that category you'll be ex empt from paying the extortionate entry fee Butterflies are nice, but at this price remem ber you'll see lots of species *gratis* (free) in the jungle proper.

Puerto Capitanía
POR
This dock close to the Plaza de Armas is a cheap way of seeing a little of the action on a major Peruvian jungle river (the Río Madre de Dios), which is about 500m wide at this point. River traffic is colorful – *peki-pekis* (canoes powered by two-stroke motorcycle engines with outlandishly long propeller shafts) leave from the dock – but vastly re duced since the opening of Puente Guiller mo Billinghurst (Puente Intercontinental), the bridge now carrying the Transoceanic Highway across the river a few hundred meters to the northwest. Gone are the days when a furor of decrepit catamarans ferried

Amazon Basin Highlights

1 Travel overland through a smorgasbord of Peruvian scenery via mountains, cloud forest and jungle to **Parque Nacional Manu** (p453)

2 Spot Amazonian animals and birds at the upper echelons of the **Río Tambopata** (p451) and the **Reserva Nacional Pacaya-Samiria** (p471)

3 Embark on a memorable voyage to visit the Asháninka people from **Puerto Bermúdez** (p463)

4 Swing in a hammock on a riverboat from **Pucallpa** (p463) or **Yurimaguas** (p469) to **Iquitos** (p471)

5 Rise and shine for a trip to Peru's premier jungle market

in the floating district of **Belén** (p474) in Iquitos

6 Tuck into the diverse, wondrous and often downright weird eating scene of **Iquitos** (p471)

7 Admire world-class art in the depths of the rainforest at the gallery of Francisco Grippa in **Pevas** (p485)

Brazil-bound drivers and the vehicles across the river alongside a constant tirade of smaller craft coming and going to this-or-that port amid a splutter of wheezing engines. *Bienvenido* to the 21st century.

Infierno INDIGENOUS CULTU...

About an hour southeast of Puerto Mald... nado is Infierno (Hell!), home and hub of a... tivity for the Ese'eja tribespeople. It's a live... spread-out settlement, which is establishi...

Puerto Maldonado

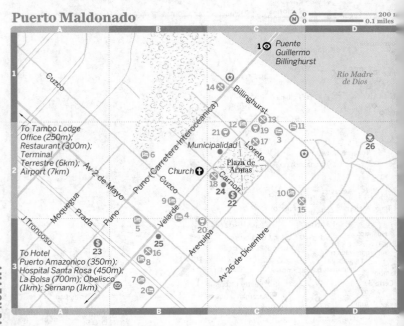

Puerto Maldonado

◎ Sights

1 Puente Guillermo Billinghurst
  (Puente Intercontinental) C1
  Puerto Capitania (Madre de Dios
  Dock) .... (see 26)
  Tambopata Hostel .... (see 10)

🛏 Sleeping

2 Cayman Lodge Amazonie Office B3
3 Corto Maltes Office C2
  Estancio Bello Horizonte Office ... (see 17)
4 Hospedaje Rey Port B2
5 Hospedaje Royal Inn B3
6 Inkaterra office B2
7 Libertador Tambopata Lodge
  Office B3
8 Paititi Hostal B3
9 Señora Leny Mejía Lodge Office B2
10 Tambopata Hostel C2
11 Wasai Lodge C2
12 Yakari Canopy Adventure
  Office C2

✖ Eating

13 Burgos's House C1
14 Burgos's House C1
15 El Catamaran C2
16 La Casa Nostra B3
17 Los Gustitos del Cura C2
18 Pizzería El Hornito/Chez Maggy C2

🍸 Drinking

19 Discoteca Witite C2
20 Gecko's B3
21 Tsaica C2

ℹ Information

22 BCP C2
23 Casa de Cambio A3
24 Locutorio C2

ℹ Transport

25 LAN Peru B3
26 Madre de Dios Ferry Crossing
  Dock D2

TRANSOCEANIC HIGHWAY: ROAD TO RICHES & RUIN

Few events in history have had such an immediate effect on the Amazon rainforest as the construction of the Transoceanic Highway (Carretera Interoceánica) seems likely to have: following its completion in July 2011, it now links the Pacific coast of Peru with the Atlantic coast of Brazil via paved road. At a cost of more than US$2800 million, the road is now a massive export opportunity for both countries (former Peruvian president Alejandro Toledo estimated the road would signify a 1.5% annual increase in Peru's GDP). The 2500km-plus of newly constructed road breaches the dual hazards of the Andes and the rainforest to link the Peruvian coast at San Juan de Marcona near Nazca via Cuzco to the southern Amazon, through Puerto Maldonado, to the Brazilian border at Iñapari. From there the road runs to Rio Branco in Brazil and feeds into the Brazilian road system.

The effects of the road, good and bad, are already being felt. Thousands of new jobs have been created and Puerto Maldonado, the main city on the route not previously connected by asphalted highway, is thriving from the increased tourism (Cuzco is now only 10 hours away by road) and commerce.

But for the estimated 15 uncontacted tribes that inhabit the once-isolated southeastern corner of Peru, the road now cutting through their territory brings risk of disease, and of loss of hunting grounds. According to one NGO, Survival International, the possibility of migration a road creates without the facilities to back up such a migration would, along with the destruction of natural habitat, have a disastrous effect on such peoples. And if there are 15 human groups at risk, there are infinitely more species of plants and animals. The total area of destroyed rainforest as a result of the Transoceanic's construction equates to a third of the size of the UK and, according to various studies on roads in the Brazilian Amazon, is likely to have a significant effect on rainforest deforestation for 40km to 60km on either side.

Yet the devastation the building of the road has caused is less significant than the devastation that people who now have improved access to the remote rainforest could bring. Newspapers from the *Peruvian Times* to the *Guardian* have reported on the 'prosibars' (bars with often underage prostitutes) springing up along routes which can now be traversed with greater ease by the prospecting miners and loggers that already posed an ecological threat to this part of the Amazon. Once, ecosystems here were renowned for being the world's most diverse and undisturbed. They still are. But, one wonders, for how much longer.

reputation, along with other Amazon locales, for its *ayahuasca* rituals, conducted by local shamans (see p442). Arrange your own transport here via car or motorbike: *mototaxis* won't make the rough journey.

Courses

Tambopata Hostel LANGUAGE COURSE
(57-4201; www.tambopatahostel.com; Av 26 de Diciembre 234) Tambopata Hostel can arrange fun salsa classes, basic Spanish lessons and Peruvian cookery classes for very reasonable prices.

Tours & Guides

Most visitors arrive with prearranged tours and stay at a jungle lodge – which is convenient but by no means the only possibility. You can also arrange a tour upon arrival by going to the lodge offices in town, where you might get a small discount on a tour that would cost more in Lima or Cuzco. You can also look for an independent guide. Bear in mind that choosing one not affiliated to a lodge, or one without a license, does give you less recourse in the event of a disastrous trip.

Choosing a guide is a lottery: they'll offer you tours for less, but stories of bad independent guides are not uncommon. Beware of guides at the airport, who often take you to a 'recommended' hotel (and collect a commission) and then hound you throughout your stay. There are crooked operators out there, too. Shop around, don't prepay for any tour and, if paying an advance deposit, insist on a signed receipt. If you agree to a boat driver's price, make sure it includes the return trip, and if quoted prices are all-inclusive or exclusive of entrance fees.

WARNING: AYAHUASCA

Throughout your travel in the Peruvian Amazon, you will come across numerous places offering the chance to partake of *ayahuasca*. This is the derivative of a hallucinogenic jungle vine, used to attain a purgative trancelike state by shamans (witch doctors) for centuries and now increasingly popular with Westerners. *Ayahuasca* is invariably taken as part of a ceremony that can last anything from hours to days, depending upon who is conducting the rituals. Be wary of taking *ayahuasca*: it can have serious side effects, including severe convulsions and dramatic rises in blood pressure. If mixed with the wrong substances, it has even been known to be fatal.

Also be sure to do your research into the ceremony you're signing up for: among some shamans offering a genuine ritualistic experience (although even so the afore-mentioned health risks still apply) there are charlatans out there who have also been known to rob and on occasion rape unsuspecting gringos under the influence. As well as a number of independently operating shamans, the vast majority of jungle lodges offer *ayahuasca* ceremonies and many of these lodges are reviewed in this chapter, although not because they offer these ceremonies. Lonely Planet does not recommend taking *ayahuasca* and those who wish to, do so at their own risk.

There are about 30 guides with official licenses granted by the local Ministerio de Industria y Turismo. Many of the best ones work full time for one of the local jungle lodges. Guides charge from S75 to S175 per person per day, depending on the destination and number of people. Going with more people reduces the cost; in fact, some guides will only take tours with a three-person minimum. Note that tours require boat rides to leave from Puerto Maldonado: boats use a lot of gas and are notoriously expensive to run; this (along with park entrance fees) influences guided tour rates.

The following are recommended:

Gerson Medina Valera　　GUIDED TOUR
(☎57-4201; www.tambopatahostel.com) Gerson has lots of experience in bird-watching tours and speaks fluent English. His one- to three-day Lago Sandoval tours (around S175 per person per day) are inclusive of all costs. He'll even let you know the chances of seeing every type of Tambopata animal and bird so you'll know what to expect on your tour. He also arranges tailored fishing trips (S175 to S300 per person).

Nilthon Tapia Miyashiro　　GUIDED TOUR
(☎982-788-174; nisa_30@hotmail.com) A well-known, experienced guide, also reachable through Tambopata Hostel.

Jony Valles Rengifo　　GUIDED TOUR
(☎982-704-736; jhovar@hotmail.com) Speaks English and French.

🛏 Sleeping

Besides the plethora of basic budget places you can now choose from pleasant backpacker accommodations or comfortable lodges and hotels. Note that not all lodges have reservations offices in Puerto Maldonado; some only have offices in Cuzco, Lima or the USA.

Outside Puerto Maldonado are a dozen jungle lodges (see p447, p450, p451 and p452).

TOP CHOICE Tambopata Hostel　　HOSTEL $
(☎57-4201; 26 de Diciembre 234; www.tambopatahostel.com; dm/s/d S25/50/80, s/d without bathroom S40/70; ☎) Puerto Maldonado finally has the backpacker accommodations it desperately needed. This clean, relaxing hostel has a mix of dorm and private rooms abutting a garden courtyard with hammocks and a huge breakfast is included in the price. There are secure lockers and the owner is one of the town's best jungle guides.

Anaconda Lodge　　LODGE $$
(☎79-2726; Av Aeropuerto Km 6; www.anacondajunglelodge.com; bungalow s/d/tr S100/160/220, bungalow without bathroom s/d S50/80; ☎) Cocooned in its own tropical garden on the edge of town, this lodge has a more remote feel than its location (Maldonado's quiet airport) would suggest. There are eight double-room bungalows with shared bathroom and four luxury bungalows with private facilities; all are mosquito netted. There's also camping space (per person S20), a small pool and a spacious two-floor restaurant-bar

rving great Thai food and pancake break-
sts.

Vasai Lodge
LODGE **$$**

☏57-2290; www.wasai.com; Billinghurst at Areq-
pa; s/d S130/170; ❄☷) This small lodge
onsists of comfortable wooden bungalows
verlooking the Madre de Dios. A few rooms
ffer air-con for an extra S30. Minifridges,
ot showers, cable TV and river views, how-
ver, are standard. The room lighting is
retty abysmal, so bring a flashlight for good
heasure. There is a good restaurant (mains
15 to S20), room service, a bar and a small
ool. The lodge arranges various trips in the
ocal area.

Hotel Puerto Amazonico
HOTEL **$$**

☏57-2170, 50-2354; www.hotelpuertoamazonico.
om.pe; León Velarde 1080; s/d incl buffet breakfast
180/240; ❄☏☷) Puerto Maldonado needed
his: it might be a little overpriced but you
an't argue that the rooms are probably the
ity's best. The more you pay, the more the
ize of your flat-screen TV increases. The
iews from the roof are some of the best
round too, although at this price you'd ex-
ect a lift.

Kapieivi Eco Village
LODGE **$$**

☏79-5650; katherinapz@hotmail.com; Carretera
ambopata Km 1.5; 1-2-person bungalow incl break-
ast S100/125; ☷) This rustic, reader-recom-
nended retreat, 2km southwest of town, lets
ackpackers experience a taste of lodge life
without the price tag, in several bungalows
for one, two or four people) enclosed within
a wild plot of jungle scrub. A renovation
neans bungalows now have private bath-
rooms, and a swimming pool has appeared
on the scene. The laid-back owners offer
vegetarian food, *ayahuasca* ceremonies and
yoga classes. Food and drink is an additional
S18 per person per day.

Hospedaje Royal Inn
GUESTHOUSE **$**

(☏57-3464; 2 de Mayo 333; s/d S35/50; ☏) A
good choice for travelers, sporting lots of
large, clean rooms with fans. The courtyard
has seen better days, but the owners have
tarted up the rooms significantly since our
last visit, making this a decent budget op-
tion. Cable TV comes with each. Get a court-
yard-facing room as street-facing rooms are
noisy.

Paititi Hostal
HOTEL **$$**

(☏57-4667; fax 57-2567; Prada 290; s/d incl breakfast S80/110; ☏) A new, relatively flash, central place, the Paititi has a series of spacious,
airy rooms, many full of attractive old wood-
en furniture, along with telephones and cable TV. A continental breakfast is included,
and there's even hot water at night – very
un-Amazon.

Hospedaje Rey Port
GUESTHOUSE **$**

(☏57-1177; Velarde 457; s/d S20/40, without bathroom S10/20) This one's for bargain hunters,
generations of which have been sniffing out
the Rey Port's 'charms.' Rooms are mostly
clean and have fans, but flash they ain't.
Ground-floor courtyard rooms with shared
bathrooms may be cheapest, but the top
floor has large (10 grubby) rooms with private bathrooms for S15 per person.

 Eating

Regional specialties include *juanes* (rice
steamed with fish or chicken in a banana
leaf), *chilcano* (a broth of fish chunks flavored with the native cilantro herb) and *parrillada de la selva* (a barbecue of marinated
meat, often game, in a Brazil-nut sauce). A

JUNGLE LODGE BEST OF

Best Amazon lodge for...

Remoteness Tahuayo Lodge (p484)

Luxury Ceiba Tops (p485)

Bird-watching Tambopata Research Center (p453), Cock-of-the-Rock Lodge (p457)

Animal spotting Manu Wildlife Center (p458)

Learning about the rainforest Otorongo Lodge (p483)

Faded colonial charm Amazonia Lodge (p457)

Budget adventure Yakari Canopy Adventure (p450)

Classy cooking Hacienda Concepción (p447)

Indigenous encounters Casa Matsiguenka Lodge (p457), Posada Amazonas (p451)

plátano (plantain) is served boiled or fried as an accompaniment to many meals.

Also consider the ambient restaurant at Wasai Lodge (p443).

La Casa Nostra
CAFE $
(Velarde 515; snacks S3-8; ⊗8am-1pm & 5-11pm) It's become a tad complacent, but this cafe is still decent enough to stand out against most: it serves varied breakfasts, tamales, great juices, snacks and Puerto Maldonado's best coffee.

Los Gustitos del Cura
DESSERTS $
(Loreto 258; snacks S3-8; ⊗11am-10pm) For a sweet treat or the best ice cream in town, drop in to this French-owned patisserie with a pleasant courtyard at the rear. Sandwiches, cakes and drinks are dished up, and local *objets d'art* are on sale.

El Catamaran
CEVICHE $$
(Jirón 26 de Diciembre 241; mains S18-30; ⊗7:30am-3pm) This is the place to feast on great freshwater ceviche (raw seafood marinated in lime juice), as the contingent of local dignitaries clearly think: there's a nice decked seating area out back with river views.

Restaurant
PERUVIAN $
(cnr Av 2 de Mayo & Madre de Dios; mains S10-15; ⊗dinner) It may have no name, street number or phone number but this place is far from unknown by the locals, who flock here for great fish with rice and *plátano*. Food is prepared on a grill outside and tables fill up fast.

Burgos's House
PERUVIAN $$
(Velarde 127; mains S15-23; ⊗11am-midnight) This has quickly developed into Puerto Maldonado's stand-out restaurant. It calls itself an exponent of novo-amazonica cuisine – that's like novo-andino, only instead making those bold culinary adaptations to food from the jungle – but this is more about dependable Peruvian Amazon staples, cooked to perfection rather than with particular innovation. It's a large, airy, courteously staffed restaurant and serves plenty of vegetarian dishes alongside its fish-focused specialties. Another branch is at Puno 106.

Pizzería El Hornito/Chez Maggy
PIZZERIA $$
(Carrión 271; pizzas S21-30; ⊗6pm-late) This popular but dimly lit hangout on the Plaza de Armas serves pasta and amply sized, wood-fired pizzas – the best in town.

Drinking & entertainment

The city's nightlife, while nothing besic Lima or Cuzco, is some of the Amazon's live liest. Discos mostly just have recorded mu sic, but bars and clubs pound away until th early hours of a weekend.

Discoteca Witite
CLU
(Velarde 153) Brightly painted Witite ha stood the test of time. The crowd is mixe and at weekends the partying here goes o all night.

Tsaica
BA
(Loreto 327; ⊗Tue-Sat) Lively, and with funk indigenous art on the walls.

Gecko's
BA
(Cuzco cuadra 2 s/n) Garishly decorated ba with a pool table and bizarre cocktails wit jungle plants; next door the ambient restau rant El Tambo dishes up wholesome day time meals for around S6.

La Bolsa
LIVE MUSI
(⊗to 2am Thu-Sat) Vast place renowned a a *peña* (bar or club featuring live folklori music) with tables fanning out along the Rí Tambopata. If you want a view while yo drink, come here.

Shopping

Proximity to local tribes means many of the lodges around town, such as Posadas Ama zonas on the Río Tambopata, are better fo purchasing local handicrafts than the towr itself.

ⓘ Information

Immigration

The border town of Iñapari (see boxed text, p445) has regular border-crossing facilities to enter Brazil.

Oficina de migraciónes (immigration office; ☑57-1069; Av 28 de Julio 467; ⊗8am-1pm Mon-Fri) To leave Peru via Puerto Heath (river) or Iberia (road) for Bolivia (see p446), get your passport stamped here. Travelers can also extend their visas or tourist cards here.

Internet Access

Internet is slower here than in other Peruvian cities, costing about S2 per hour.

Locutorio (Carrión cuadra 2) On the plaza; international calls too.

Laundry

Lavandería (Velarde 926) Wash your repulsive jungle rags here.

BORDER CROSSING: BRAZIL VIA PUERTO MALDONADO

A good paved road, part of the Transoceanic Highway, goes from Puerto Maldonado to Iberia and on to Iñapari, 233km from Puerto Maldonado, on the Brazilian border. Along the road are small settlements of people involved in the Brazil nut farming, cattle ranching and logging industries. After about 170km you reach **Iberia**, which has very basic hotels. The village of **Iñapari** is another 70km beyond Iberia.

Peruvian border formalities can be carried out in Iñapari. Stores around the main plaza accept and change both Peruvian and Brazilian currency; if leaving Peru, it's best to get rid of any nuevos soles here. Small denominations of US cash are negotiable, and hotels and buses often quote rates in US dollars. From Iñapari, you can cross over the new bridge to **Assis Brasil**, which has better hotels (starting from around US$10 per person).

US citizens need to get a Brazilian visa beforehand, either in the USA or Lima. It's 325km (six to seven hours) by paved road from here to the important Brazilian city of Rio Branco, via Brasiléia (100km, two hours).

For more detailed coverage beyond this point, pick up Lonely Planet's *Brazil*, or get *The Amazon Travel Guide* from the **Lonely Planet online shop** (http://shop.lonely planet.com).

edical Services
ospital Santa Rosa (☑57-1019, 57-1046; ajamarca 171)

oney
erhaps unsurprisingly, Brazilian reais and olivian bolivianos have become much easier exchange here since the opening of the Tran-ceanic Highway: ask where is currently giving e best exchange rate.

CP (Carrión 201) On Plaza de Armas; changes S cash or traveler's checks and has a Visa TM.

asa de Cambio (Puno at Prada) Standard ates for US dollars.

ost
ost office (Velarde) Southwest of the Plaza e Armas.

ourist Information
ernanp (☑57-3278; www.sernanp.gob.pe/ ernanp; Av 28 de Julio 875) The national park ffice gives information and collects entrance ees (in nearly all cases, guides sort this out); tandard entrance to the Tambopata reserve one is S30 but increases to S65 for visiting reas away from the riverside lodges. The vebsite is in Spanish only.

Tourist Booth (airport) Run by the Ministerio le Industria y Turismo; provides limited infor-nation on tours and jungle lodges.

❶ Getting There & Away
Most travelers fly here from Lima or Cuzco, but ous is now a viable option too. The long river rips from Manu or Bolivia are (when possible) only for hardened, adventurous travelers.

Air
The airport is 7km outside town. Scheduled flights leave every day to/from Lima via Cuzco with **LAN** (☑57-3677; www.lan.com; Velarde 503) and **Star Perú** (☑57-3564; www.starperu. com; Velarde 151). Schedules and airlines can change from one year to the next, but numerous travel agents in the town center have the latest details.

Boat
Hire boats at the Río Madre de Dios ferry dock for local excursions or to take you downriver to destinations such as Lago Sandoval, Río Heath and the Bolivian border (for more on crossing the border into Bolivia or Brazil see boxed texts this page and p446). It's difficult to find boats going up the Madre de Dios (against the current) to Manu; Cuzco is a better departure point for Manu. Occasionally, people reach Puerto Maldonado by boat from Manu (with the current) or from the Bolivian border (against the current). If you're set on the former option, Amazon Trails Peru of Cuzco (p455) can arrange boat/bus options with a Manu package. Transportation is infrequent: be prepared for waits of several days.

At the Tambopata dock, 2km south of town and reached by *mototaxis*, there are public boats up the Tambopata as far as the community of Baltimore. The *Tiburón* leaves twice a week (currently Monday and Thursday) and can drop you off at lodges between Puerto Maldonado and Baltimore. The fare is S20 or less, depending how far you go. All passengers must stop at La Torre Puesto de Control (checkpoint), where passports and Sernanp permits (S30) are need-ed. (For details on Sernanp permits, see above).

BORDER CROSSING: BOLIVIA VIA PUERTO MALDONADO

There are three ways of reaching Bolivia from the Puerto Maldonado area. One is to go to Brasiléia in Brazil (see boxed text, p445) and cross the Río Acre by ferry or bridge to **Cobija** in Bolivia, where there are hotels, banks, an airstrip with erratically scheduled flights further into Bolivia, and a rough gravel road with several river crossings to the city of **Riberalta** (seven to 12 hours depending on season). From Iberia in Peru on the Transoceanic Highway to Iñapari, a road also runs to Cobija, but public transportation mostly uses the Iñapari/Assis Brasil route.

Alternatively, hire a boat at Puerto Maldonado's Madre de Dios dock to take you to the Peru–Bolivia border at **Puerto Pardo**. A few minutes from Puerto Pardo by boat is **Puerto Heath**, a military camp on the Bolivian side. The trip takes half a day and costs about US$100 (but is negotiable) – the boat will carry several people. With time and luck, you may also be able to find a cargo boat that's going there anyway and will take passengers more cheaply.

It's possible to continue down the river on the Bolivian side, but this can take days (even weeks) to arrange and isn't cheap. Travel in a group to share costs, and avoid the dry months of July to September, when the river is too low. From Puerto Heath, continue down the Río Madre de Dios as far as Riberalta (at the confluence of the Madre de Dios and Beni, far into northern Bolivia), where road and air connections can be made: a classic (if tough) Amazon adventure the like of which no road trip can compete with. Basic food and shelter (bring a hammock) can be found en route. When river levels allow, a cargo and passenger boat runs from Puerto Maldonado to Riberalta and back about twice a month, but this trip is rarely done by foreigners. From Puerto Heath, a dirt road goes to **Chivé** (1½ hours by bus), from where you can continue to Cobija (six hours).

Get your Peruvian exit stamp in Puerto Maldonado. Bolivian entry stamps can be obtained in Puerto Heath or Cobija. Visas are not available, however, so get one ahead of time in Lima or your home country if you need it. US citizens need to pay US$135 in cash for a visa to enter Bolivia.

Formalities are generally slow and relaxed.

Boats to jungle lodges leave from both docks, depending on the lodge location. When transporting visitors upriver, some Río Tambopata lodges avoid two hours of river travel by taking the bumpy track to Infierno (about one hour), and continuing by boat from there. Travel to Infierno needs to be arranged in advance: there is nowhere to stay there and no boats await passengers.

Bus & Taxi

Trucks, minibuses and *colectivos* (shared taxis) leave Puerto Maldonado for Laberinto (1½ hours), passing the turnoff to Baltimore at Km 37 on the Cuzco road. They leave frequently during the morning and less often in the afternoon from the corner of Ica and Rivero. *Colectivos* to Iñapari (S30, three hours), near the borders with Brazil and Bolivia, leave with **Mi Nuevo Peru** (57-4325; cnr Piura & Ica) when they have four passengers. Other companies on the same block also advertise this trip. A minivan is a few soles cheaper, but the journey is a significantly more uncomfortable, protracted experience.

From the new **Terminal Terrestre** (cnr Av Elmer Faucett & Av Aeropuerto) buses ply the new (and paved) Tranoceanic Highway (Carretera Interocéanica) southwest to Cuzco and northeast to Rio Branco, Brazil. Numerous companies leave either during the morning or at night (around 8pm) to Cuzco (S50, 10 hours). Options to Rio Branco are more scant but include **Movil Tours** (989-176-309), departing Tuesday and Friday at 12:30pm (S100, nine to 10 hours). It's advisable to buy your ticket as much in advance of travel as possible.

ⓘ Getting Around

Mototaxis take two or three passengers (and light luggage) to the airport for S7. Short rides around town cost S2 or less (S1 if you bag one of the *mototaxi* Honda 90s).

You can rent motorcycles if you want to see some of the surrounding countryside; go in pairs in case of breakdowns or accident. There are several motorcycle-rental places, mainly on Prada between Velarde and Puno. They charge about S10 per hour and have mainly small, 100cc bikes. Driving one is fun, but crazed local drivers and awful road conditions can make this option intimidating. Bargain for all-day discounts.

round Puerto Maldonado

O MADRE DE DIOS

is important river flows eastward past erto Maldonado, heading into Bolivia, azil and the Amazon proper. In the wet ason it is brown colored, flows swiftly and oks very impressive, carrying huge logs d other jungle flotsam and jetsam downeam. The main reason people come here to stay for a few days in one of several ngle lodges, all of which are to be found tween 20 minutes and three hours downeam from Puerto Maldonado itself. From is river you can also access the other desnations of note downriver: Lago Sandoval, go Valencia and Río Heath (Lago Sanval and Río Heath also have lodges).

Additionally, travelers can partake in hing and nature trips, and visit beaches and digenous communities. Some excursions inolve camping or staying in simple thatched elters. Lodges often provide rubber boots r the muddy jungle paths. (For advice on hat kit to bring with you, see p437.)

Madre de Dios and Tambopata lodges uote their prices in US dollars, which inude transportation unless stated. Luggage er person is often limited but can be stored lodge offices in Puerto Maldonado.

Sights & Activities

ou can reach Lago Sandoval (p450) from ome lodges here. A couple of canopy walkays (Inkaterra Reserva Amazonica and akari Canopy Adventure) provide a distracon from normal jungle activities. The later's is approached by a 200m zipline (see akari Canopy Adventure, p450).

Hacienda Concepción
esearch Center   VISITOR CENTER
www.wcupa.edu/aceer, www.inkaterra.com) Fornerly the ITA Aceer Tambopata Research Center, Inkaterra's reconstructed lodge is an mportant research center, and of interest to cotourists, with an exhibition on conservaion, occasional lectures and a laboratory for cientists. It's built on the site of the house f one of the first doctors to practice in the \mazon. The Hacienda Concepción lodge as a good restaurant and accommodations; nkaterra's Reserva Amazonica lodge is only km away.

Sleeping

Most lodge-style accommodations are based along the rivers. Riverside lodges are listed as you travel away from Puerto Maldonado, irrespective of price.

Corto Maltes   LODGE $$$
(082-57-3831; www.cortomaltes-amazonia.com; Billinghurst 229, Puerto Maldonado; s 3 days & 2 nights US$255) The closest lodge to Puerto Maldonado is traveler friendly and upbeat. Only 5km from town, this lodge offers 15 comfortable, fully screened, high-ceilinged bungalows with solid mattresses, eyecatching Shipibo indigenous wall art, patios with two hammocks, and cheerful decorative touches in the public areas. Electricity is available from dusk until 10:30pm, and showers have hot water. The French owners pride themselves on the excellent EuropeanPeruvian fusion cuisine.

Tambo Lodge   LODGE $$$
(082-57-2227; tambojunglelodge@hotmail.com; Ancash 250, Puerto Maldonado; per person 3 days & 2 nights US$210) Just beyond Corto Maltes, this pleasant lodge offers 14 large, airy bungalows, each furnished with hot-water showers and copious supplies of fresh drinking water, around a clearing in secondary jungle. The main restaurant-bar area is convivial, with lots of board games. Included are trips to Lago Sandoval, a 5km walk away, and Monkey Island (supposedly containing each of the Amazon's monkey species).

Hacienda Concepción   LODGE $$$
(Inkaterra; www.inkaterra.com; 3 days & 2 nights s/d US$357/616, cabins s/d US$434/704) Cuzco (084-24-5314; Plaza Nazarenas 167); Lima (01-610-0400; Andalucía 174, Miraflores); Puerto Maldonado (082-57-2823; Cuzco 436;) This bright, enticing lodge is one of the southern Amazon's best. Facilities might be classic top-end Inkaterra but the big draw is that its prices are not. Its spacious rooms, fashioned out of reclaimed timber, make you feel quite the well-to-do early-20th-century traveler, and there is a securely mosquito-netted bar, chill-out area and restaurant (serving incredible food). The serene location could hardly be better, with an onsite rainforest learning center and laboratory, its own private *cocha* (an indigenous word for lagoon) nearby and Lago Sandoval barely a stone's throw away. Electricity is from 5:30am to 9:30am and 6pm to 11pm: it's one of the few jungle lodges with cell-phone reception and wi-fi. Rooms are spread around the 2nd floor surveying the forest clearing with a broad wrap-around terrace, while cabins

AMAZON BASIN AROUND PUERTO MALDONADO

Around Puerto Maldonado

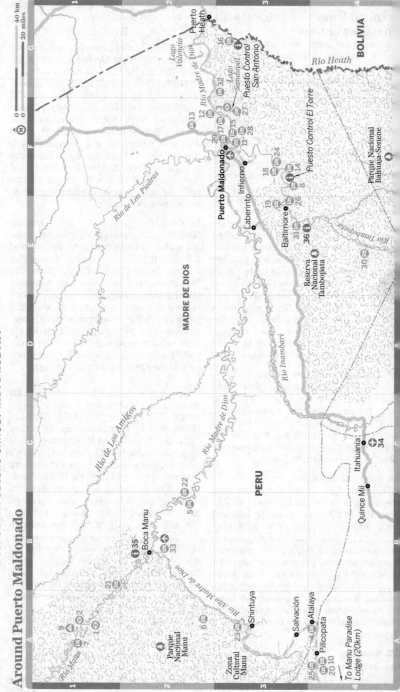

Around Puerto Maldonado

...ave secluded *cocha* views – good enough, according to staff, for celebrities such as Mick Jagger to favor. Book with Inkaterra.

Inkaterra Reserva Amazonica
LODGE $$$

(www.inkaterra.com; 3 days & 2 nights cabin s/d occupancy US$673/1082; Cuzco (☎084-24-5314; Plaza Nazarenas 167); Lima (☎01-610-0400; Andalucía 174, Miraflores); Puerto Maldonado (☎082-57-1323; Cuzco 436) Further down the Madre de Dios, almost 16km from Puerto Maldonado, this luxurious alternative offers a better look at the jungle. Tours here include 10km of private hiking trails, and a series of swaying, narrow, jungle canopy walkways up to 35m above the jungle floor for flora and fauna observation.

A huge, traditionally thatched, cone-shaped, two-story reception, restaurant, bar (built spectacularly around a fig tree), library and relaxation area greets the arriving traveler. Some of the southern Amazon's best meals are served here; travelers with special dietary needs can be accommodated. There are occasional alfresco barbecues, sitting areas upstairs for imbibing views or spotting birdlife, and a separate building housing a good interpretation center. Guides speak English, French or Italian. About 40 rustic individual cabins have bath-rooms and porches with two hammocks. Six suites boast huge bathrooms, writing desks and two queen beds each.

EcoAmazonia Lodge
LODGE $$$

(www.ecoamazonia.com.pe; per person 3 days & 2 nights US$240-260); Cuzco (☎084-23-6159; Garcilaso 210, Office 206); Lima (☎01-242-2708; Palacios 292, Miraflores); Puerto Maldonado (☎082-57-3491; Lambayeque 774) Roughly 30km from Puerto Maldonado is another lodge boasting a huge, thatch-roofed restaurant and bar, with fine river views from the 2nd floor. Guides speak English, French and Italian; the knowledgeable manager also speaks Japanese. Forty-seven rustic, completely screened bungalows each have a bathroom and a small sitting room. There are several trails from this lodge, including a tough 14km hike to a lake, and several shorter walks. Boat tours to local lakes and along the rivers are also offered, and *ayahuasca* ceremonies can be arranged by advance request.

Estancia Bello Horizonte
LODGE $$$

(☎082-57-2748, 982-720-950; www.estancia bellohorizonte.com; JM Grain 105, Puerto Maldonado; per person 3 days & 2 nights US$240; ⛱) Bello Horizonte is a superb getaway, away from the river itself. Located 20km from Puerto Maldonado on the east side of the Río Madre de Dios, the final approach to the *estancia* (ranch) is along a 6km private road through dense jungle. The accommodations, built all in local wood and poised on a ridge overlooking the rainforest, comprises bungalows with smallish, comfortable rooms with bathrooms; each has a hammock for lounging in. The main building contains a relaxing dining, reading, drinking and chill-out space, and child-friendly grounds include a soccer pitch, a volleyball court, a swimming pool and signposted jungle walks.

Yakari Canopy Adventure
LODGE $$

(☎973-978-847; www.yakaicanopyadventure.com; Velarde 144, Puerto Maldonado; 3 days & 2 nights per person US$150) More an adventure center than a lodge, with the southern Amazon's first zipline whooshing you 200m up to a hair-raising 27m-high canopy walkway. When you've got back your breath, there's kayaking on the nearest stretch of the Madre de Dios. Yakari is just beyond Lago Sandoval, set amid wildlife-rich marshlands. There's currently only room for nine people in the simple lodge, but these guys have expansion plans.

LAGO SANDOVAL

An attractive jungle lake, Lago Sandoval is surrounded by different types of rainforest and is about two hours from Puerto Maldonado down the Madre de Dios. Permits to visit the lake (included on licensed guide tours and lodge stays) are S30 for the day, or S60 for stays of up to four nights. The best way to see wildlife is to stay overnight and take a boat ride on the lake, though day trips to the lake are offered. Half the trip is done by boat and the other half on foot. For about S100 (bargain – several people can travel for this price), a boat from Puerto Maldonado will drop you at the beginning of the trail and pick you up later. The boat driver will also guide you to the lake on request. With luck, you might see caiman, turtles, exotic birds, monkeys and maybe the endangered giant river otters that live in the lake.

You can also reach the lake by hiking along a 3km trail, passable year-round, from the jungle lodges here, located between Reserva Amazonica Lodge and EcoAmazonia Lodge but on the opposite (south) side of the river. From the end of this trail, you can continue 2km on a narrower, less-maintained trail to the inexpensive Willy Mejía Cepa Lodge, or take a boat ride across the lake to Sandoval Lake Lodge, the best lod hereabouts.

Willy Mejía Cepa Lodge
LODG

(☎982-684-700; lenitokon@hotmail.com; Velar 487 interior, Puerto Maldonado; r per person arou US$25) The Mejías have been offering bas accommodations to budget travelers f two decades. The lodge can sleep 20 pe ple in bungalow-style rooms with shar bathrooms. Bottled drinks are sold. Pric include simple family meals, accommod tions and excursions (in Spanish). Roo prices vary: ask about discounts, which a frequently given according to group size ar season.

Sandoval Lake Lodge
LODGE $

(InkaNatura; www.inkanatura.com; per 3 days & nights s/d US$425/650); Cuzco (☎084-23-113 Ricardo Palma J1 Urb Santa Mónica & Plateros 36. Lima (☎01-440-2022; Manuel Bañón 461, San Is ro) This InkaNatura-owned lodge is on th other side of the lake to Willy Mejía. Gettì there is half the fun. After hiking the 3km the lake (bicycle rickshaws are available f luggage and for people with walking difficu ties), you board canoes to negotiate narro canals through a flooded palm-tree forest i habited by red-bellied macaws, then silent paddle across the beautiful lake to the lodg With luck, you may spot the endangere giant river otter, several pairs of which li in the lake (early morning is best). Variou monkey species and a host of birds and re tiles can also be seen. Hikes into the fore are offered, and the knowledgeable guide are multilingual.

The spacious lodge is built on a hillto about 30m above the lake and surrounde by primary forest. The lodge was built fro salvaged driftwood; the owners pride then selves on the fact that no primary forest wa cut during construction (this is also true c some other lodges, though not always me tioned). The rooms, with heated shower and ceiling fans, are the best in the are. The restaurant-bar area is huge, airy an conducive to relaxing and chatting. Boo with InkaNatura.

LAGO VALENCIA

Just off the Río Madre de Dios and nea the Bolivian border, Lago Valencia is abou 60km from Puerto Maldonado. At least tw days are needed for a visit here, thoug three or four days are recommended. Thi lake reportedly offers the region's best fish ing, as well as good bird-watching an dlife-watching (bring your binoculars). ere are trails into the jungle around the e. Lodges nearer Puerto Maldonado can ange tours, as can independent guides.

O HEATH

out two hours south of the Río Madre Dios and along the Río Heath (the lat- forming the Peru-Bolivia border), the rque Nacional Bahuaja-Sonene (admis- n S30) has some of the best wildlife in Pe- s Amazon region, including such rarities the maned wolf and spider monkey, al- ough these are not easily seen. Infrastruc- re in the park, one of the nation's largest, limited, and wildlife-watching trips are in eir infancy here. Bahuaja-Sonene compris- part of the vast Tambopata-Madidi wil- rness reserve that spans a nigh-on 14,000 km tract across Peru and Bolivia. Park en- ance fees should be paid at Sernanp (p445) Puerto Maldonado: checkpoints along the ay don't sell tickets.

The simple, 10-room **Heath River Wild- e Center** (s/d 4 days & 3 nights US$725/1150) owned by the Ese'eja indigenous people Sonene, who provide guiding and cul- ral services. Trails into Parque Nacional ahuaja-Sonene are available, and field bi- ogists have assessed this area as one of the ost biodiverse in southeastern Peru: it's o early to tell if the Tranoceanic Highway's nstruction could change this. Capybaras e frequently seen, and guided tours to a arby *colpa* (clay lick), a popular attrac- on for macaws and parrots, are arranged. ot water is provided and park entrance es are included. The first and last nights tours are spent at Sandoval Lake Lodge 450). Contact **InkaNatura** (www.inkanatura. m; Cuzco 084-23-1138; Ricardo Palma J1 Urb nta Mónica & Plateros 361; Lima 01-440-2022; anuel Bañón 461, San Isidro).

ÍO TAMBOPATA

he Río Tambopata is a major tributary of e Río Madre de Dios, joining it at Puerto aldonado. Boats go up the river, past sev- al good lodges, and into the **Reserva Na- ional Tambopata** (admission up to 4 nights 100), an important protected area divided to the reserve itself and the **zona de am- rtiguamiento** (buffer zone). The park en- ance fee needs to be paid at the Sernanp ffice (p445) in Puerto Maldonado unless s is nearly always the case) you are on a uided tour, in which case you will pay at e relevant lodge office. An additional fee is required if you are heading into the reserve proper (such as to the Tambopata Research Center) rather than just the buffer zone.

Travelers heading up the Río Tambopata must register their passport numbers at **Puesto Control El Torre** (Guard Post) next to Explorer's Inn and show their national-park entrance permits obtained in Puerto Maldonado. Visiting the reserve is only re- ally possible if you book a guided stay at one of the lodges within it. One of the reserve's highlights is the Colpa de Guacamayos (Ma- caw Clay Lick), one of the largest natural clay licks in the country. It attracts hundreds of birds and is a spectacular sight.

Lodges are listed in the order in which you would arrive at them if traveling from Puerto Maldonado. In addition to those be- low, check out the association of Tambopata homestays: small-scale lodges usually in the homes of local families with whom you can stay (three days and two nights per person US$100 to US$350) at http://tambopataeco tours.com. Several are located near the small community of Baltimore, just after the Re- fugio Amazonas lodge. The river is plied, as far as Baltimore, by twice-weekly passenger boat from Puerto Maldonado, or by bus and foot. Take any vehicle from Puerto Maldo- nado heading to Laberinto, and ask to get off at Km 37. From there, a footpath goes to Baltimore (two to three hours). No public transport exists to points further upriver.

Posada Amazonas LODGE $$$ (Rainforest Expeditions; www.perunature.com; s/d 3 days & 2 nights US$485/750) Cuzco (084-24- 6243; cusco@rainforest.com.pe; Portal de Carnes 236); Lima (01-421-8347; postmaster@rainforest. com.pe; Aramburu 166, Miraflores); Puerto Maldo- nado (082-57-2575; pem@rainforest.com.pe; Av Aeropuerto Km 6, CPM La Joya) The first of three lodges on the Tambopata owned by Rainfor- est Expeditions, Posada Amazonas is about two hours from Puerto Maldonado along Río Tambopata, followed by a 10-minute uphill walk. The *posada* is on the land of the Ese'eja community of Infierno, and tribal members are among the guides. (Several other lodges use 'native' guides, but these are often *mes- tizos* rather than tribe members.) There are excellent chances of seeing macaws and parrots on a small salt lick nearby, and gi- ant river otters are often found swimming in lakes close to the lodge. Guides at the lodge are mainly English-speaking Peruvian natu- ralists with varying interests. Your assigned

AMAZON BASIN AROUND PUERTO MALDONADO

guide stays with you throughout the duration of your stay. Visits are also made to the Centro Ñape ethnobotanical center, where medicine is produced for the Ese'eja community. There is a medicinal-plant trail and a 30m-high observation platform giving superb views of the rainforest canopy. The lodge has 30 large double rooms with private showers and open (unglazed) windows overlooking the rainforest. Mosquito nets are provided. Electricity is available at lunchtime and from 5:30pm to 9pm.

Explorer's Inn   LODGE $$$

(www.explorersinn.com; s/d 3 days & 2 nights US$238/396) Cuzco (☎084-23-5342; Plateros 365); Lima (☎01-447-8888, 01-447-4761; sales@explorersinn.com; Alcanfores 459, Miraflores); Puerto Maldonado (☎082-57-2078) About 58km from Puerto Maldonado (three to four hours of river travel) and featuring 15 rustic double and 15 triple rooms, all with bathrooms and screened windows. Around since the 1970s, it's a more open lodge than the others previously mentioned, in a pleasant grassy clearing. The central lodge room has a restaurant, a bar and a small museum; outside is a soccer pitch and a medicinal garden. The lodge is located in the former 55-sq-km Zona Preservada Tambopata (itself now surrounded by the much larger Reserva Nacional Tambopata). More than 600 species of bird have been recorded in this preserved zone, which is a world record for bird species sighted in one area. Despite such (scientifically documented) records, the average tourist won't see much more here than at any of the other Río Tambopata lodges during the standard two-night visit. The 38km of trails around the lodge can be explored independently or with naturalist guides. German, English and French are spoken. Four-night tours include a visit to the macaw clay lick (single/double US$620/1040).

Cayman Lodge Amazonie   LODGE $$$

(☎082-57-1970; www.cayman-lodge-amazonie.com; Arequipa 655, Puerto Maldonado; s/d 3 days & 2 nights US$400/560) Some 70km from Puerto Maldonado, this lodge is run by the effervescent French Anny and her English-speaking Peruvian partner, Daniel, and boasts an open, relaxing environment with banana, *cocona* (peach tomato) and mango trees in a lush tropical garden. Activities include visits to the oxbow Lagunas Sachavacayoc and Condenado, and there is also a five- to seven-day shamanism program, where you can learn about tropical medicine and ev be treated for ailments. There is a large b and restaurant area. The rooms are a lit on the small side, but are more than co fortable; windows have mosquito mesh One of its more arresting features is t hammock house, from where you can wat the sun set over the Río Tambopata. Reser entrance fees are not included.

Libertador Tambopata Lodge   LODGE $

(☎082-57-1726, 082-968-0022; www.tambopa lodge.com; Prada 269, Puerto Maldonado; s/d days & 2 nights US$417/676) Set mainly ne secondary forest, this considerably mc luxurious lodge is still within the Reser Tambopata. A short boat ride from here w get you into primary forest. Tours to near lakes and to the salt lick are included tours of four days or longer (single/doub from US$688/1160), and naturalist guid are available. There are 12km of well-mark trails, which you can wander at will witho a guide. The lodge consists of a series of sp cious individual bungalows, some of whi have solar-generated hot water. Each enjo a tiled patio with a table and chairs, and look out onto a lush tropical garden. The is the mandatory restaurant and a cozy se arate bar complex: the overall effect is like set from the TV series *Lost*.

Refugio Amazonas   LODGE $

(Rainforest Expeditions; www.perunature.com; days & 3 nights s/d US$695/1070) Cuzco (☎08 24-6243; cusco@rainforest.com.pe; Portal Carnes 236); Lima (☎01-421-8347; postmaster rainforest.com.pe; Aramburu 166, Miraflores); Pue to Maldonado (☎082-57-2575; pem@rainfore com.pe; Av Aeropuerto Km 6, CPM La Joya) Th lodge is better for a longer stay, as it is fairly lengthy boat ride up the river. It's bu on a 20-sq-km private reserve in the buff zone of the Reserva Nacional Tambopat While it feels just that little more isolate the lodge is not lacking in creature comfort with a large reception, dining and drinkir area. Rooms are comfortable and similar i style to those of its sister lodge, the Posac Amazonas. Activities include a Brazil-nt trail and camp and, for children, a dedicate rainforest trail. The increased remotenes usually means better opportunities for spo ting wildlife. Book with Rainforest Exped tions.

Wasai Tambopata Lodge   LODGE $

(☎082-57-2290; www.wasai.com; Billinghur at Arequipa, Puerto Maldonado; s/d per da

PUNK CHICKENS

Listen carefully as your boat passes the banks of the Río Tambopata. If you hear lots of hissing, grunting and sounds of breaking vegetation, it is likely that you have stumbled upon the elaborate mating ritual of one of the Amazon's weirdest birds, the hoatzin. This is an oversized wild chicken with a blue face and a large crest on its head (hence the nickname 'punk chicken'). Scientists have been unable to classify this bird as a member of any other avian family, mainly due to the two claws the young have on each wing. To evade predators, hoatzin chicks will fall out of the nest to the river and use their claws to help them scramble back up the muddy banks. The clawed wing is a feature no other airborne creature has possessed since the pterodactyl. The hoatzin's appearance is out-done by its terrible smell (caused by an exclusively leaf-based diet, which necessitates their having multiple micro-organisms in their stomachs to aid digestion), which may well be the first indication they are nearby. Good news for the hoatzin: their odd odor makes their flesh taste bad, so they are rarely hunted. In this age of rainforest depletion, they are one of the few native birds with a flourishing population.

$80/160) Just after Baltimore, this is the ...ultimate lodge on the river and, unlike ...e others, it does not feature programmed ...oactivities. So if you just want to relax, ...ad a book, enjoy a beer or amble around ...e 20km of well-signed trails yourself, this ... the place to do it. Fishing and canoe pad-...ing are other options. The lodge consists ... four large bungalows and two smaller ...es, and can accommodate a maximum of ... guests. There is a tall observation tower ...om where you get good views of the sur-...unding jungle. Transportation is not in-...uded in the price. The four-day, three-night ...urs (doubles US$504) take in Tambopata ...d Lago Sandoval, but not the Tambopata ...served zone.

Tambopata Research
...enter   LODGE $$$
...ainforest Expeditions; www.perunature.com; s/d 5 ...ays & 4 nights US$1015/1590) Cuzco (☎084-24-...243; cusco@rainforest.com.pe; Portal de Carnes ...6); Lima (☎01-421-8347; postmaster@rainforest. ...m.pe; Aramburu 166, Miraflores); Puerto Maldo-...ado (☎082-57-2575; pem@rainforest.com.pe; Av ...eropuerto Km 6, CPM La Joya) Finally, about ...even hours' river travel from Puerto Mal-...onado, this important research facility and ...dge is known for a famous salt lick nearby ...at attracts four to 10 species of parrots and ...acaws on most mornings. Research here ...ocuses on why macaws eat clay, their migra-...ion patterns, their diet, nesting macaws and ...echniques for building artificial nests. The ...dge itself is fairly simple, with 18 double ...ooms sharing four showers and four toilets, ...ut because of the distances involved, rates ...re higher than the other places. If you're

interested in seeing more macaws than you ever thought possible, it's worth the expense, although the owners point out that occasionally, due to poor weather or other factors, macaws aren't found at the lick. A stopover is usually made at Refugio Amazonas on the first and last nights of a trip here. The last section of the ride is through remote country, with excellent chances of seeing capybaras and maybe more unusual animals. Have your passport ready at the Puesto Control Malinowsky. Book with Rainforest Expeditions.

MANU AREA

The Manu area encompasses the Parque Nacional Manu and much of the surrounding jungle and cloud forest. Covering almost 20,000 sq km (about the size of Wales), the park is one of the best places in South America to see a wide variety of tropical wildlife. The park is divided into three zones. The largest sector is the *zona natural,* comprising 80% of the total park area and closed to unauthorized visitors. Entry to this sector is restricted to a few indigenous groups, mainly the Matsiguenka (also spelled Machiguenga), some of whom continue to live here as they have for generations; some groups have had almost no contact with outsiders and do not seem to want any. Fortunately, this wish is respected. A handful of researchers with permits are also allowed in to study the wildlife. The second sector, still within the park proper, is the *zona reservada,* where controlled research and tourism are permitted. There are a couple of official accommodation options here. This is the northeastern sector, comprising about 10% of the park area. The third sector, covering the southeastern area, is the *zona cultural,* where most other visitor activity is concentrated. To travel between the *zona cultural* and the *zona reservada,* you'll need to take the Río Madre de Dios to the park's main transit village, Boca Manu. Finally, outside the national park boundaries southeast of Boca Manu are, ironically, some of the very best wildlife-watching opportunities, especially at the macaw and tapir licks around the Manu Wildlife Center (p458).

Tours to the Manu Area

It's important to check exactly where the tours are going: Manu is a catchall word that includes the national park and much of the surrounding area. Some tours, such as to the Manu Wildlife Center, don't actually enter Parque Nacional Manu at all (although the wildlife center is recommended for wildlife-watching, nonetheless). Some companies aren't allowed to enter the park, but offer what they call 'Manu tours' outside the park or act as agents for other operators. Other companies work together and share resources such as lodges, guides and transportation services. This can mean the agency in whose office you sign up for the tour isn't the agency you end up going with. Most will combine a Manu experience with a full Peru tour on request. Confusing? You bet!

The companies listed in this section are all authorized to operate within Manu by the national park service and maintain some level of conservation and low-impact practices. The number of permits to operate tours into Parque Nacional Manu is limited; only about 3000 visitors are allowed in annually. Intending visitors must book well in advance. Be flexible with onward travel plans as delays are common. Entering by bus and boat and returning by flight is the best means of seeing Manu.

Tour costs depend on whether you camp or stay in a lodge, whether you arrive and depart overland or by air and whether you enter the *zona reservada.* A tour inside the zone won't necessarily get you better wildlife viewing – although, since it's virgin jungle here, chances of seeing larger animals are greater. If your budget allows, the more expensive companies really are worth considering. They offer more reliable and trained

multilingual guides, better equipment, wider variety of food, suitable insura and emergency procedures. Perhaps m importantly, there are more guarantees t your money is going partly toward prese ing Manu, as many of these companies fu conservation costs.

All companies provide transportatic food, purified drinking water, guides, p mits and camping equipment or scree in lodge rooms. Personal items such as sleeping bag (unless staying in a lodg insect repellent, sunblock, flashlight w spare batteries, suitable clothing and bottl drinks are the traveler's responsibility. Bi oculars and a camera with a zoom lens a highly recommended.

All lodges and tour operators in the bi money business of Manu excursions quo prices in US dollars.

Crees
ADVENTURE TO
(www.crees-manu.org) Cuzco (26-2433; U Mariscal Garmarra B-5, Zona 1); UK (0044-2(581-2932; 7-8 Kendrick Mews, London) Crees ru 'voluntourism' one-week trips into the *zor reservada* (US$1150; departing every Satu day April to December) where participar can help with projects such as reforestatic and jaguar monitoring, while at the sam time getting to see parts of the jungle th tourist otherwise couldn't reach. If one wee isn't enough for you, it also runs long-ter volunteer projects (up to 16 weeks).

Bonanza Tours
ADVENTURE TO
(084-50-7871; www.bonanzatoursperu.com; Suec 343, Cuzco) This local family-operated cor pany is run by Ryse Choquepuma and h brothers, who grew up in Manu and know better than most. Tours are arranged to th family home, which has been converted int a well-appointed lodge. The land here virt ally backs onto the park proper and ther are trails as well as a clay lick that attrac plenty of wildlife. Swims in hot springs an coconut-cutting lessons are included, as a special late-night creepy-crawly-huntin sojourn. The four-day/three-night optic with two nights at the family lodge and on at their new lodge near Pilcopata is US$43 Bonanza also runs longer tours into th *zona reservada.*

Pantiacolla Tours
ADVENTURE TOU
(084-23-8323; www.pantiacolla.com; Garcilas 265 interior, 2nd fl, Cuzco) Pantiacolla own

ee lodges in the Manu region and is frequently recommended by a variety of travel- for its knowledgeable and responsibly ecuted tours, helped by the fact that its ff members were raised in the area. It offers a variety of tours, including the opportunity to study Spanish at its jungle lodge. It o helps fund conservation of Manu, so ecogically, there's no better bet. Trips start at $1275 per person for seven days, all over- d, and include a mixture of camping and lge accommodations. The agency works th local indigenous groups in its Yine oject, which is outlined on its website.

Manu Expeditions ADVENTURE TOUR
084-22-5990, 084-22-4235; www.manuexpe ions.com; Clorinda Matto de Turner 330, Urb gisterial, Cuzco) Manu Expeditions are ners of the only tented camp within the tional park, and co-owners of Manu Wild- e Center, with more than two decades of anu experience. Its guides are excellent, t if you are lucky enough to go with the ner, British ornithologist and long-time zco resident, Barry Walker, you will really in excellent hands, particularly if birding your interest. A popular trip leaves Cuzco ery Sunday (except January to March, hen it's the first Sunday of the month only) d lasts nine days, including overland ansportation to Manu with two nights of mping at the company's Cocha Salvador nted Camp, three nights at Manu Wild- e Center, three nights at other lodges and flight back to Cuzco. This costs US$2445 er person, based on two people sharing a om. The overland section can include a ountain-biking descent if arranged in ad- nce. Shorter, longer and customized trips e offered.

Manu Nature Tours ADVENTURE TOUR
084-25-2721; www.manuperu.com; Pardo 1046, zco) This outfit operates the respected anu Lodge, the only fully appointed lodge ithin the reserve and open year-round. A 0km network of trails and guided visits lakes and observation towers are also rovided. A five-day tour, flying in or out, US$1628 per person, double occupancy, ith fixed departures every Thursday. The ip has a bilingual naturalist guide and all eals are provided. For an extra fee, moun- in biking or river running (white-water afting) can be incorporated into the road escent. Longer tours are also available. The

company also has departures to its Manu Cloud Forest Lodge (p456).

Amazon Trails Peru ADVENTURE TOUR
(084-43-7374, 984-714-148; www.amazontrails peru.com; Tandapata 660, Cuzco) This outfit comes reader-recommended and has a growing reputation for providing the best service among the cheaper tour operators. Tours provide a great deal of quirky insider information on places en route. Less obvious itineraries, such as one of the supposed sites of legendary Inca city El Dorado, can be accommodated, and if you're heading on to Puerto Maldonado, onward boat/bus transport can be arranged to save backtracking to Cuzco. High-power binoculars are also provided, increasing chances of decent wildlife sightings. Six-day tours to the *zona reservada* start from US$1370.

InkaNatura ADVENTURE TOUR
(www.inkanatura.com) Cuzco (084-25-5255; Ricardo Palma J1 Urb Santa Mónica & Plateros 361); Lima (01-440-2022; Manuel Bañón 461, San Isidro); USA (Tropical Nature Travel; 1-877-888-1770, 1-352-376-3377; POB 5276, Gainesville FL 32627-5276) InkaNatura is a highly respected international agency and co-owner of the Manu Wildlife Center. The operators can combine a visit here with trips to other parts of the southern Peruvian rainforest, including Pampas del Heath near Puerto Maldonado, where it also has a lodge.

Cuzco to Manu

This spectacular journey provides opportunities for some excellent bird-watching at the lodges en route, as well as some of Peru's most dramatic scenery changes. The route runs from bare Andean mountains into cloud forest before dropping into a steamy tangle of lowland jungle. You can get as far as Boca Manu, an hour before the entrance point for the *zona reservada,* independently. This is challenging but possible, although to either enter the *zona reservada* or maximize your chances of seeing wildlife, you will need a guide and therefore a tour. Most lodges en route will let you stay, but giving them advance notice is advised.

If traveling overland, the first stage of the journey involves taking a bus or truck (or minivan if you are on a tour) from Cuzco via Paucartambo to Shintuya. Buses run by **Gallito de las Rocas** (084-22-6895; Av Diagonal

AMAZON BASIN CUZCO TO MANU

Angamos 1952, Cuzco) leave at 5am on Monday, Wednesday and Friday for Pilcopata (S20, 10 to 12 hours in good weather), returning from Pilcopata on the same days at 6pm. Get a taxi to the departure point – it's difficult to find independently. Cheaper trucks also leave sporadically from the Coliseo Cerrado in Cuzco for Shintuya (about 24 hours in the dry season). Breakdowns, extreme overcrowding and delays are common, and during the rainy season (even during the dry) vehicles slide off the road. It's safer, more comfortable and more reliable to take the costlier tourist buses offered by Cuzco tour operators. Many tour companies in Cuzco offer trips to Manu.

Sights & Activities

After Paucartambo, the road continues for 1½ hours to the entrance to Parque Nacional Manu (*zona cultural;* admission S10 for independent travelers at the turnoff to Tres Cruces, a further 13km). The next six hours to Pilcopata are through spectacular cloud forest, occupying a humid elevation of some 1600m and home to thousands of bird species, many of which are yet to be officially identified. There are several lodges at which you can enjoy phenomenal bird-watching (including, if you are lucky, the rarely glimpsed cock-of-the-rocks, with striking scarlet plumage and elaborate mating dances).

The next village, Pilcopata, is the end of the public bus route and indeed contact with the outside world of all kinds: the last public phone (and cell-phone reception) before Manu is here, along with Manu's main police station. There are basic hotels (beds around S15) and stores too. Pickup trucks leave early every morning for Atalaya (45 minutes) and Shintuya (three hours).

The road beyond Pilcopata can be nigh-on impassable in wet season, which is why most vehicles give up the ghost at Atalaya, and switch to boat (all Manu tour agencies continue by boat from here). To continue by rough, rough road beyond here to Salvación (where there is a national park office) and Shintuya (with limited basic accommodations) is possible, but slightly pointless, as there are more boats available for continuing downriver in Atalaya. Just past Shintuya, Itahuanía has Manu's emergency hospital.

The long boat journey down the Río Alto Madre de Dios from Atalaya to Boca Manu, at the junction with the Río Manu, can take almost a day. Boca Manu village has ba facilities and is known for building the gion's best riverboats: it is interesting to these vessels in various stages of constr tion. Independent travelers: again, bear mind that if you are not on a tour with licensed Manu tour agency you will not permitted entry into the *zona reservac* although continuing on down the Río Ma to the Manu Wildlife Center and Puerto M donado *may* be possible. The Boca Ma airstrip is currently only accessible by p vate plane. Because of this, many compan are using the other route to Manu (a flig into Puerto Maldonado followed by a ro trip toward Iñapari and a trip *up* the Mac de Dios).

🛏 Sleeping

There are several good lodges on this rou While none are in the *zona reservada* the *zona natural* of Parque Nacional Mar they nevertheless can provide great wildli watching opportunities. Don't assume e tering the *zona reservada* is an automa guarantee of seeing better wildlife. Lodg are congregated either in the cloud forest on the Río Alto Madre de Dios after Atalay most let independent tourists stay, but to groups on lodge-affiliated tours get priori If you are set on staying at one of the follo ing, it's advisable to reserve at least a nig in advance. For simplicity, lodges are liste in distance order from Cuzco.

CLOUD FOREST

Manu Paradise Lodge   LODGE $
(☎084-22-4156; www.manuparadiselodge.com; U Magisterio 2da etapa, Cuzco; s/d incl mea US$85/140) Around six hours from Cuzco an overlooking the scenic Río Kosñipata va ley, this lodge sleeps 16 people in spaciou rooms with private hot-water bathrooms. looks quite modern, unlike the more rust lodges further into the park. Among its a sets are an attractive dining room-bar with fireplace and telescopes for wildlife viewin It advertises its wide variety of tours (thre to six nights) on its website. Rafting an mountain-biking tours can be arranged, bu the primary attraction is bird-watching.

Manu Cloud Forest Lodge   LODGE $$
(☎084-25-2721; www.manuperu.com; Pardo 104 Cuzco; per person s/d 3 days & 2 night US$748/1096) Manu Cloud Forest Lodge i on the same stretch of road as Cock-of-the

ck. The 16- to 20-bed lodge provides six
⸱ms with hot showers, a restaurant and
d-watching opportunities in the high
ud forest. Transportation and use of the
ına cost extra. Rates include activities:
⸱m and full board only costs US$120 per
rson per night. Book with Manu Nature
.urs.

ck-of-the-Rock Lodge LODGE $$$
ww.inkanatura.com; s/d incl meals 3 days & 2
hts US$785/1270) Cuzco (084-25-5255;
ardo Palma J1 Urb Santa Mónica & Plateros 361);
1a (01-440-2022; Manuel Bañón 461, San Isid-
This option is a few minutes' walk from a
⸱c (mating ground) for cocks-of-the-rocks.
iis lodge offers exceptional cloud-forest
⸱rd-watching at 1600m elevation. The own-
s claim you can get photos of male cocks-
⸱the-rock displaying about 7m from your
⸱mera. The InkaNatura-owned lodge has a
staurant and 12 rustic double cabins with
ivate bathrooms and hot water. Rates in-
1de round-trip transportation from Cuzco,
hich takes on average eight hours (with
⸱ints-of-interest stops).

iinforest Lodge LODGE $$
⸱084-50-7871; www.bonanzatoursperu.com; Sue-
⸱ 343, Cuzco; per person incl meals US$40) A
1uch cheaper option, and a good journey-
⸱eaker, is this rustic lodge near Pilcopata
⸱ou could hit the village nightlife from here
⸱you wanted). There are eight cabins here
⸱eeping up to 18 people, with shared bath-
⸱oms. It's at the base of the cloud forest
ne hour's drive from the best cloud forest
⸱rd-watching).

ÍO ALTO MADRE DE DIOS

is harder to stay at some of these lodges
idependently, as there are few available
⸱ats not affiliated with a particular tour
gency.

mazonia Lodge LODGE $$
084-23-1370; www.amazonialodge.com; Matará
34, Cuzco; r per person incl meals US$85) In an
ld colonial hacienda in the foothills of the
ndes, Amazonia provides travelers with
ightly different environs to bed down (al-
1ough a refurbishment is overdue). Expect
lean, comfortable beds and communal hot
nowers. The lodge has forest trails, excellent
ird-watching (guided tours are offered),
lissfully few mosquitoes and no electricity.
he lodge can make transportation arrange-
1ents, or tour agencies in Cuzco can make
eservations. As it's just across the river from

Atalaya, you can usually charter a local boat
to ferry you across.

Pantiacolla Lodge LODGE $$
(084-23-8323; www.pantiacolla.com; Garcilaso
265 interior, 2nd fl, Cuzco; s/d US$145/180, with
shared bathroom US$125/150, all incl meals) There
are 14 double rooms here, 11 with shared
bathrooms and three with private ones.
Rates include meals but not transportation
or tours, though right near the lodge are forest trails (some re-ascending into cloud forest
at 900m), a parrot lick and hot springs. Various transportation and guided-tour options
are available. It is necessary to give advance
notice for the boat to the lodge, which is on
the fringe of the national park, just before Itahuanía village. Book with Pantiacolla Tours.

Bonanza Ecological Reserve LODGE $$
(084-50-7871; www.bonanzatoursperu.com; Suecia
343, Cuzco; per person incl meals US$85) Past Ita-
huanía toward the community of Bonanza,
Bonanza Tours' family-run lodge has eight
double cabins abutting a large clearing that
also has a large restaurant area and a two-
floor hammock-strung chill-out zone; bath-
rooms are shared and there's solar-paneled
electricity. From here trails lead off into
dense jungle which backs onto the *zona
natural*. The highlight here is the treehouse
peeping out on a clay lick which tapirs visit.

Yine Lodge LODGE $$$
(084-23 8323; www.pantiacolla.com; Garcilaso
265 interior, 2nd fl, Cuzco; s/d US$145/180, with
shared bathroom US$125/150, all incl meals) A sim-
ple lodge offering the best accommodations
in Boca Manu itself (it's near the airstrip). It
has six double rooms sharing showers and
toilets, run by the Yine people in conjunction with Pantiacolla Tours through whom
you should make reservations.

Parque Nacional Manu

This national park starts in the eastern
slopes of the Andes and plunges down into
the lowlands, hosting great diversity over
a wide range of cloud forest and rainforest
habitats. The most progressive aspect of the
park is the fact that so much of it is very
carefully protected – a rarity anywhere in
the world.

After Peru introduced protection laws in
1973, Unesco declared Manu a Biosphere
Reserve in 1977 and a World Natural Heritage site in 1987. One reason the park is so

AMAZON BASIN PARQUE NACIONAL MANU

successful in preserving such a large tract of virgin jungle and its wildlife is that it is remote and relatively inaccessible to people, and therefore has not been exploited by rubber tappers, hunters and the like (although there is an ongoing dispute between local Amazonians and Hunt Oil, to whom the government gave a concession for hydrocarbon extraction in Manu's *zona cultura*).

It is illegal to enter the park without a guide. Going with an organized group can be arranged in Cuzco (see p212) or with international tour operators. It's an expensive trip; budget travelers should arrange their trip in Cuzco and be flexible with travel plans. Travelers often report returning from Manu several days late. Don't plan an international airline connection the day after a Manu trip!

Permits, which are necessary to enter the park, are arranged by tour agencies. Transportation, accommodations, food and guides are also part of tour packages. Most visits are for a week, although three-night stays at a lodge can be arranged.

The best time to go is during the dry season (June to November); Manu may be inaccessible or closed during the rainy months (January to April), except to visitors staying at the two lodges within the park boundaries.

Virgin jungle lies up the Río Manu northwest of Boca Manu. At the Puesto Control Limonal (guard post), about an hour from Boca Manu, a park entrance fee of S150 per person is payable (usually included in your tour). Continuing beyond is only possible with a guide and a permit. Near Limonal are a few trails.

Two hours upstream is the oxbow lake of **Cocha Juárez** where giant river otters are often encountered. About four hours further, **Cocha Salvador**, one of the park's largest, most beautiful lakes, has guided camping and hiking possibilities. Half an hour's boat ride away is **Cocha Otorongo**, another oxbow lake with a wildlife-viewing observation tower. These are not wide-open habitats like the African plains. Thick vegetation will obscure many animals, and a skilled guide is very useful in helping you to see them.

During a one-week trip, you can reasonably expect to see scores of different bird species, several monkey species and possibly a few other mammals. Jaguars, tapirs, giant anteaters, tamanduas, capybaras, peccaries

and giant river otters are among the co mon large Manu mammals. But they elusive, and you can consider a trip very s cessful if you see two or three large ma mals during a week's visit. Smaller ma mals you might see include kinkajous, p as, agoutis, squirrels, brocket deer, ocel and armadillos. Other animals include riv turtles and caiman (which are frequen seen), snakes (which are less often spotte and a variety of other reptiles and amph ians. Colorful butterflies and less pleasi insects also abound.

There are two lodges within the park.

At **Manu Lodge**, a row of 12 simple do ble rooms is screened and has comfortab beds; a separate building has cold showe and toilets. The lodge is on Cocha Juáre about 1km from the Río Manu. For an ext fee, you can climb up to a canopy platfor river running can also be arranged. A 20k network of trails from the lodge around t lake and beyond provides ample opportu ties for spotting wildlife. The lodge has double rooms plus a bar-cum-dining roo next to a lake that's home to giant otte Contact **Manu Nature Tours** (☎084-25-27: www.manuperu.com; Pardo 1046, Cuzco).

Cocha Salvador Safari Camp lies b yond Manu Lodge. This camp has raise platforms supporting large walk-in screene tents containing cots and bedding. Mode: showers, toilets and meals are availabl Manu Expeditions occasionally uses t more rustic **Casa Matsiguenka Lodg** (☎084-22-5990, 084-22-4235; www.manuexpe tions.com; Clorinda Matto de Turner 330, Urb Ma isterial, Cuzco) built in traditional style by th Matsiguenka tribespeople.

More primitive camping, usually on th sandy beaches of the Río Manu or on th foreshore of a few of the lakes, is anothe possibility. Tour operators can provide a necessary equipment. During the rain season (January to April) these beaches ar flooded and the park is closed to campin; Campers should come prepared with plen of insect repellent.

Manu Wildlife Center & Around

A two-hour boat ride southeast of Boc Manu on the Río Madre de Dios takes yo to **Manu Wildlife Center** (s/d 4 days & 3 night US$1345/2190). The center is a jungle lodg owned by **InkaNatura Travel** (☎084-25

5; www.inkanatura.com; Cuzco Ricardo Palma
Urb Santa Mónica & Plateros 361; Lima ☏01-
)-2022; Manuel Bañón 461, San Isidro) and
nu Expeditions (☏084-22-5990, 084-22-
5; www.manuexpeditions.com; Clorinda Matto
Turner 330, Urb Magisterial, Cuzco), both of
ich take reservations. Although the lodge
not in the Manu Biosphere Reserve, it is
ommended for its exceptional wildlife-
tching and birding opportunities. There
22 screened double cabins with hot
owers, a dining room and a bar-hammock
om. The lodge is set in tropical gardens.
te that some tours, including the option
oted above, start with a flight into Puerto
aldonado and travel up the Río Madre de
os to reach Manu Wildlife Center from
ere. This is a great opportunity to explore
little-plied section of this majestic river.
her options can also include one/two
ghts camping within the park itself.

There are 48km of trails around the wild-
e center, where 12 species of monkey, as
ell as other wildlife, can be seen. Two cano-
platforms are a short walk away, and one
always available for guests wishing to view
e top of the rainforest and look for birds
at frequent the canopy.

A 3km walk through the forest brings you
a natural salt lick, where there is a raised
atform with mosquito nets for viewing the
ghtly activities of the tapirs. This hike is
r visitors who can negotiate forest trails by
ashlight. Chances to see animals are excel-
nt if you have the patience, although visi-
rs may wait for hours. Note that there isn't
uch happening at the lick during the day.

A short boat ride along the Madre de
os brings visitors to another well-known
lt lick that attracts various species of par-
t and macaw. Most mornings you can see
ocks in the hundreds. The largest flocks
e seen from late July to September. As the
iny season kicks in, the numbers diminish
d in June birds don't visit the salt lick at
l. May and early July aren't reliable either,
ough ornithologists report the presence
f the birds in other nearby areas during
ese months, which birders can usually
ot.

The macaw lick is visited on a floating
atamaran blind, with the blind providing
concealed enclosure from which 20 peo-
le can view the wildlife. The catamaran is
table enough to allow the use of a tripod
nd scope or a telephoto lens, and gets about
alfway across the river. Boat drivers won't
bring the blind too close to avoid disturbing
the birds.

In addition to the trails and salt licks,
there are a couple of nearby lakes accessible by catamaran where giant otters may be
seen (as well as other wildlife). If you wish to
see the macaw and tapir lick, the lakes and
the canopy, and hike the trails in search of
wildlife, you should plan on a three-night
stay at the Manu Wildlife Center. Shorter
and longer stays are workable.

Near the Manu Wildlife Center, rustic
Tambo Blanquillo Lodge has rooms with
shared and private bathrooms. Some companies in Cuzco combine this cheaper option with a tour including other lodges in
the Manu area, but prices vary. Staying just
at Blanquillo isn't possible. Tour operators
include **Pantiacolla Tours** (☏084-23-8323;
www.pantiacolla.com; Saphy 554, Cuzco).

If you continue down the Madre de Dios
past gold-panning areas to Puerto Maldonado, you won't see much wildlife. Amazon
Trails Peru (p455) can also organize onward
boat/bus transportation, but transportation
to Puerto Maldonado is infrequent; almost
all visitors return to Cuzco.

CENTRAL AMAZON

For a quick Amazon fix on long weekends
and holidays, *limeños* (inhabitants of Lima)
usually head for this relatively accessible
Amazon region, reachable in eight hours by
bus. The tropical Chanchamayo province is
as different to the coastal desert strip or the
Andean mountains as can be. The last hour
of the journey here is particularly remarkable for the rapid change in vegetation and
climate as you slip down the Andes into the
vibrant green of La Selva Central, as it is
known in Spanish. Comprising the two main
towns of La Merced and San Ramón, plus
a scattering of remoter communities, the
area is noted for coffee and fruit production.
Despite its popularity with Peruvian holidaymakers, the region offers the traveler a
good insight into Amazon life. Better transportation links mean there are more opportunities here for interacting with rainforest
tribes than elsewhere in the Amazonas. Two
rough, adventurous back routes also await:
forging via Satipo and Puerto Bermúdez
through Peru's central belt of Amazon to the
port of Pucallpa, jumping-off point for river
trips deeper into the jungle.

AMAZON BASIN MANU WILDLIFE CENTER & AROUND

La Merced & San Ramón

☑064 / POP 40,000 / ELEV 800M

San Ramón is 295km east of Lima and La Merced is 11km further along. Chanchamayo's two key settlements are quite likable in a languid sort of way. Resistance to colonists by the local Asháninka people meant that these towns were not founded until the 19th century. Today they are popular Peruvian holiday destinations, and great bases for exploring the luxuriant countryside nearby, characterized by photogenic forested hills and waterfalls that tumble into the Río Chanchamayo valley. Accommodation bookings are recommended at busy periods, when room rates almost double.

◉ Sights & Activities

The stairs at the northwest end of **Avenida 2 de Mayo** afford a good view of La Merced, and from the balcony at the southwest end there's a photogenic river view.

Around San Ramón are many impressive **waterfalls**. A much-visited 35m cascade, **Catarata El Tirol**, lies 5km east of San Ramón off the La Merced road. You can take a taxi the first 2km; the last 3km is along shady forest paths and streams. Off the Pichanaqui road at Puente Yurinaki are the higher waterfalls of **Catarata Velo de la Novia** and **Catarata Bayoz**. Agencies in La Merced or Tarma arrange tours.

There is a colorful **daily market** in La Merced. An interesting **weekend market** visited by local *indígenas* (people of indigenous descent) is held at San Luis de Shuaro, 22km beyond La Merced. Asháninka tribespeople occasionally come into La Merced to sell handicrafts.

🛏 Sleeping

La Merced has most of the decent digs; San Ramón sports some luxury hotels.

LA MERCED

You don't have to look far in the central blocks to find a cheap *hospedaje* for S20 per person or less. A clean option is **Hospedaje Santa Rosa** (Av 2 de Mayo 447).

TOP CHOICE **Hotel Heliconia** HOTEL $$
(☑53-1394; http://heliconiahotel.blogspot.co.uk; Junín 922; s/d incl breakfast S90/130; ❄🛜) The best of two decent new hotels opened in central La Merced, the air-conditioned rooms

here are ginormous and all come w fridges and sparkling bathrooms. Breakf is enjoyed in a cheerful setting and views mostly onto Parque Integración.

Hostal Fanny GUESTHOU
(☑77-5530, 964-879-547; Tarma, cuadra 1; S40/80) Clean, pleasant option with si able, well-decorated, airy rooms and a r taurant. Two doubles have actual baths.

Hotel Elio's HOT
(☑53-1229; Palca 281; s/d S40/60) Just off t plaza with spacious rooms that make t beds look almost lost; there are writi desks, fans, cable TV and spotless ba rooms. Street-facing rooms are very noisy

Hotel Rey HOT
(☑53-1185; www.hotelrey.net; Junín 103; s S60/80) A popular place, and the owne know it. Bright, inviting hallways lead rooms with fans, cable TV and hot showe A top-floor restaurant serves decent fo while offering good town views.

SAN RAMÓN

The town itself is unexceptional. Howev the best places to stay in this region lie o side, on the La Merced road.

 TOP CHOICE **Rio Grande Inn** INN
(☑33-2193, 95-71-3316; www.riogrande-bungalo com; Carretera Central Km 97; s/d incl breakfa S90/120; 🛜❄) This smart and well-appoin ed hotel is set in verdant grounds by the R Chanchamayo. Rooms have wood paneli and minifridges along with the usual to end hotel facilities. There is a gorgeous po and a restaurant serving light meals and r freshments. Single travelers will pay doub room rates at peak times.

🍴 Eating

Options are pretty basic.

Restaurant Shambari Campa PERUVIAN
(Tarma 389, La Merced; mains S18-27; ⏲6:30ar 12:30am) On the plaza, this famous hol in-the-wall restaurant provides a menu s extensive you can be lost for choice, bu includes sensational *chancho* (rainfore wild pig).

Los Koquis PERUVIAN
(Tarma 376, La Merced; mains S16-25; ⏲11ar 11pm) Set back from the plaza down a lea passageway, Los Koquis lures punters i with jungle specialties.

ifa Felipe Siu   CHINESE **$**
ogreso 440, San Ramón; meals around S12;
11am-2pm & 6:30-11pm) Locals say this is
e best place to eat Chinese food in the
nazon.

Shopping

anchamayo Highland Coffee   COFFEE
53-1198; http://highlandproducts.com.pe) This
the only place around where you can
mple and buy the coffee for which Chan-
amayo is famous. (Peru is one of the
rld's largest coffee producers but nearly
gets exported.) It's gimmicky but enjoy-
le, and besides the shop, you can browse
splays on coffee production and check out
d coffee-producing machinery. It's 1km
rtheast of the bus terminal on the Satipo
ad. These days it does a good range of lo-
l jams and ice creams too.

Information

th towns have a BCP with an ATM, and plenty
public telephones. La Merced has better
cilities.

ospital (53-1002; Tarma, cuadra 1; La
erced) Small.

ternet Cafe (Palca Cuadra 2 s/n, La Merced)

olice station (Julio Piérola at Passuni, La
erced)

ost office (Av 2 de Mayo, La Merced)

elecentro (cnr Palca & Junín, La Merced) On
e Plaza de Armas.

Getting There & Away

ir

ne Chanchamayo airstrip is a 30-minute walk
om San Ramón. *Mototaxis* will take you there
round S3). Small planes can theoretically be
artered to almost anywhere in the region but
e strip is virtually deserted most days.

us

he bus terminal is a 1km downhill walk east of the
enter of La Merced; most buses arrive and leave
om here. This is well-organized, but as much
ansportation relies on *colectivo* taxis (that leave
hen full) schedules are haphazard – go down
ere as early as possible and ask around.

Direct buses go from Lima to Chanchamayo,
hough many travelers break the journey at
arma. Try to travel the 70km stretch from Tar-
na to San Ramón in daylight for the views during
he spectacular 2200m descent. Companies
oing to Lima (S25 to S35, eight hours) from the
a Merced terminal include **Junín** (in Tarma
2-1234), which also has luxury Lima-bound
ight buses (S70).

Other companies such as Transportes
Salazaar also go to Lima, with several daily
and nightly departures. Their offices are all
located at the terminal or across the road on
Prolongación Tarma. Selva Tours has an office
in the terminal and charges S25 for the 4½-hour
journey to Huancayo (with stops at Tarma and
Jauja), departing almost hourly throughout the
day. Frequent buses from various companies go
to Tarma (around S10, 2½ hours).

Transportation into the jungle is by large minibus or pickup truck. *Colectivos* ply some routes
for a slightly higher price. Minibuses leave for
Pichanaqui (S5, 1½ hours) and Satipo (S8, 2½
hours) about every half-hour. Empresa Santa
Rosa has frequent minibuses to Oxapampa (S10,
three hours), where you can change for services
to Pozuzo (four hours further on). Pickup trucks
to Puerto Bermúdez (S30, eight to 10 hours)
leave from outside the terminal when full: be
there ready at 4am. Journey time depends on
road conditions but this is always an arduous
trip, especially if you travel on top (in which case
bring sunglasses, a waterproof jacket and gloves
to prevent blisters caused by clinging on).

Taxi

Colectivos seating four passengers go to Tarma
(S20, 1¾ hours), Oxapampa (S18, two hours),
Pichanaqui (S10, one hour) and Satipo (S20, two
hours) from marked stands within the terminal
complex.

Getting Around

Minibuses linking La Merced with San Ramón
and the hotels in between leave every few minutes (S1.50, 15 minutes) from outside the bus
terminal. Drivers try charging more if they think
you're staying at one of these hotels. *Mototaxis*
charge S1 to drive you from the terminal up into
La Merced center.

Satipo

064 / POP 15,700 / ELEV 630M

This amiable jungle town is the center of
a coffee- and fruit-producing region about
130km by road southeast of La Merced. This
road was paved in 2000 to provide an outlet for produce, and accordingly Satipo is
growing quickly. It's of interest to travelers
primarily as the start of a way-off-the-beat-
en-path track and river journey to Pucallpa
(although few foreigners undertake the journey).

The attractive main plaza has a BCP
(ATM) and lots of ice-cream/cake shops.

The picks of Satipo's mushrooming accommodations scene are extremely tourist-
friendly, comfortable **Hostal El Palmero**

(☎54-5020; Manuel Prado 228; s/d S20/30) and top dog **Hostal San Luis** (☎54-5319; cnr Grau 173 & Leguía; s/d S40/60), where decent-sized rooms are served by a cafeteria downstairs. Hostal El Palmero can help arrange guided tours to nearby waterfalls and petroglyphs. Satipo's best eatery is **El Bosque** (Manuel Prado 554; mains around S15), a lovely courtyard restaurant (food served from 8am to 5pm).

It's possible to charter light aircraft at Satipo's nearby airport. Minibuses and *colectivos* leave regularly for Pichanaqui, where you can change for La Merced, or head direct to La Merced less frequently. Larger buses leave every morning and evening for La Merced (S10), some continuing on to Lima, including **Turismo Central** (☎964-101-123; Los Incas 339), which has Lima (S56) and Huancayo (S26) buses. The spectacular, but difficult back road to Huancayo via Comas is rarely used by public transportation.

Bunched around the corner of Francisco Irazola and Bolognesi, *colectivo* vehicles leave for Mazamari (S5, 30 minues), Puerto Ocapa (S25, two hours) and eventually, via an ever-deteriorating road, to Atalaya, at the intersection of Ríos Urubamba, Tambo and Ucayali. From here, it's possible to find boats heading to Pucallpa, 450km downstream (a trip taking up to three days). If undertaking this trip, be aware that this is remote jungle and not without dangers, one of which is armed plantation saboteurs.

Oxapampa

☎063 / POP 7800 / ELEV 1800M

There is a distinctly alpine feel to this pretty ranching and coffee center, 75km north of La Merced. Perhaps this was why during the mid-19th century it attracted some 200 settlers from Germany, the descendants of which (many still blonde haired and blue eyed) inhabit Oxapampa and smaller, lower, still more Germanic **Pozuzo** (four hours north of Oxapampa by daily minibus; longer in the wet season), and have preserved many of their old customs. Buildings have a Tyrolean look, Austrian-German food is prepared and an old-fashioned form of German is still spoken by some families. Oxapampa has a BCP on the main plaza and decent accommodation options.

◉ Sights

North of Oxapampa rear the cloud-capped hills of little-visited **Parque Nacional Ya-**nachaga-Chemillén. The park preser' some spectacular cloud forest and dive' flora and fauna, including the rare spectac' bear. Visiting the park is complicated. Fi' get permission from the **INRENA Off** (☎46-2544; San Martín, cuadra 2). Then take a ' zuzo-bound minibus for 60km to Yuritung' where there is a *guardabosque* (park-ran' booth). Pay the park entrance fee of S30 he' There are basic bungalows to stay in near' Bring your own bedroll and provisions. C' the Oxapampa office to radio ahead so th' the guards know you're coming.

🎎 Festivals & Events

Selvámanos LOD'
(www.selvamanos.org, Spanish only) Held Parque Nacional Yanachaga-Chemillén eve' June, is fast becoming one of Peru's m' talked-about festivals since its appearance 2010. It's a great showcase of Peruvian co' temporary music: in case you thought it w' all Andean pipes, get ready for innovative ne' rock, electronica, reggae and whacky takes ' *cumbia*. It's also a force behind simultaneou' ly run *semana kultura* where various mu' cal/cultural events occur in towns hereabou'

🛌 Sleeping & Eating

D'Palma Lodge LODGE '
(☎46-2123; www.depalmalodge.com; end of Th' mas Schauss; 2-person cabins S200) This gagg' of Swiss-style lodges is extremely conduci' to relaxation, set into a lush hillside abo' town. Several lodges are for self-cateren' and there's a stylishly rustic restaurant-ba'

Hostal Papaquell GUESTHOUSE
(☎33-7070; Bolognesi 288; s/d S45/60) P' paquell fronts the plaza with large, comfor' able rooms that have chunky wooden furn' ture and lovely hot-water bathrooms.

TOP CHOICE Das Tee Haus CAFE
(Bolivar 473; snacks & light meals S3-12; ⊙8:30an' 12:30pm & 4:40-8:30pm) For a bite to eat loo' no further: this is about the only place t' sample a really good coffee in the whole ' Peru's main coffee-producing region, bu' that's not all: this wonderful German-owne' teahouse has great homebaked cakes, ic' creams and tasty lasagnas. A giant culinar' step forward for Oxapampa.

❶ Getting There & Away

Pozuzo buses run at 6am, 10am and 1pn' from Oxapampa's Plaza de Armas along '

igh road. Oxapampa's pleasant bus sta-
on is eight blocks from the center on the
ostly paved La Merced road. La Merced
insportation (buses S10, *colectivo* taxis
8) leaves from here, and there are also di-
ct Lima buses in the evenings.

uerto Bermúdez

063 / POP 1000 / ELEV 500M

ooking at the huddle of dugout canoes tied
to the mud bank of the Río Pachitea flow-
g past sleepy Puerto Bermúdez, it is dif-
cult to imagine that one could embark on
river journey here that would eventually
ad down the Amazon to the Atlantic.

Times were not always so peaceful. The
ea southeast of Puerto Bermúdez is home
the Ashaninka tribespeople, Peru's larg-
t indigenous Amazon group. During the
eyday of the Sendero Luminoso (Shin-
g Path; see p467) guerrillas attempted to
doctrinate the Ashaninka to become fight-
s. When this didn't succeed, they tried in-
midation by massacring dozens. Today it's
ossible to visit the Ashaninka from Puerto
ermúdez: this is one of the best places in
e Amazon to interact with indigenous
ibes. Contact Albergue Humboldt to ar-
nge Ashaninka visits.

Located near the river, **Albergue Hum-**
oldt (☑83-0020, 963-722-363; www.albergue
imboldt.com; r without bathroom S19; ☺) is the
est place to stay. There are small rustic
ooms with shared cold showers, hammocks
r camping in the secure, secluded garden.
here is no electricity in the mornings.
reakfast and dinner, plus tea and coffee, are
n extra S20 per day. Chilled beer is avail-
ble, as is a well-stocked book/DVD library
nd internet access. Hospitable Basque-born
wner Jesús López de Dicastillo arranges
ekking and cultural expeditions deep into
shaninka territory with local guides from
bout S100 per person per day, depending
n group size and distance traveled and
cluding food, boats and accommodations
n simple shelters. Sometimes, you can
elp tribes with day-to-day activities such
s boat-building. Highly recommended for
udget adventurers!

The town's main street has simple eater-
es and even an internet cafe.

Trucks to La Merced leave around 6am;
his arduous journey has been improved to
round six hours with the new 'semi-paved'
oad. Continuing north, the road deterio-

rates, although this too has undergone an
upgrade. The rough ride to Pucallpa via
Ciudad Constitución and Puerto Inca is by
truck (12 hours) and now by *colectivo* taxi
(six to eight hours). During the dry season,
the river may be too low for passage, and the
road is a better bet. During the wet months,
the road can still be nigh-on impassable,
and boats are better. There are no flights to
Puerto Bermúdez anymore.

Pucallpa

☑061 / POP 205,000 / ELEV 154M

The busy port of Pucallpa has a distinctly
less jungle-like appearance than other
Amazonian towns. Although this is an important distribution center for goods along
the broad, brown Río Ucayali, which sweeps
past the city en route to join the Río Amazonas, the rainforest feels far away. After
all those miles of tropical travel to get here,
Pucallpa seems underwhelming and bland,
and hasty modern development in the center barely disguises the shantytown simplicity a few blocks further out. Still, it's a starting point for a spectacular river adventure
north to Iquitos and, if time and inclination
allow, on to Brazil and the Atlantic.

Beyond the city sprawl, there is a reason
for the traveler to linger: the lovely Lago
Yarinacocha, with river lodges to relax at
and interesting indigenous communities to
visit.

◉ Sights

Many travelers visit nearby Yarinacocha,
which is more interesting than Pucallpa and
has some good accommodation options.

About 4km from the center of Pucallpa,
off the airport road, is **Parque Natural**
(adult/child S3/1; ◉9am-5pm). This is an Amazon zoo set in lush grounds, with a museum
displaying Shipibo pottery and a few other
objects, a small children's playground and
a snack bar. Buses heading to the airport
can drop you here, or take a *mototaxi* for
about S4.

🛏 Sleeping

All the following have rooms with bathrooms, fans and cable TV.

TOP CHOICE Antonio's Hotel HOTEL $$
(☑57-3721; www.hotelantonios.com; Progreso 545;
s/d S100/120; ❄❸❄) Rooms here are huge
and have hot showers, nice tiled bathrooms,

Pucallpa

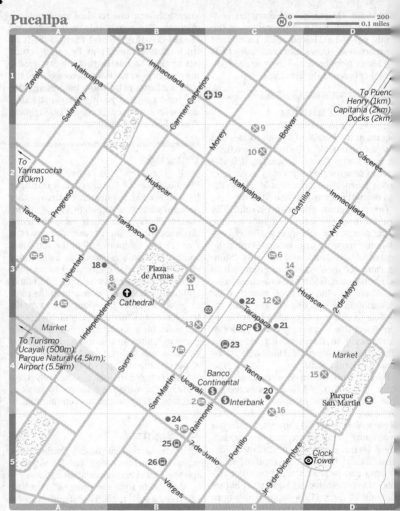

$\overset{\bigoplus}{N}$ 0 _____ 200
0 _____ 0.1 miles

To Puenc
Henry (1km)
Capitania (2km)
Docks (2km)

To
Yarinacocha
(10km)

Plaza
de Armas

Cathedral

Market

To Turismo
Ucayali (500m);
Parque Natural (4.5km);
Airport (5.5km)

BCP

Banco
Continental

Interbank

Market

Parque
San Martín

Clock
Tower

comfortable mattresses and minifridges. One of Pucallpa's best swimming pools now awaits in the garden. Higher rates cover airport pickup and air-con.

Grand Hotel Mercedes   HOTEL **$$**
(☎57-5120; www.grandhotelmercedes.com; Raimondi 610; s S90-110, d S130-160; ✳ ☼) Pucallpa's first good hotel has recently had a sprucing up. All rooms now have air-con and minifridges. There is a dated elegance to this clean, comfortable place, with its gorgeous garden courtyard and swimming pool (also open to nonguests, S3).

Hotel Luz de Luna   HOTEL **$**
(☎57 1729, www.hotelluzdelunaegirl.com; San Marti 283; s/d/ste incl breakfast S130/150/300; ✳ @ This offering sports ample rooms wit plump beds, minifridges, telephones an 21-inch TVs with DVD players. The top-floo restaurant boasts great views; there is also roof terrace and a cafe. Several suites wit Jacuzzis are available.

Hospedaje Komby   GUESTHOUSE
(☎57-1562; hostalkomby@hotmail.com; Ucaya 360; s S50-70, d S65-95; ✳ ☎ ☼) Clearly in quandary about whether to aim for budg et or luxury, Komby has rooms that vee

Pucallpa

between the two brackets. Accommodations overall are clean but basic, brightened by the small pool.

Hostal Arequipa GUESTHOUSE $$
(☎57-1348; www.hostal-arequipa.com; Progreso 573; s/d S50/65, with air-con S80/100; ✻) This is a popular, professional and often full midrange choice, and has hot water, minifridges, a restaurant, and attractive public areas decorated with Shipibo art. The pricier rooms with air-con also include a continental breakfast.

Hospedaje Barbtur GUESTHOUSE $
(☎57-2532; Raimondi 670; s/d S30/40, without bathroom S20/30) This family-run hotel has the best budget digs: small, friendly and well maintained, with cold showers.

Hotel Sol del Oriente HOTEL $$$
(☎57-5510; www.soldelorientehoteles.com; San Martín 552; s/d/ste S230/285/460, s/d with Jacuzzi S285/320; ✻@☀) This is about the best you'll get in Pucallpa proper. It's not that flash but it's comfortable. The somewhat old-fashioned rooms are of a decent size and have cable TV, minifridges and good, always-hot showers. You get a welcome cocktail on arrival.

Eating & Drinking

Pucallpa does cafes and ice-cream parlors well, but has few noteworthy restaurants. The heat in the middle of the day means that restaurants tend to open by 7am for breakfast.

Delicious cakes and ice cream can be found at cafes such as **Fuente Soda Tropitop** (Sucre 401). If you are planning a longer trip, stock up at **Supermercado Los Andes** (Portillo 545).

C'est Si Bon CAFE $
(Independencia 560; snacks S7-15) This bright plaza-abutting spot does Pucallpa's best coffee. Also head here for breakfasts, good ice cream, sandwiches and many other tasty snacks.

Restaurant Kitty PERUVIAN $
(Tarapaca 1062; menús S5-15; ⊙7am-11pm Mon-Sat, to 5pm Sun) The Kitty is clean and popular, and brings in local lunch crowds for a wide variety of Peruvian culinary classics. Join 'em!

Chez Maggy PIZZA $$
(Inmaculada 643; medium pizza S21-23) Maggy serves up pizzas nothing short of superb, and from a wood-burning oven. The interior is modern and not plasticized like some neighboring restaurants. The unusual, tropical-tasting sangria goes down well with all dishes.

Restaurant El Golf SEAFOOD $$
(Huáscar 545; mains S20; ⊙10am-5pm Tue-Sun; ✻) This upscale fish restaurant has a variety of ceviche made with freshwater fish – try

AMAZON BASIN PUCALLPA

the local *doncella* rather than the endangered *paiche*.

Chifa Mey Lin
CHINESE $$

(Inmaculada 698; mains S15-27; ⊘closed Sun) This place gets the gong for being the best of Pucallpa's *chifas* (Chinese restaurants). A spacious, convivial eating environment, and to top it off there is also karaoke next door.

Araguana
PUB

(Inmaculada cuadra 2) Of the few half-decent nightlife options to be found along Inmaculada on the endearingly named 'pizza strip,' this pub-disco seems liveliest.

🛍 Shopping

The local Shipibo tribespeople wander the streets of town selling souvenirs. More of their work is seen near Yarinacocha. For details on their handicrafts, see p467.

ℹ Information

Internet *cabinas* abound on every block, including several on cuadra 3 of Tacna. Several banks have ATMs and change money and traveler's checks. Foreign-exchange bureaus are found along the fourth, fifth and sixth *cuadras* (blocks) of Raimondi. For jungle guides, go to Yarinacocha.

Centro de Llamadas (Tacna 388) Call center; international calls possible.

Clínica Monte Horeb (☎57-1689; Inmaculada 529; ⊘24hr)

Lavandería Gasparin (Portillo 526; ⊘9am-1pm & 4-8pm Mon-Sat) Self-service or drop-off laundry.

Viajes Laser (☎57-1120; fax 57-3776; www.laserviajes.pe; Raimondi 399) Western Union is here, at one of Pucallpa's better travel agencies.

ℹ Getting There & Away

Air

Pucallpa's decent-sized airport is 5km northwest of town. **LAN Peru** (☎1-213-8200, ext 3; Tarapaca 805) has two flights daily to and from Lima, leaving the capital at the very inconvenient times of 5am and 8:30pm and returning from Pucallpa at 6:45am and 10:10pm. **Star Perú** (☎59-0586; Jirón 7 de Junio 865) has an alternative similarly priced direct flight leaving at 7am and 5pm and returning at 11:50am and 7:50pm. The morning flight from Lima usefully continues to Iquitos.

Other towns and settlements (including Atalaya – the Atalaya on the Río Ucayali, Contamaná, Tarapoto and Yurimaguas) are served by small local airlines using light aircraft; some have offices at the airport: ask. Luggage on these flights is limited to 10kg per passenger.

Boat

Pucallpa's port moves depending on water levels. During high water (January to April) boats moor at the dock abutting Parque San Martín in central Pucallpa itself.

As water levels drop, the port falls back to several spots along the banks, including **Puerto Henry** (Manco Cápac s/n) and eventually to about 3km northeast of the town center, reached by *mototaxi* (S3). The town port stretches some way: different boats for different destinations depart from different areas, usually referred to by the name of the nearest intersecting road.

Wherever the port is, riverboats sail the Río Ucayali from Pucallpa to Iquitos (S100, slinging your own hammock and with basic meals, three to five days). Cabins with two or four bunks and private bathrooms come with better food service and cost up to S400.

Boats announce their departure dates and destinations on chalkboards on the boats themselves, but these can be unreliable. Talk to the captain or the cargo loadmaster for greater dependability. They must present boat documents on the morning of their departure day at the **Capitanía** (M Castilla 754) – come here to check for the latest reliable sailing information. Many people work here, but only the official in charge of documents knows the real scoop and can give you accurate sailing information. Passages are daily when the river is high, but in the dry season low water levels result in slower, less frequent passages.

The quality of the boats varies greatly both in size and comfort. Choose a boat that looks good. The *Henry V*, when it is in port, is one of the better-equipped outfits, with a 250-passenger capacity.

This is not a trip for everyone; see p548 for more details on boat travel. Come prepared – the market in Pucallpa sells hammocks, but mosquito repellent may be of poor quality. Bottled drinks are sold on board, but it's worth bringing some large bottles of water or juice.

When negotiating prices for a riverboat passage, ask at any likely boat, but don't pay until you and your luggage are aboard your boat of choice, then pay the captain and no one else. Always get to the port well in advance of when you want to leave: it can take hours hunting for a suitable vessel. Most boats leave either at first light, or in late afternoon/evening.

The river journey to Iquitos (about S100, two to four days from Pucallpa) can be broken at various communities, including Contamaná (S30, 15 to 20 hours) and Requena, and continued on the

AMAZON TRIBESPEOPLE

The vast Amazon Basin, with its inaccessible jungle and hidden river tributaries, is a refuge for many different tribes. In Peru there are an estimated 15 tribes who have rarely or never had contact with the outside world. Across the Peruvian Amazon, there are several chances for foreign travelers to see something of the varied indigenous culture: indeed neither Brazil nor Bolivia can provide equivalently authentic opportunities for such interaction. Offering excursions to see tribespeople in the Amazon is problematic, as with elsewhere in the world. Communities risk being exploited and the travel experience is often tacky and geared toward mass tourism. Below are some of the Peruvian Amazon's indigenous people whom it is possible to visit and interact with safely and with a degree of authenticity.

TRIBE	CHARACTERISTICS	LOCATION TO VISIT THEM
Shipibo	Habitation in small tributaries; women craft delicate pots and textiles with distinctive geometric designs. Most accustomed to contact with the outside world	Santa Clara, Yarinacocha near Pucallpa. Also along Río Ucayali in simple thatched platform houses
Matsiguenka	They wear distinctive Cushmas (white tunics with red stripes, vertical stripes for men and horizontal for women). They are some of the more integrated tribal peoples living in Manu, but live near several others that live in voluntary isolation and have rarely had contact with outsiders	*Zona Reservada*, Parque Nacional Manu
Asháninka	Known historically for their fierce resistance to the Spanish conquistadors and more recently the Sendero Luminoso (Shining Path); they paint their faces with vivid dyes such as the extract of *achiote* seeds. Many accustomed to contact with the outside world	Puerto Bermúdez, Central Amazon

ext vessel coming through (although there's precious little to do in these villages). Alternatively, ask around for speedboats to Contamaná (about S100, five hours), which depart at 6am most days. The return trip (six to seven hours) goes against the current.

Smaller boats occasionally head upriver toward Atalaya; ask at the Capitanía or the town port.

Jungle 'guides' approaching you on the Pucallpa waterfront are not recommended. For jungle excursions, look for a reliable service in Yarinacocha.

Bus

A direct bus to/from Lima (S70 to S100) takes 18 to 20 hours in the dry season; the journey can be broken in Tingo María (S20, nine hours) or Huánuco (12 hours). The road is paved but vulnerable to flooding and erosion. This journey has become safer since the posting of armed police units along the parts of the route formerly prone to armed robbery: still, it's better to do the Pucallpa–Tingo María section in daylight.

León de Huánuco (☑57-5049; Tacna 765) serves Lima at 8:30am, 1pm (*bus-cama*, bed bus) and 5:30pm. Another good company is **Turismo Central** (☑59-1009; Raimondi 768), which has one morning departure and two afternoon departures.

Turismo Ucayali (☑57-2735; Centenario 150) has cars to Tingo María (S45, 4½ hours) leaving hourly throughout the day.

Several companies on cuadra 7 of Raimondi have trucks and buses to more remote Amazon towns like Puerto Bermúdez and Puerto Inca.

ⓘ Getting Around

Mototaxis to the airport or Yarinacocha are about S6; taxis are S10.

Yarinacocha

About 10km northwest of central Pucallpa, Yarinacocha is a lovely oxbow lake where you can go canoeing, observe wildlife, and visit indigenous communities and purchase their handicrafts. The lake, once part of the Río Ucayali, is now entirely landlocked, though a small canal links the two bodies of water during the rainy season. Boat services are provided here in a casual atmosphere. It's well worth spending a couple of days here.

The lakeside village of **Puerto Callao** is a welcome relief from the chaos of downtown Pucallpa's streets. It's still a ramshackle kind of place with only a dirt road skirting the busy waterfront. Buzzards amble among pedestrians, and *peki-peki* boats come and go to their various destinations all day.

Here you'll find a limited choice of generally good accommodations, as well as some decent food. You can also hire **boats** here – in fact, you'll be nabbed as soon as you turn up by boat touts seeking to lure you to their vessel. Choose your boat carefully: make sure it has new-looking life jackets and enough petrol for the voyage, and pay at the end of the tour. Wildlife to watch out for includes freshwater pink dolphins, sloths and meter-long green iguanas, as well as exotic birds such as the curiously long-toed wattled jacana (which walks on lily pads) and the metallic-green Amazon kingfisher. If you like **fishing**, the dry season is apparently the best time.

Tours & Guides

Lots of *peki-peki* boat owners offer tours. Take your time in choosing; the first offer is unlikely to be the best. Guides are also available for walking trips into the surrounding forest, including some overnight hikes.

A recommended guide is **Gilber Reategui Sangama** (☎57-9018; junglesecrets@yahoo.com), who owns the boat *La Normita* in Yarinacocha. He has expedition supplies (sleeping pads, mosquito nets, drinking water) and is both knowledgeable and environmentally aware. He speaks some English, is safe and reliable, and will cook meals for you. He charges about S125 per person per day, or S25 per hour, with a minimum of two people, for an average of three to five days. Gilber lives at the lakeside village of Nueva Luz de Fátima, and offers tours to stay with his family; his father is a shaman with 50 years' experience. Another good guiding outfit is reader-recommended father-and-son-operated **Ucayali Tours** (☎961-728-108; http://ucayali-tour.blogspot.co.uk) which charges around S90 for guided tours of Yarinacocha and the more distant waterways of the Río Ucayali. Another good guide with his own boat is **José Selva** (☎961-740-671); ask him along the Puerto Callao waterfront.

Other guides, however, will claim t above are unavailable or no longer wo there. Don't believe all you hear: a good bo driver will float slowly along, so that you c look for birdlife at the water's edge, or *pe ezosos* (sloths) in the trees. Sunset is a go time to be on the lake.

Boat trips to the Shipibo villages of eith **San Francisco** (also now reached by roa or, better, **Santa Clara** (reached only boat), are also popular. For short trips, bo drivers charge around S20 an hour for t boat; these can carry several people. Ba gaining over the price is acceptable.

Sleeping & Eating

Several inexpensive restaurants and live bars line the Puerto Callao waterfront. Tl better ones are toward the right-hand si as you face the lake, where you'll find I Maloka and nearby **Anaconda**, a floatir restaurant, among other choices.

La Maloka Ecolodge　LODGE $ (☎59-6900; lamaloka@gmail.com; Puerto Calla s/d S120/180; ❄) This is the only decent plac to stay in Puerto Callao. It is worth fork ing out the extra cash for the comfort. I Maloka Ecolodge is located at the right-han end of the waterfront. It is built right out o the water, with the amply sized but una dorned rooms sitting on stilts over the lak There is a relaxing outdoor restaurant an bar area overlooking the lake; pink dolphir regularly flash their flippers for guests. Th only downside is a small menagerie of sad looking caged animals.

La Jungla　BUNGALOW (☎57-1460; bungalows per person S70-80) Thi enthusiastically run place on Yarinacocha far shore northeast of the Puerto Calla dock has several rustic bungalows ope to guests, each sleeping up to four people There is a zoo, a resident tapir and a spa cious bar-restaurant. The owner's father ca guide you in the surrounding jungle.

Pandisho Amazon Ecolodge　LODGE $$ (☎59-1597, 961-65-9596; www.amazon-ecolodge com; 2 days & 1 night incl meals per person S310 About 40 minutes from Puerto Callao, thi place has eight rooms with bathrooms, an electricity for three hours in the evening Its bar is popular with locals on weekends hen there's music, but it's quiet otherwise. ♪urs include transportation from the air-♪rt to the lake, a welcome cocktail and a ll program of walks to visit wildlife and ♪digenous communities, as well as piranha shing! Ask about cheaper, room-only ♪tions.

NORTHERN AMAZON

aw, vast and encapsulating the real spirit ' the Amazon, the northern Amazon Basin home to the eponymous river that wells ♪p from the depths of the Peruvian jungle ♪efore making its long, languorous passage ♪rough Brazil to the distant Atlantic Ocean. ♪ttlements are scarce in this remote region: ♪urimaguas in the west and Iquitos in the ♪ortheast are the only two of any size.

Yurimaguas

♪065 / POP 45,000 / ELEV 181M

♪his sleepy, unspectacular port is one of the ♪eruvian Amazon's best-connected towns ♪nd the gateway to the northern tract of the ♪mazonas. It's visited by travelers looking ♪r boats down the Río Huallaga to Iquitos ♪nd the Amazon proper or by those want-♪ng to experience one of Peru's most animal-♪ch paradises, the Pacaya-Samiria reserve, ♪hich is accessible from here. There is little ♪ detain visitors from continuing their Am-♪zon adventure. Go to Lagunas for a jungle ♪uide, although touts will approach you in ♪urimaguas. A paved road connects Yurim-♪guas with Tarapoto to the south.

Sleeping & Eating

♪ew hotels have hot water. Other budget ho-♪els flank *cuadra* 3 of Arica and *cuadra* 4 of ♪áuregui. For eating, choices are limited: try ♪he hotel restaurants.

TOP CHOICE Hostal El Naranjo HOTEL $
(♪35-2650; http://hostalelnaranjo.com.pe; Arica ♪18; s/d S40/60; ❈@☎) This clean, quiet ♪otel has rooms with ceiling fans and cable ♪V. Some more expensive rooms have air-♪on. Internal courtyard rooms face the tiny, ♪leasant pool. There's hot water and inter-♪et access (S2 per hour), plus it has a good ♪restaurant.

Yacuruña GUESTHOUSE $
(♪965-735-767; Malecón Shanusi 200; r without bathroom S25) This is a great rustic retreat

right by the river. Four simple, nicely deco-rated rooms share a bathroom. Tours are offered both to local sites and the Pacaya-Samiria reserve. Access it via steps from the plaza.

Río Huallaga Hotel & Business Center BUSINESS HOTEL $$
(♪35-3951; www.riohuallagahotel.com; Arica 111; s/d S150/200; ❈☎) Exploding onto the scene in 2010 with just the kind of impec-cable service Yurimaguas previously lacked: spacious well-designed rooms, a swim-ming pool/bar, three restaurants (the best in town) and even its own tour agency. Río Huallaga views are of course included.

Porta Péricos HOTEL $$
(♪35-3462; www.puertopalmeras.com.pe; San Miguel 820; s/d incl breakfast from S125/155; ☎) On the northern outskirts, overlooking the Río Paranapura; the staff claim this hotel's breezy location negates the necessity for air-con. Recent renovations included adding 20 separate bungalows and giving the pool that essential Jacuzzi.

La Prosperidad PERUVIAN $
(Progreso 107; mains S10; ◷Tue-Sun) With tropical juices, burgers and chicken, this is popular as a hangout for young families and jungle guides.

Shopping

Stores selling hammocks for river journeys are on the north side of the market.

Information

The **Consejo Regional** (Plaza de Armas) can give information, as can **Kumpanamá Tours** (♪50-2472; Jáuregui 934). It is better to ar-range Pacaya-Samiria tours in Lagunas. Banco Continental (with a Visa ATM) and BCP will change US cash and traveler's checks. Internet and phone booths come and go frequently but there are a few around the plaza.

Getting There & Around

Air
No airline company currently serves Yurim-aguas. The nearest mainline airport is at Tarapoto.

Boat
The main port 'La Boca' is 13 blocks north of the center. Cargo boats from Yurimaguas follow the Río Huallaga onto the Río Marañón and Iquitos, taking between three and five days with numer-ous stops for loading and unloading cargo. There

are usually departures daily, except Sunday. Passages cost about S80 to S100 on deck (sling your own hammock and receive basic food) or S150 to S180 for a bunk in double or quadruple cabins on the top deck, where the food is better and your gear safer. Bottled water, soft drinks and snacks are sold on board. Bring insect repellent and a hat. Boat information is available from the **Bodega Dávila store** (☑35-2477) by the dock. The Eduardo boats (of which there are five) are considered the best (although readers have reported graphic animal cruelty on these). The journey can be broken at Lagunas (S20 to S30, 10 to 12 hours), just before the Río Huallaga meets the Marañón.

Smaller slow boats and fast boats to Lagunas (S100, 3½ to 4½ hours) leave from the more convenient town port 200m northwest of the Plaza de Armas.

Cruise ships sometimes dock at Yurimaguas, bound for Iquitos. Ask around at 'La Boca' to see about scheduled departures.

Bus

The new paved road makes Yurimaguas easily accessible by Amazon standards. Buses and taxis arrive and depart from offices 2km southwest of the center. For Tarapoto (S15, 2½ hours), several companies leave from offices on the Tarapoto road including **Trans Gilmer Tours** (☑942-627-415; Victor Sifuentes s/n), which has departures every two hours. Likewise, there are multiple companies nearby with *colectivos* to Tarapoto (S25, two hours) from *cuadras* 5 and 6 of Sifuentes. There is nothing to choose between them: it's a matter of which one leaves first, which will happen only when they've touted four passengers.

Taxi

Mototaxis charge S1.50 to take you anywhere around town.

Lagunas

☑065 / POP 4500 / ELEV 148M

Travelers come to muddy, mosquito-rich Lagunas because it is the best point from which to begin a trip to the Reserva Nacional Pacaya-Samiria. It's a spread-out, remote place; there are stores but stock (slightly pricier than elsewhere in Peru) is limited, so it's wise to bring your own supplies as backup. There are no money-changing facilities and hardly any public phones.

☞ Tours & Guides

Spanish-speaking guides are locally available to visit Pacaya-Samiria. It is illegal to hunt within the reserve (though fishing for the pot is OK). The going rate is a rath_ steep S120 to S150 per person per day for guide, a boat and accommodations in hu_ tents and ranger stations. Food and pa_ fees are extra, although the guides can co_ for you.

Several years ago, there was such a plet_ ora of guides in Lagunas that to avoid ha_ assment and price-cutting, an official guid_ association was formed. This then split in_ two separate organizations with the high_ regarded **Estypel** (☑40-1080; www.estyp_ com.pe; Jr Padre Lucero 1345), headed by th_ reputable guide Juan Manuel Rojas Aréval_ considered the best. The office is locate_ near the market. The other organizatic_ formed from the original guiding associ_ tion is **Etascel** (☑40-1007; etascel@hotma_ com; Fiscarrald 530), found down a side stre_ near the market. Both organizations giv_ guides jobs in turn, so it is hard to get _ particular guide. Juan Guerro, working fc_ Estypel, and Etascel's Kleber Saldaña are e_ perienced guides getting good reports fror_ travelers. However, you don't know who yo_ will get until you arrive.

In addition to these two association_ there's also **Huayruro Tours** (www.peruselv_ com; Lagunas ☑40-1186; Alfonso Aiscorbe 2; Yurin_ aguas ☑35-3951; Río Huallaga Hotel, Arica 111), a_ increasingly prominent association that i_ great for helping plan tours (agency sta_ speak English; their guides are Spanish_ speaking but know the reserve extremel_ well). They offer tours of up to 22 days an_ are involved in programs like turtle reintro_ duction within the reserve.

🛏 Sleeping & Eating

Accommodations are improving, but stil_ very basic. Hostels provide cheap meals; i_ you like chicken and fried banana, try the_ basic restaurant on the plaza.

Hostal Eco　　　　　　　　　　GUESTHOUSE $
(☑50-3703; hospeco@hotmail.com; r S25-40) Sev_ en simple, clean rooms here flank a small_ courtyard. All have private bathrooms and_ nightlights for when the power cuts out.

Hostal Samiria　　　　　　　　　GUESTHOUSE $
(☑40-1061; Fitzcarrald; r S25-40) This is prob_ ably Lagunas' best option. Rooms are_ smallish but clean enough, with Spanish-language TV and OK bathrooms. The best_ feature is the secluded central courtyard_ that the rooms face onto, which includes a_ hammock area. Situated near the market.

Getting There & Away

…ats downriver from Yurimaguas to Lagunas …ke about 10 to 12 hours and leave Yurimaguas …tween 7am and 8am most days. Times are …sted on boards at the port in both Yurimaguas …d Lagunas for a day in advance. To continue … Iquitos or return to Yurimaguas, ask which …dio station is in contact with the boat captains …case of problems. Fast boats to Yurimaguas …rive in Lagunas between noon and 2pm for the …ur- to five-hour trip against the current.

Reserva Nacional Pacaya-Samiria

…t 20,800 sq km, this is the largest of Peru's …arks and reserves. Pacaya-Samiria (www. …acaya-samiria.com) provides local people …ith food and a home, and protects ecologi-…ally important habitats. More than 40,000 …eople live on and around the reserve; jug-…ling the needs of human inhabitants while …rotecting wildlife is the responsibility of 20 …o 30 rangers. Staff also teach inhabitants …ow to best harvest the natural renewable …esources to benefit the local people and to …naintain thriving populations of plants and …nimals. Three rangers were murdered by …oachers in late 1998.

The reserve is the home of aquatic animals …uch as Amazon manatees, pink and gray …iver dolphins, two species of caiman and gi-…nt South American river turtles alongside …round 450 bird species and numerous oth-…r animals. The area close to Lagunas has …uffered from depletion: allow several days …o get deep into the least-disturbed areas. …Vith 15 days, you can reach Lago Cocha …Pasto, where there are reasonable chances …of seeing jaguars and larger mammals. Oth-…er noteworthy points in the reserve include …Quebrada Yanayacu, where the river water …s black from dissolved plants; Lago Pante-…an, where you can check out caimans and go …nedicinal-plant collecting; and Tipischa de …Huana, where you can see the giant *Victo-ria regia* waterlilies, big enough for a small …child to sleep upon without sinking. Official …information is available at the reserve office …in Iquitos.

The best way to visit the reserve is to go …by dugout canoe with a guide from Lagunas …(see p470) and spend several days camp-…ing and exploring. Alternatively, comfort-…able ships visit from Iquitos (see p474). The …nearest lodge is the Hatuchay Hotel Pacaya-…Samiria (p484).

If coming from Lagunas, Santa Rosa is the main entry point, where you pay the park entrance fee (per person S20 per day).

The best time to go is during the dry season, when you are more likely to see animals along the riverbanks. Rains ease off in late May; it then takes a month for water levels to drop, making July and August the best months to visit (with excellent fishing). September to November isn't too bad, and the heaviest rains begin in January. The months of February to May are the worst times to go. February to June tend to be the hottest months.

Travelers should bring plenty of insect repellent and plastic bags (to cover luggage), and be prepared to camp out.

Iquitos

☑065 / POP 430,000 / ELEV 130M

Linked to the outside world by air and by river, Iquitos is the world's largest city that cannot be reached by road. It's a prosperous, vibrant jungle metropolis teeming with the usual, inexplicably addictive Amazonian anomalies. Unadulterated jungle encroaches beyond town in full view of the air-conditioned, elegant bars and restaurants that flank the riverside; motorized tricycles whiz manically through the streets yet locals mill around the central plazas eating ice cream like there is all the time in the world. Mud huts mingle with magnificent tiled mansions; tiny dugout canoes ply the water alongside colossal cruise ships. You may well arrive in Iquitos for the greater adventure of a boat trip down the Amazon but whether it's sampling rainforest cuisine, checking out the buzzing nightlife or exploring one of Peru's most fascinating markets in the floating shantytown of Belén, this thriving city will entice you to stay awhile. Because everything must be 'imported', costs are higher than in other cities.

History

Iquitos was founded in the 1750s as a Jesuit mission, fending off attacks from indigenous tribes that didn't want to be converted. In the 1870s the great rubber boom boosted the population 16-fold and for the next 30 years, Iquitos was at once the scene of ostentatious wealth and abject poverty. Rubber barons became fabulously rich, while rubber tappers (mainly local tribespeople and poor *mestizos*) suffered virtual enslavement and sometimes death from disease or harsh treatment.

Iquitos

0 | 200 m
0 | 0.1 miles

Yavari
Loreto
Callao
Pevas
Nauta
Nanay
Ocampo
Yavari
Loreto
Condamine

To Boats to Frio y Fuego (100m);
Puerto Embarcadero (150m);
Amazon Yarapa River Lodge
Office (300m); Bucanero (300m);
Explorama Lodges Office (500m);
Clínica Ana Stahl (1km);
Aqua Expeditions Office (1.5km);
La Casa Fitzcarraldo (2km)

Pedro Rosell

Tavara

⊗ 30

El Refugio
(1.5km)

Moore
Tacna
Pevas
Nauta

Fitzcarrald
20
4
Plaza
Castilla
● 44
34

41 🅿
⊗ 28
6
42 💲
Napo
11 @
Putumayo
Araujo
31 ⊗
35 🅿
12

40 ℹ

19

37 ✚

18
✚ 36

● 45
13
16
39 ● 1
⊗ 29

Raimondi

9
📠 3
10

Plaza de
Armas

Iglesia de
San Juan
Bautista

🛈 **Casa de
Fierro**

23
38
25
33
Malecón Maldonado

Tacna
Araujo
To Tourism
Police (150m)

24
Lores

5
22

43

17
7

To Chifa Long
Fung (400m)

To Parrilladas
El Zorrito
(150m)

Morona
Huallaga

27 ⊗
26
21

32 ⊗

To Plaza 28
de Julio
(100m)

Brasil
Arica
14

2
🏛

Ricardo Palma
Prospero

📠 15

To Complejo CNI (500m);
Pacaya-Samiria Reserve
Office (1km); Oficina de
Migraciones (1km)

8
Malecón Tarapaca

To Amazon Apart
Hotel (250m);
Airport (6km)

To Belén
(300m)

Río
Amazonas

Iquitos

AMAZON BASIN IQUITOS

By WWI, the bottom fell out of the rubber boom as suddenly as it had begun. A British entrepreneur smuggled some rubber-tree seeds out of Brazil, and plantations were seeded in the Malay Peninsula. It was much cheaper and easier to collect the rubber from orderly rubber tree plantations than from wild trees scattered in the Amazon Basin.

Iquitos suffered subsequent economic decline, supporting itself with a combination of logging, agriculture (Brazil nuts, tobacco, bananas and *barbasco* – a poisonous vine used by indigenous peoples to hunt fish and now exported for use in insecticides) and the export of wild animals to zoos. Then, in the 1960s, a second boom revitalized the area. This time the resource was oil, and its discovery made Iquitos a prosperous modern town. In recent years tourism has

also played an important part in the area's economy.

◉ Sights

Iquitos' cultural attractions, while limited, dwarf those of other Amazon cities. On the Malecón, at the corner with Morona, is an old building housing the **Biblioteca Amazónica** (the largest collection of historical documents in the Amazon Basin) and the small **Museo Etnográfico**. Both are open on weekdays (admission for both S3). The museum includes life-sized fiberglass casts of members of various Amazon tribes.

Casa de Fierro   HISTORIC BUILDING
(cnr Putumayo & Próspero, Plaza de Armas) Every guidebook tells of the 'majestic' Casa de Fierro (Iron House), designed by Gustave

Eiffel (of Eiffel Tower fame). It was made in Paris in 1860 and imported piece by piece into Iquitos around 1890, during the opulent rubber-boom days, to beautify the city. It's the only surviving one of three different iron houses originally imported here. It looks like a bunch of scrap-metal sheets bolted together, was once the location of the Iquitos Club and is now, in humbler times, a general store.

Azulejos
HISTORIC BUILDING

Other remnants of the rubber-boom glory days include *azulejos,* handmade tiles imported from Portugal to decorate the mansions of the rubber barons. Many buildings along Raimondi and Malecón Tarapaca are lavishly decorated with *azulejos.* Some of the best are various government buildings along or near the Malecón.

Belén
NEIGHBORHOOD

At the southeast end of town is the floating shantytown of Belén, consisting of scores of huts, built on rafts, which rise and fall with the river. During the low-water months, these rafts sit on the river mud and are dirty and unhealthy, but for most of the year they float on the river – a colorful and exotic sight. Seven thousand people live here, and canoes float from hut to hut selling and trading jungle produce. The best time to visit the shantytown is at 7am, when people from the jungle villages arrive to sell their produce. To get here, take a cab to 'Los Chinos,' walk to the port and rent a canoe to take you around.

Belén mercado, located within the city blocks in front of Belén, is the raucous, crowded affair common to most Peruvian towns. All kinds of strange and exotic products are sold here among the more mundane bags of rice, sugar, flour and cheap household goods. Look for the bark of the *chuchuhuasi* tree, which is soaked in rum for weeks and used as a tonic (it's served in many of the local bars). *Chuchuhuasi* and other Amazon plants are common ingredients in herbal pain-reducing and arthritis formulas manufactured in Europe and the USA. The market makes for exciting shopping and sightseeing, but do remember to watch your wallet.

🏃 Activities
Golf
Amazon Golf Club
GOLF

(📞963-1333, 975-4976; Quistacocha; admission per day incl club rental S60; ⊙6am-6pm) Amazing as it may seem, you can play a round or two on the nine holes of the only course in the e tire Amazon. Founded in 2004 by a bunch nostalgic expats, the 2140m course was bu on bushland just outside Iquitos and boas apart from its nine greens, a wooden clu house. Hole 4 is a beauty: you tee onto an land surrounded by piranha-infested water Don't go fishing for lost balls! When ful completed the clubhouse will also include bar (it already has a fridge full of beer) and th grounds will feature a swimming pool and tennis court. Meantime, see cofounders Mil Collis or Bill Grimes at the course city offi for information on how to get swinging.

River Cruises

Cruising the Amazon is an expensive bus ness: the shortest trips can cost more tha US$1000. It's a popular pastime, too, and a vance reservations are often necessary (an often mean discounts). Cruises natural focus on the Río Amazonas, both downr ver (northeast) toward the Brazil–Colombi border and upriver to Nauta, where the Río Marañón and Ucayali converge. Beyon Nauta, trips continue up these two rivers t the Pacaya-Samiria reserve. Trips can als be arranged on the three rivers surround ing Iquitos: the Itaya, the Amazonas and th Nanay. Operators quote prices in US dollar A useful booking website for most of the fo lowing is www.amazoncruise.net.

Dawn on the Amazon
Tours & Cruises
CRUIS

(📞22-3730, 965-939-190; www.dawnontheamazon com; Malecón Maldonado 185, Iquitos; day trips inc lunch per person US$74.75, multiday cruises pe person per day US$199) This small outfit offer the best deal for independent travelers. The *Amazon I* is a beautiful 11m wooden craf with modern furnishings, available for ei ther day trips or longer river cruises up to two weeks. Included are a bilingual guide, al meals and transfers. You can travel with host Bill Grimes and his experienced crew along the Amazon, or along its quieter tributaries (larger cruise ships will necessarily stick to the main waterways). While many cruise operators have fixed departures/itineraries, Bill's can be adapted to accommodate individual needs. The tri-river cruise is a favorite local trip: while on board, fishing and bird-watching are the most popular activities.

Aqua Expeditions
CRUISE

(📞60-1053, 965-83-2517; www.aquaexpeditions. com; Prolongación Iquitos 1187; 3-night Marañón & Ucayali cruise per person in suite US$2685) Aqua the operator of luxury riverboats *MV Aria* and *MV Aqua* which have twice-weekly departures into the Pacaya-Samiria reserve. The 40m *MV Aqua* has 12 vast, luxury suite cabins (each over 22 sq meters) while the *MV Aria,* launched in 2011, has equally splendid accommodations but in 16 similar-sized suites and an onboard Jacuzzi. Both boats have beautiful observation lounges to watch the waters drifting by. Cruises last three, five or seven days.

Cruise boats come with plenty of deck space for river-watching, a full crew and bilingual guides. Meals are included and small lunches are carried for side trips. Activities can involve visiting indigenous communities (for dancing and craft sales), hikes, and bird- and pink dolphin-watching (on big ships, don't expect to see too much rare wildlife).

GreenTracks CRUISE
(in the USA 970-884-6107, 800-892-1035; www.greentracks.com; 416 Country Rd 501, PMB 31 Bayfield, CO81122; 7 days & 6 nights s/d US$2750/5000) With three luxury ships plying the Peruvian Amazon, GreenTracks offers four- to seven-day excursions into the Pacaya-Samiria reserve. The *Ayapua* is a 30-passenger, rubber-boom-era boat used for seven-day/six-night voyages, with air-conditioned rooms, a bar and even a library. The *Clavero* is a smaller boat offering the same excursion. *Delfín I* is a more modern vessel accommodating 12 passengers and operates four- and five-day cruises to the reserve. Contact the company in the USA for details.

✷✷ Festivals & Events

San Juan TRADITIONAL MUSIC
(Jun 22-27) This is the big annual debauch, a festival that has grown around the saint's day of San Juan Bautista (St John the Baptist) on June 24 (the main party day). It's celebrated in most Amazon towns but Iquitos honors the saint most fervently with dancing, cockfights, and above all feasting and frivolity. *Juanes* (turmeric-smeared rice blended with chicken, olives or sliced egg and wrapped in a jungle leaf) are the typical food consumed. On the night of the 23rd locals partake in the river dunk, as this is the day of the year when the waters of the Itaya have healing properties.

Great Amazon River Raft Race SPECTATOR SPORT
(www.grarr.org) Held in September or October, this is an annual race down the river between Nauta and Iquitos in hand-built craft.

🛏 Sleeping

There's a broad range of accommodation choices in Iquitos, from basic budget to five-star comfort. Mosquitoes are rarely a serious problem in town, so mosquito netting is not always provided.

The best hotels tend to be booked up on Friday and Saturday, and on major festivals such as San Juan. The busiest season is from May to September, when prices may rise slightly.

Most budget hotels have bathrooms and fans unless otherwise indicated; midrange places have air-con and private bathroom, normally with hot water. Walk-in rates for standard rooms are given here; holiday rates may be higher.

TOP CHOICE **La Casa Fitzcarraldo** GUESTHOUSE $$
(60-1138/39; http://lacasafitzcarraldo.com; Av La Marina 2153; r S180-350; ✳🐱) Sequestered within a serene walled garden away from the city chaos, this is the most interesting accommodation option. The house takes its title from Werner Herzog's film – Herzog and co stayed here during the filming of *Fitzcarraldo* (see p479). Stay in the mahogany-floored Mick Jagger room, the luxuriantly green Klaus Kinski suite or five other individually designed rooms. There is a tree house (with wi-fi!), a lovely swimming pool (nonresidents S5) and a huge breakfast included in the price, as well as a bar-restaurant, minicinema and several four-legged residents to check out.

Casa Morey BOUTIQUE HOTEL $$$
(23-1913; www.casamorey.com; Loreto 200; s/d incl breakfast S155/260; ✳🐱) This former mansion of the rubber baron Luis F Morey dates from 1910 and has been renovated to its former elegance, with 14 suites each large enough to house a fair few hotels in their entirety. There are plenty of original *azulejos*, voluminous bathrooms with baths, river views, a courtyard with a small pool, a library with a stupendous collection of Amazon-related literature and a grandiose dining area (though the tiling here isn't original) to enjoy breakfast in.

Camiri HOSTEL $
(965-982-854; marcelbendayan@hotmail.com; end of Pevas cuadra 1; dm/d S30/100) For a memorable dose of relaxed, rustic Iquitos living, come to crash at this floating hostel-bar, accessed by boardwalks over the river. Dorms sleep either six or 10. River views are

exquisite and the owner is a mine of intriguing information. After a recent expansion, the bar has to be the most atmospheric place for a riverside drink in Iquitos. Nights can get pretty wild. Camiri now also has a jungle lodge, Ilaquipayay, in the Pacaya-Samiria reserve buffer zone 260km from Iquitos and runs three- to five-day tours there.

Amazon Apart Hotel
APARTMENT **$$**
(☎26-6262; www.amazonaparthotel.com; Aguirre 1151; s/d S150/180, ste S144-221; ❋@≋) This bright, new, well-appointed hotel is a little out of the way – but this is its only disadvantage. There are several levels of vast colorful rooms here. Rooms all have air-con and minifridges; many also have their own kitchenettes, so that you can self-cater in style. There is also internet, a restaurant doing mean ceviche and an attractive swimming pool.

Flying Dog Hostel
HOSTEL **$**
(☎in Lima 01-445-6745; http://flyingdogperu.com; Malecón Tarapaca btwn Brasil & Ricardo Palma; dm/d S30/75) The Flying Dog, part of the same hostel chain you'll find in Lima and Cuzco, is another good budget option: clean, bright rooms, hot water and kitchen facilities. The doubles are a tad pricey but some have private bathrooms.

Posada del Cauchero
GUESTHOUSE **$$**
(☎22-2914; ermivaya@yahoo.es; Raimondi 449; s/d/ste S100/120/180; ❋❋≋) Above the restaurant of the same name lurk 12 massive, chalet-style rooms (seven with air-con), some of which are suites. All are decorated with tribal-themed art. There is a pool and some of the best river views in Iquitos.

Hotel El Dorado Plaza
LUXURY HOTEL **$$$**
(☎22-2555; www.grupo-dorado.com; Napo 258; r incl breakfast from S575; ❋🛜≋) With a prime plaza location, this modern hotel is the town's best, with 64 well-equipped, spacious rooms (some with plaza views, others overlooking the pool). Jacuzzi, sauna, gym, restaurant, several suites, 24-hour room service, two bars and attentive staff make this a five-star hotel. Rates for rooms are often discounted when the hotel is not busy. The same group runs the slightly cheaper El Dorado Hotel & Suites (☎23-2574; Napo 362; s/d/ste S230/273/410), where you can still use the plaza hotel facilities.

Hotel Acosta
HOTEL **$$**
(☎23-1761; www.hotelacosta.com; cnr Araujo & Huallaga; s/d S165/195; ❋🛜) Owned by the same people as the Victoria Regia; you ca be sure you're in good hands at this sma hotel. Rooms are large and finished in de cate earthy tones; they all come with mir fridges, air-con, minisafes and writing desk There is a ground-floor restaurant.

La Casa Del Francés
GUESTHOUSE
(☎23-1447; info@lacasadelfrances.com; Raimon 183; dm/s/d S20/40/45) A secure, hammoc strung courtyard leads back to this pleasa budget choice offering several large, sin ple, colonial-style rooms with spotless tile bathrooms.

Mad Mick's Bunkhouse
HOSTEL
(☎965-754-976; michaelcollis@hotmail.com; P tumayo 163; dm S15) A stone's throw from th Plaza de Armas, this is the city's cheape accommodations: a dark, eight-bed dor (four bunks) with one bathroom (interestin graffiti) that attracts shoestringers in drove

Hospedaje La Pascana
GUESTHOUSE
(☎23-5581, 23-1418; www.pascana.com; Peva 133; s/d/tr S40/50/65) This safe and friendl place with a small, verdant garden has bee going three decades, is deservedly popular with travelers and is often full. A book ex change and a charming cafe serving fresh brewed coffee add to the attraction. Cont nental breakfast is S7.50.

Hostal El Colibrí
GUESTHOUSE
(☎24-1737; http://hostalelcolibri.net; Nauta 172 s S45-60, d S60-80; ❋) A very good budge choice close to the river and the mai square, with pleasant, airy rooms sportin fans and TVs. The traveler-friendly folk run ning this place added three more floors o rooms in 2009. Higher tariffs are for air-con

Hostal Florentina
GUESTHOUSE **$**
(☎23-3591; Huallaga 212; s S55-75, d S75-85, t S120-140) Rooms in this old colonial house are smallish but very quiet. They come with cable TV, mosquito nets and sparkling bath rooms, and are tucked well back from the road with a lovely courtyard for hammocks at the rear. Lower rates are for rooms with fans, higher rates for air-con.

Hotel Victoria Regia
HOTEL **$$$**
(☎23-1983; www.victoriaregiahotel.com; Ricardo Palma 252; s/d incl breakfast S231/264, ste S300-400; ❋❋≋) A blast of icy, air-conditioned air welcomes guests to this comfortable hostelry. It has excellent beds and sizeable rooms that include fancy reading lights and minifridges, plus hairdryers and baths in the

throoms. One of the suites has a Jacuzzi. The indoor pool and fine restaurant-bar attract upscale guests and businesspeople, though in reality this is not significantly better than several city hotels that charge about S100 less.

arañón Hotel
HOTEL $$

(24-2673; www.hotelmaranon.com; Nauta 289; 'd incl continental breakfast S99/130; ✱@ ✈ ✻)
his place has light tiles everywhere and a estaurant with room service. The rooms ave good-sized bathrooms, minibars and deed all the usual amenities. Good value.

otel Europa
HOTEL $$

(23-1123; www.europahoteliquitos.net; Próspero 94; s/d S100/150; ✱) One of the best midange bargains, the canary-yellow Europa s a homey hotel and ticks all the boxes you ould expect for the price range: large neat ooms, air-con, minifridges, a good restaurant and laundry service.

🍴 Eating

he city has great restaurants but sadly many regional specialties feature endangered animals, such as *chicharrón de lagarto* (fried alligator) and *sopa de tortuga* turtle soup). *Paiche*, a local river fish, is making a comeback thanks to breeding programs. More environmentally friendly dishes include ceviche made with river fish, *chupín de pollo*, a tasty soup of chicken, egg and rice, and *juanes*.

For self-catering supplies, visit **Supermercado Los Portales** (Próspero at Morona).

TOP
CHOICE **Frio y Fuego**
FUSION $$

(965-607-474; Embarcadero Av La Marina 138; mains S15-35; ⊘noon-4pm & 7-11pm Tue-Sat, noon-5pm Sun) Take a boat out to this floating foodie paradise in the middle of the mouth of the Río Itaya to sample the city's best food. The emphasis is on river fish dishes (anything with Peru's Amazon-abiding *doncella* is delectable) but the *parrillas* are inviting too: tender beef medalions with a mozzarella and pepper-stuffed *bijao* leaf, for example. Come here at night for the best overall view of Iquitos, beautifully lit up as you initiate the evening with a glass of Chilean red by the restaurant's very own swimming pool. The address given is the boat embarkation point.

TOP
CHOICE **Belén Mercado**
MARKET $

(cnr Próspero & Jirón 9 de Diciembre) There are great eats at Iquitos' markets, particularly the Belén *mercado* where a set *menú* here, including *jugo especial* (jungle juice) is less than S5. Look out for specialties including meaty Amazon worms, *ishpa* (simmered sabalo fish intestines and fat) and *sikisapa* (fried leafcutter ants; abdomens are supposedly tastiest) and watch your valuables. Another good market for cheap eats is **Mercado Central** (Lores cuadra 5).

Amazon Bistro
INTERNATIONAL $$

(Malecón Tarapaca 268; breakfasts S12, mains S15-40; ⊘6am-midnight) Of the new restaurants, this is best: laid out with TLC by the Belgian owner with a New York–style breakfast bar (OK, Amazon version of!) and upper-level mezzanine seating looking down on the main eating area. Pizzas here are tasty but the cuisine refuses to be pinned down: there's Argentine steaks not to mention the Belgian influence, which creeps across in the crepes, and with the L'escargot and the range of Belgian beers... oh, and the city's best coffee. It's also a good evening drinking spot.

El Sitio
PARRILLA $

(cnr Lores & Huallaga; parrillas from S3; ⊘dinner) Wide varieties of delicious grilled meats with the added novelty of seeing them cooked up by the jovial Argentinian outside. It stays open until it's all gone.

Dawn on the Amazon Café
INTERNATIONAL $$

(Malecón Maldonado 185; mains about S20; ⊘7:30am-10pm) Something of a traveler magnet on the Malecón now, this new cafe sports a menu divided up into North American, Peruvian, Spanish and (logically) Chinese. Travel wherever your taste buds desire but bear in mind that the steamed fresh fish is very good. Ingredients are all non-MSG and those on *Ayahuasca* diets are catered for.

Ari's Burger
AMERICAN $$

(Próspero 127; meals S10-25; ⊘7am-3am) On the corner of the Plaza de Armas, this clean, chirpy and brightly lit joint is known locally as *'gringolandia.'* Two walls are open to the street, allowing great plaza- and people-watching. It's almost always open, serves American-style food as well as local plates and ice creams, changes US dollars and is popular with tourists and locals alike. Desserts in Iquitos don't get gooier.

Parrilladas El Zorrito
PARRILLA $

(Fanning 355; mains S5-10) Food is cooked outside on a grill at this lively, ambient and

AMAZON BASIN IQUITOS

immensely popular local joint. *Juanes* and river fish are the things to go for. Portions are huge. There is great live music at weekends.

Antica
ITALIAN **$$**

(Napo 159; mains S22-24; ⊙7am-midnight) The Antica is the best Italian restaurant in town. Primarily a pizza place – there's an impressive wood-fired pizza oven – pasta also takes a predominant spot on the menu with the lasagna being an excellent choice. Chow down at solid wooden tables and choose from the range of fine imported Italian wines.

Ivalú
PERUVIAN **$**

(Lores 215; snacks from S2; ⊙breakfast & lunch) One of the most popular local spots for juice and cake in the city, this place does a handy sideline in tamales (chicken or fish in corn dough, wrapped in jungle leaves). It normally opens at 8am; go sooner rather than later if you want a seat.

La Vecina
CEVICHE **$**

(Tavara West 352; small/large ceviche S8/15; ⊙lunch) There's nothing else but ceviche on the menu at this homey place, but it doesn't disappoint.

Bucanero
SEAFOOD **$$**

(Av Marina 124; mains S25; ⊙11am-5pm; ❄) For great river views in civilized air-conditioned environs, this restaurant with a fish-dominated menu is a great lunch stop. *Pescado a la plancha* (grilled river fish) with *chicharrones* (fried chunks of pork) goes down remarkably well with an icy Iquiteña (Iquitos beer).

Gran Maloca
PERUVIAN **$$**

(Lores 170; menú S15, mains S25-42; ⊙noon-10pm; ❄) Enter the bygone world of the rubber-boom glory days at this atmospheric Amazonian restaurant. Expect silk tablecloths, wall-length mirrors and imaginative regional delicacies such as *chupín de pollo*, Amazon venison with toasted coconut and the scrumptious Loretan omelet with jungle leaves.

Chifa Long Fung
CHINESE **$**

(San Martín 454; mains S10-20; ⊙noon-2.30pm & 7pm-midnight) There are several inexpensive *chifas* and other restaurants near the Plaza 28 de Julio, of which the Long Fung is a little more expensive but worth it.

Fitzcarraldo Restaurant-Bar
INTERNATIONAL **$$**

(Napo 100; mains S15-40; ⊙noon-late; ❄) The Fitzcarraldo is an upscale option on the riverside strip, with good food and serv-ice. It does good pizzas (delivery availabl) and various local and international dishe Watch out for that icy air-con.

Kikiriki
FAST FOO

(☑23-2020; Napo 159; quarter-chicken from S7.5 ⊙dinner) How does a Peruvian cock crow 'Kikiriki.' This is a great place for grille chicken. Have it served on a bed of fried b nana, the jungle way, with a dash of the le endary hot green sauce. Delivery is possibl

La Noche
INTERNATIONAL **$**

(Malecón Maldonado 177; sandwiches S10, main S20; ⊙7am-late) Past its best, but still goo with a prime location and a choice of stree front or upper balcony Malecón dinin (there's an upstairs chill-out lounge, too There's real espresso and a host of gourme sandwiches for lunch while river fish an crisp salads grace the dinner menu.

🍷 Drinking & Entertainment

Iquitos is a party city. The Malecón is th cornerstone of the lively nightlife scene.

Arandú Bar
BA

(Malecón Maldonado 113; ⊙late) This is th liveliest of several thumping Malecón bars great for people-watching and always churn ing out loud rock-and-roll classics.

Musmuqui
BA

(Raimondi 382; ⊙to midnight Sun-Thu, to 3am Fr & Sat) Locally popular lively bar with twe floors and an extensive range of aphrodisia cocktails concocted from wondrous Amazon plants.

Complejo CNI
LIVE MUSIC

(Caceres cuadra 10; ⊙Thu-Sat) Well-known local group Illusion play here at Iquitos' best disco, where hundreds and hundreds of *iquiteños* end up dancing on a weekend evening.

El Refugio
BAR

(⊙to 3am Thu-Sat) The upbeat atmosphere and the location beside an oxbow lake on the Río Nanay in the west of town are appealing even if the decor (scantily clad women) may not thrill you.

🔒 Shopping

There are a few shops on the first cuadra of Napo selling jungle crafts, some of high quality and pricey. A good place for crafts is **Mercado de Artesanía San Juan**, on the road to the airport – bus and taxi drivers

HERZOG'S AMAZON

Eccentric German director Werner Herzog, often seen as obsessive and bent on filming 'reality itself,' shot two movies in Peru's jungle: *Aguirre, the Wrath of God* (1972) and *Fitzcarraldo* (1982). Herzog's accomplishments in getting these movies made at all – during havoc-fraught filming conditions – are in some ways more remarkable than the finished products.

Klaus Kinski, the lead actor in *Aguirre*, was a volatile man prone to extreme fits of rage. Herzog's documentary *My Best Fiend* details such incidents as Kinski beating a conquistador extra so severely that his helmet, donned for the part, was all that saved him from being killed. Then there was the time near the end of shooting when, after altercations with a cameraman on the Río Nanay, Kinski prepared to desert the film crew on a speedboat. Herzog had to threaten to shoot him with a rifle to make him stay. (To tell both sides of the story, however, *My Best Fiend* also reveals that Herzog admitted to once trying to firebomb Kinski in his house and according to other members of the film crew Herzog often over exaggerated.) Kinski's biography, *Kinski Uncut* (albeit partly ghostwritten by Herzog) paints a picture of the director as a buffoon who had no idea how to make movies.

Filming *Fitzcarraldo*, the first choice for the lead fell ill and the second, Mick Jagger, abandoned the set to do a Rolling Stones tour. With a year's filming already wasted, Herzog called upon Kinski once more. Kinski soon antagonized the Matsiguenka tribespeople being used as extras: one even offered to murder him for Herzog. While filming near the Peru–Ecuador frontier, a war between the two nations erupted and soldiers destroyed the film set. Then there was the weather: droughts so dire that the rivers dried and stranded the film's steamship for weeks, followed by flash floods that wrecked the boat entirely. (Some of these are chronicled in *Conquest of the Useless: Reflections from the Making of Fitzcarraldo*, Herzog's film diaries, translated into English in 2009.) To hear another side to events during filming, chat to the folks at La Casa Fitzcarraldo (see p475), owned by the daughter of the executive producer of *Fitzcarraldo* the movie.

Herzog could certainly be a hard man to work with, filming many on-set catastrophes and using them as footage in the final cut. The director once said he saw filming in the Amazon as 'challenging nature itself.' The fact that he completed two films in the Peruvian jungle against such odds is evidence that in some ways, Herzog did challenge nature – and triumphed.

know it. Don't buy items made from animal bones and skins, as they are made from jungle wildlife. It's illegal to import many such items into the US and Europe.

You can buy, rent or trade almost anything needed for a jungle expedition at **Mad Mick's Trading Post** (965-75-4976; michaelcollis@hotmail.com; Putumayo 163; 8am-8pm). Don't need it afterwards? Mick will buy anything back (if it's in good nick) for half-price.

🛈 Information

Dangers & Annoyances

Street touts and self-styled jungle guides tend to be aggressive, and many are both irritatingly insistent and dishonest. They are working for commissions, and usually for bog-standard establishments. There have been reports of these guides robbing tourists. It is best to make your own decisions by contacting hotels, lodges and tour companies directly. Exercise particular caution around Belén, which is very poor and where petty thieving is quite common. That said, violent crime is almost unknown in Iquitos.

Emergency
National police (23-1123; Morona 126) Most central police station.
Tourism police (POLTUR; 24-2081; Lores 834)

Immigration
If arriving/leaving from Brazil or Colombia, get your entry/exit stamp at the border.
Brazilian Consulate (23-5151; Lores 363)
Colombian Consulate (23-1461; Araujo 431; 9am-12:30pm & 2-4:30pm Mon-Fri)
Oficina de migraciónes (23-5371; Cáceres, cuadra 18)

Internet Access
Places charge about S3 per hour; the wi-fi in hotels usually offers a better connection.

AMAZON BASIN IQUITOS

BORDER CROSSING: THE PERU-COLOMBIA-BRAZIL BORDER ZONE

Even in the middle of the Amazon, border officials adhere to formalities and will refuse passage if documents are not in order. With a valid passport and visa or tourist card, border crossing is not a problem.

When leaving Peru for Brazil or Colombia, you'll get an exit stamp at a Peruvian guard post just before the border (boats stop there long enough for this; ask the captain).

The ports at the three-way border are several kilometers apart, connected by public ferries. They are reached by air or boat, but not by road. The biggest, nicest border town, **Leticia**, in Colombia, boasts by far the best hotels and restaurants, and a hospital. You can fly from Leticia to Bogotá on almost-daily commercial flights. Otherwise, infrequent boats go to **Puerto Asis** on the Río Putumayo; the trip takes up to 12 days. From Puerto Asis, buses go further into Colombia.

The two small ports in Brazil are **Tabatinga** and **Benjamin Constant**; both have basic hotels. Tabatinga has an airport with flights to Manaus. Get your official Brazilian entry stamp from the Tabatinga police station if flying on to Manaus. Tabatinga is a continuation of Leticia, and you can walk or take a taxi between the two with no immigration hassles, unless you are planning on traveling further into Brazil or Colombia. Boats leave from Tabatinga downriver, usually stopping in Benjamin Constant for a night, then continuing on to Manaus, a week away. It takes about an hour to reach Benjamin Constant by public ferry. US citizens need a visa to enter Brazil. Make sure you apply in good time – either in the USA or in Lima.

Peru is on the south side of the river, where currents create a constantly shifting bank. Most boats from Iquitos will drop you at the small village of Santa Rosa, which has Peruvian immigration facilities. Motor canoes reach Leticia in about 15 minutes. For travelers to Colombia or Brazil, Lonely Planet has guidebooks for both countries.

If you are arriving from Colombia or Brazil, you'll find boats in Leticia and Tabatinga for Iquitos. You should pay US$10 to US$15 for the nigh-on two-day trip on a cargo riverboat, or US$75 for a *mas rápido* (fast boat; 12 to 14 hours), which leave daily. Prices and departures are the same for the opposite journey too, although downriver from Iquitos to the tri-border is quicker. Up or down river, you may be able to get passage on a cruise ship, but note that this will make stops en route.

Remember that however disorganized things may appear, you can always get meals, money changed, beds and boats simply by asking around.

Cyber (Putumayo 374) Lots of machines; serves beer; almost always open – why not?

Laundry
Lavandería Imperial (Nauta cuadra 1; ☺8am-8pm Mon-Sat) Coin-operated; S12 per load.

Medical Services
Clinica Ana Stahl (☎25-2535; www.caas.peru.org; Av La Marina 285; ☺24hr) Good private clinic.

Dr Carlos Vidal Ore (☎975-3346; Fitzcarrald 156)

HappyDent (Putumayo 786) Dentist.

Money
Several banks change traveler's checks, give advances on credit cards or provide an ATM, including **BCP** (cnr Próspero & Putumayo), which has a secure ATM. All have competitive rates. For changing US cash quickly, street moneychang-ers are located on Próspero between Lores and Brasil. Most are OK, but a few run scams where they replace a S100 note with a S20 note. Exercise caution when changing money on the street Also see p536 for further information on counterfeit money. Changing Brazilian or Colombian currency is best done at the border. Transfer money at **Western Union** (Napo 359).

Post
Post office (Arica 402; ☺8am-6pm Mon-Fri, to 4:30pm Sat) Central.

Tourist Information
Apart from the places listed here, various jungle guides and jungle lodges give tourist information, obviously promoting their services, which is fine if you are looking for them but otherwise rarely helpful.

iPerú Airport (☎26-0251; Main Hall, Francisco Secada Vignetta Airport; ☺whenever flights e arriving/departing); City Center (☎23-44; Napo 161; ☻9am-6pm Mon-Sat, 9am-m Sun) English spoken at the airport branch.

uitos Times (www.iquitostimes.com) A free onthly newspaper in English, aimed at tour-s, is delivered to all hotels and restaurants. r the latest on what's going down, ask editor ad' Mick Collis at his office at Putumayo 163.

eserva Nacional Pacaya-Samiria Office ☎22-3555; Chávez 930-942, Pevas 339; 8am-4pm Mon-Fri) Entry to the reserve for ree days costs S60.

Getting There & Away

ir

uitos' small but busy airport, 7km from the enter, currently receives flights from Lima, ucallpa, Tarapoto and Panama City.

LAN Peru (☎23-2421; Próspero 232) operates e most expensive flights, with two morning ad two afternoon flights to Lima. **Star Perú** ☎23-6208; Napo 256) also operates flights to nd from Lima via Tarapoto or Pucallpa. Fares e about US$120 to Lima and slightly less Pucallpa or Tarapoto. **Copa Airlines** (☎in anama 1-800-359-2672; www.copaair.com) ow operates twice-weekly flights to Panama ity (Wednesday and Saturday).

Charter companies at the airport have five-assenger planes to almost anywhere in the mazon, if you have US$500 going spare.

oat

quitos is Peru's largest, best-organized river ort. You can theoretically travel all the way rom Iquitos to the Atlantic Ocean, but most oats out of Iquitos today only ply Peruvian aters, and voyagers necessarily change boats t the Colombian–Brazilian border (see p480). If ou choose to arrive by river, you'll end up at one f three ports, which are between 2km and 3km orth of the city center.

Three main ports are of interest to travelers.

Puerto Masusa (Av La Marina), about 3km orth of the town center, is where cargo boats o Yurimaguas (upriver; three to six days) and ucallpa (upriver; four to seven days) leave from. ares cost S100 for hammock space and up to 180 for a tiny (often cell-like) cabin. Boats leave nost days for both ports: there are more frequent departures for the closer intermediate ports. The Eduardo boats to Yurimaguas are quite comfort-able, although there have been reports from read-ers of them mistreating transported animals.

Downriver boats to the Peruvian border with Brazil and Colombia leave from Puerto Masusa too. There are about two or three departures weekly for the two-day journey (per person S50 to S80). Boats will stop at Pevas (hammock space S20, about 15 hours) and other ports en route. Boats may dock closer to the center if the water is very high (from May to July).

The Henry Boats ply the Iquitos–Pucallpa route and have their own more organized **port** (☎965-67-8622; ☻7am-7pm) on Av La Marina, closer to the center.

At both ports chalkboards tell you which boats are leaving when, for where, and whether they are accepting passengers. Although there are agen-cies in town, it's usually best to go to the dock and look around; don't trust anyone except the captain for an estimate of departure time. Be wary: the chalkboards have a habit of changing dates over-night! Boats often leave hours or even days late.

You can often sleep aboard the boat while waiting for departure, and this enables you to get the best hammock space. Never leave gear unattended – ask to have your bags locked up when you sleep.

Finally, there is tiny Puerto Embarcadero, for speedboats to the tri-border (with Colombia and Brazil). These depart at 6am daily except Mon-day. You'll need to purchase your ticket in ad-vance. Speedboat offices are bunched together on Raimondi near the Plaza Castilla. Standard fares are S170 to Pevas or S200 for the 10- to 12-hour trip to Santa Rosa, on the Peruvian side, including meals.

You *may* be able to book a berth on a Leticia-bound cruise ship (see p480) if space is avail-able, although this is more likely coming from Leticia to Iquitos (the captain is more likely to take pity on you if you're stranded in Leticia).

❶ Getting Around

Squadrons of busy *mototaxis* are the bona fide transport round town. They are fun to ride, though they don't provide much protection in an accident. Always enter *mototaxis* from the sidewalk side – passing traffic pays scant heed to embarking passengers – and keep your limbs inside at all times. Scrapes and fender bending are common. Most rides around Iquitos cost a standard S1.50; to the airport it's about S7 for a *mototaxi* and S15 for the harder-to-spot cabs.

Buses and trucks for several nearby destina-tions, including the airport, leave from near Plaza 28 de Julio. Airport buses are marked Nanay-Belén-Aeropuerto: they'll head south down Arica to the airport.

A paved road extends 102km through the jungle as far as Nauta on the Río Marañón, near its confluence with the Río Ucayali. Riverboat passengers from Yurimaguas can now alight at Nauta and pick up a local bus to Iquitos, thus making the journey shorter by some six hours. Boats from Pucallpa do not stop at Nauta. Mini-vans to Nauta take two hours and depart from the corner of Próspero and José Gálvez. There are swimming opportunities at the creeks and beaches en route.

Around Iquitos

NEARBY VILLAGES & LAKES

About 16km from town, past the airport, Santo Tomás is famous for its pottery and mask making, and has a few bars overlooking Mapacocha, a lake formed by an arm of the Río Nanay. You can rent boats by asking around (motorboat with driver about S30). Santa Clara is about 15km away, on the banks of the Río Nanay. There are white-sand beaches during low water (July to October), and boats are available for rent. Both villages can be reached by *mototaxi* (about S15) or a S2 minivan ride from the Nauta van stop.

Corrientillo is a lake near the Río Nanay. There are a few bars around the lake, which is locally popular for swimming on weekends and has good sunsets. It's about 15km from town; a *mototaxi* will charge about S15.

Pilpintuwasi Butterfly Farm   FARM
(☎065-23-2665; www.amazonanimalorphanage.org; Padre Cocha; admission S20; ☉9am-4pm Tue-Sun) A visit to the fascinating Pilpintuwasi Butterfly Farm is highly recommended. Ostensibly this is a conservatorium and breeding center for Amazonian butterflies. Butterflies aplenty there certainly are, including the striking blue morpho *(Morpho menelaus)* and the fearsome-looking owl butterfly *(Caligo eurilochus)*. But it's the farm's exotic animals that steal the show. Raised as orphans and protected within the property are several mischievous monkeys, a tapir, an anteater and Pedro Bello, a majestic jaguar. To get there, take a boat from Bellavista-Nanay, a small port 2km north of Iquitos, to the village of Padre Cocha. Boats run all day. The farm is signposted: a 15-minute walk through the village from the Padre Cocha boat dock.

Laguna Quistacocha   LAKE
This lake, 15km south of Iquitos, is served by minibuses several times an hour from near Plaza 28 de Julio (corner of Bermúdez and Moore; S2), as well as *mototaxis* (S12). There is a small zoo of local fauna here, much improved of recent years, and an adjoining fish hatchery, which has 2m-long *paiche,* now an endangered river fish due to loss of habitat and its popularity as a food. An attempt to rectify the situation is being made with the breeding program here. A pedestrian walk circles the lake, swimming is possible and paddleboats are available hire (S5 to S10). There are several resta rants and a hiking trail to the Río Itaya. fairly crowded with locals on the weeke but not midweek. Admission is S3.

JUNGLE EXPEDITIONS & LODGES
Private Guides

Jungle 'guides' will approach you ever where in Iquitos. Some will be indepen ent operators, and many will be worki on behalf of a lodge. Travelers have h mixed experiences with private guides. guides should have a permit or license – they don't, check with the tourist office. G references for any guide, and proceed wi caution (also see Dangers & Annoyance p479). The better lodges often snap up t best guides quickly.

Gerson Pizango   GUIDED TO
(☎965-012-225; www.amazonjungleguide.co daily per person US$50-70) Gerson comes rea er-recommended and is renowned as on of Iquitos' best independent guides. Tou are tailored to suit tourists' needs but ca include visits to local communities aroun Gerson's home village 260km from Iquit in addition to wildlife-spotting on little-plie tributaries. Rates can be negotiated, depen ing on distances traveled.

Lodges

There are numerous lodges up and dowr river from Iquitos. Take your time choosing a bewildering variety of programs and ac tivities are available and quality varies con siderably. There is the usual mix of luxur options, where relaxation plays a key par and more rustic lodges offering camping hiking, fishing (July to September are th best months) and other adventurous sid trips. Most lodges have offices in Iquitos.

Many of these lodges can be reserve from abroad or in Lima, but if you shov up in Iquitos without a reservation you ca certainly book a lodge or tour and it'll cos you less. Bargaining is usually acceptable even though operators show you fixed pric lists. If planning on booking after you arrive avoid major Peruvian holidays, when places swarm with local holidaymakers. June to September (the dry months and summer vacation for North American/European visitors) is also busy.

Lodges are some distance from Iquitos, so river transport is included in the price. Most of the area within 50km of the city is not gin jungle. Chances of seeing big mammals here are remote and interaction with al tribespeople is geared toward tourists. vertheless, much can be seen of the jun- way of life, and birds, insects and small mmals can be observed. More-remote lges have more wildlife.

A typical two-day trip involves a river urney of two or three hours to a jungle lge with reasonable comforts and meals, ungle lunch, a visit to an indigenous vilge to buy crafts and to see dances (where urists often outnumber tribespeople), an ening meal at the lodge, maybe an afterrk canoe trip to look for caiman by searchght, and jungle walks to search for other ildlife. A trip like this will set you back out US$300, depending on the operator, e distance traveled and the comfort of the dge. On longer trips you'll get further away om Iquitos and see more of the jungle, and e cost per night drops.

There are many good lodges in this northn tract of the Peruvian jungle accessible om Iquitos that will give you a rewarding inforest experience. All prices quoted here re approximate; bargaining is often acceptble, and meals, tours and transportation om Iquitos should be included. Lodges will rovide containers of purified water for you drink when there, but bring extra water r the journey. The following lodges are sted in order of distance from Iquitos.

aseos Amazonicos
LODGE **$$$**

www.paseosamazonicos.com; 3 days & 2 nights per erson US$220-260) Iquitos (☎065-23-1618; Pevas 46); Lima (☎01-241-7576; Office 4, Bajada Balta 31, Miraflores) This company runs three lodgs. One of the best established is Amazonas inchicuy Lodge, on a small tributary of the mazon 30km northeast of Iquitos. The 32 ooms, which can sleep up to four, have private cold showers and are lantern-lit. Some ooms are wheelchair accessible. This lodge an be visited on a day trip from Iquitos. The palm-thatched Tambo Yanayacu Lodge, 0km northeast of Iquitos, has 10 rustic ooms with private bathrooms. The staff ere can supply tents for jungle expeditions. tays at these two lodges can be combined nto one trip, including visits to local Yagua communities. Finally, the Tambo Amazonico Lodge is about 160km upriver on the Río Yarapa. It is more a camping place, with two open-air dormitories sleeping up to 20 people, with beds and mosquito nets. Camp-

ing trips can be arranged, including into the Pacaya-Samiria reserve.

Cumaceba Lodges
LODGE **$$$**

(www.cumaceba.com) Iquitos (☎065-23-2229; Putumayo 188; 3 days & 2 nights s US$260-370, d US$210-260); Cuzco (☎084-25-4881; Portal Panes 123 off 107) This company has been in business since 1995 and operates three lowerend lodges. Guides speak English, French and even Japanese. The lodges are all aimed at providing budget travelers with an Amazon experience.

First up, Cumaceba Lodge is about 35km downriver from Iquitos. This has 15 screened rooms with private showers, and can arrange more adventurous trips locally. At 90km downstream from Iquitos, Amazonas Botanical Lodge places an emphasis on studying rainforest plants, in addition to wildlife-watching. Rustic en suite bungalows are right near primary jungle and there's a botanical garden (and a big swimming pool). *Ayahuasca* ceremonies and a trip to a *paiche* farm are also offered. Finally, about 180km upstream past Nauta is Piranha Ecoexplorer Lodge, offering a variety of adventurous activities. The five-day program includes fishing with spears, camping and a trip to see stupendously sized *Victoria regia* lilies. Accommodations are rustic, much like other Cumaceba lodges.

TOP CHOICE Otorongo Lodge
LODGE **$$$**

(☎065-22-4192, 965-75-6131; www.otorongoex peditions.com; Departamento 203, Putumayo 163, Iquitos; 5 days & 4 nights per person d US$761) Travelers have been giving great feedback about this relatively new, rustic-style lodge, 100km from Iquitos. It's a down-to-earth place, with 12 rooms with private bathrooms and a relaxing common area, set back down a magical tributary off the Amazon and surrounded by walkways to maximize appreciation of the surrounding wildlife. Otorongo is run by a falconer who can imitate an incredible number of bird sounds and get you up close and personal to a huge variety of wildlife. This lodge comes recommended for a magical, personal experience of the Amazonian wilderness. The five-day option can include lots of off-the-beaten-path visits to nearby communities, and camping trips deeper in the jungle. Otorongo offers passersby (!) en route to the Colombian border a daily rate of US$50. Ask about its 'extreme fishing' trips: the owner is an expert on this.

Amazon Yarapa River Lodge   LODGE $$$
(☎065-993-1172; www.yarapa.com; Av La Marina 124, Iquitos; 4 days & 3 nights s/d US$1020/1840, s/d without bathroom US$940/1680; @) Approximately 130km upriver from Iquitos on the Río Yarapa, this lodge is simply stunning. It has a huge and well-designed tropical biology laboratory, regularly used by Cornell University (USA) for research and postgraduate classes. The lab has solar-powered electricity; there are also satellite phone connections. Facilities are beautifully maintained: elaborate woodcarvings in the restaurant-bar and even on the bed heads were made by local artists, and fully screened rooms are linked by screened walkways. Eight huge bedrooms with oversized private bathrooms are available (professors stay here when Cornell is in residence) and 16 comfortable rooms share a multitude of well-equipped bathrooms. With its scientific agenda, the lodge offers top-notch guides for its jungle tours, which visit remote areas. The boats take about three to four hours from Iquitos but have a bathroom aboard. Recommended.

Tahuayo Lodge   LODGE $$$
(☎1-813-907-8475, 1-800-262-9669; www.perujungle.com; 10305 Riverburn Dr, Tampa, Florida 33647, USA; 8 days & 7 nights per person US$1295) You'll hear the phrase 'Pacaya-Samiria' bandied around a lot in these parts but this is only one of several reserves in the northern jungle. This lodge, 140km from Iquitos, has exclusive access to the 2500-sq-km Tamshiyacu-Tahuayo reserve, an area of pristine jungle where a record 93 species of mammal have been recorded. The 15 lodge cabins are located 65km up an Amazon tributary, built on high stilts and connected by walkways; half have private bathrooms. There is a laboratory with a library here, too. Wildlife-viewing opportunities are among the best of any lodge listed: they usually include a peek at the pygmy marmosets that nest near the lodge. Visitors can also stay at the nearby Tahuayo River Research Center, which boasts an extensive trail network.

Muyuna Amazon Lodge   LODGE $$$
(☎065-24-2858; www.muyuna.com; ground fl, Putumayo 163, Iquitos; 3 days & 2 nights s/d US$485/805) About 140km upriver from Iquitos on the Río Yanayacu, this intimate lodge is surrounded by 10 well-conserved lakes in a remote area less colonized than jungle downriver, which makes for a great rainforest experience. Ten stilted, thatch bungalows here each sleep between two a six people and have a private cold show and a balcony with a hammock. All a fully screened. The helpful owners live Iquitos and have a very hands-on approa to maintaining their lodge, ensuring th recycling occurs, staff set an ecofrienc example to visitors, and guests are hap During high water, the river rises up the bungalows, which are connected to tl lodge's dining building with covered, rais walkways. Lighting is by kerosene lanterr The bilingual guides are excellent and th guarantee observation of monkeys, slot and dolphins, as well as rich avian faur typical of the nearby Amazonian *varz* (flooded forest), including the *piuri* – tl wattled curassow *(crax globulosa)*, a cri cally endangered bird restricted to weste Amazonia, which can only be seen in Pe at Muyuna.

Hatuchay Hotel Pacaya-Samiria   LODGE $
(www.hatuchayhotelsperu.com; per 1/2 people days & 3 nights US$640) Iquitos (☎065-22-5769 Lima (☎1-446-2739; Av José Pardo 601, off 60 703, Miraflores) About 190km upriver on th Marañón, this excellent lodge (the forme Pacaya-Samiria Amazon Lodge) is past Nau ta on the outskirts of the Pacaya-Samiri reserve (the only lodge within the reserv buffer zone), four hours from Iquitos. It ca arrange overnight stays within the reserve Rooms feature private showers and porche with river views, and the lodge has electric ity in the evening. There are special bird watching programs.

Explorama Lodges   LODGE $$
(☎065-25-2530; www.explorama.com; Av La Marin 340, Iquitos) This well-established and recom mended company owns and operates lodge and is an involved supporter of the Amazo Conservatory of Tropical Studies (ACTS) It has a lab at the famed canopy walkway which is suspended 35m above the fores floor to give visitors a bird's-eye view of th rainforest canopy and its wildlife. You coul arrange a trip to visit one or more lodge (each of which is very different) combined with a visit to the walkway. Sample rates are given; contact Explorama for other option and combinations. Explorama serves all-you-can-eat lunch and dinner buffets, ha fast boats (50km/h) and half-price rates for under 12s. Ask about group discounts. The well-trained, friendly and knowledgeable

ides are locals who speak English (other
languages on request). The following lodges
e operated by Explorama:

CTS Field Station   LODGE **$$$**
madigosky@widener.edu; per person US$115)
ear the Canopy Walkway, the 20 rooms
re are in buildings similar to those at Ex-
orama Lodge. Book ahead, because accom-
odations are often used by researchers and
orkshop groups. Scientists and researchers
ishing to use the accommodations here
ould contact head of scientific research
r S Madigosky at the email address above.
ne station is nearly always visited as part of
program including nights at other lodges.

Ceiba Tops   LODGE **$$$**
days & 2 nights per person s/d US$515/910;
@) About 40km northeast of Iquitos
n the Amazon, this is Explorama's and the
rea's most well-appointed lodge and resort.
here are 75 luxurious rooms and suites, all
eaturing comfortable beds and furniture,
ins, screened windows, porches and spa-
ous bathrooms with hot showers. Land-
caped grounds surround the pool complex,
omplete with hydromassage, waterslide
nd hammock house. The restaurant (with
etter meals than at Explorama's other
odges) adjoins a bar with live Amazon mu-
ic daily. Short guided walks and boat rides
re available for a taste of the jungle; there
s primary forest nearby containing *Victoria regias*. This lodge is a recommended
ption for people who really *don't* want to
ough it. It even hosts business incentive
neetings.

Explorama Lodge   LODGE **$$$**
3 days & 2 nights per person s/d US$475/850)
About 80km away on the Amazon, near its
junction with the Río Napo, this was one of
he first lodges constructed in the Iquitos
area (1964) and remains attractively rustic.
The lodge has several large, palm-thatched
buildings; the 55 rooms have private cold-
water bathrooms. Covered walkways join
the buildings and lighting is by kerosene
lantern. Guides accompany visitors on sev-
eral trails that go deeper into the forest.

ExplorNapo Lodge   LODGE **$$$**
5 days & 4 nights per person s/d US$1095/1990)
On the Río Napo, 157km from Iquitos, this
simple lodge has 30 rooms with shared
cold-shower facilities. The highlights are
guided trail hikes in remote primary forest,
bird-watching, an ethnobotanical garden of
useful plants (curated by a local shaman)
and a visit to the nearby Canopy Walkway
(half-hour walk). Because of the distance involved, you spend the first and last night of
a five-day/four-night package at the Explorama Lodge. Another Explorama property,
ExplorTambos Camp, is a two-hour walk
from here. It's a self-declared 'primitive'
camp sleeping a maximum of 16: ask when
booking if you fancy staying at the camp,
which has better wildlife-watching than at
any of the lodges.

Flycatcher Tours   ADVENTURE TOURS
(065-24-1228; www.flycatchertours.com; Putumayo 155, Iquitos; 7-day wilderness adventure per
person US$999) This outfit, formerly Amazon
Adventure Expeditions, is recommended
for providing lengthy excursions into the
jungle. These are true (guided) adventures
where you can catch your own food and survive in the wild for up to two weeks. The operator has a basic lodge, the Yarapa, 220km
from Iquitos, a starting point for trips out to
its wilderness camp, 450km from Iquitos on
the Aucayacu tributary. Prices are tailored
according to distances traveled and time
spent.

Pevas

Pevas, about 145km downriver from Iquitos,
is Peru's oldest town on the Amazon. Founded by missionaries in 1735, Pevas boasts
about 5000 inhabitants but no cars, post
office or banks (or attorneys!); the first telephone was installed in 1998. Most residents
are *mestizos* or indigenous people from one
of four tribes. Pevas is the most interesting
town between Iquitos and the border and is
visited regularly (if briefly) by cruise boats
traveling to Leticia. Independent travelers
are a rarity.

The main attraction in Pevas is the studio-
gallery of one of Peru's best-known living
artists, **Francisco Grippa**. Grippa hand-
makes his canvases from local bark, similar
to that formerly used by local tribespeople
for cloth. The paintings on view are the out-
come of Grippa's two decades' observation
of Amazonian people, places and customs.
You can't miss the huge house with its red-
roofed lookout tower on the hill above the
port.

The best accommodations are at **Hospedaje Rodríguez** (83-0296; Brasil 30; s/d
with shared shower S20/25), just down from

the Pevas Plaza. Rooms face onto a pleasant courtyard.

The rustic but attractive **Casa de la Loma** on a hill in the Pevas outskirts offers Amazon views and activities including night walks, piranha fishing and visiting nearby indigenous communities (mostly part acculturated). Reservations are notoriously problematic; the owner is contactable only by rarely functioning cell phone. Prices are not fixed, but start at around S15 for a bed in one of five dark, screened rooms sharing shower facilities. This is a place to get to know the town's inhabitants by joining in a fiesta or shopping at the market. Be adventurous and show up: heading down from the plaza to the river, take the first left down to a bridge. A path then leads up through woods to the entrance.

Francisco Grippa also has basic rooms his house at the top of town that are son times offered to visitors.

Meals are available at **Hospedaje R dríguez** and the more popular pool ha restaurant **El Amigo** (☉lunch).

Leticia-bound cargo boats make reque stops at Pevas, as do daily (except Monda fast boats to the tri-border (the same a plies if you are coming from Leticia). The slow cargo boats (S20, around 15 hour or fast boats (S170, downriver/upriver 3 five hours) also connect Pevas with Iquito Tour operators can also incorporate a Pev trip into packages. Arriving independent there's an element of risk – you might g stuck here for a while – but a boat *will* eve tually turn up.

Understand
Peru

population per sq km

PERU   US   UK

👤 ≈ 25 people

Peru Today

Unparalleled Boom

Between the violence of the Conquest, the chaos of the early republic and the succession of dictatorships that swallowed up much of the 20th century, stability has been a rare commodity in Peru. But the first decade of the new millennium has treated the country with uncharacteristic grace. Peru's economy has grown every year since 2003. Foreign investment is up and the country's exports – in the areas of agriculture, mining and manufacturing – have been strong. Tourism is also big: the number of foreign travelers going to Peru doubled between 2003 and 2011 from 1.3 to 2.6 million, according to Mincetur, the government's tourism authority.

In addition, since 2000, a succession of peaceful elections has provided political stability. In 2011, former army officer Ollanta Humala was elected to the presidency. The son of a Quechua labor lawyer from Ayacucho, he has made social inclusion a theme of his presidency. One of his early acts was to make it a legal requirement for native peoples to be consulted on mining or other extractive activities in their territories.

Cultural Renaissance

The good times have resulted in a surge of cultural productivity – much of it revolving around food. Once considered a place to avoid, Lima is now a foodie bastion, where gastronomic festivals attract visitors from all over the world. La Mistura, an annual culinary gathering organized by celebrity chef Gastón Acurio drew more than 400,000 people in 2011.

The relentless focus on food has had a ripple effect on other aspects of the culture. Young fashion designers produce avant-garde clothing lines with alpaca knits. Innovative musical groups fuse folk and electronica. And the contemporary arts scene has been refreshed: the country's most important museum, the Museo de Arte de Lima (MALI) recently re-

Top Books

The Last Days of the Inca (2007) Chronicles the history-making clash between civilizations.
Aunt Julia & the Scriptwriter (1977) Mario Vargas Llosa's classic novel about a scriptwriter in love with a much older woman.

Cradle of Gold: the Story of Hiram Bingham, a Real-Life Indiana Jones, and the Search for Machu Picchu (2010) The title sums it up – a highly readable bio.
At Play in the Fields of the Lord (1965) Novel inspired by conflicts in the Amazon.

Top Albums

Arturo 'Zambo' Cavero (1993) Legendary crooner.
Canela Fina (2005) Ballads by the 1940s trio Los Morochucos.
Coba Coba (2009) Afro-Peruvian classics with a dash of electronica.

elief systems
(▸ of population)

81
Roman Catholic

13
Evangelical

6
Other

if Peru were 100 people

45 would be indigenous
37 would be mestizo (mixed indigenous & white)
15 would be white
3 would be black or Asian

▸ened after a top-to-bottom renovation, and a handful of galleries have ▸ossomed in Lima's bohemian quarters.

▪ Ways to Go

one of this means there aren't serious challenges. Though the coun-▸y's poverty rate plummeted a staggering 23% since 2002, the economic ▸oom has not benefited everyone: rural poverty, for one, is nearly double ▪e national average.

In addition, Sendero Luminoso (Shining Path), the Maoist guerilla ▸roup that took the country to the brink of civil war in the 1980s has ▸en a comeback – occasionally launching attacks on police and high-▸rofile industrial projects in the central Andes. While the group isn't ▪reatening the government's hold on power (it is estimated to have only ▸00 members), it is funding itself with money from the cocaine trade ac-▸ording to the US Drug Enforcement Agency. (Peru now rivals Colombia ▪ terms of cocaine production.) Moreover, a botched government raid ▸n one of Sendero's highland strongholds led to the deaths of 10 police ▸fficers in April of 2012, generating an avalanche of criticism for the Hu-▪ala administration.

Above all, there are environmental pressures to contend with. At the ▪ime of writing, the northern city of Cajamarca had been racked by months ▸f civil unrest over a proposed gold-mining concern in the region – with ▸ocals protesting the mine's possible effect on the water supply. And, of ▸ourse, there is the Amazon – now bisected by the Interoceanic Highway, ▪n important overland trade route that will connect Peru and Brazil physi-▪ally and economically. While it's an engineering marvel, the road has gen-▸rated deep apprehension among scientists about the impact it will have ▸n one of the world's last great wilderness areas.

Top Films

▪a Teta Asustada (The Milk of Sorrow, 2009) Claudia Llosa's ▪eature film examines the life of a girl suffering from a trauma-▸elated affliction.

Undertow (2009) A married fisherman coming to terms with ▪is dead boyfriend's ghost.

Dos & Don'ts

» Peruvians are very well-mannered. No transaction begins without a formal greeting of *buenos días* or *buenas tardes*.

» Seek permission before photographing people in indigenous communities – and don't be suprised if payment is requested.

» It is illegal to buy pre-Columbian antiquities and take them out of the country.

History

In 1532, when Francisco Pizarro disembarked on the Peruvian coast wi the intention of conquering the area in the name of God and the Spa ish crown, the Andes had already been witness to the epic rise and fa of civilizations. There had been Chavín, dating back to 1000 BC – n a civilization in the classic sense, but an era when people in the And began sharing a cultural iconography. There were the militaristic Wa who, starting at about AD 600, took over an area that stretched fro Chiclayo to Cuzco, building a network of roadways in the process. An of course, there were the Incas who administered a sprawling kingdo that began somewhere in southern Colombia and ended in the midd of present-day Chile.

The arrival of Pizarro would see the beginning of one of Peru's mo protracted shifts. The conquest changed everything about life in the A des: the economics, the political systems, the religion and the languag To some degree, Peru's modern history has been a series of aftershock from that seismic clash between Inca and Spaniard. It is a conflict tha remains deeply embedded in the Peruvian psyche. Yet, its circumstance have produced incredible things: new cultures, new races, new voice new cuisine – ultimately, a new civilization.

Earliest Settlers

There is some debate about how long, exactly, there has been a huma presence in Peru. Some scholars have suggested that humans occupie the Andes as far back as 14,000 BC (with at least one academic reportin that it could precede even that early date). The most definitive archaeo logical evidence, however, puts humans in the region at around 8000 BC Caves in Lauricocha (near Huánuco) and Toquepala (outside of Tacna bear paintings that record hunting scenes from that era. The latter show a group of hunters cornering and killing what appears to be a group o camelid animals.

TIMELINE

8000 BC	c 3000 BC	3000 BC
Hunting scenes are painted in caves by hunter-gatherers near Huánuco in the central highlands and in Toquepala in the south – early evidence of humans in Peru.	Settlement of Peru's coastal oases begins; some of the first structures are built at the ceremonial center of Caral, north of present-day Lima.	Potatoes, squash, cotton, corn, *lúcuma* fruit and quinoa begin to be domesticated; at this point, llamas, alpacas and guinea pigs had likely been tamed for 1000 years

At 4000 BC, taming of llamas and guinea pigs began in the highlands – llowed by the domestication of potatoes, gourds, cotton, *lúcuma* (a type fruit), quinoa, corn and beans. By 2500 BC, once-nomadic hunters and therers clustered into settlements along the Pacific, surviving off of hing and agriculture. These early Peruvians lived in simple one-room vellings, but also built many structures for ceremonial or ritual pur-ses. Some of the oldest – raised temple platforms facing the ocean and ntaining human burials – date from the third millennium BC.

In recent years, studies at some of these archaeological sites have re-aled that these early societies were far more developed than previously agined. Along with Egypt, India and China, Peru is considered one of e six cradles of civilization (a site where urbanization accompanied ag-cultural innovation) – the only one located in the southern hemisphere. ngoing excavations at Caral (p308), on the coast about 200km north of ma, continue to uncover evidence of what is the oldest civilization in e Americas.

Roughly contemporary to these developments on the coast, a group the highlands built the enigmatic Temple of Kotosh (p303) near Huá-uco, whose structures are an estimated 4000 years old. The site features vo temple mounds with wall niches and decorative friezes. It represents me of the most sophisticated architecture produced in the highlands uring the period.

Clay & Cloth

a the centuries from 1800 BC to about 900 BC, ceramics and a more so-histicated textile production came into being. Some of the earliest pot-ery from this time comes from coastal archaeological sites at Las Hal-as in the Casma Valley, south of Chimbote, and the Huaca La Florida, n unmapped temple structure in the heart of Lima. During this time, eramics developed from basic undecorated bowls to sculpted, incised essels of high quality. In the highlands, the people of Kotosh produced killed pieces fashioned from black, red or brown clay.

The epoch also saw the introduction of looms, which were used to roduce plain cotton cloths, as well as improvements in agriculture, in-luding early experimentation with the terrace system.

Chavín Horizon

asting roughly from 1000 BC to 300 BC, and named after the site of havín de Huántar (p396), this was a rich period of development for ndean culture – when artistic and religious phenomena appeared, erhaps independently, over a broad swath of the central and north-rn highlands, as well as the coast. The salient feature of this era is the epeated representation of a stylized feline deity, perhaps symbolizing

BIBLIOPHILES

It is possible to browse original research materials dating back to the colony (from simple text to scanned communiqués) on the website of the Biblioteca Nacional (National Library). Logon to www.bnp. gob.pe and click on the link that says 'Biblioteca Virtual.'

1000 BC	200 BC	AD 1	200
The Chavín Horizon begins, a period in which various highland and coastal communities share uniform religious deities.	The Nazca culture on the coast starts construction on a series of giant glyphs that adorn the desert to this day.	The southern coast sees the rise of the Paracas Necropolis culture, known for its intricate textiles that depict stylized images of warriors, animals and gods.	The Tiwanaku begin their 400-year domination of the area around Lake Titicaca, into what is today Bolivia and northern Chile.

spiritual transformations experienced under the influence of hallucigenic plants. One of the most famous depictions of this many-head figure can be found on the Raimondi Stela, a bas relief carving whi resides at the Museo Nacional de Antropología, Arqueología e Histo del Perú in Lima (p65).

Chavín's feline also figures prominently in ceramics of the era, p ticularly the stark, black-clay specimens referred to as Cupisnique, a st that flourished on the northern coast.

Methods of working with gold, silver and copper were also develop during this time, and there were important advances in weaving a architecture. In short, this was a period when culture truly began to blo som in the Andes.

For more on Chavín, see p512.

Birth of Local Cultures

After 300 BC, numerous local settlements achieved importance at a r gional level. South of Lima, in the area surrounding the Paracas Peni sula, lived a coastal community whose most significant phase is referre to as Paracas Necropolis (AD 1–400), after a large burial site. It is he that some of the finest pre-Columbian textiles in the Americas have bee unearthed: colorful, intricate fabrics that depict oceanic creatures, felir

---

THE MAKING OF PERU'S SAINTS

The first century of the Peruvian colony produced an unusual number of Catholic saints – five in all. There was the highly venerated Santa Rosa of Lima (1556–1617), a devout *criolla* (Spaniard born in Peru) who took a vow of chastity and practiced physical mortification. (She wore a cilice and slept on a bed of broken glass and pottery.) In addition, there was San Juan Macías (1585–1645), who counseled the needy, and San Martín de Porres (1579–1639), the New World's first black saint.

Why so many? A lot of it had to do with the Spanish program to systematically replace the old indigenous order with its own traditions. Catholic authorities, through a process known as the Extirpation, aimed to eradicate indigenous religious belief by prohibiting ancestor worship and holding ceremonies in which pre-Columbian religious idols were burned. The whole process gave rise to a crop of holy figures that Catholic officials could hold up as examples of piousness. Priests preached the wonders of everyday people who rejected worldly possessions and displayed extreme humility – qualities that the Church was eager to cultivate in its newfound flock. Countless figures were canonized during this time, and those that attained sainthood remain an integral part of Peruvian spiritual culture to this day.

You can see relics from these saints at the Iglesia de Santo Domingo in Lima, p57.

» A gold Moche mask

500

In the north, the Moche culture begins construction on the Huaca del Sol y de la Luna, adobe temples situated outside of present-day Trujillo.

600

The Wari emerge from the Ayacucho area and consolidate an empire that covers a territory from Cuzco to Chiclayo; they are closely linked, stylistically, to the Tiwanaku culture of Bolivia.

c 800

The fiercely independent Chachapoyas buil Kuélap, a citadel in the northern highlands composed of upwards of 400 constructions – including their trademark circula dwellings

rriors and stylized anthropomorphic figures. (For more on Paracas, n to p513.)

To the south, the people of the Nazca culture (200 BC–AD 600) carved nt, enigmatic designs into the desert landscape that can only be seen m the air. Known as the Nazca Lines (p122), these were mapped early the 20th century – though their exact purpose remains up for debate. e culture is also known for its fine textile and pottery works, the latter which utilized – for the first time in Peruvian history – a polychrome ulticolored) paint technique.

During this same time, the Moche culture settled the area around ujillo between AD 100 and 800. This was an especially artistic group ey produced some of the most remarkable portrait art in history), ving behind important temple mounds, such as the Huacas del Sol de la Luna (Temples of the Sun and Moon; p325), near Trujillo, and e burial site of Sipán (p339), outside Chiclayo. The latter contains a ries of tombs that have been under excavation since 1987 – one of e most important archaeological discoveries in South America since achu Picchu.

A catastrophic drought in the latter half of the 6th century may have ntributed to the demise of the Moche as a culture. For more on this oup, see p514.

The Tiwanaku were a pre-Inca culture that settled the area around Lake Titicaca and are, in many ways, closely linked with the Wari. Margaret Young-Sanchez's *Tiwanaku: Ancestors of the Inca*, provides a lushly illustrated compendium of their art and history.

Wari Expansion

the influence of regional states waned, the Wari, an ethnic group from e Ayacucho Basin, emerged as a force to be reckoned with for 500 years ginning in AD 600. They were vigorous military conquerors who built d maintained important outposts throughout a vast territory that cov ed an area from Chiclayo to Cuzco. Though their ancient capital lay tside of present-day Ayacucho – the ruins of which can still be visited 298) – they also operated the major lowland ceremonial center of Pach amac, just outside of Lima (p99), where people from all over the region me to pay tribute.

As with many conquering cultures, the Wari attempted to subdue her groups by emphasizing their own traditions over local belief. Thus om about AD 700 to 1100, Wari influence is noted in the art, technol y and architecture of most areas in Peru. These include elaborate, tie ved tunics, and finely-woven textiles featuring stylized human figures d geometric patterns, some of which contained a record-breaking 398 reads per linear inch. They are most significant, however, for devel ping an extensive network of roadways and for greatly expanding the rrace agriculture system – an infrastructure that would serve the Incas ell when they came into power just a few centuries later.

For more, see p514.

Photographer Martín Chambi (1891–1973) was known for his beguiling black and white photographs of Cuzco in the early 20th century. These provide a revealing portrait of the city before the age of mass tourism. To see images, log on to www.martin chambi.org.

c 850	1100-1200	1438-71	1492
The Chimú begin development of Chan Chan, outside of present-day Trujillo, a sprawling adobe urban center.	The Incas emerge as a presence in Cuzco; according to legend, they were led to the area by a divine figure known as Manco Cápac and his sister Mama Ocllo.	The reign of Inca Yupanqui – also known as Pachacutec – represents a period of aggressive empire-building for the Incas; during this time, Machu Picchu and Saqsaywamán are built.	Funded by the Spanish crown, Genoa-born explorer Christopher Columbus arrives in the Americas.

Regional Kingdoms

The Wari were eventually replaced by a gaggle of small nation-states t thrived from about 1000 until the Inca conquest of the early 15th centu One of the biggest and best studied of these are the Chimú of the Truj area, whose capital was the famed Chan Chan (p323), the largest ad city in the world. Their economy was based on agriculture and they ha heavily stratified society with a healthy craftsman class, which produc painted textiles and beautifully fashioned pottery that is distinctive its black stain.

Closely connected to the Chimú are the Sicán from the Lambayec area, renowned metallurgists who produced the *tumi* – a ceremon knife with a rounded blade used in sacrifices. (The knife has since come a national symbol in Peru and replicas can be found in crafts m kets everywhere.)

To the south, in the environs of Lima, the Chancay people (1000–15(produced fine, geometrically patterned lace and crudely humorous p tery, in which just about every figure seems to be drinking.

In the highlands, several other cultures were significant during t time. In a relatively isolated and inaccessible patch of the Utcubam Valley, in the northern Andes, the cloud-forest-dwelling Chachapoy people (p515) erected the expansive mountain settlement of Kuél (p424), one of the most intriguing and significant highland ruins in t country. To the south, several small *altiplano* (Andean plateau) kingdo situated near Lake Titicaca left impressive *chullpas* (funerary tower The best remaining examples are at Sillustani (p179) and Cutimbo (p17!

The formation of chiefdoms in the Amazon began during tl period, too.

Enter the Incas

According to Inca lore, their civilization was born when Manco Cáp and his sister Mama Ocllo, children of the sun, emerged from Lake Ti caca to establish a civilization in the Cuzco Valley. Whether Manco Cáp was a historical figure is up for debate, but what is certain is that the In civilization was established in the area of Cuzco at some point in the 12 century. The reign of the first several *incas* (kings) is largely unremar able – and for a couple of centuries, they remained a small, regional sta

Expansion took off in the early 15th century, when the ninth king, In Yupanqui, defended Cuzco – against incredible odds – from the invadir Chanka people to the north. After the victory, he took on the boastf new name of 'Pachacutec' ('Transformer of the Earth') and spent the ne 25 years bagging much of the Andes. Under his reign, the Incas gre from a regional fiefdom in the Cuzco Valley into a broad empire of abo

The portrayal of indigenous people in pop culture tends to be that of benign stewards of vast wilderness. But Charles C Mann's *1491: New Revelations of the Americas Before Columbus* reveals that the continent was a place of great urbanization and high technological skill. The Incas are prominently featured.

Guns, Germs & Steel, the Pulitzer Prize-winning book by Jared Diamond is a thoughtful, biological examination of why some European societies triumphed over so many others. The battle for Cajamarca and Atahualpa's capture by the Spanish is discussed at length.

1493	1532	1572
Inca Huayna Cápac begins his reign, pushing the empire north to Colombia; his untimely death in 1525 – probably from small pox – would leave the kingdom fatally divided.	Atahualpa wins a protracted struggle for control over Inca territories; at virtually the same time, the Spanish land in Peru – in less than a year, Atahualpa is dead.	Túpac Amaru, the monarch who had established an Inca state independent of the Spanish at Vilcabamba, is captured and beheaded by colonial authorities.

» Sacsaywamán (p232)

million people known as Tawantinsuyo (Land of Four Quarters). The gdom covered most of modern Peru, in addition to pieces of Ecuador, ivia and Chile. All of this was made more remarkable by the fact that Incas, as an ethnicity, never numbered more than about 100,000.

Pachacutec allegedly gave Cuzco its layout in the form of a puma and lt fabulous stone monuments in honor of Inca victories, including saywamán (p232), the temple-fortress at Ollantaytambo (p242) and ssibly Machu Picchu (p250). He also improved the network of roads t connected the empire, further developed terrace agricultural sys-ns and made Quechua the lingua franca.

tahualpa's Brief Reign

her Inca kings would continue the expansions. Pachacutec's grandson, ayna Cápac, who began his rule in 1493, took over much of modern-y Ecuador all the way into Colombia. Consequently, he spent much of life living, governing and commanding his armies from the north, her than Cuzco.

By this time, the Spanish presence was already being felt in the Andes. all pox and other epidemics transmitted by European soldiers were eeping through the entire American continent. These were so swift, fact, that they arrived in Peru before the Spanish themselves, claim-g thousands of indigenous lives – including, in all likelihood, that of ayna Cápac, who succumbed to some sort of plague in 1525.

Without a clear plan of succession, the emperor's untimely death left power vacuum. The contest turned into a face-off between two of his any children: the Quito-born Atahualpa, who commanded his father's my in the north, and Huáscar, who was based in Cuzco. The ensuing ruggle plunged the empire into a bloody civil war, reducing entire cit-s to rubble. Atahualpa emerged as the victor in April of 1532. But the cious nature of the conflict left the Incas with a lot of enemies through-t the Andes – which is why some tribes were so willing to cooperate th the Spanish when they arrived just five months later.

he Spanish Invade

1528, explorer Francisco Pizarro and his right-hand-man Diego de Al-agro landed in Tumbes, a far-flung outpost on the north coast of Peru. here, a crew of welcoming natives offered them meat, fruit, fish and rn beer. To their delight, a cursory examination of the city revealed an undance of silver and gold. The explorers quickly returned to Spain to urt royal support for a bigger expedition.

They returned to Tumbes in September of 1532, with a shipload of ms, horses and slaves, as well as a battalion of 168 men. Tumbes, the ch town he had visited just four years earlier had been devastated by

Most Influential Writers

» El Inca Garcilaso de la Vega, chronicler

» Ricardo Palma, folklorist

» Abraham Valdelomar, essayist

» César Vallejo, poet

» José Carlos Mariategui, political theorist

» Mario Vargas Llosa, novelist

1609	1611	1613	1671
Mestizo writer and thinker El Inca Garcilaso de la Vega publishes *Los Comentarios Reales* (The Royal Commentaries), a celebrated narrative of Inca life before and after the conquest.	Diego Quispe Tito, one of the most renowned painters of the so-called 'Cuzco School' movement of religious painting is born in the southern highlands.	Guamán Poma de Ayala pens a 1200-page missive to the Spanish king detailing poor treatment of natives; it lies forgotten until 1908, when it's discovered in a Danish archive.	Santa Rosa de Lima, the patron saint of Peru and the Americas, is canonized by Pope Clement X.

epidemics, as well as the recent Inca civil war. Atahualpa, in the metime, was in the process of making his way down from Quito to Cu:
to claim his hard-won throne. When the Spanish arrived, he was in
highland settlement of Cajamarca, enjoying the area's mineral baths.

Pizarro quickly deduced that the empire was in a fractious sta
He and his men charted a course to Cajamarca and approached A
hualpa with royal greetings and promises of brotherhood. But the w
mannered overtures quickly devolved into a surprise attack that I
thousands of Incas dead and Atahualpa a prisoner of war. (Between th
horses, their armor and the steel of their blades, the Spanish were prac
cally invincible against fighters armed only with clubs, slings and wicl
helmets.)

In an attempt to regain his freedom, Atahualpa offered the Spanisl
bounty of gold and silver. Thus began one of the most famous ranso
in history – with the Incas attempting to fill an entire room with the p
cious stuff in order to placate the unrelenting appetites of the Spanis
But it was never enough. The Spanish held Atahualpa for eight mont
before executing him with a garrote at the age of 31.

The Inca empire never recovered from this fateful encounter. The a
rival of the Spanish brought on a cataclysmic collapse of indigenous so
ety. One scholar estimates that the native population – around 10 milli
when Pizarro arrived – was reduced to 600,000 within a century.

Tumultuous Colony

Following Atahualpa's death, the Spanish got to work consolidating the
power. On January 6, 1535, Pizarro sketched out his new administrati
center in the sands that bordered the Río Rímac on the central coa
This would be Lima, the so-called 'City of Kings' (named in honor
Three Kings' Day), the new capital of the viceroyalty of Peru, an empi
that for more than 200 years would cover much of South America.

It was a period of great turmoil. As elsewhere in the Americas, tl
Spanish ruled by terror. Rebellions erupted regularly. Atahualpa's ha
brother Manco Inca (who had originally sided with the Spanish ar
served as a puppet emperor under Pizarro) tried to regain control
the highlands in 1536 – laying siege to the city of Cuzco for almost
year – but was ultimately forced to retreat. He was stabbed to death by
contingent of Spanish soldiers in 1544.

Throughout all of this, the Spanish were doing plenty of fightir
among themselves, splitting up into a complicated series of rival fa
tions, each of which wanted control of the new empire. In 1538, De A
magro was sentenced to death by strangulation for an attempt to tal
over Cuzco. Three years later, Pizarro was assassinated in Lima by a ban
of disgruntled De Almagro supporters. Other conquistadors met equal

In Lima, from the 16th to 19th centuries, many women donned head scarves that obscured everything but one eye, leading locals to dub them *las tapadas* (the covered ones). The origins of the tradition are unclear (some say it is Moorish), but the practice allowed women to venture out alone public.

1717	1781	1810	182
The Spanish crown establishes the Viceroyalty of New Granada, covering modern-day Ecuador, Colombia and Panama – reducing the Peruvian viceroyalty's power and reach.	Inca noble Túpac Amaru II (born José Gabriel Condorcanqui) is brutally executed by the Spanish in Cuzco after leading an unsuccessful indigenous rebellion.	Painter Pancho Fierro, a watercolorist known for recording daily life, is born in Lima; his paintings helped define a uniquely Peruvian identity.	José de San Mart declares Per independent, but tru sovereignty doesn come until Simón Bc livar's forces vanquis the Spanish in battle at Junín and Ayacuch three years late

)lent fates. Things grew relatively more stable after the arrival of Fran-
:sco de Toledo as viceroy, an efficient administrator who brought some
der to the emergent colony.

Until independence, Peru was ruled by a series of these Spanish-born
:eroys, all of whom were appointed by the crown. Immigrants from
)ain held the most prestigious positions, while *criollos* (Spaniards born
the colony) were confined to middle management. *Mestizos* – people
ho were of mixed blood – were placed even further down the social
ale. Full-blooded *indígenas* resided at the bottom, exploited as *peones*
xpendable laborers) in *encomiendas,* a feudal system that granted
)anish colonists land titles that included the property of all the indig-
ious people living in that area.

Tensions between *indígenas* and Spaniards reached a boiling point
the late 18th century, when the Spanish crown levied a series of new
xes that hit indigenous people the hardest. In 1780, José Gabriel Con-
)orcanqui – a descendant of the Inca monarch Túpac Amaru – arrested
id executed a Spanish administrator on charges of cruelty. His act un-
ashed an indigenous rebellion that spread into Bolivia and Argentina.
ondorcanqui adopted the name Túpac Amaru II and traveled the region
)menting revolution.

The Spanish reprisal was swift – and brutal. In 1781, the captured in-
igenous leader was dragged to the main plaza in Cuzco, where he would
atch his followers, his wife and his sons killed in a day-long orgy of vio-
nce, before being drawn and quartered himself. Pieces of his remains
ere displayed in towns around the Andes as a way of discouraging fur-
ier insurrection.

ndependence

ly the early 19th century, *criollos* in many Spanish colonies had grown
icreasingly dissatisfied with their lack of administrative power and the
rown's heavy taxes – leading to revolutions all over the continent. In
'eru, the winds of change arrived from two directions. Argentine revo-
Jtionary José de San Martín led independence campaigns in Argentina
ind Chile, before entering Peru by sea at the port of Pisco, in 1820. With
:an Martín's arrival, royalist forces retreated into the highlands, allowing
aim to ride into Lima unobstructed. On July 28, 1821, independence was
leclared. But real independence wouldn't materialize for another three
/ears. With Spanish forces still at large in the interior, San Martín would
leed more men to fully defeat the Spanish.

Enter Simón Bolívar, the Venezuelan revolutionary who had been
eading independence fights in Venezuela, Colombia and Ecuador. In
l823, the Peruvians gave Bolívar dictatorial powers (an honor that had
)een bestowed on him in other countries). By the latter half of 1824, he

**Important
Inca
Emperors**

» Manco Cápac
(c 1100s), Cuzco's
founder

» Mayta Cápac
(1200s), began
expansion

» Inca Yupanqui
(1400s), 'Pacha-
cutec'

» Huayna Cápac
(1400–1500s),
expanded north

» Atahualpa
(1497–1533), last
sovereign

1826	1845	1872	1879-83
The last of the Spanish military forces depart from Callao, after which the country descends into a period of anarchy.	Ramón Castilla begins the first of four nonconsecutive presidential terms, bringing some degree of stability to Peru.	Scholar Ricardo Palma publishes the first of a series of books – known as the *Tradiciones Peruanas* – that chronicle a distinctly *criollo* (creole) folklore.	Chile wages war against Peru and Bolivia over nitrate-rich lands in the Atacama Desert; Peru loses the conflict – in addition to its southernmost region of Tarapacá.

and his lieutenant, Antonio José de Sucre, had routed the Spanish decisive battles at Junín and Ayacucho. The revolutionaries had face staggering odds, but nonetheless managed to capture the viceroy and negotiate a surrender. As part of the deal, the Spanish would retire all their forces from Peru and Bolivia.

New Republic

The lofty idealism of the revolution was soon followed by the hars reality of having to govern. Peru, the young nation, proved to be ju as anarchic as Peru, the viceroyalty. Between 1825 and 1841, there wa a revolving door of regime changes (two dozen!) as regional *caudillo* (chieftains) scrambled for power. The situation improved in the 184(with the mining of vast deposits of guano off the Peruvian coast, th nitrate-rich bird droppings that reaped unheard-of profits as fertilizer o the international market. (Nineteenth-century Peruvian history is – lite ally – rife with poop jokes.)

The country would find some measure of stability under the goverm ance of Ramón Castilla (a *mestizo*), who would be elected to his first term in 1845. The income from the guano boom – which he had been key i exploiting – helped Castilla make needed economic improvements. H abolished slavery, paid off some of Peru's debt and established a publi school system. Castilla served as president three more times over th course of two decades – at times, by force; at others, in an interim capac ity; at one point, for less than a week. Following his final term, he wa exiled by competitors who wanted to neutralize him politically.

He died in 1867, in northern Chile, attempting to make his way back t(Peru. (Visitors can see his impressive crypt at the Panteón de los Procere in Central Lima, p62.)

War of the Pacific

With Castilla's passing, the country once again descended into chaos. A succession of *caudillos* squandered the enormous profits of the guan(boom and, in general, managed the economy in a deplorable fashion Moreover, military skirmishes would ensue with Ecuador (over border issues) and Spain (which was trying to dominate its former South Ameri can colonies). The conflicts left the nation's coffers empty. By 1874, Peru was bankrupt.

This left the country in a weak position to deal with the expanding clash between Chile and Bolivia over nitrate-rich lands in the Atacama Desert. Borders in this area had never been clearly defined and esca lating tensions eventually led to military engagement. To make matters worse for the Peruvians, President Mariano Prado abandoned the coun-

A full scan of Guamán Poma de Ayala's 17th century manuscript (complete with illustrations), in which he documents colonial atrocities against indigenous people, can be found on the Danish National Library's website at www.kb.dk/permalink/2006/poma/info/en/frontpage.htm.

1892	1895	1911	1924
Poet César Vallejo is born in the highlands; he lives for only 46 years, but his spare phrasing and socially-conscious themes make him one of the continent's transformative literary figures.	Nicolás de Piérola is elected president, beginning a period of relative stability buoyed by a booming world economy.	US historian Hiram Bingham arrives at the ruins of Machu Picchu; his 'discovery' of the ancient city is chronicled in *National Geographic*.	Northern political leader Victor Raúl Haya de la Torre founds APRA, a populist, anti-imperialist political party that is immediately declared illegal.

y for Europe on the eve of the conflict. The war was a disaster for Peru
every level (not to mention Bolivia, which lost its entire coastline).

Despite the very brave actions of military figures like Navy Admiral
iguel Grau, the Chileans were simply better organized and had more
esources, including the support of the British. In 1881, they led a land
ampaign deep into Peru, occupying the capital of Lima, during which
me they ransacked the city, making off with the priceless contents of
e National Library. By the time the conflict came to a close in 1883,
eru had permanently lost its southernmost region of Tarapacá – and it
ouldn't regain the area around Tacna until 1929.

A New Intellectual Era

s the 20th century loomed, things would look up for Peru. A buoyant
orld economy helped fuel an economic recovery through the export of
ugar, cotton, rubber, wool and silver. And, in 1895, Nicolás de Piérola
as elected President – beginning an era known as the 'Aristocratic Re-
ublic.' Hospitals and schools were constructed and de Piérola under-
ok a campaign to build highways and railroads.

This period would witness a sea change in Peruvian intellectual
ought. The late 19th century had been an era in which many thinkers
primarily in Lima) had tried to carve out the notion of an inherently
eruvian identity – one largely based on *criollo* experience. Key among
hem was Ricardo Palma, a scholar and writer renowned for rebuilding
ima's ransacked National Library. Beginning in 1872, he published a
eries of books on *criollo* folklore known as the *Tradiciones Peruanas*
Peruvian Traditions) – now required reading for every Peruvian school-
hild.

But as one century gave way to the next, intellectual circles saw the
ise of *indigenismo* (Indianism), a continent-wide movement that advo-
ated for a dominant social and political role for indigenous people. In
eru, this translated into a wide-ranging (if fragmented) cultural movement. Historian Luis Valcárcel attacked his society's degradation of the
ndigenous class. Poet César Vallejo wrote critically acclaimed works that
ook on indigenous oppression as themes. And José Sabogal led a genera-
ion of visual artists who explored indigenous themes in their paintings.
n 1928, journalist and thinker José Carlos Mariátegui penned a seminal
Marxist work – *Seven Interpretive Essays on Peruvian Reality* – in which
e criticized the feudal nature of Peruvian society and celebrated the
ommunal aspects of the Inca social order. (It remains vital reading for
he Latin American left to this day.)

In this climate, in 1924, Trujillo-born political leader Victor Raúl Haya
le la Torre founded the Alianza Popular Revolucionaria Americana
(American Popular Revolutionary Alliance) – otherwise known as APRA.

GUANO WEALTH

Peru's exports of guano in the mid-19th century totaled more than US$20 million a year – more than US$517 million a year by today's standards. In 1869, the country was exporting more than half a million tons of the nitrate-rich fertilizer per year.

1928	1932	1948	1962
Journalist and thinker José Carlos Mariátegui publishes the *Seven Interpretive Essays on Peruvian Reality*, which heavily critiques the feudal nature of his country's society.	More than a thousand APRA party followers are executed by the military at the ancient ruins of Chan Chan, following an uprising in Trujillo.	General Manuel Odría assumes power for eight years, encouraging foreign investment and cracking down on the APRA movement.	Mario Vargas Llosa publishes *La ciudad y los perros* (*The Time of the Hero*), an experimental novel set at a military academy in Lima.

The party espoused populist values, celebrated 'Indo-America' and ra
lied against US imperialism. It was quickly declared illegal by the aut
cratic regime of Augusto Leguía – and remained illegal for long stretch
of the 20th century. Haya de la Torre, at various points in his life, live
in hiding and in exile and, at one point, endured a 15-month stint as
political prisoner.

Dictatorships & Revolutionaries

After the start of the Great Depression in 1929, the country's histo
becomes a blur of dictatorships punctuated by periods of democrac
Leguía, a sugar baron from the north coast, ruled on a couple of occ
sions: for his first period in office (1908–1912) he was elected; for tf
second (1919–1930), he made it in via coup d'état. He spent his first ter
dealing with a morass of border conflicts and the second, stifling pre:
freedoms and political dissidents.

Legúia was followed by Colonel Luis Sánchez Cerro, who served
couple of short terms in the 1930s. (Though his time in office was tu
bulent, Sánchez would be celebrated in some sectors for abolishing
conscription law that required able-bodied men from having to labor o
road-building projects. The law affected poor indigenous men dispropo
tionately, since they couldn't afford to pay the exemption fee.) By 194
another dictator had taken power: former army colonel Manuel Odrí;
who spent his time in office cracking down on APRA and encouragir
US foreign investment.

The most fascinating of Peru's 20th-century dictators, however, is Jua
Velasco Alvarado, the former commander-in-chief of the army who too
control in 1968. Though he was expected to lead a conservative regime
Velasco turned out to be an inveterate populist – so much so that som
APRA members complained that he had stolen their party platforn
away from them. He established a nationalist agenda that included 'Pe
ruvianizing' (securing Peruvian majority ownership) various industrie:
In his rhetoric he celebrated the indigenous peasantry, championed
radical program of agrarian reform and made Quechua an official lan
guage. He also severely restricted press freedoms, which drew the wratf
of the power structure in Lima. Ultimately, his economic policies were
failures – and in 1975, in declining health, he was replaced by anothei
more conservative military regime.

Internal Conflict

Peru returned to civilian rule in 1980, when President Fernando Be
laúnde Terry was elected to office – the first election in which leftist par
ties were allowed to participate – including APRA, which was now legal
Belaúnde's term was anything but smooth. Agrarian and other socia'

SHINING PATH

Shining Path founder Abimael Guzmán took the name 'Sendero Luminoso' – 'Shining Path' – from a maxim by writer and Communist Party founder José Carlos Mariátegui: 'Marxism-Leninism will open the shining path to revolution.'

1968	1970	1980	1980
General Juan Velasco Alvarado takes power in a coup d'etat; in his seven years in office, he promulgates a populist agenda that involves 'Peruvianization' of all industry.	A 7.7-magnitude earthquake in northern Peru kills almost 80,000 people, leaves 140,000 injured, and another 500,000 homeless.	Guerilla group Sendero Luminoso (Shining Path) takes its first violent action – burning ballot boxes – in the Ayacucho region; the incident draws little notice from the press.	Fernando Belaúnde Terry becomes the first democratically elected president after a 12-year military dictatorship, but his term is plagued by economic instability and violence in the Andes.

forms took a back seat as the president tried desperately to jump-start the moribund economy.

It was at this time that a radical Maoist group from the poor region of Ayacucho began its unprecedented rise. Founded by philosophy professor Abimael Guzmán, Sendero Luminoso (Shining Path) wanted nothing less than an overthrow of the social order via violent armed struggle. Over the next two decades, the situation escalated into a phantasmagoria of violence, with the group assassinating political leaders and community activists, carrying out attacks on police stations and universities and, at one point, stringing up dead dogs all over downtown Lima. (Its actions earned the group a place on the US State Department's list of foreign terrorist organizations.) At the same time, another leftist guerrilla group also sprang into action – the Movimiento Revolucionario Túpac Amaru (MRTA), which focused its attacks to the police and the armed forces.

To quell the violence, the government sent in the military, a heavy-handed outfit that knew little about handling a guerilla insurgency. There was torture, rape, disappearances and massacres, none of which did anything to put a stop to Sendero Luminoso. Caught in the middle were tens of thousands of poor *campesinos* who bore the brunt of the casualties.

In the midst of this, Alan García was elected to the presidency in 1985. Initially, his ascent generated a great deal of hope. He was young, he was a gifted public speaker, he was popular – and he was the first member of the storied APRA party to win a presidential election. But his economic program was catastrophic (his decision to nationalize the banks and suspend foreign-debt payments led to economic ruin), and, by the late 1980s, Peru faced a staggering hyperinflation rate of 7500%. Thousands of people were plunged into poverty. There were food shortages and riots. Throughout all of this, Sendero Luminoso and MRTA stepped up attacks. The government was forced to declare a state of emergency.

Two years after completing his term, García fled the country after being accused of embezzling millions of dollars. He would return to Peru in 2001, when the statute of limitations on his case finally ran out.

Fujishock

With the country in a state of chaos, the 1990 presidential elections took on more importance than ever. The contest was between famed novelist Mario Vargas Llosa and Alberto Fujimori, a little-known agronomist of Japanese descent. During the campaign, Vargas Llosa promoted an economic 'shock treatment' program that many feared would send more Peruvians into poverty, while Fujimori positioned himself as an alternative to the status quo. Fujimori won handily. But as soon as he got into office, he implemented an even more austere economic plan that, among other

Forgotten Continent: The Battle for Latin America's Soul is an acclaimed (if dense) political tome by *Economist* contributor Michael Reid. Published in 2009, it examines the continent's strained relations with the US and Europe, as well as its economic and political development in the last three decades.

1983	1985	1987	1990
In one of the more high-profile massacres of the Internal Conflict, eight journalists are murdered in the Andean town of Uchuraccay.	Alan García becomes president, but his term is marked by hyperinflation and increased attacks by terrorist groups; he flees the country in 1992, clouded by allegations of embezzlement.	Archaeologists working near Lambayeque uncover a rare, undisturbed tomb of a Moche warrior-priest known as El Señor de Sipán.	Alberto Fujimori is elected president; his authoritarian rule leads to improvements in the economy, but charges of corruption plague his administration.

A NOBEL FOR PERU

In 2010, Mario Vargas Llosa (b 1936), Peru's most famous living writer, was awarded the Nobel Prize in literature for work that explored the vagaries of love, power and corruption. The honorific caps an extraordinary life: as a young man, Vargas Llosa had an affair with an uncle's sister-in-law, whom he later married (an incident he fictionalized in *Aunt Julia and the Scriptwriter*). In the '70s, he came to blows with Colombian Nobel Laureate Gabriel García Márquez for reasons that have never been revealed. The following decade he ran for the presidency – and lost. Over his life he has produced novels, short stories, plays and political essays. Upon winning the Nobel, he told a reporter: 'Death will find me with my pen in hand.'

things, drove up the price of gasoline by 3000%. The measures, known ... 'Fujishock,' ultimately succeeded in reducing inflation and stabilizing th economy – but not without costing the average Peruvian dearly.

Fujimori followed this, in April of 1992, with an *autogolpe* (coup from within). He dissolved the legislature and generated an entirely new co: gress, one stocked with his allies. Peruvians, not unused to *caudillo* tolerated the power grab, hoping that Fujimori might help stabilize th economic and political situation – which he did. The economy grew. An by the end of the year, leaders of both Sendero Luminoso and MRTA ha been apprehended (though, not before Sendero Luminoso had brutal assassinated community activist María Elena Moyano and detonated l thal truck bombs in Lima's tony Miraflores district).

The Internal Conflict, however, wasn't over. In December of 1996, 1 members of MRTA stormed the Japanese ambassador's residence an hundreds of prominent people were taken hostage, demanding that th government release imprisoned MRTA members, among other thing Most of the hostages were released early on, though 72 men wer held until the following April – at which point, Peruvian commandc stormed the embassy, killing every last captor and releasing the surviv ing hostages.

By the end of his second term, Fujimori's administration was plague by allegations of corruption. He ran for a third term in 2000 (which wa technically unconstitutional) and remained in power despite the fac that he didn't have the simple majority necessary to claim the electior Within the year, however, he was forced to flee the country after it wa revealed that his security chief Vladimiro Montesinos had been embe zling government funds and bribing elected officials and the media (Many of these acts were caught on film: the 'Vladivideos' – all 2700 c them – riveted the nation when they first aired in 2001.) Fujimori for

For dedicated students of Peruvian history, *The Peru Reader*, by Orin Starn, Carlos Iván Degregori and Robin Kirk provides an indispensable collection of articles covering every historical era – from excerpts of Spanish chronicles to essays on the cocaine economy.

1992	1992	1994	199(
Sendero Luminoso detonates truck bombs in Miraflores, Lima, killing 25 and wounding scores more; following this act, public opinion turns decisively against the guerrillas.	Abimael Guzmán, the founder of Sendero Luminoso, is captured in Lima after he is found hiding out above a dance studio in the well-to-do neighborhood of Surco.	Chef Gastón Acurio opens Astrid y Gastón in the Lima neighborhood of Miraflores; the restaurant helps catapult Peruvian cuisine to international levels.	Guerrillas from th Movimiento Revolu cionario Túpac Amar (MRTA) storm the Jap anese ambassador': residence in Lima an hold 72 hostages fo four months

ılly resigned the presidency from abroad, but the legislature rejected
e gesture, voting him out of office and declaring him 'morally unfit' to
vern.

Peru, however, hadn't heard the last of Fujimori. In 2005, he returned
South America, only to be arrested in Chile on long-standing charges
corruption, kidnapping and human-rights violations. He was extra-
ted to Peru in 2007 and, that same year, was convicted of ordering an
egal search. Two years later, he was convicted of ordering extra-judicial
llings, and three months after that, was convicted of channeling mil-
ns of dollars in state funds to Montesinos. In 2009, he also pleaded
ilty to wiretapping and bribery. He is currently serving 25 years in
ison. Montesinos, in the meantime, is doing 20 – for bribery and sell-
g arms to Colombian rebels.

he 21st Century

ıe new millennium has, thus far, been pretty good to Peru. In 2001,
ıoeshine-boy-turned-Stanford-economist Alejandro Toledo became the
ʼst person of Quechua ethnicity to ever be elected to the presidency.
Jntil then, Peru had had *mestizo* presidents, but never a full-blooded *in-
ígena.*) Unfortunately, Toledo inherited a political and economic mess.
his was amplified by the fact that he lacked a majority in congress,
ımpering his effectiveness in the midst of an economic recession.

Toledo was followed in office by – of all people – the APRA's Alan
arcía, who was re-elected in 2006. His second term was infinitely more
able than the first. The economy performed well and the government

> A classic of the genre, John Hemming's *The Conquest of the Incas,* first published in 1970, is a must-read for anyone wanting to understand the rise and fall of the short-lived Inca empire.

HISTORY THE 21ST CENTURY

IN THE WAKE OF THE INTERNAL CONFLICT

One of the most remarkable things to come out of Alejandro Toledo's presidency (2001–06) was the establishment of the country's Comisión de la Verdad y Reconciliación (Truth & Reconciliation Commission), which examined the innumerable acts of mass violence from the Internal Conflict (1980–2000). Though the panel wasn't endowed with prosecutorial powers, its public hearings nonetheless proved to be an emotional and cathartic act. Men and women of all ages and races came forward to testify to the massacres, rapes and disappearances that had occurred at the hands of the military and various guerrilla groups during this terrible period.

In August of 2003, the commission issued its final report, revealing that the death toll from that era was more than twice the original estimate: almost 70,000 people had been killed or disappeared. Along with the final report, the commission also staged an exhibit of photography called *Yuyanapaq* ('to remember' in Quechua) that is now housed at Lima's Museo de la Nación (p64). Even as the years pass, this poignant installation remains a profoundly moving experience.

2000

Fujimori flees to Japan after videos surface showing his intelligence chief bribing officials and the media; the Peruvian legislature votes him out of office.

2001

Alejandro Toledo becomes the first indigenous person to govern an Andean country.

2003

The country's Truth & Reconciliation Commission releases its final report on Peru's Internal Conflict: estimates of the dead reach 70,000.

» Plaza Bolívar

invested money in upgrading infrastructure such as ports, highways a
the electrical grid. But it wasn't without problems. For one, there w
the issue of corruption (García's entire cabinet was forced to resign
2008 after widespread allegations of bribery) and there has been t
touchy issue of how to manage the country's mineral wealth. In 20(
García signed a law that allowed foreign companies to exploit natu
resources in the Amazon. The legislation generated a backlash amo
various Amazon tribes and led to a fatal standoff in the northern city
Bagua in 2009.

The Peruvian congress quickly revoked the law, but this issue remai
a challenge for the new president, Ollanta Humala. Elected in 2011, t
former army officer was initially thought to be a populist in the Hu;
Chávez vein (the Lima stock exchange dropped precipitously when
was first elected). But his administration has been quite friendly to bu
ness. Though the economy has functioned well under his governan(
civil unrest over a proposed gold mine in the north, as well as a botch
raid on a Sendero Luminoso encampment in the highlands, sent his a
proval rating into a tailspin by the middle of 2012.

2005	2006	2009	201⟩
Construction of the Interoceanic Hwy, which opens an overland trade route between Peru and Brazil, begins in the southern Amazon Basin.	Alan García is elected to a second, nonconsecutive term as president after a run-off contest.	Fujimori is convicted of embezzling; this is in addition to prior convictions for authorizing an illegal search and ordering military death squads to carry out extrajudicial killings.	Populist former arm; officer Ollanta Humal assumes the Presi dency after winning tight run-off electio against Fujimori's daughter Keiko

Life in Peru

ith a geography that encompasses desert, highland and jungle, Peru relentlessly touted as a land of contrasts. This also applies to the lives its people: the country is a mix of rich and poor, modern and ancient, gricultural and urban, indigenous and white. Day-to-day existence can e difficult – but it can also be profoundly rich. For centuries, this has een the story of life in Peru.

Population

eru is essentially a bicultural society: the part that is indigenous, and e part that is European-influenced. The largest cohort consists of Pe-vians who speak Spanish and adhere to *criollo* tradition, the cultural gacy of the Peru-born Spaniards who administered the colony. This roup is a racial mix of those who are white (15% of the population) and ose who are *mestizo,* people of mixed indigenous and European herit-ge (another 37%). The country's positions of leadership and affluence re generally occupied by individuals from this group, especially those ho are white and fair-skinned.

About 45% of Peru's population is pure *indígena* (people of indigenous escent), making it one of three countries in Latin America to have such igh indigenous representation. A disproportionate share of *indígenas* habit rural areas in the Andes and work in agriculture. (For a more -depth look at this population, turn to p517.)

Afro-Peruvians, Asians and other immigrant groups are also repre-ented, but cumulatively make up only 3% of the population.

More than 75% of Peruvians live in cities. This represents a significant hift from the 1960s, when more than half of the population inhabited e countryside. This has put a strain on municipal infrastructure, par-cularly in the capital, and issues of effective sanitation and electrifica-on remain challenges – especially for the informal squatter settlements nown as *pueblos jovenes* (young towns).

It was a Peruvian priest, Gustavo Gutiérrez, who first articulated the principles of liberation theology – the theory that links Christian thought to social justice – in 1971. He now teaches in the United States.

VIVA EL PERÚ...!/¡CARAJO!

With vastly different peoples inhabiting such an extreme landscape, national identity has always been a slippery concept in Peru. Yet if there's something that binds its people together, it's a sturdy sense of defiance. In the 1950s, Peruvian journalist Jorge Donayre Belaúnde penned a poem to his homeland called *'Viva el Perú...¡Carajo!'* (Long Live Peru...Damn It!). The verse is an epic, warts-and-all tribute to Peru, depicting life in Andean villages as well as sprawling urban shantytowns. Peruvians, wrote Donayre, aren't scared off by difficult circumstances – not by cataclysmic earthquakes, difficult geography or the corrupt habits of their politicians. In the face of adversity, there is an intractable sense of assurance. In the half century since Donayre first wrote those words, that hasn't changed one bit.

Viva el Perú...!/¡Carajo!

Lifestyle

Though the recent economic boom has been good to the country, there
still a yawning disparity between rich and poor. The minimum month
wage stands at less than US$200. And, according to a UN report from 20
almost one-third of the population lives below the poverty line, while one
10 survive on less than US$1 a day. Though the official national unemplo
ment rate is only 7.9%, underemployment is rampant, especially in citi
In Lima, underemployment is estimated to affect 42.5% of the populatio

In rural areas, the poor survive largely from subsistence agricultu
living in traditional adobe or tin houses that often lack electricity a
indoor plumbing. In cities, the extreme poor live in shantytowns, wh
the lower and middle classes live in concrete, apartment-style housi
or small stand-alone homes. More affluent urban homes consist of lar
stand-alone houses, often bordered by high walls.

Across the board, homes are generally shared by more than o
generation.

Social Graces

Peruvians are polite, indeed formal, in their interactions. Handshak
are appropriate in business settings, but among good friends an *abra*
(back-slapping hug) is in order. Women will often greet each other wi
a kiss, as will men and women. Indigenous people don't kiss and the
handshakes, when offered, tend to have a light touch.

Locals are used to less personal space than some Western travele
may be accustomed to: expect seating on buses to be thisclose.

Religion

Though there is freedom of religion, Peru remains largely Roman Cathol
More than 81% of the population identifies as such (though only 15%
them attend services on a weekly basis). The Church enjoys support fro
the state: it has a largely tax-exempt status and Catholicism is the offici
religion of the military. Moreover, all of the Church's bishops, and up to a
eighth of its overall clergy, receive monthly government stipends. This ha
generated outcries from some evangelical groups that do not receive th
same generous treatment. Even so, evangelicals and other Protestants a
a growing force, representing up to 13% of the nation's population.

Women in Peru

Women can vote and own property, but the situation remains challengin
in a country that is informally ruled by machismo. The female illiterac
rate of more than 16% is almost three times that of men. In additio
women, on average, make only 56 cents to every dollar a man earn
That said, the overall situation has improved. A number of laws barrin
domestic violence and sexual assault have been passed, and women no
make up 28% of the country's professional class (senior officials, manag
ers and legislators) and almost a third of the congress.

Spectator Sports

Fútbol (soccer) is the most sanctified spectator sport. The season run
from late March to November. Though there are many teams, their abili
ties aren't always exceptional: Peru hasn't qualified for the World Cu
since 1982 – though it did take home the Copa América trophy in 200
The best teams are from Lima, and the traditional *clásico* is the match
between Alianza Lima and the Universitario de Deportes (La U).

Bullfighting is also well attended, particularly in Lima, where it i
most popular. The traditional season runs from October to early Decem
ber, when Lima's Plaza de Acho (p92) attracts international matadors.

FÚTBOL

Everything you
ever needed
to know about
every regional
Peruvian soccer
team – large
and small – is
available at www.
peru.com/futbol
(in Spanish).

Peru's Cuisine

Peru has long been a place where the concept of 'fusion' was a part of everyday cooking. Over the course of the last 400 years, Andean stews mingled with Asian stir-fry techniques, and Spanish rice dishes absorbed flavors from the Amazon, producing the country's famed *criollo* (creole) cooking. In the past decade, a generation of experimental young innovators has pushed this local fare to gastronomic heights.

Peru, once a country where important guests were treated to French meals and Scotch whisky, is now a place where high-end restaurants spotlight deft interpretations of Andean favorites, including quinoa and *cuy* (guinea pig). The dining scene has blossomed. And tourism outfits have swept in to incorporate a culinary something as part of every tour. In 2000, the country became the site of the first Cordon Bleu academy in Latin America, and in 2009, *Bon Appétit* magazine named Lima the 'next great food city.'

The foodie fever has infected Peruvians at every level, with even the most humble *chicharrón* (fried pork) vendor hyper-attentive to the varaties of preparation and presentation. No small part of this is due to mediagenic celebrity chef Gastón Acurio, whose culinary skill and business acumen (he owns more than 30 restaurants around the globe) have given him rock-star status.

The short of it is that you will never go hungry in Peru: from humble spots in Moyobamba to trendy boîtes in Miraflores, this is a country devoted to keeping the human palate entertained.

Most Influential Chefs

» Gastón Acurio, Astrid y Gastón

» Pedro Miguel Schiaffino, Malabar

» Rafael Osterling, Rafael

» Rafael Piqueras, Fusión

» Virgilio Martínez, Central Restaurante

NOVOANDINA & THE PERUVIAN NEW WAVE

The current Peruvian gastronomic renaissance has its roots in the 1980s. The country was in turmoil. The economy was in a free-fall. And newspaper publisher Bernardo Roca Rey was experimenting with Andean ingredients in his kitchen – roasting *cuy,* utilizing rare strains of potatoes and producing risottos made with quinoa (a dish now known as *quinotto*). At the same time, Cucho La Rosa, the chef at El Comensal (since closed), was upgrading Peruvian recipes by improving cooking techniques: gentle steaming instead of boiling; searing instead of frying. These early figures detailed their discoveries in newspaper articles and recipe booklets. The cuisine was dubbed *novoandina* – but given the challenges of that period, it never quite ignited as a full-blown movement.

By 1994, however, circumstances had changed. The economy was in recovery and the political situation was beginning to improve. When Gastón Acurio (who studied cooking at Le Cordon Bleu in Paris) opened Astrid y Gastón in Lima, he applied many of the same principles as the *novoandina* pioneers before him: interpreting Peruvian cooking through the lens of haute cuisine. The restaurant quickly became a place of pilgrimage. Other innovative new wave chefs have since followed, including Rafael Piqueras and Pedro Miguel Schiaffino. Collectively, they have expanded the definition of *novoandina,* adding European, Chinese and Japanese ingredients and influences – in the process, transforming Peruvian food into a global cultural phenomenon.

Staples & Specialties

Given the country's craggy topography, there are an infinite number
regional cuisines. But at a national level much of the country's cookin
begins and ends with the humble potato – which originally hails fro
the Andes. (All potatoes can be traced back to a single progenitor fro
Peru.)

Standout dishes include *ocopa* (potatoes with a spicy peanut sauc
papa a la huancaína (potato topped with a creamy cheese sauce) ar
causa (mashed potato terrines stuffed with seafood, vegetables or chic
en). Also popular is *papa rellena,* a mashed potato filled with groun
beef and then deep-fried. Potatoes are also found in the chowder-lik
soups known as *chupe* and in *lomo saltado,* the simple beef stir-fries th
headline every Peruvian menu.

Other popular items include tamales, which are made in various r
gional variations – such as *humitas* (created with fresh corn) and *juan*
(made from cassava).

Coast

The coast is all about seafood – and ceviche, naturally, plays a starrin
role. A chilled concoction of fish, shrimp or other seafood marinated i
lime juice, onions, cilantro and chili peppers, it is typically served wit
a wedge of boiled corn and sweet potato. The fish is cooked in the citru
juices through a process of oxidation. (Some chefs, however, have begu
to cut back on their marinating time, which means that some ceviche
are served at a sushi-like consistency.) Another popular seafood cockta
is *tiradito,* a Japanese-inflected ceviche consisting of thin slices of fis
served without onions, sometimes bathed in a creamy hot pepper sauc

Cooked fish can be prepared dozens of ways: *al ajo* (in garlic), *frit*
(fried) or *a la chorrillana* (cooked in white wine, tomatoes and onions
the latter of which hails from the city of Chorrillos, south of Lima. Soup
and stews are also a popular staple, including *aguadito* (a soupy risotto
picante (a spicy stew) and *chupe* (bisque) – all of which can feature fish
seafood and other ingredients.

Other items that make a regular appearance on seafood menus ar
conchitas a la parmesana (scallops baked with cheese), *pulpo al oliv*
(octopus in a smashed olive sauce) and *choros a la chalaca* (chilled mus
sels with fresh corn salsa). On the north coast, around Chiclayo, omelet
made with manta ray *(tortilla de manta raya)* are a typical dish.

None of this means that pork, chicken or beef aren't popular. *Aji d*
gallina (shredded chicken-walnut stew) is a Peruvian classic. In th
north, a couple of local dishes bear repeat sampling: *arroz con pato a l*
chiclayana (duck and rice simmered in cilantro, typical of Chiclayo) anc
seco de cabrito (goat stewed in cilantro, chilis and beer).

Along the coast, where the Asian presence is most significant, you wil
also find the Peruvian-Chinese restaurants known as *chifas.* The cuisine
is largely Cantonese-influenced: simple dishes low on heavy sauces.

Highlands

In the chilly highlands, it's all about soups – which tend to be a generous
gut-warming experience, filled with vegetables, squash, potatoes, locally
grown herbs and a variety of meats. *Sopa a la criolla* (a mild, creamy
noodle soup with beef and vegetables) is a regular item on menus, as is
caldo de gallina (a nourishing chicken soup with potatoes and herbs)
In the area around Arequipa, *chupe de camarones* (chowder made from
river shrimp) is also a mainstay.

The highlands are also known as the source of all things *cuy* – guinea
pig. It is often served roasted or *chactado* (pressed under hot rocks). It

First published in
2001, *The Exotic
Kitchens of Peru,*
by Copeland
Marks, is not only
a comprehensive
guide to tradi-
tional cooking,
but a good source
of insight into the
history of many
dishes.

Sumptuous
photographs and
recipes are availa-
ble in Tony Custer
and Miguel
Etchepare's hard-
back tome *The
Art of Peruvian
Cuisine.* Log on to
www.artperu
cuisine.com for a
delicious preview.

A PISCO PRIMER

It is the national beverage: pisco, the omnipresent grape brandy served at events from the insignificant to the momentous. Production dates back to the early days of the Spanish colony in Ica, where it was distilled on private haciendas and then sold to sailors making their way through the port of Pisco. In its early years, pisco was the local firewater: a great way to get ripped – and wake up the following morning feeling as if you had been hammered over the head.

By the early 20th century, the pisco sour (pisco with lime juice and sugar) arrived on the scene, quickly becoming the national drink. In recent decades, as production has become more sophisticated, piscos have become more nuanced and flavorful (without the morning-after effects).

The three principal types of Peruvian pisco are Quebranta, Italia and acholado. Quebranta (a pure-smelling pisco) and Italia (slightly aromatic) are each named for the varieties of grape from which they are crafted, while acholado is a blend of varietals that has more of an alcohol top-note (best for mixed drinks). There are many small-batch specialty piscos made from grape must (pressed juice with skins), known as *mosto verde*. These have a fragrant smell and are best sipped straight.

The most common brands include Tres Generaciones, Ocucaje, Ferreyros and La Botija, while Viñas de Oro, Viejo Tonel, Estirpe Peruano, LaBlanco and Gran Cruz are among the finest. Any pisco purchased in a bottle that resembles the head of an Inca will make for an unusual piece of home decor – and not much else.

astes very similar to rabbit and is often served whole. River trout – prepared myriad ways – is also popular.

Arequipa has a particularly dynamic regional cuisine. The area is renowned for its *picantes* (spicy stews served with chunks of white cheese), *rocoto relleno* (red chilis stuffed with meat) and *solterito* (bean salad).

For special occasions and weddings, families will gather to make *pachamanca:* a mix of marinated meats, vegetables, cheese, chilis and fragrant herbs baked on hot rocks in the ground.

Amazon

Though not as popular throughout the entire country, Amazon ingredients have begun to make headway in recent years. This includes the increased use of river snails and fish (including paiche and doncella), as well as produce such as *aguaje* (the fruit of the moriche palm), *yuca* (cassava) and *chonta* (hearts of palm). *Juanes* (a bijao leaf stuffed with rice, yuca, chicken and/or pork) is a savory area staple.

Desserts

Desserts tend to be hypersweet concoctions. *Suspiro limeña* is the most famous, consisting of *manjar blanco* (caramel) topped with sweet meringue. Also popular are *alfajores* (cookie sandwiches with caramel) and *crema volteada* (flan). Lighter and fruitier is *mazamorra morada,* a purple-corn pudding of Afro-Peruvian origin that comes with chunks of fruit.

During October, bakeries sell *turrón de Doña Pepa,* a sticky, molasses-drenched cake eaten in honor of the Lord of Miracles.

The dessert *turrón de Doña Pepa* was first made by a slave woman, in 1800, to honor the Christ of Miracles after she regained the use of her paralyzed arms.

Drinks

The main soft drink brands are available, but locals have a passion for Inca Kola – which tastes like bubble gum and comes in a spectacular shade of nuclear yellow. Fresh fruit juices are also popular, as are traditional drinks such as *chicha morada,* a refreshing, nonalcoholic beverage made from purple corn.

Though the country exports coffee to the world, many Peruvian drink it instant: some restaurants dish up packets of Nescafé or a inky coffee reduction that is blended with hot water. In cosmopolita and touristy areas, cafes serving espresso and cappuccino have pr liferated. Tea and *mates* (herbal teas) are also widely available. Th latter includes *manzanilla* (chamomile), *menta* (mint) and *mate d coca* (coca-leaf tea). The latter will not get you high, but it can sooth stomach ailments.

Beer & Wine

The best-known brands of beer are Pilsen Callao, Brahma, Cristal an Cusqueña, all of which are light lagers. Arequipeña and Trujillana are r gional brews served in and around those cities. In the Andes, homemad *chicha* (corn beer) is very popular. It tastes lightly sweet and is low i alcoholic content. In rural Andes villages, a red flag posted near a do indicates that *chicha* is available.

Local wines have improved greatly over the years. The best local label are Tabernero, Tacama, Ocucaje and Vista Alegre. Also very popular pisco (see the boxed text, p509).

> The culinary website Yanuq (www.yanuq.com) has an extensive online database of Peruvian recipes in English and Spanish.

Where to Eat & Drink

For the most part, restaurants in Peru are a community affair, and lo cal places will cater to a combination of families, tourists, teenager and packs of chatty businessmen. At lunch time, many eateries offer *menú* – a set meal consisting of two or three courses. This is generally good value. (Note: if you request the *menú*, you'll get the special. If yo want the menu, ask for *la carta*.)

Cevicherías – places where ceviche is sold – are popular along th coast. In the countryside, informal restaurants known as *picanterías* ar a staple. In some cases these operate right out of someone's home.

TOP EATS

Collectively, the writers on this guidebook spent months on the road and ate hundreds of meals. Herewith, a list of the places so good they brought tears to our eyes and unbridled joy to our palates:

Arequipa At Zig Zag, the succulent combination meat plate of alpaca, beef and lamb – cooked over hot volcanic rocks – is a carnivore's delight (p151).

Cuzco Cicciolina's fresh-charred octopus and crisp polenta squares (not to mention lovely service) make for a winning dinner (p221).

Huancayo Dip into the creamiest *papas a la huancaína* (steamed potatoes served with a cheese sauce) in a flower-filled courtyard at Huancahuasi (p282).

Huaraz: At Mi Chef Kristof, the chatty namesake chef serves up Belgian-Peruvian fusion that includes belly-warmers such as beef stew simmered in black beer (p372).

Iquitos Set at the mouth of the Río Itaya, Frío y Fuego has excellent night-time views of Iquitos and scrumptious dishes crafted from Amazon river fish (p477).

Lima El Verídico de Fidel has ceviches so aphrodisiacal you might find yourself making out with a waiter after your meal (p82).

Máncora Hyperfresh yellowfin tuna drawn straight from the Pacific is worth the price at La Sirena d'Juan Seafood (p353).

Tarapoto At La Patarashca don't miss the namesake dish – traditional platters of fresh-grilled Amazon fish or shrimp doused in tomatoes, garlic and cilantro (p433).

Trujillo The bamboo-lined Mar Picante is known for serving up behemoth orders of divine *ceviche mixto,* piled high with shrimp, fish, crab and scallops (p319).

Quick Eats

Peru has a vibrant street food culture. The most popular items are *an-ticuchos* (beef heart skewers), ceviche, tamales, boiled quail eggs and *choclo con queso* (boiled corn with cheese). Also popular, and quite delicious, are *picarones* (sweet doughnut fritters).

For a cheap and tasty meal, check out the many *pollerías* (spit-roasted chicken joints) found just about everywhere.

Vegetarians & Vegans

In a country where many folks survive on nothing but potatoes, there can be a general befuddlement over why anyone would choose to be vegetarian. This attitude has started to change, however, and some of the bigger cities have restaurants that cater exclusively to vegetarians.

It is possible, however, to find vegetarian dishes at a regular Peruvian restaurant. Many of the potato salads, such as *papas a la huancaína, ocopa* and *causa* are made without meat, as is *palta a la jardinera,* an avocado stuffed with vegetables. *Sopa de verduras* (vegetable soup), *tortilla* (Spanish omelet) and *tacu tacu* (beans and rice pan-fried together) are other options. *Chifas* can also be a good source of vegetarian meals. Before ordering, however, ask if these are *platos vegetarianos* (vegetarian dishes). The term *sin carne* (without meat) refers only to red meat or pork, so you could end up with chicken or seafood instead.

Vegans will have a harder time. Peruvian cuisine is based on eggs and dairy and infinite combinations thereof. Self-catering is the best option.

Cuy – otherwise known as guinea pig – was an important source of protein for pre-Columbian people all over the Andes. In recent years, Peru has begun testing the export market: the guinea pig is high in protein, but low in fat and cholesterol.

PERU'S CUISINE WHERE TO EAT & DRINK

Ancient Peru

A *pachacuti,* according to the Incas, was a cataclysmic event that divide the different ages of history. For the indigenous cultures that inhabite Peru in the 16th century, the arrival of the Spanish was the most eart shattering *pachacuti* imaginable. As conquerors are wont to do, th Europeans went about obliterating native history: melting gold object immolating religious icons and banning long-held traditions.

This has left historians to piece together Peru's pre-Columbian his tory largely by examining grave goods. (Not a single Andean culture le behind a written language.) Thankfully, the physical legacy is bountifu This area has been home to civilizations large and small, each with it own distinctive deities and traditions. Travelers to Peru can see sumptu ous textiles, striking ceramics and monumental structures so well eng neered they have not only survived conquest, but centuries of calamitou earthquakes as well.

For the *Indiana Jones* set, the adventure begins here.

Top Ruins Sites

» Machu Picchu, Sacred Valley

» Chan Chan, Trujillo

» Sillustani, Puno

» Chavín de Huántar, Huaraz

» Huacas del Sol y de la Luna, Trujillo

» Kuélap, Chachapoyas

Caral

Just a couple of hundred kilometers north of Lima lies one of the mos exciting archaeological sites in Peru. It may not look like much – half dozen dusty temple mounds, a few sunken amphitheaters and remnant of structures crafted from adobe and stone – but it is. This is the oldes known city in the Americas: Caral (p308).

Situated in the Supe Valley, this early society developed almost si multaneously with the cultures of Mesopotamia and Egypt about 500(years ago, and it predates the earliest civilizations in Mexico by abou 1500 years. Little is known about the people that built this impressiv 626-hectare urban center. But archaeologists, led by Ruth Shady Solís the former director of Lima's Museo Nacional de Antropología, Arque ología e Historia del Perú (p65), have managed to unearth a few preciou details.

Caral was a religious center that venerated its holy men and pai tribute to unknown agricultural deities (at times, with human sacrifice) They cultivated crops such as cotton, squash, beans and chilies, collect ed fruits and were knowledgeable fishers. Archaeological finds include pieces of textile, necklaces, ceremonial burials and crude, unbaked clay figurines depicting female forms. The first serious digs began in the area in 1996 and much of the complex has yet to be excavated – expect furthe discoveries.

The book *Tejidos Milenarios del Perú: Ancient Peruvian Textiles* is a sumptuously illustrated encyclopedia of just about every type of textile to emerge from Peru between Chavín and the Incas. The legacy is so rich, in fact, that this book spans more than 800 pages and weighs more than 10kg.

Chavín

If Caral is evidence of early urbanization, then Chavín de Huántar (p396), near Huaraz, represents the spread of a unified religious and artistic iconography. In a broad swath of the northern Andes, from roughly 1000 BC to 300 BC, a stylized feline deity began to appear on carvings, friezes, pottery and textiles from the era. As with Caral, there is only tchy information available about the era's societies, but its importance without question: in Peru, this moment heralds the true birth of art.

It is still debated whether the temple at Chavín de Huántar repre-nted a capital or merely an important ceremonial site, but what is ithout doubt is that the setting is extraordinary. With the stunning Cor-illera Blanca as a backdrop, the remnants of this elaborate ceremonial mplex – built over hundreds of years – include a number of temple ructures, as well as a sunken court with stone friezes of jaguars. Here, rchaeologists have found pottery from all over the region filled with *rendas* (offerings), including shells from as far away as the Ecuadorean ast, and carved bones (some human) featuring supernatural motifs. he site's most remarkable feature is a maze of disorienting galleries be-eath the temple complex, one of which boasts a nearly 5m-tall rock carv-ıg of a fanged anthropomorphic deity known as the Lanzón – the sort of erce-looking creature that is bound to turn anyone into a believer.

aracas & Nazca

he Chavín Horizon was followed by the development of a number of naller, regional ethnicities. Along the country's south coast, from about 00 BC to AD 400, the Paracas culture – situated around modern-day a – produced some of the most renowned textiles ever created. The lost impressive of these were woven during the period known as the aracas Necropolis (AD 1 to 400), so named for a massive gravesite on he Paracas Peninsula uncovered by famed Peruvian archaeologist Julio ello in the 1920s (see boxed text below).

The historical data on the culture is thin, but the magnificent tex-iles recovered from the graves – layers of finely woven fabrics wrapped round mummy bundles – provide important clues about day-to-day life nd beliefs. Cloths feature flowers, fish, birds, knives and cats, with some nimals represented as two-headed creatures. Also significant are the uman figures: warriors carry shrunken trophy heads and supernatural nthropomorphic creatures are equipped with wings, snake tongues and ots of claws. (See some fantastic examples at the Museo Larco in Lima, 65.) Many of the mummies found at this site had cranial deformations,

Published by Harvard University's Peabody Museum, *The Moche of Ancient Peru: Media and Messages,* by Jeffrey Quilter, is an outstanding introduction to the history, art and architecture of the Moche culture of the north coast.

ANCIENT PERU

FATHER OF PERUVIAN ARCHAEOLOGY

Much of what we know about some of Peru's most important pre-Columbian cultures we owe to a single man: Julio C Tello (1880–1947), the acclaimed 'Father of Peruvian Archaeol-ogy.' A self-described 'mountain Indian,' Tello was born in the highland village of Huarochirí, in the mountains east of Lima. He earned a medical degree at the Universidad Nacional Mayor de San Marco Lima and later studied archaeology at Harvard University – no small achievement for a poor, indigenous man in turn-of-the-20th-century Peru.

In the 1920s, he undertook a series of ground-breaking archaeological studies of the Wari centers around Ayacucho and the temple complex at Chavín de Huántar, where an ornate stela – the Tello Obelisk – is named in his honor. (Find it on view at the Museo Nacional de Chavín, p396.) He also discovered hundreds of mummy bundles on the Paracas Peninsula in 1927 – one of the most important sources of information about this pre-Inca culture. Most significantly, Tello brought scientific rigor to Peru's burgeoning archaeological efforts. In the 19th century, digs often resulted in more destruction than conservation, and looting was widely accepted. Tello helped get laws passed that offered legal protection to important archaeological sites.

For more on this charismatic figure, pick up a copy of *The Life and Writings of Julio C Tello: America's First Indigenous Archeologist,* published by University of Iowa Press – which, for the first time, gathers his key writings.

most of which showed that the head had been intentionally flattene using two boards.

During roughly the same period, the Nazca culture (200 BC to A 600), to the south, was producing an array of painted pottery, as we as incredible weavings that showcased everyday objects (beans, bir and fish), in addition to supernatural cat- and falcon-men in an array explosive colors. The Nazca were skilled embroiderers: some weavin; feature tiny dangling figurines that must have induced blindness in the creators. (Well-preserved examples can be seen at the Museo Andrés d Castillo in Lima, p62.) The culture is best known, however, for the Naze Lines (p122), a series of mysterious geoglyphs carved into a 500-sq-k. area in the southern Peruvian desert.

Moche

When it comes to ceramics, there is no Andean civilization that compare to the Moche (p327), a culture that inhabited the Peruvian north coa. from about AD 100 to AD 800. Though not inherently urban, they bui sophisticated ceremonial centers, such as the frieze-laden Huacas del S(y de la Luna (p325), outside of modern-day Trujillo, and the elabora burial site of Sipán (p339), near Chiclayo. They had a well-maintaine network of roads and a system of relay runners who carried message, probably in the form of symbols carved onto beans.

But it's their portrait pottery that makes the Moche a standout: lifelik depictions of individuals (scars and all) are so skillfully rendered the seem as if they are about to speak out. Artisans often created multipl portraits of a single person over the course of a lifetime. One schola in fact, recorded 45 different pieces depicting the same model. Othe ceramics showcase macho activities such as hunting, combat and ritua sacrifice. This doesn't mean, however, that the Moche didn't know thing or two about love – they are famous for their downright acrobati depictions of human sex (on view at Lima's Museo Larco, p65).

Wari

From about AD 600 to 1100, the Andes saw the rise of the first truly ex pansive kingdom. The Wari (p296) were avid empire builders, expandin; from their base around Ayacucho to a territory that occupied most of the highlands, in addition to a piece of the northern coast. Expert agricultur alists, they improved production by developing the terrace system an creating complex networks of canals for irrigation.

Like many conquering cultures in the region, the Wari built on wha was already there, usurping and adding to extant infrastructure createc by smaller regional states. The coastal ceremonial center of Pachacama (p99), for instance, was originated by the Lima culture, but was expand ed by the Wari. This doesn't mean that there aren't definitive Wari sites to be seen. The remains of what was once a 1500-hectare city (p298 is located outside of Ayacucho, and there is a Wari ceremonial cente in Piquillacta (p258), near Cuzco. Unfortunately, the Wari's architecture was cruder than that of the Incas, which means that the buildings have not aged gracefully.

In the area of weaving, however, the culture was highly skilled, pro ducing elegant fabrics with elaborate, stylized designs. The Wari were masters of color, using as many as 150 distinct shades which they incor porated into both woven and tie-dyed patterns. Many textiles feature ab stract, geometric designs, as well as supernatural figures – most common is a winged deity holding a staff.

For an excellent primer to all of Peru's pre-Hispanic art, pick up Ferdinand Anton's *The Art of Ancient Peru*. The descriptions are concise and accessible and the book comes laden with almost 300 large-scale photographic images.

ARCHAEOLOGY

Chimú & Chachapoyas

Following the demise of the Wari, a number of small nation-states emerged in different corners of the country. They are too numerous to detail here (for more, see p494), but there are two that merit discussion because of the art and architecture they left behind.

The first of these is the Chimú culture, once based around present-day Trujillo. Between about AD 1000 and AD 1400, this sophisticated society built the largest known pre-Columbian city in the Americas. Chan Chan (p323) is a sprawling, 36-sq-km complex, which once housed an estimated 60,000 people. Though over the centuries this adobe city has been worn down by the elements, parts of the complex's geometric friezes have been restored, giving a small inkling of what this metropolis must have been like in its heyday. The Chimú were accomplished artisans and metallurgists – producing, among other things, some absolutely outrageous-looking textiles covered top-to-bottom in tassels.

In the interior of the northern highlands is the cloud-forest citadel of Kuélap (p424), built by the Chachapoyas culture in the remote Utcubamba Valley beginning around AD 800. It is an incredible structure – or, more accurately, series of structures. The site is composed of more than 400 circular dwellings in addition to unusual, gravity-defying pieces of architecture, such as an inverted cone known as El Tintero (The Inkpot). The compound caps a narrow ridge and is surrounded, on all sides, by a 6m- to 12m-high wall, making the city practically impenetrable. This has led at least one historian to theorize that if the Incas had made their last stand against the Spanish here, rather than outside Cuzco, history might have been quite different.

Incas

Peru's greatest engineers were also its greatest empire builders. Because the Incas made direct contact with the Spanish, they also happen to be the pre-Columbian Andean culture that is best documented – not only through Spanish chronicle, but also through narratives produced by descendants of the Incas themselves. (The most famous of these scribes is El Inca Garcilaso de la Vega, who lived in the 16th century.)

The Incas were a Quechua civilization descended from alpaca farmers in the southern Andes. Over several generations, from AD 1100 until the arrival of the Spanish in 1532, they steadfastly grew into a highly organized empire that extended over more than 37° latitude from Colombia to Chile. This was an absolutist state with a strong army, where ultimate power resided with the *inca,* or emperor. (The political history is fascinating. Turn to p494 for more.)

The society was bound by a rigid caste system: there were nobles, an artisan and merchant class, and peasants. The latter supplied the manpower for the Incas' many public-works projects. Citizens were expected to pay tribute to the crown in the form of labor – typically three months

The website www.arqueologia.com.ar/peru/ gathers useful links (in Spanish) related to archaeology news in Peru. The site contains timelines as well as some basic photo galleries devoted to different cultural groups.

BEST ARCHAEOLOGICAL MUSEUMS

» Museo Nacional de Antropología, Arqueología e Historia del Perú (p65), Lima
» Museo Larco (p65), Lima
» Museo Inka (p202), Cuzco
» Museo Nacional de Chavín (p396), Chavín de Huántar
» Museo Santury (p140), Arequipa
» Museo Tumbas Reales de Sipán (p340), Lambayeque
» Museo Nacional Sicán (p341), Ferreñafe

INCA
EMPIRE

At its acme, the Inca empire was larger than imperial Rome and boasted 40,000km of roadways. A network of *chasquis* (runners) kept the kingdom connected, relaying fresh-caught fish from the coast to Cuzco in 24 hours.

of the year – enabling the development and maintenance of monumen canals and roadways. The Incas also kept a highly efficient communic tions system consisting of a body of *chasquis* (relay runners), who cou make the 1600km trip between Quito and Cuzco in just seven days. (I comparison, it takes the average traveler three to four days to hike t Inca Trail from Ollantaytambo to Machu Picchu – a mere 43km!) As br tal as the regime was (bloody wars, human sacrifice), the Incas also had notable social-welfare system, warehousing surplus food for distributic to areas and people in need.

On the cultural front, the Incas had a strong tradition of music, or literature and textiles. Their fabrics were generally composed of bol solid colors in an array of abstract, geometric prints. But they are be known for their monumental architecture. The capital of Cuzco (p194 along with a series of constructions at Sacsaywamán (p232), Pis; (p234), Ollantaytambo (p242) and the fabled Machu Picchu (p250), a all incredible examples of the imperial style of building. Carved pieces rock, without mortar, are fitted together so tightly that it is impossib to fit a knife between the stones. Most interestingly, walls are built at a angle and windows in a trapezoidal form, so as to resist seismic activit The Incas kept the exteriors of their buildings austere, opting to put th decoration on the inside, in the form of rich wall hangings made of pr cious metal.

Nestled into spectacular natural locales, these structures, even in thei ruined state, are an unforgettable sight. Their great majesty was som thing the Spanish acknowledged, even as they prised them apart to buil their own monuments. 'Now that the Inca rulers have lost their powe wrote Spanish chronicler Pedro Cieza de León in the 16th century, 'a these palaces and gardens, together with their other great works, hav fallen, so that only the remains survive. Since they were built of goo stone and the masonry is excellent, they will stand as memorials for cen turies to come.' León was right. The Inca civilization did not survive th Spanish *pachacuti*, but its architecture did – a reminder of the man grand societies we are just beginning to understand.

ndigenous Peru

hile Peru's social order has been indelibly stamped by Spanish custom,
s soul remains squarely indigenous. According to the country's census
ureau, this crinkled piece of the South American Andes harbors 52 dif-
rent ethnicities, 13 distinct linguistic families and 1786 native commu-
ties. In fact, almost half of Peru's population of more than 29 million
entifies as Amerindian. Together, these groups account for an infinite
umber of rituals, artistic traditions and ways of life – a cultural legacy
at is as rich as it is long-running.

ost-Conquest Life

the wake of the Spanish conquest, colonial authorities transformed
e ways in which people lived in the Andes. Indigenous people who
ad only ever known an agricultural life were forced to live on *reduc-
'ones* by colonial authorities. These urbanized 'reductions' provided the
hurch with a centralized place for evangelism and allowed the Span-
h to control the natives politically and culturally. In these, indigenous
eople were often prohibited from speaking their native languages or
earing traditional dress.

By the 17th century, after the Spanish had consolidated their power,
any indigenous people were dispersed back to the countryside. But
ather than work in the self-sustaining collectives *(ayllus)* that had exist-
d in pre-Columbian times, *indígenas* were forced into a system of debt
eonage. For example: a native family was granted a subsistence plot on
Spanish landowner's holdings. In exchange, the *campesino* (peasant)
rovided labor for the *patrón* (boss). In many cases, *campesinos* were not
llowed to leave the land on which they lived.

This system remained firmly in place into the 20th century.

20th-Century Shift

he last 100 years have marked a number of significant steps forward.
ince the indigenist social movements of the 1920s, various constitutions
nd laws have granted legal protection to communal lands (at least on
aper, if not always in practice). In 1979, the Peruvian constitution of-
icially recognized the right of people to adhere to their own 'cultural
dentities,' and the right to bilingual education was officially established.
Until then, the public school system had made a systematic effort to
liminate the use of native languages and pressured indigenous people
o acculturate to Spanish *criollo* society.) And, the following year, literacy
voting restrictions were finally lifted – allowing indigenous people to
ully participate in the political process.

In 2011, President Humala passed a law that requires native peoples to
be consulted on all mining and extraction activities on their territories.

English Words Derived from Quechua

» Coca
» Condor
» Guano
» Llama
» Pampa
» Puma
» Quinoa

In Spanish, *indígena* (indigenous) is the appropriate term. The word *indio* – 'Indian' in English – can be insulting, especially when used by outsiders. The slang *cholo* (translating roughly to 'Indian peasant') has long been considered derogatory, though some Peruvians use it as a term of empowerment.

Pressures of Poverty & Environment

Even as *indígenas* continue to make strides, there are obstacles. Ind enous people make up almost twice as many of the country's extrem poverty cases as Peruvians of European descent. In addition, access basic services is problematic. Nearly 60% of indigenous communities not have access to a health facility, and the country has a high materr mortality ratio (higher than Iraq or the Gaza Strip). This affects ind enous women disproportionately.

Perhaps the biggest issue facing some ethnicities is the loss of lan The exploitation of natural resources in ever more remote areas putting increased pressure on indigenous communities whose territor are often ill-defined and whose needs are poorly represented by the fe eral government in Lima. According to AIDESEP, a Peruvian indigeno organization representing various rainforest ethnic groups, oil prospec ing and extraction is occurring in more than 80% of indigenous territ ries in the Amazon.

Racism remains a potent societal force in Peru. In a study conducted by the country's National Agrarian University in the 1990s, 81% of indigenous people living in Lima reported having been the victims of discrimination – especially in matters of work.

Multitude of Cultures

Indigenous cultures are identified by their region or name, such as th Arequipa or Chachapoya. But with more than a thousand highly loca ized regional cultures in the Peruvian Andes alone, it is easiest to identi groups by the language they speak. Quechua – the lingua franca of th Incas – is predominant. It is the most commonly spoken native languag in the Americas and is heard all over the Andes. In Peru, more than 13 of the national population claims it as a birth language.

Aymara is the second-most spoken indigenous language – with near 2% of Peruvians speaking it from birth, primarily in the area aroun Lake Titicaca. Nearly 1% of Peruvians speak one of another 50 or s smaller, regional dialects. These include the numerous Amazon culture that inhabit the rainforest.

Quechua

The descendants of the Incas (along with the myriad peoples the Inca conquered) inhabit much of Peru's Andean spine, representing the big gest indigenous cohort in the country. The department of Cuzco, how ever, remains the symbolic center of Quechua life. Traditional Quechu refer to themselves as *runakuna* and refer to mixed-raced *mestizos* o

---

OLLANTAY: QUECHUA'S GREAT LITERARY EPIC

Ollantay tells the story of a pair of star-crossed lovers: Ollanta, a celebrated warrior of humble birth, and Cusi Cuyllur, a captivating Inca princess. Because Ollanta is not a noble, societal mores dictate that he cannot marry his beloved. But he nonetheless draws up the courage to ask Emperor Pachacutec for his daughter's hand in marriage. The emperor becomes enraged at the audacity of the young lovers and expels Ollanta from Cuzco and throws his daughter in jail. Battles ensue, a child is born and after much palace intrigue, the lovers are reunited.

Ollantay is a work of classic Quechua – the version of Quechua spoken at the time of the conquest. But because the Incas didn't leave behind a written language, its origins are quite murky: no one knows who composed it, or when. Its first recorded appearance is in the manuscripts of an 18th-century priest named Antonio Valdés, who worked in the department of Cuzco. Some scholars have surmised that Valdés may have written *Ollantay*. Others say that it was one of the many epic poems transmitted orally among the Incas, and that Valdés simply recorded it. Others figure Valdés may have tailored an indigenous work to suit Spanish tastes. Regardless, it is a popular theater drama in Peru – and remains one of the great works of art in Quechua.

digenous people who adopt Spanish Peruvian culture as *mistikuna*. ...e ritual chewing of coca is regarded as a major point of self-identifi-...tion among *runakuna*. However, such distinguishing characteristics ...e becoming increasingly blurred as more indigenous people adopt at ...ast some *criollo* customs in order to participate in the greater economy.

Regardless, many people continue to speak the language, chew coca ...d wear traditional dress. For men, this generally consists of brightly wo-...n ponchos and the ear-flap hats known as *chullos*. Women's outfits are ...ore elaborate and flamboyant: a bowler or flat-topped hat accompanies ...me sort of woven wrap or sweater, and multiple layers of hand-woven ...shiny skirts. (The layered skirt look is considered very feminine.) Ele-...ents of traditional and Western dress are often combined.

...ymara

...hough subjugated by the Quechua-speaking Incas in the 15th century, ...e Aymara have maintained a distinct language group and identity. Tra-...tionally an agricultural society, they were reduced to near-slave status ...rough debt peonage and, later, in the silver mines of Bolivia. Within ...ru, they are clustered in the area around Puno and Lake Titicaca.

While identification with indigenous custom is strong, Spanish ele-...ents are present in spiritual life. *Indígenas* have largely adapted Catho-...c deities to their own beliefs. Like the Quechua, many Aymara practice ...ncretic religious beliefs that closely link indigenous custom to Catholic ...ought. In Puno, there is a large festival in honor of La Virgen de la ...andelaria every February 2 (Candlemas). The Virgin, however, is closely ...entified with Pachamama, as well as natural elements such as light-...ing and fertility.

...ultures of the Amazon

...he vast Peruvian Amazon is home to more than 330,000 indigenous ...eople, representing more than five dozen different ethnicities – some of ...hich are closely related, others of which couldn't be more different in ...erms of tradition and language.

Within this group, the biggest demographic is comprised of the ...sháninka people (also known as Campa). Comprising roughly a quar-...er of the indigenous population in the Peruvian Amazon, they inhabit ...umerous river valleys east of the central highlands. (Because of this ...ocation, the Asháninka suffered mightily during the Internal Conflict, ...hen the *Sendero Luminoso* (Shining Path) made incursions to the east.)

The second-largest Amazon group is the Aguaruna, who occupy the ...Marañón, Nieva and Santiago River valleys to the north. The group not ...nly resisted Inca attempts at conquest, they also fended off the Spanish. ...n fact, they still occupy their pre-conquest lands, and survive by practic-...ng horticulture, hunting and fishing.

There are countless other smaller ethnic groups, including the Shipi-...o, Matsiguenka, and the small, so-called 'uncontacted tribes' that have ...made headlines in recent years. These groups are extremely vulnerable ...o land loss and pollution caused by oil and mineral extraction. For the ...most remote groups, the biggest problem can boil down to simple im-...munity: in the 1980s, more than half of the Nahua people in the southern ...Amazon died after contracting diseases from loggers and oil-company ...agents.

For more on Amazon cultures, see p467.

INDIGENOUS PERU MULTITUDE OF CULTURES

QUECHUA LIFE

For a well-written examination of Quechua life in Peru, pick up a copy of Catherine Allen's *The Hold Life Has: Coca and Cultural Identity in an Andean Community*. This intriguing ethnography, last updated in 2002, covers everything from belief systems to the rituals of daily life in the southern highlands.

Music & the Arts

The country that has been home to empires both indigenous and European has a wealth of cultural and artistic tradition. Perhaps the most outstanding achievements are in the areas of music (both indigenous and otherwise), painting and literature — the latter of which receives plenty of attention in 2010, when Peruvian novelist Mario Vargas Llosa won the Nobel Prize.

Music

Like its people, Peru's music is an intercontinental fusion of elements. Pre-Columbian cultures contributed bamboo flutes, the Spaniard brought stringed instruments and the Africans gave it a backbone of fluid, percussive rhythm. By and large, music tends to be a regional affair. African-influenced *landós* with their thumbing bass beats are predominant on the coast, high-pitched indigenous *huaynos,* heavy on bamboo wind instruments, are heard in the Andes and *criollo* waltzes are a must at any dance party on the coast.

Over the last several decades, the *huayno* has blended with surf guitars and Colombian *cumbia* (a type of Afro-Caribbean dance music) to produce *chicha* – a danceable sound closely identified with the Amazon region. (Well-known *chicha* bands include Los Shapis and Los Mirlos. *Cumbia* is also popular. Grupo 5, which hails from Chiclayo, is currently a favorite in the genre.

On the coast, guitar-inflected *música criolla* (*criollo* music) has its roots in both Spain and Africa. The most famous *criollo* style is the *vals peruano* (Peruvian waltz), a three-quarter-time waltz that is fast moving and full of complex guitar melodies. The most legendary singers in this genre include singer and composer Chabuca Granda (1920–83), Lucha Reyes (1936–73) and Arturo 'Zambo' Cavero (1940–2009). Cavero, in particular, was revered for his gravelly vocals and soulful interpretations. *Landó* is closely connected to this style of music, but features the added elements of call-and-response. Standout performers in this vein include singers Susana Baca (b 1944) and Eva Ayllón (b 1956).

Of the infinite varieties of music that exist all over Peru, the Afro-Peruvian tunes from the coast are perhaps the grooviest. For an excellent primer, pick up – or download – the David Byrne-produced compilation *Afro-Peruvian Classics: The Soul of Black Peru.*

Visual Art

The country's most famous art movement dates to the 17th and 18th centuries, when the artists of the Cuzco School produced thousands of religious paintings, the vast majority of which remain unattributed. Created by native and *mestizo* artists, the pieces frequently feature holy figures laced in gold paint and rendered in a style inspired by mannerist and late Gothic art – but bearing traces of an indigenous color palette and iconography. Today, these hang in museums and churches throughout Peru and reproductions are sold in many crafts markets.

One of the most well-known artistic figures of the 19th century is Pancho Fierro (1807–79), the illegitimate son of a priest and a slave, who painted highly evocative watercolors of the everyday figures that

TRADITIONAL CRAFTS

Peru has a long tradition of producing extraordinarily rendered crafts and folk art. Here's what to look for:

» **Textiles** You'll see intricate weavings with elaborate anthropomorphic and geometric designs all over Peru. Some of the finest can be found around Cuzco (p227).

» **Pottery** The most stunning pieces of pottery are those made in the tradition of the pre-Columbian Moche people of the north coast. But also worthwhile is Chancay-style pottery: rotund figures made from sand-colored clay. Find these at craft markets in Lima (p92).

» **Religious Crafts** These abound in all regions, but the *retablos* (three-dimensional dioramas) from Ayacucho (p297) are the most spectacular.

occupied Lima's streets: fishmongers, teachers and Catholic religious figures clothed in lush robes.

In the early 20th century, an indigenist movement led by painter José Sabogal (1888–1956) achieved national prominence. Sabogal often painted indigenous figures and incorporated pre-Columbian design in his work. As director of the National School of Arts in Lima, he influenced a whole generation of painters who looked to Andean tradition for inspiration, including Julia Codesido (1892–1979), Mario Urteaga (1875–1957) and Enrique Camino Brent (1909–60).

Literature

Mario Vargas Llosa (b 1936) is Peru's most famous writer, hailed alongside 20th-century Latin American luminaries such as Gabriel García Márquez, Julio Cortázar and Carlos Fuentes. His novels evoke James Joyce in their complexity, meandering through time and shifting perspectives. Vargas Llosa is also a keen social observer, casting a spotlight on the naked corruption of the ruling class and the peculiarities of Peruvian society. His more than two dozen novels are available in translation. The best place to start is *La ciudad y los perros* (The Time of the Hero), based on his experience at a Peruvian military academy. (The soldiers at his old academy responded to the novel by burning it.)

Another keen observer includes Alfredo Bryce Echenique (b 1939), who chronicles the ways of the upper class in novels such as *El huerto de mi amada* (My Beloved's Garden), which recounts an affair between a 33-year-old woman and a teenage boy in 1950s Lima. Demonstrating a distinctly Peruvian penchant for dark humor is Julio Ramón Ribeyro (1929–94). Though never a bestselling author, he is critically acclaimed for his insightful works, which focus on the vagaries of lower-middle-class life. His work is available in English in *Marginal Voices: Selected Stories* (1993). If you are just learning to read Spanish, his clearly and concisely written pieces are an ideal place to start exploring Peruvian literature.

Also significant is rising literary star Daniel Alarcón (b 1977), a Peruvian-American writer whose award-winning short stories have appeared in the *New Yorker* magazine. His debut novel, *Lost City Radio,* about a country recovering from civil war, was published to wide acclaim in 2007.

If Vargas Llosa is the country's greatest novelist, then César Vallejo (1892–1938) is its greatest poet. In his lifetime, he published only three slim books – *Los heraldos negros* (The Black Heralds), *Trilce* and *Poemas humanos* (Human Poems) – but he has long been regarded as one of the most innovative Latin American poets of the 20th century. Vallejo frequently touched on existential themes and was known for pushing the language to its limits, inventing words when real ones no longer suited him.

CÉSAR VALLEJO

César Vallejo is one of the world's most renowned poets, influencing writers all over the West. Now his complete works – in English and Spanish – are available in a single volume, *The Complete Poetry of César Vallejo: A Bilingual Edition.*

The Natural World

Few countries have topographies as rugged, as forbidding and as wild, diverse as Peru. The third-largest country in South America – at 1,285,22 sq km – it is five times larger than the UK, almost twice the size of Texa and one-sixth the size of Australia. It lies in the tropics, south of th equator, straddling three strikingly different geographic zones: the ari Pacific coast, the craggy Andes mountain range and a good portion the Amazon Basin.

Regardless of which part of the country you're visiting, it's a guarantee you will never travel a straight line. Between snaking rivers, plung ing canyons and all the zigzagging mountain roads, navigating Peru landscape is about circumventing natural obstacles – but with plenty excitement and jaw-dropping beauty in between.

The Land

On the coast, a narrow strip of land, which lies below 1000m in eleva tion, hugs the country's 3000km-long shoreline. Consisting primaril of scrubland and desert, it eventually merges, in the south, with Chile Atacama Desert, one of the driest places on earth. The coast include Lima, the capital, and several major agricultural centers – oases watere by dozens of rivers that cascade down from the Andes. These settle ments make for a strange sight: barren desert can give way to bursts o green fields within the course of a few meters. The coast contains som of Peru's flattest terrain, so it's no surprise that the country's best road the Carretera Panamericana (Pan-American Hwy), borders much of th Pacific from Ecuador to Chile.

The Andes, the world's second-greatest mountain chain, form th spine of the country. Rising steeply from the coast, and growing sharp ly in height and gradient from north to south, they reach spectacula heights of more than 6000m just 100km inland. Peru's highest peak Huascarán (6768m), located northeast of Huaraz, is the world's highes tropical summit and the sixth-tallest mountain in the Americas. Though the Peruvian Andes resides in the tropics, the mountains are laced with a web of glaciers above elevations of 5000m. Between 3000m and 4000m lie the agricultural highlands, which support more than a third of Peru's population.

The eastern Andean slopes receive much more rainfall than the dry western slopes and are draped in lush cloud forests as they descend into the lowland rainforest of the Amazon. Here, the undulating landscape rarely rises more than 500m above sea level as various tributary systems feed into the mighty Río Amazonas (Amazon River), the largest river in the world. Weather conditions are hot and humid year-round, with most precipitation falling between December and May.

Top Protected Areas

» Cañón del Colca, Arequipa

» Cordillera Blanca, Ancash

» Lake Titicaca, Puno

» Parque Nacional Manu, Amazon

» Islas Ballestas, Pisco

The origin of the word 'Andes' is uncertain. Some historians believe it comes from the Quechua *anti*, meaning 'east,' or *anta*, an Aymara-derived term that signifies 'copper-colored.' Interestingly, the mountains don't stop at the Pacific coast; 100km offshore there is a trench that is as deep as the Andes are high.

...ildlife

...th its folds, bends and plunging river valleys, Peru is home to countless ...osystems, each with its own unique climate, elevation, vegetation and ...l type. As a result, it boasts a spectacular variety of plant and animal ...e. Colonies of sea lions occupy rocky outcroppings on the coast, while ...ucous flocks of brightly colored macaws descend on clay licks in the ...mazon. In the Andes, rare vicuñas (endangered relatives of the alpaca) ...t about in packs as condors take to the wind currents. Peru is one of ...ly a dozen or so countries in the world considered to be 'megadiverse.'

...nimals

...ildlife enthusiasts come to Peru to see a rainbow of birds, as well as ...melids, freshwater dolphins, butterflies, jaguars, anacondas, macaws ...d spectacled bears – to name but a few...

...irds

...ru has more than 1800 bird species – that's more than the number of ...ecies found in North America and Europe together. From the tiniest ...ummingbirds to the majestic Andean condor, the variety is colorful and ...emingly endless; new species are discovered regularly.

Along the Pacific, marine birds of all kinds are most visible, especially ... the south, where they can be found clustered along the shore. Here ...u'll see exuberant Chilean flamingos, oversized Peruvian pelicans, ...lump Inca terns sporting white-feather mustaches and bright orange ...eaks, colonies of brown boobies engaged in elaborate mating dances, ...ormorants and endangered Humboldt penguins, which can be spotted ...addling around the Islas Ballestas (p112).

In the highlands, the most famous bird of all is the Andean condor. ...eighing up to 10kg, with a 3m-plus wingspan, this monarch of the air ...a member of the vulture family) once ranged over the entire Andean ...ountain chain from Venezuela to Tierra del Fuego. Considered the larg-...st flying bird in the world, the condor was put on the endangered spe-...ies list in the 1970s, due mostly to loss of habitat and pollution. But it ...as also hunted to the brink of extinction because its body parts were ...elieved to increase male virility and ward off nightmares. Condors usu-...lly nest in impossibly high mountain cliffs that prevent predators from ...natching their young. Their main food source is carrion and they're ...ost easily spotted riding thermal air currents in the canyons around ...requipa (p163).

Other prominent high-altitude birds include the Andean gull (don't ...all it a seagull!), which is commonly sighted along lakes and rivers as

One of the most engagingly written books on rainforest life is Adrian Forsyth and Ken Miyata's *Tropical Nature: Life and Death in the Rain Forests of Central and South America.* Partially re-searched in the Amazon Basin, it is an essential, highly enjoyable primer on life in the lowland tropics.

FOR THE DOGS: PERUVIAN HAIRLESS

Visit many of the ancient sites around coastal Peru and you'll be greeted by a strangely awesome canine sight: hairless dogs – some with small mohawks on the crown of their heads – bounding about the ruins. A pre-Inca breed whose roots in the Andes date back almost 3000 years, the *perro biringo* or *perro calato* (naked dog), as it is known, has been depicted in Moche, Chimú and Chancay pottery.

Over the centuries, as cutesy breeds from abroad have been introduced to Peru, the population of Peruvian hairless has declined. But, in recent years, they've started to make a comeback, with dedicated Lima breeders working to keep the species alive, and the government employing them as staple attractions at pre-Columbian sites. In 2009 they were even awarded with their own commemorative stamp. The dogs may not be pretty, but they are generally very friendly. And they do have one thing going for them: no fur means no fleas.

high as 4500m. The mountains are also home to several species of il
such as the puna ibis, which inhabits lakeside marshes, as well as roug
ly a dozen types of cinclodes, a type of ovenbird (their clay nests resem
ovens) endemic to the Andes. Other species include torrent ducks, whi
nest in small waterside caves, Andean geese, spotted Andean flicke
black-and-yellow Andean siskins and, of course, a panoply of hummin
birds (see boxed text opposite).

Swoop down toward the Amazon and you'll catch sight of the worl
most iconic tropical birds, including boisterous flocks of parrots an
macaws festooned in brightly plumed regalia. You'll also see clusters
aracaris, toucans, parakeets, toucanets, ibises, regal gray-winged tru
peters, umbrella birds donning gravity-defying feathered hairdos, crin
son colored cocks-of-the-rock, soaring hawks and harpy eagles. The li
goes on.

A comprehensive overview of the country's avian life is contained in the 656-page Princeton Field Guide *Birds of Peru*, by Thomas Schulenberg.

BIRDS OF PERU

Mammals

The Amazon is also home to a bounty of mammals. More than two doze
species of monkeys are found here, including howlers, acrobatic spide
monkeys and wide-eyed marmosets. With the help of a guide, you ma
also see sloths, bats, piglike peccaries, anteaters, armadillos and coati
(ring-tailed members of the raccoon family). And if you're really luck
you'll find giant river otters, capybaras (a rodent of unusual size), rive
dolphins, tapirs and maybe one of half a dozen elusive felines, includir
the fabled jaguar.

Toward the west, the cloud forests straddling the Amazon and th
eastern slopes of the Andean highlands are home to the endangere
spectacled bear. South America's only bear is a black, shaggy mamma
known for its white, masklike face markings, that grows up to 1.8m i
length.

The highlands are home to roving packs of camelids: llamas and al
pacas are the most easily spotted since they are domesticated, and use
as pack animals or for their wool; vicuñas and guanacos live exclusive
in the wild. On highland talus slopes, watch out for the viscacha, whic
looks like the world's most cuddly rabbit. Foxes, deer and domesticate
cuy (guinea pigs) are also highland dwellers, as is the puma (cougar o
mountain lion).

On the coast, huge numbers of sea lions and seals are easily seen o
the Islas Ballestas (p112). Dolphins are commonly seen offshore, bu

---

WATCHING WILDLIFE IN PERU

Sea lions, vicuñas, scarlet macaws and monkeys – a lot of travelers come to Peru specifically to observe the extraordinary animal life. A few tips on making the most of your wildlife-watching:

» be willing to travel – the coast has limited fauna and some highland areas have been hunted out; remote is the way to go

» hire a knowledgeable local guide – they know what to look for and where

» get up *really* early – animals tend to be most active at dawn and dusk

» bring a pair of lightweight binoculars – they will improve wildlife observation tremendously

» be quiet: animals tend to avoid loud packs of chatty humans, so keep chit-chat to a whisper; in the Amazon, opt for canoes instead of motorboats – you'll see much more

» have realistic expectations: vegetation can be thick and animals shy – you're not going to see everything in a single hike

FREQUENT FLYERS

For many bird enthusiasts in Peru, the diminutive hummingbirds are among the most delightful to observe. More than 100 species have been recorded in the country, and their exquisite beauty is matched by their extravagant names. There's the 'green-tailed goldenthroat,' the 'spangled coquette,' the 'fawn-breasted brilliant' and 'amethyst-throated sunangel.' Species such as the red-headed Andean hillstar, living in the *puna* (high Andean grasslands), have evolved an amazing strategy to survive a cold night. They go into a state of torpor, which is like a nightly hibernation, by lowering their body temperature by up to 30°C, thus drastically slowing their metabolism.

One of the most unusual species of hummingbird is the marvelous spatuletail, found in the Utcubamba Valley in northern Peru. Full-grown adult males are adorned with two extravagant feathery spatules on the tail, which are used during mating displays to attract females.

hales very rarely. In the coastal desert strip, there are few unique species of land animals. One is the near-threatened Sechuran fox, the smallest of the South American foxes (found in northern Peru), which has a black-tipped tail, pale, sand-colored fur and an omnivorous appetite for small rodents and seed pods.

Reptiles, Amphibians, Insects & Marine Life

The greatest variety of reptiles, amphibians, insects and marine life can be found in the Amazon Basin. Here, you'll find hundreds of species, including toads, tree frogs and thumbnail-sized poison dart frogs (indigenous peoples once used the frogs' deadly poison on the points of their blow-pipe darts). Rivers teem with schools of piranhas, *paiche* and *doncella* (various types of freshwater fish), while the air buzzes with the activity of thousands of insects: armies of ants, squadrons of beetles, as well as katydids, stick insects, caterpillars, spiders, praying mantis, transparent moths, and butterflies of all shapes and sizes. A blue morpho butterfly in flight is a remarkable sight: with wingspans of up to 10cm, their iridescent-blue coloring can seem downright hallucinogenic.

Naturally, there are all kinds of reptiles, too, including tortoises, river turtles, lizards, caimans and, of course, that jungle-movie favorite: the anaconda. An aquatic boa snake that can measure more than 10m in length, it will often ambush its prey by the water's edge, constrict its body around it and then drown it in the river. Caimans, tapirs, deer, turtles and peccaries are all tasty meals for this killer snake; human victims are almost unheard of (unless you're Jennifer Lopez and Ice Cube in a low-rent Hollywood production). Far more worrisome to the average human is the bushmaster, a deadly, reddish brown viper that likes to hang out inside rotting logs and among the buttress roots of trees. Thankfully, it's a retiring creature, and is rarely found on popular trails.

Travellers' Wildlife Guides: Peru, by David Pearson and Les Beletsky, helpfully lists the country's most important and frequently seen birds, mammals, amphibians, reptiles and ecosystem habitats.

Plants

At high elevations in the Andes, especially in the Cordilleras Blanca and Huayhuash, outside Huaraz, there is a cornucopia of distinctive alpine flora and fauna. Plants encountered in this region include native lupins, spiky tussocks of ichu grass, striking quenua *(Polylepis)* trees with their distinctive curly, red paperlike bark, in addition to unusual bromeliads (see p526). Many alpine wildflowers bloom during the trekking season, between May and September.

In the south, you'll find the distinctive *puna* ecosystem. These areas have a fairly limited flora of hard grasses, cushion plants, small herbaceous plants, shrubs and dwarf trees. Many plants in this environment

GIANT FLOWERS OF THE MOUNTAINS

Reaching the staggering height of more than 10m, with an explosive, flower-encrusted cigar shape that looks to be straight out of a Dr Seuss book, the *Puya raimondii* certainly takes the award for most unusual flora. The world's tallest flowering plant is a member of the pineapple family and can take up to a century or more to mature. In full bloom, each plant flaunts up to 8000(!) white flowers, each resembling a lily. It blooms only once in its lifetime, after which the plant dies. Some of the most famous stands of *Puya raimondii* can be found in the Peruvian Andes, in the rocky mountainscape outside Huaraz, near Catac (p394) and Punta Winchus (p392).

have developed small, thick leaves that are less susceptible to frost ar radiation. In the north, there is some *páramo,* which has a harsher cl mate, is less grassy and has an odd mixture of landscapes, including pe bogs, glacier-formed valleys, alpine lakes, wet grasslands and patches scrubland and forest.

Vegetation of the Cloud & Rainforest

As the eastern Andean slopes descend into the western Amazon upland the scenery once again changes. Here, tropical cloud forests – so name because they trap (and help create) clouds that drench the forest in fine mist – allow delicate forms of plant life to survive. Cloud forest tree are adapted to steep slopes, rocky soils and a rugged climate. They ar characterized by low, gnarled growth, dense small-leafed canopies an moss-covered branches supporting a host of plants such as orchids, fern and bromeliads. The mist and the dense vegetation give the cloud fores a mysterious, fairy-tale appearance.

In the Amazon rainforest, the density is astonishing: tens of thousand of species of plant can be found living on top of and around each othe There are strangler figs (known as *matapalos*), palms, ferns, epiphyte bromeliads, flowering orchids, fungi, mosses and lianas, to name a fev Some rainforest trees – such as the 'walking palm' – are supported b strange roots that look like stilts. These are most frequently found wher periodic floods occur; the stilt roots are thought to play a role in keepin the tree upright during the inundation.

One thing that often astounds visitors is the sheer immensity of man; trees. A good example is the *ceiba* (also called the 'kapok' or cotton sil tree), which has huge flattened trunk supports, known as buttresses around its base. The trunk of a ceiba can easily measure 3m across and will grow straight up for 50m before the first branches are reached These spread out into a huge crown with a slightly flattened appearance The staggering height of many Amazon trees, some reaching a height o 80m-plus, creates a whole ecosystem of life at the canopy level, inhabited by creatures that never descend to the forest floor.

Andean Botanical Information System (www. sacha.org) is a veritable online encyclopedia of flowering plants in Peru's coastal areas and the Andes.

Desert Coast

In stark contrast to the Amazon, the coastal desert is generally barren of vegetation, apart from around water sources, which may spring into palm-fringed lagoons. Otherwise, the limited plant life you'll glimpse wil consist of cacti and other succulents, as well as *lomas* (a blend of grasses and herbaceous species in mist-prone areas). On the far north coast, in the ecological reserves around Tumbes (p356), is a small cluster of mangrove forests, as well as a tropical dry forest ecosystem, of which there is little in Peru.

National Parks

Peru's vast wealth of wildlife is protected by a system of national parks and reserves with 60 areas covering almost 15% of the country. The newest is the Sierra del Divisor Reserve Zone, created in 2006 to protect 5 million hectares of rainforest on the Brazilian border. All of these protected areas are administered by the **Instituto Nacional de Recursos Nacionales** (Inrena; www.inrena.gob.pe), a division of the Ministry of Agriculture.

Unfortunately, resources are lacking to conserve protected areas, which are subject to illegal hunting, fishing, logging and mining. The government simply doesn't have the funds to hire enough rangers and provide them with the equipment necessary to patrol the parks. That said, a number of international agencies and not-for-profit organizations contribute money, staff and resources to help with conservation and education projects.

Environmental Issues

Peru faces major challenges in the stewardship of its natural resources, with problems compounded by a lack of law enforcement and its impenetrable geography. Deforestation and erosion are major issues, as is industrial pollution, urban sprawl and the continuing attempted eradication of coca plantations on some Andean slopes (see boxed text below). In addition, the Inter-Oceanic Hwy through the heart of the Amazon may imperil thousands of square kilometers of rainforest.

A Neotropical Companion, by John Kricher, provides an introduction to the wildlife and ecosystems of the New World tropics, including coastal and highland regions.

Deforestation & Water Problems

At the ground level, clear-cutting of the highlands for firewood, of the rainforests for valuable hardwoods, and of both to clear land for agriculture, oil drilling and mining has led to severe erosion. In the highlands, where deforestation and overgrazing of Andean woodlands and *puna* grass is severe, soil quality is rapidly deteriorating. In the Amazon rainforest, deforestation has led to erosion and a decline in bellwether species such as frogs. Erosion has also led to decreased water quality in this area, where silt-laden water is unable to support microorganisms at the base of the food chain.

COCA CULTIVATION PAST & PRESENT

Cultivation of the coca plant dates back at least 5000 years and its traditional uses have always included the practical and the divine. In pre-Hispanic times, chewing coca was a traditional treatment for everything from a simple toothache to exhaustion. It has also long been used in religious rituals as a sacred offering. When the Spaniards arrived in the 15th century, they attempted to outlaw the 'heathen' practice of cultivating this 'diabolical' plant. However, with coca-chewing an essential part of life for the colony's indigenous labor pool (it is a mild appetite suppressant and stimulant – on par with coffee), the Spanish ultimately reversed their policies.

Today, there continues to be a struggle surrounding coca, but it has to do with its derivative product, cocaine (in which a paste derived from coca leaves is treated with kerosene and refined into a powder). In an attempt to stem the flow of this narcotic, the US has led eradication programs of coca plants in Peru. These programs appear to have done little to curb coca's cultivation (or the cocaine trade), but the herbicides employed have damaged some agricultural lands in indigenous communities. Critics of the US-sponsored programs – including Peruvian *cocaleros* (coca growers' associations) and President Evo Morales of Bolivia – have called for regulation of eradication. The issue, however, remains far from resolved.

Other water-related problems include pollution from mining in t
highlands. Sewage contamination along the coast has led to many bea
es around some coastal cities being declared unfit for swimming. In t
south, pollution and overfishing have led to the continued decline of t
Humboldt penguin (its numbers have declined by more than a thi
since the 1980s).

Protective Steps

In the early 1990s, Peru took steps to formulate a national environment
and natural resource code, but the government (occupied with a bloo
guerrilla war in the highlands) lacked the funding and political will
enforce it. In 1995 Peru's congress created a National Environment
Council (CONAM) to manage the country's national environmental p
icy. Though there have been some success stories (eg flagrant pollute
being fined for poor practices), enforcement remains weak.

Some positive measures are being taken to help protect the country
environment. For example, the Peruvian government and private inte
ests within the tourism industry have come together to develop sustai
able travel projects in the Amazon. In 2005, Peru became one of 17 Lat
American countries, along with Spain, to sign the Amazon River Declar
tion, which calls for environmental safeguards to ensure biodiversity an
for the development of tourism strategies that will fight rural pover
and spur regional development in sustainable ways.

Monga Bay (www.
mongabay.com)
is an excellent
online resource
for news and in-
formation related
to the Amazon
and rainforests
around the world.

Survival Guide

Directory A–Z

Accommodations

Peru has accommodations to suit every budget, especially in tourist hubs and cities. Listings are organized in order of our preference, considering value for cost. All prices listed are high-season rates for rooms that include private bathroom, unless otherwise specified.

Many lodgings offer laundry service and free short-term luggage storage (ask for a receipt). *Habitación simple* refers to a single room. A *habitación doble* features twin beds while a *habitación matrimonial* has a double or queen-sized bed.

Street noise can be an issue in any lodging, so select your room accordingly. It's always OK to ask to see a room before committing.

Homestays are sometimes offered by Spanish schools. Campgrounds are few.

Rates

Rates in this book are for high season. Note that prices may fluctuate with exchange rates.

Foreigners do not have to pay the 18% hotel tax (sometimes included in rates quoted in soles), but may have to present their passport and tourist card to photocopy. A credit-card transaction surcharge of 7% or more does not include the home bank's foreign-currency exchange fee. US dollars may be accepted, but the exchange rate may be poor.

In the remote jungle lodges of the Amazon and in popular beach destinations such as Máncora, all-inclusive resort-style pricing is more the norm.

In Cuzco, demand is very high during the high season (June to August). Other busy times include Inti Raymi, Semana Santa and Fiestas Patrias (see p534), when advance reservations are a must. In Lima, prices remain steady throughout the year; look for last-minute specials online. Paying cash always helps; ask for discounts for long-term stays.

Apartments

A limited number of short-term rentals, primarily in Lima, attend mid- to high-end needs. Check www.vrbo. com and www.cyberrentals. com for listings.

Hostels

Hostelling International (www.hihostels.com) has hostels in the country's main tourist areas, including Lima, Cuzco and Arequipa. Beyond that, principal tourist towns (especially Lima) have a wide range of options, from party hostel to mellow ones. Most feature the gamut of amenities. Rates vary from S10 to S35 per person.

Hotels

BUDGET

Hostales, hospedajes and *albergues* are Peru's cheapest accommodations. In this price range, expect to find small rooms, with a shared or private bathroom. In the major cities, these options will generally include hot showers; in more rural and remote areas, they likely will not. Some budget inns will include a very simple breakfast in the rate, such as instant coffee with toast.

Avoid rooms appearing insecure; test the locks on doors and windows. Shopping around makes a difference.

MIDRANGE

Rooms generally have private bathrooms with hot-water showers and small portable heaters or fans. Some are also equipped with air-conditioning. Amenities

---

ACCOMMODATIONS PRICES

Price ranges for this book are:

Budget Dorm rooms and doubles up to S85

Midrange From S85 to S250 per double room

Top End More than S250 per double room

ay include cable TV, in-room telephones and safes. ontinental or American-tyle breakfasts are usually ncluded.

OP END

eru's top hotels are gener-ly equipped with en suite athrooms with bathtubs, nternational direct dial hones, handy dual-voltage utlets, central heating or r-conditioning, hairdry-rs, in-room safes, cable TV nd internet access (either hrough high-speed cable or vi-fi); some may come with ninifridges, microwaves or offee makers. A large high-nd spot may also feature bar, cafe or restaurant (or everal), as well as room ervice, concierge services nd an obliging, multilingual taff. Expect the biggest laces (particularly in Lima) o come with business enters, spas and beauty alons. In the Amazon, where onditions tend to be iso-ated, high-end lodgings have ewer amenities and are more ustic.

Reservations

Since many flights into Lima rrive late at night, it's inad-visable to begin searching or a place to sleep upon ar-ival. Reserve your first night ahead; most hotels also can arrange airport pickup. Around the country, reser-vations are a necessity for stays during a major festival (such as Inti Raymi in Cuzco) or a holiday such as Semana Santa (Easter Week), when all of Peru is on vacation. In

the Amazon, reservations are needed at remote lodges. In smaller villages and areas off the beaten path, service tends to be on a first-come, first-served basis.

Cheap budget places may not honor a reservation if you arrive late. Even if you've made a reservation, it is best to confirm your arrival time. Late check-in is not a prob-lem at many midrange and top-end hotels, in which case a deposit may be required. Some lodges, especially in the Amazon, may also require all or part of the payment up front. Make sure your travel plans are firm if you are paying in advance, as securing refunds can be a challenge.

Reserving online is convenient, but off-season walk-in rates may be lower. At top-end hotels, however, last-minute online deals are the norm, so always check a hotel's website for discounts and special promotional packages.

Business Hours

Hours are variable and li-able to change, especially in small towns, where regular

hours are irregular. Posted hours are a guideline, not gospel, and services can be slow.

Most cities have 24-hour ATMs. Lima has the most continuity of services. In other major cities, taxi driv-ers often know where the late-night stores and phar-macies are.

Reviews in this book only list opening hours which vary from the standard given here.

Shops 9am-6pm, some 9am-6pm Sat

Government offices & businesses 9am-5pm Mon-Fri

Banks 9am-6pm Mon-Fri, 9am-1pm Sat

Restaurants 10am to 10pm, many close between 3-6pm

Museums Often close on Monday

Customs Regulations

Peru allows duty-free impor-tation of 3L of alcohol and 20 packs of cigarettes, 50 cigars or 250g of tobacco. You can import US$300 of gifts. Legally, you are allowed to bring in such items as a lap-top, camera, portable music player, kayak, climbing gear, mountain bike or similar items for personal use.

It is illegal to take pre-Columbian or colonial artifacts out of Peru, and it is illegal to bring them into most countries. If purchasing reproductions, buy only from a reputable dealer and ask for a detailed receipt. Purchasing animal products made from endan-gered species or even just

HOT SHOWERS

Peru's budget accommodations don't always have hot water, and some only have it for certain hours of the day. Early birds often use up all the hot water, so plan accordingly.

Electric showerheads require care. Switch them on for a hot shower and wait a few minutes. Water is hotter if the pressure is low. Don't fiddle with the heating unit while the water is on or you may get a shock. Tall travel-ers: keep your eyes peeled.

transporting them around Peru is also illegal.

Coca leaves are legal in Peru, but not in most other countries, even in the form of tea bags. People subject to random drug testing should be aware that coca, even in the form of tea, may leave trace amounts in urine.

Check with your own home government about customs restrictions and duties on any expensive or rare items you intend to bring back. Most countries allow their citizens to import a limited number of items duty-free, though these regulations are subject to change.

Discount Cards

An official International Student Identity Card (ISIC), with a photograph, can get you a 50% discount at some museums and attractions and for organized tours. Senior discount cards are not recognized.

Electricity

Peru uses the following electrical plugs.

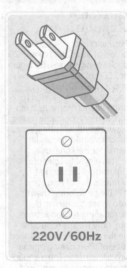

220V/60Hz

220V/60Hz

Embassies & Consulates

Most foreign embassies are in Lima, with some consular services in major tourist centers such as Cuzco.

It is important to realize what your embassy can and can't do if you get into trouble. Your embassy will not be sympathetic if you end up in jail after committing a crime, even if such actions are legal in your own country. If all your money and documents are stolen, the embassy can help you get a new passport.

Call in advance to double-check operating hours or schedule an appointment. While many consulates and embassies are staffed during regular business hours, attention to the public is often more limited. Public operating hours are listed below. For after-hours and emergency contact numbers, check individual websites.

Australia (☑01-630-0500; www.embassy.gov.au/peru; Suite 1301, Av La Paz 1049, piso 10, Miraflores, Lima; ☺9am-5pm Mon-Fri)

Belgium (☑01-241-7566; www.diplomatie.be/lima; Av Angamos Oeste 380, Miraflores, Lima; ☺8:30am-4pm Mon-Fri)

Bolivia Lima (☑01-440-209 Los Castaños 235, San Isidro; ☺8am-4pm); Puno (☑/fax 051-35 1251; 2nd fl, Jirón Arequipa 136; ☺8am-2pm Mon-Fri

Brazil (☑01-512-0830; www embajadabrasil.org.pe; Av José Pardo 850, Miraflores, Lima; ☺9:30am-noon & 4-5pm Mon-Fri)

Canada (☑01-319-3200; www.canadainternational. gc.ca/peru-perou/; Bolognesi 228, Miraflores, Lima; ☺8am-12:30pm & 1:15-5pm Mon-Thu 8am-12:30pm Fri)

Chile (☑01-710-2211; chile abroad.gov.cl/peru; Av Javier Prado Oeste 790, San Isidro, Lima; ☺9am-5pm Mon-Thu, 9am-2pm Fri)

Colombia Lima (☑01-441-0954; Av Jorge Basadre 1580, San Isidro; ☺8:30am-1pm & 2:30-5:30pm Mon-Fri); Iquitos (☑065-23-6246; Araujo 431; ☺9am-12:30pm & 2-4:30pm Mon-Fri)

Ecuador Lima (☑01-212-417 www.mecuadorperu.org.pe; Las Palmeras 356, San Isidro; ☺9am-1pm Mon-Fri); Tumbes (☑072-525-949; 3rd fl, Jirón Bolívar 129, Plaza de Armas; ☺9am-1pm & 4-6pm Mon-Fri)

France (☑01-215-8400; www ambafrance-pe.org; Av Arequipa 3415, San Isidro, Lima; ☺9am-noon)

Germany (☑01-203-5940; www.lima.diplo.de; Av Arequipa 4210, Miraflores, Lima; ☺8:30-11:30am Mon-Fri)

Ireland (☑01-449-6289; irishconsulperu@yahoo.ca; Miguel Alegre Rodríguez 182, Miraflores, Lima) Lima has only an honorary consul with limited services.

Israel (☑01-418-0500; lima. mfa.gov.il; Centro Empresarial Platinum Plaza II, Av Andres Reyes 437, piso 13, San Isidro, Lima; ☺9am-12:30pm Mon-Fri)

Italy (☑01-463-2727; www. amblima.esteri.it; Av Guiseppe Garibaldi 298, Jesús María, Lima; ☺8:30-11am Mon-Fri)

Netherlands (☑01-213-9800; www.nlgovlim.com; 13th fl, Torre Parque Mar, Ave José Larco 1301, Miraflores, Lima;

8:30am-12:45pm & 1:30-5pm
on-Thu, 8:30am-1pm Fri)

pain (☎01-513-7930; www.
aec.es/subwebs/Consulados/
ma; Calle Los Pinos, San
idro, Lima; ☺8:30am-1pm
on-Fri)

witzerland (☎01-264-
305; www.eda.admin.ch/lima;
v Salaverry 3240, San Isidro,
ma; ☺8am-1pm & 2-4:30pm
on-Thu, 8am-2pm Fri)

K (☎01-617-3000; ukinperu.
o.gov.uk; 22nd fl, Torre
arque Mar, Av José Larco 1301,
iraflores, Lima; ☺9am-4pm
on-Thu, 9am-1pm Fri)

SA (☎01-618-2000; lima.
sembassy.gov; Av La Encalada
n, cuadra 17, Monterrico,
ma; ☺8-11:30am Mon-Fri)
his place is a fortress – call
efore showing up in person.
or up-to-date visa informa-
on on travel to Peru, visit
www.lonelyplanet.com.

If you need to extend your
tay in Peru, receive an exit
tamp or secure a new entry
ard, see p540 for *oficinas*
e migraciónes (immigration
ffices).

Gay & Lesbian Travelers

Peru is a strongly conserva-
ive, Catholic country. While
many Peruvians will tolerate
omosexuality on a 'Don't
sk; don't tell' level when
ealing with foreign travelrs, gay rights in a political or
egal context does not exist
s an issue. When it does
rise in public, hostility is
most often the response. As
a result, many gays in Peru
don't publicly identify as
homosexual, and some men,
in keeping with the macho
nature of Peruvian culture,
will identify as straight,
even if they have sex with
other men or transvestite
prostitutes. Effeminate men,
even if they are straight, may
be called *maricón* (which
roughly translates as 'fag-
got'), although this word has
come to be a catch-all insult
that is also used in jest.

Public displays of affection
among homosexual cou-
ples is rarely seen. Outside
gay clubs, it is advisable to
keep a low profile. HIV/AIDS
transmission, both homo-
sexual and heterosexual, is a
growing problem. Lima is the
most accepting of gay people, but this is on a relative
scale. Beyond that, the tourist towns of Cuzco, Arequipa
and Trujillo tend to be more
tolerant than the norm.

FYI: the rainbow flag seen
around Cuzco and in the
Andes is *not* a gay pride flag –
it's the flag of the Inca empire.

Several organizations
provide resources for gay
and lesbian travelers:

Deambiente.com (www.
deambiente.com, www.
introspektivo.com) Spanish-
language online magazine
about politics and pop culture, along nightlife listings.

Gay Lima (lima.queercity.
info) A handy guide to the
latest gay and gay-friendly
spots in the capital, along
with plenty of links.

Gayperu.com (www.gayperu.
com) A modern, Spanish-
language online guide that
lists everything from bars
to bathhouses; also runs a
multilingual travel agency
(www.gayperutravel.com).

Global Gayz (www.glo
balgayz.com) Excellent,
country-specific information
about Peru's gay scene and

PRACTICALITIES

» Peru's government-leaning *El Comercio* (www.
elcomercioperu.com.pe) is the leading daily. There's
also the slightly left-of-center *La República* (www.
larepublica.com.pe) and *Peruvian Times* (www.peruvi
antimes.com) in English.

» The most well-known political and cultural weekly is
Caretas (www.caretas.com.pe), while *Etiqueta Negra*
(etiquetanegra.com.pe) focuses on culture. A good
bilingual travel publication is the monthly *Rumbos*
(www.rumbosdelperu.com).

» Cable and satellite TV are widely available for a fix of
CNN or even Japanese news.

» Helpful online resources in English are expatperu.
com and www.theperuguide.com.

» Electrical current is 220V, 60Hz AC. Standard
outlets accept round prongs, some have dual-voltage
outlets which take flat prongs. Even so, your adapter
may need a built-in surge protector.

» Peru uses the metric system but gas (petrol) is
measured in US gallons.

FOOD PRICES

Restaurant listings are organized according to author
preference, considering value for cost. Mid- to high-end
restaurants charge a 10% service fee and a 19% tax.
See p508 for more on Peruvian cuisine. Price ranges for
this book are:

Budget Mains less than S20

Midrange Mains between S20 to S45

Top End Mains more than S45

politics, with links to international resources.

Lima Tours (Map p58; ☎01-619-6901; www.limatours.com.pe; Jirón Belén 1040, Central Lima) A travel agency that is not exclusively gay, but that organizes gay-friendly group trips around the country.

Movimiento Homosexual de Lima (☎01-332-2945; www.mhol.org.pe; Mariscal Miller 822, Jesús María) Peru's best-known gay and lesbian activist organization.

Purpleroofs.com (www.purpleroofs.com) Massive GLBT portal with links to a few tour operators and gay-friendly accommodations in Peru.

Rainbow Peruvian Tours (Map p76; ☎01-215-6000; www.perurainbow.com; Río de Janeiro 216, San Isidro, Lima) Gay-owned tour agency based in Lima, with a multilingual website.

Holidays

Major holidays may be celebrated for days around the official date.

Fiestas Patrias (National Independence Days) is the biggest national holiday, when the entire nation seems to be on the move. Major national, regional and religious holidays include the following:

New Year's Day January 1
Good Friday March/April
Labor Day May 1
Inti Raymi June 24

IMPORTANT DOCUMENTS

All important documents (passport, credit cards, travel insurance policy, driver's license etc) should be photocopied before you leave home. Leave one copy at home and keep another with you, separate from the originals.

Feast of Sts Peter & Paul June 29
National Independence Days July 28-29
Feast of Santa Rosa de Lima August 30
Battle of Angamos Day October 8
All Saints Day November 1
Feast of the Immaculate Conception December 8
Christmas December 25

Insurance

Having a travel-insurance policy to cover theft, loss, accidents and illness is highly recommended. Many policies include a card with toll-free or collect-call hotlines for 24-hour assistance (carry it with you). Not all policies compensate travelers for misrouted or lost luggage. Check the fine print to see if it excludes 'dangerous activities,' which can include scuba diving, motorcycling and even trekking. Also check if the policy coverage includes worst-case scenarios, such as evacuations and flights home. A variety of travel-insurance policies are available. Those handled by STA Travel (www.statravel.com) and other budget travel organizations are usually good value.

You must usually report any loss or theft to local police (or airport authorities) within 24 hours. Make sure you keep all documentation to make any claim.

Internet Access

Most regions have excellent internet connections and reasonable prices; it is typical for hotels and hostels to have wi-fi or computer terminals. Family guesthouses, particularly outside urban areas, lag behind in this area. Internet cafes can be found pretty well everywhere, even in villages where they provide the only Friday-night entertainment for youth. Rates start

at S1 per hour, with very high rates only in remote areas.

In this book, @ indicates computer terminals and 🛜 indicates wi-fi access.

Language Course

Peru has schools in Lima, Cuzco, Arequipa, Huaraz, Puerto Maldonado and Huancayo. You can also study Quechua with private teachers or at one of the various language institutes in Lima, Cuzco and Huancayo.

Legal Matters

Your own embassy is of limited help if you get into trouble with the law in Peru, where you are presumed guilty until proven innocent. you are the victim, the *policía de turismo* (tourist police; Poltur) can help, with limited English. Poltur stations are found in major cities.

Be aware that some police officers (even tourist police) have a reputation for corruption, but that bribery is illegal. Since most travelers won't have to deal with traffic police, the most likely place you'll be expected to pay officials a little extra is (sometimes) at land borders This too is illegal, and if you have the time and fortitude to stick to your guns, you'll eventually be allowed in without paying a fee.

Avoid having any conversation with someone who offers you drugs. In fact, talking to any stranger on the street can hold risks. There have been reports of travelers being stopped soon after by plainclothes police officers and accused of talking to a drug dealer. Should you be stopped by a plainclothes officer, don't hand over any documents or money. Never get into a vehicle with someone claiming to be a police officer, but insist on going to a bona fide police station on foot. Peru has draconian penalties for possessing ever

small amount of drugs;
minimum sentences are
several years in jail.

If you are imprisoned for
any reason, make sure that
someone else knows about it
as soon as possible. Extended pre-trial detainments are
not uncommon. Peruvians
bring food and clothing to
family members who are in
prison, where conditions are
extremely harsh.

If you think that you were
ripped off by a hotel or
tour operator, register your
complaint with the **National
Institute for the Defense
of Competition and the
Protection of Intellectual
Property** (Indecopi; ☎01-224-
7800; www.indecopi.gob.pe, in
Spanish) in Lima.

Maps

The best road map of Peru
is the 1:2,000,000 *Mapa
Vial* published by Lima 2000
and available in better bookstores. The 1:1,500,000 *Peru
South and Lima* country
map, published by International Travel Maps, covers the
country in good detail south
of a line drawn east to west
through Tingo María, and has
a good street map of Lima,
San Isidro, Miraflores and
Barranco on the reverse side.

For topographical maps, go
to the **Instituto Geográfico
Nacional** (IGN; ☎01-475-3030,
ext 119; www.ign.gob.pe; Aramburu 1190-98, Surquillo, Lima;
☺8am-6pm Mon-Fri, to 1pm
Sat), with reference maps and

others for sale. In January, the
IGN closes early, so call ahead.
High-scale topographic maps
for trekking are available,
though sheets of border areas
might be hard to get. Geological and demographic maps
and CD-ROMs are also sold.

Topographic, city and
road maps are also at the
South American Explorers'
clubhouses in Lima (see the
boxed text, p96) and Cuzco
(p229).

Up-to-date topo maps are
often available from outdoor
outfitters in major trekking
centers such as Cuzco,
Huaraz and Arequipa. If you
are bringing along a GPS
unit, ensure that your power
source adheres to Peru's
220V, 60Hz AC standard and
always carry a compass.

Money

Peru uses the *nuevo sol* (S).
For exchange rates, see p17.

Carrying cash, an ATM
card, as well as a credit card
that can be used for cash advances in case of emergency,

is advisable. When receiving
local currency, always ask
for *billetes pequeños* (small
bills), as S100 bills are hard
to change in small towns or
for small purchases. Carry
as much spare change as
possible, especially in small
towns. Public bathrooms
often charge a small fee for
use and getting change for
paper money can be darn
near impossible.

The best places to ex-
change money are normally
casas de cambio (foreign-
exchange bureaus), which
are fast, have longer hours
and often give slightly better rates than banks. Many
places accept US dollars. Do
not accept torn money as
it will likely not be accepted
by Peruvians. It is best not
to change money on the
street as counterfeits are a
problem. See the boxed text,
p536, for more.

See also p16 for informa-
tion on costs and money.

ATMs

Cajeros automáticos (ATMs)
are found in nearly every
city and town in Peru, as
well as at major airports,
bus terminals and shopping
areas. ATMs are linked to the
international Plus (Visa), Cirrus (Maestro/MasterCard)
systems, American Express
and other networks. They will
accept your bank or credit
card as long as you have a
four-digit PIN. To avoid problems, notify your bank that
you'll be using your ATM card
abroad.

ATMs are a convenient
way of obtaining cash, but

rates are usually lower than at *casas de cambio*. Both US dollars and *nuevos soles* are readily available from Peruvian ATMs. Your home bank may charge an additional fee for each foreign ATM transaction.

ATMs are normally open 24 hours. For safety reasons, use ATMs inside banks with security guards, preferably during daylight hours.

Cash

The *nuevo sol* ('new sun') comes in bills of S10, S20, S50, S100 and (rarely) S200. It is divided into 100 *céntimos*, with copper-colored coins of S0.05, S0.10 and S0.20, and silver-colored S0.50 and S1 coins. In addi-

tion, there are bimetallic S2 and S5 coins with a copper-colored center inside a silver-colored ring.

US dollars are accepted by many tourist-oriented businesses, though you'll need *nuevos soles* to pay for local transportation, meals and other incidentals.

Changing Money

Carrying cash enables you to get the top exchange rates quickly. The best currency for exchange is the US dollar, although the euro is increasingly accepted in major tourist centers. Other hard currencies can be exchanged, but usually with difficulty and only in major cities. All

foreign currencies must be flawless condition.

Cambistas (money-changers) hang out on street corners near banks and *casas de cambio* and give competitive rates (there's only a little flexibility for bargaining), but are not always honest. Officially, they shou wear a vest and badge identifying themselves as legal. They're useful after regular business hours or at border where there aren't any othe options.

Credit Cards

Many top-end hotels and shops accept *tarjetas de crédito* (credit cards) but usually charge you a 7% (or greater) fee for using them. The amount you'll eventual pay is not based on the poir of-sale exchange rate, but the rate your bank chooses to use when the transactior posts to your account, som times weeks later. Your ban may also tack on a surcharg and additional fees for each foreign-currency transactio

The most widely accepte cards in Peru are Visa and MasterCard, although Ame can Express and a few othe are valid in some establishments, as well as for cash advances at ATMs. Before you leave home, notify your bank that you'll be using yo credit card abroad.

Taxes, Tipping & Refunds

At Peruvian airports, interna tional departure tax (p543) is payable in US dollars or *nuevos soles* (cash only), though it may be included ii the ticket price. Expensive hotels will add a 19% sales tax and 10% service charge the latter is generally not included in quoted rates. No Peruvians may be eligible fo a refund of the sales tax only (see p530). A few restauran charge combined taxes of more than 19%, plus a servi charge (*servicio* or *propina* of 10%. At restaurants that don't do this, you may tip 1C

FUNNY MONEY

Counterfeiting of both US and local-currency bills has become a serious problem in Peru. Merchants are extremely careful about accepting large-denomination notes; you should be, too. Everyone has their own technique for spotting a fake – some can feel the difference in paper quality, while others will sniff out counterfeit ink. You should look for a combination of signs; new forgeries simulate some security features, but never all of them. Politely refuse to accept *any* worn, torn or damaged bills, even small-denomination notes, since many businesses will not accept these.

Watch out for the following issues:

» Check the watermark – most fake bills have these, but real bills will have a section where the mark is made by discernibly thinner paper.

» The writing along the top of the bill should be embossed – run your finger to see that it is raised from the paper and test the back for an impression.

» The line underneath this writing is made up of tiny words – if it's a solid line, then it's a fake.

» The value of the bill written on the side should appear metallic and be slightly green, blue and pink at different angles – fake bills are only pink and have no hologram.

» The metal strip running through the note has the word 'Peru' repeatedly written along its length in tiny letters when held up to the light – fake bills also have this, but the letters are messier and difficult to read.

» The tiny pieces of colored thread and holographic dots scattered on the bill should be embedded in the paper, not glued on.

by Rafael Wlodarski

r good service. Taxi drivers
o not generally expect tips
unless they've assisted with
eavy luggage), but porters
nd tour guides do. There is
o system of sales-tax re-
nds for shoppers.

ost

he privatized postal system
run by **Serpost** (www.
erpost.com.pe). Its service is
airly efficient and reliable,
ut surprisingly expensive.
lost international mail will
ake about two weeks to
rrive from Lima; longer from
he provinces.

Lista de correos (general
elivery or poste restante)
an be sent to any major
ost office. Bring your
assport when picking up
nail and ask the post-office
lerk to check alphabeti-
ally under the initial letter
f each of your first, last and
niddle names, as well as
nder 'M' (for Mr, Ms et al).
sk your correspondents to
nake sure that your name is
learly printed and to capital-
ze and underline your last
ame to avoid confusion. For
xample:

  Margarita SILVA
  Lista de Correos
  Correo Central
  Lima
  Peru

or express mail and pack-
ges, international couriers
uch as **Federal Express**
www.fedex.com.pe) and **DHL**
www.dhl.com.pe) are more
eliable than post offices, but
nay only have drop-off cent-
rs in Lima or other major
ities. They are also more
xpensive than Serpost.

Safe Travel

There is no shortage of wild
stories about traveling in
Peru, including periodic pro-
ests, thefts and bus drivers
who act as if every bend in
he road should be assaulted
at Autobahn speeds. Cer-
ainly, the country is not for
he faint of heart. Buses are

filled to overflowing – and
then some. Violent political
protests and roadblocks can
shut down arterial highways
for days, even weeks. And
Peru's grinding poverty –
more than half of the country
lives under the poverty line –
means that petty crime is
rampant. The biggest an-
noyance most travelers will
experience, however, is a
case of the runs, so don't let
paranoia ruin your holiday.

As with every other place
on earth, a little common
sense goes a very long way.

Thefts, Muggings & Other Crime

The situation has improved
significantly since the 1980s,
especially in Lima. Yet street
crimes such as pickpock-
eting, bag-snatching and
muggings are still common.
Sneak theft is by far the most
widespread type of crime,
while muggings happen with
less regularity. Even so, they
do happen.

Use basic precautions
and a reasonable amount of
awareness, however, and you
probably won't be robbed.
Some tips:
» crowded places such as
bus terminals, train stations,
markets and fiestas are the
haunts of pickpockets; wear
your day pack in front of you
or carry a bag that fits snugly
under your arm
» thieves look for easy targets, such as a bulging wallet
in a back pocket or a camera
held out in the open; keep
spending money in your front

pocket and your camera
stowed when it's not in use
» passports and larger sums
of cash are best carried in
a money belt or an inside
pocket that can be zipped
or closed – or better yet,
stowed in a safe at your hotel
» snatch theft can occur
if you place a bag on the
ground (even for a few seconds), or while you're asleep
on an overnight bus; never
leave a bag with your wallet
and passport in the overhead
rack of a bus
» don't keep valuables in
bags that will be unattended
» blending in helps: walking
around town in brand-new
hiking gear or a shiny leather
jacket will draw attention;
stick to simple clothing
» leave jewelry and fancy
watches at home
» hotels – especially cheap
ones – aren't always trust-
worthy; lock valuables inside
your luggage, or use safety
deposit services
» walk purposefully wherever
you are going, even if you are
lost; if you need to examine
your map, duck into a shop
or restaurant
Some thieves work in pairs or
groups. One person creates a
distraction as another robs.
This can take the form of a
bunch of kids fighting in front
of you, an elderly person 'accidentally' bumping into you
or perhaps someone spilling
something on your clothes.
Some razor-blade artists
may slit open your bag,

whether it's on your back or on the luggage rack of a bus.

In some cases, there have been robberies and armed muggings of trekkers on popular hiking trails around Huaraz (p374), and jungle treks in the south (p263). Going as part of a group with a local guide may help prevent this. In addition, the area around Tingo María (p306), on the eastern edge of the central highlands, is a renowned bandit area, with armed robberies and other crimes regular occurrences. Keep any activities in the area, including bus rides, to daylight hours.

Armed taxi robberies and rapes have been reported in Cuzco. Always take an official taxi at night and from the airport or bus terminals. If threatened, it's better just to give up your goods than face harm.

In recent years, 'express' kidnappings have been recorded, particularly in some of the unsavory neighborhoods that surround the airport in Lima. An armed attacker (or attackers) grabs someone out of a taxi or abducts them off the street, then forces them to go to the nearest bank to withdraw cash using their ATM cards. Victims who do not resist their attackers generally don't suffer serious physical harm.

The *policía de turismo* (tourist police, aka Poltur) can be found in major cities and tourist areas and can be helpful with criminal matters. If you are unsure how to locate them, contact the main office in Lima. If you are the victim of a crime, file a report with the tourist police immediately. At some point, inform your country's embassy about what has happened. They won't be able to do much, but embassies do keep track of crime geared at foreigners as a way of alerting other travelers to potential dangers.

If you have taken out travel insurance and need to make a claim, Poltur will provide you with a police report. Airlines may reissue a lost ticket for a fee (though this is increasingly unnecessary, since most airlines use electronic tickets). Stolen passports can be reissued at your embassy, though you may be asked for an alternative form of identification first. After receiving your new passport, go to the nearest Peruvian immigration office to get a new tourist card. For more on legal issues, see p534.

For issues of safety affecting female travelers, turn to p541.

Corruption & Scams

The military and police (even sometimes the tourist police) have a reputation for corruption. While a foreigner may experience petty harassment (usually to procure payment of a bribe), most police officers are quite courteous to tourists, or just leave them alone.

Perhaps the most pernicious thing travelers face are the persistent touts that gather at bus stations, train stations, airports and other tourist spots to offer everything from discounted hotel rooms to local tours. Many touts – among them, many taxi drivers – will say just about anything to steer you to places they represent. They will tell you the establishment you've chosen is a notorious drug den, it's closed down or is overbooked. Do not believe everything you hear. If you have doubts about a place you've decided to stay at, ask to see a room before paying up.

Moreover, it is not advisable to book hotels, travel arrangements or transportation through these independent agents. Often, they will demand cash up-front for services that never materialize. Stick to reputable, well-recommended agencies and you'll be assured a good time.

Transport Issues

When taking buses, choose operators carefully. The cheapest companies will be the most likely to employ reckless drivers and have roadside breakdowns. Overnight travel by bus can get brutally cold in the highlands (take a blanket or a sleeping bag). In some parts, nighttime trips are also subject to the vagaries of roadside bandits, who create impromptu road blocks, then relieve passengers of their valuables. For more on overland transport in Peru, see p548.

Environmental Hazards

Some of Peru's natural hazards include earthquakes and avalanches. Rescues in remote regions are often done on foot because of the inability of helicopters to reach some of the country's more challenging topography. Perhaps the most common hazard is travelers' diarrhea, which comes from consuming contaminated food or water. Other problems include altitude sickness, animal and insect bites, sunburn, heat exhaustion and even hypothermia. You can take precautions for most of these. See p551 for medical advice.

Protests & Other Conflict

During the Internal Conflict, through the 1980s and into the 1990s, terrorism, civil strife and kidnappings mean that entire regions were off limits to both foreign and domestic travelers. Thankfully, the situation has improved dramatically and travelers visit much of the country without ever encountering problems. Even so, Peru remains a politically volatile place and public protests are a familiar sight. Generally speaking, these have little effects on tourists, other than blocking roads, but on some occasions they do turn violent. It is worth staying

ware of current events while
 the country; and if a road
 blocked or an area cut off,
espect the situation. Being
 foreigner will not grant you
nmunity from violence.

In the news, a Sendero
uminoso (Shining Path; see
 292) resurgence has
rought isolated incidents of
iolence in rural areas in the
rovinces of Ayacucho, Cuzco,
luancavelica, Huánuco,
unín and San Martín. These
re generally directed at the
'eruvian military or the police.
ven so, it is worth exercising
aution: avoid transit through
solated areas in these regions
t night and always check
vith reputable tour opera-
ors before heading out on a
emote trekking route.

Likewise, drug trafficking
reas can be dangerous,
especially at night. Travelers should avoid the upper
Río Huallaga valley between
Tingo María and Juanjui and
he Río Apurímac valley near
Ayacucho, where the majority
of Peru's illegal drug-growing
akes place. Exercise similar
aution near the Colombian
border, where trafficking also
goes on. For more informa-
ion on drug-related legal
natters, see p534.

Landmines

A half century of armed
conflict over the Cordillera
del Condor region on Peru's
northeastern border with Ecuador was finally resolved in
1998. However, unexploded
ordinance (UXO) in the area
has not been completely
cleaned up. Only use official
border crossings and don't
stray from the beaten path
when traveling in this region.

Shopping

Arts and crafts are inevitably sold wherever tourists
gather. Popular souvenirs
include alpaca wool sweaters
and scarves, woven textiles,
ceramics, masks, gold and
silver jewelry and the backpacker favorite: Inca Kola
T-shirts. While Lima offers a

wealth of crafts, highly specialized regional items may
be difficult to find.

Expensive foreign-language
books and magazines are
stocked at better bookstores,
especially in Lima and Cuzco.

Bargaining is the norm
at street stalls and markets,
where it's cash only. Prices
are fixed in upscale stores,
which may add a surcharge
for credit card transactions.

Solo Travelers

Peru's top tourist spots are
good places for solo travelers. Inexpensive hostels with
communal kitchens encour-
age social exchange, while
a large number of language
schools, tours and volunteer
organizations provide every
traveler with plenty of opportunities to meet others.

Outside popular areas,
this type of infrastructure
may be limited, in which case
you might be spending a lot
more time by yourself. It is
not recommended to under-
take long treks in the wilderness on your own.

For more specific advice
for women travelers, see
p541.

Telephone

A few public pay phones
operated by **Movistar**
(www.movistar.com.pe) are
still around, especially in
small towns. They work with
phone cards which can be
purchased at supermarkets
and groceries. Often internet
cafes have 'net-to-phone' and
'net-to-net' capabilities (such
as Skype), to talk for pennies
or even for free.

When calling Peru from
abroad, dial the international
access code for the country
you're in, then Peru's country
code (51), then the area code
without the 0 and finally, the
local number. When making
international calls from Peru,
dial the international access
code (00), then the country
code of where you're calling

to, then the area code and finally, the local phone number.

In Peru, any telephone
number beginning with a 9 is
a cell-phone number. Num-
bers beginning with 0800
are often toll-free only when
dialed from private phones.
To make a credit card or
collect call using AT&T,
dial ☎0800-50288. For an
online telephone directory,
see www.paginasamarillas.
com.pe.

Cell Phones

It's possible to use a tri-band
GSM world phone in Peru
(GSM 1900). Other systems
in use are CDMA and TDMA.
This is a fast-changing field,
so check the current situation before you travel: just
do a web search and browse
the myriad products on the
market. In Lima and other
larger cities, you can buy
cell phones in stands at
the supermarket that use
SIM cards for about S48,
then pop in a SIM card that
costs from S14. Claro is a
popular pay-as-you-go plan.
Cell-phone rentals may be
available in major cities and
tourist centers. Cell-phone
reception may be poor in the
mountains or jungle.

Phone Cards

Called tarjetas telefónicas,
these cards are widely available and are made by many
companies in many price
ranges. Some are designed
specifically for international
calls. Some have an elec-
tronic chip that keeps track
of your balance when the
card is inserted into an appropriate phone. Other cards
use a code system whereby
you dial your own personal
code to obtain balances and
access; these can be used
from almost any phone.

Time

Peru is five hours behind
Greenwich Mean Time
(GMT). It's the same as East-
ern Standard Time (EST) in
North America. At noon in

Lima, it's 9am in Los Angeles, 11am in Mexico City, noon in New York, 5pm in London and 4am (following day) in Sydney.

Daylight Saving Time (DST) isn't used in Peru, so add an hour to all of these times between the first Sunday in April and the last Sunday in October.

Punctuality is not one of the things that Latin America is famous for, so be prepared to wait around. Buses rarely depart or arrive on time. Savvy travelers should allow some flexibility in their itineraries. Bring your own travel alarm clock – tours and long-distance buses often depart before 6am.

Toilets

Peruvian plumbing leaves something to be desired. There's always a chance that flushing a toilet will cause it to overflow, so you should avoid putting anything other than human waste into the toilet. Even a small amount of toilet paper can muck up the entire system – that's why a small, plastic bin is routinely provided for disposing of the paper. This may not seem sanitary, but it is definitely better than the alternative of clogged toilets and flooded floors. A well-run hotel or restaurant, even a cheap one, will empty the bin and clean the toilet daily. In rural areas, there may be just a rickety wooden outhouse built around a hole in the ground.

Public toilets are rare outside of transportation terminals, restaurants and museums, but restaurants will generally let travelers use a restroom (sometimes for a charge). Those in terminals usually have an attendant who will charge you about S0.50 to enter and then give you a miserly few sheets of toilet paper. Public restrooms frequently run out of toilet paper, so always carry extra with you.

Travelers with Disabilities

Peru offers few conveniences for travelers with disabilities. Features such as signs in Braille or phones for the hearing-impaired are virtually nonexistent, while wheelchair ramps and lifts are few and far between, and the pavement is often badly potholed and cracked. Most hotels do not have wheelchair accessible rooms, at least not rooms specially designated as such. Bathrooms are often barely large enough for an able-bodied person to walk into, so few are accessible to wheelchairs. Toilets in rural areas may be of the squat variety.

Nevertheless, there are Peruvians with disabilities who get around, mainly through the help of others. It is not particularly unusual to see mobility-impaired people being carried bodily to a seat on a bus, for example. If you need assistance, be polite and good-natured. Speaking Spanish will help immeasurably. If possible, bring along an able-bodied traveling companion.

Organizations that provide information for travelers with disabilities:

Access-Able Travel Source (www.access-able.com) Partial listings of accessible transportation and tours, accommodations, attractions and restaurants.

Apumayo Expediciones (☑/fax 084-24-6018; www.apumayo.com; Interior 3, Calle Garcilaso 265, Cuzco) An adventure-tour company that takes disabled travelers to Machu Picchu and other historic sites in the Sacred Valley.

Conadis (☑01-332-0808; www.conadisperu.gob.pe; Av Arequipa 375, Santa Beatriz, Lima) Governmental agency for Spanish-language information and advocacy for people with disabilities.

Emerging Horizons (www.emerginghorizons.com) Travel magazine for the mobility impaired, with handy advice columns and news articles.

Mobility International USA (MIUSA; ☑/TTY 541-343-1284; www.miusa.org; Suite 343, 132 E Broadway, Eugene, OR 97401, USA) International development and exchange programs for people with disabilities.

Society for Accessible Travel & Hospitality (SATH; ☑212-447-7284; www.sath.org; Suite 610, 347 Fifth Ave, New York, NY 10016, USA) A good resource for general travel information.

Visas

With a few exceptions, visas are not required for travelers entering Peru. Tourists are permitted a 30- to 90-day stay, stamped into passports and onto a tourist card called a Tarjeta Andina de Migración (Andean Immigration Card). Keep it – it must be returned upon exiting the country. The length of stay is determined by the immigration officer at the point of entry.

If you lose your tourist card, visit an *oficina de migraciónes* (immigration office; www.digemin.gob.pe) for a replacement. Extensions can be obtained at immigration offices in Lima, Arequipa, Cuzco, Iquitos, Puerto Maldonado, Puno and Trujillo, as well as near the Chilean and Ecuadorian borders. Forms and information in English can be found online. For extensions, click on Foreigners and Extension of Stay. Cost is S12.25 for a right of paperwork and an additional US$20 for the 30-day extension. Two extensions are allowed per year.

Anyone who plans to work, attend school or reside in Peru for any length of time must obtain a visa in advance. Do this through the Peruvian embassy or consulate in your home country.

Carry your passport and tourist card on your person at all times, especially in

mote areas (it's required
y law on the Inca Trail). For
ecurity, make a photocopy
both documents and keep
em in a separate place
om the originals.

olunteering

eneral advice for finding
olunteer work is to ask
t language schools; they
sually know of several
rograms suitable for their
tudents. South American
xplorers (SAE) has an
nline volunteer database
nd also folders with reports
ft by foreign volunteers at
e SAE clubhouses in Lima
see the boxed text, p96) and
uzco (p229).

Both nonprofit and for-
rofit organizations can
rrange volunteer opportuni-
es, if you contact them in
dvance. These include the
ollowing:

ction Without Borders
www.idealist.org) Online
atabase of social work-
riented jobs, internships
nd volunteer opportunities.

ross-Cultural Solutions
(☎in USA 800-380-4777, in UK
845-458-2781; www.crosscul
uralsolutions.org) Educational
nd social-service projects in
ima and Ayacucho; program
ees include professional in-
ountry support.

arthwatch Institute (☎in
JSA 800-776-0188; www.
arthwatch.org) Pay to help
cientists on archaeological,
cological and other real-life
xpeditions in the Amazon
Basin and the Andes.

lobal Crossroad (☎in USA
66-387-7816, in UK 0800-310-
821; www.globalcrossroad.
om) Volunteer, internship
and job programs in the
Andes. Summer cultural
mmersion programs for
8- to 29-year-olds include
anguage instruction, homestays, volunteer work and
sightseeing.

Global Volunteers (☎in
USA 800-487-1074; www.
globalvolunteers.org; 375 E
Little Canada Rd, St Paul, MN

55117, USA) Offers short-term
volunteer opportunities
helping orphans in Lima.

HoPe Foundation (☎084-
24-9885, in the Netherlands
0413-47-3666; www.stichting
hope.org; Casilla 59, Correo
Central, Cuzco) Provides
educational and healthcare
support in the Andes.

**Kiya Survivors/Peru
Positive Action** (☎1273-
721902; www.kiyasurvivors.
org; 1 Sussex Rd, Hove BN3
2WD, UK) Organizes two- to
six-month volunteer placements for assistant teachers
and therapists to work with
special-needs children in
Cuzco, Urubamba in the
Sacred Valley and Máncora
on the north coast.

ProWorld Service Corps
(☎in USA 877-429-6754, in UK
018-6559-6289; www.my
proworld.org) This highly
recommended organization
offers two- to 26-week cultural, service and academic
experiences, including in the
Sacred Valley and the Amazon. It has links with affiliated
NGOs throughout Peru and
can organize placements for
individuals or groups.

**Teaching & Projects
Abroad** (☎01903-708300;
www.teaching-abroad.co.uk;
Aldsworth Pde, Goring, Sussex
BN12 4TX, UK) For summer,
gap-year and career breaks,
this UK-based organization
has opportunities for community care and English
teaching in the Sacred Valley
and conservation in the
Amazon jungle.

Volunteers for Peace (VFP;
☎802-259-2759; www.vfp.org;
1034 Tiffany Rd, Belmont, VT
05730, USA) Places volun-
teers in short-term work-
camp programs, usually in
Lima or Ayacucho. Program
fees are more than reasonable and may be partially
paid directly to local communities.

Working Abroad (www.
workingabroad.com) Online
network of grassroots
volunteer opportunities (eg
social development, environmental restoration, indig-

enous rights, traditional art
and music) with trip reports
from the field.

Women Travelers

Machismo is alive and well in
Latin America. Most female
travelers to Peru will experience little more than shouts
of *mi amor* (my love) or an
appreciative hiss. If you are
fair-skinned with blond hair,
however, be prepared to be
the center of attention. Peruvian men consider foreign
women to have looser morals
and be easier sexual con-
quests than Peruvian women
and will often make flirtatious
comments to single women.

Staring, whistling, hissing
and catcalls in the streets
are run-of-the-mill – and
should be treated as such.
Many men make a pas-
time of dropping *piropos*
(cheeky, flirtatious or even
vulgar 'compliments'). However, these are generally not
meant to be insulting. Most
men rarely, if ever, follow up
on the idle chatter (unless
they feel you've insulted their
manhood). Ignoring all prov-
ocation and staring ahead is
generally the best response.
If someone is particularly
persistent, try a potentially
ardor-smothering phrase
such as *soy casada* (I'm married). If you appeal directly to
locals, you'll find most Peruvians to be protective of lone
women, expressing surprise
and concern if you tell them
you're traveling without your
family or husband.

It's not uncommon for
fast-talking charmers, especially in tourist towns such
as Cuzco, to attach them-
selves to gringas. Known in
Peru as *bricheros*, many of
these young Casanovas are
looking for a meal ticket, so
approach any professions of
undying love with extreme
skepticism. This happens to
men too.

Use common sense when
meeting men in public places.
In Peru, outside of a few big
cities, it is rare for a woman

to belly up to a bar for a beer, and the ones that do tend to be prostitutes. If you feel the need for an evening cocktail, opt for a restaurant instead. Likewise, heavy drinking by women might be misinterpreted by some men as a sign of promiscuity. When meeting someone, make it very clear if only friendship is intended. This goes double for tour and activity guides. When meeting someone for the first time, it is also wise not to divulge where you are staying until you feel sure that you are with someone you can trust.

In highland towns, dress is generally fairly conservative and women rarely wear shorts, opting instead for long skirts. Slacks are fine, but note that shorts, miniskirts and revealing blouses may draw unwanted attention.

As in any part of the world, the possibilities of rape and assault do exist. Use your big city smarts (even in small towns). A few tips:

» skip the hitchhiking

» do not take unlicensed taxis, especially at night (licensed taxis have an authorization sticker on the windshield)

» avoid walking alone in unfamiliar places at night

» if a stranger approaches you on the street and asks a question, answer it if you feel comfortable – but *don't* stop walking as it could allow potential attackers to surround you

» avoid overnight buses through bandit-ridden areas, since women have been known to be raped during robberies

» be aware of your surroundings; attacks have occurred in broad daylight around well-touristed sites and popular trekking trails

» when hiring a private tour or activity guide, seek someone who comes from a recommended or reliable agency

Travelers who are sexually assaulted can report it to the nearest police station or to the tourist police. However, Peruvian attitudes toward sexual assaults favor the attackers, not the survivors. Rape is often seen as a disgrace, and it is difficult to prosecute. Because the police tend to be unhelpful, we recommend calling your own embassy or consulate (p532) to ask for advice, including on where to seek medical treatment, which should be an immediate priority.

On a far more mundane note: tampons are difficult to find in smaller towns, so stock up in major cities. Birth-control pills and other contraceptives (even condoms) are scarce outside metropolitan areas and not always reliable, so bring your own supply from home. Rates of HIV infection are on the rise, especially among young women. Abortions are illegal, except to save the life of the mother.

These organizations provide useful information for female travelers:

Centro de La Mujer Peruana Flora Tristán (☎01-433-1457; www.flora.org. pe; Parque Hernán Velarde 14, Lima; ☉1-5pm Mon-Fri) Feminist social and political advocacy group for women's and human rights in Peru, with a Spanish-language website and a library in Lima.

Instituto Peruano de Paternidad Responsable (Inppares; ☎01-640-2000; www.inppares.org.pe) Planne Parenthood-affiliated organization that runs a dozen sexual and reproductive health clinics for both women and men around the country, including in Lima.

Work

It's increasingly difficult to obtain residence and work permits for Peru, and likewise to get jobs without a proper work visa. Some jobs teaching English in language schools may not require one but this is illegal. Occasionally, schools advertise for teachers, but more often, jobs are found by word of mouth. Schools expect you to be a native English speaker, and the pay is low. If you have teaching credentials, so much the better.

American and British schools in Lima sometimes hire teachers of math, biology and other subjects, but usually only if you apply in advance. They pay much better than the language schools, and might possibly be able to help you get a work visa if you want to stay. In Lima, the South American Explorers clubhouse and international cultural centers may have contacts with schools that are looking for teachers.

Most other jobs are obtained by word of mouth (eg bartenders, hostel staff, jungle guides), but the possibilities are limited. For internships and short-term job opportunities through volunteer organizations, see p541.

Transportation

GETTING THERE & AWAY

Entering the Country

Arriving in Peru is typically straightforward, as long as your passport is valid for at least six months beyond your departure date. When arriving by air, US citizens must show a return ticket or open-jaw onward ticket – don't show up with just a one-way ticket to South America. For information on Peruvian visas, see p540.

When arriving by air or overland, immigration officials may only stamp 30 days into your passport (though 90 days is standard); if this happens, explain how many more days you need, supported by an exit ticket for onward or return travel.

Bribery (known colloquially as *coima*) is illegal, but some officials may try to procure extra 'fees' at land borders.

Air

Peru (mainly Lima) has direct flights to and from cities all over the Americas, as well as

continental Europe. Other locations require a connection. An international departure tax of US$31 is now usually included in ticket costs.

Airports & Airlines

Located in the port city of Callao, Lima's **Aeropuerto Internacional Jorge Chávez** (airline code LIM; ☎01-517-3100; www.lap.com. pe; Callao) has remodeled terminals sparkling with ample shopping and services. A major hub, it's serviced by flights from North, Central and South America, and two regular direct flights from Europe (Madrid and Amsterdam). Check the airport website or call ☎01-511-6055 for updated departure and arrival schedules for domestic and international flights. See p96 for details of airport services and p98 for transportation options to/from the airport. Cuzco (p229) has the only other airport with international service, to La Paz, Bolivia.

AIRLINES FLYING TO/FROM PERU

The phone numbers and addresses listed here are for airline offices in Lima; add

☎01 if calling from outside the capital.

If you plan to visit an office, call before you go or check a phone directory under 'Líneas Aéreas,' as they change addresses frequently.

Aerolineas Argentinas (airline code ARG; ☎513-6565; www.aerolineas.com.ar/ar/pe)

Aeroméxico (airline code AMX; ☎705-1111; www.aero mexico.com)

Air Canada (airline code ACA; ☎626-0900; www.aircanada. com)

Air Europa (airline code AEA; ☎652-7373; www.aireuropa. com)

Air France (airline code AFR; ☎213-0200; www.airfrance. com)

Alitalia (airline code AZA; ☎241-1026; www.alitalia.it)

American Airlines (airline code AAL; ☎211-7000; www. aa.com)

Avianca (airline code AVA; ☎440-4104; www.avianca. com)

Copa Airlines (airline code CMP; ☎610-0808; www. copaair.com)

Delta Airlines (airline code DAL; ☎211-9211; www.delta. com)

Iberia (airline code IBE; ☎411-7800; www.iberia.com.pe)

KLM (airline code KLM; ☎213-0200; www.klm.com)

LAN (airline code LPE; ☎213-8200; www.lan.com)

Spirit Airlines (airline code SIP; ☎517-2563; www.spirit. com)

TACA (airline code TAI; ☎511-8222; www.taca.com)

TAM (airline code TAE; ☎202-6900; www.tam.com.br)

United Airlines (airline code UAL; ☎712-9230; www.united. com)

Tickets

From most places in the world, South America can be a relatively costly destination. The high season for air travel to and within Peru is late May to early September, as well as around major holidays. Look for lower fares outside peak periods.

Contacting a travel agent that specializes in Latin American destinations and shopping around for competing online fares can turn up cheaper tickets. Students with international student ID cards (ISIC is one widely recognized card) and anyone under 26 can often get discounts with budget or specialty travel agencies. A good option to check out is **STA Travel** (www.stat ravel.com), which has offices around the globe. The agency also supports Planeterra, a foundation for community development.

Tickets bought in Peru are subject to a 19% tax. It is essential to reconfirm all flights 72 hours in advance, either by phone or online, or you may get bumped off the flight. If you are traveling in remote areas, have a reputable travel agent do this for you.

ROUND-THE-WORLD TICKETS

Some of the best deals for travelers visiting many countries on different continents are round-the-world tickets. Itineraries from the USA, Europe or Australasia typically require at least five stopovers, possibly including unusual destinations such as Tahiti. Fares vary widely, but check **Air Treks** (www. airtreks.com) and **Air Brokers** (www.airbrokers.com). These types of tickets have restrictions, so read the fine print carefully.

Australia & New Zealand

Santiago, Chile tends to be the most common gateway city from Australia and New Zealand, though some carriers connect through the US as well.

In Australia, agency **South American Travel Centre** (☏03-9642-5353; www.satc. com.au) specializes in travel to Latin America.

Canada

There are direct flights to Lima from Toronto, but most trips require a connection in the US or Mexico City.

Continental Europe

There are direct flights from Amsterdam and Madrid, but connections through the USA, Central America or Colombia are often cheaper.

Latin America

There are direct flights from a large number of Latin American cities to Peru, including Bogotá, Buenos Aires, Caracas, Guayaquil, La Paz, Mexico City, Panama City, Quito, Rio de Janeiro, San José (Costa Rica), Santiago (Chile) and São Paulo. LAN, Copa and TACA are the principal Latin American airlines that fly to Lima.

Recommended agencies in Latin America:

ASATEJ Viajes (www.asatej. com, in Spanish) In Mexico, Argentina and Uruguay.

Student Travel Bureau (STB; ☏11-3038-1551; www.stb. com.br) In Brazil.

UK & Ireland

Flights from the UK or Ireland connect through gateway cities in continental Europe, North America and Brazil.

In the UK, the following agencies specialize in travel to Latin America:

Austral Tours (☏020-7233-5384; www.latinamerica.co.uk)

Journey Latin America (JLA; ☏020-8747-3108; www. journeylatinamerica.co.uk)

North-South Travel (☏0125 608 291; www.north southtravel.co.uk) Donates a portion of its profits to projects all over the developing world.

South American Experience (☏0845-277-3366; www. southamericanexperience. co.uk)

USA

There are direct (nonstop) flights to Lima from Atlanta, Dallas-Fort Worth, Houston, Los Angeles, Miami and New York. In other cases, flights will connect either in the US or in Latin American gateway cities such as Mexico City and Bogotá.

US travel agencies that specialize in travel to Latin America:

Exito Travel (☏800-655-4053; www.exitotravel.com)

Latin America for Less (☏1-817-230-4971; latinameri caforless.com)

Land & River

Because no roads bridge the Darien Gap, it is not possible to travel to South America by land from the north (unless you spend a week making your way through swampy, drug-dealer-infested jungle). Driving overland from neighboring Bolivia, Brazil, Chile, Colombia and Ecuador requires careful logistical planning. See p540 for important information on visas, immigration offices and other border-crossing formalities.

Ormeño (☏01-472-1710; www.grupo-ormeno.com.pe) is the main international bus company that goes to Chile, Ecuador, Colombia, Bolivia and Argentina. Smaller regional companies do cross-border travel, but on a more-limited basis. The only rail service that crosses the Peru border is the train between Arica, Chile, and Tacna on Peru's south coast.

With any form of transport, it may be a bit cheaper to buy tickets to the border, cross over and then buy onward tickets on the other side, but it's usually much easier, faster and safer to buy a cross-border through ticket. When traveling by bus, check carefully with the company about what is included in the price of the ticket, and whether the service is direct or involves a transfer, and possibly a long wait, at the border.

Getting to Peru by boat is possible from points on the Amazon River in Brazil and from Leticia, Colombia, as well as to the port cities on Peru's Pacific coast.

The following sections outline the principal points of entry to and exit from Peru.

Bolivia

Peru is normally reached overland from Bolivia via Lake Titicaca (see the boxed text, p180); the border crossing at Yunguyo is much safer and a lot less chaotic than its counterpart at Desaguadero. There are many transportation options for both of these routes, most of which involve changing buses at the Peru–Bolivia border before reaching Puno. It's possible, but a logistical feat, to cross into Bolivia from Puerto Maldonado (see the boxed text, p446).

Brazil

You can travel overland between Peru and Brazil via Ñapari (see the boxed text, p445). Traveling from Iquitos, it's more straightforward to go along the Amazon to Tabatinga in Brazil via Leticia, Colombia. For more information on boat trips, see the boxed text, p480.

Chile

Traveling on the Pan-American Hwy, the major crossing point is between Arica, Chile, and Tacna on Peru's south coast (see the boxed text, p133). Long-distance buses to Tacna depart from Lima, Arequipa and Puno. Colectivo (shared) taxis are the fastest and most reliable way to travel between Tacna and Arica. It's also possible to make the crossing, albeit much slower, by train; border formalities are done at the respective stations. Flights to Tacna from Arequipa are cheap but book up quickly. Alternatively, Ormeño runs through buses from Lima all the way to Santiago, Chile. From Arequipa, Ormeño goes to Santiago, Chile, and Buenos Aires.

Colombia

It is easiest to travel between Peru and Colombia via Ecuador. Ormeño has through buses between Lima and Bogotá via Ecuador. This long-haul trip is better done in stages, though.

If you are in the rainforest, it is more straightforward to voyage along the Amazon by boat between Iquitos and Leticia, Colombia, from where there are flights to Bogotá. For more details on border formalities there, see the boxed text, p480.

Ecuador

The most common way to get to or from Ecuador is along the Pan-American Hwy via Tumbes (see the boxed text, p357). Another route is via La Tina to Loja in Ecuador (see the boxed text, p348). A third way is via Jaén (see the boxed text, p420). Cifa (072-52-5120) runs buses between Tumbes in Peru and Machala or Guayaquil in Ecuador. Transportes Loja (073-30-5446) runs buses between Piura in Peru and Machala or Loja in Ecuador. Ormeño has weekly through buses between Lima and Quito.

Tours

Travelers who prefer not to travel on their own, or have a limited amount of time have ample tours to choose from. Travel with knowledgeable guides comes as a premium. It's worth it for highly specialized outdoor activities like river running, mountaineering, bird-watching or mountain biking.

If you want to book a tour locally, Lima, Cuzco, Arequipa, Puno, Trujillo, Huaraz, Puerto Maldonado and Iquitos have the most travel agencies offering organized tours. For more specialized, individual or small-group tours, you can generally hire a bilingual guide starting at US$20 an hour or US$80 a day plus expenses (keep in mind exchange rates may affect this); tours in other languages may be more expensive. Some students or unregistered guides are cheaper, but the usual caveat applies – some are good, others aren't. A few local guides are listed in this book.

For more guide listings, check out www.leaplocal.org, a resource promoting socially responsible tourism. For listings of gay-friendly tour operators, see p533.

From Australia & New Zealand

Aspiring Adventures (1-877-438-1354, 643-489-7474; www.aspiringadventures.com) A small, enthusiastic outfit that's Kiwi-Australian run with extensive experience in Cuzco and the Sacred Valley. Does biking, classic trips and food-focused tours.

Peregrine Adventures (03-8601-4444; www.peregrine.net.au; 380 Lonsdale St, Melbourne, VIC 3000) Hotel-based and trekking trips in Peru.

Tucan Travel (1300-769-249, in Cuzco 084-24-8691; www.tucantravel.com; 217 Alison Rd, Randwick, NSW 2031) Long-running tour operator specializing in Latin America provides a wide variety of options in Peru; also has an office in Cuzco.

From Canada & the USA

With easy flight connections, the USA has more companies offering tours of Peru than the rest of the world.

Adventure Center (510-654-1879, 800-228-8747; www.adventurecenter.com; Suite 200, 1311 63rd St, Emeryville, CA 94608) A clearinghouse for tour operators offering various trips.

Adventure Life (406-541-2677, 800-344-6118; www.adventure-life.com; Suite 1, 1655 S 3rd St W, Missoula, MT 5980) Andean trekking, Amazon exploring and multisport itineraries; reputable agency that uses bilingual guides, family-run hotels and local transportation.

Exodus (☎44-208-675-5550; www.exodus.co.uk; Grange Mills, Weir Rd, London SW12 0NE, England) Award-winning responsible-travel operator offering long-distance overland trips and shorter cultural and trekking adventures.

Explorations (☎239-992-9660, 800-446-9660; www.explorationsinc.com; 27655 Kent Rd, Bonita Springs, FL 34135) Amazon trips include biologist-escorted cruises, lodge-based expeditions and fishing trips in the Reserva Nacional Pacaya-Samiria.

GAP Adventures (☎888-800-4100; www.gap.ca; 19 Charlotte St, Toronto, ON M5V 2H5) The premier Canadian agency with offices in Vancouver, Boston, USA, and London, UK. Budget-priced tours include hotel-based, trekking, Amazon and cultural trips.

International Expeditions (☎205-428-1700, 800-234-9620; www.ietravel.com; One Environs Park, Helena, AL 35080) Offers Amazon tours, staying in jungle lodges or on river boats, with an emphasis on natural history and bird-watching.

Mountain Travel Sobek (☎510-594-6000, 888-831-7526; www.mtsobek.com; 1266 66th St, Emeryville, CA 94608) Luxury trekking tours along the Inca Trail or in the Cordillera Blanca, and occasional rafting trips on the Río Tambopata.

Sacred Rides (☎647-999-7955, 888-423-7849, sacredrides.com; 261 Markham St, Toronto, ON M6J 2G7) A mountain-biking specialist that organizes various multiday bike tours throughout the Peruvian Andes.

Southwind Adventures (☎303-972-0701, 800-377-9463; www.southwindadventures.com; PO Box 621057, Littleton, CO 80162) Peruvian-American tour operator with trekking, cycling, rafting and

boat-cruise itineraries in the Andes, the Amazon and the Galapagos Islands.

Tropical Nature Travel (☎352-376-3377, 877-888-1770; www.tropicalnaturetravel.com; PO Box 5276, Gainesville, FL 32627) Organizes multiday itineraries in the Amazon, as well as trekking, river running and archaeological and cultural tours.

Wilderness Travel (☎510-558-2488, 800-368-2794; www.wildernesstravel.com; 1102 Ninth St, Berkeley, CA 94710) Offers luxury treks, from four nights to two weeks, throughout the highlands and the Amazon.

Wildland Adventures (☎206-365-0686, 800-345-4453; www.wildland.com; 3516 NE 155th St, Seattle, WA 98155) Environmentally sound, culturally sensitive treks around the Sacred Valley and the Cordillera Blanca, as well as Amazon tours.

From the UK & Continental Europe

Andean Trails (☎44-131-467-7086; www.andeantrails.co.uk; 33 Sandport St, Lieth, Edinburgh, Scotland EH6 5QG) Mountain-biking, climbing, trekking and rafting tours in some unusual spots.

Guerba Adventure & Discovery Holidays (☎01373-826-611; www.guerba.co.uk; Wessex House, 40 Station Rd, Westbury, Wiltshire BA13 3JN, UK) Trekking, activity and family-focused tours of the Andes and the Amazon.

Hauser Exkursionen (☎89-235-0060; www.hauser-exkursionen.de, in German; Spiegelstrasse 9, D-81241 Munich, Germany) Among the best German companies offering Andean treks.

Huwans Clubaventure (☎08-2688-2080; www.clubaventure.fr; 18 rue Séguier, 75006 Paris, France) A reputable French company organizing treks and tours.

Journey Latin America (☎020-3432-1507; www.journeylatinamerica.co.uk; 12

& 13 Heathfield Tce, Chiswick, London W4 4JE, UK) Cultural trips and treks in the Cordilleras Blanca and Huayhuash and to Machu Picchu.

GETTING AROUND

Peru has a constant procession of flights and buses connecting the country. In particular, driving routes to the jungle have improved drastically. Keep in mind, poor weather conditions can cancel flights and buses. Strikes can be another obstacle in regional travel – consult travel experts on the routes you will be taking.

Air

Domestic-flight schedules and prices change frequently. New airlines open every year, as those with poor safety records close. Most big cities are served by modern jets, while smaller towns are served by propeller aircraft.

Airlines in Peru

Most airlines fly from Lima to regional capitals, but service between provincial cities is limited. The following domestic airlines are the most established and reliable:

LAN (airline code LPE; ☎01-213-8200; www.lan.com) Peru's major domestic carrier flies to Arequipa, Chiclayo, Cuzco, Iquitos, Juliaca, Piura, Puerto Maldonado, Tacna, Tarapoto and Trujillo. Additionally it offers link services between Arequipa and Cuzco, Arequipa and Juliaca, Arequipa and Tacna, Cuzco and Juliaca, and Cuzco and Puerto Maldonado.

Peruvian Airlines (airline code PVN; ☎716-6000; www.peruvianairlines.pe) Flies to Lima, Arequipa, Cuzco, Piura, Iquitos and Tacna.

Star Perú (airline code SRU; ☎01-705-9000; www.starperu.com) Another domestic carrier, flying to Ayacucho, ajamarca, Cuzco, Iquitos, ucallpa, Puerto Maldonado, alara and Tarapoto; with nk service between Tarapoto and Iquitos.

ACA (airline code TAI; ☎01-511-8222; www.taca.com) entral American airline that ffers service between Lima nd Cuzco.

Most domestic airlines ave offices in Lima (p96). maller carriers and charters re listed under destinations hroughout this book. The most remote towns may require connecting flights, and smaller towns are not served every day. Many airports for these places are often no more than a dirt strip.

Be at the airport two hours before your flight departs. Flights may be overbooked, baggage handling and check-in procedures tend to be chaotic, and flights may even leave *before* their official departure time because of predicted bad weather.

Tickets

Most travelers travel in one direction overland and save time returning by air. The peak season for air travel within Peru is late May to early September, as well as around major holidays. Buy tickets for less popular destinations as far in advance as possible, as these infrequent flights book up quickly.

Buying tickets and reconfirming flights is best done at airline offices in remote areas; otherwise, you can do so online or via a recommended travel agent. You can sometimes buy tickets at the airport on a space-available

Peru Air Routes

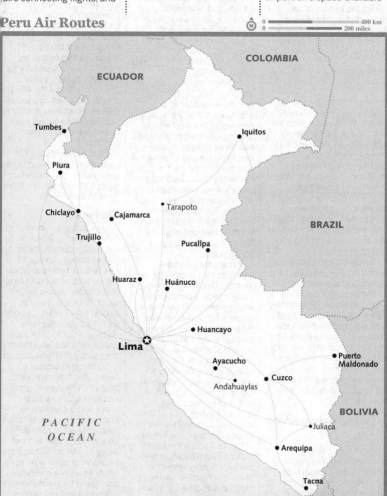

basis, but don't count on it. It's almost impossible to buy tickets for just before major holidays (p534), notably Semana Santa (the week leading up to Easter) and Fiestas Patrias (the last week in July). Overbooking is the norm.

Ensure all flight reservations are *confirmed and reconfirmed* 72 and 24 hours in advance; airlines are notorious for overbooking and flights are changed or canceled with surprising frequency, so it's even worth calling the airport or the airline just before leaving for the airport. Confirmation is especially essential during the peak travel season.

Bicycle

The major drawback to cycling in Peru is the country's bounty of kamikaze motorists. On narrow, two-lane highways, drivers can be a serious hazard to cyclists. Cycling is more enjoyable and safer, though very challenging, off paved roads. Mountain bikes are recommended, as road bikes won't stand up to the rough conditions. See p34 for more about mountain biking and cycling in Peru.

Reasonably priced rentals (mostly mountain bikes) are available in popular tourist destinations, including Cuzco, Arequipa, Huaraz and Huancayo. These bikes are rented to travelers for local excursions, not to make trips all over the country. For long-distance touring, bring your own bike from home.

Airline policies on carrying bicycles vary, so shop around.

Boat

There are no passenger services along the Peruvian coast. In the Andean highlands, there are boat services on Lake Titicaca. Small motorized vessels take passen-

gers from the port in Puno to visit various islands on the lake, while catamarans zip over to Bolivia.

In Peru's Amazon Basin, boat travel is of major importance. Larger vessels ply the wider rivers. Dugout canoes powered by outboard engines act as water taxis on smaller rivers. Those called *peki-pekis* are slow and rather noisy. In some places, modern aluminum launches are used.

Some travelers dream of plying the Amazon while swinging in a hammock aboard a banana boat with cargo on the lower deck. It's possible to travel from Pucallpa or Yurimaguas to Iquitos and on into Brazil this way (see p480).

At ports, chalkboards with ships' names, destinations and departure times are displayed; these are usually optimistic. The captain has to clear documents with the *capitanía* (harbor master's office) on the day of departure, so directly ask the captain for updates. Nobody else really knows. Departure time often depends on a full cargo. Usually, you can sleep on the boat while waiting if you want to save on hotel bills. Never leave your luggage unattended.

Bring your own hammock, or rent a cabin for the journey. If using a hammock, hang it away from the noisy engine room and not directly under a light, as these are often lit late at night, precluding sleep and attracting insects. Cabins are often hot, airless boxes, but are lockable. Sanitary facilities are basic and there's usually a pump shower on board.

Basic food is usually included in the price of the passage, and may be marginally better on the bigger ships, or if you are in cabin class. Finicky eaters or people with dietary restrictions should bring their own food. Bottled soft drinks are usually available.

Bus

Buses are the usual form of transportation for most Peruvians and many travelers. Fares are cheap and services are frequent on the major long-distance routes, but buses are of varying quality. Remote rural routes are often served by older, worn-out vehicles. Seats at the back of the bus yield a bumpier ride.

Many cities do not have a main bus terminal. For a rundown of major companies with offices in Lima, see p97. Buses rarely arrive or depart on time, so the average trip times quoted throughout this book are best-case scenarios. Buses can be significantly delayed during the rainy season, particularly in the highlands and the jungle. From January to April journey times may double or face indefinite delays from landslides and bad road conditions.

Fatal accidents are not unusual in Peru. Avoid overnight buses, on which muggings and assaults are more likely to occur.

Classes

Luxury buses are invariably called Imperial, Royal, Business or Executive. These higher-priced express services feature toilets, snacks, videos and air-conditioning. *Bus-camas* feature seats which recline halfway or almost fully. For trips under six hours, you may have no choice but to take an *económico* bus, and these are usually pretty beaten up.

Better long-distance buses stop for bathroom breaks and meals in special rest areas. Luxury buses serve paltry snacks and don't stop. Rest areas feature inexpensive but sometimes unappetizing fare. Almost every bus terminal has a few kiosks with basic provisions. While *económico* services don't stop for meals, vendors will board and sell snacks.

osts & Reservations

chedules and fares change equently and vary from ompany to company; erefore, the prices quoted this book are only ap-oximations. You can check chedules online (but not ake reservations, at least ot yet) for the major play-s, including **Cruz del Sur** ww.cruzdelsur.com.pe), rmeño (www.grupo-ormeno. m), **Transportes Línea** vww.transporteslinea.com.pe, Spanish) and **Oltursa** (www. tursa.com.pe, in Spanish).

Fares fluctuate during eak and off-peak travel mes. For long-distance or vernight journeys, or travel o remote areas with only mited services, buy your cket at least the day before. 1ost travel agencies offer eservations but shockingly vercharge for the ticket. xcept in Lima, it's cheaper o take a taxi to the bus erminal and buy the tickets ourself.

uggage

Vatch your luggage in bus erminals very carefully. 5ome terminals have left-uggage facilities.

Bags put into the luggage ompartment are generally afe. Hand luggage is a dif-erent matter. Items may be aken while you sleep. For his reason, never use the verhead compartments nd bring only items which an fit below your legs or on our lap.

Car & Motorcycle

Distances in Peru are long so it's best to bus or fly to a egion and rent a car from here. Hiring a taxi is often cheaper and easier.

At roadside checkpoints police or military conduct meticulous document checks. Drivers who offer an officer some money to smooth things along con-sider it a 'gift' or 'on-the-spot fine' to get on their way. For more advice on legal mat-ters, see p534.

Driver's License

A driver's license from your own home country is suf-ficient for renting a car. An International Driving Permit (IDP) is only required if you'll be driving in Peru for more than 30 days.

Rental

Major rental companies have offices in Lima (p98) and a few other large cities. Rent-ing a motorcycle is an option mainly in jungle towns, where you can go for short runs around town on dirt bikes, but not much further.

Economy car rental starts at US$25 a day without the 19% sales tax, 'super' collision-damage waiver, per-sonal accident insurance and so on, which together can climb to more than US$100 per day, not including excess mileage. Vehicles with 4WD are more expensive.

Make sure you completely understand the rental agree-ment before you sign. A credit card is required, and renters normally need to be over 25 years of age.

Road Rules & Hazards

Bear in mind that the condi-tion of rental cars is often poor, roads are potholed (even the paved Pan-Amer-ican Hwy), gas is expensive, and drivers are aggressive, regarding speed limits, road signs and traffic signals as mere guides, not the law. Moreover, road signs are often small and unclear.

Driving is on the right-hand side of the road. Driving at night is not recommended because of poor conditions, speeding buses and slow-moving, poorly lit trucks.

Theft is all too common, so you should not leave your vehicle parked on the street. When stopping overnight, park the car in a guarded lot (common in better hotels).

Gasoline or petrol stations (called *grifos*) are few and far between.

Hitchhiking

Hitchhiking is never entirely safe in any country in the world and is not recommend-ed. Travelers who decide to hitchhike should understand that they are taking a serious risk. Hitchhikers will be safer if they travel in pairs and let someone know where they are planning to go. In Peru hitchhiking is not very practi-cal, as there are few private cars, buses are so cheap and trucks are often used as paid public transportation in remote areas.

Local Transportation

In most towns and cities, it's easy to walk everywhere or take a taxi. Using local buses, *micros* and *combis* can be tricky, but is very inexpensive.

Bus

Local buses are slow and crowded but cheap. Ask locals for help, as there aren't any obvious bus lines in most towns.

A faster, more hair-raising alternative is to take *mic-ros* or *combis,* sometimes called *colectivos* (though the term usually refers to taxis). Typically, *micros* and *combis* are minibuses or minivans stuffed full of passengers. They can be identified by stickers along the outside panels and destination plac-ards in the front windows. You can flag one down or get off anywhere on the route. A conductor usually leans out of the vehicle, shouting out destinations. Once inside, you must quickly squeeze into any available seat, or be prepared to stand. The con-ductor comes around to col-lect the fare, or you can pay when getting off. Safety is not a high priority for *combi* drivers. The only place for a passenger to safely buckle up is the front seat, but in the event of a head-on collision (not an unusual occurrence), that's the last place you'd want to be.

Taxi

Taxis seem to be everywhere. Private cars that have a small taxi sticker in the windshield aren't necessarily regulated. Safer, regulated taxis usually have a lit company number on the roof and are reached by phone. These are more expensive than taxis flagged down on the street, but are more reliable.

Always ask the fare in advance, as there are no meters. It's acceptable to haggle; try to find out what the going rate is before taking a cab, especially for long trips. The standard fare for short runs in most cities is around S5. Tipping is not the norm, unless you have hired a driver for a long period or he has helped you with luggage or other lifting.

Hiring a private taxi for long-distance trips costs less than renting a car and takes care of many of the problems outlined earlier. Not all taxi drivers will agree to drive long distances, but if one does, you should carefully check the driver's credentials and vehicle before hiring.

Train

The privatized rail system, **PeruRail** (📞084-58-1414), has daily services between Cuzco and Aguas Calientes, aka Machu Picchu Pueblo, and services between Cuzco and Puno on the shores of Lake Titicaca three times a week; see p231 for details of both services. Passenger services between Puno and Arequipa have been suspended indefinitely, but will run as a charter for groups. Two other competing companies now also have service between Cuzco and Aguas Calientes.

Train buffs won't want to miss the lovely **Ferrocarril Central Andino** (📞01-226-6363; www.ferrocarrilcentral.com.pe), which reaches a head-spinning altitude of 4829m. It usually runs between Lima and Huancayo weekly from mid-April through October. In Huancayo, cheaper trains to Huancavelica leave daily from a different station. See p285 for details of both services. Another charmingly historic railway makes inexpensive daily runs between Tacna on Peru's south coast and Arica, Chile (see p135).

Health

iseases found in Peru
clude mosquito-borne
fections such as malaria,
ellow fever and dengue
ver, although these are rare
temperate regions.

The only required vac-
ine for Peru is yellow fever,
nd that's only if you're
rriving from a yellow-fever-
fected country in Africa or
he Americas. It is strongly
dvised, though, for those
isiting the jungle, as are
alaria pills.

Medical Checklist

» antibiotics
» antidiarrheal drugs (eg operamide)
» acetaminophen (Tylenol) or aspirin
» anti-inflammatory drugs (eg ibuprofen)
» antihistamines (for hay ever and allergic reactions)
» antibacterial ointment (eg Bactroban; for cuts and abrasions)
» steroid cream or cortisone (for poison ivy and other allergic rashes)
» bandages, gauze, gauze rolls
» adhesive or paper tape
» scissors, safety pins, tweezers
» thermometer
» pocketknife
» insect repellent containing DEET (for the skin)
» insect spray containing permethrin (for clothing, tents and bed nets)
» sunblock
» oral rehydration salts
» iodine tablets (for water purification)
» acetazolamide (Diamox; for altitude sickness)

Websites

World Health Organization (www.who.int/ith/) Free download *International Travel and Health*.

MD Travel Health (www.mdtravelhealth.com) Travel-health recommendations.

Availability of Health Care

Lima has high-quality 24-hour medical clinics, and English-speaking doctors and dentists. See the guide at the website for the **US embassy** (lima.usembassy.gov/acs_peru.html). Rural areas may have the most basic medical services. You may have to pay in cash, regardless of whether you have travel insurance.

Life-threatening medical problems may require evacuation. For a list of medical evacuation and travel insurance companies, see the website of the **US State Department** (travel.state.gov/travel/tips/brochures/brochures_1215.html).

Pharmacies are known as *farmacias* or *boticas*, identified by a green or red cross. They offer most of the medications available in other countries.

Infectious Diseases

Many of the following diseases are spread by mosquitoes. Take precautions to minimize your chances of being bitten (p552). These precautions also protect against other insect-borne diseases like Baronellois (Oroya fever), Leishmaniasis and Chagas' disease.

Cholera

An intestinal infection, cholera is acquired through contaminated food or water, resulting in profuse diarrhea, which may cause life-threatening dehydration. Treatment includes oral rehydration solution and possibly antibiotics.

Dengue Fever

A viral infection, dengue is transmitted by mosquitoes which breed primarily in puddles and artificial water containers. It is especially common in densely populated, urban environments, including Lima and Cuzco.

Flu-like symptoms include fever, muscle aches, joint pains, headaches, nausea and vomiting, often followed by a rash. The body aches may be quite uncomfortable, but most cases resolve in a few days.

Take analgesics such as acetaminophen/paracetamol (Tylenol) and drink plenty of fluids. Severe cases may require hospitalization.

Malaria

Malaria is transmitted by mosquito bites, usually between dusk and dawn. High spiking fevers may be accompanied by chills, sweats, headache, body aches, weakness, vomiting or diarrhea. Severe cases may lead to seizures, confusion, coma and death.

Taking malaria pills is strongly recommended for all areas in Peru except Lima and its vicinity, the coastal areas south of Lima, and the highland areas (including around Cuzco, Machu Picchu, Lake Titicaca and Arequipa). Most cases in Peru occur in Loreto in the country's northeast, where transmission has reached epidemic levels.

Typhoid Fever

Caused by ingestion of food or water contaminated by *Salmonella typhi*, fever occurs in virtually all cases. Other symptoms may include headache, malaise, muscle aches, dizziness, loss of appetite, nausea and abdominal pain. Either diarrhea or constipation may occur. Possible complications include intestinal perforation or bleeding, confusion, delirium or, rarely, coma.

The vaccine is usually given orally, but is also available as an injection. The treatment drug is usually a quinolone antibiotic such as ciprofloxacin (Cipro) or levofloxacin (Levaquin).

Yellow Fever

A life-threatening viral infection, yellow fever is transmitted by mosquitoes in forested areas. Flu-like symptoms may include fever, chills, headache, muscle aches, backache, loss of appetite, nausea and vomiting. They usually subside in a few days, but one person in six enters a second, toxic phase characterized by recurrent fever, vomiting, listlessness, jaundice, kidney failure and hemorrhage which can lead to death. There is no treatment except for supportive care.

Yellow-fever vaccine is strongly recommended for all those who visit any jungle areas of Peru at altitudes less than 2300m (7546ft). Most cases occur in the departments in the central jungle. Get vaccinated at least 10 days before any potential exposure; it remains effective for about 10 years.

Environmental Hazards

Altitude Sickness

Altitude sickness may result from rapid ascents to altitudes greater than 2500m (8100ft). In Peru, this includes Cuzco, Machu Picchu and Lake Titicaca. Being physically fit offers no protection. Symptoms may include headaches, nausea, vomiting, dizziness, malaise, insomnia and loss of appetite. Severe cases may be complicated by fluid in the lungs (high-altitude pulmonary edema) or swelling of the brain (high-altitude cerebral edema). If symptoms persist for more than 24 hours, descend immediately by at least 500m and see a doctor.

The best prevention is to spend two nights or more at each rise of 1000m. Diamox may be taken starting 24 hours before ascent. A natural alternative is ginkgo.

It's also important to avoid overexertion, eat light meals and abstain from alcohol. Altitude sickness should be taken seriously; it can be life threatening when severe.

Hypothermia

To prevent hypothermia, dress in layers: silk, wool and synthetic thermals are all good insulators. Essentials include a hat and a waterproof outer layer. Carry food and lots of fluid. An emergency space blanket can be highly useful.

Symptoms are exhaustion, numbness (particularly toes and fingers), shivering, slurred speech, irrational or violent behavior, lethargy, stumbling, dizzy spells, muscle cramps and violent bursts of energy.

To treat, go indoors and replace wet clothing with dry. Take hot liquids – no alcohol and some high-calorie, easily digestible food. Do not rub victims, as rough handling may cause cardiac arrest.

Mosquito Bites

The best prevention is wearing long sleeves, long pants, hats and shoes (rather than sandals). Use insect repellent with 25% to 35% DEET. Protection usually lasts about six hours. Children age two to 12 should use formulas with 10% DEET or less, which lasts about three hours.

Insect repellents containing certain botanical products, including oil of eucalyptus and soybean oil, are effective but last only 1½ to two hours.

If sleeping outdoors or in accommodations where mosquitoes can enter, use a mosquito net with 1.5mm mesh, preferably treated with permethrin, tucking edges in the mattress.

Sunburn & Heat Exhaustion

Stay out of the midday sun, wear sunglasses and a wide-brimmed sun hat, and use sunblock with high SPF, UVA and UVB protection. Be aware that the sun is more intense at higher altitudes.

Dehydration or salt deficiency can cause heat

haustion. Drink plenty of ids and avoid excessive cohol or strenuous activity hen you first arrive in a hot mate. Long, continuous pe- ods of exposure can leave u vulnerable to heatstroke.

Water

p water in Peru is not safe drink. Vigorous boiling of ater for one minute is the most effective means of wa- ter purification. At altitudes over 2000m (6500ft), boil for three minutes.

You can also disinfect water with iodine or water- purification pills or use a water filter or Steripen. Con- sult with outdoor retailers on the best option for your travel situation.

Women's Health

Travel to Lima is reasonably safe if you're pregnant, but finding quality obstetric care outside the capital may be difficult. It isn't advis- able for pregnant women to spend time at high altitudes. The yellow-fever vaccine should not be given during pregnancy.

WANT MORE?

For in-depth language information and handy phrases, check out Lonely Planet's *Latin American Spanish Phrasebook* and *Quechua Phrasebook*. You'll find them ʑ **shop.lonelyplanet.com**, or yo can buy Lonely Planet's iPhoɾ phrasebooks at the Apple Apɾ Store.

Language

Latin American Spanish pronunciation is easy, as most sounds have equivalents in English. Read our colored pronunciation guides as if they were English, and you'll be understood. Note that kh is a throaty sound (like the 'ch' in the Scottish *loch*), v and b are like a soft English 'v' (between a 'v' and a 'b'), and r is strongly rolled. There are also some variations in spoken Spanish across Latin America, the most notable being the pronunciation of the letters *ll* and *y*. In our pronunciation guides these are represented with y because they are pronounced like the 'y' in 'yes' in much of Latin America. Note, however, that in some parts of Peru (and the rest of the continent) they sound like the 'lli' in 'million'. The stressed syllables are indicated with italics in our pronunciation guides.

The polite form is used in this chapter; where both polite and informal options are given, they are indicated by the abbreviations 'pol' and 'inf'. Where necessary, both masculine and feminine forms of words are included, separated by a slash and with the masculine form first, eg *perdido/a* (m/f).

BASICS

Hello.	Hola.	o·la
Goodbye.	Adiós.	a·dyos
How are you?	¿Qué tal?	ke tal
Fine, thanks.	Bien, gracias.	byen gra·syas
Excuse me.	Perdón.	per·don
Sorry.	Lo siento.	lo syen·to
Please.	Por favor.	por fa·vor
Thank you.	Gracias.	gra·syas

| You're welcome. | De nada. | de na·da |
| Yes./No. | Sí./No. | see/no |

My name is ...
| Me llamo ... | | me ya·mo ... |

What's your name?
| ¿Cómo se llama Usted? | ko·mo se ya·ma oo·ste (pol |
| ¿Cómo te llamas? | ko·mo te ya·mas (inf) |

Do you speak English?
| ¿Habla inglés? | a·bla een·gles (pol) |
| ¿Hablas inglés? | a·blas een·gles (inf) |

I don't understand.
| Yo no entiendo. | yo no en·tyen·do |

ACCOMMODATIONS

I'd like a single/double room.
Quisiera una	kee·sye·ra oo·na
habitación	a·bee·ta·syon
individual/doble.	een·dee·vee·dwal/do·ble

How much is it per night/person?
| ¿Cuánto cuesta por | kwan·to kwes·ta por |
| noche/persona? | no·che/per·so·na |

Does it include breakfast?
| ¿Incluye el desayuno? | een·kloo·ye el de·sa·yoo·no |

Question Words

What?	¿Qué?	ke
When?	¿Cuándo?	kwan·do
Where?	¿Dónde?	don·de
Who?	¿Quién?	kyen
Why?	¿Por qué?	por ke

mpsite	terreno de cámping	te·re·no de kam·peeng
esthouse	pensión	pen·syon
tel	hotel	o·tel
uth hostel	albergue juvenil	al·ber·ge khoo·ve·neel
r-con	aire acondicionado	ai·re a·kon·dee·syo·na·do
athroom	baño	ba·nyo
d	cama	ka·ma
indow	ventana	ven·ta·na

IRECTIONS

here's ...?
Dónde está ...?   don·de es·ta ...

hat's the address?
Cuál es la dirección?   kwal es la dee·rek·syon

ould you please write it down?
Puede escribirlo, or favor?   pwe·de es·kree·beer·lo por fa·vor

an you show me (on the map)?
Me lo puede indicar en el mapa)?   me lo pwe·de een·dee·kar (en el ma·pa)

t the corner	en la esquina	en la es·kee·na
t the traffic lights	en el semáforo	en el se·ma·fo·ro
ehind ...	detrás de ...	de·tras de ...
n front of ...	enfrente de ...	en·fren·te de ...
eft	izquierda	ees·kyer·da
ext to ...	al lado de ...	al la·do de ...
pposite ...	frente a ...	fren·te a ...
ight	derecha	de·re·cha
traight ahead	todo recto	to·do rek·to

ATING & DRINKING

Can I see the menu, please?
Puedo ver el menú, or favor?   pwe·do ver el me·noo por fa·vor

What would you recommend?
Qué recomienda?   ke re·ko·myen·da

Do you have vegetarian food?
Tienen comida vegetariana?   tye·nen ko·mee·da ve·khe·ta·rya·na

I don't eat (red meat).
No como (carne roja).   no ko·mo (kar·ne ro·kha)

That was delicious!
¡Estaba buenísimo!   es·ta·ba bwe·nee·see·mo

Cheers!
¡Salud!   sa·loo

The bill, please.
La cuenta, por favor.   la kwen·ta por fa·vor

KEY PATTERNS

To get by in Spanish, mix and match these simple patterns with words of your choice:

When's (the next flight)?
¿Cuándo sale (el próximo vuelo)?   kwan·do sa·le (el prok·see·mo vwe·lo)

Where's (the station)?
¿Dónde está (la estación)?   don·de es·ta (la es·ta·syon)

Where can I (buy a ticket)?
¿Dónde puedo (comprar un billete)?   don·de pwe·do (kom·prar oon bee·ye·te)

Do you have (a map)?
¿Tiene (un mapa)?   tye·ne (oon ma·pa)

Is there (a toilet)?
¿Hay (servicios)?   ai (ser·vee·syos)

I'd like (a coffee).
Quisiera (un café).   kee·sye·ra (oon ka·fe)

I'd like (to hire a car).
Quisiera (alquilar un coche).   kee·sye·ra (al·kee·lar oon ko·che)

Can I (enter)?
¿Se puede (entrar)?   se pwe·de (en·trar)

Could you please (help me)?
¿Puede (ayudarme), por favor?   pwe·de (a·yoo·dar·me) por fa·vor

Do I have to (get a visa)?
¿Necesito (obtener un visado)?   ne·se·see·to (ob·te·ner oon vee·sa·do)

I'd like a table for ...	Quisiera una mesa para ...	kee·sye·ra oo·na me·sa pa·ra ...
(eight) o'clock	las (ocho)	las (o·cho)
(two) people	(dos) personas	(dos) per·so·nas

Key Words

appetisers	aperitivos	a·pe·ree·tee·vos
bottle	botella	bo·te·ya
bowl	bol	bol
breakfast	desayuno	de·sa·yoo·no
children's menu	menú infantil	me·noo een·fan·teel
(too) cold	(muy) frío	(mooy) free·o
dinner	cena	se·na
food	comida	ko·mee·da
fork	tenedor	te·ne·dor
glass	vaso	va·so
hot (warm)	caliente	kal·yen·te

knife	cuchillo	koo·chee·yo
lunch	comida	ko·mee·da
main course	segundo plato	se·goon·do pla·to
plate	plato	pla·to
restaurant	restaurante	res·tow·ran·te
spoon	cuchara	koo·cha·ra
with	con	kon
without	sin	seen

Meat & Fish

beef	carne de vaca	kar·ne de va·ka
chicken	pollo	po·yo
duck	pato	pa·to
fish	pescado	pes·ka·do
lamb	cordero	kor·de·ro
pork	cerdo	ser·do
turkey	pavo	pa·vo
veal	ternera	ter·ne·ra

Fruit & Vegetables

apple	manzana	man·sa·na
apricot	albaricoque	al·ba·ree·ko·ke
artichoke	alcachofa	al·ka·cho·fa
asparagus	espárragos	es·pa·ra·gos
banana	plátano	pla·ta·no
beans	judías	khoo·dee·as
beetroot	remolacha	re·mo·la·cha
cabbage	col	kol
carrot	zanahoria	sa·na·o·rya
celery	apio	a·pyo
cherry	cereza	se·re·sa
corn	maíz	ma·ees
cucumber	pepino	pe·pee·no
fruit	fruta	froo·ta
grape	uvas	oo·vas
lemon	limón	lee·mon
lentils	lentejas	len·te·khas
lettuce	lechuga	le·choo·ga
mushroom	champiñón	cham·pee·nyon
nuts	nueces	nwe·ses
onion	cebolla	se·bo·ya
orange	naranja	na·ran·kha
peach	melocotón	me·lo·ko·ton
peas	guisantes	gee·san·tes
(red/green) pepper	pimiento (rojo/verde)	pee·myen·to (ro·kho/ver·de)

pineapple	piña	pee·nya
plum	ciruela	seer·we·la
potato	patata	pa·ta·ta
pumpkin	calabaza	ka·la·ba·sa
spinach	espinacas	es·pee·na·kas
strawberry	fresa	fre·sa
tomato	tomate	to·ma·te
vegetable	verdura	ver·doo·ra
watermelon	sandía	san·dee·a

Other

bread	pan	pan
butter	mantequilla	man·te·kee·ya
cheese	queso	ke·so
egg	huevo	we·vo
honey	miel	myel
jam	mermelada	mer·me·la·da
oil	aceite	a·sey·te
pasta	pasta	pas·ta
pepper	pimienta	pee·myen·ta
rice	arroz	a·ros
salt	sal	sal
sugar	azúcar	a·soo·kar
vinegar	vinagre	vee·na·gre

Drinks

beer	cerveza	ser·ve·sa
coffee	café	ka·fe
(orange) juice	zumo (de naranja)	soo·mo (de na·ran·kha)
milk	leche	le·che
red wine	vino tinto	vee·no teen·to
tea	té	te
(mineral) water	agua (mineral)	a·gwa (mee·ne·ral)
white wine	vino blanco	vee·no blan·ko

Signs

Abierto	Open
Cerrado	Closed
Entrada	Entrance
Hombres/Varones	Men
Mujeres/Damas	Women
Prohibido	Prohibited
Salida	Exit
Servicios/Baños	Toilets

EMERGENCIES

Help!	¡Socorro!	so·ko·ro
Go away!	¡Vete!	ve·te

Call ...!	¡Llame a ...!	ya·me a ...
a doctor	un médico	oon me·dee·ko
the police	la policía	la po·lee·see·a

I'm lost.		
Estoy perdido/a.		es·toy per·dee·do/a (m/f)
I'm ill.		
Estoy enfermo/a.		es·toy en·fer·mo/a (m/f)
I'm allergic to (antibiotics).		
Soy alérgico/a a	soy a·ler·khee·ko/a a	
(los antibióticos).	(los an·tee·byo·tee·kos) (m/f)	
Where are the toilets?		
¿Dónde están los	don·de es·tan los	
baños?	ba·nyos	

SHOPPING & SERVICES

I'd like to buy ...		
Quisiera comprar ...	kee·sye·ra kom·prar ...	
I'm just looking.		
Sólo estoy mirando.	so·lo es·toy mee·ran·do	
Can I look at it?		
¿Puedo verlo?	pwe·do ver·lo	
I don't like it.		
No me gusta.	no me goos·ta	

Numbers

1	uno	oo·no
2	dos	dos
3	tres	tres
4	cuatro	kwa·tro
5	cinco	seen·ko
6	seis	seys
7	siete	sye·te
8	ocho	o·cho
9	nueve	nwe·ve
10	diez	dyes
20	veinte	veyn·te
30	treinta	treyn·ta
40	cuarenta	kwa·ren·ta
50	cincuenta	seen·kwen·ta
60	sesenta	se·sen·ta
70	setenta	se·ten·ta
80	ochenta	o·chen·ta
90	noventa	no·ven·ta
100	cien	syen
1000	mil	meel

How much is it?		
¿Cuánto cuesta?	kwan·to kwes·ta	
That's too expensive.		
Es muy caro.	es mooy ka·ro	
Can you lower the price?		
¿Podría bajar un	po·dree·a ba·khar oon	
poco el precio?	po·ko el pre·syo	
There's a mistake in the bill.		
Hay un error	ai oon e·ror	
en la cuenta.	en la kwen·ta	

ATM	cajero automático	ka·khe·ro ow·to·ma·tee·ko
internet cafe	cibercafé	see·ber·ka·fe
market	mercado	mer·ka·do
post office	correos	ko·re·os
tourist office	oficina de turismo	o·fee·see·na de too·rees·mo

TIME & DATES

What time is it?	¿Qué hora es?	ke o·ra es
It's (10) o'clock.	Son (las diez).	son (las dyes)
It's half past (one).	Es (la una) y media.	es (la oo·na) ee me·dya

morning	mañana	ma·nya·na
afternoon	tarde	tar·de
evening	noche	no·che

yesterday	ayer	a·yer
today	hoy	oy
tomorrow	mañana	ma·nya·na

Monday	lunes	loo·nes
Tuesday	martes	mar·tes
Wednesday	miércoles	myer·ko·les
Thursday	jueves	khwe·ves
Friday	viernes	vyer·nes
Saturday	sábado	sa·ba·do
Sunday	domingo	do·meen·go

TRANSPORTATION

boat	barco	bar·ko
bus	autobús	ow·to·boos
plane	avión	a·vyon
train	tren	tren

first	primero	pree·me·ro
last	último	ool·tee·mo
ticket office	taquilla	ta·kee·ya
timetable	horario	o·ra·ryo

AYMARA & QUECHUA

The few Aymara and Quechua words and phrases included here will be useful for those traveling in the Andes. Aymara is spoken by the Aymara people, who inhabit the area around Lake Titicaca. While the Quechua included here is from the Cuzco dialect, it should prove helpful wherever you travel in the highlands too.

In the following lists, Aymara is the second column, Quechua the third. The principles of pronunciation for both languages are similar to those found in Spanish. An apostrophe (') represents a glottal stop, which is the 'nonsound' that occurs in the middle of 'uh-oh.'

Hello.	Kamisaraki.	Napaykullayki.	food	manka	mikiuy
Please.	Mirá.	Allichu.	river	jawira	mayu
Thank you.	Yuspagara.	Yusulipayki.	snowy peak	kollu	riti-orko
Yes.	Jisa.	Ari.	water	uma	yacu
No.	Janiwa.	Mana.			
			1	maya	u'
How do you say ...?	Cun saña-sauca'ha ...?	Imainata nincha chaita ...?	2	paya	iskai
			3	quimsa	quinsa
It's called ...	Ucan sutipa'h ...	Chaipa'g sutin'ha ...	4	pusi	tahua
			5	pesca	phiska
Please repeat.	Uastata sita.	Ua'manta niway.	6	zo'hta	so'gta
How much?	K'gauka?	Maik'ata'g?	7	pakalko	khanchis
			8	quimsakalko	pusa'g
father	auqui	tayta	9	yatunca	iskon
mother	taica	mama	10	tunca	chunca

bus stop	parada de autobuses	pa·ra·da de ow·to·boo·ses
train station	estación de trenes	es·ta·syon de tre·nes
A ... ticket, please.	Un billete de ..., por favor.	oon bee·ye·te de ... por fa·vor
1st-class	primera clase	pree·me·ra kla·se
2nd-class	segunda clase	se·goon·da kla·se
one-way	ida	ee·da
return	ida y vuelta	ee·da ee vwel·ta

Does it stop at ...?
¿Para en ...? pa·ra en ...

What stop is this?
¿Cuál es esta parada? kwal es es·ta pa·ra·da

What time does it arrive/leave?
¿A qué hora llega/sale? a ke o·ra ye·ga/sa·le

Please tell me when we get to ...
¿Puede avisarme pwe·de a·vee·sar·me
cuando lleguemos a ...? kwan·do ye·ge·mos a ...

I want to get off here.
Quiero bajarme aquí. kye·ro ba·khar·me a·kee

I'd like to hire a ...	Quisiera alquilar ...	kee·sye·ra al·kee·lar ...
4WD	un todo-terreno	oon to·do·te·re·no
bicycle	una bicicleta	oo·na bee·see·kle·ta
car	un coche	oon ko·che
motorcycle	una moto	oo·na mo·to
helmet	casco	kas·ko
hitchhike	hacer botella	a·ser bo·te·ya
mechanic	mecánico	me·ka·nee·ko
petrol/gas	gasolina	ga·so·lee·na
service station	gasolinera	ga·so·lee·ne·ra
truck	camion	ka·myon

Is this the road to ...?
¿Se va a ... por se va a ... por
esta carretera? es·ta ka·re·te·ra

Can I park here?
¿Puedo aparcar aquí? pwe·do a·par·kar a·kee

The car has broken down.
El coche se ha averiado. el ko·che se a a·ve·rya·do

I have a flat tyre.
Tengo un pinchazo. ten·go oon peen·cha·so

GLOSSARY

albergue – family-owned inn

altiplano – literally, a high plateau or plain; specifically, it refers to the vast, desolate Andean flatlands of southern Peru, Bolivia, northern Chile and northern Argentina

aluvión – fast-moving flood of ice, water, rocks, mud and debris caused by an earthquake or the bursting of a dam in a mountainous region

arequipeño – inhabitant of Arequipa

arriero – animal driver, usually of *burros* or *mulas* (mules)

avenida – avenue (abbreviated Av)

ayahuasca – potent hallucinogenic brew made from jungle vines and used by shamans and traditional healers

barrio – neighborhood

bodega – winery, wine shop, wine cellar or tasting bar

boleto turístico – tourism ticket

bruja/brujo – shaman, witch doctor, or medicine woman or man

burro – donkey

bus-cama – long-distance, double-decker buses with seats reclining almost into beds; toilets, videos and snacks are provided on board

caballito – high-ended, cigar-shaped boat; found near Huanchaco

calle – street

campesino – peasant, farmer or rural inhabitant

cañón – canyon

carretera – highway

casa – home, house

casa de cambio – foreign-exchange bureau

cerro – hill, mountain

chullpa – ancient Andean burial tower, found around Lake Titicaca

cocha – lake, from the indigenous Quechua language; often appended to many lake names, eg Conococha

colectivo – shared transportation; usually taxis, but sometimes minibuses, minivans or even boats

combi – minivan or minibus (usually with tiny seats, cramming in as many passengers as possible)

cordillera – mountain chain

criolla/criollo – Creole or native of Peru; also applies to coastal Peruvians, music and dance; *criollo* food refers to spicy Peruvian fare with Spanish, Asian and African influences

cuadra – city block

curandera/curandero – traditional healer

cuzqueño – inhabitant of Cuzco (also spelled Cusco or Qosq'o)

escuela cuzqueña – Cuzco school; colonial art movement that combined Spanish and Andean artistic styles

feria – street market with vendor booths

garúa – coastal fog, mist or drizzle

grifo – gas (petrol) station

gringa/gringo – generally refers to all foreigners who are not from South or Central America and Mexico

guanaco – large, wild camelid that ranges throughout South America, now an endangered species in Peru

hospedaje – small, family-owned inn

hostal – guesthouse, smaller than a hotel and with fewer amenities

huaca – sacred pyramid, temple or burial site

huaquero – grave robber

huayno – traditional Andean music using instrumentation

with roots in pre-Columbian times

iglesia – church

inca – king

indígena – indigenous person (male or female)

Inrena – Insituto Nacional de Recursos Naturales (National Institute for Natural Resources); government agency that administers national parks, reserves, historical sanctuaries and other protected areas

Inti – ancient Peruvian sun god; husband of the earth goddess Pachamama

isla – island, isle

jirón – road (abbreviated Jr)

lavandería – laundry

limeño – inhabitant of Lima

marinera – a typical coastal Peruvian dance involving the flirtatious waving of handkerchiefs

mestizo – person of mixed indigenous and Spanish descent

micro – a small bus used as public transport

mirador – watchtower, observatory, viewpoint

mototaxi – three-wheeled motorcycle rickshaw taxi; also called *motocarro* or *taximoto*

museo – museum

nevado – glaciated or snow-covered mountain peak

nuevo sol – the national currency of Peru

oficina de migraciónes – immigration office

Pachamama – ancient Peruvian earth goddess; wife of the sun god Inti

pampa – large, flat area, usually of grasslands

Panamericana – Pan-American Highway (aka Interamericana); main route joining Latin American countries

parque – park

peña – bar or club featuring live folkloric music

playa – beach

pongo – narrow, steep-walled, rocky, jungle river canyon that can be a dangerous maelstrom during high water

pueblo – town, village

puna – high Andean grasslands of the *altiplano*

puya – spiky-leafed plant of the bromeliad family

quebrada – literally, a break; often refers to a steep ravine or gulch

quero – ceremonial Inca wooden drinking vessel

río – river

selva – jungle, tropical rainforest

sillar – off-white volcanic rock, often used for buildings around Arequipa

soroche – altitude sickness

taximoto – see *mototaxi*

terminal terrestre – bus station

totora – reed of the papyrus family; used to build the 'floating islands' and traditional boats of Lake Titicaca

turismo vivencial – homestay tourism

vals peruano – Peruvian waltz, an upbeat, guitar-driven waltz played and danced to in coastal areas

vicuña – threatened wild relative of the alpaca; smallest living member of the camelid family

behind the scenes

SEND US YOUR FEEDBACK

We love to hear from travelers – your comments keep us on our toes and help make our books better. Our well-traveled team reads every word on what you loved or loathed about this book. Although we cannot reply individually to postal submissions, we always guarantee that your feedback goes straight to the appropriate authors, in time for the next edition. Each person who sends us information is thanked in the next edition – the most useful submissions are rewarded with a selection of digital PDF chapters.

Visit **lonelyplanet.com/contact** to submit your updates and suggestions or to ask for help. Our award-winning website also features inspirational travel stories, news and discussions.

Note: We may edit, reproduce and incorporate your comments in Lonely Planet products such as guidebooks, websites and digital products, so let us know if you don't want your comments reproduced or your name acknowledged. For a copy of our privacy policy visit lonelyplanet.com/privacy.

OUR READERS

Many thanks to the travelers who used the last edition and wrote to us with helpful hints, useful advice and interesting anecdotes:

Birgou Albat, Stephanie Allan, Fernando Alvarez, Melanie Anderson, Kristin Anexstad, Raja Antony, Lisa Arcobelli, Anita Armold, Marta Saenz Arranz, Josh Austin, Matt Ball, Paul & Gail Banyard, Matthew Barker, Marcelo Barucca, Irmgard Bauer, Zoe Baumgart, Josh Berk, Adrian Berteletti, Lorraine Bligh, Vera Boersting, Rick Bohn, Giovanna Botticella, Tim Brandle, Anna Lena Brischke, Chris Brooker, Maya Brunner, Michel Bruno, Dennis Brunt, Gabriele Buondonno, Leslie Burneo, Brigitte Cannuel, Janine Carger, Jose Cerf, Eirik Chambe-Eng, David Claveau, Shea Codd, Christophe R Côté, Peter Cottrell, Peter Dam, Michael Dassa, Andy De Groot, Anthony De Lannoy, Inger Dehn, Andrea Dekkers, Laurie Devault, Edwin Deventer, Karyn Dirse, Reuben Dunagan, Noelle Ehrenkaufer, Ruth Eldridge, Rosa Elena, Hila Elinav, Lars Elle, Omer Feitelson, Raquel Flecha, Margo Freistadt, Alex Fuller-Young, Amanda Fulmer, Alessandra Furlan, Barbara Gaetani, Terri Gaines, Susanne Galla, Gabriela Gardiner, David Gaviller, Daniel Geissler, Chantale Germain, Harry Geurkink, Matt Gillespie, Annie Gingras, Eric Guay, Caterina Gut, Dries Haesendonck, Lisa Hardy, Eddy Heftend, Hannah Henze, Marjolein Herweijer, Katy Hinton, Stuart Hobbs, Matthew Hodges, Lizet Hoenderdos, Esther Hoenen, Randall Holmes, Dana Howell, Magdalena, Karin, Troch & Marten Ijzerman, Anja Irmisch, Maria Isabel, Thomas Mcfarlane Jelstrom, Ron Jerome, Bonnie Johnson, Laura Joseph, Monica Kelsh, Gadi Kenny, Kathy Kieffer, Guy Kingsbury, Edward Kirk-Wilson, Timo Koivu, Wouter Krikke, John Landry, Roberto Lapalma, Sarah Larsen, Russ Lawrence, Pia Lehtonen-Davies, Elizabeth Leodler, Francesca Lewis, Meg Lewis, Larissa Liepins, Peter Lintner, Jenny Little, Imogen Lockyer, Kate Lomas, Gabriel Melo Lozano, Ralph Maclean, Francesco Maconi, Kim Macquarrie, Eleni Macrakis, Nicholas Maple, Thomas Marcilly, Hayley Markel, Stephan Marks, Santi Martí, Brian Mcfarland, Rachel Atau Mcfarland, Les Meteorites, Sasha Moazed, Nathalie Moerker, Dennis Mogerman, Gian Monteleone, Francis Moore, Patricia Moreno, Ruben Bustamante Moreno, Daina Morris, Charles Motley, Tristan Mules, Eric Neemann, Stuart Nelson, Courtney Newlon, Wang Feng Ng, Sofie Hougaard Nielsen, Mads Niemann, Pamela Nieto, Judith Nijeboer, Angela Nurse, Beth O'Leary, Michele Oechsle, Ida Oldhoff, Juan Oltra, Sandra

Otto, Alice Pajard, Nilla Palmer, Mateusz Papla, Matt Pepe, Diane Perlman, Ruth Anne Phillips, Barbara Prescott, Lauren Radebaugh, Victor Radulescu, Jonathan Rae, Jorge Ore Rebatta, Eder Reis, Marissa Rensen, Mohammad Husam Rezek, Liz Rha, Adam Rheingans, Ron Richardson, Moritz Riess, Philipp Ringgenberg, Ignacio Riveira, Alexandre Robert, Federico Rodrigo, Maïté Rolin, Bram Rouges, Solen Roussel, Darren Rubbo, Wendy Rushbrooke, Andrea Saul, Gianna U Schorno, Chip Scialfa, Max Seelhofer, Cathy Shumaker, Elizabeth Shumaker, Eva-Carol Simpson, Francois Sonnet, Veronika Stalz, Eliki Stathakopoulos, Martijn Steijn, Dave Stokes, Lionel Stoller, Jesus Tejera, Richard Thiel, Jemma Thornes, Jessica Thrall, Rolf & Sanne Tijsma, Marie Timmermans, Jaime Quiroz Tirado, Anne Tonkin, Maksim Turlov, Amy Uccello, Shirley Van Der Griendt, Bert Vanderfe, Annie Vanslambrouk, Jan Verendel, Pierre Verkerk, Margaret Vile, Felix Wagner, Susan Waldock, Leora Walter, Milo Wende, Wayo Whilar, Mirjam Wildeboer, Kristina Willas, Jana Wille, Rachel Wright, Shellene Wyrick, Kai Xue, Hillary Yacobucci, Jenipher Young-Hall, Jan Zapal, Allen Zhang, Roland Zimmermann.

AUTHOR THANKS

Carolyn McCarthy

Many thanks go out to all the Peruvian chefs and street vendors who played a key role in my contentment. I am also grateful for the friendship, advice and assistance of Daniel Fernandez Davila, Milton, Michael and Illa Liendo, Arturo Rojas, Jorge Riveros-Cayo, Louise Norton, Edgar in Puno, Elizabeth Shumaker, Marco Palomino, John Leivers and Paolo Greer. To my hardworking co-authors, a chilled pisco sour for starters.

Carolina A Miranda

Thanks to my husband, who tolerates my wandering (and all my related stomach illnesses), and also to Arturo Rojas, who always teaches me something new about Peruvian food. I also wish to thank Juan Cincunegui, the patient librarian at the Monastery of Santo Domingo in Cuzco, for turning me on to so many wonderful books. And to the people of Peru, who are always gracious and generous, thank you! Y que!/!Viva el Perú Carajo!

Kevin Raub

Special thanks to my wife, Adriana Schmidt Raub, who didn't see me much at all in 2012. At Lonely Planet, Kathleen Munnelly, as always! On the road, Carolyn McCarthy, Carolina Miranda, Camille Ulmer and all at SAE, Moche Tours, Julio and Mauro Olaza, Chris Benway, Kristof Van Den Bussche, Bruni Frampton, Dr John Rick, Charlie Good, Alberto Cafferata, Daniel Fernandez-Davila, Fidel Elera, Lluis Dalmau, Maya Ortiz, and Susan van der Wielen.

Brendan Sainsbury

Thanks to all the untold bus drivers, tourist-information volunteers, restaurateurs, pan-pipe blowers, weather forecasters, novoandina chefs and innocent bystanders who helped me during my research. Thanks especially to guide and mountaineer, Carlos Zárate, for his time and interesting insights in Arequipa and Colca Canyon.

Luke Waterson

Gracias to all the boat captains and colectivo/combi drivers, who, apart from (generally) making arduous Andean and Amazonian trips possible and even enjoyable, rarely stopped smiling or recommending incredible places for me to explore. Ryse, you're next: thanks for saving me from drowning! Special acknowledgement is also due to my wonderful parents who tolerated me during write-up, to Huancayo's Lucho Hurtado for the umpteenth time, to Pauline in Ayacucho, to Gerson in Puerto Maldonado and Bill and Marcel in Iquitos.

ACKNOWLEDGMENTS

Climate map data adapted from Peel MC, Finlayson BL & McMahon TA (2007) 'Updated World Map of the Köppen-Geiger Climate Classification', Hydrology and Earth System Sciences, 11, 163344.

Cover photograph: Island of Ticonata, Lake Titicaca, Jean-Pierre Degas / Hemis©.

his Book

iis 8th edition of Lonely
anet's *Peru* guidebook was
searched and written by
arolyn McCarthy, Carolina A
iranda, Kevin Raub, Brendan
ainsbury and Luke Waterson.
he previous edition was writ-
en by Carolina A Miranda and
uke Waterson, along with Aimée
owl, Katy Shorthouse and Beth
illiams. This guidebook was
ommissioned in Lonely Planet's
akland office, and produced by
he following:

ommissioning Editors
athleen Munnelly, Catherine
raddock-Carrillo

Coordinating Editors
Justin Flynn, Ross Taylor
**Coordinating
Cartographer** Andy Rojas
**Coordinating Layout
Designer** Carol Jackson
Managing Editors Sasha
Baskett, Bruce Evans
Senior Editor Andi Jones
Managing Cartographers
Mark Griffiths, Alison Lyall
**Managing Layout
Designer** Chris Girdler
Assisting Editors Kate
Evans, Carly Hall, Helen Koehne,
Anne Mulvaney, Christopher
Pitts, Erin Richards

Assisting Cartographers
Valeska Cañas, Jacqueline
Nguyen, Jolyon Philcox
Cover Research Naomi
Parker
Internal Image Research
Kylie McLaughlin
Illustrator Michael Weldon
Language Content
Branislava Vladisavljevic

Thanks to Ryan Evans, Larissa
Frost, James Hardy, Bella Li,
Annelies Mertens, Trent Paton,
Kirsten Rawlings, Raphael
Richards, Kerrianne Southway,
Gerard Walker

BEHIND THE SCENES

index

how to use this book

These symbols will help you find the listings you want:

👁	Sights	👉	Tours	🍷	Drinking
🏖	Beaches	🎊	Festivals & Events	⭐	Entertainment
🏃	Activities	🛏	Sleeping	🔒	Shopping
🎓	Courses	🍴	Eating	ℹ	Information/Transport

These symbols give you the vital information for each listing:

📞	Telephone Numbers	📶	Wi-Fi Access	🚌	Bus
⏱	Opening Hours	🏊	Swimming Pool	⛴	Ferry
P	Parking	🥗	Vegetarian Selection	M	Metro
⊖	Nonsmoking	📖	English-Language Menu	S	Subway
❄	Air-Conditioning	👶	Family-Friendly	🚋	Tram
@	Internet Access	🐾	Pet-Friendly	R	Train

Reviews are organised by author preference.

Look out for these icons:

TOP CHOICE	Our author's recommendation
FREE	No payment required
🌿	A green or sustainable option

Our authors have nominated these places as demonstrating a strong commitment to sustainability – for example by supporting local communities and producers, operating in an environmentally friendly way, or supporting conservation projects.

Map Legend

Sights
- 🏖 Beach
- 🛕 Buddhist
- 🏰 Castle
- ✝ Christian
- 🕉 Hindu
- ☪ Islamic
- ✡ Jewish
- 🗿 Monument
- 🏛 Museum/Gallery
- 🏚 Ruin
- 🍇 Winery/Vineyard
- 🦁 Zoo
- ◉ Other Sight

Activities, Courses & Tours
- 🤿 Diving/Snorkelling
- 🛶 Canoeing/Kayaking
- ⛷ Skiing
- 🏄 Surfing
- 🏊 Swimming/Pool
- 🚶 Walking
- 🏄 Windsurfing
- ⊙ Other Activity/Course/Tour

Sleeping
- 🛏 Sleeping
- ⛺ Camping

Eating
- 🍴 Eating

Drinking
- ☕ Drinking
- ☕ Cafe

Entertainment
- 🎭 Entertainment

Shopping
- 🛍 Shopping

Information
- 💲 Bank
- 🏢 Embassy/Consulate
- ➕ Hospital/Medical
- @ Internet
- 👮 Police
- ✉ Post Office
- ☎ Telephone
- 🚻 Toilet
- ℹ Tourist Information
- ● Other Information

Transport
- ✈ Airport
- 🛂 Border Crossing
- 🚌 Bus
- ⊶⊕⊷ Cable Car/Funicular
- 🚲 Cycling
- ⛴ Ferry
- 🚝 Monorail
- P Parking
- ⛽ Petrol Station
- 🚕 Taxi
- 🚆 Train/Railway
- 🚋 Tram
- M Underground Train Station
- ● Other Transport

Routes
- Tollway
- Freeway
- Primary
- Secondary
- Tertiary
- Lane
- Unsealed Road
- Plaza/Mall
- Steps
-)═(Tunnel
- Pedestrian Overpass
- Walking Tour
- Walking Tour Detour
- Path

Geographic
- 🏠 Hut/Shelter
- 🗼 Lighthouse
- 👁 Lookout
- ▲ Mountain/Volcano
- 🌴 Oasis
- 🌳 Park
-)(Pass
- 🧺 Picnic Area
- 💧 Waterfall

Population
- ● Capital (National)
- ◉ Capital (State/Province)
- ● City/Large Town
- ○ Town/Village

Boundaries
- — — — International
- — — State/Province
- — - Disputed
- — - Regional/Suburb
- Marine Park
- Cliff
- Wall

Hydrography
- River, Creek
- Intermittent River
- Swamp/Mangrove
- Reef
- Canal
- Water
- Dry/Salt/Intermittent Lake
- Glacier

Areas
- Beach/Desert
- + + + Cemetery (Christian)
- × × × Cemetery (Other)
- Park/Forest
- Sportsground
- Sight (Building)
- Top Sight (Building)

Brendan Sainsbury

South Coast, Arequipa & Canyon Country An expat-Brit now living [in] Canada, Brendan first visited Peru as part of an epic South America[n] odyssey in the early 2000s; a trip that involved getting hailed on in M[achu Pic]chu, getting lost in the middle of the Bolivian salt pans, and teaching [Uru]guayans how to do the 'Madness dance' in Punta del Este. He has sin[ce written] numerous Spanish-speaking countries for Lonely Planet including Cu[ba, P]uerto Rico and Spain.

Luke Waterson

Central Highlands, Amazon Basin Two near-death experiences (includin[g nearly] drowning in Río Madre de Dios) made for a poignant sixth trip to Peru for [this book.] He's been traveling (hiking/hitching/boating on vessels of dubious qualit[y) around] across the country since 2004. His writing about close encounters with bi[g wilder-] ness in Latin America, Cuba and central Europe has graced several publica[tions] including 15 Lonely Planet guidebooks and the UK magazine, *Real Travel*, w[hich] [h]e helped relaunch. This is the second time he's worked on *Peru*. Tweet him (@lukewaterson1[) about] anything South/Central America–related.

OUR STORY

A beat-up old car, a few dollars in the pocket and a sense of adventure. In 1972 that's all Tony and Maureen Wheeler needed for the trip of a lifetime – across Europe and Asia overland to Australia. It took several months, and at the end – broke but inspired – they sat at their kitchen table writing and stapling together their first travel guide, *Across Asia on the Cheap*. Within a week they'd sold 1500 copies. Lonely Planet was born.

Today, Lonely Planet has offices in Melbourne, London and Oakland, with more than 600 staff and writers. We share Tony's belief that 'a great guidebook should do three things: inform, educate and amuse'.

OUR WRITERS

Carolyn McCarthy

Coordinating author; Lima, Lake Titicaca, Cusco & the Sacred Valley
Author Carolyn McCarthy first discovered *cumbia* camping on the Inca Trail many years ago. For this trip, she sampled hundreds of Peruvian delicacies, climbed Wayna Picchu and visited one medical clinic. Some of her other Lonely Planet titles include *Argentina*, *Panama*, *Yellowstone & Grand Teton National Parks*, *USA*, *The Travel Book*, *Best in Travel* and *Trekking in the Patagonian Andes*. She has also written for *National Geographic*, *Outside* and *Lonely Planet Magazine*, among other publications. You can follow her Americas blog at www.carolynswildblueyonder.blogspot.com.

Carolina A Miranda

Understand Peru The daughter of a Peruvian father, Carolina has spent her life making pilgrimages to Peru to eat ceviche and sip pisco sours. An avid student of Peruvian history (she has a degree in Latin American Studies), she has read Mario Vargas Llosa novels in Spanish, danced to Peruvian waltzes and spent countless hours studying the arts and textiles of the Andes. She also makes a mean *aji de gallina*. Find her at C-Monster.net or on Twitter at @cmonstah.

Read more about Carolina at:
lonelyplanet.com/members/carolinamiranda

Kevin Raub

North Coast, Huaraz & the Cordilleras, Northern Highlands Kevin Raub grew up in Atlanta and started his career as a music journalist in New York, working for *Men's Journal* and *Rolling Stone* magazines. He ditched the rock 'n' roll lifestyle for travel writing and moved to Brazil. Working on *Peru* he logged over 2500km in his beige Renault tank, canvassing up and down the North Coast. He even stood his ground on a shakedown from Policía Nacional on one of the nine times they stopped him. After that, he opted for buses in the Northern Highlands and Huaraz areas. This is Kevin's 20th Lonely Planet guide. You can find him at www.kevinraub.net.

Read more about Kevin at:
lonelyplanet.com/members/kraub

OVER MORE
PAGE WRITERS

Published by Lonely Planet Publications Pty Ltd
ABN 36 005 607 983
8th edition – April 2013
ISBN 978 1 74179 921 7
© Lonely Planet 2013   Photographs © as indicated 2013
10 9 8 7 6 5 4 3 2 1
Printed in China

Best-selling guide to Peru – source: Nielsen BookScan, Australia, UK and USA, September 2011 to August 2012.